Handbook of Research on Artificial Immune Systems and Natural Computing:
Applying Complex Adaptive Technologies

Hongwei Mo
Harbin Engineering University, China

Medical Information Science REFERENCE

MEDICAL INFORMATION SCIENCE REFERENCE

Hershey · New York

Director of Editorial Content:	Kristin Klinger
Director of Production:	Jennifer Neidig
Managing Editor:	Jamie Snavely
Assistant Managing Editor:	Carole Coulson
Cover Design:	Lisa Tosheff
Printed at:	Yurchak Printing Inc.

Published in the United States of America by
    Medical Information Science Reference (an imprint of IGI Global)
    701 E. Chocolate Avenue
    Hershey PA 17033
    Tel: 717-533-8845
    Fax: 717-533-8661
    E-mail: cust@igi-global.com
    Web site: http://www.igi-global.com

and in the United Kingdom by
    Information Science Reference (an imprint of IGI Global)
    3 Henrietta Street
    Covent Garden
    London WC2E 8LU
    Tel: 44 20 7240 0856
    Fax: 44 20 7379 0609
    Web site: http://www.eurospanbookstore.com

Copyright © 2009 by IGI Global. All rights reserved. No part of this publication may be reproduced, stored or distributed in any form or by any means, electronic or mechanical, including photocopying, without written permission from the publisher.

Product or company names used in this set are for identification purposes only. Inclusion of the names of the products or companies does not indicate a claim of ownership by IGI Global of the trademark or registered trademark.

    Library of Congress Cataloging-in-Publication Data

Handbook of research on artificial immune systems and natural computing : applying complex adaptive technologies / Hongwei Mo, editor.

    p. ; cm.

  Includes bibliographical references and index.

  Summary: "This book offers new ideas and recent developments in Natural Computing, especially on artificial immune systems"-- Provided by publisher.

  Summary: "This book offers new ideas and recent developments in Natural Computing, especially on artificial immune systems"-- Provided by publisher.

  ISBN 978-1-60566-310-4 (hardcover)

  1. Natural computation--Handbooks, manuals, etc. 2. Immunoinformatics--Handbooks, manuals, etc. 3. Immunology--Computer simulation--Handbooks, manuals, etc. I. Mo, Hongwei, 1973-

  [DNLM: 1. Computer Simulation. 2. Immune System. 3. Artificial Intelligence. QW 504 H2367 2009]

  QA76.9.N37H36 2009

  006.3--dc22

                2008037502

British Cataloguing in Publication Data
A Cataloguing in Publication record for this book is available from the British Library.

All work contributed to this book is original material. The views expressed in this book are those of the authors, but not necessarily of the publisher.

If a library purchased a print copy of this publication, please go to http://www.igi-global.com/agreement for information on activating the library's complimentary electronic access to this publication.

Editorial Advisory Board

Carlos A. Coello Coello
CINVESTAV-IPN, Mexico

Fabio Freschi
CINVESTAV-IPN, Mexico

Maurizio Repetto
CINVESTAV-IPN, Mexico

Mahdi Mahfouf
The University of Sheffield, UK

Sławomir T. Wierzchoń
Polish Academy of Sciences, Poland

Jiao Licheng
Xidian University, China

Bo-Suk Yang
Pukyong National University, South Korea

Georgios Ch. Sirakoulis
Democritus University of Thrace, Greece

Lenka Lhotska
BioDat Research Group, Czech Republic

Eugene Eberbach
Rensselaer Polytechnic Institute at Hartford, USA

James F. Peters
University of Manitoba, Canada

List of Contributors

Table of Contents

Section I
Artificial Immune Systems

Section I.I
Immune Optimization Algorithms

Section I.II
Artificial Immune Systems and Agents

Section I.VI
The Other Applications of Artificial Immune Systems

Section II
Natural Computing

Section II.I
Evolutionary Computing

Section II.II
Ant Colony

Detailed Table of Contents

Section I
Artificial Immune Systems

Section I.I
Immune Optimization Algorithms

 Fabio Freschi, Politecnico di Torino, Italy
 Carlos A. Coello Coello, CINESTAV-IPN, Evolutionary Computation Group, Mexico
 Maurizio Repetto, Politecnico di Torino, Italy

The chapter provides a thorough review of the state of the art in multi-objective optimization with artificial immune system(MOAIS). The basic ideas and implementations of different kinds of algorithms of MOAIS are introduced. They had been used in different fields, such as power systems, control theory and so on.

 Jun Chen, The University of Sheffield, UK
 Mahdi Mahfouf, The University of Sheffield, UK

This chapter introduces a population adaptive based immune algorithm (PAIA) and its modified version for engineering optimization applications. It is argued that PAIA and its variations embody some new features recognized nowadays as the key to success for any stochastic algorithms dealing with continuous optimization problems. PAIA is used for a real-world problem besides some test suites in the chapter.

 Licheng Jiao, Xidian University, China
 Maoguo Gong, Xidian University, China
 Wenping Ma, Xidian University, China

In this chapter, the authors build a general computational framework simulating immune response process, a population-based artificial immune dynamical system, termed as PAIS, and it isapplied to numerical optimization problems. Based on it, a dynamic algorithm, termed as PAISA, is designed and tested on many benchmark functions and a real opmtization problem. It shows high performance in these problems.

Section I.II
Artificial Immune Systems and Agents

Małgorzata Lucińska, Kielce University of Technology, Poland
Sławomir T. Wierzchoń, Polish Academy of Sciences, Poland & University of Gdańsk, Poland

In this chapter, clonal selection algorithm, inspired by the real mechanism of immune response, is proposed to solve the problem of learning strategies in the pursuit-evasion problem. It compares game theory with artificial immune systems by using multi-agent system as platform. The obtained results show that mutual interactions of individuals in the system have a great influence on its effectiveness.

Luis Fernando Niño Vasquez, National University of Colombia, Colombia
Fredy Fernado Muñoz Mopan, National University of Colombia, Colombia
Camilo Eduardo Prieto Salazar, National University of Colombia, Colombia
José Guillermo Guarnizo Marín, National University of Colombia. Colombia

This is a survey chapter within which single and multi-agent systems (MAS) inspired by immunology concepts are presented and analyzed. Classical immune theories and mechanisms, including clonal selection, idiotypic immune network and even negative selection had been used in this field. Most of them are embodied in robotics system.

Section I.III
Artificial Immune System and Scheduling

Xingquan Zuo, Beijing University of Posts and Telecommunications, P.R. China
Hongwei Mo, Harbin Engineering University, P.R. China

Inspired from the robust control principle, a robust scheduling method is proposed to solve uncertain scheduling problems. A variable neighborhood immune algorithm (VNIA) is used to obtain an optimal robust scheduling scheme. It is an immune algorithm with two immune networks. Experiments show its insensitive characteristics to uncertain disturbances in scheludling environment.

Fabio Freschi, Politecnico di Torino, Italy
Maurizio Repetto, Politecnico di Torino, Italy

A method of artificial immune systems is applied to energy production systems management. The energy system is seen as a living body reacting to stimulation and satifing internal requirements. Immune based scheduling method is proposed for exploiting the optimal state of the power energy system. It is compared to classicial linear programming. The results show the effectiveness of the proposed immune scheduling algorithm.

Krzysztof Ciesielski, Polish Academy of Sciences, Poland
Mieczysław A. Kłopotek, Polish Academy of Sciences, Poland
Sławomir T. Wierzchoń, Polish Academy of Sciences, Poland & University of Gdańsk, Poland

In this chapter, artificial immune network algorithm-aiNet- is used to extract the clusters structure in large collection of documents. It combines document map and visualization to realize document clustering. And it evaluates clustering performance based on the initialization of immune network.

Xiangrong Zhang, Xidian University, P.R. China
Fang Liu, Xidian University, P.R. China

Clonal selection algorithm is used to feature selection in this chapter. Feature selection can be considered as an optimization problem and aims to find an optimal feature subset from the available features according to a certain criterion function. Three kinds of clonal operators are designed to speed up the covegence to gloabl optimum. It is desmonstrated by UCI data and radar image classifcation in practice. The results show its promising performance.

Yong-Sheng Ding, Ministry of Education, China
Xiang-Feng Zhang, Ministry of Education, China & Shanghai Dianji University, China
Li-Hong Ren, Ministry of Education, China

A bio-network simulation platform which has the capability of service emergence, evolution is developed. The simulation platform can be used to simulate some complex services and applications for Internet or distributed network. As a demonstration, two immune network computation models are proposed to generate the emergent services through computer simulation experiments on the platform. The bio-network architecture provides a novel way to design new intelligent Internet information services and applications.

Tao Gong, Donghua University, China & Central South University, China

Static Web immune system is an important application of artificial immune system. On the Static Web system, a normal model is proposed with the space property and the time property of each component, in order to identify the normal state of the system that the artificial immune system protects. It is showed that the static web immune system is effective and useful for both theory and applications.

Immunocomputing is now an important concept with sound mathmatic foundation in the field of Artificial Immune System. Based on mathematical models of immunocomputing, this chapter describes an approach to spatio-temporal forecast (STF) by intelligent signal processing. Real-world application is demonstrated on data of space monitoring of the Caspian, Black, and Barents Sea.

Based on the biological immune mechanism and artificial immune model, this chapter attempts to study the immune controller design and application in traditional control system. Three kinds of artificial immune controller are proposed based on the T-B cells immunity, simple double-cell immune dynamics model, and the Varela immune network model.

In this chapter, a kind of immune algorithm named immune programming is used for image processing. The test results show that immune programming is a feasible and effective image segmentation algorithm.

A framework of a hardware immune system for the error detection of MC8051 IP core is designed in this chapter. The system designed in this chapter is implemented on an FPGA development board and the results are given as waveforms of the implemented circuit.

Section II
Natural Computing

Section II.I
Evolutionary Computing

Different classes of evolutionary automata (evolutionary finite automata, evolutionary Turing machines and evolutionary inductive Turing machines) are introduced and studied. It is demonstrated that evolutionary algorithms are more expressive than conventional recursive algorithms, such as Turing machines. Expressiveness and generality of the introduced classes of evolutionary automata are investigated.

Chapter XVII

This chapter presents an evolutionary approach utilizing both fuzzy logic and GAs that provides both path and trajectory planning. It has the advantage of considering diverse terrain conditions when determining the optimal path. The terrain conditions are modeled using fuzzy linguistic variables. The method is robust, allowing the robot to adapt to dynamic the environment.

Section II.II
Ant Colony

Chapter XVIII

The aim of this chapter is to provide the reader with a Content Based Image Retrieval (CBIR) system which incorporates AI through ant colony optimization and fuzzy logic. In order to speed up the whole process, the designed algorithm is implemented by hardware and hardware implmentation analysis of thw whole system is provided.

Chapter XIX

The chapter concentrates on the use of ant-inspired swarm intelligence in data mining. It focuses on the problem of medical data clustering. Important applications and results recently achieved are provided.

Section II.III
Artificial Life, Optimizing Society, and Ethology

Chapter XX

This chapter describes a hybrid artificial life optimization algorithm (ALRT) based on emergent colonization to compute the solutions of global function optimization problem. It focuses on the searching for the optimum solution in the location of emergent colonies and can achieve more accurate global optimum. The optimized results are compared with those of genetic algorithm and successive quadratic programming to identify the optimizing ability.

A novel binary optimization technique called Social Impact Theory based Optimizer (SITO), is introduced, which is based on social psychology model of social interactions. It tries to demonstrate different aspects of the SITO's behavior and to give some suggestions for potential users.

The problem considered in this chapter is how the observed behaviour of organisms provides a basis for machine learning. The proposed approach to machine learning leads to novel forms of the well-known Q-learning algorithm. It proposes a complete framework for an ethology-based study of approximate adaptive learning.

Section II.IV
Parallel Computing and Neural Networks

Nature Inspired Parallel Computing(NIPC) is proposed and used for designing virtual city. NIPC is inspired by some parallel phenomena of nature. NIPC is designed and used based on four dimensions. The four dimensions can be organized into different decomposition and communication schemes of NIPC. The architecture of NIPC is given in the chapter and its performance is illustrated by many examples.

This chapter is focused on the new ways of fuzzy neural networks construction and its application based on the existing achievement of this field. Four types of fuzzy chaotic neural networks are introduced. The new established self-evolution fuzzy neural network can work under two kind of active statuses and complete different functions.

Foreword

As a relatively new research field in computer science and engineering, natural computing (NC) deals with intelligent methods inspired from nature, especially biological and physical systems, and has made great progress in both theory and applications over recent years, as evidenced by the large number of publications in books, journals, and conferences. In particular, the joint International Conference on Natural Computation (ICNC) and the International Conference on Fuzzy Systems and Knowledge Discovery (FSKD), which I founded in 2005, has been attracting over 3,000 submissions world-wide every year since the very beginning. New ideas and methods continue to emerge.

The artificial immune system (AIS) is a new branch within NC. Professor Hongwei Mo, the Editor of the present book, has previously published two books on the AIS (in Chinese). What is different in the present book is that he combines the AIS with other NC methods by cooperating with experts in NC from different countries and the present book is published as a handbook, thereby providing a good tool for NC researchers.

The book is divided into two parts. The first part is a collection of achievements from researchers, some being quite famous, mainly on AIS theory and applications in optimization, agent, scheduling, data processing, spatio-temporal, internet, image processing, and control. It embodies the richness of AIS research, such as internet and control theory inspired by the immune network and immune multi-objective optimization algorithms, with characteristics which are different from other NC methods. In the second part, many kinds of nature inspired computing methods or theories are presented, including evolutionary computing, ant colony, artificial life, social theory, ethology, nature-inspired parallel computing, and artificial neural networks. Applications of these methods are mainly on optimization. This part shows how diverse nature phenomena have inspired researchers to develop theories and methods for solving engineering problems.

These research results will help readers not only understand many approaches in the AIS and other NC methods, but also compare the AIS with other NC methods.

In conclusion, it is a good book full of new ideas and recent developments in NC, especially the AIS. It should motivate researchers to cultivate new theories and methods, and thus advance the field even further. The book can also arouse beginners' interests and bring many young minds into this field.

Lipo Wang
August 2008
Singapore

Lipo Wang *received a BS degree from the National University of Defense Technology (China) in 1983 and a PhD from Louisiana State University (USA) in 1988. In 1989, he worked at Stanford University as a postdoctoral fellow. In 1990, he was a faculty member in the Department of Electrical Engineering, University College, ADFA, University of New South Wales (Australia). From 1991 to 1993 he was on the staff of the Laboratory of Adaptive Systems, National Institutes of Health (USA). From 1994 to 1997 he was a tenured faculty member in computing at Deakin University (Australia). Since*

1998, he has been associate professor at the School of Electrical and Electronic Engineering, Nanyang Technological University (Singapore). Wang's research interest is in natural computation with applications to data mining, bioinformatics, multimedia, and optimization. He has published over 200 papers in journals and conferences. He holds a U.S. patent in neural networks. Dr. Wang has authored two monographs and edited 20 books. He was keynote/plenary/panel speaker for several international conferences. Dr. Wang is associate editor for IEEE Transactions on Neural Networks *(since 2002),* IEEE Transactions on Evolutionary Computation *(since 2003),* IEEE Transactions on Knowledge and Data Engineering *(since 2005). He is area editor of the* Soft Computing *journal (since 2002). He serves on the editorial board of 12 additional international journals and was on the editorial board of three other journals. Dr. Wang was vice president for technical activities (2006-2007) and chair of the Emergent Technologies Technical Committee (2004-2005), IEEE Computational Intelligence Society. He has been on the governing board of the Asia-Pacific Neural Network Assembly (APNNA) since 1999 and served as its president in 2002/2003. He won the 2007 APNNA Excellent Service Award. He was founding chair of both the IEEE Engineering in Medicine and Biology Chapter Singapore and IEEE Computational Intelligence Chapter Singapore. Dr. Wang serves/served as general/program/steering committee chair for 15 international conferences and as a member of steering/advisory/organizing/program committees of over 150 international conferences.*

Preface

Today, no one will doubt that nature is the teacher of human beings. Nature is now being used as a source of inspiration or metaphor for the development of new techniques for solving complex problems in various domains, from engineering to biology; and new material and means with which to compute are currently being investigated. We have developed many kinds of technologies, theories, and methods inspired by nature. And then we use them to change the world and become more adapt to it. In one word, not only have we got sources and food from nature, but also ideas and thought.

Natural computing (NC) or nature inspired computing (NIC) is such a kind of technology. Of course, there are series of theories and methods relating to it. As we know, NC was developed with artificial intelligence, because genetic algorithm, artificial neural network, fuzzy theories, which are classical methods of NC, were developed with AI. Now they are called biologically inspired computing (BIC), which is an important type of NC. The other kinds of NC are social inspired NC, physical inspired computing and chemical inspired computing. Most methods of NC belong to BIC. Besides the classical ones, there are so many kinds of BIC developed today, such as DNA Computing, Membrane Computing, Bacterial Computing, Ant Colony, Swarm Intelligence, and Artificial Immune System (AIS), which is also one of the main topics of this book. So, here we can see that AIS is also a part of NC. That is why we can discuss NC and AIS in one book.

Artificial immune systems are adaptive systems inspired by theoretical immunology and observed immune functions, principles, and models, which are applied to complex problem domains; they are relatively recent examples of using the real world as computational inspiration. Immune system, particularly a human being's immune system, is a very complex system, so it has many special characteristics and physiology processes which the other biology systems do not own, such as recognizing virus by pattern, keeping memory by immune cells, learning by responding to invaders, clone selection, negative selection, and so on.

In the past ten years, researchers from different fields have investigated immune system from different angles for different aims. In the field of computer science, we mainly focus on the computational ability of it.

In addition to obvious security metaphor, many other application areas of AIS have been developed, including anomaly detection, optimization, fault tolerance, machine learning, data mining, automation control, Internet, and so on. Although AIS do not break all the classic computational paradigms, for example, they do not use concepts from quantum physics, they do challenge some of the major paradigms. That is why they are worthy to be researched.

As a whole, AIS is one of a whole array of novel approaches for computation. In fact, these separate areas are not independent. Rather, their results and insights should provide valuable groundwork for the overarching challenge. Thus they are to produce a fully mature science of all forms of computation unifying the classical and non-classical computing paradigms.

THE OVERALL OBJECTIVE OF THE BOOK

First, it is a good reference book for researchers in the field of NC because it provides latest empirical researching achievements for them. They can learn the main developing tendency, ideas, methods, and technologies of AIS.

Second, it will make the research of the field be more active and absorb much more attention. Because AIS is a relative new research direction in the field of NC, this book will enhance the position of AIS in the field of NC or biologically inspired computing (BIC). It will enhance many more applications of AIS in the near future. It makes researchers learn that in the field of AIS, immune system should not only be used as metaphor for solving computer security or designing optimization algorithms based on clonal selection theory and immune network theory from immunology. It has many potential abilities to be developed, such as its detecting ability and distinct ways of information processing relative to brain. And the applications of AIS could extend to many broad fields besides security, optimization, such as Internet, control, forecast, and so on. Many more theories should be paid attention to for their long-term developing.

Third, as comparison, people can also learn more about the other paradigms of NC in the same book because immune system is only one kind of inspiration source. Researchers can understand the main differences among those different inspiration sources and where they are adaptive to respectively. It is written for professionals who want to improve their understanding of the strategic role of NC in different fields. What is more important, it can be seen that the inspiration resources of NC are so diverse, that is why NC has had such a strong living ability for so many years. Based on these, it can inspire more researchers to develop advanced technologies or theories to solve practice problems. This is the main objective of the handbook.

THE TARGET AUDIENCE

The contents of this book will be attractive for graduate students, doctoral candidates, lecturers, academic or professionals, researchers and industry parties in biology, computing, engineering, computer science, artificial intelligence, information technology, especially those who are interested in developing and applying alternative problem solving techniques inspired by immune system, and also the other ways inspired by biology or nature.

INTRODUCTION

The book is mainly divided into two section: The first one is mainly on AIS. Some new ideas, methods are proposed by using metaphor or mechanisms of immune system to solve problems of engineering and science. After reading this part, the readers can know recent applications of AIS in different fields, so they can open their mind much more broadly. There are 15 chapters in this section.

The first three chapters focus on the application of optimization of AIS.

Chapter I is a review of multi-objective optimization (MOP) with AIS (MOAIS). This chapter provides a thorough review of the literature on MOAIS algorithms based on the emulation of the immune system for the readers who are interested in this topic. MOP had been given much more attention in recent years. Many different methods had been designed to solve many types of problems of MOP, such as evolutionary algorithm, neural networks and so on. The algorithms of MOAIS were also used for MOP problems recently and showed their strengths or weaknesses in solving these problems. There are roughly 17 algorithms of MOAIS reviewed in this chapter. Most of them are from the papers before 2007.

The multi-objective immune system algorithm (MISA) is considered the real first proposal of MOAIS. After it, many different algorithms of MOAIS were developed, most of which are based on the two main theories of immunology: clonal selection theory and immune network theory.

In this review, we can learn that MOAIS has four features, including elitism, adaptive population, clone size, and memory. Algorithms of MOAIS are designed distinctly based on these common features to adapt to their concrete tasks. They had been applied to power systems, electromagnetism, computer science, biomedicine, control theory, networking, and so on. Although some comparison work proved that neither MOAIS performs better nor is it inferior to the other kinds of MOP, for any class of problems, and such results sounds to be frustration to our researchers, just as the author said, these considerations opens the research trends to study if there is a class of problems which is well suited to be solved by immune inspired algorithms.

Chapter II tells us a new algorithm of MOAIS and its engineering applications in practice. A population adaptive based immune algorithm (PAIA) and its modified version for MOP are put forward and tested in this chapter. In this chapter, at first, it reviews previous research work about single and multi-objective optimization of the existing immune algorithms. Then, the drawbacks of immune algorithms are analyzed, and also those of the other evolutionary algorithms and the modified PAIA are compared with many important evolutionary algorithms on ZDT and DTLZ test suites. Based on the comparison research work, it presents a general framework from the modified PAIA.

In fact, the main contribution of the new algorithm is that it adapts a multi-stage optimization procedure, which reduces the number of evaluation significantly. The algorithm has its own strengths, including adaptive population, good jumping-off point, good and fast convergence, which make it compete with EA. And what is more important, the proposed algorithm is used to solve a real engineering problem. The results show that it is efficient in real application. So far, since the real applications of MOAIS are few, we are pleased to see in the chapter that it proves that the algorithm of MOAIS can be useful in some real problems.

Chapter III tells us a new kind of optimization algorithm called population-based artificial immune dynamical system(PAIS). But it is not for MOP. It is mainly for solving the problems of numerical optimization(NO). Some general descriptions of reaction rules including the set of clonal selection rules and the set of immune memory rules are introduced in PAIS. Thus, a general model of AIS, which models the dynamic process of human immune response and is particularly used for NO, is established. Based on the model, a dynamic algorithm, termed as PAISA, is designed for solving NO problems. The performance of PAISA is tested on nine benchmark functions with 20 to 10000 dimensions and a practical optimization problem, optimal approximation of linear systems, successively. The experiment results indicate that PAISA is good at optimizing some benchmark functions and practical optimization problems, especially large search space problems.

The main contribution of this chapter lies in that it proposes a general model combing the main mechanisms of immune system and then designs dynamic algorithm to solve problem. Based on the model or a platform, many different algorithms for NO can be proposed. And its validation experiments are very sound relative to the other similar researches. This chapter also proves that AIS can solve practice problem of optimization, and embodies the strength of immune-inspired dynamic algorithm.

So till now, we can see that algorithms of AIS can be used to solve optimization problems, though there are some disadvantages waiting for being improved, at least, it is proved by so much hard work that immune optimization algorithms has become an important and competitive branch in the field of NC. But it is clear that the applications of AIS are not limited to optimization since there are so many problems from the other fields waiting for being solved. So, let us see another important application aspect of AIS, that is, Agent, which is a well known field in computer science. The following three chapters are mainly on AIS and Agent.

In Chapter IV, the authors tell us an interesting game solving plan by using immune inspired algorithm. Basically, it is interesting because a classical problem of multi-agent encounters-pursuit-evasion problems is researched, and the immune system is considered as a multi-agent system. Then, some parallel relation can be established between the two different systems. There are two kinds of pursuit-evasion problems—two player and multi-player. The immune approach is used for the both. In the problem, the interactions between a pursuer and an evader are modeled by those between an antigen and an antibody. And the interactions between antibodies help choose more and the most suitable pursuer. The well known clonal selection algorithm(CSA) is extended to Multi-Agent Immune System Algorithm(MISA) for solving the problem. It is scalability and can be on-line learning, resistance to errors.

The simulation results show that MISA outperforms the other solution both in a number of training epochs and the number of steps, necessary for the goal achievement.

The main contribution of the chapter is that it uses the paradigm of reinforcement learning method in the proposed immune algorithm. And it can solve the complex problem combining with game theory. Although there is no sound theoretic explanation of the approach, just as the authors say: it seems that bridging a gap between traditional, mathematically motivated models and novel, unconventional paradigms can be very fruitful for both parties, producing a kind of stimulating feedback.

Chapter V is a detail review about artificial immune systems and agents. In fact, AIS had been used in the field of Agents for many years (since middle 90's in last century). Most of the work focused on robotic applications. The chapter briefly introduces the background of AIS applied in robotics from the angle of view of single and multi-agent. Then, some single and multi-agent systems based on the principles of immunology and applied in robotics are introduced in detail, including artificial immune network based cooperative control in collective autonomous mobile robots, AIS based multilayered cognitive model for autonomous navigation, AIS based cooperative strategies for robot soccer competition, AIS for a multi-agent robotics system, AIS based intelligent multi-agent model and its applications to a mine detection problem, idiotypic immune network for mobile robot control, a gait acquisition of a 6-legged robot using immune networks, and the application of a dendritic cell algorithm to a robotic classifier. At last, two projects implementing immune inspired multi-agent systems are presented.

We can see that most of the work is usually based on the adaptive immune response characteristics, especially the idiotypic immune networks or immune network theory, the innate immune response has been neglected and there is not much work where innate metaphors are used as inspiration source to develop multi-agent robotic systems.

The contribution of the chapter is that it shows a relative full picture of AIS applied in the field of Agent. And the immune network theory plays an important role in these applications. It is mainly because immune system has basic features of agent. Immune cells are active agents. It is relative easy to make a connection between immune system and agents. But what is disappointed is that there is no general theory about immune agent proposed till now.

Now we turn to another topic to which AIS is applied. As we know, scheduling is a kind of general problem in engineering. Chapter VI proposes an immune algorithm based robust scheduling method to solve uncertain scheduling problem. The model of workflow simulation scheduling is used to model uncertain scheduling problem. In fact, it is a complex optimization problem to find an optimal robust scheduling scheme. A workflow simulation can be executed by using a workflow model. A variable neighborhood immune algorithm(VNIA) is proposed to find the optimal robust scheduling scheme. The VNIA is based on the immune network theory and uses variable neighborhood strategy to balance the conflict of local and global searches. A two-level immune network is designed to maintain a large diversity of populations during the optimization process.

It is compared with definitive scheduling schemes on 4 problems.. Experimental results show that the method is very effective for generating a robust scheduling scheme and has satisfactory performances under uncertain scheduling environments.

The contribution of the chapter is that it succeeds in solving uncertain scheduling problem by immune inspired method.

In Chapter VII, another important scheduling problem--the management of complex small scale cogeneration systems is solved by immune algorithm.

The energy management problem is called the Combined Heat and Power(CHP). Such a problem is to minimize the management costs of power system and fulfill all loads requirements. It is defined as a scheduling period (e.g. one day, one week etc.) with loads, costs, fares changing.

In the chapter, after describing the classical formulation of energy management problem in complex energy nodes, it uses the classical clonal selection algorithm to solve the problem. The problem is coded by binary. And special immune mutation operator is designed to generate feasible solutions. The modified immune algorithm is called artificial immune system-linear programming (AIS-LP). It is compared with mixed integer linear programming (MILP) on a simple but effective energy management problem. The result shows that AIS can efficiently solve such problem.

The contribution of the chapter lies in modifying existing immune algorithm to be adaptive to new problem and get relative good result.

These two chapters let us see that immune inspired algorithms, either new developed ones or existing ones, can be used to solve the complex scheduling problems. Of course, all of them must be specific to problem being solved.

In the following two chapters, we learn something about AIS used for data mining or information retrieval.

Document clustering is a common problem in the field of data mining. In Chapter VIII, it uses the modified aiNet to solve the problem of document clustering. In the background, it introduces a method named document map and a research project BEATCA, which is a fully-fledged search engine capable of representing on-line replies to queries in graphical form on a document map.

After that, it introduces how to use aiNet to realize document clustering. The initialization of immune network is the first important step, which starts from random document drawn. The other improvements include robust constructing antibodies by new mutation approach, defining time-dependent parameters to stabilize the size of memory M, and global research replaced by modified local research to find robust antibodies. For the performance validation, it focused more on the structural properties of the immune network obtained and the impact of initialization strategies on document clustering. And some meaningful results are observed.

The contribution of the chapter is that it proposes some effective strategies to modify aiNet to be adaptive to the problem of document clustering, and it is combined with many technologies, such as document map, visualization, to solve the problem. And the modified aiNet for document clustering is computational savings as well as the resulting slow evolution of clusters compared to the alternative "from scratch".

In Chapter IX, an important topic of pattern recognition-feature selection, which is also an important step in data mining, is discussed. Clonal selection algorithm, which is an important and representative algorithm, is used to solve this problem. In order to solve feature selection problem, an antibody represents a given feature subset and a binary bit denoted the presence or absence of the feature at the corresponding location. The affinity function takes both the separability and the dimension of feature subset into consideration. New clonal operators, including clonal proliferation, affinity maturation, clonal selection are implemented.

The algorithm is tested by three different ways. The first one is datasets from UCI repository. The second one is brodatz textures classification, the last one is SAR image classification. All of these test results prove the good performance in solving the problem of feature selection.

The contribution of the chapter lies in that the clonal selection algorithm is used for feature selection and tested on real problem. It testifies that clonal selection algorithm, with the characteristics of local optimization and global searching, is a good choice for finding an optimal feature subset for classifier. Of course, this algorithm had been developed into many different versions and used for different tasks.

As we have seen, most of the algorithms of AIS solving engineering problems in the above chapters are based on a few immune algorithm developed earlier, such as aiNet and clonal selection algorithm. But AIS should be limited here. In the following four chapters, we can some different immune inspired methods to solve more broad problems.

In Chapter X, the researchers propose immune based bio-network architecture. It is inspired by the resemble features between the immune systems and future Internet, and uses some key principles and mechanisms of the immune systems to design a bio-network architecture to address the challenges of future Internet. In such architecture, network resources are represented by various bio-entities, while complex services and application can be emerged from the interactions among bio-entities. The authors designs a bio-network simulation platform with the capability of service emergence, evolution etc. It can be used to simulate some complex services and applications for Internet or distributed network. Two immune network computation models, mutual-coupled immune network model and immune symmetrical network model, are developed to generate the emergent services through computer simulation experiments on the platform. They are used to simulate web service simulator and peer to peer service model respectively. The feasibility of the two models is demonstrated through computer simulation experiments on the platform.

The main contribution of the chapter lies in that the researchers design two new immune network models inspired by immunology theories and use them to address the challenges from Internet. It let us believe in that classical immune network theory is not the only choice for inspiring or solving engineering problems. There should be more new ideas inspired by immune system.

Chapter XI is more interesting than the chapters above because of the problem in it. It is not solved by existing immune algorithms. But a new algorithm based on mathematical models of immuncomputing. In the chapter, the key model is the formal immune network (FIN) including apoptosis (programmed cell death) and immunization both controlled by cytokines (messenger proteins). It is used for spatio-temporal forecast (STF). For the task, FIN can be formed from raw signal using discrete tree transform (DTT), singular value decomposition (SVD). The performance of the model is demonstrated on real application, that is, data of space monitoring of the Caspian, Black, and Barents Sea. And it gets surprising results by using this model.

The contribution of the chapter is great. One hand, the work in the chapter makes AIS application extend to the field of forecast in practice. On the other hand, what is more important, the work is based on a relative complete mathematic theory of AIS, named immunocomputing, which was proposed by the author. The core of theory is the model of FIN. Although it is not new to researchers in the field of AIS, it is deserved to be paid attention to.

As we know, one of the disadvantages of AIS is that it has no general theory itself. Immunocomputing brings promise to us.

In Chapter XII, the mechanisms of immune system are used for controller, which is important component in control system. It is not surprised that immune based controller can be developed out because similar ideas and technologies inspired by biology exist for a long time, for example neural network.

In the chapter, three kinds of artificial immune controller are researched. The first one is based on the principle of T cells and B cells immunity. The second one is based on a simple double-cell immune dynamics model. And the third one is based on varela immune network model, which is a famous model in the field of theory immunology.

All of them are verified by simulations. At last, the authors propose a general structure of artificial immune controller based on the comparison results of the three controllers.

AIS had been used in field of automation control for a long time. But the earlier researches mainly focused on using immune algorithm to optimize classical PID controller. So the contribution of the chapter lies in that the mechanisms and theories of immunology are used to the design new type of controllers. Not only does the research bring fresh thought to the field of control theory, but also broad mind and new research content to the field of AIS.

In Chapter XIII, a kind of immune algorithm--immune programming is applied in image segmentation. It combines immune mechanism with that of evolution to form a global optimization algorithm. Two types of IP algorithms, the immune image threshold segmentation algorithm based on the maximum information entropy theory and the immune image segmentation algorithm based on the expense function minimization, are proposed in the chapter. All of them are tested on image segmentation. And the results show that IP can retain the image details perfectly.

The main contribution of the chapter is that it proposes two types of IP algorithm to solve the problem of image processing. It proves that IP can be used as a new tool for image processing.

The research content of Chapter XIV is different from that of any chapter above. All of the researches above are realized by computer programming or simulation. They can be seen as software artificial immune systems in general meaning. While in this chapter, a kind of hardware immune system for MC8051 IP Core is developed out.

A framework of a hardware immune system is designed and used for the error detection of MC8051 IP core.

The principle of negative selection, which is an important mechanism keeping health of body, is realized in the design. The normal state of MC8051 is collected as self set and detectors are generated by negative selection algorithm. After this phase, the error of the system can be detected.

The system designed in this chapter is tested on an FPGA development board and the detail hardware system including circuits is shown. The experiment results are given as waveforms of the implemented circuit.

Although a few kinds of hardware immune systems are designed in recent years, more attention should paid to them. Immunotronics had been an important concept and research topic in the field of AIS. The contribution of this chapter is that the hardware immune system is used detecting errors of hardware system in practice. It is still a system with simple functions, but it will be improved in further and play more important role in similar task.

As we can see, the researches in chapters above are mainly for real engineering applications, while Chapter XV proposes a general platform of AIS. A Static Web Immune System(SWIS) is presented in it. It can also be looked as an important application of artificial immune system. According to the chapter, on the static web system, a normal model is proposed with the space property and the time property of each component, in order to identify the normal state of the system that the artificial immune system protects. There are three tiers, including the innate immune tier, the adaptive immune tier and the parallel immune tier, which are inspired by immune system. Such a system can be used as a general tool or platform to execute the task of detecting abnormal states of systems. It is useful for both theories and applications.

The contribution of the chapter is that it presents a general platform inspired by immune system and can be used for theories and applications researches. Such work can promote the development of AIS.

AIS is only one of a whole array of NC available. The second section is mainly on the other methods of natural computing.

Chapter XVI focuses on the mathematical foundation of evolutionary computation based on an evolutionary automata approach. Three classes of evolutionary automata, including evolutionary finite automata, evolutionary

Turing machines and evolutionary inductive Turing machines, are studied. And they are proved to have universal automata—evolutionary automata(EA). An important property of evolutionary automata is their expressiveness. Based on the models, universal evolutionary algorithms and automata are proposed. All four basic kinds of evolutionary computation, including GA,ES, EP and GP, can be modeled by it.

The contribution of the chapter is that it proposes a new theory of evolutionary computation with sound mathematics foundation, which is meaningful to this field. And it also provides means to study many important evolutionary algorithms because the EA approach is very general and allows one to capture all currently known areas of evolutionary computation. The potential ability of this approach is so big that it will allow one to accommodate future areas of evolutionary computation as well, including algorithms of AIS.

Optimal motion planning is critical for the successful operation of an autonomous mobile robot. In Chapter XVII, it proposes a concrete application of evolutionary algorithm (EA)--genetic algorithm--for this problem. It is an evolutionary path planning for robot navigation under varying terrain conditions. It has the advantages of dealing with diverse terrain conditions when determining the optimal path. The key point of the method is that it combines GA with fuzzy logic. The later is used to model terrain conditions. The simulation results show that this method is robust and makes the robot adapt to environment where conditions are dynamic.

The contribution of the chapter is that the proposed genetic algorithm can make the autonomous objects deal with dynamic environment robustly. And in fact, it is a kind of hybrid algorithm for using fuzzy linguistic variables.

The two chapters discussed above are mainly on evolutionary algorithm. The following chapters turns to another important method of BIC-Ant Colony Optimization(ACO).

In Chapter XVIII, ACO is used for content based image retrieval. Similar to Chapter XVII, it is also a hybrid method, which combines ACO with fuzzy logic. It has two stages to deal with problem. In this first stage of the algorithm, a comparison is performed using all the bins of the three features, that is, the whole population of the ants, and an initial ranking of the images takes place. The second stage is initiated after classifying image database. The experiment results prove that it is a more efficient means compared to popular and contemporary methods. In order to speed up the process, hardware implementation analysis of the whole system is designed and analyzed. The increase in speed is phenomenal.

The main contribution of the chapter is that it deals with image processing by ACO and fuzzy logic and get better results. What is more important and meaningful, hardware system is designed for speeding up processing. Similar work is few to see in the applications of NC.

In Chapter XIX, Ant Colony is applied in the field of data mining. It focuses on the problem of medical data clustering. After introducing some basic concepts of data mining and ant colony, it presents a clustering method based on ant colony for processing biomedical data- electrocardiogram. The method is called ACO DTree, because ACO works with classifier trees—decision tree(DT) like structure. Creation of the trees is driven by a pheromone matrix, which uses the ACO paradigm, while DT is evolved by PSO and the fittest one is selected as classifier. The data are divided into subgroups having similar properties and the classes are different. It thus finishes the task of clustering data. This method is compared with the other nature inspired methods and some classical methods. It is comparable to them.

The main contribution of the chapter is that it proposes a hybrid method of NC to solve clustering problem. This chapter and the chapters above inspire us that single method of NC may not be enough to deal with some complex problem. Hybrid one may be a good choice according to different problems.

In Chapter XX, a well known and interesting NC method is introduced and used for optimization. It is a hybrid artificial life optimization algorithm (ALRT) based on emergent colonization. In this method, the emergent colony is a fundamental mechanism for searching the optimum solution. It can be formed by the metabolism, movement and reproduction among artificial organisms appearing at the optimum locations in the artificial world. In this case, the optimum locations mean the optimum solutions of the optimized problem. Thus, the ALRT can search the location of emergent colonies and achieve more accurate global optimum. The experiment results are compared with those of genetic algorithm and successive quadratic programming and show the optimizing ability of ALRT.

The main contribution of this chapter is that it uses hybrid AL method to solve optimization problem. Its idea is fresh because AL is known to be an important research field of NC, not a optimizing method.

If it is not enough, the ideas of following two chapters give us more surprises.

In Chapter XXI, a new method of optimization—so called Social Impact Theory based Optimizer—SITO—is presented. It is a kind of optimizer based on the social impact theory.

The main source of inspiration for SITO comes from the models of social interactions. The individuals or agents participating social activity forms an artificial society. The individuals are scattered over a grid defining their environment. Each individual changes their properties based on some rules involving the individual's neighborhood. Each individual is represented by four parameters: the individual's attitude, two indicators of strength (persuasiveness and supportiveness) and the individual's location in the social structure. It is used to binary optimization problems. The experiment results show that the new optimizing technology is valid.

The main contribution of the chapter is that it presents a social-psychology-inspired, stochastic and population based method, SITO algorithm, which can be used for optimization of generally non-linear, multimodal and analytically, unoptimizable binary functions. It brings fresh technology for the field of optimization and also the field of NC.

In Chapter XXII, a machine learning technology- ethology-based approximate adaptive learning is proposed. Ethology-based form of machine learning is presented by the author before. Fundamental to the proposed approach to adaptive learning is the notion of perception. Near sets is a theory which can be used to solve the problem of ethology-based machine learning. It can be viewed as an extension of rough set. A near set approach approximating the sets of behaviours of organisms forms the basis for approximating adaptive learning. The principles of near set and adaptive learning are given in detail in the chapter.

Adaptive learning algorithms are used in the simulation of the behaviour of a single species of fish. The results show that short-term memory model provides an efficacious basis of for adaptive learning.

The contribution of this chapter is that a complete framework for an ethology-based study of approximate adaptive learning is proposed. And it acquires some interesting results from the simulation.

Parallel computing becomes more and more important for science and engineer because the problems faced by people become more and more complex. Nature has prepared such paradigms for us. In Chapter XXIII, Nature Inspired Parallel Computing (NIPC) is proposed. The parallelism mainly exists in five dimensions including horizontal, vertical, application, time, and user. The four dimensions can be organized into different decomposition and communication schemes of NIPC.

Four schemes of NIPC are introduced in detail. Based on these schemes, the architecture of NIPC is constructed and composed of four layers, corresponding to the four schemes. It is also tested on three examples.

NIPC is tested on three examples, such as detecting illegal buildings in a city and so on The results show that it can speed up the generation and simulation of digital city.

The contribution of the chapter is that the working way of NIPC regards parallel computing just as a simulation of the parallel way in nature based on computing technology and electronic information technology. Such a new nature inspired parallel computing can promote the efficiency of parallel programming and parallel applications.

The last chapter is also a hybrid NC method—fuzzy chaotic neural networks, which integrates fuzzy logic, chaotic, neural network in one model. It tries to mimic the function of brain to design new kind of neural network. Four types of fuzzy chaotic neural networks are introduced, including chaotic recurrent fuzzy neural networks, cooperation fuzzy chaotic neural networks, fuzzy number chaotic neural networks and self-evolution fuzzy chaotic neural networks. Analysis to them shows that fuzzy number chaotic neuron not only has fuzzy number but also chaos characteristic. Such neurons can be used to construct fuzzy number chaotic neural networks. At last, a self-evolution fuzzy chaotic neural network is proposed according to the principle of self-evolution network. It unifies the fuzzy Hopfield neural network constitution method. The new model can work under two kind of active statuses and complete different function.

The main contribution of the chapter is that it establishes a series of new neural network models, which have some new characteristics and may be used to tackle more complex problem.

So far, we can see that AIS has some characteristics which are different from the other methods, for example, it has many inspiration sources, like the mechanisms of it, and theories from immunology. All of them can inspire researchers to develop new algorithms for different tasks. While the inspiration source of the other NC methods is single. And readers can compare the backgrounds and performances of different NC methods through the excellent researching work in the book, especially the applications of AIS and other methods, for example, in the field of optimizations. In the aspect of applications, AIS can be used for many different fields, as we have seen in the chapters, but not limited to them, while most of the other NC methods can mainly be used in optimization, except neural networks. Note that the book doesn't cover all kinds of NC methods, such as DNA computing, membrane computing, and also the other excellent research work..

So, we hope the book brings some new and fresh ideas to the readers.

For the editing of the book, I must acknowledge the following people:

All the authors join in the book, sorry for not listing them one by one here. You can see them in each chapter. And especially those who I have never seen before, most of them are from outside of China. All of them have a warm heart, serious attitude and are patient to join the hard work for one and a half year. And all the authors from China, thanks for their supporting very much!

I must thank all IGI Global staff for their great work in publishing the book, particular thanks go to Rebecca Beistline, Christine Bufton, Jeff Ash, and Jamie Snavely. And I must say thank to my teacher, Prof. Yao Sun, who always supports me in so many years since I become a teacher and always encourage me to challenge myself. And also Prof. Lipo Wang, Prof. Licheng Jiao help me so much in editing the book.

At last, thanks to my parents, my wife and my lovely daughter!

Hongwei Mo
August 2008
Harbin, China

Section I
Artificial Immune Systems

Section 1.1
Immune Optimization Algorithms

The first three chapters of the book mainly focus on the applications of immune algorithm (IA) used in the field of multi-objective optimization. Many immune algorithms are developed to solve this problem. Some special characteristics make immune algorithms well suited for multi-objective optimization and be more adaptive to dynamic problem. Two kinds of immune algorithms-PAIA and PAIS demonstrate their validation by different experiments.

Chapter I
Multiobjective Optimization and Artificial Immune Systems:
A Review

Fabio Freschi
Politecnico di Tornio, Italy

Carlos A. Coello Coello
CINESTAV-IPN, Evolutionary Computation Group, Mexico

Maurizio Repetto
Politecnico di Tornio, Italy

ABSTRACT

This chapter aims to review the state of the art in algorithms of multiobjective optimization with artificial immune systems (MOAIS). As it will be focused in the chapter, Artificial Immune Systems (AIS) have some intrinsic characteristics which make them well suited as multiobjective optimization algorithms. Following this basic idea, different implementations have been proposed in the literature. This chapter aims to provide a thorough review of the literature on multiobjective optimization algorithms based on the emulation of the immune system.

INTRODUCTION

Many real world problems involve the simultaneous optimization of various and often conflicting objectives. Evolutionary algorithms seem to be the most attractive approaches for this class of problems, because they are usually population based techniques that can find multiple compromise solution in a single run, and they do not require any hypotheses on the objective functions (e.g. unimodality and convexity). Among other techniques, in the last decade a new paradigm based on the emulation of the immune system behaviour has been proposed. Since the pioneer works, many different implementations have been proposed in literatures. The aim of this chapter is to review the most significant works in this field, giving a common framework for classification and showing strengths and weaknesses of artificial immune systems metaphor in multiobjective optimization with respect to other bio-inspired algorithms.

Copyright © 2009, IGI Global, distributing in print or electronic forms without written permission of IGI Global is prohibited.

The chapter is structured as follows. Section 3 gives a background on the immune system and multiobjective optimization terminology used in the chapter. Section 4 explains the methodology used to select the reference list used for the review, while in section 5 the papers are reviewed according to their research field. Finally in Section 6 future and emerging trends in multiobjective optimization with artificial immune systems are drawn.

BACKGROUND

Immune System Overview

Our immune system has as its main task the detection of the infectious foreign elements (called pathogens) that attack us, and defend us from them (in other words, its main task is to keep our organism healthy). Examples of such pathogens are bacteria and viruses. Any molecule that can be recognized by our immune system is called antigen. Such antigens provoke a specific response from our immune system. Lymphocytes are a special type of cells that play a major role in our immune system. Two types of lymphocytes exist: B cells (or B lymphocytes) and T cells (or T lymphocytes). Upon detection of an antigen, the B cells that best recognize (i.e., match) the antigen are cloned. Some of these clones will be differentiated into plasma cells, which are the most active antibodies secretors, while others will act as memory cells. These cloned cells are subject to a high somatic mutation rate (normally called hypermutation) in order to increase their affinity level (i.e., their matching to the antigens). These mutations experienced by the clones are proportional to their affinity to the antigen. The highest affinity cloned cells experiment the lowest mutation rates, whereas the lowest affinity cloned cells have high mutation rates. Due to the random nature of this mutation process, some clones could be dangerous to the body and are, therefore, eliminated by the immune system itself. Plasma cells are capable of secreting only one type of antibody, which is relatively specific for the antigen. Antibodies play a key role in the immune response, since they are capable of adhering to the antigens, in order to neutralize and eliminate them.

These cloning and hypermutation processes are collectively known as the clonal selection principle. It is worth noting, however, that the immune response is certainly more complex than the above explanation, in which we only focused on the B cells, in order to keep our discussion very short.

Once the antigens have been eliminated by the antibodies, the immune system must return to its normal conditions, eliminating the in-excess cells. However, some cells remain in our blood stream acting as memory cells, so that our immune system can 'remember' the antigens that have previously attacked it. When the immune system is exposed again to the same type of antigen (or a similar one), these memory cells are activated, presenting a faster (and perhaps improved) response, which is called secondary response.

Based on the previous (oversimplified) explanation of the way in which our immune system works, we can say that, from a computer science perspective, the immune system can be seen as a parallel and distributed adaptive system. Clearly, the immune system is able to learn; it has memory, and is able of tasks such as associative retrieval of information. These features make immune systems very robust, fault tolerant, dynamic and adaptive. All of these properties make it very attractive to be emulated in a computer.

Artificial Immune Systems (AIS) are composed of the following basic elements:

- A representation for the components of the system (e.g., binary strings, vectors of real numbers, etc.).
- A set of mechanisms to evaluate the interaction of individuals with their environment and with each other. Such an environment is normally simulated through an affinity function, which is based on the objective function(s) in the case of optimization problems.
- Procedures of adaptation, that indicates the way in which the behavior of the system changes over time. These procedures of adaptation consist of, for example, mutation operators.

AIS are population-based meta-heuristics, and have been widely used for a wide variety of optimization and classification tasks.

Multiobjective Optimization

Multiobjective optimization refers to the simultaneous optimization of two or more objectives, which are normally in conflict with each other. Formally, we are interested in the solution of problems of the form:

$$\text{minimize} \left[f_1(\vec{x}), f_2(\vec{x}), \dots, f_k(\vec{x}) \right] \qquad (1.1)$$

subject to the m inequality constraints:

$$g_i(\vec{x}) \leq 0 \quad i = 1, 2, \dots, m \qquad (1.2)$$

and the p equality constraints:

$$h_i(\vec{x}) = 0 \quad i = 1, 2, \dots, p \qquad (1.3)$$

where k is the number of objective functions $f_i : \Re^n \to \Re$. We call $\vec{x} = [x_1, x_2, \dots, x_n]^T$ the vector of decision variables. We wish to determine from among the set F of all vectors which satisfy (1.2) and (1.3) the particular set of values $x_1^*, x_2^*, \dots, x_n^*$ which yield the best compromise solutions among all the objective functions.

Pareto Optimality

The most commonly notion of optimality adopted in multiobjective optimization is the so-called Pareto optimality (Pareto, 1896), which is the following:

We say that a vector of decision variables $\vec{x}^* \in F$ is Pareto optimal if there does not exist another $\vec{x} \in F$ such that $f_i(\vec{x}) \leq f(\vec{x}^*)$ for all $i = 1, \dots, k$ and $f_j(\vec{x}) < f(\vec{x}^*)$ for at least one j (assuming minimization).

In words, this definition says that $\vec{x}^*$ is Pareto optimal if there exists no feasible vector of decision variables $\vec{x} \in F$ which would decrease some criterion without causing a simultaneous increase in at least one other criterion. Unfortunately, this concept almost always gives not a single solution, but rather a set of solutions called the Pareto optimal set. The vectors $\vec{x}^*$ corresponding to the solutions included in the Pareto optimal set are called nondominated. The image of the Pareto optimal set under the objective functions is called Pareto front.

The aim in multiobjective optimization is to find the elements of the Pareto optimal set (normally, as many different elements, as possible). In the Operations Research literature, a number of mathematical programming techniques have been proposed to solve multiobjective optimization problems. However, such techniques normally require an initial point to trigger the search, and tend to produce a single element of the Pareto optimal set per run. Additionally, they are normally susceptible to the shape and continuity of the Pareto front. On the other hand, population-based metaheuristics (such as evolutionary algorithms and artificial immune systems), are less affected by the features of the Pareto front and can generate several elements of the Pareto optimal set in a single run, departing from a randomly generated population.

For a good motivation for multiobjective optimization and a thorough description of the multiobjective optimization algorithms cited in this chapter, the reader should refer to the suggested readings included at the end of the chapter. The bibliography is limited to the reviewed papers, only.

METHODOLOGY

The selection of reviewed papers has been done by accessing to Compendex and Inspect scientific databases, using as keywords

a)   multiobjective (or multi-objective) AND immun* (* is truncation wildcard),
b)   multiobjective (or multi-objective) AND clonal.

Only papers in English language published by December 2007 have been considered. In addition references from the EMOO repository (http://delta.cs.cinvestav.mx/~ccoello/EMOO) have been selected by searching with immune and clonal as keywords. Finally, results have been manually filtered to avoid false positive matching. The total number of reference found so far is 80. The distributions of the references by year and by category are shown in Figure 1 and Figure 2, respectively.

It is worth noting that the distribution by year of Figure 1, approximately reflects the same trend of the distribution of references on multiobjective optimization available on the EMOO repository, with a peak delay of one year (2005 EMOO repository, 2006 this work), testifying the more recent development of MOAIS with respect to other evolutionary multiobjective heuristics.

CLASSIFICATION

In the present analysis, references are classified by their research field (see Figure 3):

*   Survey papers (SUR): general reviews or review on some specific field
*   Algorithmic papers (ALG): papers describing the implementation of AIS for multiobjective optimization
*   Theoretical papers (THE): theoretical works on multiobjective AIS optimization
*   Papers on hybrid algorithms (HYB): propose hybridization of other heuristics by AIS
*   Application paper (APP): show the application of MOAIS to some specific topic
*   Analogy papers (ANA): show analogies between Artificial Immune System and other metaphors;

The reference list collects two PhD Theses (Chueh, 2004; Freschi, 2006) and one Master Thesis (Haag, 2007a).

Figure 1. Distribution of the references by year (MTH: Master thesis, PHD: PhD Thesis, CNF: Conference Paper, JNL: Journal Paper)

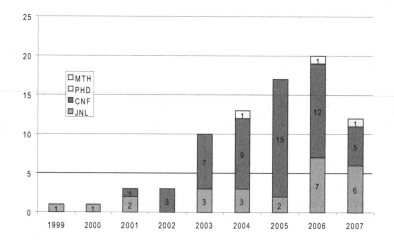

Figure 2. Distribution of the references by category (MTH: Master thesis, PHD: PhD Thesis, CNF: Conference Paper, JNL: Journal Paper)

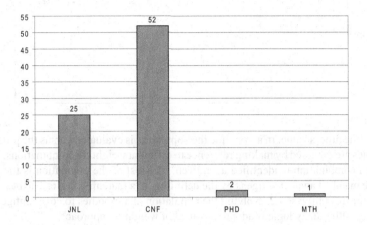

Figure 3. Distribution of references by application field (see text for abbreviations). Note that one paper may belong to different fields.

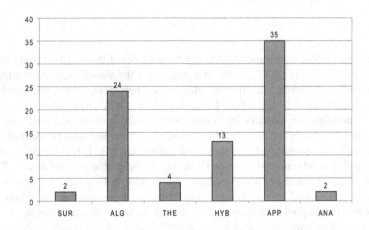

MOAIS Surveys

The work classifying the state of the art of MOAIS starts very recently. Two works only appear within the selected references. Campelo, Guimarães and Igarashi (2007) provided a common framework for the description and analysis of MOAIS, presenting canonical MOAIS algorithms from which other algorithms can be reviewed. Darmoul, Pierreval and Gabouj (2006) propose a more specific review reporting the use of single and MOAIS for scheduling problems. With respect to these interesting reviews, our work tries to take into account not only original MOAIS algorithms but also their different fields of application.

MOAIS Algorithms

The first direct use of the immune system for multiobjective optimization goes back to Yoo and Hajela (1999). In their work they use a standard genetic algorithm where the immune principle of antibody-antigen affinity is

Figure 4. Outline of the canonical MOAIS (Adapted from (Campelo, Guimarães, & Igarashi, 2007)

```
0.  define search space Ω, population size N, objectives and constraints
1.  initialize population
2.  initialize memory
3.  while stop criterion is not met
    a.      evaluate objectives and constraints
    b.      evaluate avidity (scalar index for ranking)
    c.      select clone set
    d.      cloning and mutation
    e.      suppression (diversity enforcement)
    f.      update population
    g.      update memory
```

employed to modify the fitness value. In a first time the population is evaluated versus the problem objectives and different scalar values are obtained by making reference to different weighting combinations. The best individual with respect to each combination is identified as antigen. The rest of the population is the pool of antibodies. Then antibodies are matched against antigens by the definition of a matching score. The best matching antibody fitness is added by this matching score, evolving the population of antibodies to cover antigens. In a subsequent work (Yoo & Hajela, 2001) fuzzy logic is adopted instead of weighting approach.

Besides the importance of pioneer work of Yoo and Hajela, their algorithm cannot be properly considered as a MOAIS.

For the following classification we adopt the common outline of the canonical MOAIS proposed in (Campelo, Guimarães, & Igarashi, 2007), reported in Figure 4.

MISA

The multiobjective immune system algorithm (MISA) can be considered the real first proposal of MOAIS in literature (Coello Coello & Cruz Cortés, 2002). In the first proposal of the algorithm, authors attempted to follow the clonal selection principle very closely, then the algorithm performances have been improved in a successive version (Cruz Cortés & Coello Coello 2003a, 2003b; Coello Coello & Cruz Cortés, 2005) sacrificing some of the biological metaphor. The population is encoded by binary strings and it is initialized randomly. The algorithm does not use explicitly a scalar index to define the avidity of a solution but some rules are defined for choosing the set of antibodies to be cloned. The ranking scheme uses the following criteria: 1) first feasible and nondominated individuals, then 2) infeasible nondominated individuals, finally 3) infeasible and dominated. The memory set (called secondary population) is updated by the nondominated feasible individuals. Because of this repository being limited in size, an adaptive grid is implemented to enforce a uniform distribution of nondominated solutions. The number of clones for the pool of best antibodies depends on the antibody-antibody affinity. These best antibodies are selected for a uniform mutation, with mutation probability proportional to antibody-antigen affinity, according to the ranking scheme previously described, while the remaining population undergoes a nonuniform mutation. Again, the ranking scheme is used as criterion to reduce the population to its original cardinality.

MOIA

Luh, Chueh & Liu (2003) develop the multiobjective immune algorithm (MOIA). In MOIA antibodies are encoded as binary strings with a distinction of light chains (least significant bits) and heavy chains (most significant bits). Objectives are evaluated and the rank index, which measures the dominance level, is defined. Nondominated antibodies are chosen for hypermutation, which takes place only in light chain, to ensure only local mutations. After this phase, nondominated cells are stored into memory. Suppression and generation of the new antibody population is a complex step in MOIA. Firstly a cumulative scalar index, named avidity, is evaluated as a product of antibody-antigen affinity (reciprocal of rank index) and antibody-antibody affinity (reciprocal of a distance measure). This combined index is used to select antibodies for the construction of germ-line DNA libraries, that requires also a predefined percentage of memory cells. Then, through a recombination/diversification stage the population for the next iteration is created.

Authors extend their work for handling constraints in a successive paper (Luh & Chueh, 2004). The problem is transformed into an unconstrained one by associating to each antibody an interleukine value. In biological processes interleukine can either stimulate or suppress the promotion of antibodies. In their in silicon experiments, the interlukine is a global index of constraint violation which is summed to the rank index.

MOCSA

Multiobjective clonal selection algorithm (MOCSA) is the real coded multiobjective version of clonalg (Campelo, Guimarães, Saldanha, Igarashi, Noguchi, Lowther & Ramirez, 2004). Antibodies are evaluated over the objectives and classified by a nondominated sorting, i.e. individuals are ranked into successive nondominated fronts. Then clones are generated for whole population; the number of clones for each antibody is inversely proportional to its ranking index. A random perturbation with fixed standard deviation is then added to clones, in order to locally explore the search space. The whole population of original antibodies and mutated clones is ranked in fronts and copied into memory. Then suppression is applied, according to a niching procedure in objective space. At each iteration s given percentage of randomly generated antibodies are allowed to replace the lower ranked antibodies, ensuring the maintenance of diversity in the population.

VIS

Freschi & Repetto (2005, 2006) extend the optimization ability of opt-aiNet to multiobjective problems. Their algorithm, named vector immune system (VIS), has two nested loops: the clonal selection stage is repeated a certain number of times, before evaluating interactions in the antibody network.

The scalar index is based on simple a Pareto ranking: avidity of each antibody is the number of antibody by which it is dominated. Since VIS deals with real coded variables, the hypermutation operator is obtained by a random perturbation with standard deviation that depends on the avidity value and it is adapted by the 1/5 success rule. The selection mechanism does not consider the whole population, but each time the best antibody among a parent and its progenies is selected. It is worth noting that in this stage a dominated solution has opportunities to evolve, preventing a faster convergence to local optimal fronts. Memory is updated at this stage by copying nondominated cells into memory. Diversity is enforced after a predefined number of cloning/selection steps into the memory pool, by evaluating antibody-antibody affinity in objective space and then removing most affine solutions from memory by using an adaptive suppression threshold. As in MOCSA, at each iteration a fixed number of newcomers is allowed to enter the population. In addition Authors suggest an original constraint handling technique which maintains the feasibility of solutions during mutation, which can be adopted any time the constraint evaluation is not time consuming.

IDCMA

The immune dominance clonal multiobjective algorithm (Jiao, Gong, Shang, Du & Lu, 2005) introduces the concept of immune differential degree as measure of antibody-antibody affinity. This index is used to reduce the size of nondominated antibodies in the memory before the cloning stage. One random antibody is selected from the memory and it is used to activate a new population of random antibodies generated at each iteration. These antibodies are sorted by their affinity with the activation antibody (based on the degree of matching bits in strings) and are split into two sets: dominance clonal antibody population and immune anergy antibody population. The former set undergoes to recombination and binary mutation and it is recombined with the latter set and to memory to provide the population for the next iteration. Since variables are coded as binary strings, the extension to combinatorial problems is straightforward and presented successively in Ma, Jiao, Gong & Liu (2005).

IFMOA

The same Authors of IDCMA propose the immune forgetting multiobjective optimization algorithm (IFMOA) (Lu, Jiao, Du & Gong, 2005) for problems with real variables. In this case avidity is a scalar index which contains both Pareto dominance and density information. Antibody-antigen affinity is measured by Pareto strength, as in the strength Pareto evolutionary approach, while antibody-antibody affinity is inversely proportional to the sum of two smallest Euclidean distances between an antibody and the rest of population. The immune forgetting operator is introduced to emulate the non activation of certain cells when exposed to antigens. Part of the evolved population is suppressed (according to the avidity value) and replaced by antibodies from the memory.

CSADMO/ICMOA

A further work of Shang, Jiao, Gong & Lu (2005) extends the previous ideas to continuous dynamic multiobjective optimization problems. The clonal selection algorithm for dynamic multiobjective optimization (CSADMO) implements the nonuniform mutation, which combines the mutation operator with information on the evolutionary generation: the more the algorithm approaches to its termination, the smaller the mutation amplitude. To enforce diversity, when nondominated antibodies exceed a fixed threshold, suppression operator is applied to the population according to the crowding distance criterion already proposed for the nondominated sorting genetic algorithm (NSGA-II). It is important to notice that in CSADMO no particular strategies are adopted to solve dynamic problems, but the algorithm only exploits the natural ability of the immune system to adapt dynamically to the problem.

Immune clonal multiobjective algorithm (ICMOA) is very similar to CSADMO and it is proposed to study ZDT problems (Shang & Ma, 2006) and 0/1 knapsack problems (Shang, Ma & Zhang, 2006).

Tan & Mao's MOIA

Tan & Mao (2005) propose the use of an aggregating function based on compromise programming (Miettinen, 1998) to solve multiobjective optimization problems. The aggregating function adopted requires the maximum and minimum values in each objective, and it is not clear from the paper if they adopt the local maxima and minima of each iteration, or if they require the user to obtain the ideal vector (i.e., the optimum values for each objective, considered separately). If such an ideal vector is required, that increases the computational cost of the algorithm, since additional single-objective optimizations need to be performed. This approach uses immune network theory for the search engine, and it is appropriately called multi-objective optimization based on immune algorithm (MOIA). The authors advocate for the advantages of their approach over traditional Pareto ranking and density estimation schemes. However, the authors provide no discussion regarding two parameters introduced: suppression threshold and decay scale.

PAIA

In their population adaptive based immune algorithm (PAIA), Chen & Mahfouf (2006) emulate the adaptivity of antibody concentration in the blood with an adaptive population size in their algorithm. The main characteristic of PAIA is the activation process. Starting from one random antibody chosen in the population, two affinity measures are calculated for dominated and nondominated solutions. These values are related to the distance from the identified antibody in the search space and they are defined to ensure that nondominated antibodies always have smallest affinity. The index defined so far couple information about antibody-antibody and antibody antigen affinities. The clone set is selected with reference to affinity, then a variable number of clones is generated, specifying the total number of clones allowed. The unselected antibodies are cloned once. Mutation is a random perturbation with standard deviation proportional to the parents' affinity. At the end of the iteration suppression is applied to the population for antibodies whose distance from other solutions is greater than a predefined network threshold.

PAIA does not implement an external offline population to collect memory cells, but evolve nondominated antibodies by maintaining them in the population, dynamically adapted to the complexity of the problem.

omni-aiNet

Coelho & Von Zuben (2006) put their algorithm, based on immune network theory, within the framework of an omni-optimization, where the same algorithm can solve single and multiobjective optimization, both constrained and unconstrained. omni-aiNet works with a real coded population and it incorporates two genetic variation techniques: polynomial mutation and gene duplication. Polynomial mutation is the mechanism that governs the hypermutation mechanism with a mutation rate inversely proportional to the avidity. Avidity is evaluated according to the constrained ε-dominance rank index. The selection process make reference to a grid procedure for selecting antibodies with a good spread in the objective space, contributing to the diversity of solutions in the population. Then gene duplication is applied to the population: a random coordinate is selected and its value is used to replace other coordinate whenever this replacement improves the performance of the antibody. The suppression is based on the Euclidean distance in variable space, applying binary tournament for too close antibodies. The rules for binary tournament are based on constraint violation. Finally random newcomers are introduced at each iteration. The cardinality of the population is not defined a priori, but it is dynamically adjusted by the algorithm during the evolution, according to the suppression threshold.

ACSAMO

In their adaptive clonal selection algorithm for multiobjective optimization (ACSAMO), Wang & Mahfouf (2006) keeps trace of two best solutions that act as antigens: the best previous population and the best overall solution in the actual population. To identify these best solutions it is used a dynamically adjusted weighted approach, with weights randomly changed at each iteration. The avidity of an antibody is then defined as the sum of its Euclidean distances from antigens (best previous population and the best overall solution) measured in the search space. This index is used also to drive the mutation amplitude, so that the best the individual, the shorter the mutation. The selection of cells for the next generation is based on nondominated sorting and, with the eventual suppression of exceeding antibodies by the light of the crowding distance indicator. The offline memory is added by the nondominated antibodies

CNMOIA

In his constrained nonlinear multiobjective optimization immune algorithm (CNMOIA), Zhang (2006, 2007) computes two scalar indicators for each antibody: antibody-antigen affinity and antibody density. The first value measures the proximity to nondominated solutions by means of the definition of an inner product and it is suitably coupled with the constraint violation degree. The second one counts the number of solutions in the proximity of the antibody. This information contributes to create also a scalar index which measures the stimulation level of an antibody. The number of clones for each antibody and its mutation probability are evaluated according to the affinity value, while antibodies are dynamically selected for the next generation with a probability which depends on the stimulation level. In CNMOIA, the memory coincide witht the antigen population.

QUICMOA

Li & Jiao (2007) propose to merge quantum theory with the immune metaphor in their quantum inspired immune clonal multiobjective optimization algorithm. They use a novel probabilistic representation of antibodies, based on the concept of quantum bits (qubits). One qubit is defined with a pair of complex numbers that give the probability that the qubit will be found in the 0 or 1 state. A qubit may be in the 1 state, in the 0 state, or in a linear superposition of the two. The rationale of this encoding is that qubits have better characteristic of diversity than binary encoding, since a single qubit is enough to represent four states, when two bits are needed in the classical representation. The additional expense is the decoding phase of qubits given by the observing operator. According to the solution representation, Authors propose recombination update and chaos update strategy as search technique. The rest of the algorithm is similar to ICMOA and other algorithm based on clonal selection with binary variables.

Discussion

In this section, the main features which have been recognized by authors as additional strength of MOAIS over other bio inspired algorithms are presented.

Diversity enforcement. Basically MOAIS algorithms belong to two macro-groups: algorithms based on the clonal selection principle and algorithms based on immune network theory. The latter are structured in order to make independent parallel searches of optimal solutions, leaving to an upper level of the algorithm the management of suppression of similar configurations. This feature prevents genetic drift toward a portion of the Pareto front. Population based algorithms must introduce *ad hoc* tricks to prevent premature convergence, such as niching, fitness sharing, etc.

Elitism. In population based algorithms, the population is usually replaced by offspring after mating. Elitism must be introduced to preserve good solutions and not lose them during iterations. Elitism is inherently embedded in the selection scheme of AIS, whichever set is chosen for selection (parent, clones, memory cells, or union of these sets). This is a common feature of almost all implementation of MOAIS.

Adaptive population. State-of-the-art multiobjective optimization algorithms work with a population of fixed size. One peculiarity of MOAIS is the possibility of adjust the cardinality of the population with the problem (Coelho & Von Zuben, 2006 and Chen & Mahfouf, 2006), according to a predefined suppression threshold. The presented results show that whatever initial size is used, the population is adaptively adjusted to a reasonable size for the specific problem. This feature leads to two advantages: the population size is not a crucial parameter and the number of objective function calls is reduced to the minimum.

Clone size. In a similar way, also the hypermutation operator can be designed in such way that the number of clones for each antibody can be variable, depending on the Pareto ranking (as in MISA, VIS, PAIA).

Memory. The archive of best solutions found during iterations is considered as a key point for the success of multiobjective algorithms. While other evolutionary algorithms have to artificially introduce a fictitious repository for nondominated solutions, the memory mechanism is already defined in MOAIS and optimal solutions are simultaneously preserved once located. Memory can be external (as in MISA, MOIA, VIS) or part of the population, after having applied the suppression operator. This issue could be very effective in tackling dynamic optimization problems.

Comparisons of MOAIS

Comparisons among different MOAIS algorithms and among MOAIS and other bio inspired metaphors are not a standardized task and it is difficult to perform. Most of the source codes of reviewed algorithms are not available for the scientific community neither by request to the authors. Obviously in most of the papers some comparisons are carried out with other state-of-the-art algorithms, using standard test functions and standard metrics. In some cases these comparisons seem to be unfair, e.g it is not clear whether the number of objective function calls is equal for all algorithms.

By a deep analysis of all tests reported by developers, it comes out that only low dimensional test cases have been analyzed (up to four objective functions) but also with very high decision spaces (up to 750 binary variables). The overall performances are shown to be good (MOAIS are capable to converge to the true Pareto front) but no final conclusions can be drawn.

Theory of MOAIS

Despite the considerable effort in developing algorithms based on the IS metaphor, both single and multi objective, there is little work on theory of convergence in literature. To our best knowledge, the very first attempt to provide a mathematical background of convergence of a MOAIS algorithm is (Villalobos-Arias, Coello Coello & Hernandez-Lerma, 2004). The main result is the mathematical proof with Markov chains theory of convergence of MISA (with binary representation of variables and uniform mutation operator) under the hypothesis of using elitism, a secondary population which stores the nondominated solutions in their specific case. In (Villalobos-Arias, Coello Coello & Hernandez-Lerma, 2005) the same authors removed some constraints on the way of transition from one state to another, giving a more general proof of convergence of a MOAIS. Zhang (2006, 2007) provided the proof of weak convergence of CNMOIA (with real or binary encoding and nonlinear constraints) for any initial antibody population distribution by using inhomogeneous Markov chains.

Hybridization of MOAIS

Some immune principles are often used in literature to hybridize other metaheuristics, in order to best-fit a particular problem or to increase a particular feature during the evolution.

Cui, Li & Fang (2001) proposes the emulation of the self adaptive mechanism that keeps immune balance, i.e. control the production of similar antibodies to preserve diversity. They propose a strategy based on immunity and entropy to evaluate affinity among antibodies and penalize more similar individuals by exponential fitness rescaling which reduce their reproduction probability. They apply the methodology to a multiobjective genetic algorithm for the solution of a flow shop scheduling problem.

The hypermutation mechanism seems to be very attractive to increase the exploitation phase during the evolution. Cutello, Narzisi, & Nicosia, (2005) for example, improve the performances of the (1+1) Pareto archived evolutionary algorithm (PAES) by two hypermutation operators, used together in the affinity maturation phase: the first one may change dramatically the individual by randomly replacing one variable, the second one performs a local search in the proximity of the parent. Results show that the hybrid approach outperforms the standard PAES, with a computational effort similar to single objective state-of-the-art approaches for the Protein Structure Prediction problem. Zhang.; Meng & Jiao (2005a, 2005b) and Meng, Zhang & Liu (2005) hybridize a multiobjective particle swarm algorithm by the use of clonal selection operator. The balance between competition and clonal selection is designed to provide an appropriate selection pressure to the swarm population. Comparisons are performed versus the multiobjective particle swarm optimization (MOPSO) algorithm on standard metrics with better performances. Kurapati & Azarm (2000), couple the immune network simulation with a multiobjective genetic algorithm in a two level algorithm. During the first step the system is hierarchical decomposed in subsystems, which handles a portion of the overall design vector. Each system is solved for the same set of objective functions, but optimize different variables. The immune network simulation is used to provide a coordination strategy for subsystems by evaluating affinity among nondominated solutions in each subsystem.

The concept of vaccination is used by Meng & Liu (2003) to restrain degeneracy of the evolution process. At each iteration, through a detailed analysis of nondominated solutions, common information are extracted and used to modify some individuals produced by the standard strength pareto evolutionary algorithm.

Balicki & Kitowski (2003) and Balicki, (2004, 2005), present an hybridization of a tabu search algorithm with a model of the immune system to handle constraints in multicriteria optimization problems. A negative selection algorithm is used to handle constraints by subdividing the population into two groups: feasible-antigens and infeasible-antibodies. The amount of similarity at the genotype level between antibodies and a randomly chosen antigen is used as fitness of a internal procedure, responsible of producing feasible individuals for the external tabu search algorithm. The procedure is proposed to solve the task assignment in distributed computer system problem, improving the quality of the outcomes obtained by the standard algorithm.

The reverse hybridization process is also present in literature, i.e. using features from other metaphors to hybridize AIS algorithms. In Ahuja, Das & Pahwa (2007) a multiobjective clonal selection algorithm is combined by ant colony optimization: to exploit the information gathered from previous iterations, Authors use a pheromone-based hypermutation method to improve the balance between exploration and exploitation, but no

Figure 5. Fields of application of MOAIS

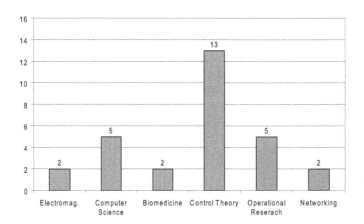

comparisons are presented neither with a pure AIS nor with other algorithms. Tavakkoli-Moghaddam, Rahimi-Vahed & Mirzaei (2007a, 2007b) hybridize the clonal mutation operator by borrowing antibodies improvement methods from bacterial optimization. Bacterial mutation and gene transfer are applied as mutation operators.

Application Fields of MOAIS

Application of MOAIS algorithms to real world problems largely diffused in the reviewed references. In the following these papers are organized by their field of application, as shown in Figure 5.

Power Systems

Distribution power system reconfiguration is the process of changing the topology of the distribution network by altering the open/closed status of the switches in consequence of a fault in the system. It is a complex, combinatorial optimization problem with constraints. Lin, Chen, Wu & Kang (2003) formulate the problem with two objectives 1) power losses, 2) transformer load balancing, while voltage deviation is considered as constraint. Objectives are normalized by referring them to their minimum and maximum value (obtained by a preliminary optimization phase), then a minmax approach is adopted. A Pareto-based multiobjective formulation is proposed in (Ahuja, Das & Pahwa 2007), transforming voltage deviation in the third objective.

Xiong & Cheng (2006), Xiong, Cheng, Zhang, Xu & Jia (2006) and Huang, Hsiao, Chen & Chang (2006) deal with the problem of compensating the reactive power in distribution networks.

By a proper encoding/decoding, specific generation of antibodies, and a new affinity definition, in (Xiong & Cheng, 2006) the multiobjective optimal power flow with 1) minimization of power losses and 2) maximization of voltage stability margin is solved by MOIA. The same approach is adopted in (Xiong, Cheng, Zhang, Xu & Jia, 2006) for choosing the optimal compensatory sites. Huang, Hsiao, Chen & Chang (2006) make use of fuzzy logic to normalize four objectives: 1) minimization of total costs of capacitors, 2) minimization of power losses, 3) minimization of voltage deviations and 4) maximization of system security margin of transformers.

Then a two stage procedure is applied: firstly four single objective problems are solved, by optimizing with respect to one objective and converting the others into constraints. These optimal values are used to define the utopia point for a goal programming-based AIS optimization.

The reference (Liu, Ma, Liu & Lan, 2006), faces the problem of environmental/economic dispatch, defined as the scheduling of the electrical power of a generating unit that match the local power demand with the minimum operating cost and emissions, satisfying some network equality and inequality constraints. The two objectives are aggregated by a weighted sum and solutions with different weights. The problem is solved by a genetic algorithm with immune diversity operator to improve its local search ability.

Electromagnetism

A benchmark problem in electromagnetism (TEAM 22) deals with the optimization of a superconducting magnetic energy storage system. The objectives are to maintain a prescribed level for the stored energy on the device and to minimize the stray field evaluated along fixed lines, while not violating the quench condition that assures the superconductivity state. Guimarães, Campelo, Saldanha, Igarashi, Takahashi & Ramirez, (2006) approach the problem with three objectives: 1) minimize the stray field, 2) minimize the deviation from the prescribed value for the stored energy and 3) minimize the distance of the working point from the limit of the quench condition, with a better use of the superconducting material. Two problems are presented, with three and eight parameters.

In (Canova, Freschi & Tartaglia, 2007), a multiobjective combinatorial optimization algorithm is applied to the optimal sequence of parallel cables in a multi conductor three phase system. The objective function is built in order to minimize the magnetic stray field and the current unbalance of a bunch of rectilinear power cables. Encoding, mutation and suppression have been customized in order to fit the structure of the problem, which is similar to a multiobjective traveling salesman problem with nonlinear objectives.

Computer Science

Most of attention in this area is devoted to the defense of the informatics system from an outsider attack. An analogy can be easily drawn from the biological immune system and the artificial one which should provide recognition for possible harmful pieces of information.

Anchor, Zydallis, Gunsch & Lamont (2002) introduce the computer defense immune system as an artificial immune system for virus and computer intrusion detection. In this work, the main concepts of AIS are used to define two objective functions: one objective is the antibody-antigen affinity (non-self detection) while another one is the antibody-antibody affinity (self detection). These objectives are then optimized by a multiobjective evolutionary program. Jackson, Grunsch, Claypoole & Lamont (2003) apply immune concepts to the problem of steganalysis, that is the recognition of hidden messages in ordinary files. Starting from a wavelet decomposition of graphic files Authors develop a computational immune system (CIS) able to distinguish between stego and clean images. Evolution of CIS classifier is driven by a genetic algorithm. Haag, Lamont, Williams & Peterson (2007b, 2007c) presents the need to bypass deterministic recognition of harmful information and propose a stochastic way of recognition based on evolutionary technique. Authors use a combination of immune inspired algorithms: REALGO (retrovirus algorithm) for its ability to escape local minima and MISA for handling multi-objective problems. Two objectives are considered: best classification and size of classifier hypervolume.

Another field of application, proposed by Zhang, Lu, Gou & Jiao (2006), is the learning issue. In this paper Authors face the problem of unsupervised feature selection. By use of fuzzy logic, this problem is treated like clustering by improving two different objectives: cluster quality and clusters number. Immune operators are clonal selection, updating of Ab archive and of forgetting pool. Results are presented on an artificial data set.

Biomedicine

In (Cutello, Narzisi & Nicosia 2005) a multiobjective version of the protein structure prediction problem is presented. The problem of predicting the native conformation of a protein is to give the amino acid sequence. Objectives are two potential energy functions: bonded (stretching, bending, torsion, Urey-Bradley, impropers) and non-bonded (van-der-Valls, electrostatics) atom energies. The problem has no constraints, with the exception of the variable bounds.

Li, Pu and Mastorakis (2006) introduce the principles of unwounded blood pressure measuring. It puts forward the application of MOIA to the identification of the values of the pulse wave crests.

Control Theory

The paper (Guimarães, Palhares, Campelo & Igarashi, 2007) proposed a multiobjective solution of the mixed H2/H∞ control problem. Given a linear time invariant dynamic system subject to exogenous disturbances, the optimization procedure aims to determine the parameters of the controller that minimizes both the H2 and H∞ of the closed loop matrices of the system. The problem is characterized by 1) nonlinear and multimodal search space, 2) non convexity and 3) search space with many continuous variables with large range size. It is shown that the proposed approach provides Pareto optimal solutions which dominate the ones obtained by a classical LMI approach for and systems with and without uncertainties.

Several works by Kim & colleagues (Kim & Hong, 2003; Kim, 2003a, 2004, 2005; Kim & Cho, 2004a, 2004b, 2005) addresses the optimal choice of a PID controller parameters in order to have a robust tuning of its dynamic response. Targets for settling time, rise time, overshoot, gain margin and phase margin are defined and fuzzy membership function are used to scalarize and aggregate the deviation from these values. Comparisons are provided with results obtained by a fuzzy logic based neural network. In (Kim, 2003b) and (Kim & Lee, 2004; Kim, Jo & Lee, 2004) the procedure is applied to the PID controller of a thermal power plant.

Concepts from immune network theory are employed to design autonomous navigation system of mobile robots in (Michelan & Von Zuben, 2002; Cazangi & Von Zuben, 2006). In the former work the robot must find and collect garbage, without colliding with obstacles and return to the base before it runs out of energy. Control actions of the robot are described by network nodes and correspond to antibodies, whereas antigens are the current states of the robot. In the latter work, the system must deal with simultaneous purposes of capturing targets and avoiding obstacles in unknown environment. Concepts from immune network theory are applied to create a network of classifiers, given rise to a so called connectionist autonomous navigation system. Both the elementary behaviors (classifiers) and their coordination dynamics (immune network) are evolved during the robot navigation. The evolutionary steps take place independently and do not require any a priori knowledge. The connectionist autonomous navigation system is shown to be capable of escaping from local minima, created by some configurations of obstacles and targets, while pure reactive navigation systems are not able to deal properly with such hampering scenarios.

Operations Research

Flow shop scheduling problems addresses the determination of sequencing a number of jobs that have to be processed on a number of machines so that performance measures, e.g. makespan, tardiness, etc. are optimized.

Mori, Kitamura & Shindo (2004) propose a simulation-based scheduling method to solve the scheduling of a semiconductor test facility in presence of multiple objectives as minimization of energy consumption, makespan and tardiness and subject to different technical constraints typical of a testing process. A non automatic investigation of the nondominated solutions produced, allows the choice of the best alternatives among them. Qualitative (not quantitative) results are provided.

Extensive tests with small-sized and large sized flow shop scheduling problem problems (up to 500 jobs and 20 machines) are conduced in (Tavakkoli-Moghaddam, Rahimi-Vahed & Mirzae, 2007a, 2007b) The paper deals with a bi-criteria, where weighted mean completion time and weighted mean tardiness are minimized. Because more than one workpiece must be produced in practical production, the work of Zhou, Li, Yang, & Wang (2006) consider batch during scheduling. After having provided a methodology for deciding the starting time of jobs on machines under different move ways, an illustrative example of multiobjective batch job shop problem is solved by a MOAIS.

In (Chan, Swarnkar, & Tiwari, 2005) the problem of machine tool operation allocation of a flexible manufacturing system having as objectives 1) total machine cost, 2) total set-up cost and 3) total material handling cost and many constraints which take into account magazine capacity, tool life and machine capacity. The problem is formulated with binary variable and it is solved by a single objective AIS algorithm where objectives are fuzzy-fied and constraints are incorporated into the aggregated fitness function by penalty functions.

Networking

Stevens, Natarajan & Das, (2004) propose to design of spreading codes for a DS-CDMA with a MOAIS algorithm. The problem requires generating complex spreading codes with a wide range of auto as well as cross-correlation properties. Three ad-hoc hypermutation operators are designed to provide a faster convergence to better solutions. Results are drastically better than those produced by standard NSGA-II. Authors theorize that this is partly because the crossover operator is not well suited for the production of solutions with high cross correlation, and additionally because of the application of specific operators.

Multicast routing is an effective way to communicate among multiple hosts in a network, with several Quality of Service indicators. In (Wang, Qin & Kang, 2006) paper end-to-end delay, cost of multicast tree and minimum bandwidth utilization are chosen as objectives (differently from previous works where single objective optimization is adopted, considering other objective as bounded constraints). To obtain solutions available for real time application, a gene library is introduced to produce better quality initial paths, rather than starting from a random population.

Analogies

Are considered as analogy papers those works which do not directly deal with MOAIS, but make reference to AIS because of some similarities with other meta-heuristics.

Ahmed, & Elettreby, (2006) propose an analogy between extremal optimization and the way the immune system renews its cells. If B cells are able to recognize antigens then they are preserved

for longer period. Otherwise they are replaced randomly. This dynamics is called extremal dynamics and it can explain the long range memory of the immune system even without the persistence of antigens. The reason is that if a system evolves according to such dynamics then the annihilation probability for a clone (a type of cells) that has already survived for time t is inversely proportional to t.

Efatmaneshnik, & Reidsema, (2007) give a description of complex systems based on the analogy of immunity where the environment of a system or nonself represents the set of input and outputs with the self of the system as the resulting effect. A multiobjective approach is then adopted to find a globally robust design of a system as characteristic of the system's self and not its environment.

CONCLUSION

From the analysis of the reviewed literature, it is possible to draw some considerations on MOAIS algorithms. AIS have some intrinsic characteristics which make them well suited as multiobjective optimization algorithms. Following this basic idea, different implementations have been proposed in the literature.

One key point is the inherently ability to maintain population diversity, ensuring a good exploration of the search space. In other bio-inspired algorithms this feature must be enforced with proper strategies (e.g. niching and fitness sharing). This characteristic is particularly desired in multiobjective optimization, when multiple optimal solutions have to be found simultaneously. The more recent implementations of MOAIS algorithms have also the capability of automatically adapting the size of the population at each iteration, according to the demand of the application. The comparisons performed versus other metaphors seems to put forward that this can be a key point for real world, computationally expensive optimizations. Finally the memory mechanism, naturally presented by the immune system (the so called vaccine effect), is deeply exploited in multiobjective optimization to preserve optimal solutions, once they are located. It has been also theoretically proved that the presence of a memory set guarantees the elitism of the algorithm and the convergence to the optimal solutions. The dynamicity of the immune system, which is able to cope with always changing intruders, is a particularly desired characteristic in multiobjective optimization. In these problems the fitness landscape is based on Pareto dominance, thus it has to be recomputed at each time the population involved in the optimization process changes.

Future Research Directions

From the application point of view, it seems that the progresses obtained in MOAIS algorithm have not yet exploited, with the exception of a few cases. It could be fruitful to bridge the gap among theories, algorithms and the applicative fields, by using state of the art MOAIS algorithms to solve real world application in a more effective way.

Despite these qualitative considerations, comparisons carried out versus other algorithms have proved neither AIS performances better nor they inferiority for any class of problems. This last consideration opens the research trends to study if there is a class of problems which is well suited to be solved by immune inspired algorithms. Our opinion is that dynamic multiobjective problems could take advantage of the peculiar characteristics of MOAIS algorithms.

REFERENCES

Ahmed, E., & Elettreby, M. F. (2006). On combinatorial optimization motivated by biology. *Applied Mathematics and Computation, 172*(1), 40-48.

Ahuja, A., Das, S., & Pahwa, A. (2007). An AIS-ACO hybrid approach for multi-objective distribution system reconfiguration. *IEEE Transactions on Power Systems, 22*(3), 1101-1111.

Anchor, K. P., Zydallis, J. B., Gunsch, G. H., & Lamont, G. B. (2002). Extending the Computer Defense Immune System: Network Intrusion Detection with a Multiobjective Evolutionary Programming Approach. In J. Timmis, & P.J. Bentley (Ed.) *1st International Conference on Artificial Immune Systems* (pp. 12-21).

Balicki, J. (2005). Immune systems in multi-criterion evolutionary algorithm for task assignments in distributed computer system. In *3rd International Atlantic Web Intelligence Conference* (pp. 51-56).

Balicki, J. (2004). Multi-criterion Evolutionary Algorithm with Model of the Immune System to Handle Constraints for Task Assignments. In L. Rutkowski, J.H. Siekmann, R. Tadeusiewicz, & L.A. Zadeh (Ed.), *7th International Conference on Artificial Intelligence and Soft Computing* (pp. 394-399).

Balicki, J., & Kitowski, Z. (2003). Model of the Immune System to Handle Constraints in Evolutionary Algorithm for Pareto Task Assignments. In M.A. Klopotek, S.T. Wierzchon, & K. Trojanowski (Ed.), *International Intelligent Information Processing and Web Mining* (pp. 3-12).

Campelo, F., Guimarães, F. G., & Igarashi, H. (2007). Overview of artificial immune systems for multi-objective optimization. In *4th International Conference on Evolutionary Multi-Criterion Optimization* (pp. 937-951).

Campelo, F., Guimarães, F. G., Saldanha, R. R., Igarashi, H., Noguchi, S., Lowther, D. A., & Ramirez, J. A. (2004). A novel multiobjective immune algorithm using nondominated sorting. In *11th International IGTE Symposium on Numerical Field Calculation in Electrical Engineering*.

Canova, A., Freschi, F., & Tartaglia, M. (2007). Multiobjective optimization of parallel cable layout. *IEEE Transactions on Magnetics, 43*(10), 3914-3920.

Cazangi, R. R., & Von Zuben, F. J. (2006). Immune Learning Classifier Networks: Evolving Nodes and Connections. In *IEEE Congress on Evolutionary Computation* (pp. 7994-8001).

Chan, F. T. S., Swarnkar, R., & Tiwari, M. K. (2005). Fuzzy goal-programming model with an artificial immune system (AIS) approach for a machine tool selection and operation allocation problem in a flexible manufacturing system. *International Journal of Production Research, 43*(19), 4147-4163.

Chen, J., & Mahfouf, M. (2006). A population adaptive based immune algorithm for solving multi-objective optimization problems. In *5th International Conference on Artificial Immune Systems* (pp. 280-293).

Choi, B. K., & Yang, B. S. (2001). Multiobjective optimum design of rotor-bearing systems with dynamic constraints using immune-genetic algorithm. *Journal of Engineering for Gas Turbines and Power, 123*(1), 78-81.

Chueh, C. H. (2004). *An Immune Algorithm for Engineering Optimization*. Unpublished doctoral dissertation, Department of Mechanical Engineering, Tatung University, Taipei, Taiwan.

Coelho, G. P., & Von Zuben, F. J. (2006). omni-aiNet: an immune-inspired approach for omni optimization. In *5th International Conference on Artificial Immune Systems* (pp. 294-308).

Coello Coello, C. A., & Cruz Cortés, N. (2005). Solving multiobjective optimization problems using an artificial immune system. *Genetic Programming and Evolvable Machines, 6*(2), 163-190.

Coello Coello, C. A., & Cruz Cortés, N. (2002). An Approach to Solve Multiobjective Optimization Problems Based on an Artificial Immune System. In J. Timmis, & P.J. Bentley (Ed.), *1st International Conference on Artificial Immune Systems* (pp. 212-221).

Cruz Cortés, N., & Coello Coello, C. (2003a). Multiobjective Optimization Using Ideas from the Clonal Selection Principle. In. E. Cantú-Paz (Ed.), *Genetic and Evolutionary Computation* (pp. 158-170).

Cruz Cortés, N., & Coello Coello, C. A. (2003b). Using Artificial Immune Systems to Solve Optimization Problems. In A. Barry (Ed.), *Workshop Program of Genetic and Evolutionary Computation Conference* (pp. 312-315).

Cui, X., Li, M., & Fang, T. (2001). Study of population diversity of multiobjective evolutionary algorithm based on immune and entropy principles. In *IEEE Conference on Evolutionary Computation* (pp. 1316-1321).

Cutello, V., Narzisi, G., & Nicosia, G. (2005). A class of Pareto Archived Evolution Strategy algorithms using immune inspired operators for Ab-Initio Protein Structure Prediction. In F Rothlauf (Ed.), *EvoWorkshops* (pp. 54-63).

Darmoul, S., Pierreval, H., & Gabouj, S. H. (2006). Scheduling using artificial immune system metaphors: a review. In *International Conference on Service Systems and Service Management* (pp. 1150-1155).

Das, S., Natarajan, B., Stevens, D., & Koduru, P. (2008). Multi-objective and constrained optimization for DS-CDMA code design based on the clonal selection principle. *Applied Soft Computing Journal, 8*(1), 788-797.

Efatmaneshnik, M., & Reidsema, C. (2007). Immunity as a design decision making paradigm for complex systems: A robustness approach. *Cybernetics and Systems, 38*(8), 759-780.

Freschi, F. (2006). *Multi-Objective Artificial Immune Systems for Optimization in Electrical Engineering*. Unpublished doctoral dissertation, Department of Electrical Engineering, Politecnico di Torino, Torino, Italy.

Freschi, F., & Repetto, M. (2006). VIS: an artificial immune network for multi-objective optimization. *Engineering Optimization, 38*(8), 975-996.

Freschi, F., & Repetto, M. (2005). Multiobjective optimization by a modified artificial immune system algorithm, In *4th International Conference on Artificial Immune Systems* (pp. 248-261).

Guimarães, F. G., Campelo, F., Saldanha, R. R., Igarashi, H., Takahashi, R. H. C., & Ramirez, J. A. (2006). A multiobjective proposal for the TEAM benchmark problem 22. *IEEE Transactions on Magnetics, 42*(4), 1471-1474.

Guimarães, F. G., Palhares, R. M., Campelo, F., & Igarashi, H. (2007). Design of mixed H_2/H_∞ control systems using algorithms inspired by the immune system. *Information Sciences, 177*(29), 4368-4386 .

Haag, C. R. (2007a). *An Artificial Immune System-inspired Multiobjective Evolutionary Algorithm with Application to the Detection of Distributed Computer Network Intrusions*. Unpublished master's thesis, Department of

Electrical and Computer Engineering, Graduate School of Engineering and Management, Air Force Institute of Technology, Dayton, Ohio, USA.

Haag, C. R., Lamont, G. B., Williams, P. D., & Peterson, G. L. (2007b). An artificial immune system-inspired multiobjective evolutionary algorithm with application to the detection of distributed computer network intrusions. In *6th International Conference on Artificial Immune Systems* (pp. 420-435).

Haag, C. R., Lamont, G. B., Williams, P. D., & Peterson, G. L. (2007c). An artificial immune system-inspired multiobjective evolutionary algorithm with application to the detection of distributed computer network intrusions, *In Genetic and Evolutionary Computation Conference* (pp. 2717-2724).

Huang, T. Y., Hsiao, Y. T., Chen, C. P., & Chang, C. H. (2006). Fuzzy modeling with immune multi-objective algorithm to optimal allocate of capacitors in distribution systems. *In 9th Joint Conference on Information Sciences* (pp. 289-292).

Jackson, J. T., Grunsch, G. H., Claypoole, R. L., & Lamont, G. B. (2003). Blind Steganography Detection Using a Computational Immune System: A Work in Progress. *International Journal of Digital Evidence, 4*(1), 1-19.

Jiao, L., Gong, M., Shang, R., Du, H., & Lu, B. (2005). Clonal selection with immune dominance and anergy based multiobjective optimization. In *3rd International Conference on Evolutionary Multi-Criterion Optimization* (pp. 474-489).

Kim, D. H. (2005). Tuning of PID controller for dead time process using immune based multiobjective. In *IEEE Mid-Summer Workshop on Soft Computing in Industrial Applications* (pp. 63-68).

Kim, D. H. (2004). Robust PID control using gain/phase margin and advanced immune algorithm. *WSEAS Transactions on Systems, 3*(9), 2841-2851.

Kim, D. H. (2003a). Tuning of PID controller of dead time process using immune based on multiobjective. In *7th IASTED International Conference on Artificial Intelligence and Soft Computing* (pp. 368-373).

Kim, D. H. (2003b). Intelligent 2-DOF PID control for thermal power plant using immune based multiobjective. In *IASTED International Conference on Neural Networks and Computational Intelligence* (pp. 215-220).

Kim, D. H., & Cho, J. H. (2005). Robust control of power plant using immune algorithm. In *2nd IASTED International Multi-Conference on Automation, Control, and Information Technology* (pp. 105-110).

Kim, D. H., & Cho, J. H. (2004a). Robust PID controller tuning using multiobjective optimization based on clonal selection of immune algorithm. In *8th International Conference on Knowledge-Based Intelligent Information and Engineering Systems* (pp. 50-56).

Kim, D. H., & Cho, J. H. (2004b). Robust tuning for disturbance rejection of PID controller using evolutionary algorithm. In *Annual Conference of the North American Fuzzy Information Processing Society* (pp. 248-253).

Kim, D. H., & Hong, W. P. (2003). Tuning of PID controller of dead time process using immune based on multiobjective. In *IASTED International Conference on Neural Networks and Computational Intelligence* (pp. 221-226).

Kim, D. H., Jo, J. H., & Lee, H. (2004). Robust power plant control using clonal selection of immune algorithm based multiobjective. In *4th International Conference on Hybrid Intelligent Systems* (pp. 450-455).

Kim, D. H., & Lee, H. (2004). Intelligent control of nonlinear power plant using immune algorithm based multiobjective optimization. In *IEEE International Conference on Networking, Sensing and Control* (pp. 1388-1393).

Kurapati, A., & Azarm, S. (2000). Immune network simulation with multiobjective genetic algorithms for multidisciplinary design optimization, *Engineering Optimization, 33*(2), 245-260.

Li, X., Pu, Q., & Mastorakis, N. (2006). The immune algorithm and its application to blood pressure measuring. *WSEAS Transactions on Electronics, 3*(5), 288-292.

Li, Y., & Jiao, L. (2007). Quantum-inspired immune clonal multiobjective optimization algorithm. In *11th Pacific-Asia Conference on Advances in Knowledge Discovery and Data Mining* (pp. 672-679).

Lin, C. H., Chen, C. S., Wu, C. J., & Kang, M. S. (2003). Application of immune algorithm to optimal switching operation for distribution-loss minimisation and loading balance. *IEE Proceedings: Generation, Transmission and Distribution, 150*(2), 183-189.

Liu, H., Ma, Z., Liu, S., & Lan, H. (2006). A new solution to economic emission load dispatch using immune genetic algorithm. In *IEEE Conference on Cybernetics and Intelligent Systems* (pp. 1-6).

Lu, B., Jiao, L., Du, H., & Gong, M. (2005). IFMOA: immune forgetting multiobjective optimization algorithm. In *1st International Conference on Advances in Natural Computation* (pp. 399-408).

Luh, G., Chueh, C., & Liu, W. (2003). MOIA: Multi-Objective Immune Algorithm. *Engineering Optimization, 35*(2), 143-164.

Luh, G. C., & Chueh, C. H. (2004). Multi-objective optimal design of truss structure with immune algorithm. *Computers and Structures, 82*(11-12), 829-844.

Ma, W., Jiao, L., Gong, M., & Liu, F. (2005). An novel artificial immune systems multi-objective optimization algorithm for 0/1 knapsack problems. In *International Conference on Computational Intelligence and Security* (pp. 793-798).

Meng, H., & Liu, S. (2003). ISPEA: improvement for the strength Pareto evolutionary algorithm for multiobjective optimization with immunity. In *5th International Conference on Computational Intelligence and Multimedia Applications* (pp. 368-372).

Meng, H., Zhang, X., & Liu, S. (2005). Intelligent multiobjective particle swarm optimization based on AER model. In *12th Portuguese Conference on Artificial Intelligence* (pp. 178-189).

Michelan, R., & Von Zuben, F. J. (2002). Decentralized control system for autonomous navigation based on an evolved artificial immune network. In *Congress on Evolutionary Computation* (pp. 1021-1026).

Mori, K., Kitamura, S., & Shindo, S. (2004). Simulation-based scheduling system for saving energy consumptions. In *SICE Annual Conference* (pp. 657-660).

Shang, R., Jiao, L., Gong, M., & Lu, B. (2005). Clonal selection algorithm for dynamic multiobjective optimization. In *International Conference on Computational Intelligence and Security* (pp. 846-851).

Shang, R., & Ma, W. (2006). Immune clonal MO algorithm for ZDT problems. In *2nd International Conference on Advances in Natural Computation* (pp. 100-109).

Shang, R., Ma, W., & Zhang, W. (2006). Immune clonal MO algorithm for 0/1 knapsack problems. In *2nd International Conference on Advances in Natural Computation* (pp. 870-878).

Stevens, D., Natarajan, B., & Das, S. (2004). Multiobjective artificial immune systems based complex spreading code sets for DS-CDMA. In *4th IASTED International Multi-Conference on Wireless and Optical Communications* (pp. 364-368).

Tan, G. X., & Mao, Z. Y. (2005). Study on Pareto front of multi-objective optimization using immune algorithm. In *International Conference on Machine Learning and Cybernetics* (pp. 2923-2928).

Tan, K. C., Goh, C. K., Mamun, A. A., & Ei, E. Z. (2008). An evolutionary artificial immune system for multi-objective optimization. *European Journal of Operational Research, 187*(2), 371-392.

Tavakkoli-Moghaddam, R., Rahimi-Vahed, A., & Mirzaei, A. H. (2007a). Solving a bi-criteria permutation flow shop problem using immune algorithm. In *IEEE Symposium on Computational Intelligence in Scheduling* (pp. 49-56).

Tavakkoli-Moghaddam, R., Rahimi-Vahed, A., & Mirzaei, A. H. (2007b). A hybrid multi-objective immune algorithm for a flow shop scheduling problem with bi-objectives: Weighted mean completion time and weighted mean tardiness. *Information Sciences, 177*(22), 5072-5090.

Villalobos-Arias, M., Coello Coello, C. A., & Hernández-Lerma, O. (2005). Asymptotic convergence of some metaheuristics used for multiobjective optimization. In *Revised Selected Papers of 8th International Workshop on Foundations of Genetic Algorithms* (pp. 95-111).

Villalobos-Arias, M., Coello Coello, C. A., & Hernández-Lerma, O. (2004). Convergence analysis of a multiobjective artificial immune system algorithm. In *3rd International Conference on Artificial Immune Systems* (pp. 226-235).

Wang, J. Q., Qin, J., & Kang, L. S. (2006). A new QoS multicast routing model and its immune optimization algorithm. in *3rd International Conference on Ubiquitous Intelligence and Computing* (pp. 369-378).

Wang, X. L., & Mahfouf, M. (2006). ACSAMO: An Adaptive Multiobjective Optimization Algorithm using the Clonal Selection Principle. In *2nd European Symposium on Nature-Inspired Smart Information Systems* (pp. 1-12).

Xiong, H. and Cheng, H. (2006). Multi-objective optimal reactive power flow incorporating voltage stability. *WSEAS Transactions on Power Systems, 1*(3), 613-618.

Xiong, H., Cheng, H., Zhang, W., Xu, Y., & Jia, D. (2006). Optimal reactive power compensation planning with improving voltage stability margin in deregulated environment. *WSEAS Transactions on Circuits and Systems, 5*(1), 104-110.

Yoo, J., & Hajela, P. (2001). Fuzzy Multicriterion Design Using Immune Network Simulation. *Structural and Multidisciplinary Optimization, 22*(3), 188-197.

Yoo, J., & Hajela, P. (1999). Immune network simulations in multicriterion design. *Structural Optimization, 18*, 85-94.

Zhang, X., Lu, B., Gou, S., & Jiao, L. (2006). Immune multiobjective optimization algorithm for unsupervised feature selection. In *10th Pacific-Asia Conference on Advances in Knowledge Discovery and Data Mining* (pp. 484-494).

Zhang, X., Meng, H., & Jiao, L. (2005a). Improving PSO-based multiobjective optimization using competition and immunity clonal. In *International Conference on Computational Intelligence and Security* (pp. 839-845).

Zhang, X., Meng, H., & Jiao, L. (2005b). Intelligent particle swarm optimization in multiobjective optimization. In *IEEE Congress on Evolutionary Computation* (pp. 714-719).

Zhang, Z. (2007). Immune optimization algorithm for constrained nonlinear multiobjective optimization problems. *Applied Soft Computing Journal, 7*(3), 840-857.

Zhang, Z. (2006). Constrained Multiobjective Optimization Immune Algorithm: Convergence and Application. *Computers and Mathematics with Applications, 52*(5), 791-808.

Zhou, Y., Li, B., Yang, J., & Wang, Q. (2006). An immune algorithm for batch job-shop scheduling with multi-objectives. In *International Technology and Innovation Conference* (pp. 1642-1646).

KEY TERMS

Antibody: Antibodies are the candidate solutions of the problem to be optimized.

Antigen: In optimization problems, antigens are the optimal configurations of the problem.

Antibody-Antibody Affinity: Affinity among antibodies is defined as a measure of the distance among candidate solutions. In accordance with the antibody representation, it is possible to define different distances (e.g. Euclidean for continuous representation, Hamming for binary representation, etc.), both in variable and in objective spaces.

Antibody-Antigen Affinity: Scalar index adopted as measure for the goodness of a solution with respect to the objective to be optimized. It is usually related to the objective value to be minimized/maximized, with or without the use of scaling or correcting factors. In multiobjective optimization this index (also referred to as avidity) is usually obtained by ranking solutions in accordance to Pareto optimality conditions.

Avidity: See Antibody-Antigen affinity.

Memory: Memory is an offline repertoire of optimal solutions found during the evolution of the algorithm. Memory has a key role for proof of convergence of a multiobjective algorithm because it ensures the survival of the best configurations (elitism).

Suppression: In order to preserve diversity in the solutions at each iteration, antibodies which are very affine to each other (see antibody-antibody affinity) are deleted and eventually randomly replaced. Suppression can be applied either to online population or to offline memory.

Chapter II
Artificial Immune Systems as a Bio-Inspired Optimization Technique and Its Engineering Applications

Jun Chen
The University of Sheffield, UK

Mahdi Mahfouf
The University of Sheffield, UK

ABSTRACT

The primary objective of this chapter is to introduce Artificial Immune Systems (AIS) as a relatively new bio-inspired optimization technique and to show its appeal to engineering applications. The advantages and disadvantages of the new computing paradigm, compared to other bio-inspired optimization techniques, such as Genetic Algorithms and other evolution computing strategies, are highlighted. Responding to some aforementioned disadvantages, a population adaptive based immune algorithm (PAIA) and its modified version for multi-objective optimization are put forward and discussed. A multi-stage optimization procedure is also proposed in which the first stage can be regarded as a vaccination process. It is argued that PAIA and its variations are the embodiments of some new characteristics which are recognized nowadays as the key to success for any stochastic algorithms dealing with continuous optimization problems, thus breathing new blood into the existing AIS family. The proposed algorithm is compared with the previously established evolutionary based optimization algorithms on ZDT and DTLZ test suites. The promising results encourage us to further extract a general framework from the PAIA as the guild to design immune algorithms. Finally, a real-world engineering problem relating to the building of a transparent fuzzy model for alloy steel is presented to show the merits of the algorithm.

Copyright © 2009, IGI Global, distributing in print or electronic forms without written permission of IGI Global is prohibited.

INTRODUCTION

Bio-Inspired Computing lies within the realm of Natural Computing, a field of research that is concerned with both the use of biology as an inspiration for solving computational problems and the use of the natural world experiences to solve real world problems. The increasing interest in this field lies in the fact that nowadays the world is facing more and more complex, large, distributed and ill-structured systems, while on the other hand, people notice that the apparently simple structures and organizations in nature are capable of dealing with most complex systems and tasks with ease. Artificial Immune Systems (AIS) is one among such computing paradigms, which has been receiving more attention recently.

AIS is relatively a new research area which can be traced back to Farmer *et al.*'s paper published in 1986 (Farmer, J. D. & Packard, N. H., 1986). In this pioneering paper the author proposed a dynamical model for the immune systems based on the Clonal Selection Principle (Bernet, F. M, 1959) and Network Hypothesis (Jerne, N. K., 1974; Perelson, A. S., 1989). However, there were only a few developments since then until 1996 when the first international conference based on artificial immune systems was held in Japan. Following this event, the increasing number of researchers involved in this field indicated the emergence of the new research field: Artificial Immune Systems. But hitherto, no new formal framework based on AIS has been proposed.

There are three main application domains which AIS research effort has focused on, viz. fault diagnosis, computer security, and data analysis. The reason behind this is that it is relatively easy to create a direct link between the real immune system and the aforementioned three application areas, e.g. in the applications of data analysis, clusters to be recognized are easily related to antigens, and the set of solutions to distinguish between these clusters is linked to antibodies. Recently, a few attempts to extend AIS to the optimisation field have been made (de Castro & Von Zuben, 2002; Kelsey, J. & Timmis, J., 2003). However, as mentioned by Emma Hart and Jonathan Timmis (2005), maybe by historic accident, many of the AIS practitioners arrive in the optimisation field by way of working in other biologically inspired fields such as Evolutionary Computing (EC), and thus in terms of optimisation the distinctive line between EC and AIS is vague. In other words, there is not a formal distinctive framework for AIS applied to optimisation. The situation is even worse when it comes to multi-objective optimisation (MOP) case since it is hard to find a way to define Antigen and the *affinity* due to the implicit Antigen population to be recognized (Chen J. & Mahfouf, M., 2006). Based on such an understanding, this chapter will present a systematic AIS framework to solve MOP with clear definitions and roles of the immune metaphors to be employed, and will highlight the difference between AIS and traditional EC to finally discover the extra advantages which are exclusively inherent in AIS.

The structure of the chapter is organized as follows: Backgrounds and Previous Research Work provides a detailed review and a background of the existing AIS algorithms, as well as the main challenges for both single and multi-objective optimizations. The Main Thrust of the Chapter consists of five parts: firstly, the advantages and disadvantages of the existing developments compared to other evolutionary algorithms are given in Part 1; responding to some disadvantages of the existing AIS algorithms and drawbacks of other evolutionary algorithms, a detailed description of the modified PAIA (Chen J. & Mahfouf, M., 2006) and its variants can be found in Part 2, where the newly proposed algorithms are compared with NSGAII (Deb, K., 2001), SPEA2 (Zitzler, E. & Laumanns, M., 2001) and VIS (Freschi, F. & Repetto, M., 2005) using ZDT (Deb, K., 2001) and DTLZ (Deb, K., *et al.* 2001) test suites; following this, a general framework extracted from the modified PAIA is presented as a guild to design AIS-based optimization algorithms; some characteristics which are commonly admitted nowadays as the key contributions to the success of continuous optimization are also included in this part; in Part 4, a multi-stage optimization procedure is proposed, in which a single objective optimization algorithm is utilized in the first stage which can be regarded as a vaccination process, followed by the modified PAIA in the second stage to push the set of solutions along the whole Pareto front; the number of evaluations is reduced significantly due to this multi-stage procedure; a real-world engineering problem relating to the building of a transparent fuzzy model for alloy steel is presented in Part 5 to show how the algorithm can be efficiently applied in such a real-world application. Concluding Remarks concludes the whole chapter with the special emphasis on: 1) the difference between AIS and traditional evolutionary algorithms, 2) the extra advantage that are exclusively inherent to AIS; finally, the future directions are addressed in Future Research Directions. The terms and definitions, as well as an additional reading list, can be found at the end of the chapter.

BACKGROUNDS AND PREVIOUS RESEARCH WORK

Bio-inspired optimization concerns mainly the way in which to extract useful metaphors from biology to provide sound structures for solving engineering problems. The most successful and visible work belongs to the realm of Evolutionary Algorithms through the simulation of biological evolution. Within this realm, three independently developed methodologies exist, viz. Genetic Algorithms (GA) (Holland, J. H., 1975), Evolution Strategies (ES) (Back, T., 1996) and Genetic Programming (GP) (Koza, J. R., 1999). Apart from these three schools, AIS represents an alternative line of this type of research through the simulation of vertebrate immune mechanisms. In the following subsections, three themes are explored, namely single objective optimization (SOP), multi-objective optimization (MOP) and immunological models. A brief literature review of the existing AIS-based optimization algorithms is also presented.

Single Objective Optimization: A Springboard to Multi-Objective Optimization

Despite the apparent focus on MOP in this chapter SOP is the basis of all types of the optimization. Hence, in this subsection, four important issues are addressed, which relate to the local search, the global search, the uni-modal optimization and the multi-modal optimization. Due to such different emphases, a special attention should be given to each individual, which brings various challenges to the design stage of a specific algorithm for any one of the aforementioned research directions. In the following discussion, only minimization is considered without any loss of generality.

The most famous local search algorithms fall into the category of gradient-based optimization. In this case, the search is directed by the derivative of the objective function. Since the direction always leads the candidate solution to the place which results in a smaller objective value than the previous position does, this kind of optimization represents obviously a local search mechanism. The disadvantage of such a mechanism is obvious: once the solution is trapped at a local minimum there is no way to come out of it. Another concomitant disadvantage lies in the fact that the objective function should be derivatively possible. However, the gradient-based search is fast and accurate. The Nelder-Mead Simplex search (Nelder, J. A. & Mead, R., 1965) represents another type of the local search mechanism. It is derivative-free and can be categorized as the simplest version of the heuristic search method. Due to its heuristic nature, any new move of the vertices may not always minimize the objective function. Through the consecutive employments of *reflection, expansion, contraction* and *shrink*, all vertices of the simplex gradually converge to a locally optimal solution. The main difference between the Simplex and other stochastic search methods is that there is no mechanism in the design of the Simplex to ensure that the vertices escape from the local optimum.

In most situations, the search space contains several minima. Thus, a good balance between exploitation and exploration in the search space is the only insurance to locate the global area. For example, a legitimate step to extend Simplex to the global version is to restart the algorithm with a new simplex starting at the current best value. Restarting with a new simplex can be viewed as exploration, and preserving the current best value is a type of exploitation and elitism. In this sense, the above approach can be seen as the rudiment of a population-based GA, despite the fact that in the latter case a pool of individuals parallel searching for the optimum replaces the sequential restarting of the algorithm. By using a pool of individuals, a GA parallel explores more of the search space and thus increases the chance of finding the global optimum. Another mechanism to enhance the global search capability of GA is to utilize a mutation operator. Despite the greate success in the early stage of the development of GA, single-point and two-point crossover are only feasible in the binary case. The stagnation of finding a feasible crossover operator in the real-valued situation is the main reason for the denouncements of GA, such as premature convergence, slow convergence and low accuracy especially, when it is applied to continuous optimization problems. Many research endeavors which specifically targeted at solving continuous optimization problems have been proliferating. Most of these share some common features if one looks into the meaning behind their variation operators. More details can be found in the fourth part of the body of the chapter.

In the presence of the coexistence of many local optima, designers are often more interested in obtaining as many local optima as possible rather than the global one, and in doing so they increase their choices for decision making. This is where the multi-modal optimization comes in. Under this scenario, keeping the diversity of the candidate solutions plays a key role in preserving a set of solutions. In GA, this has been achieved by introducing the sharing mehtod (Goldberg, D. E., 1989). In this way, different species can format and co-exist in the final population. However, two associated problems with the sharing method and GA are: 1) it is sensitive to the setting of the sharing parameters; 2) it depends highly on the population size to preserve the diveristy of the population.

Bio-Inspired Multi-Objective Optimization

Many real-world problems are inherently of a multi-objective nature with often conflicting goals. Generally, MOP consists of minimizing/maximizing the following vector function:

$$f(x) = [f_1(x), f_2(x), ..., f_m(x)]^T \qquad (1)$$

subject to J inequality and K equality constraints as follows:

$$g_j(x) \geq 0 \quad j = 1, ...J; \quad h_k(x) = 0 \quad k = 1, ...K \qquad (2)$$

where $x = [x_1, x_2, ..., x_n]^T \in \Omega$ is the vector of decision variables and Ω is the feasible region. Classical methods to deal with MOP often use a higher-level of information about the problem to be optimized to choose a preference vector so that multiple objectives can be aggregated into a single objective. In doing so, MOP is actually transformed into a SOP. However, because of its high dependence on the preference information this approach is sometimes subjective and impractical. Facing the possibility of lacking the problem information, the idea of simultaneously finding a set of uniform-distributed optimal solutions through a single run, rather than several runs receives more and more attention. Bio-inspired optimization algorithms are very ideal for the implementation of this idea due to the following reasons: first, they are population based search methods; second, they are derivative-free search methods; third, they effectively use previous knowledge.

Hitherto, many well-known implementations of this concept were proposed (Deb, K., 2001; Zitzler, E. & Laumanns, M., 2001; Fonseca, C. M. & Fleming, P. J., 1993; Knowles, J. D. & Corn, D. W., 2000; Jin, Y., Olhofer, M. & Sendhoff, B., 2001), and two text books (Deb, K., 2001; Coello Coello, Carloa A., *et al.*, 2002) are available. One web repository http://www.lania.mx/~ccoello/EMOO/ is maintained by Dr. Carlos A. Coello Coello.

By carefully studying the differences of the existing MOP algorithms, it is possible to group them into three categories, viz. the Weighted-aggregation-based method, the Pareto-based method and the Archive-based method. The idea of the *weighted-aggregation-based method* is to randomly change weight combinations of the objectives during each generation so that the population can approach the different locations of the Pareto front. Schaffer's work-VEGA (Schaffer, J. D. & Grefenstette, J. J., 1985), which is normally regarded as the first implementation of GA applied to MOP, falls into this family by implicitly performing a linear combination of the objectives where the weights depend on the distribution of the population at each generation. The problem associated with this method is that it suffers from the curse of 'concave Pareto front'. In such a situation, solutions tend to converge to some portion of the front rather than residing on the whole front. The *Pareto-based method* relates mainly to how to assign fitness values to individuals in the population according to the concept of Pareto dominance. The first proposal was made by Goldberg (1989) as a means of assigning an equal probability of reproduction to all non-dominated individuals in the population. The method consisted of assigning ranks to the non-dominated individuals and removing them from contention, then repeating the same operations until the remaining population is empty. Following this idea, Deb *et al.* (2001) proposed the Non-dominated Sorting Algorithm II (NSGAII). In such an implementation, solutions were classified into different ranks according to the aforementioned procedures. Some newly developed features were included in NSGA-II, such as elitism. The algorithm employs a crowded tournament selection operator to keep diversity so that it does not need to specify any niching parameters. The main problem associated with NSGAII is that individuals with the same rank have the same fitness; in the later runs, all individuals will be classified in rank 1 and thus have the same fitness; in such a situation the selection pressure will diminish. SPEA2 was later proposed as an improved version of SPEA (Zitzler, E. & Laumanns, M., 2001). It distinguishes itself from other algorithms by using a different fitness assignment procedure, which for each individual takes into account how many individuals that it dominates and it is dominated by in the union of internal and external population; density estimation is also incorporated into the algorithm to calculate the fitness of each individual. In doing so, SPEA2 successfully resolved the problem associated with NSGAII as mentioned above. An enhanced archive truncation method was developed to guarantee the preservation of the boundary solutions and the diversity of the population. The main problem with SPEA2 is its high computational cost in the fitness assignment procedure and the archive truncation process. Both NSGAII and SPEA2 highly depend on their initial population size. Knowles and Corne (2000) proposed a new baseline for approximating the Pareto front which can be viewed as the gestation of the *Archive-based method*. The Pareto Archived Evolutionary Strategy (PAES) was developed by introducing the concept of archiving. PAES does not use the dominance concept to carry out the fitness assignment. The Pareto concept is only used to compare the mutated individuals against the existing archive consisting of non-dominated solutions previously found. An adaptive grid partition method is applied to the archive to preserve the diversity of the solutions so far found. Traditionally, the weighted aggregation method could not solve the concave problem. However, using the concept of archiving to record any non-dominated solutions so far found, it is possible to find solutions on the concave front. Jin *et al.* (2001) discussed this issue and demonstrated how a single objective optimization method combined with a dynamic change of a weighed aggregation plus an archive can deal with both convex and concave problems. The advantage of the archive-based method lies in the simplification of the fitness assignment procedure.

Immunological Models: Inspirations for Alternative Bio-Inspired Optimization

The vertebrate immune system is highly complex and possesses multi layers. Here, what one is interested in is the third layer, namely, the adaptive immune system, which can learn and adapt to most previously unseen antigens, and can respond to such patterns quickly in the next sample. Among many immunological models, the *Clonal Selection* (Bernet, F. M, 1959) and the *Immune Network theories* (Jerne, N. K., 1974; Perelson, A. S., 1989) are the two branches which have proved to be the sources of inspiration for many people working in the AIS-based optimization field and were emulated in this work. Another immune metaphor which was exploited for the algorithm developed in this chapter is the way that the immune system controls its antibodies' (Abs) concentration.

The *Clonal Selection Principle* describes the basic features of an immune response to an antigenic stimulus, and establishes the idea that only those cells that recognize the antigen are selected to proliferate. The key procedures are: 1) Selection: the B-cell with a higher affinity than a threshold is selected to clone itself; 2) Proliferation: the selected B-cells produce many offspring with the same structure as themselves; the clone size is proportional to the individual's affinity; 3) Affinity Maturation: this procedure consists of *Hypermutation* and *Receptor Editing*; in the former case, clones are subjected to a high-rate mutation in order to differentiate them from their parents; the higher the affinity, the lower the mutation rate; in the latter case, cells with a low affinity, or self-reactive cells, can delete their self-reactive receptors or develop entirely new receptors; 4) Reselection: after affinity maturation, the mutated clones and edited cells are reselected to ensure that only those cells with a higher affinity than a certain threshold survive. The whole process is performed iteratively until a certain stable state is achieved. *Fig. 1* describes the previous steps graphically.

Immune Network Theory tells the story that Abs not only include paratopes but also epitopes. This results in the fact that Abs can be stimulated by recognizing other Abs, and for the same reason can be suppressed by being recognized. Consequently, the immunological memory can be acquired by this self-regulation and mutual reinforcement learning of B-cells. The suppression function is a mechanism that allows to regulate the over-stimulated B-cells to maintain a stable memory and thus serves as the inspiration to control the over-crowed population during the optimization process.

The way that the immune system controls its *Abs' concentration* represents an interesting phenomenon from the perspective of the optimization practitioners. Initially, only a small number of B-cells cruise in the body. If they encounter foreign antigens (Ags), some of them are activated and then they proliferate. This process is adaptive, i.e. the number of clones that are proliferated during the activation process and how many of them are maintained at each iteration step and at the end in order to neutralize Ags is adaptive. This makes sense since if a large number of initial B-cells is available then undoubtedly it can kill any Ags at the cost of spending more energy to activate B-cells and secrete Abs. However, only an optimal number of B-cells during each step is

Figure 1. The schematic diagram of the Clonal Selection Principle ©2008 Jun Chen. Used with permission.

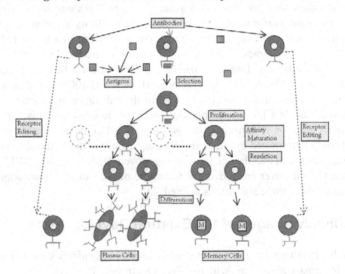

necessary (less means more time is needed to reach the required concentration; more means redundant B-cells are introduced).

A Review of Existing AIS-Based Optimization Algorithms

It is noting that most AIS-based research which relates to SOP identified the diversity of the population as the main advantage of AIS over conventional evolution algorithms and the slow convergence as its drawback. In the early days, AIS was mainly integrated into other evolutionary algorithms to overcome the well known problem of premature convergence in searching for the global optimum. In those developments, GA was combined with AIS to model the somatic mutation and gene recombination by means of two GA operators, viz. crossover and mutation in order to maintain the diversity of the population (Wang, X., Gao, X. Z. & Ovaska, S. J., 2004). More recently, some newly developed optimization algorithms, which are solely based on the immune mechanisms, were proposed. Most of these algorithms establish the single objective multi-modal optimization problem as a target. It is the diversity that gestates the motivation of using the immune based algorithms for solving multi-modal problems. Toyoo F. *et al.* (1998) proposed an Immune Algorithm (IA) which is based on the somatic theory and network hypotheses. The somatic theory contributes to increasing the diversity of antibodies and as a result to increasing the possibility of finding a global solution as well as local optimal solutions. The network hypotheses contributes to the control of the proliferation of clones. Opt-aiNet is an augmented version of ClONAG (de Castro, L. N., & Von Zuben, F. J., 2002; de Castro, L. N., & Timmis, J., 2002) by combining Network hypothesis with the Clonal Selection Principle. The main features of Opt-aiNet include dynamically adjustable population size, balance between exploitation and exploration of the search space and the ability of locating the multiple optima.

Freschi and Repetto (2005) argued that AIS has, in its elementary structure, the main features required to solve MOP. Their vector artificial immune system (VIS) is mainly based on immune network theory. Unlike other immune algorithms, the clonal selection of the fittest antibodies is not based on the calculation of affinity, instead, it is based on a ranking scheme which is a modified version of the scheme adopted by SPEA2. The diversity of the antibody's population is maintained via the network suppression and the newcomers inserted in the outer-loop. Since in the clonal selection step, the best mutated clone for each cell replaces the original parent rather than selecting the best mutants from the union of all parents and clones, the speed of convergence of this algorithm may be slower than that of the one adopting the latter selection scheme. Carlos A. Coello Coello *et al.*'s Multi-objective Immune System Algorithm (MISA) (2005) mainly takes ideas from the Clonal Selection Principle. Antibodies in their algorithms are encoded into binary strings. The algorithm sacrifices some biological metaphors in exchange for a better performance. There is no explicit affinity calculation within the algorithm, and thus both the selection and clone processes cannot be based on it. Apart from this, due to the binary encoding scheme, both the convergence and accuracy are deteriorated when it is used to deal with continuous optimization problems. Both the aforementioned algorithms fix the number of clones that each parent can proliferate. Pareto-optimal Neighbor Immune Algorithm (PNIA) (Gong, M. G. *et al.*, 2006) adopts a new way in defining affinity. The fitness (affinity) is calculated according to the crowding-distance proposed in NSGAII and is only assigned to the dominant individuals. Clone, recombination and hypermutation are only applied to the dominant individuals. Non-dominated selection is performed on the union of all kinds of the population. The clone size in this algorithm is adaptively determined by the corresponding affinity. Due to the selection scheme adopted in PNIA, both the convergence speed and the accuracy are improved. It seems that in PNIA there is no explicit diversity mechanism except that the over-crowed antibodies are removed from the population. It is worth noting that the population size in all these three algorithms is fixed.

Advantages and Disadvantages of the Existing Developments

From the descriptions in the first two parts of the last section, one can easily identify the following disadvantages related to the existing evolutionary algorithms with the GA as their representative.

- Premature convergence and low accuracy.
- The population size is problem-contingent and crucial for the search capability.
- Slow convergence.
- The sharing parameters are problem-contingent.

From the discussions of the fourth part of the last section, the following problems associated with the already developed AIS-based MOP algorithms are exposed.

- No formal systematic framework (each algorithm has its own structure and is very much different from the others).
- Not consistent with the immune mechanisms, e.g. 1) the clone size in most algorithms is fixed; however, in real immune systems, the clone size is proportionate to the corresponding affinity; 2) the population size is fixed; however, in real immune systems, the Ab's concentration is adaptively changing.
- Not effectively using the information from the decision variable space. In most cases affinity is only related to the dominance of each solution in the objective space.
- Coupled with other evolutionary mechanisms.

All the previous considerations justify the 'rationale' behind a Population Adaptive Based Immune Algorithm (PAIA) (refer to Chen, J. and Mahfouf, M. 2006 for further details). PAIA is the synthesis of the three immune metaphors (refer to the third part of last section), where the Clonal Selection Principle is used to provide a selection pressure to effectively drive the population towards the Pareto front over many iteration steps; the Network Theory is used to regulate the dynamics of the population; and the last immune metaphor is the main inspiration for the design of the PAIA's structure so that the population is adaptive at each iteration step. PAIA aims to provide a generic AIS framework for MOP solving, to make the population size adaptive to the problem and to reduce the number of evaluation times so that only the necessary evaluations are carried-out (speed up the convergence). Despite the great success in achieving the above three aims, PAIA was found to be converging slowing when applied to problems with many local optima such as DTLZ1 and DTLZ3 (refer to *Table 2.*). Thus, a refined hypermutation and a crossover operator are incorporated into the original algorithm. The effect of such a modification is to reinforce the local search capability of PAIA so that both the convergence speed and the accuracy of the solutions are improved. The detailed steps of the modified PAIA are described in the next part of this section.

The Modified Algorithm – PAIA2

It is recognized that when the test problem includes many local optima PAIA generally uses more evaluations to finally converge compared to other GA algorithms, e.g. SPEA2 (refer to Simulation Studies for the comparative results). Furthermore, when PAIA is applied to DTLZ test suite, it fails to converge fully to the Pareto fronts of DTLZ1 and DTLZ3, both having many local optima. Generally speaking, PAIA has no problem in finding the global trade-offs provided enough evaluations are given (i.e. with the sacrifice of using more evaluations). This is recognized as the problem associated with the mutation operator which is not adequately designed so that many evaluations may be wasted on evaluating the local optima. In light of the above observations, a modified PAIA with the Simulated Binary Crossover (SBX) (Deb, K. and Agrawal, B. R., 1994) as the recombination operator and a modified mutation operator is proposed. Density information is also incorporated to calculate the affinity of each Antibody in order to allow a more uniformed distribution of the final population. The basic idea of the modified mutation operator is to let the mutation rate of each antibody decrease when the optimization process evolves so that a more focused search is introduced in the later iterations. The decreasing rate can be controlled through a predefined parameter. SBX is a real-code GA crossover and is similar to a mutation operator in the way that it allocates two children alongside their parents by a calculated distance (the only difference is that it uses two solutions to calculate the distance to mutate). The reason for choosing this operator is that in the later iterations solutions are normally close to each other in the decision variable space (especially, when the problem has many local optima), in this case, the modified mutation operator is not good enough to produce an adequate mutation rate (it is either too small or too large). On the other hand, SBX uses two solutions to calculate the distance to mutate, in other words, it takes into account the crowding information in the decision variable space. The mutation operator is very good at finding directions and strengths to mutate in the early iterations and SBX is very good at fine tuning the distance to mutate in the later iterations. By combining them both, one can reach a very fast convergence and a good accuracy. In the implementation of SPEA2, the author used an adaptation of the *k-th* nearest neighbor method to calculate the density at any point, which is an inverse of the distance to the *k-th* nearest neighbor. In PAIA2, the density estimation is also added to each Ab so that the calculated affinity can reflect this kind of information as well.

Description of the Algorithm

The terms and definitions used in this subsection can be found at the end of the chapter. The modified algorithm-PAIA2 can be described via the following steps:

1. **Initialization:** a random Ab population is first created.
2. **Identify_Ab:** one random Ab in the first non-dominated front is identified.
3. **Activation:** the identified Ab is used to activate the remaining dominated Abs. The dominated Abs' affinity value (NB: affinity is the inverse of affinity value) is calculated according to Equation (3), where n is the dimension of the decision variables.

$$aff\_val_d = \sum_{i=1}^{n} \left(x_{identified}(i) - x_d(i) \right) / n + D(d) \tag{3}$$

The non-dominated Abs' affinity value is calculated as follows: **I.** if the size of dominated Abs is not zero, the affinity value equals the minimum affinity value of the dominated Ab divided by two; **II.** otherwise, the affinity value is calculated according to Equation (4), where N is the size of non-dominated Abs.

$$aff\_val_{nd} = \sum_{j=1}^{N} \left(\sum_{i=1}^{n} \left(x_{identified}(i) - x_j(i) \right) / n \right) / N + D(j) \tag{4}$$

In this way, Ag-Ab affinity is indirectly embedded in Abs' affinity since the non-dominated Abs always have the smallest affinity value (the highest affinity). $D(j)$ is the density of the *j*th antibody and can be calculated by Equation (5).

$$D(i) = \frac{1}{\sigma_j^k + 2} \tag{5}$$

Where σ_j^k is the distance between point j and the k-*th* nearest point of j. k is set to 2.

4. **Clonal Selection:** Clonal selection consists of three steps: **I.** Abs with the smallest affinity value are selected, i.e. the non-dominated Abs are always selected; **II.** The Abs in the remaining population with an affinity value smaller than a threshold (δ) are selected; **III.** the unselected Abs are kept in a different set.

5. **Clone: I.** for the selected Abs, a maximum clone size (N_{cmax}) is pre-defined; then a fraction of N_{cmax} is allocated to each selected Ab according to its affinity percentage, i.e. the higher the percentage the larger the fraction is assigned; **II.** Unselected Abs are cloned once regardless of their affinity.

6. **Affinity Maturation: I.** the selected Abs are subjected to *hypermutation*, i.e. one dimension of the Ab is randomly chosen to mutate; the mutation rate is proportional to the affinity value (inversely proportional to affinity); the whole process is calculated using Eqs. (6). **II.** the unselected Abs are submitted to *receptor editing* which means more than one dimensions (two, in PAIA) are randomly chosen to mutate; the mutation rate is calculated using Equation (6).

$$x_{new}(i) = x_{old}(i) + \alpha \cdot N(0,1) \quad i = 1,\ldots,n; \quad \alpha = r \times \exp(aff\_val)/\exp(1) \tag{6}$$

where $N(0, 1)$ is a Gaussian random variable with zero mean and standard deviation 1. i represents the dimension that has been chosen to mutate. r is an decreasing rate and is calculated according to Eqs. (7).

$$r = 1 - rand \wedge ((1 - G/Gen) \wedge b) \tag{7}$$

Where G is the current iteration and Gen is the predefined total number of iterations. b is a control parameter and equals to 1. The selected Abs are also submitted to *recombination* which is implemented using SBX.

7. **Reselection:** the mutated, edited and recombined clones and their corresponding parents are mixed together and reselected: **I.** all non-dominated Abs are selected; **II.** if the number of current non-dominated Abs (NCR) is less than the initial population size (IN), the Abs from the next non-dominated front are selected according to their recalculated Abs' affinity value (the ones with smaller affinity values are favoured) to fill the difference between these two; this process continues until the difference is filled; **III.** only when NCR is greater than IN and the number of non-dominated Abs in the last iteration (NPR) can *Network Suppression* be invoked to suppress too-close Abs.

8. **Network Suppression:** the *Euclidian* distance in objective space between any two Abs is calculated; if it is less than a predefined network threshold (σ) the one with larger affinity value is suppressed and deleted; this operator is invoked in step 7 when certain conditions are satisfied.

9. **Iteration:** the process is repeated from step 2 until certain conditions are met.

Simulation Studies

The benchmark functions used in this chapter are ZDT1~ZDT4, ZDT6 and DTLZ1~DTLZ7. The ZDT series problems have two objectives and represent the same type of problems with a large decision variable space, a concave and discrete Pareto front, many local optima and variable density of the decision variable space and the objective space. The DTLZ problems are scalable test problems with three or more objectives and are characterized by a concave (DTLZ2~DTLZ4) and a discrete (DTLZ7) Pareto front, a variable density of the decision variable space and the objective space (DTLZ4, DTLZ6) and many local optima (DTLZ1, DTLZ3). The definitions about these two test suites can be found in *Tables 1* and *2*.

Two performance metrics, namely the Generational Distance (GD) and the Spread Δ are employed to evaluate the convergence and distribution of the final solutions, which are defined as follows.

Table 1. ZDT test problems

Problems	Definition
ZDT1	30-variable problem with a convex Pareto front. $f_1 = x_1 \qquad g = 1 + \dfrac{9}{n-1}\sum_{i=2}^{n} x_i \qquad f_2 = g\left(1 - \sqrt{f_1/g}\right) \qquad 0 \le x_i \le 1 \qquad n = 30$
ZDT2	30-variable problem with a concave Pareto front. $f_1 = x_1 \qquad g = 1 + \dfrac{9}{n-1}\sum_{i=2}^{n} x_i \qquad f_2 = g\left(1 - (f_1/g)^2\right) \qquad 0 \le x_i \le 1 \qquad n = 30$
ZDT3	30-variable problem with disconnected Pareto fronts. $f_1 = x_1 \qquad g = 1 + \dfrac{9}{n-1}\sum_{i=2}^{n} x_i \qquad f_2 = g\left(1 - \sqrt{f_1/g} - (f_1/g)\sin(10\pi f_1)\right) \qquad 0 \le x_i \le 1 \qquad n = 30$
ZDT4	10-variable problem with 100 local Pareto fronts. $f_1 = x_1 \qquad g = 1 + 10(n-1) + \sum_{i=2}^{n}\left(x_i^2 - 10\cos(4\pi x_i)\right) \qquad f_2 = g\left(1 - \sqrt{f_1/g}\right) \qquad n = 1$ $0 \le x_1 \le 1 \quad -5 \le x_i \le 5 \quad i = 2,3,\dots,n$
ZDT6	10-variable problem with a concave and non-uniform distributed Pareto front. $f_1 = 1 - \exp(-4x_1)\sin^6(6\pi x_1) \qquad g = 1 + 9\left(\left(\sum_{i=2}^{n} x_i\right)/9\right)^{0.25} \qquad f_2 = g\left(1 - (f_1/g)^2\right) \qquad 0 \le x_i \le 1 \qquad n = 10$

- **Generational Distance:** GD measures the closeness of the obtained Pareto solution set Q from a known set of Pareto-optimal set P^*.

$$GD = \frac{\left(\sum_{i=1}^{|Q|} d_i^m\right)^{1/m}}{|Q|} \qquad (8)$$

For a two-objective problem ($m=2$), d_i is the *Euclidean* distance between the solution $i \in Q$ and the nearest member of P^*. A set of $|P^*|=500$ uniformly distributed Pareto-optimal solutions is used to calculate GD.

- **Spread:** Δ measures the diversity of the solutions along the Pareto front in the final population. where d_i is the distance between the neighbouring solutions in the Pareto solution set Q. d is the mean value of all d_i. d_m^e is the distance between the extreme solutions of P^* and Q along the mth objective. It is worth noting that for ZDT3 Δ is calculated in each continuous region and averaged.

$$\Delta = \frac{\sum_{m=1}^{M} d_m^e + \sum_{i=1}^{|Q|} \left| d_i - \overline{d} \right|}{\sum_{m=1}^{M} d_m^e + |Q|\, \overline{d}} \qquad (9)$$

A. Experimental Study on the ZDT Series Problems

In this experiment, the proposed PAIA2 is compared to two well-known algorithms-NSGAII and SPEA2, and one immune-based algorithm-VIS. By comparing with NSGAII and SPEA2, it is shown that the modified PAIA is a valuable alternative to standard algorithms; by comparing with VIS, the difference between these two immune algorithms is identified. For a fair comparison, the experiments configuration refers to the experiments in Deb's book (2001). The maximum function evaluation for NSGAII and SPEA2 is set to 25000. For PAIA and its variations, although the population is adaptive the final population can be controlled by σ. Hence, one can set an adequate value for σ so that the final population size and evaluation times are around 120 and 25000 respectively. The results of SPEA2, PAIA and PAIA2 shown in *Tables 3* and *4* are obtained after 10 independent runs. The results of NSGAII are from Deb (2001) and the results of VIS are from Chen, J. *et al.* (2006).The parameter settings for different algorithms is listed as follows:

Table 2. DTLZ test problems

DTLZ1: this test problem is a *M*-objective problem with a linear Pareto-optimal front.	**DTLZ2**: this problem is its concave Pareto-optimal area.

Minimize $\quad f_1(X) = \frac{1}{2}x_1 x_2 \cdots x_{M-1}(1 + g(X_M))$,

Minimize $\quad f_2(X) = \frac{1}{2}x_1 x_2 \cdots (1 - x_{M-1})(1 + g(X_M))$,

$\vdots$

Minimize $\quad f_{M-1}(X) = \frac{1}{2}x_1(1 - x_2)(1 + g(X_M))$,

Minimize $\quad f_M(X) = \frac{1}{2}(1 - x_1)(1 + g(X_M))$,

subject to $\quad 0 \le x_i \le 1$, for $i = 1,2,\ldots,n$,

where $\quad g(X_M) = 100\left[|X_M| + \sum_{x_i \in X_M}(x_i - 0.5)^2 - \cos(20\pi(x_i - 0.5))\right]$.

Minimize $\quad f_1(X) = (1 + g(X_M))\cos(x_1\frac{\pi}{2})\cdots\cos(x_{M-2}\frac{\pi}{2})\cos(x_{M-1}\frac{\pi}{2})$,

Minimize $\quad f_2(X) = (1 + g(X_M))\cos(x_1\frac{\pi}{2})\cdots\cos(x_{M-2}\frac{\pi}{2})\sin(x_{M-1}\frac{\pi}{2})$,

Minimize $\quad f_3(X) = (1 + g(X_M))\cos(x_1\frac{\pi}{2})\cdots\sin(x_{M-2}\frac{\pi}{2})$,

$\vdots$

Minimize $\quad f_{M-1}(X) = (1 + g(X_M))\cos(x_1\frac{\pi}{2})\cdots\sin(x_2\frac{\pi}{2})$,

Minimize $\quad f_M(X) = (1 + g(X_M))\sin(x_1\frac{\pi}{2})$,

subject to $\quad 0 \le x_i \le 1$, for $i = 1,2,\ldots,n$,

where $\quad g(X_M) = \sum_{x_i \in X_M}(x_i - 0.5)^2$.

DTLZ3: this problem has 3^k-1 local Pareto-optimal fronts and one global Pareto-optimal front. *k* is the decision variable's dimension.	**DTLZ4**: this problem has more dense solutions near f₃-f₁ and f₁-f₂ planes.

Minimize $\quad f_1(X) = (1 + g(X_M))\cos(x_1\frac{\pi}{2})\cdots\cos(x_{M-2}\frac{\pi}{2})\cos(x_{M-1}\frac{\pi}{2})$,

Minimize $\quad f_2(X) = (1 + g(X_M))\cos(x_1\frac{\pi}{2})\cdots\cos(x_{M-2}\frac{\pi}{2})\sin(x_{M-1}\frac{\pi}{2})$,

Minimize $\quad f_3(X) = (1 + g(X_M))\cos(x_1\frac{\pi}{2})\cdots\sin(x_{M-2}\frac{\pi}{2})$,

$\vdots$

Minimize $\quad f_{M-1}(X) = (1 + g(X_M))\cos(x_1\frac{\pi}{2})\cdots\sin(x_2\frac{\pi}{2})$,

Minimize $\quad f_M(X) = (1 + g(X_M))\sin(x_1\frac{\pi}{2})$,

subject to $\quad 0 \le x_i \le 1$, for $i = 1,2,\ldots,n$,

where $\quad g(X_M) = 100\left[|X_M| + \sum_{x_i \in X_M}(x_i - 0.5)^2 - \cos(20\pi(x_i - 0.5))\right]$.

Minimize $\quad f_1(X) = (1 + g(X_M))\cos(x_1^\alpha\frac{\pi}{2})\cdots\cos(x_{M-2}^\alpha\frac{\pi}{2})\cos(x_{M-1}^\alpha\frac{\pi}{2})$,

Minimize $\quad f_2(X) = (1 + g(X_M))\cos(x_1^\alpha\frac{\pi}{2})\cdots\cos(x_{M-2}^\alpha\frac{\pi}{2})\sin(x_{M-1}^\alpha\frac{\pi}{2})$,

Minimize $\quad f_3(X) = (1 + g(X_M))\cos(x_1^\alpha\frac{\pi}{2})\cdots\sin(x_{M-2}^\alpha\frac{\pi}{2})$,

$\vdots$

Minimize $\quad f_{M-1}(X) = (1 + g(X_M))\cos(x_1^\alpha\frac{\pi}{2})\cdots\sin(x_2^\alpha\frac{\pi}{2})$,

Minimize $\quad f_M(X) = (1 + g(X_M))\sin(x_1^\alpha\frac{\pi}{2})$,

subject to $\quad 0 \le x_i \le 1$, for $i = 1,2,\ldots,n$,

where $\quad g(X_M) = \sum_{x_i \in X_M}(x_i - 0.5)^2$.

DTLZ5: this problem has a Pareto front which is a curve.	**DTLZ6**: this problem has variable density in decision variable space and objective space.

Minimize $\quad f_1(X) = (1 + g(X_M))\cos(\theta_1\frac{\pi}{2})\cdots\cos(\theta_{M-2}\frac{\pi}{2})\cos(\theta_{M-1}\frac{\pi}{2})$,

Minimize $\quad f_2(X) = (1 + g(X_M))\cos(\theta_1\frac{\pi}{2})\cdots\cos(\theta_{M-2}\frac{\pi}{2})\sin(\theta_{M-1}\frac{\pi}{2})$,

Minimize $\quad f_3(X) = (1 + g(X_M))\cos(\theta_1\frac{\pi}{2})\cdots\sin(\theta_{M-2}\frac{\pi}{2})$,

$\vdots$

Minimize $\quad f_{M-1}(X) = (1 + g(X_M))\cos(\theta_1\frac{\pi}{2})\cdots\sin(\theta_2\frac{\pi}{2})$,

Minimize $\quad f_M(X) = (1 + g(X_M))\sin(\theta_1\frac{\pi}{2})$,

subject to $\quad 0 \le x_i \le 1$, for $i = 1,2,\ldots,n$,

where $\quad g(X_M) = \sum_{x_i \in X_M}(x_i - 0.5)^2$,

and $\quad \theta_i = \frac{\pi}{4}(1 + g(r))(1 + 2g(r)x_i)$, *for* $i = 2,\ldots,(M-1)$.

Minimize $\quad f_1(X) = (1 + g(X_M))\cos(\theta_1\frac{\pi}{2})\cdots\cos(\theta_{M-2}\frac{\pi}{2})\cos(\theta_{M-1}\frac{\pi}{2})$,

Minimize $\quad f_2(X) = (1 + g(X_M))\cos(\theta_1\frac{\pi}{2})\cdots\cos(\theta_{M-2}\frac{\pi}{2})\sin(\theta_{M-1}\frac{\pi}{2})$,

Minimize $\quad f_3(X) = (1 + g(X_M))\cos(\theta_1\frac{\pi}{2})\cdots\sin(\theta_{M-2}\frac{\pi}{2})$,

$\vdots$

Minimize $\quad f_{M-1}(X) = (1 + g(X_M))\cos(\theta_1\frac{\pi}{2})\cdots\sin(\theta_2\frac{\pi}{2})$,

Minimize $\quad f_M(X) = (1 + g(X_M))\sin(\theta_1\frac{\pi}{2})$,

subject to $\quad 0 \le x_i \le 1$, for $i = 1,2,\ldots,n$,

where $\quad g(X_M) = \sum_{x_i \in X_M}x_i^{0.1}$,

and $\quad \theta_i = \frac{\pi}{4}(1 + g(r))(1 + 2g(r)x_i)$, *for* $i = 2,\ldots,(M-1)$.

DTLZ7: this problem has 2^{M-1} disconnected Pareto-optimal regions in the search space.

Minimize $\quad f_1(X_1) = x_1$, *Minimize* $f_2(X_2) = x_2,\ldots$,

Minimize $\quad f_{M-1}(X_{M-1}) = x_{M-1}$, *Minimize* $f_M(X) = (1 + g(X_M))h(f_1, f_2, \ldots, f_{M-1}, g)$,

subject to $\quad 0 \le x_i \le 1$, for $i = 1,2,\ldots,n$,

where $\quad g(X_M) = 1 + \frac{9}{|X_M|}\sum_{x_i \in X_M}x_i$, $\quad h(f_1, f_2, \ldots, f_{M-1}, g) = M - \sum\left[\frac{f_i}{1+g}(1 + \sin(3\pi f_i))\right]$.

Figure 2. Pareto solutions of the modified PAIA2 on ZDT1~ZDT4 and ZDT6 ©*2008 Jun Chen. Used with permission.*

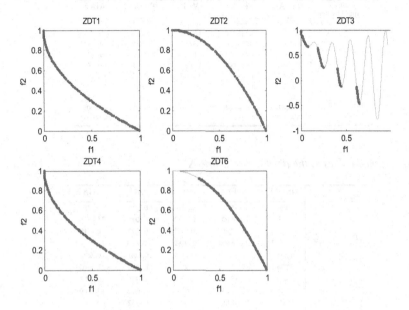

- **SPEA2:** Population size 100, archive size 100, mating pool size 100, the distribution index for crossover 20, the distribution index for mutation: 20, maximum generation 250; crossover probability 1 and mutation probability 1/ (the dimension of the decision variable).
- **NSGA II:** Population size 100, maximum generation 250, crossover probability 0.9 and mutation probability 1/(string-length). 30 bits are used to code variable.
- **PAIA2:** IN = 7, δ = 0.4, N_{cmax} = 95, σ = 0.004, the distribution index for SBX 20.
- **PAIA and VIS:** Refer to Chen, J. *et al.* (2006).

Fig. 2 shows the Pareto fronts obtained by PAIA2, where the continuous lines represent the true Pareto fronts and the dots represent the obtained fronts using PAIA2.

From the above figure, one can see that the PAIA2 approaches the true Pareto fronts with very good diversity and accuracy. The results shown in *Table 3* indicate that PAIA2 reached a better performance than any of other four algorithms in terms of the convergence. Results of SPEA2 are comparatively as good as those results obtained using PAIA2. Generally, PAIA2 produces a slightly better convergence, while SPEA2 produces a slightly better distribution as one can see from *Table 4*. As already stated in the first part of this section, the original PAIA needs more evaluations to finally converge for problems consisting of many local minima. This is confirmed by the experiment and can be observed through *Table 3*. For ZDT4, while PAIA did not quite converge to the true Pareto front using 25000 evaluations, the enhanced PAIA2 had no problem in finding the true Pareto front within 25000 evaluations with the aid of the new mutation operator and SBX. Due to the inclusion of the density information in the calculation of the affinity, PAIA2 slightly improved the performance as far as the diversity is concerned.

Fig. 3 shows the results from the original PAIA and PAIA2 under the same number of evaluations when they are applied to ZDT4.

The original PAIA failed to fully converge to the Pareto front in this case, which justifies the new proposed mutation operator and the incorporation of SBX.

To examine how efficient PAIA2 is compared to VIS and SPEA2, all three algorithms are run as many evaluations as necessary until adequate convergence and diversity (this means that both metrics cannot be significantly

Table 3. Mean and variance values of the convergence measure GD

Test problems/Algorithms		NSGAII	SPEA2	VIS	PAIA P	AIA2
ZDT1	GD	8.94e-4	2.64e-004	1.81e-3	1.43e-4	2.45e-4
	σ^2	0	4.68e-010	1.97e-7	1.56e-9	4.44e-10
ZDT2	GD	8.24e-4	1.05e-004	1.21e-3	1.04e-4	9.34e-005
	σ^2	0	1.21e-011	1.04e-6	2.2e-11	3.69e-011
ZDT3	GD	4.34e-2	1.69e-004	1.58e-3	1.58e-4	1.55e-004
	σ^2	4.20e-5	1.74e-010	2.26e-7	4.60e-10	1.89e-010
ZDT4	GD	3.228	4.68e-004	0.1323	1.20e-3	2.43e-004
	σ^2	7.3076	1.36e-008	4.20e-2	1.88e-7	7.86e-010
ZDT6	GD	7.8067	1.81e-004	-	1.02e-4	9.41e-005
	σ^2	1.67e-3	6.65e-011	-	6.04e-12	1.87e-011

Table 4. Mean and variance values of the diversity measure Δ

Test problems/Algorithms		NSGAII	SPEA2	VIS	PAIA P	AIA2
ZDT1	Δ	0.4633	0.1575	0.5420	0.3368	0.3289
	σ^2	4.16e-2	1.44e-004	8.25e-3	1.10e-3	7.05e-004
ZDT2	Δ	0.4351	0.1523	0.6625	0.3023	0.3345
	σ^2	2.46e-2	1.31e-004	2.58e-2	7.07e-4	3.55e-004
ZDT3	Δ	0.5756	0.1638	0.6274	0.4381	0.3292
	σ^2	5.08e-3	2.90e-2	1.60e-2	1.50e-3	2.61e-004
ZDT4	Δ	0.4795	0.1555	0.1011	0.3316	0.3310
	σ^2	9.84e-3	4.34e-004	1.37e-3	1.20e-3	4.18e-004
ZDT6	Δ	0.6444	0.3248	-	0.4932	0.3210
	σ^2	3.50e-2	1.29e-004	-	3.56e-4	2.58e-004

Figure 3. Pareto solutions of the modified PAIA (left) and PAIA (right) on ZDT4 ©2008 Jun Chen. Used with permission.

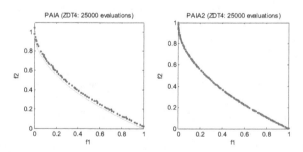

improved by only increasing the number of evaluations) are obtained. *Table 5* summarizes the results after 10 independent runs.

It can be seen that for all the five test problems, PAIA2 generally uses a fewer evaluations than VIS does. While on the other hand results of PAIA2 are comparatively as good as those obtained by SPEA2. It is worth noting that PAIA2 only used 3900 evaluations for ZDT6 compared to 18000 evaluations used by SPEA2. Such a big difference lies in the fact that PAIA2 uses information from both the objective space and the decision variable space to calculate the affinity. For the problem having a variable density in both the decision variable space and the objective space, the aforementioned scheme seems very effective. A similar observation is encountered in the experiment B for DTLZ6. The big difference in the needed evaluations of PAIA2 and VIS indicates that there must be some fundamental differences in the design of the algorithms, which are summarised below.

Table 5. Evaluation times of PAIA2, VIS and SPEA2 when they are fully converged

Test suite	Evaluation Times		
	PAIA2 (GD/Δ)	VIS (GD/Δ)	SPEA2(GD/Δ)
ZDT1	7500 (2.48e-4/0.2990)	28523 (1.32e-4/0.3142)	8000 (2.66e-4/0.1814)
ZDT2	7000 (9.12e-5/0.3567)	29312 (1.10e-4/0.2123)	11000 (9.50e-5/0.1589)
ZDT3	7500 (1.81e-4/0.4201)	32436 (1.23e-4/0.3451)	9000 (1.69e-4/0.1489)
ZDT4	20000 (2.90e-4/0.3140)	46899(1.23e-3/0.0834)	20000 (5.56e-4/ 0.1879)
ZDT6	3900 (1.40e-4/0.4569)	-	18000 (2.65e-4/0.3172)

Figure 4. Adaptive population size and adaptive clone size (the assigned maximum clone size among all Abs) Vs iteration ©2008 Jun Chen. Used with permission.

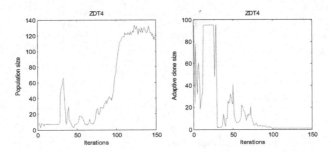

1)   PAIA2 only preserves the necessary Abs during each iteration step so that only the necessary evaluations are carried out.

2)   PAIA2 uses an adaptive clone size so that only the necessary clone size is assigned to each selected Ab.

Fig. 4 only takes results from ZDT4 as an example to provide a graphical explanation about the aforementioned two differences. From the figure, one can see that the clone size is adaptively decided by the population size and their corresponding affinities. If the population size is small, each selected Ab can be assigned a large clone size so that the size of the activated clones is large enough to explore the objective space. Most previous research endeavours, like VIS, fixes the clone size (4 in VIS), which generally leads to two main problems: 1) in the early stage, a fixed clone size may not be large enough to speed up the convergence; 2) in the later stage, a fixed clone size may be too large so that at each iteration step many unnecessary clones are produced.

In PAIA2, the population size is not fixed. It is regulated by the network suppression threshold σ so that any too-close Abs are suppressed. It will be finally stabilized, which is a sign for the convergence of the algorithm. Due to the nature of the adaptive population as one can see from *Fig. 4*, irrespective of the initial size used the population can be adaptively adjusted to a reasonable size according to the need of the problem. *Fig. 5* and *Table 6* take ZDT2 and ZDT3 as examples, without any loss of generality, to show that even with 1 as the initial size the algorithm can still find the Pareto front.

Although the initial size is not crucial to the success of PAIA2, *Table 6* clearly indicates that in the case of 1 as the initial size more evaluations are needed compared to the one with 7 as the initial size. Hence, an optimal initial size does influence the computation load.

B. Experimental Study on the DTLZ Series Problems

In this experiment, PAIA2 is compared to SPEA2. To make the comparison fair, the experiment configuration refers to those in Deb *et al.* (2001). The maximum function evaluations and the number of decision variables are shown in *Table 7*. All the parameter settings for SPEA2 are kept unchanged expect for the maximum generations. For PAIA2, all the parameters are kept the same as the last experiment expect for the network suppression

Figure 5. PAIA2 with 1 as the initial population size ©2008 Jun Chen. Used with permission.

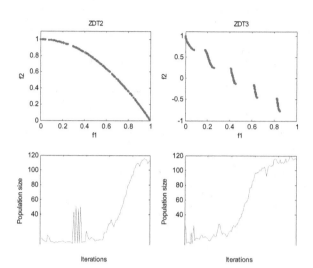

Table 6. PAIA2 with 7 and 1 as the initial population size

Test suite	Evaluation Times	
	PAIA2 (GD/Δ) with 7 as the initial size	PAIA2 (GD/Δ) with 1 as the initial size
ZDT2	7000 (9.12e-5/0.3567)	12000 (9.28e-5/0.3340)
ZDT3	7500 (1.81e-4/0.4201)	14000 (1.47e-4/0.2860)

Table 7. The maximum function evaluations and the number of decision variables

Test suite	The maximum function evaluations	The number of decision vairables	The number of objectives
DTLZ1	30000	7	3
DTLZ2	30000	12	3
DTLZ3	50000	12	3
DTLZ4	20000	12	3
DTLZ5	20000	12	3
DTLZ6	50000	12	3
DTLZ7	20000	22	3

threshold which will be shown along with the corresponding plots. *Figures 6* to *12* show the results of PAIA2 and SPEA2 in different angles of view.

For all seven problems, PAIA2 consistently produced better results than SPEA2. For DTLZ1 and DTLZ3, SPEA2 cannot quite converge to the true Pareto front although the results are very close to the front. For DTLZ4, since the density of the decision variable is different, SPEA2 has a tendency to converge to the verge of the whole front. As one can see from *Fig. 9*, SPEA2 led to two outcomes: 1) converged to any one verge out of three verges; 2) converged to the whole Pareto front. Which outcome it finally reaches highly depends on the initial population to decide upon. On the other hand, PAIA2 had no problem in finding the spread solutions on the whole Pareto front. For DTLZ6, SPEA2 encountered two problems: 1) it cannot converge to the Pareto front and 2) the Pareto front is not a curve due to the variable density of the solutions in the objective space. For the same problem, PAIA2 produced very good approximation of the Pareto front.

Figure 6. The results of PAIA2 (σ = 0.03) and SPEA2 on DTLZ1   ©2008 Jun Chen. Used with permission.

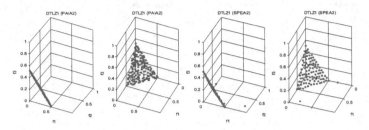

Figure 7. The results of PAIA2 (σ = 0.03) and SPEA2 on DTLZ2   ©2008 Jun Chen. Used with permission.

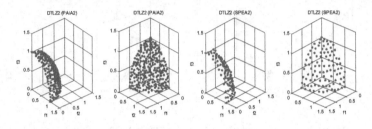

Figure 8. The results of PAIA2 (σ = 0.03) and SPEA2 on DTLZ3   ©2008 Jun Chen. Used with permission.

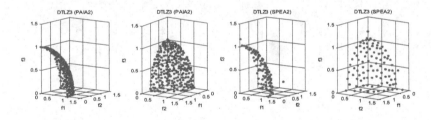

Figure 9. The results of PAIA2 (σ = 0.03) and SPEA2 on DTLZ4   ©2008 Jun Chen. Used with permission.

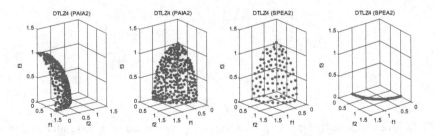

Figure 10. The results of PAIA2 (σ = 0.004) and SPEA2 on DTLZ5 ©2008 Jun Chen. Used with permission.

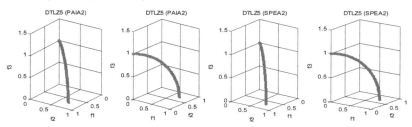

Figure 11. The results of PAIA2 (σ = 0.004) and SPEA2 on DTLZ6 ©2008 Jun Chen. Used with permission.

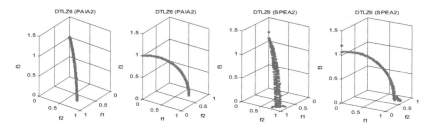

Figure 12. The results of PAIA2 (σ = 0.01) and SPEA2 on DTLZ7 ©2008 Jun Chen. Used with permission.

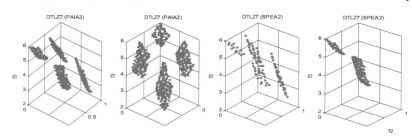

Fig. 13. The results of PAIA2 on DTLZ6 using 5000 evaluations ©2008 Jun Chen. Used with permission.

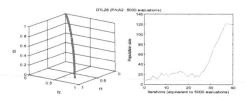

For DTLZ7, SPEA2 occasionally leads to partial fronts (e.g. two fractions among four discontinued Pareto fronts). PAIA2 had no problem in maintaining discontinued Pareto fronts for DTLZ7.

It is worth recalling that, for DTLZ6, PAIA2 can use much less evaluations than SPEA2 does (less than 5000 evaluations compared to 50000 evaluations in SPEA2). *Fig. 13* shows the results of PAIA2 using 5000 evaluations. As already mentioned in Experiment A, and in contrast to SPEA2, PAIA2 utilizes information from both the decision variable space and the objective space. Hence, it is very good at dealing with problems having variable

Figure 14. (a) σ = 0.01, 18432 evaluations; (b) σ = 0.02, 18452 evaluations ©2008 Jun Chen. Used with permission.

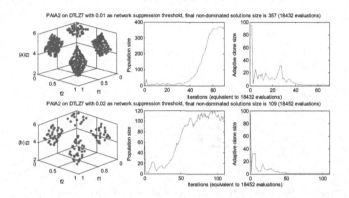

Figure 15. Generic AIS framework for MOP solving (NCR: the number of current non-dominated Abs; NPR: the number of non-dominated Abs in the last iteration; IN: the initial Abs size; Stop: at least one iteration step is executed) ©2008 Jun Chen. Used with permission.

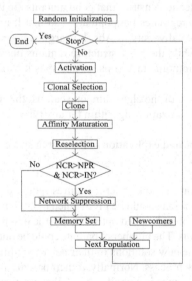

density both in the objective and decision variable spaces (e.g. DTLZ4 and DTLZ6). Another promising property of PAIA2 is that it generally finds more solutions (which can be tuned with Network threshold) with similar or less evaluations than those used in SPEA2. By tuning Network threshold, one can obtain more options in a single run without increasing the number evaluations dramatically. *Fig. 14* shows that even without increasing the number of evaluations, the obtained non-dominated solutions increased from 109 to 357!

The Generic AIS Framework

Although PAIA2 is a specific MOP algorithm, the main structure of the algorithm can be extracted as a generic AIS framework for MOP solving, as shown in *Fig. 15*.

Figure 16. Decreasing rate r vs. Iterations ©2008 Jun Chen. Used with permission.

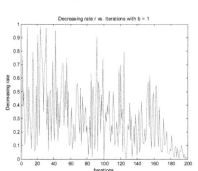

Two kinds of activation are emulated, namely Ag-Ab activation and Ab-Ab activation, so that one obtains information from both the objective space (Ag-Ab affinity) and the decision variables space (Abs' affinity) to select Abs. The Clonal Selection and Clone prefer good Abs by providing them with more chances to be cloned so that they always dominate the whole population. On the other hand, the Clone itself contributes a lot to the diversity of the population. Affinity Maturation includes hypermutation, receptor editing and recombination, the former two of which increase the diversity of the population so that more objective landscape can be explored, and the last one of which efficiently uses the information contained in the solutions so that fine search can be executed in the late stage of the optimization. Reselection ensures that good mutants are inserted into the memory set and bad Abs *apoptosis*. Network Suppression regulates the population so that it is adaptive to the search process. Newcomers are used to further increase the diversity of Abs. It is argued here that each part of the framework can be implemented by various means; while the basic structure remains unchanged. The framework is more consistent with the previously discussed immune mechanisms, and thus it can serve as a guild to design AIS-based optimization algorithms.

From the framework and the description of the algorithm, one can list the following two points as the most important parts when implementing an optimization algorithm for any type of the optimization problems.

- A good balance between exploitation and exploration of the search space.
- The diversity of the population.

Although the aforementioned two points are the general features required by any type of the optimization problems, one should note that special attention should be given when embodying these two points for a specific kind of optimization problems. In the field of real-valued optimization, the first point is normally implemented by generating the offspring around their parents. The number of parents could be one, two, or any number depending on the implementation. The distance of the new solutions to their corresponding parents depends on how good their parents are and the stage of the search process. Normally, if their parents are very good in terms of their fitness or in the late stage of the search the distance is a small value so that a focused search can be carried out, and vice versa. In this way, a good balance between exploitation and exploration is achieved. In this sense, as far as real-valued optimization is concerned, the distinctive line between mutation and crossover diminishes since they all tend to allocate their children to the places according to the calculated distances. The naive crossover operator (Goldberg, D. E., 1989) is not applicable in this case any more. There are many ways to maintain the diversity of the population, e.g. random mutation, large population size, or the insertion of new random individuals. PAIA2 is the embodiment of the above features via the following implementations:

1) Hypermutation maintains a good balance between exploitation and exploration of the search space by providing a small mutation rate to the good Abs and vice versa.

2) The decreasing rate r (refer to Equation (6)) allows a fine search to be executed in the late stage of the optimization process. *Fig. 16* depicts the change of r against the iteration step. 200 iterations are used in this case.

3) The recombination operator-SBX allows a more focused search in the late stage of the optimization. In this case solutions are normally close to each other, and thus the calculated distance is small.

4) Receptor editing explores more search space by employing mutations in more positions with large mutation rates.

5) Adaptive clone size ensures the diversity of the Ab population.

A Multi-Stage Optimization Procedure

In this section, a new procedure has been proposed, which aims at reducing the computational cost in the case of dealing with the problems with many local optima. The procedure is enlightened by the vaccination process and the secondary response of the immune systems. It is well known that if the vaccine (which is very similar as the real antigens in terms of their structures) is available and first applied to the immune systems, the immune systems can remember it and can respond quickly in the successive encounter of the similar antigens. Such a response is called the secondary response in the immune community. The same mechanism can be emulated in the MOP algorithm by first obtaining a solution which can be viewed as the vaccine, and then invoking the immune algorithm with the vaccine as one of the initial population to find the rest solutions. Here, the problem is how to acquire the vaccine in the first place without any knowledge about the problem to be solved. The process of obtaining the vaccine should be computationally inexpensive otherwise there is no point of adding this additional mechanism. In this chapter, a multi-stage optimization procedure is proposed, which divides the whole search procedure into two separate stages with the first one as the vaccination process. In the first stage, a single objective optimization method is used to quickly find a solution on the Pareto front, and in the second stage, PAIA2 is used as a post-processing algorithm to approximate the rest trade-offs along the Pareto front. In the following space, the reason why the first stage can reduce the computational cost of the whole optimization process is explained.

In the MOP context, the direction information is not fully used. As far as the dominance-based method is concerned, partial order of the candidates according to their dominance is given; in such a case candidates can only progress in a general direction (in the sense of dominance concept rather than a fixed direction leading to a more optimized front). In the weighted aggregation method, the weight combination is adaptively changed; hence candidates always change their directions to minimize the current weight combination. Both the aforementioned cases result in an ineffective search due to many searches being wasted to find more dominant solutions in the current non-dominated front rather than progress to a more optimized front. On the other hand, most single objective optimization algorithms use directional information in a more order fashion since there is only one objective to deal with. The effect of this is that single objective optimization algorithms are more efficient in terms of approaching the solution on the true Pareto front although only one at each run. *Fig. 17* is a graphical

Figure 17. (a) Single objective optimization; (b) two-objective optimization with candidate solutions far from the true Pareto front; (b) two-objective optimization with solutions close to the Pareto front ©2008 Jun Chen. Used with permission.

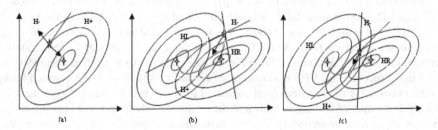

Figure 18. Results from multi-stage optimization procedure on DTLZ1: (a) solution found by the first stage; (b) adaptive population size vs. iterations using PAIA2; (c) non-dominated solutions found by the second stage; (d) adaptive population size vs. iterations using multi-stage optimization procedure, the second stage ©2008 Jun Chen. Used with permission.

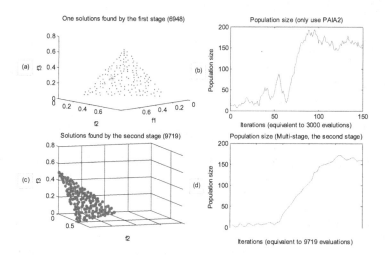

explanation of the above arguments via a two dimensional problem with one or two objectives without any loss of generality.

In this figure, pentacles are the start points from which new solutions will be produced. The stars in the middle of the ellipses are the global optimum of each objective. In stochastic search methods, pentacles can move in any direction with equal opportunity. In a single objective optimization case, the pentacle has 50% chance to choose the right direction, represented by H+ half plane in *Fig. 17 (a)*, to move. In the two-objective case, this is more involved as *Fig. 17 (b)* and *(c)* indicate. The lines connecting two stars are the Pareto solutions that one wishes to approach. Again, H+ plane represents the right direction to go since if the newly generated solution falls into this area it will simultaneously optimize two objectives. However, as one can see from the figure, the probability of choosing the right direction becomes smaller in this case as compared to the single-objective case. More often than not, there is a greater probability of choosing a direction which falls into HL and HR planes so that only trade-offs can be found rather than better solutions. The situation becomes more severe when the candidates are close to the Pareto solutions. In such a case many searches are wasted by moving from one place to another place on the same trade-off front. This is the reason why for most evolutionary algorithms it becomes inefficient to progress any further to the true Pareto front in the later iterations.

From the above discussions, it is argued that the most efficient way to deal with MOP problem is to divide the search process into two separate stages. In the first stage, a single objective optimization algorithm is used to find any solution on the Pareto front. The solution found in the first stage serves as the vaccine in the second stage to quickly find the rest solutions on the Pareto front. In doing so, one maximizes the possibility of choosing the right direction in both stages. Due to the space limitation, only graphical results of DTLZ1 are shown in *Fig. 18*.

In the first stage, PAIA2 is used as a single objective optimizer to find an optimum corresponding to a fixed weight combination of the objectives (*Fig. 18 (a)*). The solution found in the first step is then fed into PAIA2 as the initial population to find the rest solutions. From *Fig. 18*, one can see that in the first stage 6948 evaluations are executed, and in the second stage 9719 evaluations are needed for the rest solutions, which leads to 16667 evaluations in total to cover the whole Pareto front compared to 30000 evaluations in Experiment B. With the solution found in the first stage, PAIA2 can quickly find the remaining solutions on the Pareto front as shown in *Fig. 18 (d)*, which corresponds to the secondary response in the immune systems. *Fig. 18 (b)* shows the variation curve of the population size by only using the PAIA2. The curve fluctuates with each peak corresponding to a local Pareto front. More evaluations are needed to finally stabilise the population size in this case.

Engineering Applications

To validate the proposed algorithm and the multi-stage optimization procedure, it is applied to the modeling of tensile strength (TS) of alloy steels. The aim of the modeling is to build a fuzzy logic based model with a very good prediction and a certain level transparency (interpretability). However, it is well known that the prediction accuracy and the transparency of the fuzzy model are often conflicting objectives (principle of incompatibility). Thus, MOP plays an important role in this type of a problem.

In this work, 3760 TS data are collected. 75% of the data are used for training and the remaining data are used for checking. Another 12 samples are used as unseen data set to validate the generality of the model. The TS data includes 15 inputs and one output. The inputs consists of the weight percentages for the chemical composites, the test depth, the size of the specimen and the site where is has been produced, the cooling medium, the quenching and tempering temperatures. The output is the tensile strength itself. The Singleton fuzzy model (Jang, J. R. 1993) and the multi-stage optimization procedure are adopted. In the first stage, the back-propagation algorithm with momentum terms (Passino, K. M. *et al.*, 1998) is used to train the fuzzy singleton model. The trained model is then used to seed the initial population of PAIA2 in the second stage to obtain a set of fuzzy models with improved transparency by removing redundant rules and merging similar fuzzy sets and rules in the rule base. The objectives used in the first stage and second stage are as follows.

$$Objective1: \quad RMSE = \sqrt{\frac{\sum_{k=1}^{m} \left(y_{prediction} - y_{real}\right)^2}{m}}$$

$$Objectiv2: \quad Nrule + Nset + RL \quad (10)$$

Figure 19. The prediction performance of the vaccine model of the first stage with 12 rules ©2008 Jun Chen. Used with permission.

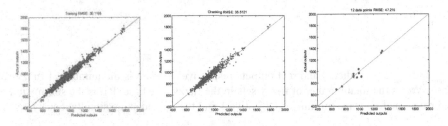

Figure 20. The Pareto fronts of the second stage using PAIA2 ©2008 Jun Chen. Used with permission.

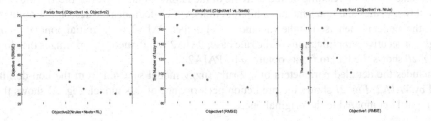

Table 8. The parameters of a 9-rule fuzzy model

9-rule fuzzy model	Parameters
The number of fuzzy rules	9
The number of fuzzy sets in each inputs	Inputs: [7; 6; 6; 6; 5; 7;6; 8; 7; 6; 2; 6; 6; 9; 9]
RMSE for training	36.013
RMSE for checking	39.767
RMSE for validation	48.619

Figure 21. The prediction performance of the optimized 9-rule model ©2008 Jun Chen. Used with permission.

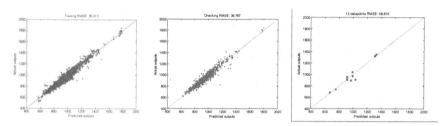

Figure 22. The fuzzy sets of input 11: (right) the 12-rule model; (left) the optimized 9-rule model ©2008 Jun Chen. Used with permission.

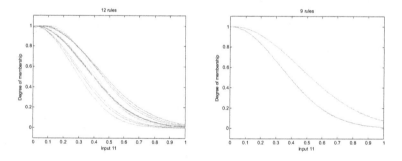

where, $y_{prediction}$ and y_{real} are predicted and real outputs respectively; *Nrule* is the number of fuzzy rules in the fuzzy rule base; *Nset* is the total number of fuzzy sets in the fuzzy rule base; RL is the summation of the rule length of each rule. The first stage minimizes Objective 1 and the second stage simultaneously optimizes both objectives.

Fig. 19 shows the results obtained from the first stage. The obtained fuzzy rule base consists of 12 rules. The training root mean squared error (RMSE) is 30.12. The checking RMSE is 35.51 and the validation RMSE is 47.22. The obtained fuzzy model has very good prediction accuracy and generality as one can see from *Fig. 19*, which represents a solution residing on the extreme of the Pareto front. However, the 12-rule model contains many redundant fuzzy rules and fuzzy membership functions, which degrades the descriptive ability of the fuzzy model. Hence, the model is then used as the vaccine model to feed PAIA2 as the initial population in the second stage. Through consecutive simplifications of the rule base, PAIA2 simultaneously optimizes the aforementioned objectives. *Fig. 20* shows the Pareto fronts obtained by PAIA2.

Table 8 includes the detailed parameters of a 9-rule fuzzy model selected from the non-dominated fuzzy models found by PAIA2. *Fig. 21* shows the prediction performance of this model. *Fig. 22* shows the simplified fuzzy sets in input 11 compared to the original one.

The models obtained from the multi-stage optimization procedure provide the user with more options on the chosen model. The complexity of the rule base and the prediction accuracy are taken into account at the same time. Details about this modelling methodology can be found in Jun Chen & Mahdi Mahfouf (2008).

CONCLUDING REMARKS

In this chapter, an enhanced version of PAIA and a multi-stage optimization procedure are proposed. A real engineering application relating to the building of an accurate and a transparent fuzzy model for alloy steels is also presented. For all experiments, significant results, either improving the convergence or reducing the computational cost, are observed. Such superiority is based on the fact that AIS is inspired by a different regime of natural mechanisms. Thus, it is important to clarify the difference between AIS and other evolutionary-based algorithms (with GA as their representative) to finally discover the extra advantages that AIS can deliver. The fundamental differences are summarized as follows:

1. **Reproduction mechanism:** AIS represents a type of asexual reproduction; while on the other hand, a population-based GA represents the counterpart. Through the latter, the offspring is produced by crossing the chromosomes of both parents. Through the former, each Ab copies itself to produce many clones.
2. **Selection scheme:** for a population-based GA, good solutions are selected into the mating pool with a high probability. For AIS, good solutions are always selected.
3. **Evolution strategy:** for a population-based GA, the whole population evolves by using crossover. The hypothesis is if both parents are the good ones their crossed offspring would have a high probability to become even better solutions; mutation is only used to jump out of the local optima hence the diversity is very important, otherwise, GA is likely to reach premature convergence; for AIS, since clones are duplicates of their predecessor the evolution of the population depends mainly on the mutation of the clones. Recombination is also applied to the clones. Only in the later stages of the search can this operator takes effect.
4. **Elitism:** for a population-based GA, during each generation, the whole population is replaced with the offspring after mating; hence 'elitism' has to be introduced to preserve good solutions found hitherto, otherwise they would be lost during successive generations; for AIS, the mutated clones and their predecessors are mixed together to compete for survival, so the 'elitism' is inherently embedded in AIS.
5. **Population control:** for a population-based GA, since one has to specify the size of the mating pool in the first place the population size is thus fixed during each generation; if one only selects good solutions into the mating pool and makes the pool size flexible to the number of selected solutions GA could reach premature convergence due to its evolutionary strategy; a reasonable pool size is necessary so that in the early stage sub-optimal solutions can also get into the pool to increase population diversity; for AIS, a mating pool does not exist hence the population should be flexible and finally controlled by the mutual influences of Abs.
6. **Diversity preservation:** for a population-based GA, diverity is maintianed through the mutation and an adequate population size; obviously, the population size is problem-contingent; for AIS, diversity is maintianed through a prolific mechanism, affinitiy maturation, network suppression and the insertion of the newcomers.
7. **Fitness (affinity) assignment.** For conventional evolutionary algorithms, ranking and fitness assignment are only based on the information from the objective space; for AIS, it combines both to calculate affinity. So, it effectively uses the information from both the objective and decision variable space.

Based on such differences, it can be concluded that AIS, specifically PAIA2, possesses further strengths which cannot be found in the conventional evolutionary algorithms.

1. **Adaptive population.** Due to point 5 mentioned above, PAIA2 posses an adaptive population size which can adjust to an adequate size according to need of the problem under investigation. This adaptive rather

than a fixed population leads to the following three advantages: 1) Initial population size is not problem dependent; 2) more solutions can be obtained without significantly increasing the number of evaluations by tuning the network suppression threshold; 3) only necessary evaluations are exercised because only necessary population and clones are maintained and produced in each iteration step.

2. **Good jumping-off point.** By using the multi-stage optimization procedure, an optimized solution can be included in the initial population to bias the search process, which reduces the computational load of the whole optimization process.

3. **Good convergence.** Due to points 3 and 7, a good balance between exploitation and exploration of the search space is achieved, especially when the problem has variable density in the objective and decision variable spaces.

4. **Fast convergence.** The slow convergence observed in the previous works is eliminated, and fast convergence is claimed as one advantage of the proposed algorithm instead. In PAIA2, even a small initial size (e.g. 7) can give a very fast convergence because one only select good Abs and let them reproduce with an adaptive clone size. In the early iteration this can not only provide sufficient Abs to support the search but also accelerate the convergence speed.

FUTURE RESEARCH DIRECTIONS

Here, three possible directions to extend the current work presented in this chapter are identified, which are considered as deserving more attentions for the interested readers.

1. In the current implementation, newcomers are not included. However, it is reckoned that the diversity of the population can be further improved by inserting newcomers during the search process. Previous reported research findings normally insert randomly generated individuals at each iteration step. In this way, individuals may be generated in an area which has already been searched and classified as the not-so-good region. Hence, investigations into generating a more subtle way of forming newcomers deserves more research together with the negative selection principle (Espond, F. and Forrest, S., 2004) which may also play a significant role.

2. A more computationally efficient single objective optimization algorithm is needed to replace the current implementation of the first stage of the multi-stage optimization procedure.

3. Based on the neural-fuzzy models obtained in the last part of the body of the chapter, one can use AIS based MOP algorithm, such as PAIA2, to find and control the 'best' processing parameters and the corresponding chemical compositions to achieve certain pre-defined mechanical properties of steels.

REFERENCES

Burnet, F. M. (1959). *The Clonal Selection Theory of Acquired Immunity*. UK: Cambridge at the University Press,

Chen, J., & Mahfouf, M. (2006). A Population Adaptive Based Immune Algorithm for Solving Multi-objective Optimization Problems. In H. Bersini and J. Carneiro (Ed.), *ICARIS 2006, LNCS 4163* (pp. 280-293). Springer Berlin/Heidelberg.

Chen, J., & Mahfouf, M. (2008). An Immune Algorithm Based Fuzzy Predictive Modeling Mechanism using Variable Length Coding and Multi-objective Optimization Allied to Engineering Materials Processing. In *Proceedings of the 2009 IEEE International Conference on Granule Computation (GrC 2008)*. China.

Coello Coello, C. A., David, A., Van, V., & Lamont, G. B. (2002). *Evolutionary Algorithms for Solving Multi-objective Problems*. London, New York: Kluwer Academic.

Coello Coello, C. A., & Cruz Cortes, N. (2005). Solving Multiobjective Optimization Problems Using an Artificial Immune System. *Genetic Programming and Evolvable Machines, 6*(2), 163-190. Springer Netherlands.

de Castro, L. N., & Von Zuben, F. J. (2002). Learning and Optimization Using the Clonal Selection Principle. *IEEE Transactions on Evolutionary Computation, 6*(3), 239-251.

de Castro, L. N., & Timmis, J. (2002). An Artificial Immune Network for Multimodal Function Optimization. *Proc. of the IEEE Congress on Evolutionary Computation (CEC' 2002), 1,* 699-704. Honolulu, Hawaii.

Deb, K., & Agrawal, B. R. (1994). *Simulated Binary Crossover for Continuous Search Space* (Technical Reports IITK/ME/SMD-94027). Convenor: Indian Institute of Technology, Department of Mechanical Engineering.

Deb, K. (2001). *Multi-Objective Optimization using Evolutionary Algorithms*. Chichester, UK: Wiley.

Deb, K., Thiele, L., Laumanns, M., & Zitzler, E. (2001). *Scalable Test Problems for Evolutionary Multi-Objective Optimization* (TIK-Technical Report 112). Zurich: Swiss Federal Institute of Technology (ETH), Computer Engineering and Networks Laboratory (TIK).

Eberhart, R. C., & Kennedy, J. (1995). A New Optimizer Using Particle Swarm Theory. *The 6th International Symposium on Micro Machine and Human Science* (pp. 39-43).

Esponda, F., Forrest, S., & Helman, P. (2004). A Formal Framework for Positive and Negative Detection Scheme. *IEEE Transaction on Systems, Man, and Cybernetics, 34*(1), 357-373.

Farmer, J. D., & Packard, N. H. (1986). The Immune System, Adaptation, and Machine Learning. *Physica, 22D,* 187-204. North-Holland, Amsterdam.

Fonseca, C. M., & Fleming, P. J. (1993). Genetic Algorithms for Multi-objective Optimization: Foundation, Discussion, and Generalization. *Proc. Of the 5th International Conference on Genetic Algorithms* (pp. 416-423).

Freschi, F., & Repetto, M. (2005). Multiobjective Optimization by a Modified Artificial Immune System Algorithm. In: Christian Jacob et al. (eds.), *ICARIS 2004, LNCS 3627* (pp. 248-261). Springer Berlin/Heidelberg.

Fukuda, T., Mori, K., & Tsukiyama, M. (1998). Parallel Search for Multi-Modal Function Optimization with Diversity and Learning of Immune Algorithm. *Artificial Immune Systems and Their Applications* (pp. 210-220). Springer Berlin/Heidelberg.

Goldberg, D. E. (1989). *Genetic Algorithms for Search, Optimization, and Machine Learning*. MA: Addison-Wesley.

Gong, M. G., Jiao, L. C., Du, H. F., & Bo, L. F. (2006). *Multi-objective Immune Algorithm with Pareto-optimal Neighbor-based Selection* (Technical Report (IIIP-06-05)). China: Xiandian University, Institute of Intelligent Information Processing.

Hart, E., & Timmis, J. (2005). Application Areas of AIS: The Past, The Present and The Future. In C. Hacob et al. (Ed.), *ICARIS 2005, LNCS 3527* (pp. 483-497). Springer-Verlag Berlin/Heidelberg.

Jang, J. R. (1993). ANFIS: Adaptive-Network-Based Fuzzy Inference System. *IEEE Transaction on Systems, Man and Cybernetics, 23*(3), 665-685.

Jerne, N. K. (1974). Towards a Network Theory of the Immune System. *Ann. Immunology (Inst. Pasteur), 125C,* 373-389.

Jin, Y., Olhofer, M. & Sendhoff, B. (2001). Dynamic Weighted Aggregation for Evolutionary Multi-Objective Optimization: Why Does It Work and How? *Proc. GECCO 2001 Conf.* (pp. 1042-1049).

Kelsey, J., & Timmis, J. (2003). Immune Inspired Somatic Contiguous Hypermutation for Function Optimization. In Cantupaz, E. et al. (ed.), *Proc. Of Genetic and Evolutionary Computation Conference (GECCO).* Lecture Notes in Computer Science, *2723*, 207-218. Springer Berlin/Heidelberg.

Knowles, J. D., & Corne, D. W. (2000). Approximating the Nondominated Front Using the Pareto Archived Evolution Strategy. *Evolutionary Computation*, *8*(2), 149-172.

Mahfouf, M., Chen, M., & Linkens, D. A. (2005). Design of Heat-treated Alloy Steels Using Intelligent Multi-objective Optimization. *ISIJ International*, *45*(5), 694-699.

Nelder, J. A., & Mead, R. (1965). *Computer Journal*, *7*, 308-313.

Passino, K. M., & Yurkovich, S. (1998). *Fuzzy Control*. MA: Addison-Wesley.

Perelson, A. S. (1986). Immune Network Theory. *Immunological Review*, *110*, 5-36.

Schaffer, J. D., & Grefenstette, J. J. (1985). Multi-objective Learning via Genetic Algorithms. *Proc. Of the Ninth International Joint Conference on Artificial Intelligence*. Morgan Kaufmann (pp. 593-595).

Wang, X., Gao, X. Z., & Ovaska, S. J. (2004). Artificial Immune Optimization Methods and Applications-A Survey. *2004 International Conference on Systems, Man and Cybernetics*.

Zitzler, E., Laumanns, M., & Thiele, L. (2001). *SPEA2: Improving the Strength Pareto Evolutionary Algorithm* (TIK-Report 103). Zurich: Swiss Federal Institute of Technology (ETH), Computer Engineering and Networks Laboratory (TIK).

KEY TERMS

Ab-Ab Affinity (Abs' affinity): Is defined as the distance (refer to Eqs. (3)) in the decision variable space between one randomly chosen Ab in the first non-dominated front and the one in the remaining population.

Ab-Ab Suppression (Abs' suppression/Network suppression): When two Abs are very close to each other, they can be recognized by each other. The result is that one of them is suppressed and deleted. Unlike Abs' affinity, this term is defined as the *Euclidian* distance in the objective space.

Ag-Ab Affinity: For SOP, it is defined as the objective value (fitness value); for MOP, it is determined by using non-dominance concept, i.e. solutions in the first non-dominated front have the highest affinity, then the second front and so on.

Antibody (Ab): Ab is the candidate solutions of the problem to be optimized.

Antigen (Ag): Ag is the problem to be optimized.

Pareto Front: The plot of the objective functions whose non-dominated vectors are in the Pareto optimal set is called the Pareto front.

Transparency of the Fuzzy Model: A fuzzy model is regarded as having a better transparency if it contains less fuzzy rules, less fuzzy sets and less overlapped fuzzy sets.

Chapter III
An Artificial Immune Dynamical System for Optimization

Licheng Jiao
Xidian University, China

Maoguo Gong
Xidian University, China

Wenping Ma
Xidian University, China

ABSTRACT

Many immue-inspired algorithms are based on the abstractions of one or several immunology theories, such as clonal selection, negative selection, positive selection, rather than the whole process of immune response to solve computational problems. In order to build a general computational framework by simulating immune response process, this chapter introduces a population-based artificial immune dynamical system, termed as PAIS, and applies it to numerical optimization problems. PAIS models the dynamic process of human immune response as a quaternion (G, I, R, Al), where G denotes exterior stimulus or antigen, I denotes the set of valid antibodies, R denotes the set of reaction rules describing the interactions between antibodies, and Al denotes the dynamic algorithm describing how the reaction rules are applied to antibody population. Some general descriptions of reaction rules, including the set of clonal selection rules and the set of immune memory rules are introduced in PAIS. Based on these reaction rules, a dynamic algorithm, termed as PAISA, is designed for numerical optimization. In order to validate the performance of PAISA, 9 benchmark functions with 20 to 10,000 dimensions and a practical optimization problem, optimal approximation of linear systems are solved by PAISA, successively. The experimental results indicate that PAISA has high performance in optimizing some benchmark functions and practical optimization problems.

Copyright © 2009, IGI Global, distributing in print or electronic forms without written permission of IGI Global is prohibited.

INTRODUCTION

Biological inspiration can successfully be transferred into novel computational paradigms, as shown in the development and successful use of concepts such as artificial neural networks, evolutionary algorithms, swarm algorithms, and so on. Many bio-inspired algorithms are based on populations of agents trained to perform some task or optimization. The most obvious one is the area of evolutionary algorithms, based on analogy to populations of organisms breeding and selecting to become "fitter" (Stepney, Smith, Timmis, & Tyrrell, 2004).

In recent years, **Artificial Immune Systems** (AIS) have received a significant amount of interest from researchers and industrial sponsors. Some of the first work in applying human immune system (HIS) metaphors was undertaken in the area of fault diagnosis (Ishida, 1990). Later work applied HIS metaphors to the field of computer security (Forrest, Perelson, Allen, & Cherukuri, 1994), which seemed to act as a catalyst for further investigation of HIS as a metaphor in such areas as Anomaly Detection (Gonzalez, Dasgupta, & Kozma, 2002), Pattern Recognition (Carter, 2000; Timmis, Neal, & Hunt, 2000; White, & Garrett, 2003), Job shop Scheduling (Hart, & Ross, 1999; Coello Coello, Rivera, & Cortes, 2003), optimization (Jiao &Wang, 2000; de Castro & Von Zuben, 2002) and Engineering Design Optimization (Hajela, Yoo, & Lee, 1997; Gong, Jiao, Du, & Wang, 2005).

In order to build a general computational framework by simulating the whole process of immune response, this chapter introduces a model for population-based Artificial Immune Systems, termed as PAIS. PAIS models the dynamic process of human immune response as a quaternion (*G, I, R, AI*), where *G* denotes exterior stimulus or antigen, *I* denotes the set of valid antibodies, *R* denotes the set of reaction rules describing the interactions between antibodies, and *AI* denotes the dynamic algorithm describing how the reaction rules are applied to antibody population. PAIS can be considered as a general architecture of population-based artificial immune systems rather than an immune algorithm. Many immune phenomena, such as clonal selection, immune memory, negative selection, passive selection, can be modeled as corresponding reaction rules and added to the set of reaction rules *R*. Based on the PAIS, our final aim is to build a self-adaptive dynamical system by simulating all the possible interactions between antibodies during immune response. Then the PAIS can automatically select reaction rules depending on antigen *G*, and thereby the pending problems could be solved automatically. In order to solve numerical optimization problems, the set of clonal selection rules and the set of immune memory rules are introduced. Consequently, a dynamic algorithm based on these heuristic rules is designed, which can effectively solve numerical optimization problems even when the number of variable parameters is as many as 10 000.

The rest of the paper is organized as follows: Section 2 describes some related background. Section 3 describes the population-based artificial immune dynamical system architecture. Section 4 describes the experimental study on nine benchmark functions. Section 5 describes the experimental study on the optimal approximation of linear systems. Finally, concluding remarks are presented in Section 6.

RELATED BACKGROUND

The human immune system (HIS) is a highly evolved, parallel and distributed adaptive system. Human immune response relies on the prior formation of an incredibly diverse population of B cells and T cells (Abbas, Lichtman, & Pober, 2000). The specificity of both the B-cell receptors and T-cell receptors, that is, the epitope to which a given receptor can bind, is created by a remarkable genetic mechanism. Each receptor is created even though the epitope it recognizes may never have been present in the body. If an antigen with that epitope should enter the body, those few lymphocytes able to bind to it will do so. If they also receive a second co-stimulatory signal, they may begin repeated rounds of mitosis. In this way, clones of antigen-specific lymphocytes (B and T) develop providing the basis of the immune response. This phenomenon is called clonal selection (Burnet, 1978; Berek & Ziegner, 1993; Abbas, Lichtman, & Pober, 2000). In fact, besides the clonal selection, during the initial expansion of clones, some of the progeny cells neither went on dividing nor developed into plasma cells. Instead, they reverted to small lymphocytes bearing the same B-cell receptor on their surface that their ancestors had. This lays the foundation for a more rapid and massive response the next time the antigen enters the body, i.e. immune memory.

The information processing abilities of HIS provide important aspects in the field of computation. This emerging field is referring to as the Immunological Computation, Immunocomputing or **Artificial Immune Systems** (Tarakanov, & Dasgupta, 2000) which can be defined as computational systems inspired by theoretical immunology and observed immune functions, principles and models, which are applied to problem solving (de Castro, & Timmis, 2002). The first immune optimization algorithm may be the work of Fukuda, Mori and Tsukiyama (1993) that included an abstraction of clonal selection to solve computational problems (Garrett, 2005). But the AIS for optimization have been popularized mainly by de Castro and Von Zuben's CLONALG (de Castro & Von Zuben, 2002). CLONALG selects part fittest antibodies to clone proportionally to their antigenic affinities. The hypermutation operator performs an affinity maturation process inversely proportional to the fitness values generating the matured clone population. After computing the antigenic affinity of the matured clone population, CLONALG creates randomly part new antibodies to replace the lowest fitness antibodies in current population and retain best antibodies to recycle. de Castro and Timmis proposed an artificial immune network called opt-aiNet (de Castro, & Timmis, 2002) for multimodal optimization. In opt-aiNet, antibodies are part of an immune network and the decision about the individual which will be cloned, suppressed or maintained depends on the interaction established by the immune network. Kelsey and Timmis (2003) proposed the B Cell Algorithm (BCA). Through a process of evaluation, cloning, mutation and selection, BCA evolves a population of individuals (B cells) towards a global optimum. Each member of the B cell population can be considered as an independent entity. Garrett has presented an attempt to remove all the parameters from clonal selection algorithm (Garrett, 2004). This method, which is called ACS for short, attempts to self-evolve various parameters during a single run. Cutello and Nicosia proposed an immune algorithm for optimization called opt-IA (Cutello, Nicosia, & Pavone 2004; Cutello, Narzisi, Nicosia, & Pavone, 2005). Opt-IA uses three immune operators, cloning, hypermutation and aging. In hypermutation operator, the number of mutations is determined by mutation potential. The aging operator eliminates old individuals to avoid premature convergence. Opt-IA also uses a standard evolutionary operator, $(\mu + \lambda)$-selection operator. Meanwhile, the clonal selection has also been successfully applied to multi-objective optimization field (Coello Coello, & Cortes, 2005; Jiao, Gong, Shang, et al., 2005; Freschi, & Repetto, 2006; Gong, Jiao, Du, & Bo, 2007). Furthermore, negative Selection (Ji, & Dasgupta, 2007), danger theory (Aickelin, & Cayzer, 2002) and some other immune theories have also been frequently applied as computational paradigms. However, few of them have been applied to optimization.

The majority immune-inspired optimization algorithms mentioned above are concentrated on the clonal selection while the immune memory is only a concomitant which is simply modeled as the elitist selection. Furthermore, these algorithms encoded the parameters into individuals where each individual represents a search point in the space of potential solutions. A large number of parameters would result in a large search space (Cheng & Hwang, 2001). Nowadays, there is no report about AIS algorithms effectively solving numerical optimization problems with more than 100 parameters.

A POPULATION-BASED ARTIFICIAL IMMUNE DYNAMICAL SYSTEM

HIS incorporates mechanisms that enable antibodies (lymphocytes) to learn the structures of specific foreign proteins. Essentially, HIS evolves and reproduces antibodies that have high affinities for specific antigens. In this chapter, we introduce a model for population-based Artificial Immune Systems, termed as PAIS. PAIS models the dynamic process of human immune response as a quaternion (G, I, R, Al) (Gong, Jiao, Liu, & Du, 2005), where G denotes exterior stimulus or antigen, I denotes the set of valid antibodies, R denotes the set of reaction rules describing the interactions between antibodies, and Al denotes the dynamic algorithm describing how the reaction rules are applied to antibody population.

Quaternion Model of PAIS

Among the four elements of the PAIS model (G, I, R, Al), antibody space I and dynamic algorithm Al depend on the antigen G, and the practical design of reaction rules in Set R depend on the antigen G and the representation method of antibodies.

Antigen G

In immunology, an antigen is any substance that causes immune system to produce antibodies against it. In PAIS, antigens refer to the pending problems. Taking optimization problem (*P*) for example

$$(P) \begin{cases} \text{minimize} & f(x) \\ \text{subject to} & g_i(x) < 0 \quad i = 1, 2, \cdots, p \\ & h_j(x) = 0 \quad j = p+1, p+2, \cdots, q \end{cases} \tag{1}$$

where $x = (x_1, x_2, \ldots, x_m)$ is called the decision vector, antigen is the function of objective function $f(x)$, i.e. $G(x) = g(f(x))$. Similar to the effect of antigen in immunology, it is the initial factor of artificial immune response.

Antibody Space I

In PAIS, an antibody represents a candidate solution of an antigen. The antibody $a = a_1 a_2 \cdots a_l$ is the coding of variable x, denoted by $a = e(x)$, and x is called the decoding of antibody a, expressed as $x = e^{-1}(a)$. The representation of antibody a varies with antigen G, can be binary string, real number sequence, symbolic sequence, and characteristic sequence. In this study, we adopt real-coded presentation, i.e. $a = e(x) = x$.

Set I is called antibody space, where $a \in I$. An antibody population $A = \{a_1, a_2, \cdots, a_n\}, a_k \in I, \ 1 \le k \le n$, is an n-dimensional group of antibody a, where the positive integer n is the antibody population size.

In order to explain the concepts of antibody and antibody population, we give a simple example as follows. For the optimization problem in equation (1), if a vector $x_1 = (0.5, 0.2, 4, 5)$ belongs to the feasible region, then x_1 is a candidate solution of the optimization problem (*P*), the corresponding real-coded antibody is denoted by $a_1 = (0.5, 0.2, 4, 5)$. If $a_1 = (0.5, 0.2, 4, 5)$, $a_2 = (0.7, 0.6, 4, 7)$, and $a_3 = (0.2, 0.6, 6, 1)$, are three antibodies, then the set $A = \{a_1, a_2, a_3\}$ is an antibody population with size 3.

The Set of Reaction Rules R

The set R describes all the possible interactions between antibodies in antibody space I. For antibody population $A = \{a_1, a_2, \cdots, a_n\}$, a rule $R \in R$ can be expressed as

$$R(A) = R(a_1 + a_2 + \cdots + a_n) = a_1' + a_2' + \cdots + a_m' \tag{2}$$

where n, m are positive integers, the value of m depends on rule R, and the representation '+' is not the arithmetical operator, but only separates the antibodies on either side in Equation (2). Equation (2) shows that the n antibodies of A evolve into m antibodies on the right-hand side by the work of reaction rule R. For simulating biologic immune response in detail, it is necessary to design enough rules inspired by biologic immune system.

Dynamic Algorithm AI

AI is the algorithm simulating the process of antibody evolution and dominating interactions among antibodies during artificial immune response, including the format of the set R acting on antibody space I, the calculation of antibody-antibody affinity and antibody-antigen affinity, the termination judgment, and so on.

Antibody-antigen affinity reflects the total combination power locales between antigen and antibodies. In PAIS, it generally indicates values of objective functions or fitness measurement of the problem. Antibody-antibody affinity reflects the total combination power locales between two antibodies. In PAIS, it generally indicates the distance between two antibodies. Especially, Hamming distance is adopted for binary coding and Euclidian distance is adopted for decimal coding. The termination criterion can be set as a limited number of iterations or the best solution cannot be further improved in successive given iterations or some others.

Reaction Rules Designed for PAIS

In this chapter, we design the set $\boldsymbol{R}$ composed of two subsets, namely, the set of clonal selection rules $\boldsymbol{R}_{CS}$ and the set of immune memory rules $\boldsymbol{R}_M$, then $\boldsymbol{R} = \boldsymbol{R}_{CS} \cup \boldsymbol{R}_M$.

The Set of Clonal Selection Rules R$_{CS}$

The clonal selection theory is used in immunology to describe the basic features of an immune response. Its main idea lies in that the antibodies can selectively react to the antigens, which are the native production and spread on the cell surface in the form of peptides. The reaction leads to cell clonal proliferation and the colony has the same antibodies. Some clonal cells divide into the eventual production of a pool of plasma cells, and others become immune memory cells to boost the secondary immune response (Abbas, Lichtman, & Pober, 2000).

Inspired by the clonal selection principle, the set of clonal selection rules $\boldsymbol{R}_{CS}$ include Clonal Proliferation Rule (R_P^C), Affinity Maturation Rule (R_M^A) and Clonal Selection Rule (R_S^C) on the antibody population $A(k)$, where the antibody population at time k is represented by the time-dependent variable matrix $A(k) = \{a_1(k), a_2(k), \cdots, a_n(k)\}$. The evolution process can be described as:

$$A(k) \xrightarrow{R_P^C} Y(k) \xrightarrow{R_M^A} Z(k) \cup A(k) \xrightarrow{R_S^C} A(k+1) \tag{3}$$

The main operations of $\boldsymbol{R}_{CS}$ is shown in Figure 1.

Clonal Proliferation Rule R_P^C: Define

$$Y(k) = R_P^C(A(k)) = [R_P^C(a_1(k)), R_P^C(a_2(k)), \cdots, R_P^C(a_n(k))]^T \tag{4}$$

where $Y_i(k) = R_P^C(a_i(k)) = I_i \times a_i(k)$, $i = 1, 2, \cdots, n$, I_i is a q_i-dimensional identity column vector. $q_i \in [1, n_c]$, termed as clonal scale, is a self-adaptive parameter, or set as a constant, n_c is a given value related to the upper limit of clonal scale.

After Clonal Proliferation, the population becomes:

Figure 1. The main operational process of $\boldsymbol{R}_{CS}$

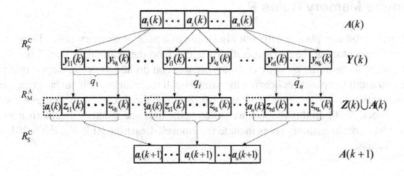

$$Y(k) = \{Y_1(k), Y_2(k), \cdots, Y_n(k)\} \tag{5}$$

where

$$Y_i(k) = \{y_{ij}(k)\} = \{y_{i1}(k), y_{i2}(k), \cdots, y_{iq_i}(k)\} \text{ and } y_{ij}(k) = a_i(k), \; j = 1, 2, \cdots, q_i \; \; i = 1, 2, \cdots, n \tag{6}$$

Affinity Maturation Rule R_M^A: Inspired by immune response process, the Affinity Maturation Operation R_M^A is diversified basically by two mechanisms: hypermutation (Berek & Ziegner, 1993) and receptor editing (George & Gray, 1999).

Random changes are introduced into the genes, i.e. mutation, such changes may lead to an increase in the affinity of the clonal antibody occasionally.

Antibodies had deleted their low-affinity receptors (genes) and developed entirely new ones through recombination, i.e. receptor editing (de Castro & Von Zuben, 2003). Receptor editing offers the ability to escape from local optima on an affinity landscape.

After Affinity Maturation Operation, the population becomes:

$$Z(k) = \{Z_1(k), Z_2(k), \cdots, Z_n(k)\} \tag{7}$$

where

$$Z_i(k) = \{z_{ij}(k)\} = \{z_{i1}(k), z_{i2}(k), \cdots, z_{iq_i}(k)\} \text{ and } z_{ij}(k) = R_M^A\left(y_{ij}(k)\right), \; j = 1, 2, \cdots, q_i \; \; i = 1, 2, \cdots, n \tag{8}$$

Clonal Selection Rule R_S^C: $\forall \; i = 1, 2 \cdots n$, if $b_i(k) \in Z_i(k)$ is the best antibody (the antibody with the highest Affinity) in $Z_i(k)$, then

$$a_i(k+1) = R_S^C\left(Z_i(k) \bigcup a_i(k)\right) = \begin{cases} b_i(k) & \text{if } b_i(k) \text{ is better than } a_i(k) \\ a_i(k) & \text{else} \end{cases} \tag{9}$$

The new population is

$$
\begin{aligned}
A(k+1) &= R_S^C\left(Z(k) \bigcup A(k)\right) \\
&= \left[R_S^C\left(Z_1(k) \bigcup a_1(k)\right), \quad R_S^C\left(Z_2(k) \bigcup a_2(k)\right), \quad \cdots, \quad R_S^C\left(Z_n(k) \bigcup a_n(k)\right) \right]^{\mathrm{T}} \\
&= \{a_1(k+1), a_2(k+1), \cdots, a_n(k+1)\}
\end{aligned}
\tag{10}
$$

where $a_i(k+1) = R_S^C\left(Z_i(k) \bigcup a_i(k)\right) \; \; i = 1, 2 \cdots n.$

The Set of Immune Memory Rules R$_M$

Clonal selection not only produces plasma cells but also leads to a pool of memory cells. These memory cells are B lymphocytes with receptors of the same specificity as those on the original activated B cell. During the initial expansion of clones, some of the progeny cells neither went on dividing nor developed into plasma cells. Instead, they reverted to small lymphocytes bearing the same B-cell receptor on their surface that their ancestors had. This lays the foundation for a more rapid and massive response the next time the antigen enters the body (Abbas, Lichtman, & Pober, 2000). In this chapter, we simulate the immune memory mechanism by setting up a memory population. The immune memory rules include the Nonself-Learning Rule R_M^N, the Self-Learning Rule R_M^S and the Feedback Rule R_M^F.

Nonself-Learning Rule R_M^N: If the memory population is $M = \{m_1, m_2, m_3, \cdots, m_s\}$, and a_0 is an antibody outside M, then the Nonself-Learning Rule R_M^N can be written in the form of

$$R_M^N (M + a_0) = \{m_1' + m_2' + m_3' + \cdots + m_s'\} \tag{11}$$

where R_M^N designed as follows: calculating the antibody-antibody affinities between a_0 and all the antibodies in M. Antibody-antibody affinities embody the relative distribution of antibodies in antibody space I, the larger the value, the bigger difference of genes the two antibodies have, contrariwise, it is still right. If the antibody-antibody affinity between $m_i \in M$ and a_0 is the minimum one, and its value is δ_{i0}, then there are two cases to be considered: if $\delta_{i0} \leq \delta_0$, where δ_0 is the minimum distance between every two individuals of M, then

$$m_i' = \begin{cases} a_0 & \text{if } a_0 \text{ is better than } m_i \\ m_i & \text{else} \end{cases} \tag{12}$$

Otherwise, if $\delta_{i0} > \delta_0$, it means that the distance between a_0 and any individual of M is greater than the minimum distance between every two individuals of M, therefore, a_0 is a relative isolate individual, at least is not the most crowded one. Under this condition, we add a_0 into M, meanwhile, in order to keep the memory population size unchanged, we delete the worst antibody of M. In this way, the Nonself-Learning of M is absorbed in maintaining the population diversity.

Self-Learning Rule R_M^S: Memory population does not only learn external information pattern by R_M^N, but also learning new pattern in the form of hypermutation (Berek, Ziegner, 1993) and receptor editing (George & Gray, 1999). References (Zhong, Liu, Xue, & Jiao, 2004) and (Kazarlis, Papadakis, Theocharis, & Petridis, 2001) use small scale GAs as the local searchers and obtain good performances. Enlightened by their idea, we propose the Self-Learning Rule R_M^S of memory population which uses a small scale clonal selection rules $R_{CS} = \{R_P^C, R_M^A, R_S^C\}$ to realize the local search in the surrounding of excellent antibodies (memory antibodies). The Self-Learning Rule R_M^S on $M = \{m_1, m_2, m_3, \cdots, m_s\}$ can be written as

$$R_M^S (M) = \{m_1' + m_2' + m_3' + \cdots + m_s'\} \tag{13}$$

In this way, the Self-Learning of M is absorbed in local search in the surrounding of excellent antibodies.

Feedback Rule R_M^F: The antibodies of memory population can retroact at antibody population, which is denoted as the Feedback Rule R_M^F of Memory population. The Feedback Rule R_M^F of $M = \{m_1, m_2, \cdots, m_s\}$ on antibody population $A(k) = \{a_1(k), a_2(k), \cdots, a_n(k)\}$ can be described as:

$$R_M^F (M + A(k)) = M + A'(k) \tag{14}$$

R_M^F means that randomly select $l = \lfloor T\% \times s \rfloor$ antibodies of M to replace the worst l antibodies of $A(k)$, $T\%$ is a constant, termed as feedback ratio, and s is the memory population size.

Dynamic Algorithm Driving the Population Evolution

Dynamic algorithm AI is the algorithm dominating the interactions between antibodies and driving the antibody population evolution in PAIS, including the format of the set R acting on antibody populations, the affinity assignment, the termination judgment, and so on. ALGORITHM 1 describes the details of the population-based **artificial immune system** algorithm (PAISA) for numerical optimization. See Algorithm 1.

Algorithm 1.

ALGORITHM 1 Population-based AIS Algorithm (PAISA)

   Step 1) Initialization: Give the termination criterion.

   Randomly generate the initial antibody population:
$$A(0) = \{a_1(0), a_2(0), \cdots a_n(0)\} \in I^n .$$

   Randomly generate the memory population:
$$M(0) = \{m_1(0), m_2(0), \cdots, m_s(0)\} \in I^s .$$

   Calculate the antibody-antigen affinities of all antibodies of $A(0)$ and $M(0)$. $k=0$.

   Step 2) Perform R_{CS}:

   Step 2.1) Clonal Proliferation: Get $Y(k)$ by applying R_P^C to $A(k)$.

   Step 2.2) Affinity Maturation: Get $Z(k)$ by applying R_M^A to $Y(k)$.

   Step 2.3) Evaluation: Calculate the antibody-antigen affinities of all antibodies of $Z(k)$.

   Step 2.4) Clonal Selection: Get $A(k+1)$ by applying R_S^C to $Z(k)$ and $A(k)$.

   Step 3) Perform R_M:

   Step 3.1) Nonself-Learning: Update the memory population $M(k)$ by applying R_M^N to $M(k)$ and the best antibody of $A(k+1)$.

   Step 3.2) Self-Learning: Get $M(k+1)$ by applying R_M^S to $M(k)$.

   Step 3.3) Feedback: Update $A(k+1)$ by applying the Feedback Rule R_M^F of $M(k+1)$ to $A(k+1)$.

   Step 4) Termination Judgment: If a stopping condition is satisfied, stop the algorithm. Otherwise, $k=k+1$, go to **Step 2)**.

Analysis of PAIS and PAISA

In this chapter, in order to solve numerical optimization problems, the dynamic algorithm PAISA adopts two sets of rules, namely, the clonal selection rules and the immune memory rules. Hereinto, the clonal selection rules are highly inspired from the works mentioned in Section 1, including CLONALG and opt-IA. However, the Clonal Selection Rule R_S^C is different from the truncation selection in CLONALG and opt-IA. R_S^C selects the best one individual $a_i(k+1)$ from the sub-population $Z_i(k) \cup a_i(k)$, respectively, and all the best individuals $a_i(k+1)$ $i = 1, 2, \cdots n$ constitute the new population. Therefore, single individuals will be optimized locally by the clonal proliferation rule, the affinity maturation rule, and the clonal selection rule. Furthermore, PAISA is unique in its immune memory rules. Essentially, PAISA performs on two populations, i.e. the antibody population $A(k)$ and the memory population $M(k)$. The evolutionary process of $A(k)$ can be described as

$$A(k+1) = R_M^F \left(R_S^C \left(R_M^A \left(R_P^C (A(k)) \right) \right) + M(k+1) \right) \tag{15}$$

The evolutionary process of $M(k)$ can be described as

$$M(k+1) = R_M^S \left(R_M^N \left(M(k) + a_0 \right) \right) \tag{16}$$

where a_0 is the best antibody of $A(k+1)$. The evolution of $A(k)$ pays more attention to global search and accelerate the convergence speed, while the evolution of $M(k)$ is absorbed in local search in the surrounding of excellent antibodies and maintaining the population diversity.

Definition 1. *For antibody set* B, $\vartheta(B) \triangleq \left| B \cap B^* \right|$, *where* B^* *is the set of global optimums,* $|\cdot|$ *denotes the cardinality of a set.*

The function $\vartheta(B)$ means the number of global optimum in B, $\vartheta(B) \geq 1$ means that there is at least one global optimum in the antibody population B.

Based on the concepts above and (Rudolph, 1994; Dinabandhu, Murthy, & Sankar, 1996), we have Definition 2.

Definition 2. *For random state* B_0, *the PAISA can converge to global optimum, if and only if*

$$\lim_{k \to \infty} p\left\{ B(k) \cap B^* \neq \varnothing \middle| B(0) = B_0 \right\} = \lim_{k \to \infty} p\left\{ \vartheta(B(k)) \geq 1 \middle| B(0) = B_0 \right\} = 1 \tag{17}$$

This leads to:

Theorem 1. *The population-based artificial immune system algorithm PAISA can converge to global optimum.*
Proof: Let $p_0(k) = p\left\{ \vartheta\left(A(k) \cup M(k)\right) = 0 \right\} = p\left\{ (A(k) \cup M(k)) \cap B^* = \varnothing \right\}$, from Bayes's Theorem (Swinburne, 2002), we get

$$p_0(k+1) = p\left\{ \vartheta\left(A(k+1) \cup M(k+1)\right) = 0 \right\} =$$
$$p\left\{ \vartheta(A(k+1) \cup M(k+1)) = 0 \middle| \vartheta(A(k) \cup M(k)) \neq 0 \right\} \times p\left\{ \vartheta(A(k) \cup M(k)) \neq 0 \right\}$$
$$+ p\left\{ \vartheta(A(k+1) \cup M(k+1)) = 0 \middle| \vartheta(A(k) \cup M(k)) = 0 \right\} \times p\left\{ \vartheta(A(k) \cup M(k)) = 0 \right\} \tag{18}$$

$\forall Z(k) \in I^{\sum q_i}$, if $\vartheta(Z(k)) \geq 1$ or $\vartheta(A(k)) \geq 1$, then $p\left\{ \vartheta(R_S^C(Z(k) \cup A(k))) \geq 1 \right\} = 1$.

Consequently,

$$p\left\{ \vartheta\left(A(k+1) \cup M(k+1)\right) = 0 \middle| \vartheta(A(k) \cup M(k)) \neq 0 \right\} = 0 \tag{19}$$

Therefore, Equation (18) can be simplified as

$$p_0(k+1) = p\left\{ \vartheta\left(A(k+1) \cup M(k+1)\right) = 0 \middle| \vartheta(A(k) \cup M(k)) = 0 \right\} \times p_0(k) \tag{20}$$

Each elements of the state space can be regard as an integer number in binary representation. The projection $b_i(k) \in A(k) \cup M(k)$ picks up the i-th bit segment of length l from the binary representation of the state at time k and used to identify single individuals from the population $A(k) \cup M(k)$. Suppose that the hamming distance between b_i and $b^* \in B^*$ is l_1. From reference (Rudolph, 1994) the probability of generating b^* from b_i by mutation, marked as $p\left\{ b_i \to b^* \right\}$, satisfies $p\left\{ b_i \to b^* \right\} = \left(p_m^{l_i}(1 - p_m)^{l - l_i} \right)^{qt} > 0$, where p_m is the mutation probability. Thus,

$$p\left\{ \vartheta\left(A(k+1) \cup M(k+1)\right) = 1 \middle| \vartheta(A(k) \cup M(k)) = 0 \right\}_{\min} \geq \min_i p\left\{ b_i \to b^* \right\} > 0 \tag{21}$$

Let $\zeta = \min_k p\left\{ \vartheta\left(A(k+1) \cup M(k+1)\right) = 1 \middle| \vartheta(A(k) \cup M(k)) = 0 \right\}_{\min}$, $k = 0, 1, 2 \cdots$ then

$$p\left\{\vartheta\left(A(k+1)\cup M(k+1)\right)\geq 1\,\middle|\,\vartheta\left(A(k)\cup M(k)\right)=0\right\}\geq \zeta>0. \tag{22}$$

Consequently,

$$P\left\{\vartheta\left(A(k+1)\cup M(k+1)\right)=0\,\middle|\,\vartheta\left(A(k)\cup M(k)\right)=0\right\}$$
$$=1-P\left\{\vartheta\left(A(k+1)\cup M(k+1)\right)\neq 0\,\middle|\,\vartheta\left(A(k)\cup M(k)\right)=0\right\}$$
$$=1-P\left\{\vartheta\left(A(k+1)\cup M(k+1)\right)\geq 1\,\middle|\,\vartheta\left(A(k)\cup M(k)\right)=0\right\}\leq 1-\zeta<1 \tag{23}$$

Therefore,

$$0\leq p_0(k+1)\leq\left(1-\zeta\right)\times p_0(k)\leq\left(1-\zeta\right)^2\times p_0(k-1)\cdots\leq\left(1-\zeta\right)^{k+1}\times p_0(0). \tag{24}$$

Notes that $\lim\limits_{k\to\infty}\left(1-\zeta\right)^{k+1}=0, 1\geq p_0(0)\geq 0$, thus,

$$0\leq\lim_{k\to\infty}p_0(k)\leq\lim_{k\to\infty}\left(1-\zeta\right)^{k+1}\times p_0(0)=0. \tag{25}$$

Therefore, $\lim\limits_{k\to\infty}p_0(k)=0$. Consequently,

$$\lim_{k\to\infty}p\left\{\left(A(k)\cup M(k)\right)\cup B^*\neq\varnothing\,\middle|\,A(0)\cup M(0)=B_0\right\}=1-\lim_{k\to\infty}p_0(k)=1. \tag{26}$$

Thus, the population-based artificial immune system algorithm PAISA can converge to global optimum.

EXPERIMENTAL STUDIES ON BENCHMARK FUNCTIONS

In order to test the performance of PAISA, nine benchmark functions showed in Table 1 have been used. The nine benchmark functions were examined in (Gonzalez, Dasgupta, & Kozma, 2002), f_1–f_5 are multimodal functions where the number of local minima increases with the problem dimension. f_6–f_9 are unimodal functions.

We use experiments to evaluate the performance of PAISA by comparing with some existing **Evolutionary Algorithms** (EAs) including BGA (Mühlenbein, & Dirk, 1993), AEA (Pan & Kang, 1997), OGA/Q (Leung & Wang, 2001), IEA (Ho, Shu, & Chen, 2004) and MAGA (Zhong, Liu, Xue, & Jiao, 2004). The existing results reported in (Mühlenbein & Dirk, 1993; Pan & Kang, 1997; Leung & Wang, 2001; Ho, Shu, & Chen, 2004; Zhong, Liu, Xue, & Jiao, 2004) can be used for direct comparisons. We first give a brief description of the five algorithms.

1) BGA: It is based on artificial selection similar to that used by human breeders, and is a recombination of evolution strategies (ES) and GAs. BGA uses truncation selection as performed by breeders. This selection scheme is similar to the (μ, λ)-strategy in ES. The search process of BGA is mainly driven by recombination, making BGA a genetic algorithm.
2) AEA: This is a modified version of BGA. Besides the new recombination operator and the mutation operator, each individual of AEA is coded as a vector with components all in the unit interval, and inversion is applied with some probability to the parents before recombination is performed.
3) OGA/Q: This is a modified version of the classical **genetic algorithm**. It uses the quantization technique and the orthogonal design to generate the initial population and the offspring of the crossover operator.

Table 1. Benchmark functions used in this study

Test functions	x domain	Optimum
$f_1(x) = -\sum_{i=1}^{D} x_i \sin\left(\sqrt{|x_i|}\right)$	[-500, 500]	-412.9829D (min)
$f_2(x) = 10D + \sum_{i=1}^{D}(x_i^2 - 10\cos(2\pi x_i))$	[-5.12, 5.12]	0 (min)
$f_3(x) = -20\exp\left(-0.2\sqrt{\frac{1}{D}\sum_{i}^{D} x_i^2}\right)$ $-\exp\left(\frac{1}{D}\sum_{i=1}^{D}\cos(2\pi x_i)\right) + 20 + e$	[-32, 32]	0 (min)
$f_4(x) = \sum_{i=1}^{D}\frac{x_i^2}{4000} - \prod_{i=1}^{D}\cos(\frac{x_i}{\sqrt{i}}) + 1$	[-600, 600]	0 (min)
$f_5(x) = \frac{1}{D}\sum_{i=1}^{D}(x_i^4 - 16x_i^2 + 5x_i)$	[-5, 5]	-78.33236 (min)
$f_6(x) = \sum_{i=1}^{D} x_i^2$	[-100, 100]	0 (min)
$f_7(x) = \sum_{i=1}^{D}|x_i| + \prod_{i=1}^{D}|x_i|$	[-10, 10]	0 (min)
$f_8(x) = \sum_{i=1}^{D}\left(\sum_{j=1}^{i} x_j\right)^2$	[-100, 100]	0 (min)
$f_9(x) = \sum_{i=1}^{D} x_i^4 + random[0,1)$	[-1.28, 1.28]	0 (min)

4)   IEA: This is an **evolutionary algorithm** based on orthogonal design. IEA uses a novel intelligent gene collector (IGC) in recombination. Based on orthogonal experimental design, IGC uses a divide-and-conquer approach, which consists of adaptively dividing two individuals of parents into N pairs of gene segments, economically identifying the potentially better one of two gene segments of each pair, and systematically obtaining a potentially good approximation to the best one of all combinations using at most $2N$ fitness evaluations.

5)   MAGA: It integrates multi-agent systems and **genetic algorithm**s for solving the global numerical optimization problem. An agent in MAGA represents a candidate solution to the optimization problem in hand. All agents live in a lattice-like environment, with each agent fixed on a lattice-point. In order to increase energies, they compete or cooperate with their neighbors, and they can also use knowledge. Making use of these agent-agent interactions, MAGA realizes the purpose of minimizing the objective function value.

   In the following experiments, PAISA adopts real-coded representation. The antibody-antigen affinity is a linear mapping of the value of the objective function $f(\bullet)$ for a given antibody. We design the hypermutation and receptor editing in R_M^A as follows.

   For the antibody $y_{ij}(k)$, $i = 1, 2, \cdots, n$ $j = 1, 2, \cdots q_i$ in the antibody population $Y(k)$, replacing its certain numbers by a random integer between 0 and 9. For example, if a three-dimensional optimization problem to be solved, the antibody $y_{ij}(k) = (1.233567, 12.334567, 0.123356)$, and the second variable's fifth number is selected to mutate. Then we can randomly generate an integer between 0 and 9 to take the place of the number '4'.

   The receptor editing is designed as follows. Let $a = \{a_1, a_2, \cdots, a_l\}$ be the antibody to be recombined, $i, j \in \{1, 2, \cdots, l\}$ be two integers generated randomly, then the recombined antibody a' is $a' = \{a_1, a_2, \cdots a_{i-1}, m_i, m_{i+1}, \cdots, m_j, a_{j+1}, \cdots, a_l\}$

Table 2.Performance comparisons of PAISA, IEA and OGA/Q

f	D	Mean number of function evaluations			Mean function value (Standard deviation)		
		PAISA	IEA	OGA/Q	PAISA	IEA	OGA/Q
f_1	30	**1,984**	54,706	302,166	**-12569.49** **(1.040166×10⁻⁷)**	-12569.49 (6.079×10⁻³)	-12569.4537 (6.447×10⁻⁴)
f_2	30	**2,528**	8,420	224,710	1.705302×10⁻¹² (1.678557×10⁻¹¹)	**0** **(0)**	**0** **(0)**
f_3	30	**2,774**	8,420	112,421	3.512307×10⁻¹⁶ (2.190891×10⁻¹⁷)	**0** **(0)**	4.440×10⁻¹⁶ (3.989×10⁻¹⁷)
f_4	30	**2,612**	16,840	134,000	1.017947×10⁻¹⁵ (3.857255×10⁻¹⁶)	**0** **(0)**	**0** **(0)**
f_5	100	**4,794**	184,711	245,930	**- 78.33236** **(1.978150×10⁻⁹)**	-78.33232 (6.353×10⁻⁶)	-78.3000296 (6.288×10⁻³)
f_6	30	**3,956**	16,840	112,559	2.512062×10⁻¹⁷ (4.000892×10⁻¹⁸)	**0** **(0)**	**0** **(0)**
f_7	30	**3,206**	8,420	112,612	7.993605×10⁻¹⁴ (9.358604×10⁻¹⁵)	**0** **(0)**	**0** **(0)**
f_8	30	**7,146**	16,840	112,576	2.448395×10⁻¹¹ (1.440866×10⁻¹¹)	**0** **(0)**	**0** **(0)**
f_9	30	**2,708**	8,420	112,652	3.063671×10⁻¹¹ (1.364153×10⁻¹¹)	**0** **(0)**	6.301×10⁻³ (4.069×10⁻⁴)

where $\{m_i, m_{i+1}, \cdots, m_j\}$ is the corresponding segment of a memory antibody randomly selected from the memory population.

Furthermore, the antibody population size of PAISA is 10, memory population size is 5, clonal scale is a constant and its value is 4, feedback ratio is 0.5. The hypermutation and receptor editing in R_M^A is applied to each antibody of the antibody population $Y(k)$ with probability 1. More analysis of parameter influences is in Section 3.3.

Performance Comparisons of OGA/Q, IEA and PAISA

Table 2 shows the statistical results of PAISA, IEA and OGA/Q, where the reported results of IEA and OGA/Q are obtained from the references (Ho, Shu, & Chen, 2004; Leung & Wang, 2001). The termination criterion of PAISA is that when the given optimal value is reached or the best solution cannot be further improved in successive 30 iterations, which is the same as that in (Ho, Shu, & Chen, 2004). Each result of PAISA is obtained from 50 independent runs.

All test functions can be categorized into three classes by carefully examining the simulation results in Table 2 as follows:

1) Functions f_2, f_4, f_6, f_7, and f_8: The globally optimal solution exists in the orthogonal array based initial populations generated using the method of OGA/Q and IEA, respectively ((Ho, Shu, & Chen, 2004). Therefore, OGA/Q and IEA can obtain the optimal solution with a zero standard deviation. The solution quality of PAISA is lower than OGA/Q and IEA, but PAISA can reduce the number of function evaluations sufficiently.

2) Functions f_3 and f_9: The globally optimal solution exists in the orthogonal array based initial populations generated using the method of IEA, but not in those of OGA/Q. Therefore, IEA can obtain the optimal solution with a zero standard deviation. PAISA performs much better than IEA and OGA/Q in terms of the number of function evaluations while the solution quality of PAISA is better than OGA/Q.

3) Functions f_1 and f_5: The globally optimal solution does not exist in either the orthogonal array based initial populations generated using the method of IEA or those of OGA/Q. PAISA performs much better than OGA/Q and IEA, not only in terms of the solution quality but also in terms of the number of function evaluations.

OGA/Q and IEA apply the orthogonal design to generate an initial population of points that are scattered uniformly over the feasible solution space, so that the algorithm can evenly scan the search space once to locate good points for further exploration in subsequent iterations. They also use the recombination methods based on orthogonal design (Ho, Shu, & Chen, 2004). Therefore, OGA/Q and IEA can obtain an accurate solution but a large number of fitness evaluations are needed.

PAISA reproduces individuals and selects their improved matured progenies after the affinity maturation process, so single individuals will be optimized locally and the newcomers yield a broader exploration of the search space. Immune memory rules pay more attention to maintain the population diversity and realize the local search in the surrounding of excellent individuals. Therefore, PAISA can obtain a satisfying solution with a much smaller number of function evaluations.

Performance Comparisons of BGA, AEA, MAGA and PAISA

Because the size of the search space and the number of local minima increase with the problem dimension, the higher the dimension is, the more difficult the problem is. Therefore, this experiment studies the performance of PAISA on functions with 20~1000 dimensions. The termination criterion of PAISA is one of the objectives, $|f_{best} - f_{min}| < \varepsilon \cdot |f_{min}|$ or $|f_{best}| < \varepsilon$ if $f_{min} = 0$, is achieved, where f_{best} and f_{min} represent the best solution found until the current generation and the global optimum, respectively. $\varepsilon = 10^{-4}$ is used for all functions, which is the same as that in (Zhong, Liu, Xue, & Jiao, 2004).

Table 3. Performance comparisons of PAISA, MAGA, AEA and BGA

	f_1					f_2			
D	Mean number of function evaluations				D	Mean number of function evaluations			
	PAISA	MAGA	AEA	BGA		PAISA	MAGA	AEA	BGA
20	**957**	2,483	1,603	16,100	20	1,497	4,301	**1,247**	3,608
100	**2,787**	5,443	5,106	92,000	100	4,914	10,265	**4,798**	25,040
200	**3,618**	7,284	8,158	248,000	200	**8,937**	14,867	10,370	52,948
400	**6,285**	12,368	13,822	699,803	400	**13,728**	17,939	23,588	112,634
1000	**10,920**	22,827	23,867	/	1000	**17,585**	20,083	46,024	337,570

	f_3					f_4			
D	Mean number of function evaluations				D	Mean number of function evaluations			
	PAISA	MAGA	AEA	BGA		PAISA	MAGA	AEA	BGA
20	**1,372**	3,583	7,040	197,420	20	**1,018**	2,566	3,581	66,000
100	**3,036**	5,410	22,710	53,860	100	**3,990**	4,447	17,228	361,722
200	**4,664**	6,051	43,527	107,800	200	**4,982**	5,483	36,760	748,300
400	**6,126**	6,615	78,216	220,820	400	**5,740**	6,249	61,975	1,630,000
1000	**7,192**	7,288	160,940	548,306	1000	**6,988**	7,538	97,660	/

The statistical results of PAISA, MAGA, IEA and OGA/Q optimizing the function $f_1, f_2, f_3,$ and f_4 with various dimensions are shown in Table 3, where the reported results of MAGA, AEA and BGA are obtained from (Zhong, Liu, Xue, & Jiao, 2004; Pan & Kang, 1997; Mühlenbein & Dirk, 1993). Each result of PAISA is obtained from 50 independent runs.

As can be seen from Table 3, the number of function evaluations of PAISA is much smaller than that of BGA for all the four functions. For f_1, f_3 and f_4, the number of function evaluations of PAISA is always smaller than those of AEA and MAGA. For f_2, when $D=20$ and $D=100$, the numbers of function evaluations of PAISA are slightly greater than that of AEA, but they are much smaller than those of MAGA. In general, PAISA obtains

Figure 2. Comparisons of AEA, MAGA and PAISA on f_1 and f_2 with 20~10 000 dimensions. ©2008 Institute of Intelligent Information Processing, Xidian University, Xi'an, China. Used with permission.

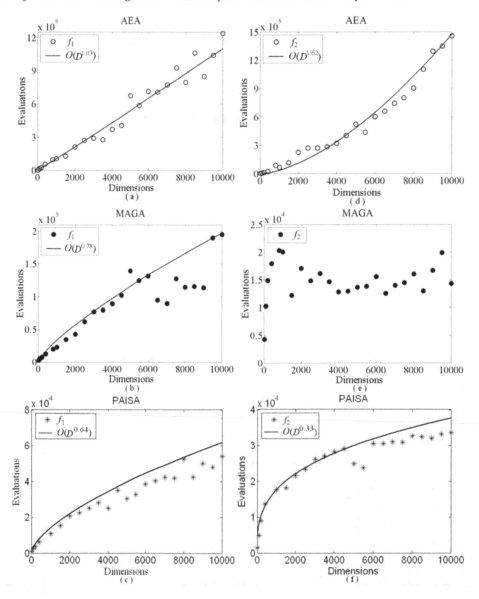

Figure 3. Comparisons of AEA, MAGA and PAISA on f_3 and f_4 with 20~10 000 dimensions. ©2008 Institute of Intelligent Information Processing, Xidian University, Xi'an, China. Used with permission.

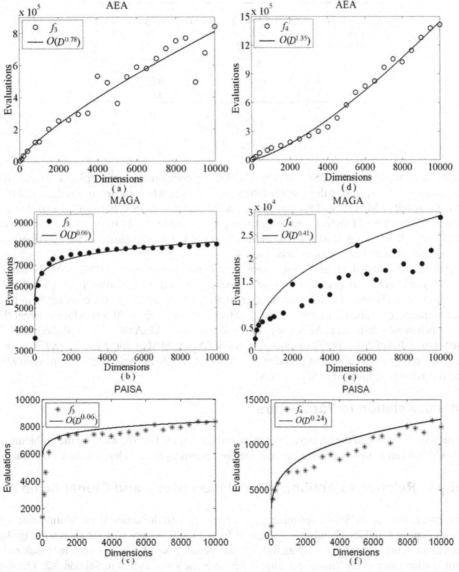

satisfying solutions at a lower computational cost than BGA, AEA and MAGA, and displays a good performance in solving large parameter optimization problems.

In order to compare the scalability of PAISA, MAGA and AEA along the problem dimension further, we use PAISA, MAGA and AEA to optimize f_1, f_2, f_3 and f_4 with higher dimensions, respectively. The problem dimension is increased from 1000 to 10 000 in steps of 500. Fig. 2 shows the mean number of function evaluations of AEA, MAGA and PAISA for f_1 and f_2. Fig. 3 shows the mean number of function evaluations of AEA, MAGA and PAISA for f_3 and f_4. The results of PAISA and MAGA are averaged over 50 independent runs and the results of AEA are averaged over ten independent runs since the running time of AEA is much longer than those of

Table 4. Comparisons of AEA, MAGA, and PAISA in the number of function evaluations for functions with 10 000 dimensions and the derived $O(D^\alpha)$

		f_1	f_2	f_3	f_4
Mean function evaluations (D=10 000)	AEA	1,239,098 1	,458,428	841,827 1	,416,717
	MAGA	195,292	14,315	7,961	28,815
	PAISA	54,039	33,523	8,358 1	1,980
$O(D^\alpha)$	AEA	$O(D^{1.03})$	$O(D^{1.62})$	$O(D^{0.78})$	$O(D^{1.35})$
	MAGA	$O(D^{0.78})$	/	$O(D^{0.06})$	$O(D^{0.41})$
	PAISA	$O(D^{0.64})$	$O(D^{0.33})$	$O(D^{0.06})$	$O(D^{0.24})$

MAGA and PAISA. The results of PAISA, AEA and MAGA for each function are depicted in three figures. The figures in the same column represent the results of the same function, where the top one is the result of AEA, the middle one is the result of MAGA, and the bottom one is the result of PAISA. In order to study the complexity of them further, the number of function evaluations is approximated by $O(D^\alpha)$ ($0 < \alpha < 2$). For more clarity, the comparisons of PAISA, MAGA and AEA in the mean number of function evaluations for functions with 10 000 dimensions and the derived $O(D^\alpha)$ are shown in Table 4.

As can be seen from Table 4, Figure 2 and Figure 3, for f_1, the complexities of PAISA, MAGA and AEA are $O(D^{0.64})$, $O(D^{0.78})$ and $O(D^{1.03})$, respectively, and the number of function evaluations of PAISA is only 54 039 even when D is 10 000, which is much smaller than those of MAGA and AEA. For f_2, the complexity of PAIS is only $O(D^{0.33})$, and the number of function evaluations is 33 523 when D increases to 10 000, which is larger than that of MAGA but is much smaller than that of AEA. For f_3, the complexities of PAISA and MAGA are both $O(D^{0.06})$, which are much better than that of AEA. For f_4, the complexities of PAISA, MAGA and AEA are $O(D^{0.24})$, $O(D^{0.41})$ and $O(D^{1.35})$, respectively, and the number of function evaluations of PAISA is only 11 980 even when D is 10 000, which is much smaller than those of MAGA and AEA.

Sensitivity in Relation to Parameters

In order to study the influence of the main parameters when running the PAISA, we solve the problems f_1, f_2, f_3 and f_4 by PAISA with various antibody population size, memory population size, clonal scale and feedback ratio.

Sensitivity in Relation to Antibody Population Size n and Clonal Scale nc

The experimental results of PAISA on optimizing f_1, f_2, f_3 and f_4 with the antibody population size n increased from 5 to 30 in steps of 5 and the clonal scale increased from 2 to 20 in steps of 3 are shown in Fig. 4(a), (b), (c) and (d). The values of other parameters are as follows: the memory population size is 5, feedback ratio is 50%, and the problem dimension is 20. The termination criterion is the same as that in Section 3.2. The data are the statistical results of the number of function evaluations obtained from 50 independent runs.

The results in Fig. 4 show that, antibody population size and clonal scale have a large effect on the number of function evaluations. After approximating the number of function evaluations by $O(\mu \times n \times n_c)$, we find that the average numbers of function evaluations on optimizing functions f_1, f_2, f_3, f_4 increase about $\mu_{f_1} \approx 13.1543$, $\mu_{f_2} \approx 25.6400$, $\mu_{f_3} \approx 37.1429$, and $\mu_{f_4} \approx 34.1829$, when the antibody population size increases one. The average numbers of function evaluations on optimizing functions f_1, f_2, f_3, f_4 increase about $\mu_{f_1} \approx 13.0019$, $\mu_{f_2} \approx 20.2648$, $\mu_{f_3} \approx 27.4926$, and $\mu_{f_4} \approx 26.0778$, respectively, when the clonal scale increases one. Thus, increasing the clonal scale will result in a less increment in the number of function evaluations than increasing the antibody population size. In addition, the bigger clonal scale helps to extend the searching scope, while the lager antibody population size improves the population diversity.

Sensitivity in Relation to Memory Population Size s and Feedback Ratio T%

The experimental results of PAISA on optimizing functions f_1, f_2, f_3, f_4 with the memory population size s increased from 0 to 10 in steps of 2 and feedback ratio $T\%$ increased from 0 to 1 in steps of 0.2 are shown in Fig. 5(a), (b), (c) and (d). The values of other parameters are as follows: the antibody population size is 10, the clonal scale is 3, and the problem dimension is 20. The termination criterion is the same as that in Section 3.2. The data are the statistical results of the number of function evaluations obtained from 50 independent runs.

From the results, we conclude that the influence of memory population size is weaker than those of antibody population size and clonal scale on the average number of function evaluations. For f_1, f_2, f_3 and f_4, too large or too small value of s leads an increase of the number of function evaluations. The feedback ratio has a rather weak influence on the performance when $T\% > 0.1$. Generally, when $T\%$ is set around 50%, the number of function evaluations is rather few.

EXPERIMENTAL STUDIES ON OPTIMAL APPROXIMATION OF LINEAR SYSTEMS

In this section, the problem of approximating linear systems is solved by PAISA. Optimal approximation of linear systems is an important task in the simulation and controller design for complex dynamical systems (Cheng &

Figure 4. PAISA sensitivity in relation to n and n_c. ©2008 Institute of Intelligent Information Processing, Xidian University, Xi'an, China. Used with permission.

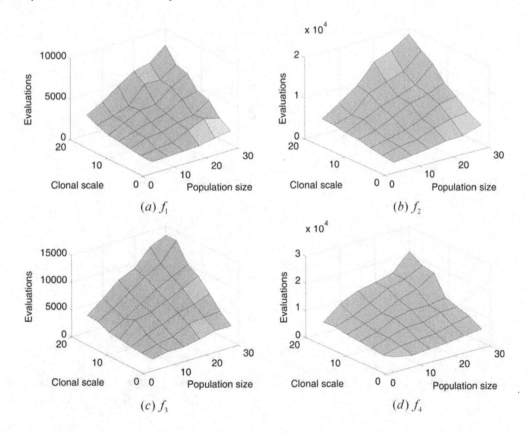

Hwang, 2001). In order to solve the model approximation problem, numerous methods have been proposed and they may be grouped into two major categories, the performance-oriented and the nonperformance-oriented approaches (Cheng & Hwang, 2001). For a performance-oriented model approximation method, approximate models are obtained by minimizing certain approximation error criteria. This class of methods relies heavily on the numerical optimization procedure (Cheng & Hwang, 2001; Dinabandhu, Murthy, Sankar, 1996).

Problem Statement

Given a high-order rational or irrational transfer function $G(s)$, it is desired to find an approximate model of the form in (27) such that $H_m(s)$ contains the desired characteristic of the original system $G(s)$.

$$H_m(s) = \frac{b_0 + b_1 s + \cdots + b_{m-1} s^{m-1}}{a_0 + a_1 s + \cdots + a_{m-1} s^{m-1} + s^m} \cdot e^{-\tau_d s} \tag{27}$$

The aim is to find an optimal approximate model $H_m(s)$ such that the frequency-domain L^2-error performance index in (28) is minimized, where the frequency points, ω_i, $i=0,1,2,3,\ldots N$, and the integer N are taken a priori.

$$J = \sum_{i=0}^{N} \left| G(j\omega_i) - H_m(j\omega_i) \right|^2 \tag{28}$$

Figure 5. PAISA sensitivity in relation to s and T%. ©2008 Institute of Intelligent Information Processing, Xidian University, Xi'an, China. Used with permission.

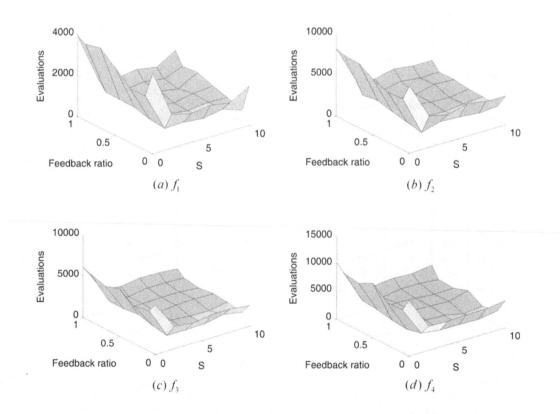

Table 5. Comparisons of PAISA, DEA and MAGA in optimal approximation of the stable linear system

Search space	Method	Approximate model	J
$[0, 10]^4$	DEA	$H_2(s) = \dfrac{0.0266114(s+6.10646821)e^{-0.4894422s}}{s^2+1.65105264s+0.25757166}$	1.4308×10^{-4}
	PAISA	$H_2(s) = \dfrac{0.021430231(s+6.130164886)e^{-0.454259829s}}{s^2+1.226172374s+0.208228229}$	$\mathbf{4.4889\times10^{-5}}$
$[0, 50]^4$	DEA	$H_2(s) = \dfrac{0.00495562(s+35.0505313)e^{-0.39077937s}}{s^2+1.7606862s+0.27531759}$	6.2568×10^{-5}
	PAISA	$H_2(s) = \dfrac{0.006473125(s+20.835707811)e^{-0.360175108s}}{s^2+1.254970252s+0.213777917}$	$\mathbf{8.2269\times10^{-6}}$
$[0, 100]^4$	DEA	$H_2(s) = \dfrac{0.00415886(s+65.9114728)e^{-0.5907097s}}{s^2+2.7140333s+0.43448690}$	1.0021×10^{-3}
	PAISA	$H_2(s) = \dfrac{0.003374488(s+39.802784056)e^{-0.332274274s}}{s^2+1.250285692s+0.212893270}$	$\mathbf{8.5147\times10^{-6}}$
$[0, 150]^4$	PAISA	$H_2(s) = \dfrac{0.006163363(s+21.914785100)e^{-0.357316587s}}{s^2+1.256812898s+0.214089609}$	$\mathbf{7.7369\times10^{-6}}$
adjustable	DEA	$H_2(s) = \dfrac{0.0025538(s+68.1706405)e^{-0.3787929s}}{s^2+1.7606862s+0.2759465}$	6.1129×10^{-5}
	MAGA	$H_2(s) = \dfrac{0.0172520(s+7.7668024)e^{-0.4346119s}}{s^2+1.2483717s+0.2123842}$	2.7180×10^{-5}
	PAISA	$H_2(s) = \dfrac{0.004717881(s+28.822747965)e^{-0.351042212s}}{s^2+1.264931127s+0.215537542}$	$\mathbf{6.5526\times10^{-6}}$

Table 6. Comparisons of the approximate models of the unstable linear system obtained by PAISA with fixed search spaces

Search space	Approximate model	J	ε
$[-500,500]^4$	$H_2(s) = \dfrac{129.283987966s - 451.269244983}{s^2+13.078500583s - 91.851175413}$	8.795 1	.381
$[-1000,1000]^4$	$H_2(s) = \dfrac{129.283365165s - 450.817260700}{s^2+13.085060426s - 91.764682717}$	8.795 1	.380
$[-2000,2000]^4$	$H_2(s) = \dfrac{129.330759446s - 450.748056298}{s^2+13.090054195s - 91.755967406}$	8.795 1	.379
$[-5000,5000]^4$	$H_2(s) = \dfrac{129.251155710s - 450.318766288}{s^2+13.082602535s - 91.687472588}$	8.795 1	.381

Table 7. Comparisons of PAISA and other algorithms in optimal approximation of the unstable linear system

Method	Approximate model	J	ε
PAISA	$H_2(s) = \dfrac{129.310457004s - 450.941328300}{s^2 + 13.088391129s - 91.794882948}$	**8.795 1**	**.380**
MAGA	$H_2(s) = \dfrac{129.315s - 451.012}{s^2 + 13.092s - 91.8129}$	8.795 1	.380
DEA	$H_2(s) = \dfrac{129.297s - 450.711}{s^2 + 13.089s - 91.7495}$	8.795 1	.449
GS	$\widehat{G}_{2,H}(s) = \dfrac{160.1(s - 3.074)}{(s + 25.84)(s - 5.000)}$	26.46 1	.194
GL1	$\widehat{G}_{2,g1}(s) = \dfrac{161.0(s - 3.155)}{(s + 24.7)(s - 5)}$	18.21 1	.122
GL2	$\widehat{G}_{2,g2}(s) = \dfrac{177.6(s - 7.183)}{(s + 24.7)(s - 12.8)}$	25.21 1	.599
BT1	$\widehat{G}_{2,\alpha}(s) = \dfrac{183.5(s - 3.099)}{(s + 27.1)(s - 5.21)}$	23.79 1	.278
BT2	$\widehat{G}_{2,n}(s) = \dfrac{205.5(s - 2.680)}{(s + 31.9)(s - 4.73)}$	32.26 1	.445

Figure 6. Error magnitude between the approximate models and the original system G(s). ©2008 Institute of Intelligent Information Processing, Xidian University, Xi'an, China. Used with permission.

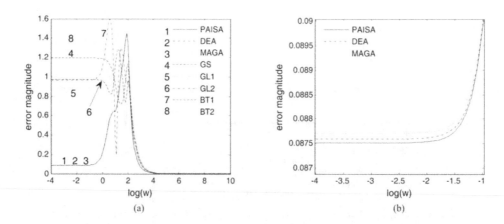

In the case where the original system $G(s)$ is asymptotically stable, the constraint, $H_m(0) = G(0)$, is placed to ensure that the steady-state responses of the original system and the approximate model are the same for the unit-step input.

The problem of minimizing given in (28) is an optimal parameter selection problem. The optimal parameters a_i, b_i, $i = 1, 2, \cdots m - 1$ and τ_d of the approximate model (27) can be found by a gradient-based method (Aplevich, 1973) or by a direct search optimization (Cheng & Hwang, 2001; Guo & Hwang, 1996; Luus, 1980; Zhong, Liu, Xue, & Jiao, 2004). In this experiment, we shall apply PAISA to find the optimal parameters a_i, b_i, $i = 1, 2, \cdots m - 1$ and τ_d.

The searches for optimal approximate models for a stable and an unstable linear system are carried out to verify the effectiveness of PAISA. The parameters of PAISA are the same as those of Section 3.1. The termination criterion of PAISA is to run 300 generations. Under this condition, the number of evaluations averaged over 30 trials of PAISA is 18015, while reference (Cheng & Hwang, 2001) needs 19800 and reference (Zhong, Liu, Xue, & Jiao, 2004) needs 19735 for approximating the stable linear system. So the computational cost of PAISA is as much as some other algorithms.

Optimal Approximation of a Stable Linear System

This system is quoted from (Cheng & Hwang, 2001) and (Zhong, Liu, Xue, & Jiao, 2004), in which a complex transfer function containing delay terms in the denominator is to be approximated by a rational transfer function with a time delay. The transfer function is given by equation (29).

$$G(S) = \frac{Y(s)}{U(s)} = \frac{k_d k_{r1} (\tau_{od} s + 1) e^{-\theta_d s}}{(\tau_r s + 1)(\tau_1 s + 1)(\tau_2 s + 1) - k_{r2} k_d (\tau_{bd} s + 1) e^{-\theta_d s}} \tag{29}$$

where $k_{r1} = 0.258$, $k_{r2} = 0.281$, $k_d = 1.4494$, $\theta_d = 0.2912$, $\tau_r = 0.3684$, $\tau_1 = 1.9624$ and $\tau_2 = 0.43256$. It is desired to find the second-order models

$$H_2(s) = \frac{k_{2,p}(s + \tau_{2,z})}{a_{2,0} + a_{2,1}s + s^2} \cdot e^{-\tau_{2,d}s} \tag{30}$$

such that the performance index given by (28) with the 51 frequency values, $\omega_i = 10^{-2 + 0.1i}, i = 0, 1, \cdots N = 50$, is minimized while it is subject to the constraint of $H_2(0) = G(0)$. Under this requirement, the unknown parameter is simply related to others by the relation

$$a_{2,0} = \frac{k_{2,p}(1 - k_{r2}k_d)}{k_d k_{r1}} \tau_{2,z} \tag{31}$$

Hence, the parameters to be determined are $a_{2,1}$, $k_{2,p}$, $\tau_{2,z}$ and $\tau_{2,d}$. Due to the fact that the original system is stable, each parameter lies in the interval $[0, +\infty)$.

We first search for the optimal parameters by using PAISA without a search-space expansion scheme. In search for the parameters, four fixed search spaces, $[0, 10]^4$, $[0, 50]^4$, $[0, 100]^4$ and $[0, 150]^4$ are tested. Then we searched the optimal parameters by using PAISA with the search-space expansion scheme in (Cheng, & Hwang, 2001) where the initial search space for the parameter vector $X_4 = [a_{2,1}, k_{2,p}, \tau_{2,z}, \tau_{2,d}]$ is set as $[0, 0.1]^4$, search-space expansion factor is fixed as 2, and search space checking period is 10. The termination criterion of PAISA is to run 300 generations. The optimal approximate models for $G(s)$ and the corresponding performance indices obtained by PAISA are compared with other algorithms in Table 5.

As can be seen from Table 5, when the search space is set as $[0, 10]^4$, $[0, 50]^4$, $[0, 100]^4$ and adjustable, the performance indices of the models obtained by PAISA are much better than those of DEA. When the search pace is as large as $[0, 100]^4$, the optimal model obtained by DEA has a bad performance index due to DEA drops into a local optimum while PAISA performs much better. Even when the search space is set as $[0,150]^4$, PAISA can also find the approximate model with the performance index 7.7369×10^{-6}. So a too-large search space does not influence the performance of PAISA in approximating the stable linear system. The performance index of the model obtained by PAISA is also much better than that of MAGA.

Optimal Approximation of an Unstable Linear System

The second system is quoted from (Cheng & Hwang, 2001; Guo & Hwang, 1996; Zhong, Liu, Xue, & Jiao, 2004). Given the 4th-order unstable and nonminimum phase transfer function

$$G(s) = \frac{60s^3 + 25850s^2 + 685000s - 2500000}{s^4 + 105s^3 + 10450s^2 + 45000s - 500000} \tag{32}$$

It is desired to approximate this transfer function by the second-order model

$$H_2(s) = \frac{c_{2,1}s + c_{2,0}}{s^2 + b_{2,1}s + b_{2,0}} \qquad\qquad (33)$$

such that the performance index defined in (28) with $\omega_i = 10^{-2+0.2i}, i = 0,1,\cdots N = 60$, is minimized. The allowable interval for each parameter is $(-\infty, +\infty)$.

We first search for the optimal parameters by using PAISA without a search-space expansion scheme. In search for the parameters $X_4 = [c_{2,1}, c_{2,0}, b_{2,1}, b_{2,0}]$, four fixed search spaces, $[-500,500]^4$, $[-1000,1000]^4$, $[-2000,2000]^4$ and $[-5000,5000]^4$ are tested. The termination criterion of PAISA is to run 300 generations. The optimal approximate models for $G(s)$ and the corresponding performance indices obtained by PAISA are listed in Table 6. Table 6 also shows the L^∞-norm of the approximation error, $\varepsilon = |G(j\omega) - H_2(j\omega)|$ for each model. Then we searched the optimal parameters by PAISA with the search-space expansion scheme in (Cheng & Hwang, 2001) where the initial search space for the parameter vector $X_4 = [c_{2,1}, c_{2,0}, b_{2,1}, b_{2,0}]$ is set as $[-0.1, 0.1]^4$, search-space expansion factor is fixed as 2, and search space checking period is 10. The optimal approximate models for $G(s)$ and the corresponding performance indices obtained by PAISA are compared with other algorithms in Table 7.

As can be seen from Table 6 that all the performance indices J converges to 8.795 with the four fixed search spaces. So a too-large search space does not influence the performance of PAISA in approximating the unstable linear system either.

The plots of error magnitude $|G(j\omega) - R(j\omega)|$ versus frequencies, where $R(s)$ denotes an approximate model, for these approximate models in Table 7 are shown in Fig. 6. It can be seen from Table 7 that the performance index of the model obtained by PAISA is as good as those of MAGA and DEA, but the L^∞-norm of the approximation error of the models obtained by PAISA and MAGA are better than DEA. From Fig. 6 (a), we can see that all the models obtained by PAISA, MAGA and DEA fit well the original system over the $[10^{-4}, 10^{0.6}]$ and $[10^2, 10^{10}]$ frequency ranges. But the local amplificatory figure, i.e. Fig. 6(2) shows that the model obtained by PAISA has the least error magnitude $|G(j\omega) - R(j\omega)|$ among all the models over the most frequency ranges.

CONCLUSION

In this chapter, we introduced the population-based architecture of an Artificial Immune System, PAIS, and proposed a novel dynamic algorithm, PAISA, for Global Numerical Optimization. PAIS modeled the dynamic process of human immune response as a quaternion (G, I, R, AI), where G denotes exterior stimulus or antigen, I denotes the set of valid antibodies, R denotes the set of reaction rules describing the interactions between antibodies, and AI denotes the dynamic algorithm describing how the reaction rules are applied to antibody population. PAISA was a specific AI based on the set of clonal selection rules and the set of immune memory rules. Theoretical analyzes showed that PAISA can converge to the global optimum. In section 3, PAISA was tested on nine benchmark functions with 20 to 10 000 dimensions and compared with five existing **evolutionary algorithm**s. The experiments indicated that PAISA outperformed the five algorithms in computational cost. In order to study the scalability of PAISA along the problem dimension, PAISA was used to optimize the functions with 1000 to 10 000 dimensions. The results indicated that PAISA obtained high quality solutions with lower computation cost than some existing algorithms. In section 4, PAISA was applied to a practical optimization problem, the approximation of linear systems. A stable linear system and an unstable one were used to test the performance of PAISA. Experiments showed that a too-large search space does not influence the performance of PAISA in approximating these linear systems and the performance indices of the approximate models obtained by PAISA were much better than those of some other algorithms. It is shown empirically that PAISA has high performance in optimizing some benchmark functions and practical optimization problems. Just as evolutionary optimization algorithms, PAISA can not guarantee for their performance. So in practical applications, we should set appropriate termination criterion, run the algorithm many times and select the best result to avoid occasional loss of a single trial.

FUTURE RESEARCH DIRECTIONS

The PAIS modeled the immune response process as a quaternion. It can be considered as a general architecture of population-based artificial immune systems rather than an immune algorithm. Many immune phenomena, such as clonal selection, negative selection, passive selection, immune memory, can be modeled as corresponding reaction rules and added to the set of reaction rules *R*. Based on the PAIS, our final aim is to build a self-adaptive dynamical system by simulating all the possible interactions between antibodies during immune response. Then the PAIS can select reaction rules automatically depending on antigen *G*, and thereby the pending problems could be solved automatically. Obviously, this chapter only introduced the general architecture of PAIS. It is far from the final aim. One issue should be addressed in the future research is to design sufficient rules simulating the immune phenomena. Another issue is the model self-adaptive strategy, such as the automatically rule-selection strategy and the population size self-adaptive strategy.

ACKNOWLEDGMENT

This work was supported by the National Natural Science Foundation of China (Grant No. 60703107), the National High Technology Research and Development Program (863 Program) of China (Grant No. 2006AA01Z107), the National Basic Research Program (973 Program) of China (Grant No. 2006CB705700) and the Program for Cheung Kong Scholars and Innovative Research Team in University (Grant No. IRT0645).

REFERENCES

Abbas, A. K., Lichtman, A. H., & Pober, J. S. (2000). *Cellular and Molecular Immunology*. 4th edn. W B Saunders Co., New York.

Aplevich, J. D. (1973). Gradient methods for optimal linear system reduction. *International Journal of Control, 18*(4), 767-772.

Berek, C., & Ziegner, M. (1993). The maturation of the immune response. *Immunology Today, 14*(8), 400-402.

Beyer, H. G. & Schwefel, H. P. (2002). Evolution Strategies: A Comprehensive Introduction. *Natural Computing, 1*(1), 3-52.

Burnet, F. M. (1978). Clonal selection and after. *Theoretical Immunology*. New York: Marcel Dekker. (pp. 63-85).

Carter, J. H. (2000). The Immune System as a model for Pattern Recognition and classification. *Journal of the American Medical Informatics Association, 7*(3), 28-41.

Cheng, S. L. & Hwang, C. (2001). Optimal Approximation of Linear Systems by a Differential Evolution Algorithm. *IEEE Transactions on systems, man, and cybernetics-part A, 31*(6), 698-707.

Coello Coello, C. A., Cortes Rivera, D., & Cruz Cortes, N. (2003). Use of an Artificial Immune System for Job Shop Scheduling. In *Proceeding of Second International Conference on Artificial Immune Systems*, Napier University, Edinburgh, UK.

Cutello, V., Narzisi, G., Nicosia, G., & Pavone, M. (2005). Clonal Selection Algorithms: A Comparative Case Study Using Effective Mutation Potentials. In *Proceedings of 4th International Conference on Artificial Immune Systems, Lecture Notes in Computer Science, 3627*, 13-28.

Cutello, V., Nicosia, G., & Pavone, M. (2004). Exploring the Capability of Immune Algorithms: A Characterization of Hypemutation Operators. In *Proceedings of Third International Conference on Artificial Immune Systems, Lecture Notes in Computer Science, 3239*, 263-276.

Dasgupta, D.(1999). Artificial Immune Systems and Their Applications. Springer-Verlag.

de Castro, L. N. & Timmis, J. (2002). *Artificial Immune Systems: A New Computational Intelligence Approach.* Springer-Verlag, Berlin Heidelberg New York.

de Castro, L. N. & Von Zuben F.J. (2002). Learning and Optimization Using the Clonal Selection Principle. *IEEE Transactions on Evolutionary Computation, 6*(3), 239-251.

Dinabandhu, B., Murthy, C. A., & Sankar, K. P. (1996). Genetic algorithm with elitist model and its convergence. *International Journal of Pattern Recognition and Artificial Intelligence, 10*(6), 731-747.

Dong, W. S., Shi, G. M., Zhang, L. (2007). Immune memory clonal selection algorithms for designing stack filters. *Neurocomputing, 70(4-6)*, 777-784.

Du, H. F., Gong, M. G., Jiao, L. C., & Liu, R. C. (2005). A novel artificial immune system algorithm for high-dimensional function numerical optimization. *Progress in Natural Science, 15*(5), 463-471.

Forrest, S., Perelson, A. S., Allen, L., & Cherukuri, R. (1994). Self-nonself discrimination in a computer. In *Proceedings of the IEEE Symposium on Research in Security and Privacy.* Los Alamitos, CA: IEEE Computer Society Press. (pp. 202-212).

Fukuda, T., Mori, K., & Tsukiyama, M. (1993). Immune networks using genetic algorithm for adaptive production scheduling. In Proceedings of the 15th IFAC World Congress. (pp. 57-60).

García-Pedrajas, N., & Fyfe, C. (2007). Immune network based ensembles. *Neurocomputing, 70*(7-9), 1155-1166.

Garrett, S. M. (2004). Parameter-free, Adaptive Clonal Selection. In *Proceedings of IEEE Congress on Evolutionary Computing, CEC 2004*, Portland, Oregon. (pp. 1052-1058).

Garrett, S. M. (2005). How Do We Evaluate Artificial Immune Systems. *Evolutionary Computation, 13*(2), 145-178.

George, A. J. T., & Gray, D. (1999). Receptor editing during affinity maturation. *Immunology Today, 20*(4), 196.

Glover, K. (1984). All optimal Hankel-norm approximations of linear multivariable systems and their L^{∞} − error bounds. *International Journal of Control, 39*(6), 1115-1193.

Gong, M. G., Du, H. F., & Jiao, L. C. (2006). Optimal approximation of linear systems by artificial immune response. Science in China. *Series F Information Sciences, 49*(1), 63-79.

Gong, M. G., Jiao, L.C., Liu, F., & Du, H.F. (2005). The Quaternion Model of Artificial Immune Response. In *Proceedings of the fourth international conference on Artificial Immune Systems, Lecture Notes in Computer Science, 3627*, 207-219.

Gonzalez, F., Dasgupta, D., & Kozma, R. (2002). Combining Negative Selection and Classification Techniques for Anomaly Detection. In *Proceedings of the special sessions on artificial immune systems in Congress on Evolutionary Computation*, Honolulu, Hawaii.

Guo, T. Y., & Hwang, C. (1996). Optimal reduced-order models for unstable and nonminimum-phase systems. *IEEE Transactions on Circuits and Systems-I, 43*(9), 800-805.

Hajela, P., Yoo, J., & Lee, J. (1997). GA Based Simulation of Immune Networks-Applications in Structural Optimization. *Journal of Engineering Optimization.*

Hart, E., & Ross, P. (1999). The Evolution and Analysis of a Potential Antibody Library for Use in Job-Shop Scheduling. In *New Ideas in Optimization*. McGraw-Hill.

Hart, E., & Timmis, J. (2005). Application Areas of AIS: The Past, The Present and The Future. In *Proceedings of the 4th International Conference on artificial immune systems, Lecture Notes in Computer Science, 3627,* 483-497.

Ho, S. Y., Shu, L. S., & Chen, J. H. (2004). Intelligent Evolutionary Algorithms for large Parameter Optimization Problems. *IEEE Transactions on Evolutionary Computation, 8*(6), 522-540.

Ishida, Y. (1990). Fully Distributed Diagnosis by PDP Learning Algorithm: Towards Immune Network PDP Model. In *Proceedings of International Joint Conference on Neural Networks*, San Diego, 777-782.

Jiao, L. C., & Wang, L. (2000). A novel genetic algorithm based on immunity. *IEEE Transactions on Systems, Man and Cybernetics, Part A, 30(*5), 552-561.

Kazarlis, S. A., Papadakis, S. E., Theocharis, J. B., & Petridis, V. (2001). Microgenetic algorithms as generalized hill-climbing operators for GA optimization. *IEEE Transactions on Evolutionary Computation, 5*(2), 204-217.

Kelsey, J., & Timmis, J. (2003). Immune inspired somatic contiguous hypermutation for function optimisation. In *Proceedings of the Genetic and Evolutionary Computation Conference*, 207-218.

Leung, Y. W., & Wang, Y. P. (2001). An Orthogonal Genetic Algorithm with Quantization for Global Numerical Optimization. *IEEE Transactions on Evolutionary Computation, 5*(1), 41-53.

Luus, R. (1980). Optimization in model reduction. *International Journal of Control, 32*(5), 741-747.

Mühlenbein, H., & Dirk, S. (1993). Predictive Models for the Breeder Genetic Algorithm. *Evolutionary Computation, 1*(1), 25-49.

Pan, Z. J., & Kang, L. S. (1997). An adaptive evolutionary algorithms for numerical optimization. In *Proceedings of the International Conference on Simulated Evolution and Learning*, Berlin, Germany, 27-34.

Parker, P. J., & Anderson, B. D. (1987). Unstable rational function approximation. *International Journal of Control, 46(*5), 1783-1801.

Rudolph, G. (1994). Convergence analysis of canonical genetic algorithms. *IEEE Transactions on Neural Networks, 5,* 96-101.

Stepney, S., Smith, R. E., Timmis, J., & Tyrrell, A. M. (2004). Towards a Conceptual Framework for Artificial Immune Systems. In *Proceedings of Third International Conference on Artificial Immune Systems*, 53-64.

Swinburne, R. (2002). *Bayes's Theorem*. Oxford: Oxford University Press.

Tarakanov, A., & Dasgupta, D. (2000). A formal model of an artificial immune system. *BioSystems, 55*(1/3), 151-158.

Timmis, J., Neal, M., & Hunt, J. (2000). An artificial immune system for data analysis. *Biosystems, 55*(1/3), 143-150.

White, J. A. & Garrett, S. M. (2003). Improved Pattern Recognition with Artificial Clonal Selection. In *Proceedings of Second International Conference on Artificial Immune Systems*, Napier University, Edinburgh, UK.

Zhong, W. C., Liu, J., Xue, M. Z., & Jiao, L. C. (2004). A multiagent genetic algorithm for global numerical optimization. *IEEE Transactions on Systems, Man and Cybernetics, Part B, 34*(2), 1128-1141.

ADDITIONAL READING

Carter, J.H.(2000). The Immune System as a model for Pattern Recognition and classification. Journal of the American Medical Informatics Association, 7(3), 28-41.

Cutello, V., Narzisi, G., Nicosia, G., & Pavone, M. (2005). Clonal Selection Algorithms: A Comparative Case Study Using Effective Mutation Potentials. In: Proceedings of 4th International Conference on Artificial Immune Systems, Lecture Notes in Computer Science, 3627, 13-28.

Cutello, V., Nicosia, G., Pavone, M. (2004). Exploring the Capability of Immune Algorithms: A Characterization of Hypemutation Operators. In: Proceedings of Third International Conference on Artificial Immune Systems, Lecture Notes in Computer Science, 3239, 263-276.

Dasgupta, D.(1999). Artificial Immune Systems and Their Applications. Springer-Verlag.

de Castro, L.N. & Timmis, J. (2002). Artificial Immune Systems: A New Computational Intelligence Approach. Springer-Verlag, Berlin Heidelberg New York.

de Castro, L.N. & Von Zuben F.J. (2002). Learning and Optimization Using the Clonal Selection Principle. IEEE Transactions on Evolutionary Computation, 6(3), 239-251.

Freitas, A.A. & Timmis, J. (2007). Revisiting the Foundations of Artificial Immune Systems for Data Mining. IEEE Transactions on Evolutionary Computation, 30(5), 551-540.

Garrett, S.M. (2004). Parameter-free, Adaptive Clonal Selection. In: Proceedings of IEEE Congress on Evolutionary Computing, CEC 2004, Portland, Oregon, 1052-1058.

Garrett, S.M. (2005). How Do We Evaluate Artificial Immune Systems. Evolutionary Computation, 13(2), 145-178.

Ho, S.Y., Shu, L.S., & Chen, J.H. (2004). Intelligent Evolutionary Algorithms for large Parameter Optimization Problems. IEEE Transactions on Evolutionary Computation, 8(6), 522-540.

Jiao, L.C., Wang, L. (2000). A novel genetic algorithm based on immunity. IEEE Transactions on Systems, Man and Cybernetics, Part A, 30(5), 552-561.

Leung, Y.W. & Wang, Y.P. (2001). An Orthogonal Genetic Algorithm with Quantization for Global Numerical Optimization. IEEE Transactions on Evolutionary Computation, 5(1), 41-53.

Tarakanov, A. & Dasgupta, D. (2000). A formal model of an artificial immune system. BioSystems, 55(1/3), 151-158.

Timmis, J., Neal, M., & Hunt, J. (2000). An artificial immune system for data analysis. Biosystems, 55(1/3), 143-150.

KEY TERMS

Artificial Immune Systems: Artificial immune systems are adaptive systems inspired by theoretical immunology and observed immune functions, principles and models, which are applied to complex problem domains.

Clonal Selection: Human immune response relies on the prior formation of an incredibly diverse population of B cells and T cells. The specificity of both the B-cell receptors and T-cell receptors, that is, the epitope to which a given receptor can bind, is created by a remarkable genetic mechanism. Each receptor is created even though the epitope it recognizes may never have been present in the body. If an antigen with that epitope should enter the body, those few lymphocytes able to bind to it will do so. If they also receive a second co-stimulatory signal, they may begin repeated rounds of mitosis. In this way, clones of antigen-specific lymphocytes (B and T) develop providing the basis of the immune response. This phenomenon is called clonal selection

Dynamical System: A means of describing how one state develops into another state over the course of time. A dynamical system is a smooth action of the reals or the integers on another object.

Evolutionary Algorithms: Evolutionary algorithms are search methods that take their inspiration from natural selection and survival of the fittest in the biological world.

Immune Memory: Besides the clonal selection, during the initial expansion of clones, some of the progeny cells neither went on dividing nor developed into plasma cells. Instead, they reverted to small lymphocytes bearing the same B-cell receptor on their surface that their ancestors had. This lays the foundation for a more rapid and massive response the next time the antigen enters the body, i.e. immune memory.

Natural Computation: Natural computation is the study of computational systems that are inspired from natural systems, including biological, ecological, physical, chemical, economical and social systems.

Optimization: Find values of the variables that minimize or maximize the objective function while satisfying the constraints.

Section I.II
Artificial Immune Systems and Agents

Immune system has similar features with multi-agent systems (MAS). So it is easy to relate immune individuals and immune mechanisms to multi-agents. The main immune mechanisms including clonal selection, idiotypic network, and negative selection had been used MAS and solved different interesting problems.

Chapter IV
An Immune Inspired Algorithm for Learning Strategies in a Pursuit-Evasion Game

Małgorzata Lucińska
Kielce University of Technology, Poland

Sławomir T. Wierzchoń
Polish Academy of Sciences, Poland & University of Gdańsk, Poland

ABSTRACT

Multi-agent systems (MAS), consist of a number of autonomous agents, which interact with one-another. To make such interactions successful, they will require the ability to cooperate, coordinate, and negotiate with each other. From a theoretical point of view such systems require a hybrid approach involving game theory, artificial intelligence, and distributed programming. On the other hand, biology offers a number of inspirations showing how these interactions are effectively realized in real world situations. Swarm organizations, like ant colonies or bird flocks, provide a spectrum of metaphors offering interesting models of collective problem solving. Immune system, involving complex relationships among antigens and antibodies, is another example of a multi-agent and swarm system. In this chapter an application of so-called clonal selection algorithm, inspired by the real mechanism of immune response, is proposed to solve the problem of learning strategies in the pursuit-evasion problem.

INTRODUCTION

Multi-agent system problems involve several agents attempting, through their interaction, to jointly solve given tasks. The central issue in such systems is an agent conjecture about the other agents and their ability to adapt to their teammates' behavior. Due to the interactions among the agents, the problem complexity can rise rapidly with the number of agents or their behavioral sophistication. Moreover, as all the agents are trying to find simultaneously the optimal strategy, the environment is no longer stationary. Also in real-world systems it is necessary to address agents' limitations, which make them not always being capable of acting rationally. To sum up, scalability, adaptive dynamics and incomplete information are the most challenging topics, which have to be coped with by any techniques applied to multi-agent encounters.

Copyright © 2009, IGI Global, distributing in print or electronic forms without written permission of IGI Global is prohibited.

Game theory is already an established and profound theoretical framework for studying interactions between agents (Rosenschein, 1985). Although originally designed for modeling economical systems, game theory has developed into an independent field with solid mathematical foundations and many applications. It tries to understand the behavior of interacting agents by looking at the relationships between them and predicting their optimal decisions. Game theory offers powerful tool, however the issues of incomplete information and large state spaces are still hard to overcome.

Artificial immune systems (AIS) are computational systems inspired by theoretical immunology, observed immune functions, principles and mechanisms in order to solve problems (de Castro & Timmis, 2002). The fundamental features of the natural immune system, like distribution, adaptability, learning from experience, complexity, communication, and coordination have decided that immune algorithms have been applied to a wide variety of tasks, including optimization, computer security, pattern recognition, mortgage fraud detection, aircraft control etc. – consult (de Castro & Timmis, 2002) for details.

The above mentioned features indicate a natural parallel between the immune and multi-agent systems, which suggests that immune metaphor constitutes a compelling model for agents' behavior arbitration. Examples of successful utilization of immune metaphor to multi-agent systems include works of Lee, Jun, & Sim (1999), Sathyanath & Sahin (2002), and Singh & Thayer (2002), to name but a few. In the chapter an original algorithm MISA (Multi-Agent Immune System Algorithm) is proposed for a multi-agent contest (Lucińska & Wierzchoń, 2007). Solutions presented in the above mentioned papers as well as the MISA algorithm perform better than traditional techniques (i.e. dynamic programming, reinforcement learning, etc.) for given problem domains. Despite promising results in a wide range of different applications there remain however many open issues in the field of AIS. Being a relatively new perspective, they are deficient in theoretical work to study their dynamic behavior in order to explain the results obtained by computational models.

In this chapter, an attempt is made to compare game theory and artificial immune systems by using multi-agent system as intersection platform. We try to extract commonalities between the two methods, in order to indicate possible directions of their future development. The chapter is organized as follows. In section 2 the pursuit-evasion problem is introduced and different attempts to cope with it are discussed. Section 3 presents an immune-based algorithm proposed to solve such a problem. Both algorithmic details and numerical results are given in this section. In section 4 a short discussion of possible extension of this work is given and section 5 concludes the paper.

BACKGROUND

In order to concentrate on the immune and game theoretic techniques, the rest of the chapter will focus on one class of the multi-agent encounters, i.e. pursuit-evasion problems. They are among the most widespread, challenging, and important multi-agent scenarios and represent some of the most significant potential applications for robots and other artificial autonomous agents. In a typical contest of this sort, one or more pursuers chase one or more evaders around until all preys are captured. Models in which pursuit-evasion problems are examined differ in: environment, number of players, agents' limitations, definition of capture, optimality criterion, space structure etc. (Isler, Kannan, & Khanna, 2004). Various aspects of pursuit-evasion as well as extensive bibliography on this subject can be found in (Sheppard, 1996).

Two-Player Pursuit-Evasion Games

In the literature, most studies on pursuit-evasion games have concentrated on two-player games, with a single pursuer and a single evader. Under the game theoretic framework a number of formal solutions regarding optimal strategies have been achieved (Isaacs, 1965, Basar & Olsder, 1998). Some of the most representative solutions will be introduced below.

For the sake of simplicity, both the space and time are discrete: the field of action is assumed to be a two-dimensional grid and at every time-step the players can move to new positions as shown in Fig. 1.

Figure 1. Player's moves on a greed. ©2008 Malgorzata Lucińska. Used with permission.

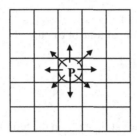

According to Nash (1950), a game is a set consisting of: *n* players, or positions, each with an associated set of strategies; and corresponding to *i*-th player, a payoff function, p_i, which maps the set of strategies into the real numbers.

The following assumptions are made in order to model the pursuit-evasion game as a finite non-cooperative game (Khan 2007):

1.   Set of players $N = \{p, e\}$, where *p* stands for the pursuer and *e* for the evader.

A position of the pursuer at time *t* is represented by his coordinates on the grid $r_t^p = (x_t^p, y_t^p)$, similarly for the evader location r_t^e. The position of both players at time *t* is denoted by $r_t = (r_t^p, r_t^e)$.

2.   Action profile $A = \{A_p, A_e\}$.

A_p represents an action (strategy) set of the pursuer and is defined as $\{a_1^p, ..., a_k^p\}$, where a_i^p stands for the *i*-th action of the pursuer; similarly for the set A_e. Both action sets consist of finite numbers of pure strategies.

In spite of pure strategies players can also execute mixed strategies, which are understood as probability distributions over a set of pure strategies. A mixed strategy s_i of the *i*-th player is given by:

$$s_i = \sum_k c_{ik} a_{ik} \qquad (2.1)$$

where c_{ik} stands for the probability of choosing *k*-th action by *i*-th player, i.e. $c_{ik} \geq 0$ and $\sum_k c_{ik} = 1$.

Generally a state of the game at time *t*+1 can be described in the following way:

$$r_{t+1} = f(r_t, a_i^p, a_i^e) \qquad (2.2)$$

where the function $f: \mathbf{R} \times A \to \mathbf{R}$ is a function which maps the positions and actions of both players at time *t* to the positions at the next instant.

3.   Payoff function $u(u_p, u_e)$

A purpose of players' credit assignment is to lead to better performance in terms of the goal achievement. To establish the payoff function, the termination of the game should be defined. If the evader is considered as being caught when it is close enough to the pursuer, the game ends under the following condition:

$$d(r_t^p, r_t^e) < d_{min} \qquad (2.3)$$

where d_{min} is a given threshold and $d(r_t^p, r_t^e)$ denotes the distance between the pursuer and the evader.

In case the definition of capture involves herding the evader to a pen, the game is over when:

$$d\left(\boldsymbol{r}^{pen}, \boldsymbol{r}_t^e\right) < d_{min} \tag{2.4}$$

where $\boldsymbol{r}^{pen}$ denotes coordinates of the pen on the grid.

As the criterion of optimality concerns the minimal time of capture, the payoff function for the pursuer can be defined as:

$$u_p\left(Z\right) = \sum_t -d_t \tag{2.5}$$

where Z is termination of the game and d_t a distance at time t from the termination state.

Worth noticing is a fact, that the objectives of the evader and the pursuer are opposite to each other, what means that they play a zero-sum game and their payoff functions fulfill the following equation:

$$u_e(Z) = -u_p(Z) \tag{2.6}$$

The pursuer at each moment in time should try to minimize the distance to the capture-state, and the evader should try to maximize it. A solution to the game is an equilibrium among the players, in which no player can improve their current strategy in terms of maximizing their payoff. An equilibrium is understood as a Nash equilibrium point and defined in the following way:

Considering an n player game, an n-tuple of strategies $a \in A$ is a Nash equilibrium point if for each player i, $i \in N$, and for each strategy a^i* of player i:

$$u_i(a|a^i*) \leq u_i(a) \tag{2.7}$$

where the strategy $a|a^i*$ is derived from a by substituting a^i* for a^i, denoting a strategy of the i-th player.

Thus each player's strategy is optimal against those of the others.

According to the Nash theorem (Nash, 1950), any n-person, non-cooperative game (zero-sum or nonzero-sum) for which each player has a finite number of pure strategies has at least one equilibrium set of strategies.

The above theorem guarantees reaching equilibrium in the simplest case of pursuit-evasion game as a direct consequence of modeling it as a non-cooperative finite game with perfect information.

A two-player pursuit-evasion game can also be modeled as a repeated game (Khan, 2007), which consists of some number of repetitions of the basic game (called a stage game). An assumption is made that at each time instant players play a (reduced) two-step extensive form game and the definition of the payoff is modified accordingly. It can be proved with a help of folk theorem (Shoham & Leyton-Brown, 2008), that for such games a Nash equilibrium exists and corresponds to the Nash equilibrium of each stage of the game.

Traditional game theory has focused on games with discrete moves, however one of the earliest and most popular analyses of the pursuit-evasion problem describes positions of the pursuer and the evader as continues time variable. The solution is given by Isaacs (1965), who utilizes differential game theory to solve such problems like aerial combat or a missile and a plane. Changes in states of the players, being results of their actions, are given in a form of partial differential equations (later called Hamilton-Jacobi-Isaacs equations). In order to find the optimal strategy Isaacs developed the method tenet of transition. It specifies that players must optimize the transitions between states, leading towards a goal-state. In other words a solution should be found, which can be represented as optimizing the temporal derivatives of the relevant state variables.

Multi-Player Pursuit-Evasion Games

Much more interesting from both practical and theoretical point of view are pursuit-evasion problems with multiple pursuers and multiple evaders. Unfortunately despite the wide amount of research on two-agent pursuit-evasion problems, there is not much work to study their multi-agent extension.

In the previous section, the pursuit-evasion problem is modeled as a non-cooperative game. In a presence of many pursuers a need for co-operation arises, so that they act more efficiently. Levy & Rosenschein (1992) suggest a method for solving the pursuit-evasion problem by mixing cooperative games with non-cooperative games. They focus on a team of four pursuers, attempting to surround a randomly moving evader. In addition to a global goal of the system each player may have some local, private goals, which can contradict the common goal and the other players' goals. To achieve a compromise a payoff function is a sum of two components. The first one encourages a pursuer to get closer to the evader and the second one to coordinate their actions with other pursuers. The solution utilizes theory of cooperative games (with side-payments), which assumes coalitions between players and deals with sharing the payments earned by the coalition. The authors define the cooperative game in coalitional form with side payments as a pair (N, v), where N is a set of players and $v(T)$ is a payoff function of the coalition T. For every move of the strategy s each player i first calculates his share $\psi^i(v_s)$ of the payoff function $v_s(T)$, that corresponds to the "local" cooperative game. Then he returns to the "global" problem and uses the payoff $\psi^i(v_s)$ in order to solve the non-cooperative game. As these authors state such a game has at least one equilibrium point, depending on the specific scenario. In order to bind the "local" solutions with the global ones a concept of "optimal points" is introduced, which represent moves that are best for the system as a whole. The proof is given, that each equilibrium point of the non-cooperative game constitutes also an optimal point. The assumed payoff policy guarantees coordination of the players, although none of them cares about it explicitly.

Experimental results show however, that some scenarios are not covered by the model and the agents are not sufficiently motivated by the above described payoff function. Another drawback of the proposed solution is a large computer power necessary for finding equilibrium in the presence of many players.

Another interesting approach to the pursuit-evasion problem is presented by Hespanha, Prandini, & Sastry (2000). In order to comply with real world situations the model takes into consideration limitations of the players. As the assumption of perfect knowledge of all the players' states and actions is hardly realistic, the authors model uncertainty, affecting actions of the players. The scene, on which the players move, contains obstacles, preventing them from occupying some cells on the grid. Uncertainty corresponds to incomplete knowledge of the obstacles configuration and inaccuracy in observing other players' positions.

The authors describe the problem as a partial information stochastic game in order to integrate map-learning and pursuit. The system consists of many pursuers and one evader. All the players effectively reach a chosen next position with some probability. At each time instant the pursuers' team and the evader chose their stochastic actions so as to respectively maximize and minimize the probability of finishing the game at the next time instant. Action is assumed as stochastic if a player selects it according to some probability distribution.

In the worst case, the evader has access to all information available to the pursuers. As the evader and pursuers have different sets of information, this one-step game is a nonzero-sum static game. The evader, contrary to the pursuers, could calculate the expected payoff used by the pursuers in addition to its own and therefore find a Nash equilibrium of the game. In order to overcome the pursuers' limitation, a solution is found, by treating the problem as a fictitious zero-sum game, in which the pursuers' estimate of the evader's cost is considered to be correct. Such assumption reveals an additional advantage: choosing the one-step Nash equilibrium policy the team of pursuers forces the rational evader to select a stochastic action corresponding to a Nash equilibrium for the original non-zero sum game. In other words, thanks to the players' rationality, the less informed pursuers can influence the best achievable evader's payoff without knowing its value.

By complying with the real-world conditions, the model constitutes a great novelty among many traditional approaches from the game theoretic perspective. However, it is not free from some drawbacks. It should be emphasized that this approach would not work if the evader did not have access to all information held by the pursuers or the pursuers could not share information. The authors' discussion about computational expenditure of the simulations shows that the complexity of the problem increases exponentially with a size of the grid and linearly with a number of pursuers' team positions. Another problem from the multi-player game perspective seems to be a formal reduction of many pursuers to one player. Such an approach simplifies the solution by omitting the pursuers' interactions.

Possibility of real world application is one of the most important factors, taken into account while assessing different solutions to the pursuit-evasion problem and generally all the multi-players contests. Unfortunately, traditional game theory does not provide convenient tools, which can be used in practical problems. One of the main obstacles, which should be overcome, is the assumption of perfect rationality of the players. In real life situations players seldom act rationally, due to their limitations, both physical and rational, which are unavoidable.

The static Nash concept does not reflect the dynamic nature of real problems. Players usually lack perfect information but they should be capable of learning. While acquiring new information, they may change their equilibrium strategies. In such systems, static solutions are rather not very useful and need to be extended to more feasible models, allowing for evolution in time.

Some of the above mentioned problems are addressed by evolutionary game theory, which offers solid basis for rational decision making in an uncertain environment. The theory does not require assumption, that all players are sophisticated and think the others are also rational. Instead, the notion of rationality is replaced with the much weaker concept of reproductive success: strategies that are successful on average will be used more frequently and thus prevail in the end. The dynamics, called replication dynamics, are based on an assumption that each strategy is played by a certain fraction of individuals. Then, given this distribution of strategies, individuals with better average payoff will be more successful than others, so that their proportion in the population increases over time. This, in turn, may affect which strategies are better than others.

The traditional static equilibrium concept has been replaced by evolutionary stable strategy introduced by Maynard-Smith (1982). The author considers a population of agents playing the same strategy, which is invaded by a different strategy, initially played by a small number of agents. If the new strategy does not overrule the original one and disappears after some time, the old strategy is regarded as evolutionary stable against the new one.

This view originates from biology and utilizes a core learning process from evolution. From the computer science perspective, such an approach adopts mechanisms typical for genetic algorithms.

Unfortunately, to the authors' knowledge, application of evolutionary game theory to pursuit-evasion contests has been strangely overlooked, despite its obvious relevance to such problems.

IMMUNE APPROACH TO THE MULTI-PLAYER PURSUIT-EVASION PROBLEM

In this section, a quite different view, than the game theoretic perspective, is presented. This approach is based on an immune metaphor, derived from theoretical biology. The considered system includes as many real elements as possible: agents have limitations, they do not know strategies of their opponents, and learn from experience. There is a lack of central control in the system. The proposed MISA, i.e. Multi-Agent Immune System Algorithm, was designed in such a way to fulfil the next requirements:

- scalability (effectiveness for both small and large problems with many players),
- on-line learning (the process of learning strategy accompanies the task execution),
- resistance to errors (fulfillment of the system goal in spite of misrepresented data).

Such a set of assumptions allows for true examination of the proposed immune algorithm and emphasizes great potential of the used mechanisms. The objective of this simulation is indeed to make a step towards extracting aggregated properties of two different approaches that may result in an achievement of a new, powerful tool.

The model is a broaden version of a system used for the herding problem behaviour, studied e.g. in (Aditya, 2001 and Kachroo, 2001). On the $l \times l$ grid there are r pursuers and v evaders. The pursuers' task is to locate evaders in a given place on the grid. For the sake of clarity an assumption is made, that it is the field with the coordinates (0, 0). There could be a few agents of the same type in the same field of the grid. The minimum distance between a pursuer and an evader is $d_{min} = 1$ unit.

Using similar formalism as in section 2. a set of players is given:

$N = \{p1, .. pr, e1, ...ev\}$.

An action set should be also determined for each player:

A_p – action set for a pursuer, consisting of moves in eight directions and staying at the same place; possible moves are shown in Fig. 2a.

Figure 2. The dynamics of: (a) pursuer P and (b) evader located at the distance of 2 units from the pursuer P. ©2008 Malgorzata Lucińska. Used with permission.

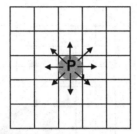 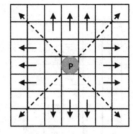

A_e – action set for an evader; possible moves are shown in Fig. 2b.

Evader's moves can be 2 units long (Fig. 2b) and are determined by the distance from the pursuer – the former tries to keep the maximum distance. If he observes a pursuer from the distance of d_{max} units he stays in place. If the distance is smaller he goes away to the safe distance d_{max}. Evaders' moves are explicitly defined according to each pursuer's position. If in the neighbourhood of an evader there are several pursuers his move is a vector sum of the shifts caused by each of the pursuers.

In order to model a real situation, the pursuers do not know their payoff functions. They get to know them in an on-line process of learning and save in the system memory.

Distances between agents are measured in the Tchebyshev metric:

$$d_{ij} = \max(|x_i - x_j|, |y_i - y_j|) \tag{3.1}$$

where x_i, y_i are Cartesian coordinates of the i-th agent and x_j, y_j are Cartesian coordinates of the j–th agent.

Perception of both, pursuers and evaders, is limited to the distance $d_{max} = 3$ units. An area, which a pursuer can "see" constitutes his local domain.

The Model Components

The natural immune system is composed of lymphocytes, i.e. white blood cells. We distinguish between lymphocytes of type B, B-lymphocytes for short, and T-lymphocytes. The later initialize immune response, while the former are responsible for binding invading antigens and for destroying them, (de Castro & Timmis, 2002). In our model, like in many other approaches used in the AIS, the B-cells are identified with their antibodies and we focus on the immediate reactions among antibodies and antigens only. The following assumptions are made:

- Presence of an evader within perception range of a pursuer plays a role of an antigen in the immune system.
- Presence of a pursuer corresponds to an antibody.
- Both antigens and antibodies are described by a pair of coordinates $(x, y) = (x_p - x_e, y_p - y_e)$, where x_p, y_p (x_e, y_e) denote the coordinates of the pursuer (evader) relative to the bottom left corner of the grid.
- In case of evader's absence, coordinates of an antibody are calculated relative to any chosen point, the same for all pursuers, who can "see" each other.

In the presented model, antibodies and antigens are associated with the two opposing types of players. In spite of the fact they are described in the same way. If an evader is visible by several pursuers, the antigen connected with him is described by different coordinates for each pursuer. The same coordinates correspond to antibodies, connected with the appropriate pursuers.

Figure 3. Part of the system with the evader at the origin of coordinates: (a) the antigen with coordinates (2, -2) and (b) antibodies making up a set of potential answers to the antigen. ©2008 Malgorzata Lucińska. Used with permission.

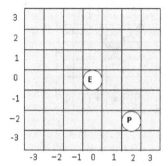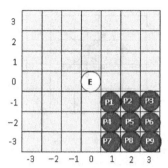

The Interactions

Interactions play crucial role in the natural immune system, determining its correct operation. Although they are still not fully understood, there exist a few models explaining some of the phenomena, observed in natural immunology. Jerne (1974) proposed so-called idiotypic network theory, according to which antibodies form a highly complex interwoven system, where they recognize not only foreign antigens, but are capable of recognizing each other. The system components react with certain other constituents to form a complex network.

In the presented multi-agent system interactions between artificial molecules (i.e. antigens and antibodies) are responsible for pursuers' dynamics, governing their movements. To describe these interactions the following assumptions are made:

- The antibody Ab can interact with (recognize) the antigen Ag if the distance between the antibody Ab and the antigen Ag is not bigger than the threshold value $a_{min}=1$. Such a threshold value results from limitation of the pursuers' moves. In the figure 3 there are the antigen with coordinates (2, -2) and antibodies, which interact with the antigen. The latter ones correspond to the states, which can be obtained in one step, made by the pursuer. Because of the players' moves limitation only these states are possible, which match up the following nine antibodies with coordinates: (1, -1), (2, -1), (3, -1), (1, -2), (2, -2), (3, -2), (1, -3), (2, -3), (3, -3).
- The interaction threshold for two antibodies, i.e. the maximum distance between them, for which they can interact with each other, equals the agents perception threshold – d_{max}. Such a choice seems to be a natural consequence of the fact that any interactions are possible only in case when agents can "see" each other.
- The total stimulation/suppression s_i of the antibody i equals a sum of stimulations/suppressions from other antibodies and antigens, interacting with it:

$$s_i = \sum_j \sigma_{ij} + \sum_k S_{ik} \qquad (3.2)$$

where σ_{ij} stands for stimulation/suppression of the i-th antibody by the j-th antigen and S_{ik} is the stimulation/suppression of the i-th antibody by the k-th antibody. In other words, the first part of this formula represents interactions between the given antibody and the antigens, whereas the second part represents interactions among the set of antibodies.
- The stimulation σ_{ij} of the i-th antibody by the j-th antigen is equal to a length of the evader's move, under the influence of the pursuer, that is $\sigma_{ij} = \Delta x + \Delta y$. Δx, Δy are components of the evader's displacement vector (relative to the bottom left corner of the grid), being a result of the pursuer's presence, which corresponds to the antibody i.
- In case when no antigen is present stimulation of the antibody i equals σ_0 (a parameter).

Figure 4. Illustration of stimulation value of the antibody with coordinates (2, -2)

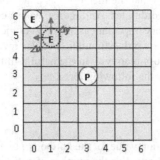

If a pursuer moves an evader closer to its target position (the bottom left corner of the grid), the antibody stimulation has a positive value. Otherwise, in case when an evader gets away from the target position, the antibody stimulation is negative and corresponds to suppression. Figure 4 illustrates stimulation value of an antibody by an antigen. The antibody with coordinates (2, -2), corresponding to the pursuer's position relative to the evader's position (marked with dotted line), causes the last one's move closer by 1 unit along the *OX*-axis and away by 1 unit along the *OY*-axis from the bottom left corner of the grid. The antibody stimulation equals 1-1=0.

The pursuer's position related to the first position of the evader (represented by a doted circle) corresponds to an antibody (2, -2). The evader moves to the next field (white circle) according to its dynamic.

The strength S_{ik} of interaction between the *i*-th and *k*-th antibody is defined in the following way:

$$S_{ik} = -\frac{c\sum_{j}\sqrt{|\sigma_{jk}\sigma_{ji}|}}{d_{ik}} \tag{3.3}$$

where σ_{ji} is the stimulation/suppression of the *i*-th antibody by the *j*-th antigen, σ_{jk} is the stimulation/suppression of the *k*-th antibody by the *j*-th antigen, d_{ik} is Tchebyshev distance between the antibodies *i* and *k*, and *c* is a coefficient.

In the above formula, contributions from all the antigens, interacting with both the antibody *k* and the antibody *i*, are aggregated. It is assumed, that only suppression is possible between two antibodies. The role of the coefficient *c* will be discussed in the next section.

In the natural immune system, the higher is the level of the antibody stimulation the more intense its proliferation is and – as a result – its concentration. Similarly in the presented model, the level of stimulation, given by the already introduced formulas, corresponds to probability of the antibody choice and reproduction. For each antigen, the most activated antibody is chosen from the group of antibodies interacting with it.

Interactions between an antigen and an antibody enable to choose the relatively best pursuer's position, so that the evader moves in a desirable direction. Interactions between antibodies aim at a choice of the most suitable pursuer, who is able to control the evader. As a result of antibodies mutual suppression, the pursuers, whose positions relative to the evader, are less effective or even improper, are forced to move away. Furthermore, interactions between antibodies prevent unnecessary gathering of pursuers, enabling better exploration of the grid. It can be assumed that antibodies create a network of locally interacting cells, that leads to global self-organization of the system.

The System Memory

An important feature of the immune memory is that it is associative: antibodies adapted to a certain type of antigen present a faster and more efficient secondary response not only to the same intruder but also to another similar one. This phenomenon is called cross-reactive response (de Castro & Timmis, 2002).

The system possesses a memory, in which antibodies stimulations from antigens are saved during the learning process. The presented model assumes that the memory has a network structure. A place of each antibody in the network is strictly defined by its coordinates. Antibodies, whose coordinates values differ by 1 unit, are adjacent to each other in the memory. A very important assumption of the model is the similarity of the stimulation values for adjacent antibodies. In other words, stimulation values reveal continuous distribution for ordered memory cells. The idea corresponds to cross-reactivity in the natural immune system. This postulate is crucial for defining network stimulation, given by the following formula:

$$u_{ij} = \sigma_{ij} + \frac{1}{2N} \sum_{k=1}^{N} \sigma_{kj} \tag{3.4}$$

Here u_{ij} stands for the network stimulation value for the antibody i by the antigen j, σ_{ij} is the stimulation/suppression of the antibody i by the antigen j, and N is the number of antibodies with known stimulation from the antigen j, adjacent in the memory to the antibody i.

Network stimulation can be used in the following situations:

- Rough estimation of unknown antibody stimulation value, on the basis of adjacent antibodies stimulations. In such a case the second part of the last formula is used.
- Diversification of quality of antibodies with equal stimulation values. In Figure 5 an example of the system memory is shown. The stimulation values for the antibodies Ab_1 with coordinates (-3, 0) and Ab_2 with coordinates (-3, 2) are the same. However their network stimulations differ from each other. The antibody Ab_2 with higher network stimulation constitutes indeed the better choice, taking into consideration longer time perspective. The field (0, 0) in Fig. 5 corresponds to the position of the evader and is not available for the pursuer.

Mutation

The MISA algorithm belongs to the class of on-line working algorithms, i.e. the process of learning strategy accompanies the task execution. Antibodies stimulations can be saved in the system memory only after being previously chosen in the experiment. The value of stimulation is calculated on the basis of the observed evader's positions. Incorrect move of a pursuer decreases efficiency of the whole system. In such a situation, an effective mutation mechanism is necessary, that enables generation of the possibly best solutions. The use of the memory network structure together with stimulation continuity makes possible to direct the mutation process in order to obtain the best cells.

Figure 5. Example of the system memory including antibodies stimulation values. ©2008 Malgorzata Lucińska. Used with permission.

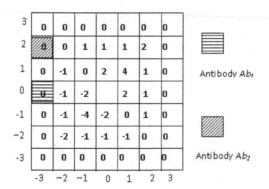

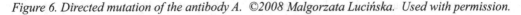

Figure 6. Directed mutation of the antibody A. ©2008 Malgorzata Lucińska. Used with permission.

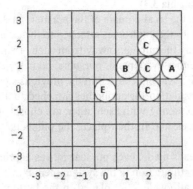

Figure 6 illustrates the directed mutation process of the antibody A with coordinates (3, 1). At the beginning, we search the memory of the system to identify the most stimulated antibody, which interacts with the given antibody A. In the presented example, the antibody B with coordinates (1, 1) meets the above mentioned conditions. Afterwards, new antibodies C are created. They are adjacent to the antibody A and as close as possible to the antibody B from the system memory. The antibody A corresponds to the position of the pursuer relative to the evader E. Because each pursuer can make a move only 1 unit long, the mutated cells must lie in the immediate vicinity of the antibody A.

Thanks to the mechanism of directed mutation, the number of clones, of a given antibody can be rather low (in our experiments this number was not greater than three). Moreover avoiding repetitions of the same cells choices leads to the increase of exploitation capabilities of the system.

The Algorithm

The MISA algorithm is in some sense an extension of the well known clonal selection algorithm (CSA) proposed by de Castro & Von Zuben (2000). It utilizes similar processes as the previous solution: clonal selection and affinity maturation.

In CSA first a set of candidate cells is generated, in which memory cells are included. After antigen presentation the best individuals are selected, in terms of their affinity with a given antigen. They are reproduced, giving rise to a temporary population of clones. Further, the clones undergo hypermutation. The number of clones, produced by a given antibody, and a size of hypermutation are respectively an increasing and decreasing functions of the antibody affinity with the antigen. In next step, the improved individuals are re-selected to compose a memory set. Afterwards, some antibodies with the lowest affinity are replaced by novel ones in order to assure diversity of cells. The steps are repeated for the next generation.

The main steps of the CSA are also repeated in the MISA algorithm, i.e. antigen presentation, antibody selection, affinity maturation, and memory reorganization. The differences between the two solutions are a natural consequence of the MISA adaptation to on-line learning. They include directed mutation, interactions between antibodies, and structured memory. Inclusion of network interactions causes that the MISA is an instance of a hybrid immune algorithm rather than an instance of the CSA.

The initial state of the multi-agent system is generated randomly – the evaders and pursuers are placed on the $l \times l$ grid at random. Players of different types are not allowed in the same field of the grid. In the subsequent steps each pursuer collects information concerning the evaders and the other pursuers he can "see"; this corresponds to antigens presentation.

When some evaders are visible, the pursuer looks into the system memory in order to find the most suitable solution (antibody selection). The antibody A, which corresponds to the current pursuer's position, undergoes the process of directed mutation. Afterwards the most stimulated clone of the antibody A is chosen, according to the clonal selection principle (affinity maturation). In order to choose the most suitable antibody in the memory and to evaluate the mutated clones, formula (3.4) is used.

If the pursuer can "see" other pursuers in his local domain, the antibody attached to him interacts with antibodies attached to the other agents (formula 3.3).

In case there are not any evaders in the local domain of the pursuer but there are other pursuers, the antibody is chosen on the basis of interaction with the antibodies attached to the other players. According to the formula (3.3) the antibodies, which cause getting the pursuers away from each other, are more stimulated.

When the pursuer cannot "see" neither evaders nor pursuers, no new cell appears in the system. Thus, it is assumed that interactions between cells, which occurred in the previous step, continue in this step.

After determining the level of stimulation for antibodies attached to all the pursuers, the most stimulated ones, from the group of antibodies interacting with each other, are chosen. Cells with stimulation smaller than zero (formula 3.3) are subject to suppression. In their place, the pursuers, to whom they are attached, have to choose better antibodies.

When the final choice of antibodies is made, each pursuer moves appropriately and then, after noticing the evader's action, he updates antibodies stimulation in the system memory.

After each epoch, i.e. every time all evaders are placed in the bottom left corner of the grid, the system memory is modified (memory reorganization). The maximum σ_{max} and the minimum σ_{min} values of stimulation

Figure. 7. Pseudo-code of the MISA. ©2008 Malgorzata Lucińska. Used with permission.

```
1. (Initialisation) Put the pursuers and evaders at random on the
grid
2. Until the termination condition is not met do:
  2.1 For each pursuer P do:
    2.1.1 Find other pursuers visible to P.
    2.1.2 (Antigens presentation) Determine antigens coordinates on
    the basis of the visible evaders.
    2.1.3 For each antigen A do:
        (Clonal selection) If within the distance of d_max from the
        antigen A there are not any antibodies in the memory
          choose antibody at random
      else
        (Affinity maturation) for each antigen:
          Find in the memory the most stimulated antibody, within
          a distance of d_max from A
          Mutate the antibody in the direction to the most
          stimulated antibody
        (Clonal interactions) for each mutated clone:
          Find stimulation from all antigens
        (Clonal suppression) choose the best antibody
  2.2 For each pursuer:
    2.2.1 (Network interaction) determine stimulation of the chosen
          antibody from other agents' antibodies.
    2.2.2 (Network suppression) choose the best antibody and make the
          move
  2.3 Find new positions of all evaders.
  2.4 Update antibodies stimulations on the basis of the evaders'
      moves.
3. (Memory reorganization) choose the antibodies with the extreme
      values of stimulation and save into the memory.
```

are determined. Only the antibodies with the extreme stimulation from antigens – not smaller than $\sigma_{max}/2$ and not higher than $\sigma_{min}/2$ – are left.

The algorithm for the system learning is presented in Fig 7.

Results

The above algorithm has been implemented in the JDK1.4.1 environment (http://java.sun.com). The grid size l, the number of pursuers r, and the number of evaders v are parameters. The program has been tested for a wide range of parameters values from $l=4$, $r=1$, $v=1$ to $l=100$, $r=300$, $v=350$ and the only limitation for increasing the parameters values is the time the program runs. It increases proportionally to the number of players, that arises from the necessity of determining all players' moves but is not a result of more complicated action choice in larger systems. The complexity of the MISA algorithm in terms of players number is of the order $O(rs)$, where r indicates a number of pursuers and s a number of other players the one can "see". Because of the players' limited perception and implemented repulsion, s hardly depends on the total number of players. The system is scalable.

The presented model is used for determining dependence between the system efficiency and players' mutual relations. The coefficient c in the formula (3.3) has the biggest influence on players' interactions. There are possible two diametrically opposed behaviours:

- Independence – each pursuer's actions do not depend directly on states of the other pursuers. Each player individually tries to execute the system task, without paying attention to the others. Such a behaviour is obtained by neglecting interactions among antibodies in the formula 3.2, i.e. assuming that $S_{ik} = 0$ and $c = 0$.
- Greed – interactions between players are nothing else but only repulsion. In case of evaders' absence, pursuers get away from each others. If an evader is visible, only one pursuer leads him, and the other pursuers go away. Such a behaviour corresponds to large values of the coefficient c (e.g. $c \geq 10$) in the formula (3.3).

Efficiency of independent and greedy players has been compared for two different systems: the one with a small grid edge and high pursuer's density (Fig. 8) and the other with a bigger grid edge and lower pursuers density (Fig. 9). In the second case the independent players reveal much worse effectiveness than the greedy ones, which is a result of weaker grid foraging. However, in systems with smaller grid and high density of players, the results for independent agents are by 15% better in comparison to greedy ones.

The above effects indicate that the best solution is an introduction of the coefficient c (in the formula 3.3), which depends on the number of interacting antibodies. In the MISA algorithm, the following relation is assumed:

$$c = \frac{1}{g} \tag{3.5}$$

where g is a local density of antibodies.

For each antibody, attached to the pursuer, the local density of antibodies equals the number of other antibodies, attached to the other visible pursuers, interacting with the same antigen. As the result of such assumption concerning the coefficient c, only a part of the pursuers gathers around the evader whereas the rest is responsible for foraging. In other words, the players co-operate with each other dividing up different tasks, that leads to self-organisation of the system. Extreme players' behaviours – independence or greed – perform well only in some specific conditions. The best results, irrespective of system parameters, are achieved for co-operating agents.

Relation between time of the task execution and values of the system parameters has been examined. In all the experiments, the initial states of the players are generated at random and the number of training epochs equals 10. The time of task execution is represented by the number of steps, which the algorithm makes in order to achieve the system goal. In the first case, the number of evaders v and the grid edge l are constant, whereas the number of pursuers r changes beginning from one to seventy – see Fig. 10. At the initial stage of the experiment, when the number of pursuers is approximately as big as the number of evaders and their average density on grid not too high, the number of steps dramatically decreases with an increase of the parameter r. Later the system reaches

Figure 8. Comparison of effectiveness of independent and greedy agents in a system with parameters l = 8, r = 14 and v = 13. ©2008 Malgorzata Lucińska. Used with permission.

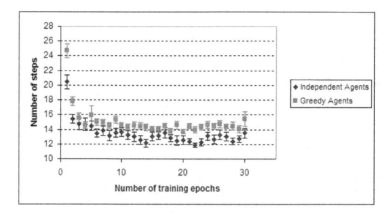

Figure 9. Comparison of effectiveness of independent and greedy agents in a system with parameters l = 10, r = 4 and v = 3. ©2008 Malgorzata Lucińska. Used with permission.

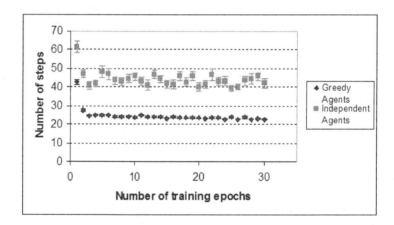

the state of saturation, when the number of steps depends on the parameter *r* very weakly. Such an effect results from limitation of the evaders' moves. Involvement of a large number of pursuers in herding one evader can also lead to an "escape" of the last one from the local domains of the pursuers. Too large number of pursuers in the system has little influence on its effectiveness.

In Fig. 11, the relation between the time of the task execution and the number of evaders is shown. In this case, the initial change in the number of steps is not as rapid as it was in the previous experiment. At the later stage, the number of steps increases very slowly with the evaders' number, similarly as for pursuers. Explanation of the effect becomes simple after looking at evaders' distribution during the initial stage. Evaders reveal tendency for gathering in a few fields on the grid. Independently on their number, about 70% of all evaders occupies several (3-4) fields on the grid after a few steps of the algorithm. The fields are usually situated in corners and at the

Figure 10. Relation between the number of steps and number of pursuers (l=10, v=3). ©2008 Malgorzata Lucińska. Used with permission.

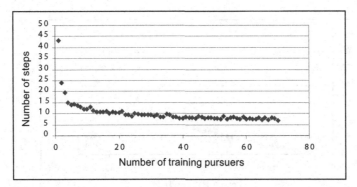

Figure 11. Relation between the number of steps and number of evaders (l=10, r=3). ©2008 Malgorzata Lucińska. Used with permission.

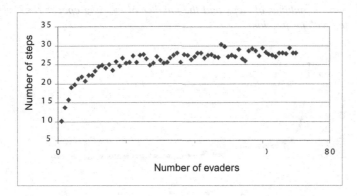

edges of the grid. The reason for this is that while pursuers search, evaders try to hide in resultant niches. With an increase of the evaders' number the number of the tasks for execution changes very slowly. Moreover, the number of steps devoted for foraging decreases.

As there is shown in Fig. 12, a number of steps is approximately proportional to the square of the grid edge length. The relation is quite intuitive as a number of fields to be searched increases as the square of the parameter l. The complexity of the MISA algorithm in terms of the parameter l is of the order $O(l^2)$.

The number of steps, which are necessary to accomplish the system goal, decreases dramatically at the very beginning of the system training (Fig. 13). The effect is similar to the secondary response phenomenon in the natural immune system.

The MISA algorithm was inspired by a work of Aditya (2001), who also has used immune metaphor for the herding problem solution. Despite a few similarities like the antigen model or the way of establishing antibody stimulation, the two algorithms are different. The Aditya's proposal does not include antibodies mutation and interactions between cells are foreordained. After comparing results obtained for the two systems, it is easy to see that MISA outperforms the other solution both in a number of training epochs (about ten times faster proc-

Figure 12. Relation between number of steps and length of the grid edge (r=4, v=3). ©2008 Malgorzata Lucińska. Used with permission.

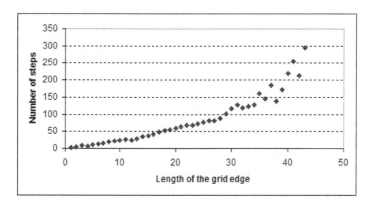

Figure 13. Relation between the number of steps and the number of training epochs (l=7, r=3, v=1). ©2008 Malgorzata Lucińska. Used with permission.

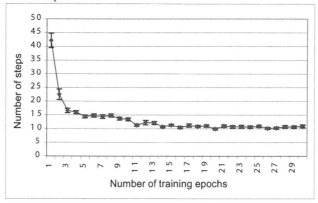

ess of learning) and the number of steps, necessary for the goal achievement (about ten times smaller number of steps).

The introduced immune algorithm uses the paradigm of reinforcement learning method. Random exploitation of solution space is replaced by directed moves, chosen on the basis of saved information. The memory network structure allows for additional differentiation of the system states quality. Thanks to the implementation of interactions, observed in the natural immune system, the algorithm leads to self-organization of players' activities, without any central control. The obtained results show that mutual interactions of individuals, of whom the system consists, have a great influence on its effectiveness. A very important observation seems to be the possibility of compensation for the players' limitations by their co-operation. In spite of sometimes incorrect perception, the system goal is always achieved, that proves resistance to errors.

Unfortunately, the above described methods, used for optimisation of the agent behaviour, are base on very fragile theoretic fundamentals. Being quite intuitive ones, they lack any proofs of convergence or even guarantees of finding a solution. Their appealing flexibility in modelling real situation and good simulation results, however, encourage extending them to other approaches.

CONCLUSION

The proposed algorithm is scalable, capable to learn on-line, and resistant to errors connected with agents' limitations. Moreover it is decentralized and allows for modeling different behaviors of the players.

Despite representing a biology inspired solution, the MISA algorithm does share some fundamental concepts with more formal models, originating from game theory.

The final choice of the best antibody in the algorithm, or rather the pursuer with the most stimulated cell, resembles the game theoretic leadership model proposed by Stackelberg (1952). In such a strategic game, the decision making of players has a hierarchy. The leader moves first, enforcing strategy of the other players (followers), who then move sequentially, reacting to the leader's decisions. In the described system at each time step a leader-pursuer is chosen, who has a privilege of making the first move. The other pursuers, who can "see" the leader, accommodate to his action. Otherwise, they would not only harm themselves, but also harm the leader, as it is also in the Stackelberg model.

Both approaches allow generating some types of co-operation between players without communication. Players can use game theoretic techniques to predict what others will do, considering their perfect rationality. The immune metaphor implies certain rules, which govern behaviour of the whole system and its elements. Imitation of complex adaptive system features results in players' coordination. Moreover, the immune solution seems to be a feasible tool for modelling different behaviours of the players and observing their influence on the system efficiency.

Even further similarities between AIS and game theory had been indicated by Alonso, Nino, & Velez (2004). In this work a well-known evolutionary dynamics, replicator dynamics (mentioned in the section 2.), is used to model the behaviour of an immune network. In order to introduce the game theoretic model, elements of the immune network are thought to be involved in interactions, which may be seen as pair-wise interactions between them, such as in evolutionary game theory, where agents are paired to play. An antibody i corresponds to an individual programmed to play a pure strategy a_i. A network of interacting cells represents a mixed strategy (defined in the section 2.), whereas a stimulation level of a cell can be thought of as a payoff, earned by a player with a pure strategy, when confronted with mixed strategy. In addition, replicator dynamics takes care of modeling metadynamics of the immune network. Using such a model, the authors investigate conditions, under which the immune network is expected to stabilize, i.e. reach a Nash equilibrium state.

The objective of this chapter is to present research done in the area of multi-agent encounters, focusing on the relation to artificial immune systems and game theory. To serve this purpose, an overview of basic game theoretic concepts, terminology and notation has been provided, and some specific approaches to dealing with the pursuit-evasion problem are surveyed. In addition an attempt to address some open research questions is made.

Handling complex, dynamic, and uncertain problems produces many challenges, independently of the techniques used. Although artificial immune systems and game theory have been established on quite different basis, they have to cope with the same problems, which constitute an increasing cross-fertilization among these fields.

FUTURE RESEARCH DIRECTIONS

The unquestionable advantages of both game theoretic and immune models represent a promising field for future research. It seems that bridging a gap between traditional, mathematically motivated models and novel, unconventional paradigms can be very fruitful for both parties, producing a kind of stimulating feedback.

In this chapter, an example of evolutional game theory should be quoted, which has been originated as an application of the mathematical theory of games to biological contexts. It successfully utilizes concepts used also in genetic algorithms. As there is an intuitive analogy between biological evolution and learning, why not to employ a bit sophisticated models, like a natural immune system, in order to obtain complex behaviours. The most appealing features of such hybrid models include: security, reliability, distribution, adaptability.

This chapter has argued that exploration of the pursuit-evasion problem constitutes a perfect arena for inter-disciplinary studies. It is a very realistic model, integrating important issues of complex dynamic systems, which can be explored in diverse aspects. According to Tefatsion (2001), decentralized market economies are complex adaptive systems. AIS models represent a convenient tool for studying the basic features of such systems, like aggregation, flows, diversity or non-linearity. Combining immune metaphor with game theory, which has its roots in economics, will allow for exploration of broader economic issues rather than focusing on local behavior of limited dimension. This paper provides an example of agent's behavior modeling (greed an independence), which results in emergence of macro-level changes in the system performance.

Pursuit-evasion contests have many other applications: military uses, video games, computer application, wireless ad hoc routing, medical operations, intelligent buildings etc. These fields may also encourage researches to explore their potentials with a use of game theory and AIS.

REFERENCES

[1]   Aditya, G. (2001). *Learning strategies in multi-agent systems - applications to the herding problem.* Un-published master's thesis, Virginia Polytechnic Institute and State University.

[2]   Alonso, O. M., Nino, F., & Velez, M. (2004). A game-theoretic approach to artificial immune networks. In G. Nicosia et al, (Ed.), *Third International Conference on Artificial Immune Systems, number 3239 in LNCS* (pp. 143-151). U.K.: Springer-Verlag.

[3]   Basar, T., & Olsder, G. J. (1998). *Dynamic non-cooperative game theory.* New York: Academic Press.

[4]   de Castro, L. N. & Von Zuben, F. J. (2000). The clonal selection algorithm with engineering applications. In L. D. Whitley; D. E. Goldberg; E. Cantú-Paz; L. Spector; I. C. Parmee, & H. Beyer (Ed.), *GECCO'00, Workshop on Artificial Immune Systems and Their Applications* (pp. 36-37). Las Vegas, USA: Morgan Kaufmann.

[5]   de Castro, L. N. & Timmis, J. (2002). *Artificial immune systems: A new computational approach.* London, UK: Springer-Verlag.

[6]   Hespanha, J., Prandini, M., & Sastry, S. (2000). Probabilistic pursuit-evasion games: A one-step Nash approach. In *IEEE Conference on Decision and Control: Vol. 3* (pp. 2272–2277). Sydney: IEEE Press.

[7]   Isaacs, R. (1965). *Differential games,* New York: John Wiley & Sons, Inc.

[8]   Isler, V., Kannan, S., & Khanna, S. (2004). Randomized pursuit-evasion with limited visibility. In J. I. Munro (Ed.), *ACM-SIAM Symposium on Discrete Algorithms (SODA)* (pp. 1053– 1063). New Orleans, USA: SIAM.

[9]   Jerne, N. K. (1974). Towards a network theory of the immune system. *Annals of Institute Pasteur/Immunology, 125C,* 373-389.

[10]   Kachroo, P. (2001). Dynamic programming solution for a class of pursuit evasion problems: the herding problem. *IEEE Transactions on Systems, Man, and Cybernetics, Part C: Applications and Reviews, 31*(1), 35–41.

[11]   Khan, M. E. (2007). *Game theory models for pursuit evasion games* (Tech. Rep. No. 2). Vancouver, University of British Columbia, Department of Computer Science.

[12]   Lee, D. W., Jun, H. B., & Sim, K. B. (1999). Artificial immune system for realization of cooperative strategies and group behavior in collective autonomous mobile robots. In *Fourth International Symposium on Artificial Life and Robotics* (pp. 232-235). Oita, Japan.

[13]   Levy, R. & Rosenschein, J. S. (1992). A game theoretic approach to distributed artificial intelligence and the pursuit problem. In Y. Demazeau & E. Werner (Ed.), *Decentralized Artificial Intelligence III* (pp. 129-146). North-Holland: Elsevier Science Publishers B.V.

[14]   Lucińska, M., & Wierzchoń, S. T. (2007). An immune-based system for herding problem. In T. Burczyński, W. Cholewa, & W. Moczulski (Ed.), *Recent Developments in Artificial Intelligence Methods* (pp. 107-121). Gliwice: Silesian University of Technology.

[15]   Maynard-Smith, J. (1982). *Evolution and the theory of games*. U.K.: Cambridge University Press.

[16]   Nash, J. F. Jr. (1950). Equilibrium points in n-person games. *Proceedings of the National Academy of Sciences, 36*(1), 48–49.

[17]   Rosenschein, J. S. (1985). *Rational interaction: Cooperation among intelligent agents*. Unpublished doctoral dissertation, Stanford University, CA.

[18]   Sathyanath, S., & Sahin, F. (2002). AISIMAM – An artificial immune system based intelligent multi agent model and its application to a mine detection problem. In *International Conference on Artificial Immune Systems* (pp. 3-11), U.K.: Canterbury Printing Unit.

[19]   Sheppard, J.W. (1996). Multi-Agent Reinforcement Learning in Markov Games, Ph.D. Dissertation, The Johns Hopkins University, Baltimore, Maryland.

[20]   Shoham, Y., & Leyton-Brown, K. (2008). *Multi agent systems*. U.K.: Cambridge University Press.

[21]   Singh, S., & Thayer, S. (2002). A foundation for kilorobotic exploration. In *IEEE World Congress on Evolutionary Computational Intelligence*: *Vol. 2*. Honolulu: IEEE Press.

[22]   Stackelberg, H. (1952). *The theory of the market economy*. London, U.K.: Oxford University Press.

[23]   Tefatsion, L. (2001). Economic agents and markets as emergent phenomena. *Proceedings of the National Academy of Sciences of the United States of America, 99(10),* 7191-7192.

ADDITIONAL READING

1)   Alonso, O. M., Nino, F., & Velez, M. (2004). A robust immune based approach to the Iterated Prisoner's Dilemma. In G. Nicosia (Ed.), *Third International Conference on Artificial Immune Systems, number 3239 in LNCS* (pp. 113-121). U.K.: Springer-Verlag.

2)   Baird, L. C. (1995). Residual algorithms: Reinforcement learning with function approximation. In A. Prieditis & S. Russell (Ed.), *Machine learning: Proceedings of the Twelfth International Conference*. San Francisco, CA: Morgan Kaufman Publishers.

3)   Baird, L.C. (1993). *Advantage updating* (Tech. Rep. No. WL-TR-93-1146). Alexandria, VA, Defense Technical Information Center.

4)   Barto, A. G., Sutton, R. S., & Watkins, C. J. (1989). *Learning and sequential decision making* (Tech. Rep. No. 89-95). Massachusetts, Amherst, University of Massachusetts, Department of Computer and Information Science. Also published (1991) in M. Gabriel & J. Moore (Ed.), *Learning and computational neuroscience: Foundations of adaptive networks*. Cambridge, U.K.: MIT Press.

5)   Brandt, F., Fischer F., Harrenstein P., & Shoham Y. (2007). A game-theoretic analysis of strictly competitive multiagent scenarios. In M. Veloso (Ed.), *International Joint Conference on Artificial Intelligence (IJCAI)* (pp. 1199-1206).

6)   Brandt, F., Fischer, F., & Holzer, M. (2007). Symmetries and the complexity of pure Nash equilibrium. In W. Thomas & P. Weil (Ed.), *International Symposium on Theoretical Aspects of Computer Science (STACS): Vol. 439. Lecture Notes in Computer Science (LNCS)* (pp. 212-223). U.K.: Springer-Verlag.

7)   Carmel, D., & Markovitch, S. (1999). Exploration strategies for model-based learning. *Multi-agent systems. Autonomous agents and multi-agent systems, 2*(2), 141-172.

8)   Fogel, D. B. (1993). Evolving behaviours in the iterated prisoner's dilemma. *Evolutionary Computation, 1*(1), 77-97.

9)   Fudenberg, D., & Levine, D. (1998). *The theory of learning in games*. Cambridge, MA: MIT Press.

10)   Guibas, L. J., Latombe, C., LaValle, S. M., Lin, D., & Motwani, R. (1999). Visibility-based pursuit-evasion in a polygonal environment. *International Journal of Computational Geometry and Applications, 9*(5), 471—494.

11)   Harmon, M. E., Baird, L. C, & Klopf, A. H. (1995). Advantage updating applied to a differential game. In G. Tesauro, D. S. Touretzky, & T. K. Leen (Ed.), *Advances in Neural Information Processing Systems: Vol. 7 (pp. 353-360)*. Cambridge, MA: MIT Press.

12)   Holland, J. H. (1992). *Adaptation in natural and artificial systems: An introductory analysis with applications to biology, control, and artificial intelligence, 2nd edition*. Cambridge, MA: MIT Press.

13)   Hu, J. & Wellman, M. (2003). Nash Q-learning for general-sum stochastic games. *The Journal of Machine Learning Research, 4*, 1039–1069.

14)   Kian, A., Cruz, J. B., & Simaan, M. (2002). Stochastic discrete-time Nash games with constrained state estimators. *Journal of Optimization Theory and Applications, 1*(114), 171–188.

15)   Lagevardi, M. & Lewis, J. (2006). Artificial immune system for discovering heuristics in Othello. In *Genetic and Evolutionary Computation Conference (GECCO)*. Seattle, Washington, USA: ACM.

16)   LaValle, S. M., & Hinrichsen, J. (2001). Visibility-based pursuit-evasion: The case of curved environments. *IEEE Transactions on Robotics and Automation, 17*, 196–201.

17)   Li, D., Cruz, J. B. Jr., Chen, G., & Chang, M. H. (2005). A hierarchical approach to multi-player pursuit-evasion differential games. In *IEEE Conference on Decision and Control, 2005 and 2005 European Control Conference CDC-ECC* (pp. 5674- 5679). IEEE Press.

18)   Nash, J. (1951). Non-cooperative Games. *Annals of Mathematics Journal, 54*, 286-295.

19)   Osborne M. & Rubinstein A. (1994). *A course in game theory*. Cambridge, MA: MIT Press.

20)   Papadimitriou, C. H. & Roughgarden, T. (2005). Computing equilibria in multi-player games. In *Annual ACM-SIAM Symposium on Discrete Algorithms (SODA)* (pp. 82–91). USA: SIAM.

21)   Paruchuri, P., Pearce, J. P., Tambe, M., Ordonez, F., & Kraus, S. (2007). An efficient heuristic approach for security against multiple adversaries. In *International Conference on Autonomous Agents and Multiagent Systems, AAMAS*. Honolulu, Hawaii.

22)   Schenato, L., Oh, S., & Sastry, S. (2005). Swarm coordination for pursuit evasion games using sensor networks. In *Barcelona International Conference on Robotics and Automation* (pp. 2493–2498). Barcelona, Spain.

23)   Trianni, V., Ampatzis, C., Christensen, A. L., Tuci, E., Dorigo, M., & Nolfi, S. (2007). From solitary to collective behaviours: Decision making and cooperation. In F. Almeida, E Costa et al. (Ed.), *Advances in Artifi-*

cial Life. Proceedings of the 9th European Conference on Artificial Life (ECAL 2007): Vol. 464. Lecture Notes in Artificial Intelligence (pp. 575-584). Berlin, Germany: Springer Verlag.

24) Turetsky, V. & Shinar J. (2003). Missile guidance laws based on pursuit-evasion game formulations. *Automatica, 39*(4), 607–618.

25) Tuyls, K. & Nowe, A. (2005). Evolutionary game theory and multi-agent reinforcement learning. *The Knowledge Engineering Review, 20*(01), 63–90.

26) Vidal, R., Rashid, S., Sharp, C., Shakernia, O., Kim, H. J., & Sastry, S. (2001). Pursuit-evasion games with unmanned ground and aerial vehicles. In *IEEE International Conference on Robotic & Automation: Vol 3* (pp. 2948-2955). IEEE Press.

27) Vidal, R., Shakernia, O., Kim, H. J., Shim, D. H., & Sastry, S. (2002). Probabilistic pursuit-evasion games: Theory, implementation, and experimental evaluation. *IEEE Transactions on Robotics and Automation, 18*, 662-669.

28) von Neumann, J. & Morgenstern, O. (1947). *The theory of games and economic behavior.* USA: Princeton University Press.

29) Weibull, J. W. (1995). *Evolutionary game theory.* Cambridge, MA: MIT Press.

30) Wiegand, R. P., Liles, W., & De Jong, K. (2002). Analyzing cooperative coevolution with evolutionary game theory. In D. B. Fogel, M. A. El-Sharkawi, X. Yao, G. Greenwood, H. Iba, P. Marrow, & M. Shackleton (Ed.), *Congress on Evolutionary Computation CEC2002* (pp. 1600–1605). IEEE Press.

31) Wooldridge, M. (2002). *An introduction to multi agent systems.* Chichester, England: John Wiley & Sons, Inc.

32) Yamaguchi, H. (2002). A distributed motion coordination strategy for multiple non-holonomic mobile robots in cooperative hunting operations. In *IEEE Conference on Decision and Control* (pp. 2984-2991). IEEE Press.

KEY TERMS

Pursuit-Evasion Game: A game in which, predators, or pursuers, chase preys (evaders) around until the preys are captured. Solution constitutes chasing agents' optimal strategy, which guarantees execution of their task.

Agent: An entity, that perceives its environment and acts upon it in order to realize a given set of goals or tasks.

Multi-Agent System: A system consisting of many agents, who can perform tasks individually or co-operate in order to achieve a system goal. A very important factor in such systems are agents' interaction. Agents' limitations - anything that prevent agents from acting optimally, e.g. limited perception, limited speed.

Repeated Game: A game consisting of a series of interactions among two or more players. After each interaction players may receive some payoff. Unlike a game played once, a repeated game allows for a strategy to be contingent on past moves.

Stochastic Game: A game, where at any point in time the game is in some state. The game transitions to a new state depend on a stochastic function of the previous state and the interactions among the agents.

On-Line Learning: A process, in which a system learns and acts simultaneously.

Adaptability: The ability to cope with internal or external changes or to adjust itself to dynamic environments or unexpected events.

Directed Mutation: A process that is aimed at creating cells with particular features rather then a random set of cells. First the best cell (in terms of interaction strength with the present antigen) is found and afterwards cells with similar features are created.

Chapter V
Applications of Artificial Immune Systems in Agents

Luis Fernando Niño Vasquez
National University of Colombia, Colombia

Fredy Fernando Muñoz Mopan
National University of Colombia, Colombia

Camilo Eduardo Prieto Salazar
National University of Colombia, Colombia

José Guillermo Guarnizo Marín
National University of Colombia, Colombia

ABSTRACT

Artificial Immune Systems (AIS) have been widely used in different fields such as robotics, computer science, and multi-agent systems with high efficacy. This is a survey chapter within which single and multi-agent systems inspired by immunology concepts are presented and analyzed. Most of the work is usually based on the adaptive immune response characteristics, such as clonal selection, idiotypic networks, and negative selection. However, the innate immune response has been neglected and there is not much work where innate metaphors are used as inspiration source to develop robotic systems. Therefore, a work that involves some interesting features of the innate and adaptive immune responses in a cognitive model for object transportation is presented at the end of this chapter.

Copyright © 2009, IGI Global, distributing in print or electronic forms without written permission of IGI Global is prohibited.

INTRODUCTION

In this chapter, a revision of different applications in agents inspired by the vertebrate immune system is developed. Among different applications, there are cases where artificial immune systems (AISs) have been used for either single or multiple-agents. Some applications like computer vision, agent navigation or agent cognitive models have been designed and developed.

Most of applications are inspired by the adaptive immune response but there has not been much work including metaphors of the innate immune response.

Along this chapter different projects where innate and adaptive immune responses are emulated will be presented.

The main goal of this chapter is to present different works where AISs are applied to robotics and multi-agent systems. At the end, three projects that implement immune inspired multi-agent systems are presented; the first one is a prospective project that uses cognitive models based on immunology for object recognition and classification in a multi-agent system where all the agents have similar features. The second work deals with adaptive strategies in robot-soccer using metaphors from immunology and the last work presents a cognitive model inspired by the innate and adaptive immune responses for object transportation. The prospective project is being developed in the Intelligent Systems Research Laboratory (LISI) at National University of Colombia and the last two ones were also developed in LISI and recently presented on international conferences.

BACKGROUND

AISs have been used in robotics since middle 90's, where Akio Ishiguro, S. Ichikawa and Yoshiki Uchikawa (Ishiguro et al., 1994) developed a gait acquisition of a 6-legged walking robot using immune networks. Later other works developed by Ishiguro et al involved concepts of biological immune system for robotic mechanisms in single-agent and multi-agent systems (Ishiguro et al., 1997), (Watanabe et al., 1998).

Among the projects that dealt with single-agent systems, AISs have been widely used for navigation in unknown environments. In the work by Whitbrook (Whitbrook, 2005), an idiotypic network for mobile robot control is proposed. D.A. Romero and F. Nino (Romero & Niño, 2006), proposed an immune cognitive model combined with neural networks for autonomous navigation. In both cases, the models were inspired by the adaptive immune response. Another work in the field of single-agent systems was done by Mark Neal (Neal et al., 2006). In this work, an artificial innate immune response was used in order to supervise and control the internal state of an agent.

In the field of multi-agent systems based on immunology, several works have been applied to cooperation among agents, for example, the work by W. Lee and K. B. Sim (Lee & Sim, 1997), which is based on metaphors from swarm systems and immunology in order to solve different tasks in a distributed autonomous robotic system (DARS). In another work developed by Srividhya Sathyanath and Ferat Sahin (Sathyanath & Sahin, 2002), an artificial immune system is applied to a mine detection problem. Among the multi-agent system applications, one of the most popular problems is robot-soccer; however, no much work based on immunology metaphors in this field has been carried out so far. In the work by Guan-Chun Luh, Chun-Yin Wu and Wei-Wen Liu (Luh et al., 2006, p. 76), they implemented an artificial immune system, specifically; they used an idiotypic network proposed by Jerne, in order to build up strategies for multi-agent systems.

In the multi-agent systems mentioned above, metaphors from innate response are not considered, but in the work by Chingtham Tejbanta Singh, and Shivashankar B. Nair (Singh & Shivashankar, 2005, p. 308), both innate and adaptive responses are used in order to make an outer robot help an inner robot to always follow a predefined path.

Table 1. A parallel between DARS and AISs

DARS	AISs
Robot's environment	Antigens
Action strategy	Antibody
Robot	B cell
Adequate	Stimulus
Inadequate	Suppression
Excellent Robot	Plasma cell
Inferior Robot	Inactivation Cell

SINGLE AND MULTI AGENT SYSTEMS BASED ON IMMUNOLOGY

In this section, some artificial immune systems in multi-agent systems and robotics are presented.

Artificial Immune Network Based Cooperative Control in Collective Autonomous Mobile Robots

This work was developed by Dong Wook Lee and Kwee Bo Sim at the Robotics and Intelligent Information System laboratory, Department of control and instrumentation engineering, Chung Ang University, and published by IEEE international workshop on Robot and Human communication, 1997.

In this work, the authors proposed an artificial immune system for control behavior in a Distributed Autonomous Robotic System (DARS); this AIS is based on clonal selection, and idiotypic networks.

In DARS every agent component of the system is a robot (Asama, 1994). An individual robot has rules, a goal, and it makes its own decisions based on the neighboring environmental situations, communications among agents, and its programmed rules. An agent cooperates with other agents, search of a global goal, and maintain certain order in whole system. In this case, the robots must spread out on the environment; depending on the local environment information (task), every agent selects a strategy, such strategy is then transmitted to other robots (Weiss, 1999). The robots will be stimulated and suppressed, and the most stimulated strategy is selected as the global strategy and is adopted by every robot. Under these conditions, the authors proposed an algorithm inspired on clonal selection and idiotypic network hypothesis, this algorithm can be achieved well using sensing and local communication system for autonomous mobile developed by authors (Kim et al., 1997), the metaphor between DARS and AISs is presented in table 1.

Depending on task distributions, the density of task is classified on four levels: 1.high, 2.medium, 3.low and 4.nothing. Robot strategies are respectively: a. aggregation, b. random search, c. dispersion and d. homing, Last strategies are the antibodies for the respective antigen. Aggregation is the robots´ ability to gather expecting to establish and maintain some maximum inter-agent distance. Random search is the ability to find tasks by moving in random directions. Dispersion consists of the ability to spread out to establish and maintain some maximum inter-agent distance. Homing is the ability to find and go to particular regions.

In this work, they proposed a swarm-immune algorithm, implemented in each robot, which is summarized next.

Step 1: Initialize stimulus value and concentrations of antibody for all action strategies. These values are initialized:

$t = 0$, $S_i(0) = s_i(0) = 0.5$ for $i = 0, ..., N - 1$ where N is the number of action strategies.

Step 2: Select and execute strategy (antibody) with higher antibody concentration (s_i), Random search is selected by default.

Step 3: When a robot encounters another robot, they stimulate and suppress each other using local communication. The B cell stimulus value and antibody concentration are calculated by the following equations:

$$S_i(t) = S_i(t-1) + \left(a \frac{\sum_{j=0}^{N-1} \gamma_{ij} s_i(t-1)}{N} + \beta g_i - k_i \right) s_i(t) \tag{1}$$

$$s_i(t) = \frac{1}{1 + \exp(0.5 - S_i(t))} \tag{2}$$

Where $i, j = 0, ..., N-1$, s_j is of the other robots' antibody concentration; γ_{ij} is the mutual stimulus coefficient antibody i and j (see Table 2); α, β are response rate parameters of other robots and antigens. If a given robot's strategy stimulus is above the upper threshold $(\bar{\tau})$, the robot becomes an excellent robot; furthermore, if an excellent robot finds an inferior robot, the excellent robot can transmit its strategy to it.

If a robot's strategies were stimulated below lower threshold $(\underline{\tau})$, then the robot becomes an inferior robot. The thresholds are:

$$\bar{\tau}(upper\_threshold) = 0.622\left(-\frac{1}{1 + e^{-0.5}} \right) \tag{3}$$

$$\underline{\tau}(lower\_threshold) = 0.378\left(-\frac{1}{1 + e^{0.5}} \right) \tag{4}$$

Step 4: If an inferior robot encounters an excellent robot, it receives all strategies and renews the concentration of each strategy.

Step 5: $t = t + 1$, and go to step 2.

Next, an example of mutual stimulus coefficient between antibody i and j (Lee & Sim, 1997) (See Table 2).

Simulations and Results

In fig.1, a simulated environment, and the process of swarm strategy decision in cooperative search problem are shown; the simulation conditions are set as follows:

Table 2. Example of mutual stimulus coefficient (γ)

Robot j Robot i	Aggregation	Search	Dispersion	Homing
Aggregation	1	-0.4	-0.2	-0.4
Search	-0.4	1	-0.4	-0.2
Dispersion	-0.2	-0.4	1	-0.4
Homing	-0.4	-0.2	-0.4	1

Figure 1. DARS based on immune systems. ©2008 Fredy Fernando Munoz. Used with permission.

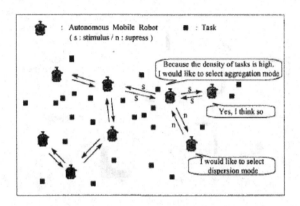

Number of robots: 50.

Working area: 10mX10m.

Objective of the system: find and execute given spread task.

Communication radius: 75 cm.

Sensing radius: 32.5 cm.

Parameter values: $\alpha = 0.5$, β : 0.0005, $k = 0.002$.

Antigen evaluation time: 100 unit time, in 1 time, the robot can change its direction or can move 2.5 cm.

Number of task:

Case 1 tasks 10

Case 2 tasks 100

Case 3 tasks 200

Case 4 tasks 500.

Experimentation was carried out with and without the AIS algorithm. In all cases, without the immune algorithm, the robot makes the decision based upon only local information; consequently, it selects the strategy individually. Finally, the number of robots which select a specific strategy is uniform. In the simulations, the AIS algorithm is used; in this case, strong strategy is selected and adopted as a swarm strategy by the global system of robots. More implementation details can be found at the paper.

An Immune-Based Multilayered Cognitive Model for Autonomous Navigation

This work was developed by Diego Romero and Fernando Niño, Department of Electrical and Electronics engineering, and Department of computing and systems engineering National University of Colombia, and published at the IEEE Congress on Evolutionary Computation, 2006.

The work developed in this paper consisted of an agent's multilayered cognitive model for an autonomous navigation system. The computational techniques used were neural networks (Haykin, 1994), an immune algorithm based on immune networks (De Castro &Von Zuben, 2001), and a reinforcement learning technique (Holland et al., 1989).

Problem Definition

A two dimension environment with distributed obstacles is given; the obstacles are geometrically different, and a number of storage locations for the obstacles are available. A mobile agent with ultrasonic sensors around and photo sensors in its front and the environment is depicted in Fig.2.

Figure 2. Mobile agent's environment. ©2008 Fredy Fernando Munoz. Used with permission.

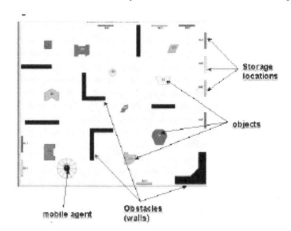

The related problem has three interrelated tasks

- **Basic navigation:** The agent does not know the environment, the object locations, the obstacles; the only information the agent knows is storage locations, with respect to a global coordinate position system. The agent must go on the environment for the exploration, ensuring its physical integrity, for example, the agent must avoid obstacles in the recognition of the environment.
- **Object identification:** When the agent finds an object, the agent must identify it and transport it to the respective storage location.
- **Trajectory optimization:** Once the agent has learned to match the identified objects in their respective location, it is required to minimize the trajectory to transport the objects to their storage location.

Proposed Solution

For everyone task is associated a cognitive layer, according to specific environment information received. The next layers were developed:

Basic navigation: This layer is activated so the agent moves around the environment; it is the most elementary layer. In this layer, a multilayer perceptron is used, which is trained with the backpropagation algorithm (Haykin, 1994),. Training patterns for the navigation stage correspond to local conditions detected by sensors; thus, 48 training patterns were generated. There are 12 inputs, which belong to ultrasonic sensors of the mobile, six neurons in the hidden layer, and three neurons in the output layer, correspond to three outputs, S_1, S_2, S_3; if S_1 is activated with +1, the agent should move forward, if S_1 is zero, the agent should turn back; if S_2 is enable (takes the value +1), the agent should turn, the turning direction is determined by S_3, for S_3, if its value is one, it means the agent turns left 30°, if its value is zero, the agent turns right 30°. For more details, see (Romero & Niño, 2006).

Object identification: For this layer, a model based on immunology, called Artificial Cognitive Immune System (ACIS) , was used. This algorithm combines the structure of Artificial Immune Network (AiNet) (De Castro &Von Zuben, 2001) and its capabilities to perform data clustering and optimization; also, a reinforcement learning mechanism is proposed. The ACIS is used in the object identification layer and in the optimization layer.

Figure 3. Scanning an object perimeter in order to determine the input information to the ACIS. ©2008 Fredy Fernando Munoz. Used with permission.

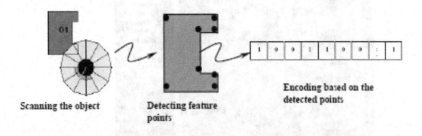

Scanning the object   Detecting feature   Encoding based on the
                             points   detected points

Figure 4. Antigen encoding, this information may be thought of as an internal representation of a sensed object. ©2008 Fredy Fernando Munoz. Used with permission.

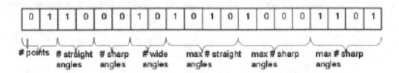

points   # straight   # sharp   # wide   max # straight   max # sharp   max # sharp
            angles   angles   angles   angles   angles   angles

The inputs to the ACIS are encoded in binary form. An example is presented in Fig. 3.

For every point, the coordinates for the ACIS are given. The antibody consists of two binary substrings; the first substring is the paratope section compared to the distance from the antigen. The second string corresponds to an epitope, this contains information about the response of the antibody to the stimulus generated by the antigen. For this layer, an example of an antigen is shown in Fig. 4 (taken from Romero & Niño, 2006).

ACIS algorithm: It is based on the Artificial Immune Network architecture, AiNet, is combined with a reinforcement learning mechanism, particularly the "Bucket Brigade" algorithm (Holland et al., 1989). This works throughout a set of binary strings named classifiers; each one of those has a strength parameter (S_i) that represents the classifier's fitness to respond to certain stimulation (antigen). A brief explanation of the algorithm is as follows. A random repertory of antibodies is created, the affinity with external antigens is determined by fitness function (S_i), the distance between antibody and antigen is a Hamming Distance. Each antibody is matched with the antigen, then a clonal repertoire is created with the best antibodies matched, by means of clonal selection. Each clonal antibody repertoire places a bet, based on its strength (S_i), the better (S_i) has the best probability to win the bet. The selected antibody is executed into the environment. The other antibodies not executed are penalized, simulating a natural death mechanism. According to the environmental reinforcement, the antibody is rewarded or punished. If the reinforcement is positive, the antibody is reproduced at high rate with low mutation, otherwise, it mutates at higher rate. If the antibody has an adequate response in various learning cycles, and two or more antibodies exceed the similar threshold, then antibodies with higher fitness will survive, others will disappear.

Trajectory optimization layer: When the ACIS for identification layer is used, and the object is classified, the agent must transport the classified object at its storage location. For more details see (Romero & Niño, 2006).

In the experiments, ACIS was compared with compared with a Holland Classifier System (LCS), learning convergence was considered. ACIS shown a faster convergence than (LCS), due to space limitations, the experiments are not shown. For further details see (Romero & Niño, 2006).

Figure 5. Simurosot middle league platform. ©2008 Fredy Fernando Munoz. Used with permission.

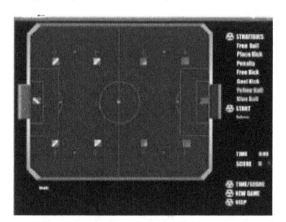

Figure 6. The architecture of the proposed layered immune networks. ©2008 Fredy Fernando Munoz. Used with permission.

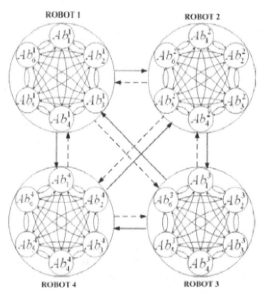

Artificial Immune System Based Cooperative Strategies for Robot Soccer Competition

In this paper, the Artificial Immune System technique to deal with the robot soccer problem was used. It specifically dealt with soccer strategies. The strategy enables robots to select behavior between 'pass', 'kick', 'shoot', 'chase', 'guard' and 'track'. Although, there are different robot soccer tournaments, in this work, the proposed strategies were evaluated on Simurosot Middle League, a 5-vs-5 simulation platform in FIRA (see Fig. 5).

A robot soccer player makes its decision based on the immune network model proposed by Jerne (Luh et al., 2006). In this work, the antigen is represented by environment information and each robot has 6 antibodies to be

Figure 7. The Helper and Learner on their respective traces. ©2008 Fredy Fernando Munoz. Used with permission.

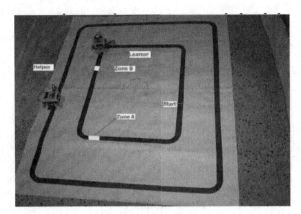

executed which are: chase, pass, kick, shoot, guard and track (see Fig. 6). The antigen-antibody affinity is presented by the best decision a robot can make. Each affinity value is fuzzified using fuzzy sets (Kosko, 1997): one is associated with the distance between ball and robot, the other one with distance between robots and the last one with distance to opponents. Depending on the average of these three affinities the finally decision is made. This decision represents the stimulation and suppressive interaction between antibodies. In other words, each robot's antibody with the highest concentration is selected to activate its corresponding behavior to the world.

In this paper, a hybrid system is used, this system mixes components of AIS and fuzzy logic for making decision; it is a valid approach to apply in other engineering fields.

An Artificial Immune System for a Multiagent Robotics System

This paper explores an application of an adaptive learning mechanism for robots based on the natural immune system.

Most of the research carried out so far are based either on the innate or adaptive characteristics of the immune system, they present a combination of such features to achieve behavior arbitration wherein a robot learns to detect vulnerable areas of a track and adapts to the required speed over such portions. The test bed comprises two Lego robots deployed simultaneously on two predefined near concentric tracks with the outer robot capable of helping the inner one when it misaligns. The helper robot works in a damage-control mode by realigning itself to guide the other robot back onto its track, the environment is showed in Fig. 7.

The panic-stricken robot records the conditions under which it was misaligned and learns to detect and adapt under similar conditions thereby making the overall system immune to such failures.

They use AIS for 2 robots: the helper (outner) and the learner (inner), to keep the learner robot on a black track. If the learner goes out of the track, the helper robot will go to the place where the learner misaligned and help it to go back on the track. Every time the learner robot misaligns, it will store the information received from its sensors at that time, thus the learner can associate the misalignment with the stored information and learn from its own experience. In this way, it is expected that the learner will need the helper robot less and less each time. The learner robot's behavior was inspired by the immune system, specifically a clonal selection mechanism was used as its cognitive model. The reward received by the learner robot is gotten from the helper robot: the first time the learner robot misaligns; it tries for 10 seconds to get back to the track and continues on its path if successful. This constitutes the first layer of the immune system (the innate immune response), if it fails, it panics and starts transmitting SOS signals continuously via its IR port to the Helper robot. The learner robot creates

Figure 8. Speed vs. track distance (Antibody formation by Somatic hyper mutation of the Paratope). ©2008 Fredy Fernando Munoz. Used with permission.

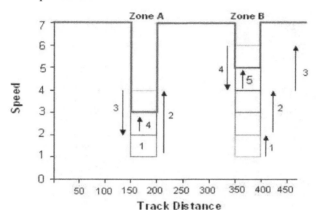

antibodies with the velocity 1 and the Helper detects the SOS when it comes within the range of the Learner and aligns itself in such a manner that it can guide the former back to the inner track. The second time the learner misaligns, it hypermutates the antibody to a new randomly value and if the learner gets help from the helper robot then the learning process has not yet finished, otherwise, the learner robot has finished its learning process and has the information of the antibody (the correct speed value), which can be used to avoid the dangerous zone on the track (see Fig.8).

There were 2 dangerous zones: zone A (which is yellow color) and zone B (which is white color) and the track was black color.

In this paper, the interaction between the innate and adaptive immune responses are emulated, nevertheless the approach was good enough to achieve the goal, bearing in mind that there is not much research carried out so far that are based on the innate immune response.

An Artificial Immune System Based Intelligent Multi Agent Model and Its Applications to a Mine Detection Problem

This work was developed by Srividhya Sathyanath and Ferat Sahin, Department of Electrical engineering, Rochester Institute of Technology, and published at ICARIS 2002.

In this work, the authors propose an Artificial Immune System based Intelligent Multi Agent Model (AISIMAM), applied to a mine detection and diffusion problem.

Problem Definition

An approach for mine detection and diffusion is presented. Given a two dimensional environment, there are a determinate number o mines, deployed in a uniform and unknown distribution. The mines are static. Some number of agents must find the mines, and communicate its coordinate locations to other agents; the agents deactivate the mines when some agents go around the mine.

AISIMAM Artificial Immune Network System Based Intelligent Multi Agent Model

The AISIMAM is a computational model, which imitates the behaviour of artificial immune systems, in terms of feature and functions in multi-agent system. Both models share some characteristics, like decentralization, multiples autonomous entities, individual and global goals. Both learn from their experience and are adaptable.

Figure 9. Representation of AISIMAM. ©2008 Fredy Fernando Munoz. Used with permission.

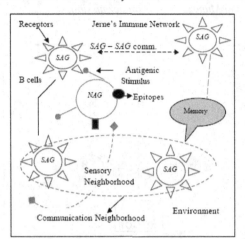

They sense the charges in the environment and act accordingly. Both systems communicate and work coordinately. Both possess knowledge and can make decisions. In Fig. 9, a representation of AISIMAM is depicted.

The antigens are modelled as non-self agents (NAGs), and lymphocytes are modelled as self-agents (SAGs); such agents operate in a matrix (determined by a coordinate system), this matrix is the environment. Then, it is assumed that there is an information vector for each non-self agent, that information vector corresponds to the epitopes of the antigen. Each self-agent has information vectors defines as self-goals, and it corresponds to receptor of lymphocytes. SAGs have sensory capability to identify the NAG within a region named sensory neighbour-hood, also SAGs can transmit the information about NAG to other SAG, within a region called communication neighborhood. The agent model describes five stages of processing namely pattern recognition, where SAGs recognize the presence of antigens by stimulation function, and identifier function. In the binding process is calculated an affinity value between the actions of self and non-self agents, by affinity function, this could be a distance metric such as Euclidean distance. Subsequently in the activation process, is chosen the affinity value greater in a set activation threshold, the process helps the agents to find out the highest affinity actions named mature actions that are closer to the desired goal. The post activation process involves cloning, where the agents are reproduced with mature actions. In the suppression function, the agents networks are suppressed, for more details see (Sathyanath & Sahin, 2002).

The mathematical representation of AISIMAM is presented in (Sathyanath & Sahin, 2002), and it will not be considered in this section.

Application to AISIMAM to a Mine Detection Problem

Using the last model in the problem described above, is proposed one model solution.

The antigen of Nonself agent NAG is the mine, the location of the mine correspond to epitope or the receptor of the antigen, the mines are stationary. The B cell to be the self agent SAG, they are in a distribution within the environment. The initial locations of the SAG correspond to the receptors of B cells. The SAGs can sense and communicate the position of the mines, to other SAGs, by a Jerne's network.

In this problem memory is not used, there is not usefulness in remembering the location of the mine once it is detected and diffused.

Figure 10. The starting conditions for each experiment. Cylinder A is the 'dangerous' obstacle, cylinder B is the 'safe' obstacle. ©2008 Fredy Fernando Munoz. Used with permission.

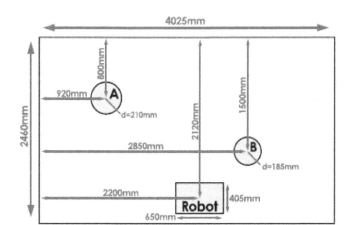

Simulations and Results

In the experiments, it is necessary to know the number of the mines, different experiments were realized changing the mine population between 10 and 70, accordingly the robots population between 40 and 100. The observations of the experiments were the number of mines and agents. The convergence rate is slightly greater, when the sensory and communication rate is increased, the number of steps to algorithm converge is reduced. In all cases, all mines are diffused. For more details see the paper.

The Application of a Dendritic Cell Algorithm to a Robotic Classifier

The security and robotics are areas in which this paper takes an inspiration in order to implement an algorithm based on the behavior of dendritic cells. An immune inspired technique for processing time-dependant data is used. Based on "behavioral models" proposed by Brooks, a robotics system is developed. A robotic dendritic cell algorithm as a stand-alone module that walks around by an inspection area and to identify anomalous obstacles is implemented.

The main problem in robotic security system is to classify normal events from anomalous events; specifically, in order to solve this problem a dendritic cell algorithm (DCA) is used. This algorithm emulates the dendritic cell behavior which is responsible for controlling and leading the immune response, basically it takes the signals across the population of artificial dendritic Cells and the asynchronous correlation of signals with antigen in order to make the classification process. The DCA used in this paper uses '3-signal' model, three input signals: Danger, Safe and PAMP signals, three output signals: Co-stimulatory, IL-10 (safe signal alone) and IL-12(PAMP and danger) signals. By using an image processing module the PAMP input signal is obtained. The Safe and Danger signals are obtained from sonar sensors. The generation of antigen is based on the current location of the robot. With the information of linear and rotational velocities of the robot, the amount of antigen added to the environment is calculated.

$$W\left(v,\dot{\theta}\right)=75\left(1-\left|\frac{v}{v_{max}}\right|\right)+1+25\left(1-\left|\frac{\dot{\theta}}{\dot{\theta}_{max}}\right|\right)+1 \tag{5}$$

Figure 11. Environment of mobile robot. ©2008 Fredy Fernando Munoz. Used with permission.

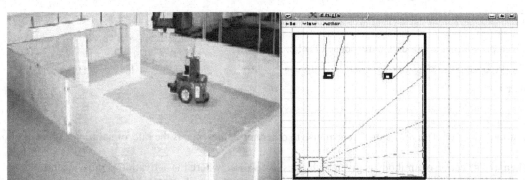

In this equation v is the velocity of the robot, θ is the rotational velocity of the robot and W is the amount of antigen added to the environment. The antigen is sampled and given to population of dendritic cells, if output IL-12 is greater than IL-10 means the antigen is potentially anomalous. By testing the DCA on a robotic system, a robot is placed inside 4025mm x 2460mm area, with two obstacles (safe and dangerous); the dangerous obstacle is of pink color, see Fig.10 a, this figure is taken from (Oates et al., 2007). The experimental results show that this DCA is capable of identifying anomalous events from normal events. In noisy environments, the DCA performance is high.

In this paper, the Dendritic Cell Algorithm is used in order to solve security problems but its analogy with biological part is not deeply showed. Although DCA is an interesting model, different environments and tests are necessary in order to implement it into several engineering areas. As it was mentioned in this paper, the next step is to compare it with other techniques such fuzzy and neural systems.

An Idiotypic Immune Network for Mobile Robot Control

This thesis dissertation was developed by Amanda Marie Whitbrook, in partial fulfilment of the conditions of the award of the degree M.Sc. School of computer Science and Information Technology University of Nottingham.

In this work, a robot mobile was simulated, and subsequently implemented, the team of this work, in a rectangular environment, a robot must go inside two columns, where used sonar sensors for detection off ambient situations, the environment is presented in Fig. 11.

In the solution proposed for this problem, an idiotipyc immune network as a mobile control for the robot is presented. The environment situations are modelled as antigens (signal sensors vector) $[y_1, y_2, ..., y_n]$, the robot response is modelled as antibodies (signal control of motors), it selects the antibody in response to a set of antigens. For this step, given N set of antibodies $[x_1, x_2, ..., x_N]$, the antibody is selected according to highest match affinity. Alter match affinity according to idiotypic effects. Change in the concentration of a particular antibody is calculated using the following farmer equation (Farmer et al., 1986, p 187):

$$x_i' = c\left[\sum_{j=1}^{N} m_{ji} x_i x_j - k_1 \sum_{j=1}^{N} m_{ij} x_i x_j + \sum_{j=1}^{n} m_{ji} x_i y_j\right] - k_2 x_i \tag{6}$$

Where

$$\sum_{j=1}^{N} m_{ji} x_i x_j$$

represent the stimulations of the antibodies in response of other antibodies,

$$k_1 \sum_{j=1}^{N} m_{ji} x_i x_j$$

model suppression of antibodies in response of other antibodies,

$$\sum_{j=1}^{n} m_{ji} x_i y_j$$

is the stimulations of other antibodies in response to other antibodies, $k_2 x_i$ is the rate of natural death of antibodies.

Then, the selection of antibody is given by highest activation, where the activation is the concentration multiplied by the strength. For the learning of the artificial immune network (AIN), initially was created a set of a paratope mapping (matrix of antibodies). Afterwards are stimulated and suppressed by learning reinforcement, the behaviours are scored using an evaluation (reward or penalty) function. Winning antibody selected every second, the reinforcement learning carried out half a second later, increase degree of match to dominant antigen for successful antibodies, decreases degree of match for unsuccessful antibodies, also remove any concentration increases. For more details, you can see (Whitbrook, 2005)

A Gait Acquisition of a 6-Legged Robot Using Immune Networks

It was the first application of AIS in robotics. The goal is to find the coordination for 6 legged walking robot, given the robot shown en Fig. 12, an AIS for the walk control is initialized, where the notation from R1 to R3 denote the legs located on right hand side of the body, and the ones from L1 to L3 are the legs on the left hand side of the body.

Each shaded circle located at each leg represents the unit which corresponds to B-lymphocyte in immune system. And each arrow represents the testing relation. For example, the arrow from R2 to R1 denotes that the test of the unit RI carried out by the unit R2. The test outcome, in this case, authors describe T[R2][RI]. In Ishida's method, the values of test outcome were limited to only binary values, namely 1.0 and -1.0. Therefore, in this study we expand the values of test outcome to real values instead of integer values as mentioned later. To make the problem simpler, we assume that each leg moves in the same way, namely the stance widths and duration of the leg movements are all the same. As mentioned before, authors have defined the test and chosen the structure

Figure 12. AIS for 6 legged walking robot. ©2008 Fredy Fernando Munoz. Used with permission.

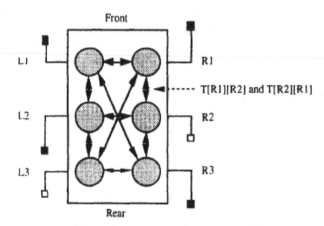

Figure 13. The proposed deciding method of the test outcome. ©2008 Fredy Fernando Munoz. Used with permission.

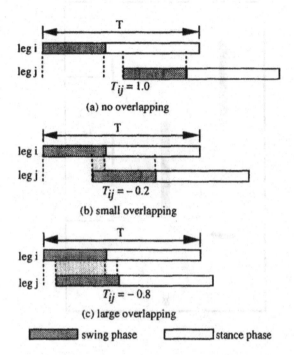

of the immune network suitable for the defined test to make the robot successfully walk. Authors determine the value of the test outcome in the following way:

If the swing phase of the tested unit j and that of the testing unit i do no overlap, then the value of the test outcome is set to 1.0. Otherwise, the value of the test outcome is set to the real values between -1.0 and 0.0 in accordance with the overlapping ratio between i and j.

In fig.13, the schematic method is show. The notation T denotes the duration of the leg movement, and the shaded and empty bars represents the swing and stance phases, respectively. The figure (a) is the case that the swing phases of the testing unit i and the tested unit j do not overlap. Thus authors determine the value of the test outcome set to I .O. The figures (b) and (c) are both the cases that small and large overlapping between swing phases of leg i and j exist. In these cases, the values of the test outcome are set to -0.2 and -0.8, respectively.

The authors proposed an algorithm. The results obtained by test outcome are modelled by mathematical model.

Several Models of Agent System Based on AIS

In this section, we present two models for multi-agent systems and one model for a mobile agent. The three projects use AISs and have been developed in the Intelligent Systems Research Laboratory (LISI) at the National University of Colombia by the authors.

Model for Object Recognition and Classification Using AIS

The following work is still being developed and the problem consists in a robot that wanders in a two dimensional world and has to classify objects and transport them to a storage room. Thus, the model is presented as follows.

Figure 14. Environment simulation. ©2008 Fredy Fernando Munoz. Used with permission.

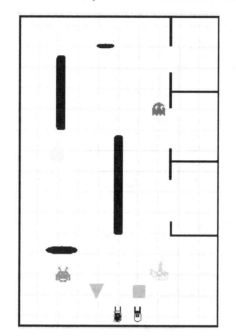

When the robot is activated, it navigates waiting for an object to recognize it; the world is presented in Fig.14. For a primary selection, an artificial innate response is used as follows, when the mobile finds an object with its center laser sensor, it must detect whether the object is self or non self; self objects are walls and other mobiles, when the mobile detects an object in its front, it activates the bars code reader (every robot is identified by a bar code), if there is a positive lecture, the object is self, and the wandering process by the agent will continue, otherwise, the robot's camera (its blob finder camera for color recognition) is activated; in the environment, the wall, structures and other things are black, then if the object is black, it is classified as self, and the search continues, if it is not, it may be classified as non self object, and the recognition layer is activated.

The recognition will be developed in two different ways for future comparison; with Kohonen network (Haykin, 1994) and with AIS. The former method is a self organized neural network, the inputs of the NN will be the signal laser sensors of the mobile, a determinate number of neurons will be assigned, the training consists of input patterns which activate one neuron, this neuron will indicate the object recognized, to do this, it is necessary a previously offline training, with enough input-output pattern combinations. Once the NN is trained, given an unknown object, the NN will activate the most similar neuron, but it does not allow the insertion of a new object and in order to achieve recognition, it is necessary to train the NN once again, with more neurons, old patterns and new patterns of the new object.

The NN does not allow an online training, thus, an AIS for the problem of pattern recognition is proposed, therefore if a new object is detected, it is possible to build a new class to the recognized object. Initially the artificial immune system must be trained and to do that, we represent the environment information as antigens, in this case, the signal sensors, and the antibodies as the information stored to identify a given object. For instance, it is presented in Fig. 15. an object that is found by the agent and it is necessary to train the AIS for future recognitions, the agent stops at a specific distance away from the object, and it scans the object by means of its laser sensor, obtains a data vector (epitope), the robot moves 10 degrees (it moves on a circle trajectory) and repeats the procedure, finally 36 epitopes are obtained, which will be stored in an internal matrix, to be used as paratopes for future recognitions, thus the initial paratope is obtained; later on, similar objects are put in the room and the

Figure 15. Model for pattern recognition. ©2008 Fredy Fernando Munoz. Used with permission.

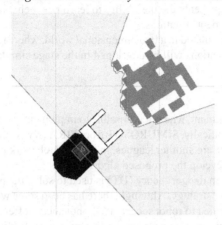

Figure 16. Simurosot game field used in this work. ©2008 Fredy Fernando Munoz. Used with permission.

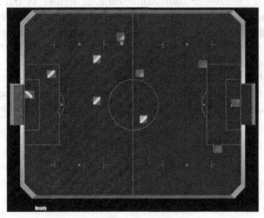

process is repeated, each antigen is compared against each antibody, using a length metric, the antibody with highest affinity to detect the antigen, is selected and mutated, activating the clonal selection algorithm, repeat the process in order to improve the affinity between antigens and antibodies, the last process is repeated for every class of object to be identified. Once the recognition layer is trained and activated, the mobile can go to recognize objects, now it will just need to take 3 antigens in 3 places separate 180 degrees each other; the mobile can get closer to the object to be recognized from any direction but it must stay away from the object to a given distance. Three antigens are compared with all antibodies, and the three antibodies with highest affinities are selected, if the three affinities are equal or higher than a threshold, the object is classified, if not, the mobile makes a second process recognition (the mobile rounds the object one more time). If the second process recognition does not give a positive response, which means the three affinities were lesser than the threshold, the object will be considered as a new one, and the process of trained is initialized as were explained. The simulations are being made using *Player Project* (Player Project, 2007)

In this chapter was presented an explanation about the Artificial Immune Networks, and some applications to robotics. In these applications, the AIS presents the possibility to learn new behaviors online, presents strongly capability to adaptation in new environment situations.

In future works, this model will be simulated in a two dimensional world, where robots must identify and classify objects to be transported. The simulations will be developed in the stage simulator of the player project.

AIS Applied to Robot Soccer

Robot soccer presents a dynamic environment, where it is possible to implement and test diverse and new computational techniques. In robot soccer, specifically, SIMUROSOT from FIRA (www.fira.net), there are two leagues: middle and large leagues. Although there are another leagues, in the research work in the LISI we use the Middle League (simulated league) in order to develop the proposed algorithm.

In this research, an approach based on danger theory (DT) is used to solve the problem of designing a robot soccer strategy, specifically, a goalkeeper strategy. Although, there has been some work related to danger theory, there has not been work where DT is applied to robot soccer. The robot soccer offers a platform based on human soccer whose rules are widely known and easy to understand. The main objective is that robot players can identify its environment and respond quickly and adequately, exhibiting a coordinated behavior. The SIMUROSOT game field is shown in figure 16. The simulated league is the abstraction from MIROSOT league, where the real robot players match in a field game.

In 1994, Matzinger introduced DT (Matzinger, 2001), which caused controversy and gained some acceptance among immunologists. DT suggests that human immune system acts in response to the combination of danger signals, thus, it is capable of distinguishing between danger and safe elements, no matter whether they belong to self or non-self. From a computational point of view, this characteristic is very useful to solve engineering problems and is currently being subject of extensive research in the AIS field.

In this research work, an algorithm inspired by danger theory is developed to implement the behavior of the goalkeeper. The main goal of the proposed algorithm is to detect elements that represent danger for a system. Some of essential features were modeled in order to implement the proposed algorithm. Although the biological

Figure 17. Natural immune system. ©2008 Fredy Fernando Munoz. Used with permission.

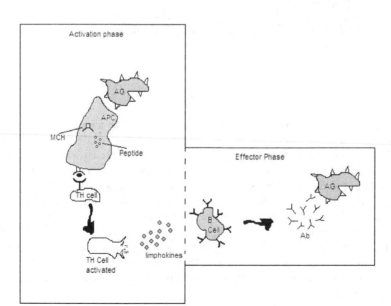

Figure 18. The Th1 activates the infected macrophage for internal bacteria destruction. ©2008 Fredy Fernando Munoz. Used with permission.

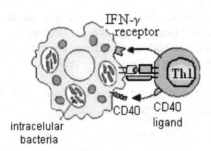

Table 3. A comparison of some relevant immunology components and AIS components used in this work

IMMUNOLOGY	AIS COMPONENTS
Th1	Th Agent (ThA)
T Cell Receptor (TCR)	Th Agent Receptor (ThAR)
IFN-γ	Signals from the ThA to activate the MA
Macrophage	Macrophage Agent (MA)
Toll-Like Receptor (TLR)	Artificial TLR (ATLR)
MHCII Molecules	Communication Protocol
CD80 and CD86 molecules	MA reasserts the infection to the ThA
Antigen	Non-self object (possible object to be transported)
PAMP	Artificial PAMP (APAMP)
Antigenic Peptide	Feature vector extracted from the non-self object by the MA

Figure 19. ©2008 Fredy Fernando Munoz. Used with permission.

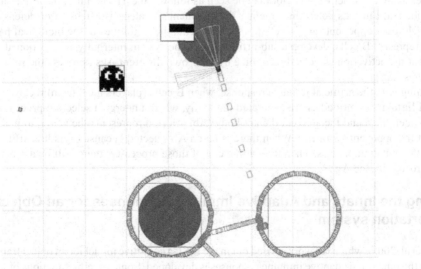

response presented after recognizing danger signals may be more complex, in this model, it is assumed that an antigen recognized inside the danger zone is a dangerous element; therefore, in order to eliminate it, the activated lymphocyte is a natural killer cell (NKC).

The proposed model is tested and analyzed in robot soccer; specifically, simulated FIRA (FIRA, 2007) middle league. The developed algorithm is used to implement a goalkeeper strategy. As in its biological inspiration, the purpose of the immune system is to protect the body against dangerous entities and to prevent disease or tissue damage. In a goalkeeper strategy, the purpose is to protect or to defend a team from the opponent's dangerous moves.

Several tests were made in this work obtaining good results, besides this algorithm offers a good scenario for future research in this area. For more details, see (Prieto et al, 2008).

FUTURE DIRECTIONS

As a future work, a learning mechanism, to implement robot soccer strategies that are adaptable to the way the opponent plays, may be developed as follows.

Among various computational intelligence techniques that currently exist (De Castro, N., & Timmis, 2002), it was chosen an artificial immune system due to its adaptability to unknown environments. Because soccer game is a very dynamic system it must possess a system that is able to adapt to the gaming system of the opponent in order to win the match or at least not lose it. Based on the natural immune system, the artificial immune system used in this work attempts to follow as close as possible to their biological inspiration. In Fig.17, how the human system detects and removes an antigen is shown; where Ag is the antigen, APC is an antigen presenting cell, MHC is major histocompatibility complex and TH cell is a T helper cell.

The artificial immune response has been classified into 2 stages: activation and effecter stages. But as the natural immune system, effecter stage can be activated without the activation stage. In this work, the antigen is the opponent's strategy; the concept of strategy used in this study is defined as the formation of the opponent with respect both to the ball and the court within a window of time. Due to the necessity of sampling the opponent's strategy, it is essential to have a history of the opponent's movements, the data from all 5 opponent robots are used to predict their next move according to that history.

The routine that represents the APC behavior is as follows: first of all, the APC takes the Ag information and processes it with information from the robot's local team (information that mimics an MHC molecule); this information mixed and processed corresponds to the MCH-Peptide complex in the biological part, this means that the algorithm can identify the robots that are closer to the ball and hence the ones that may be dangerous. On the other hand, the T helper behavior may be seen as follows: the Th cell takes information provided by the MCH-Peptide and can thus determine whether the opponent's strategy is offensive or defensive, and tells the players which robot opponents are in action; this represents the linfokines in the biological part. Players local team, who represent B cells, develop a sub-artificial immune system internally, as mentioned above, they can work without the activation stage and recognize by their own different Ags , process the information and thus eliminate those Ags.

Continuing with the artificial immune response, when B cells (players local team) receive information such as artificial linfokines, antibodies are generated randomly, which undergo a selection process according to the affinity between them and the antigen, the antibody (Ab) selected represents the action to make in order to argue against the opponent's strategy. When there is no an Ab selected because of its low affinity, a random Ab undergoes the mutation process. Therefore, at the end of those processes, there will be a repertory of Abs that are able to recognize the Ag .

Modelling the Innate and Adaptive Immune Responses for an Object Transportation system

In (Munoz et al, 2008), which is a work carried out in the LISI, a cognitive model for an object transportation agent inspired by the innate and adaptive immune responses is developed. Some specific functions of macrophages and

Th1 cells are modeled and incorporated in this artificial immune system; particularly the function of a Toll-Like Receptor on a macrophage to detect pathogen-associate molecular patterns on an antigen and the function of a T cell receptor on a Th1 cell in activating an infected macrophage, see figure 18.

Based on the fact that immunology has traditionally divided the immune system into innate and adaptive components with distinct functional roles (Aickelin and Twycross, 2005) and most of the research carried out so far in the field of AIS are based on the adaptive characteristics of the immune system, this work presents a cognitive model that combines the innate and adaptive immune responses in an object transportation agent, presenting a new perspective of how metaphors of the innate immune response can be used as inspiration to develop applications in robotics. This work also presents how a basic feature vector that represents an object can be used in the pattern recognition process. The proposed model was implemented and tested using the Player Project and Stage simulator.

Table 3 presents the immune components that were modelled in this work and how they were emulated in the AIS in order to deal with the specific object transportation problem.

Figure 19 depicts the mobile agent transporting a big blue circle to a specific location within the indoor environment. This transportation process was made by the macrophage agent (MA) after some pattern recognition stages that the MA and the Th agent had to deal with.

In future work, a cognitive model inspired by some features of a B cell behavior will be incorporated into the model presented in this paper in order to add learning and memory mechanisms to the agent. Some other pattern recognition techniques such as moment invariants and Fourier descriptors will be implemented with the expectation that the agents can cope with the recognition of more complex objects. The use of a neural network such as a Self Organized Map (SOM) may be a good possibility for the classification process instead of the statistical analysis that was performed in this work.

CONCLUSION

Several works in the field of single and multi-agent systems were presented. In those works, AIS were used as mechanisms in order to solve different tasks such as navigation, robot-soccer, network security (Galeano et al., 2002) , among others; and not only common techniques such as idiotypic network, clonal selection were used but also authors developed new AIS algorithms.

Some applications used hybrid techniques; this means AIS along with techniques such as NN and fuzzy logic in order to deal with specific goals.

It can be seen that most of the applications are inspired by some features of the adaptative immune response but there are few works whose cognitive models are based on the vertebrate innate immune response which has a fast response as an important feature to be explore.

REFERENCES

Asama, A. (1994) *Distributed Autonomous Robotic Systems I , 0,* Springer-Verlag,

De Castro, Leandro, N., & Timmis, J. (2002). *Artificial Immune System: A New Computational Intelligence Approach.* 1st ed. 2002, Springer-Verlag.

De Castro, Leandro, N., & Von Zuben, F. (2001) *aiNET: An Artificial Immune Network for Data Analysis, in Data Mining: A Heuristic Approach.* (Eds). Idea Group Publishing.

Farmer, J. D., Packard, N. H., & Perelson, A. S., (1986). The immune system, adaptation, and machine learning. *Physica, 22D,* 187-204.

FIRA official Web page. (2007) (*www.fira.net*)

Galeano, C., Veloza, A., & Gonzales, F. (2005). *A Comparative Analysis of Artificial Immune Network Models.* GECCO '05: Proceedings of the 2005 conference on Genetic and evolutionary computation. Washington, DC, USA.

Haykin, S. (1994). *Neural Networks a comprehensible Foundation.* Ed College Publishing Company.

Holland, J., Holyoak, K., Nisbett, R., & Thagard, P. (1989). *Induction, Processes of Inference, Learning and Discovery. MA:* MIT Press.

Ishiguro, A., Ichikawa, S., & Uchikawa, Y, (1994). A gait acquisition of 6-legged walking robot using immune networks. *Proceedings of the IROS'94, 2,* 1034-1041.

Ishiguro, A., Watanabe, Y., Kondo, T., Shirai, Y., & Uchikawa (1997). *A robot with decentralized concensus-making mechanism based on the immune system.* Proceeding of the ISADS'97, (pp. 231-237).

Kosko, B. (1997). *Fuzzy Engineering.* Prentice Hall, Upper Saddle River, NJ.

Lee, D.-W., & Sim, K.-B. (1997) *Artificial immune network-based cooperative control in collective autonomous mobile robots.* Proceedings of the IEEE International Workshop on Robot and Human Communication. (pp. 58-63).

Luh, G., Wu, Ch., & Liu, W. (2006) *Artificial Immune System based Cooperative Strategies for Robot Soccer Competition.* Strategic Technology, The 1st International Forum on. (pp. 76-79).

Kim, D. J., Lee, D. W., & Sim, K. B. (1997). Development of Communication System for Cooperative Behavior in Collective Autonomous Mobile Robots. *Puoc. of 2nd ASCC.*

Matzinger, P. (2001). The Danger model in its historical context. *Scandinavian Journal of Immunology, 54.*

Munoz, F., Nino, L., & Quintana, G. (2008). Object Transportation with an Agent Inspired by the Innate and Adaptive Immune Responses. *ISA'08: Proceedings of the Intelligent Systems and Agents 2008 Conference.* Amsterdam, The Netherlands. (pp. 135-142).

Neal, M., Feyereisl, J., Rascunà, R., & Wang, X. (2006). *Don't Touch Me, I'm Fine: Robot Autonomy Using an Artificial Innate Immune System.* ICARIS 349-361.

Oates, R., Greensmith, J., Aickelin, U., Garibaldi, J., & Kendall, G. (2007). The application of a dendritic cell algorithm to a robotic classifier. In *ICARIS 2007.*

Player project official web page. (2006) (http://playerstage.sourceforge.net/)

Prieto, C., Nino, F., & Quintana, G. (2008). A Goalkeeper Strategy in Robot Soccer Based on Danger Theory. In *2008 IEEE World Congress on Computational Intelligence*, Hong Kong.

WCCI 2008 Proceedings (2008). 2008 IEEE Congress on Evolutionary Computation. *IEEE Computational Intelligence Society.* ISBN: 978-1-4244-1823-7

Romero, D. A., & Niño, L. F. (2006). An Immune-based Multilayered Cognitive Model for Autonomous Navigation. *Proceedings of the IEEE Congress on Evolutionary Computation* (pp. 1115–1122).

Sathyanath, S., & Sahin, F. (2002). *AISIMAM – An Artificial Immune System Based Intelligent Multi Agent Model and its Application to a Mine Detection Problem.* ICARIS 2002, Session I, pp. 22-31.

Singh, Ch., & Fair, Sh. (2005). An Artificial Immune System for a MultiAgent Robotics System. *Transactions on Engineering, C V6*, 308-311.

Watanabe, Y., Ishiguro, A., Shirai, Y., & Uchikawa, Y. (1998). Emergent Construction of a Behavior Arbitration Mechanism Based on Immune System. *Advanced Robotics, 12*(3), *227-242.*

Weiss, G. (Ed). (1999). *Multiagent Systems.* The MIT Press

Whitbrook. A., M. (2005). *An Idiotypic Immune Network For Mobile Robot Control.* School of Computer Science and information and Information Technology, University of Nottingham. (www.cs.nott. ac.uk/~uxa/papers/05amanda_thesis.pdf)

KEY TERMS

Adaptive Immune Response: The antigen-specific response of T and B cells. It includes antibody production and the killing of pathogen-infected cells, and is regulated by cytokines such as interferon-alfa. The immune cells are able to learn and improve immune defenses when they encounter the same pathogen several times. This is based on the concept of "memory" in certain immune cells such as T and B cells.

Agent: A computer system, situated in some environment, that is capable of flexible autonomous action in order to meet its design objectives. The flexible autonomous action means the ability to act without the direct intervention of humans and they are capable to perceive their environment and response to changes to occur in it.

Artificial Immune Systems Algorithms: They are algorithms used in AIS which attempt to extract concepts from natural immune system.

Clonal Selection Algorithm: The clonal selection theory has been used as inspiration for the development of AIS that perform computational optimization and pattern recognition tasks. In particular, inspiration has been taken from the antigen driven affinity maturation process of B-cells, with its associated hypermutation mechanism. These AIS also often utilize the idea of memory cells to retain good solutions to the problem being solved. Castro and Timmis highlight two important features of affinity maturation in B-cells that can be exploited from the computational viewpoint. The first of these is that the proliferation of B-cells is proportional to the affinity of the antigen that binds it, thus the higher the affinity, the more clones are produced. Secondly, the mutations suffered by the antibody of a B-cell are inversely proportional to the affinity of the antigen it binds. Utilizing these two features, de Castro and Von Zuben developed one of the most popular and widely used clonal selection inspired AIS called CLONAG, which has been used to performed the tasks of pattern matching and multi-modal function optimization.

Cognitive Model: A cognitive model may comprise a "circle & arrow theory" of how some aspect of cognition is structured (e.g. information processing stages), or a set of equations with the proper input-output specifications and some internal structure that is believed to represent some aspect of cognition. In studying a cognitive model, one considers issues such as predictive power and model uniqueness. In other words, one examines whether the model can foresee any traits of the aspect of cognition it claims to govern, and also whether success of the model logically excludes other possible models with the proper I/O mapping.

Immune Network Algorithm: The premise of immune network theory is that any lymphocyte receptor within an organism can be recognized by a subset of the total receptor repertoire. The receptors of this recognizing set have their own recognizing set and so on, thus an immune network of interactions is formed. Immune networks are often referred to as idiotypic networks. In the absence of foreign antigen, Jerne concluded that the immune system must display a behavior or activity resulting from interactions with itself and from these interactions immunological behavior such as tolerance and memory emerge.

Immune System: A body system that is made up of specialized cells that keep you healthy. It works by getting rid of organisms that cause infections.

Innate Immune Response: It responses to certain general targets very quickly. This response is crucial during the early phase of host defence against infection by pathogens, before the antigen-specific adaptive immune response is induced.

Negative Selection Algorithm: It is inspired by the main mechanism in the thymus that produces a set of mature T-cells capable of binding only non-self antigens. The starting point of this algorithm is to produce a set of self strings, S, that define the normal state of the system. The task then is to generate a set of detectors, D, that only bind/recognize the complement of S. These detectors can then be applied to new data in order to classify them as being self or non-self, thus in the case of the original work by Forrest , highlighting the fact that data has been manipulated.

Single and Multi Agent System: When there is only one agent in a defined environment, it is named Single-Agent System (SAS). This agent acts and interacts only with its environment. If there are more than one agent and they interact with each other and their environment, the system is called Multi-Agent System.

Section I.III
Artificial Immune System and Scheduling

Scheduling problem is an important engineering problem in the real-world. Artificial immune systems can also be used to solve such problem since immune system can solve its own scheduling problem in the process of protecting body from invading. Many different kinds of immune algorithms had been used for the problem. The following two chapters tell us how to use immune algorithms to solve the scheduling problem in practice.

Chapter VI
An Immune Algorithm Based Robust Scheduling Methods

Xingquan Zuo
Beijing University of Posts and Telecommunications, P.R. China

Hongwei Mo
Harbin Engineering University, P.R. China

ABSTRACT

Inspired from the robust control principle, a robust scheduling method is proposed to solve uncertain scheduling problems. The uncertain scheduling problem is modeled by a set of workflow simulation models, and then a scheduling scheme (solution) is evaluated by the results of workflow simulations that are executed by using the workflow models in the set. A variable neighborhood immune algorithm (VNIA) is used to obtain an optimal robust scheduling scheme that has good performances for each model in the model set. The detailed steps of optimizing robust scheduling scheme by the VNIA are given. The antibody coding and decoding schemes are also designed to deal with resource conflicts during workflow simulation processes. Experimental results show that the proposed method can generate robust scheduling schemes that are insensitive for uncertain disturbances of scheduling environments.

INTRODUCTION

In this paper, we proposed a robust scheduling method for uncertain scheduling problems. The method is based on workflow simulation models and an immune algorithm. We introduced the method of modeling uncertain scheduling problems by a set of workflow simulation models, and gave the detailed steps of optimizing the problems by the immune algorithm. In simulation experiments, we compared the proposed method with the definitive scheduling method, and experimental results shown that the robust scheduling method can improve the robustness of scheduling schemes and generate robust scheduling schemes that are insensitive to uncertain disturbances of scheduling environments.

Copyright © 2009, IGI Global, distributing in print or electronic forms without written permission of IGI Global is prohibited.

BACKGROUND

Scheduling problems exist widely in actual production processes, and are very important for improving enterprise efficiency, reducing the labor of workers, and enhancing the competitive power of enterprises. In recent years, many scheduling methods are proposed, and most of them are used to solve definitive scheduling problems (Brucker, 1998; Hajri, 2000; Yang, 2001). But in actual production scheduling, there are a lot of uncertainties such as the uncertainty of process time and the failure of machines, which would lead the primary scheduling scheme become worst or even infeasible. Dynamic scheduling methods (Suresh, 1993) can solve such uncertain scheduling problems effectively, i.e., when dynamic events occur, a new scheduling scheme can be generated by rescheduling to deal with the changed scheduling environment.

Dynamic scheduling methods can generate feasible scheduling schemes, but for some trades such as civil aviation, frequent rescheduling is not a good idea and may cause some problems for airliners and passengers. When an accidental event occurs, we hope that the event would not influence the whole scheduled flight. In this condition, a "robust" flight scheduling is welcome that would still maintain good performances when the scheduling environment changes.

Along with the increasing requirement of robust scheduling method, researches on robust scheduling arouse much attention in recent years (Lin, 2004). Compared with dynamic scheduling, robust scheduling is a new research area, and there are still many problems needed to be solved, and the definition of robust scheduling has not been given explicitly until now. General speaking, robust scheduling can be considered as a suboptimum scheduling scheme that is not sensitive to noise environments, and it emphasizes on the stability of scheduling schemes. Byeon et al decomposed a scheduling problem into several sub-problems, and a heuristic algorithm was used to solve each sub-scheduling problem to obtain a robust scheduling scheme (Byeon, 1998). Jensen proposed a robust scheduling method based on robust optimization (Jensen, 2003). His method used a disconnected chart model to construct a scheduling neighborhood, all of the scheduling solutions in the neighborhood are used to evaluate scheduling schemes, and an optimal robust scheduling scheme is obtained by a genetic algorithm. Leon et al proposed a robust scheduling method based on genetic algorithm, and scheduling schemes was evaluated by the weighted sum of the expectation values and variances of the performance index "Makespan" (Leon, 1994).

Inspired from the ideas of robust control, a robust scheduling method is proposed in this paper. The method uses a set of workflow simulation models to describe an uncertain scheduling problem, and a robust scheduling scheme is obtained by a variable neighborhood immune algorithm. Scheduling solutions are evaluated by many workflow simulations that are executed by using the workflow models in the set. Different from other robust scheduling methods, the proposed method focuses on finding a global robust solution whose scheduling results are stable for uncertain scheduling environments, not just a local robust solution that is only robust for small uncertain disturbances. The proposed method is also different from those robust scheduling methods based on robust optimization: it tries to find a scheduling scheme (solution) that has stable scheduling results when the scheduling environment changes; while the robust optimization based methods try to obtain a scheduling scheme (solution) whose variety would not cause a large variety of scheduling results for a given scheduling environment.

MODEL OF UNCERTAIN SCHEDULING PROBLEMS

Workflow simulation scheduling model is a universal scheduling model that has good model description capability for large scale complex scheduling problems and their uncertain disturbances (Fan, 2001; Zuo, 2006). Hence, this paper uses the workflow simulation scheduling model to model uncertain scheduling problems. The scheduling model is composed of process model, resource model, and transaction model etc, and is capable of describing all kinds of scheduling problems.

(1) **Process model:** The process model consists of multi-processes that are independent one another. Each of these processes describes the manufacturing procedures of a classification of jobs. The process model can describe the manufacturing procedures of all classifications of jobs, including job shop, flow shop, and hybrid scheduling problems etc. Each process of the model has several activities, and each activity denotes

an operation of a job. The logic relationship of activities in a process defines restrictions of operation processing order for a job.

(2) **Resource model:** Resource model describes resource entities used in a manufacturing process, and defines the resource restriction of a scheduling problem. The resource entities mainly include manufacture devices, transportation devices, and storage devices etc. Two kinds of resources are defined, i.e., resource entities and resource pools. The resource entities refer to real equipments and a resource pool is a classification of resource entities that has same functions. The resource model is related to the process model by the mapping between the activities in the process model and the resource entities in the resource model.

(3) **Transaction model:** Jobs are considered as transactions. The scheduling system generates transactions and enables many process instances to execute on the workflow simulation scheduling model.

Figure 1 gives a workflow simulation scheduling model of a job shop problem with n job and m machines. The "Job $x.y$" in the figure means the yth operation of the xth job. The process model includes n processes, and each process represents the processing of a job. The resource model consists of m machines, and each machine can handle n operations, for example, the 2th machine can process Job 2.1, Job 1.2, …, and Job $n.m$. The processing of n jobs is described by n workflow processes, and each activity in the processes needs to be handled by a fixed machine. So that the job shop problem is converted to a resource allocation problem, and resource allocation schemes are needed to allocate a machine for each activity during the process of multi-process workflow simulation.

When some dynamic events occur, the scheduling environment of a scheduling problem is changed. We call the scheduling environment without dynamic events as the nominal scheduling environment, which can be modeled by a workflow simulation model defined as the nominal scheduling model. A workflow simulation can be executed by using the nominal scheduling model. During each simulation process, some dynamic events are mimicked, so that a changed workflow simulation model can be obtained. If n workflow simulations are executed, then n changed models are produced that reflect the uncertain scheduling environment. Hence, the uncertain scheduling problem can be modeled by a set of changed workflow simulation models.

For an uncertain scheduling problem x, assume its nominal scheduling model is $M(x)$ and the scheduling environment disturbance caused by dynamic events is denoted by Δ_i, then the actual scheduling model is expressed by

Figure 1. The workflow model of a job shop problem with n jobs and m machines

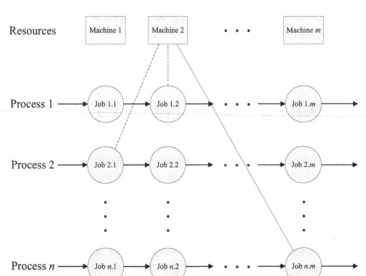

$$M_i(x) = M(x) + \Delta_i \tag{1}$$

The uncertain scheduling problem can be modeled by

$$U(x) = \left\{ M_i(x) \middle| \ i = 1, \cdots, n \right\} \tag{2}$$

If we can find a scheduling scheme that has satisfactory performances for each model in the set, then the scheduling scheme is robust for the uncertain scheduling environment. In this paper, a scheduling scheme (solution) is a priority list for all operations of the scheduling problem, and is used to allocate resources for each activity during workflow simulations. A workflow simulation is executed by using each model in the set $U(x)$. During the n workflow simulations, the resources are allocated by the scheduling scheme to avoid the phenomenon of resource conflicts.

Suppose the scheduling scheme is expressed by s, and $f(s, M_i(x))$ is the performance index obtained by the workflow simulation, during which the ith workflow model is used and resources are allocated by the scheduling scheme s. The average value $A(s, x)$ and standard deviation $D(s, x)$ of the performance indexes obtained by n workflow simulations are

$$A(s,x) = \frac{1}{n} \sum_{i=1}^{n} f\left(s, M_i(x)\right) \tag{3}$$

$$D(s,x) = \sqrt{\frac{1}{n-1} \sum_{i=1}^{n} \left(f\left(s, M_i(x)\right) - A(s,x)\right)^2} \tag{4}$$

The evaluation value of the scheduling scheme s can be calculated by

$$E(s,x) = \frac{1}{k_1 \times A(s,x) + k_2 \times D(s,x)} \tag{5}$$

where the coefficients k_1 and k_2 are used to balance the weights of average value and standard deviation of scheduling results.

OPTIMIZATION OF UNCERTAIN SCHEDULING PROBLEMS

Finding an optimal robust scheduling scheme is a complex optimization problem, so a global optimization algorithm is required to solve the problem. In paper (Zuo, 2007), we propose a variable neighborhood immune algorithm (VNIA) that shows good performances for complex function optimization problems. In this chapter, the VNIA is used to find an optimal robust scheduling scheme as shown in Figure 2.

Antibody Coding

Each antibody represents a scheduling scheme, which is a set of priorities for all operations of a scheduling problem. The representation of an antibody is based on random keys, i.e., each gene of an antibody is a random number in the interval [0, 1], corresponding to the priority of an operation. An antibody is evaluated by workflow simulations that are executed by using the workflow model set.

For an uncertain job shop problem with m machines $M1, M2, ..., Mm$ and n jobs $J1, J2, ..., Jn$, the antibody coding can be shown in figure 3, where $0 \le P_{Mq,Jp} \le 1$ ($q = 1, \cdots m; \ p = 1, \cdots, n$) is the priority of the operation of the job Jp, which need to be processed on the machine Mq.

Figure 2. Finding a robust scheduling scheme by VNIA

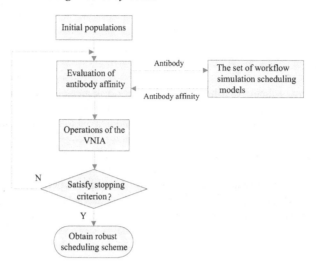

Figure 3. Antibody coding

$$\left\{ \ \underbrace{P_{M1,\,J1} \quad P_{M1,\,J2} \quad \cdots \quad P_{M1,\,Jn}}_{M1} \ \underbrace{P_{M2,\,J1} \quad P_{M2,\,J2} \quad \cdots \quad P_{M2,\,Jn}}_{M2} \quad \cdots \quad \underbrace{P_{Mm,\,J1} \quad P_{Mm,\,J2} \quad \cdots \quad P_{Mm,\,Jn}}_{Mm} \ \right\}$$

Antibody Decoding

A workflow simulation can be executed by using a workflow model. During the simulation, an antibody is used to allocate resources for each activity in the model to generate a feasible schedule. So the antibody can be decoded into a feasible schedule for each model in the set U, and n schedules can be obtained by using the n models in the set. The antibody affinity is calculated by the n simulations according to the equations (3), (4) and (5). The process of antibody decoding is described as follows.

(1) Initialization: a workflow model is given; the system clock is set to 0; the event list and resource list is set to empty;

(2) Each activity in the process model is assigned a priority according to the given antibody;

(3) The first activity of each process in the process model is added into the resource list used by the activity;

(4) The activities in the resource lists are moved to the event list, and the activities in event list are sorted according to their completed time;

(5) While the number of activities in the event list is not zero, repeat the following steps:

- The system clock is set to the completed time of the earliest completed activity in the event list;
- The earliest completed activity is executed, and the state of the activity in the process model is changed;
- If the resource list used by the completed activity is empty, then the source state is set to idle; otherwise, an activity is moved from the resource list to the event list. If there are several activities in the resource list (i.e., resource conflicts), the activity with the highest priority is selected to move from the resource list to the event list;

- For the next activity of the completed activity, if the resource used by the activity is idle, then the activity is added into the event list; otherwise the activity is added into its resource list;
- The activities in the event list are sorted according to their completed time.

(6)   The simulation process stops, and a feasible schedule is generated.

Optimizing Uncertain Scheduling Problems by VNIA

Human immune system can recognize antigens by immune response. For a long time, immunology has been dominated by the idea of clonal selection theory, which provides the main concepts to account for the adaptive immune response. More recently, immunologists have discovered that an adaptive immune response is a cooperative phenomenon involving the interactions between antigen and B cells. This discovery has led to a question of the simplicities of the classical clonal selection theory. Jerne explained the interaction between B cells by an immune network (Jerne, 1974), which is an expanding theory of clonal selection. He suggested that immune cells and molecules can play the role of antigens, and the immune system is composed of a regulated network of cells and molecules that recognize one another even in the absence of antigens. The antigen portion that is recognized by B cell receptors is called epitope, and the epitopes displayed by the variable regions of a B cell receptor is defined as idiotype. An antigen may have several different types of epitopes, and can be recognized by several different antibodies. The antibody portion responsible for recognizing an antigen is called paratope. A B cell recognizing antigens can stimulate the B cell, and a B cell being recognized by other antibodies will suppress the B cell. The strength of stimulating and suppressing is measured by the match degree (affinity) between paratopes and epitopes. If a B cell is stimulated to a certain degree, then the B cell begins to clone to generate antibodies.

Based on the immune network theory, the VNIA uses variable neighborhood strategy to balance the conflict of local and global searches, and a two-level immune network is suggested to maintain a large diversity of populations during the optimization process. Multi-population is used in the algorithm and these populations act on one another to form the first level immune network. The B cells in each population interact mutually to form the second level immune network. The first level immune network is to make each populations distribute in different parts of the solution space, and the second level immune network is used to disperse the antibodies in each population widely.

First Level Immune Network

Assume the VNIA have Pop_num populations, denoted by $Population = \{Pop_1, Pop_2, \cdots, Pop_{Pop\_num}\}$. Each population Pop_i ($i = 1, 2, \cdots, Pop\_num$) consists of Pop_size antibodies expressed by $Pop_i = \{Ab_1^i, Ab_2^i, \cdots, Ab_{Pop\_size}^i\}$. Each antibody Ab_j^i ($i = 1, 2, \cdots, Pop\_num$; $j = 1, 2, \cdots, Pop\_size$) is a real-coded string as shown in figure 3, and denoted by $Ab_j^i = \{gene_1^{i,j}, gene_2^{i,j}, \cdots, gene_N^{i,j}\}$, where $gene_k^{i,j} \in [0,1]$ ($k = 1, 2, \cdots, N$). For a job shop problem with n jobs (each job consists of m operations), the length of antibody is $N = m \times n$. The Pop_num populations interact to form the first level immune network.

(1)   **Population affinity:** The affinity of the highest affinity antibody in a population is considered as the population affinity. The affinity of population Pop_i is expressed as

$$Pop\_Aff(i) = \max_{j=1,2,\ldots,Pop\_size} \{Ab\_aff(i,j)\} \tag{6}$$

where $Ab\_aff(i,j)$ is the affinity of the jth antibody in the population i.

(2)   **Population center:** The center vector C_i for each population Pop_i is denoted by $C_i = (c_i^1, c_i^2, \cdots, c_i^N)$, where

$$c_i^k = \sum_{j=1}^{Pop\_size} gene_k^{i,j} \Big/ Pop\_size, \, k = 1, ..., N \tag{7}$$

(3) **Population distance:** The Euclidean distance between the centers of any two populations is calculated. The distance between population Pop_i and Pop_j can be denoted by $Pop\_dis(i, j)$, and the average distance of all populations is calculated and denoted by Ave_dis.

(4) **Population stimulating level:** tThe stimulating level of a population is determined by its affinity and the distance from other populations. A population is stimulated by its affinity and the populations that are far from it, and is suppressed by those populations near it. So the stimulating level of population Pop_i can be calculated by

$$Pop\_stimul(i) = Pop\_Aff(i). \frac{\displaystyle\sum_{j=1}^{pop\_num, j \neq i} Pop\_dis(i, j) \Big/ Ave\_dis}{(Pop\_num - 1)} \qquad (8)$$

From equation (8), it can be seen that if $Pop\_dis(i, j) > Ave\_dis$, then the population j is a stimulating population that would increase the stimulating level of population i. Otherwise, the population j would reduce the stimulating level of population i. So the stimulating and suppressive populations can be distinguished by the average distance Ave_dis.

Second Level Immune Network

In each population Pop_i, an antibody is stimulated by the antibodies far from it and is suppressed by the antibodies near it. The antibodies in the population interact to form the second level immune network, which is described as follows.

(1) **Antibody affinity:** The affinity of each antibody Ab_j^i is denoted by $Ab\_aff(i, j)$, and is calculated according to equations (3), (4), and (5) by the simulation process.

(2) **Antibody distance:** tTe Euclidean distance between any two antibodies in the population is calculated. The distance between the antibody j and k in the population Pop_i is denoted by $Ab\_dis(i, j, k)$.

(3) **Antibody stimulating level:** The simulating level of an antibody is determined by its affinity, as well as by the stimulating and suppressive effects from other antibodies in the same population. Each antibody Ab_j^i is given a neighborhood whose size is $Neigh_j^i$, denoted by $Neigh_j^i(x)$. The antibodies locating in its neighborhood are considered as suppressive antibodies, and the antibodies outside its neighborhood as stimulating antibodies. So the stimulating effect of the antibody Ab_j^i can be calculated by

$$Stimul(i, j, Neigh_j^i) = \sqrt{\sum_{m \in \left\{k \mid Ab_k^i \notin Neigh_j^i(x), k=1,\ldots,Pop\_size\right\}} \left(Ab\_dis(i, j, m) - Neigh_j^i\right)^2} \qquad (9)$$

and the suppressive effect of the antibody can be calculated by

$$Suppress(i, j, Neigh_j^i) = \sqrt{\sum_{m \in \left\{k \mid Ab_k^i \in Neigh_j^i(x), k=1,\ldots,Pop\_size, k \neq j\right\}} \left(Neigh_j^i - Ab\_dis(i, j, m)\right)^2} \qquad (10)$$

It can be seen from equations (9) and (10) that a stimulating antibody far from the antibody would have a large stimulating effect, and a suppressive antibody with a small distance from the antibody would have a large suppressive effect. The antibody stimulating level is the synthesis of antibody affinity, stimulating, and suppressive effects from other antibodies, so it can be calculated by

$$Ab\_stimul(i, j, Neigh_j^i) = Ab\_aff(i, j) \cdot \frac{Stimul(i, j, Neigh_j^i)}{Stimul(i, j, Neigh_j^i) + Suppress(i, j, Neigh_j^i)} \qquad (11)$$

From equation (11), it can be seen that if all other antibodies are outside the antibody neighborhood, the stimulating level is maximal (equates to the antibody affinity). If there are antibodies in the antibody neighborhood, then the stimulating level would be reduced. An antibody with a high affinity and far from other antibodies would have a large stimulating level.

Clone, Mutation, and Selection

Suppose the total number of clones generated for the *Pop_num* populations is *Clone_num*. By using the population stimulating level, the proportional selection scheme is used to calculate the number of clones for each population Pop_i $(i = 1, 2, \cdots, Pop\_num)$, denoted by $Pop\_Clonenum(i)$. Furthermore, by using the obtained $Pop\_Clonenum(i)$ and the antibody stimulating level, the number of clones for each antibody Ab_j^i $(j = 1, 2, \cdots, Pop\_num)$ in population Pop_i, expressed by $Ab\_clonenum(i, j)$, can also be calculated by using the proportional selection scheme.

(1) **Antibody elimination:** if $Ab\_clonenum(i, j) = 0$, it means that the antibody Ab_j^i is non-stimulated and would be eliminated, and it is replaced by a random antibody. This is caused by several reasons, including low affinity, large neighborhood or too many other antibodies around it.

(2) **Antibody proliferation:** if $Ab\_clonenum(i, j) \neq 0$, each antibody Ab_j^i clones to generate $Ab\_clonenum(i, j)$ clones, denoted by $C_j^i = \left\{ Clone_1^{i,j}, Clone_2^{i,j}, \cdots, Clone_{Ab\_clonenum(i,j)}^{i,j} \right\}$.

(3) **Antibody hypermutation:** Each clone of antibody Ab_j^i mutates to generate a new antibody in its neighborhood. Suppose the mutated clones of the antibody Ab_j^i is $M_j^i = \left\{ Muta_1^{i,j}, Muta_2^{i,j}, \cdots, Muta_{Ab\_clonenum(i,j)}^{i,j} \right\}$, where $Muta_k^{i,j}$ ($k = 1, 2, \cdots, Ab\_clonenum(i, j)$) is a random antibody in the neighborhood of Ab_j^i.

(4) **Antibody selection:** The affinities of mutated clones for each antibody Ab_j^i are calculated according to equations (3), (4), and (5), and the highest affinity antibody $Muta\_best_j^i$ is selected

$$Ab\_aff(Muta\_best_j^i) = \max_{k=1,2,\ldots,Ab\_clonenum(i,j)} \left\{ Ab\_aff(Muta_k^{i,j}) \right\} \qquad (12)$$

(5) **Antibody updating:** If $Ab\_aff(Muta\_best_j^i) > Ab\_aff(Ab_j^i)$, then let $Ab_j^i = Muta\_best_j^i$; otherwise the antibody Ab_j^i is replaced by $Muta\_best_j^i$ according to a given small probability.

Crossover

A special crossover operation is applied to each of the selected antibodies to exchange genes. For an antibody Ab_j^i in the population Pop_i, choice an antibody Ab_k^i from the set $Pop_i \setminus Ab_j^i$ randomly. Construct a new antibody $Ab\_new_j^i$ by making each gene of the antibody come form Ab_k^i in the probability *Exch_rate*, and from Ab_j^i in the probability (1- *Exch_rate*). If the affinity of the new antibody is higher than the antibody Ab_j^i, then let $Ab_j^i = Ab\_new_j^i$; otherwise the antibody Ab_j^i is kept unchanged.

Variable Neighborhood Strategy

Neighborhoods are used in the process of antibody clone and mutation. In this paper, a variable neighborhood strategy is introduced to change the neighborhood size of each antibody from N_min to N_max by a step N_step adaptively. The variable neighborhood strategy is given as follows.

(1)   **Neighborhood initialization:** Each antibody Ab_j^i is given a neighborhood that is denoted by

$$Neigh_j^i(x) = \left\{ x \mid \ \left\| x - Ab_j^i \right\| \leq Neigh_j^i, x \in R^N \right\} \tag{13}$$

The initial neighborhood sizes of all antibodies are all given by N_min.

(2)   In each generation, the neighborhood size of each antibody is changed adaptively. The pseudocode of the variable neighborhood strategy can be described as follows.

Let Ab_j^i is an arbitrary antibody in populations.
If $Ab\_clonenum(i,j) = 0$, then
　　The antibody is replaced by a random new antibody
　　Let $Neigh_j^i = N\_min$
Else if the antibody is replaced by its mutated clone $Muta\_best_j^i$, then
Let $Neigh_j^i = N\_min$
　Else
　　Let $Neigh_j^i = Neigh_j^i + N\_step$
　　If $Neigh_j^i > N\_max$, then
Let $Neigh_j^i = N\_min$
　　End if
End if

Immigration Operation

In order to exchange information between different populations, immigration operation is used in the VNIA. Firstly, two populations are selected from the *Population* randomly. Then, two antibodies are randomly chosen from the two selected populations respectively to exchange, and the neighborhood sizes of the two antibodies are exchanged also. The immigration operation is carried out every several generations. The operation can bring genes from one population to another population, and makes these populations cooperate to evolve.

The Steps of VNIA

The steps of VNIA can be summarized as follows:

(1)   Initialization: generate *Pop_num* populations randomly and give the initial neighborhood for each antibody in these populations.
(2)   Using the first level immune network to calculate the stimulating degree for each population.
(3)   The stimulating degree of each antibody is calculated by using the second level immune network.
(4)   The number of clones generated by each antibody is calculated by using the two-level immune network.
(5)   For each population Pop_i (i=1,2,…, *Pop_num*), repeat the following steps:
　　•   Each antibody in the population clone;
　　•   The generated clones mutate in its neighborhood;
　　•   Each antibody is replaced by its mutated clone or kept unchanged according to a certain probability;
　　•   Variable neighborhood strategy is applied to each antibody;
　　•   Each antibody is carried out crossover operation.
(6)   The *Pop_num* populations perform immigration operation very several generations.
(7)   Return to the step (2) until the stop criterion is fulfilled.

Table 1. The benchmark job shop problems

Job shop Problems	Job number	Operation number	Machine number
FT06	6	6	6
FT10	10	10	10
LA20	10	10	10
MT20	20	5	5

EXPERIMENTAL RESULTS

To verify the effectiveness of the proposed robust scheduling method, it is used to solve 4 uncertain scheduling problems whose nominal models are FT06, FT10, LA20, and MT20 respectively, as shown in Table 1. For each of these problems, the processing time of an operation of each job varied randomly in a given range, and the nominal processing time of each operation of these problems equals to that of their nominal models. The processing time uncertainty of operations is considered as uncertain disturbances. The uncertain degree of processing time is defined by its variety range, for example, if t_i is the nominal processing time of the operation o_i, then the actual processing time can by expressed by $t_i' \in [t_i - \alpha t_i, t_i + \alpha t_i]$, where $\alpha \in [0,1]$ expresses uncertain degree of processing time.

A model set is constructed for each scheduling problem. For the problem FT06, the model set includes 200 models; for other scheduling problems, each model set consists of 50 models. Each model in the sets is generated by a workflow simulation process, during which some dynamic events (processing time varieties) occur. The performance index considered in this paper is C_{max}. For the problems FT06 and FT10, the k_1 and k_2 in equation (5) are given by 0.01 and 0.05 respectively; for the problems LA20 and MT20, the two coefficients are given by 0.01 and 0.02 respectively. For all scheduling problems, the parameters of VNIA are given by *Subpop_num*=4, *Subpop_size*=5, *Clone_num*=100, *N_max*=0.05, *N_min*=0.005, and *N_step*=0.005.

For each scheduling problem, several uncertain degrees are given and for each uncertain degree the VNIA is run for 30 generations to obtain a robust scheduling scheme. To compare with definitive scheduling method, the VNIA is also run for 30 generations to optimize definitive scheduling problems FT06, FT10, LA20, and MT20 to get definitive scheduling schemes. For each uncertain degree of a scheduling problem, 100 random scheduling instances are generated and scheduled by the robust scheduling scheme and definitive scheduling scheme respectively. The experimental results are given in Table 2-5. In these Tables, "Average" expresses the average value of the 100 scheduling results to reflect the scheduling quality. "Deviation" is the standard deviation of scheduling

Table 2. The comparison results for the problem FT06

Uncertainty degree α	Robust scheduling scheme				Definitive scheduling scheme			
	Average	Best	Worst	Deviation	Average	Best	Worst	Deviation
10%	58.126	56.492	60.263	0.549	58.612	56.599	65.592	1.844
20%	59.155	56.479	62.246	0.910	59.350	56.006	69.002	2.556
30%	59.674	56.038	74.223	1.668	60.165	55.761	72.690	3.400
40%	60.488	54.926	65.438	1.984	60.505	55.453	71.887	3.513
50%	60.633	55.272	69.944	2.399	61.306	54.641	71.023	3.713
60%	61.436	54.627	71.931	2.849	62.168	54.033	73.571	4.020
70%	61.121	54.614	73.874	3.368	62.858	55.416	78.005	4.495
80%	60.378	52.000	72.405	3.493	63.426	52.508	78.263	5.023

Table 3. The comparison results for the problem FT10

Uncertainty	Robust scheduling scheme				Definitive scheduling scheme			
degree α	Average	Best	Worst	Deviation	Average	Best	Worst	Deviation
5%	1080.1	1069.5	1126.4	13.64	1088.3	1015.6	1208.5	80.48
10%	1088.1	1067.8	1122.6	6.86	1130.8	1015.8	1213.3	75.64
15%	1078.0	1045.4	1170.4	18.92	1132.5	1007.5	1217.5	72.58
20%	1110.0	1054.0	1193.6	21.44	1135.2	1016.2	1232.0	74.20
25%	1085.9	1047.2	1211.1	27.84	1138.3	1011.2	1227.4	67.91
30%	1129.1	1094.9	1229.1	24.85	1152.0	1015.4	1249.0	61.67
35%	1094.7	1026.6	1250.2	36.23	1138.6	1004.2	1278.4	72.07
40%	1106.8	1050.1	1239.5	25.76	1150.8	1012.7	1260.3	61.84
45%	1123.1	1039.6	1259.2	33.26	1156.9	1018.6	1260.9	61.51
50%	1110.2	1027.1	1228.8	35.49	1150.1	1012.0	1256.4	62.20

Table 4. The comparison results for the problem LA20

Uncertainty	Robust scheduling scheme				Definitive scheduling scheme			
degree α	Average	Best	Worst	Deviation	Average	Best	Worst	Deviation
5%	1011.7	997.4	1079.1	7.31	986.9	961.5	1099.2	30.43
10%	976.9	956.2	1064.8	10.45	988.5	944.2	1197.1	44.09
15%	1016.1	966.8	1105.7	26.95	993.7	943.1	1153.0	51.90
20%	1019.1	957.8	1094.2	27.61	1000.6	937.7	1200.8	52.95
25%	991.9	946.0	1078.7	23.79	1001.2	926.3	1196.3	60.38
30%	973.3	929.1	1049.0	24.33	1000.3	928.7	1208.0	55.58
35%	989.3	921.7	1131.9	41.59	1012.1	927.5	1189.7	62.86
40%	1022.2	940.5	1188.6	51.35	1007.1	925.8	1189.3	61.95
45%	1006.5	929.3	1074.0	30.73	1013.7	940.6	1202.3	58.09
50%	1003.8	942.4	1132.7	33.03	1022.7	938.0	1220.0	68.47

Table 5. The comparison results for the problem MT20

Uncertainty	Robust scheduling scheme				Definitive scheduling scheme			
degree α	Average	Best	Worst	Deviation	Average	Best	Worst	Deviation
5%	1240.4	1221.7	1259.9	7.71	1258.1	1237.0	1280.1	12.95
10%	1240.9	1204.5	1309.7	21.74	1267.6	1236.8	1341.4	21.72
15%	1248.8	1216.0	1295.4	17.09	1281.7	1233.9	1371.4	26.27
20%	1210.5	1160.6	1288.1	19.44	1290.5	1228.0	1351.7	27.64
25%	1263.5	1195.9	1329.0	27.40	1295.3	1236.0	1387.2	31.10
30%	1272.8	1214.8	1361.6	28.44	1298.6	1232.3	1367.0	29.86
35%	1310.7	1258.4	1361.4	23.17	1314.3	1255.1	1459.4	34.54
40%	1254.7	1203.6	1367.4	34.32	1308.3	1242.1	1407.1	35.57
45%	1249.7	1182.2	1365.9	33.66	1313.7	1225.7	1431.9	39.03
50%	1259.1	1147.2	1356.1	38.88	1316.7	1228.2	1490.6	42.58

results and denotes the stability of the scheduling results. "Best" and "Worst" are the best and worst scheduling results among the 100 scheduling. The worst scheduling result is very important for evaluating a robust scheduling scheme, since it must be considered in actual scheduling problems.

It can be seen from these Tables that the robust scheduling scheme has better robustness as scheduling FT06, and when the uncertain degree is large, the advantage of the robust scheduling scheme appears more clearly. For FT10, the robust scheduling scheme obtains better scheduling results and shows better performances when the uncertain degree is small. This is because the problem FT10 is very complex and the 50 models can not adequately describe its uncertainty when the uncertain degree is large. For LA20, the average scheduling results obtained by the two schemes are similar, but the robust scheduling scheme is more robust for uncertain disturbances and can get better "Worst" scheduling results. For MT20, the robust scheduling scheme obtains better average scheduling results obviously.

To compare robust scheduling schemes with definitive scheduling schemes in same scheduling environments, 10 definitive scheduling instances are generated for each of 3 uncertain degrees and scheduled by the two schemes respectively. The scheduling results are given in Table 6-9. It can be seen from these Tables that the average scheduling results obtained by robust scheduling schemes are better than that of definitive scheduling schemes. Robust scheduling schemes can obtain more stable scheduling results, while the results of definitive scheduling schemes are not stable and sometimes the results are very bad.

The VNIA is a kind of stochastic optimization algorithm, so scheduling results for each uncertain degree of a scheduling problem may be different. The coefficients k_1 and k_2 in equation (5) can balance the "optimality" and "robustness" of scheduling results, and it is important to give the two coefficients properly for obtaining satisfactory scheduling results. It can be seen that for simple scheduling problem FT06, robust scheduling schemes are better than definitive scheduling schemes slightly, but for complex scheduling problems FT10, LA20, and MT20, the advantages of the robust scheduling schemes appear obviously. The robust scheduling method is more effective for complex uncertain scheduling problems.

Table 6. The comparison of optimizing definitive scheduling problems for FT06

| Experiments | Uncertainty degree α | | | | | |
| | 40% | | 60% | | 80% | |
	Robust	Definitive	Robust	Definitive	Robust	Definitive
1	59.054	60.054	61.804	60.568	59.770	58.000
2	62.526	58.898	59.775	55.873	59.438	61.764
3	60.814	58.772	63.291	64.274	56.422	70.211
4	57.427	58.000	62.398	58.367	59.270	67.444
5	59.616	57.879	64.146	70.355	59.000	63.041
6	61.438	62.494	60.704	57.049	59.593	62.649
7	61.078	67.044	60.230	59.594	62.910	67.910
8	58.352	68.194	63.250	67.206	62.950	71.132
9	58.645	60.891	61.479	68.608	65.055	60.788
10	60.475	69.475	62.488	65.946	62.575	61.905
Average	**59.943**	**62.170**	**61.956**	**62.784**	**60.698**	**64.484**
Worst	**62.526**	**69.475**	**64.146**	**70.355**	**65.055**	**71.132**

Table 7. The comparison of optimizing definitive scheduling problems for FT10

Experiments	Uncertainty degree α					
	10%		20%		40%	
	Robust	Definitive	Robust	Definitive	Robust	Definitive
1	1088.9	1065.0	1123.7	1224.5	1113.3	1190.0
2	1094.4	1185.9	1101.6	1177.7	1104.4	1058.3
3	1079.4	1205.0	1121.0	1020.0	1089.5	1142.9
4	1093.3	1167.0	1065.7	1006.3	1113.6	1020.4
5	1092.8	1140.0	1082.1	1182.2	1102.5	1159.4
6	1084.5	1020.4	1085.9	1189.9	1120.1	1170.6
7	1086.1	1123.1	1121.2	1177.5	1119.0	1217.2
8	1083.9	1171.1	1105.7	1172.8	1075.0	1180.1
9	1085.6	1175.8	1115.0	1020.0	1072.4	1181.1
10	1094.5	1179.8	1097.3	1196.6	1087.7	1135.7
Average	**1088.3**	**1143.3**	**1101.9**	**1136.7**	**1099.7**	**1145.6**
Worst	**1094.5**	**1205.0**	**1123.7**	**1224.5**	**1120.1**	**1217.2**

Table 8. The comparison of optimizing definitive scheduling problems for LA20

Experiments	Uncertainty degree α					
	10%		30%		50%	
	Robust	Definitive	Robust	Definitive	Robust	Definitive
1	984.8	966.1	980.5	1019.3	1015.9	1195.1
2	975.6	970.5	987.3	973.4	1059.2	1136.9
3	975.0	973.8	947.4	971.4	987.6	960.4
4	973.0	985.0	944.9	968.9	1042.3	979.7
5	970.9	1096.6	957.7	1188.9	994.4	990.8
6	970.1	967.8	936.3	960.3	980.4	1006.2
7	972.1	961.5	965.5	1011.4	970.1	967.9
8	971.2	971.2	988.2	1022.2	983.8	974.8
9	982.1	1043.1	981.1	988.6	992.4	965.0
10	975.0	1036.0	1067.1	969.8	1003.0	1020.7
Average	**975.0**	**997.2**	**975.6**	**1007.4**	**1002.9**	**1019.7**
Worst	**984.8**	**1096.6**	**1067.1**	**1188.9**	**1059.2**	**1195.1**

Table 9. The comparison of optimizing definitive scheduling problems for MT20

| Experiments | Uncertainty degree α | | | | | |
| | 10% | | 30% | | 50% | |
	Robust	Definitive	Robust	Definitive	Robust	Definitive
1	1281.5	1256.2	1251.4	1313.2	1224.0	1327.3
2	1245.6	1310.3	1257.8	1309.1	1261.0	1363.2
3	1274.5	1247.2	1275.1	1306.2	1227.6	1364.4
4	1233.5	1264.6	1281.7	1284.8	1240.8	1306.9
5	1249.9	1251.5	1264.8	1270.0	1304.1	1355.4
6	1222.0	1276.3	1263.9	1254.2	1249.2	1276.0
7	1215.3	1267.4	1286.4	1318.5	1237.6	1273.5
8	1233.9	1319.4	1231.6	1295.7	1270.6	1301.3
9	1230.8	1258.9	1248.2	1329.0	1272.5	1346.4
10	1253.1	1285.2	1267.3	1256.5	1229.1	1276.1
Average	**1244.0**	**1273.7**	**1262.8**	**1293.7**	**1251.7**	**1319.1**
Worst	**1281.5**	**1319.4**	**1286.4**	**1329.0**	**1304.1**	**1364.4**

CONCLUSION

In this paper, a robust scheduling method is proposed. In the method, a set of workflow models is utilized to model uncertain scheduling problems and a variable neighborhood immune algorithm is used to obtain an optimal robust scheduling scheme. Scheduling schemes are evaluated by multi-process workflow simulations that are executed by using the workflow models in the model set. Antibody coding and decoding methods are designed to deal with the resource conflicts during workflow simulation processes. Experimental results show that the robust scheduling method is very effective for generating a robust scheduling scheme that has satisfactory performances under uncertain scheduling environments.

FUTURE DIRECTIONS

Robust scheduling is still a new research direction in the field of production scheduling. Like dynamic scheduling, robust scheduling can also deal with uncertain scheduling problems. Dynamic scheduling deals with uncertain scheduling problems by real-time rescheduling when uncertain dynamic events occur, while robust scheduling only generate a robust scheduling scheme that is insensitive to dynamic events. In future study, we will focus on the following topics:

(1) In our method, the evaluation of scheduling schemes will cost much time, which is also the common shortage of simulation based evaluation methods. In future, we will improve the evaluation method to reduce the evaluation time largely.

(2) The robustness of any robust scheduling schemes is within a boundary, when uncertain disturbances are very large, the robust scheduling scheme may not schedule perfectly. In future, we will study online robust scheduling algorithms to generate new robust scheduling schemes when uncertain disturbances become very large.

(3)   Several scheduling objectives are concerned for robust scheduling problems, such as "optimization" and "robustness" etc. In future, we will develop multi-objective robust scheduling methods to balance the several objectives by selecting a pareto solution for an uncertain scheduling problem.

ACKNOWLEDGMENT

This work was granted financial support from the National Natural Science Foundation of China (No. 60504028).

REFERENCES

Brucker, P. (1998). *Scheduling algorithms.* Berlin, Heidelberg: Springer-Verlag.

Byeon, E. S., David, W. S., & Robert, H. S. (1998). Decomposition Heuristics for Robust Job-shop Scheduling. *IEEE Transactions on Robotics and Automation, 14*(2), 303-313.

Fan, Y. S., Luo, H. B., & Lin, H. P. (2001). *Workflow management technology foundation.* Beijing: Tsinghua University Press, Springer-Verlag.

Hajri, S., Liouane, N., Hammadi, S., & Borne, P. (2000). A controlled genetic algorithm by fuzzy logic and belief functions for job-shop scheduling. *IEEE Transactions on System, Man, and Cybernetics Part B: Cybernetics, 30*(5), 812-818.

Jensen, M. T. (2003). Generating robust and flexible job shop schedules using genetic algorithms. *IEEE Transactions on Evolutionary Computation, 7*(3), 275-288.

Jerne, N. K. (1974). Towards a network theory of the immune system. *Annual Immunology, 125C,* 373-389.

Leon, V. J., Wu, S. D., & Storer, R. H. (1994). Robustness measures and robust scheduling for job shops. *IIE Transactions, 26*(5), 32-43.

Lin, X. X., Janak, S. L., & Floudas, C. A. (2004). A new robust optimization approach for scheduling under uncertainty: I bounded uncertainty. *Computers and Chemical Engineering, 28,* 1069-1083.

Pierre, H., & Nenad, M. (2001). Variable neighborhood search: principles and applications. *European Journal of Operational Research, 130,* 449-467.

Shutler, P. M. E. (2004). A priority list based heuristic for the job shop problem: part 2 tabu search. *Journal of Operational Research Society, 55*(7), 780-784.

Yang, S. X., & Wang, D. W. (2001). A new adaptive neural network and heuristics hybrid approach for job-shop scheduling. *Computer & Operations Research, 28,* 955-971.

Suresh, V., & Chandhuri, D. (1993). Dynamic scheduling--A survey of research. *International Journal of Production Economics, 32*(1), 53-63.

Zuo, X. Q., Fan, Y. S. et al. (2006). Workflow simulation scheduling model with application to a prototype system of cigarette factory scheduling. In Koji, K., Shinasuke, T., & Osamu, O. (Ed.), *Systems Modeling and Simulation: Theory and Applications* (pp. 158-162). Springer-Verlag.

Zuo, X. Q., Fan, Y. S., & Mo, H. W. (2007). Variable neighborhood immune algorithm. *Chinese Journal of Electronics, 16*(3), 503-508.

Willy, H., & Roel, L. (2005). Project scheduling under uncertainty: survey and research potentials. *European Journal of Operational Research, 165*, 289-306.

ADDITIONAL READING

AI-Fawzan, M. A., & Haouari, M. (2005). A bi-objective model for robust resource-constrained project scheduling. *International Journal of Production Economics, 96*, 175-187.

Anglani, A., Grieco, A., Guerriero, E., & Musmanno, R. (2005). Robust scheduling of parallel machines with sequence-dependent set-up costs. *European Journal of Operational Research, 161*, 704-720.

Artigues, C., Billaut, J. C., & Esswein, C. (2005). Maximization of solution flexibility for robust shop scheduling. *European Journal of Operational Research, 165*, 314-328.

Catherine, A. P., Leonardo, B. H., Philippe, B., Serge, D., & Luc, P. (1998). A two-stage methodology for short-term batch plant scheduling: discrete-event simulation and genetic algorithm. *Computers & Chemical Engineering, 22*(10), 1461-1481.

Honkomp, S. J., Mockus, L., & Reklaitis, G. V. (1997). Robust scheduling with processing time uncertainty. *Computers & Chemical Engineering, 21*, 1055-1060.

Sahinidis, N. V. (2004). Optimization under uncertainty: state-of-the-art and opportunities. *Computers & Chemical Engineering, 28*, 971-983.

Shafaei, R., & Brunn, P. (1999). Workshop scheduling using practical (inaccurate) data part2: an investigation of the robustness of scheduling rules in a dynamic and stochastic environment. *International Journal of Production Research, 37*(18), 4105-4117.

Shafaei, R., & Brunn, P. (2000). Workshop scheduling using practical (inaccurate) data part3: a framework to integrate job releasing, routing and scheduling functions to create a robust predictive schedule. *International Journal of Production Research, 38*(1): 85-99.

Wang, J. (2004). A fuzzy robust scheduling approach for product development projects. *European Journal of Operational Research, 130*, 449-467.

KEY TERMS

Dynamic Scheduling: For an uncertain scheduling problem, when some dynamic events occur, a new scheduling scheme is generated to deal with the uncertain disturbances by identifying the stochastic disturbances and rescheduling.

Immune Algorithm: A kind of algorithms that is developed based on human's immune principles.

Job Shop Scheduling: Suppose m machines have to process n jobs, and each job consists of a set of operations that have to be processed in a special sequence; each operation has to be processed on a definite machine and has a deterministic processing time. The objective is to find the optimal schedule, i.e., the schedule of the operation order and starting time on each machine such that one or more optimization objectives are optimal.

Optimization Algorithms: is a kind of algorithms that are used for solving optimization problems.

Robust Scheduling: For an uncertain scheduling problem, the goal of robust scheduling is to generate a sub-optimum scheduling scheme that is not sensitive to stochastic disturbances, i.e., robust scheduling emphasizes on the stability of scheduling schemes.

Scheduling: Scheduling concerns the allocation of limited resources to tasks over time, and is a decision-making process with the goal of optimizing one or more objectives.

Scheduling Scheme: Can be considered as a solution of a schedule problem.

Workflow: The automation of a business process, in whole or part, during which documents, information or tasks are passed from one participant to another for action, according to a set of procedural rules.

Chapter VII
Artificial Immune System in the Management of Complex Small Scale Cogeneration Systems

Fabio Freschi
Politecnico di Torino, Italy

Maurizio Repetto
Politecnico di Torino, Italy

ABSTRACT

The increasing cost of energy and the introduction of micro-generation facilities and the changes in energy production systems require new strategies to reach their optimal exploitation. Artificial Immune System (AIS) metaphor can be used to reach this aim. In this kind of management, the energy system can be seen as a living body which must react to external stimuli (cost of fuel, energy prices, fares, etc.) fulfilling its internal requirements (user loads, technical constraints, etc.). In this chapter, a developed procedure based on AIS is described and applied to this problem. Its performance is compared with the mixed integer linear programming on the same test. The result shows that AIS based method obtained better results, in terms of computational efficiency, compared with classical energy production management procedures based on Mixed Integer Linear Programming.

INTRODUCTION

Energy costs and concerns about its availability are an important issue at present. Recently, a growing interest in problems concerning energy distributed generation has emerged. This fact can be explained with two reasons: failures of centralized power grids with events of power delivery interruption, not always short, involving a large number of users (black-outs in USA and in Europe), and impact of energy market deregulation for industrial and civil uses. At the same time, the attention to a larger energy efficiency and to the environment contributes to the diffusion of renewable or combined energy sources to be used together with the energy furnished by the power stations connected to the grid has grown.

Copyright © 2009, IGI Global, distributing in print or electronic forms without written permission of IGI Global is prohibited.

At present, many American and European institutions (U. S. Department of Energy, 2000, 2001; EU, 2003) are suggesting the realization of small distributed energy networks, usually called micro-grids, aiming at supplying, partially or totally, a small number of users. Thus they are able to operate in grid connected and stand alone modes. Such a twofold possibility allows to be disconnected from the grid if power peaks requirements occur or, if an excess of energy is produced by the sources connected to the micro-grid, to sell this power to the network.

Designing and optimizing of the energy local network are quite different from those of the classical energy grid, because the micro grid includes both sources and loads, so it is active in nature. A large number of small or medium size generators are often present in the grid: this makes their intermitted working during the day possible.

Another problem occurring in the micro-grid design stage is the sizing and sitting of the generators with respect to the loads, in order to reduce transmission losses and improve the dynamic response of the grid with respect to load power requirements. Moreover, very often loads need both electric and thermal power, so that the micro-grid must be of Combined Heat and Power (CHP) type.

One of the main peculiarities of these networks is that it often combines production of electric with thermal energy using in a positive way. The thermal energy is wasted in the thermodynamic cycle for thermal loads both in domestic or industrials. Since heat cannot be efficiently moved over long distances, its source must be located close to the load. In order to meet the specific needs of loads, the following factors, including generators with different nominal powers, reliability and pollution levels, the presence of storage units in conjunction with fuel cells and super-capacitors, must be taken into account in the micro-grid. These devices must be optimally controlled. And they add more degrees of freedom in the micro grid management.

The high complexity of the micro grid structure, the heterogeneity of sources, loads and backup units require an advanced management system. The use of new network strategies, for instance, can accumulate part of the energy produced in a given time instant. It needs to be exploited when favorable cost/price conditions are needed. Experience has taught us that decision making procedures, driven by low standards criteria, can lead to sub-optimal solutions both on the energy and operational standpoint.

The aim of maximizing performance indicators can be pursued by putting at the heart of the system. An energy manager (Energy Management System, EMS) which can optimally manage power flows inside the system and toward an external energy network. This management must be carried out by considering in each instant, the satisfaction of load requests, prices/costs of energy, operational constraints of the power units and optimizing different indicators, such as minimizing costs, minimizing emissions, keeping each power unit work at its best.

The interest of the research community toward this kind of problems is testified by several publications (Lasseter, 2002; Lasseter & Paigi, 2004; Georgakis, Papathanassiou, Hatziargyriod, Engle, & Hardt, 2004, Hernandez-Aramburo, Green, & Mugniot, 2005).

In the literature, micro grids optimization often concerns sizing and sitting of distributed energy sources with respect to loads (Vallem, & Mitra, 2005; Mardaneh, & Gharehpetian, 2004; Carpinelli, Celli, Mocci, Pilo, & Russo, 2005; Celli, Ghiani, Mocci, & Pilo, 2005; Gandomkar, Vakilian, & Ehsan, 2005; El-Khattam, Bhattacharya, Hegazy, & Salama, 2004; El-Khattam, Hegazy, & Salama, 2005), but the system management is seldom faced. Heuristic software tools are often used for the optimization and work on a set of objective functions, including constraints expressing costs, reliability with respect to parametric uncertainties, probability of faults occurrence, distribution energy losses, voltage and power quality, harmonic distortion and so on. Simple analytic models of generators, transmission lines, storage units and loads are used to express objectives and constraints with respect to design parameters. The energy management problem of an energy system subjected to time-varying constraints is also interesting under the algorithmic point of view when it becomes the test field of different innovative optimization procedures.

In this state of the art, the use of innovative optimization algorithms can give an important boost to the energy system. AIS based procedures can be efficiently used in the solution of this problem. As testified by several decades of use of optimization algorithms (Michalewitz, 2002), their efficiency in problem solving comes by the algorithm itself but, more often, by its intimate integration with the problem under analysis.

In the following section, the AIS procedure is integrated with an energetic system analysis. The energy management aspect is taken into account, while planning of the energy site, its optimal adaptation to the size of the load is left to an external procedure. Due to this hypothesis, no investment costs are taken into account in this study. A more complete analysis of the method containing both planning and management phases can be found in (Canova, Cavallero, Freschi, Giaccone, Repetto, & Tartaglia, 2007).

Suitable and characteristic degrees of freedom of the energy system are defined and an analysis method to extract system performances complying with system technical constraints is designed. Afterwards, this forward analysis method is coupled with AIS procedure to drive the system management towards the minimization of system costs.

In order to assess the performance of the proposed procedure, another optimal management procedure based on classical deterministic mixed integer linear programming is implemented. The results of both optimization procedures are compared on an industrial test case and performances shows benefits of immune based management.

BACKGROUND

As stated in the introduction, the efficiency of energy production nodes is becoming more and more actual. One of the most promising way of reaching this objective is the use of combined production of electrical and thermal energy, usually called co-generation. In particular, starting from the fact that loads very often requires both electric and thermal power. The local system can be of Combined Heat and Power type.

The combined production of electric and thermal energy leads to the use, in a positive way, of the thermal energy which is usually wasted in the thermodynamic cycle. This energy can be efficiently employed to satisfy the requirements of thermal loads from both domestic and industrials. Since heat cannot be efficiently transferred to far away sites, its source must be located close to the load and thus this characteristic also requires that energy is produced in a distributed way all over the network.

The energy management of this system needs to take into account local loads and generators, with different nominal powers, marginal cost levels etc. and the possible presence of energy storage units. In addition, all these characteristics and requirements change with time, such as load profiles, price of energy bought from or sold to the electrical network etc.

An accurate scheduling of the system must ensure the use of the most economical power sources, fulfilling operational constraints and load demand. The management of the energy system requires the definition of the on/off status of the machines and the identification of their optimal production profile of them. When the start-up/shut-down profile is set, the problem can be approached by means of Linear Programming (LP), as it will be explained in detail in the next section.

The definition of the on/off status of the sources is referred to as scheduling and it requires the introduction of logical variables, which are defined in each time interval (e.g. one hour, one quarter of an hour etc.) the power source status. The complete problem must deal with both continuous (power levels) and integer (on/off status) variables.

This problem has been solved many times in the management of large power grids. Pang & Chen (1976) proposed a dynamic technique which managed the commitment of power utilities minimizing the total running cost of the system taking also into account several technical constraints. From this pioneer work, research activity stemmed and interest on this topic is still high, as testified, for instance, by the work of Bakirtzis, Ziogos, & Tellidou (2007) which, with similar mathematical techniques, deals with new technical problems coming out of the deregulation of energy markets.

In most of the classical approaches to unit commitment, the problem is stated as a Mixed Integer Linear Programming problem (MILP) (Arroyo, & Conejo, 2000). Even if this approach guarantees to find out the global minimum of the cost function, the use of MILP needs the application of branch-and-bound techniques, whose computational cost exponentially increases with the number of branches.

Instead of a full LP approach, some of the authors of this chapter have proposed (Carpaneto, Freschi, & Repetto, 2005) an heuristic optimization algorithm used to define the on/off status of the power sources, leaving to an inner LP module the optimization of a particular configuration. An AIS algorithm can be efficiently employed in this phase and its use is shown to be quite efficient if all operational constraints are embedded inside the scheduling

Figure 1. Outline of the CHP system

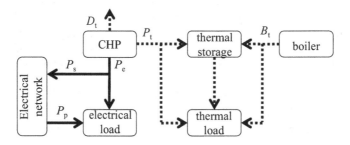

interval definition. In the following chapter the mathematical definition of the problem will be highlighted.

CLASSICAL FORMULATION OF THE ENERGY MANAGEMENT PROBLEM IN COMPLEX ENERGY NODES

A complex energy node is made up of different modules both of generation and user type. In this chapter an idealized energy node is considered: even if this structure is not referring to a specific installation, all the most important components are here considered.

The main module is the CHP, that is, the machine can produce electrical power and useful heat for industrial or domestic uses at the same time. From the technological viewpoint, this machine can be a micro-turbine or an internal combustion engine. These machines can be fed by both natural gas and oil as primary fuel. While these machines are frequently used at the micro-generation level (rated power lower than some megawatts) and on larger power scale, steam turbines should be used. An energy management system cannot neglect technical constraints associated to the CHP. These constraints are mostly related to "good practice" rules and prevent EMS from making unnecessary maneuvers on machines, for instance, repeated starting and switching off of the generator stress the systems and increase the need for maintenance.

If generators are the heart of the energy node, then user loads determine the way of running the system. User loads, both electrical and thermal, are function of the kind of installation with which energy node is associated. For instance, hospitals, commercial centers, office or residential buildings have different energy requirements. And the energy node must, as primary functioning constraint, supply load requirements.

Besides generation and load, energy storage systems are important components of energy node. By accumulating energy produced at a given instant for later use, they allow a decoupling of generation and load, for instance, increasing electrical power production during peak hours, when selling electrical power to the grid is economically convenient, and using thermal power in evening hours when it is required for heating purposes.

The energy node not only must handle load requirements but also take advantage by energy prices changing through the hours of the day. Since deregulation of electrical networks, energy market rules the exchanges of electrical power on the grid. Different levels of power demand change energy price which is usually higher during the day and lower during the night when electrical power request is mainly of industrial type running on a whole day production basis. This dynamical price system must be taken into account by EMS in order to maximize revenues from the running of the system.

Starting from this preliminary assumption, a system containing all the relevant issues is defined. The outline of the system under study is represented in Figure 1, where:

- P_e is the electrical power produced by the CHP;
- P_t is the thermal power produced by the CHP;
- B_t is the heat produced by a boiler which fulfils the thermal load when production of electric power is neither needed nor economically convenient;

- D_t is the heat produced in the thermodynamic cycle which is not used by the thermal load and it is thus released into the atmosphere;
- P_p and P_s are the electrical power purchased from or sold to the external network respectively;
- S_t is the stored thermal energy;
- U_e and U_t are the electrical and thermal power required by the load.

In each time interval (i), thermal and electrical power of a CHP are linked by a linear relation, such as:

$$P_t(i) = k_t P_e(i) \tag{1}$$

The energy management problem of the CHP system regards the definition of the best arrangement of production levels of the power unit to minimize the management costs and fulfilling all loads requirements. The problem is defined over a scheduling period (e.g. one day, one week etc.) where loads, costs, fares etc. can change. The scheduling period is subdivided in $N_{intervals}$ time intervals of length Δt. During each interval all CHP characteristics and load data are assumed to be constant.

Besides plant data, some operational constraints have to be imposed on the power source like:

- Minimum On Time (MOT): minimum time interval during which CHP must be on when it is switched on;
- Minimum Shut-down time (MST): minimum time interval which CHP must be off since it was turned off;
- Maximum ramp rate: maximum power rate of the source.

The unit production costs of the node, expressed in €/kWh, are:

- c_e: cost coefficient of electric energy produced by the CHP;
- c_t: cost coefficient of thermal energy produced by the boiler;
- $c_p(i)$, $c_s(i)$: prices of purchased and sold energy at ith time interval.

By using the previous definitions it is possible to write a global cost function (in €) over the scheduling period

$$f_{CHP} = \sum_{i=1}^{N_{intrvals}} \left(c_e P_e(i) + c_t B_t(i) - c_{si} P_s(i) + c_{pi} P_p(i) \right) \tag{2}$$

The optimization problem can be stated as

$$\min f_{CHP} \tag{3}$$

subject to operational constraints electrical balance:

$$P_e(i) + P_p(i) - P_s(i) = U_e(i) \tag{4}$$

thermal balance:

$$P_t(i) + B_t(i) - D_t(i) + \frac{S_t(i-1) - S_t(i)}{\Delta t} = U_t(i) \tag{5}$$

dissipation of thermal power produced by CHP:

$$D_t(i) - P_t(i) \le 0 \tag{6}$$

thermal and electrical CHP characteristic (1):

$$k_t P_e(i) - P_t(i) = 0 \tag{7}$$

MOT, MST and ramp limit satisfaction.
Variables are bounded by their upper and lower bounds.

$$P_e^{\min} \le P_e(i) \le P_e^{\max},$$
$$0 \le B_t(i) \le P_t^{\max} t,$$
$$0 \le P_s(i),$$
$$0 \le P_p(i),$$
$$0 \le D_t(i),$$
$$0 \le S_t(i) \le S_t^{\max}. \tag{8}$$

The first bound comes out of the technological limits on real machines where produced power cannot be lower than a prescribed limit, usually around 50% of maximum power. Obviously, this constraint does not hold during the starting-up and shutting-down phases.

MIXED INTEGER SCHEDULING APPROACH

The scheduling problem can be directly formulated as a MILP (Arroyo, & Conejo, 2000; Gomez-Villalva, & Ramos, 2003). It means that the problem is still linear, but its variables are continuous and integer. This class of problems can be solved by exact methods like Branch and Bound technique (Wolsey, & Nemhauser, 1999). The MILP approach requires defining the on/off status of the CHP as a logical variable $\delta(i)$ defined for all ith time intervals. Moreover, two additional sets of logical variables must be considered to take into account MOT/MST constraints and up/down ramps (Carpaneto, Freschi & Repetto, 2005) (see Figure 2)

$$y(i) = \begin{cases} 1 \text{ if CHP turns on at } i\text{th time interval} \\ 0 \text{ otherwise} \end{cases} \tag{9}$$

$$z(i) = \begin{cases} 1 \text{ if CHP turns off at } i\text{th time interval} \\ 0 \text{ otherwise} \end{cases} \tag{10}$$

The complexity of the problem depends on time discretization, because the finer the discretization, the higher the number of integer variables is. The model of ramp limits, MOT and MST introduce several additional constraints which must be explicitly added to the model. In (Arroyo, & Conejo, 2004) it is shown that it is possible to model start-up and shut-down power trajectories with eleven constraints. Finally, it is common to define an upper limit to the number of turns on and off during the scheduling period $N_{on} = N_{off} = N_{change}$

$$\sum_{i=1}^{N_I ntervals} y(i) \le N_{change}$$

$$\sum_{i=1}^{N_{ntervalsI}} z(i) \le N_{change} \tag{11}$$

Figure 2. On/off status of generator and its logical state variables δ, y and z

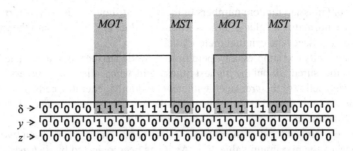

Figure 3. opt-aiNet flowchart

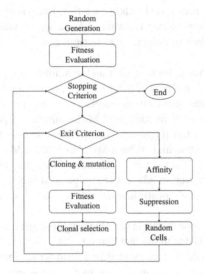

For instance, for a one-day scheduling period with the CHP in one day, and $N_{on} = N_{off} = 1$, this means that CHP can be turned on and off just once.

IMMUNE SCHEDULING APPROACH

The proposed immune scheduling method is based on the opt-aiNet version (de Castro, & Timmis, 2002) of the clonal selection algorithm. It combines artificial immune system with linear programming. It is named artificial immune system-linear programming (AIS-LP) in later section.

The algorithm has two nested loops (Figure 3). In the inner loop, two operators are applied to the population: cloning & mutation and clonal selection. The individuals of the previous iteration, called memory cells, are reproduced in N_{clones} copies of the original. Then, each clone is locally mutated by a random perturbation, in order to find a high-affinity (high-fitness) cell. The amplitude of mutation decreases when the fitness of the original memory cell increases, according to (12) (de Castro, & Timmis, 2002)

$$\mathbf{x}_{new} = \mathbf{x}_{old} + \alpha \mathbf{x}_{random}$$
$$\alpha = \sigma \exp(-f*) \tag{12}$$

where $\mathbf{x}_{random}$ is a vector of Gaussian random numbers of mean 0 and standard deviation 1, σ is a parameter normally set to 0.01, $f*$ is the normalized value of fitness from the values $[f_{min}, f_{max}]$ into the range [0,1]. The best mutated clone for each cell replaces the original memory cell.

In the outer cycle, the affinity and suppression operators are applied to the population. The Euclidean distance between memory cells is measured; all but the highest fitness cells whose distances are less than a threshold are suppressed. The suppressed cells are then replaced with new randomly generated cells. In order to maintain the diversity of solutions and to obtain a good exploration of the space of the parameters, at each iteration, a minimum number of new cells is guaranteed.

Both loops finish if the average fitness of the memory cells does not improve between two iterations or if the number of iterations reaches the maximum value N_{max}. As it has been reported by de Castro, & Timmis (2002) "evolution in the immune system occurs within the organism and, thus it can be viewed as a micro-evolutionary process". For what concerns a comparison with GA, it can be said that the key interest in diversity is implemented directly within the basic algorithm and it is not introduced as an upgrade like in GA.

The optimization procedure AIS-LP is divided into two nested stages: the inner one is the LP problem derived in section 2, which defines the optimal production levels at each time interval once the on/off profiles are defined. The outer stage is responsible for defining the on/off status of the generation units.

It is useful to use degrees of freedom of optimizing the time amplitudes of the on and off intervals τ_j of the CHP (Figure 4).

These values are treated as integer variables representing the number of on and off intervals of each control period. The variables are then decoded in terms of 0-1 strings representing, for each utility, its on/off status. This assumption drastically simplifies the optimization search. The number of available solutions is in fact equal to M^N, where N is the number of degrees of freedom and M the number of possible values assumed by each variable. A fine discretization does not affect the number of variables but only their range of values M, thus the overall complexity of the problem is polynomial. With a MILP approach, M is always equal to 2, because the problem is modeled by binary variables. The time discretization affects the value of N, giving rise to an exponential complexity of the problem. Moreover, in AIS-LP, the value of M is restricted when including MOT/MST constraints. Thus the modeling of technical constraints reduces the search space and converges to the optimal solution faster (Table 1).

The definition of on/off intervals τ as optimization variables requires using an optimization algorithm without complex operators. This consideration is due to the fact that it is not easy to keep the feasibility of solutions.

In the present case, mutation operator is implemented in a form which implicitly satisfies the feasibility of solution, that is if ith interval τ_i is increased of an interval Δ, its following interval amplitude τ_{i+1} is decreased of the same quantity. Particular cases of intervals of null amplitude are handled by dynamically reducing the number of intervals. For the same reason, algorithms requiring binary operators, like crossover and recombination, such as Genetic Algorithm and Evolution Strategy must be excluded a priori. The AIS has the advantage of using the mutation operator, and its memory capability will be exploited in future work to handle the time varying scenarios in real time optimization. The performances of AIS-LP can be enhanced by using problem-specific information:

- creation of feasible initial population which satisfies the equality constraints;
- modified mutation operator to generate feasible-only clones.

For these reasons, some immune operators must be customized to solve the specific problem. Particularly, the mutation operator is not related to the actual fitness of the parent cell. Algorithms 1 relative to the generation of the first completely random generation and Algorithm 2 relevant to the generation of mutated configurations automatically complying with time-line constraints are reported in form of pseudo codes.

The use of problem-specific information drastically decreases the dimension of the search space (Carpaneto, Freschi, & Repetto, 2005), making the AIS-LP approach more suited for high dimensional or fine discrete pro-

Figure 4. Translation of logical states in on and off time intervals τ_1, τ_2, τ_3, τ_4

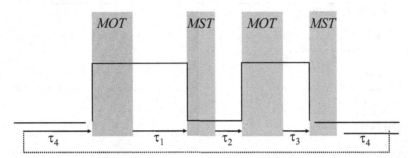

Table 1. Number of available configurations for two time discretizations

	$\Delta t = 1$ hour		$\Delta t = 0.25$ hour	
	MILP	AIS-LP	MILP	AIS-LP
M	2	24	2	96
N	24	2	96	2
M^N	16.8×10^6	576	79.2×10^{27}	9216

blems. Similar conclusions are drawn also by other researchers working on genetic algorithm. It can be found in (Deb, Reddy, & Singh, 2003).

EXPERIMENTAL RESULTS

MILP and AIS-LP are tested on a simple but effective energy management problem. The structure of the CHP node is the one of Figure 1; the operational data of the devices are reported in Table 1. The thermal storage unit is considered to have a maximum capacity of 300 kWh. Energy price profiles during one regular week day are shown in Figure 5.

Several scheduling instances are solved with a quarter of hour time sampling ($\Delta t = 0.25$ hours), thus a one day scheduling period has $N_{\text{intervals}} = 96$, two days scheduling $N_{\text{intervals}} = 192$ etc. Results are compared in terms of convergence time and number of objective function calls. It must be remarked that a comparison in terms of the mere number of objective function calls can be misleading because the linear problem solved by MILP and AIS-LP are different. These differences can be explained by noting that the number of variables, number of constraints and number of non zero elements in coefficients matrix are not the same for two formulations. The main differences in the LP formulation between AIS-LP and MILP are summarized in Table 3. The larger MILP model is due to the fact that operational constraints (ramp limits and MOT and MST constraints) have to be taken into account directly in the linear model whereas AIS-LP approach manage these limits in the external loop, as described in Section 4. In Figure 6, an example of a branch and bound tree obtained by the commercial software Xpress-Optimizer (Dash, 2008) is reported.

The parameter setting of AIS-LP is:

population cardinality: 10;
number of clones: 5;
number of inner iterations: 5;
convergence criterion: the search ends if the objective function value does not improve for more than ten external generations.

Algorithm 1 New cells generation

1: **for all** newcells **do**
2:     $sum \leftarrow 0$
3:     **for** $i \leftarrow 1, N_{\text{intervals}}$ **do**   ▷ Random initialization
4:         $cell(i) \leftarrow \text{random}()$
5:         $sum = sum + cell(i)$
6:     **end for**
7:     **for** $i \leftarrow 1, N_{\text{intervals}}$ **do**   ▷ Normalization and interization
8:         $cell(i) \leftarrow \text{INT}(N_{\text{free}} \times cell(i)/sum)$
9:     **end for**
10: **end for**

Algorithm 2 Mutation

1: **for all** clones **do**
2:     **for** $i \leftarrow 1, N_{\text{intervals}}$ **do**
3:         $mutaz(i) \leftarrow \text{random}()$
4:         **if** $0 \leq mutaz(i) \leq 1/3$ **then** $mutaz(i) \leftarrow -1$
5:         **if** $1/3 \leq mutaz(i) \leq 2/3$ **then** $mutaz(i) \leftarrow 1$
6:         **if** $2/3 \leq mutaz(i) \leq 1$ **then** $mutaz(i) \leftarrow 0$
7:     **end for**
8:     **for** $i \leftarrow 1, N_{\text{intervals}}$ **do**
9:         $clone(i) = parent(i) + mutaz(i) - mutaz(i-1)$ ▷ Feasible mutation
10:         **if** $clone(i) \leq xlow(i)$ **then**   ▷ Fix mutation to the lower bound
11:             $clone(i) \leftarrow xlow(i)$
12:             $mutaz(i) \leftarrow 0$
13:         **end if**
14:         **if** $clone(i) \geq xup(i)$ **then**   ▷ Fix mutation to the upper bound
15:             $clone(i) \leftarrow xup(i)$
16:             $mutaz(i) \leftarrow 0$
17:         **end if**
18:     **end for**
19: **end for**

Table 2. Main operational data used in the test case

	P_{min}	P_{max}	MOT	MST	Ramp limit
	kW	kW	hour	hour	kW/hour
CHP	200	600	5	4	170
Boiler	0	800	none	none	none

A study on the effects of these values on results accuracy and on convergence has been described in (Freschi, Carpaneto, & Repetto, 2005). Results are averaged on 10 independent runs to take into account the statistical variation of performances due to the stochastic nature of the algorithm.

DISCUSSION

In Figure 7 MILP and AIS-LP are compared with respect to the computational time (in seconds) to converge to the optimal value on a Pentium IV 2.8 GHz. These data are displayed versus dimension of problem, represented by the value of $N_{intervals}$.

Figure 5. Energy price profiles

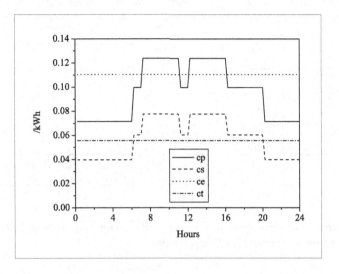

Figure 6. Branch and Bound tree obtained with Xpress-Optimizer software

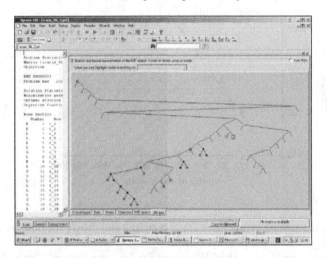

Figure 7 shows two important properties. Firstly, there is a crossing point between the two curves of MILP and AIS-LP. This fact leads to the consideration that the computational time of MILP approach becomes impracticable for large instances, i.e. for fine discretization and/or long period managements.

Secondly, by analyzing each curve, it is possible to find that MILP has an exponential dependence of the computational time on the cardinality of the problem, while AIS-LP has a quadratic rule.

The previous considerations are confirmed by the analysis of Figure 8 which shows the number of LP problems solved by the two techniques. In this case, the number of LP problem is linearly dependent on the cardinality of the problem. It is also worth noting that the solutions found by AIS-LP and MILP models share the same objective function values, or are slightly different. This fact shows that AIS-LP procedure converges to the exact solution.

Figure 9 shows the electrical, thermal power and energy storage profiles of a one day scheduling. The following remarks can be made:

Table 3. Comparison of dimensions of different LP problems (N_{MOT}: number of minimum on time intervals, N_{MST}: number of minimum shutdown time intervals, N_{up} : number of time intervals needed to reach P_{min} during start-up phases, N_{dw} : number of time intervals needed to reach zero power during shut-down phases)

	AIS-LP	MILP
Nr. of constraints	$6N_{intervals}$	$21N_{intervals}+2$
Nr. of variables	$7N_{intervals}$	$10N_{intervals}$
Matrix elements	$35N_{intervals}^2$	$210N_{intervals}^2$
Non zeros	$14N_{intervals}$	$(48+N_{MOT}+N_{MST}+8N_{dw}+8N_{up})N_{intervals}$

Figure 7. Computational time of the two procedures versus number of time intervals. AIS-LP computational time has a quadratic dependence on the cardinality of the problem.

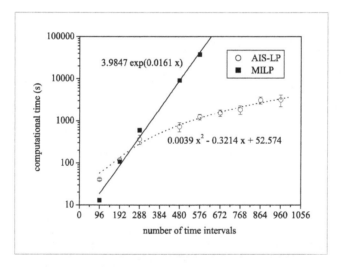

the CHP starts early in the morning in order to store heat energy and satisfy the first thermal load peak of the day. Excess electrical power is sold to the external network;

the electrical load is always supplied by the CHP except for few time intervals; by looking at Figure 9 it is possible to note that CHP production never follows thermal load. This fact is explained by the role of thermal storage;

the boiler is requested to produce thermal power only during night hours, when the CHP electrical production is neither needed nor economical;

during night hours, thermal storage reaches its upper limit for some time intervals. This fact means that the possibility of storing more thermal energy would be useful to reduce costs.

The effectiveness of the optimal scheduling is evidenced by referring the optimal objective function to the cost of a non cogeneration system, where the electrical load is supplied by the external network and the thermal power is produced by the boiler only. In this case

Figure 8. Number of objective function calls of the two procedures versus number of time intervals. The number of LP problems solved by AIS-LP is linearly dependent on time discretization.

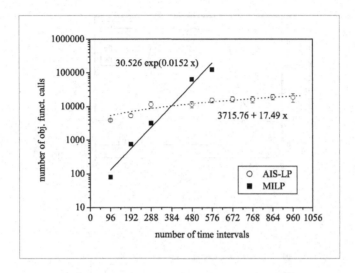

$$f_{conventional} = \sum_{i=1}^{N_{intervals}} \left[c_p(i)U_e(i) + c_t U_t(i) \right]$$

$$f_{\%} = \frac{f_{CHP}}{f_{conventional}} 100 \tag{13}$$

The one day scheduling allows saving money of about 34% ($f_{\%} = 66\%$)

FUTURE RESEARCH DIRECTIONS

There are some further research directions on this particular topic, as follows:

- on one side, the method will be applied to the on-line management of cogeneration system that will be implemented in the frame of different research projects funded by European Community (Polycity, 2006, Hegel 2006);
- on the other side, the application of optimization algorithms to multi-objective energy management problems is foreseen. In fact, not only does the energy management problem require minimizing the economic revenue from a plant, but also taking into account several other issues such as environmental impact, reliability, etc. In the case of immune algorithm, it seems to be suited to the specific task.

More in general, the substitution of deterministic procedures with stochastic one is a common feature with other engineering problems that will be continued.

Figure 9. Daily profiles of electrical and thermal power and of stored thermal energy: (a) electrical power, (b) thermal power, (c) thermal storage

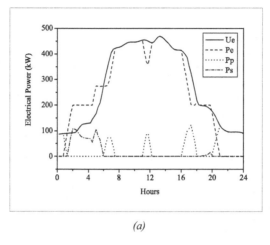

(a)

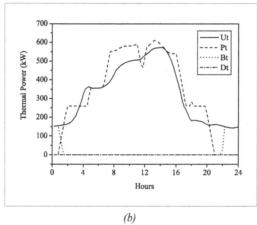

(b)

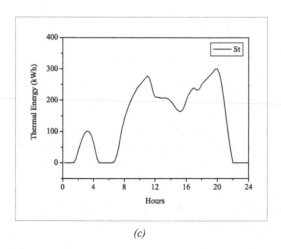

(c)

CONCLUSION

The increasing complexity of energy networks makes their management always more difficult. The satisfaction of user, technical constraints, dynamics required by evolution of energy prices and costs make the deterministic enumeration of the whole set of possibilities impossible to perform. The computational cost of MILP techniques is unbearable when the dimension of the problem becomes large. Thus, the management strategy moves from deterministic management to stochastic approximated one, which is able to deal with the problem in polynomial time.

The proposed method AIS-LP shows that AIS can efficiently solve this problem. In particular, the application of immune algorithm to the energy management problem has allowed highlighting some useful characteristics of this metaphor. In particular:

a suitable translation of technical constraints in a particular mutation operator has allowed to reduce the number of degrees of freedom of the optimization;

the intrinsic mutation operator in AIS algorithm which does not require any other way to generate new individuals with more than one configuration involved (like cross-over in Genetic Algorithm) is efficient in the search for the optimal configuration;

the energy production system is able to react to external stimuli, such as energy prices/cost keeping all user loads satisfied, or a biological being which reacts to external attacks trying to preserve its life functions.

REFERENCES

Arroyo, J. M., & Conejo, A. J. (2000). Optimal Response of a Thermal Unit to an electricity Spot Market. IEEE Transaction on Power Systems, 15(3), 1098-1104.

Arroyo, J. M., & Conejo, A. J. (2004). Modeling of Start-up and Shout-down Power Trajectories of Themal Units. IEEE Transaction on Power Systems, 19(3), 1562-1568.

Bakirtzis, A., Ziogos, N., & Tellidou, G. (2007). Electricity Producer Offering Strategies in Day-Ahead Energy Market With Step-Wise Offers. IEEE Transaction on Power Systems, 22(4), 1804-1818.

Caire, R., Retiere, N., Morin, E., Fontela, M., & Hadjsaid, N. (2003). Voltage management of distributed generation in distribution networks. In IEEE Power Engineering Society General Meeting, 1, 282-287..

Caldon, A. T. R. (2004). Optimisation algorithm for a virtual power plant operation. In 39th International Universities Power Engineering Conference, 3,1058-1062.

Canova, A., Cavallero, C., Freschi, F., Giaccone, L., Repetto, M., & Tartaglia, M. (2007). Comparative Economical Analysis of a Small Scale Trigenerative plant: A Case Study. In Conference Record of IEEE 42nd IAS Annual Meeting (pp. 1456-1459).

Carpaneto, E., Freschi, F., & Repetto, M. (2005). Two stage optimization of a single CHP node. In Symposium on Power Systems with Dispersed Generation: Technologies, Impacts on Development, Operation and Performances.

Carpinelli, G., Celli, G., Mocci, S., Pilo, F., & Russo, A. (2005). Optimisation of embedded generation sizing and siting by using a double trade-off method. IEE Proceedings-Generation, Transmission and Distribution, 152(4), 503-513.

Celli, G., Ghiani, E., Mocci, S., & Pilo, F. (2005). A multiobjective evolutionary algorithm for the sizing and siting of distributed generation. IEEE Transactions on Power Systems, 20(2), 750-757.

Dash (2008). Xpress [computer software]. http://www.dashoptimization.com.

de Castro, L. N., & Timmis, J. (2002). An Artificial Immune Network for Multimodal Function Optimization. In Congress on Evolutionary Computation, 1, 699-704.

Deb, K., Reddy, A., & Singh, G. (2003). Optimal scheduling of casting sequences using genetic algorithms. Journal of Materials and Manufacturing Processes 18(3), 409-432.

El-Khattam, W., Bhattacharya, K., Hegazy, Y., & Salama, M. M. A. (2004). Optimal investment planning for distributed generation in a competitive electricity market. IEEE Transactions on Power Systems, 19(3), 1674-1684.

El-Khattam, W., Hegazy, Y. G., & Salama, M. M. A. (2005). An integrated distributed generation optimization model for distribution system planning. IEEE Transactions on Power Systems, 20(2), 1158-1165.

EU (2003). Directive 2003/54/Ec of the European Parliament and of the Council of 26 June 2003 concerning common rules for the internal market in electricity and repealing Directive 96/92/EC, Retrieved February 11, 2008, from http://eur-lex.europa.eu/en/index.htm.

Freschi, F., Carpaneto, E., & Repetto, M. (2005). Application of a Double Stage Optimization to Integrated Energy Management In 22nd IFIP TC 7 Conference on System Modeling and Optimization (pp. 30).

Gandomkar, M., Vakilian, M. & Ehsan, M. (2005). Optimal Distributed Generation Allocation in Distribution Network Using Hereford Ranch Algorithm. In 8th International Conference on Electrical Machines and Systems, 2, 916-918.

Georgakis, D., Papathanassiou, S., Hatziargyriod, N., Engle, A., & Hardt, C. (2004). Operation of a prototype microgrid system based on micro-sources quipped with fast-acting power electronics interfaces. In 35th Annual IEEE Power Electronics Specialists Conference, 4 2521-2526.

Gomez-Villalva, E., & Ramos, A. (2003). Optimal energy management of an industrial consumer in liberalized markets. IEEE Transactions on Power Systems, 18(2), 716-723.

Hegel (2006). Official website of the EU sponsored research Project HEGEL, Retrieved February 11, 2008, from http://www.hegelproject.eu.

Hernandez-Aramburo, C. A., Green, T. C. & Mugniot, N. (2005). Fuel Consumption Minimization of a Microgrid. IEEE Transaction on Industry Applications, 41(3), 673-681.

Lasseter, R. H. (2002). Microgrids. In IEEE Power Engineering Society Winter Meeting, 1, 305-308).

Lasseter, R. H., & Paigi, P. (2004). Microgrid: A Conceptual Solution. In 35th Annual IEEE Power Electronics Specialists Conference, 6,4285-4290.

Lasseter, R., Akhil, A., Marnay, C., Stephens, J., Dagle, J., & Guttromson, R., et al. (2002). The CERTS MicroGrid concept. Retrieved February 11, 2008, from http://certs.lbl.gov/certs-der-micro.html.

Mardaneh, M., & Gharehpetian, G. B. (2004). Siting and sizing of DG units using GA and OPF based technique. In IEEE Region 10 Conference, 3, 331-334.

Michalewicz, Z. (2002). Genetic algorithms + data structure = evolution programs. New York, NY, USA: Springer-Verlag.

Nehrir, H., Caisheng, W., & Shaw, S. R. (2006). Fuel cells: promising devices for distributed generation. IEEE Power and Energy Magazine, 4(1), 47-53.

Pang, C. K., & Chen, H. C. (1976). Optimal short-term thermal unit commitment. IEEE Transaction on Power Apparatus and Systems, 95(4), 1336-1346.

Polycity (2006). Official website of the EU sponsored research Project Polycity, Retrieved February 11, 2008, from http://www.polycity.net.

Sedghisigarchi, A. (2006). Impact of Fuel Cells on Load-Frequency Control in Power Distribution Systems. IEEE Transactions on Energy Conversion, 21(1), 250-256.

U. S. Department of Energy, (2000). Strategic Plan for Distributed Energy Resources.

U. S. Department of Energy, (2001). Transmission Reliability Multi-Year Program Plan FY2001-2005.

Vallem, M., & Mitra, J. (2005). Siting and sizing of distributed generation for optimal microgrid architecture. In 37th Annual North American Power Symposium (pp. 611-616).

Wolsey, L. A., & Nemhauser, G. L. (1999). Integer and Combinatorial Optimization. New York, NY, USA: Wiley-Interscience.

KEY TERMS

Cogeneration: Cogeneration is the production of electricity and useful thermal energy simultaneously from a common fuel source. The rejected heat from industrial processes can be used to power an electric generator. Surplus heat from an electric generator can be used for industrial processes, or for heating purposes.

Combined Heat and Power (CHP) Generation: Combined Heat and Power (CHP) is a highly fuel-efficient energy technology, which puts to use waste heat produced as a by-product of the electricity generation process. CHP can increase the overall efficiency of fuel utilization to more than 75% Gross Calorific Value – compared with around 40% achieved by fossil fuel electricity generation plants in operation today, and up to 50% from modern Combined Cycle Gas Turbines – and has the potential to save substantially on energy bills. CHP is the simultaneous generation of usable heat and power (usually electricity) in a single process. Most new CHP schemes use natural gas, but a significant proportion burn alternative, renewable fuels and some, such as those bio-fuels that are suitable for use, qualify for additional support (e.g. under the Renewable Obligation). CHP is not only more efficient through utilization of heat, but it also avoids transmission and distribution losses and can provide important network services such as "black start", improvements to power quality, and the ability to operate in "island mode" if the distribution network goes down.

Distributed Generation: Distributed Generation (DG) is a new trend in electric power generation. The basic concept sees an electricity "consumer", who is generating electricity for his/her own needs, to send surplus electrical power back into the power grid. An example of DG are factories, offices and especially hospitals which require extremely reliable sources of electricity and heating for air conditioning and hot water. To safeguard their supply and reduce costs, some have installed cogeneration or CHP facilities, often using waste material, such as wood waste, or surplus heat from an industrial process to generate electricity. In some cases electricity is generated from a locally supplied fuel such as natural gas or diesel oil and the waste heat from the generator's thermal energy source is then used to provide hot water and industrial heating as well. It is often economic to have a co-generation plant when an industrial process requires large amounts of heat that are generated from non-electric sources such as fossil fuels or biomass.

Energy Management System (EMS): An energy management system is usually a collection of computer-aided tools used by operators of electric facilities to monitor, control, and optimize the performance of the generation and/or transmission system. Different computer aided tools are implemented from short time control modules to scheduling or commitment of power production units on a day/week basis. EMS has the objective of maximizing system performances by monitoring and control functions which require a centralized system of data collection and a decision making procedure.

Minimum On Time (MOT) Constraint: Minimum on time constraint is the minimum time interval during which CHP must be on when it is switched on. This constraint is set because the switching on of the machine has some costs on its own and so it is justified only if the working time interval is sufficiently long. In addition, some technologies, like micro-turbines of aeronautical derivation, have a limited number of switching on before maintenance must be applied.

Minimum Shutdown Time (MST) Constraint: Minimum on shutdown constraint is the minimum time interval which CHP must be off since it was turned off (see *Minimum On Time (MOT) constraint*).

Primary Fuel Cost: The cost of fuel used by the primal engine moving the electrical generator. Usually this fuel is natural gas but could be also oil. The fuel cost is taken into account inside the production cost coefficient and it is expressed in €/kWh or $/kWh.

Ramp Limit Constraint: Inner dynamics of power generator does not always allow to change instantaneously power production level and so a maximum rate of change of produced power must be set. Usually generators with larger rated power have more strict ramp limits.

Selling and Purchasing Energy Costs: Electrical energy is exchanged with the power grid, operated by an external utility, with different purchasing and selling costs set by Authorities and Facilities. Due to the different request of electrical power by user, these cost coefficients, expressed in €/kWh or $/kWh, are changing through the day and during the week. Dynamics of energy costs is ruled by free energy market which originated by de-regulation process started during '90s.

Section I.IV
Artificial Immune System and Data Processing

Data processing is a general concept here. Artificial immune systems had been designed to process data for different aims, such as data clustering in machine learning. In this section, immune network algorithm and clonal selection algorithm are used for document clustering and feature selection respectively. They are the important data processing step of data mining and pattern reorganization respectively.

Chapter VIII
Applying the Immunological Network Concept to Clustering Document Collections

Krzysztof Ciesielski
Polish Academy of Sciences, Poland

Mieczysław A. Kłopotek
Polish Academy of Sciences, Poland

Sławomir T. Wierzchoń
Polish Academy of Sciences, Poland & University of Gdańsk, Poland

ABSTRACT

In this chapter the authors discuss an application of an immune-based algorithm for extraction and visualization of clusters structure in large collection of documents. Particularly a hierarchical, topic-sensitive approach is proposed; it appears to be a robust solution, both in terms of time and space complexity, to the problem of scalability of document map generation process. The approach relies upon extraction of a hierarchy of concepts, that is almost homogenous groups of documents described by unique sets of terms. To represent the content of each context a modified version the aiNet algorithm is employed; it was chosen because of its flexibility in representing natural clusters existing in a training set. To fasten the learning phase, a smart method of initialization of the immune memory was proposed as well as further modifications of the entire algorithm were introduced. Careful evaluation of the effectiveness of the novel text clustering procedure is presented in section reporting experiments.

1. INTRODUCTION

Information retrieval is a topic devoted to developing tools providing fast and efficient access to unstructured information in various corporate, scientific and governmental domains, consult e.g. (Manning, Raghavan, & Schütze, 2008). Recent attempts to explain and to model information seeking behavior in humans compare it

Copyright © 2009, IGI Global, distributing in print or electronic forms without written permission of IGI Global is prohibited.

to food searching activity performed by the animals. A fusion of the optimal foraging theory (developed in the frames of ecological biology) with theories of human cognition resulted in so-called information foraging theory proposed to understand how strategies and technologies for information seeking are (and should be) adapted to a user's information needs (Pirolli, 2007). One of the most intriguing observations done within this theory is that seeking information, humans follow so-called information scent. If the scent is sufficiently strong, a user will continue to go on that trail, but if the scent is weak, he/she goes back until another satisfactory trace will appear. This process, called three-click rule (Barker, 2005), is repeated usually until the user will be satisfied. If so, Web pages should be equipped with sufficiently strong information scent. This is a lesson for home page designers. Another problem is how to present the content of the home pages, and in general the content of Web resources, to the users with different information needs. `WebBook` and `WebForager` are examples of how to implement in an interactive visualization the theories of information foraging (Card, Robertson & York, 1996). Both these systems try to visualize the content of the WWW in a smart way by using the concepts of clustering (i.e. grouping) and visualization of huge collection of data.

The idea of grouping documents takes its roots in so-called Cluster Hypothesis (Rijsbergen, 1979) according to which relevant documents tend to be highly similar to each other (and therefore tend to appear in the same clusters). Thus, it is possible to reduce the number of documents that need to be compared to a given query, as it suffices to match the query against cluster representatives first. In case of documents collections pertaining different themes one can imagine a hierarchical clustering, according to which we identify rough categories first and next we refine these categories into sub-categories, sub-sub-categories, and so-on. However such an approach offers only technical improvement in searching relevant documents, as we obtain something like "nested index" representing the content of the whole collection.

A more radical solution can be gained by using so-called document maps, (Becks, 2001), where a graphical representation allows to convey information about the relationships of individual documents or group of documents. This way, apart of clusters presentation, we gain additional "dimension": visualization of a certain similarity among the documents. The well-known representative of such formalism is `WEBSOM` – a system for organizing collection of text documents onto meaningful maps for exploration and search[1] (Kohonen et al., 2000). The system uses Kohonen's (2001) `SOM` (Self-Organizing Map) algorithm that automatically organizes the documents onto a two-dimensional grid so that related documents appear close to each other. Although it allows analyzing collections of up to one million documents, its main drawback are large time and space complexity what raises questions of scaling and updating of document maps.

The problem of document map creation is closely related to Web mining activity (Chakrabarti, 2002). Its nature can be characterized as extracting nontrivial, previously unknown, and potentially useful information from a given set of Web sites. Document maps are developed in the framework of Information Visualization, or IV for brevity – a process that "aims at an interactive visualization of abstract non-spatial phenomena such as bibliographic data sets, web access patterns, etc.", (Börner, Chen & Boyack, 2003). The principal idea in IV relies upon displaying inter-document similarity by representing the entire documents collection as 2-dimensional points on a plane in such a way that the relative distance between the points represents similarity between the corresponding documents[2].

Observed advances of information visualization were significantly driven by IR research. A central problem for IR researchers and practitioners is how to improve the efficiency and effectiveness of the entire retrieval process. It is trivial to say that the more a user knows about his/her search space, the more likely that his or her search will become more effective. The IV systems are oriented towards user friendly representation of the overall semantic structure of a collection of documents. Such a structural visualization is exploited by the users to satisfy their information needs.

Aside from of competitive learning methods, like `SOM` or `GNG` (Fritzke, 1995) used in IV systems supporting information retrieval other learning paradigms are employed, particularly that one based on immune metaphor (de Castro and Timmis, 2002). Immune-based algorithms join, at least conceptually, evolutionary mechanisms together with self-organization. Hence they can be viewed as multi-agent systems designed to solve cooperatively complex tasks. In this paper, we study a clustering immune-based algorithm to the problems of information extraction and visualization.

The chapter is organized as follows: document maps are briefly reviewed in Section 2. And in Section 3, our original idea of contextual processing of textual data is presented. A basic tool for extracting contexts, i.e. immune-based clustering algorithm is described in Section 4. Numerical results are discussed in Section 5. The last two sections present conclusions from our research and future research directions.

2. DOCUMENT MAPS: AN OVERVIEW

The idea of document maps dates back to Doyle (1961) who proposed so-called semantic road maps for graphical representation of the concepts and relationships among these concepts. When restricting to the concepts occurring in a given database only the roadmap acts like a graphical presentation and communication of the content of this database. Usually the distance on the map between certain items reflects their semantic relationship.

Doyle's intention was "to increase the mental contact between the searcher and the information store" in such a way that he/she can "home in on the relevant documents just as one would in a supermarket". Although he referred to some similarities between semantic road map and "psychological map" in the brain, he argued that "it is very difficult to represent any associative maps two dimensionally".

This last difficulty has been overcome when Kohonen (2001) has introduced his SOM, i.e. a kind of self-organizing map inspired by "topographic maps" forming in the brain. This idea appeared to be computationally simple and attractive tool enabling unsupervised clustering and topological ordering of input patterns onto a 2-dimensional grid with fixed topology. It has two attractive features (Lin et al., 1991):

- It preserves the most important neighborhood relationships between the input data, and makes such relationships geographically explicit.
- It allocates different numbers of nodes to inputs based on their occurrence frequencies. The more frequent input patterns are mapped to larger domains at the expense of the less frequent ones.

Lin et al. (1991) suggested an application of SOM to displaying and browsing the content of a collection of documents pertaining "Artificial Intelligence" from the LISA database. Another interesting application for browsing large collection of documents was proposed by Lesteven, Poincot, and Murtagh (1996). Scholtes (1993), mentions a number of deficiencies of the entire SOM algorithm. Among them, the most important are: incompatibility between the semantic space and 2-dimensional grid (what distort clusters content), scalability, unreliability of convergence, and lack of clear evaluation procedures.

At least a partial solution to these deficiencies offer another competitive learning algorithms like e.g. GNG (Fritzke, 1995). In all these algorithms we start with a very small network, adapt it to the pattern space, grow the network in regions where this is needed and prune the network of spurious nodes. One of the first applications of GNG in IR was proposed by Zavrel (1995) who observed that in this case

- the "true" structure of the data set will be reflected in the cluster structure more accurately, including cluster boundaries, and
- final networks are much less likely to get stuck in local minima, because they start out ordered and do not get tangled easily.

Other approaches to different visualization techniques are discussed in (Becks, 2001).

In our research project BEATCA, (Kłopotek et al., 2007a, 2007b), oriented towards exploration and navigation in large collections of documents, a fully-fledged search engine capable of representing on-line replies to queries in graphical form on a document map has been designed and constructed. BEATCA extends the main goals of WEBSOM by a multilingual approach, and new forms of geometrical representation (besides rectangular maps, projections onto sphere and torus surface are possible). Further we experimented with various modifications of the entire clustering process by using the SOM, GNG and immune algorithms.

The process of document map creation, depicted in Figure 1, consists of the following main stages: (1) document crawling – collecting documents from the Inter- or intranet, (2) indexing – preparing documents for

Figure 1. BEATCA system: Phases of document map creation process. ©2008 Krzysztof Ciesielski. Used with permission.

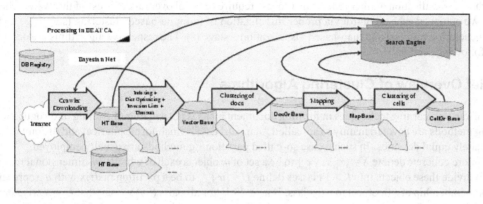

Figure 2. BEATCA system: Graphical user interface. ©2008 Krzysztof Ciesielski. Used with permission.

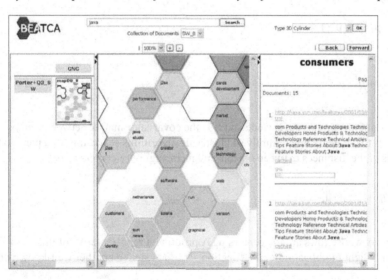

retrieval by turning HTML representation of a document into a vector-space model representation, (3) context identification, yielding major topic of the document map, (4) document grouping, done within the contexts and between contexts, (5) group-to-map transformation, (6) map region identification, (7) group and region labeling, and finally, (8) visualization, associated with the query processor responding to user's queries.

At each of theses stages various decisions can be made implying different views of the document map. For instance, the indexing process involves dictionary optimization, which may reduce the documents collection dimensionality and restrict the subspace in which the original documents are placed. The topics identification establishes basic dimensions for the final map and may involve such techniques as SVD analysis (Berry, 1992), fast Bayesian network learning (Kłopotek, 2003), etc. Document grouping may involve various variants of network-based clustering paradigms, such as GNG or immune-based approaches. The group-to-map transformation, used in BEATCA, is based on SOM ideas, (Kohonen, 2001), but with variations concerning dynamic mixing of local and global search, based on diverse measures of local convergence. The visualization involves 2D and 3D variant (see Figure 2). For more details on this multi-stage process, cf. (Kłopotek, et al. 2007a).

With a strongly parameterized map creation process, the user of BEATCA can accommodate map generation to his particular needs, or even generate multiple maps covering different aspects of document collection. However, such a personalization of map generation process requires control over randomness of the overall clustering process. We achieved such a control via proper initialization of immune-based clustering (stages (3) and (4) of the map generation process) and map-based visualization – stage (8). The respective algorithms are described in the two following sections.

2.1 Brief Overview of Clustering Algorithms

The use of various learning techniques in forming document maps is not a matter of coming into vogue. Standard clustering methods are devoted mainly to so-called "standard data" which form spherical and disjoint clusters of approximately equal densities. In such a case so-called partitioning methods are usually employed.

To be more concrete denote $X = \{x_1, \ldots, x_m\}$ to be a set of m objects each of which is n-dimensional real-valued vector. To divide these objects into $K > 1$ classes define $U = [u_{ij}]_{m \times K}$ to be a partition matrix with u_{ij} representing a degree of membership of i-th object to j-th class. If $u_{ij} \in \{0,1\}$ for all pairs (i, j) we say that U is a crisp partition. On the other hand, if $u_{ij} \in [0,1]$ – U is a fuzzy partition. To compute this partition, define $\mu = (1/m)\sum_{i=1,\ldots,m} x_i$ to be the center of gravity of whole collection of objects and $\mu_j = (1/m_j)\sum_{i=1,\ldots,m} u_{ij}x_i$ to be the center of gravity of j-th class (m_j stands for the cardinality of this class). Now we can define two matrices – see e.g. (Everitt, 1993)

$$\mathbf{W} = \sum_{i=1}^{m}\sum_{j=1}^{K} u_{ij}(x_i - \mu_j)(x_i - \mu_j)^T$$

$$\mathbf{B} = \sum_{j=1}^{K} (\mu_j - \mu)(\mu_j - \mu)^T$$

$\mathbf{W}$ is the matrix of intra-groups covariance and $\mathbf{B}$ is the covariance matrix between groups. Minimization of the trace of $\mathbf{W}$ leads to the well known family of clustering algorithms searching for a partition that minimizes the sum of squares of the distances between objects and nearest gravity centers

$$J(U,M) = \sum_{i=1}^{m}\sum_{j=1}^{K} u_{ij} \| x_i - \mu_j \|^2$$

where M is the matrix whose rows are the centers μ_j. A prominent representative of this family of algorithms is K-means algorithm. Slight modification of the function $J(U, M)$ leads to another well-known criterion

$$J_F(U,M) = \sum_{i=1}^{m}\sum_{j=1}^{K} u_{ij}^{\alpha} \| x_i - \mu_j \|^2$$

where $\alpha > 1$ controls fuzziness of resulting partition. Minimization of $J_F(U, M)$ leads to so-called Fuzzy-ISODATA, a generalization of K-means algorithm (Bezdek & Pal, 1992). In both cases the resulting matrix U is determined through sequential improvements of an initial matrix U^0.

These algorithms, although simple from conceptual and implementation point of view, suffer on a number of drawbacks. First of all they pretty perform on standard (in the sense mentioned earlier) data. Further we must know in advance the number K of classes. Moreover final classification hardly depends on initialization of the matrix U^0.

The techniques referring to competitive learning lead to more elaborated algorithms, like SOM, GNG, etc.

Artificial immune networks offer another successful paradigm for designing clustering algorithms. It refers to the idea of "internal image" recovered by a population of evolved antibodies[3] – consult (de Castro, & von Zuben, 2001) for details. Here, according to the general recipe, the set of data to be clustered is treated as a set of antigens and the role of the algorithm is to produce the set of antibodies located in crucial positions among these antigens. This way the antibodies represent the most important features of the set of antigens.

The most successful representative of the clustering immune algorithms is aiNet proposed by de Castro and von Zuben (2002). The algorithm implements ideas from clonal selection theory, according to which a set of antigens is presented to the evolved set of antibodies. Most efficient (in terms of assumed similarity measure) antibodies are subjected clonal explansion (i.e. they copy proportionally to their quality) and the clones are subjected hypermutation (in the rate inversely proportional to their quality). Next the authors refer to so-called idiotypic interactions according to which unique and most successful clones are identified and these clones compete for survival with current set of antibodies. The final set of antibodies can be clustered and their mutual relationships can be represented by so-called idiotypic network representing crucial characteristics of the set of antigens. An interested reader is referred to the original papers by de Castro and von Zuben (2001, 2002) as well as to the monograph (de Castro & Timmis, 2002) for details. A number of other immune-based clustering algorithms is reviewed by Galeano, Veloza-Suan & González (2005). Our modifications to the original algorithm are mentioned in further parts of this chapter. It is interesting to mention that the antibodies play a role similar to the leaders in a simple clustering algorithm known as "leaders algorithm".

2.2 Initialization of the Immune Network

In is commonly known that the results of almost all clustering algorithms are sensitive to the initialization concerning cluster centers in case of standard K-means algorithm, or codebook vectors in case of SOM algorithm, or antibodies in case of immune-based algorithm. Thus, we proposed new initialization method, especially designed for the purpose of clustering huge collections of textual documents. The method is inspired by the boosting algorithm (Freund & Schapire, 1997) and it is especially useful when processing large datasets, since it clusters only a sample of objects and re-clustering is performed when there are objects which do not fit to the existing partition.

The initialization algorithm starts from a random sample of documents drawn, according to the uniform distribution, from the set D in case of global, i.e. "plain", clustering, or from a contextual group C in case of contextual clustering. The sample size is $S = \min(1000, 0.1n)$, where n is the total number of documents. The sample is clustered into K groups, where K is a user defined parameter. Usually, the fuzzy clustering is applied here, such as Fuzzy K-Means (Bezdek & Pal, 1992) or our own Fuzzy C-Histograms (Ciesielski & Kłopotek, 2007).

Having initial groups, the degree of membership $m_{d,C}$ of each document d to each group C is determined; it reflects the typicality of the document for a given topical group of documents as well as the similarity to other documents in this group.

In subsequent steps, new samples of documents are drawn randomly, but this time the probability of including drawn document d into new sample equals to $P(d) = 1 - \max_{C \in \mathbf{C}} m_{d,C}$, where $\mathbf{C}$ stands for the set of groups computed in previous steps. This way new sample is formed by the documents with low degree of membership to the existing set of clusters. The aim of such a procedure is recurrent improvement of the partition which should represent all the themes from the collection D of documents.

The procedure terminates after a given number of steps or when the set $\mathbf{C}$ stabilizes, i.e. no cluster is modified and no new cluster is added. For the details on this method, as well as the concept of histogram-based clustering, confer (Ciesielski, Kłopotek, 2007) and (Ciesielski, Kłopotek & Wierzchoń, in press).

2.3 Initialization of the Map-Based Visualization

One of our design principles, implemented successfully within BEATCA project, was to separate network-based clustering process in high-dimensional vector space from the 2D map visualization of the clustering structure.

However, in such a setting, also the visualization part needs to be properly initialized to obtain human-readable presentation of the relationships among clusters and individual documents. The initialization of the SOM-like grid, i.e. phase (8) above, relies upon five steps:

- Identify *k* main topics in a given collection of documents. Here *k* is a parametr. To identify the topics naive Bayesian classifier can be used as well as more elaborated tools, like Bayesian networks – consult (Kłopotek et al., 2007a).
- Choose *k* cells, called fixpoints, on the grid. These fixpoints should uniformly cover the entire grid.
- Order the topics according their mutual similarity (measured e.g. in terms of the cosine measure).
- Assign the codebook vectors[4] to each of the distinguished points on the grid. These vectors are initialized with terms[5] characteristic to the corresponding topics.
- Initialize remaining cells by assigning weights proportional to the distance between a given cell and nearest fix point. Random noise is added to each codebook vector.

Numerical experiments prove that the maps initialized in such a way are not only more stable and human-readable, but – what is more important – are constructed much faster than in case of "standard" competitive learning (Kłopotek *et al.*, 2007a, 2007b). The term stability refers here to the repeatability of final form of the map under different initializations.

The above idea was an inspiration for "contextual document processing" relying upon: (a) hierarchical decomposition of the set of documents and (b) identification of terms specific to each of the subgroups of documents. In this approach, identified groups of homogenous documents form so-called context and each context is characterized by specific set of terms. The main advantage of such an approach is dimensionality reduction of the general, very huge, space of terms. Since only fragments of the term space are appropriate to describe particular contexts, we can say about the adaptive clustering. Note that in this procedure contexts determine subsets of terms, and the terms decided as important to a given context influence its physical content.

3. CONTEXTUAL DOCUMENTS PROCESSING

Text documents are usually described by the vectors of the form $\mathbf{w}_d = (w_{d,1}, \ldots, w_{dT})$, where the subscript *d* refers to a particular document, *T* stands for the number of terms, and $w_{d,t}$ is a weight representing importance of the term for the document *d*. Usually $w_{d,t}$ is expressed as so-called `tfidf` weight (*Singhal, 2001)* computed as the product of term frequency (the number of occurrences of the term *t* in the document *d*) and inverted document frequency (the logarithm of the total number of documents divided by the number of documents containing the term *t*). The main disadvantage of such a representation is its inability to cope with problems like polysemy and synonymy. The former reduces precision of an IR system since different documents containing a word identical with a given word may pertain absolutely different domains (e.g. the term "operation" may be used in medical, military, or mathematical context) and the later reduces recall (only the documents containing the words identical with user's query are retrieved and returned).

That is why our contextual approach has been introduced (Ciesielski & Kłopotek, 2007). Here the global weighting scheme is replaced by an assessment procedure taking into account local distribution of words and phrases in a subset of documents pertaining similar topic. Terms weights are modified now by using heuristic criteria resembling human perception and analysis of the documents. More precisely, one can identify (automatically, semi-automatically or even manually, taking into account user's background knowledge on the structure of a given document collection) groups containing similar documents as the preprocessing step in document maps creation process (cf. Figure 1). Such a cluster of document will be called a *contextual* group or a *context*. If a term *t* occurs in a context *C*, then its specificity $s_{t,C}$ is defined as

$$s_{t,C} = |C| \cdot \frac{\sum_{d \in C} f_{t,d} \cdot m_{d,C}}{f_{t,D} \cdot \sum_{d \in C} m_{d,C}} \tag{1}$$

where $f_{t,d}$ stands for the term frequency in the document *d*, $f_{t,D}$ is the global term frequency (i.e. total number f occurrences of the term *t* in the whole set of documents *D*, $m_{d,C}$ is (non-normalized) degree of membership of

Figure 3. BEATCA System: hierarchy of contextual maps. ©2008 Krzysztof Ciesielski. Used with permission.

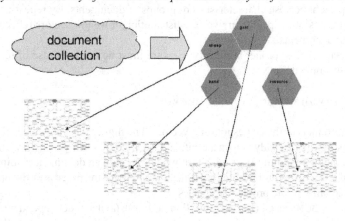

the document d to the context C, and $|C|$ stands for the cardinality of the group C. Finally, the term weight in the context C is computed as

$$w_{t,d}(C) = s_{t,C} \cdot f_{t,d} \cdot \log\left(\frac{|C|}{f_t^C}\right) \tag{2}$$

where f_t^C stands for the term frequency in the context C. Finally the vector $\mathbf{w}_d(C)$ with the components $w_{t,d}(C)$ is normalized in such a way that $\|\mathbf{w}_d(C)\| = 1$. If for some term t the weight $w_{t,d}(C)$ is less than a pre-specified threshold for all the documents belonging to the context C, then such a term can be removed from the set of terms specific for C.

For each contextual group, separate maps are generated. From the user's point of view, contextual model is viewed as a hierarchy of maps, where on the top level a labeled map of contexts is placed (see Figure 3). Further details of this procedure can be found in (Ciesielski, Wierzchoń & Kłopotek, 2006) and (Kłopotek *et al.* 2007a).

4. ADAPTIVE CLUSTERING

Clustering and content labeling are the crucial issues for understanding the two-dimensional map by a user. In SOM algorithm, each unit of an $m \times m$ grid contains the codebook, or reference vector $\mathbf{v}_i$, whose dimension agrees with the dimension of training examples. The training examples are repeatedly presented to the network until a termination criterion is satisfied. When an example $\mathbf{x}(t)$ is presented at time t to the network, its reference vectors are updated according to the rule

$$\mathbf{v}_i(t + 1) = \mathbf{v}_i(t) + \alpha_i(t) \cdot [\mathbf{x}(t) - \mathbf{v}_i(t)], \; i = 1, ..., m \cdot m \tag{3}$$

where $\alpha_i(t)$ is so-called neighborhood function varying according to the equation

$$\alpha_i(t) = \varepsilon(t) \cdot \exp\left(-\frac{dist(i, w)}{\sigma^2(t)}\right) \tag{4}$$

Here $\varepsilon(t)$ and $\sigma(t)$ are two user defined monotonically decreasing functions of time called, respectively, learning rate and neighborhood radius. The symbol $dist(i, w)$ stands for the distance (usually Manhattan distance) between i-th unit and so-called winner unit w (i.e. the unit which reference vector is most similar to the example $\mathbf{x}(t)$).

In case of information retrieval the examples $\mathbf{x}(t)$ correspond to the vector representation of documents, $\mathbf{w}_d(t)$, and the weights $\mathbf{v}_i(t)$ represent concise characteristics of groups of documents. By repeating the presentation of learning vectors several times, we expect to arrive at a distribution of weight vectors reflecting semantical relationships among the real documents.

To discover these relationships, proper similarity measure must be used. In case of textual documents the cosine measure is usually applied, i.e.

$$sim(\mathbf{w}_d(t), \mathbf{v}_i(t)) = \cos(\mathbf{w}_d(t), \mathbf{v}_i(t)) = <\mathbf{w}_d(t), \mathbf{v}_i(t)>/(\|\mathbf{w}_d(t)\|\cdot\|\mathbf{v}_i(t)\|) \qquad (5)$$

where $<\cdot,\cdot>$ denotes dot-products of the corresponding vectors. The higher the *sim* value is the more similar both the items are. This measure can be easily converted into a distance δ by setting $\delta(\mathbf{w}_d(t), \mathbf{v}_i(t))$ $1 - \cos(\mathbf{w}_d(t), \mathbf{v}_i(t))$. Now it is easy to define the winner unit w as such a unit which, for a given document d, minimized the distance $\delta(\mathbf{w}_d(t), \mathbf{v}_i(t))$ over all the reference vectors. Note that time complexity of the process of the winner determination increases as the dimensionality of the problem increases.

The main deficiencies of SOM are, cf. (Baraldi and Blonda, 1999): (a) it is order dependent, i.e. the components of final weight vectors are affected by the order in which training examples are presented, (b) the components of these vectors may be severely affected by noise and outliers, (c) the size of the grid, the step size as well as the size of the neighborhood must be tuned individually for each dataset to achieve useful results, (d) high computational complexity, and (e) the final map hardly depends on the codebook vectors initialization.

While an immune algorithm is able to generate the reference vectors (called antibodies), each of them can summarize basic properties of a small group of documents treated here as antigens. The way that the clusters in the immune network spanned over the set of antibodies will serve as internal images, responsible for mapping existing clusters in the document collection into network clusters. In essence, this approach can be viewed as a successful instance of exemplar-based learning giving an answer to the question "what examples to store for use during generalization, in order to avoid excessive storage and time complexity, and possibly to improve generalization accuracy by avoiding noise and overfitting" (Willson and Martinez, 2000).

4.1 aiNet Algorithm for Data Clustering

The immune-based clustering algorithm aiNet (de Castro and von Zuben, 2001) mimics the processes of clonal selection, maturation and apoptosis observed in the natural immune system. Its aim is to produce a set of antibodies binding a given set of antigens (i.e. documents). The efficient antibodies form a kind of immune memory capable to bind new antigens sufficiently similar to these from the training set.

Like in SOM, the antigens are repeatedly presented to the memory cells (being matured antibodies) until a termination criterion is satisfied. More precisely, a memory structure $\mathbf{M}$ consisting of matured antibodies is initiated randomly with few cells. When an antigen ag_i is presented to the system, its affinity $aff(ag_i, ab_j)$ to all the memory cells is computed. The value of $aff(ag_i, ab_j)$ expresses how strongly the antibody ab_j binds the antigen ag_i. From a practical point of view $aff(ag_i, ab_j)$ can be treated as a degree of similarity between these two cells, and in typical applications it is related to a dissimilarity measure. In our case, *aff* equals the cosine similarity measure defined in equation (5).

The idea of clonal selection and maturation translates into next steps (here σ_d and σ_s are parameters, described below). The cells with the highest affinity to the antigen are subjected clonal selection (i.e. each cell produces a number of copies proportionally to the degree of its stimulation measured by the degree of affinity), and each clone is subjected to mutation (the intensity of mutation is inversely proportional to the degree of stimulation of the mother cell). Only clones cl which can cope successfully with the antigen (i.e. $aff(ag_i, cl) > \sigma_d$) survive. They are added to a tentative memory, $\mathbf{M}_t$, and the process of clonal suppression starts: an antibody ab_j too similar to another antibody ab_k (i.e. $aff(ab_j, ab_k) > \sigma_s$) is removed from $\mathbf{M}_t$. Remaining cells are added to the global memory $\mathbf{M}$. These steps are repeated until all antigens are presented to the system. Next the degree of affinity between all pairs $ab_j, ab_k \in \mathbf{M}$ is computed and again too similar (in fact: redundant) cells are removed from the memory. This step represents network suppression of the immune cells. Lastly $r\%$ (one more parameter) of worst individuals in $\mathbf{M}$ is replaced by freshly generated cells. This epoch ends after the step and next epoch begins until a termination condition is met.

Among all the parameters mentioned above the crucial one seems to be the σ_s as it critically influences the size of the global memory. Each memory cell can be viewed as an exemplar which summarizes important features of "bundles" of antigens stimulating it.

4.2 Improvements to the aiNet

Below some modifications of the entire algorithm are described. Their aim is to reduce the impact of the "curse of dimensionality" on the numerical complexity of the algorithm.

4.2.1 Robust Construction of Mutated Antibodies

First of all, the complexity of an immune algorithm can be significantly reduced if we could restrict the number of required expensive recalculations of stimulation level. The direct, high-dimensional calculations can be replaced by operations on scalar values on the basis of the simple geometrical observation that a stimulation of a mutated antibody clone can be expressed in terms of original antibody stimulation.

Dually, it is possible to estimate mutation intensity in order to get sufficient level of stimulation. More precisely, we can find mutation threshold so that mutated antibody clone stimulation $aff(m,d)$ is less than the predefined threshold σ_d. The advantage of such an approach is the reduction of the number of inefficient (too specific) antibodies, which would be created via mutation process and immediately removed from the clonal memory.

Such an optimization, based on the generalized Pythagoras theorem, was described in (Ciesielski, Wierzchoń and Kłopotek, 2006).

4.2.2 Stabilization via Time-Dependent Parameters

Typical problem with immune based algorithms is the stabilization of the size of the memory **M**. Particularly, the diversity of the memory cells and their number depend hardly on the suppression threshold σ_s and slightly on the death threshold σ_d.

We decided to use time dependent parameters. For each parameter p, we defined its initial value p_0 and the final value p_f as well as the time-dependent function $f_p(t)$, such that $p(t) = f_p(t)$ and $p(0) = p_0$, $p(T) = p_f$, where T is the number of learning iterations.

In particular, both σ_s and σ_d are increased with time, while $m_b(t)$ – the number of clones produced by a cell is increased with time, i.e.

$$\sigma(t) = \sigma_0 + (\sigma_f - \sigma_0)\frac{(t-1)(T+1)}{tT} \tag{6}$$

where $\sigma_0 = 0.05$, $\sigma_f = 0.25$ in case of the suppression and $\sigma_0 = 0.1$, $\sigma_f = 0.4$ for the death threshold. On the other hand the intensity of mutation decreases in time according to the equation

$$m_b(t) = m_0 + (m_f - m_0) \cdot t/T \tag{7}$$

with $m_0 = 3$ and $m_f = 1$.

4.2.3 Robust Antibody Search in Immune Network

Finding the best fitted (most stimulated) antibodies is – from a computational point of view – the most time consuming part of the algorithm. This is especially true, in application to web documents, where both the text corpus size and the number of immune cells is huge. The cost of even a single global search phase in the network is prohibitive. Numerical experiments proved that neither local search method (i.e. searching through the graph edges of the idiotypic network from last-iteration's starting cell) nor joint-winner search method (our own approach devoted to SOM learning (Kłopotek et al., 2004) are directly applicable to idiotypic networks.

We propose a replacement of a global search approach with a modified local search (i.e. searching for current iteration's most stimulated antibody through the graph edges of the idiotypic network, starting from the last iteration's most stimulated antibody). The modification relies upon remembering most stimulated cell for more than one connected component of the idiotypic network and to conduct in parallel a single local-winner search thread for each component. Obviously, it requires one-for-iteration recalculation of connected components, but this is not very expensive: the complexity of this process is of order $O(V+E)$, where V is the number of cells and E is the number of connections (graph edges).

A special case is the possibility of an antibody removal. When the previous iteration's most stimulated antibody for a particular document (antigen) has been removed from the system's memory, we activate search processes (in parallel threads) from each of its direct neighbors in the graph.

We have developed another, slightly more complicated method, but as the experiments show, more accurate. It exploits well-known Clustering Feature Tree (CF-Tree, (Zhang, Ramakrishan, and Livny, 1997) to group similar network cells in dense clusters. Antibody clusters are arranged in the hierarchy and stored in a balanced search tree. Thus, finding most stimulated (similar) antibody for a document requires $O(\log_t V)$ comparisons, where t is the tree branching factor. Amortized tree structure maintenance cost (insertion and removal) is also proportional to $O(\log_t V)$.

4.2.4 Adaptive Visualization of the AIS Network

Despite many advantages over SOM approach, AIS networks have one serious drawback: high-dimensional networks cannot be easily visualized. In our approach, the immune cells are projected onto a regular Kohonen grid. To initialize such a grid properly, a given group of documents is divided into small number of disjoint group (main topics) by using fast ETC Bayesian tree (Kłopotek et al., 2007a).

After its initialization, the map is learned with the standard Kohonen algorithm. Finally, we adopt attraction-repelling algorithm (Timmis, 2001) to adjust the position of AIS antibodies on the SOM projection map, so that the distance on the map reflects as close as possible the similarity of the adjacent cells. The topical initialization of the map is crucial here to assure the stability of the final visualization (Kłopotek et al., 2004). The resulting map visualizes AIS network with resolution depending on the SOM size (a single SOM cell can gather more than one AIS antibody).

5. NUMERICAL EXPERIMENTS

A number of experiments concerning applicability of the immune approach to textual document processing has been reported in (Ciesielski, Wierzchoń and Kłopotek, 2006). Subject of the investigation was first of all the model quality as well as scalability of the algorithms. The model quality of contextual approach, measured in terms of cluster purity, cluster entropy, mutual information between clusters and labels, proved to be superior to e.g. SOM approach to document clustering. as well as compared to non-contextual immune network version. The contextual approach seems also to perform well in terms of scalability, as the model creation time was significantly reduced (faster convergence to a stable set of antibodies) along with reduction of spatial complexity. Also possibility of parallel and distributed processing became obvious with that study.

As the study required manually labeled documents, those experiments were executed on a widely-used 20 Newsgroups document collection[6] containing approximately 20 thousands newsgroup messages, partitioned into 20 different newsgroups (about 1000 messages each).

The data preprocessing step in BEATCA system consists in entropy-based dimensionality reduction (Kłopotek et al., 2004). Its application to the training data yielded dimensionality (the number of distinct terms used) reduced to 4419.

In the study reported here, we experimented more on the structural properties of the immune network obtained (Section 5.1.) and on the impact of initialization strategies (Section 5.2).

We use here the same data set and the same preprocessing procedures so that the results will be consistent with earlier one.

Each immune model has been trained for 100 iterations, using algorithms and methods mentioned in Section 4.

To make the factual comparisons, a number of quality measures were used. Particularly, to measure the quality of clustering at the level of a single cell c the quantization error

$$Q = \frac{1}{|C|} \sum_{c \in C} \left(\frac{1}{D_c} \sum_{d \in D_c} aff(d,c) \right) \tag{8}$$

was introduced. Here D_c stands for the number of documents assigned to the cell c. Obviously, $Q \in [0, 1]$ and lower values of Q correspond to more "compact" and "smoother" clusters.

In (Ciesielski, Wierzchoń and Kłopotek, 2006) we presented experimental results, comparing contextual aiNet model (C-aiNet) with other clustering paradigms such as SOM, hierarchical SOM as well as contextual SOM. C-aiNet significantly outperforms other models both in terms of computation time and final clustering structure quality. In the same paper, we have also presented comparison of basic aiNet model with its contextual variant and impact of time-dependent parametrization (described in section 4.2.2) on stability and quality of the idiotypic network. In general, there is no recipe which allows to tune both the parameters to a given dataset. In original approach by deCastro and Zuben, a trial-and-error method was suggested. We observed that in highly dimensional space the value of σ_d is almost as critical as the value of σ_s. Hence, we propose a "consistent" tuning of these parameters, independent for each contextual group. The general recipe is: carefully (i.e. not to fast) remove weakly stimulated and too specified antibodies and splice redundant (too similar) antibodies.

In the next two sections, we present brief discussion on the analysis of the structure of the idiotypic network based on aiNet clustering model and more detailed results on the impact of topical initialization on the stability and quality of the contextual aiNet (C-aiNet) model.

5.1 Evaluation of the Idiotypic Network Structure

Typical (common) measures of cluster quality, like cluster purity, cluster entropy, mutual information, treat the clusters as separate entities, without any interest for the interrelations between them. However, an idiotypic network is a much richer structure, in which also the usually neglected interrelationships are revealed, so that also their quality is an interesting research topic.

To get a further insight into the quality of the immune network, distribution of edge lengths in the minimal spanning tree built over the set of antibodies in the immune memory was examined. Here an edge length is proportional to the dissimilarity measure between the cells joined by a given edge. After the average length u of the edges was computed together with its standard deviation s, five labels of the length l were proposed: shortest with $l \leq u - s$, short with $l \in (u - s, u - s/2]$, medium with $l \in (u - s/2; u + s/2]$, long with $l \in (u + s/2; u + s]$, and very long: $l > u+s$.

We studied such topics like:

- An impact of the time-dependent (versus constant) parameters on the quality of final immune network. This quality was measured in terms of edge-length variance, network size, quantization error, and learning time.
- An impact of hierarchical and contextual model on the learning time in comparison to "flat" models used in traditional text processing. Particularly, scalability issues were examined in (Ciesielski, Wierzchoń and Kłopotek, 2006).

It was observed that in "standard" immune network medium and long edges prevail and the number of such edges increases in time. This attest to fuzzy nature of the resulting clusters. On the contrary, in case of the contextual models medium edges prevail. In both types of models, the number of short edges diminishes with subsequent iterations. This can be explained by referring to a gradual elimination of redundant cells. However, such elimination is much slower in case of the global model, what is another reason of slow convergence and high learning time. Also in case of SOM model, which has a static topology and no removal of inefficient cells is pos-

Figure 4. Quantization error in consecutive phases of immune network training: (a) topic-based initialization (b) random initialization. Axis X represents the training iteration, axis Y represents the quantization error. ©2008 Krzysztof Ciesielski. Used with permission.

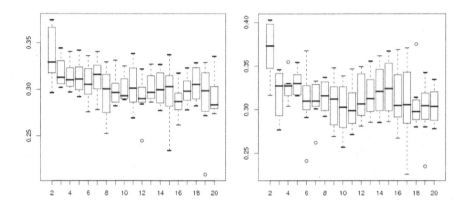

Figure 5. The total number of antibodies in each phase of immune network training: (a) topic-based initialization (b) random initialization. Axis X represents the training iteration, axis Y represents network size in terms of the number of antibodies. ©2008 Krzysztof Ciesielski. Used with permission.

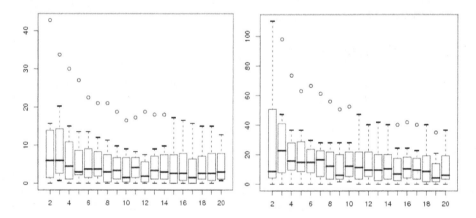

sible, we can see that the model slowly reduces the number of redundancies, represented by too similar referential vectors. More detailed discussion can be found in (Ciesielski, Wierzchoń and Kłopotek, 2006).

5.2 Impact of Topical Initialization on the Stability of aiNet

In the next experiment, we examined the influence of the boosting-like initialization, described in Section 2.2, on the aiNet algorithm. The number of topical clusters identified by initalization algorithm was less than the total number of newsgroups in the 20 Newsgroups collection. However, a single cluster gathered documents from newsgroups which are closely related thematically (e.g. related to religion, computer issues as well as sport-related, motorization-related and science-related clusters). So the initial network consisted of antibodies, each of which was a tentative "main" theme of discussion.

On the other hand, in the non-initialized case, starting set of antibodies consists of randomly generated vectors.

Figure 6. Processing time of a single phase of immune network training: (a) topic-based initialization (b) random initialization. Axis X represents the training iteration, axis Y represents time in seconds. ©2008 Krzysztof Ciesielski. Used with permission.

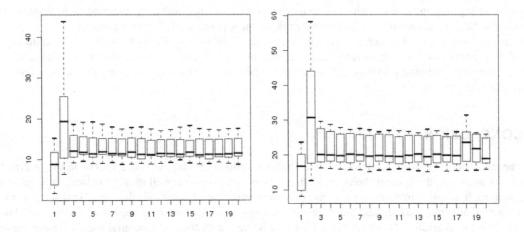

In both cases of initialized and non-initialized learning, the network was trained 10 times. Each time data was randomly split into training and testing samples, in proportion of 10:1 (ten-fold cross validation).

Figures below show box-and-whisker plots of the results. A single box presents the distribution of some measure (respectively – quantization error in Figure 4, immune network size in Figure 5 and processing time in Figure 6) in a single phase (interation step) of the learning process. Each measure is thus characterized by its median (he horizontal bar), 25% and 75% quartiles (the lower and upper sides of the box); lastly the "whiskers" represent lower and upper extreme values and the dots – the outliers. The distribution of the measure at each step was obtained by running the cross-validation process, splitting the data into training and test sets (the evaluation is of the test set, not used in the training).

Each measure is depicted at consecutive steps of the learning process, so one can get an impression how the algorithm converges to the final values.

Left column in these figures illustrates the behavior of the learning process when the topic based initialization is applied, and the right column illustrates the effect of the common method of random initialization.

Results presented in these figures show clear improvements of the resulting immune networks in case of the proper, topical initialization, promoted in this chapter:

- final idiotypic networks are smaller, i.e. they contain lower number of antibodies (it means higher level of data compression),
- the network size has lower variance during training process and the set of antibodies is more stable (less antibodies die or is replaced by other ones),
- the quality of the initialized model is higher, i.e. the quantization error (average of the cosine distance between each document and its closest antibody) is lower. It should be noted that the quantization error depends on the size of the network, so it is additional advantage that is was achieved for smaller network.
- the variance of the quantization error for cross-validated networks is lower
- the processing time in each iteration of the training process is lower. Primarily, it is due to the lower number of antibodies which has to be processed in each iteration. But one should also note that the set of antibodies is more stable during training and less of them is replaced - it also reduces complexity of the process.

However, it should be noted here that the differences between initialized and non-initialized network are not as large as in case of the other clustering approaches, examined e.g. in (Ciesielski, Kłopotek, and Wierzchoń,

173

in press). Taking into account high level of randomness, incorporated in the learning of the immune model and introduced mainly by mutation, it is not surprising that the initialization, which affects only a few initial antibodies, hasn't got prominent impact on the subsequent phases of network maturation during training.

On the other hand, after close inspection of the set of antibodies, present in each of the 10 cross-validated networks during training process, one can notice that initialized antibodies, representing main themes of the document collection, remain in the idiotypic network throughout the whole learning process.

It shows that the level of maturity of the antibody depends on its proper initialization and can influence the rate of the convergence to the stable set of universal antibodies. This claim is supported by the observation, that in the random, non-initialized network, antibodies were replaced more frequently and the network was less stable and required more time to converge.

6. CONCLUSION

The capability of the immune networks to cluster the documents in an adaptive way seems to be a very attractive feature for analyzing the dynamic behavior of the Internet as a whole (as well as of its topical, regional or any other subset). It is also of interest for managers of typical intranets. The methods described in this chapter have the additional advantageous feature: computational savings as well as the resulting slow evolution of clusters compared to the alternative "from scratch". This may be very attractive for potential users of document-map based content management systems.

In this chapter we pointed to a number of aspects of immune system based structural clustering, addressing among others the issues of

- cluster set visualization,
- learning parameter tuning,
- immune network initialization,
- dimensionality reduction,
- document context,
- scalability.

We proposed (partial) solutions to these issues and demonstrated their validity for standard document sets. Essentially they concentrate around balancing global and local look at the data (when searching for best cluster, when computing document context statistics etc.)

Let us note that some document classification methods like ones based on ID3 of Quinlan use in some sense "contextual" information when selecting the next attribute (term) for split of document collection. Our contextual method exploits the split much more thoroughly, extracting more valuable local information about the term in the collection.

We can conclude that aiNet clustering methodology is a promising one in general terms for next generation (map-based) content management systems, while detailed solutions should take into account the problems we raised and eventually built on solutions we proposed here.

7. FUTURE RESEARCH DIRECTIONS

While supplying some answers, we have to acknowledge that a number of issues needs to be still resolved.

First, it is still a very grieving problem that a good tuning of parameters is important for proper performance of the model. Our approach, consisting in letting these parameters vary over time and hopefully hit the optimal zone for the given collection, though successful, is only a partial solution. So a large-scale investigation for determining their most promising initial setting based on varying sizes of document collections would be useful. Further, or alternatively, one could seek promising ways of updating of learning parameters for growing document collections depending of emergence of new topics and declining old ones.

Also the idea of contexts of documents needs a more thorough exploration. How quickly should the impact of other contexts decline with distance? What are the limits of dimensionality reduction?

Many document clustering techniques, including the original `aiNet`, suffer from the tendency of forming spherical clusters. The histogram-based characterization of clusters (Ciesielski, 2007) allows for departing from this shortcoming not only in case of artificial immune systems. An in-depth research is still needed, what are the advantages and limits of such characterizations and to what extent the immune network based on them comes closer to the intrinsic informational structure of document collection.

An acute problem remains the dimensionality of the document processing problem. High-dimensional computations require high processing time. Tang (2005) integrates Principal Component Analysis (PCA) with the original `aiNet` to reduce the time complexity, with results preferential to hierarchical agglomerative clustering and K-means. However, in our opinion, classical dimensionality reduction techniques can actually lead to dimensionality increase, as many zero coordinates become non-zero. So dimensionality reduction, possibly via feature selection or zero-preserving transformations should remain of interest in the future.

Last not least, the networked clustering methods lack generally good measures of quality. Neither the supervised (external) quality measures nor unsupervised (internal) ones derived for independent clusters reflect the quality of link structure between the clusters. Kohonen (2001) proposed therefore map continuity measures, based on differences between neighboring map points. Immune networks differ in structure from the SOM networks, hence proper extensions of Kohonen measures would be needed.

ACKNOWLEDGMENT

This research has been partly supported by Polish state scientific budget for scientific research under grant No. N516 01532/1906 and co-financed by the European Commission and by the Swiss Federal Office for Education and Science with the 6FP project REWERSE no. 506779

REFERENCES

Baraldi, A., & Blonda, P. (1999). A survey of fuzzy clustering algorithms for pattern recognition, *IEEE Transactions on Systems, Man and Cybernetics, 29B*, 786-801.

Barker, I. (2005). *Information scent: helping people find the content they want.* Retrieved February 7, 2008, from http://www.steptwo.com.au/papers/kmc_informationscent/index.html

Becks, A. (2001). Visual knowledge management with adaptable document maps. Sankt Augustin, *GMD Research Series, 15.*

Berry, M.W. (1992). Large scale singular value decompositions. *International Journal of Supercomputer Applications, 6*(1), 13-49.

Bezdek, J. C., & Pal, S. K. (1992). *Fuzzy models for pattern recognition: Methods that search for structures in data.* New York: IEEE.

Börner, K., Chen, Ch., & Boyack, K. (2003). Visualizing knowledge domains. In B. Cronin (Ed.), *Annual Review of Information Science & Technology, 37,* 179-255. Medford, NJ: Information Today, Inc./American Society for Information Science and Technology.

Card, S. K., Robertson, G. G., & York, W. (1996). The WebBook and the WebForager: An information Workspace for the World Wide Web. Retrieved February 7, 2008, from http://www.sigchi.org/chi96/proceedings/acmcopy.htm

de Castro, L. N. & Von Zuben, F. J. (2002). Learning and optimization using the clonal selection principle, *IEEE Transactions on Evolutionary Computation, 6*(3), 239-251.

de Castro, L. N., & von Zuben, F. J. (2001). `aiNet`: An artificial immune network for data analysis. In: H. A. Abbass, R.A. Sarker, and Ch.S. Newton (Eds.), *Data mining: A heuristic approach* (pp. 231-259). Hershey, PA: Idea Group Publishing.

de Castro, L. N., & Timmis, J. (2002). *Artificial immune systems: A new computational intelligence approach.* London Berlin Heidelberg, Springer.

Chakrabarti, S. (2002) *Mining the Web: Analysis of hypertext and semi structured data.* San Fransisco, CA: Morgan Kaufmann.

Ciesielski, K., Wierzchoń, S. T., & Kłopotek, M. A. (2006). An immune network for contextual text data clustering. In H. Bersini, J. Carneiro (Eds.), *Artificial immune systems. Proceedings of the 5th International Conference, ICARIS-2006* (pp. 432-445) LNCS 4163, Berlin Heidelberg, Springer.

Ciesielski, K., & Kłopotek, M. A. (2007). Towards adaptive Web mining. Histograms and contexts in text data clustering. In M.R. Berthold, J. Shawe-Taylor, N. Lavrac (Eds.), *Advances in Intelligent Data Analysis* VII IDA 07 (pp. 284-295), LNCS 4723, Berlin Heidelberg, Springer.

Ciesielski, K., Kłopotek, M. A., & Wierzchoń, S. T. (in press). Term distribution-based initialization of fuzzy text clustering. In *The Seventeenth International Symposium on Methodologies for Intelligent Systems (ISMIS'08)*, Toronto, Canada, LNCS, Springer.

Doyle, L. B. (1961). Semantic road maps for literature searchers. *Journal of ACM, 8*, 553-578.

Everitt, B. S. (1993). *Cluster analysis.* Halsted Press.

Freund, Y., & Schapire, R. E. (1997). A decision-theoretic generalization of on-line learning and an application to boosting. *Journal of Computer and System Sciences, 55*(1), 119-139.

Fritzke, B. (1995). *Some Competitive Learning Methods.* Draft available from http://www.neuroinformatik.ruhr-uni-bochum.de/ini/VDM/research/gsn/JavaPaper/.

Galeano, J. C., Veloza-Suan, A., & González, F. A. (2005). A comparative analysis of artificial immune network models. In *Proceedings of the 2005 Conference on Genetic and Evolutionary Computation, GECO2005*, (pp. 361-368) Washington DC, USA.

Kłopotek, M. A. (2003). Reasoning and learning in extended structured Bayesian networks. *Fundamenta Informaticae, 58*(2)2003, 105-137.

Kłopotek, M. A., Dramiński, M., Ciesielski, K., Kujawiak, M., & Wierzchoń, S. T. (2004). Mining document maps. In M. Gori, M. Celi, M. Nanni (Eds.), *Proceedings of Statistical Approaches to Web Mining Workshop (SAWM) at PKDD'04* (pp. 87-98), Pisa, 2004.

Kłopotek, M. A., Wierzchoń, S. T., Ciesielski, K., Dramiński, M., & Czerski, D. (2007a). Techniques and technologies behind maps of Internet and Intranet document collections. In J., Lu, D. Ruan, G., Zhang (Eds.), *E-Service intelligence – Methodologies, Technologies and Applications* (pp. 169-190). Series: Studies in Computational Intelligence, 37, Berlin Heidelberg, Springer.

Kłopotek, M. A., Wierzchoń, S. T., Ciesielski, K., Draminski, M., & Czerski, D., (2007b). *Conceptual Maps of Document Collections in Internet and Intranet. Coping with the Technological Challenge.* IPI PAN Publishing House, Warszawa, 139 pages.

Kohonen, T. (2001). Self-organizing maps. *Springer Series in Information Sciences, 30.* Berlin, Heidelberg, New York, Springer.

Kohonen, T., Kaski, S., Lagus, K., Salojärvi, J., Honkela, J., Paatero, V., & Saarela, A. (2000). Self organization of a massive document collection. *IEEE Transactions on Neural Networks, 11*(3), 574-585.

Lesteven, S., Poincot, P., & Murtagh, F., (1996). Neural networks and information extraction in astronomical information retrieval. *Vistas in Astronomy, 40*(3), 395-400.

Manning, C. D., Raghavan, P., & Schütze, H. (2008). *Introduction to Information Retrieval,* New York: Cambridge University Press.

Pirolli, P. (2007). *Information Foraging Theory: Adaptive interaction with information.* Oxford: Oxford University Press.

van Rijsbergen, C. J. (1979). *Information retrieval.* London: Butterworths.

Singhal, A. (2001). Modern information retrieval: A brief overview. *Bulletin of the IEEE Computer Society Technical Committee on Data Engineering, 24*(4), 35-43.

Scholtes, J. C. (1993). *Neural networks in natural language processing and information retrieval.* Unpublished doctoral dissertation, University of Amsterdam.

Tang, N., & Vemuri, V. R. (2005). An artificial immune system approach to document clustering. In *Proceedings of the 2005 ACM Symposium on Applied Computing* (pp. 918-922), Santa Fe, New Mexico.

Timmis, J. (2001). aiVIS: Artificial immune network visualization. In *Proceedings of EuroGraphics UK 2001 Conference,* (pp. 61-69), London, University College London,

Trepes, D. (2008). *Information foraging theory.* Retrieved 1 February, 2008 from Interaction-Design.org: http://www.interaction-design.org/encyclopedia/information_foraging_theory.html

Wilson, D. R., & Martinez, T. R. (2000). Reduction techniques for instance-based learning algorithms. *Machine Learning, 38,* 257-286.

Zavrel, J. (1995). *Neural information retrieval - An experimental study of clustering and browsing of document collections with neural networks.* Unpublished doctoral dissertation, University of Amsterdam.

Zhang, T., Ramakrishan, R., & Livny, M. (1997). BIRCH: Efficient data clustering method for very large databases, in: *Proceedings ACM SIGMOD International Conference on Data Management* (pp. 103-114).

ADDITIONAL READINGS

Bezerra, G. B. P., Barra, T.V., Hamilton, M.F., & von Zuben, F.JOURNAL, (2006). A hierarchical immune-inspired approach for text clustering. In: *Proceedings of the 11th Information Processing and Management of Uncertainty in Knowledge-Based Systems International Conference,* IPMU'2006, (pp. 2530-2537, Paris, France, July 2-7, 2006.

Card, S.K., Mackinlay, JOURNALD., Shneiderman, B., (1999). *Readings in information visualization: Using vision to think.* Morgan Kaufmann Publishers.

Cayzer, S., & Aickelin, U. (2005). A recommender system based on idiotypic artificial immune networks. *Journal of Mathematical Modelling and Algorithms, 4*(2), 181-198.

Dodge, M., & Kitchin, R. (2000). *Mapping Cyberspace.* London, Routledge.

Frawley, W. J., Piatetsky-Shapiro, G., & Matheus, C. J., (1991). Knowledge discovery in databases: An overview. In: G. Piatetsky-Shapiro and W. J. Frawley (eds.) *Knowledge Discovery in Databases* (p. 1-30), Cambridge, MA, AAAI Press/MIT Press.

Herman I, Melançon G, Marshall M.S. (2000) Graph visualization and navigation in information visualization: a survey. *IEEE Transactions on Visualization and Computer Graphics, 6*(1), 24-43.

Knight, T., & Timmis, J., (2001). AINE: An immunological approach to data mining. In: N. Cercone, T. Y. Lin and X. Wu: *Proceedings of the 2001 IEEE International Conference on Data Mining*, (pp. 297 – 304), 29 November - 2 December 2001, San Jose, California, USA.

Liu, X., & Zhang, N., (2006). Incremental immune-inspired clustering approach to behavior-based anti-spam technology. *International Journal of Information Technology, 12*(3), 2006, 111-120.

Leake, D. B., Maguitman, A., & Canas, A., (2002). Assessing conceptual similarity to support concept mapping. In: *Proceedings of the 15th International Florida Artificial Intelligence Research Society Conference* (pp. 186-172). AAAI Press, Menlo Park.

Li, Z.H. & Tan, H.Z., (2006). A combinational clustering method based on artificial immune system and support vector machine. In: B. Gabrys, R.J. Howlett, L.C. Jain (Eds.): *Knowledge-Based Intelligent Information and Engineering Systems*, 10th International Conference, KES 2006 (pp. 153-162), Bournemouth, UK, October 9-11, 2006, Lecture Notes in Computer Science 4251, Berlin Heidelberg, Springer 2006.

Nasraoui, O., Cardona-Uribe, C., & Rojas-Coronel, C., (2003). Tecno-streams: Tracking evolving clusters in noisy data streams with a scalable immune system learning model. In: *IEEE International Conference on Data Mining*, Melbourne, Florida, Nov. 2003, (pp. 235 - 242).

Paulovich, F.V.; Minghim, R. (2006) Text map explorer: A tool to create and explore document maps. In: *Proceedings of the 10th International Conference on Information Visualization* (pp. 245 – 251), Washington, DC,: IEEE Computer Society.

Sahan, S., Polat, K., Kodaz, H., & Gunes, S., (2007). A new hybrid method based on fuzzy-artificial immune system and k-nn algorithm for breast cancer diagnosis. *Computers in Biology and Medicine, 37*(3), 415-423.

Secker, A., Freitas, A.A., & Timmis, J., (2003). *AISEC: an artificial immune system for e-mail classification*. The 2003 Congress on Evolutionary Computation (pp. 131 - 138), Vol. 1, IEEE.

Tufte, E. R. (1983). *The Visual Display of Quantitative Information*. Cheshire, CT: Graphics Press.

Tufte, E. R. (1990). *Envisioning Information*. Cheshire, CT: Graphics Press.

Tufte, E. R. (1997). *Visual Explanations*. Cheshire, CT: Graphics Press.

Wang, L., Jiao, L., (2001). An immune neural network used for classification. In: N. Cercone, T.Y. Lin and X. Wu, eds., *Proceedings of the 2001 IEEE International Conference on Data Mining*, ICDM'2001, (pp. 657-658). IEEE Computer Society.

X. Yue, Abraham, A., Chi, Z.-X., Hao, Y.-Y., & Mo, H., (2007). Artificial immune system inspired behavior-based anti-spam filter. *Soft Computing*, 11, 729–740.

KEY TERMS

Adaptive Clustering: Clustering approach which is able to dynamically modify document representation and similarity measure, on the basis of local contexts discovered in the document collection.

Competitive Learning: A paradigm used in structured (networked) environments, based on the psychological assumption by Hebb, 1949, that neurons that are stimulated by similar effectors, have stronger functional relationship. In neural clustering models (e.g. SOM, GNG) this assumption means that during training process not only a single neuron weights are modified, but also weights of its neighboring neurons.

Context: Sufficiently large (for statistics sake) set of documents with sufficiently uniform topics. Each document can belong to several different contexts, depending on topics it covers.

Document Map: A 2D map representing relationships among the documents from a given collection. Usually the closer the items on the map surface, the more (semantically) similar their contents.

Fuzzy Clustering: Clustering which splits data into overlapping clusters, where each object can belong, in some degree, to more than one cluster. Thus each cluster is treated as a fuzzy subset of objects and the membership function defining this subset represents the degrees of membership of each item to the subset. Major algorithm based on fuzzy paradigm is Fuzzy *K*-Means (Bezdek & Pal, 1992)

Immune-Based Clustering: It exploits immune-based principles of producing antibodies binding antigens. Here the antigens correspond to the input data and antibodies are workable characteristics of the groups of data. In so-called idiotypic network paradigm, antibodies bind not only antigenes, but also similar antibodies, creating a structure of clusters. It is an example of self-organizing evolutionary algorithm. Contrary to many existing clustering algorithms it does not require prior number of classes and it easily adapts to the problems of incremental learning.

Information Visualization: A discipline devoted to the problems of human oriented representation and exploration of large data sets. The tools developed here offer graphical means supporting quick and efficient solutions to these problems.

Topic: A label (or label vector) describing common characteristics of a subset of documents (e.g. suitability of texts for different age groups). Equivalently it refers to thematic homogeneity of the subset of documents.

Vector Space Model: One of classical representations of document content. The documents are points (or vectors rooted in coordinate origin) in this high-dimensional space (spanned by terms being coordinate axes) , with the point (vector) coordinates reflecting frequencies of different terms (linearly or in a more complex manner) in a given document.

ENDNOTES

[1] See also http://websom.hut.fi/websom for additional material.

[2] Quick introduction to the main themes of IV can be found on the page http://www.pnl.gov/infoviz. See also http://personalpages.manchester.ac.uk/staff/m.dodge/cybergeography for a review of different specific techniques.

[3] Intuitively by antigen we understand any substance threatening proper functioning of the host organism while antibodies are protein molecules produced to bind antigens. A detailed description of these concepts can be found in (de Castro and Timmis, 2002).

[4] See section 4.

[5] Documents representation is discussed in next section.

[6] Available from http://people.csail.mit.edu/jrennie/20Newsgroups.

Chapter IX
Feature Selection Based on Clonal Selection Algorithm:
Evaluation and Application

Xiangrong Zhang
Xidian University, P.R. China

Fang Liu
Xidian University, P.R. China

ABSTRACT

The problem of feature selection is fundamental in various tasks like classification, data mining, image processing, conceptual learning, and so on. Feature selection is usually used to achieve the same or better performance using fewer features. It can be considered as an optimization problem and aims to find an optimal feature subset from the available features according to a certain criterion function. Clonal selection algorithm is a good choice in solving an optimization problem. It introduces the mechanisms of affinity maturation, clone, and memorization. Rapid convergence and good global searching capability characterize the performance of the corresponding operations. In this study, the property of rapid convergence to global optimum of clonal selection algorithm is made use of to speed up the searching of the most appropriate feature subset among a huge number of possible feature combinations. Compared with the traditional genetic algorithm-based feature selection, the clonal selection algorithm-based feature selection can find a better feature subset for classification. Experimental results on datasets from UCI learning repository, 16 types of Brodatz textures classification, and synthetic aperture radar (SAR) images classification demonstrated the effectiveness and good performance of the method in applications.

1. INTODUCTION

Feature selection is an active research area in pattern recognition, machine learning, and data mining. In the workshop of NIPS 2003 on feature extraction and feature selection challenge, feature selection is studied extensively. And there is a workshop on feature selection in NIPS 2006. Also, FSDM 2006 is an international workshop on feature selection for data mining. At present, a great deal of research on feature selection has been carried out. **Feature selection** is defined as the process of choosing a subset of the original predictive variables by eliminating redundant features and those with little or no predictive information. If we extract as much information as

Copyright © 2009, IGI Global, distributing in print or electronic forms without written permission of IGI Global is prohibited.

possible from a given dataset while using the smallest number of features, we can not only save a great amount of computing time and cost, but also improve the generalization ability to unseen points.

The majority of classification problems require supervised learning where the underlying class probabilities and class-conditional probabilities are unknown, and each instance is associated with a class label. In these situations, relevant features are often unknown a priori. Therefore, many candidate features are introduced to better represent the domain. Unfortunately, many of these are either partially or completely irrelevant to the target concept. Reducing the number of irrelevant features drastically reduces the running time of a learning algorithm and yields more general concept. This helps in getting better insight into the underlying concept of a real-world classification problem (Kohavi, & Sommereld, 1995; Koller, & Sahami, 1994). Feature selection methods try to pick a subset of features that are relevant to the target concept (Blum, & Langley, 1997).

Recently, natural computation algorithms get widely applications in feature selection (Yang, & Honavar, 1998) and synthesis (Li, Bhanu, & Dong, 2005; Lin, & Bhanu, 2005) to improve the performance and reduce the feature dimension as well. Among them, genetic algorithm (GA) is one of the most popularly used in feature selection (Oh, Lee, & Moon, 2004; Raymer, Punch, Goodman, Kuhn, & Jain, 2000; Zio, Baraldi, & Pedroni, 2006). In this chapter, instead of using GA to search for the optimal feature subset for classification, an effective global optimization technique, the clonal selection algorithm (de Castro, & Von Zuben, 1999, 2000, 2002; Du, Jiao, & Wang, 2002) in artificial immune systems (AISs) is applied in feature selection. AISs are proving to be a very general and applicable form of bio-inspired computing. To date, AISs have been applied to various areas (Bezerra, de Castro, & Zuben, 2004; Dasgupta, & Gonzalez, 2002; de Castro, & Timmis, 2002; de Castro, & Zuben, 2002; Forrest, Perelson, Allen, & Cherukuri, 1994; Nicosia, Castiglione, & Motta, 2001; Timmis, & Neal, 2001; Zhang, Tan, & Jiao, 2004) such as machine learning, optimization, bioinformatics, robotic systems, network intrusion detection, fault diagnosis, computer security, data analysis and so on. **Clonal selection algorithm** was proposed as a computational realization of the clonal selection principle for pattern matching and optimization. It has become perhaps the most popular in the field of AISs. This chapter will investigate the performance of the clonal selection algorithm in the feature selection.

When we design a feature selection approach based on the clonal selection algorithm, the nature of the problem space should be taken into account. Representation, affinity function, and clonal selection operators are described according to the feature selection problem. An antibody in the population represents a given feature subset and each binary bit is used to denote the presence or absence of the feature at the corresponding location. In the clonal selection algorithm, the evolution process is induced by the affinity. To realize the purpose of feature selection, achieving the same or better performance with fewer features, the definition of the affinity function takes both the separability measure and the dimension of feature subset into consideration. Inspired by the clonal selection theory, the clonal proliferation (T_c^C), affinity maturation (T_m^C) and clonal selection (T_S^C) are implemented iteratively on the antibody population. The selected optimal feature subset is the antibody with the maximal affinity value in the last evolutionary generation.

The remainder of this chapter is organized as follows: the next section describes the related background of feature selection techniques including generation procedure and evaluation function. In section III, after reviewing the clonal selection algorithm, we describe the feature selection approach based on clonal selection algorithm. Section IV evaluates the performance of the algorithm on datasets from UCI learning repository, Brodatz textures, and SAR images classification. The future research directions are given in Section V. And finally, concluding remarks are given.

2. RELATED BACKGROUND

Feature selection is motivated for three-fold: improve generalization error, determine the relevant features and reduce the dimensionality of the input space. It is defined by looking at it from various angles, but many of those are similar in intuition and/or content. Dash and Liu (1997) summarized the definitions into the following ones:

1. **Idealized:** Find the minimally sized feature subset that is necessary and sufficient to the target concept (Kira, & Rendell, 1992).

2. **Classical:** Select a subset of d features from a set of D features, $d \leq D$, such that the value of a criterion function is optimized over all subsets of size d (Narendra, & Fukunaga, 1977).
3. **Improving prediction accuracy:** The aim of feature selection is to choose a subset of features for improving prediction accuracy of the classifier built using only the selected features (John, Kohavi, & Peger, 1994).
4. **Approximating original class distribution:** Select a small subset such that the resulting class distribution, given only the values for the selected features, is as close as possible to the original class distribution given all feature values (Koller, & Sahami, 1994).

Ideally feature selection methods search through the subsets of features and try to find the best one among the competing $\sum_{i=1}^{D} C_D^i$ (or can be $2^D - 1$, minus 1 means that we have to choose one feature at least) candidate subsets according to some evaluation function. But this procedure is exhaustive as it tries to find only the best one. Other methods based on heuristic or random search methods attempt to reduce computational complexity by compromising performance. These methods need a stopping criterion to prevent an exhaustive search of subsets. There are four basic steps in a typical feature selection method, including a generation procedure to generate the next candidate subset; an evaluation function to evaluate the subset under examination; a stopping criterion to decide when to stop; a validation procedure to check whether the subset is valid.

The generation procedure is a search procedure (Doak, 1992; Langley, 1994; Liu, & Yu, 2005; Siedlecki, & Sklansky, 1988). It can start (i) with no features, (ii) with all features, or (iii) with a random subset of features. In the first two cases, features are iteratively added/removed, whereas in the last case, features are either iteratively added/removed or produced randomly thereafter. An evaluation function measures the goodness of a subset produced by some generation procedure. If it is found to be better, then it replaces the previous best subset. A suitable stopping criterion is needed to stop the feature selection process. Generation procedures and evaluation functions can influence the choice for a stopping criterion. Stopping criteria based on a generation procedure include: (i) whether a predefined number of features are selected, and (ii) whether a predefined number of iterations reached. Stopping criteria based on an evaluation function can be: (i) whether addition (or deletion) of any feature does not produce a better subset, and (ii) whether an optimal subset according to some evaluation function is obtained.

2.1 Generation Procedures

If the original feature set contains D features then the total number of competing candidate subsets is $2^D - 1$. This is a huge number even for medium-sized D. There are different approaches of solving this problem, namely: complete, heuristic, and random.

- **Complete.** This generation procedure does a complete search for the optimal subset according to the evaluation function used. To reduce the computation cost, different heuristic functions are used to reduce the search without missing the chances of finding the optimal subset. In this way, a fewer subsets are evaluated. The branch and bound feature selection (Narendra, & Fukunaga, 1977) belongs to this kind of method. It can be used to find the optimal subset of features much more quickly than exhaustive search.
- **Heuristic.** In each iteration of this generation procedure, all remaining features are considered for selection (rejection). There are many variations to this simple process, but generation of subsets is basically incremental (either increasing or decreasing). These procedures are very simple to implement and very fast in producing results because the search space is only quadratic in terms of the number of features. Many heuristic algorithms can be used, such as the sequential forward, backward, or floating selections.
- **Random.** Optimality of the selected feature subset depends on the resources available. Each random generation procedure would require values of some parameters. Assignment of suitable values to these parameters is an important task for achieving good results. Simulated annealing (Meiri, & Zahavi, 2006), GA and clonal selection algorithm based feature selections use this kind of generation scheme.

2.2 Evaluation Functions

An optimal feature subset is always relative to certain evaluation function. Typically, an evaluation function tries to measure the capability of a feature subset to distinguish among different class labels. Langley (1994) grouped different feature selection methods into two broad groups, i.e., filter and wrapper, based on their dependence on the learning algorithm that will finally use the selected subset. Filter methods are independent of the learning algorithm whereas wrapper methods use the learning algorithm as the evaluation function. Doak (1992) divided the evaluation functions into three categories: data intrinsic measures, classification error rate, and estimated or incremental error rate, where the third category is basically a variation of the second category. The data intrinsic category includes distance, entropy, and dependence measures.

In generally, the selection of evaluation function is related to the characteristics of the subsets chosen, different evaluation functions may acquire different feature sets. According to whether adopt the accuracy of classifier as the evaluation function, here we main introduce the two categories of feature selection methods: Filter and Wrapper.

2.3 Framework for Feature Selection

2.3.1 Filter Approaches to Feature Selection

Intuitively, removing some irrelevant features before inductive step will improve the performance. For this purpose, an approach to feature selection introduces a separate process that occurs before the basic learning step. This approach can be considered as a preprocessing for classification. For this reason, John, Kohavi, & Peger (1994) have termed them filter methods, because they filter out irrelevant attributes before learning occurs. The preprocessing step uses general characteristics of the training set to select some features and exclude others. Thus, filter methods are independent of the learning algorithm that will use their output, and they can be combined with any learning method. The procedure is shown in Fig.1.

The simplest filtering scheme is to evaluate each feature individually based on its correlation with the target function (e.g., using a mutual information measure) and then to select the d features with the highest value. The best choice of d can be determined by testing on a hold out set.

2.3.2 Wrapper Approaches to Feature Selection

Another approach for feature selection occurs outside the basic learning method but uses that method as a subroutine, rather than as a postprocessor (see Fig.2). Kohavi and John (1997) referred to these as wrapper approaches. The typical wrapper algorithm searches the same space of feature subsets as filter methods, but it evaluates feature subsets by running a given learning algorithm on the training data which will be used in the inductive step, and using the estimated accuracy of the resulting classifier as the evaluation criterion.

The wrapper approach uses the same learning algorithm in feature selection step as that in inductive step, which should provide a better estimate of accuracy than a separate measure. The major disadvantage of wrapper methods over filter methods is the former's computational cost, which results from calling the learning algorithm for evaluating each feature set considered.

3. CLONAL SELECTION ALGORITHM BASED FEATURE SELECTION

In this section, we will introduce a filter feature selection with random generation procedure because the wrapper approach to feature selection is time consuming.

Feature selection can be considered as an optimization problem. GA has been widely used in feature subset searching (Yang, & Honavar, 1998, Oh, Lee, & Moon, 2004; Raymer, Punch, Goodman, Kuhn, & Jain, 2000; Zio, Baraldi, & Pedroni, 2006). However, GA displayed a tendency towards premature convergence in feature selec-

Figure 1. Filter approaches to feature selection

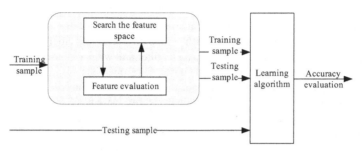

Figure 2. Wrapper approaches to feature selection

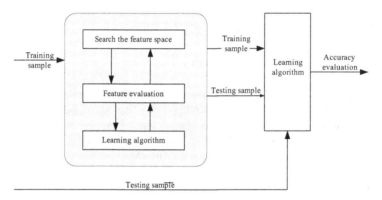

tion (Jain, & Zongker, 1997). Clonal selection algorithm overcomes the shortcoming of GA to some degree. It is based on the artificial immune system, and the competition and cooperation coexist. Clonal selection algorithm demonstrates the self-adjustability function by accelerating or restraining the generation of antibodies, which enhances the diversity of the population. Accordingly, a new feature selection method based on clonal selection algorithm (CSA-FS) is proposed.

3.1 Clonal Selection Algorithm

The clonal selection theory, proposed by Burnet (1959), is used in immunology to describe the basic features of an immune response to an antigenic stimulus. It establishes the idea that the cells are selected when they recognize the antigens and proliferate (de Castro, & Von Zuben, 1999). When exposed to antigens, immune cells that may recognize and eliminate the antigens can be selected in the body and mount an effective response against them during the course of the clonal selection.

Above description clearly sounds like a selective and stochastic-based adaptive process. Based on the clonal selection theory, some new optimization algorithms have been proposed (de Castro, & Von Zuben, 1999; Du, Jiao, & Wang, 2002; Gong, Du, & Jiao, 2006; Du, Jiao, Gong, & Liu, 2004). The clonal selection functioning of the above optimization algorithms can be interpreted as a remarkable microcosm of Charles Darwin's theory of evolution, with three major principles such as repertoire diversity, genetic variation, and natural selection (de Castro, & Von Zuben, 2002). Clonal selection algorithm is characterized by the representation of the antibody, the evaluation function, and the population dynamics such as population size, immune genetic operators, clonal selection. In the clonal selection algorithm, the antigen means the problem to be optimized and its constraints, while the antibodies are the candidate solutions of the problem. The antibody-antigen affinity indicates the matching between solution and the problem. The algorithm performs the selection of antibodies based on affinity either by matching against an antigen pattern or via evaluation of a pattern by a cost function.

Inspired by the clonal selection theory, the clonal selection operator implements clonal proliferation (T_s^C), affinity maturation operation (T_c^C) and clonal selection (T_m^C) on the antibody population $A(k)$, where the antibody population at k-th generation is represented by the time-dependent variable matrix $A(k) = \{a_1(k), a_2(k), \cdots, a_n(k)\}$, in which n is the size of the antibody population. The evolution process can be described as follows.

$$\mathbf{A}(k) \xrightarrow{T_c^C} \mathbf{Y}(k) \xrightarrow{T_m^C} (\mathbf{Z}(k) \cup \mathbf{A}(k)) \xrightarrow{T_s^C} \mathbf{A}(k+1) \tag{1}$$

According to the affinity function f, an antibody $a_i(k) \in \mathbf{A}(k)$, $i = 1, 2, \cdots n$ in the solution space will be divided into q_i same points $y_{ij}(k) \in \mathbf{Y}(k)$, $j = 1, 2, \cdots, q_i$ by performing clonal proliferation. After affinity maturation operation and clonal selection operation, we get the new antibody population $\mathbf{A}(k+1)$. The **clonal selection algorithm** can be implemented as follows (Du, Jiao, & Wang, 2002):

Clonal Selection Algorithm

Step1 $k=1$, randomly generate the original antibody population $A(1) = \{a_1(1), a_2(1), \dots a_n(1)\} \in I^n$

. Set the initial parameters, and calculate the affinity of $A(1)$.

Step2 Do clonal proliferation operation according to clonal size: $Y(k) = T_c^c(A(k))$;

Step3 Do affinity maturation operation to $Y(k)$: $Z(k) = T_m^c(Y(k))$;

Step4 Calculate the affinity: $\{f(Z(k))\}$;

Step5 Do clonal selection operation and update the antibody population:

$A(k+1) = T_s^c(A(k) \cup Z(k))$;

Step6 $k=k+1$. The algorithm will be halted when the restricted iterative number is satisfied, otherwise, return to Step2.

The corresponding diagrammatic presentation of the main operations is shown in Fig. 3 and the major operations are defined as follows.

Clonal Proliferation Operation T_c^C:

$$\mathbf{Y}(k) = T_c^C(\mathbf{A}(k)) = [T_c^C(a_1(k)) \quad T_c^C(a_2(k)) \quad \cdots \quad T_c^C(a_n(k))]^T$$

in which, $T_c^C(a_i) = a_i \otimes I_i$ ($i = 1, 2, \cdots n$), I_i is a q_i-dimension row vector and usually the clonal size:

$$q_i = Int\left(n_c \times f(a_i) \middle/ \sum_{j=1}^{n} f(a_j)\right)$$

where $n_c > n$ is a given value, and $Int(x)$ returns the minimum integer larger than x. After clonal proliferation, the antibody population becomes:

$$\mathbf{Y}(k) = \{Y_1(k), Y_2(k), \cdots, Y_n(k)\}$$

where $Y_i(k) = \{y_{i1}(k), y_{i2}(k), \cdots, y_{iq_i}(k)\}$, and $y_{ij}(k) = a_i(k)$, $j = 1, 2, \cdots q_i$, $i = 1, 2, \cdots, n$.

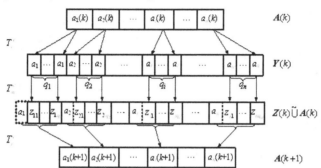

Figure 3. Operation process of clonal selection algorithm

Affinity Maturation Operation T_m^C:

The hypermutation is performed in this operation. T_m^C is implemented on the population Y(k) obtained by clonal proliferation, namely $\mathbf{Z}(k) = T_m^C(\mathrm{Y}(k))$, which changes each of the bits with the mutation probability P_m^i. Generally, $P_m^i = 1/l$, where l is the length of the antibody.

For binary encoding, mutation operation can be done as follows: each gene in an antibody is replaced by its opposite number (i.e. 0-1, and 1-0).

After the affinity maturation operation, the population becomes:

$$\mathbf{Z}(k) = \{Z_1(k), Z_2(k), \cdots, Z_n(k)\}$$

where $Z_i(k) = \{z_{i1}(k), z_{i2}(k), \cdots, z_{iq_i}(k)\}$ and $z_{ij}(k) = T_m^c(y_{ij}(k))$, $j = 1, 2, \cdots q_i, i = 1, 2, \cdots, n$

Clonal Selection Operation T_s^C:

Suppose $\forall\ i = 1, 2, \dots n, b_i(k) = \{z_{ij}^*(k) \mid f(z_{ij}^*(k)) = \max f(z_{ij}(k)), j = 1, 2, \cdots, q_i\}$ is the best antibody in $Z_i(k)$, then the new population is

$$
\begin{aligned}
\mathrm{A}(k+1) &= T_s^c(\mathrm{A}(k) \cup \mathrm{Z}(k)) \\
&= [T_s^c(a_1(k) \cup Z_1(k)), T_s^c(a_2(k) \cup Z_2(k)), \cdots, T_s^c(a_n(k) \cup Z_n(k))] \\
&= \{a_1(k+1), a_2(k+1), \dots a_n(k+1)\}
\end{aligned}
$$

where $a_i(k+1) = \begin{cases} b_i(k), & \text{if } f(b_i(k)) > f(a_i(k)) \\ a_i(k), & \text{otherwise} \end{cases}$.

T_s^C selects the best individual from the sub-population $a_i(k) \cup Z_i(k)$, $i = 1, 2, \dots, n$, respectively, and all the best individuals constitute the new population.

3.2 Feature Selection Based on Clonal Selection Algorithm

In the application of the clone selection algorithm, three problems must be solved according to a given task: how to represent a solution of the problem as an antibody, how to define the affinity function to evaluate the performance of antibody, and how to implement the operations and determine the parameters in the clonal selection algorithm.

Feature selection based on clonal selection algorithm can be used to identify the *d* most discriminative features out of a set of *D* potentially useful features, where $d \leq D$, namely, to find the antibody which is used for representing a feature subset whose affinity is the maximum. The affinity corresponds to the value of evaluation function for measuring the efficiency of the considered feature subset.

3.2.1 Representation

A binary encoding scheme is used to represent the presence or absence of a particular feature of the samples. An antibody is a binary string whose length equals to the number of all available features, *D*. Let $(a_{i1}, a_{i2}, \cdots, a_{iD})$, $i = 1, 2, \cdots, n$ denote an antibody, where $a_{ij} = 0$, $j = 1, 2, \cdots, D$ denotes the associated feature is absent, and $a_{ij} = 1$, $j = 1, 2, \cdots, D$ denotes the associated feature is present. Each antibody represents a feature subset. As an illustration, let us consider the following example.

Example 1. Suppose the feature dimension of dataset **X** is 8. Then antibody $a_i(k) = (1, 1, 0, 0, 1, 0, 1, 0)$ represents that the first, second, fifth, and seventh features are chosen to consist the considered feature subset.

Unlike the sequential feature selection, this method does not attempt to find the best feature subset with a specified dimension. Its search space encompasses all the subsets. Therefore, we need not set the expected number of features in the selection procedure. Regardless of the dimension of the feature subset, the feature subset with the highest affinity will be selected as the optimal subset by the algorithm.

3.2.2 Affinity Function for Feature Subsets Evaluation

For pattern classification, Bayes classification error minimization criterion is the ideal evaluation function. However, it is difficult to be evaluated and analysed because the probability distribution of data is unknown in application. An alternative method is using the accuracy as the evaluation function, which is typically the wrapper approach to feature selection (Jolliffe, 1986). However, using the accuracy as the evaluation function is time-consuming because the learning algorithm must be used to evaluate every feature subset generated during the course of feature selection, and its generalization is not good because the feature selection must be performed again when the learning algorithm is changed. Here, we apply a filter approach to feature selection. Feature selection is considered as an independent procedure and distance measure is exploited to be separability criteria. It is well know that the Bhattacharyya distance determines the upper bound of Bayes classification error. So it is appropriate to be used as the separability measure for classes. In addition, because the goal of feature selection is to achieve the same or better performance using fewer features, the evaluation function should contain the number of features also (Sun, Yuan, Bebis, & Louis, 2002). Combining the distance measure and the dimension of considered feature subset, the affinity function is given as:

$$f = 10^3 J - 0.7 \times d, \tag{2}$$

where *f* is the affinity of an antibody, *d* the dimension of the considered feature subset, and *J* the distance separability criteria. For two classes indexed by *i* and *j*, the Bhattacharyya distance is defined by:

$$B_{ij} = \frac{1}{8}(\mu_i - \mu_j)^T \left[\frac{\Sigma_i + \Sigma_j}{2} \right]^{-1} (\mu_i - \mu_j) + \frac{1}{2} \ln \frac{\left| \frac{1}{2}(\Sigma_i + \Sigma_j) \right|}{\left[|\Sigma_i||\Sigma_j| \right]^{\frac{1}{2}}} \tag{3}$$

where μ_i, μ_j are the feature mean vectors and Σ_i, Σ_j denote the class covariance matrices for classes *i* and *j* respectively. Class mean vector and covariance are estimated from the available training data.

For multi-class problems, the average Jeffreys-Matusita Distance (JMD) is used as the separability criteria. For C classes, the average JMD is defined as

$$J = \frac{2}{C(C-1)} \sum_{i=1}^{C} \sum_{j=1}^{i-1} J_{ij},$$ (4)

where $J_{ij} = 2(1 - e^{-B_{ij}})$.

Formula (2) ensures that the higher the distance measure, the higher the affinity. And in the case that two subsets achieve the same performance, the subset with low dimension is preferred. Between the distance measure and the dimension of feature subset selected, the former is the major concern. Example 2 gives an example of evaluation procedure for a given subset represented by an antibody.

Example 2. Let $X_i \in \mathrm{X}$, $i = 1, 2, \cdots, N$ be one of N samples in the original 8-dimension dataset X. When we evaluate the feature subset represented by a given antibody (1, 1, 0, 0, 1, 0, 1, 0), the new dataset is gotten by removing the third, fourth, sixth and eighth features. Then the 4-dimension new dataset X' with $X_i' = (x_{i1}, x_{i2}, x_{i5}, x_{i7})$, $i = 1, 2, \cdots, N$ is gotten. In this case, $d = 4$, and J can be calculated according to formula (4). The affinity of the antibody is gotten with equation (2).

3.2.3 Feature Selection Procedure Based on Clonal Selection Algorithm

With the evaluation function for feature subset, feature selection is reduced to find an antibody Ab^* by the clonal selection algorithm so that $f(Ab^*) = \max f(Ab)$. The feature selection procedure can be summarized as follows.

Step1: Initialization. Let $k = 1$, the initial population $\mathbf{A}(1)$ with n antibodies is generated randomly, and each binary string with D bits of n antibodies represents a feature subset.

Step2: Affinity Evaluation. Each antibody is decoded to the corresponding features combination and the new training sample sets are gotten. The affinity $\{f(\mathbf{A}(1))\}$ is evaluated with equation (2).

Step3: Determine the Iterative Termination Condition. The termination condition can be either a threshold of the affinity or the maximum number of generations. Here, the termination in the cloanl selection algorithm is triggered whenever the maximum number of generations is attained. If it holds, the iteration stops and then the optimal antibody in current population is the final solution. Otherwise, it continues.

Step4: Clone. Implement the clonal proliferation operation on the current parent population $\mathbf{A}(k)$, then $\mathbf{Y}(k) = \{Y_1(k), Y_2(k), \cdots, Y_n(k)\}$. The clonal size q_i of each antibody can be determined proportionally by the affinity between antibody and antigen or be a constant integer for convenience.

Step5: Affinity Maturation Operation. The clonal mutation operation is implemented on $\mathbf{Y}(k)$ with the mutation probability $P_m = 1/D$, and then $\mathbf{Z}(k)$ is achieved.

Step6: Affinity Evaluation. The corresponding feature subset is gotten based on each antibody of current population $\mathbf{Z}(k)$, and the new training datasets are obtained. The affinity $\{f(\mathbf{Z}(k))\}$ is evaluated with (2).

Step7: Clonal Selection. In i-th (i = 1, 2, ..., n) subpopulation, if there exists a mutated antibody $b_i(k) = \{z_{ij}^*(k) \mid f(z_{ij}^*(k)) = \max f(z_{ij}(k)), j = 1, 2, \cdots, q_i\}$, and $f(b_i(k)) > f(a_i(k))$, $a_i \in A(k)$, $b_i(k)$ replaces the antibody a_i and is added to the new population of next generation $A(k + 1)$.

Step8: Affinity Evaluation. Based on each antibody of current population, corresponding feature subset is obtained and the new training sample sets are gotten. The affinity $\{f(A(k + 1))\}$ is evaluated with equation (2).

Step 9: $k = k + 1$, return to **Step3**.

4. EXPERIMENTAL RESULTS

4.1 Results on Datasets from UCI Repository

To elucidate relative advantages of the proposed feature selection, the results of different feature selection algorithms on six datasets from UCI machine learning repository (Blake, Keogh, & Merz, 1998) are presented. Table 1 summarizes the characteristics of the used datasets. According to the categorization of problem sizes described by Kudo and Sklansky (2000), small with $0 < D \leq 19$, medium with $20 \leq D \leq 49$, and large with $50 \leq D$, the used small-sized datasets include wine, heart, and Australia, WDBC and ionosphere are medium-sized, and the last dataset, sonar is large-sized.

After feature selection, the nearest neighbor algorithm is carried out as classifier here, and classification rate is used to evaluate the performance of selected feature subsets. In the experiments, each dataset was randomly partitioned into training and testing sets with equal size (50% of the data used for training and the remaining 50% for testing).

The GA-based feature selection (GA-FS) is carried out on each dataset for comparison. The same encoding scheme and evaluation function as those also used in CSA-FS are used in GA-FS. Over a given data partition, 5 runs of GA are carried out and the average and maximum accuracy rates are recorded. 'Mean (Std. dev.)' of GA-FS listed in Table 2 represents the mean and the standard deviation over 50 runs of GA (10 partitions of the dataset, 5 runs for each partition), while 'Best (Std. dev.)' of GA-FS represents the mean and the standard deviation of the best results by GA-FS over 10 partitions of each dataset among the 5 independent runs of GA. In the experiments, the parameters of GA are set as follows. The population size is 20. The stopping criterion is set to be the maximum number of evolutionary generations. It is set to be 50. The crossover rate is 0.6, and the mutation rate is 0.01.

Similar to GA-FS, in CSA-FS, 5 runs of the clonal selection algorithm are performed over a given data partition for each dataset. The mean and the standard deviation of average and the best results over 10 partitions of each dataset are listed in Table 2. The parameters of clonal selection algorithm are set as follows. The antibody population size is 20. For each dataset, the length of the antibody is the feature dimension. The clonal size is set to be a constant, 5. The stopping criterion is set to be the maximum number of evolutionary generation, 50. And the mutation rate is set to be $1/D$.

As we can see from Table 2, both feature selection methods, GA-FA and CSA-FS, improved the classification performance, compared with classification using all features. In comparison to the results of GA-FS, CSA-FS performs better on these datasets in terms of the classification rate. We also find that both feature selection methods did not reduce the dimension of features a lot on the small-scale datasets, such as wine, heart, and Australia. But on the middle-scale and large-scale datasets, such as WDBC, ionosphere, and sonar, the dimension of the selected feature subset is reduced greatly. Also, compared with GA-FS, smaller standard deviations of the classification rate given by CSA-FS demonstrate that the solution quality is quite stable.

Table 1. UCI datasets used in the experiments

Dataset	Size	Features	Class	Normalize
wine	178	13	3	Yes
heart	270	13	2	Yes
Australia	690	14	2	Yes
WDBC	569	30	2	Yes
ionosphere	351	34	2	No
sonar	208	60	2	No

Table 2. Comparison of results by nearest neighbor classifier with different feature selection algorithms

Dataset	All features		GA-FS				CSA-FS			
			Mean (Std. dev.)		Best (Std. dev.)		Mean (Std. dev.)		Best (Std. dev.)	
	Dim	Rate	Dim	Rate	Dim	Rate	Dim	Rate	Dim	Rate
wine	13	94.94 (1.78)	12.12(0.42)	95.43(1.26)	11.90(0.74)	96.77(1.30)	12.16(0.34)	96.31(1.37)	12.10(0.74)	97.41(1.20)
heart	13	74.06 (4.16)	12.40(0.21)	74.16(3.77)	12.00(0.47)	75.95(3.83)	12.30(0.26)	75.35(3.26)	12.50(0.71)	76.88(3.54)
Australia	14	80.28 (1.95)	12.98(0.27)	80.34(1.45)	12.50(0.53)	81.60(1.33)	12.72(0.51)	80.38(1.47)	12.70(1.16)	81.75(1.40)
WDBC	30	94.59 (1.10)	12.06(1.22)	92.85(0.88)	13.50(4.64)	94.63(0.74)	13.94(0.35)	93.18(0.89)	14.40(0.70)	94.73(0.91)
ionosphere	34	80.05 (3.11)	16.18(0.61)	82.07(1.79)	16.00(0.67)	84.70(1.98)	15.06(0.89)	83.49(3.47)	15.20(1.03)	86.35(2.17)
sonar	60	79.99 (3.55)	42.88(1.11)	80.79(2.86)	42.40(3.13)	81.76(2.66)	45.30(1.66)	81.38(2.08)	44.40(2.55)	83.64(2.01)

* Dim is the dimension of features used. Rate is the classification rate (%).

4.2 Brodatz Textures Classification

In many applications, such as image classification, feature selection is often performed on the basis of feature extraction. We first extract some potential features, and then implement the feature selection and classification. In this experiment, we choose 16 similar textures from the Brodatz texture database for classification, they are D006, D009, D019, D020, D021, D024, D029, D053, D055, D057, D078, D080, D083, D084, D085, D092, as shown in Fig.4.

For each type of texture, we have 25 sub-images with size of 128×128 pixels. In the experiment, 10 sub-images of each texture are used for training and the remaining 15 sub-images are used for testing.

For the **texture classification**, an efficient description of image texture is needed. Here, we extract 14-dimensiton statistic features which are derived from gray-level co-occurrence matrix (Haralick, Shanmugam, & Dinstein, 1973) and 10-dimension energy features from the undecimated wavelet decomposition (Fukuda, & Hirosawa, 1999). Brief introductions of both texture feature extraction methods are given in the next sub-section. We first extract these features for training samples, and then make use of the feature selection method to choose an optimal subset from the above extracted 24-dimension features. Finally, the nearest neighbor algorithm is applied to classify the 16 types of textures.

Figure 4. 16 types of Brodatz textures

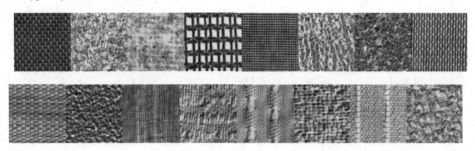

In the clonal selection algorithm, the antibody population size is 10 and the length of each antibody is 24. The maximum number of generations is 20. The clonal size is 5, and the mutation rate is set to be $P_m = 1/24$. We also compared the results with GA-FS. The parameters of GA are set as follows. The population size is 10, the maximum number of evolutionary generations is 20, the mutation rate is 0.01 and the crossover rate is set to be 0.8. The average and best values over 20 independent runs of each method are recorded in Table 3.

From Table 3, it is found that the feature selection method based on clonal selection algorithm is better than GA in terms of the dimension of the selected feature subset and the classification accuracy. Especially, among the 20 experiments, the best classification accuracy based on the selected feature subsets by GA and clonal selection algorithm are both up to 99.58%, but the dimension of the selected feature subsets by the clonal selection algorithm is 11, while that by GA is 19.

4.3 SAR Image Classification

Synthetic aperture radar (SAR) images find increasingly wide applications because SAR sensors can penetrate clouds and work in bad weather conditions and the night when optical sensors are inoperable. One of the most important problems in SAR image applications is land covers classification.

Texture is an important characteristic used for identifying objects or regions of interest in an image (Haralick, Shanmugam, & Dinstein, 1973). Especially, for single-band and single-polarized **SAR image classification**, texture may provide abundant useful information. It contains significant information about the structural arrangement of surfaces and their relationship to the surrounding environment. It can be considered that texture is an innate property of all surfaces. There exist various methods in extracting textural information based on statistic methods, for example, the histogram statistic method, auto correlation function algorithm, energy spectrum and correlation frequency method etc. More recently, the texture features based on the gray-level co-occurrence matrix (Haralick, Shanmugam, & Dinstein, 1973; Solberg, & Jain, 1997) and the methods of multi-channel or multi-resolution have received much attention (Peleg, Naor, Hartley, & Avnir, 1984). Obviously, combining different texture features above is helpful to improve the classification accuracy. However, the resulting redundancy and the additive computation time is usually contaminated the performance of classifiers. Accordingly, it is necessary to find the most suitable feature subset for **SAR image classification**. The new feature selection method based on clonal selection algorithm is applied to search the optimal texture feature subset here. And support vector machine (SVM) (Vapnik, 1995), a learning machine with good generalization performance, is applied to SAR image classification using the selected features.

4.3.1 Texture Feature Extraction

In this section, we investigate the performance of texture features derived from the gray-level co-occurrence matrix (GLCM) and the gray-gradient co-occurrence matrix (GGCM), and the energy measures of the undecimated wavelet decomposition (Fukuda, & Hirosawa, 1999) for land covers classification of SAR images.

Table 3. 16 types of Brodatz textures classification by nearest neighbor classifier with different selected features

Methods	All features	GA-FS		CSA-FS	
		Mean	Best	Mean	Best
Dimension	24	13.6	19	9.8	11
Accuracy (%)	98.75	96.45	99.58	97.59	99.58

GLCM Based Statistic Features

GLCM method is frequently used in texture analysis and texture feature extraction for SAR images. Texture features are demonstrated by the statistics over the GLCM. In this work, 14 statistics suggested by Haralick et. al (1973) are used, including angular second moment, contrast, correlation, sum of squares: variance, inverse difference moment, sum average, sum variance, sum entropy, entropy, difference variance, difference entropy, information measure of correlation I, information measure of correlation II and maximal correlation coefficient.

There are four parameters that must be indicated to generate a GLCM, i.e. the interpixel orientation, distance, grey level quantization, and window size (Clausi, & Zhao, 2002). Here we set the interpixel orientation to 0^0 for convenient calculation. Short interpixel distances typically generate the preferred texture features in SAR image analysis (Barber, & LeDrew, 1991), so we set interpixel distance to 1. The role of different values for gray levels and windows size with respect to statistics from GLCM has been investigated in many literatures (Clausi, 2002; Clausi, & Yue, 2004). According to their analysis and fine-tune experiments, in this study, we set the image quantization to 16 and the window size to 9×9.

GGCM Based Statistic Features

GLCM based texture features have achieved considerable success in texture classification in that it characterizes effectively the gray-tone spatial dependencies. However, GLCM based method cannot provide the edge information. A solution is to combine the features extracted from gray-level co-occurrence matrix with those extracted from gray-gradient co-occurrence matrix that concerns the associated statistic distribution of the gray and the edge gradient. From the GGCM, 15 features are computed including little gradient dominance, large gradient dominance, gray heterogeneity, gradient heterogeneity, energy, gray average, gradient average, gray mean square error, gradient mean square error, correlation, gray entropy, gray entropy, hybrid entropy, inertia and inverse difference moment.

Wavelet Energy Features

Wavelet transform has the ability to examine a signal at different scales. In this study, the undecimated wavelet based texture feature set composed by the energies of the subband coefficients is used. A multiresolution feature extraction with 2 or 3 levels is preferable to a local analysis. Here we implement 3-level wavelet decomposition on each square local area with size of 16×16. The features of each pixel can be represented as a 10-dimension vector $(e_{LL-1}, e_{LH-1}, e_{HL-1}, e_{HH-1}, e_{LH-2}, e_{HL-2}, e_{HH-2}, e_{LH-3}, e_{HL-3}, e_{HH-3})$, in which, for example e_{LL-1} denotes the energy of the LL subimage in the first level.

4.3.2 SAR Image Classification Based on Clonal Feature Selection

Experiment 1. X-SAR Image

The first experiment is carried out on a 3-look X-band SAR sub-image of Switzerland obtained by Space Radar Laboratory Missions in 1994, as shown in Fig. 5 (a). The image consists of three types of land covers: water, urban area and mountain. Left part of this image is the mountain area, the water is on the top right, and the bottom middle is the urban area. The training set consists of 658 representative samples, including 277 water samples, 115 urban area samples, and 316 mountain samples. The test set with 616 samples is used to evaluate the performance of different methods. It includes 213 water samples, 98 urban area samples, and 305 mountain samples. 29-dimension features are extracted from GLCM and GGCL for the center pixel in a certain window region. In the clonal selection algorithm, the antibody population size is set to be 10, and the length of each antibody is 29. The maximum number of generations is 50. And the clonal size is 5. SVM with Gaussian kernel function is used for classification. The classification results are shown in Fig.5.

In the classification result with features from GLCM, as shown in Fig.5 (b), a part of mountain area is misclassified into urban area seriously. In the classification result with features from GGCM, shown in Fig.5 (c), the mountain area in the bottom left is misclassified to water. The result with the combination of two kinds of features, shown in Fig.5 (d), improves the classification performance. Especially, the misclassified regions in the mountain area in Fig. 5(b) and Fig.5 (c) are correctly classified. The best result is obtained by using the 9-dimension features selected by CSA-FS. The water and the mountain areas are well distinguished.

Also, the results using different features are compared in terms of the classification accuracy and kappa coefficient on the test samples. The results are listed in Table 4. From the results, it is clear that CSA-FS gets the best results in terms of the classification accuracy and kappa coefficient.

Figure 5. X-SAR image classification (a) original image, (b) classification with the 14-dimension features extracted from GLCM, (c) classification with the 15-dimension features extracted from GGCM, (d) classification with combination of two kinds of features (29-dimension), (e) classification with 9-dimension features selected by CSA-FS

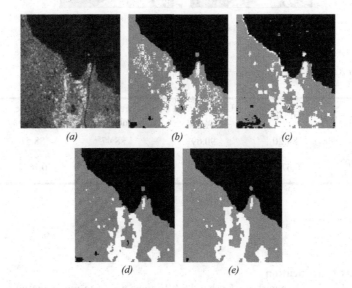

Table 4. Comparison of X-SAR image classification results

	GLCM	GGCM	Feature combination	CSA-FS
Accuracy (%)	80.03	71.59	88.47	92.21
Kappa coefficient	0.7018	0.5817	0.8193	0.8773

Figure 6. Ku-band SAR image classification (a) original image, (b) classification with the 14-dimension features extracted from GLCM, (c) classification with the 10-dimension energy measures of the undecimated wavelet decomposition, (d) classification with combination of two kinds of features (24-dimension), (e) classification with 4-dimension features selected by CSA-FS

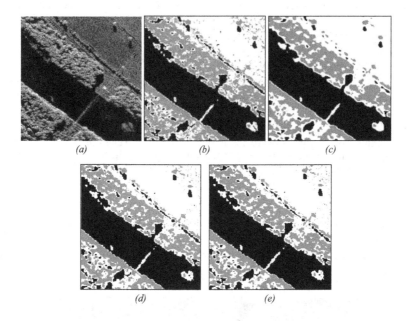

Table 5. Comparison of Ku-SAR image classification results

	GLCM	Undecimated wavelet	Feature combination	Feature selection
Accuracy (%)	84.20	90.69	88.47	88.51
kappa coefficient	0.6789	0.7897	0.7651	0.7655

Experiment 2. Ku-SAR Classification

The image, as shown in Fig. 7 (a), is a part of a Ku-band SAR image with one-meter spatial resolution in the area of Rio Grande River near Albuquerque, New Mexico. This image consists of three types of land-cover: water, vegetation, and crop.

We select 50 samples from each class to compose the training set. The 24-dimension texture features are extracted from GLCM and the undecimated wavelet decomposition. In clonal selection algorithm, the antibody population size is 10 and the length of each antibody is 24. The maximum number of generations is 50, and the clonal size is set to be 5. SVM with Gaussian kernel function is used for classification. Classification results are shown in Fig.6. A test set, including 957 vegetation samples, 352 river samples, and 968 crop samples, is used to evaluate the performance of different methods. In Table 5, the average classification accuracy and Kappa coefficient of different methods are listed.

Figure 7. One-meter X-SAR image classification (a) original image, (b) classification with the 14-dimension features extracted from GLCM, (c) classification with the 10-dimension energy measures of the undecimated wavelet decomposition, and (d) classification with 8-dimension features selected by CSA-FS. ©2008 Institute of Intelligent Information Processing, Xidian University, Xi'an, China. Used with permission.

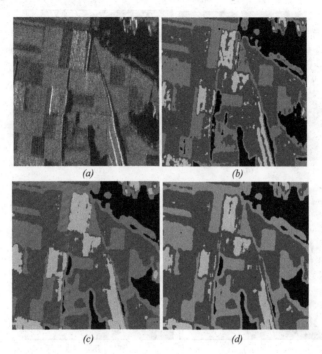

(a)   *(b)*

(c)   *(d)*

The classification result with 14-dimension features extracted from GLCM is shown in Fig. 6 (b). The crop on the upper right is misclassified as the vegetation. The classification result with the 10-dimension energy measures of the undecimated wavelet decomposition, as shown in Fig. 7 (c), improves the uniformity in the crop region. However, it loses details such as the pipeline on the river. The classifications with the combination of two kinds of features and with the selected feature subset by CSA-FS get the similar results as shown in Fig.7 (d) and Fig.7 (e). Both methods preserved the detail. But the latter used much fewer features than the former. The feature dimensions used in the two methods are 24 and 4 respectively.

Furthermore, we compared the GA-FS with CSA-FS in this SAR image classification. For both algorithms, the termination condition is set to be the maximum number of generations, 50. Two methods take the approximately same time 9 seconds for feature selection. But the CSA-FS converges to the stable affinity 1995.72287 at the 20th generation, and the dimension of the selected feature subset is 4; while the GA-FS gets to the affinity 1994.59083 when the iteration stops, and the dimension of the selected feature subset is 7.

Experiment 3. X-SAR Image Classification

We also performed the experiments on other three X-band SAR images. Fig.7 is an X-SAR image with one-meter resolution, and it contains four types land covers: river and three kinds of vegetations. Fig.8 is an X-SAR image with three-meter resolution, and consists of four different land covers: city, river and two kinds of crops. Fig.9 is an X-SAR image with five-meter resolution and contains four land covers: city, river and two kinds of crops. The parameters set in the experiments are the same as those set in Experiment 2. From the classification results, we

Figure 8. Three-meter X-SAR image classification (a) original image, (b) classification with the 14-dimension features extracted from GLCM, (c) classification with the 10-dimension energy measures of the undecimated wavelet decomposition, and (d) classification with 6-dimension features selected by CSA-FS. ©2008 Institute of Intelligent Information Processing, Xidian University, Xi'an, China. Used with permission.

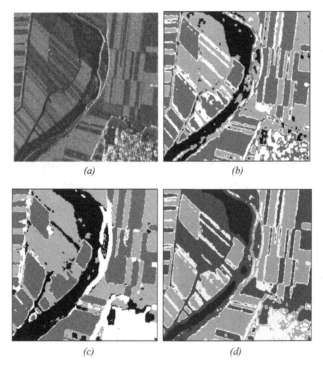

(a)   *(b)*

(c)   *(d)*

find that CSA-FS improve the SAR classification performance, and can get better classification for SAR images with selected fewer features.

5. CONCLUDING REMARKS

Feature selection is an important task in pattern recognition, and various methods have been proposed and applied in applications, such as text categorization, image retrieval, gene selection, and so on. Feature selection can be considered as an optimization problem. Because the clonal selection algorithm combines the local optimization and the global searching simultaneously, it is a good choice for finding an optimal feature subset for classifier. In this work, we proposed a filter feature selection approach based on the clonal selection algorithm. Experimental results on some datasets from UCI learning repository demonstrated the effectiveness of the method. And results on SAR image classifications demonstrated the good performance of the method in applications. Also, feature selection is usually performed on the extracted features in practice. Therefore, feature extraction is important as well.

Figure 9. Five-meter X-SAR image classification (a) original image, (b) classification with the 14-dimension features extracted from GLCM, (c) classification with the 10-dimension energy measures of the undecimated wavelet decomposition, and (d) classification with 6-dimension features selected by CSA-FS. ©2008 Institute of Intelligent Information Processing, Xidian University, Xi'an, China. Used with permission.

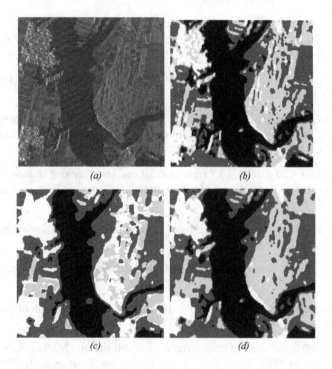

6. FUTURE RESEARCH DIRECTIONS

In the feature selection, how to evaluate the selected feature subset is seriously relevant to the performance of the classification. Therefore, the definition of the affinity function in the feature selection based on clonal selection algorithm is an important problem. In order to improve the classification performance, to define an effective evaluation function for a given task should be studied.

Feature selection for classification, or supervised feature selection is a popular work, and has been successfully applied to various applications because it can improve the accuracy and lighten or even avoid the dimension curse as well. Compared with supervised learning, however, feature selection for unsupervised learning, or unsupervised feature selection received little attention. Unsupervised feature selection is more difficult because one has not effective guidance for finding relevant features without class labels. The task is made more challenging when the number of clusters is unknown. Feature selection for unsupervised learning using optimization algorithms in AISs is worth being studied in the future research.

ACKNOWLEDGMENT

This work was supported by the National Natural Science Foundation of China (Grant No. 60672126, 60673097, 60703107), the National High Technology Research and Development Program (863 Program) of China (Grant

No. 2008AA01Z125), the Key Project of Ministry of Education of China (No.108115), and the National Basic Research Program (973 Program) of China (Grant No. 2006CB705700).

REFERENCES

Almuallim, H., & Dietterich, T. G. (1991). Learning with many irrelevant features. In *Proceedings of the Ninth National Conference on Artificial Intelligence*, (pp. 547-552). San Jose, CA: AAAI Press.

Barber, D. G., & LeDrew, E. F. (1991). SAR sea ice discrimination using texture statistics: a multivariate approach. *Photogrammetric Engineering & Remote Sensing, 57*(4), 385–395.

Bezerra, G. B., de Castro, L. N., & Zuben, F. J. V. (2004). A hierachical immune network applied to gene expression data. In Nicosia, G., Cutello, V., Bentley, P., & Timmis, J. (Eds.), *Proc. 3rd Int. Conf. Artif. Immune Syst.*, Catania, Italy, (pp. 14–27).

Blake, C., Keogh, E., & Merz, C. J. (1998). *UCI repository of machine learning databases* [http://www.ics.uci.edu/~mlearn/MLRepository.html], Department of Information and Computer Science, University of California, Irvine, CA.

Blum, A. L., & Langley, P. (1997). Selection of relevant features and examples in machine learning. *Artificial Intelligence, 97*(2), 245–271.

Burnet, F. M. (1959). *The Clonal Selection Theory of Acquired Immunity*. Cambridge, MA, UK: Cambridge Univ. Press.

Clausi, D. A. (2002). An analysis of co-occurrence texture statistics as a function of grey level quantization. *Canadian Journal of Remote Sensing, 28*(1), 45–62.

Clausi, D. A., & Yue, B. (2004). Comparing cooccurrence probabilities and Markov Random Fields for texture analysis of SAR sea ice imagery. *IEEE Trans. Geoscience and Remote Sensing, 42*(1), 215-228.

Clausi, D. A., & Zhao, Y. (2002). Rapid extraction of image texture by co-occurrence using a hybrid data structure. *Computers & Geosciences, 28*(6), 763–774.

Dasgupta, D., & Gonzalez, F.A. (2002). An immunity-based technique to characterize intrusions in computer networks. *IEEE Trans. Evol. Comput., 6*, 281–291.

Dash, M., & Liu, H. (1997). Feature selection for classification. *Intelligent Data Analysis, 1*(3), 131–156.

de Castro, L. N., & Timmis, J. (2002). *Artificial Immune Systems: A New Computational Intelligence Paradigm*. London, UK: Springer-Verlag.

de Castro, L. N., & Von Zuben, F. J. (1999). *Artificial Immune Systems: part I-basic theory and applications*. FEEC/Univ. Campinas, Campinas, Brazil.

de Castro, L. N., & Von Zuben, F. J. (2000). Clonal selection algorithm with engineering applications. In *Proc GECCO's* (pp. 36–37). Las Vegas, NV.

de Castro, L. N. & Von Zuben, F. J. (2002). Learning and optimization using the clonal selection principle. *IEEE Trans. Evol. Comput., 6*. 239–251.

Doak, J. (1992). *An evaluation of feature selection methods and their application to computer security* (Tech. Rep.). Davis, CA: University of California, Department of Computer Science.

Du, H. F., Jiao, L. C., Gong, M. G., & Liu, R. C. (2004). Adaptive dynamic clone selection algorithms. In Shusaku Tsumoto, Roman Sowiński, Jan Komorowski, et al, (Ed.), *Proceedings of the Fourth International Conference on Rough Sets and Current Trends in Computing* (pp. 768–773). Uppsala, Sweden.

Du, H. F., Jiao, L.C., & Wang, S. A. (2002). Clonal operator and antibody clone algorithms. In Shichao, Z., Qiang, Y. & Chengqi, Z. (Ed.), *Proceedings of the First International Conference on Machine Learning and Cybernetics* (pp. 506-510). Beijing.

Forrest, S., Perelson, A. S., Allen, L., & Cherukuri, R. (1994). Self-nonself discrimination in a computer. In *Proc. IEEE Symp. Research in Security and Privacy*, Oakland, CA, (pp. 202–212).

Fukuda, S., & Hirosawa, H. (1999). A Wavelet-Based Texture Feature Set Applied to Classification of Multifrequency Polarimetric SAR Images. *IEEE Trans. on Geoscience and Remote Sensing, 37,* 2282–2286.

Gong, M. G., Du, H. F., & Jiao, L. C. (2006). *Optimal approximation of linear systems by artificeal immune response*, Science in China: Series F Information Sciences. Science in China Press, co-published with Springer-Verlag *GmbH, 49*(1), 63-79.

Haralick, R. M., Shanmugam, K., & Dinstein, I. (1973). Textural Features for Image Classification. *IEEE Trans. on System, Man, and Cybernetics, 3,* 610–621.

Il-Seok Oh, Jin-Seon Lee, & Byung-Ro Moon (2004). Hybrid genetic algorithms for feature selection, *IEEE Trans. Pattern Analysis and Machine Intelligence, 26*(11), 1424-1437.

Jackson, J. (1994). An efficient membership-query algorithm for learning DNF with respect to the uniform distribution. In *proceedings of the IEEE Symposium on Foundations of Computer Science.*

Jain, A. K., & Zongker, D. (1997). Feature selection: evaluation, application, and small sample performance. *IEEE Trans. Pattern Analysis and Machine Intelligence, 19*(2), 153-158.

John, G. H., Kohavi, R., & Peger, K. (1994). Irrelevant features and the subset selection problem. In *proceedings of the Eleventh International Conference on Machine Learning* (pp. 121-129). New Brunswick, NJ: Morgan Kaufmann.

Kira, K., & Rendell, L. A. (1992). The feature selection problem: Traditional methods and a new algorithm (pp. 129-134). In *proceedings of Ninth National Conference on AI.*

Kohavi, R., & John, G. H. (1997). Wrappers for Feature Subset Selection. *Artificial Intelligence Journal, 97,* 273–324.

Kohavi, R., & Sommereld, D. (1995). Feature subset selection using the wrapper method: Overtting and dynamic search space topology. In *proceedings of First International Conference on Knowledge Discovery and Data Mining* (pp. 192-197). Morgan Kaufmann.

Koller, D., & Sahami, M. (1994). Toward optimal feature selection. In *proceedings of International Conference on Machine Learning* (pp. 171-182).

Kira, K., & Rendell, L. (1992). A practical approach to feature selection. In *proceedings of the Ninth International Conference on Machine Learning* (pp 249-256). Aberdeen, Scotland: Morgan Kaufmann.

Langley, P. (1994). Selection of relevant features in machine learning. In *Proceedings of the AAAI Fall Symposium on Relevance* (pp. 1-5).

Li, R., Bhanu, B., & Dong, A. (2005). Coevolutionary Feature Synthesized EM Algorithm for Image Retrieval. In *proceedings of the Application of Computer Multimedia* (pp. 696–705).

Lin, Y., & Bhanu, B. (2005). Evolutionary Feature Synthesis for Object Recognition. *IEEE Trans. on Systems, Man, and Cybernetics–Part C, 35,* 156–171.

Liu, H., & Yu, L. (2005). Toward Integrating Feature Selection Algorithms for Classification and Clustering. *IEEE Trans. Knowledge and Data Engineering, 17*(4), 491–502.

Meiri, R., & Zahavi, J. (2006). Using simulated annealing to optimize the feature selection problem in marketing applications. *European Journal of Operational Research*, *171*(3), 842–858.

Narendra P. M., & Fukunaga K. (1977). A branch and bound algorithm for feature subset selection. *IEEE Trans. on Computers*, C-*26*(9), 917–122.

Nicosia, G., Castiglione, F., & Motta, S. (2001). Pattern recognition by primary and secondary response of an artificial immune system. *Theory in Biosciences*, *120*(2), 93–106.

Peleg, S., Naor, J., Hartley, R., & Avnir, D. (1984). Multiple Resolution Texture Analysis and Classification. *IEEE Trans. on Pattern Analysis and Machine Intelligence*, *6*, 518–523.

Raymer, M.L., Punch, W.F., Goodman, E.D., Kuhn, L.A., & Jain, A.K. (2000). Dimensionality reduction using genetic algorithms. *IEEE Trans. Evolutionary Computation*, *4*(2), 164–171.

Schlimmer, J. C. (1993). Efficiently inducing determinations: A complete and systematic search algorithm that uses optimal pruning. In *proceedings of Tenth International Conference on Machine Learning* (pp. 284–290).

Siedlecki, W. & Sklansky, J. (1988). On automatic feature selection. *International Journal of Pattern Recognition and Artificial Intelligence*, *2*, 197–220.

Solberg, A. H. S., & Jain, A. K. (1997). Texture Fusion and Feature Selection Applied to SAR Imagery. *IEEE Trans. on Geoscience and Remote Sensing*, *35*, 475–479.

Sun, Z. H., Yuan, X. J., Bebis, G., & Louis, S. J. (2002). Neural-Network-based Gender Classification Using Genetic Search for Eigen-Feature Selection. *IEEE International Joint Conference on Neural Networks*, *3*, 2433–2438.

Timmis, J., & Neal, M. (2001). A recourse limited artificial immune system for data analysis. *Knowledge Based Systems*, *14*(3–4), 121–130.

Vapnik, V. (1995). *The Nature of Statistical Learning Theory*. Springer-Verlag, New York.

Yang, J., & Honavar, V. (1998). Feature Subset Selection Using a Genetic Algorithm. *IEEE Trans. on Intelligent Systems*, *13*, 44–49.

Zhang, X., Tan, S., & Jiao, L. (2004). SAR Image Classification Based on Immune Clonal Feature Selection. In Proceedings of International Conference on Image Analysis and Recognition (pp. 504–511).

Zio, E., Baraldi, P., & Pedroni, N. (2006). Selecting features for nuclear transients classification by means of genetic algorithms, *IEEE Trans. Nuclear Science*, *53*(3), 1479–1493.

ADDITIONAL READING

Almullim H., & Dietterich T.G. (1991). Learning with many irrelevant features. In Proc. Ninth National Conf. on Artificial Intelligence (pp. 547–552).

Bruzzone L. (2000). An approach to feature selection and classification of remote sensing images based on the Bayes rule for minimum cost. *IEEE Trans. Geoscience and Remote Sensing*, *38*(1), 429–438.

Caruana, R. A., & Freitag, D. (1994). Greedy attribute selection. In *Proceedings of the Eleventh International Conference on Machine Learning* (pp. 28–36). New Brunswick, NJ: Morgan Kaufmann.

Casillas, J., Cordon, O., et al. (2001). Genetic feature selection in a fuzzy rule-based classification system learning process for high dimensional problems. *Information Sciences*, *136*(1-4), 135–157.

Chakraborty, B. (2002). Genetic algorithm with fuzzy fitness function for feature selection. In *Proceedings of the 2002 IEEE International Symposium on Industrial Electronics* (pp. 315–319).

Dash, M., & Liu, H. (1997). Feature selection for classification. *Intelligent Data Analysis, 1*(3), 131–156.

Dietterich, T. (1997). Machine learning research: Four current directions. *AI Magazine, 18*(4), 97–136.

Frohlich, H., Chapelle, O., & Scholkopf, B. (2003). Feature selection for support vector machines by means of genetic algorithms. In *Proceedings of the 15th IEEE International Conference on Tools with Artificial Intelligence* (pp. 142–148). Sacramento, USA.

Hall, M. A. (1999). *Correlation-based feature selection for machine learning.* Unpublished doctoral dissertation, The University of Waikato, Hamilton, Newzealand.

NIPS 2003 workshop on feature extraction and feature selection challenge, Dec.11-13, 2003, Whistler, British Columbia, CA, http://www.clopinet.com/isabelle/Projects/NIPS2003/.

Huber, R., & Dutra, L. V. (1998). Feature selection for ERS-1/2 InSAR classification: high dimensionality case. In *Proceedings of International Geoscience and Remote Sensing Symposium*, Seattle (pp. 1605–1607).

Kittler, J. (1978). Feature set search algorithms. *Pattern Recognition and Signal Processing*, 41–60.

Last, A., Kandel, A., & Maimon, O. (2001). Information-theoretic algorithms for feature selection. *Pattern Recognition Letters, 22*(6–7), 799-811.

Littlestone, N. (1988). Learning quickly when irrelevant attributes abound: A new linear-threshold algorithm. *Machine Learning, 2*, 285-318.

Liu, H., & Motoda, H. (1998). *Feature selection for knowledge discovery and data mining.* Kluwer Academic Publishers.

Liu, H., & Setiono, R. (1998). Incremental feature selection. *Applied Intelligence, 9*(3), 217–230.

Mucciardi, A. N., & Gose, E. E. (1971). A comparison of seven techniques for choosing subsets of pattern recognition propertied. *IEEE Trans. Computers*, C-20, 1023–1031.

Pudil, P., Novovicova, J., & Kittler, J. (1994). Floating search methods in feature selection. *Pattern Recognition Letters, 15*, 1119–1125.

Serpico, S. B., & Bruzzone L. (2001). A new search algorithm for feature selection in hyperspectral remote sensing images. *IEEE Trans. Geoscience and Remote Sensing, 39*(7), 1360–1367.

Weston, J., Mukherjee, S, et al. (2000). Feature selection for SVMS. *Advances in Neural Information Processing Systems, 13*, 668–674.

Wettschereck, D., Aha, D. W., & Mohri, T. (1997). A review and empirical evaluation of feature weighting methods for a class of lazy learning algorithms. *Artificial Intelligence Review, 10*, 1–37.

Zhang, L. X., Zhao, Y. N., Yang, Z. H., & Wang, J. X. (2003). A novel hybrid feature selection algorithm: using Relief Estimation for GA-Wrapper Search. In *Proceeding of the 2nd International Conference on Machine Learning and Cybernetics* (pp. 380–386).

KEY TERMS

Artificial Immune Systems: Artificial immune systems are adaptive systems inspired by theoretical immunology and observed immune functions, principles and models, which are applied to complex problem domains.

Clonal Selection: Human immune response relies on the prior formation of an incredibly diverse population of B cells and T cells. The specificity of both the B-cell receptors and T-cell receptors, that is, the epitope to which a given receptor can bind, is created by a remarkable genetic mechanism. Each receptor is created even though the epitope it recognizes may never have been present in the body. If an antigen with that epitope should enter the body, those few lymphocytes able to bind to it will do so. If they also receive a second co-stimulatory signal, they may begin repeated rounds of mitosis. In this way, clones of antigen-specific lymphocytes (B and T) develop providing the basis of the immune response. This phenomenon is called clonal selection.

Feature Selection: Feature selection attempts to select the minimally sized of features without performance loss or even with performance improvement comparing with using all features.

Natural Computation: Natural computation is the study of computational systems that are inspired from natural systems, including biological, ecological, physical, chemical, economical and social systems.

Optimization: Find values of the variables that minimize or maximize the objective function while satisfying the constraints.

Pattern Classification: Pattern classification is a sub-topic of machine learning. It is concerned with the automatic discovery of regularities in data through the use of learning algorithms.

SAR Image Classification: SAR image classification is to use machine learning algorithms to classify the land covers via SAR images.

Texture Classification: Texture is a fundamental property of surfaces. Texture classification is one of the four problem domains in the field of texture analysis. The other three are texture segmentation, texture synthesis, and shape from texture. Texture classification process involves two important phases: efficient description of image texture, and learning and recognition.

Section I.V
Some New Types of Artificial Immune Networks

Immune network theory is an important and classical theory in immunology. But by using metaphor, the other kinds of immune network can also work in solving engineering problems. Several kinds of immune networks are developed for special aim or general model.

Chapter X
Immune Based Bio–Network Architecture and its Simulation Platform for Future Internet

Yong-Sheng Ding
Ministry of Education, China

Xiang-Feng Zhang
Ministry of Education, China & Shanghai Dianji University, China

Li-Hong Ren
Ministry of Education, China

ABSTRACT

Future Internet should be capable of extensibility, survivability, mobility, and adaptability to the changes of different users and network environments, so it is necessary to optimize the current Internet architecture and its applications. Inspired by the resemble features between the immune systems and future Internet, the authors introduce some key principles and mechanisms of the immune systems to design a bio-network architecture to address the challenges of future Internet. In the bio-network architecture, network resources are represented by various bio-entities, while complex services and application can be emerged from the interactions among bio-entities. Also, they develop a bio-network simulation platform which has the capability of service emergence, evolution, and so forth. The simulation platform can be used to simulate some complex services and applications for Internet or distributed network. The simulators with different functions can be embedded in the simulation platform. As a demonstration, this chapter provides two immune network computation models to generate the emergent services through computer simulation experiments on the platform. The experimental results show that the bio-entities on the platform provide quickly services to the users' requests with short response time. The interactions among bio-entities maintain the load balance of the bio-network and make the resources be utilized reasonably. With the advantages of adaptability, extensibility, and survivability, the bio-network architecture provides a novel way to design new intelligent Internet information services and applications.

INTRODUCTION

The development of Internet technologies enables more and more man-made devices to access Internet and act as its components, which shows us a bright prospect of Internet. The future Internet will be the core of the worldwide

Copyright © 2009, IGI Global, distributing in print or electronic forms without written permission of IGI Global is prohibited.

information infrastructure and the general service platform with computation, communication, entertainment, e-business, and so on. So future Internet should configure and reconfigure its network services dynamically to satisfy demanders, and Internet applications can adapt to the change of different network environments. Internet nodes also should be secure and can survive failures and attacks. Obviously, the future Internet should be capable of extensibility, survivability, mobility, and adaptability to network environments. It is necessary to optimize the current Internet architecture and its applications to address the challenges of the above requirements.

Biological systems such as human beings can be regarded as sophisticated information processing systems, and can be expected to provide inspiration for various ideas to science and engineering. Artificial immune systems (AIS), one of biologically-motivated information processing systems, have recently received much attention of researchers (Castro & Timmis, 2002; Ding & Ren, 2000). Immunized computational systems combining a prior knowledge with the adaptive capabilities of immune systems can provide a powerful alternative to currently available techniques for intelligent systems. AIS are adaptive systems based upon the models of natural systems in which learning takes place by evolutionary mechanisms similar to biological evolutions. AIS do not precisely model the human immune system or provide an explanation of how the immune system works. They provide problem-solving methods to some complex problems. However, the recent studies of AIS are mainly focusing on the intelligent control, fault diagnose, optimization, pattern recognition, associative memory, computer security, and so on. All of these models are referred to one or two aspects of biological immune system, and its complex behaviors and systemic intelligence have not been developed yet.

Inspired by the resemble features between future Internet and the immune systems, we can introduce some key principles and mechanisms of the immune systems into the design for future Internet. So we can apply these theories and mechanisms, particularly the emergent behaviors, to design a novel bio-network architecture (Ding & Ren, 2003), which provides for future Internet application environments. And we can further build a bio-network simulation platform which has the capability of service emergence, evolution etc. (Gao et al., 2004; Ren & Ding, 2002). The platform can be used to simulate some complex services and applications for Internet or distributed systems.

In this chapter, we discuss the design and implementation of the bio-network architecture and its simulation platform, particularly, how the bio-entities, the society-entities, and the interactions among the society-entities are designed to emerge some complex services and applications for Internet or distributed systems. We also provide two examples of bio-network simulators to generate the emergent services from the immune network computation models to demonstrate the feasibility of the bio-network architecture through computer simulation experiments on the platform.

BACKGROUND

The Requirements of Future Internet

Future Internet should exhibit a strong sense of automation: 1) Support for survivability from massive failures and attacks; 2) Ability to configure and reconfigure system dynamically; 3) Awareness of Internet system environment; 4) Seeking of behavior optimization to achieve its goal; and 5) Requirement to detailed knowledge of system components and status.

The requirements of future Internet resemble the self-organizing and the self-healing properties of biological systems. There is a strong similarity between the complex interaction of organisms in biological systems and that of components in a networked system (Bhalla & Lyengar, 1999; Girvan & Newman, 2002). This makes us to study the relationships among components in the Internet environment by associating it with biological systems, especially with some key concepts and principles in biological immune systems. As such, we can introduce some immune mechanisms to study evolutionary Internet systems with those desirable properties.

Immune Emergent Computation for Future Internet

Emergent computation is generally characterized by the interaction of relatively simple entities, forming a system that as a whole is said to exhibit emergent properties (Harada & Kinoshita, 2003; Pagello et al., 2003; Read, 2003). Emergent computation has three aspects: self-organization, aggregative behavior, and cooperative behavior. Self-organization means that emergent behavior is produced spontaneously in an original random system. Aggregative behavior shows that many entities interact with each other in the system but the whole behavior is emphasized. Cooperative behavior shows that the whole behavior is more than summation of each entity.

The biological immune system is a secure and survivable system and can still be active even if invaders or accidents destroy some issues (Hoffmann, 1986; Jerne, 1973; Jerne, 1974; Perelson, 1989). The whole behavior of the immune system is an emergent behavior of many local components' interactions (Vertosick & Kelly, 1989). We summarize the key features of the immune system related to the emergent computation as follows:

1) Emergent behavior. The immune system consists of many lymphocytes (such as, T cells and B cells) and every lymphocyte has several simple behavior rules, while a group of individuals (immune network) can behavior a complex emergent behavior (i.e. adaptability, evolution, security, and self-maintenance). These mechanisms can be applied to realize a secure, adaptive, self-healing, and survivable bio-network and its services for optimization of the future Internet.

2) Evolution. The immune system evolves through diversity and natural selection. The bio-entities in the bio-network are designed with evolutionary mechanisms to make their behaviors more efficient.

3) Diversity. There are various types of elements that together perform the role of identifying the body and protecting it from malefic invaders and malfunctioning cells. Various bio-entities provide different services and perform different functions in the bio-network.

4) Distributed Detection. The immune system is inherently distributed. The immune cells undergo constant recalculation through the blood, lymph, lymphoid organs, and tissue spaces. They will simulate specific immune responses if they encounter antigenic challenges. These mechanisms can be used to design the security of the future Internet.

5) Interaction of individuals. The interaction caused by stimulation and suppression adjusts the immune network to be in a stable state.

6) Autonomy. There is no central "element" to control the immune system. The immune system does not require outside intervention or maintenance. It works through autonomously classifying and eliminating pathogens and it is capable of partially repairing itself by replacing damaged or malfunctioning cell.

DESIGN OF THE IMMUNE-BASED BIO-NETWORK ARCHITECTURE

In order to study the complex Internet services and applications, particularly its emergent behaviors, we design the bio-network architecture by combining the mechanisms of the biological immune system with multi-agent systems (Tchikou & Gouraderes, 2003; Valckenaers et al., 2003), as shown in Fig. 1. The biological immune system is a set of active computational components interacting in a dynamic and unpredictable environment. Then, Its behaviors can be modeled in terms of bio-entities and society-entities. Bio-entities in the bio-network architecture are regarded as autonomous agents and possess the characteristics such as interaction, no central control, diversity, mobility, and evolution. The bio-network architecture will make it possible to emerge the complexity of the biological immune system from the interactions of bio-entities. We only need design simple biological behaviors of bio-entities, while complex behaviors are the emergence of bio-entities behaviors.

The layered infrastructure of the bio-network architecture consists of bio-entities, bio-entity survivable environment, bio-network core services, bio-network low-level functional modules, and bio-network simulators, as shown in Fig. 1.

Figure 1. The bio-network architecture

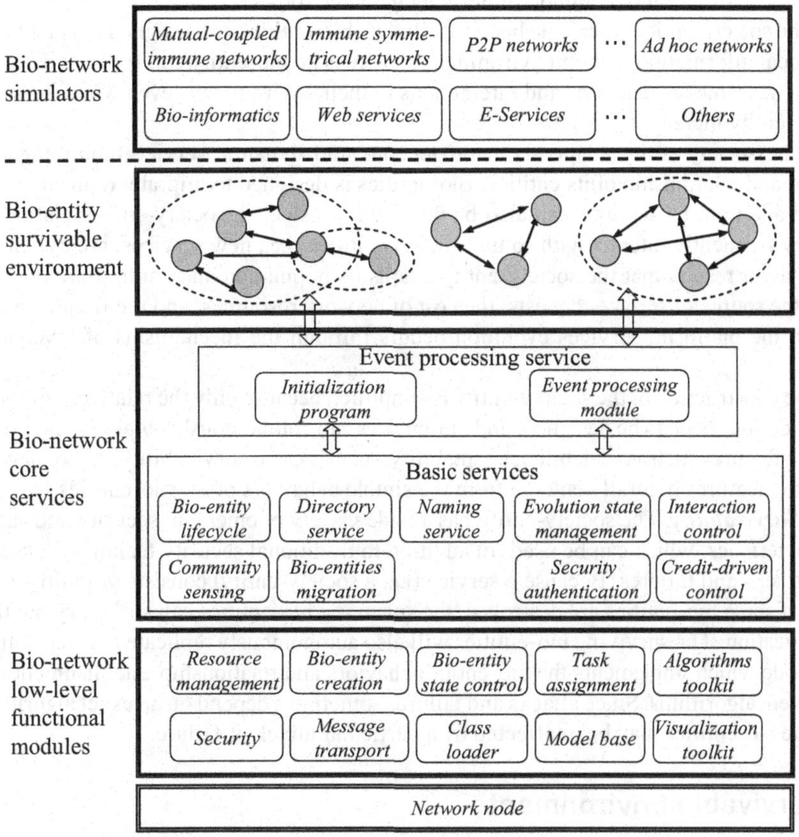

Bio-Entity and Society-Entity

A bio-entity is the least component in the network applications. The bio-entity consists of three main parts: attributes, body, and behaviors.

Attributes. Attributes of the bio-entity include bio-entity ID, relationship, bio-entity type, and stored energy level. Its relationship signifies how the bio-entity is related to the others in its environment. Its relationship includes the relationship type (e.g., society-entity, community, local), strength of the relationship, information about the bio-entities that it has relationship with (e.g. their IDs, locations, service types). The relationship is useful for interaction among bio-entities.

Body. Body contains materials relevant to the service that the bio-entity provides, such as data or user profiles (non-executable data), or application code (executable code).

Behavior. Behavior includes some autonomous actions of the bio-entities. The behavior can be defined according to the requirements of applications. The behaviors related to evolution mechanism include: migration, replication, reproduction, interaction, death, and so on.

In the bio-network architecture, a group of bio-entities establish the relationships among them, and they interact to form a society-entity. Actually, the society-entity is not an entity, but an emergent behavior based on interactions and relationships. They can provide some services through the emergence behaviors among the interaction of bio-entities.

The society-entity and the society-entity network are dynamic and changeable. The society-entity makes the preponderant bio-entities live and removes the inferior bio-entities so that the bio-network architecture can satisfy with the users' dynamic self-adaptability. The society-entity (that is, services and applications) based on the immune network shares a set of common important characteristics:

Scalability. The society-entity is scalable because all of its bio-entities are designed to act autonomously and locally based on local information in their environments. There is no bio-entity controlling all other bio-entities. Bio-entities repeat the same local actions and interactions in their environments even when the size and population of the society-entity increases.

Adaptation. The society-entity adapts to heterogeneous and dynamic service requirements through the emergent behavior and relationship of its entities. Bio-entities is designed to migrate, replicate or die according to the demand. In addition, bio-entities can also be designed to establish society-entity relationships with the bio-entity that they frequently interact with so that society-entities (i.e., new services) are dynamically created. The emergent behavior results that the society-entity adapts its population and configuration to the amount of service requests, the source of service requests, the cost of network resources, and the frequency of interaction.

Evolution. On the platform, services evolution occurs through the mechanisms of diversity and natural selection.

Simplicity. The construction of the society-entity is simplified because only the relatively simple behaviors of the individual bio-entities need to be designed, and bio-entities can autonomously obtains society-entity relationship. The other key features such as scalability, adaptability, security, and survivability, do not have to be directly designed. These key features naturally emerge from the simple behaviors of the bio-entities.

Security and Survivability. The society-entity has a wide variety of emergent security and survivability behaviors and characteristics, which can be used, in addition to traditional security techniques, as extra layers of defense against attacks and failures. Because a service (i.e. a society-entity) consists of multiple and replicated bio-entities, even if some bio-entities are destroyed, the surviving bio-entities can still carry out the function of the service or application. The surviving bio-entities will also autonomously replicate to re-establish their initial population. The code which implements the bio-entity behaviors and relationship establishment may be implemented with different algorithms. Since attacks and failures sometimes depend on an exact algorithmic sequence or parameter, some bio-entities may be unaffected by a particular attack or failure.

Bio-Entity Survivable Environment

The bio-entity survivable environment is a runtime environment for deploying and executing bio-entities and protects the node from attacking with some security policies.

In the bio-entity survivable environment, different bio-entities may be available to the bio-network architecture and they may contribute to different services. Information carried by bio-entities may or may not be accessible to other bio-entities at different levels. Therefore, the availability of a bio-entity depends on its relationship to the survivable environment, with very relevant bio-entities providing services quickly and irrelevant bio-entities interacting loosely or not at all. In this way, the survivable environment determines the interaction behaviors among bio-entities.

Bio-Network Core Services

The bio-network core service layer provides a set of general-purpose runtime services that are frequently used by bio-entities. They include event processing service and some basic services such as lifecycle service, directory service, naming service, community sensing service, bio-entities migration service, evolution state management service, interaction control service, credit-driven control service, security authentication service, and application service.

Bio-Network Low-Level Functional Modules

Bio-network low-level functional modules layer is a bridge to maintain access to various resources. It includes local resource management, bio-entity creation, bio-entity state control, local security, message transport, class loader, task assignment, model base, algorithms toolkit, visualization toolkit, etc.

Figure 2. The main components of the bio-network simulation platform

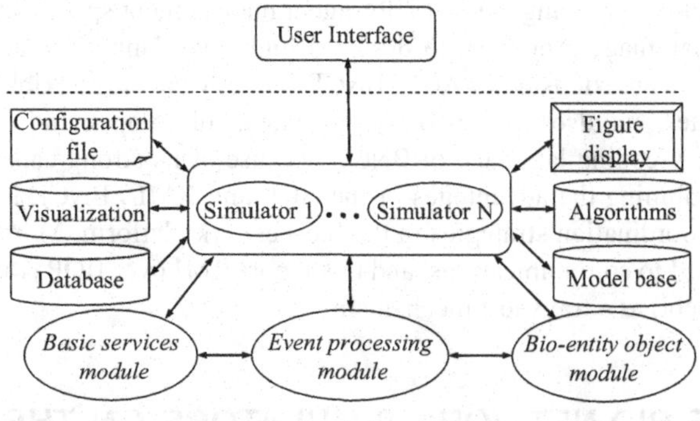

Bio-Network Simulators

Based on the bio-network architecture, we can build various simulators to study complex network services and applications. We only need design simple behaviors of bio-entities, and complex behaviors are the emergence of bio-entities behaviors. Also, we can seek the mapped relationships among bio-entity behaviors and emergent behaviors. The various simulators are helpful to describe complex biological systems of interacting bio-entities, and explore various possible applications in complex Internet system.

DEVELOPMENT OF THE BIO-NETWORK SIMULATION PLATFORM

Based on the bio-network architecture, the bio-network simulation platform is developed through utilizing multi-agent systems. The ideal model can place the bio-network platform on each device as a network node. Bio-network low-level functional modules layer is a bridge to maintain access to local resources.

The bio-network simulation platform is a software framework fully implemented by Java language, and its main components are as shown in Fig. 2. The platform includes simulators, configuration file, database, figure display, algorithms toolkit, and visualization toolkit. Where, algorithms toolkit includes various traditional intelligent algorithms and can be loaded by the bio-network platform. Visualization toolkit includes various visual methods to demonstrate the results in the bio-network platform.

The platform also includes some main modules such as basic services module, event processing module, and bio-entity object module. Basic services module implements the services designed in the bio-network platform. Event processing includes initialization program and event processing service. Event processing module is the core of connecting all the bio-network services. This module controls other services and coordinates relative components to provide services according to different service requests. Bio-entity object module implements the construct of a bio-entity, including the bio-entity's attributes and behaviors. It also implements simple services (tasks) that can be used by the simulator module.

Several mechanisms are adopted in the control and management of the bio-network platform. We provide two main mechanisms in the following.

Energy-driven mechanism. The livings of all bio-entities depend on energy, which is an important concept inspired from natural ecosystem. Bio-entities must store and consume energy for their livings. They expend energy for their usage of resources. In order to gain energy from users or other bio-entities, a bio-entity may perform a service. In addition, the changes of the bio-entity actions and the transitions of the bio-entity evolution states are driven by energy. For instance, the more abundant energy a bio-entity owns, the higher demand it needs. If the energy expenditure of a bio-entity is more than its energy earning by providing a service, the bio-entity will be lack of energy and not be permitted to use resources. As thus, it dies from its wasteful energy performances.

Bio-network communication mechanism. Society-entities implement the construction of various complex services. Searching, assembling, organizing and coordinating of bio-entities to form a society-entity depend on effective communication and cooperation mechanism. And, it is the foundation of using message communication to realize the flexible and complicated coordination tactics. We reuse "FIPA (Foundation for Intelligent Physical Agents) ACL (Agent Communication Language)" (FIPA agent management specification; Labrou et al., 1999), an abstract communication language protocols, to design a high-level language called BNCL (Bio-Network Communication Language). As an extension of ACL, BNCL not only enables flexible communications among bio-entities and society-entities, but also satisfies our requirements of an open and future-proof environment. Also, we use XML as primary coding language of BNCL because of its strong capability of data description and metadata aspect. By combining the advantages of the ACL and XML, BNCL is simple, flexible and can implement the complicated coordination strategies in the bio-network platform. Moreover, through BNCL, we are able to define a generic API to communications, and to support RMI over IIOP (Remote Method Invocation over Internet Inter-Orb Protocol) as a transport mechanism.

TWO EXAMPLES OF BIO-NETWORK SIMULATORS ON THE PLATFORM

On the bio-network simulation platform, we can simulate large-scale complex network services and applications. Also, we can seek the mapped relationships among basic behaviors, bio-entity behaviors, and emergent behaviors. The Internet services and applications would be easily created using this method because we only need to design simple behaviors of bio-entities. Others requirements, e.g. self-adaptation and evolution, would be implemented through the emergence of bio-entities behaviors.

Some immune network simulators designed on the platform can be applied to complex applications. Following, we provide two examples of the emergent services generated from the immune network computation models. One is the mutual-coupled immune network computation model to satisfy various users' requirements of Web service. The other one is the peer to peer (P2P) network service model based on the immune symmetrical network theory. The feasibility of the two models is demonstrated through computer simulation experiments on the platform.

A Web Service Simulator Based on Mutual-Coupled Immune Network

A. Mutual-Coupled Immune Network Model

The mutual-coupled immune network hypothesis shows that the immune systems are constructed by forming large-scale immune networks with the interactions among small-scale networks (Ishiguro et al., 1996). According to the hypothesis, we consider that each small-scale network has a specific task, and can be regarded as a local immune network (LIN). The interactions among the small-scale networks form a global network, and the global

Figure 3. The mutual-coupled immune network model

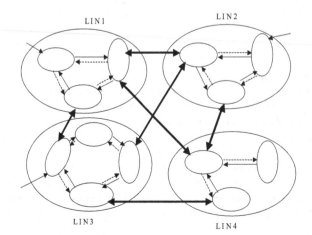

Figure 4. The emergent computation model for providing services

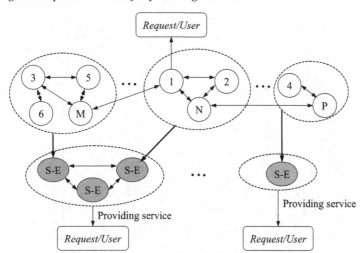

network has remarkable ability to accomplish a complex task. We demonstrate that LINs mutually communicate and form a global immune network in Fig. 3.

B. Web Service Simulator

Based on the emergent computation model of the mutual-coupled immune network in Fig. 3, a Web service simulator is designed as shown in Fig. 4. In the simulator, a bio-entity is regarded as an anti-body, while a user's request or other bio-entity is regarded as an antigen. When a user sends a request message to the platform, a bio-entity will provide services to the user if it has this specific function. If no bio-entity can provide complex service, the bio-entities on the same platform will interact with each other, such as bio-entities 3, 5, 6, and *M* to develop a society-entity (S-E in Fig. 4). They will mutually communicate and interact to finish the service emergence for the request. Several society-entities also communicate to form a society-entity network. The society-entity and the society-entity network are dynamic in the bio-network architecture. The society-entity makes the superior bio-entities live and removes the inferior bio-entities from the bio-network so that the bio-network can satisfy the users' variable requirements.

When the simulation begins, the simulator calls the configuration file to set parameters and proper circumstance first. Then, we configure the information about network nodes and network topology. The bio-entities will migrate from the nodes that they host to other nodes in order to provide services if these nodes send requests. Thus these bio-entities on different nodes will form a society-entity to provide much more complex services like the LIN in the mutual-coupled immune network. Once a bio-entity migrates and provides services to the users, its attribute information, such as its credit (energy) units, will change. And the information is stored to database each period of time. When the simulation ends, the simulator calls the display program and show the simulation results to the users.

During the running period of a simulator, there are three processes to finish a kind of service: requesting service, providing service, and receiving service.

Requesting service. A bio-entity sends a request to the other bio-entities that can provide some specific services. It knows which service can be received or which society-entity can provide the service. If it sends the request to the other bio-entities, these bio-entities will automatically provide services, and it will choose the service that it needs.

Providing service. A society-entity in the bio-network can actively or inactively provides a service to a bio-entity or a user who send a request message. If there is no proper society-entity to provide the service, the bio-entities will interact with others and form a new society-entity to provide service.

Figure 5. Bio-entities' response time for complex requests

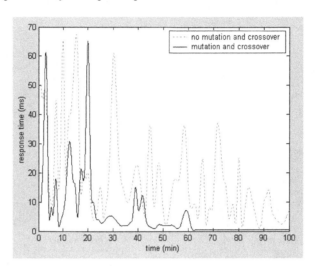

Receiving service. After the bio-entities receive the services, they record the society-entities' ID and build up much stronger relationship with it in order to request it to provide the service again.

C. Simulation Results

We can simulate complex network services, which are implemented through emergence behaviors of bio-entities' interaction. According to the simulator based on the mutual-coupled immune network, some experiments are made about an application case of "Web personalization browse service", and evaluate the theories and emergence services.

Suppose that the bio-network platform runs in a network node and credit units for resource cost are the same in the bio-network platform. A user needs Web browse service while a Web server includes more than one Web page and can provide these functions. Static Web servers cannot meet the user's requirement because of user's individual requirements; these static Web servers should adapt and evolve to provide proper services.

First we assume that the user's requests are few and simple, bio-entities can meet the request quickly. They need not form a society-entity, so the response time is very short. Then we simulate more complex network services and distribute different Webs to ten Web servers and 200 user's requests to 216 nodes. Each bio-entity represents a Web page or a specific user request, while a Web server represents a society-entity. Bio-entities browse pages and pay other bio-entities for providing services according to user requirements.

The simulation results show that emergent services can adapt and evolve to meet user's requests, as shown in Fig. 5. We compare different bio-entities' production behaviors. If the bio-entities mutate or crossover with others during reproduction process, they will provide services quickly, that is, the response time is shorter. However, the response time is longer without mutation and crossover. From the simulation results, we can see that bio-entities can optimize network services and network applications. The services emerged by interactions of bio-entities adapt and survive the changes of network environments.

A Peer-to-Peer Service Model Based on Immune Symmetrical Network

A. Immune Symmetrical Network Model

Hoffmann (1986) has proposed a symmetrical network theory for the immune system. The principle lymphocytes fall into just two specificity classes. The first class is the antigen-binding set, denoted T_+ and B_+ for T cells and B cells, respectively. The second set is minus or anti-idiotypic set, T_- and B_-. There are three types of interaction

Figure 6. The P2P network model based on immune symmetrical network

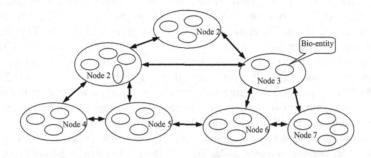

between the plus and minus sets as follows: stimulation, inhibition, and killing. Stimulation can occur when two lymphocytes encounter each other. The receptors of one lymphocyte ('+') can cross-link the receptors of a second lymphocyte ('-'), the converse is also true. So stimulation is assumed to be symmetrical in both directions between the two sets. Specific T cells factors could inhibit receptors. Finally, antibody molecules are assumed to be killed in a symmetrical fashion. According to the interaction among B cells and T cells, we can receive a set of four stable steady states for the system of T_+, B_+, T_- and B_- cells. The steady states are the initial state, the suppressed or unresponsive state, the immune state and the anti-immune state.

B. P2P Network Simulation Environment

Although the traditional client-server model first established the Internet's backbone, more and more clients enter the Internet, and the load on the servers is steadily rising, resulting in long access times and server breakdowns. The users' requirements and communications among users are completed through application server. While P2P systems offer an alternative to such traditional systems for a number of application domains. Different applications of P2P systems have been developed to support searching, file sharing, distributed computing, collaboration, instant messaging and mobile devices (Ripeanu et al., 2002). In P2P systems, every node (peer) of the system acts as both client and server, and provides part of the overall resources/information available from the system. In a pure P2P system, no central coordination or central database exists and no peer has a global view of the system. The participating peers are autonomous and self-organize the system's structure, i.e., global behavior emerges from local interactions. Peers will not always be available but still all existing data and services should be accessible which should be addressed by sufficiently high replication.

The P2P network model is implemented on the designed bio-network simulation platform according to the symmetrical network theory of immune systems. The network can provide services and applications to users.

Figure 7. Interaction of two peers in P2P network based on immune symmetrical network

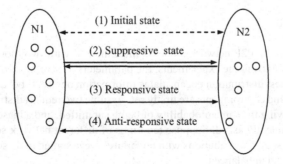

Because of complexity and heterogeneity of future Internet, the network structure is very changeable, from just few nodes to incalculable nodes. Users can communicate directly, share resources and collaborate with each other.

Users or services, represented by bio-entities in the network nodes, can be regarded as antibodies or anti-antibodies in the immune system. The bio-entities in different nodes interact equally. They have three actions between two neighbor nodes and keep four steady states. A P2P network model is provided with a few nodes only to show the network structure as shown in Fig. 6. There are several bio-entities on the nodes to provide network services. The inter-connecting nodes are called symmetrical nodes, such as node 1 and node 2, node 2 and node 4. As an example, node 1 (N1) and node 2 (N2) are regarded as two sets and the bio-entities in the bio-network are regarded as antibodies in the symmetrical immune network, thus three interactions of the bio-entities in these two nodes are stimulation, inhibition, and killing. The two nodes have four stable states: initial state, suppressive state, responsive state, and anti-responsive state, as shown in Fig. 7. These states are shown in details as follows.

Initial state. When user requests towards nodes are few, the bio-entities in the node can provide enough services to the users so that the users need not send requests to other nodes. At the same time, bio-entities have not enough credits to provide services to the other nodes.

Suppressive state. With the increment of user requests, bio-entities require more and more credits to reward their services and they will evolve to produce next generations. At the same time, bio-entities in the node cannot provide enough services to the request users towards the node. For instance, the bio-entities on N1 have not enough credits for some users; while the bio-entities on N2 suppress the users of N1 to access their services because they have to provide services to their own users. The two nodes suppress each other to use their own resources and services, so the bio-entities in the nodes keep suppressive state.

Responsive state. When the requests towards N1 are increasing while the requests towards N2 are decreasing, a lot of unused resources or bio-entities exist on N2, bio-entities on N1 stimulus bio-entities on N2 and the latter provides services directly or migrates to N1 to provide services. When the services are provided, the bio-entities return their nodes and establish relationship with N1. The state of the two nodes is in responsive state. With the decrement of bio-entities on N2, the services to N2 are reduced and the credit level of N1 is higher than that of N2 so that N1 and N2 cannot keep the relationship, they will look for new nodes, and return the initial state. But the relationship between these nodes still exits and the bio-entities on the nodes interact with each other to provide services.

If a bio-entity, denoting user requests, needs network services on other nodes, it sends a request to all of its known neighbors. The neighbors then check to see whether they can reply to the request by matching it to the service type. If they find a match, they will reply; otherwise, they will forward the query to their own neighbors and increase the message's hop count. For instance, there are three bio-entities A, B, and C hosting on N1, N2, and N3 respectively. Bio-entity A sends requests to other bio-entities of its neighbors. If bio-entity B can provide service, it replies to bio-entity A. At the same time, bio-entity B acquires credits from bio-entity A and establishes a relationship with bio-entity B. If bio-entity B cannot provide services to bio-entity A, it sends the request to bio-entity C, and bio-entity C will migrate to N1 to provide service for bio-entity A. Then bio-entity C returns its node and establishes a relationship with bio-entity A. At the same time, bio-entity A and C announce their relationships to other bio-entities on N1. Bio-entities on N1 may access services on N3 directly and save time because of the decrease of the hops next time.

Anti-responsive state. The state is opposite to responsive state. The bio-entities on N1 provide services to requests from N2 and receive the credits.

C. Simulation Results

On the simulation platform, the P2P network model is implemented with two thousand nodes and the service access is simulated. Before starting the experiments, the parameters are configured as follows: 1) service information distribution; 2) request distribution encapsulates information on users' behavior.

Simulation parameters and environments are firstly set. Assume two request distributions: an unbiased distribution, with all requests having the same probability of being submitted, and a biased distribution, with a small number of requests are frequently asked. Suppose ten kinds of different network services distribute randomly on different nodes. Static resource distributions with no failures are assumed in these experiments. The resource distributions are balanced and unbalanced.

Figure 8. Average number of hops per request with the change of simulation time

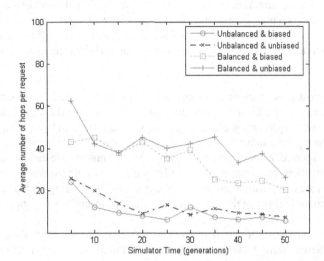

Average number of hops per request with time is shown in the Fig. 8. We can see that biased user request can access services more easily than biased user request under unbalanced or balanced resource distribution. As to a type of user request, bio-entities can migrate to resource nodes more efficiently and achieve resource services more easily under the unbalanced resource distribution. The nodes are in four stable states just as the immune symmetrical network model. Different distribution of requests affects the average number of hops. The interaction of bio-entities maintains the balance of the bio-network and makes the resources utilized reasonably, as such optimizes the bio-network architecture.

CONCLUSION

A novel bio-network architecture based on immune emergent computation is proposed to address the challenges of future Internet. The bio-network architecture combines the mechanisms of immune systems with agent approaches. It is competent for future Internet requirements, such as extensibility, survivability, mobility, and adaptability to the changes of different users and network environments. We develop the bio-network simulation platform for simulating complex network services and applications. We also provide two examples of bio-network simulators to generate the emergent services from the immune network computation models. One is the mutual-coupled immune network computation model to satisfy various Web users' requirements. The other one is the network service model in a P2P network environment based on the immune symmetrical network theory. The feasibility of the two models is demonstrated through computer simulation experiments on the platform.

The bio-network architecture provides a novel way to study future Internet, and is a good simulation environment for studying the network theory and practical applications. On the simulation platform, further researches can be done to design new Internet information services and applications.

Future Research Directions

The bio-network architecture provides a novel way to study future Internet, and is a good simulation environment for network theory researches and practical applications. Further researches can be done to extend the frame of the bio-network architecture and design new Internet information services and applications.

(1) We have recently extended the bio-network architecture and re-built the bio-network platform for service emergence inspired by the systemic emergence and self-evolution of neuroendocrine-immune system. Some mechanisms from other complex systems have also been borrowed to develop the bio-network architecture, such as ecological systems, social networks, small-world networks, post-office networks, etc.

(2) The bio-network architecture and its simulation platform should be further applied to Grid and Web service environment.

- **Grid computing.** Next generation grid systems are heading for globally collaborative, service-oriented and live information systems. The next generation grid systems have the hallmarks of complex systems, namely, adaptation, self-organization and emergence. More attempts on how to impose the ability of solving complexity deriving from natural complex systems on complex grid systems should be enhanced.

- **Web service.** Web service, as next generation promising infrastructure established in the Internet, has caused extensive attention from industry and academy circles around the world. Some novel methods for automatic Web service composition and management should be developed through Web services emergence. The issues about improving the efficiency of both the bio-entities negotiation and the Web service emergence should be developed.

- **E-service.** With the explosive growth of Internet, more enterprises are providing various E-services for collaborative commerce online to achieve competitive advantages. The bio-network architecture has the true potential of E-services to dynamically compose some new services that provide more sophisticated functionalities. It adapts well to the changes of dynamic environments.

- **Pervasive service.** Some composition methods of service emergence in pervasive service environments should be studied by the inspiration from the characteristics of system emergence and self-evolution in the bio-network architecture. The pervasive service composition is provided by emergent network of bio-entities to adapt to dynamic environment.

ACKNOWLEDGMENT

This work was supported in part by the Key Project of the National Nature Science Foundation of China (No. 60534020), the National Nature Science Foundation of China (Nos. 60474037, 60004006), and Program for New Century Excellent Talents in University from Ministry of Education of China (No. NCET-04-415).

REFERENCES

Bhalla, U. S., & Lyengar, R. (1999). Emergent properties of networks of biological signaling pathways, *Science*, *283*(5400), 381-387.

de Castro, L. N., & Timmis, J. (2002). *Artificial immune systems: A new computational intelligence approach.* Springer-Verlag, London.

Ding, Y. S., & Ren, L. H. (2000). Artificial immune systems: Theory and applications. *Pattern Recognition and Artificial Intelligence*, *13*(1), 52-59. (in Chinese).

Ding, Y. S., & Ren, L. H. (2003). Design of a bio-network architecture based on immune emergent computation. *Control and Design*, 18(2), 185-189. (in Chinese)

FIPA agent management specification, http://www.fipa.org/specs/fipa00023/XC00023H.html.

Gao, L., Ding, Y. S., & Ren, L. H. (2004). A novel ecological network-based computation platform as grid middleware system. *Int. J. Intelligent Systems,* *19*(10), 859-884.

Girvan, M., & Newman, M. E. (2002). Community structure in social and biological networks. *Proc. Natl Acad. Sci.*, *99*, 7821-7826.

Harada, K., & Kinoshita, T. (2003). The emergence of controllable transient behavior using an agent diversification strategy. *IEEE Transactions on Systems, Man and Cybernetics - Part A: Systems and Humans, 33*(5), 589-596.

Hoffmann, G. W. (1986). A neural network model based on the analogy with the immune system. *J. Theoretical Biology, 122*, 33-67.

Ishiguro, A., Kuboshiki, S., Ichikawa, S., & Uchikawa, Y. (1996). Gait control of hexapod walking robots using mutual-coupled immune networks. *Advanced Robotics, 10*(2), 179-195.

Jerne, N. K. (1973). The immune system. *Scientific American, 229*(1), 52-60.

Jerne, N. K. (1974). Towards a network theory of the immune system. *Annual Immunology, 125C*, 373-389.

Labrou, Y., Finin, T., & Peng, Y. (1999). Agent communication languages: The current landscape. *IEEE Intelligent Systems, 14*(2), 45-52.

Pagello, E., D'angelo, A., Ferrari, C., Polesel, R., Rosati, R., & Speranzon, A. (2003). Emergent behaviors of a robot team performing cooperative tasks. *Advanced Robotics, 17*(1), 3-19.

Perelson, A. S. (1989). Immune network theory. *Immunological Review, 10*, 5-36.

Read, D.W. (2003). Emergent properties in small scale societies. *Artificial life, 9*(4), 419-428.

Ren, L. H., & Ding, Y. S. (2002). A new network simulation platform based on ecological network computation. *J. System Simulation, 14*(11), 1497-1499, 1503. (in Chinese).

Ripeanu, M., Foster, I., & Iamnitchi, A. (2002). Mapping the Gnutella network: Properties of large-scale peer-to-peer systems and implications for system design. *IEEE Internet Computing Journal, 6*(1).

Tchikou, M., & Gouraderes, E. (2003). Multi-agent model to control production system: A reactive and emergent approach by cooperation and competition between agents. *Lecture notes in computer sciences, 2606*, 105-118.

Valckenaers, P., Brussel, H., Hadeli, O., Bochmann, B., Germain, S. and Zamfirescu, C. (2003). On the design of emergent systems: An investigation of integration and interoperability issues, *Engineering applications of artificial intelligence, 16*(4), 377-393.

Vertosick, F. T., & Kelly, R. H. (1989). Immune network theory: A role for parallel distributed processing? *Immunology, 66*, 1-7.

KEY TERMS

Bio-Network Architecture: We consider the biological immune system as a set of active computational components interacting in a dynamic and often unpredictable environment. Then, the behaviors of the biological immune systems can be modeled in terms of bio-entities and society-entities. Bio-entities in the bio-network architecture are regarded as autonomous agents and possess the characteristics such as interaction, no central control, diversity, mobility, and evolution. The bio-network architecture will make it possible to emerge the complexity of the biological immune systems from the interactions of bio-entities. We only need design simple behaviors of bio-entities, while complex biological behaviors are the emergence of bio-entities behaviors. The layered infrastructure of the bio-network architecture consists of bio-entities, bio-entity survivable environment, bio-network core services, bio-network low-level functional modules, and bio-network simulators.

Bio-Network Platform: The bio-network simulation platform is a software framework fully implemented by Java language based on the bio-network architecture by utilizing multi-agent systems. The ideal model would place the bio-network platform on every device as a network node. The bio-network simulation platform has the capability of service emergence, evolution etc.. The platform can be used to simulate some complex services and applications for Internet or distributed systems.

Biological Immune Systems: The biological immune system in our body is an efficient adaptive system. According to the immunologists, the components such as cells, molecules and organs in the biological immune system can prevent the body from being damaged by pathogens, known as antigens. The basic components of the immune system are lymphocytes that have two major types, B cells (B lymphocytes) and T cells (T lymphocytes). Biological immune systems are adaptive systems and their learning behaviors take place through evolutionary mechanisms similar to biological evolutions. They are distributed systems without central control. They can survive local failures and external attacks and maintain balance because of emergent behaviors of the interactions of many local elements, like immune cells. In the immune systems, the whole is more than the sum of the systems' parts because of the interactions among the parts, just as emergent behaviors in other complex systems.

Emergent Computation: Emergent computation is generally characterized by the interaction of relatively simple entities, forming a system to exhibit emergent properties. Emergent computation has three aspects: self-organization, aggregative behavior, and cooperative behavior.

Future Internet: The future Internet will be the core of the worldwide information infrastructure and the general service platform with computation, communication, entertainment, e-business, and so on. Future Internet should configure and reconfigure its network services dynamically to satisfy demanders and Internet application can adapt to the change of different network environments. Internet nodes also should be secure and can survive failures and attacks. Obviously, future Internet should be capable of extensibility, survivability, mobility, and adaptability to the changes of different users and network environments.

Immune Symmetrical Network: The symmetrical network theory for the immune system is a tractable first approximation. The principle lymphocytes fall into just two specificity classes. The first class is the antigen-binding set, denoted T+ and B+ for T cells and B cells respectively. The second set is minus or anti-idiotypic set, T- and B-. There are three types of interaction between the plus and minus sets as follows: stimulation, inhibition, and killing. Stimulation can occur when two lymphocytes encounter each other. The receptors of one lymphocyte ('+') can cross-link the receptors of a second lymphocyte ('-'), the converse is also true. So stimulation is assumed to be symmetrical in both directions between the two sets. Specific T cells factors could inhibit receptors. Finally, antibody molecules are assumed to be killed in a symmetrical fashion. According to the interaction among B cells and T cells, we can receive a set of four stable steady states for the system of T+, B+, T- and B- cells. The steady states are the initial state, the suppressed or unresponsive state, the immune state and the anti-immune state.

Mutual-Coupled Immune Network: The mutual-coupled immune network hypothesis shows that the immune systems are constructed by forming large-scale immune networks with the interactions among small-scale networks. According to the hypothesis, we consider that each small-scale network has a specific task, and can be regarded as a local immune network (LIN). The interactions among the small-scale networks form a global network, and the global network has its remarkable ability to accomplish a complex task.

P2P Network: In P2P network, every node (peer) of the system acts as both client and server and provides part of the overall resources/information available from the system. In a pure P2P system, no central coordination or central database exists and no peer has a global view of the system. Participating peers are autonomous and self-organize the system's structure, i.e., global behavior emerges from local interactions. P2P technologies have many applications, such as file sharing and exchanging, distributed computing, collaborative system, P2P computing, and enterprise applications.

Web Service: Web services are self-contained, modular applications that can be described, published, located, and accessed over network by using open standards. The functionality of the individual Web service is limited and cannot satisfy some practical requirements. The potential of Web services can only be achieved if they are used to dynamically compose some new Web services that provide more sophisticated functionalities compared to existing ones. The Web service composition is a highly complex task, and it is already beyond the human capability to deal with the whole process manually. Some methods for automatic composition and management of Web services have been proposed. They are conducted to fall into the realm of workflow composition or artificial intelligence planning methods.

Chapter XI
A Static Web Immune System and Its Robustness Analysis

Tao Gong
Donghua University, China & Central South University, China

ABSTRACT

Static Web immune system is an important applicatiion of artificial immune system, and it is also a good platform to develop new immune computing techniques. On the Static Web system, a normal model is proposed with the space property and the time property of each component, in order to identify the normal state of the system that the artificial immune system protects. Based on the normal model, the Static Web immune sytsem is modelled with three tiers, that is the innate immune tier, the adaptive immune tier and the parallel immune tier. All the three tiers are inspired from the natural immune system. On the tri-tier immune model, the self detection mechanism is proposed and programmed based on the normal model, and the non-self detection is based on the self detection. Besides, the recognition of known non-selfs and unknown non-selfs are designed and analyzed. It is showed that the Static Web immune system is effective and useful for both theory and applications.

A.1 INTRODUCTION

Human immune system is very important for human health, because it is able to detect, recognize, memorize and eliminate foreign viruses and inner faults, which are sometimes unknown and even quite complex (Perelson, Hightower & Forrest, 1996; Fauci, 2003; Chao, Davenport & Forrest, et al, 2004). Inspired from nature, artificial immune system is very important for computer world, because it is used to detect, recognize, learn, memorize and eliminate special objects, which are possibly unknown and even quite complex, such as computer viruses,

Copyright © 2009, IGI Global, distributing in print or electronic forms without written permission of IGI Global is prohibited.

faults and so on (De Castro & Timmis, 2002; Jerne, 1974; De Castro & Von Zuben, 2002). However, due to incomplete theories of immunology, one of bottlenecks for detecting the unknown non-selfs prevents the artificial immune system from developing. First, traditional detection approaches against viruses and faults are based on matching the features of the viruses and faults, and the features of unknown viruses and unknown faults are possibly unknown, thus 100% detection is impossible in theory (Balachandran, 2005; Gonzalez & Dasgupta, 2003). Second, the faulty mechanism for detecting viruses and faults causes lower possibility for recognizing the viruses and faults, and affects ability and efficiency for repairing the damaged computer system. To overcome the bottleneck of research on the artificial immune system and improve research on the basis of the anti-worm application and software fault diagnosis, a normal model of the static web immune system is proposed and built with the space-time properties of the components, and the normal model is used to represent the selfs.

A.2 BACKGROUND

Web system is popular on the Internet now and useful for many web users, and web security has become a serious problem due to viruses, worms and faults (Balthrop, Forrest & Newman, et al., 2004; Orman, 2003). To solve the security problem, some detecting techniques are used to recognize the non-selfs such as viruses and faults by matching the features of the non-selfs, but the traditional techniques have a difficult bottleneck in detecting unknown non-selfs especially such as brand-new viruses. To overcome the bottleneck, a new strategy for detecting the unknown non-selfs has been proposed with the normal model of the system that the artificial immune system protects. Current work has been done on the static web system and in fact many static web systems are useful and popular on the Internet, such as the webpage system for many companies and universities.

A.2.1 Space Property of Component

Suppose a static web system S is comprised of m web directories and n files in the cyberspace, and the system can be represented with the set

$$\{p_{ij}, d_k \mid \sum_{i=1}^{m} n_i = n; p_{ij} \in S; j = 1, \cdots, n; k = 1, \cdots, m\}.$$

Here, p_{ij} denotes the jth file in the ith directory of the system S, dk denotes the kth directory in the system S, and ni denotes the sum of all files in the ith directory of the system S.

The components of the static web system are software parts, and the software is used to simulate the physical world in the cyberspace. In the physical world, every object has unique 3-dimension space coordinates and 1-dimension time coordinate, so that the state of the object is uniquely identified by its space-time coordinates (Einstein, 1920). Alike in the cyberspace, every software part has unique location for storing the space property because the storage of the software is based on the hardware in the physical world. The absolute pathname pi is used to represent the location information for storing the file and/or the directory, and the pathname consists of the name ri of the disk or the URL, the name di of the directory and the full name ni of the file ci, shown in Figure A.1. The full name of the file includes the file-name of the file and the suffix name of the file, and the suffix name of the file is one of features that are useful for classifying the files.

According to the basic rules of the operating systems for managing the files, the absolute pathname of the file c_i uniquely identifies the location of the file in the computer. One absolute pathname belongs to only one file at a certain time, and at that time the file has only one absolute pathname.

A.2.2 Time Property of Component

Time property of every object in both the physical world and the software world only has one dimension, and each time variable has four parts: date part, hour part, minute part and second part. However, the time property of natural object in the physical world is not changeable, but the time properties of files in the current operating

Figure A.1 3-dimension information of the absolute pathname for files. ©2008 Tao Gong. Used with permission.

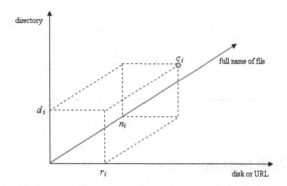

Figure A.2. External change of the component c_i. ©2008 Tao Gong. Used with permission.

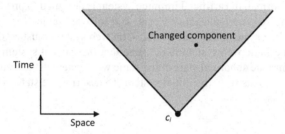

system are changeable. The operating system is a kind of complex dynamic system in which the normal model is difficult to build. For simplification, the normal model is built for the static web system and the artificial immune system is designed to protect the static web system, because the normal model can be built on the condition that the time property in the static system is unchangeable to keep the normal state.

In general, according to the representing method of time, the data of time includes the data of the date, the data of hour, the data of minute and the data of second. Moreover, if the accuracy for representing the data of time is higher, the data of time may include the data of microsecond and so on.

When a component is changed, the time point of the cyberspace is certainly changed and the change on the component can be external or internal. The external change of the component can be shown with the space property of the component, but the internal change of the component must be detected by the operating system and represented with the time property. In some current operating systems, the change of the component such as file or directory is detected with the function for representing the time that the component has been changed for the last time. The approach may be imperfect, but it is feasible in the static web system on the condition that the operating system is robust. The external change of the component may occur on the disk name of the component, the directory name of the component or the file name of the component, and the future change of the component c_i is shown in Figure A.2 (Hawking & Penrose, 1996).

On the other hand, the internal change of the component is affected by many factors such as the structure of the component, the length of the component, the special unit of the component and so on. For example, from the time point t_1 to t_2, the component c_i is changed with its structure into a new component c_j, shown with bigger scale in Figure A.3, and the functions of the component will be also changed.

Figure A.3. Internal change of the component c_i. ©2008 Tao Gong. Used with permission.

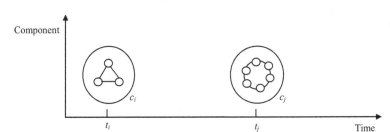

A.2.3 State of Static Web System

The state of the static web system is either normal or abnormal, and the normal state of the static web system is static. When the static web system is set up for usage, the initial state of the system is normal and the normal state of the static web system can not be transformed into another different normal state. In this chapter, suppose the operating system is always normal, the artificial immune system is designed to protect the static web system so that the static web system can keep normal against worms and software faults.

To keep the normal state of the system, the state of the static web system must be defined as normal or abnormal. The normal state of the static web system is the state that the current system has same structure and components as the initial system. The abnormal state of the static web system is the state that the current system has different structure and components from the initial system. To describe the state of the static web system, a normal function $N(x)$ is defined as such.

$$N(x) = \begin{cases} 1 & , x \text{ is normal,} \\ 0 & , x \text{ is abnormal.} \end{cases} \tag{A.1}$$

Here, x is an object in the static web system or the system itself.

Considering the composition of the static web system, the state of the static web system is uniquely identified by the states of the components for the system, and the components of the static system include files and directories. Suppose the state of the component c_i is represented as $N(c_i)$, the state of the system S can also be represented as such.

$$N(S) = \prod_{i=1}^{m+n} N(c_i), \ c_i \in S. \tag{A.2}$$

A.2.4 Normal Model of Normal Static Web System

When and only when all the components of the system are normal, the system is normal. If one component among them is abnormal, the system is abnormal. Therefore, if and only if every component of the static normal web system is identified uniquely, the normal state of the static web system can be identified uniquely. The following theorem proves that the normal state of the static web system can be detected with the space-time properties of the components in the system.

Theorem A.1 Suppose a static web system S is comprised of $m+n$ components, each of which has its unique absolute pathname (space property) and unique last revision time (time property). Let the absolute pathname of a component c_i be p_i and the last revision time of the component c_i be t_i. On the condition that the space-time properties of the static web system are correct, the absolute pathnames and last revision time of all the normal components in the normal static web system uniquely identify the normal state of the system.

[Proof] In the static web system there are n+m components of web pages and directories, which uniquely identify the system. Therefore, the normal state of every component in the static web system should be identified with its space property and time property before the whole web system is identified. For a certain absolute pathname p_i, the corresponding component c_i is unique. Moreover, if the last revision time t_i of the component c_i is certain, the current state of the component c_i is also unique. The revision time t_i is recorded when the static web system is normal, so that the component c_i is also normal at that time. Thus, the absolute pathname p_i and the last revision time t_i identify the normal state of the unique component c_i in both the space and time dimensions. For a certain component c_i of the web system S, the absolute pathname p_i of the component is unique, because this is kept by the rules for managing files and directories with the operating system. Besides, the revision time of the component c_i is also unique, because the last revision time of every thing should be unique. All in all, the absolute pathname and last revision time of every normal component in the normal static web system identify the normal state of the component. Based on the unique identification between the static web system and its components, the normal state of the static web system is uniquely identified with the absolute pathnames and last revision time of its all normal components. Theorem 1 is correct. ■

The last revision time is a representing parameter for the operating system and the parameter is different in the physical world. When a copy of a component is made in the cyberspace, the copy has same revision time (time property) as the component, so that the copy is called same to the component. In fact, the physical storage of the copy is different from that of the component. In the physical world, no two objects are completely same and the concept of sameness is local and partial. Therefore, the time property of the component shows the partial computing feature of the operating system in the cyberspace.

According to Theorem 1, the normal state of the static web system has three examples. The first example is the initial static web system, and the conclusion is self-evident. The second is the unchanged system after a period, and the space properties and the time properties of all the components in the system are unchanged. Therefore, the state of the current system is same as the initial system, so that the current system is also normal. The third example is the repaired system that was damaged and ever abnormal but now has been repaired by the artificial immune system. When the damaged components are being repaired, the backup components are copied to replace the damaged ones and the backup components have same last revision time as the components that were damaged. Thus, all the components of the repaired system have same space properties and time properties as those of the initial system, and the repaired system has the same state as the initial system.

The normal model of the static web system is a new attempt to build the normal model of the selfs and increase the probability for detecting the non-selfs by detecting the selfs. This work can establish a basis for investigating the approaches to build the normal model of the dynamic system and design more intelligent and effective immune algorithms for real complex systems. To update the normal model for the dynamic systems, the normal models must be adjusted according to some rules and protected by some security techniques.

A.3 TRI-TIER IMMUNE MODEL OF STATIC WEB SYSTEM

In biological immune systems, the innate immunity and the adaptive immunity are two main types of immunity, which are provided by many immune cells such B-cells and T-cells. The innate immunity is responsible for discriminating the selfs from the non-selfs and recognizing the known non-selfs. The adaptive immunity is responsible for learning unknown non-selfs and memorizing the new known non-selfs that were ever unknown but now known after learning. Based on the mapping model of natural computation, the two types of immunity are mapped to the first tier and the second tier of the immune computing model for the static web immune system. Considering another important trait of processing information in a parallel and distributed way in the biological immune systems, the parallel immune cells is an infrastructure for the immune system. Alike, the parallel computer can provide a powerful computing infrastructure for some complex artificial immune systems, and the parallel computer is used as the third tier of the immune computing tier for the static web immune system.

Figure A.4. Tri-tier immune computing model of static web immune system. ©2008 Tao Gong. Used with permission.

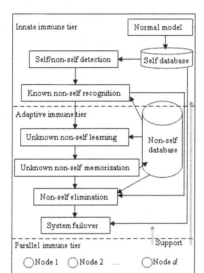

A.3.1 Tri-Tier Immune Structure

The tri-tier immune computing model of the static web immune system is based on the normal model of the static web system, and the normal model is built with both the space property and the time property of each component in the system. The tri-tier immune computing model is inspired from some natural immune theories, and includes inherent immune tier, adaptive immune tier and parallel immune tier, shown in Figure A.4. The parallel immune tier is built on the parallel computing theorems, and used to increase efficiency (Gong & Cai, 2003).

In Figure A.4, when the foreign object enters the static web system, the random detectors begin to detect whether the foreign object is self or non-self, by matching the features of the foreign object with the self information in the self database. The self is the part of the static web system, such as the webpage files of the static web system. And the non-self is not any part of the static web system or compatible with the static web system. The self information is used to define the features of the self and represent the normal state of the static web system. And all self information is stored in the self database. During the immune process of the artificial immune system, the percent of the selfs is maximized and the amount of the non-selfs in the static web system is minimized. When a foreign object is determined as a non-self, pattern recognition of the non-self is started in two ways. One is the way of matching features, and the other is the way of matching rules. The former is done through querying records in the database and matching the feature information of the detected non-self with the record information in the non-self database, where the entire known non-selfs store. The latter is done in a random way through searching some antibodies in the rule base. If the non-self is known by the artificial immune system, then the destroyer is called to eliminate the non-self. For computer viruses and software faults, the deletion command in the operating system is a kind of destroyer. Otherwise, the rule matching is used to recognize the non-self by the antibody and the rule-base on the adaptive immune tier. The rule includes two parts: the first one is the condition of the non-self feature, and the second one is the conclusion of the rule-based reasoning, which shows the type of the non-self and the elimination approach of the non-self. The rule matching is similar to the combination of DNA genes. And the immune algorithm is built on the random search of the rules. If the random search is done through evolutionary algorithm, then the immune algorithm is built on the evolutionary algorithm (Jiao & Wang, 2000; Deng & Korobka, 2001; Bell, 1970). Cooperative co-evolutionary adaptive genetic algorithm (CCAGA) is suitable for parallel computation, which is convenient to solve complicated problems (Cai & Peng, 2002).

In the immune computing model of the static web immune system, the immune computation has the threshold that is alike in the immune response of many biological immune systems. And the threshold is caused by the long-time cost of the random search. Moreover, the antibody search and rule matching are large-scaled in the chaos state.

A.3.2 Innate Immune Tier

The innate immune tier of the artificial immune system is inspired from the innate immunity of the biological immune system, and this tier is responsible for detecting all the selfs & non-selfs and recognizing the known non-selfs whose features have been stored in the non-self database. The normal model provides a certain representation of selfs and is useful for modeling the static web immune system. The normal model is the information basis of the model for detecting selfs and non-selfs with the space-time properties of the selfs, and the probability for detecting the selfs and the non-selfs can attain 100% in theory.

In the innate immune tier, recognition of foreign objects is relatively simple and quick, because this operation is only based on matching the feature information of the foreign objects and the records of the known non-selfs in the non-self database, and the operation for matching them can be done by the operator for querying. According to the results for querying, the corresponding methods for eliminating the non-selfs may be called from the records, for example some methods is used to delete the files that have been infected by some viruses. In the innate immune tier, there are also the operators for capturing the features of the non-selfs and querying, the non-self database, and so on. If a record of the feature information in the non-self database is matched with the features of the non-self that is being recognized, then the non-self is classified as a known non-self, otherwise it is a unknown non-self.

A.3.3 Adaptive Immune Tier

The adaptive immune tier of the artificial immune system is inspired from the adaptive immunity, and the adaptive immune tier is used to recognize the unknown non-selfs that can not be matched with any record on the feature information in the non-self database. The feature information of all the known non-selfs in the non-self database is represented on the dimension of features in the multi-dimension space, as called the feature space of the non-selfs, and the feature space is used to learn unknown features and types of the unknown non-selfs. By random searching and reasoning in the feature space, the most similar known non-selfs in features are found for the unknown non-selfs. These conclusions are memorized into the non-self database with the operator for memorizing the unknown non-selfs, so that the unknown non-selfs are transformed into new known non-selfs, which shows an immune memory of the artificial immune system. The advantage of such intelligence is to quickly recognize the same type of non-selfs in the innate immune tier as the memorized non-self for the next time and need no recognition in the adaptive immune tier, as the second immune response is much quicker than the first immune response.

The algorithm that is used to recognize the unknown non-selfs is called as artificial antibody, and many parallel antibodies are searching in the feature space.

A.3.4 Parallel Immune Tier

The parallel immune tier is inspired from the parallel immune response of many immune cells in the biological immune system, and parallel immune computation is used to break through the bottleneck of efficiency in the artificial immune system. The parallel immune tier provides a high-performance computing infrastructure for the innate immune tier and the adaptive immune tier, and can be used for solving the problems of limited computing and load balance. The computing capability and resource for one host may be limited for complex immune computation, and computing with overload is unsafe, easy to wither and of high risk. When information that the static web system processes is overload for single processor, the parallel immune tier is called and data are backed up and repaired in multi-threads.

The artificial immune system for the static web system eliminates the non-selfs such as some viruses and abnormity with immune agents and destroyers, but the capability for an immune agent is limited. When a large amount of unknown evil non-selfs attack the static web system, the speed for detecting recognizing and eliminating the non-selfs may be smaller than the speed for the non-selfs to clone transport and attack the system. Therefore, some parts of the artificial immune system may be infected by the non-selfs, and the load for immune computing will be increased. In this way, the speed for immune computing will be smaller and smaller, and then much smaller than the speed for the non-selfs to clone and attack the system. On the other hand, more parts of the artificial immune system will be infected and damaged by the non-selfs and in the end the static web system will be destroyed completely. Moreover, when the artificial immune system is quite abnormal, the immune computation and some destroyers may quicken damage to the static web system.

A.4 SELF/NON-SELF DETECTION OF STATIC WEB IMMUNE SYSTEM

The normal model is a new technique for the artificial immune system, and the model has powerful functions. Therefore, the static web immune system based on the normal model has some new traits, and one of them is the self/non-self detection based on the normal model. Many traditional approaches for detecting abnormity attain low probability for detecting some unknown abnormity, so that many researchers do not believe that there is probability for detecting all the non-selfs in a system. But the normal artificial immune system based on the normal model can detect all the selfs and all the non- selfs in the static web system, in theory.

A.4.1 Self Detection Based on Normal Model

The model for detecting selfs based on the normal model is comprised of the operator for visiting components, the operator for reading the space-time properties, the operator for querying, the static web system and the set of detecting results, shown in Figure A.5. First, the operator for visiting components selects a component of the static web system as the object that is being detected in one turn. For the object that has been selected, both the space property and the time property of the object is measured with the operator for reading the space-time properties, and the space-time properties are encapsulated as an immune object. Next, the operator for querying is used to query whether there is any record that matches the immune object. If yes, then the object is determined as a self. Such is repeated until all the components in the static web system are all detected. At last, the results for detecting the selfs are stored into the set of detecting results.

A.4.2 Non-Self Detection Based on Self Detection

The algorithm for detecting the non-selfs is based on the model for detecting the selfs and the recursive logic. For a component that is being detected, the space property and the time property of the component are used to deter-

Figure A.5. Model for detecting selfs based on the normal model. ©2008 Tao Gong. Used with permission.

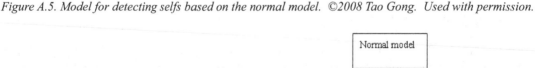
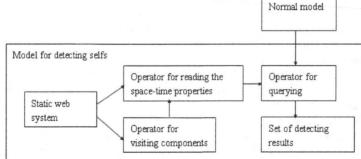

Figure A.6. Algorithm for detecting the non-selfs by detecting the selfs. ©2008 Tao Gong. Used with permission.

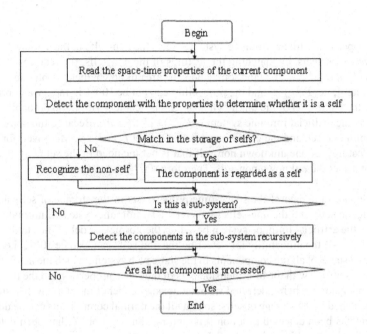

mine whether the component is a self, at first. For a sub-system, the sub-system is checked recursively to detect whether any component of the sub-system is not a self. Suppose the current static web system has *l* components that are being detected, the algorithm for detecting the non-selfs is show in Figure A.6.

A.4.3 Probability for Detecting Selfs and Non-Selfs

According to the unique relationship between the state of the components and the space-time properties of the components, the function can be established between the state set $\{s(c_i)\}$ of the components and the bi-dimension set $\{(p_i, t_i)\}$ of the space-time properties as such.

$$s(c_i) = f((p_i, t_i)) = g(p_i, t_i). \tag{A.3}$$

Here, $f(.)$ represents the mapping from the vector (p_i, t_i) to the state $s(c_i)$ and $g(.)$ represents the mapping from the space property p_i and the time property t_i to the state $s(c_i)$.

To investigate how to improve the approach for detecting the non-selfs, some definitions should be given on the probability for detecting the non-selfs.

Definition A.1 Self/non-self detection of the artificial immune system is a random event, and the event is denoted with D. The measurement on the probability of the random event is called as the probability for detecting the selfs and the non-selfs, and the probability is denoted with $P(D)$. Suppose the number of the selfs that have been detected during immunizing is n_s, the number of the non-selfs that have been detected during immunizing is n_n, the sum of selfs before immunizing is s_s, the sum of non-selfs before immunizing is s_n, then the probability $P(D_s)$ for detecting the selfs can be represented as such.

$$P(D_s) = \frac{n_s}{s_s}. \tag{A.4}$$

The probability $P(D_n)$ for detecting the non-selfs can be represented as such.

$$P(D_n) = \frac{n_n}{s_n}. \tag{A.5}$$

Theorem A.2 Suppose an artificial immune system detects the non-selfs in the static web system, which the artificial immune system protects, by matching the features of the non-selfs, the feature set of the known non-selfs is denoted with $U=\{u_i, i=1, 2, ..., C\}$, and some non-selfs are unknown, then the probability for detecting the non-selfs is smaller than 1, i.e. $P(D_n)<1$, and the probability can not be 100% in theory and real applications.

[Proof] Suppose the feature set of the unknown non-selfs is denoted with I, the probability for detecting the unknown non-selfs by the artificial immune system is $P(D_n)=|U|/|I|=C/|I|$. Because the non-selfs are unknown, the set I can be an unlimited set, and the element number of the set I can be ∞. Moreover, for any limited set U, there is at least one feature r of one unknown non-self that is not included in the set U, so that the artificial immune system can not detect the unknown non-self. Therefore, $P(D_n)<1$. ∎

Theorem A.3 Suppose the data of the space-time property set in the storage of selfs are correct, and the operator for detecting the selfs and the non-selfs by the artificial immune system is normal, the probability for detecting the selfs by the artificial immune system based on the normal model of the static web system can be 100% in theory, i.e. $P(D_s)=1$; the probability for detecting the non-selfs can also be 100%, i.e. $P(D_n)=1$.

[Proof] The normal states of all the components in the static web system, which the artificial immune system protects, are uniquely identified with the bi-dimension data of the space properties and the time properties. Thus, when the normal components are being detected with the normal model of the static web system, all the normal components can be matched in the storage of selfs, so that all the normal components can be detected. Therefore, no normal component has been detected as a non-self, and no abnormal object has been detected as a normal component. Hence, all the non-selfs can be detected.

$$P(D_s) = \frac{n_s}{s_s} = \frac{\sum_{i=1}^{n+m} N(s(c_i))}{s_s} = \frac{s_s}{s_s} = 1,$$

$$P(D_n) = \frac{n_n}{s_n} = \frac{l-s_s}{s_n} = \frac{s_n}{s_n} = 1.$$

In conclusion, with the artificial immune system and the normal model of the static web system, the probability for detecting the selfs can be 100%, and the probability for detecting the non-selfs can also be 100%. ∎

The complete detection of the non-selfs can detect more non-selfs from unknown non-selfs, so that the next step for recognizing the non-selfs will have more non-selfs to learn.

A.4.4 Experiments for Detecting Selfs and Non-Selfs

To test the approach for detecting non-selfs by detecting the selfs with the normal model, a web demo system was infected by some unknown worms and then its immune mechanism was activated. The unknown worms mean that the worms can not be matched in the storage of worms for the artificial immune system, and there are three variants of known worms and two complete-unknown worms among the unknown worms. The three variants are respectively modified from the loveletter worm, the happy-time worm and the Jessica worm (Levy, 2005; Arce & Levy, 2003; Zou, Gong & Towsley, 2002). The worms copy themselves into the file system of the static web system, overwrite the system files and the registration data of the operating system, and spread themselves via the e-mail system. If the static web system is attacked and affected by the worms, the users will feel that the system becomes much slower and more unstable, and the other computers or movable memorizers that connect the static web system may also be affected by the worms.

The experiment was setup on the web demo system of robots, as shown in Figure A.7, and the machine was with double CPUs and 2GB memory. First, the selfs of the web demo system were represented with the normal

Figure A.7. Initial web demo system when the system is normal. ©2008 Tao Gong. Used with permission.

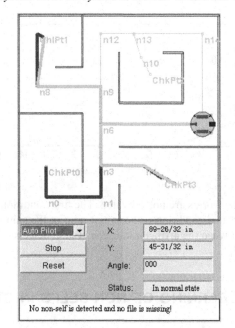

model of the system, and the normal model was uniquely identified by the space-time properties of all the normal components when the initial system was normal. The system was a part of web-based e-learning system, which was developed by some web programming languages such as HTML JSP, Java and JDBC. The system was used to show how a fire-fighting robot searches a path to find the fire and put out the fire, and the initial system was normal. Therefore, at the initial normal state the normal model of the system was built and used to represent the selfs.

To detect and eliminate the worms and the variants in the web demo system, the immune programs were tested in 50 experiments on the machine. The experiments of immune computation show that the non-self percent p decreases from the initial value to zero, and the non-self percent may increase first and then decreases due to the spread of the worms, as shown in Figure A.8. The time is denoted as T and the unit of the time is second. The minimization of the non-self percent means that the elimination of the worms is accomplished and the danger from the worms disappears. The non-self percent means the ratio of the sum of current worms to the sum of components in the current system, and different curves represent different immunization against different worms. The first condition for the first curve is that some files are lost in the Web system; the second condition is that the initial ratio of the sum of worms to the sum of files is 1.1%; and the third condition is that when the artificial immune system detects and eliminates the worms, the worms are activated to copy themselves and produce new worms, until the process of the worm is closed, and then the worms are eliminated. The first condition for the second curve is that no file is lost in the Web system; the second condition is that the initial ratio of the sum of worms to the sum of files is 1%; and the third condition is that when the artificial immune system detects and eliminates the worms, the worms are activated to produce new worms, until the process of the worm is closed, and then the worms are eliminated. The first condition for the third curve is that no file is lost in the Web system; the second condition is that the initial ratio of the sum of worms to the sum of files is 1%; and the third condition is that when the artificial immune system detects and eliminates the worms, the worms are activated to infect some self files, until the process of the worm is closed, and then the worms are eliminated. The first condition for the fourth curve is that some files are lost in the Web system; the second condition is that the initial ratio of the sum of worms to the sum of files is 1.1%; and the third condition is that when the artificial immune system

Figure A.8. Non-self percent of immune computation. ©2008 Tao Gong. Used with permission.

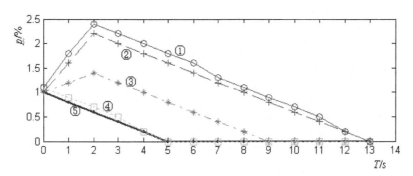

detects and eliminates the worms, the worms are not activated. The first condition for the fifth curve is that no file is lost in the Web system; the second condition is the initial ratio of the sum of worms to the sum of files is 1%; and the third condition is that when the artificial immune system detects and eliminates the worms, the worms are not activated.

A.5 RECOGNITION AND LEARNING OF NON-SELFS IN STATIC WEB IMMUNE SYSTEM

For the artificial immune system, the recognition of the non-selfs is classified into two types according to the difference among the non-selfs, and the two approaches for recognizing the non-selfs are inspired from the innate immunity and the adaptive immunity in the biological immune system. The first approach is used to recognize the known non-selfs by matching the features of the known non-selfs in the storage of non-selfs. The second approach is used to recognize some unknown non-selfs by the random search for finding the most similar known non-selfs to the unknown non-selfs in the feature space of the non-selfs and learning the unknown non-selfs.

A.5.1 Recognition of Known Non-Selfs

Before designing the algorithm for recognizing the known non-selfs on the model for recognizing the known non-selfs, the storage of non-selfs must be designed. The storage of non-selfs is used to represent and store the feature information of all the known non-selfs, and the feature information includes the space information of the non-selfs, the feature string of the non-selfs, the copying behavior of the non-selfs, the modifying behavior of the non-selfs to the registration data, the calling behavior of the non-selfs to the e-mails and so on.

The multi- dimension feature information of the non-selfs is encapsulated into the feature objects of the non-selfs, and the feature objects of the non-selfs consist of the set of feature information for the non-selfs. The set of feature information is called as the feature space of the non-selfs, shown in Table A.1.

In Table A.1, the feature information of the known non-selfs should be input into the storage of non-selfs first, and the software of database management can be used to import the data. For example, for the loveletter worms, if the worms are known for the artificial immune system, then the data of the loveletter worms can be input into the storage of non-selfs. The data include 1) Non-self No.: w00001, 2) Space information of the non-selfs (File-extension): vbs, 3) Feature string of the non-selfs: loveletter, 4) Copying behavior of the non-selfs: .Copy, 5) Modifying behavior of the non-selfs to the registration data: .RegWrite, 6) Calling behavior of the non-selfs to the e-mails: Outlook.Application, 7) Non-self name: loveletter worm, 8) Type of the non-self: worm, 9) Eliminating schema of the non-self: delete and so on.

At first, the algorithm for recognizing the known non-selfs queries the space information of the non-self in the feature space, which is represented in the storage of non-selfs. If a record is matched with the space feature of the non-self that is being recognized, then other features of the non-self are recognized for the next steps,

Table A.1. Dimension of the feature space for the non-selfs

Dimension No.	Dimension of non-selfs' features	Description of non-selfs' features
1	u_1	Non-self No.
2	u_2	Space information of the non-selfs
3	u_3	Feature string of the non-selfs
4	u_4	Copying behavior of the non-selfs
5	u_5	Modifying behavior of the non- selfs to the registration data
6	u_6	Calling behavior of non-selfs to the e-mails
7	u_7	Non-self name
8	u_8	Type of the non-self
9	u_9	Eliminating schema of the non-self
...	...	...

otherwise the non-self is regarded as an unknown non-self. Afterwards, the feature string, the information on the copying behavior, the information on the modifying behavior to the registration data and the information on the calling behavior to the e-mails are extracted from the non-selfs. If the features of the non-selfs can be matched with any samples in the feature space that has been built with all the known non-selfs, then the non-self is a new sample of known non-selfs.

In the static web demo system, the algorithm for recognizing the known non-selfs reads the file extension of the non-self file at first. If at least one record is matched on the file extension, then the algorithm for recognizing the known non-selfs continues to recognize the other features of the non-self and classifies the non-self into an existing type of the known non-selfs; otherwise, the file is regarded as a unknown non-self, and the algorithm for learning the unknown non-selfs is used to recognize the unknown non-self. After the matching record is found, the information of the record is read according to the feature string, the copying behavior, the modifying behavior to the registration data, and the calling behavior to the e-mails and so on. For example, the loveletter worm has been recorded as a known non-self in the storage of non-selfs, and the No. of the worm is w00001, so the result for recognizing the loveletter worm is shown in Figure A.9.

In Figure A.9, the file that has been infected by the loveletter worm has been detected as a non-self. Afterwards, the algorithm for recognizing the known non-selfs is used to recognize the file's features such as the file extension, the feature string, the copying behavior of the file, the modifying behavior of the file to the registration data, the calling behavior of the file to the e-mails and so on. By matching the features of the non-self with the records in the storage of non-selfs, the non-self is recognized as a known non-self, and the type of the non-self is worm. The name of the non-self is Loveletter Worm, and the schema of deleting can be used to eliminate the non-self.

A.5.2 Feature Space That is Built with all the Known Non-Selfs

Suppose the feature dimension of all the known non-selfs is q, the feature vector of the non-self c_j among the known non-selfs is denoted with $(u_{j1}, u_{j2}, ..., u_{jq})$, the feature space of the non-selfs is represented with $\{(u_{j1}, u_{j2},$

Figure A.9 Recognition of the known non-selfs by the algorithm. ©2008 Tao Gong. Used with permission.

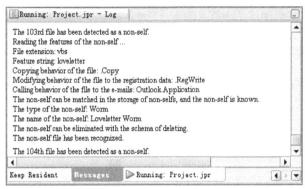

Figure A.10. Feature space of non-selfs with unlimited class expending. ©2008 Tao Gong. Used with permission.

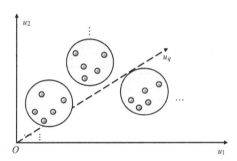

..., u_{jq})}, shown in Figure A.10, j=1, 2, ..., M, and M denotes the sum of the known non-selfs. The known non-selfs are classified into many classes, and the number of the classes is limited and numerable at any time. After the process for learning the unknown non-selfs, the unknown non-selfs are classified into the type of the most similar known non-selfs to the unknown ones or given new classes, according to the feature vector of the unknown non-selfs. Sometimes, the unknown non-selfs can not be classified into any type of known non-selfs, and new classes must be created for the unknown ones at that time. With creation of new class repeated, the classes of unknown non-selfs may be unlimited but numerable.

In Figure A.10, the dimension coordinate of the feature space for the non-selfs is represented with u_i, i=1, 2, ..., q, small balls are used to denote the non-selfs, and the big circles represent the classes of the non-selfs. For the problem for learning unknown non-selfs with unlimited class, current approaches of machine learning are not quite suitable, so that the class of unknown non-selfs is regarded as a limited variable in some applications.

A.5.3 Learning of Unknown Non-Selfs

Suppose the current static web system that the artificial immune system protects has l components, among which the algorithm for recognizing known non-selfs has regarded l_2 components as unknown non-selfs. There is some feature information for K known non-selfs in the storage of non-selfs, and each non-self has q features that are coded in some tables. The problem for recognizing the unknown non-selfs can be solved by finding the most similar known non-self to the unknown non-self and/or creating a new class for the unknown non-self, and the problem for finding the most similar known non-self to the unknown non-self is a constrained optimization problem. Suppose the difference between the unknown non-self c_u and the known non-self c_i is represented with the function $f(c_u, c_i)$, the constrained optimization problem is described as such (Cai & Wang, 2006).

$$\text{minimize} \quad f(c_u, c_i) \qquad c_u = (u_{u1}, x_{u2}, \cdots, x_{uq}) \in \Re^q \qquad\qquad\qquad (A.6)$$
$$c_i = (u_{i1}, x_{i2}, \cdots, x_{iq}) \in \Re^q$$

subject to: $\quad f(c_u, c_i) < r$

Here, r represents the threshold that is used to determine if the unknown worm belongs to any class of known non-selfs.

The constrained optimization problem for finding the most similar known non-self to the unknown non-self can be solved with some evolutionary algorithms, and the algorithm for recognizing the unknown non-selfs is designed with immune memory, shown in Figure A.11. The immune memory means that the unknown non-self can be transformed into a known one after learning, and the immune learning is enhanced.

Step 1. Select some known non-selfs with random probability from the storage of known non-selfs, and build the first colony for evolutionary computation with the feature vectors of the selected non-selfs.

Step 2. Read the measurable features of unknown non-self c_u, and build its feature vector.

Step 3. Compute the distance between the feature vectors of the unknown non-self c_u and each known non-self in the colony, and sort the distances that represent the difference between the unknown non-self and the known non-selfs. Select the minimal distance and keep the relevant feature vector and known non-self.

Step 4. Mutate and cross in the colony of feature vectors with the feature vectors of other known non-selfs and the feature vector of the unknown non-self.

Step 5. Match the new vector with the feature vectors of all the known non-selfs. If the new vector belongs to any other known non-self, call step 3 to continue the random search; otherwise end the loop, and select the feature vector that has the minimal distance. Then compute unknown features of the unknown non-self with the feature vector that has the minimal distance.

Step 6. Determine whether the minimal distance is smaller than r. If yes, then the unknown non-self belongs to the type of the known non-self whose feature vector has the minimal distance; otherwise, the unknown non-self is regarded as a new class of non-selfs and a new class is created for the unknown non-self.

Step 7. Memorize the feature vector of the unknown non-self, and then the unknown non-self becomes a new known non-self.

A.5.4 Probability for Learning Non-Selfs

Before the algorithm for recognizing the unknown worms is used, the unknown worms must be detected. The algorithm for detecting selfs and non-selfs on the normal model is used to detect whether the object is a self or non-self, and the algorithm for recognizing the known non-selfs is used to determine whether the non-self is a known non-self or unknown non-self. For recognizing more unknown non-selfs the stage for detecting selfs and non-selfs is very crucial, and the stage for recognizing known non-selfs is relatively simple.

With the space properties and the time properties of the components, the normal model uniquely identifies the normal state of each component and the normal state of the whole static web system that the artificial immune system protects. Therefore, based on Theorem A.3, the following theorem shows the advantages of the normal model to the algorithm for recognizing the unknown non-selfs.

Theorem A.4 Suppose the event that the artificial immune system detects the non-selfs by matching the features of the non-selfs is denoted with D_T, the event that the artificial immune system detects the non-selfs is denoted with D_N, the probability for recognizing the unknown non-selfs based on the normal model is represented with $P(R|D_N)$, the probability for recognizing the unknown non-selfs only based on matching the features of the non-selfs is represented with $P(R|D_T)$, then $P(R|D_N) > P(R|D_T)$.

Figure A.11. Algorithm for recognizing the unknown non-selfs with immune memory. ©2008 Tao Gong. Used with permission.

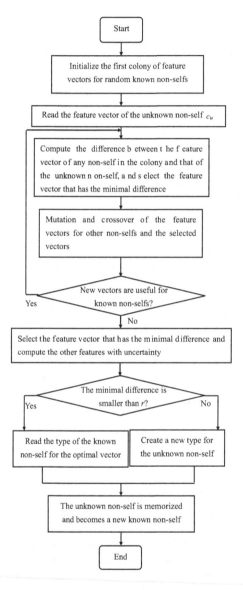

[Proof] The artificial immune system recognizes the unknown non-selfs after the system detects some non-selfs as the unknown non-selfs. Thus, the probability for recognizing the unknown non-selfs is a conditional probability $P(R|D)$, which is the probability of the event that unknown non-selfs are recognized on the condition that the non-selfs are detected.

$\because P(D_N) = 1$, $P(D_T) < 1$, $\therefore P(D_N) > P(D_T)$.

$\therefore P(R|D_N) = P(R) > P(R|D_T)$. ∎

Figure A.12. Density of the offspring produced with three-parent SPX. ©2008 Tao Gong. Used with permission.

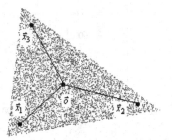

A.5.5 Experiments for Learning Non-Selfs

After the experiment for detecting selfs and non-selfs were done, the experiment for learning non-selfs was activated. The algorithm for detecting selfs and non-selfs on the normal model was used to detect whether the object is a self or non-self, and the algorithm for recognizing the known non-selfs was used to determine whether the non-self is a known non-self or unknown non-self.

In the web demo system shown in Figure A.7, 50 independent trials for learning the non-selfs are executed with MATLAB offline. In the algorithm for learning unknown worms with evolutionary computation, the common recombination operator involve simulated binary crossover (SBX), simplex crossover (SPX) (Tsutsui, Yamamure & Higuchi, 1999) etc. In this test, the algorithm adopts SPX, which generates offspring based on uniform probability distribution and does not need any fitness information, as the recombination operator. In $\Re^n$, μ mutually independent parent vectors $(\overrightarrow{x_i}, i = 1, \cdots, \mu)$ form a simplex, and Figure A.12 illustrates the density of the offspring produced with three-parent SPX.

The production of an offspring consists in: 1) employing a certain ratio to expand the original simplex in each direction $\overrightarrow{x_i} - \overrightarrow{o}$ ($\overrightarrow{o}$ is the center of μ vectors, $\overrightarrow{o} = (1)/(n+1)\sum_{i=1}^{\mu} \overrightarrow{x_i}$) and forming a new simplex; and 2) choosing one point form the new simplex as an offspring.

The evolutionary search was tested with some benchmark functions such as g1, g2, g3, g10, g11, g12 (Cai & Wang, 2006), and the evolutionary algorithm in the static web immune system showed good optimum and performance, shown in Table A.2. For example, when the benchmark function g10 was tested with 100 experiments, the convergence curves of the two experiments among them are shown in Figure A.13. At first, the evolutionary search with some constraints jumped up and down beside the optimum and then found much closer solutions to the optimum than before until the convergence of the algorithm was accomplished.

Table A.2. Results of evolutionary searching for learning the non-selfs

fcn	optimal	best	median	mean	st. dev	worst	average percentage
g01	-15.000	-15.000000	-15.000000	-15.000000	2.522E-08	-15.000000	95
g02	-0.803619	-0.803241	-0.802556	-0.801258	3.832E-03	-0.792363	86
g03	-1.000	-1.000000	-1.000000	-1.000000	1.304E-12	-1.000000	91
g10	7049.248	7049.248020	7049.248020	7049.248020	1.502E-12	7049.248020	92
g11	0.750	0.750000	0.750000	0.750000	1.546E-12	0.750000	56
g12	-1.000000	-1.000000	-1.000000	-1.000000	0.000E+00	-1.000000	100

Figure A.13. Convergence of the two evolutionary searching curves. ©2008 Tao Gong. Used with permission.

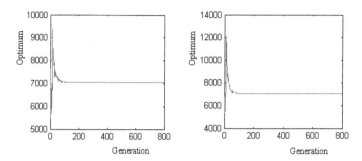

The immune memory is a kind of rote learning, and the memory part can be regarded as a function $m(\cdot)$ in mathematics. The input vector of the memory function is $(u_{ji_1}, u_{ji_2}, \cdots, u_{ji_o})$, and the output vector of the memory function is the combination of unknown features and unknown type of the unknown worm, as denoted with $(u_{jl_1}, u_{jl_2}, \cdots, u_{jl_{q-o}}, T)$. The immune memory can be searched directly and easily, and no repeated immune computation is needed for learning unknown features and type, when the memory function $m(u_{ji_1}, u_{ji_2}, \cdots, u_{ji_o})$ is called (Cai & Xu, 2004).

$$(u_{ji_1}, \cdots, u_{ji_o}) \xrightarrow{\ m\ } (u_{jl_1}, \cdots, u_{jl_{q-o}}, T) \xrightarrow{\ \text{storing}\ } (u_{ji_1}, \cdots, u_{ji_o})\, (u_{jl_1}, \cdots, u_{jl_{q-o}}, T) \qquad (A.7)$$

In this example, the three variants v_1, v_2, v_3 are recognized to belong to three classes of the loveletter worms, the happy-time worms, and the Jessica worms respectively, and the three classes are known, shown as the real-line circle in Figure A.14. The other unknown worms w_1, w_2 are recognized as two brand-new unknown worms, and two new classes are created for them, shown as the dashed circle.

The web demo system is immunized by the artificial immune system and is now immune from some worms. When many known worms and the unknown worms attack the demo system that the artificial immune system protects, the innate immune tier is activated to detect the worms and recognized the known worms. Detection of all the worms and recognition of the unknown worms are both quick because of the normal model and the storage of known worms, shown as the curve from the time point 0 to t_2 in Figure A.15. After the innate immune tier confirms that the unknown worms are not any known worms, the adaptive immune tier begins to learn the unknown worms with random evolutionary search, shown as the curve from the time point t_2 to t_3 in Figure A.15,

Figure A.14. Learning results of the unknown worms in the feature space. ©2008 Tao Gong. Used with permission.

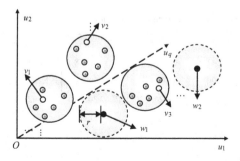

Figure A.15. Immune response to the known worms and the unknown worms. ©2008 Tao Gong. Used with permission.

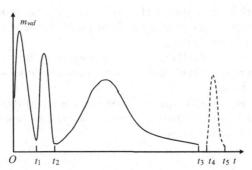

and the most similar known worm is found to decide whether the unknown worms belong to any type of known worms or are really new type of worms. The learning results are memorized so that the unknown worms are transformed into new known worms in the end. If another variant of the loveletter worm attacks the demo system, the artificial immune system recognizes the variant as a known worm now and the immune response is quick from the time point t_4 to t_5 in Figure A.15. Here, m_{wd} represents the sum of the worms that have been processed, and t represents the time coordinate.

In Figure A.15, the primary immune response includes the self/non-self detection and recognition of the known worms, and the detection is accomplished from the time point 0 to t_1. The secondary immune response is from the time point t_2 to t_3, which is much longer than the primary immune response. In fact, the hypothetic immune response from the time point t_4 to t_5 is a part of the primary immune response after the secondary immune response.

The experiments are made on the web-based course system, and the web demo system is a part. Over a hundred of worms attack the web system, and many files are infected. The artificial immune system detects all the worms successfully with the normal model and the approach for detecting selfs and non-selfs. But only with some intelligent techniques such as the artificial neural network, the probability for detecting the non-selfs is smaller, and such result affects the process of recognizing the worms. With the immune learning algorithm after detecting the worms with the normal model, the artificial immune system recognizes the unknown worms with the higher probability than the result with the artificial neural network with the BP algorithm.

A.6 CONCLUSION

The tri-tier immune computing model is a useful and effective model for the static Web immune system. The first tier is the innate immune computing tier, the second tier is the adaptive immune computing tier, and the last tier is the parallel immune computing tier.

The theorems prove that, on the condition that the time property is correct, the normal model and the tri-tier immune computing model are useful for increasing the probability of detecting selfs and non-selfs in the static web system. Many anti-worm experiments of immunization validate effectiveness and advantages of the static web immune system and the immune algorithms. The static web immune system can eliminate worms and repair itself with higher probability for detecting non-selfs than traditional approaches.

A.7 FUTURE DIRECTIONS

This work emphasized on static web immune system, and this is new try of new techniques for immune computing. But this is just a beginning, the next work is emphasizing and will emphasize on dynamic web immune system.

The related issues abut the dynamic web immune system can be shown in the following:

1) Normal model of dynamic web immune system. How to build the normal model for the dynamic web immune system and how to transform the normal model from a normal state to another normal state are the difficult bottlenecks for representing the selfs.

2) Adaptive learning of unknown non-selfs. If the viruses are designed by the most intelligent programmers, how to design the adaptive learning mechanism of complete-unknown non-selfs is really a difficult problem for other most intelligent programmers.

3) Design of artificial immune system for the operating systems. It is very difficult to build a normal model for a Windows operating system, because the designers for the Windows operating system do not really know when the system is normal or abnormal.

ACKNOWLEDGMENT

This work was supported in part by the Shanghai Natural Science Foundation under Grant 08ZR1400400, the Shanghai Educational Development Foundation under Grant 2007CG42 and Donghua Univ. Foundation under Grant #104-10-0044017.

REFERENCES

Arce, I., & Levy, E. (2003). An analysis of the Slapper worm. *IEEE Security & Privacy, 1*(1), 82-87.

Balachandran, S. (2005). *Multi-shaped detector generation using real-valued representation for anomaly detection*. Masters Thesis, University of Memphis.

Balthrop, J., Forrest, S., & Newman, M. E. J., et al. (2004). Technological Networks and the Spread of Computer Viruses. *Science, 304*(5670), 527-52.

Bell, G. I. (1970). Mathematical model of clonal selection and antibody production. *J Theor Biol, 29*(2), 191-232.

Cai, Z. X., & Peng, Z. H. (2002). Cooperative coevolutionary adaptive genetic algorithm in path planning of cooperative multi-mobile robot systems. *Journal of Intelligent and Robotic systems, 33*(1), 61-71.

Cai, Z. X., & Wang, Y. (2006). Multiobjective optimization based evolutionary algorithm for constrained optimization. *IEEE Trans. on Evolutionary Computation, 10*(6), 658-675.

Cai, Z. X., & Xu, G. Y. (2004). Artificial Intelligence: Principles and Applications (Third Edition, Graduate Book), Beijing: Tsinghua University Press.

Chao, D. L., Davenport, M. P., & Forrest, S., et al. (2004). Modelling the impact of antigen kinetics on T-cell activation and response. *Immunology and Cell Biology, 82*(1), 55-61.

De Castro, L. N., & Timmis, J. (2002). *Artificial Immune Systems: A New Computational Intelligence Approach*. London: Springer-Verlag.

De Castro, L. N., & Von Zuben, F. J. (2002). Learning and optimization using the clonal selection principle. *IEEE Trans on Evolutionary Computation, 6*(3), 306-313.

Deng, Y., & Korobka, A. (2001) Performance of a supercomputer built with commodity components. *Parallel Processing, 27*(12), 91-108.

Einstein, A. (1920). *Relativity: the Special and General Theory*. Three Rivers Press, New York.

Fauci, S. A. (2003). HIV and AIDS: 20 years of science. *Nature Medicine, 9*(7), 839-843.

Gong, T., & Cai, Z. X. (2003) Parallel evolutionary computing and 3-tier load balance of remote mining robot. *Trans Nonferrous Met Soc China, 13*(4), 948-952.

Gonzalez, F., & Dasgupta, D. (2003). Anomaly detection using real-valued negative selection. *Journal of Genetic Programming and Evolvable Machines, 4*(4), 383-403.

Hawking, S., & Penrose, R. (1996). *The nature of space and time*, Princeton University Press.

Jerne, N. K. (1974). Towards a network theory of the immune system. *Ann Immunol, 125C*, 373-389.

Jiao, L. C., & Wang, L. (2000) Novel genetic algorithm based on immunity. *IEEE Trans on Systems, Man and Cybernetics — Part A: Systems and Humans, 30*(5), 552-561.

Levy, E. (2005). Worm Propagation and Generic Attacks. *IEEE Security and Privacy, 3*(2), 63- 65.

Orman, H. (2003). The Morris Worm: A Fifteen-Year Perspective. *IEEE Security & Privacy, 1*(5): 35-43.

Perelson, A., Hightower, R., & Forrest, S. (1996). Evolution (and learning) of v-region genes. *Research in Immunology, 147*, 202-208.

Tsutsui, S., Yamamure, M., & Higuchi, T. (1999). Multi-parent recombination with simplex crossover in real coded genetic algorithms. in *Proc. Genetic and Evol. Comput. Conf.*, 657–664.

Zou, C. C., Gong, W., & Towsley, D. (2002). Code Red Worm Propagation Modeling and Analysis. In: Atluri V. eds. *Proc of the 9th ACM Conf on Computer and Communications Security*, ACM Press, New York, 138-147.

KEY TERMS

Adaptive Immune Tier: The immune computing tier, which learn and recognize the unknown non-selfs, is called as the adaptive immune tier of the artificial immune system.

Immune Memorization: The process for remembering the unknown non-selfs to transform the non-self into the known ones is called as the immune memorization.

Innate Immune Tier: The immune computing tier, which detects the selfs & non-selfs and recognize all the known non-selfs, is called as the innate immune tier of the artificial immue system.

Non-Self Database: The database that stores the feature information of the known non-selfs is called as the non-self database.

Normal Model of Normal Static Web System: The set of space-time properties for all the normal components of the normal static web system is called as the normal model of the normal static web system.

Parallel Immune Tier: The immune computing tier, which uses parallel computing to increase efficiency and load balance of immune computation, is called as the parallel immune tier of the artificial immune system.

Probability for Detecting Non-Selfs: The measurement on the probability of the random event that the artificial immune system detects the non-selfs is called as the probability for detecting the non-selfs.

Probability for Learning Unknown Non-Selfs: The measurement on the probability of the random event that the artificial immune system learns the unknown non-selfs is called as the probability for learning the unknown non-selfs.

Self Database: The database that stores the space-time information of the selfs is called as the self database.

Self/Non-Self Detection: The process for detecting the object to decide whether the object is a self or non-self is called as the self/non-self detection.

Section I.VI
The Other Applications
of Artificial Immune Systems

In this section, artificial immune systems are used in forecast, control, image segmentation, and hardware detection. Different immune mechanisms are used for solving these problems. The applications in this section show the flexibility of artificial immune systems when solving the problems in different fields.

Chapter XII
Immunocomputing for Spatio–Temporal Forecast

Alexander O. Tarakanov
Russian Academy of Sciences, Russia

ABSTRACT

Based on mathematical models of immunocomputing, this chapter describes an approach to spatio-temporal forecast (STF) by intelligent signal processing. The approach includes both low-level feature extraction and high-level ("intelligent") pattern recognition. The key model is the formal immune network (FIN) including apoptosis (programmed cell death) and immunization both controlled by cytokines (messenger proteins). Such FIN can be formed from raw signal using discrete tree transform (DTT), singular value decomposition (SVD), and the proposed index of inseparability in comparison with the Renyi entropy. Real-world application is demonstrated on data of space monitoring of the Caspian, Black, and Barents Sea. A surprising result is strong negative correlation between anomalies of sea surface temperature (SST) and sunspot number (SSN). This effect can be utilized for long-term STF.

1 INTRODUCTION

Artificial immune systems (AISs) (Dasgupta 1999; de Castro & Timmis 2002) and immunocomputing (IC) (Tarakanov et al. 2003; Zhao 2005) are developing with the branches of computational intelligence (Tarakanov & Nicosia 2007; Dasgupta & Nino 2008; Tarakanov 2008) like genetic algorithms (Tarakanov A. & Tarakanov Y. 2005) and artificial neural networks (ANNs) also called neurocomputing (Tarakanov A. & Tarakanov Y. 2004). Recent advances in AISs include a stochastic model of immune response (Chao et al. 2004), an aircraft fault detection (Dasgupta et al. 2004), intrusion detection (Dasgupta & Gonzalez 2005) and computational models based on the negative selection process that occurs in the thymus (Dasgupta 2006; Dasgupta & Nino 2008). Recent advances in IC include a concept of biomolecular immunocomputer as a computer controlled fragment of

Copyright © 2009, IGI Global, distributing in print or electronic forms without written permission of IGI Global is prohibited.

the natural immune system (Goncharova et al. 2005). A connection of IC with brain research leads to promising results in understanding of basic principles of organization of molecular networks and receptor mosaics which are common for the brain and immunity (Agnati et al. 2005ab, 2008; Goncharova & Tarakanov 2007, 2008b). A connection of IC with cellular automata (CA) (Adamatzky 1994) leads to encouraging results in three-dimensional (3D) computer graphics (Tarakanov and Adamatzky 2002) and inspires a novel method of identification of CA (Tarakanov & Prokaev 2007). Recent advances in real-world applications of the IC (Tarakanov 2007a) include signal processing and intrusion detection (Atreas et al. 2003, 2004; Tarakanov et al. 2005b, 2007a) as well as intelligent simulation of hydro-physical fields (Tarakanov et al. 2007bc).

In such general perspective, the objective of this chapter is to develop the IC approach to spatio-temporal forecast (STF) by intelligent signal processing. According to (Cheng & Wang 2007), STF can be considered as data mining or the extraction of unknown and implicit knowledge, structures, spatio-temporal relationships, or patterns not explicitly stored in spatio-temporal data. In this chapter, the IC approach is applied to real-world data of space monitoring of the Caspian, Black, and Barents Sea (NASA 2007). A surprising and controversial result of this application is rather strong negative correlation between anomalies of sea surface temperature (SST) and an index of solar activity – sunspot number (SSN). This effect may be utilized for long-term STF.

2 BACKGROUND

According to (Tarakanov et al. 2003), IC is based on the principles (especially, mathematical models) of information processing by proteins and immune networks. Some analogies between neurocomputing and IC are shown in Tab. 1. Since ANN represents a "hardwired" network of artificial neurons, essential difference of IC is that formal immune network (FIN) represents a network of free bindings between formal proteins. For example, the IC approach to pattern recognition is abstracted from the principle of molecular recognition between proteins, including antibody (also called immunoglobulin: Ig) of natural immune system and any other antigen (including another antibody). Let Ig1 and Ig2 be two antibodies, while Ag be antigen. The strength of biophysical interaction between any pair of proteins can be measured by their binding energy. Let FIN[1] and FIN[2] be values of binding energy between Ag and Ig1, Ig2, correspondingly. Then any protein (including antibody) can be represented and recognized by the corresponding couple of numbers FIN[1] and FIN[2] in such two-dimensional immune network of interactions that is formed by two antibodies Ig1 and Ig2. Accordingly, any high-dimensional input vector Ag (antigen which can include several Ig-binding sites – epitopes) can be projected to such low-dimensional space of FIN and recognized by the class (or some value f) of the nearest point of FIN (Fig. 1).

In such background, the key model of the IC approach to STF is the FIN. In the training mode, FIN is formed from the raw spatio-temporal signal using discrete tree transform (DTT) (Atreas et al. 2003, 2004) and singular value decomposition (SVD) (Horn & Johnson 1986). After the procedures of apoptosis (programmed cell death) and immunization both controlled by cytokines (messenger proteins) (Tarakanov et al. 2005a), the result of such feature extraction by FIN is estimated by the proposed index of inseparability (Tarakanov 2007b) in comparison with the Renyi entropy (Renyi 1961). In the recognition mode, the current SST signal is processed by DTT, mapped to the FIN, and forecasted by a "cytokine value" of the nearest cell (point) of the FIN.

Table 1. Analogies between neurocomputing and immunocomputing

Approach	Neurocomputing	Immunocomputing
Basic Element	Artificial Neuron	Formal Protein
Network	Artificial Neural Network	Formal Immune Network
Hardware	Neurochip	Immunochip

Figure 1. Immunocomputing approach to pattern recognition. ©2008 Alexander Tarakanov. Used with permission.

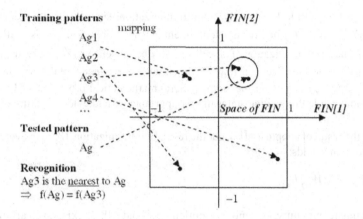

3 MATHEMATICAL MODELS OF IMMUNOCOMPUTING

3.1 Formal Immune Network

Let vector-matrix transposing be designated by upper stroke ($[\ ]'$). For example, if X is column vector then X' is row vector.

Definition 1. Cell is a pair $V = (f, P)$, where f is real value ("cytokine value") $f \in R$, whereas $P = (p_1, ..., p_q)$ is a point of q-dimensional space: $P \in R^q$, and P lies within unit cube: $\max\{|\ p_1\ |, ..., |\ p_q\ |\} \le 1$.

Let distance ("affinity") $d_j = d(V_i, V_j)$ between cells V_i and V_j is defined by the following (Tchebyshev) norm:

$$d_{ij} = \left\| P_i - P_j \right\|, \ \|P\| = \max\left\{ \left| p_1 \right|, ..., \left| p_q \right| \right\}.$$

Fix some finite non-empty set of cells ("innate immunity"): $W_0 = (V_1, ..., V_m)$.

Definition 2. FIN is a set of cells: $W \subseteq W_0$.

Definition 3. Cell V_i recognizes cell V_k if the following conditions are satisfied:

$$|f_i - f_k| < \rho, \ d_{ik} < h, \ d_{ik} < d_{ij}, \ \forall V_j \in W, \ j \ne i, \ k \ne j,$$

where $\rho \ge 0$ and $h \ge 0$ are non-negative real values ("recognition threshold" and "affinity threshold").
Let us define the behavior of FIN by the following two rules.

Rule 1 (apoptosis). If cell $V_i \in W$ recognizes cell $V_k \in W$ then remove V_i from FIN.

Rule 2 (immunization). If cell $V_k \in W$ is nearest to cell $V_i \in W_0 \setminus W$ among all cells of FIN: $d_k < d_j$, $\forall V_j \in W$, whereas $|f_i - f_k| \geq \rho$, then add V_i to FIN.

Note that the immunization in Rule 2 is actually "auto-immunization" since the immunizer cell belongs to the set of "innate immunity" W_0. Let W_A be FIN as a consequent of application of apoptosis to all cells of W_0. Let W_I be FIN as a consequence of immunization of all cells of W_A by all cells of W_0. Note that the resulting sets W_A and W_I depend on the ordering of cells in W_0. Further it will be assumed that the ordering is given. It will be also assumed that $d_{ij} \neq 0$, $\forall i \neq j$. Consider some general mathematical properties of FIN. The following Properties 1-3 look obvious while Proposition states more important and less evident feature of FIN.

Property 1. Neither the result of apoptosis W_A nor the result of immunization W_I can overcome W_0 for any innate immunity and both thresholds:

$$W_A \subseteq W_0, \quad W_I \subseteq W_0, \quad \forall W_0, h, \rho.$$

Property 2. For any innate immunity W_0 and recognition threshold ρ there exists such affinity threshold h_0 that apoptosis does not change W_0 for any h less than h_0: $W_A = W_0$, $\forall h < h_0$.

Property 3. For any innate immunity W_0 and affinity threshold h there exists such recognition threshold ρ_0 that apoptosis does not change W_0 for any ρ less than ρ_0: $W_A = W_0$, $\forall \rho < \rho_0$.

Proposition. For any innate immunity W_0 and recognition threshold ρ there exists affinity threshold h_1 such that consequence of apoptosis and immunization $W_1 = W_I(h_1)$ provides the minimal number of cells $|W_1| > 0$ for given W_0 and ρ and any h: $|W_1| \leq |W_I(h)|$, $\forall h$, $\forall W_I \subseteq W_0$.

The proof of this Proposition can be found in (Tarakanov 2007a). Actually, the Proposition states that the minimal number of cells after apoptosis and immunization is a kind of "inner invariant" of any FIN, which depends on the innate immunity and the recognition threshold but does not depend on the affinity threshold. Practically, it means that such invariant can be found for any FIN by apoptosis and immunization without considering any affinity threshold (in Definition 3) at all.

Now we can define a model of molecular recognition in terms of FIN. Let "epitope" (antigenic determinant) be any point $P = (p_1, ..., p_q)$ of q-dimensional space: $P \in R^q$. Note that any cell of FIN also contains an epitope, according to Definition 1.

Definition 4. Cell V_i recognizes epitope P by assigning him value f_i if the distance $d(V_i, P)$ between the cell and the epitope is minimal among all cells of FIN: $d(V_i, P) = \min\{d(V_j, P)\}$, $\forall V_j \in W$.

If value f (in Definition 1) is natural number $f = c$, $c \in N$ (i.e. "cytokine class"), whereas recognition threshold (in Definition 3) $\rho < 1$, then we obtain a special case of cytokine FIN proposed by Tarakanov et al. (2005a) and applied to pattern recognition. Note that innate immunity W_0 and its ordering of cells are determined by the set and the order of raw data of a particular application. For example, this order is naturally determined by time series in signal processing (Tarakanov & Nicosia 2007; Tarakanov 2008) and spatio-temporal forecast.

3.2 Singular Value Decomposition

Let pattern ("molecule") be any n-dimensional column-vector $Z = [z_1,...,z_n]$, where $z_1,...,z_n$ are real values. Let pattern recognition be mapping $Z \to P$ of the pattern to a q-dimensional epitope, and recognition of the epitope by the value f of the nearest cell of FIN. Consider a mathematical model of such mapping of any pattern: $R^n \to R^q$. Let $Z_1,...,Z_m$ be n-dimensional training patterns with known values $f_1,...,f_m$. Let $A = [Z_1,...,Z_m]'$ be training matrix of dimension $m \times n$. Consider SVD of this matrix:

$$A = s_1 X_1 Y_1' + s_2 X_2 Y_2' + s_3 X_3 Y_3' + ... + s_r X_r Y_r', \tag{1}$$

where r is rank of the matrix, s_k are singular values and X_k, Y_k are left and right singular vectors with the following properties:

$$X_k' X_k = 1, \ Y_k' Y_k = 1, \ X_k' X_i = 0, \ Y_k' Y_i = 0, \ i \neq k, \ k = 1,...,r. \tag{2}$$

Consider the following map $P(Z): R^n \to R^q$, where Z is any n-dimensional pattern $Z \in R^n$ and $Y_1,...,Y_q$ are left singular vectors of SVD (1):

$$p_k = \frac{1}{s_k} Y_k' Z, \ k = 1,...,q. \tag{3}$$

According to (Tarakanov et al. 2003), formula (3) can be computed as the binding energy between two formal proteins: Z("antigen") and Y_k ("antibody").

Property 4. Any epitope $P(Z_i)$ obtained by the application of formula (3) to any training pattern Z_i, $i = 1,...,m$, lies within unit cube of FIN (see Definition 1).

This property can be proved using the properties (2) of singular vectors.

3.3 Discrete Tree Transform

Consider the mathematical model of forming pattern from any one-dimensional signal (time series). Let $T = \{t_1,...,t_n\}$ be a fragment of signal, where $t \in R$ be real value in general case, $n = 2^{N_0}$ and N_0 is some number exponent so that n is a power of 2. Let $u = 2^{N_1}$, $N_1 \leq N_0$. According to (Atreas et al. 2003), the dyadic DTT of T is the following map:

$$T \to \{a_{u,k}\}, a_{u,k} = \frac{1}{n} \sum_{1+(k-1)u}^{ku} t_i, \ k = 1,...,2^{N_0-N_1}.$$

Let $l = N_1$ be DTT level: $0 \leq l \leq N_0$. Let us denote the DDT map as follows:

$$T \to T^{(l)}, \ T^{(l)} = \{t_1^{(l)},...,t_n^{(l)}\}, \ t_i^{(l)} = a_{u,k}, \ 1 + (k-1)u \le i \le ku. \tag{4}$$

Consider the values $z_j = t_j^{(l)}$, $j = 1,...,n$, as the pattern (vector) $Z = [z_1,...,z_n]'$ obtained by the processing of any fragment T of the signal.

According to (Atreas et al. 2003, 2004), the proposed approach to signal processing is inspired by a mode of biomolecular computing (Goncharova et al. 2005) where immune cells chop unknown antigen to its local epitopes and expose them to the immune system. Analogously, the DTT approach represents unknown signal as a tree of data, and chop the branches of the tree at the level l to detect local features of the signal.

3.4 Index of Inseparability

According to the above models, the feature extraction method by the IC is as follows.

1.   Extract m training patterns from the signal.

2.   Form q-dimensional FIN1 with $m_1 = m$ cells (using DTT and SVD).

3.   Find its inner invariant FIN2 with $m_2 \le m_1$ cells (using apoptosis and immunization).

As the result, the q-dimensional points of FIN2 $P_1,..., P_{m_2}$ can be considered as the feature vectors that represent the signal.

The following task is to estimate a quality of such feature extraction. This can be done using the special entropy proposed in (Renyi 1961) and proved to be rather useful metric of very large networks regarding the task of intrusion detection (Johnson 2005). According to (Renyi 1961; Johnson 2005), the Renyi entropy of j-th dimension of FIN can be defined as follows:

$$[I_R]_j = -\frac{1}{m}\sum_{i=1}^{m}\log_2(p_{ij}^2), \tag{5}$$

where $p_{1j},..., p_{jm}$ are the values of j-th coordinate of the points of FIN $P_1,..., P_m$. According to (Tarakanov 2007b), let us consider the maximal entropy as the Renyi entropy of FIN:

$$I_R = \max\{[I_R]_j\}, \ j = 1,..., q. \tag{6}$$

Usually, entropy represents a measure of disorder. The lower is entropy the lower is disorder of the system and vice versa. Consider another metric which is more specific to FIN. According to (Tarakanov 2007b), the index of inseparability of FIN2 can be defined as follows:

$$I_2 = \ln\left(\frac{m_2}{m_1 h_{\min}}\right), \tag{7}$$

where m_1 is number of cells in FIN1 and m_2 is number of cells in FIN2 (after apoptosis and immunization), whereas $h_{\min}$ is the minimal distance between any pair of cells of FIN with different values of f:

$$h_{\min} = \min\{d_{ij}\}, \ i \ne j, \ |f_i - f_j| > \rho. \tag{8}$$

Consider that $m_2 = m_1$ for FIN1. Then the index of FIN1 can be derived from (7) as follows:

$$I_1 = -\ln(h_{\min}).$$

(9)

Thus, the greater is minimal distance $h_{\min}$ the lower is the index and the better is the separability between different cells of FIN.

4 SIGNAL FORECAST BY IMMUNOCOMPUTING

The IC scheme of signal forecast is shown in Fig. 2. In both training and recognition modes, the fragment is extracted from the signal and processed by DTT to form the pattern (antigen).

Steps 1-11 below describe the IC algorithm of signal forecast, where Steps 1-8 form the training, whereas Steps 9-11 form the forecast by recognition.

Step 1. Fix the real-valued recognition threshold ρ and the integers n, m, l, q, g, where $n \geq 1$ is the number of previous counts of signal ("history") to be considered for the temporal forecast of the next count $n + 1$, or the number of signals to be considered for the spatial forecast of another signal; $m \geq 1$ is the number of training fragments in the signal; $l \geq 0$ is the level of DTT so that $l = 0$ means no DTT; $q \geq 1$ is the dimension of FIN; $g \geq 1$ is the number of nearest points of FIN to be considered for the forecast.

Step 2. Compute DTT (4) of each fragment of the training signal: $(t_i, \ldots, t_{i+n+1})$, $i = 1, \ldots, m$.

Step 3. Form training vector $Z_i = [z_{i1}, \ldots, z_{in}]'$, where $z_{ij} = t_{i+j}^{(l)}$, $j = 1, \ldots, n$, and assign him the value:

$$f(Z_i) = t_{i+n+1}^{(l)}.$$

Step 4. Form training matrix $A = [Z_1 \ldots Z_m]'$ of the dimension $m \times n$.

Step 5. Compute first q singular values $s_1, \ldots, s_q$ and corresponding right singular vectors $Y_1, \ldots, Y_q$ by SVD (1) of the training matrix, where $q \leq r$ and r is rank of the matrix: $r \leq \min\{m, n\}$.

Step 6. Form the points of FIN1 $P_1, \ldots, P_q$ by mapping (3) of each training vector Z_i, $i = 1, \ldots, m$ to the q-dimensional space of FIN:

$$p_{i1} = \frac{1}{s_1} Y_1' Z_i, \ldots, p_{iq} = \frac{1}{s_q} Y_q' Z_i.$$

Step 7. Compute the index of inseparability of FIN1 (9). If $I_1 > 50$ then go to Step 9 without apoptosis and immunization at Step 8. This means that $h_{\min} < 10^{-21}$ and, thus, the training data are conflicting so that at least a couple of actually coincident patterns has different values of f:

$$|f(Z_i) - f(Z_j)| > \rho, \quad Z_i \cong Z_j, \quad i \neq j.$$

Figure 2. Immunocomputing scheme of signal forecast. ©*2008 Alexander Tarakanov. Used with permission.*

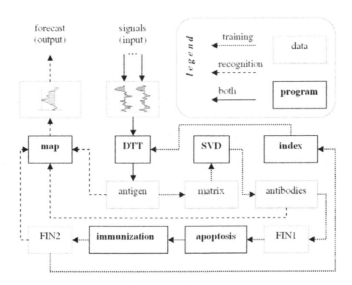

Step 8. Using the apoptosis and immunization, reduce $m_1 = m$ training points of FIN1 to $k = m_2$ points of FIN2, where the number of the points k is self-defined by the inner invariant of FIN (see Proposition).

Step 9. Compute DTT of the fragment of test signal, form n-dimensional vector Z and compute its mapping (3) to the q-dimensional space of FIN (FIN1 or FIN2, depending on Step 7):

$$p_1 = \frac{1}{s_1} Y_1' Z \,,\, \ldots \,,\, p_q = \frac{1}{s_q} Y_q' Z \,.$$

Step 10. Among the training points of FIN $P_1, \ldots, P_k$ (where $k = m_1$ or $k = m_2$, depending on Step 7), determine g nearest to $P(Z)$ points $P_1, \ldots, P_g$ and their distances:

$$d_1 = \left\| P_1 - P(Z) \right\|, \ldots, d_g = \left\| Y_g - P(Z) \right\|.$$

Step 11. Interpolate $f(Z)$ by the following sum:

$$f = \sum_{i=1}^{p} w_i f_i \,,$$

where $f_i = f(P_i)$ are the training values, which correspond to the nearest points of FIN, whereas coefficients w_i are determined by the distances:

$$w_i = \cfrac{1}{1 + d_i \sum\limits_{j \neq i}^{g} \cfrac{1}{d_j}}.$$

It can be shown that

$$\sum_{i=1}^{g} w_i = 1.$$

Note the following important property of the IC algorithm.

Property 5. If test vector is equal to any training vector: $Z = Z_i$, $i = 1, ..., m$, then exactly $f(Z) = f(Z_i)$.

The proof of this property can be found in (Tarakanov 2007a). Thus, the IC algorithm recognizes exactly any pattern it has been trained. Simply say, the IC approach does not make mistakes on any non-conflicting training set.

Main idea of the IC algorithm is the mapping of any high-dimensional vector (antigen) to low-dimensional space of FIN using binding energies between the antigen and antibodies. Also apoptosis and immunization essentially reduce the number of storing cells of FIN without loss of the accuracy of recognition. Due to these mathematically rigorous features, the IC algorithm outperforms state-of-the-art approaches of computational intelligence (Tarakanov 2008).

5 NUMERICAL EXAMPLES

5.1 Data Description and Signal Computation

Data for the numerical experiments have been obtained from space monitoring of the Caspian, Black, and Barents Sea during 2003-2006 (NASA 2007). These raw data form twelve arrays of monthly average SST in centigrade degree (T°C) for each year and each sea. For example, a fragment of such data is shown in Tab. 2. Note that the points where $T = -5.0$ either do not belong to the Caspian Sea or the corresponding SST may be unavailable due to the cloud clusters or other causes.

Let $N = 48$ be the number of months during 2003-2006. Consider the following signal (time series) t_i, where $T(lat, lon)$ is the value of SST in the point with the coordinates (lat, lon):

$$t_i(lat, lon) = T_i(lat, lon) - T_{0i}(lat, lon),$$

$$T_{0i}(lat, lon) = \frac{1}{4} \sum_{j=1}^{4} T_{k(i,j)}(lat, lon),$$

$$k(i, j) = mnth + 12(j-1)$$

$$mnth = \text{imod}(12),$$

$$i = 1, ..., N.$$

Table 2. Fragment of SST of the Caspian Sea for December 2005

Longitude (E) Latitude (N)	49.5	50.0	50.5	51.0	51.5	52.0	52.5
41.5	8.6	10.5	10.7	10.4	11.0	12.0	12.5
41.0	-5.0	10.2	11.4	10.9	10.7	12.1	13.2
40.5	-5.0	-5.0	-5.0	11.1	11.2	12.3	14.1
40.0	-5.0	11.7	11.4	11.4	12.5	13.7	15.2
39.5	-5.0	12.5	12.4	13.1	13.0	14.1	14.9
39.0	12.5	13.6	14.3	14.6	14.2	15.6	15.4
38.5	14.2	14.5	14.9	15.1	15.0	15.5	16.1
38.0	14.3	15.2	15.4	14.9	15.2	15.5	15.7

In other words, T_{0i} is the mean (over 2003-2006) value of SST for the month $mnth = \{Jan, ..., Dec\}$ in the point (lat, lon), while the value of the signal t_i is the difference ("anomaly") between the actual and mean SST. Example of the computation of such SST signal for the year 2005 in the point with $lat = 38.0$ and $lon = 51.5$ (Caspian Sea) is shown in Fig. 3. The corresponding values of the computed signal $(t_{25}, ..., t_{36})$ are given in Tab. 3:

5.2 Temporal Forecast

Let the recognition threshold (see Definition 3 and Step 1) be everywhere considered as $\rho = 0.1\,°C$. Consider the temporal forecast of SST signal in any point with given coordinates (lat, lon). Let 2003-2005 be the training years with the training values of the signal: $t_1, ..., t_{36}$. Let the task be to forecast the values of SST signal for the year 2006: $f_{37}, ..., f_{48}$, and to compare them with the actual values of the signal: $t_{37}, ..., t_{48}$. Let us consider two previous months for the temporal forecast: $n = 2$. Then the number of training vectors is equal to $m = 34$:

$$Z_1 = [t_1, t_2]', \ f(Z_1) = t_3, \ ... \ , \ Z_{34} = [t_{34}, t_{35}]', f(Z_{34}) = t_{36}.$$

Table 3. Example of signal computation (Fig. 3)

Month	SST	mean SST	Signal	Month	SST	mean SST	Signal
Jan	11.7	12.2	−0.5	Jul	27.2	26.2	1.0
Feb	11.0	11.6	−0.6	Aug	29.3	28.1	1.2
Mar	11.1	11.6	−0.5	Sep	26.3	26.2	0.1
Apr	14.4	13.9	0.5	Oct	22.2	23.0	−0.8
May	20.7	18.9	1.8	Nov	18.2	19.0	−0.8
Jun	24.6	23.7	0.9	Dec	15.2	14.9	0.3

Figure 3. Example of signal computation: black curve – daily SST for 2005; gray curve –mean SST for 2003-2006; small graphic – SST signal computed for 2005. ©2008 Alexander Tarakanov. Used with permission.

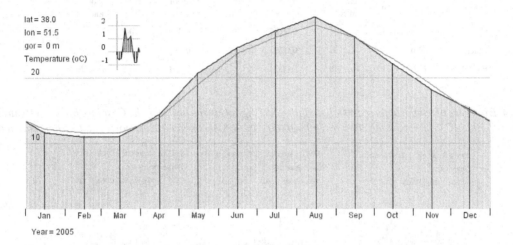

The number of test vectors is equal to $N - n - m = 12$:

$$Z_{35} = [t_{35}, t_{36}]', Z_{36} = [t_{36}, f_{37}]', Z_{37} = [f_{37}, f_{38}]', \dots, Z_{46} = [f_{46}, f_{47}]'.$$

The task is to forecast consequently the following values (note that f_{37} is the first value that can be forecasted by two previous values t_{35}, t_{36} in Z_{35}):

$$f_{37} = f(Z_{35}), \dots, f_{48} = f(Z_{46}).$$

The quality of the forecast can be estimated by the following error:

$$\delta_k = f_k - t_k, \tag{10}$$

and the following mean square error (MSE):

$$\sigma = \sqrt{\frac{1}{12} \sum_{k=37}^{48} \delta_i^2}, \tag{11}$$

The obtained results are shown in Tab. 4 and visualized in Fig. 4. The values of the remaining parameters (see Step 1) are as follows: no DTT $l = 0$ and two-dimensional FIN $q = 2$ with one nearest point for the interpolation (see Step 11) $g = 1$. Note that the MSE (11) of the forecast is less than 0.5°C while the maximal error (10) (absolute) is less than 1°C for the considered points of the Caspian and Barents Sea (Tab. 4).

5.3 Spatial Forecast

Consider the task to forecast the values of the signal for the year 2006 $f_{37}, \dots, f_{48}$ in the point with (lat_0, lon_0) using the measured values of the synchronous signals in several other points with (lat_j, lon_j): $t_{37,j}, \dots, t_{48,j}$, $j = 1, \dots, n$. Consider that the training values of the signals for the years 2003-2005 are known in all points,

Table 4. Example of temporal forecast (Fig. 4)

Sea	lat	lon	entropy of FIN	d min of FIN	index of FIN	MSE of forecast	max error	month of max error
Caspian	38.0	51.5	8.4	0.0185	3.9	0.434	−0.7	Sep
Black	44.0	31.0	7.6	0.0263	3.6	0.663	1.2	Jan
Barents	73.0	31.0	7.1	0.0000	∞	0.451	−0.9	Jun

Figure 4. Examples of temporal forecast (left to right – SST signals in the points of the Caspian, Black, and Barents Sea; gray "2006 IC" – forecast for 2006 by 2003-2005). ©2008 Alexander Tarakanov. Used with permission.

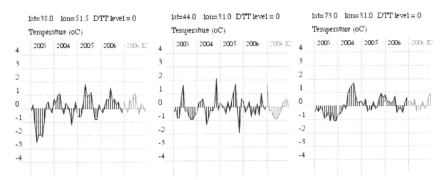

including the forecasting one: $t_{1,j},...,t_{36,j},\ j = 0,...,n$. Then the number of training vectors is equal to $m =$ 36:

$$Z_i = [t_{i,1}...t_{i,n}]',\ f(Z_i) = t_{i,0},\ i = 1,...,m.$$

The number of test vectors is equal to $N - m = 12$:

$$Z_k = [t_{k,1}...t_{k,n}]',\ f_k = f(Z_k),\ k = 37,...,48.$$

The obtained results are shown in Tab. 5 and visualized in Fig. 5. The values of the SST signal in the point $(lat_0 = 38.0,\ lon_0 = 51.5)$ of the Caspian Sea have been forecasted by the measured values of the signal in the following three points $n = 3$ of the same sea: $(lat_1 = 37.0,\ lon_1 = 52.5),\ (lat_2 = 38.5,\ lon_2 = 51.5),\ ($ $lat_3 = 37.5,\ lon_3 = 51.5)$. The values of the remaining parameters are as follows: no DTT $l = 0$ and one-dimensional FIN $q = 1$ with two nearest points for the interpolation $g = 2$. The Renyi entropy (5, 6) of the obtained FIN1 (no Step 8 for apoptosis and immunization) is $I_R = 7.6$, while the index of inseparability (9) is $I_1 = 11.3$. The MSE (11) of the forecast is less than 0.2°C while the absolute value of maximal error (10) is 0.5°C for June 2006 (Tab. 5).

5.4 Spatio-Temporal Forecast

Similar to the spatial forecast (Section 5.3), consider the task to forecast the values of the signal for the year 2006 $f_{37},...,f_{48}$ in a given point, but for the month ahead $k + 1$ using the measured values of the signals for the previous month k in several other points. Then the number of training vectors is equal to $m = 35$:

Table 5. Example of spatial forecast (Fig. 5)

Month	SST forecast	SST actual	error	Month	SST forecast	SST actual	error
Jan	0.2	−0.1	0.3	Jul	0.4	0.5	−0.1
Feb	−0.2	−0.3	0.1	Aug	0.6	0.7	−0.1
Mar	0.0	0.2	−0.2	Sep	0.4	0.3	0.1
Apr	0.4	0.7	−0.3	Oct	0.4	0.5	−0.1
May	0.6	0.6	0.0	Nov	−0.1	0.0	−0.1
Jun	1.0	1.5	−0.5	Dec	−0.3	−0.3	0.0

Figure 5. Example of spatial forecast (left to right – SST anomalies in the points of the Caspian Sea; gray "2006 IC" – forecast of the right signal by three synchronous left signals). ©2008 Alexander Tarakanov. Used with permission.

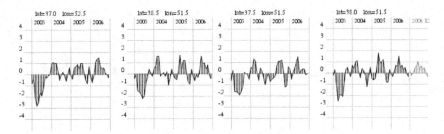

$$Z_i = [t_{i,1} \ldots t_{i,n}]', \ f(Z_i) = t_{i,0}, \ i = 1, \ldots, m.$$

The number of test vectors is equal to $N - 1 - m = 12$:

$$Z_k = [t_{k,1} \ldots t_{k,n}]', \ f_{k+1} = f(Z_k), \ k = 36, \ldots, 47.$$

The obtained results are shown in Tab. 6 and visualized in Fig. 6 for the same points of the Caspian Sea as for the spatial forecast. The values of the remaining parameters are also the same as those in the spatial forecast. The Renyi entropy of the obtained FIN1 tends to infinity $I_R = \infty$, while the index of inseparability is $I_1 = 8.8$ The MSE of the forecast is less than 0.5°C while the absolute maximal error is 1.1°C for April 2006 (Tab. 6).

5.5 Parameters and Quality of Forecast

The dependence of the forecast upon apoptosis and immunization of FIN1 is shown in Tab. 7 for the above examples of temporal (Section 5.2), spatial (Section 5.3) and spatio-temporal forecast (Section 5.4). The temporal forecast in Tab. 7 is given for the corresponding points of the Caspian, Black, and Barents Sea (see Tab. 4). Note that the training data are conflicting for the point of the Barents Sea in Tab. 4 and Tab. 7 so that the apoptosis and

Table 6. Example of spatio-temporal forecast (Fig. 6)

Month	SST forecast	SST actual	error	Month	SST forecast	SST actual	error
Jan	0.6	−0.1	0.7	Jul	0.7	0.5	0.2
Feb	−0.2	−0.3	0.1	Aug	0.6	0.7	−0.1
Mar	0.3	0.2	0.1	Sep	0.4	0.3	0.1
Apr	−0.4	0.7	−1.1	Oct	−0.1	0.5	−0.6
May	−0.2	0.6	−0.8	Nov	0.2	0.0	0.2
Jun	1.1	1.5	−0.4	Dec	−0.3	−0.3	0.0

Figure 6. Example of spatio-temporal forecast (left to right – SST signals in the points of the Caspian Sea; gray "2006 IC" – forecast of the right signal for month ahead by three left signals). ©2008 Alexander Tarakanov. Used with permission.

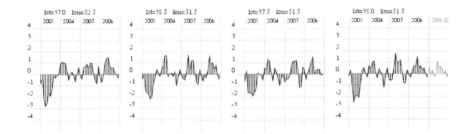

immunization (Step 8) have been canceled by the value of the index of inseparability (Step 7).

The dependence of the temporal forecast upon the parameters of FIN1 is shown in Tab. 8 for the same point of the Caspian Sea as in Tab. 4 and Tab. 7.

Other numerical experiments (not presented in the Tabs) also show that DTT level $l > 0$ worsens quality of the forecast. However, this parameter may be useful for discovering long-term spatio-temporal trends and relations. For example, Tab. 9 and Fig. 7 clearly demonstrate negative correlation between SSN and SST. Such correlation becomes especially evident for the DTT level $l = 4$. The SSN data has been taken from (SIDC 2007).

6 COMPARISON

Consider the temporal forecast in Section 5.2. The IC results of the forecast for the corresponding point of the Caspian Sea are given in 1st row of Tab. 4. Table 10 shows results of the same forecast but by ANN. This ANN (trained by the error back propagation method) has been taken from our previous work (Tarakanov & Tarakanov 2004; Tarakanov 2008). The temporal forecast was performed with the parameters of ANN in the following diapasons: number of hidden neurons: 2-10; value of learning constant: 0.002-0.25. The results of best runs of the ANN are shown in Tab. 10.

Table 11 presents results of the same forecast but by the support vector machine (SVM) with several kernels (Joachims 2003). This SVM has been taken from (Joachims 2004).

Table 12 selects best results of the temporal forecast by ANN (Tab. 10) and SVM (Tab. 11) together with the

Table 7. Parameters of FIN1/FIN2 and quality of forecast

Forecast	Sea	Cells	Entropy	Index	MSE	max error
Temporal	Caspian	34/32	8.4/8.6	4.0/3.9	0.43/0.43	−0.7/−0.7
Temporal	Black	34/32	7.6/7.8	3.6/3.6	0.66/0.82	1.2/1.3
Temporal	Barents	34/34	7.1/7.1	∞/∞	0.45/0.45	−0.9/−0.9
Spatial	Caspian	36/31	7.6/7.6	11.3/11.2	0.19/0.48	−0.5/−1.0
Spatio-Temporal	Caspian	35/30	7.6/7.6	8.8/8.6	0.48/0.72	−1.1/−1.3

Table 8. Parameters of FIN1 and quality of forecast

Previous months (n)	Dimension of FIN (q)	Nearest points (g)	Entropy	Index	MSE	max error
1	1	4	∞	∞	0.48	−1.0
2	2	1	8.4	4.0	0.43	−0.7
4	3	3	7.2	3.1	0.47	−1.0
6	2	2	6.9	3.9	0.45	−0.9
12	3	2	6.7	2.7	0.76	−1.2

Table 9. Negative correlations between SSN and SST (Fig. 7)

Sea	lat	lon	DTT level	correlation	DTT level	correlation
Caspian	41.5	50.5	0	−0.50	4	−0.94
Black	45.5	30.0	0	−0.38	4	−0.97
Barents	74.0	41.0	0	−0.62	4	−0.99

same forecast by IC (Tab. 4) as well as the forecast by mean values of test vectors and by the nearest neighbor method (NNM: Cover & Hart 1967; Tarakanov 2008). The results of comparison in Tab. 12 show that the accuracy of the forecast by IC is the best among all other methods considered in this section. Also note relatively big training time of the ANN (Tab. 10 for AMD 1.5 GHz) while the training time of all other methods in Tab. 12 is less than 1 second.

7 DISCUSSION

The reverse trend between SSN and SST signals that has been demonstrated above by the IC approach looks rather surprising and contradictory. For example, Reid (1991) found a striking similarity between SST anomalies and the 11-year running mean of SSN. At the same time, Varotsos et al. (1992) identified a strong negative correlation between the 11-year solar cycle and the sea surface pressure. A possible physical mechanism of the reverse trend between SSN and SST may be explained and specified using an intermediate factor like cloudiness (Svensmark & Friis-Christensen 1997; Tsiropoula 2003). According to Bates & Gautier (1989), correlations between cloud and SST fields show a high day-to-day variability. The monthly mean correlation, however, shows large positive values. A sign of relation of clouds with solar irradiance and cosmic rays looks also contradictory. For example, Palle et al. (2004) reported a strong correlation between low cloud and the cosmic ray flux for extensive regions

Figure 7. Reverse trends between SSN and SST of the Caspian, Black, and Barents Sea (in the corresponding points marked by "+")

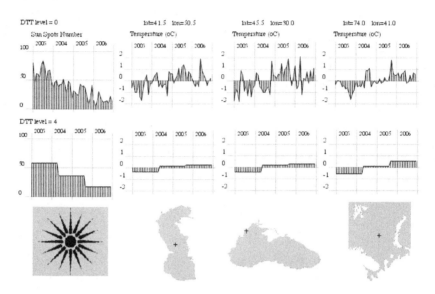

Table 10. Temporal forecast by ANN

hidden neurons	learning constant	training time (sec)	MSE	max error	month
2	0.25	1	0.60	−1.4	Jun
3	0.25	28	0.70	1.6	Jan
4	0.25	6	0.54	1.1	Jan
5	0.25	6	0.53	1.1	Jan
7	0.002	154	0.52	−1.1	Apr
10	0.02	25	0.54	−1.1	Apr

Table 11. Temporal forecast by SVM

Kernel	MSE	max error	month
Linear	0.76	1.3	Jul
Polynomial	0.54	1.0	Jan
Radial	0.71	−1.3	Jun
Sigmoid	0.74	1.4	Jul

Table 12. Comparison of several methods

Method	MSE	max error	month
IC	0.43	−0.7	Sep
mean	0.48	−0.8	Jul
ANN	0.52	−1.1	Apr
SVM	0.54	1.0	Jan
NNM	0.70	−1.8	Apr

of the Earth. However, Gupta & Hubble (2002) mentioned just the reverse results that showed negative correlation of cloud amount with both galactic cosmic ray flux and SSN over the U.S. The reverse trend between winter SST and SSN can be also selected from (Oguz et al. 2006) for the Black Sea during 1993-1996. Based on negative correlations between SST and low cloud cover, a mechanism was suggested by Kristjansson et al. (2002) whereby solar irradiance variations were amplified by interacting with SST, and subsequently low cloud cover.

Other results of this chapter also show that the IC approach can be useful for STF. The essence of the approach can be interpreted as follows. The IC takes the nearest "history" of the signal (e.g., two months, like in Section 5.2), looks for (i.e., recognizes) the most similar situation over the training data (e.g., during three previous years 2003-2005), and then forecasts the signal by this nearest analogy. Such forecast by analogy can be clearly seen in Fig. 4 where the forecasted signals (2006 IC gray) actually represent different fragments of the previous signals. However, the nearest analogies become so apparent only for the forecast by two previous months and a single nearest point of FIN. For example, the forecasted signal shows no clear similarity with any previous fragment when the forecast considers more that one point of FIN and, thus, represents a running linear combination of several nearest analogies (e.g., see 2006 IC gray in Fig. 6).

Unfortunately, the real-world data for the numerical experiments above (Section 5) cover rather short time lag (2003-2006). Probably, this explains some evident weak points of the considered applications. For example, the quality of the temporal forecast for one year may be not so good (Fig. 4) because the choice of the nearest analogies is rather restricted by the poor training data (three years only). Such poor choice may also cause rather inefficient apoptosis and immunization of FIN (Tab. 7) as well as no clear relations between the entropy, the index of inseparability of FIN and the quality of forecast (Tab. 7, Tab. 8). On the other hand, the quality of STF demonstrated by the IC approach can be estimated as not so bad regarding so poor training data. In addition, the apoptosis-immunization and index of inseparability of FIN proved to be rather useful for another application – intrusion detection in computer networks (Tarakanov et al. 2005a,b; Tarakanov 2007a,b; Tarakanov 2008). The training sets for that application are ranging from several hundreds to tens hundreds network connection records, while the feature extraction by FIN provides more than hundred compression rate (Tarakanov 2007b).

Another mathematically rigorous property of FIN is the exact recognition of any pattern it has been trained. This property allows using FIN to disclose the ambiguities in any data, e.g., like in the task of identification of cellular automata (Tarakanov & Prokaev 2007). Such possibility, by the way, is beyond the capabilities of ANN due to irreducible training errors and the known effect of overtraining when the attempts to reduce the errors may lead to their drastic increase (Tarakanov A. & Tarakanov Y. 2004). Therefore, FIN demonstrates the combination of faultless recognition with rather low training time. This looks unobtainable for its main competitors in the field of intelligent signal processing. For example, a comparison in (Tarakanov et al. 2007b) shows that FIN needs just 20 seconds to determine its optimal parameters where ANN trained by the error back propagation needs about 24 hours (!) for the similar purpose. The above properties of FIN may be also useful for STF but this needs rather representative set of training data.

It is also worth noting that the proposed IC approach to STF has nothing common with a statistical analysis technique. Moreover, it is well-known that statistical methods (e.g. Markov chains, Bayesian networks etc.) are too slow and inaccurate to cope with real-world signals. For example, several comparisons (Tarakanov et al. 2002, 2003) show that the IC works at least ten time faster and much more accurate than conventional statistics. At the same time, the IC is able to sharply focus attention at most dangerous situations (like the forecast of plague outburst, e.g., see: Tarakanov et al. 2003), which is beyond the capabilities of the traditional statistics. No wonder that more and more of modern approaches to signal processing turn to wavelet analysis, where the dyadic DTT (Section 3.3) is also a wavelet-type transform (Kozyrev 2002; Atreas et al. 2004).

8 CONCLUSION

The proposed IC approach to STF by signal processing belongs to the field of computational intelligence (Tarakanov 2008). This approach is based essentially on the mathematical models of information processing by proteins and immune networks (Tarakanov et al. 2003). On such background, the mathematical model of FIN with apoptosis and immunization controlled by cytokines (Tarakanov et al. 2005a) represents the key model of the IC approach to intelligent signal processing and STF. This means that the other models described here (DTT, SVD, Renyi entropy) are not so critical for feature extraction and pattern recognition since they were utilized just to provide a kind of convenient zero-approach ("innate immunity" for Definition 2) to be optimized then by FIN using apoptosis and immunization. On the other hand, let us note once again that the SVD (Section 3.2) can model the binding energy between two proteins (Tarakanov et al. 2003), whereas the dyadic DTT (Section 3.3) can model an immune-type antigen processing (Atreas et al. 2003, 2004).

9 FUTURE RESEARCH DIRECTIONS

The discovered reverse trend between SSN and SST may be utilized for long-term STF. This needs more careful study of such controversial question over long time lag. The developed IC approach to STF also needs further study over more representative data sets. However, such data sets on SST may be rather problematic to obtain. Another opportunity may be an application of the IC approach to forecasting emergent and critical financial situations like default, currency fall, market collapse, collusion of brokers etc.

The results of numerical experiments reported in (Tarakanov et al. 2005b, 2007b) suggest that the speed and accuracy of the IC approach is probably unobtainable for other robust methods of computational intelligence (in particular, neurocomputing and evolutionary algorithms). These advances of the IC approach together with its biological nature probably mean a further step toward placing more of the intelligent functions on the chip. Such hardware implementation of the IC may be completed in two steps: 1) implementation in a chip architecture available from the market (like DSP SHARC: digital signal processor of super Harvard architecture, or FPGA: field programmable gate array) and then 2) developing a proper architecture of an intelligent immunochip in-silicon (Tarakanov 2007b).

It is also worth highlighting that the IC helps to discover at least three deep functional similarities and the fundamental communicative mechanisms the neural and immune synapse have in common: 1) cytokine networks (Goncharova & Tarakanov 2007), 2) receptor assemblies (Agnati et al. 2008; Goncharova & Tarakanov 2008b), and 3) nanotubes (Goncharova & Tarakanov 2008a). Understanding these issues could lead to new therapeutic targets and tools, especially in neurodegenerative disorders related to microglia.

REFERENCES

Adamatzky, A. (1994). *Identification of Cellular Automata*. London: Taylor & Francis.

Agnati, L. F., Tarakanov, A. O., & Guidolin, D. (2005a). A simple mathematical model of cooperativity in receptor mosaics based on the "symmetry rule". *BioSystems, 80*(2), 165-173.

Agnati, L. F., Tarakanov, A. O., Ferre, S., Fuxe, K., & Guidolin, D. (2005b). Receptor-receptor interactions, receptor mosaics, and basic principles of molecular network organization: possible implication for drug development. *Journal of Molecular Neuroscience, 26*(2-3), 193-208.

Agnati, L. F., Fuxe, K. G., Goncharova, L. B., & Tarakanov, A. O. (2008). Receptor mosaics of neural and immune communication: possible implications for basal ganglia functions. *Brain Research Reviews,* (in press).

Atreas, N., Karanikas, C., & Polychronidou, P. (2004). Signal analysis on strings for immune-type pattern recognition. *Comparative and Functional Genomics, 5*, 69-74.

Atreas N., Karanikas, C., & Tarakanov, A. (2003). Signal processing by an immune type tree transform. *Lecture Notes in Computer Science, 2787*, 111-119.

Bates, J., & Gautier, C. (1989). Interaction between net shortwave flux and sea surface temperature. *Journal of Applied Meteorology, 28(1)*, 43-51.

Chao, D. L., Davenport, M. P., Forrest, S., & Perelson, A. S. (2004). A stochastic model of cytotoxic T cell responses. *Journal of Theoretical Biology, 228*, 227-240.

Cheng, T., & Wang, J. (2007). Application of a dynamic recurrent neural network in spatio-temporal forecasting. *Lecture Notes in Geoinformation and Cartography, XIV*, 173-186.

Cover, T. M., & Hart, P. E. (1967). Nearest neighbor pattern classification. *IEEE Transactions on Information Theory, 13(1)*, 21-27.

Dasgupta, D. (Ed.). (1999). *Artificial Immune Systems and Their Applications*. Berlin: Springer.

Dasgupta, D., Krishna-Kumar, K., Wong, D., & Berry, M. (2004). Negative selection algorithm for aircraft fault detection. *Lecture Notes in Computer Science, 3239*, 1-13.

Dasgupta, D., & Gonzalez, F. (2005). Artificial immune systems in intrusion detection. In V. Rao Vemuri (Ed.), *Enhancing Computer Security with Smart Technology* (pp. 165-208). Boca-Raton, FL: Auerbach Publications.

Dasgupta, D. (2006). Advances in artificial immune systems. *IEEE Computational Intelligence Magazine, 1(4)*, 40-49.

Dasgupta, D., & Nino, F. (2008). *Immunological Computation: Theory and Applications*. Auerbach Publications.

De Castro, L. N., & Timmis, J. (2002). *Artificial Immune Systems: A New Computational Intelligence Approach*. London: Springer.

Goncharova, L. B., Jacques, Y., Martin-Vide, C., Tarakanov, A. O., & Timmis, J. I. (2005). Biomolecular immune-computer: theoretical basis and experimental simulator. *Lecture Notes in Computer Science, 3627*, 72-85.

Goncharova, L. B., & Tarakanov, A. O. (2007). Molecular networks of brain and immunity. *Brain Research Reviews, 55(1)*, 155-166.

Goncharova, L. B., & Tarakanov, A. O. (2008a). Nanotubes at neural and immune synapses. *Current Medicinal Chemistry, 15(3)*, 210-218.

Goncharova, L. B., & Tarakanov, A. O. (2008b).Why chemokines are cytokines while their receptors are not cytokine ones? *Current Medicinal Chemistry, 15(13)*, 1297-1304.

Gupta, S.K., & Hubble, J.M. (2002). Minutes from the CERES science team meeting. *The Earth Observer, 14(1)*, 1-13.

Horn, R., & Johnson, Ch. (1986). *Matrix Analysis*. London: Cambridge University Press.

Joachims, T. (2003). *Learning to Classify Text Using Support Vector Machines: Methods, Theory, and Algorithms*. Kluwer Academic Publishers.

Joachims, T. (2004). *SVM-light: Support Vector Machine*, from http://svmlight.joachims.org

Johnson, J. E. (2005). Networks, Markov Lie monoids, and generalized entropy. *Lecture Notes in Computer Science, 3685,* 129-135.

Kozyrev, S.V. (2002). Wavelet theory as p-adic spectral analysis. *Izvestia: Mathematics, 66(2),* 367-376.

Kristjansson, J.E., Staple, A., Kristiansen, J., & Kaas, E. (2002). A new look at possible connections between solar activity, clouds and climate. *Geophysical Research Letters, 29(23),* 2107-2110.

NASA (2007). *Ocean Color Time-Series Online Visualization and Analysis,* from http://reason.gsfc.nasa.gov/Giovanni

Oguz, T., Dipper, J.W., & Kaymaz, Z. (2006). Climatic regulation of the Black Sea hydro-meteorological and ecological properties at interannual-to-decadal time scales. *Journal of Marine Systems, 60,* 235-254.

Palle, E., Butler, C.J., & O'Brien, K. (2004). The possible connection between ionization in the atmosphere by cosmic rays and low level clouds. *Journal of Atmospheric and Solar-Terrestrial Physics, 66,* 1779-1790.

Reid, G.C. (1991). Solar total irradiance variation and the global sea surface temperature record. *Journal of Geophysical Research, 96,* 2835-2844.

Renyi, A. (1961). On measures of entropy and information. *Fourth Berkeley Symposium on Mathematics, Statistics and Probability: Vol. 1* (pp. 547-561). London: Cambridge University Press.

SIDC (2007). *Solar Influences Data Analysis Center,* form http://sidc.oma.be

Svensmark, H., & Friis-Christensen, E. (1997). Variation of cosmic ray fux and global cloud coverage – a missing link in solar-climate relationships. *Journal of Atmospheric and Solar-Terrestrial Physics, 59,* 1225-1232.

Tarakanov, A. O. (2007a). Formal immune networks: self-organization and real-world applications. In M. Prokopenko (Ed.), *Advances in Applied Self-Organizing Systems* (pp. 269-288). Berlin: Springer.

Tarakanov, A. O. (2007b). Mathematical models of intrusion detection by an intelligent immunochip. *Communication in Computer and Information Science, 1,* 308-319.

Tarakanov, A. O. (2008). Immunocomputing for intelligent intrusion detection. IEEE Computational Intelligence Magazine, *3*(2), 22-30.

Tarakanov, A., & Adamatzky, A. (2002). Virtual clothing in hybrid cellular automata. *Kybernetes, 31*(7-8), 394-405.

Tarakanov, A., & Nicosia, G. (2007). Foundations of immunocomputing. *First IEEE Symposium on Foundations of Computational Intelligence (FOCI'07)* (pp. 503-508). Madison, WI: Omnipress.

Tarakanov, A., & Prokaev, A. (2007). Identification of cellular automata by immunocomputing. *Journal of Cellular Automata, 2*(1), 39-45.

Tarakanov, A. O., & Tarakanov, Y. A. (2004). A comparison of immune and neural computing for two real-life tasks of pattern recognition. *Lecture Notes in Computer Science, 3239,* 236-249.

Tarakanov, A. O., & Tarakanov, Y. A. (2005). A comparison of immune and genetic algorithms for two real-life tasks of pattern recognition. *International Journal of Unconventional Computing, 1*(4), 357-374.

Tarakanov, A., Goncharova, L., Gupalova, T., Kvachev, S., & Sukhorukov, A. (2002). Immunocomputing for bioarrays. In: Timmis, J., & Bentley, P. (Eds.), *Proceedings of the 1st International Conference on Artificial Immune Systems ICARIS'02* (pp. 32-40). University of Kent at Canterbury, UK.

Tarakanov, A. O., Goncharova, L. B., & Tarakanov, O. A. (2005a). A cytokine formal immune network. *Lecture Notes in Artificial Intelligence, 3630,* 510-519.

Tarakanov, A. O., Kvachev, S. V., & Sukhorukov, A.V. (2005b). A formal immune network and its implementation for on-line intrusion detection. *Lecture Notes in Computer Science, 3685*, 394-405.

Tarakanov, A., Kryukov, I., Varnavskikh, E., & Ivanov, V. (2007a). A mathematical model of intrusion detection by immunocomputing for spatially distributed security systems. *RadioSystems, 106*, 90-92 (in Russian).

Tarakanov, A., Prokaev, A., & Varnavskikh, E. (2007b). Immunocomputing of hydroacoustic fields. *International Journal of Unconventional Computing, 3*(2), 123-133.

Tarakanov, A. O., Sokolova, L. A., & Kvachev, S. V. (2007c). Intelligent simulation of hydrophysical fields by immunocomputing. *Lecture Notes in Geoinformation and Cartography, XIV*, 252-262.

Tarakanov, A. O., Skormin, V. A., & Sokolova, S. P. (2003). *Immunocomputing: Principles and Applications.* New York: Springer.

Tsiropoula, G. (2003). Signatures of solar activity variability in meteorological parameters. *Journal of Atmospheric and Solar-Terrestrial Physics, 65*, 469-482.

Varotsos, C., Dris, N., Asimakopoulos, D., & Cartalis, C. (1992). On the relationship between the 10.7 cm solar flux, surface pressure and air temperature over Greece. *Theoretical and Applied Climatology, 46(1)*, 27-32.

Zhao, W. (2005). Review of "Immunocomputing: Principles and Applications". *ACM SIGACT News, 36*(4), 14-17.

KEY TERMS

Apoptosis: Programmed cell death.

Cytokines: Messenger proteins that provide intercellular communication within the immune system.

Discrete Tree Transform (DTT): Mapping of signal to the tree structure.

Formal Immune Network (FIN): Mathematical model of information processing by natural immune network.

Immunization: Training of immune network.

Immunocomputing (IC): Mathematical models of information processing by proteins and immune networks.

Singular Value Decomposition (SVD): Matrix decomposition by singular values and singular vectors.

Spatio-Temporal Forecast (STF): Prediction of values of a parameter (e.g. sea surface temperature) over time and/or space.

Chapter XIII
Research of Immune Controllers

Fu Dongmei
University of Science and Technology, Beijing, P.R. China

ABSTRACT

In engineering application, the characteristics of the control system are entirely determined by the system controller once the controlled object has been chosen. Improving the traditional controller or constructing the new controller is an unfading study field of control theory and application. The control system is greatly enriched and developed by this way. As a complicated self-adaptable system, the biological immune system can effectively and smoothly stand against antigens and viruses intruded into organism. It is possible to improve the self-learning, adaptive and robustness capability of the control system through embedded an artificial immune controller in control system. Based on the biological immune mechanism and artificial immune model, this chapter attempts to study the immune controller design and application in traditional control system..First, a kind of artificial immune controller is proposed based on the T-B cells immunity. The boundedness and the stability of SISO control systems, which constructed by the artificial immune controller, are proved by the little gain theorem. A general controller structure frame based on the T-B cells immunity is proposed, which includes the same kind of controller proposed previously. The validity of this artificial immune controller is verified by simulation. Second, a new type of artificial immune controllers is constructed according to a simple double-cell immune dynamics model. The non-error characteristic of SISO control systems, which constructed by the artificial immune controller, is proved by the nonlinear theory in this chapter. The I/O stability and no-error characteristic of the system are verified by simulations, which show that the kind of artificial immune system have good anti-lag capability. Third, the Varela immune network model has been improved based on which an artificial immune system is proposed. The odd linearization method of the non-linear system is used to prove the stability and non-error characteristic of the SISO system constructed by the artificial immune control system. Its I/O stability, non-error characteristic and strong anti-lag capability are also verified by simulation. Finally, based on the comparison of the three kinds of immune controllers, a general structure of the artificial immune controller is proposed. The further study on this field is indicated in this chapter lastly.

Copyright © 2009, IGI Global, distributing in print or electronic forms without written permission of IGI Global is prohibited.

INTRODUCTION

In engineering application, once the controlled object and the measuring components have been determined, the performance of linear control systems will depend on controllers. For example, (1) One of the most important purpose of studying the theory of fuzzy control is to design fuzzy controller with better adaptability and robustness. (2) The major concern of neural network control is to get neural network controller, which is often composed of two neural networks, one playing the part of the traditional controller, the other dealing with real-time identification of the object model (3) In expert control system, the function of the its expert knowledge and the reasoning is used to adjust the parameters of the controllers, such as PID. Even with the widely used simple PID controller, there are also many people engaged in a wide variety of intelligent study. Thus, the study of the control system is centered on the controller.

Controller is designed to improve the quality of the control system, allowing the system to serve the required control purposes. Once the controlled object is chosen, the design of the controller is the key to guarantee the quality and property of the whole control system, so the design and analysis of the controller is the focus of the entire control field. Traditional controller design methods fall into two categories: one is the design method based on the classical control theory, including linear methods such as root-locus correction, frequency correction, PID regulation as well as non-linear methods such as phase plane and description function; another category is the design methods based on modern control theory, including state-feedback controller, adaptive correction controller, variable structure controller, controller based on H or Lyapunov stability theory and so on. Although the controller design and implementation are based on a series of relatively complete and thorough theoretical approach, there are still shortcomings to overcome, for example, the restrictions on the controlled object are rather rigid and the object model is required to be linear.

Biological immune system can handle the disturbance and uncertainty in human body easily. If an artificial immune controller can be embedded in the control system, the system will undoubtedly possess such intelligence characteristics as self-learning, adaptive, robust and so on. This chapter will study the immune controller design and application in traditional control system based on the biological immune mechanism and artificial immune model.

BACKGROUND

In real applications, once the controlled object and the measuring components have been determined, the performance of linear control systems will depend on controllers. Therefore, designing and constructing new types of controllers or improving traditional controllers have been being a fascinating topic in the theory of control systems. For instance, one of the important applications of fuzzy control theory is to design and construct controllers which have great adaptability and robustness(Jingzhen & Zengji, 1997), so is the neural network (Dongqiang & Yaqing, 2001) and expert system. Even the widely used **PID controllers** are also studied by many individuals to make it more intelligent. The study and application of intelligent controllers has extraordinarily enriched and developed the theory of control systems.

Intelligent controllers fall into four levels according to the designing complexity: simple robust feedback control, parameter adaptive control based on error criterion, adaptive control based on optimization of objective function and adaptive control based on global optimization of objective function varied with environment conditions. Corresponding with these, biologic immune system fall into four similar levels: firstly, the innate immune system is corresponding to robust feedback control; secondly, T cells stimulate B cells to resist antigens; thirdly, microphages present antigens to T cells and activate B cells; lastly, microphages have some changes against certain antigens. Studies have found that biologic immune system has a series of excellent control characteristics, such as adaptability, distributed control and coordination, dynamic, robust, self-organization, self-learning etc. So a further study of immune system on its mechanism and strategies will provide some ideas for constructing advanced intelligent controllers.

Immune mechanism has been introduced into the research field of control systems for many years. One example is the immune algorithm proposed by Ishida(Watanabe et al., 2004) based on the agent structure to suppress noises in a control system. Ishiguro(Kesheng et al., 2000; Kim, 2001) applied Ishida's immune discrimination network to adjust the walking of a hexapod robot. By corresponding each foot of the robot to a node in the network, the algorithm can achieve a coordinated walk of the robot through identifying and correcting a particular inconsistent foot. Lee(Kim & Lee, 2002) proposed an immune network based method for the cooperative control of decentralized autonomous robots, with each robot treated as a B cell, each environment state as an antigen, and the robot's behavior decision as an antibody. When the environment changes, every robot will yield a certain behavior decision, causing B cells (robots) to stimulate or suppress each other, which will end up confirming every robot's behavior decision. D. H. Kim, coming from South Korea, together with his colleagues and students, has published a series of articles about how to use immune algorithms for designing and tuning parameters of PID controller(Dongmei & Deling, 2005; Yongsheng & Lihong, 2006; Takahashi & Yamada, 1997; Sasaki et al., 1999). Ding Yongsheng and Ren Lihong(Ansheng & Chanying, 1998) advanced a controller structure based on the immune feedback mechanism. Tan Yingzi(Weibing, 1988) and others has applied such controller for the automatic tuning of PID to controlling the superheated steam temperature. In recent years, Prof. Fu Dongmei in University of Science and Technology Beijing has constructed many kinds of immune mechanism based immune controllers; meanwhile conducted theoretical analysis and simulation research for these controllers(Takahashi & Yamada, 1998; Yingzi et al., 1993; Zixing, 2004; Kim & Cho, 2004; Kim & Horg, 2004; Sergei & Yuri, 2003; Lydyard et al., 2001; Dasgupta & Forrest, 1999). However, in general, applications or theoretical researches of artificial immune system in the control field are still very limited, a lot of problems remain to be studied and solved.

Note that we don't have as much knowledge of immune system as neural network, so we cannot yet build up a thorough and precise model of artificial immune system. The focus of studying AIS control strategy is to solve the learning and adaptability problems in a control system by using immune mechanism.

The two important points in modern intelligent control are control law without modeling and robustness of a control system. Control law model-free does not mean there is no model in a control law, but to build a control law model without knowledge about the object's model. Robustness of a system refers to the fact that the whole system could still run properly even when the system's model has undergone some changes. In the adjustment of natural immune system, these two problems have been solved effectively, reasonably and coordinately. Through their own immune systems, creatures can recover from infection of outside viruses. These innate robust and model-free properties have fascinated many experts to study the immune mechanism based control method, thus provide new ideas for the development of modern control theories and applications.

Definition 1.1 Artificial immune control is the process to detect, control or manage the applications, such as controlled objects, production procedures, or managements, by constructing immune models or algorithms suitable for control systems through reference of measures and regulars extracted from immune mechanisms, models and the cooperation between immune factors.

Definition 1.2 Artificial immune controller is a man-made controller that based on measures and regulars of macro immune mechanisms, models or micro cooperation between immune factors to improve the performance of a control system. Artificial immune controllers mostly are nonlinear dynamic models or algorithms with iteration process.

1.1 A Class of Artificial Immune Controllers Based on T-B Cells

1.1.1 T-B_AIC Model

Biologic immune system is a system with great robust and adaptability even in an environment with considerable uncertainty and disturbance. Immune response is triggered by invaded antigens (Ag). Antigen presenting cells absorb antigens and activate CD4+T cells. At the initial stage of the immune response, CD4+T cells will activate helper T cells (T_h) which can further activate B cells, which will produce antibodies (Ab) to eliminate antigens. At the final stage of immune response, CD4+T cells can activate suppressor T cells (T_s), which will play a role in the negative feedback regulation to restore the organism's immune balance. Fig.1.1 shows the mechanism of immune response.

Figure 1.1. Sketch map of immune response

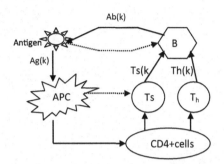

In a immune system T_h cells have stimulating effect on antibodies $A_b(k)$, while T_s cells have inhibiting effect on $A_b(k)$, suppose that in kth generation the concentration of $A_b(k)$ is determined by the concentration margin between T_h cells and T_s cells (Tarakanov & Dasgupta, 2000; Zhengshan, 2003):

$$A_b(k) = T_h(k) - T_s(k) \tag{1.1}$$

For the sake of simplicity, merge the two dashed lines in Fig. 1.1 into the solid line where APC has effect on CD4+T cells, and suppose the concentration of the kth generation's T_h cells is determined by:

$$T_h(k) = P_h(A_g(k)) \tag{1.2}$$

Where $P_h(\bullet)$ refers to a kind of nonlinear relationship, $A_g(k)$ is the quantity of invaded antigens in kth generation.

Assume the concentration of kth generation's T_s cells have relation with the antibodies' concentration margin before dth generation $\square A_b(k\text{-}d)$, and is decided by:

$$\nabla A_b(k-d) = A_b(k-d) - A_b(k-d-1) \tag{1.3}$$

$$T_s(k) = f_s(\nabla A_b(k-d)) \tag{1.4}$$

Take the substitution (1.2), (1.4) in (1.1):

$$A_b(k) = P_h(A_g(k)) - f_s(\nabla A_b(k-d)) = P_h(A_g(k)) \cdot (1 - \frac{f_s(\nabla A_b(k-d))}{P_h(A_g(k))}) \tag{1.5}$$

Define:

$$f_h(A_g(k)) = P_h(A_g(k))^{-1} \tag{1.6}$$

Then

$$A_b(k) = P_h(A_g(k)) \cdot (1 - f_h(A_g(k)) \cdot f_s(\nabla A_b(k-d))) \tag{1.7}$$

Figure 1.2. Curve of normalized Hill function

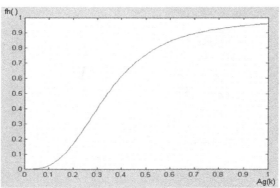

Figure 1.3. Curve with respect to $e(k) \sim f_h(e(k))$

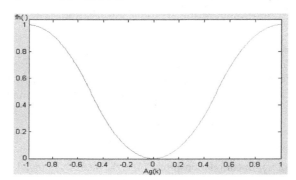

From Eq. (1.2) and (1.6), it can be inferred that the selection of $f_h(A_g(k))$ can reflect the relation between the concentration of T_h cells and antigens to some extent. According to the theoretical immune response model proposed by M. Kaufman and J. Urban, the above relation satisfies Hill function(Isidori et al., 2005) :

$$f_h(A_g(k)) = \frac{A_g^2(k)}{(\theta^2 + A_g^2(k))} \tag{1.8}$$

Where θ^2 is a threshold constant, which is related to the categories of antigens and different T_h cells.

If the control system error $e(k)$ is an antigen, controller output $u(k)$ is an antibody, then Eq. (1.7) can be expressed as:

$$u(k) = P_h(e(k)) \cdot (1 - f_h(e(k)) \cdot f_s(\nabla u(k-d))) \tag{1.9}$$

Eq. (1.9) is a discrete **artificial immune controller** based on the immune mechanism of T-B cells, simply recorded as **T-B_DAIC**.

Define $d = 0$, and express Eq. (1.9) in continuous form:

$$u(t) = P_h(e(t)) \cdot (1 - f_h(e(t)) \cdot f_s(\dot{u}(t))) \tag{1.10}$$

Eq. (1.10) is a continuous **artificial immune controller** based on T-B cells immune mechanism (**T-B_CAIC**).

$P_h(e(k))$ in Eq. (1.9) and (1.10) can be selected (such as PID etc.) under the practical control system.

In a control system, error $e(k)$ has positive or negative changes, so negative and positive error $e(k)$ can be taken as two kinds of different antigens, Ag_+ and Ag_-. There also exist two kinds of T_h cells corresponding to the above antigens, T_{h+} and T_{h-}, whose concentrations are respectively:

$$f_{h+}(A_{g+}(k)) = \frac{A_{g+}^2(k)}{(\theta^2 + A_{g+}^2(k))}, \quad f_{h-}(A_{g-}(k)) = \frac{A_{g-}^2(k)}{(\theta^2 + A_{g-}^2(k))}.$$

Considerate the concentration relationship of the two T_h cells, a curve is shown in Fig. 1.3 with respect to $e(k) \sim f_h(e(k))$.

In order to facilitate physical realization, define $P_h(e(k))=K_p$, $f_h(e(k))$ can be simplified as follows, i.e. the nonlinear relationship shown in the dashed box in Fig. 1.4:

$$f_h(e(k)) = \begin{cases} 0 & |e(k)| \leq \dfrac{e_0}{k_p} \\[3mm] k_1 |e(k)| & \dfrac{e_0}{k_p} < |e(k)| \leq \dfrac{f_0}{k_p k_1} \\[3mm] f_0 & |e(k)| > \dfrac{f_0}{k_p k_1} \end{cases} \tag{1.11}$$

$f_s(\dot{u}(t))$ in Eq. (1.10) reflects the relation between concentration of T_s cells and the concentration change rate of antibodies, which can be approximately expressed as:

$$f_s(\dot{u}(t)) = k_2 \cdot \left(\frac{1}{1+e^{-\dot{u}(t)}} - 0.5\right) \tag{1.12}$$

The structure diagram of TB_CAIC in Fig. 1.4 is obtained from Eq. (1.10), (1.11) and (1.12).

Figure 1.4. Block diagram of TB_CAIC

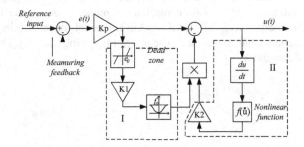

1.1.2 Characteristic Analysis of T-B_CAIC

(1)   Immune P Controller

We can acquire the model of **T-B_CAIC** according to Fig. 1.4:

$$u(t) = k_p e(t) - f_h(e(k)) f_s(\dot{u}(t)) = \begin{cases} k_p e(t) & |e(t)| \le \dfrac{e_0}{k_p} \\ k_p e(t) - k_1 k_2 (\dfrac{1}{1+e^{-\dot{u}(t)}} - 0.5)|e(t)| & \dfrac{e_0}{k_p} < |e(t)| < \dfrac{f_0}{k_1 k_p} \\ k_p e(t) - f_0 k_2 (\dfrac{1}{1+e^{-\dot{u}(t)}} - 0.5) & |e(t)| \ge \dfrac{f_0}{k_1 k_p} \end{cases}$$

(1.13)

If

$$|e(t)| \le \frac{e_0}{k_p},$$

T-B_CAIC model is simply a linear relationship; if

$$\frac{e_0}{k_p} < |e(t)| < \frac{f_0}{k_1 k_p},$$

T-B_CAIC model is a linear relationship with variable proportional coefficient, whose proportional coefficient is effected by the change rate of control variable $\dot{u}(t)$; if

$$|e(t)| \ge \frac{f_0}{k_1 k_p},$$

T_B-CAIC model is a nonlinear relationship with argument

$$f_0 k_2 (\frac{1}{1+e^{-\dot{u}(t)}} - 0.5).$$

To sum up, **T-B_CAIC** is a controller with adaptive varying structure and changing proportional coefficient in natural. In the designing and constructing of the controller no consideration is given to the structure and form of the object's model. From this perspective, T-B_CAIC is a kind of model-free controller. However, the controller does not have an integral function, which is doomed to be inferior in setting tracking. This is why such controller is called artificial immune P controller.

(2)   Immune **PID controller**

Substitute PID for $p_h(e(k))$:

$$u(t) = \begin{cases} k_p[PID] & |e(t)| \le \dfrac{e_0}{k_p} \\[3mm] k_p[PID] - k_1 k_2(\dfrac{1}{1+e^{-u(t)}} - 0.5)|PI| & \dfrac{e_0}{k_p} < |e(t)| < \dfrac{f_0}{k_1 k_p} \\[3mm] k_p[PID] - f_0 k_2(\dfrac{1}{1+e^{-u(t)}} - 0.5) & |e(t)| \ge \dfrac{f_0}{k_1 k_p} \end{cases}$$

(1.14)

Where,

$$PID = e(t) + \frac{1}{T_i}\int e(t)dt + T_D \frac{de(t)}{dt}$$.

In essence, the controller is a cascade of PID controller and immune P controller, which has fused the adaptive varying structure of immune P controller, integral function and derivative function of PID controller to eliminate static error and speed up system response.

1.1.3 Characteristic Analysis of SISO System with TB_CAIC by Using Small Gain Theorem

In control systems, a broad category of feedback control systems can be represented by Fig.1.5, where u_1, u_2 are external inputs; y_1, y_2 are outputs; e_1 is the system error, e_2 is the control variable on the object, H_1 is the controller, H_2 is the object's model.

In the system shown in Fig. 1.6, assume $H_1, H_2: L_e \rightarrow L_e$, $e_1, e_2 \in L_e$, eliminate y_1 and y_2:

$$\begin{cases} u_1 = e_1 + H_2 e_2 \\ u_2 = e_2 - H_1 e_1 \end{cases}$$

(1.15)

Eliminate e_1, e_2, there is:

$$\begin{cases} y_1 = H_1(u_1 - y_2) \\ y_2 = H_2(u_2 + y_1) \end{cases}$$

(1.16)

This kind of feedback system has follow I/O stable definition.

Construct the SISO immune control system as shown Fig. 1.5 with T-B_CAIC and controlled object. It can be seen that Fig .1.5 and Fig. 1.6 are the same in structure; therefore **Small Gain Theorem** that can analyze the control system shown in Fig. 1.5 can be equally used to analyze the stable property of the control system shown in Fig.1.6.

Figure 1.5. Block diagram of immune control system

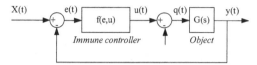

Figure 1.6. General block diagram of control system

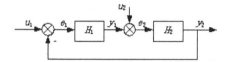

Definition 1.3 If operator H satisfies:

(1) $Hf(t) \in L_p$, while $f \in L_p$;
(2) Exist limited constant k and b , make

$$\| Hf \|_p < k \| f \|_p + b, \quad \forall f \in L_p \tag{1.17}$$

Then operator H is called L_p stable, also called operator H is L_p bounded. If H is linear, then $b = 0$.

Definition 1.4 For general operator H: $L_{pe} \to L_{pe}(L^n_{pe} \to L^n_{pe})$, $g=Hf$, if existed real β and $\zeta > 0$, make:

$$\| (Hf)_T \| \leq \zeta \| f_T \| + \beta, \quad \forall f, \quad \forall T > 0 \tag{1.18}$$

Then operator H can be defined as:

$$r = \inf\{\zeta\} \tag{1.19}$$

Definition 1.5 If $u_i \in L_p$, $y_i \in L_p$, and exist constant k and b, for arbitrary $u_i \in L_p$ and corresponding y_i, there is:

$$\begin{cases} \| y_1 \|_p \leq k(\| u_1 \|_p + \| u_2 \|_p) + b \\ \| y_2 \|_p \leq k(\| u_1 \|_p + \| u_2 \|_p) + b \end{cases} \tag{1.20}$$

Then system (1.20) is called L_p stable, or I/O stable.

Lemma 1.1 (Small Gain Theorem): For general control system (1.18)

$$\begin{cases} u_1 = e_1 + H_2 e_2 \\ u_2 = e_2 - H_1 e_1 \end{cases}$$

If the gains of operator H_1 and H_2, r_1 and r_2 satisfy:

$$r_1 r_2 < 1 \tag{1.21}$$

Then the system is I/O stable with respect to L$_p$.
First, proof operator T-B_CAIC shown in Fig. 1.4 is bounded.

Theorem 1.1 Immune P controller (1.14) is an I/O stable controller.
Proof: Known from Eq. (1.14) the output of artificial immune controller $u(t)$ is

$$u(t) = k_p e(t) - f_h(e(t)) f_s(\dot{u}(t)) \tag{1.22}$$

Where $f_h(e(t))$ is a nonlinear function satisfying Eq. (1.11), $f_s(\dot{u}(t))$ is a nonlinear function satisfying Eq. (1.12). In essence, $u(t)$ is a function with respect to $e(t)$, so $\dot{u}(t)$ is also a function with respect to $e(t)$, therefore Eq. (1.27) can be expressed as:

$$u(t) = k_p e(t) - f(e(t)) \tag{1.23}$$

According to Eq. (1.12), obviously $|f_h(e(t))| \le f_0$, pay attention to Eq. (1.14), there is $|f(\dot{u}(t))| \le 0.5|k_2|$, so $|f(e(t))| \le 0.5 f_0 |k_2|$, thus Eq. (1.28) can be expressed as:

$$||u(t)|| \le k_p ||e(t)|| + 0.5 f_0 |k_2| \tag{1.24}$$

Because of operator stabilization **definition 1.3**, operator T-B_CAIC is stable.

Theorem 1.2 If $k_p > 0$, all poles of $G(s)$ have negative real part, and the gain of operator G is k_G, then while

$$|k_1 k_2| < \frac{2}{f_0} \left(\frac{1}{k_G k_p} - 1 \right),$$

the immune control system shown in Fig. 1.5 is I/O stable.
Proof: According to the conditions of operator gain **definition 1.4**, the gain of operator G is k_G, i.e.:

$$|| y(t) || < k_G || q(t) || \tag{1.25}$$

Where $q(t)$ is the input of $G(s)$, $y(t)$ is the output of $G(s)$.
The follow equation is obtained from Eq. (1.13):

$$||u(t)|| < k_p (1 + 0.5 f_0 |k_1 k_2|) ||e(t)|| + 0.5 f_0 |k_2| \tag{1.26}$$

According to operator gain **definition 1.4**, operator gain of artificial immune controller $f(e, u)$ is:

$$k_f = k_p (1 + 0.5 f_0 |k_1 k_2|) \tag{1.27}$$

Table 1.1. Several immune P controllers

	$P_h(\bullet)$	$f_h(\bullet)$	$f_s(\bullet)$
Artificial immune controller in this article	$P_h(\bullet) = K_p$	$f_h(e(k)) = \begin{cases} 0 & |e(k)| \le \dfrac{e_0}{k_p} \\[2mm] k_1|e(k)| & \dfrac{e_0}{k_p} < |e(k)| \le \dfrac{f_0}{k_p k_1} \\[2mm] f_0 & |e(k)| > \dfrac{f_0}{k_p k_1} \end{cases}$	$f_s(\dot{u}(t)) = k_2 \cdot (\dfrac{1}{1+e^{-\dot{u}(t)}} - 0.5)$
Artificial immune controller in literature (Dasgupta & Forrest, 1999)	$P_h(\bullet) = K_p$	$f_h(\bullet) = \gamma$	$f_s(\bullet) = (u(t-d) - u(t-d-1))^2$
Artificial immune controller in literature (Tarakanov & Dasgupta, 2000)	$P_h(\bullet) = K_p$	$f_h(\bullet) = \eta$	$f_s(\bullet) = 1 - \dfrac{2}{\exp(-a\dot{u}(t)) + \exp(a\dot{u}(t))}$
Artificial immune controller in literature (Zhengshan, 2003)	$P_h(\bullet) = K$	$f_h(\bullet) = \eta_0$	$f_s(\bullet) = 1 - \exp(-u(t)^2 / a)$

According to **Small Gain Theorem**, while $k_f k_G = k_p(1 + 0.5 f_0 |k_1 k_2|) k_G < 1$, i.e. while

$$|k_1 k_2| < \frac{2}{f_0}(\frac{1}{k_G k_p} - 1) \tag{1.28}$$

The immune system is I/O stable.

Note that the I/O stable condition obtained by **Small Gain Theorem** is just sufficient condition. Nevertheless, the significance of **Theorem 1.2** is that it has proposed the condition of I/O stable, thus **Theorem 1.2** is an important guide for choosing parameters of artificial immune controller.

1.1.4 General Structure of Immune P Controller

The T-B_CAIC model described by Eq. (1.13) has some extensive meanings, from which the general structure of this kind of artificial immune system is obtained as in Fig.1.7. While $P_h(e(t))$, $f_h(e(t))$ and $f_s(e(t))$ have different forms, we can get a series of artificial immune controllers listed in table 1.1.

Figure 1.7. General form of immune P contoller

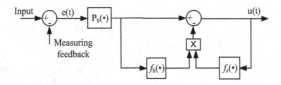

Figure 1.8. Block diagram of motor control system constructed by T-B_DIC *and* PI

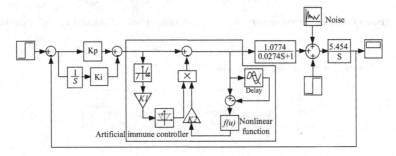

1.1.5 Simulation Study of T-B_AIC in a SISO System

Using Simulink as the simulation tool, treating a motor as the controlled object, linear model of the motor near the working point is:

$$n(s) = \frac{1.0774}{0.0274s+1} \cdot \frac{5.464}{s} u(s) - \frac{5.464}{s} i(s) \tag{1.50}$$

Where $n(s)$ is the motor's output speed, $u(s)$ is the driving voltage, $i(s)$ is the variation of armature current.

Assume the motor load has reduced 20%; consider a white noise varying in the range [-0.2, 0.2], and the load joined in the system within 2 seconds, meanwhile maintain the object's parameters unchanged, parameters of the controller shown in Fig. 1.8 and 1.9.

It can be observed from the simulation result: motor control system without controller or with only immune P controller can not eliminate the output change caused by the change of the load, but motor control system composed of PI controller or immune PI controller can finally make the system output achieve the setting value. Even so, it is also obvious that PI controller needs too much regulation time, while immune PI controller could nearly realize smooth transition.

1.2 A Class of Artificial Immune Controllers Based on R-K Immune Cells

T-B cell based artificial immune controller proposed in the last section doesn't have the ability of setting tracking, because the artificial immune model for constructing T-B_DAIC is so simple that the constructed controller is only an adaptive varying structure proportional controller.

Sergei G. and Yuri M.(Jerne, 1973) proposed a model of the double-cell nonlinear immune feedback based on recognizers and killers in 2003. The model is a bilinear model, which can give a better description of the relationship between recognizers, killers and antigens in an organism to some extent. Based on the model, and carefully thinking about similarities and differences between biologic immunity and artificial immune applica-

Figure 1.9. Simulation curves when the load and disturbance ore changing

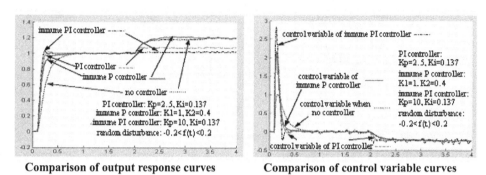

Comparison of output response curves　　**Comparison of control variable curves**

Figure 1.10. Sketch map of macro immune mechanism

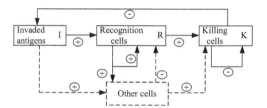

tions, a class of double-cell artificial immune models for using as controller will be constructed and analyzed in this section. The study shows this controller has good characteristics such as the first-order setting tracking, anti-lag and so on.

1.2.1 Basic Double-Cell Tuned Immune Dynamic Equation

Adaptive immune system is a very complex system whose mechanism has not been fully clarified in medical science yet, thus it is impossible to precisely describe the operation law of immune system by using dynamic equations. However, it is roughly clear about the immune mechanism on macro and parts on micro in medical science. As to adaptive immunity, its approximate mechanism on macro is: after invasion, antigens are firstly recognized by recognizers (such as APC) and promote a proliferation of recognizers as well, then recognizers will activate a series of cells and finally make killers (such as Th2) activated, killers are capable of killing antigens, and recognizers will decrease with the decreasing of antigens, which will also cause a reduction of killers to maintain the safety and balance of an organism. The above process can be roughly represented by Fig.1.10, where ⊕ the promotion effect,Θ is the suppression effect.

Suppose $I(t)$ denotes number of the intruders at time t; Number of the recognizers is denoted as $R(t)$ and number of the killers as $K(t)$ at time t. We assume that after initial infection the intruders reproduce themselves within the organism with efficiency $\alpha > 0$. Then the additional amount of intruders produced by the amount $I(t)$ during time interval $\Box t$ is:

$$\Delta I_1(t) = \alpha I(t)\Delta t \tag{1.51}$$

Where $\Box I_1(t)$ is the additional number of intruders during time interval Δt. Meanwhile, if an intruder encounters with a killer, the intruders is destroyed with some probability. Frequency of such events is proportional to the numbers of the intruders and killers at the moment of time. Thus the decreased amount of intruders during time interval Δt caused by the presence of the number $I(t)$ of intruders and the number $K(t)$ of killers in the organism is:

$$\Delta I_2(t) = -\eta I(t)K(t)\Delta t \tag{1.52}$$

Where $\eta > 0$ is the coefficient determined by the probability of one intruder to meet one killer and the probability of intruder destruction in this case. According to Eq. (1.51), (1.52), the additional number of intruders produced during interval Δt is:

$$\Delta I(t) = \Delta I_1(t) - \Delta I_2(t) = (\alpha I(t) - \eta I(t)K(t))\Delta t$$

i.e.

$$\dot{I}(t) = \alpha I(t) - \eta I(t)K(t) \tag{1.53}$$

Recognizers are present in the organism before the attack of intruders, thus the initial value of recognizers should not be 0 (otherwise, the immune system will lose effect for disability of recognizing antigens). The amount of recognizers in an organism is always greater than zero, suppose it is $R(0) = R_0 > 0$. According to immunology, when a recognizer meets an intruder and recognizes it, two processes(Lydyard et al, 2001) are launched: (1) the recognizer starts to reproduce itself much more faster than the intruder, (2) recognizer triggers proliferation of killers. Assume the varied amount of recognizers is proportional to the square of the amount of intruders during interval Δt:

$$\Delta R(t) = \kappa I^2(t)\Delta t \tag{1.54}$$

Expressed in derivative form:

$$\dot{R}(t) = \kappa I^2(t), \quad R(0) = R_0 \tag{1.55}$$

As to killers, on one hand they are proliferating triggered by recognizers; on the other hand they are self-destroyed in the same time. With regard to the first aspect, assume that in the unit time the amount of triggered killers is proportional to the amount of recognizers during the same interval, the proportional coefficient is $v > 0$:

$$\Delta K_1(t) = v R(t)\Delta t \tag{1.56}$$

For short, v is called triggered efficiency of killers. With regard to the second aspect, assume that natural destroyed efficiency is $\mu > 0$, destroyed efficiency caused by killing intruders is $\lambda > 0$, then in the moment time the amount of destroyed killers is:

$$\Delta K_2(t) = (-\mu K(t) - \lambda I(t))\Delta t \tag{1.57}$$

Merge Eq. (1.56), (1.57), and express in derivative form:

$$\dot{K}(t) = -\mu K(t) - \lambda I(t) + v R(t) \tag{1.58}$$

At this point, the double-cell feedback dynamic equations of adaptive immunity are obtained.

$$\begin{cases} \dot{I}(t) = \alpha I(t) - \eta I(t)K(t) \\ \dot{R}(t) = \kappa I(t)^2 \quad R(0) = R_0 \\ \dot{K}(t) = \nu R(t) - \lambda I(t) - \mu K(t) \end{cases}$$

$$(1.59)$$

Where, η is the killing efficiency of killers against intruders; κ is the proliferation efficiency of recognizers; ν is the activating efficiency of killers; μ is natural destruction efficiency of killers; λ is the destroyed efficiency of killers for killing intruders; R_0 is the initial amount of recognizer.

According to immunology, parameters in Eq. (1.59) should satisfy $\alpha > 0$, $\eta > 0$, $\kappa > 0$, $\nu > 0$, $\mu > 0$, $R_0 > 0$, and $I(t) \geq 0$, $K(t) \geq 0$, $R(t) > 0$.

1.2.2 Designing and Realizing of Double-Cell Artificial Immune Controller

What are described in Eq. (1.59) are the changes of intruders after invading into an organism. Suppose the error of a control system $e(t)$ is the antigen $I(t)$, the control variable $u(t)$ is the killer $K(t)$, then the following equations of the double-cell artificial immune controller is obtained:

$$\begin{cases} \dot{e}(t) = \alpha e(t) - \eta e(t)u(t) \\ \dot{R}(t) = \kappa e(t)^2 \quad R(0) = R_0 \\ \dot{u}(t) = \nu R(t) - \lambda e(t) - \mu u(t) \end{cases}$$

$$(1.60)$$

Since the model has seven adjustable parameters totally, it is not convenient to construct a practical artificial immune controller. When constructing a new type of artificial immune controller, it should be firstly clarified what in the immune model is similar to the control system that can be used for references, and what is the different that needs improving The similarities between double-cell immune dynamic model and a control system that can also used for references are: (1) if the antigen $I(t)$ is treated as the error $e(t)$ in a control system, the killer $K(t)$ as the control variable $u(t)$, then the inhibiting effect of antibodies on antigens described in the immune dynamic model (1.60) can be treated as inhibiting effect of the control variable on the error. (2) The immune dynamic model (1.60) contains recognizers, whose existence has proved to be one of the most important reasons of the memory property of an immune system in medical science, thus recognizers should be preserved when constructing a new type of artificial immune controller.

The differences between the double-cell immune dynamic model and a control system is as follows: (1) in $\dot{I}(t) = \alpha I(t) - \eta I(t)K(t)$, the first item represents the reproduction of antigens, the second item represents the killing efficiency of killers against antigens, while the error in a control system does not reproduce itself. (2) In an immune system, the amounts of antigens, killers and recognizers are all greater than zero, while in a control system, the error or the control variable can be either positive or negative. (3) Since the antigen $I(t) \geq 0$, and $\dot{R}(t) = \kappa I^2(t)$, thus the recognizer $R(t)$ can only increase with time increasing, if $I(t)$ can not achieve zero at last, then $R(t)$ will be infinite, which is impossible either in an immune system or in a control system.

When the construct of an artificial immune controller is obtained by referencing to the double-cell immune model, it should not only inherit main features from the double-cell immune model, but also consider real applications. Thus reconstruct Eq. (1.60) as follows:

(1)   Because reproducing and magnifying of the error is not expected in real applications, so omit the item represented reproducing of antigens in Eq. (1.60). Meanwhile the error in real applications can be either positive or negative, so define:

$$\dot{I}(t) = \eta \left| K(t) \right| I(t) \tag{1.61}$$

(2)   Recognizer in Eq. (1.60) can not be always greater than zero, thus define:

$$\dot{R}(t) = \kappa \left| I(t) \right| I(t) \tag{1.62}$$

Therefore, after proper reconstruction, Eq. (1.60) has changed into the following dynamic model:

$$\begin{cases} \dot{I}(t) = \eta \left| K(t) \right| I(t) \\ \dot{R}(t) = \kappa \left| I(t) \right| I(t) \quad R(0) = R_0 \\ \dot{K}(t) = v\,R(t) - \lambda I(t) - \mu K(t) \end{cases} \tag{1.63}$$

Definition 1.6 Define

$$P(t) = I(t) + R(t) \tag{1.64}$$

$P(t)$ is called generalized recognizer of immune system.
Define $v = \lambda$, and consider Eq. (1.64), the following model is obtained from Eq. (1.63):

$$\begin{cases} \dot{P}(t) = (\kappa \left| I(t) \right| + \eta \left| K(t) \right|) I(t), P(0) = P_0 \\ \dot{K}(t) = -\mu K(t) + v\,P(t) \end{cases} \tag{1.65}$$

Define $e(t) = I(t)$, $u(t) = K(t)$, and the following model is obtained:

$$\begin{cases} \dot{P}(t) = (\kappa \left| e(t) \right| + \eta \left| u(t) \right|) e(t), P(0) = P_0 \\ \dot{u}(t) = -\mu u(t) + v\,P(t) \end{cases} \tag{1.66}$$

Where $\kappa > 0$, $\eta > 0$, $\mu > 0$, $v > 0$. The first equation in Eq. (1.66) has assured the existence of generalized recognizer. The second equation has described the immune mechanism, in which control variable is stimulated or operated by the generalized recognizer.
Merge Eq. (1.66) into a differential equation:

$$\ddot{u}(t) = -\mu \dot{u}(t) + (\gamma \left| e(t) \right| + \beta \left| u(t) \right|) e(t), u(0) = u_0 \tag{1.67}$$

Eq. (1.67) is the model of Basic Double-Cell Artificial Immune Controller (**BDC_AIC**).

Definition 1.7 If the controller model satisfies Eq. (1.67), this kind of controller can be called BDC_AIC. Where, γ denotes the error recognition coefficient, β denotes the immune feedback coefficient, and μ denotes the stability coefficient of immune control.

1)   Extended Double-Cell Artificial Immune Controller (**EDC_AIC**)

According to the immunology, if stimulated by the invasion of antigen, the number of recognition factor will increase much faster than the proportion rate(Jerne, 1974; Lydyard et al., 2001), but so far this kind of increase rate hasn't been quantitatively described. Assuming using $\dot{R}(t) = \kappa I(t)^3, R(0) = R_0$ instead of $\dot{R}(t) = \kappa I(t)^2, R(0) = R_0$ in Eq. (1.59), then Eq. (1.66) will be changed into Eq. (1.68) as follows:

$$\begin{cases} \dot{P}(t) = (\kappa e^2(t) + \eta |u(t)|)e(t), P(0) = P_0 \\ \dot{u}(t) = -\mu u(t) + \nu P(t) \end{cases} \tag{1.68}$$

So there is no need of joining absolute value in Eq. (1.62) forcefully.
Merge Eq. (1.68) into a differential equation:

$$\ddot{u}(t) = -\mu \dot{u}(t) + (\gamma e^2(t) + \beta |u(t)|)e(t), u(0) = u_0 \tag{1.69}$$

Eq. (1.69) is called **EDC_AIC**, where, $\gamma = \nu\kappa > 0$ denotes the error recognition coefficient, $\beta = \nu\eta > 0$ denotes the immune feedback coefficient, and μ denotes the stability coefficient of immune control.

Definition 1.8 If the controller model satisfies Eq. (1.69), this kind of controller can be called **EDC_AIC**. Where, γ denotes the recognition rate coefficient of deviation, β denotes the immune positive feedback coefficient, and μ denotes the stability coefficient of immune control.

2)   Simplify Double-Cell Artificial Immune Controller (**SDC_AIC**)

If μ is small, or in the actual control system the mortality of self-destruction factor is not taken into consideration, Eq. (1.68) can be further simplified into Eq. (1.70):

$$\begin{cases} \dot{P}(t) = (\kappa e^2(t) + \eta |u(t)|)e(t), P(0) = P_0 \\ u(t) = \nu P(t) \end{cases} \tag{1.70}$$

Eq. (1.70) can be called the model of **SDC_AIC** in Eq. (1.66). Compare Eq. (1.70) with Eq. (1.66) and Eq. (1.68), the biggest feature of Eq. (1.70) is that the role of generalized recognition factor has been strengthened, but the mortality of self-destruction has been neglected, then the model order has been reduced. Merge Eq. (1.69), then a differential equation can be got as follows:

$$\dot{u}(t) = (\gamma e^2(t) + \beta |u(t)|)e(t), u(0) = u_0 \tag{1.71}$$

Where, $\gamma = \nu\kappa$, $\beta = \nu\eta$. The structure diagram of **SDC_AIC** is shown in Fig. 1.11 as follows.

Figure 1.11. The structure of SDC_AIC

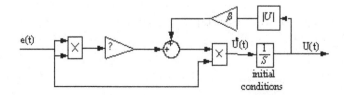

Figure 1.12. The ERDC_AIC and its control system structure

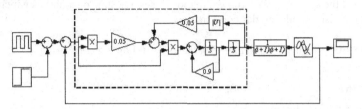

Definition 1.9 If the controller model satisfies Eq. (1.71), this kind of controller can be called **SDC_AIC**. Where, γ denotes the error recognition rate coefficient, β denotes the immune positive feedback coefficient.

The 3 immune controllers given above are collectively called Double-Cell Artificial Immune Controller.

1.2.1 One-Order Tracking Performance of DC_AIC

The general structure of SISO immune control system is shown in Fig.1.5 where $f(e, u)$ represents a certain immune controller, and $G(s)$ represents the controlled object.

On one order fixed tracking performance, DC_AIC is equivalent with PID, but on the mechanism and method, they are different. When the controller is nonlinear, whether it has one order fixed tracking performance (integral properties) is very important. However, this form of nonlinear controller performance will be more extensive in mathematics. The following is a definition of one order fixed tracking performance of a nonlinear controller SISO on the basis of steady-state response.

Definition 1.10 If the SISO control system, as shown in Fig.1.5, consisting of nonlinear controllers is internal

stable, while the external input of the system is constant $x(t) = r$, $v(t) = z$, the output is $y(t)$, then:

(1)   While $v(t) \equiv 0$, and $\lim_{t \to \infty} \|y(t) - r\| = 0$, then this nonlinear control system has one order fixed tracking performance.

(2)   While $x(t) \equiv 0$, and $\lim_{t \to \infty} \|y(t)\| = 0$, then this nonlinear control system with constant interference z has invariance.

If the controlled object $G(s)$ is a strictly positive real model of 0-type, so obviously the tracking performance of the system is caused by the nonlinear controller $f(e, u)$ shown in Fig.1.5. Similar methods can be used to define high-order tracking performance.

Definition 1.11 General nonlinear control systems can be expressed as follow:

$$\dot{X}(t) = F(X(t), U(t)) \tag{1.72}$$

$X \in R^n$ denotes the state vector, $U \in R^m$ denotes the control vector. The stationary means the state of the system does not change with time, just the state while:

$$\dot{X}(t) = F(X(t), U(t)) = \mathbf{0} \tag{1.73}$$

The stationary of the control system means the static point in the phase space. The physical meaning of the stationary refers to the point (one or more) whose generalized phase velocity in the phase space is zero. Another physical meaning is: while $t \to \infty$, the state that the system will reach.

In the qualitative study of Nonlinear Science, if the number of the stationary and their respective properties are known, the evolution of the system will be known. In most cases, the state of solutions which meet Eq. (1.27) is often called equilibrium, also called singular point in math.

Theorem 1.3 If the SISO system shown in Fig.1.5 satisfies the following conditions:

(1)   The control input $u(t) = r$ (r is a constant);

(2)   The system state can tend to stationary X° ;

(3)   The system output corresponding with the stationary is $y^\circ = r$.

Then the SISO system will have one order fixed tracking performance corresponding with the control input.

Proof: According to the condition (2)): $\lim_{t \to \infty} X(t) = X^\circ$

Yet $\because y^\circ = r$, and system output y(t) is confirmed just only by the system state, thus the output of the system is gradually tending to r. Then, $\lim_{t \to \infty} \|y(t) - r\| = 0$,and the SISO system has one order fixed tracking performance according to **Definition 1.6**.

Assuming the controlled object model is transfer function of 0-type in Fig.1.5:

$$G(s) = \frac{b_m s^m + b_{m-1} s^{m-1} + \cdots + b_1 s + b_0}{a_n s^n + a_{n-1} s^{n-1} + \cdots + a_1 s + a_0} \tag{1.74}$$

Where, $a_0 \neq 0, b_0 \neq 0, m < n$, and the unstable pole does not exist in G(s), at the same time suppose that there is no zero-pole cancellation. Not losing general, define: $a_n = 1, m = n - 1$. The state equation form is:

$$\begin{cases} \begin{bmatrix} \dot{x}_1 \\ \dot{x}_2 \\ \vdots \\ \dot{x}_n \end{bmatrix} = \begin{bmatrix} 0 & 1 & 0 & \cdots & 0 \\ 0 & 0 & 1 & \cdots & 0 \\ \vdots & \vdots & \vdots & \cdots & \vdots \\ 0 & 0 & 0 & \cdots & 1 \\ -a_0 & -a_1 & -a_2 & \cdots & -a_{n-1} \end{bmatrix} \begin{bmatrix} x_1 \\ x_2 \\ \vdots \\ x_n \end{bmatrix} + \begin{bmatrix} 0 \\ \vdots \\ 0 \\ 1 \end{bmatrix} u \\ y = \begin{bmatrix} b_0 & b_1 & \cdots & b_{n-1} \end{bmatrix} X \end{cases} \tag{1.75}$$

Now we only take the BDC_AIC as an example for discussion, others are in the similar situations. The control system model which controller is **BDC_AIC** shown in Fig.1.5 can be expressed as:

$$
\begin{cases}
\begin{bmatrix} \dot{x}_1 \\ \dot{x}_2 \\ \vdots \\ \dot{x}_n \end{bmatrix} =
\begin{bmatrix}
0 & 1 & 0 & \cdots & 0 \\
0 & 0 & 1 & \cdots & 0 \\
\vdots & \vdots & \vdots & \cdots & \vdots \\
0 & 0 & 0 & \cdots & 1 \\
-a_0 & -a_1 & -a_2 & \cdots & -a_{n-1}
\end{bmatrix}
\begin{bmatrix} x_1 \\ x_2 \\ \vdots \\ x_n \end{bmatrix} +
\begin{bmatrix} 0 \\ \vdots \\ 0 \\ 1 \end{bmatrix} u(t) = AX + Bu \\[4pt]
y(t) = \begin{bmatrix} b_0 & b_1 & \cdots & b_{n-1} \end{bmatrix} X = CX \\[4pt]
\ddot{u}(t) = -\mu \dot{u}(t) + (\gamma|e(t)| + \beta|u(t)|)e(t) \quad , \quad u(0) = u_0 \\[4pt]
e(t) = r - y(t) = r - CX
\end{cases}
\tag{1.76}
$$

Where, r denotes the constant control input of the control system.

Theorem 1.4 The immune control system in Eq. (1.76) has a singular point (stationary):

$$
\left(\begin{bmatrix} \dfrac{r}{b_0} & 0 & \cdots & 0 & \dfrac{a_0 r}{b_0} & 0 \end{bmatrix}^T \right)_{(n+3)\times 1}.
$$

Proof: Set $x_{n+1} = u(t)$, $x_{n+2} = \dot{u}(t)$, $x_{n+3} = e(t)$, then Eq.(16) can be expressed as follow:

$$
\begin{cases}
\underline{\dot{X}} = A^* \underline{X} + \Theta \\
y = C^* \underline{X}
\end{cases}
$$

Where, $\underline{X} = (x_1, x_2, \cdots x_n, x_{n+1}, x_{n+2}, x_{n+3})^T$, $C^* = (b_0, b_1, \cdots b_{n-1}, 0, 0, 0)$

$$
A^* =
\begin{bmatrix}
0 & 1 & \cdots & 0 & 0 & 0 & 0 \\
0 & 0 & \cdots & 0 & 0 & 0 & 0 \\
\vdots & \vdots & \cdots & \vdots & \vdots & \vdots & \vdots \\
0 & 0 & \cdots & 1 & 0 & 0 & 0 \\
-a_0 & -a_1 & \cdots & -a_{n-1} & 1 & 0 & 0 \\
0 & 0 & \cdots & 0 & 0 & 1 & 0 \\
0 & 0 & \cdots & 0 & 0 & -\mu & 0 \\
-a_0 b_{n-1} & b_0 - a_1 b_{n-1} & \cdots & b_{n-2} - a_{n-1} b_{n-1} & -b_{n-1} & 0 & 0
\end{bmatrix}_{(n+3)\times(n+3)}
$$

$$
\Theta = \begin{pmatrix} 0 & \cdots & 0 & \gamma(r-CX)^3 + \beta|x_{n+1}|(r-CX) & 0 \end{pmatrix}^T_{(n+3)\times 1}
$$

From $A^* \underline{X} + \Theta = 0$, the singular point is:

$$\mathbf{X}^0 = \left(\left[\frac{r}{b_0} \quad 0 \quad \cdots \quad 0 \quad \frac{a_0 r}{b_0} \quad 0 \right]^T \right)_{(n+3)\times 1}$$

Theorem 1.5: If the singular point

$$\left(\left[\frac{r}{b_0} \quad 0 \quad \cdots \quad 0 \quad \frac{a_0 r}{b_0} \quad 0 \right]^T \right)_{(n+3)\times 1}$$

of the immune control system (1.76) is stable, the system will have no error while given a constant control input r.

Proof: $\therefore$ Singular point

$$\left(\left[\frac{r}{b_0} \quad 0 \quad \cdots \quad 0 \quad \frac{a_0 r}{b_0} \quad 0 \right]^T \right)_{(n+3)\times 1} \text{ is stable,}$$

$\therefore$ While $t \to \infty$, then

$$x(t) \to \left[\frac{r}{b_0} \quad 0 \quad \cdots \quad 0 \quad \frac{a_0 r}{b_0} \quad 0 \right]^T .$$

$\therefore \lim_{t\to\infty} y(t) = \lim_{t\to\infty} CX = r$

$\therefore \lim_{t\to\infty} e(t) = \lim_{t\to\infty}(r - y(t)) = 0$.

According to **Theorem 1.3**, the control system (1.76) has one order fixed tracking performance.

When the controlled object in a control system which is controlled by a immune controller is 0-type linear system, the performance of one order fixed tracking is acquired from the immune controller.

According to (1.75) and (1.76), we can easy get immune control systems which include SDC_AIC or RDC_AIC. Then the similar theorems like **Theorem 1.4** and **Theorem 1.5** can be gained.

1.2.2 The Simulation Study of SISO System DC_AIC

Assuming the controlled object model is:

$$G_0(s) = \frac{e^{-\tau s}}{(s+1)(s+1)} \tag{1.77}$$

While pure lag is large relatively, the system will be difficult to control. The Simulink simulation map of the control system is shown in Fig. 1.12.

In order to display memory characteristics of the EDC_AIC, we choose a square-wave signal as control signal, the high threshold of the square-wave signal is 0.5, -0.5 for the low limits, nonzero initial value $u_0=0$. Calibration parameters are shown in Fig.1.13. In the course of simulation we set the controlled object's pure delay parameter τ respectively as 0, 1, 2, 4, 6, without outside interference. The simulation result is shown in Fig.1.13.

Fig. 1.13. Basic double-cell artificial immune system be controlled by square wave signal

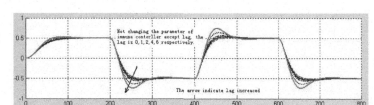

From Fig.1.13 which shows the simulation curve of the system output, the second response speed is faster than the first one, mainly because of the first control study, when doing control response to the second step EDC_AIC implements the reaction rate, and at this point it is same with the memory characteristics of the initial response and second response of the artificial immune system, that are the results of immune learning and immune memory. While the system response is a slow one, such an implementation of the reaction speed will help improving the dynamic quality; while the system response is a rapid response process concussion, it may not be conducive to improve the system quality.

Yet from the output simulation curve showed in Fig. 1.13, with the pure delay time constant $\tau = 0$, 1, 2, 4, 6 gradually increasing, although the control quality of the system has dropped, the system remains stable. But if using a PID controller, and ensuring the open-loop amplification coefficient of system remains unchanged, then the system will be not stable while $\tau > 3$. It shows the SISO control system composed of EDC_AIC has a good anti-lag capacity.

Also from the curve, EDC_AIC has no differential tracking capability to constant input, or has one order fixed tracking performance. Compared with P-type artificial immune controller referred in the second chapter, the Double-Cell Artificial Immune Controller in this section can be called PI-type immune controller.

1.3 An Immune Controller Based on the Immune Network Model

Varela Immune Network Model (VINM)(Kim, 2002) belongs to a kind of the idiotypic network models, it is usually considered as the second generation of the idiotypic network models after Jerne's, it is also a kind of continuous network model. On the basis of VINM, this section will propose an improved Varela immune network model, and by simplifying the improved Varela immune network model another immune controller with capability of learning will be constructed.

1.3.1 Varela Immune Network Model (Kim, 2002; Kim 2003)

Basic assumptions of the Varela immune network model are:

(1) Just consider B cells and the free antibodies produced by them, and the type of cells and antibodies belonging to a same type can be called a clone or a unique characteristic. Antibodies can be produced only by mature B cells.

(2) Interactions between different kinds of clones are expressed by a connection matrix *m*, in which the values are *0*s or *1*s.

(3) New B cells are produced continuously, while the old ones are dying. The probability of maturation and propagation of B cells are determined by the interactions among clones in the network.

Varela immune network model includes the following two equations:

Fig. 1.14. Function shape of M(σ) and P(σ)

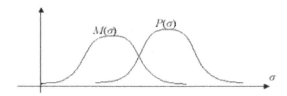

$$\begin{cases} \dot{T} = -k_{ttd}\sigma_i T - k_{td}T_i + k_{bv}M(\sigma_i)B_i \\ \dot{B} = -k_{bd}B_i + k_{bl}P(\sigma_i)B_i + k_{bn} \end{cases} \tag{1.78}$$

where T_i and B_i represents the quantity of the ith kind of the cloned free antibodies and the B-cells respectively; k_{ttd} represents the antibodies' mortality due to the interactions among antibodies; k_{td} represents the natural mortality of the antibodies; k_{bv} represents the velocity of B cells to produce antibodies; k_{bd} represents the B cells' mortality; k_{bl} represents the reproductive rate of B cells; k_{bn} represents the new B cells produced from the bone marrow; $M(\sigma_i)$ is mature function of B_i cells; $P(\sigma_i)$ is the propagation function of the B_i cell produced T_i antibody.

The mature function and the propagation function are both bell shape functions as shown in Fig.1.14; σ_i is the sensitivity of the ith kind clones against the network.

$$\sigma_i = \sum_{j=1}^{n} m_{i,j}T_i \tag{1.79}$$

where $m_{i,j}$ is a Boolean value of the affinity effect between the ith kind clones and the jth kind clones, in which *1* means there exist an affinity, while 0 is none. n is the kinds of the B-cell and the T_i antibodies, i = 1, 2, ... n.

The bell shape function can reflect a basic fact in the artificial immune process: inadequate or excessive sensitivity will suppress both the differentiation of B cells and their capabilities of producing T antibodies(Kim, 2002).

Eq. (1.78) and (1.79) reflects the dynamic interaction process between B cells and T-antibodies in the artificial immune process in some extent, but there still exist some demerits when realizing an artificial immune controller in a control system by directly using Eq. (1.78) and (1.79) , the most prominent is: Varela immune network model can not reflect the effects of the antigens, while designing an artificial immune controller is used to treat the system error as an antigen, and one of the ultimate results of controlling is the elimination or minimization of the error.

1.3.2 Improved Varela Immune Network Model (IVINM)

There will be two different responses after the antigens enter the organism. One is the self-reproduction and propagation of the antigens, the other is the antigens will be impacted by phagocytes and killing cells which can eliminate antigens.

The above two kinds of interaction effect can be descript by the following dynamic equation [19]:

$$\dot{Ag}_i = q'Ag - H(T_i)Ag_i \tag{1.80}$$

Where q' is the multiplication rate of the antigens while there is no immune response, $H(T_i)$ is the function about antibodies removing antigens, define(Lydyard et al., 2001):

$$H(T_i) = h + K_e T_i \tag{1.81}$$

Where h is the killing rate of non-peculiar response; K_e is the approximate peculiar removing velocity of the antigens. Suppose $q = q' - h$, now put equation (1.79) into equation (1.78), then we can get the following equation:

$$\dot{A}g_i = qAg_i - K_e T_i Ag_i \tag{1.82}$$

Where q is the multiplication rate of the antigens; K_e is the removing rate of the antigens, here we assume that the removing of antigens are mostly realized by the encountering and combining between antibodies and antigens, which can be represented by the product of the numbers of antibodies and antigens, i.e. $T_i Ag_i$ (Jerne, 1973).

In a practical biologic immune system, even there is no outside invasion of antigens into the organism, there will still exist a little quantity of antibodies inside the body[27], which means T cells have a little initial value: $T(0) = T_0$, which is equal to the memory effect of antibodies against antigens.

Given the multiplication rate of B cells is affected by antigens, assuming the effect is linearity. Meanwhile, pay attention to the Eq. (1.78) and (1.82), then we can get the Improved Varela Immune Network Model(**IVINM**):

$$\begin{cases} \dot{A}g_i = qAg_i - K_e T_i Ag_i \\ \dot{T}_i = -k_{ttd}\sigma_i T_i + k_{bv}M(\sigma_i)B_i \qquad \dot{T}(0) = T_0 \\ \dot{B}_i = -k_{bd}B_i + k_{bl}P(\sigma_i)B_i + k_{bn} - K_{Ag}Ag_i \end{cases} \tag{1.83}$$

where $T(0)$ represents the little amount of memory antibodies without invasion of antigens. K_{Ag} represents the propagation rate of B cells caused by the existing of antigens; Ag_i, q, K_e is the same as in Eq. (1.82); $k_j, j = ttd, td, bv, bd, bl, bn$, T_i B_i is the same as in Eq. (1.78); $M(\sigma_i)$, $P(\sigma_i)$, σ_i is the same as in Eq. (1.79). Eq. (1.83) can be called as the improved Varela immune network model (IVINM).

1.3.3 The Designing and Implementation of the Varela Artificial Immune Contoller

Similarly, when using IVINM as a reference to construct a new kind of artificial immune controllers, it is necessary to clarify the similarities between the IVINM and control systems as well as the differences to be improved. The similar points which can be used as references are: firstly, if the invasion antigens Ag is regarded as the deviation $e(t)$ of a system, B cells as the control variable $u(t)$, then Eq. (1.83) has described the immune inhibition process of B cells against the invasion antigens, thus the whole can be used as references; secondly, Eq. (1.83) includes B cells and antibodies, where B cells are the key cells for recognition, remembering antigens and excreting antibodies. It has proved in medicine that the phlogocyte in a B cell is one of the most important reasons for immune system possessing memory characteristic. The differences are: (1) in an SISO system, only one controller is required; (2) in Eq. (1.83), the variable rate of the invaded antigens is composed of two parts, the self-reproduction rate of antigens and the killing rate of antibodies against antigens. But in a control system error can not reproduce itself, only the second item about the variable rate of antigen is needed to consider; (3) in an immune system, the quantities of antigens, antibodies and B cells are all greater than zero, while in a control system the deviation, the control variable have either positive or negative changes.

Figure 1.15. The curve of maturation function M(σ)

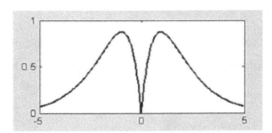

For the above differences, Eq. (1.84) is needed to be simplified and improved when constructing an artificial immune controller.

(1) Because only one controller is needed in an SISO system, the following equation can be obtained from Eq. (1.83):

$$\begin{cases} \dot{Ag} = qAg = K_e TAg \\ \dot{T} = -k_{ttd}\sigma T - k_{td}T + k_{bv}M(\sigma)B \qquad T(0) = T_0 \\ \dot{B} = -k_{bd}B + k_{5N}P(\sigma) + k_{bn} - K_{Ag}Ag \end{cases}$$

(1.84)

where the parameters is the same as in Eq. (1.83).

(2) Omit the self-reproducing item in Eq. (1.84);

(3) Make the mature function $M(\sigma)$ has the following form:

$$M(\sigma) = K_m(e^{p_1|\sigma|} - e^{p_2|\sigma|})$$

(1.85)

Where $K_m > 0$ is a constant, $p_2 < p_1 < 0$ are all constants, then the function has the shape as shown in Fig.1.15. The curve in Fig.1.15 has a left part and a right part that are all similar to the bell shape in Fig.1.14, which are used to adjust positive and negative variables in a control system. Parameters p_1 and p_2 can reflect the basic features of a "bell" shape. For the sake of simplicity, define $K_m = 1$ in the following applications. The propagation function $P(\sigma)$ is also adopt form as Eq. (1.85).

(4) Merge the first two items in Eq. (1.84), and define Ag is the error in a setting value adjustment system, B is the control variable $u(t)$. The following control model based on improved Varela immune model can be obtained:

$$\begin{cases} \dot{e}(t) = -k_e T(t)e(t) \\ \dot{T}(t) = -k_T T(t) + k_{bv}M(\sigma)u(t) \qquad T(0) = T_0 \\ \dot{u}(t) = -ku(t) + k_{bl}p(\sigma)u(t) + k_{bn} - K_{bn}e(t) \end{cases}$$

(1.86)

Where $k_T = k_{ttd}\sigma + k_{td}$

It is too complex to use Eq. (1.86) as practical controller, because there are totally 11 variable parameters. Thus Eq. (1.86) needs a further simplification to construct a practical artificial immune controller.

Figure 1.16. Structure diagram of VINM_AIC

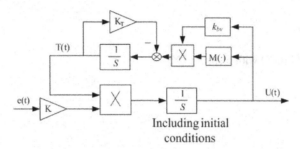

Including initial
conditions

(1)   Assume that the coefficients of the propagation rate of B cells are $k_{bl} = 0$, $k_{bn} = 0$, i.e. $u(t)$ and $e(t)$ has the following simple proportional relationship:

$$u(t) = -K_{ee}e(t) \tag{1.87}$$

The biologic meaning of Eq. (1.87) is: the number of B cells is determined by the number of invaded antigens, more invaded antigens, more B cells, and vice versa.

(2)   For the sake of simplicity, define the free variable in $M(\sigma)$ is $u(t)$.

Then Eq. (1.86) can be simplified as:

$$\begin{cases} \dot{e}(t) = -K_e T(t)e(t) \\ \dot{T}(t) = -k_e T(t) + k_{bv} M(u(t))u(t) \qquad T(0) = T_0 \\ u(t) = -k_{ee}e(t) \end{cases} \tag{1.88}$$

Find the first derivative of the third equation in Eq. (1.88), and merge it with the first equation:

$$\begin{cases} \dot{T}(t) = -k_T T(t) + k_{bv} M(u(t))u(t) \qquad T(0) = T_0 \\ \dot{u}(t) = -kT(t)e(t) \end{cases} \tag{1.89}$$

Where $k = K_{ee}K_e$ is called immune amplification coefficient; $M(\bullet)$ is the mature function of B cells. Eq. (1.89) is the Artificial Immune Controller based on the Improved Varela Immune Network Model (**IVINM_AIC**). The structure of the artificial immune controller has been shown in Fig.1.16. The integral part with the initial condition in the figure reflects the initial T cells, T_0.

IVINM_AIC totally includes 7 adjustable parameters: k_T is the mortality of T cells, k_{bv} is the velocity of mature B cells to produce antibodies, k is the coefficient of the immune magnification, the initial value is T_0 and. P1, P2 and K_m in $M(\cdot)$ can reflect the shape feature of the bell shape function.

1.3.4 Improve Varela Artificial Immune System Controller and the Control of SISO Analysis

Observing Eq. (1.89), if P_1, P_2 is confirmed in advance, and note the product relationship between k_{bv} and K_m, then only one parameter needs to be adjusted, thus the simplified Varela artificial immune controller has only 4 adjustable parameters left. Likewise, replace $f(e,u)$ with IVINM_AIC, a new immune control system can be constructed.

Definition 1.12(the first order approximation of the nonlinear system)(Kim & Cho, 2002)For a nonlinear system

$$\dot{X} = F(t, X), \; F(t, 0) = 0 \tag{1.90}$$

Consider Jacobi matrix of F(t, X) with respect to X:

$$\left. \frac{\partial F(t, X)}{\partial X} \right|_{x=0} = A(t) \tag{1.91}$$

If $A(t)$ and t are unrelated, then nonlinear system (1.90) can_be expressed as:

$$\dot{X} = AX + G(t, X), \quad A \in R^{n \times n} \tag{1.92}$$

Where $G(t, X)$ is called a higher-order power function with respect to X, so the linear time-invariant system:

$$\dot{X} = AX \tag{1.93}$$

is generally called the first order approximation of nonlinear system (1.90) or (1.92)

Lemma 1.2(Kim & Cho, 2002) If the zeros of the system (1.93) are asymptotically stable, and $G(t, X)$ satisfies Eq. (1.94), then the zeros of Eq. (1.90) or (1.92) are locally exponentially asymptotically stable.

$$\lim_{\|X\| \to 0} \frac{G(t, X)}{\|X\|} = 0 \tag{1.94}$$

Lemma 1.3(Kim & Cho, 2002) If the zeros of Eq. (1.93) are not stable in essence, the zeros of Eq. (1.90) or (1.92) are unstable for any $G(t, X)$ that satisfies Eq. (1.94).

Lemma 1.4 (Kim & Cho, 2002) If the zeros of Eq. (1.93) are critical stable and $G(t, X)$ satisfies Eq. (1.94), then the zeros of Eq. (1.90) or (1.92) <u>are</u> locally critical stable.

$$\lim_{\|X\| \to 0} \frac{G(t, X)}{\|X\|^{1+a}} = 0, \alpha > 0 \tag{1.95}$$

The proofs of lemma 1.2, 1.3, 1.4 are shown in Ref.(Kim & Cho, 2002)

Not lose general, if the controlled object's model shown in Fig.1.5 is a 0 type linear transfer function.

$$G(s) = \frac{b_{n-1}s^{n-1} + b_{n-2}s^{n-2} + \cdots + b_1 s + b_0}{s^n + a_{n-1}s^{n-1} + \cdots + a_1 s + a_0} \tag{1.96}$$

where $a_0 \neq 0, b_0 \neq 0$ and no instable pole in Eq.(1.96). Assume that zeros and poles are not cancelled out. The state equation can be expressed as follows:

$$
\left\{
\begin{array}{l}
\begin{bmatrix} \dot{x}_1 \\ \dot{x}_2 \\ \vdots \\ \dot{x}_n \end{bmatrix} =
\begin{bmatrix}
0 & 1 & 0 & \cdots & 0 \\
0 & 0 & 1 & \cdots & 0 \\
\vdots & \vdots & \vdots & \cdots & \vdots \\
0 & 0 & 0 & \cdots & 1 \\
-a_0 & -a_1 & -a_2 & \cdots & -a_{n-1}
\end{bmatrix}
\begin{bmatrix} x_1 \\ x_2 \\ \vdots \\ x_n \end{bmatrix} +
\begin{bmatrix} 0 \\ \vdots \\ 0 \\ 1 \end{bmatrix} u \\
y = \begin{bmatrix} b_0 & b_1 & \cdots & b_{n-1} \end{bmatrix} X
\end{array}
\right.
$$

(1.97)

Assume that $r(t)=r$ in the SISO system as shown in Fig. 1.5, then the system model whose controller is **IVINM_AIC** can be expressed as follows:

$$
\left\{
\begin{array}{l}
\begin{bmatrix} \dot{x}_1 \\ \dot{x}_2 \\ \vdots \\ \dot{x}_n \end{bmatrix} =
\begin{bmatrix}
0 & 1 & 0 & \cdots & 0 \\
0 & 0 & 1 & \cdots & 0 \\
\vdots & \vdots & \vdots & \cdots & \vdots \\
0 & 0 & 0 & \cdots & 1 \\
-a_0 & -a_1 & -a_2 & \cdots & -a_{n-1}
\end{bmatrix}
\begin{bmatrix} x_1 \\ x_2 \\ \vdots \\ x_n \end{bmatrix} +
\begin{bmatrix} 0 \\ \vdots \\ 0 \\ 1 \end{bmatrix} u(t) = AX + Bu \\
y(t) = \begin{bmatrix} b_0 & b_1 & \cdots & b_{n-1} \end{bmatrix} X = C^T X \\
\dot{T}(t) = -k_T T(t) + k_{bv} M(u(t)) u(t) \quad T(0) = T_0 \\
\dot{u}(t) = -kT(t)e(t) \\
e(t) = r - y(t) = r - C^T X
\end{array}
\right.
$$

(1.98)

Theorem 1.6 The immune control system (1.98) has two singular points: $X_1^0 = \begin{bmatrix} 0 & \cdots & 0 \end{bmatrix}^T_{(n+2)\times 1}$ and

$$
X_2^0 = \begin{bmatrix} \dfrac{r}{b_0} & 0 & \cdots & 0 & \dfrac{a_0 r}{b_0} & \dfrac{k_{bv}}{k_T} M(\dfrac{a_0 r}{b_0}) \dfrac{a_0 r}{b_0} \end{bmatrix}^T_{(n+2)\times 1}.
$$

Proof: Define $x_{n+1} = u(t)$, $x_{n+2} = T(t)$, Eq. (1.98) can be expressed as follows:

$$
\left\{
\begin{array}{l}
\underline{\dot{X}} = \underline{A}\,\underline{X} + \Theta \\
y = \underline{C}^T \underline{X}
\end{array}
\right.
$$

(1.99)

where $\underline{X} = (x_1, x_2, \cdots x_n, x_{n+1}, x_{n+2})^T$, $\underline{C}^T = (b_0, b_1, \cdots b_{n-1}, 0, 0)$

$$\underline{A} = \begin{bmatrix} 0 & 1 & 0 & \cdots & 0 & 0 & 0 \\ 0 & 0 & 1 & \cdots & 0 & 0 & 0 \\ \vdots & \vdots & \vdots & \cdots & \vdots & \vdots & \vdots \\ 0 & 0 & 0 & \cdots & 1 & 0 & 0 \\ -a_0 & -a_1 & -a_2 & \cdots & -a_{n-1} & 1 & 0 \\ 0 & 0 & 0 & \cdots & 0 & 0 & -kr \\ 0 & 0 & 0 & \cdots & 0 & k_{bv}M(\bullet) & -k_T \end{bmatrix}_{(n+2)\times(n+2)}$$

$$\Theta = (0 \quad \cdots \quad 0 \quad kx_{n+2}\underline{C}^T\underline{X} \quad 0)^T_{(n+2)\times 1}$$

From $\underline{A}\underline{X} + \Theta = \mathbf{0}$ obtain:

$$\begin{cases} x_2 = x_3 = \cdots = x_n = x_{n+2} = 0 \\ x_{n+1} = -a_0 x_1 \\ kx_{n+2}(r - b_0 x_1) = 0 \\ k_{bv}M(x_{n+1})x_{n+1} - k_T x_{n+2} = 0 \end{cases}$$

(1.100)

Solve Eq. (1.100):

$$\underline{X}_1^0 = \begin{bmatrix} 0 & \cdots & 0 \end{bmatrix}^T_{(n+2)\times 1}$$

(1.101)

$$X_2^0 = \begin{bmatrix} \dfrac{r}{b_0} & 0 & \cdots & 0 & \dfrac{a_0 r}{b_0} & \dfrac{k_{bv}}{k_T}M(\dfrac{a_0 r}{b_0})\dfrac{a_0 r}{b_0} \end{bmatrix}^T_{(n+2)\times 1}$$

(1.102)

By analyzing characteristics of every singular point, we can infer the characteristics of the immune control system (1.98).

1) Stability analysis of the singular point $\underline{X}_1^0 = \begin{bmatrix} 0 & \cdots & 0 \end{bmatrix}^T_{(n+2)\times 1}$

The first order linear approximation of Eq. (1.98) at $\underline{X}_1^0 = \begin{bmatrix} 0 & \cdots & 0 \end{bmatrix}^T_{(n+2)\times 1}$ can be expressed as:

$$\begin{cases} \begin{bmatrix} \underline{\dot{x}}_1 \\ \vdots \\ \underline{\dot{x}}_n \\ \underline{\dot{x}}_{n+1} \\ \underline{\dot{x}}_{n+2} \end{bmatrix} = \begin{bmatrix} 0 & 1 & 0 & \cdots & 0 & 0 & 0 \\ 0 & 0 & 1 & \cdots & 0 & 0 & 0 \\ \vdots & \vdots & \vdots & \cdots & \vdots & \vdots & \vdots \\ 0 & 0 & 0 & \cdots & 1 & 0 & 0 \\ -a_0 & -a_1 & -a_2 & \cdots & -a_{n-1} & 1 & 0 \\ 0 & 0 & 0 & \cdots & 0 & 0 & -rk \\ 0 & 0 & 0 & \cdots & 0 & k_{bv}M(\bullet) & -k_T \end{bmatrix} \begin{bmatrix} \underline{x}_1 \\ \underline{x}_2 \\ \vdots \\ \underline{x}_{n-1} \\ \underline{x}_n \\ \underline{x}_{n+1} \\ \underline{x}_{n+2} \end{bmatrix} = \underline{A}\underline{X} \\ y = (b_0, b_1, \cdots b_{n-1}, 0, 0)\underline{X} = \underline{C}^T\underline{X} \end{cases}$$

(1.103)

The corresponding high-order power function $G(t, \underline{X})$ is:

$$G(t, \underline{X}) = \begin{bmatrix} 0 & \cdots & 0 & kx_{n+2}\underline{C}^T\underline{X} & 0 \end{bmatrix}^T_{(n+2)\times 1} \tag{1.104}$$

Obviously, Eq. (1.104) satisfies the conditions of Eq. (1.94) (See Appendix for the solution). According to Lemma 1.2, 1.3 and 1.4, we can analyze the linear system (1.103) in order to indirectly know the stability at the singular point $\underline{X}^0_1 = \begin{bmatrix} 0 & \cdots & 0 \end{bmatrix}^T_{(n+2)\times 1}$.

Theorem 1.7 With regard to the nonlinear system expressed as Eq. (1.99) and shown in Fig.1.5, if the controlled object is stable and satisfies the condition:

$$k_T > 0, \quad rkk_{bv}M(\bullet) > 0 \tag{1.105}$$

Then the immune control system (1.99) is asymptotical stable near singular point

$$\underline{X}^0_1 = \begin{bmatrix} 0 & \cdots & 0 \end{bmatrix}^T_{(n+2)\times 1}.$$

Proof: The characteristic polynomial of Eq.(1.103) is:

$$|(sI - \underline{A})| = \begin{vmatrix} s & -1 & 0 & \cdots & 0 & 0 & 0 \\ 0 & s & -1 & \cdots & 0 & 0 & 0 \\ \vdots & \vdots & \vdots & \cdots & \vdots & \vdots & \vdots \\ 0 & 0 & 0 & \cdots & -1 & 0 & 0 \\ a_0 & a_1 & a_2 & \cdots & s+a_{n-1} & -1 & 0 \\ 0 & 0 & 0 & \cdots & 0 & s & rk \\ 0 & 0 & 0 & \cdots & 0 & -k_{bv}M(\bullet) & s+k_T \end{vmatrix}$$

$$= (s+k_T)\begin{vmatrix} s & -1 & 0 & \cdots & 0 & 0 \\ 0 & s & -1 & \cdots & 0 & 0 \\ \vdots & \vdots & \vdots & \cdots & \vdots & \vdots \\ 0 & 0 & 0 & \cdots & -1 & 0 \\ a_0 & a_1 & a_2 & \cdots & s+a_{n-1} & -1 \\ 0 & 0 & 0 & \cdots & 0 & s \end{vmatrix} + (k_{bv}M(\bullet))\begin{vmatrix} s & -1 & 0 & \cdots & 0 & 0 \\ 0 & s & -1 & \cdots & 0 & 0 \\ \vdots & \vdots & \vdots & \cdots & \vdots & \vdots \\ 0 & 0 & 0 & \cdots & -1 & 0 \\ a_0 & a_1 & a_2 & \cdots & s+a_{n-1} & 0 \\ 0 & 0 & 0 & \cdots & 0 & rk \end{vmatrix}$$

$$= (s^2 + k_T s + rkk_{bv}M(\bullet))\begin{vmatrix} s & -1 & 0 & \cdots & 0 \\ 0 & s & -1 & \cdots & 0 \\ \vdots & \vdots & \vdots & \cdots & \vdots \\ 0 & 0 & 0 & \cdots & -1 \\ a_0 & a_1 & a_2 & \cdots & s+a_{n-1} \end{vmatrix}$$

$$= (s^2 + k_T s + rkk_{bv}M(\bullet))(s^n + a_{n-1}s^{n-1} + \cdots + a_1 s + a_0) \tag{1.106}$$

- The controlled object is stable.

- All eigenvalues of Eq. $(s^n + a_{n-1}s^{n-1} + \cdots + a_1 s + a_0) = 0$ are located at the left part of S-plane.

- Only if the Eigen values of Eq. $(s^2 + k_T s + rkk_{bv}M(\bullet)) = 0$ are located at the left part of S-plane (except image axis), then the system is stable. Obviously, when $k_T > 0, \quad rkk_{bv}M(\bullet) > 0$, the system (1.103) is asymptotical stable.

According to Lemma 1.2, nonlinear system (1.100) is asymptotical stable near singular point

$$\underline{X}_1^0 = \begin{bmatrix} 0 & \cdots & 0 \end{bmatrix}_{(n+2)\times 1}^{T.}.$$

Usually, it is not expected that system output $y(t)=0$ when the system is under a constant input $r(t) = r$.

2) Stability Analysis of the singular point

$$\underline{X}_2^0 = \begin{bmatrix} \dfrac{r}{b_0} & 0 & \cdots & 0 & \dfrac{a_0 r}{b_0} & \dfrac{k_{bv}}{k_T}M(\dfrac{a_0 r}{b_0}) & \dfrac{a_0 r}{b_0} \end{bmatrix}_{(n+2)\times 1}^{T}$$

Move the coordinate origin to $\underline{X}_2^0$. For that, difine:

$$\underline{\underline{X}} = \underline{X} - \underline{X}_2^0 \tag{1.107}$$

Put Eq. (1.107) into Eq.(1.99), then obtain:

$$\underline{\dot{\underline{X}}} = \begin{bmatrix} 0 & 1 & 0 & \cdots & 0 & 0 & 0 \\ 0 & 0 & 1 & \cdots & 0 & 0 & 0 \\ \vdots & \vdots & \vdots & \cdots & \vdots & \vdots & \vdots \\ 0 & 0 & 0 & \cdots & 1 & 0 & 0 \\ -a_0 & -a_1 & -a_2 & \cdots & -a_{n-1} & 1 & 0 \\ b_0^* & b_1^* & b_2^* & \cdots & b_{n-1}^* & 0 & 0 \\ 0 & 0 & 0 & \cdots & 0 & k_{bv}M(\bullet) & -k_T \end{bmatrix} \underline{\underline{X}} + \begin{bmatrix} 0 \\ \vdots \\ 0 \\ kM(\bullet)\underline{x}_{n+2}C^T\underline{\underline{X}} \\ 0 \end{bmatrix}$$

$$\tag{1.108}$$

Where

$$b_i^* = k\dfrac{k_{bv}}{k_T}M(\bullet)\dfrac{a_0 r}{b_0}b_i.$$

It is easy to see that the nonlinear term $\underline{\underline{\Theta}}$ satisfies the condition given in Eq. (1.94) (Refer to the certification in the addendum). According to Lemma 1.$\overline{2}$, 1.3 and 1.4, the stability of the singular point

$$\underline{X}_2^0 = \begin{bmatrix} \dfrac{r}{b_0} & 0 & \cdots & 0 & \dfrac{a_0 r}{b_0} & \dfrac{k_{bv}}{k_T}M(\dfrac{a_0 r}{b_0}) & \dfrac{a_0 r}{b_0} \end{bmatrix}_{(n+2)\times 1}^{T}$$

in the nonlinear system (1.101) can be analyzed indirectly by analyzing the stability of the linear system

$$\underline{\dot{X}} = \underline{A}\,\underline{X}\ .$$

Theorem 1.8 The model of the nonlinear system shown in Fig. 1.5 is Eq. (1.99). If the controlled object is stable, when the poles of the following characteristic equation

$$(s + k_T)(s^{n+1} + a_{n-1}s^n + (a_{n-2} - b_{n-1}^*)s^{n-1} + (a_{n-3} - b_{n-2}^*)s^{n-2}$$
$$+ \cdots + (a_{i-1} - b_i^*)s^i + \cdots + (a_0 - b_1^*)s - b_0^*) = 0$$

$$b_i^* = k\frac{k_{bv}}{k_T}M(\bullet)\frac{a_0 r}{b_0}b_i, \quad i = 0,1,2,\cdots n-1$$

(1.109)

are all located in the left half of S-plane, then the system is asymptotically stable on the singular point

$$\underline{X}_2^0 = \left[\frac{r}{b_0}\quad 0\quad \cdots\quad 0\quad \frac{a_0 r}{b_0}\quad \frac{k_{bv}}{k_T}M(\frac{a_0 r}{b_0})\frac{a_0 r}{b_0}\right]_{(n+2)\times 1}^T .$$

Proof: The characteristic equation of the linear system (1.108) is:

$$|(sI - \underline{A})| = \begin{vmatrix} s & -1 & 0 & \cdots & 0 & 0 & 0 \\ 0 & s & -1 & \cdots & 0 & 0 & 0 \\ \vdots & \vdots & \vdots & \cdots & \vdots & \vdots & \vdots \\ 0 & 0 & 0 & \cdots & -1 & 0 & 0 \\ a_0 & a_1 & a_2 & \cdots & s+a_{n-1} & -1 & 0 \\ -b_0^* & -b_1^* & -b_2^* & \cdots & -b_{n-1}^* & s & 0 \\ 0 & 0 & 0 & \cdots & 0 & -k_{bv}M(\bullet) & s+k_T \end{vmatrix}$$

$$= (s + k_T)\begin{vmatrix} s & -1 & 0 & \cdots & 0 & 0 \\ 0 & s & -1 & \cdots & 0 & 0 \\ \vdots & \vdots & \vdots & \cdots & \vdots & \vdots \\ 0 & 0 & 0 & \cdots & -1 & 0 \\ a_0 & a_1 & a_2 & \cdots & s+a_{n-1} & -1 \\ -b_0^* & -b_1^* & -b_2^* & \cdots & -b_{n-1}^* & s \end{vmatrix}$$

$$= s(s+k_T)\begin{vmatrix} s & -1 & 0 & \cdots & 0 \\ 0 & s & -1 & \cdots & 0 \\ \vdots & \vdots & \vdots & \cdots & \vdots \\ 0 & 0 & 0 & \cdots & -1 \\ a_0 & a_1 & a_2 & \cdots & s+a_{n-1} \end{vmatrix} + (s+k_T)\begin{vmatrix} s & -1 & 0 & \cdots & 0 \\ 0 & s & -1 & \cdots & 0 \\ \vdots & \vdots & \vdots & \cdots & \vdots \\ 0 & 0 & 0 & \cdots & -1 \\ -b_0^* & -b_1^* & -b_2^* & \cdots & -b_{n-1}^* \end{vmatrix}$$

$$= s(s + k_T)(s^n + a_{n-1}s^{n-1} + \cdots + a_1 s + a_0)$$

$$-b_{n-1}^*(s + k_T)\begin{vmatrix} s & -1 & 0 & \cdots & 0 \\ 0 & s & -1 & \cdots & 0 \\ \vdots & \vdots & \vdots & \cdots & \vdots \\ 0 & 0 & 0 & \cdots & -1 \\ 0 & 0 & 0 & \cdots & s \end{vmatrix} + (s + k_T)\begin{vmatrix} s & -1 & 0 & \cdots & 0 \\ 0 & s & -1 & \cdots & 0 \\ \vdots & \vdots & \vdots & \cdots & \vdots \\ 0 & 0 & 0 & \cdots & -1 \\ -b_0^* & -b_1^* & -b_2^* & \cdots & -b_{n-2}^* \end{vmatrix}$$

$$= (s + k_T)(s^{n+1} + a_{n-1}s^n + (a_{n-2} - b_{n-1}^*)s^{n-1} + (a_{n-3} - b_{n-2}^*)s^{n-2}$$
$$+ \cdots + (a_{i-1} - b_i^*)s^i + \cdots + (a_0 - b_1^*)s - b_0^*)$$

Where

$$b_i^* = k\frac{k_{bv}}{k_T}M(\bullet)\frac{a_0 r}{b_0}b_i, \quad i = 0, 1, 2, \cdots n-1.$$

Obviously, when the poles of the characteristic equation above are all located in the left half of S-plane, linear system (1.109) is asymptotically stable. According to Lemma 1.2, the immune control system (1.99) is asymptotically stable by the singular point in this condition:

$$\underline{X}_2^0 = \begin{bmatrix} \dfrac{r}{b_0} & 0 & \cdots & 0 & \dfrac{a_0 r}{b_0} & \dfrac{k_{bv}}{k_T}M(\dfrac{a_0 r}{b_0})\dfrac{a_0 r}{b_0} \end{bmatrix}^T_{(n+2)\times 1} .$$

According to Routh Criterion, the necessary condition of the stability of the linear system is that all the coefficients of the characteristic equation (1.110) should be greater than zero. Suppose that $a_i > 0$, $i = 0, 1, 2, \cdots n-1$, and the controlled object is stable. Consider a special condition:

$$b_i^* = k\frac{k_{bv}}{k_T}M(\bullet)\frac{a_0 r}{b_0}b_i < 0, \quad i = 0, 1, 2, \cdots n-1 \tag{1.110}$$

Then the coefficients of the polynomial:

$$s^{n+1} + a_{n-1}s^n + (a_{n-2} - b_{n-1}^*)s^{n-1} + (a_{n-3} - b_{n-2}^*)s^{n-2} + \cdots + (a_{i-1} - b_i^*)s^i + \cdots + (a_0 - b_1^*)s - b_0^* = 0 \tag{1.111}$$

could be guaranteed greater than zero. If the poles of Eq. (1.111) are all located in the left half of S-plane, it can be inferred that the immune control system (1.98) is asymptotically stable with the poles:

$$\underline{X}_2^0 = \begin{bmatrix} \dfrac{r}{b_0} & 0 & \cdots & 0 & \dfrac{a_0 r}{b_0} & \dfrac{k_{bv}}{k_T}M(\dfrac{a_0 r}{b_0})\dfrac{a_0 r}{b_0} \end{bmatrix}^T_{(n+2)\times 1} .$$

Note **Theorem 1.8**, when the immune system (1.98) satisfies $k_T > 0$, $rkk_{bv}M(\bullet) > 0$, it will be stable at $\underline{X}_1^0 = \begin{bmatrix} 0 & 0 & \cdots & 0 \end{bmatrix}_{(n+2)\times 1}^T$. When $k > 0, k_{bv} > 0$, the conditions of **Theorem 1.8** can be explained as that r and $M(\bullet)$ must have the same sign. Then consider Eq. (1.111), for $k > 0$, $k_{bv} > 0$, $k_T > 0$, $a_0 > 0$, $b_0 > 0$, if $b_i^* < 0$ is guaranteed, r and $M(\bullet)$ must have opposite signs. Accordingly, the following inference can be found:

Inference 1.1 If the immune control system (1.99) satisfies Theorem 1.8 and the parameter b_i^* satisfies Eq. (1.111), the immune control system (1.98) will be stable on the singular point

$$\underline{X}_2^0 = \begin{bmatrix} \dfrac{r}{b_0} & 0 & \cdots & 0 & \dfrac{a_0 r}{b_0} & \dfrac{k_{bv}}{k_T}M(\dfrac{a_0 r}{b_0})\dfrac{a_0 r}{b_0} \end{bmatrix}_{(n+2)\times 1}^T,$$

while its stability will not be guaranteed on the singular point $\underline{X}_2^0 = \begin{bmatrix} 0 & 0 & \cdots & 0 \end{bmatrix}_{(n+2)\times 1}^T$.

Theorem 1.9 If the singular point of the immune control system (1.98):

$$\underline{X}_2^0 = \begin{bmatrix} \dfrac{r}{b_0} & 0 & \cdots & 0 & \dfrac{a_0 r}{b_0} & \dfrac{k_{bv}}{k_T}M(\dfrac{a_0 r}{b_0})\dfrac{a_0 r}{b_0} \end{bmatrix}_{(n+2)\times 1}^T$$

is stable, the system's response to a constant control input r will be free of steady error.

Proof: The singular point of the immune control system (1.100)

$$\underline{X}_2^0 = \begin{bmatrix} \dfrac{r}{b_0} & 0 & \cdots & 0 & \dfrac{a_0 r}{b_0} & \dfrac{k_{bv}}{k_T}M(\dfrac{a_0 r}{b_0})\dfrac{a_0 r}{b_0} \end{bmatrix}_{(n+2)\times 1}^T \quad \text{is stable,}$$

When $x(t)$ is close to $\underline{X}_2^0$, we have:

$$\lim_{t \to \infty} x(t) = \begin{bmatrix} \dfrac{r}{b_0} & 0 & \cdots & 0 & \dfrac{a_0 r}{b_0} & \dfrac{k_{bv}}{k_T}M(\dfrac{a_0 r}{b_0})\dfrac{a_0 r}{b_0} \end{bmatrix}_{(n+2)\times 1}^T \tag{1.112}$$

Then there is:

$$\lim_{t \to \infty} y(t) = \underline{C}^T \begin{bmatrix} \dfrac{r}{b_0} & 0 & \cdots & 0 & \dfrac{a_0 r}{b_0} & \dfrac{k_{bv}}{k_T}M(\dfrac{a_0 r}{b_0})\dfrac{a_0 r}{b_0} \end{bmatrix}_{(n+2)\times 1}^T = r \tag{1.113}$$

The deviation is:

$$\lim_{t \to \infty} e(t) = \lim_{t \to \infty}(r - y(t)) = 0 \tag{1.114}$$

So the immune control system (1.99) has the first-order tracing character under a constant control input.

Theorem 1.10: For the nonlinear system as shown in Eq.(1.99),if it can be proved that

$$\lim_{\|\underline{X}\| \to 0} \frac{\grave{\mathbf{E}}}{\|\underline{X}\|} = \mathbf{0},$$

then it is obvious from lemma 1.2 that the zero values local exponentially asymptotic stability of the nonlinear system shown in Eq.(1.108) is determined by that of the linear system ignoring $\grave{\mathbf{E}}$.

Proof: it is known from the problem that:

$$\lim_{\|\underline{X}\| \to 0} \frac{\grave{\mathbf{E}}}{\|\underline{X}\|} = \mathbf{0}$$

which has the following equation: $\lim\limits_{\|\underline{X}\| \to 0} \dfrac{k x_{n+2} \mathbf{C}^T \mathbf{X}}{\|\mathbf{X}\|} = 0$.

Because $\underline{\mathbf{C}} \in \mathrm{R}^{n+2}$ is a constant vector, $\mathrm{k} \in \mathrm{R}$ is a constant, $\underline{\mathbf{X}} \in \mathrm{R}^n$ is a vector, there is:

1) $\|\underline{\mathbf{X}}\| \to 0$ hence there exists $\|x_i\| \to 0$

$$\because \left\{ x_1^2 + x_2^2 + \cdots + x_i^2 + \cdots x_{n+2}^2 \right\}^{\frac{1}{2}} > |x_i| > 0 \tag{1.115}$$

$$\|\underline{\mathbf{X}}\| > |x_i| > 0 \tag{1.116}$$

$\|\underline{\mathbf{X}}\| \to 0$ hence there exists $|x_i| \to 0$, i=1$\cdots$n+2

2) $|(\alpha \bullet \beta)| \le |\alpha| |\beta|$

$$0 < |c_1 x_1 + \cdots + c_{n+2} x_{n+2}| \le \sqrt{c_1^2 + \cdots c_{n+2}^2} \bullet \sqrt{x_1^2 + \cdots x_{n+2}^2} = \underline{\mathbf{C}}^T \bullet \|\underline{\mathbf{X}}\| \tag{1.117}$$

3)   if $\|\underline{\mathbf{X}}\|$ is bounded, which means $\|\underline{\mathbf{X}}\|$ changes in a limited scope, from 1 we can see that $k x_i$ is bounded, that is $|k x_n| < K'$ $K' > 0$

From 2 it can be proved that: while $\|\underline{\mathbf{X}}\| \to 0$, there must exist $|x_i| \to 0$, i=1$\cdots$n+2

$$\lim_{\|\underline{\mathbf{X}}\| \to 0} \frac{k x_{n+2} \mathbf{C}^T \mathbf{X}}{\|\underline{\mathbf{X}}\|} = 0 \tag{1.118}$$

Figure 1.17. The block diagram of the IVINM_AIC system with long time-delay

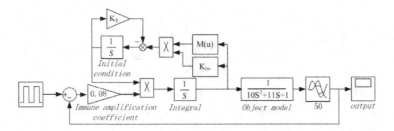

$$\lim_{\|\underline{\mathbf{X}}\| \to 0} \frac{\grave{\mathbf{E}}}{\|\underline{\mathbf{X}}\|} = \mathbf{0} \tag{1.119}$$

The proof is completed.

Theorem 1.11: For the nonlinear system as shown in Eq.(1.99), if it can be proved that

$$\lim_{\|\underline{\mathbf{X}}\| \to 0} \frac{\grave{\mathbf{E}}}{\|\underline{\mathbf{X}}\|} = \mathbf{0},$$

it is obvious from lemma 1.2 that the zero values local exponentially asymptotic stability of the nonlinear system shown in Reference 3 is determined by that of the linear system ignoring $\grave{\mathbf{E}}$.

Proof: Comparing $\underline{\grave{\mathbf{E}}}$ with $\grave{\mathbf{E}}$, we get that the differences between the two variables just exist in the equation $M(\bullet) = K_m(e^{p_1|u(t)|} - e^{p_2|u(t)|})$. While $K_m > 0$, $p_2 < p_1 < 0$, and K_m, p_1, p_2 are finite values, known from the Fig.4.2 that whatever $u(t)$ is, $K_m(e^{p_1|u(t)|} - e^{p_2|u(t)|}) < Q$ always exists, where Q is a constant. so:

$$\left| kM(\bullet)\underline{\underline{x}}_{n+2}\underline{\underline{\mathbf{C}}}^T \underline{\underline{\mathbf{X}}} \right| < \left| kQ\underline{\underline{x}}_{n+2}\underline{\underline{\mathbf{C}}}^T \underline{\underline{\mathbf{X}}} \right| \text{ comes into existence.}$$

Define $\underline{\underline{\Theta}}^* = (0 \quad \cdots \quad 0 \quad kQ\underline{\underline{x}}_{n+2}\underline{\underline{\mathbf{C}}}^T\underline{\underline{\mathbf{X}}} \quad 0)^T_{(n+2)\times 1}$, then while

$$\lim_{\|\underline{\mathbf{X}}\| \to 0} \frac{\underline{\grave{\mathbf{E}}}^*}{\|\underline{\mathbf{X}}\|} = \mathbf{0}, \text{ exists that } \lim_{\|\underline{\mathbf{X}}\| \to 0} \frac{\underline{\grave{\mathbf{E}}}}{\|\underline{\mathbf{X}}\|} = \mathbf{0}.$$

The proof is completed.

1.3.5 The simulation Results of Varela Artificial Immune Controller

In practical applications, an object with a great inertia and a long time-delay is difficult to control. Assume that the controlled object is as follow:

Figure 1.18. The simulation output curves of the great inertia and long time-delay Varela immune control system after resisting pure time delay

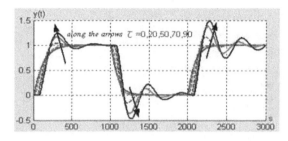

$$G_0(s) = \frac{e^{-\tau s}}{(10s+1)(s+1)} \qquad (1.120)$$

Fig.1.17 shows the block diagram based on Matlab Simulink.

Fig.1.17 shows **IVINM_AIC** parameters. The values of the pure time-delay parameters are: $\tau=0, 20, 50, 70,$ and 80. The simulation results are shown in Fig.1.18. Two points can be concluded from it: (1) the secondary response of the output is verified to be faster than the primary. If the primary response is fast enough, the oscillations and overshoot of the secondary will be more serious. (2) IVINM_AIC can maintain the stability of the system despite substantial changes in the pure time-delay parameters of the object, which is a clear evidence of IVINM_AIC's strong resistance to anti-time-delay.

1.4 The Design Principles of the Three Kinds of Artificial Immune Controllers and the General Structure of Artificial Immune Controller

A close examination of Fig. 1.4, Fig.1.11, Fig. 1.16 will reveal that this three artificial immune controllers have several common features as follows: (1) They are all nonlinear controllers, in which there are product operators; (2) They all have a feedback channel in order to coordinate the internal balances of the controllers; (3) all of the artificial immune controllers take deviations as invading antigens, and the outputs of the controllers as antibodies.

Integrating the features mentioned above, the general structure of the **artificial immune controller** is shown in Fig.1.19. The general structure of this kind of artificial immune controllers for SISO-system consists of five modules:

* Immune recognition module: It mainly realizes the recognition preprocessing for invading antigens, viz. the deviations.
* Immune assistant module: It mainly realizes the preprocessing, such as the assistant recognition calculation for invading antigens, viz. the deviations.
* Immune control module: It mainly converts immune calculation module outputs to immune antibodies via mathematic transformation ----- the control output of artificial immune controller.
* Immune monitor module: It mainly realizes the internal monitoring and control of the immune processing. It is an internal feedback control, and the control strategy could be negative-feedback control in some conditions. It can also make an instantaneous positive-feedback control in some special conditions, in order to promote or inhibit the production of antibodies.
* Immune calculation module: It mainly realizes the mathematic operations such as addition, subtraction, product, and so on.

Figure 1.19. The general structure block diagram of artificial immune controller in the system

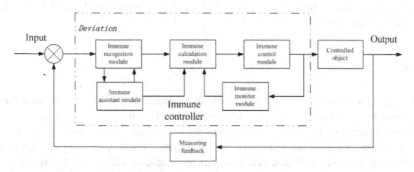

Figure 1.20. The modularized partition of general artificial immune controlers

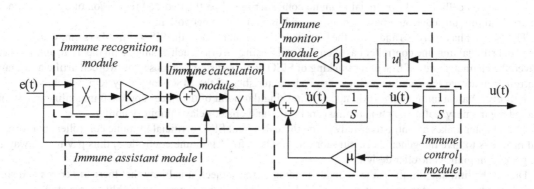

Fig.1.20 shows the details of each modularized part in the SISO artificial immune control system by using the **EDC_AIC** as an example.

FUTURE RESEARCH DIRECTION

Compared with the intelligent method such as neural networks and genetic algorithms, the study of AIS is still in a very preliminary stage, despite rapid development in Artificial Immune in recent years. The main areas that call for further in-depth study are:

1) The intensive studying about the self-adaptability and robustness of the immune controller; the effective choice and method of regulating online of immune parameters of the controller; the practical engineering application of immune controller; MIMO immune controller model and the stability, robustness, and other issues of MIMO control system.
2) Further studying immune mechanism and develop of new artificial immune model and algorithm.
3) Study and develop artificial immune controller with self-learning, self-tolerance, self-healing, recognition and memory features on the basis of the artificial immune model.
4) Proving the convergence of various immune learning algorithms and make theoretical analysis of the performance such as the learning algorithm efficiency.
5) Integrating AIS and intelligent method such as fuzzy logic, neural networks and genetic algorithms to develop new types of intelligent information processing and control system.
6) Further developping the application of AIS in other areas of science and engineering.

In short, the current application of artificial immune in the area of control is still very limited and just in the initial stage. Many problems remain to be studied and resolved. But judging from the results of the present application, it is obvious that artificial immune will have a good prospect.

CONCLUSION

Biological immune system is a complicated self-adaptive system, which can effectively and smoothly handle the disturbance and uncertainties within human body and environment. Based on the current immunization theory, a number of models and algorithms have been put forward and the concept of immunity has been introduced in many engineering study and has achieved some satisfactory results. This chapter is an attempt to improve the immune kinetic model and its controller for the system design and implementation. The following major achievements are what have been achieved.

Three different structural artificial immune controllers are designed and they are: the artificial immune controller based on cells T-B, the artificial immune controller based on the two-cell regulation of dynamic model, the artificial immune controller based on improved Varela immune network model.

This chapter has analyzed and prove the boundedness and stability of the SISO control system, which is composed of artificial immune controller based on T-B cells, using theories such as small gain theorem; analyzed and proved the characteristics of first order tracking of SISO control system composed of two-cell artificial immune controller; analyzed the stability and non-error characteristics of the SISO control system, which is based on the improved Varela immune network model, using singular point of the linear approach in nonlinear systems; studied the memory features, anti-jamming capabilities and object-delay inhibitory ability.

This chapter makes a contrastive study of the three different SISO artificial immune controllers put forward and proceeds to give the general structure for the SISO artificial immune controllers, thus paving the way for the general immune controller design.

Due to the limitation in the author's understanding of the subject, it is likely that there are errors and slips. Therefore advice and recommendations from readers, colleagues and experts are highly appreciated.

REFERENCES

Ansheng Q., & Chanying D. (Ed.) (1998). *Nonlinear Model of Immunology*. Shanghai, CN: Science and Technology Education Press Shanghai.

Dasgupta D., & Forrest S. (1999). *Artificial Immune Systems in Industrial Applications*. Paper presented at the 2nd International Conference on Intelligent Processing and Manufacturing of Materials, Honolulu.

Dongmei F., & Deling Zh. (2005). *The Analysis of Stability of Immune Control System Based on Small Gain Theorem*. Paper presented at the International Conference on Communications, Circuits and Systems, HKUST, Hong Kong, China.

Dongmei F., & Deling Zh. (2005). *Design and Analysis of a Biological Immune Controller Based on Improved Varela Immune Network Model*. Paper presented at the 2005 international Conference on Machine Learning and Cybernetics.

Dongmei F., & Deling Zh. (2006). An Anamnestic and Integral Two-cell Immune Controller and Its Characteristic Simulation. *Journal of University of Science and Technology Beijing, 27*(2), 190-193.

Dongmei F., Deling Zh., & Yaoguang W. (2006). Design,Realization and Analysis of Immune Controller Based on Two-cell Adjustment. *Information and Control, 35*(4), 526-531.

Dongmei F., Deling Zh., Yaoguang W., Ying Zh., & Lei J. (2004). Design for Biological Immune Controllers and Simulation on Its Control Feature. *Journal of University of Science and Technology Beijing, 26*(4), 442.

Dongmei F., Deling Zh., & Ying C. (2005). *Design and Simulation of a Biological Immune Controller Based on Improved Varela Immune Network Model. Artificial Immune Systems.* Paper presented at the 4th International Conference, ICARIS 2005.

Dongqiang Q., & Yaqing T. (2001). Present Situation and Future Development of Neural Network-based Control. *Journal of Automation & Instrumentation,* 27(1), 1-7.

Isidori A., Ben W., & Shengxian Zh Translation. (Ed.) (2005). *Nonlinear Control System.* Beijing, CN: Electronic Publishing Industry.

Jerne N. K. (1973). The Immune System. *Scientific American,* 229(1), 52-60.

Jerne N. K. (1974). Towards a Network Theory of the Immune System. *Annual Immuno- logy,* 125C, 373-389.

Jingzhen Zh., & Zengji H. (1997). Development of Fuzzy Control Theory and its Applications. *Journal of Technological advances,* 19(3), 156-159.

Kesheng L., Jun Zh., & Xianbing C. (2000). An Algorithm Based on Immune Principle Adopted in Controlling Behavior of Autonomous Mobile Robots. *Computer Engineering and Applications,* 36(5), 30-32.

Kim D. H. (2001). *Tuning of a PID Controller Using an Artificial Immune Network Model and Local Fuzzy Set.* Paper presented at the meeting of IEEE International Symposium on Industrial Electronics, Seoul Korea.

Kim D. H., & Lee K. Y. (2002). *Neural Networks Control by Immune Network Algorithm Based Auto-Weight Function Tuning.* Paper presented at the International Joint Conference on Neural Networks, Hawaii USA.

Kim D.W. (2002). *Parameter Tuning of Fuzzy Neural Networks by Immune Algorithm.* Paper presented at the 2002 IEEE International Conference on Fuzzy Systems, Japan.

Kim D.W. (2003). Intelligent 2-DOF PID Control for Thermal Power Plant Using Immune Based on Multiobjective. *Neural Network and Computational Intelligence, 22(2), 215-220.*

Kim D.W., & Cho J. H. (2002). *Auto-tuning of Reference Model Based PID Controller Using Immune Algorithm.* Paper presented at the meeting of Evolutionary Computation, CEC '02. Honolulu, HI, USA.

Kim D.W., & Cho J. H. (2004). *Intelligent Tuning of PID Controller with Robust Disturbance Rejection Function Using Immune Algorithm.* Paper presented at the 8th International Conference on Knowledge-Based Intelligent Information & Engineering System KES, Wellington, New Zealand.

Kim D.W., & Horg W. P. (2004). *Tuning of PID Controller of Deal Time Process Using Immune Based on Multiobjective.* Paper presented at the 8th International Conference on Knowledge-Based Intelligent Information & Engineering System KEMS, Wellington, New Zealand.

Lydyard P M., Whelan A., & M.W.Panger. (Ed.) (2001). *Instant Notes in Immunology.* Beijing, CN: Science Press (The introduction of photoprint).

Sasaki M., & Kawakuku M., & Takahashi K. (1999) *An Immune Feedback Mechanism Based Network controller.* Paper presented at the 6th IEEE International Conference on Neural Information Processing(ICONIP '99), Perth, Australia.

Sergei G., & Yuri M. (2003). A Simple Non-linear Model of Immune Response[J]. *Chaos. Solitons and Fractals,* 16 (1), 125-132.

Takahashi K., & Yamada T. (1997). *A Self-Tuning Immune Feedback Controller for Controlling Mechanical System.* Paper presented at the meeting of IEEE Advanced Intelligent Mechatronics, USA.

Takahashi K., & Yamada T. (1998). Application of an Immune Feedback Mechanism to Control Systems. *JSME International Journal, Series C*, 41(2), 184-191.

Tao L. (Ed.) (2004). *Computer Immunology.* Beijing, CN: Electronic Publishing Industry.

Tarakanov A., & Dasgupta D. (2000). A Formal Model of an Artificial Immune System. *Biosystems,* 55(8), 151-158.

Watanabe Y., Ishiguro A., Shirai Y., & Uchikawa Y. (1998). Emergent Construction of Behavior Arbitration Mechanism Based on the Immune System. Paper presented at the meeting of ICEC'98, Seoul, Korea.

Varela F.J. (1994). The Immune Learning Mechanisms: Reinforcement, Recruitment and Their Application. *Computing with Biological Metaphors,* 1(1), 37-45.

Varela F.J., & Stewart J. (1990). Dynamics of a Class of Immune Networks- I: Global Behavior. *Theory Biology,* 144(1), 93-101.

Weibing G. (Ed.) (1988). *Nonlinear Control System Introduction.* Beijing, CN: Science Press.

Yingqi X., & Jie C. (Ed.) (2002). *Nonlinear Dynamics Mathematical Methods.* Beijing, CN: Meteorological Press.

Yingzi T., Jiong S., & Zhengzhong L. (2003). A Study of the Immune Evolutionary Algorithm-based Self-tuning PID Control of Superheated Steam Temperature. *Power Engineering Department,* 18(1), 58-62.

Yongsheng D., & Lihong R. (2006). An Algorithm Based on Immune Principle Adopted in Controlling Behavior of Autonomous Mobile Robots. *Journal of Control And Decision.*

Zixing C. (Ed.) (2004) *Intelligent Control* (pp. 312-318). Beijing, CN: Electronic Publishing Industry.

Zhengshan L. (Ed.) (2003). *The Study of Non-linearity Science and its Application in the Geosciences.* Beijing, CN: Meteorological Press.

KEY TERMS

Antibody: Antibodies are protein substances produced in the blood or tissues to response to a specific antigen, such as a bacterium or a toxin. Antibodies destroy or weaken bacteria and neutralize organic poisons, thus forming the basis of immunity.

Antigen: The antigen is a substance which stimulate the person or animal body to produce sensitized antibodies or lymphocytes, these products arose specific responses in the person or animal body. Antigens include toxins, bacteria, foreign blood cells, the cells of transplanted organs and so on.

Artificial Immune Control: Artificial immune control is similar ordinary control except Artificial immune algorithm and model in it. Artificial immune control is the process to detect, control or manage the applications, such as controlled objects, production procedures, or managements, by constructing immune models or algorithms suitable for control systems through reference of measures and regulars extracted from immune mechanisms, models and the cooperation between immune factors.

Artificial Immune Models: Artificial Immune models are a kind of mathematical models which are constructed by macro-biological or micro-biological immune mechanism.

Artificial Immunity: The algorithms or dynamics models which are founded by men imitate the part or all of the biological immune mechanism to gain some special features or peculiar functions. Those algorithms or the dynamics models are usually known as the artificial immunity.

Immune Controller: Immune controller is a man-made controller that based on measures and regulars of macro immune mechanisms, models or micro cooperation between immune factors to improve the performance of a control system. Immune controllers mostly are nonlinear dynamic models or algorithms with iteration process. Artificial immune controller is similar ordinary controller except immune algorithm and model in it.

Immune Factor: The immune factors are a sort of small molecule polypeptide which mainly were secreted the biological activity immunocyte, such as transfer factor, distinguishing factor and so on. Immune factors mainly make regulative roles in the immune recognition and immune responses.

Chapter XIV
Immune Programming Applications in Image Segmentation

Xiaojun Bi
Harbin Engineering University, P.R. China

ABSTRACT

In fact, image segmentation can be regarded as a constrained optimization problem, and a series of optimization strategies can be used to complete the task of image segmentation. Traditional evolutionary algorithm represented by Genetic Algorithm is an efficient approach for image segmentation, but in the practical application, there are many problems such as the slow convergence speed of evolutionary algorithm and premature convergence, which have greatly constrained the application. The goal of introducing immunity into the existing intelligent algorithms is to utilize some characteristics and knowledge in the pending problems for restraining the degenerative phenomena during evolution so as to improve the algorithmic efficiency. Theoretical analysis and experimental results show that immune programming outperforms the existing optimization algorithms in global convergence speed and is conducive to alleviating the degeneration phenomenon. Theoretical analysis and experimental results show that immune programming has better global optimization and outperforms the existing optimization algorithms in alleviating the degeneration phenomenon. It is a feasible and effective method of image segmentation.

INTRODUCTION

Based on the research of the characteristics mechanism of Artificial Immune System (AIS), the feasibility of applying Immune Programming (IP) into the digital image processing is further discussed. The IP mechanism is successfully used into **image segmentation**, and the image threshold segmentation algorithm based on the maximum information entropy theory and the **image segmentation** algorithm based on the **expense function** minimization are proposed in this paper, At the same time give out definite algorithm design and operation steps. We also do simulation experiment both on image threshold segmentation based on the maximum entropy

Copyright © 2009, IGI Global, distributing in print or electronic forms without written permission of IGI Global is prohibited.

theory and **image segmentation** based on cost function minimization, and compare them with classical genetic algorithm, analysis and summarize the segmentation result and experiment data.

The structure of the chapter is organized as follows: **Backgrounds and Previous Research Work** provides a detailed review and a background of the existing methods of image segmentation, as well as the main challenges for these methods and the advantages of IP. The Main Thrust of the Chapter consists of two parts: firstly, the image threshold segmentation based on the **maximum entropy** theory is introduced, and the advantages and disadvantages of this method are demonstrated by several groups experiment; in the second part, the **image segmentation** based on cost function minimization is introduced, and simulation experiment results is given . **Concluding Remarks** concludes the whole chapter with the special emphasis on: The IP mechanism is successfully introduced into **image segmentation**, and the image threshold segmentation algorithm based on the maximum information entropy theory and the image segmentation algorithm based on the **expense function** minimization are proposed in this paper. This method is fit for not only the images with double-peak-shaped histogram, but also those of complicated-shaped histogram. finally, the future directions are addressed in **Future Research Directions**. The terms and definitions, as well as an additional reading list, can be found at the end of the chapter.

BACKGROUNDS AND PREVIOUS RESEARCH WORK

Image segmentation is a technical process which can divide an image into regions with certain and special characteristics and extract the objectives interested from them. Classic image segmentation is to construct a differential operator that is sensitive to pixel gray-level's step changing, such as Laplace operator, Roberts gradient operator, Sobel gradient operator, etc.

The speed of edge detection based on operators is high, but the results obtained are always intermittent and incomplete information. And this kind of methods is sensitive to noises, so the influence of edge feature from noises is great. For the image with significant double peak and comparative deep valley-bottom histogram, the acceptable segmentation can be got with traditional evolutionary algorithm quickly. Contrarily for the image without such features, in the complex cases such as the target and background are multi or close gray levels, or the gray histogram is multi-peak or single peak but no main valley-bottom, traditional evolutionary algorithm is easy to get into the local optimum, and can not get acceptable segmentation.

Immune Programming (IP) combining immune mechanism and evolution mechanism, is a novel idea of utilizing Artificial Immune System (AIS) into engineering application. As a global optimization algorithm with strong robustness, immune programming absorbs the advantage of genetic algorithm——parallel searching. It can construct immune operator by utilizing local characteristic information. By vaccinating and immune selecting, it can intervene the parallel global searching with certain intensity, and effectively restrain the degenerative phenomena in the existing evolution algorithms. The constructed algorithm shows wonderful global convergence capability, and keeps certain individual **diversity** under the guiding of the **affinity**, which helps to avoid premature convergence and greatly improve the algorithm global performance. The more complex the problems to be settled , the more superior that IP will show. However, complexity and great computation is two characteristics that image segmentation originally have, which can make the advantages of IP be fully used in **image segmentation**. Hence, more accurate segmentation results can be got by IP than other evolutionary algorithms.

Based on the research of the characteristics mechanism of AIS, the feasibility of applying IP into the digital image processing is further discussed in this paper. The IP mechanism is successfully used into **image segmentation**, and the image threshold segmentation algorithm based on the maximum information entropy theory and the image segmentation algorithm based on the **expense function** minimization are proposed in this paper. This algorithm is fit for not only the images with double-peak-shaped histogram, but also those of complicated-shaped histogram. Theoretical analysis and experimental results show that immune programming has better global optimization and outperforms the existing optimization algorithms in alleviating the degeneration phenomenon. It is a feasible and effective method of image segmentation.

Image Threshold Segmentation Based on the Maximum Entropy Theory

The difficulty of gray-level image threshold segmentation is how to choose the threshold. Because of complexity and great computation of the image itself, the present heuristic search algorithms are all have the disadvantages of low processing speed and easy to get immature convergence more or less. Therefore, IP is considered to be applied in the threshold choosing of **image segmentation**. By combining with the entropy of quantified grey image, an image threshold segmentation algorithm based on the **maximum entropy** was proposed. The implementing processes are as follows:

(1) Breaking Antigen and Coding Mode

Image can be regarded as breaking **antigen** set $x = \{x_1, x_2, ..., x_n\}$, where the whole image is represented by x, and the image regions for segmentation is represented by x_i (1, 2, ..., n). The optimal threshold by IP can be regarded as **antibody** that immune system produced correspondingly to the breaking **antigens** x_i. In image threshold segmentation, when calculate the **affinity** using binary coding, the segmentation threshold needs to be decoded and changed into decimal data, which results in the prolonging of running time. In order to save storage space and improve algorithm efficiency, decimal coding scheme is used in segmentation threshold in the proposed algorithm.

(2) Initialization

Setting parameters: the population size is $n = 10$; the maximum iteration number is $Gen_{max} = 50$; and k=0. Initializing **antibody** population means randomly generating 10 integers between 0-255 as an initial **antibody** population.

(3) Vaccine Extraction

In this paper, automatic method is used in vaccine extraction which is proposed in 3.3.3, that is, the effective information is extracted from the best individual gene of every generation to make vaccine.

(4) Suspend Judgment

The constrain of suspend judgment, which is defined in proposed algorithm, is whether the generations achieve the maximum. If so, suspend, and output the optimal segmentation threshold; otherwise, turn to step (5).

(5) Fitness Calculation

Here, we choose the maximum function as the fitness function.

(6) Operating on the Genetic Operator of Antibody Population

a. adaptive suppression and promote selection operator based on individual density The regulation mechanism of biological immune system is taken based on the individual density: the higher individual density is, the lower probability of genetic operator is chosen. The individual density C_i is defined as:

C_i =the number of individual i in solution population/size of solution population　　**(1)**

Calculate the density of every individual and use selection operator to regulate individual promotion and suppression. The selection probability (p) is decided by the fitness probability (p_f) and density probability (p_d), that is

$$p = p_f \cdot p_d \tag{2}$$

p_f= fitness of individual i in solution population/ sum fitness of all individuals in solution population

$$p_d = \exp\left(- \hat{a} \cdot C_i\right)\!/\acute{a} \quad (\acute{a}, \hat{a} \text{ are constants, in this paper the value is 1})$$

From (2) we can see that: on the basis of traditional fitness selection operator, regulate probability factor based on density is added into the proposed selection operator, that is immune regulation mechanism is introduced. Thus, the greater individual fitness is, the greater the selection probability is (Promotion); the greater individual density is, the lower selection probability is (Suppression). By this way, the algorithm not only remains the individuals with high fitness, but also ensures the **diversity** of individual in population and avoids premature phenomena.

b. Crossover operator
Decimal-coded is used in optimizing parameters in the proposed algorithm, so redefining the crossover operator and mutation operator is necessary. Crossover operator is defined as

$$\begin{cases} x' = x + r(x - y) \\ y' = y + (1 - r)(x - y) \end{cases} \tag{3}$$

where, r is a random number between [0, 1]. If the value of x' or y' goes beyond the range of the image gray level, a new random number will be produced and x' and y' will be calculated again till it meets the requirement.

c. Mutation operator
Most of the present mutation operators is based on the mutation of random number, and individual fitness information is not introduced. Therefore, a new adaptive mutation operator is used in this paper, which makes the variation extent of individual is proportional to the difference between the optimal individual and that in father generation. That is, mutation operator is defined as

$$x' = x + r(x_{max} - x) \tag{4}$$

where, x_{max} is the one who has the optimal fitness of father generation (optimal individual); r is a random number between [0, 1]. New individual x' has the same feasibility conditions with crossover operator.

(7) Immune Operating

Immune operating is implemented according to the steps shown in this paper and the simulated annealing used in this paper is geometric annealing scheme. Although it can't strictly guarantee gradual converge to global optimal solution as the algorithm annealing scheme does, it can be proved that its convergent speed is much faster and it can get quite good solution.

(8) Population updating. Set $k = k + 1$, then turn to step(4)

Table 1.The optimal segmentation threshold of the ten independent experiments

	1	2	3	4	5	6	7	8	9	10	Mean value	Best solution
(a)	171	173	173	175	172	173	172	174	173	173	173.1	173
(b)	122	124	121	122	122	123	121	122	124	122	122.3	122
(c)	83	83	85	82	83	81	81	83	82	84	82.7	83
(d)	168	191	168	166	166	190	168	168	169	167	168.1	168

The simulation experiments of the **maximum entropy** threshold segmentation based on IP and quantization image gray-level histogram were taken below. Ten times independent experiments are taken on the image for processing, the results of which are shown as table 1.

The segmentation results based on optimal segmentation threshold are shown in table 1. From the image for segmentation, it is shown that there are too many object regions of the original image and in some of them the contrast gradient is weak. From the segmentation results, it is shown that the details are kept perfectly by the algorithm, the object region is got precisely, and the result has good object shape and clear edge. The searching speed of the method is high, and there aren't any differences between the results after 20 times and 50 times.

Another analysis is taken from the gray-level histogram. The histogram of fig.2 is a multi-peak-shaped histogram without obvious valley-bottom; the histogram of fig.3 is double-peak-shaped but the valley-bottom is too mild; the histograms of fig.4 and fig.5 are one-peak-shaped. But the image for the general segmentation is asked to be obviously double-peak-shaped, otherwise the result is not acceptable.

The image threshold segmentation algorithm based on IP can search the suitable threshold. Moreover, the algorithm has good compatibility. It can be used in the images with not only double-peak-shaped histogram but also complex shaped histogram.

To confirm the high effectiveness of immune programming in image threshold **Image segmentation** application, a comparison has been carried between immune programming algorithm and the classic genetic algorithm. A kind of threshold segmentation algorithm based on the classic genetic algorithm is designed correspondingly. The segmentation threshold is set as 8-bit binary coding. The size of population is n=10. Mutation probability is set as $P_m=0.08$. Selection probability is set as $P_c=0.7$. And the fitness function is chosen as follows:

$$f(M) = W_1(M) \cdot W_2(M) \cdot [U_1(M) - U_2(M)]^2 \qquad (5)$$

where, $W_1(M)$ is the pixel amount of the object image, and $W_2(M)$ is the pixel amount of the background image; $U_1(M)$ is the mean gray-level of all the pixels in the object image, and $U_2(M)$ is the mean gray-level of all the pixels in the background image.

In the experiments, the immune programming algorithm and classic genetic algorithm is used separately in the Lena image and cameraman **image segmentation**. With the same generations of genetic algorithm and immune programming algorithm, the optimal segmentation threshold got from the genetic algorithm is worse. So, the generations of genetic algorithm is set to 100, while the generations of immune programming algorithm is set to 50. The changing process of the optimal solution and the population mean value is shown as fig.6. The segmentation results are shown as fig.7 and fig.8, and the gray histograms of corresponding primitive images are shown as fig.9 and fig.10.

Considering the segmentation effect, the immune programming retains the image detail perfectly, and segments the object more precisely. However classical genetic algorithm exists over-segmentation phenomenon (such as the lawn in cameraman image).The precision of optimal segmentation threshold is inferior to the immune programming. In the search processing, the optional segmentation threshold which the genetic algorithm obtains every time fluctuates more seriously, but comparing with genetic algorithm, the optimal segmentation threshold is stable. While it obtains satisfaction segmentation threshold, the iteration number which immune programming needs is the smallest. That is, both stability and convergence of the immune programming are better than the genetic algorithm. Comparing the experimental results□we can find that it is effectively to obtain the optimal segmentation threshold using immune programming .

Image Segmentation Based on Cost Function Minimization

In the processing of image threshold segmentation based on cost function minimization, for the image to be segment, firstly it is necessary to strengthen the **diversity**, to threshold and mark the connected component. Then, it

Figure 1. The results of the maximum entropy threshold segmentation based on immune programming and quantification gray-level histogram

(a) the original image

(b) the segmentation result.
©2008 Xijun Bi. Used with permission.

(c) the original image

(d) the segmentation result.
©2008 Xijun Bi. Used with permission.

(e) the original image

(f) the segmentation result.
©2008 Xijun Bi. Used with permission.

continued on following page

Figure 1. continued

(g) the original image

(h) the segmentation result.
©2008 Xijun Bi. Used with permission.

Figure 2. The gray histogram of image (a). ©2008 Xijun Bi. Used with permission.

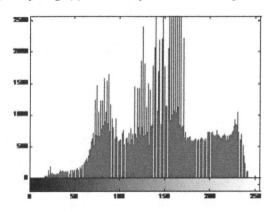

Figure 3. The gray histogram of image (c). ©2008 Xijun Bi. Used with permission.

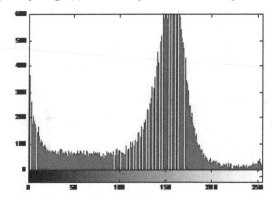

Figure 4. The gray histogram of image (e). ©2008 Xijun Bi. Used with permission.

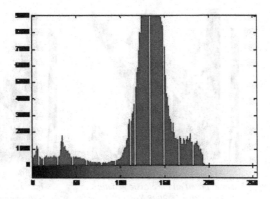

Fig.5. the gray histogram of image (g). ©2008 Xijun Bi. Used with permission.

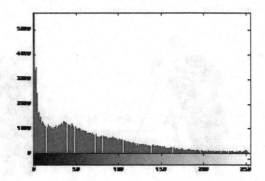

Figure 6. The changing process of the optimal solution and population mean value

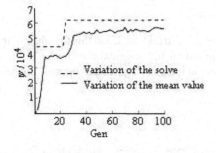

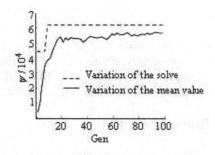

(a) Classic genetic algorithm

(b) Immune programming

311

Figure 7. The threshold segmentation result of image Lena

(a)The original Lina image

(b) the threshold segmentation result based on the classic genetic algorithm. ©2008 Xijun Bi. Used with permission.

(c) the threshold segmentation result based on immune programming algorithm. ©2008 Xijun Bi. Used with permission.

Figure 8. The threshold segmentation result of image Cameraman

(a)The original image

(b) the threshold segmentation result based on the classic genetic algorithm. ©2008 Xijun Bi. Used with permission.

(c) the threshold segmentation result based on immune programming algorithm. ©2008 Xijun Bi. Used with permission.

is naturally to obtain the initial segmentation image and it's marginal distribution. Upon this foundation, the cost function can be designed by weighting regional distribution information and marginal distribution information, and optimized using immune programming. That is, the final region image is regarded as optimal image which is satisfied constraints produced by the cost factor of all images.

Diversity Enhancement

The basic characteristic of pixels on edge of image is that it can separate the regions which are different. In the processing of **diversity** enhancement, this characteristic will be strengthened, that is, the pixels which have the above characteristic will be wighted greater. In the image $D = \{d(i,j) | 1 \le i \le M, 1 \le j \le N\}$ enhanced using **diversity** enhancement, every pixel value is proportion to the region **diversity**. The value scope of pixel is limited in the region $0 \le d(i,j) \le 1$, where, the pixels closed to 1 can be considered as candidate point. The implementing processes are as follows:Initialing all pixels $d(i,j)$ as zero;Executing step(1)and(2)for each pixels

Figure 9. The grey histogram of Lena image. ©2008 Xijun Bi. Used with permission.

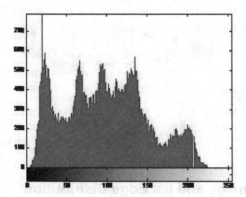

Figure 10. The grey histogram of Cameraman image. ©2008 Xijun Bi. Used with permission.

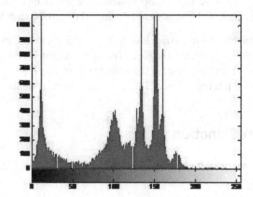

(1) Shown as image 2.1, regarding pixel (i, j) as the center, interpolating 12 edge structure in the fundamental set separately, calculating the differences of average grey-level $f(R_1, R_2)$ between region R_1 and R_2, which are in every interpolate edge structure, choosing the egde structure with maximum of $f(R_1, R_2)$ as optimal interpolate edge structure, where, 3 edge pixels are recorded as $(i, j) \square (i_1, j_1) \square (i_2, j_2)$ respectively.

(2) changing the position of the optimal edge structure and carrying on the non-maximum suppression. It's direction is decided by the edge structure. for horizontal, vertical and diagonally edge structure, moving an edge in the direction vertical to edge; for other edge structure, moving an edge in the top, bottom, left and right respectively. For every edge structure that has moved, determining the new region of R_1 and R_2, and calculating the corresponding $f(R_1, R_2)$. If $f(R_1, R_2)$ that has moved already is not bigger than the original value, then sets $d = f(R_1, R_2)/3 \square d(i, j) \square d(i_1, j_1) \square d(i_2, j_2)$ all increase δ, Otherwise, $d(i, j) \square d(i_1, j_1) \square d(i_2, j_2)$ maintain invariable.

(3) Finally, compressing all the value of $d(i, j)$ to the maximum, which will be 1, to ensure that the range of **diversity** is limited to [0,1] in the image D.

Figure 11. Edge structure in fundamental set (bright and dark shadow region represent R_1 and R_2 separately)

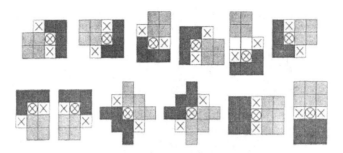

The Initial Segmentation Image and It's Edge Distribution

The binary image is obtained from image D based on iterative threshold method, while image D is an enhancement image which is obtained by deversity enhancement. The pixels in binary image are belonging to objective or background. Using the connected component labeling, the membership labeling matrix L of Initial

segmentation image is got, where, each element $L(i, j)$ denotes the region label of pixel (i, j). At last, scan the segmentation image by raster from the first pixel of the objective. If the region label of the current pixel is different from the 4 neighborhoods, then, the current pixel is the edge pixel, or else it's not. It is easy to get the initial edge distributive matrix B by this edge tracing method. In the matrix, where 1 denotes the edge pixel, 0 denotes the non-edge pixel (the inside pixel).

The Evaluation of Expense Function

The whole **expense function** of the segmentation image was consisted of the information of region distribution and edge distribution, it is defined as

Figure 12. The moving direction which was suppressed by non maximum

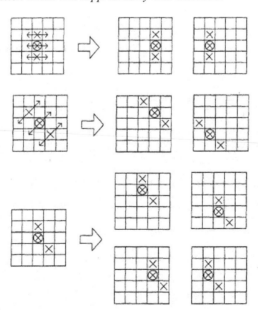

$$F = w_1 \sum_{1}^{n_R} \sigma_i^2 + w_2 F_e \tag{6}$$

σ_i^2 is the gray variance of region i, n_R is the number of the segmentation regions, so the **expense function** of the region distribution is the summation of the gray variance of all the regions. And the F_e is the **expense function** of the edge distribution. At each pixel (i, j), $F_e(i, j)$ is defined as the weighted sums of following expense factors

(1) C_d: an expense factor based on the dissimilarity of local region. The significance of the factor is to place the edge pixel at the position of which the dissimilarity is great, simultaneously the pixel position at where the gray variance is less is punished. If pixel (i, j) is a edge pixel, $C_d(i, j) = 0$, or else $C_d(i, j) = d(i, j)$.

(2) C_t: an expense factor based on the thickness of the edge. This factor would penalize the pixel which produce rough edge, at the same time□put a premium on the pixel which bring thin edge. if pixel (i, j) is rough edge pixel, $C_t(i,j) = 1$ □or $C_t(i,j) = 0$ □

(3) C_c: an expense factor based on the curvature of the edge. This factor can smooth the edge and wipe off the kinks. It will be gotten by reviewing the local edge structure of the edge pixel (at lest, there are two neighborhood edge pixel) which is not an extreme point. And if the turnover angle of the structure, which is produced by a couple of neighborhood edge pixels around edge pixel (i, j), exceeds 45°, $C_c(i,j) = 1$; in the event that the turnover angle amounts to 45°, $C_c(i,j) = 0.5$; if the angle is 0°, $C_c(i,j) = 0$.

(4) C_f: an expense factor based on the fragment of the edge. This factor can connect or wipe off the edge. If there are no neighborhood edge pixels around the edge pixel (i, j), $C_f(i,j) = 1$; if there is only one, $C_f(i,j) = 0.5$; in other conditions, $C_f(i,j) = 0$

(5) C_e: an expense factor based on the number of the edge pixels. C_d encourages the edge pixel whose $f(R_1, R_2)$ is unequal to zero, leading that too much edge pixels would be detected, and C_e can control this trend. If there is an edge pixel at (i, j), then $C_e(i,j) = 1$, otherwise $C_e(i,j) = 0$.

Expense factors should be seen as different demands settling for the usual conflicts in a final regional image, so the final regional image is the best one to fit all the constraints brought by the expense factors, namely, it is a constrained optimization problem. At each pixel position the point **expense function** is expressed as

$$F(i, j) = \sum_i w_i C_i, \quad i \in \{d, t, c, f, e\} \tag{7}$$

w_i is the weighting coefficient corresponding to each expense factor, a heuristic method should be used to choose w_i, commonly suppose $w_d = 2$, $w_e = 1$, $w_c = \{0.25, 0.50, 0.75\}$, $w_f = \{2, 3, 4\}$.

Well then the **expense function** of an image which is a $M \times N$ view picture is

$$F_e = \sum_{i=1}^{M} \sum_{j=1}^{N} F_e(i,j) \tag{8}$$

Minimization of Expense Function

We will introduce an immunization program to optimize the expense function, the implementary process are **as** follows:

1.   Chromosome Code And Fitness Evaluation

In the colony each individual's chromosome will be expressed as two dimensional matrixes, viz. the labeling matrix of membership degree of the initial segmented image L which is coded in integer and the edge distribution matrix B which is coded in binary. The fitness function of the individual can be showed as

$$f_i = (F_w - F_i)^2 \tag{9}$$

F_w denotes the worst individual expense of the current population, F_i is the *ith* individual expense.

2.   Select Operator

Combining the expectation with the elitist strategy as a parent select operator. Concretely, the expectation method is divided into two steps:

a.   If all individual fitnesses are f, $i = 1,2,\cdots N$, then the times that individual i is chosen as follow:

$$K = \text{int}[Q] + k \tag{10}$$

$$Q = N \times f_i / \sum_{j=1}^{N} f_j \tag{11}$$

If the fractional part of Q is larger than the appearance probability which is gotten by Benouli experiment later, $k = 1$, or else $k = 0$.Through the repeatedly individual experiment thus, until we get N parent individuals. And this is obviously that the larger the integer and fractional part of Q is, the more times the individual would be chose.

b.   chose the individuals which has been chose as the parent individual, then set the times of the individual as 1□

3.   Crossover Operator

Adopting the 2D window crossover operator to retain the space structure of the image. We choose the windows in the same size in the matrix L of the parent generation, interchange the windows, and then we will create the matrix L of filial generation. In order to improve the precision, we divide the image into small blocks, and then set the position and size of the square window randomly in the blocks, finally exchange the windows. The matrix B of filial generation will be gotten from L by the fringe tracking method as above.

4.   Mutation Operator

This mutation operation is dead against edge pixels only, the specific methods are as follows: With the raster scanning, the matrix L of filial generation will be scanned from top to bottom , and from right to left ,and we choose one pixel q of the 8 neighbourhood regions around the current edge pixel p,if the regional membership labels of p and q are different, replace the label of p by q's, also update the edge distribution of 4 neighborhood regions, and then scan the next pixel.

5.   Vaccine Inoculation

Vaccine inoculation is a mutation operation based on the knowledge direction of the problem, and it shows a search of the solution space which is local or insatiable. The concrete practice is as follow: Divide the matrix L of the best individual into small blocks, the square window said above will be used as a vaccine to inject several individuals which are at the top of the colony whose fitness is largest. There is an adaptive parameter p_1 in this operation, it shows the percentage of the individuals choosing vaccination. With the increase of the algebra, p_1 increases by degrees, till $p_1 =1$.

The simulation results of the image region segmentation based on the minimization of expense function are showed as follow:

A 256 gray level image which is 162×242 is chosen, the segmentation result is showed in fig.13. The content effect will be gotten in the 80th generation. The segmentation of the image will be translated into the minimization of expense function, and the available message which is gotten from the gene of the best individual will be turned adaptively to the immune vaccine, and in the vaccine inoculation, we quote another auto-adaptive parameter to shows the percentage of the individuals choosing vaccination. The whole performance of the algorithm will be improved.

The experimental results above indicate that the segmentation based on the minimization of expense function is feasible and effective. We can get the segmentation image with better edge structure.

FUTURE RESEARCH DIRECTIONS

Image segmentation is a problem which has long history and wide application prospect. In this paper **image segmentation** has been translated into a problem of optimization with constraints, we designed two optimization object functions in two different criterions, and immune programming was chosen to achieve optimization. The summation of entropy of the object and background which are segmented was defined as a objective function by the **image segmentation** based on the **maximum entropy** theory, and the weighted sums of the region distribution and edge distribution of the image which is segmented initially are defined as a objective function, and the solution we got was the global optimal solution corresponding to the objective function under the constrained conditions. The performance of immune programming was more excellent when the problem was more complicated, the complexity and heavy computation of the **image segmentation** brought the immune programming into full play.

This paper has done many researching and simulating works on immune programming applications in **image segmentation**, but it still needs further researchs on aspects as follow:

(1)   For the image that its background gray has significant change, if only one fixed global threshold is used to segment the whole image, all the situation of image would not be considered and it must influence the segmentation effect. Multi-threshold segmentation should be used to solve this problem, but with raising of segmentation threshold, the searching space of optimization parameter will extend quickly. The **diversity** and the selectivity of population are not easy to achieve simultaneously, strong selectivity must cause premature convergence, and weak selectivity must cause the bad search efficiency. How to give attention to both of them is the difficulty that evolutionary algorithms need to solve.

(2)   The designing of fitness function is one of most important aspects of imune .programming. How to design excellent fitness function and the perfect evaluation theory for fitness function is worth to research. In

Figure 13. The segmentation result based on the minimization expense function

(a)The original image

(b) the segmentation result with 20 generations. ©2008 Xijun Bi. Used with permission.

(c) the segmentation result with 50 generations. ©2008 Xijun Bi. Used with permission.

(d) the segmentation result with 100 generations. ©2008 Xijun Bi. Used with permission.

threshold segmentation processing, the evaluation function of **image segmentation** is used as the fitness function usually. The propose of evaluatation is to guide, improve and raise the segmentation result. Although a lot researches on **image segmentation** have done, there is not a perfect evaluation standard at present. So, there are many works to do on how to relate evaluation with applications of **image segmentation**.

(3)   For the different regions in an image, such as target region and background region, the pixels in the same region have the strong uniformity and the relevance on the position and the gray-level. However, the image segmentation proposed in this paper only explores the information of gray-level provided by histogram, but neglects the details of space information. When the completely different two pictures have the same histogram, even if their peak-valley are obvious, the image segmentation proposed in this paper also can not assure the reasonable threshold.

REFERENCES

Bersini H., & Varela F. J. (1990). Hints for adaptive problem solving gleaned from immune networks. *Parallel Problem Solving from Nature. Springer-Verlag,* 343-354

Gao, F., (2000). Optimal design of piezo-electric actuators for plate vibroacoustic control using genetic algorithms with immune diversity. *Smart Materials and Structures, 8,* 485-491

Gao Xiujuan, M. (2005). *The theories, methods and applications of image segmentation.* Master's thesis, Jilin University, Changchun.

Han, S., & Wang, L. (2002). A survey of thresholding methods for image segmentation. Systems Engineering and Electronics, 24(6), 91-102

Huo, F. M. (2004). *Optimal problems research based on artificial immune algorithm.* Master's thesis ,Daqing Petroleum Institute, Daqing.

Mori, K., Tsukiyama, M., & Fukuda, T. (1998). Adaptive scheduling system inspired by immune system. *1998 IEEE International Conference on System, Man and Cybernetics, 4, 3833-3837, Oct 11-14, San Diego, California, USA,* .

Takahashi, K., & Yamada, T. (1997). A self-tuning immune feedback controller for controlling mechanism systems. *IEEE/ASME International Conference on Advanced Intelligent Mechatronics'97, June 16-20, Tokyo, Japan,* 101-104

Kapur, J. N., Sahoo, P. K., & Wong, A. K. C. (1985). A new method of gray level picture thresholding using the entropy of the histogram. *Computer Vision, Graphics and Image Processing, 29(2),* 273-285

Li, Y. D. (2002). *Hybrid intelligent computing techniques and its application.* Doctoral dissertation, Xidian University, Xi'an.

Luo, X. D. (2002). *The research on artificial immune genetic learning algorithm and its application in engineering.* Doctoral dissertation, Zhejiang University, Hangzhou.

Toma, N., Endoh, S., & Yamada, K. (1999). Immune algorithm with immune network and MHC for adaptive problem solving. *Fourth International Symposium Autonomous Decentralized Systems, 4,* 271-276. March 21-23, Tokyo, Japan.

Endoh, S., Toma, N., & Yamada, K. (1998). Immune algorithm for n-TSP. *1998 IEEE International Conference on System, Man and Cybernetics, 4,* 3844-3849. Oct 11-14, San Diego, California, USA.

Huang, S. (1999). Enhancement of thermal unit commitment using immune algorithms based optimization approaches. *Electrical Power and Energy Systems, 21,* 245-252.

Huang, S. (2000). An immune-based optimization method to capacitor placement in a radial distribution system. *IEEE Transaction on Power Delivery, 15(2),* 744-749.

Huang, S. (2000). An immune-based optimization method to capacitor placement in a radial distribution system. *IEEE Transaction on Power Delivery, 5(2),*744-749.

Stewart, J., & Varela, F. J. (1990). Dynamics of a class of immune networks. Oscillatory activity of cellular and humeral component. *Theo. Biol., 144,* 103-115.

Sun, Y. D. (2004). *The research on model, algorithm and application of artificial immune system.* Doctoral dissertation, Zhejiang University, Hangzhou.

Varela, F. J., & Stewart, J. (1990). Dynamics of a class of immune networks. *Global behavior. Theo. Biol., 144,* 93-101.

Varela, F. J., & Stewart, J.(1990). Dynamics of a class of immune networks. *Global behavior. Theo. Biol., 1(144),* 93-101.

Wang Lei, D. (2004). *Immne evolutionary computation and its application.* Doctoral dissertation, Xidian University, Xi'an.

Wang, L., Pan, J. & Jiao, L. (2000). The immune algorithm. *ACTA Electronica Sinica, 28*(7),74-78

Zhang, L. M. (2004). *The research and application on artificial immune system.* Master's thesis, Nanjing University of Technology, Nanjing.

Zhou, F., & Deng, L. (2004). *Compatison of immune algorithm with genetic algorithm* (Tech. Rep. No. 6). Danjiangkou, Hubei: Yunyang Teachers College.

Zhou, Q. M. (2005). *The research on aritificial immune system theory and immune clone optimization algorithm.* Master's thesis, Hunan University, Changsha.

KEY TERMS

Antigen (Ag): Ag is the problem to be optimized.

Antibody (Ab): Ab is the candidate solutions of the problem to be optimized.

Fitness (affinity): For conventional evolutionary algorithms, ranking and fitness assignment are only based on the information from the objective space.

Diversity: For a population-based GA, diverity is maintianed through the mutation and an adequate population size; obviously, the population size is problem-contingent.

Image Segmentation: Image segmentation is a technical process which can divide an image into regions with certain and special characteristics and extract the objectives interested from them. Classic image segmentation is to construct a differential operator that is sensitive to pixel gray-level's step changing, such as Laplace operator, Roberts gradient operator, Sobel gradient operator, etc.

Immune Programming: Immune Programming (IP) combining immune mechanism and evolution mechanism, is a novel idea of utilizing Artificial Immune System (AIS) into engineering application. As a global optimization algorithm with strong robustness, immune programming absorbs the advantage of genetic algorithm——parallel searching. It can construct immune operator by utilizing local characteristic information. By vaccinating and immune selecting, it can intervene the parallel global searching with certain intensity, and effectively restrain the degenerative phenomena in the existing evolution algorithms.

Maximum entropy: Digital image consists of pixels, in which the pixels that are different intensity belong to different regions. Sequentially, different shapes are displayed, while different shapes contains of different entropy. Therefore, image entropy can describe shape. For a $M \times M$ image, assume that image intensity is nonnegative, that is $f(i, j) \geq 0$, then we define image entropy H_f as follow:

$$H_f = -\sum_{i=1}^{M}\sum_{i=1}^{M} p_{i,j} \log p_{i,j}, \text{where, } p_{i,j} = f(i, j) \bigg/ \sum_{i=1}^{M}\sum_{j=1}^{M} f(i, j)$$

When an image has the equivalent probability of every intensity, the uncertainty of shape in image will reach its max, that is, the image contains the maximum entropy.

Expense Function: The expense function of the segmentation image is consisted of the information of region distribution and edge distribution, it is defined as:

$$F = w_1 \sum_{1}^{n_R} \sigma_i^2 + w_2 F_e$$

Where, σ_i^2 is the gray variance of region i, n_R is the number of the segmentation regions, so the expense function of the region distribution is the summation of the gray variance of all the regions. And the F_e is the expense function of the edge distribution. At each pixel (i, j), $F_e(i, j)$ is defined as the weighted sums.

Chapter XV
A Hardware Immune System for MC8051 IP Core

Xin Wang
University of Science and Technology of China, China

Wenjian Luo
University of Science and Technology of China, China

Zhifang Li
University of Science and Technology of China, China

Xufa Wang
University of Science and Technology of China, China

ABSTRACT

A hardware immune system for the error detection of MC8051 IP core is designed in this chapter. The binary string to be detected by the hardware immune system is made from the concatenation of the PC values in two sequential machine cycles of the MC8051. When invalid PC transitions occurred in the MC8051, the alarm signal of the hardware immune system can be activated by the detector set. The hardware immune system designed in this chapter is implemented and tested on an FPGA development board, and the result is given in waveforms of the implemented circuits. The disadvantages and future works about the system are also discussed.

INTRODUCTION

Hardware Immune System (HwIS) is a novel branch of Artificial Immune Systems (AIS) (Castro & Timmis, 2002; Dasgupta, 2006). Inspired by mechanisms in the biological immune system, the hardware immune system is proposed as an approach to hardware fault tolerance (Bradley & Tyrrell, 2002b). Some immunological theories have been adopted to develop new technologies for hardware error detection.

Negative Selection Algorithm (NSA) proposed by Forrest and her colleagues (Forrest, Perelson, Allen, & Cherukuri, 1994), and the concept of Immunotronics proposed by Bradley and Tyrrell (Bradley & Tyrrell, 2001, 2002a, 2002b) are briefly introduced in this chapter as the necessary backgrounds. Immunotronics is the architecture of a hardware immune system for the protection of digital systems represented as finite state machines (FSM). The NSA is applied to identify faults within a FSM by distinguishing invalid state transitions from valid state transitions.

Copyright © 2009, IGI Global, distributing in print or electronic forms without written permission of IGI Global is prohibited.

Up to now, little works about the hardware immune system are concerned on real world applications. In this chapter, a hardware immune system for MC8051 IP Core is studied. The system can detect the abnormal PC (Program Counter) transitions occurred in a MC8051 single-chip microcontroller. A hardware immune system for the MC8051 IP Core is implemented and tested on a FPGA (Field Programmable Gate Array) development board, and the experimental results are given. The disadvantages and future works of the system in this chapter are also discussed.

BACKGROUNDS

This section is organized as follows. Firstly, the Negative Selection Algorithm (NSA) by Forrest and her colleagues (Forrest et al., 1994) is briefly introduced, which is the fundamental algorithm applied in the hardware immune system. Secondly, a brief introduction to the architecture of the hardware immune system proposed by Bradley and Tyrrell (Bradley & Tyrrell, 2002b) is given. Related works about NSA and hardware immune systems are also given.

A Brief Introduction to Negative Selection Algorithm

Inspired by the self-nonself discrimination mechanism of the biological immune system, the Negative Selection Algorithm is proposed by Forrest et al in (Forrest et al., 1994). The "*r*-contiguous-bits" partial matching rule is adopted to perform the matching operation between two strings. Under the "*r*-contiguous-bits" rule, two strings of equal length match each other if they are identical in at least *r* contiguous corresponding locations. As shown in Fig. 1 the negative selection algorithm mainly consists of two working phases (Forrest et al., 1994).

The negative selection algorithm is the fundamental algorithm in the artificial immune systems. A lot of extended works about the negative selection algorithms have been done by researchers. A linear time detector set generating algorithm and a greedy detector generating algorithm are proposed by D'haeseleer et al in (D'haeseleer, 1995; D'haeseleer, Forrest, & Helman, 1996), where the problem of holes in the detector space caused by the "*r*-contiguous-bits" rule is also studied. Another novel algorithm for detector generating is introduced and different procedures to generate detectors are reviewed and compared in (Ayara, Timmis, Lemos, Castro, & Duncan, 2002).

Figure 1. Negative selection algorithm proposed by Forrest et al. (1994)

Phase 1 : Detector set generating
(1)   Generate a binary string randomly as an immature detector.
(2)   Under the "*r*-contiguous-bits" rule, filter the immature detector by the self strings one by one. If the immature detector matches with any self string, reject it and go to (1).
(3)   Insert the mature detector which has passed the self filtration into the detector set. If the number of the detectors is enough, go to the phase II, or else go to (1).
Phase 2 : Non-self detecting
(1)   Applying the "*r*-contiguous-bits" rule, filter the input string by the detector set. If the input string matches with any detector string, it is claimed as a non-self string, or else go to (2).
(2)   The input string which does not match with any detector string is claimed as a self string. Get the next input string and go to (1).

A randomized real-valued negative selection algorithm is presented in (Gonzalez, Dasgupta, & Nino, 2003). And an augmented negative selection algorithm with variable coverage detectors in real-valued space is proposed in (Ji & Dasgupta, 2004). The work in (Zhang, Wu, Zhang, & Zeng, 2005) introduces a novel negative selection algorithm with r-adjustable detectors in binary space. In (Luo, Wang, Tan, & Wang, 2006), aiming at the problem of holes, a novel negative selection algorithm (i.e. r[]-NSA) is studied. Every detector in the r[]-NSA has an array of partial matching length thresholds, by which the coverage of a r[]-detector is larger than a traditional detector which has only one threshold. Moreover, the detector set generating process of r[]-NSA is more effective than traditional process. By r[]-NSA, the non-self space coverage of the detector set can be enlarged, and the problem of holes can be solved. A heuristic detector generating algorithm for the Hamming distance partial matching rule is presented in (Luo, Zhang, & Wang, 2006). Inspired by the multi-pattern matching algorithm proposed by Aho and Corasick in (Aho & Corasick, 1975), a novel fast negative selection algorithm enhanced by state graphs is proposed in (Luo, Wang, & Wang, 2007), by which the speed of matching between an input string and the detector set can be dramatically increased. A negative selection algorithm with variable length detectors is proposed in (He, Luo, & Wang, 2007), by which the presence of holes can be removed and the number of redundant detectors can be clearly decreased. In (Ji & Dasgupta, 2007), Ji and Dasgupta make a review about the progress of negative selection algorithms, and categorize various negative selection algorithms by several different criteria.

A Brief Introduction to Hardware Immune System

Fault tolerance is an important research area in digital system design (Avizienis, 1978; Lee & Anderson, 1990). Taking inspiration from the human immune system as a method of error detection, the architecture of the hardware immune system and the concept of Immunotronics are firstly presented by Bradley and Tyrrell as a novel approach to electronic hardware fault tolerance (Bradley & Tyrrell, 2001, 2002a, 2002b). In (Bradley & Tyrrell, 2001, 2002a, 2002b), it is demonstrated that the operations of the immune system can be used for developing novel error detection mechanisms for the design of reliable hardware systems. In their works, the Immunotronics is the architecture of a hardware immune system for the error detection of sequential digital systems represented as finite state machines (FSM). Since invalid transitions may occur between valid states, the hardware immune system detects state transitions rather than single states of the FSM. Negative Selection Algorithm (NSA) by Forrest et al (Forrest et al., 1994) is applied to identify faults within a FSM by distinguishing invalid state transitions from valid state transitions. The state transitions of the monitored system are represented by binary strings in form of "previous state / current state / current input". The self set consists of valid state transitions, and the detector set is generated to cover the invalid state transition string space and detect the invalid state transitions occurred in the monitored system. By applying the "*r*-contiguous-bits" rule (Forrest et al., 1994), high fault coverage can be achieved with limited memory requirements of the detector set.

A finite state machine immunization cycle is introduced by Bradley and Tyrrell (Bradley & Tyrrell, 2002b), by which any system represented as an FSM can be immunized against the occurrence of invalid operations. The immunization cycle consists of 4 steps as follows (Bradley & Tyrrell, 2002b).

(1) Data Gathering. This step collects the valid state transitions of the monitored FSM, and creates a self set that represents a complete or substantial percentage of all possible valid state transitions of the FSM.
(2) Tolerance Condition Generation. In this step, according to the Negative Selection Algorithm (Forrest et al., 1994), a detector set is generated in such a way that the detectors can only match with the invalid state transition strings of the monitored FSM.
(3) Fault Detection. This step performs partial matching operations between the state transition strings of the monitored FSM and the detector set.
(4) Fault Removal. This step removes the detected faults of the monitored FSM.

As an example of the immunization cycle, an immunized 4-bit decade counter is implemented on an FPGA platform, where the faulty state transitions can be detected in real time (Bradley & Tyrrell, 2001, 2002a, 2002b).

Based on the works of Bradley and Tyrrell (Bradley, Ortega-Sanchez, & Tyrrell, 2000; Bradley & Tyrrell, 2000, 2001, 2002a, 2002b; Tyrrell, 1999), extended works have been done by some researchers.

Based on the Embryonic Array (Mange et al., 1996; Ortega-Sanchez, Mange, Smith, & Tyrrell, 2000), a multi-layered hardware immune system with learning ability is proposed by Canham and Tyrrell (Canham & Tyrrell, 2002, 2003a, 2003b). Inspired by the multi-layered feature of the biological immune system, the learning acquired layer of the hardware immune system detects the behaviors of monitored system for abnormal activities, and the non-learning innate layer is employed to localize the location of the fault (Canham & Tyrrell, 2002, 2003a, 2003b). In (Canham & Tyrrell, 2002, 2003a, 2003b), the Negative Selection Algorithm (Forrest et al., 1994) is applied to identify unusual states at system level and only the current state is considered. In this way, the number of error states is dramatically reduced. In their example, there are more self states than non-self states. The "*r*-contiguous-bits" partial matching rule (Forrest et al., 1994) between the detectors and the current state is no longer needed, because when the "*r*-contiguous-bits" rule is adopted, the detectors are more likely to match with self states than non-self states, and the number of holes is too large to be practical. Therefore, compared to works in (Bradley & Tyrrell, 2001, 2002a, 2002b), the number of needed detectors in (Canham & Tyrrell, 2002, 2003a, 2003b) is small. Canham and Tyrrell also introduced a novel artificial immune system for robot error detection, where the detectors are defined as columns in a 2-D feature space (Canham, Jackson, & Tyrrell, 2003).

Inspired by the co-stimulation mechanism in the biological immune system (Zhou, 2000), novel self-tolerant algorithms for the hardware immune system are studied to deal with the problem of incomplete predefined self set and maintain the self-tolerance (Luo, Wang, Tan, Zhang, & Wang, 2005; Wang, Luo, & Wang, 2006b). Due to the process of the Negative Selection Algorithm (Forrest et al., 1994), an incomplete predefined self set is a threat to the self-tolerance of the hardware immune system as it can result in false positives (i.e., the detector set recognizes self individuals as non-self). The co-stimulation mechanism plays an important role in maintaining self-tolerance in human body (Zhou, 2000). Taking a T-cell as an example, the activation of an inactive T-cell needs the first signal and the second signal (the co-stimulation) at the same time. The first signal is issued by the recognition of a non-self antigen's peptide. The second signal comes from various immune cells or molecules, and it does not have specificity. A T-cell which has only obtained the first signal will become an anergy cell or die (Zhou, 2000). In (Luo et al., 2005; Wang et al., 2006b), the first signal is triggered by the detector set when it matches with a state transition string, and the second signal is provided by the Concurrent Error Detection (CED) (Zeng, Saxena, & McCluskey, 1999). In the self-tolerant algorithm studied in (Luo et al., 2005; Wang et al., 2006b), the self set and the detector set can be updated according to the co-stimulation mechanism, and the number of false positives caused by the incomplete self set can be reduced. Different strategies to maintain the self-tolerance of the hardware immune system are studied and compared in (Wang, Luo, & Wang, 2006a).

THE MC8051 IP CORE MONITORED BY HWIS

The source codes of the MC8051 IP Core used in this chapter are downloaded from the web page http://oregano. at/eng/8051.html, which are available for free under the GNU LGPL (Lesser General Public License). This MC8051 IP Core is a synthesizable VHDL microcontroller IP core (*MC8051 IP Core - User Guide*, 2002) provided by Oregano Systems – Design & Consulting GesmbH. It is binary compatible to the well known 8051 processor of Intel (*MCS®51 Microcontroller Family User's Manual*, 1994). This MC8051 IP core also offers faster program execution compared to the original Intel 8051 devices since the processor's architecture has been optimized.

In this chapter, the MC8051 IP Core (*MC8051 IP Core - User Guide*, 2002) plays the role of the system monitored by a hardware immune system. Here, the objective of the HwIS is designed to detect the error of program running out of track in MC8051. Therefore, the value of the Program Counter (PC) register of the MC8051 is treated as the state of the monitored system. Furthermore, the state transition string to be detected by the hardware immune system is made from the concatenation of two PC values in two sequential machine cycles, as shown in Fig. 2.

In other words, a state transition string in the *n*-th machine cycle is composed of the PC value of the (*n*-2)-th machine cycle and the PC value of the (n-1)-th machine cycle in the form of "PC [*n*-2] | PC [*n*-1]". The PC transition strings are treated as the detection input strings by the hardware immune system introduced in this chapter. The self strings and the detector strings are in the same format as the PC transition strings.

In normal operations, the PC transitions are limited in a certain transition space. The normal PC transition strings are collected as the self set in the HwIS. And a detector set is generated by the HwIS to cover the abnormal

Figure 2. The state transition of the MC8051 monitored by the hardware immune system

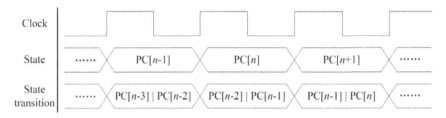

Figure 3. The structure of the hardware immune system for MC8051 IP Core

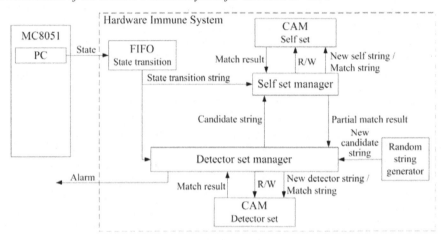

transition space. If abnormal PC transitions occur, the MC8051 will run out of track and result in error operations. The detector set is expected to match with the abnormal PC transition strings and produce alarms.

THE STRUCTURE OF THE HWIS FOR MC8051 IP CORE

The structure of hardware immune system is introduced in this section, which is introduced for the error detection of MC8051 IP Core.

The structure of the hardware immune system for the error detection of the MC8051 IP Core is depicted in Fig. 3. As shown in Fig. 2, the PC values of the MC8051 are treated as the states of the monitored system, and the PC transition strings are treated as the state transition strings to be monitored by the hardware immune system. The structure of the hardware immune system will be introduced in a form composed of 3 phases as follows.

Phase 1 : Self Set Collecting

In this phase, the MC8051 under monitoring is supposed to be running in fault free period. The state transition strings are assembled from the input states (values of the PC register of the MC8051) by the FIFO circuit, and are sent to the self set manager. The self set manager firstly check if the newly received string is same as an existent string stored in the content-addressable memory (CAM) (Kohonen, 1987) module. If it has not been stored in the

CAM, it will be treated as a new self string and be written to the CAM. This process ensures that there are no duplicate self strings stored in the CAM. Once the self set has been collected, the work flow of the system will turn to the phase 2. The work flow of this phase is depicted in Fig. 4 in detail.

To ensure the matching speed, two blocks of CAM are used for storing the self strings and detector strings, respectively. The CAM is also used in (Bradley & Tyrrell, 2001, 2002a, 2002b). The CAM (Kohonen, 1987) can search all addresses in parallel in a single clock cycle. The data stored in the CAM are a set of patterns. If the input pattern matches one of the patterns stored in the CAM, the address of the matching pattern is produced. Each pattern bit stored in the CAM can be specified as a binary "1", a binary "0", or a "don't care" bit. Comparison between a stored "don't care" bit and a corresponding input pattern bit always results in a match. The CAM can be used for any application requiring high-speed searches, such as networking, communications, data compression, and cache management.

Phase 2 : Detector Set Generating

In accordance with the detector set generating phase of the negative selection algorithm (Forrest et al., 1994), the detector set manager receives random binary candidate detector strings from the random string generator, and sends every candidate detector to the self set manager. The self set manager returns the partial matching result between the input candidate detector and the self set. If a candidate detector does not match with the self set and it is not same as any existent detector, it will be written to the CAM storing the detector set. This process also ensures that there are no duplicate detector strings in the CAM. When this phase is completed, the work flow will turn to the phase 3. The work flow of this phase is depicted in Fig. 5.

Figure 4. The work flow of the self set collecting phase. A PC transition string is represented as pt for short.

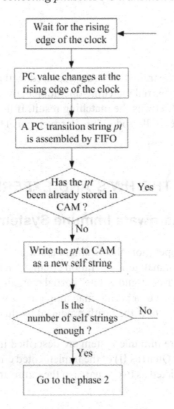

Figure 5. The work flow of the detector set generating phase

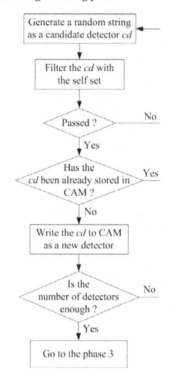

Phase 3 : Error Detecting

After the phase 2 is completed, every state transition string captured by the FIFO is sent to the detector set manager. The detector set manager performs partial matching operation between the input state transition string and the detector set stored in the CAM, and returns the matching result. If the state transition string is matched by the detector set, the detector set manager will produce an alarm signal. The work flow of this phase is depicted in Fig. 6 in detail.

THE IMPLEMENTATION OF THE HWIS AND EXPERIMENTAL RESULTS

The Implementation of the Hardware Immune System

Firstly, the circuit of partial matching operation allows single clock cycle partial matching between two input strings. The design diagram of the partial matching operation circuit which produces the partial matching result from two input strings according to the "r-contiguous-bits" partial matching rule (Forrest et al., 1994) is depicted in Fig. 7. The Fig. 7 is an example diagram of a partial matching circuit with two 8-bit input strings, where the partial matching length threshold is set as 6. If the result produced by this circuit is "1", the alarm signal of the hardware immune system is triggered.

Secondly, the circuits of the hardware immune system are described in VHDL (a hardware description language). The RTL diagram (generated by Quartus II) of the implemented circuits of the hardware immune system is shown in Fig. 8. The two modules depicted as two squares in the figure are the self set manager module (at left)

Figure 6. The work flow of the error detecting phase. A PC transition string is represented as pt.

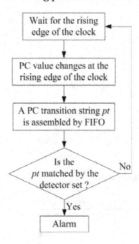

Figure 7. The diagram of the partial matching circuit

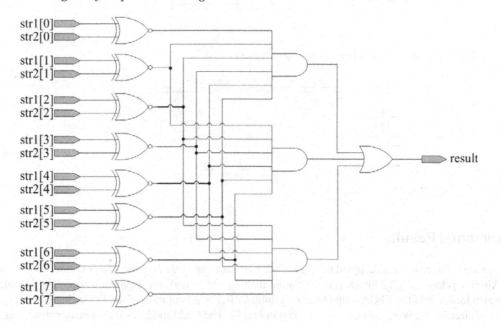

and the detector set manager module (at right). The port definition of the self set manager module is given in Fig. 9. The port definition of the detector set manager module is given in Fig. 10.

Thirdly, the VHDL description of the top module of the hardware immune system implemented in this work is listed in Fig. 11, where the main working flow of the system is described. For the limitation on the length of chapter, the details in the description are replaced with italic words. The source code package of the whole circuit design is available on request.

Figure 8. The RTL diagram of the implemented hardware immune system

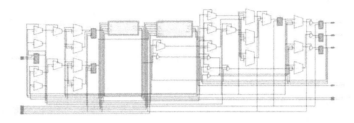

Figure 9. The definition of the self set manager module

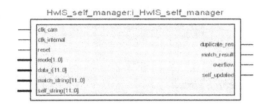

Figure 10. The definition of the detector set manager module

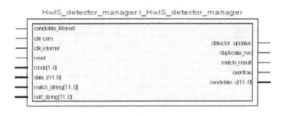

Experimental Results

The hardware immune system designed for the MC8051 IP Core (*MC8051 IP Core - User Guide*, 2002) is tested on an Altera Cyclone EP1C12 FPGA (Field Programmable Gate Array) development board[1]. The MC8051 IP Core is also loaded into the FPGA chip (Altera Cyclone EP1C12). About 85% of the FPGA logic resources are used by the circuits in this experiment, as indicated in Fig. 12. The CAM modules are resource consuming, they cost more logic resources than the ROM (Read-Only Memory) and RAM (Random-Access Memory) of the supervised MC8051 IP Core.

Invalid state transitions can be injected into the MC8051 microcontroller by setting the PC value as a random number (generated by a random generator) at every rising edge of the system clock, when the interference signal is activated by pressing down a dedicated button on the development board.

A simple microcontroller program is tested, which needs less than 64 bytes of program memory space (i.e. the ROM space) in the MC8051 microcontroller. Hence, only the lower 6 bits of the PC register are used by the program, and the length of the PC transition binary string is set as $l=12$. The upper 10 bits of the PC register are unnecessary for the program. The partial matching threshold is set as $r=8$, and the expected failure detection probability is set as $P_f=0.1$. According to the following two equations (where $m=2$), the needed size of the detector set (i.e. the number of CAM memory units needed by this application) is $N_R=196$.

Figure 11. The VHDL description of the top module of the hardware immune system for the MC8051 IP Core

```
entity HwIS_top is
        port declarations
end HwIS_top;

architecture struc of HwIS_top is
        signal declarations
begin
        FIFO : process (clk)   begin
                get state transition string with FIFO operations at every rising edge of clk
        end process FIFO;

        p_main : process (clk, reset)   begin
                if (rising_edge(clk)) then
                        if (reset = '1')   then   do reset operations
                        else
                                case   working mode   is
                                when   initial mode   =>
                                        initialize the system and go to self set collecting mode
                                when   self set collecting mode   =>
                                        if ( collecting is completed )   then   go to detector set generating mode   end if;
                                when   detector set generating mode   =>
                                        if ( generating is completed )   then   go to error detecting mode   end if;
                                when   error detecting mode   =>
                                        if ( the detector set matches with the state transition string ) then   alarm   end if;
                                when others =>
                                        null;
                                end case;
                        end if;
                end if;
        end process p_main;

        i_HwIS_self_manager : HwIS_self_manager   port map ( self set manager port mapping );
        i_HwIS_detector_manager : HwIS_detector_manager port map ( detector set manager port mapping );
end struc;
```

Figure 12. The resource allocation of the FPGA chip used in this experiment

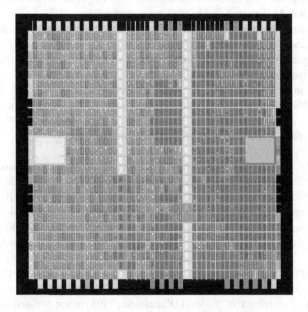

Figure 13. The waveforms of some key nodes in the circuits of the hardware immune system when an invalid state transition is occurred

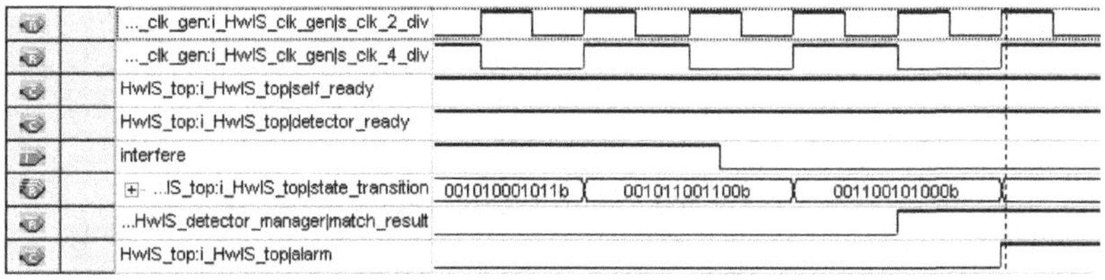

$$P_M \approx m^{-r}[(l-r)(m-1)/m+1] \text{ (Percus, Percus, \& Perelson, 1993)} \tag{1}$$

$$N_R \approx \frac{-\ln P_f}{P_M} \text{ (Forrest et al., 1994)} \tag{2}$$

The functions of the implemented circuits are able to work correctly, including self set collecting, detector set generating and error detecting. When an invalid state transition (PC transition) is occurred, the waveforms of some key nodes in the circuits captured by SignalTap II Logic Analyzer are shown in Fig. 13. The SignalTap II Logic Analyzer is a technique that can capture data from nodes in the circuits of a device in real-time and at high speed, the data captured can be viewed in waveforms.

The key nodes in the waveform of Fig. 13 are listed as follows.

s_clk_2_div : the internal clock signal of the hardware immune system.
s_clk_4_div : the main clock signal of the hardware immune system, the period is two times as long as the period of s_clk_2_div. It is synchronous to the clock of MC8051 microcontroller.
self_ready : the high enable signal to indicate that the self set collecting phase is completed.
detector_ready : the high enable signal to indicate that the detector set generating phase is completed.
interfere : the low enable signal to indicate that the interference signal is activated as the dedicated button on the development board is pressed down.
state_transition : the state transition string of the MC8051 microcontroller.
match_result : the high enable signal to indicate that a match has been found between the detector set and a state transition string.
alarm : the high enable fault alarm generated by the hardware immune system.

In the waveforms of Fig. 13, after the "interfere" input pin goes low, the "state_transition" node in the following clock cycles of "s_clk_4_div" turns to invalid state transition strings. The first invalid state transition string "001100101000" appears at the first rising edge of the clock signal "s_clk_4_div" after the "interfere" input pin goes low. Then, the "match_result" node goes high at the next rising edge of the clock signal "s_clk_2_div", to show that there is a match found between the input state transition string "001100101000" and the detector set. And at the next rising edge of the clock signal "s_clk_4_div", the "alarm" output pin goes high to indicate a fault alarm.

As the partial matching rule is adopted to perform the matching operation between the detector set and the state transition strings of the MC8051 microcontroller, some of the invalid state transition strings can not be matched by the detector set as the existence of "holes" (D'haeseleer, 1995) in the non-self space. Moreover, since the number of detectors is limited in this experiment, the coverage of the detector set is limited too. Therefore, a small number of invalid state transitions can not be detected by the detector set. In this experiment, the detection results of 360 invalid state transition strings were captured (there may have duplicate strings). The results tell that 76 of the 360 invalid strings were not detected by the detector set. In other words, about 21% of the invalid state transition strings were not detected in this experiment.

DISCUSSIONS

The hardware immune system designed and implemented in this chapter is a basic system that only has the functions of self set collecting, detector set generating and error detecting. But these functions are not enough to face the requirements of practical applications.

In a hardware immune system, the self set consists of individuals representing the normal state transitions of the monitored system. Individuals other than the self set are treated as non-self. According to the negative selection algorithm (Forrest et al., 1994), a detector set should be generated so that it can only match the non-self state transitions. Then, in the course of error detecting, if the current state transition of the monitored system is matched by a detector, a warning signal should be sent out to indicate the abnormal state of the monitored system. But in a complex environment like the MC8051 IP Core (*MC8051 IP Core - User Guide*, 2002), the predefined self set may be incomplete or noisy.

In the phase of self set collecting, it is difficult to collect all the normal state transition strings of a complex monitored system into the self set (Luo et al., 2005). Taking the MC8051 IP Core (*MC8051 IP Core - User Guide*, 2002) as an example, if the flow of the program written in the ROM is complex and is tightly dependent on the inputs signals from the peripherals, it is almost impossible to collect all the possible normal state transitions (i.e., PC transitions). And if there are interrupt service routines in the program, it will be more difficult to collect the PC transitions from every possible point in the normal flow of the program to the entrances of the interrupt service routines. In the maturation process of an initial detector set, due to the process of negative selection, an incomplete self set will result in self-reactive detectors (detectors that match with self individuals). Therefore, in a hardware immune system, a self set updating mechanism should be designed to add newly discovered self state transition strings to the incomplete self set, and a detector set updating mechanism should be designed to remove the self-reactive detectors from the detector set. The incomplete self set problem in hardware immune systems has been studied in (Luo et al., 2005; Wang et al., 2006a, 2006b).

A noisy self set is a self set that contains non-self individuals. It is possible that some non-self data are accidentally collected into the predefined self set in certain circumstances. For example, when the monitored system receives interference signals in the course of collecting the self set, the work flow of the system can be disturbed, and some non-self individuals may be collected in to the predefined self set. As for the MC8051 IP Core (*MC8051 IP Core - User Guide*, 2002), the interferences can result in unwanted or error operations. The interference signals may come from different sources, such as power supply system, peripherals, nearby electrical equipments, or the circuits of the monitored system itself. Due to the effects of interferences, the flow of the program can be disturbed, or unwanted interrupts can be triggered, etc. In fact, in most real world applications, the self set can not be collected without the effects of interferences, and some non-self individuals may be collected into the predefined self set just by man-made fault. In the process of generating the initial detector set, the candidate detectors matching any individual of the predefined self set will be deleted. Then, the non-self data in the noisy predefined self set can not be detected by the initial detector set. Therefore, a self set updating mechanism should be designed to remove the non-self data from the noisy self set, and a detector set updating mechanism should be designed to add new detectors to the detector set to cover the non-self data discovered from the noisy self set.

In future works, to deal with the incomplete self set problem and the noisy self set problem in the hardware immune systems, the self set updating mechanisms and detector set updating mechanisms should be studied and tested in real hardware.

CONCLUSION

The hardware immune systems have been studied by several researchers. Previous works about hardware immune systems are reviewed briefly in this chapter. Based on the previous works, a structure of a hardware immune system for the error detection of PC transitions in the MC8051 IP core (*MC8051 IP Core - User Guide*, 2002) is designed in this chapter. The binary string to be detected by the hardware immune system is made from the concatenation of two sequential PC values. Invalid PC transitions occurred in the MC8051can be indicated by the alarm signal triggered by the detector set of the hardware immune system. The hardware immune system designed in this chapter is implemented on an FPGA development board, and the results are given.

Since the MC8051 (*MC8051 IP Core - User Guide*, 2002) is a typical single-chip microcontroller which is binary compatible to the well known 8051 processor of Intel (*MCS®51 Microcontroller Family User's Manual*, 1994), the structure of the hardware immune system for the MC8051 IP core (*MC8051 IP Core - User Guide*, 2002) designed in this chapter can be extended and optimized to match the requirements of a wide range of applications.

In future works, the efficiency and the stability of the implemented system should be improved by optimizing the structure and the timing relationship of the circuit. And based on the structure introduced in this chapter, the incomplete self set problem and the noisy self set problem in the hardware immune systems should be studied.

ACKNOWLEDGMENT

This work is supported by National Natural Science Foundation of China (No.60404004).

REFERENCES

Aho, A. V., & Corasick, M. J. (1975). Efficient string matching: An aid to bibliographic search. *Communications of the ACM, 18*(6), 333-340.

Avizienis, A. (1978). Fault-Tolerance: The Survival Attribute of Digital Systems. *Proceedings of the IEEE, 66*(10), 1109-1125.

Ayara, M., Timmis, J., Lemos, R. d., Castro, L. N. d., & Duncan, R. (2002, September). *Negative Selection: How to Generate Detectors.* Paper presented at the 1st International Conference on Artificial Immune Systems, Canterbury, UK.

Bradley, D. W., Ortega-Sanchez, C., & Tyrrell, A. M. (2000, July). *Embryonics + Immunotronics: A Bio-Inspired Approach to Fault Tolerance.* Paper presented at the 2nd NASA/DoD Workshop on Evolvable Hardware, Silicon Valley.

Bradley, D. W., & Tyrrell, A. M. (2000, April). *Immunotronics: Hardware Fault Tolerance Inspired by the Immune System.* Paper presented at the 3rd International Conference on Evolvable Systems: from Biology to Hardware, Edinburgh.

Bradley, D. W., & Tyrrell, A. M. (2001, July 12-14). *The Architecture for a Hardware Immune System.* Paper presented at the 3rd NASA/ DoD Workshop on Evolvable Hardware, Long Beach, Cailfornia.

Bradley, D. W., & Tyrrell, A. M. (2002a). *A Hardware Immune System for Benchmark State Machine Error Detection.* Paper presented at the 2002 Congress on Evolutionary Computation, Honolulu, USA.

Bradley, D. W., & Tyrrell, A. M. (2002b). Immunotronics - Novel Finite-State-Machine Architectures with Built-In Self-Test Using Self-Nonself Differentiation. *IEEE Transactions on Evolutionary Computation, 6*(3), 227-238.

Canham, R. O., Jackson, A. H., & Tyrrell, A. M. (2003, July). *Robot Error Detection Using an Artificial Immune System.* Paper presented at the NASA/DoD Conference on Evolvable Hardware.

Canham, R. O., & Tyrrell, A. M. (2002, September). *A Multi-layered Immune System for Hardware Fault Tolerance within an Embryonic Array.* Paper presented at the 1st International Conference on Artificial Immune Systems, Canterbury.

Canham, R. O., & Tyrrell, A. M. (2003a). A Hardware Artificial Immune System and Embryonic Array for Fault Tolerant Systems. *Genetic Programming and Evolvable Machines, 4*(4), 359-382.

Canham, R. O., & Tyrrell, A. M. (2003b). *A Learning, Multi-Layered, Hardware Artificial Immune System Implemented upon an Embryonic Array*. Paper presented at the 5th International Conference on Evolvable Systems (ICES 2003), Trondheim, Norway.

Castro, L. N. d., & Timmis, J. (2002). *Artificial Immune Systems: A New Computational Intelligence Approach*. London: Springer-Verlag.

D'haeseleer, P. (1995). *Further Efficient Algorithms for Generating Antibody Strings* (No. Technical Report CS95-3). Albuquerque, New Mexico: Department of Computer Science, University of New Mexico.

D'haeseleer, P., Forrest, S., & Helman, P. (1996). *An Immunological Approach to Change Detection: Algorithms, Analysis and Implications*. Paper presented at the 1996 IEEE Symposium on Security and Privacy, Los Alamitos, CA.

Dasgupta, D. (2006, November). Advances in Artificial Immune Systems. *IEEE Computational Intelligence Magazine,* 40-49.

Forrest, S., Perelson, A. S., Allen, L., & Cherukuri, R. (1994). *Self-Nonself Discrimination in a Computer*. Paper presented at the 1994 IEEE Symposium on Research in Security and Privacy, Los Alamitos, CA.

Gonzalez, F., Dasgupta, D., & Nino, L. F. (2003, September 1-3). *A Randomized Real-Valued Negative Selection Algorithm*. Paper presented at the 2nd International Conference on Artificial Immune Systems (ICARIS 2003), LNCS 2787, Edinburgh, UK.

He, S., Luo, W., & Wang, X. (2007). A Negative Selection Algorithm with the Variable Length Detector. *Journal of Software, 18*(6), 1361-1368.

Ji, Z., & Dasgupta, D. (2004, June 19-23). *Augmented Negative Selection Algorithm with Variable-Coverage Detectors*. Paper presented at the 2004 Congress on Evolutionary Computation (CEC '04).

Ji, Z., & Dasgupta, D. (2007). Revisiting Negative Selection Algorithms. *Evolutionary Computation, 15*(2), 223-251.

Kohonen, T. (1987). *Content-Addressable Memories* (2nd ed.). Berlin, Germany: Springer-Verlag.

Lee, P. A., & Anderson, T. (1990). *Fault Tolerance Principles and Practice, Dependable Computing and Fault-Tolerance Systems* (2 ed. Vol. 3). Berlin, Germany: Springer-Verlag.

Luo, W., Wang, X., Tan, Y., & Wang, X. (2006, September 9-13). *A Novel Negative Selection Algorithm with an Array of Partial Matching Lengths for Each Detector*. Paper presented at the 9th International Conference on Parallel Problem Solving From Nature (PPSN IX), LNCS 4193, Reykjavik, Iceland.

Luo, W., Wang, X., Tan, Y., Zhang, Y., & Wang, X. (2005, September 12-14). *An Adaptive Self-Tolerant Algorithm for Hardware Immune System*. Paper presented at the 6th International Conference on Evolvable Systems (ICES 2005), LNCS 3637, Sitges, Spain.

Luo, W., Wang, X., & Wang, X. (2007, August 26-29). *A Novel Fast Negative Selection Algorithm Enhanced by State Graphs*. Paper presented at the 6th International Conference on Artificial Immune Systems (ICARIS 2007), LNCS 4628, Santos/SP, Brazi.

Luo, W., Zhang, Z., & Wang, X. (2006, September 4-6). *A Heuristic Detector Generation Algorithm for Negative Selection Algorithm with Hamming Distance Partial Matching Rule*. Paper presented at the 5th International Conference on Artificial Immune Systems (ICARIS 2006), LNCS 4163, Instituto Gulbenkian de Ciência, Oeiras, Portugal.

Mange, D., Goeke, M., Madon, D., Stauffer, A., Tempesti, G., & Durand, S. (1996). Embryonics: A new family of coarse-grained FPGA with self-repair and self-reproduction properties. In E. Sanchez & M. Tomassini (Eds.), *Toward Evolvable Hardware: The Evolutionary Engineering Approach* (pp. 197-220): Springer-Verlag.

MC8051 IP Core - User Guide. (2002). Vienna: Oregano Systems - Design & Consulting GesmbH.

MCS®51 Microcontroller Family User's Manual. (1994). Intel Corporation.

Ortega-Sanchez, C., Mange, D., Smith, S., & Tyrrell, A. (2000). Embryonics: A Bio-Inspired Cellular Architecture with Fault-Tolerant Properties. *Genetic Programming and Evolvable Machines, 1*(3), 187-215.

Percus, J. K., Percus, O. E., & Perelson, A. S. (1993). Probability of Self-Nonself Discrimination. In A. S. Perelson & G. Weisbuch (Eds.), *Theoretical and Experimental Insights into Immunology* (pp. 63-70). New York: Springer-Verlag.

Tyrrell, A. M. (1999, September). *Computer Know Thy Self!: A Biological Way to Look at Fault Tolerance*. Paper presented at the 2nd EuroMicro / IEEE Workshop Dependable Computing Systems.

Wang, X., Luo, W., & Wang, X. (2006a, September 4-6). *A Comparative Study on Self-tolerant Strategies for Hardware Immune Systems*. Paper presented at the 5th International Conference on Artificial Immune Systems (ICARIS 2006), LNCS 4163, Instituto Gulbenkian de Ciência, Oeiras, Portugal.

Wang, X., Luo, W., & Wang, X. (2006b). Research on an Algorithm with Self-Tolerant Ability in Hardware Immune System. *Journal of System Simulation, 18*(5), 1151-1153.

Zeng, C., Saxena, N., & McCluskey, E. J. (1999, September 28-30). *Finite State Machine Synthesis with Concurrent Error Detection*. Paper presented at the International Test Conference.

Zhang, H., Wu, L., Zhang, Y., & Zeng, Q. (2005). An Algorithm of r-Adjustable Negative Selection Algorithm and Its Simulation Analysis. *Chinese Journal of Computers, 28*(10), 1614-1619.

Zhou, G. (2000). *Principles of Immunology*. Shanghai: Scientific and Technical Documents Publishing House.

ADDITIONAL READING

Aickelin, U., Greensmith, J., & Twycross, J. (2004). *Immune System Approaches to Intrusion Detection - A Review*. Paper presented at the 3rd International Conference on Artificial Immune Systems (ICARIS 2004), LNCS 3239, Catania, Italy.

Avizienis, A. (1978). Fault-tolerance: The survival attribute of digital systems. *Proceedings of the IEEE, 66*(10), 1109-1125.

Ayara, M., Timmis, J., Lemos, R. d., Castro, L. N. d., & Duncan, R. (2002, September). *Negative Selection: How to Generate Detectors*. Paper presented at the 1st International Conference on Artificial Immune Systems, Canterbury, UK.

Bradley, D. W., Ortega-Sanchez, C., & Tyrrell, A. M. (2000, July). *Embryonics + Immunotronics: A Bio-Inspired Approach to Fault Tolerance*. Paper presented at the 2nd NASA/DoD Workshop on Evolvable Hardware, Silicon Valley.

Bradley, D. W., & Tyrrell, A. M. (2000, April). *Immunotronics: Hardware Fault Tolerance Inspired by the Immune System*. Paper presented at the 3rd International Conference on Evolvable Systems: from Biology to Hardware, Edinburgh.

Bradley, D. W., & Tyrrell, A. M. (2001, July 12-14). *The Architecture for a Hardware Immune System*. Paper presented at the 3rd NASA/ DoD Workshop on Evolvable Hardware, Long Beach, Cailfornia.

Bradley, D. W., & Tyrrell, A. M. (2002a). *A Hardware Immune System for Benchmark State Machine Error Detection.* Paper presented at the 2002 Congress on Evolutionary Computation, Honolulu, USA.

Bradley, D. W., & Tyrrell, A. M. (2002b). Immunotronics - Novel Finite-State-Machine Architectures with Built-In Self-Test Using Self-Nonself Differentiation. *IEEE Transactions on Evolutionary Computation, 6*(3), 227-238.

Canham, R. O., Jackson, A. H., & Tyrrell, A. M. (2003, July). *Robot Error Detection Using an Artificial Immune System.* Paper presented at the NASA/DoD Conference on Evolvable Hardware.

Canham, R. O., & Tyrrell, A. M. (2002, September). *A Multi-layered Immune System for Hardware Fault Tolerance within an Embryonic Array.* Paper presented at the 1st International Conference on Artificial Immune Systems, Canterbury.

Canham, R. O., & Tyrrell, A. M. (2003a). A Hardware Artificial Immune System and Embryonic Array for Fault Tolerant Systems. *Genetic Programming and Evolvable Machines, 4*(4), 359-382.

Canham, R. O., & Tyrrell, A. M. (2003b). *A Learning, Multi-Layered, Hardware Artificial Immune System Implemented upon an Embryonic Array.* Paper presented at the 5th International Conference on Evolvable Systems (ICES 2003), Trondheim, Norway.

D'haeseleer, P. (1995). *Further Efficient Algorithms for Generating Antibody Strings* (No. Technical Report CS95-3). Albuquerque, New Mexico: Department of Computer Science, University of New Mexico.

D'haeseleer, P., Forrest, S., & Helman, P. (1996). *An Immunological Approach to Change Detection: Algorithms, Analysis and Implications.* Paper presented at the 1996 IEEE Symposium on Security and Privacy, Los Alamitos, CA.

Forrest, S., Perelson, A. S., Allen, L., & Cherukuri, R. (1994). *Self-Nonself Discrimination in a Computer.* Paper presented at the 1994 IEEE Symposium on Research in Security and Privacy, Los Alamitos, CA.

Ji, Z., & Dasgupta, D. (2005, June 25-29). *Estimating the Detector Coverage in a Negative Selection Algorithm.* Paper presented at the Genetic and Evolutionary Computation Conference (GECCO 2005), Washington, D.C. USA.

Ji, Z., & Dasgupta, D. (2007). Revisiting Negative Selection Algorithms. *Evolutionary Computation, 15*(2), 223-251.

Kohonen, T. (1987). *Content-Addressable Memories* (2nd ed.). Berlin, Germany: Springer-Verlag.

Luo, W., Wang, X., Tan, Y., Zhang, Y., & Wang, X. (2005, September 12-14). *An Adaptive Self-tolerant Algorithm for Hardware Immune System.* Paper presented at the 6th International Conference on Evolvable Systems (ICES 2005), LNCS 3637, Sitges, Spain.

Ortega-Sanchez, C., Mange, D., Smith, S., & Tyrrell, A. (2000). Embryonics: A Bio-Inspired Cellular Architecture with Fault-Tolerant Properties. *Genetic Programming and Evolvable Machines, 1*(3), 187-215.

Percus, J. K., Percus, O. E., & Perelson, A. S. (1993). Probability of Self-Nonself discrimination. In A. S. Perelson & G. Weisbuch (Eds.), *Theoretical and Experimental Insights into Immunology* (pp. 63-70). New York: Springer-Verlag.

Tyrrell, A. M. (1999, September). *Computer Know Thy Self! A Biological Way to Look at Fault Tolerance.* Paper presented at the 2nd EuroMicro / IEEE Workshop Dependable Computing Systems.

Wang, X., Luo, W., & Wang, X. (2006a, September 4-6). *A Comparative Study on Self-tolerant Strategies for Hardware Immune Systems.* Paper presented at the 5th International Conference on Artificial Immune Systems (ICARIS 2006), LNCS 4163, Instituto Gulbenkian de Ciência, Oeiras, Portugal.

Wang, X., Luo, W., & Wang, X. (2006b). Research on an Algorithm with Self-Tolerant Ability in Hardware Immune System. *Journal of System Simulation, 18*(5), 1151-1153.

Wierzchoń, S. T. (2000). Generating Optimal Repertoire of Antibody Strings in an Artificial Immune System. In M. A. Kopotek, M. Michalewicz & S. T. Wierzchoń (Eds.), *Intelligent Information Systems* (pp. 119-133). Heidelberg New York: Physica-Verlag/Springer Verlag.

KEY TERMS

Artificial Immune System: Inspired by several immunological principles, Artificial Immune Systems (AIS) emerged in the 1990s as a new branch of Computational Intelligence. Like artificial neural networks (ANNs), evolutionary algorithms (EAs), and cellular automata, AISs also try to extract ideas from the biological mechanisms in order to develop novel computational techniques for solving science and engineering problems. A number of AIS models are applied in areas like pattern recognition, fault detection, computer security, etc. Among various AIS models, negative selection, immune network and clonal selection are the most discussed models.

Error Detection: Discovering an error operation in hardware or software. In this chapter, the error detection indicates the detection of invalid state transitions occurred in the monitored system (the MC8051 IP Core) which can be represented as an FSM.

Finite State Machine: A model of computation consisting of a set of states, a start state, an input alphabet, and a transition function that maps input symbols and current states to a next state. Computation begins in the start state with an input string. It changes to new states depending on the transition function. There are many variants, for instance, machines having actions (outputs) associated with transitions (Mealy machine) or states (Moore machine), etc. (http://www.nist.gov/dads/HTML/finiteStateMachine.html). A finite state machine can be used both as a development tool for solving problems and as a formal way of describing specific device or program interactions.

Hardware Immune System: Taking inspiration from the biological immune systems, a method of error detection for the sequential digital systems represented as finite state machines (FSM) is proposed by Bradley and Tyrrell as a novel approach to hardware fault tolerance. Negative Selection Algorithm (NSA) proposed by Forrest et al is applied to identify faults within a FSM by distinguishing invalid state transitions from valid state transitions. The state transitions of the system under monitoring are represented by binary strings in the form of "previous state / current state / current input". In particular, it is shown that by use of partial matching in NSA, high fault coverage can be achieved with limited memory requirements. Bradley and Tyrrell also introduced a generic FSM immunization cycle that allows any system that can be represented as an FSM to be "immunized" against the occurrence of faulty operations.

Immunotronics: Immunotronics is a term combined from "immunological electronics". It represents the immune-inspired hardware fault-tolerance technique proposed by Bradley and Tyrrell, i.e., the hardware immune system.

MC8051 IP Core: MC8051 IP Core is a synthesizable VHDL microcontroller IP core provided by Oregano Systems – Design & Consulting GesmbH. It is binary compatible to the well known 8051 processor of Intel, and offers faster program execution compared to the original Intel 8051 devices since the processor's architecture has been optimized. The VHDL source codes of the MC8051 IP Core are available for free under the GNU LGPL (Lesser General Public License). The source codes used in this chapter are downloaded from web page http://oregano.at/eng/8051.html.

Negative Selection Algorithm: In biological immune system, all new birth immature T-cells must undergo a process of negative selection in the thymus, where the self-reactive T-cells binding with self proteins are destroyed. When the mature T-cells are released to the blood circle, they can only bind with non-self antigens.

Inspired by the self-nonself discrimination mechanism of the biological immune system, the Negative Selection Algorithm (NSA) is proposed by Forrest et al in 1994 as a change detection algorithm. The first step of the NSA is to collect a set of self strings that defines the normal state of the monitored system. Then the second step is to generate a set of detectors that only recognize non-self strings. Finally, the detector set is used to monitor the anomaly changes of the data to be protected.

ENDNOTE

[1] The source codes of this hardware immune system are available from the authors on request. Noted that the Altera Cyclone EP1C12 FPGA development board is bought, and not developed by the authors.

Section II
Natural Computing

Section II.I
Evolutionary Computing

Evolutionary computation (EC) is an important branch of natural computing and also important optimization technology. In this section, a general model for EC is proposed and used for analyzing some important problems of EC. It is a very meaningful theoretic work. And a hybrid genetic algorithm, which is combined with fuzzy logic, is used in path planning for robot navigation. The experiment results show its effectiveness in solving path planning.

Chapter XVI
On Foundations of
Evolutionary Computation:
An Evolutionary Automata Approach

Mark Burgin
University of California, USA

Eugene Eberbach
Rensselaer Polytechnic Institute, USA

ABSTRACT

There are different models of evolutionary computations: genetic algorithms, genetic programming, etc. This chapter presents mathematical foundations of evolutionary computation based on the concept of evolutionary automaton. Different classes of evolutionary automata (evolutionary finite automata, evolutionary Turing machines and evolutionary inductive Turing machines) are introduced and studied. It is demonstrated that evolutionary algorithms are more expressive than conventional recursive algorithms, such as Turing machines. Universal evolutionary algorithms and automata are constructed. It is proved that classes of evolutionary finite automata, evolutionary Turing machines and evolutionary inductive Turing machines have universal automata. As in the case of conventional automata and Turing machines, universal evolutionary algorithms and automata provide means to study many important problems in the area of evolutionary computation, such as complexity, completeness, optimality and search decidability of evolutionary algorithms, as well as such natural phenomena as cooperation and competition. Expressiveness and generality of the introduced classes of evolutionary automata are investigated.

INTRODUCTION

In this chapter, we argue that the separation of combinatorial optimization methods into exact and heuristic classes is somewhat superficial. Natural classification of algorithms depends on the complexity of the search problem solved by an algorithm. The, so called, exact methods, can and have to be interrupted to produce approximate solutions for large search problems. As a result, these algorithms become heuristic. This is usually true when somebody tries to use dynamic programming to solve NP-complete problems for big or multidimensional

Copyright © 2009, IGI Global, distributing in print or electronic forms without written permission of IGI Global is prohibited.

systems. As we know, it is possible, for example, to use "exact" dynamic programming for 6-10 cities in traveling salesman problem, but only inexact dynamic programming solutions for hundreds and thousands cities are tractable. Although "inexact" evolutionary algorithms and simulated annealing methods can guarantee finding exact solutions for traveling salesman problem, in a general case, this is possible to do only in an infinite number of generations. However, solving a problem in an infinite number of steps goes beyond classical algorithms and Turing machines, and in spite of being common in mathematics, encounters steady resistance in finitely oriented conventional computer science.

Here we show how to achieve the same results, i.e., to find exact solutions for hard problem, in a finite number of steps (time). Namely, we can use super-recursive algorithms. They allow one to solve many problems undecidable in the realm of recursive algorithms (Burgin, 2005). We argue that it is beneficial for computer science to go beyond recursive algorithms, making possible to look for exact solutions of intractable problems or even to find solutions of undecidable problems, whereas recursive solutions do not exist. As the basic computational model, we take evolutionary automata, which extend computational power of evolutionary Turing machines introduced in (Eberbach, 2005) and parallel evolutionary Turing machines introduced in (Burgin&Eberbach, 2008). Our goal here is to study expressiveness of classes of evolutionary automata, relations between these classes, and existence of universal automata in these classes.

Our chapter is organized as follows. In section 2 we present the relevant background information on evolutionary computation and its theoretical foundations. In section 3 we propose a generic class of evolutionary automata to model evolutionary processes. In particular, evolutionary automata consist of evolutionary finite automata, evolutionary Turing machines and evolutionary inductive Turing machines. The properties of each class are investigated. The corresponding classes of universal evolutionary automata are defined. In section 4 we study the generality of evolutionary automata approach in modeling all known and future subareas of evolutionary computation. In section 5 we make conclusions and outline directions for the future work.

BACKGROUND

Evolution by natural selection is one of the most compelling themes of modern science. In evolutionary algorithms, selection operates on population of individuals represented by semiotic chromosomes, which are stored in a computer's memory. Populations of semiotic chromosomes evolve in a computational process, using mutation and/or crossover in much the same way as natural populations do. This form of computation is called Evolutionary Computation (EC). Evolutionary Computation consists of four main areas: Genetic Algorithms (GA), Genetic Programming (GP), Evolution Strategies (ES) and Evolutionary Programming (EP). Additional areas include: Ant Colony Optimization (ACO), Particle Swarm Optimization (PSO), co-evolution, Artificial Immune Systems (AIS), evolutionary robotics, evolvable hardware, Evolutionary Artificial Neural Networks (EANN), evolutionary multiobjective optimization, Artificial Life (A-Life), Classifier Systems, DNA-Based Computing and some fields in bioinformatics. Applications of Evolutionary Computing are vast and diverse. Evolutionary Computing is used for finding solutions of intractable (hard and NP-complete) optimization problems, machine learning, data mining, neural network training, evolution of technology, robotics, control, electronic circuit design, games, economics, network design, pattern recognition, genome and protein analysis, DNA-based computing, evolvable programming languages, reconfigurable hardware and many others (Back, Fogel and Michalewicz 1997; Fogel 2001; Michalewicz and Fogel, 2004).

However, in spite of a diversity of useful applications, evolutionary computation theory is still very young and incomplete (Fogel, 1995; 2001; Michalewicz, 1996; Michalewicz and Fogel, 2004). Studied theoretical topics include convergence in the limit (elitist selection, Michalewicz's contractive mapping GAs, (1+1)-ES), convergence rate (Rechenberg's 1/5 rule), Building Block analysis (Schema Theorems for GA and GP), best variation operators (No Free Lunch Theorem). Very little has been known about expressiveness, or computational power, of Evolutionary Computation and its scalability. Conventional computation has many models. One of the most popular is Turing Machine. Quantum computation has such a theoretical model as Quantum Turing Machine. However until recently, Evolutionary Computation did not have a theoretical model that represented practice in this domain. Of course, there are many results on evolutionary algorithms theory (see, e.g., Holland, 1975;

Rudolph, 1994; Wolpert, 1997; He and Yao, 2004). However, these authors do not introduce their own original models – rather they apply high-quality mathematical apparatus to existing models like Markov chains, etc. They also cover only some aspects of evolutionary computation like convergence or convergence rate, completely neglecting for example EC expressiveness, self-adaptation, or scalability. In other words, EC is not treated as a distinct and complete area with its own distinct model situated in the context of general computational models. In other words, in spite of intensive usage of mathematical techniques, EC lacks theoretical foundations. As a result, many properties of evolutionary computation processes and of evolutionary computation results could not be precisely studied or even found by researchers. Our research is aimed at filling this gap.

Based on the thorough analysis of the concept of foundation made by Simpson (2006), we suggest the following definition. The term foundations of some field of study usually means a systematic analysis of the most basic or fundamental concepts of this field, that results in demonstration of fundamentality, building theoretical (often mathematical) models, finding properties of these concepts, and establishing the rules of operation with these concepts.

That is why in this paper, we develop mathematical models that allow one to systematically analyze the most basic or fundamental concepts of evolutionary computation, such as Genetic Algorithms, Evolution Strategies, Genetic Programming, and Evolutionary Programming. We also find important properties of these models and through them properties of various types and kinds of evolutionary computation. Utilization of abstract automata (e.g., Turing machines) seems to restore this missing context, and puts EC on equal grounds with other more mature areas in computer science.

EVOLUTIONARY COMPUTATIONS IN CLASSES OF ALGORITHMS AND AUTOMATA

An evolutionary algorithm is a probabilistic beam hill climbing search algorithm directed by a fitness objective function. The beam (population size) maintains multiple search points, hill climbing means that only a current search point from the search tree is remembered, and reaching the optimum of the fitness function is very often a termination condition.

Definition 1. A generic *evolutionary algorithm* (*EA*) *A* contains the following components:

- a *representation space X*; (e.g., *X* consists of fixed binary strings for genetic algorithms (GAs), of Finite State Machine descriptions for evolutionary programming (EP), of parse trees for genetic programming (GP), of vectors of real numbers for evolution strategies (ES));
- *selection* operators s_i (e.g., *truncation, proportional selection* or *tournament*), $i = 1, 2, 3, \ldots$;
- *variation* operators v_j (e.g., *mutation, crossover* or some combination of mutations and crossover), $j = 1, 2, 3, \ldots$;
- a *fitness* function $f: X \rightarrow R$, which typically takes values in the domain of nonnegative real numbers and is extended to the subsets of the set *X* by the following rule

  if $Y \subseteq X$, then $f(Y) = \max \{f(x); x \in Y \}$

- a *termination* or *search condition* (goal of evolution) *C*.

Often the termination condition of an evolutionary algorithm is given as a subset *F* of the representation space *X*. Computation halts when an element from *F* is obtained. Another form of a termination condition is optimum (maximum or minimum) of the fitness function $f(x)$. Computation, for example, halts when a maximum of the fitness function $f(x)$ is obtained. In many cases, it is impossible to achieve or verify this optimum. Thus, another termination condition is used (e.g., the maximum number of generations or the lack of progress through several generations).

Dynamics of the evolutionary algorithm *A* can be described in the form of the functional equation (recurrence relation) working in a simple iterative loop with parts of the space *X* called generations in discrete time $t = 0, 1, 2, \ldots$ (Fogel, 1995, Michalewicz & Fogel, 2004, Fogel, 2001):

$$X[t+1] = s \, (v \, (X[t])) \quad (1)$$

Equation (1) describes how algorithm *A* taking the generation $X[t] \subseteq X$ produces the generation $X[t + 1] \subseteq X$. An *initial* population $X[0] \subseteq X$ is given as the input of the EA. Selection is based on the fitness function $f(x)$, which is often extended from elements of *X* to subsets of *X*, giving the best value on the elements in this subset as its value for this subset.

In what follows, we assume that in each class of automata, all automata work with the same alphabet.

Note that Definition 1 encompasses all typical EAs, including GA, EP, ES, GP. It is possible to use this definition to describe other emerging optimizing strategies, such as ant colony optimization or particle swarm optimization. Of course, it is possible to think and implement more complex versions of evolutionary algorithms.

The goal of evolutionary algorithms is to evolve the population $X[t]$ of solutions *x* to a given optimization problem, but algorithms themselves may be the subject of self-adaptation (like in ES) as well. As we know, evolution in nature is not static, the rate of evolution fluctuates, their variation operators are subject to slow or fast changes, its goal (if it exists at all) can be a subject to modifications. Thus, to properly model evolutionary processes, evolutionary algorithms have to be adaptive and flexible.

Formally, an evolutionary algorithm looking for the optimum of the fitness function violates some classical requirements of recursive algorithms. If its termination condition is set to the optimum of the fitness function, it may not terminate after a finite number of steps. To fit it to the old "algorithmic" approach, an artificial (or somebody can call it pragmatic) stop criterion is often added (see e.g., (Michalewicz, 1996; Koza, 1992)). Thus, to remain recursive, an evolutionary algorithm has to be stopped after a finite number of generations or when no visible progress is observable. Naturally, in a general case, evolutionary algorithms are instances of super-recursive algorithms (Burgin, 2005).

Now, we define a formal algorithmic model of Evolutionary Computation - an *Evolutionary Automaton*.

Let **K** be a class of automata/algorithms.

Definition 2. An *evolutionary automaton* (*EA*) in the class **K** is a (possibly infinite) sequence $E = \{A[t]; t = 0, 1, 2,\ldots\}$ of automata $A[t]$ from **K** each working on the population $X[t]$ in generations $t = 0, 1, 2,\ldots$ where

- each automaton $A[t]$ called a component, or more exactly, a *level automaton*, of *E* represents (encodes) an one-level evolutionary algorithm that works with the population $X[t]$ by applying the variation operators $v_j, j = 1, 2, 3, \ldots$, and selection operators $s_i, i = 1, 2, 3, \ldots$;
- only the first generation $X[0]$ is given in advance, and any other generation depends on its predecessor only, i.e., each generation $X[t + 1]$ is obtained by applying the variation operator *v* and selection operator *s* to the population $X[t]$ for all generations $t = 0, 1, 2,\ldots$;
- the goal of the EA *E* is represented by any population $X[t]$ satisfying the search condition.

The desirable search condition is the optimum of the fitness performance measure $f(x[t])$ of the best individual from the population $X[t]$. When the search condition is satisfied, then working in the recursive mode, the EA *E* halts (*t* stops to be incremented), otherwise a new input population $X[t + 1]$ is generated by $A[t + 1]$. When the search condition is satisfied and *E* is working in the inductive mode, the EA *E* stabilizes (the population $X[t]$ stops changing), otherwise a new input population $X[t + 1]$ is generated by $A[t + 1]$.

We denote the class of all evolutionary automata in the class **K**, i.e., with level automata from **K**, by **EK**.

Remark 1. Very often, researchers consider only accepting automata (cf., for example, (Davis&Weyuker, 1983) or (Hopcroft, et al, 2001)). However, in evolutionary computations all automata are transducers (Burgin, 2005), i.e., they receive input and give output. The automata $A[t]$ from an evolutionary automaton *E* perform multiple computations in the sense of (Burgin, 1983).

Remark 2. We do not consider here such evolutionary automata that change rules or memory of the components $A[t]$ or/and the fitness functions that regulate the evolutionary process. We study automata with self-transformation in another work.

Let us consider some examples of evolutionary automata.

Example 1. Evolutionary Turing Machines (Eberbach, 2005; Burgin&Eberbach, 2008).

An *evolutionary Turing machine (ETM) ET* = {TM[t]; t = 0, 1, 2, 3, ...} is a (possibly infinite) sequence of Turing machines TM[t] each working on the population $X[t]$ in generations t = 0, 1, 2,... where

- each transition function (rules) $\delta[t]$ of the Turing machine TM[t] represents (encodes) an evolutionary algorithm that works with the population $X[t]$, and evolved in generations 0, 1, 2, ... , t ;
- only the first generation $X[0]$ is given in advance, and any other generation depends on its predecessor only, i.e., the generation $X[t + 1]$ is obtained by applying recursive variation operators v_j, j = 1, 2,... , and recursive selection operators s_i, i = 1, 2,... to the population $X[t]$;
- (TM[0], $X[0]$) is the initial Turing machine operating on its input - an initial population $X[0]$;
- the goal (or halting) state of ETM *ET* is represented by any population $X[t]$ satisfying the termination condition. The desirable termination condition is the optimum of the fitness performance measure $f(x[t])$ of the best individual from the population $X[t]$;

When the termination condition is satisfied, then the ETM *ET* halts (t stops to be incremented), otherwise a new input population $X[t + 1]$ is generated by TM[$t + 1$].

We denote the class of all evolutionary Turing machines by **ETM**.

Remark 3. Variation and selection operators are recursive to ensure their realization by Turing machines. Later, we will release that restriction to allow nonrecursive solutions.

Note that an infinite sequence of Turing machines in ETM generally can work like a limit Turing machine or infinite time Turing machine. Both limit and infinite time Turing machines have more computing power than Turing machines (Burgin, 2005), thus evolutionary Turing machines have more computing power than Turing machines, i.e., it is a class of super-recursive algorithms or super-Turing models of computation (Eberbach & Wegner, 2004).

Example 2. Evolutionary Inductive Turing Machines.

Here and in what follows, we consider only evolutionary inductive Turing machines and evolutionary inductive Turing machines of the first order.

An *evolutionary inductive Turing machine (EITM) EI* = {ITM[t]; t = 0, 1, 2,...} of the first order is a (possibly infinite) sequence of inductive Turing machines ITM[t] of the first order (Burgin, 2005) each working on the population $X[t]$ in generations t = 0, 1, 2,... where

- each transition function (rules) $\delta[t]$ of the inductive Turing machine ITM[t] represents/encodes an evolutionary algorithm that works with the population $X[t]$, and evolved in generations 0, 1, 2, ... , t ;
- only the first generation $X[0]$ is given in advance, and any other generation depends on its predecessor only, i.e., the generation $X[t + 1]$ is obtained by applying recursive variation operators v_j, j = 1, 2,... , and recursive selection operators s_i, i = 1, 2,... to the population $X[t]$;
- (ITM[0], $X[0]$) is the initial inductive Turing machine of the first order operating on its input - an initial population $X[0]$;
- the goal (or stabilizing) output of the EITM *EI* is represented by any population $X[t]$ satisfying the search condition. The desirable search condition is the optimum of the fitness performance measure $f(x[t])$ of the best individual from the population $X[t]$;

When the search condition is satisfied, then the EITM *EI* stabilizes (the population $X[t]$ stops changing), otherwise a new input population $X[t + 1]$ is generated by ITM$[t + 1]$.

We denote the class of all evolutionary inductive Turing machines of the first order by **ETM**.

Remark 5. Variation and selection operators are recursive to ensure that all computing steps of machines ITM$[t]$ are recursive. Otherwise, we go beyond inductive Turing machines of the first order (Burgin, 2005). Later, we will release that restriction to allow nonrecursive solutions.

Example 3. Evolutionary Finite Automata.

An *evolutionary finite automaton (EFA)* is a (possibly infinite) sequence $G = \{G[t]; t = 0, 1, 2,...\}$ of finite automata $G[t]$ each working on the population $X[t]$ in generations $t = 0, 1, 2,...$ where

- each automaton $G[t]$ called a component of E represents (encodes) an evolutionary algorithm that works with the population $X[t]$ by applying the variation operator v and selection operator s;
- only the first generation $X[0]$ is given in advance, and any other generation depends on its predecessor only, i.e., each generation $X[t + 1]$ is obtained by applying recursive variation operators v_j, $j = 1, 2,...$, and recursive selection operators s_i, $i = 1, 2,...$ to the population $X[t]$ for all generations $t = 0, 1, 2,...$;
- the goal of the EFA E is represented by any population $X[t]$ satisfying the search condition.

We denote the class of all evolutionary finite automata by **EFA**.

It is possible to consider deterministic finite automata, which form the class **DFA**, and nondeterministic finite automata, which form the class **NFA**. This gives us two classes of evolutionary finite automata: **EDFA** of all deterministic evolutionary finite automata and **ENFA** of all nondeterministic evolutionary finite automata.

Types of evolutionary automata in the class **K**.

Definition 3. An evolutionary automaton E in the class **K** is called:

a) *constant* if all automata $A[t]$ are equal.
b) *periodic* if there is a finite sequence L of the automata $A[t]$ ($= 1, 2,...$, n) such that the whole sequence E $= \{ A[t]; t = 0, 1, 2,...\}$ of automata $A[t]$ is built as a repetition of the sequence L.
c) *almost periodic* if there is a finite sequence L of the automata $A[t]$ ($= 1, 2,$, $3, ... , n$) such that starting with some $t = k$ the infinite sequence $\{ A[t]; t = k, k+1, k+2, k+3,...\}$ of automata $A[t]$ is built as a repetition of the sequence L or when the sequence $E = \{ A[t]; t = 0, 1, 2,...\}$ is finite $E = PLL ... LLQ$ and lengths of the sequence P and Q are less than the length of L.

Remark 6. In general, when the fitness function can also be the subject of evolution, evolution is potentially an *infinite* process. Changing the transition function $\delta[t]$ of the TM can be thought as some kind of evolvable hardware, or assuming fixed hardware, we can use reprogrammable evolutionary algorithms.

The concept of a universal automaton/algorithm plays an important role in computing and is useful for different purposes. In the most general form, this concept is developed in (Burgin, 2005a).

The construction of universal in a class **A** automata and algorithms is usually based on some codification (symbolic description) **c**: **A** $\to X$ of all automata/algorithms in **A**.

Definition 4.

a) An automaton/algorithm U is *universal for the class* **A** if given a description **c**(A) of an automaton/algorithm A from **A** and some input data x for it, U gives the same result as A for the input x or gives no result when A gives no result for the input x.
b) A universal for the class **A** automaton/algorithm U is called *universal in the class* **A** if U belongs to **A**.

Example 4. Universal Turing Machines.

A Turing machine U is called *universal* if given a description $\mathbf{c}(A)$ of a Turing machine T and some input data x for it, U gives the same result as T for the input x or gives no result when T gives no result for the input x.

Existence of universal Turing machines is a well-known fact (cf., for example, Burgin, 2005).

Any universal Turing machine is universal for the class **FA** of all finite automata. However, a universal Turing machine is not universal in the class **FA** because it does not belong to this class. In essence, the class **FA** of all finite automata does not have a universal finite automaton.

Example 5. Universal Evolutionary Turing Machines.

The concept of a universal automaton immediately leads us, following Turing's ideas, to the concept of the universal Turing machine and its extension - a *Universal Evolutionary Turing Machine*. We can define a universal evolutionary Turing machine as an abstraction of all possible ETMs, in the similar way, as a universal Turing machine has been defined as an abstraction of all possible Turing machines.

Let **A** be a space of optimizing algorithms with the optimization space X and $\mathbf{c}: \mathbf{A} \to I$ be a codification (symbolic description) of all automata/algorithms in **A**. Evolutionary algorithms are series of algorithms from **A**. For instance, an evolutionary Turing machine is a series of Turing machines.

Definition 5. A *universal evolutionary Turing machine* (*UETM*) is an ETM *EU* with the optimization space $Z = X \times I$. Given a pair $(\mathbf{c}(E), X[0])$ where $E = \{TM[t]; t = 0, 1, 2,...\}$ is an ETM and $X[0]$ is the start population, the machine *EU* takes this pair as its input and produces the same population $X[1]$ as the Turing machine TM[0] working with the same population $X[0]$. Then *EU* takes the pair $(\mathbf{c}(E), X[1])$ as its input and produces the same population $X[2]$ as the Turing machine TM[1] working with the population $X[1]$. In general, *EU* takes the pair $(\mathbf{c}(E), X[t])$ as its input and produces the same population $X[t + 1]$ as the Turing machine TM[t] working with the population $X[t]$ where $t = 0, 1, 2,... $.

In other words, by a *universal evolutionary Turing machine* (*UETM*) we mean such ETM *EU* that on each step takes as the input a pair $(\mathbf{c}(TM[t]), X[t])$ and behaves like ETM E with input $X[t]$ for $t = 0, 1, 2, ...$ UETM *EU* stops when ETM E stops.

Definition 5 gives properties of a universal evolutionary Turing machine but does not imply its existence. However, as in the case of Turing machines, we have the following result.

Theorem 1 (Eberbach, 2005). In the class **ET** of all evolutionary Turing machines, there is a universal evolutionary Turing machine.

It is possible to find a proof of this theorem in (Eberbach, 2005) and (Burgin&Eberbach, 2008).

Example 6. Universal Inductive Turing Machines.

Inductive Turing machines for a broad and powerful class of super-recursive algorithms.

An inductive Turing machine U of the first order is called *universal* if given a description $\mathbf{c}(A)$ of an inductive Turing machine M of the first order and some input data x for it, U gives the same result as M for the input x or gives no result when M gives no result for the input x.

Existence of universal inductive Turing machines of the first order is proved in (Burgin, 2005).

Note that any universal inductive Turing machine of the first order is universal for the class **T** of all conventional Turing machines. However, an inductive Turing machine of the first order is not universal in the class **T** because it does not belong to this class (Burgin, 2005).

To better understand this example and to be able to prove some results for evolutionary inductive Turing machines of the first order, we give here descriptions of inductive Turing machines in general and of universal inductive Turing machines, in particular.

An inductive Turing machine M has three abstract devices: a *control device A*, which is a finite automaton and controls performance of M; a *processor* or *operating device H*, which corresponds to one or several *heads* of a conventional Turing machine; and the *memory E*, which corresponds to the *tape* or tapes of a conventional Turing machine. The memory E of the simplest inductive Turing machine consists of three linear tapes, and the operating device consists of three heads, each of which is the same as the head of a Turing machine and works with the corresponding tapes.

The *control device A* is a finite automaton. It regulates processes and parameters of the machine *M*: the state of the whole machine *M*, the processing of information by *H*, and the storage of information in the memory *E*.

The *memory E* is divided into different but, as a rule, uniform cells. It is structured by a system of relations that organize memory as well-structured system and provide connections or ties between cells. In particular, *input* registers, the *working* memory, and *output* registers of *M* are separated. Connections between cells form an additional structure *K* of *E*. Each cell can contain a symbol from an alphabet of the languages of the machine *M* or it can be empty.

In a general case, cells may be of different types. Different types of cells may be used for storing different kinds of data. For example, binary cells, which have type B, store bits of information represented by symbols 1 and 0. Byte cells (type BT) store information represented by strings of eight binary digits. Symbol cells (type SB) store symbols of the alphabet(s) of the machine *M*. Cells in conventional Turing machines have SB type. Natural number cells, which have type NN, are used in random access machines (Aho, et al, 1976). Cells in the memory of quantum computers (type QB) store q-bits or quantum bits (Deutsch, 1985). Cells of the tape(s) of real-number Turing machines (Burgin, 2005) have type RN and store real numbers. When different kinds of devices are combined into one, this new device has several types of memory cells. In addition, different types of cells facilitate modeling the brain neuron structure by inductive Turing machines.

The processor *H* performs information processing in *M*. However, in comparison to computers, *H* performs very simple operations. When *H* consists of one unit, it can change a symbol in the cell that is observed by *H*, and go from this cell to another using a connection from *K*. It is possible that the processor *H* consists of several processing units similar to heads of a multihead Turing machine. This allows one to model various real and abstract computing systems: multiprocessor computers; Turing machines with several tapes; networks, grids and clusters of computers; cellular automata; neural networks; and systolic arrays.

The *software R* of the inductive Turing machine *M* is also a program that consists of simple rules:

$$q_h a_i \rightarrow a_j q_k c \tag{1}$$

Here q_h and q_k are states of *A*, a_i and a_j are symbols of the alphabet of *M*, and *c* is a type of connection in the memory *E*. The rule (1) means that if the state of the control device *A* of *M* is q_h and the processor *H* observes in the cell the symbol a_i, then the state of *A* becomes q_k, the processor *H* writes the symbol a_j in the cell where it is situated and moves to the next cell by a connection of the type *c*. Each rule directs one step of computation of the inductive Turing machine *M*. Rules of the inductive Turing machine *M* define the transition function of *M* and describe changes of *A*, *H*, and *E*. Consequently, these rules also determine the transition functions of *A*, *H*, and *E*.

A general step of the machine *M* has the following form. At the beginning, the processor *H* observes some cell with a symbol a_i (with Λ as the symbol of an empty cell) and the control device *A* is in some state q_h. Then the control device *A* (and/or the processor *H*) chooses from the system *R* of rules a rule *r* with the left part equal to $q_h a_i$ and performs the operation prescribed by this rule. If there is no rule in *R* with such a left part, the machine *M* stops functioning. If there are several rules with the same left part, *M* works as a nondeterministic Turing machine, performing all possible operations. When *A* comes to one of the final states from *F*, the machine *M* also stops functioning. In all other cases, it continues operation without stopping.

M gives the result when *M* halts and its control device *A* is in a final state from *F*, or when *M* never stops but at some step of the computation the content of the output register becomes fixed and does not change. The result of *M* is the word that is written in the output register of *M*. In all other cases, *M* does not give the result.

The memory *E* is called *recursive* if all relations that define its structure are recursive. Here recursive means that there are some Turing machines that decide/build all naming mappings and relations in the structured memory.

Inductive Turing machines with recursive memory are called *inductive Turing machines of the first order*. The memory *E* is called *n-inductive* if its structure is constructed by an inductive Turing machine of the order *n*. Inductive Turing machines with *n*-inductive memory are called *inductive Turing machines of the order n + 1*. We denote the class of all inductive Turing machine of the order *n* by $\mathbf{IT}_n$ and take $\mathbf{IT} = \cup_{n=1}^{\infty} \mathbf{IT}_n$.

Theorem 2. In the class **IT** of all inductive Turing machines with inductive memory and a fixed alphabet, there is a universal inductive Turing machine of the first order, which works in the iterative inductive mode.

Proof. The proof is an extension of the proof for inductive Turing machines of the first order from (Burgin, 2005). That is why to make the proof simpler, we do not give all details and formal constructions.

Before describing the construction of the universal inductive Turing machine U of the first order, let us make some preliminary remarks that allow us to simplify the proof. First, we remind that a universal inductive Turing machine U of the first order has to be able to simulate any inductive Turing machine T of the first order with its arbitrary input. That is why we begin the construction of a universal inductive Turing machine U of the first order with enumeration of all inductive Turing machines of the first order.

Second, properties of the structured memory allows us to assume that the memory of T is realized in one linear tape and the processor of T contains only one head, while the memory of U contains as many linear tapes and processor of U has as many heads as we need.

Third, it is possible to assume that the common alphabet A of all machines in **IT** consists of two symbols 1 and 0, i.e., $A = \{1, 0\}$.

The iterative inductive mode of functioning of the inductive Turing machine U means that obtaining some final result in one cycle of inductive computations, the machine U can use this result in the next cycle of its computation.

Any inductive Turing machine T of the order n can be decomposed into two components: the mainframe BT of T, which consists of the control automaton A, the program (set of rules) R, and the operating device (head) H, and the structured memory E_T of the inductive Turing machine T. The mainframe BT of T is almost the same as the mainframe of any conventional Turing machine. Only the rules can contain descriptions of arbitrary moves specified by ties in the memory. It is possible to consider the mainframe BT as a machine that has everything that has the machine T but the memory of BT is a conventional linear tape, which lacks additional structure. This structure is built by a inductive Turing machine T_E of the order $n - 1$, which organizes connections in the memory E_T of T.

Codification of T as a word in the alphabet A is constructed by an inductive process similar to the process described in (Burgin, 2005). This process builds a function $\mathbf{c} : \mathbf{IT} \to A^*$, where A^* is the set of all finite words in the alphabet A. As $\mathbf{IT} = \cup_{n=1}^{\infty} \mathbf{IT}_{n'}$, we build functions $\mathbf{c}_n : \mathbf{IT}_n \to A^*$, for each component of and then combine these functions $\mathbf{c}_n$ into a function $\mathbf{c} : \mathbf{IT} \to A^*$.

The base of induction is the conventional codification of Turing machines. It is done in the following way (cf. (Burgin, 2005) or (Hopcroft, et al, 2001)).

To represent a Turing machine T as a binary string $\mathbf{c}_0(T)$, we at first assign integers to the states, tape symbols, and directions L, R, and S. If T has the states $q_1, q_2, \ldots, q_k$ for some number k, then the start state is always q_1 and we correspond to each q_i the string 0^i. To the tape symbols 0, 1, and the blank symbol B, which denotes an empty cell, we correspond 0, 00, and 000, respectively. Then we denote the direction L as D_1, direction R as D_2, and direction S, which means no move at all, as D_3, and correspond to D_1, D_2, and D_3 words 0, 00, and 000, respectively.

Once we have established an integer to represent each state, symbol, and direction, we can encode the transition rules. When we have a transition rule $\boldsymbol{q_i}, \boldsymbol{a_j} \to \boldsymbol{q_k}, \boldsymbol{a_l}, \boldsymbol{D_m}$, for some natural numbers $i, j, k, l,$ and m, we code this rule using the string $0^i 10^j 10^k 10^l 10^m$. As each number $i, j, k, l,$ and m, is larger than or equal to one, there are no occurrences of two or more consecutive 1's within the code for one transition rule. Having codes for all transition rules, we write them as one word in which they are separated by couples of 1's. For example, we have the code $0^i 10^j 10^k 10^l 10^m 110^h 10^l 10^q 10^p$ for two transition rules $\boldsymbol{q_i}, \boldsymbol{a_j} \to \boldsymbol{q_k}, \boldsymbol{a_l}, \boldsymbol{D_m}$ and $\boldsymbol{q_h}, \boldsymbol{a_t} \to \boldsymbol{q_r}, \boldsymbol{a_q}, \boldsymbol{D_p}$. This gives us the coding $\mathbf{c}_0(T)$ of the rules R of the machine T. In a similar way, we can obtain a coding $\mathbf{c}_0(R)$ for rules R of any inductive Turing machine M. As a Turing machine is completely described by its states, initial state, tape symbols, and transition rules, in such a way that we obtain a complete coding $\mathbf{c}_0(T)$ of T by a binary word. This coding is used for many purposes. For example, the coding $\mathbf{c}$ of a Turing machine allows us to give the instantaneous description (ID) of T. An instantaneous description of a Turing machine T represents the complete state of T after some step of computation. This description includes the word(s) written in the tape of T, the state of the control device of T, and the position of the head H of T. In its turn, the coding and instantaneous descriptions are used for building a universal Turing machine.

Since for each Turing machine, it is possible to assign natural numbers to its states and tape symbols in many different orders, there exist more than one encoding of the typical Turing machine. Nevertheless, any such encoding may be used by a universal Turing machine for simulating one and the same Turing machine. The only difference may be in efficiency of simulation, as some encodings give better efficiency in comparison with others.

With this base and supposing that we have a codification $\mathbf{c}_{n-1} : \mathbf{IT}_{n-1} \to A^*$, of all inductive Turing machine of the order $n - 1$, we build the function $\mathbf{c}_n : \mathbf{IT}_n \to A^*$. Taking an inductive Turing machine M of the order n, we define the code $\mathbf{c}_n(M)$ by the following formula

$$\mathbf{c}_n(M) = r(\mathbf{c}_{n-1}(M_E), \mathbf{c}_0(R_M))$$

Here M_E is the structured memory of the machine M, R_M are rules, $\mathbf{c}_0(R_M)$ is the codification of these rules described above, and r is a one-to-one function from the Cartesian product $A^* \times A^*$ onto A^*. Such function are described, for example, in (Burgin, 2005).

To simulate input and output operations of the machine T and functioning of the mainframe BT of T, the machine U has several tapes: L_1, L_0, L_1, L_2, L_3, L_4, and L_5. As usually, L_1 and L_0 are input and output tapes of U, correspondingly. The first tape L_1 is used for storing the word that represents the input w of T. The second tape L_2 is used for storing the word that represents the current state of the control automaton A of T. The third tape L_3 is used for storing the rules for operation of T. The fourth tape L_4 is used for storing the current word that is written in the tape of T. The fifth tape L_5 is used for auxiliary operations of U.

Additional tapes are used for simulating in the active mode the structured memory E_T of the machine T. The structured memory E_T of the machine T is simulated by the structured memory E_U of the machine U. Thus, the machine U has two parts: the first part simulates its mainframe BT of T and the second part simulates the structured memory of T. Simulation of the mainframe BT of T does not depend on the order of T.

To simulate input and output operations of the machine T and functioning of the mainframe of T, the machine U has several heads h_c, h_o, h_1, h_2, h_3, h_4, and h_5. The head h_c reads the input of U from its input tape, while the head h_o writes the output of U to its output tape. The first head h_1 is used for reading when it is necessary the input word w of T, which is stored in the first tape L_1. The second head h_2 is used for changing the word that represents the current state of the control automaton A of T. The third head h_3 is used for searching the rules for operation of T. The fourth head h_4 is used for simulating the work of the working head of the machine T, which is changing the word on the tape L_1 that reflects the changing memory content of T. The fifth head h_5 is used for auxiliary operations of U. In addition to this, U has a part that simulates the machine T_E that builds connections in the memory E_T of T. We consider simulation of T, assuming that its memory is already constructed by the machine U.

Given a word $r(\mathbf{c}(T), w)$ where $r : N^2 \to N$ is one-to-one function, the machine U simulates the machine T working with the word w. Simulation of the machine T is performed in several cycles. Here we give only a procedural description of these cycles. Using the technique from (Hopcroft, et al, 2001) and (Burgin, 2005), it is possible to make this description formal.

The first cycle:

The machine U examines whether the input v has the form $r(\mathbf{c}(T),w)$, finding, in particular, if the first component of the pair $r^{-1}(v)$ is a legitimate code $\mathbf{c}(T)$ for some inductive Turing machine T. This is possible to do by standard methods in a finite number of steps (cf., for example, (Hopcroft, et al, 2001) or (Ebbinghaus, *et al*, 1970)). If the answer is *yes*, that is, the input v passes the test, U goes to the second cycle of simulation. If the answer is *no*, U gives no result. It can stop without generating an output or go into an infinite resultless cycle.

The second cycle:

The machine U:

1. rewrites the word w on the first working tape L_1;
2. rewrites the word w to the fourth working tape L_4,
3. writes the initial state q_0 of T on the second working tape of U; and

4.   puts its head h_4 into the cell that contains the first symbol a_1 of the word w.

Then U goes to the third cycle.

The third cycle:

The machine U reads the symbol in the cell where the head h_1 is situated. At the beginning, it is the first symbol a_1 of the word w. If $a_1 = 0$, then U finds the first rule r with one 0 after 1 and one 0 after 11. If $a_1 = 1$, then U finds the first rule r with one 0 after 1 and two 0's after 11.

Then U goes to the fourth cycle.

The fourth cycle:

If the operations for h_1 are prescribed in the rule r that is found in the third cycle, then the machine U performs these operations. They can include:

1.   reading with the head h_1 from the first tape L_1 ;
2.   writing with the head h_0 the description of an output symbol x of T to the output tape L_0 when the rule r prescribes T to write x to its output tape;
3.   changing with the head h_2 the content of the second working tape to the number of 0's that go after 11111 in the right part of the rule r;
4.   changing with the head h_4 the content of that cell in the fourth working tape: the new content is 0 if there is one 0 that goes after 11 in the right part of the rule r and the new content is 1 if there are two 0's that go after 11 in the right part of the rule r; and
5.   moving the head h_4 according to the connection in the corresponding rule; this move simulates in a definite way the corresponding move of the head of T.

The connections between the cells of the tape L_4 are installed by the part of U that simulates the machine T_E. When T has a recursive memory, T_E is a conventional Turing machine, for which there is a universal Turing machine, which performs the same actions.

After executing the prescribed operations, U goes back to the third cycle.

If the machine T has no transition that matches the simulated state and tape symbol, then no transition will be found by U. Thus, the machine T halts in the simulated configuration, and the machine U does likewise.

In such a way, U simulates each step of the machine T. In addition, the word written in the output tape of T when it works with the input word w coincides on each step with the word written in the output tape of U when it works with the input word $(\mathbf{c}(T), w)$. Thus, when the word written in the output tape of T stops changing, the same happens to the word written in the output tape of U. In a similar way, when the word written in the output tape of U stops changing, the same happens to the word written in the output tape of T. For this reason, U gives the same result as T when T gives a result. The same argument shows that U gives no result when T gives no result.

Using mathematical induction in the number of steps the machine T make to obtain the final result, we prove that all results of the machine U working with the code $\mathbf{c}(T)$ of T and the machine T coincide. Consequently, U completely simulates functioning of T.

Theorem is proved.

Note that working in the bounded inductive mode, no inductive Turing machine of a fixed order can simulate all machines from the class **IT** because, as it is proved in (Burgin, 2003), classes do not coincide with one another and form an infinite hierarchy.

Example 7. Universal Evolutionary Inductive Turing Machines.

Let **A** be a space of optimizing algorithms with the optimization space X and $\mathbf{c}$: $\mathbf{A} \to I$ be a codification (symbolic description) of all automata/algorithms in **A**. Evolutionary algorithms are series of algorithms from **A**. For instance, an evolutionary Turing machine is a series of Turing machines.

Definition 6. A *universal evolutionary inductive Turing machine* (*UEITM*) is an EITM *EU* with the optimization space $Z = X \times I$. Given a pair $(\mathbf{c}(E), X[0])$ where $E = \{\text{ITM}[t]; t = 0, 1, 2, 3, ...\}$ is an EITM and $X[0]$ is the start population, the machine *EU* takes this pair as its input and produces the same population $X[1]$ as the inductive Turing machine ITM[0] working with the same population $X[0]$. Then *EU* takes the pair $(\mathbf{c}(E), X[1])$ as its input and produces the same population $X[2]$ as the inductive Turing machine ITM[1] working with the population $X[1]$. In general, *EU* takes the pair $(\mathbf{c}(E), X[t])$ as its input and produces the same population $X[t+1]$ as the inductive Turing machine ITM[t] working with the population $X[t]$ where $t = 0, 1, 2,...$.

In other words, by a *universal evolutionary inductive Turing machine* (*UEITM*) we mean such EITM *EU* that on each step takes as the input a pair $(\mathbf{c}(\text{ITM}[t]), X[t])$ and behaves like EITM *E* with input $X[t]$ for $t = 0, 1, 2,...$. UEITM *EU* gives a result when EITM *E* gives a result.

Definition 6 gives properties of a universal evolutionary inductive Turing machine but does not imply its existence. However, as in the case of inductive Turing machines, we have the following result.

Theorem 3. In the class **EIT** of all evolutionary inductive Turing machines, there is a universal evolutionary inductive Turing machine.

Proof. To build a universal evolutionary inductive Turing machine (UEITM), we use the structure of the universal inductive Turing machine described above and for an evolutionary inductive Turing machine (EITM) $E = \{\text{ITM}[t]; t = 0, 1, 2,...\}$, we take as its coding $\mathbf{c}(E)$ the series $\{\mathbf{c}(\text{ITM}[t]); t = 0, 1, 2,...\}$ of the code $\mathbf{c}(\text{ITM}[t])$ of the inductive Turing machines ITM[t]. There are different ways to code inductive Turing machines (cf., (Burgin, 2005)) and we take one of such consistent codes. An explicit description of a universal evolutionary inductive Turing machine is constructed in a form of a series $EU = \{\text{UEITM}[t]; t = 0, 1, 2,...\}$ of (possibly infinite) instances of universal inductive Turing machines UITM[t] working on pairs $(\mathbf{c}(\text{ITM}[t]), X[t])$ in generations $t = 0, 1, 2,...$, where

- each ITM[t], encoded by $\mathbf{c}(\text{ITM}[t])$, represents the component *t* of the evolutionary algorithm *E* with population $X[t]$ for all generations $0, 1, 2, ... , t$;
- each UITM[t] takes as an input the code $\mathbf{c}(\text{ITM}[t])$ of the inductive Turing machines ITM[t] (the component of the evolutionary algorithm *E*), the generation $X[t]$, and simulates ITM[t] working with the generation $X[t]$ for all generations $0, 1, 2, ... , t$;
- only generation $X[0]$ is given in advance, while any other generation depends on its predecessor only, i.e., the outcome of generation $t = 0, 1, 2, ...$ is obtained by applying the recursive variation *v* and selection *s* operators operating on population $X[t]$ and (possibly) on evolutionary algorithm ITM[t] as well;
- UITM[0] is the initial evolutionary algorithm operating on its input - an initial population $X[0]$,
- the goal (or halting) state of UEITM is represented by any pair $(\text{ITM}[t], X[t])$ satisfying the termination condition. The desirable termination condition is the optimum of the fitness performance measure $f(X[t])$ of the best individual from the population of solutions and evolutionary algorithms. If the termination condition is satisfied, then the UEITM *EU* halts (*t* stops to be incremented), otherwise a new pair ITM[$t+1$] and its input/population $X[t+1]$ is generated.

The described evolutionary inductive Turing machine *EU* is universal in the class of all evolutionary inductive Turing machines because any UITM[t] can simulate any inductive Turing machine.

Theorem is proved.

Example 8. Universal Evolutionary Finite Automata.

It is well known that in the class **DFA** of all deterministic finite automata, as well as in the class **NFA** of all nondeterministic finite automata, there are no universal automata. However, the extension of finite automata to evolutionary finite automata changes the situation. It becomes possible to build a universal evolutionary finite automaton.

At first, let us look for universal automata for **DFA** outside **DFA**. According to the general theory of algorithms and automata (Burgin, 2005a), it is useful to consider automata that are universal for some class **A** of automata but do not belong to the class **A**. For example, we know that any finite automaton can be simulated by an appropriate Turing machine. As in the class **T** of all Turing machines, there is a universal automaton (universal Turing machine), we have the following result.

Proposition 1. There is a Turing machine UA universal for the class **DFA** of all deterministic finite automata.

The same is true for the class **NFA** of all nondeterministic finite automata.

Theorem 3. There is an evolutionary deterministic finite automaton EU universal for the class **DFA** of all deterministic finite automata that work with an alphabet X.

Proof. To construct a universal evolutionary finite automaton (UEDFA) $EU = \{W_n ; n = 0, 1, 2,...\}$, we build a constructive enumeration of all deterministic finite automata. It is possible to use a similar technique to the technique that is used to enumerate all Turing machines (cf., for example, (Rogers, 1987) or (Burgin, 2005)). This gives us an enumeration of all deterministic finite automata $A_1, A_2, A_3,..., A_n,...$

Let us consider the set $\{A_1, A_2, A_3, ..., A_n\}$ and take a set $\{B_1, B_2, B_3, ..., B_n\}$ of all deterministic finite automata such that sets of states Q_i and Q_j of any B_i and B_j do not have common elements for all $i, j \leq n$ and $i \neq j$, while the rules R_i of each B_i are obtained by some renaming of the states in A_i so that B_i and A_i compute the same language. Then we define the automaton U_n that works with inputs of the form (k, w) where k is a natural number in some representation, e.g., k is the word that consists of k symbols 1, and w is a word in the alphabet X. The number k is the code of the automaton A_k that has to be simulated with the input W. The set of states of U_n consists of all states of the automata $B_1, B_2, B_3, ..., B_n$ taken together with the states $p_0, p_1, p_2, p_3, ..., p_n$ where all of these symbols do not belong to the states of $B_1, B_2, B_3, ..., B_n$. We assume that p_0 is the initial state of the automaton U_n.

The automaton U_n has the following rules:

$(k,w)p_i \rightarrow (k-1,w)p_{i+1}$ when $n>k>0$;
$(0,w)p_i \rightarrow wq_{0,i}$ where $q_{0,i}$ is the initial state of the automaton B_i;
all rules of the automata $B_1, B_2, B_3, ..., B_n$.

According to these rules, when the automaton U_n gets a word (k,w) with $n>k$ as its input, this automaton, at first, consumes the word k and comes to the state p_k. Then U_n starts working as the automaton B_k with the input w. Thus, U_n produces the same word as B_k with the input w. Consequently, U_n models all automata $B_1, B_2, B_3, ..., B_n$, and since automata $B_1, B_2, B_3, ..., B_n$ are equivalent to automata $A_1, A_2, A_3, ..., A_n$, the automaton U_n models all automata $A_1, A_2, A_3, ..., A_n$.

The automaton U_n is called an *n-universal deterministic finite automaton* as it can model the first n automata from the sequence $A_1, A_2, A_3, ..., A_n, ...$. Note that an *n*-universal deterministic finite automaton is not unique and depends on the enumeration of automata in **DFA**.

Now we enhance each automaton U_n with an additional structure so that receiving a word (k,w) as its input, this automaton would be able to discern whether $k \leq n$ or $k > n$. To do this, we show how it is possible to construct a memory in a finite automaton, utilizing states of this automaton. If we have a deterministic finite automaton A with the set of states $Q = \{p_0, p_1, p_2, p_3, ..., p_n\}$ and we want to be able to store in this automaton words $W = \{v_1, v_2, v_3, ..., v_m\}$, then we define a new automaton A_W with the set of states $Q_W = \{(p_i, x); p_i \in Q, x \in W \cup \{\Lambda\}\}$ where is the symbol Λ of the empty storage. All initial states $p_0, p_1, p_2, p_3, ..., p_n$ correspond to the states (p_0, Λ), (p_1, Λ), $(p_2, \Lambda),..., (p_n, \Lambda)$. When it is necessary to store in the memory a word v_m, the new automaton changes its state from p_i to (p_n, v_m) and continues to function the word stored in the memory until it is necessary to change or erase the stored word.

The automaton W_n has a memory that allows this automaton to store in it its number n. When the automaton W_n gets a word (k,w) as its input, this automaton, at first, compares the number k with the number n by writing a necessary part of k symbol after symbol to its memory. It is possible to build a memory in W_n such that any number less than or equal to n can be stored in this memory.

When the automaton W_n finds that k is less than or equal to n, then it starts working as the automaton U_n, which simulates the automaton B_k with the input w. Thus, W_n produces the same word as B_k with the input w. Since the automaton B_k is equivalent to the automaton A_k, the automaton W_n also models the automaton A_k. The output of W_n becomes the output of the whole evolutionary finite automaton *EU*. In such a way, the evolutionary finite automaton *EU* models the automaton A_k.

When the automaton W_n finds that k is larger than n, then it gives the whole word (k,w) as its output and this output goes to the next automaton W_{n+1} in the evolutionary finite automaton *EU*. The automaton W_{n+1} repeats the same procedure of the automaton W_n. This process continues until at some step the number of the automaton W_n becomes larger than k. Then the automaton W_n also models the automaton A_k. This shows that sooner or later the evolutionary deterministic finite automaton *EU* models any deterministic finite automaton A_k from the class **DFA** and thus, is universal to this class.

Theorem is proved.

As the class **DFA** does not have universal automata, Theorem 3 gives us the following result.

Corollary 1. The class of evolutionary deterministic finite automata **EDFA** is more expressive than the class of finite automata **FA**.

Let us compare evolutionary deterministic finite automata with other models of computation.

It is interesting that in spite of a much weaker computational power of deterministic finite automata in comparison with Turing machines, evolutionary deterministic finite automata can model Turing machines.

Theorem 4. For any Turing machine T, there is an evolutionary deterministic finite automaton E that models T.

Because of size limitations, the proof will be given elsewhere.

Corollary 2. There is an evolutionary deterministic finite automaton *EUT* universal for the class **T** of all Turing machines that work with an alphabet X.

Let **c**: **DFA** $\rightarrow I$ be a codification (symbolic description) of all finite automata in **DFA**. Evolutionary algorithms are series of automata from **DFA**. For instance, an evolutionary finite automaton is a series of finite automata.

Definition 7. A *universal evolutionary deterministic finite automaton* (*UEDFA*) is an EDFA *EU* = {UA[t]; t = 0, 1, 2, 3, ...} with the optimization space $Z = X \times I$. Given a pair (**c**(E), X[0]) where E = {A[t]; t = 0, 1, 2,...} is an EDFA and X[0] is the start population, the machine *EU* takes this pair as its input and produces the same population X[1] as the finite automaton A[0] working with the same population X[0]. Then *EU* takes the pair (**c**(E),X[1]) as its input and produces the same population X[2] as the finite automaton A[1] working with the population X[1]. In general, *EU* takes the pair (**c**(E),X[t]) as its input and produces the same population X[t + 1] as the finite automaton A[t] working with the population X[t] where t = 0, 1, 2, 3, ...

In other words, by a *universal evolutionary deterministic finite automaton* (*UEDFA*), we mean such EDFA *EU* that on each step takes as the input a pair (**c**(A[t]),X[t]) and behaves like EDFA E with input X[t] for t = 0, 1, 2,... UEDFA *EU* stops when EDFA E stops.

Definition 7 gives properties of a universal evolutionary finite automaton but does not imply its existence. However, as in the case of evolutionary finite automata, we have the following result.

Theorem 4. In the class **ET** of all evolutionary deterministic finite automata, there is a universal evolutionary deterministic finite automaton.

Proof. Let us take the evolutionary finite automaton *EU* = {W_n ; n = 1, 2,...} built in the proof of Theorem 3 and show that *EU* is a universal evolutionary deterministic finite automaton.

Let us take some evolutionary deterministic finite automaton E = {A[t]; t = 0, 1, 2,...} and describe how *EU* models E. By Definition 2, all A[t] are deterministic finite automata and have their numbers in the sequence A_1, A_2, A_3, ..., A_n,... That is, we assume that if A[t] = A_n, then **c**(A[t]) = n.

To explain how the automaton *EU* models the evolutionary automaton E, we show how the work of each finite automaton A[t] is modeled in *EU*. We show this using induction on the levels of the considered evolutionary automata.

In the beginning, the automaton W_1 receives a word (**c**(A[0]),w) = (i,w) where **c**(A[0]) = i as its input. Then the automaton W_1 compares the number i with the number 1 stored in its memory by writing a necessary part of i (symbol after symbol) to its memory. When the automaton W_1 finds that i is equal to 1, then it simulates the automaton A[0] with the input w. After this simulation, the output v of W_1 is transformed to the word $(\mathbf{c}(A[1]),v)$, which goes to the next level W_2 of the evolutionary finite automaton EU. When the automaton W_1 finds that i is larger than 1, then it gives the whole word $(\mathbf{c}(A[0]),w)$ as its output and this output goes to the next automaton W_2 in the evolutionary finite automaton EU. The automaton W_2 repeats the same procedure of the automaton W_n. This process continues until at some step the number of the automaton W_n becomes larger than i. When it happens, the automaton W_n models the automaton A[0] with the input w. Then the output v of W_n is transformed to the word $(\mathbf{c}(A[1]), v)$, which goes to the next level W_{n+1} of the evolutionary finite automaton EU. This forms the base for induction because it is demonstrated that EU models the first level of E.

To provide a general step of induction, we assume that an automaton W_n receives a word $(\mathbf{c}(A[t]),w) = (k,w)$ where $\mathbf{c}(A[t]) = k$ as its input. The automaton W_n has a memory that allows this automaton to store in it its number n. When the automaton W_n gets a word (k,w) as its input, this automaton, at first, compares the number k with the number n by writing k symbol after symbol to its memory. When the automaton W_n finds that k is less than or equal to n, then it simulates the automaton A[t] with the input w. After this simulation, the output v of W_n is transformed to the word $(\mathbf{c}(A[t+1]),v)$, which goes to the next level W_{n+1} of the evolutionary finite automaton EU.

When the automaton W_n finds that k is larger than n, then it gives the whole word $(\mathbf{c}(A[t]), w)$ as its output and this output goes to the next automaton W_{n+1} in the evolutionary finite automaton EU. The automaton W_{n+1} repeats the same procedure of the automaton W_n. This process continues until at some step the number of the automaton W_n becomes larger than k. Then the automaton W_n simulates the automaton A[t] with the input w. This shows that sooner or later the evolutionary deterministic finite automaton EU models the deterministic finite automaton A[t] from E. Now we can apply the principle of mathematical induction, which completes the proof of the theorem.

MODELING EVOLUTIONARY COMPUTATION BY EVOLUTIONARY AUTOMATA

The EA approach is very general and allows one to capture all currently known areas of evolutionary computation. Moreover, the potential of this approach is so big that it will allow one to accommodate future areas of evolutionary computation as well. In a natural way, evolutionary finite automata and evolutionary Turing machines give models for all four basic kinds of evolutionary computation: GA, ES, EP and GP. In each case, the n-th generation is computed by the n-th level automaton A_n from a relevant evolutionary automaton EA. The main difference is in the input representation of optimized systems in evolutionary algorithms. GA work with binary strings, ES work with vectors of real numbers, EP work with descriptions of finite automata, and GP work with parse trees. Difference in operators used by the basic kinds of evolutionary computation is reflected by utilization of the corresponding types of automata A_n in evolutionary automata EA.

In coevolutionary systems, more than one evolution process takes place: usually there are different populations which interact with each other. In coevolutionary systems that are a special case of concurrent systems, the fitness function for one population may depend on the state of the evolution processes in the other population(s). Coevolutionary systems might be important for approaching larger-scale problems, where a large problem is decomposed into smaller subproblems; there is a separate evolutionary process for each of the subproblems, however, these evolutionary processes are connected. Usually, evaluation of individuals in one population depends also on developments in other populations. In the EA approach, this feature is captured by making the fitness of the individual dependent on the whole population. This allows evolutionary automata to capture evolution/interaction of subsystems.

Particle Swarm Optimization (PSO, also called Swarm Intelligence) is a multiagent/coevolutionary technique, developed by Jim Kennedy and Russ Eberhart in 1995. A population of particles "flies" through the problem space. PSO has been inspired by bird flocking, fish schooling, buffalo herds, and swarming theory of social behaviors. A bird flock becomes swarm steering toward the center, matching neighbors' velocity, and avoiding collisions. PSO operates on a population of individuals where variation is applied, but without selection. Each individual has a position and velocity that is updated according to the relationship between the individual's parameters and the best location of the individual in the population found so far. The search is biased toward better regions of space, with the result being a sort of "flocking" toward the best solutions. The basic PSO is very simple to model in the EA approach: problem is represented by population/swarm of particles, where abstract positions are updated by of automata A_n from an appropriate evolutionary automaton EA. Level automata A_n add velocities using update equations based on previous best and global (or neighborhood) best positions.

Ant Colony Optimization (ACO also known as Ant Colony System (ACS)) is another multiagent technique, devoped by Marco Dorigo and his coauthors in 1997, where low-level interactions between artificial (i.e., simulated) ants result in a complex behavior of the larger ant colony. ACO algorithms were inspired by colonies of real ants that deposit a chemical substance (pheromone) on the ground. This substance influences the behavior of individual ants. The greater the amount of pheromone is on a particular path, the larger the probability that an ant will select that path. Artificial ants in ACO algorithms behave similarly. An abstract pheromone parameter plays a role similar to PSO position/velocity, or to Simulated Annealing temperature. It forms a communication/interaction channel between ants. In the EA approach, level automata A_n realize a simple iterative evolutionary algorithm, which builds solutions for each artificial ant/individual by applying the variation rule. This rule depends on the pheromone trail deposited and on another parameter called heuristic desirability.

Artificial Immune Systems (AIS) began in mid 80's with Farmer, Packard and Perelson's paper on immune networks in 1986. AIS are inspired by biological immune systems. Like other biologically inspired techniques, AIS try to extract ideas from a natural system, in particular the vertebrate immune system, in order to develop computational tools for solving engineering problems. AIS typically exploit the immune system's characteristics of learning and memory to solve a problem. AIS are coupled to AI and EC. Processes simulated in AIS include pattern recognition, hypermutation and clonal selection for B cells, negative selection of T cells, affinity maturation and immune network theory.

The biological immune system is a highly parallel and distributed adaptive system. It uses learning, memory, and associative retrieval to solve recognition and classification tasks. In particular, it learns to recognize relevant patterns, remembers patterns that have been seen previously, and use combinatorics to construct pattern detectors efficiently. AIS is probably the most specific form of evolutionary algorithms. However, abstract evolutionary automata can represent any adaptive system (and not only mutation, crossover and selection typical for evolutionary processes). In particular, evolutionary automata can realize pattern recognition, learning, immune phases of detection, containment, diagnosis and recovery typical for AIS.

Evolutionary Multiobjective Optimization is now an area of EC dealing with optimization of several objectives simultaneously. In the 1960s Rosenberg hinted the potential of evolutionary algorithms in multiobjective optimization, but the first actual implementation was developed in 1984 by Shaffer (VEGA). The first scheme to incorporate user's preferences into a multiobjective evolutionary algorithm (MOEA) was proposed in 1992 by Tanaka. There are two possible approaches to the solution of MOP: by converting it to a single objective using an arbitrary aggregating function taking into account the tradeoff between several objectives; or by keeping a vector of objective functions and using the notion of Pareto optimality (named after Italian economist Vilfredo Pareto, and also called Edgeworth-Pareto optimum) for nondominated solutions. Both approaches are easily captured by the EA approach using a vector of fitness functions associated with each objective and potentially combined by an aggregating function.

We will skip the description of other related areas of evolutionary computation (i.e., Evolutionary Artificial Systems, evolvable hardware, evolutionary robotics, Classifier Systems, Artificial Life, bioinformatics, or DNA-based computing). All of them can be quite efficiently modeled in the Evolutionary Automata approach.

CONCLUSION

In this paper, we elaborate a class of mathematical models for evolutionary computation. As in the case of conventional computations, these mathematical models allow us to study properties of evolutionary processes. We build universal systems for several classes of evolutionary algorithms: for evolutionary deterministic finite automata, evolutionary Turing machines, and evolutionary inductive Turing machines.

An important property of evolutionary automata is their expressiveness. Two classes of evolutionary automata have the same expressiveness if they can model the same evolutionary processes. We have demonstrated that evolutionary deterministic finite automata have much higher expressiveness than deterministic finite automata because evolutionary deterministic finite automata provide universal algorithms for the class of all deterministic finite automata and can model Turing machines. Consequently, evolutionary deterministic finite automata have more expressiveness in comparison with deterministic finite automata and have, at least, the same expressiveness as Turing machines.

FUTURE DIRECTIONS

It would be interesting to compare evolutionary deterministic finite automata to evolutionary Turing machines. Namely, we have the following problem:Is the class of all evolutionary deterministic finite automata **EDFA** as expressive as the class of evolutionary Turing machines **ET**?

It is also possible to consider other classes of evolutionary automata: the class of evolutionary nondeterministic pushdown automata **EPDA**, the class of evolutionary deterministic pushdown automata **EDPDA**, the class of evolutionary linearly bounded automata **ELBA**, the class of all evolutionary nondeterministic finite automata **ENFA**, etc., and to study their properties. In particular, it is interesting when these classes have the same expressiveness and in what situations their expressiveness is different.

One more interesting problem is to build evolutionary automata using the $-Calculus (Eberbach, 2005b).

REFERENCES

Aho, A. V., Hopcroft, J. E., & Ullman, J. D. (1976). *The Design and Analysis of Computer Algorithms*. Reading, MA: Addison-Wesley P.C.

Back, T., Fogel, D. B., & Michalewicz, Z. (Eds.) (1997). *Handbook of Evolutionary Computation*. Oxford University Press.

Bonabeau, E., Dorigo, M., & Theraulaz, G. (1999). *Swarm Intelligence: From Natural to Artificial Systems*. Oxford University Press.

Burgin, M. (1983). Multiple computations and Kolmogorov complexity for such processes. *Notices of the Academy of Sciences of the USSR*, 269(4), 793-797

Burgin, M. (2003) Nonlinear Phenomena in Spaces of Algorithms, *International Journal of Computer Mathematics*, 80(12), 1449-1476.

Burgin, M. (2005). *Superrecursive Algorithms*. Springer, New York.

Burgin, M. (2005a). *Measuring Power of Algorithms, Programs, and Automata*. In Artificial Intelligence and Computer Science. Nova Science Publishers, New York, 1-61.

Davis, M., & Weyuker, E. (1983). *Computability, Complexity and Languages*. Orlando: Academic Press.

Deutsch, D. (1985). Quantum theory, the Church-Turing principle, and the universal quantum Turing machine. *Proc. Roy. Soc.,* Ser. A, *400*, 97-117.

Eberbach, E. (2005a). Toward a theory of evolutionary computation. *BioSystems, 82*, 1-19.

Eberbach, E. (2005b). $-Calculus of Bounded Rational Agents: Flexible Optimization as Search under Bounded Resources in Interactive Systems. *Fundamenta Informaticae, 68*(1-2), 47-102.

Eberbach, E., & Wegner, P. (2003). Beyond Turing Machines, *Bulletin of the European Association for Theoretical Computer Science* (EATCS Bulletin), *81*, 279-304.

Ebbinghaus, H. -D., Jacobs, K., Mahn, F. -K., & Hermes, H. (1970). *Turing Machines and Recursive Functions*, Springer-Verlag, Berlin/Heidelberg/New York.

Fogel, D. B. (1995). *Evolutionary Computation: Toward a New Philosophy of Machine Intelligence*. IEEE Press.

Fogel, D. B. (2001). *An Introduction to Evolutionary Computation, Tutorial, Congress on Evolutionary Computation (CEC'2001)*, Seoul, Korea.

He, J., & Yao, X. (2004). A study of drift analysis for estimating computation time of evolutionary algorithms. *Nat. Comput. 3*, 21-25.

Holland, J. H. (1975). *Adaptation in Natural and Artificial Systems*. Univ. of Michigan Press, Ann Arbor: MIT Press, 2nd ed.

Hopcroft, J. E., Motwani, R., & Ullman, J. D. (2001). *Introduction to Automata Theory, Languages, and Computation*, Addison Wesley, Boston/San Francisco/New York.

Kennedy, J., & Eberhart, R. (1995). Particle Swarm Optimization. In *Proc. of the 1995 IEEE Int. Conf. on Neural Networks*, 1942-1948.

Kennedy, J., Eberhart R., & Shi Y. (2001). *Swarm Intelligence*, Morgan Kaufmann.

Koza, J. (1992). *Genetic Programming I, II, III*, MIT Press, 1992, 1994, 1999.

Michalewicz, Z. (1996). *Genetic Algorithms + Data Structures = Evolution Programs*. Springer-Verlag.

Michalewicz, Z., & Fogel D. B. (2004). *How to Solve It: Modern Heuristics*. Springer-Verlag.

Rogers, H. (1987). *Theory of Recursive Functions and Effective Computability*. Cambridge, MA: MIT Press.

Rudolph, G. (1994). Convergence analysis of canonical genetic algorithms. *IEEE Trans. Neural Networks: Special Issue on EC, 5*(1), 96-101.

Simpson, S. G. (2006). *What is Foundations of Mathematics?* (http://www.math.psu.edu/simpson/hierarchy. html)

Wolpert, D. H., & Macready, W. G. (1997). No free lunch theorems for optimization. *IEEE Trans. Evol. Comput., 1*(1), 67-82.

Wolpert, D. H., & Tumer, K. (2000). An Introduction to Collective Intelligence. In *Handbook of Agent Technology*. AAAI/MIT Press.

KEY TERMS

Completeness of an Evolutionary Algorithm: The ability of an evolutionary algorithm to find any solution.

Completeness of a Class of Evolutionary Algorithms: The ability to find any solution using algorithms from this class.

Decidability of an Evolutionary Algorithm: The ability to find whether the evolutionary algorithm can solve a specific problem or class of problems.

Decidability of a Class of Evolutionary Algorithms: The ability to find whether it is possible solve a specific problem or class of problems using algorithms from this class.

Evolutionary Automata: Class of abstract automata designed to model evolutionary processes.

Evolutionary Turing Machine: An evolutionary automaton that consists of an infinite series of Turing machines each of which computes a generation in evolution.

Evolutionary Inductive Turing Machine: An evolutionary automaton that consists of an infinite series of inductive Turing machines each of which computes a generation in evolution.

Expressiveness of an Evolutionary Algorithm: Characterized by the class of problems solvable by an evolutionary algorithm.

Expressiveness of a Class of Evolutionary Algorithms: Characterized by the class of problems solvable by evolutionary algorithms from this class.

Inductive Turing Machine: A finite-state machine associated that has an external storage or memory medium and gives its final result only when its output stops changing after a finite number of steps.

Inductive Turing Machines of the First Order: Inductive Turing machines that have recursive memory.

Inductive Turing Machines of the Order n: Inductive Turing machines that have a memory connections in which are constructed by an inductive Turing machine of the order $n - 1$.

Recursive Algorithms: Classes of algorithms that can solve the same problems (compute the same fucntions) as Turing machines.

Subrecursive Algorithms: Classes of algorithms that cannot solve all problems (compute everything) that Turing machines can solve (compute).

Super-Recursive Algorithms: Classes of algorithms that can solve more problems (compute more) than Turing machines.

Super-Turing Models of Computation: Models of computation more expressive than Turing machines.

Chapter XVII
Evolutionary Path Planning for Robot Navigation Under Varying Terrain Conditions

Terrence P. Fries
Coastal Carolina University, USA

ABSTRACT

Path planning is an essential component in the control software for an autonomous mobile robot. Evolutionary strategies are employed to determine optimal paths for their robustness and ability to solve complex problems. However, current evolutionary approaches fail to consider varying terrain conditions when determining an optimal path and offer only path planning without trajectory planning. This chapter presents an approach that determines a near optimal path while incorporating trajectory planning in the solution. Fuzzy linguistic variables are used represent the inherent imprecision and uncertainty in the terrain conditions presented to the robot. Most importantly, the method is computationally efficient and robust, providing real-time response and the ability to operate in a dynamic environment.

INTRODUCTION

Optimal path planning is critical to the successful operation of autonomous mobile robots and any application in which they are involved. An autonomous robot must be able to determine an optimal or near-optimal path and then follow it. It must also have the capability to detect unexpected obstacles in a dynamic or uncertain environment and adjust its path accordingly. Motion planning consists of two components: path planning and trajectory planning (Latombe, 1991). In many navigation methods, these two components are distinct and separate, although they are combined in some methods. Path planning computes a collision-free path through an environment. The path is optimal or near-optimal with respect to some criteria, such as shortest distance traveled, shortest time, or least hostile environment. Trajectory planning computes the actions the robot must take to follow the path. These actions include turns and straight movements. This chapter presents an evolutionary navigation approach that combines path and trajectory planning and has the capability to adapt in a dynamic environment. Fuzzy linguistic variables are used to represent uncertain terrain conditions.

Copyright © 2009, IGI Global, distributing in print or electronic forms without written permission of IGI Global is prohibited.

Figure 1. Non-monotone path between rooms

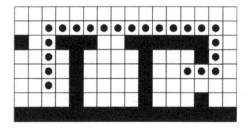

Several issues must be considered when evaluating a robot navigation scheme. Any practical navigation algorithm must be able to respond in real-time. In a real world application, it is often not practical for a robot to wait for any length of time before proceeding. Usually computational resources are limited onboard an autonomous mobile robot and must be shared with operational algorithms, such as vision and image recognition. Therefore, a useful navigation algorithm must be computationally efficient. An algorithm must be able to adapt to a dynamic environment and take into consideration the myriad of issues associated with traversing various types of terrain.

Due to the complexity and uncertainty involved in autonomous robot navigation, attempts have been made to employ evolutionary algorithms. However, the most of these approaches reduce the computational complexity by constraining the robot's operation to a static environment (Akbarzadeh, 2000; Cuesta, 2005; Fogel, 2000; Nearchou, 1999; Pratihar, 1999). This is not practical because real world environments are not isolated from external influences. Often, people move about in the environment and obstacles may be moved. When a robot interacts with these dynamic actors, it requires the ability to adjust its path. In addition, due to the nature of sensory data, especially that acquired through vision interpretation techniques, the environment information possesses some level of uncertainty and incompleteness. Most evolutionary approaches to navigation fail to account for these anomalies and assume a smooth and level terrain for the robot. Those that do address these issues are not able to respond in real-time due to computational complexity. The evolutionary navigation method presented in this chapter is sufficiently computationally efficient to provide real-time operation in all tested situations. Furthermore, the approach has the capability to adapt to dynamic and uncertain environments while addressing terrain issues.

The majority of navigation approaches that utilize evolutionary computation fail to provide real-time operation (Akbarzadeh, 2000; Cuesta, 2005; Fogel, 2000; Nearchou, 1999; Pratihar, 1999). The few methods that provide real-time operation do so by placing unacceptable restrictions on the generated path, such as limiting the possible solution paths to x-monotone or y-monotone (Sugihara, 1997). An x-monotone path is one in which the projection of the path on the x-axis is non-decreasing. This limits the robot's path to always move in the same direction relative to a given axis. Such as restriction prevents the robot from responding to an newly discovered obstacle in a dynamic environment because it is unable to backtrack in its path. A simple path between two rooms in a building is neither x-monotone nor y-monotone as shown in Figure 1.

The use of fixed-length chromosomes has also been tried to reduce the computational complexity of an evolutionary algorithm for path planning (Cordon, 2004; Sugihara, 1997). However, it has been demonstrated that fixed-length chromosomes are too restrictive to be useful in navigation (Cordon, 2004; Fogel, 2000). They place unacceptable constraints on the representation of the environment and the solution path.

More flexible approaches to path planning using evolutionary computation techniques have been proposed. Shibata and Fukuda (1993) have used an evolutionary algorithm for a point robot, however, it was limited to a static environment. Another attempt at evolutionary path planning is based on minimizing the accumulated deviation between the actual and desired path (Davidor, 1991). The major failure of this approach is that it assumes a desired path is already know and that the robot is confined to a static environment. Nearchou (1998) proposed an evolutionary approach that requires the robot's map to be converted to a graph. However, the conversion of maps in formats, such a Voronoi map, are computationally intensive. Other evolutionary approaches to path planning apply GAs to the training of neural networks (Peters, 2003), reactive navigation (deLope, 2003), potential fields

(Vadakkepat, 2003), and hierarchical structures (Urdiales, 2003). However, these approaches are only able to perform in a static environment.

Another problem with many current navigation approaches is their failure to address various terrain conditions. It is common to label map areas with one of two options: clear or blocked by an obstacle (Cordon, 2004; Pratihar, 1999). In true operational environments, especially outdoors, there may exist a myriad of varying terrains. Sandy or sloped terrain may cause slippage of the robot, changing its path or restricting its progress. Rocky terrain may force minor course adjustments and/or loss of time. Hills may increase the time and difficulty of progress while climbing or descending the slope. Although adverse terrain conditions may have costs associated with its traversal, it may yield a more optimal path than easier terrain with substantially longer paths (Fries, 2006b).

It has been proposed to measure the roughness of the terrain by its elevation changes (Iagnemma, 2004). However, the approach is more concerned with relatively large elevation changes and the impact on wheel diameter and wheel-terrain contact force and angle. This results in complex computation and is only suitable to the slow movement of a planetary rover. It does not provide the real-time response required in common applications. Other researchers (Bonnafous, 2001; Davidson, 2001; Hait, 1996; Iagnemma, 2003; Kelly, 1998; Madjidi, 2003; Pai, 1998; Seraji, 2002; Spero, 2002) have also addressed the affects of harsh terrain such as large elevation changes and rocky expanses. However, they fail to address less severe terrain features that may also have significant effect on the traversability of the terrain. A sandy or gravel surface or a shallow slope often confront mobile robots in everyday applications.

A successful navigation algorithm must address the uncertainty inherent in terrain sensing devices and mapping methods (Fries, 2004; Fries, 2005; Iagnemma, 2003; Kelly, 1998; Laubach, 1999; Lee, 2003; Tunstel, 2003). Frequently, the exact condition of terrain in an area is uncertain due sensory methods. As a result, the terrain conditions for a certain area are only approximations or, at times, guesses. Attempts to address this uncertainty using Gaussian (Iagnemma, 2004) and Kalman (Jung, 2003) filters have had varying levels of success. However, these approaches are computationally complex and, therefore, fail to provide real-time operation.

The unique contribution of this research is the inclusion of a variety of terrain conditions into the calculation of the optimal path. Although research into the use of GAs for path planning has been conducted for several years, little of it has included terrain conditions other than severe ones. The few methods that account for terrain conditions rely on elevation changes as the sole terrain criteria. This research has not only includes terrain conditions in the determination of a near-optimal path, it also provides a method of accounting for the uncertainty of those conditions through the use of fuzzy sets. The vast majority of navigation algorithms address only path planning, leaving trajectory planning for a later step by another operational part of the system. The GA coding scheme used in this research combines path planning with trajectory planning, thus, eliminating the additional step of trajectory planning once an optimal path is found and reducing the computational time to allow a real-time response. In addition, this method is robust, allowing the robot to adapt to dynamic conditions in the environment.

Section 2 presents a background on evolutionary computation, fuzzy set theory, and current work in evolutionary path planning. In Section 3, the new fuzzy genetic motion planning approach is presented including representation of the environment in a grid format, encoding of the chromosome, representation of terrain conditions using fuzzy linguistic variables, and selection of the genetic algorithm parameters. Section 4 provides a discussion of the implementation and test results of the new path planning approach. Sections 5 and 6 provide a summary of the approach and a discussion of future directions for research on this method, respectively.

BACKGROUND

Genetic Algorithms

A genetic algorithm (GA) is a form of evolutionary computation frequently used for optimization (Goldberg, 1998; Holland, 1975). Chromosomes, which represent possible solutions to a problem, comprise the population set. Each chromosome encodes a possible solution as a binary string. New chromosomes are added to the population via methods analogous to biological evolution.

Figure 2. Crossover with same size offspring

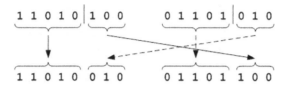

Figure 3. Crossover with different size offspring

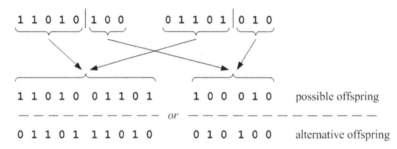

The GA starts with an initial population of randomly generated chromosomes. The fittest individuals are selected to reproduce offspring. The fitness of an individual is evaluated using some domain-specific criteria based on the problem to be solved. A fitness function computes the relative merit of a chromosome by determining how good the possible solution is. For example, in the case of path planning, the fitness function may calculate the distance traveled or the traversal time to move from the initial position to the destination. The offspring are generated by applying to the parent chromosomes various genetic operators which emulate natural evolutionary processes. Two of the most commonly used genetic operators are crossover and mutation. Once the offspring have been completely generated, their fitness is evaluated. The most fit members of the enlarged population are retained and the others are discarded. The process continues until the population converges to a solution indicated by exceeding a fixed number of generations or the changes fitness between generations falls below a specified threshold. Several components can significantly affect the performance of a genetic algorithm: encoding of the chromosome, the initial population, the genetic operators and their control parameters, and the fitness function.

The crossover operator divides two or more chromosomes and recombines the parts of different chromosomes into new ones. In single point crossover, the left section of one parent is combined with the right section of another, and then the remaining two parts of the parents are combined, thus, creating two new offspring. This produces two offspring of the same size as the parents as shown in Figure 2. In an alternate form, the crossover operator can also combine the left parts of two parents to form one offspring and the left sections to form a second offspring. This approach forms offspring of differing sizes as shown in Figure 3. Although it is quite common for the crossover point to be randomly selected, for some problems it is more appropriate to fix the crossover point. Some applications benefit from multiple point crossover which divides the chromosome into multiple strings which are recombined with those of another chromosome. Additional crossover schemes which utilize heuristics also exist, but add too much computational complexity for this application. As in biological evolution, not all chromosomes are subjected to crossover. The crossover rate, μ, specifies the percentage of parent chromosomes involved in crossover and recombination.

Another genetic operator is mutation which changes the value of one random bit in a chromosome. A single parent produces an offspring which is identical except at the randomly selected mutation point as shown in Figure 4. The mutation rate, ρ, specifies the probability that a particular chromosome is subjected to mutation.

Figure 4. Mutation operator

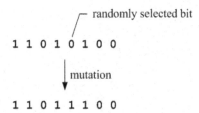

Fuzzy Sets

In many real world situations, an object cannot be solely classified into one class, while totally excluding it from all others. For example, a class of tall people cannot be defined in usual mathematical terms because there exist different degrees of tallness which are subjective. Traditionally, membership in a class is represented by a binary value using the characteristic function

$$\mu_A(x) = \begin{cases} 1 & \text{if } x \text{ is an element of set } A \\ 0 & \text{if } x \text{ is not an element of set } A \end{cases}$$

where an object x is an element of some universe A. This characteristic function provides the mapping to binary choice of 0 or 1

$$\mu_A(x) \quad : \quad X \to \{0, 1\}$$

A fuzzy set, or class, is defined by a membership function which describes an object's degree of membership in a particular set (Zadeh, 1965). The membership function provides a mapping to any real value in the range 0 to 1, inclusive,

$$\mu_A(x) \quad : \quad X \to [0, 1]$$

The characteristic function may be a ramp, a step, sigmoidal, bell-shaped, or any other continuous function over the interval [0, 1]. A commonly used characteristic function has the shape of a triangle and is referred to as a triangular fuzzy number.

A triangular fuzzy number has a membership function with a convex contour and is denoted by the tuple (a, b, c) as shown in Figure 5. The membership function is defined as

$$\mu_A(x) = \begin{cases} (x-a)/(b-a) & \text{if } a \leq x \leq b \\ (x-c)/(b-c) & \text{if } b \leq x \leq c \\ 0 & \text{otherwise} \end{cases}$$

Evolutionary Approaches to Path Planning for Robot Navigation

Path planning using standard search algorithms is NP complete. However, genetic algorithms have been proven to be capable of solving such search problems (Goldberg, 1998; Holland , 1975). In addition, traditional search

Figure 5. Triangular fuzzy number

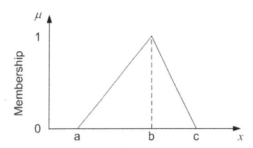

algorithms can easily get caught in a local minimum, where GAs have the inherent capability of escaping local minima. Due to the suitability of GAs, there have been many attempts at evolutionary robot path planning.

One approach describes the robot motion as a series of Euclidean transformations that rotate or move the robot (Wu, 2006). The path is a sequence of dots representing the Euclidean coordinates of the robot as it moves. These coordinates are encoded as real numbers in the chromosome. The GAs uses the crossover and mutation operators to produce new offspring. The fitness of each chromosome depends on the length and the smoothness of path. The GA requires 20 generations to converge on a solution. Wu establishes convergence to a near optimal solution when the best element in a generation produces no more than a 0.5% fitness improvement over the best element in the prior generation.

Li (2006) uses a similar representation in the chromosome. The crossover and mutation operators are used to generate new offspring, however, the fitness function is simplified to account only for the length of the path. The method improves on other GA approaches by using a self-adaptive algorithm to control crossover and mutation probabilities. The method performs well in simulations, but has not been tested in a real environment.

A method using a dual-layer GA has been proposed to address dynamic environments containing both static and dynamic obstacles (Lu, 2007). The first layer of the GA accounts for static obstacles, while the second layer handles dynamic obstacles. The path is viewed as a series of waypoints in the movement of the robot. The chromosome encodes sets of coordinates for the robot and the fitness function is based on both the length of the path and its smoothness. Offspring are generated using the crossover and mutation operators. Simulation in Visual C++ has shown acceptable results, however, the method has not been tested in a real world environment.

Hu and Vie (2007) propose a niche genetic algorithm (NGA). A niche is a heuristic that increases search efficiency by adjusting the fitness of each element in the population based on some criteria. The sharing niche decreases the fitness of each population element (chromosome) by an amount related to the number of similar individuals in the population. This maintains diversity of the population. The approach was tested on a 20 x 20 grid with 7 obstacles. The GA used the crossover and mutation operators with an initial population of 50. The probability of mutation was 0.1and the mutation rate was 0.9. The NGA converged to a near optimal solution after 9 generations, while the traditional GA required 14 generations. This method has not been tested on a larger grid so it is not possible to determine its performance for larger, higher resolution environments.

Tarokh (2008) provides one of the few attempts to consider terrain conditions in evolutionary path planning. The fitness function attempts to optimize terrain roughness and path curvature. The environment is considered to be a grid of cells with each cell containing the height of rocks in it. A contour map is created with the height of rocks in each cell expressed as a fuzzy set with 5 possible options. A unique feature is that the method adjusts the probabilities of the genetic operators based on the diversity measure of path populations and the traversability measure of the paths. The method has been successfully tested on a 16 x 16 grid, but has not been evaluated by the researchers for higher resolution grids.

An approach for a non-holonomic robot, one with joints that cannot be assumed to be a point, parameterizes the joint angles by sinusoidal functions (Xu, 2006). The GA uses the crossover and mutation operators to search for an optimal solution for the sinusoidal function parameters.

While these approaches provide satisfactory results, they fail to account for terrain conditions when searching for a path. In addition, their performance has not been tested on higher resolution grids. This brings into question the viability of any of current evolutionary approach for real world applications.

EVOLUTIONARY PATH PLANNING

In order to focus on the issues of motion planning and the impact of terrain conditions, it was necessary to reduce the complexity of the problem through several assumptions. First, the robot is assumed to be holonomic, that is, able to turn within its own radius. A nonholonomic vehicle, such as an automobile, faces difficult challenges when planning a turn or backing up. The use of a holonomic robot significantly reduces the complexity involved in navigation planning (Hait, 1996; Latombe, 1991). Second, the robot's movement has been limited to a move-stop-turn paradigm. The robot will move in a straight line, stop and turn to orient itself in the direction of its next movement, and then proceed. Using this movement paradigm eliminates the complexity of planning an arc-shaped path and the problems associated with the lateral forces induced by a curved path (Fries, 2006a). Third, localization of the robot will depend solely on dead reckoning determined by wheel odometry.

Environment Grid

An occupancy grid is commonly used to represent the range over which a robot may navigate (Elfes, 1989; Latombe, 1991). The proposed evolutionary path planning algorithm utilizes an environment grid which extends the occupancy grid by encoding the terrain characteristics for each cell within the grid itself. The algorithm defines the robot's path as the traversal of a series of moves through adjacent cells in the grid followed by a stop, and then a rotation that orients the robot toward the next movement. Since the robot movement is defined as traversal from the center of one cell to the center of an adjacent cell, the path length is easily calculated as the sum of the distances between the cells traversed. The distance $d(a,b)$ between any two adjacent cells a and b is defined as the Euclidean distance between the centers of the two cells. This representation of distance allows the map data to be stored in any efficient format, such as a quadtree. Quadtree storage of an environment provides a more compact representation by storing a large open area or large obstacle as a single grid location, rather than many uniformly sized small squares (Yahja, 1998). In addition, it allows fewer segments in the path which reduces the size of the chromosome in the GA and the time required for the GA to converge to a solution

A fuzzy value is assigned to each cell in the grid denoting the difficulty involved in traversing that cell due to its terrain conditions. Fuzzy terrain conditions allow the consideration of cells with moderately difficult terrain, such as loose sand or rocks, if the path is significantly shorter than a one with no terrain problems. This allows the GA to consider the tradeoffs of terrain conditions and distance. Cells containing obstacles are labeled with an extreme fuzzy value indicating that they are totally impassible. Further discussion of the fuzzy terrain conditions can be found in another section on this chapter. For this research, the grid will be restricted to 16 by 16 for simplicity, however, the algorithm has been successfully tested for much larger sized grids. Further discussion of this restriction and actual testing is found in the Test Results section of this chapter.

When placing obstacles in the environment grid, the boundaries of the obstacles are expanded by the radius of the robot as shown in Figure 6. This allows the algorithm to consider the robot as a holonomic point rather than a two-dimensional object. Since the obstacles have been expanded by the radius of the robot, it is not necessary to consider other cells sharing a common corner with the cell occupied by the robot. This permits navigation of the point robot along the side of an obstacle or diagonally between obstacles without concern for the adjacent cells. Figure 7 illustrates the diagonal traversal of cells. Since we know that the obstacle has been expanded by the radius of the robot, it can be concluded that the open diagonal traversal will not encounter the obstacle itself. If the actual obstacle were a hindrance to the diagonal movement, it would have been expanded to block the diagonal movement.

Figure 6. Expanding obstacles by the radius of the robot

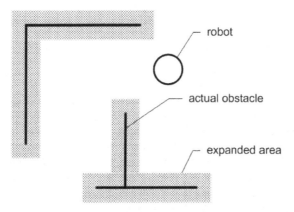

Figure 7. Diagonal traversal of cells with expanded obstacles

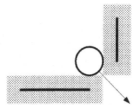

Chromosome Encoding

The speed of convergence of a genetic algorithm to a solution depends upon the gene encoding method (Wu, 2006). A successful encoding scheme accurately represents the possible solutions while minimizing the length of the binary string, or chromosome. Minimizing the length of the chromosome reduces the number of generations required to produce an acceptable solution because fewer permutations are possible. Since fixed-length chromosomes are too restrictive for path planning, as previously discussed, a variable length string was chosen. The string is composed of blocks which encode the direction and length of movement for each segment of the solution path. Consider the robot in the center of nine cells as in Figure 8 (a) having just arrived from cell 4 and facing in the direction of the arrow. Although there are eight possible directions for movement, many can be eliminated from consideration. Cell 4 can be eliminated for the next move since the robot has just traversed through that cell and returning to it would produce a non-optimal path. Cells 1, 2, 6, and 7 can be eliminated from consideration because they could have been reached from cell 4 using a shorter distance than through the center cell in which the robot currently is positioned. That leaves only three cells to be considered for possible movement. The three cells require only 2 bits to encode as in Figure 8 (b).

The largest number of cells that can be traversed in a square grid is the full width, height, or major diagonal of the square. Since the grid in our example is constrained to 16 by 16 cells, the maximum number of cells that can be traversed in a single move is 15 which requires 4 bits to encode. Thus, each movement can be encoded in a 6-bit block with 2 bits for direction and 4 bit for distance as shown in Figure 9. For larger n x n grids, the block size is denoted by $2 + \log 2n$. A chromosome composed of these 6-bit blocks contains not only the path, but also the necessary trajectory information for movement of the robot. This unique encoding provides both path planning and trajectory planning.

Figure 8. Possible movement to next cell

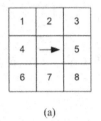 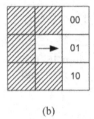

(a)   (b)

Figure 9. Block encoding of one movement

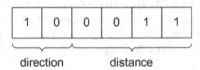

direction   distance

Figure 10. Sample path in a 16 x 16 environment grid

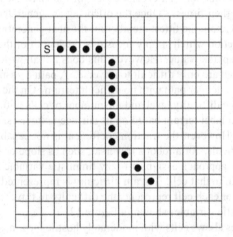

Figure 10 shows a typical path for the robot. The chromosome for the path is shown in Figure 11 with 4 blocks, one for each path segment. In this case, it is assumed that the robot is already facing in the correct direction, so it can proceed straight ahead. If a turn of more than 45 degrees clockwise or counterclockwise is needed for the first move, the other blocks would be proceeded by one or more block encoding a turn with zero cell traversals.

Genetic Operators and Parameters

Finding the optimal values for GA parameters is an entire subfield of evolutionary research. Many attempts have been made to automate the selection of parameters (Kamei, 2004; Yan, 2007). Since this lies outside the scope of this algorithm, GA parameters were determined through experimentation.

Figure 11. Chromosome encoding of solution path

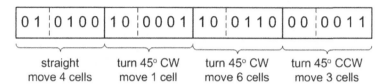

| straight | turn 45° CW | turn 45° CW | turn 45° CCW |
| move 4 cells | move 1 cell | move 6 cells | move 3 cells |

The motion planning genetic algorithm first randomly generates an initial population of chromosomes. In an attempt to direct the solution toward the shortest path, one addition chromosome is added to the initial population. It represents a straight line from the start to destination regardless of obstacles. Through the testing of various combinations of variables, it was found that a population size, $p = 20$, was sufficient to seed the chromosome base to provide rapid convergence while simultaneously minimizing computational complexity.

The algorithm uses single point crossover with a crossover rate of 0.85. The crossover rate, γ, is the percentage of parent chromosomes involved in the crossover. The mutation rate, μ, or probability that a particular bit in the string is inverted, was 0.02. The parameter values were used for all testing, including different grid sizes and different environmental configurations.

Fuzzy Terrain Conditions

The selection of an appropriate fitness function is a crucial aspect of the GA-based approach. Chromosomes are selected for reproduction based on their fitness. Once the offspring are generated, the fitness of each of the individuals in the population is used to retain the fittest member for the next generation. Current GA-based path planning approaches use a fitness function which simply measures the length of the path. If an obstacle is in the path, the fitness is set to an unacceptable value. However, this does not allow for considerations of terrain conditions which are not impassable, but are only difficult to traverse. A path crossing one or more cells with a difficult terrain may still be superior to a longer path with no difficult terrain. On the other hand, the longer path may be a better option depending on the difficulty level and the number of cells with difficult terrain.

Recent attempts have been made to label terrain based on its surface texture using a fuzzy set representing a traction coefficient (Tuntsel, 2003). However, the traction coefficient is not capable of representing many of the terrain conditions which cause difficulty for a robot's traversal, such as slope or slippage potential. Instead of a traction coefficient, the fuzzy-GA approach assigns a fuzzy linguistic variable to each cell corresponding to the difficulty in traversing the terrain in that cell. Terrain difficulty is represented a fuzzy linguistic variable (Zadeh, 1983). The terrain condition for each cell represents the difficulty in traversing the cell is expressed as a triangular fuzzy set using the linguistic variables shown in Figure 12.

The use of fuzzy linguistic variables allows cells with moderately hostile terrain, such as rocks or loose sand, to be considered in a possible solution path while being weighted by their difficulty of traversal. For any path not passing through an obstacle, the fitness function uses the Euclidean distance between the centers of the cells traversed weighted by the terrain conditions for each cell. A cell which contains an obstacle is assigned a fuzzy linguistic variables indicating it is impassable and any possible solution path containing it is unacceptable.

Problems in terrain conditions arise because it is difficult to compare different terrain conditions due to their varied nature. In addition, the difficulty of traversal may vary from one instance to another. The direction of traversal can also have significant impact on the difficulty level. The difficulties for a robot moving uphill, downhill, or across the side of a sandy hill are quite different. The side-hill traversal is usually much more difficult due to the angle and more time consuming due to slippage. When moving across the face of a slope, slippage can result in deviation from the planned path, as well as loss of forward progress. Because of the imprecision of terrain conditions and the problems in directly comparing them, fuzzy linguistic variables are very appropriate for representing terrain conditions.

Figure 12. Fuzzy representation of terrain conditions

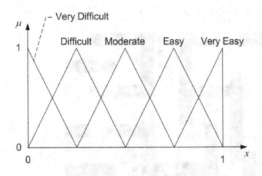

Operation of a Dynamic Environment

The evolutionary terrain-based method provides a robust navigation scheme by allowing a robot to function in a dynamic environment. If an obstacle is encountered by the robot where it is not expected, the algorithm uses the GA to recalculate a new optimal path from the current location of the robot to the destination. The robot can then continue its movement.

TEST RESULTS

The evolutionary navigation was implemented using C++ and Saphira robot control software by SRI International. It was tested first in the Saphira simulator and, then, on a Pioneer 2-DX mobile robot. The Pioneer 2-DX is a 3-wheeled holonomic robot with a 250 mm radius. It is equipped with a suite of eight sonar sensors arranged around the forward hemisphere of the robot as shown in Figure 13 and tactile bumpers in the rear hemisphere to detect collisions while backing. The robot was provided a predefined map representing the environment as a grid. All test cases were conducted using a 16 by 16 grid for the purpose of clarity. This grid size allows demonstration of the functionality of the algorithm while maintaining the readability of the images. Testing has also been conducted using much larger grids and quadtree representations of the environment with similar results.

Figure 13. Sonar sensor suite on Pioneer 2-DX robot

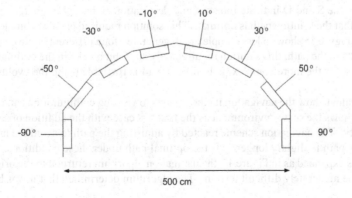

Figure 14. Path generation with no terrain problems

Figure 15. Path in alternate environment with no terrain problems

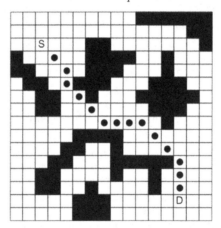

Figure 14 shows a test environment and the path generated by the evolutionary navigation. In this case, no cells were labeled with fuzzy terrain conditions. The black cells indicate expanded boundaries of actual obstacles which are impassable. The S and D indicate the start and destination cells of the robot, respectively. Manual examination confirms that the solution path is optimal. This solution required eleven 6-bit blocks in the optimal solution chromosome. Figure 15 shows a less complex path generated for a different environment grid. Because there are fewer segments in the path, this solution required only six 6-bit blocks in the optimal solution chromosome. Even the solution for the more complex path in Figure 14 is tractable using the evolutionary navigation algorithm.

It is important to evaluate how the navigation method reacts to varying configurations and severity of terrain conditions. Figure 16 shows the same environment as the first test case with the addition of several cells labeled with Moderate difficulty. The navigation scheme reacted by adjusting the path to avoid the moderately difficult terrain. While the new path is slightly longer, it is the optimal path under these conditions. When the area of Moderate difficulty was expanded as in Figure 17, the navigation algorithm returned to the original path optimal path passing through the moderately difficult terrain. The algorithm determined that it was better to traverse a

Figure 16. Path avoiding area with Moderate area of difficulty

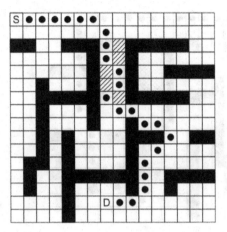

Figure 17. Path traversing area with Moderate area of difficulty

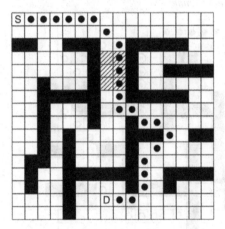

small area of moderately difficult terrain rather than take a much longer path. However, when the terrain conditions were changed to Difficult, the path generated avoided the difficult area and took a much longer route shown in Figure 18. The path provided by the evolutionary scheme matched the expected behavior in all cases.

A critical aspect of autonomous navigation is the ability to respond to a dynamic environment. Using the test environment grid with no terrain conditions, the robot calculated the optimal path and began to follow it. Figure 19 shows the planned robot path as solid circles and an unexpected obstacle blocking the path shown as an X. When the robot encountered the unexpected obstacle, it recalculated a new optimal path from its current location to the destination. The hollow circles illustrate the dynamically recalculated optimal path followed by the robot to the destination. This, along with additional tests, demonstrated the robust nature of the evolutionary navigation algorithm and its ability to respond to a dynamic environment.

The flexibility of the grid representation of the environment was also investigated by representing the environment from Figure 15 as a quadtree as shown in Figure 20. Tests confirmed that an optimal path is also generated when using a quadtree environment. The only adjustment to the method is inclusion of a heuristic to decide to which cell to move in the event several exist when moving from a large aggregate cell to one of several adjacent smaller ones as shown in Figure 21.

Figure 18. Path with Difficult terrain area

Figure 19. Navigation in a dynamic environment

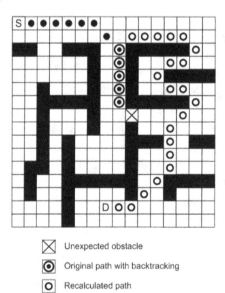

CONCLUSION

This chapter has presented a fuzzy genetic algorithm approach to navigation for an autonomous mobile robot that performs in real-time without the limitations of current methods. The primary significance of the method is its ability to include a wide variety of terrain conditions in the decision making process when determining a near optimal path. The few current method that account for terrain conditions only rank terrain based on a single-dimensional concept such as the height of rocks. This method in this chapter allows the inclusion of a wide variety of terrain conditions, including slope, soil conditions and texture, and rockiness. Varying terrain conditions are represented as fuzzy linguistic variables for inclusion in the path planning decision. The encod-

Figure 20. Quadtree representation of an environment

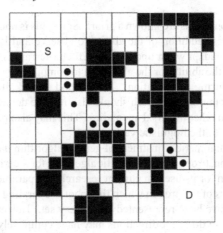

Figure 21. Movement decision for quadtrees

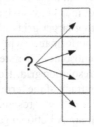

ing of the chromosome provides full motion planning capabilities and the method is capable of operation in a dynamic environment. Further research directions include the ability to observe and learn terrain conditions during movement along the path.

Another advantage of this research over many traditional path planning algorithms, such as those using search algorithms, is that it incorporates trajectory planning into the solution. Thus, once the optimal path is discovered, the trajectory information is immediately available for movement of the robot and does not require additional computation

For purposes of demonstrating its functionality and clarity of the images, this chapter has presented the algorithm using a very simplistic 16 x 16 grid. The approach has been successfully implemented using much larger grids and with quadtree representations of the environment. It has been shown through testing that the approach is scalable and continues to provide real-time response when the grid size is increased. Testing has been successful with grids as large as 512 x 512. For a 512 x 512 grid, the GA converges to a near optimal solution with acceptable performance for a real-time situation. A quadtree representation allows the environment to be represented using even larger grids while maintaining real-time performance. The use of grid abstraction discussed in the following section can also address expanded grid sizes.

This chapter has presented a genetic motion planning algorithm for autonomous robots. It is unique in that it provides the inclusion of diverse terrain conditions in determining a near optimal path. Other genetic and non-genetic methods fail to provide this flexibility. In addition, it offers real-time performance, allowing it to be used in many applications.

FUTURE RESEARCH DIRECTIONS

It has been assumed that the terrain conditions are known a priori. Since this is not realistic in many applications, further research directions will address addition of the ability to observe and learn terrain conditions during movement along the path and to then adapt when unexpected difficult terrain is discovered along the planned path. Research is planned to develop the ability for the algorithm to compute new fuzzy terrain conditions from sensory data acquired by the robot during its operation. The method should allow weighting of sensory data including vision, infrared, and laser ranging. Research should also include detection of new terrain conditions based on slippage, odometry drift, and other traversal anomalies. This may also include adjustment of the fuzzy membership functions corresponding to the linguistic variables.

Another research direction is the automatic adjustment of genetic algorithm parameters, including crossover rate, mutation rate and initial population, to optimize the genetic algorithm for the particular area in which the robot is operating or the specific application for its use. In current research, the parameters were established by trial and error and do not change regardless of the area in which the robot is operating or its intended application.

Terrain conditions for each cell have been represented by a fuzzy set. However, it has already been noted in this chapter that traversal of a cell in different directions may have completely different levels of difficulty. Further research will involve assigning multiple fuzzy sets to each cell grid based on the direction of traversal.

Perfect movement by the robot has been assumed without accounting for drift and slippage. Currently, localization is accomplished through dead reckoning. Additional research will incorporate localization to ensure the robot is on the planned path and, if it has deviated from the path, to provide the necessary adjustments to the motion plan. Localization may include the addition of inertial, visual, and other sensory data.

Further research is also planned for accommodating larger grids which represent a higher resolution of the environment. The method has provided acceptable performance with a grid as large as 512 x 512. This size requires 11-bit blocks for each movement in the chromosome. As noted earlier, larger grids can be utilized by using a quadtree representation to simplify the higher resolution grid. However, there are cases when the quadtree reduction cannot be used if we are to maintain the accuracy of the terrain representation. In this case, it may be possible to implement levels of abstraction of the grid. A lower resolution grid can be used with each cell representing the average difficulty of traversal for that area. Additional grids will represent the terrain conditions for each cell within the low resolution grid. Once the path has been planned for the low resolution grid, the high resolution grids can be used to further refine the path within each low resolution cell to be traversed.

This chapter has presented a unique method for genetic method for motion planning of an autonomous mobile robot with real-time performance. These directions for further research will improve the method and extend its usefulness to additional applications.

REFERENCES

Akbarzadeh M. R., Kumbla, K., Tunstel, E., & Jamshidi, M. (2000). Soft computing for autonomous robotic system. *Computers and Electrical Engineering*, *26*(1), 5-32.

Bonnafous, D., Lacroix, S., & Simeon, T. (2001). Motion generation for a rover on rough terrains. In *Proceedings of the IEEE/RSJ International Conference on Intelligent Robots and Systems* (pp. 784-789). New York, NY: IEEE Press.

Cordon, O., Gomide, F., Herrera, F., Hoffmann, F., & Magdalena, L. (2004). Ten years of genetic fuzzy systems: Current framework and new trends. *Fuzzy sets and Systems*, *141*(1), 5-31.

Cuesta, F., & Ollero, A. (2005). *Intelligent Mobile Robot Navigation*. Berlin: Springer.

Davidor, Y. (1991). *Genetic algorithms and Robotics: A Heuristic Strategy for Optimization*. Singapore: World Scientific.

Davidson, A., & Kita, N. (2001). 3D simulation and map-building using active vision for a robot moving on undulating terrain. In *Proceedings of the 2001 IEEE Computer Society Conference on Computer Vision and Pattern Recognition* (pp. 784-789). New York, NY: IEEE Press.

deLope, J., & Maravall, D. (2003). Integration of reactive utilitarian navigation and topological modeling. In C. Zhou, D. Maravall, & D. Ruan (Eds.), Autonomous Robotics Systems: Soft Computing and Hard Computing Methodologies and Applications (pp. 122-138) Heidelberg: Physica-Verlag.

Elfes, A. (1989). Using occupancy grids for mobile robot perception and navigation. *IEEE Computer, 22*(1), 46-57

Fogel, D. B. (2000). *Evolutionary Computation: Toward a New Philosophy of Machine Intelligence.* New York, NY: IEEE Press.

Fries, T. P. (2004). Fuzzy genetic motion planning under diverse terrain conditions for autonomous robots. In *Proceedings of the IASTED International Conference on Circuits, Signals, and Systems* (pp. 449-454). Calgary, Canada: ACTA Press.

Fries, T. P. (2005). Autonomous robot motion planning in diverse terrain using genetic algorithms. In *Proceedings of the 2005 Genetic and Evolutionary Computation Conference.* New York, NY: ACM Press.

Fries, T. P. (2006a). Autonomous robot motion planning in diverse terrain using soft computing. In *Proceedings of the 2006 IEEE SMC Workshop on Adaptive and Learning Systems.* New York, NY: IEEE Press.

Fries, T. P. (2006b). Evolutionary robot navigation using fuzzy terrain conditions. In *Proceedings of the 2006 Conference of the North American Fuzzy Information Processing Society* (pp. 535-540). New York, NY: IEEE Press.

Goldberg, D. E. (1989). *Genetic algorithms in Search, Optimization and Machine Learning.* New York, NY: Addison-Wesley.

Hait, A., & Simeon, T. (1996). Motion planning on rough terrain for an articulated vehicle in presence of uncertainties. In *Proceedings of the IEEE/RSJ International Conference on Intelligent Robots and Systems* (pp. 1126-1133). New York, NY: IEEE Press.

Holland, J. H. (1975). *Adaptation in Natural and Artificial Systems.* Ann Arbor, MI: University of Michigan Press.

Hu, X., & Vie, C. (2007). Niche Genetic algorithm for Robot Path planning. In *Proceedings of the Third International Conference on Natural Computation* (774-778). New York, NY: IEEE Press.

Iagnemma, K., & Dubowsky, S. (2004). *Mobile Robots in Rough Terrain.* New York, NY: Springer.

Iagnemma, K., Kang, S., Brooks, C., & Dubowsky, S. (2003). Multi-sensor terrain estimation for planetary rovers. In *Proceedings of the 7th International Symposium on Artificial Intelligence, Robotics, and Automation in Space* (pp. 542-549). Nara, Japan: Japan Aerospace Exploration Agency.

Jung, I.K., & Lacroix, S. (2003). High resolution terrain mapping using low altitude aerial stereo imagery. In *Proceedings of the Ninth IEEE International Conference on Computer Vision* (pp. 946-953). New York, NY: IEEE Press.

Kamei, K., & Ishikawa, M. (2004). Determination of the Optimal Values of Parameters in Reinforcement Learning for Mobile Robot Navigation by a Genetic algorithm. In *Brain-Inspired IT: Invited papers of the 1st Meeting Entitled Brain IT 2004* (pp. 193-196). New York, NY: Elsevier.

Kelly, A., & Stentz, A. (1998). Rough terrain autonomous mobility—part 2: an active vision predictive control approach. *Journal of Autonomous Robots, 5*(2), 163-198.

Latombe, J. C. (1991). *Robot motion planning*. Norwell, MA: Kluwer Academic.

Laubach, S., & Burdick, J. (1999). An autonomous sensor-based path planner for microrovers. In *Proceedings of the IEEE International Conference on Robotics and Automation* (pp. 347-354). New York, NY: IEEE Press.

Lee, T., & Wu, C. (2003). Fuzzy motion planning of mobile robots in unknown environments. *Journal of Intelligent and Robotic Systems, 37*(2), 177-191.

Li, Q., Tong, X., Xie, S., & Zhang, Y. (2006). Optimum Path planning for Mobile Robots Based on a Hybrid Genetic algorithm. In *Proceedings of the Sixth International Conference on Hybrid Intelligent Systems* (53-56). New York, NY: IEEE Press.

Lu, J., & Yang, D. (2007). Path planning Based on Double-layer Genetic algorithm. In *Proceedings of the Third International Conference on Natural Computation* (357-361). New York, NY: IEEE Press.

Madjidi, H., Negahdaripour, S., & Bandari, E. (2003). Vision-based positioning and terrain mapping by global alignment for UAVs. In *Proceedings of the IEEE Conference on Advanced Video and Signal Based Surveillance* (pp. 305-312). New York, NY: IEEE Press.

Nearchou, A. C. (1999). Adaptive navigation of autonomous vehicles using evolutionary algorithms. *Artificial Intelligence in Engineering, 13*(2), 159-173.

Nearchou, A. C. (1998). Path planning of a mobile robot using genetic heuristics. *Robotica, 16*(5), 575-588.

Pai, D., & Reissel, L. M. (1998). Multiresolution rough terrain motion planning. *IEEE Transactions on Robotics and Automation, 14*(1), 19-33.

Pratihar, D. K., Deb, K., & Ghosh, A. (1999). A genetic-fuzzy approach for mobile robot navigation among moving obstacles. *International Journal of Approximate Reasoning, 20*(2), 145-172.

Peters, J. F., Ahn, T. C., Borkowski, M., Degtyaryov, V., & Ramana, S. (2003). Line-crawling robot navigation: a neurocomputing approach. In C. Zhou, D. Maravall, & D. Ruan (Eds.) *Autonomous Robotics Systems: Soft Computing and Hard Computing Methodologies and Applications* (pp. 141-164) Heidelberg: Physica-Verlag.

Seraji, H., & Howard, A. (2002). Behavior based robot navigation on challenging terrain: a fuzzy logic approach. *IEEE Transactions on Robotics and Automation, 18*(3), 308-321.

Shibata, T., & Fukuda, T. (1993). Intelligent motion planning by genetic algorithm with fuzzy critic. In *Proceedings of the 8th IEEE Symposium on Intelligent Control* (pp. 565-569). New York, NY: IEEE Press.

Spero, D., & Jarvis, R. (2002). Path planning for a mobile robot in a rough terrain environment. In *Proceedings of the Third International Workshop on Robot Motion and Control* (pp. 417-422). New York, NY: IEEE Press.

Stafylopatis, A., & Blekas, K. (1998). Autonomous vehicle navigation using evolutionary reinforcement learning. *European Journal of Operational Research, 108*(2), 306-318.

Sugihara, K., & Smith, J. (1997). Genetic algorithms for adaptive motion planning of an autonomous mobile robot. In *Proceedings of the 1997 IEEE International Symposium on Computational Intelligence in Robotics and Automation* (pp. 138-143). New York, NY: IEEE Press.

Tarokh, M. (2008). Hybrid Intelligent Path planning for Articulated Rovers in Rough Terrain. *Fuzzy sets and Systems*, 159, 1430-1440.

Tunstel, E., Howard, A., Huntsberger, T., Trebio-Ollennu, A., & Dolan, J. M. (2003). Applied soft computing strategies for autonomous field robotics. In C. Zhou, D. Maravall, & D. Ruan (Eds.), *Autonomous Robotics Systems: Soft Computing and Hard Computing Methodologies and Applications* (pp. 75-102) Heidelberg: Physica-Verlag.

Urdiales, C., Bandera, A., Perez, E., Poncela, A., & Sandoval, F. (2003). Hierarchical planning in a mobile robot for map learning and navigation. In C. Zhou, D. Maravall, & D. Ruan (Eds.) *Autonomous Robotics Systems: Soft Computing and Hard Computing Methodologies and Applications* (pp. 165-188) Heidelberg: Physica-Verlag.

Vadakkepat, P., Lee, T. H., & Xin, L. (2003). Evolutionary artificial potential field – applications to mobile robot planning. In C. Zhou, D. Maravall, & D. Ruan (Eds.), *Autonomous Robotics Systems: Soft Computing and Hard Computing Methodologies and Applications* (pp. 217-232) Heidelberg: Physica-Verlag.

Wu, J., Qin, D.-X., & Yu, H.-P. (2006). Nonholonomic Motion planning of Mobile Robot with Ameliorated Genetic algorithm. In *Proceedings of the 2006 International Conference on Intelligent Information Hiding and Multimedia Signal Processing* (219-222). New York, NY: IEEE Press.

Xu, W., Liang, B., Li, C., Qiang, W., Xu, Y., & Lee, K. (2006). Non-holonomic Path planning of Space Robot Based on Genetic algorithm. In *Proceedings of the 2006 IEEE International Conference on Robotics and Biometrics* (1471-1476). New York, NY: IEEE Press.

Yahja, A., Stentz, A., Singh, S., & Brumitt, B. (1998). Framed-quadtree path planning for mobile robots operating in sparse environments. In *Proceedings of the IEEE International Conference on Robotics and Automation* (pp. 650-655). New York, NY: IEEE Press.

Yan, X., Wu, Q., Yan, J., & Kang, L. (2007). A Fast Evolutionary Algorithm for Robot Path planning. In *Proceedings of the IEEE International Conference on Control and Automation* (pp. 84-87). New York, NY: IEEE Press.

Zadeh, L. (1983). Commonsense knowledge representation based on fuzzy logic. *IEEE Computer, 16*(1), 61-65.

Zadeh, L. (1965). Fuzzy sets. *Information and Control, 8*(3), 338-353.

Zhang, B. T., & Kim, S. H. (1997). An evolutionary method for active learning of mobile robot path planning. In *Proceedings of the 1997 IEEE International Symposium on Computational Intelligence in Robotics and Automation* (pp. 312-317). New York, NY: IEEE Press.

ADDITIONAL READING

Adams, M. D. (1998) Sensor Modelling, *Design and Data Processing for Autonomous Navigation*. Singapore: World Scientific Publishing Company.

Al-Khatib, M., & Saade, J. J. (2003) An efficient data-driven fuzzy approach to the motion planning problem of a mobile robot. *Fuzzy sets and Systems, 134*(1), 65-82.

Ang, M., & Khatib, O. (Eds.) (2006) *Experimental Robotics IX: The 9th International Symposium on Experimental Robotics*, New York, NY: Springer.

Baeck, T., Fogel, D. B., & Michalewicz, Z. (Eds.). (2000) *Evolutionary Computation 1: Basic Algorithms and Operators*. London: Taylor & Francis.

Barraquand, J., Langlois, B., & Latombe, J.-C. (1992) Numerical potential field techniques for robot path planning. *IEEE Transactions on Systems, Man and Cybernetics, 22*(2), 224 – 241.

Berger, J., Barkaoui, M., & Boukhtouta, A. (2007) A Hybrid Genetic Approach for Airborne Sensor Vehicle Routing in Real-Time Reconnaissance Missions. *Aerospace Science and Technology, 11*, 317-326.

Cagigas, D. (2005) Hierarchical D* algorithm with materialization of costs for robot path planning. *Robotics and Autonomous Systems, 52*(2-3), 190-208.

Cameron, S., Probert, P. (1994) *Advanced Guided Vehicles: Aspects of the Oxford AGV Project*. Singapore: World Scientific Publishing Company.

Choset, H., Lynch, K. M., Hutchinson, S., Kantor, G., Burgard, W., Kavraki, L. E., & Thrun, S. (2005) *Principles of Robot Motion: Theory, Algorithms, and Implementations*. Cambridge, MA: MIT Press.

Cuesta, F., & Ollero, A. (2005) *Intelligent Mobile Robot Navigation*. Berlin: Springer.

Dario, P., & Cahtila, R. (2005) *Robotics Research: The Eleventh International Symposium*. New York, NY: Springer.

De Jong, K. A. (2002) *Evolutionary Computation*. Camgridge, MA: MIT Press.

Doh, N. L., Kim, C., Na, S., Yu, W.-P., Cho, Y., & Chung, W. K. (2006) A Practical Roadmap for the Path planning of Mobile Robots in Rectilinear Environments. In *Proceedings of the 2006 SICE-ICASE International Joint Conference* (pp. 2022-2027). New York, NY: IEEE Press.

Driankov, D., & Saffiotti, A. (Eds.). (2002) Fuzzy Logic Techniques for Autonomous Vehicle Navigation. Heidelberg: Physica-Verlag.

Dudek, G., & Jenkin, M. (2000) *Computational Principles of Mobile Robotics*. Oxford: Cambridge University Press.

Garcia, E., & de Santos, P. G. (2004) Mobile-robot navigation with complete coverage of unstructured environments. *Robotics and Autonomous Systems*, 46(4), 195-204.

Garro, B. A., Sossa, H., & Vazquez, R. A. (2007) Evolving ant colony system for optimizing path planning in mobile robots. In *Proceedings of the IEEE Conference on Electronics, Robotics and Automotive Mechanics* (pp. 444-449). New York, NY: IEEE Press.

Ge, S. S., & Lewis, F. L. (Eds.). (2006) Autonomous Mobile Robots: Sensing, Control, Decision Making and Applications. Boca Raton, FL: CRC Press.

Ge, S. S, Lai, X.-C., & Al Mamun, A. (2007) Sensor-based path planning for nonholonomic mobile robots subject to dynamic constraints. *Robotics and Autonomous Systems*, 55(7), 513-526.

Gemeinder, M., Gerke, M. (2003) GA-based path planning for mobile robot systems employing an active search algorithm. *Applied Soft Computing*, 3(2), 149-158.

Gen, M., & Cheng, R. (1999) *Genetic algorithms and Engineering Optimization*. New York, NY: Wiley-Interscience.

Goldberg, D.E. (1989) *Genetic algorithms in Search, Optimization and Machine Learning*. New York, NY: Addison-Wesley.

Hager, G. D., Christensen, H. I., Bunke, H., Klein, R. (Eds.). (2002) *Sensor Based Intelligent Robots: International Workshop*. New York, NY: Springer.

Hwang, Y. K., & Ahuja, N. (1992) Gross motion planning – A survey, *ACM Computing Surveys* 24(3), 219-291

Iyengar, S. S., & Elfes, A. (1991) *Autonomous Mobile Robots: Perception, Mapping, and Navigation*. New York, NY: IEEE Press.

Laugier, C., & Chatila, R. (Eds.). (2007) *Autonomous Navigation in Dynamic Environments*. New York, NY: Springer.

Liu, G., Li, T., Peng, Y., & Hou, X. (2005) The Ant Algorithm for Solving Robot Path planning Problem. In *Proceedings of the IEEE Third International Conference on Information Technology and Applications* (pp. 25-27). New York, NY: IEEE Press.

Lu, H.-C., & Chuang, C.-Y. (2005) The Implementation of Fuzzy-Based Path planning for Car-Like Mobile Robot. In *Proceedings of the 2005 IEEE International Conference on MEMS, NANO and Smart Systems* (pp. 467-472). New York, NY: IEEE Press.

Martínez-Alfaro, H., & Gomez-García, S. (1998) Mobile robot path planning and tracking using simulated annealing and fuzzy logic control. *Expert Systems with Applications*, 15(3-4), 421-429.

Meyer, J.-A., & Filliat, D. (2003) Map-based navigation in mobile robots:: II. A review of map-learning and path-planning strategies. *Cognitive Systems Research*, 4(4), 283-317.

Moreno, L., & Dapena, E. (2003) Path quality measures for sensor-based motion planning. *Robotics and Autonomous Systems*, 44(2), 131-150.

Mukhopadhyay, S. C., & Gupta, G. (Eds.). (2007) Autonomous Robots and Agents. New York, NY: Springer.

Niederberger, C., Radovic, D., & Gross, M. (2004) Generic Path planning for Real-Time Applications. In *Proceedings of the Computer Graphics International Conference* (pp. 299-306). New York, NY: IEEE Press.

Park, K.-S., & Choi, H.-S. (2006) Neural Network Based Path planning Plan Design of Autonomous Mobile Robot. In *Proceedings of the 2006 SICE-ICASE International Joint Conference* (pp. 3757-3761). New York, NY: IEEE Press.

Patnaik, S. (2007) *Robot Cognition and Navigation: An Experiment with Mobile Robots*. New York, NY: Springer.

Saboori, I., Menhaj, M.B., & Karimi, B. (2006) Optimal Robot Path planning Based on Fuzzy Model of Obstacles. In *Proceedings of the 32nd Annual IEEE Conference on Industrial Electronics* (pp. 383-387). New York, NY: IEEE Press.

Salichs, M. A., & Halme, A. (Eds). (1998) *Intelligent Autonomous Vehicles*. London: Pergamon Press. 1998.

Sanchez, A. (2003) A deterministic sampling approach to robot motion planning. In *Proceedings of the IEEE Fourth Mexican International Conference on Computer Science* (pp. 300-307). New York, NY: IEEE Press.

Shiller Z., & Chen, J. (1990) Optimal motion planning of autonomous vehicles in 3-dimensional terrains. In *Proceedings of the IEEE International Conference on Robotics and Automation* (198-203). New York, NY: IEEE Press.

Siegwart, R., & Nourbakhsh, I. R. (2004) *Introduction to Autonomous Mobile Robots*. Cambridge, MA: MIT Press.

Spero, D., & Jarvis, R. (2002) Path planning for a mobile robot in a rough terrain environment. In *Proceedings of the Third International Workshop on Robot Motion and Control* (pp. 417-422). New York, NY: IEEE Press.

Thrun, S., Burgard, W., & Fox, D. (2005) *Probabilistic Robotics*. Cambridge, MA: MIT Press.

Thrun, S. (1998) Learning metric-topological maps for indoor mobile robot navigation. *Artificial Intelligence*, 99(1), 21-71.

Vadakkepat, P., Tan, K. C., & Ming-Liang, W. (2000) Evolutionary artificial potential fields and their application in real time robot path planning. In *Proceedings of the 2000 Congress on Evolutionary Computation* (pp. 256-263). New York, NY: IEEE Press.

Velagic, J., Lacevic, B., & Perunicic, B. (2006) A 3-Level Autonomous Mobile Robot Navigation System Designed by using Reasoning/Search Approaches. *Robotics and Autonomous Systems*, 54, 989-1004.

Wan, T. R., Chen, H. & Earnshaw, R. (2003) Real-time Path planning for Navigation in Unknown Environment. In *Proceedings of the Conference on Theory and Practice of Computer Graphics* (pp. 138-45). New York, NY: IEEE Press.

Zhou, C., Maravall, D., & Ruan, D. (2003) *Autonomous Robotics Systems: Soft Computing and Hard Computing Methodologies and Applications*. Heidelberg: Physica-Verlag.

KEY TERMS

Autonomous Mobile Robot: A robot capable of planning and executing it own traversal of an environment without human assistance.

Chromosome: The representation of possible solutions of a problem usually using a binary string. This method is utilized by genetic algorithms to represent possible problem solutions for use in a genetic algorithm.

Environment Grid: A rectangular grid, usually square, that divides a given area into rows and columns, similar to chess board.

Fitness Function: A function in a genetic algorithm that judges which individual chromosomes are most appropriate for a problem. The criteria for judging appropriateness are based upon the particular problem.

Fuzzy Linguistic Variable: The use of English words or phrases to represent information with some degree of uncertainty or vagueness.

Genetic Algorithm: A search technique that uses the concept of survival of the fittest to find an optimal or near optimal solution to a problem. Genetic algorithms use techniques inspired by evolutionary biology to generate new possible solutions known as offspring from an existing set of parent solutions. These recombination techniques include inheritance, selection, mutation, and crossover.

Motion Planning: The process of computing an optimal or near-optimal, collision-free path and then generating the sequence of moves necessary to realize that path. This is a combination of path planning and trajectory planning.

Path Planning: The process of computing an optimal or near-optimal, collision-free path through an environment containing obstacles. The path is optimal with respect to criterion specific to the application.

Trajectory Planning: The process of generating the actions of the robot necessary to proceed along a computed path.

Section II.II
Ant Colony

Ant colony is one kind of swarm intelligence, which is also representative algorithm of natural computing. In this section, it is used for image retrieval and data mining. In these applications, it doesn't solve problems by itself, but combined with the other methods. And in nature, it is used as optimization technology.

Chapter XVIII
Ant Colony Optimization for Use in Content Based Image Retrieval

Konstantinos Konstantinidis
Democritus University of Thrace, Greece

Georgios Ch. Sirakoulis
Democritus University of Thrace, Greece

Ioannis Andreadis
Democritus University of Thrace, Greece

ABSTRACT

The aim of this chapter is to provide the reader with a Content Based Image Retrieval (CBIR) system which incorporates AI through ant colony optimization and fuzzy logic. This method utilizes a two-stage fuzzy modified ant colony algorithm employing in parallel low-level features such as color, texture and spatial information which are extracted from the images themselves. The results prove the system to be more efficient compared to popular and contemporary methods such as the histogram intersection, joint histograms and the scalable color histogram of the MPEG-7 standard. However, due to the high computational burden of the AI methods the system is quite slow when implemented in software. Thus in order to speed up the whole process the reader is also provided with the hardware implementation analysis of the whole system. The increase in speed is phenomenal.

INTRODUCTION

Due to the increase in usage and production of digital images and large volume image databases, a need has risen for organizing them according to their content so that they can easily be retrieved. A simple though effective way to index and retrieve images is through query by example, which means that the user has to present an image to the system and the latter searches for others alike by extracting features from the query image and comparing them to the ones stored in the database. The extraction of meaningful features as well as the actual retrieval of image data based on illustrative content queries is a challenging issue actively confronted by a large number of scientists (Del Bimbo, 1999). Effective retrieval of image data is important for general multimedia information

Copyright © 2009, IGI Global, distributing in print or electronic forms without written permission of IGI Global is prohibited.

management. For an image to be retrievable, it has to be indexed by its content. Color can provide significant information about the content of an image. Among the methods that use color as a retrieval feature, the most popular one is probably that of color histograms (Del Bimbo, 1999; Swain & Ballard, 2001). The color histogram is a global statistical feature which describes the color distribution for a given image (Gonzalez & Woods, 2002). Other low-level features widely used by researchers for indexing and retrieval of images, except color are texture and shape (Del Bimbo, 1999). In order to exploit the strong aspects of each of these features while constructing an optimum and robust CBIR system, a plethora of methods, introduced over time, have been based on combinations of these features (Cheng and Chen, 2003; Pass & Zabih, 1999).

In this chapter the synergy of such features, specifically color, texture, and spatial information is performed by use of a modified artificial ant colony. This specific type of insect was selected since studies showed that when in groups, the ants show self-organization as well as adaptation which are desirable attributes in image retrieval. Artificial ant colonies have previously been used in text based search engines (Kouzas et al, 2006) but also in texture classification (Ramos et al, 2002) and color matching (Huang et al, 2006). Here, a modified ant colony algorithm is applied in order to optimize the process of the retrieval of general interest images. The main thrust of the proposed method is a two stage modified ant colony algorithm employing in parallel color, texture and spatial information which are extracted from the images themselves.

The study of ant colony behavior and of their self-organizing abilities (Bonabeau et al, 2000) inspired the algorithm, although in this chapter they are approached in a more unorthodox (modified) way. Normally the ants exit their nest searching for the shortest path to the food. In this approach the nest is regarded to be the most similar image to the query one while the ants search for the closest food surrounding the nest, which are actually the images in the database. Unlike other methods which employ ant colony optimization techniques, in this case we try to establish which few, from a plethora of food, are closest to the nest by altering the position of the nest in two separate consecutive stages. In the first stage, the synergy of the low-level descriptors is considered to be a swarm of ants, seeking for the optimal path to the surrounding "food", whilst settling pheromone on each of the paths in a "high similarity" area of 1,000 images. The terrain on which the ants move is predefined through three low-level features extracted from the query image. In the second stage the terrain changes as additional queries are made by using the highest ranked images from the first stage as new nests. In each of the queries in the first and second stages the ants disperse pheromone on the paths to the food that is supposedly closest to the nest. A Mamdani inference fuzzy system (Mamdani & Assilian, 1999) is employed in order to extract the aggregate amount of pheromone in respect to each query since none of them is considered to be of the same importance to the next.

In comparison to other popular and contemporary methods such as the histogram intersection (Swain & Ballard, 1991), joint histograms (Pass & Zabih, 1999) and the scalable color descriptor of the MPEG-7 standard (Manjunath et al, 2001), the proposed system exhibits better results. In this chapter, performance is presented in the form of Precision vs. Recall graphs (Muller et al, 2001) averaged over numerous queries using two large databases which contain images of general interest, as is the case with the LabelMe database (Russel et al, 2005) and a portion of the Corel database.

One way for rendering the complex image retrieval algorithms more applicable to real-time systems is by accelerating them through hardware implementation. As an application, image retrieval belongs to the field of processing and analyzing images. Consequently, the hardware implementation of a retrieval system and in fact a Field Programmable Gate Array (FPGA) (Ali, 1996; Hamid, 1994), offers benefits to the wider field of image processing, where circuits of this kind may be used in a broader spectrum of applications such as robot vision (Chen & Li, 2004), image retrieval (Yang et al, 2007) etc. However, very little has been done in this direction. Three such cases include an FPGA image retrieval system based on the color histogram (Kotoulas & Andreadis, 2003), an FPGA application for the retrieval of a sub-image from an image database (Nakano & Takamichi, 2003), and a method for the efficient retrieval in a network of imaging devices (Woodrow & Heizelman, 2002).

In this chapter we present the design and hardware implementation of a specialized processor for image retrieval which combines three different descriptors with the use of an ant colony algorithm (Konstantinidis et al, 2007). It constitutes a tentative approach from the point of view that in the field of image retrieval, even for databases with millions of images, the process followed is more offline rather than online. This means that the descriptor extraction process usually takes place during the initial classification of the database. Subsequently, every time a new image is introduced, a simple update of the descriptors' database is performed. This approach was followed in order to examine the possibility of achieving much shorter times through a hardware processor than with the use of software programming packages; thus executing the feature extraction process concurrently and giving the user the option of searching within any database without having to wait for excessively large time intervals.

The digital circuit aims at the minimization of the required calculation times by using pipelining and parallel processing. The proposed hardware structure has the ability to execute the calculations for the extraction of the descriptors, their intermediate comparison and the final fuzzy accumulation of pheromone for color images of any size. The system architecture is generic and the modules that execute the fuzzy logic operations can be used for any image size, with any descriptors available and also in other related applications. The speed and hardware cost are factors that have been taken seriously into account during the circuit design.

BACKGROUND

In the approach discussed in this chapter we distribute the search activities over so-called "ants" that is, agents with very simple basic capabilities which, to some extent, mimic the behaviour of real insects, namely ants (Dorigo, 1992). Real ants are in some ways much unsophisticated insects. They have a very limited memory and exhibit individual behaviour that appears to have a large random component. However, acting as a collective, ants *synergize* to perform a variety of complicated tasks with great reliability and consistency (Deneubourg & Goss, 1989), such as of selecting the shortest pathway, among a set of alternative pathways, from their nests to a food source (Beckers et al, 1992). This social behaviour of ants is based on *self-organization*, a set of dynamical mechanisms ensuring that the system can achieve its global aim through low-level interactions between its elements (Goss et al, 1989). A key feature of this interaction is that the system elements use only local information. There are two ways of information transfer between ants: a direct communication (mandibular, antennation, chemical or visual contact, etc) and an indirect communication, which is called *stigmergy* [as defined by Grassé (1959)] and is biologically realized through *pheromones*, a special secretory chemical that is deposited, in many ant species, as trail by individual ants when they move (Blum, 2005). More specifically, due to the fact that ants smell pheromone, when choosing their way, they tend to choose, in probability, paths marked by strong pheromone concentrations. As soon as an ant finds a food source, it evaluates the quantity and the quality of the food and carries some of it back to the nest. During the return trip, the quantity of pheromone that an ant leaves on the ground may depend on the quantity and quality of the food. The pheromone trails will guide other ants to the food source. This behaviour is known as *'auto catalytic'* behaviour or the positive feedback mechanism in which reinforcement of the previously most followed route, is more desirable for future search.

Consider for example the experimental setting shown in Fig. 1 (Dorigo et al, 1996). The ants move along the path from food source A to the nest E, and vice versa (Fig. 1a). Suddenly an obstacle appears and the path is cut off. So at position B the ants walking from A to E (or at position D those walking in the opposite direction) have to decide whether to turn right or left (Fig. 1b). The choice is influenced by the intensity of the pheromone trails left by preceding ants. A higher level of pheromone on the right path gives an ant a stronger stimulus and thus a higher probability to turn right. The first ant reaching point B (or D) has the same probability to turn right or left (as there was no previous pheromone on the two alternative paths). Because path BCD is shorter than BHD, the first ant following it will reach D before the first ant following path BHD (Fig. 1c). The result is that an ant returning from E to D will find a stronger trail on path DCB, caused by the half of all the ants that by chance decided to approach the obstacle via DCBA and by the already arrived ones coming via BCD: they will therefore prefer (in probability) path DCB to path DHB. As a consequence, the number of ants following path BCD per unit of time will be higher than the number of ants following BHD. This causes the quantity of pheromone on the shorter path to grow faster than on the longer one, and therefore the probability with which any single ant chooses the path to follow is quickly biased towards the shorter one. The final result is that very quickly all ants will choose the shorter path.

The Ant Colony Optimization (ACO) algorithms (Dorigo, 1992; Dorigo & Stützle, 2004) are basically a colony of artificial ants or cooperative agents, designed to solve a particular problem. They are a class of heuristics based search algorithms used to solve many combinatorial optimization problems (Bonabeau et al., 1999). These

Figure 1. An example with real ants. ©2008 Konstantinos Konstantinidis. Used with permission.

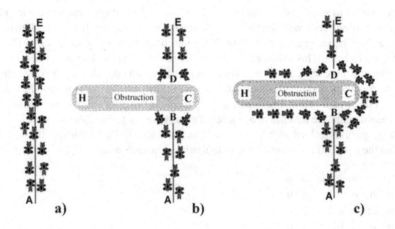

algorithms are probabilistic in nature because they avoid the local minima entrapment and provide very good solutions close to the natural solution (Bonabeau et al., 1999). The metaphor of trail laying by ants has previously been successfully applied to certain combinatorial optimization problems such as the Traveling Salesman Problem (TSP) (Dorigo & Gambardella, 1997). Even though the original ant algorithm achieved encouraging results for the TSP problem, it was found to be inferior to state-of-the-art algorithms for the TSP as well as for other CO problems. Therefore, several extensions and improvements of the original AS algorithm were introduced over the years (Dorgio & Stützle, 2004). As a result, the ACO heuristic and its extensions have been used successfully to solve a wide variety of problems such as cell placement in circuit design (Alupoaei & Katkoori, 2004), protein folding (Shmygelska & Hoos, 2005), etc.

As mentioned before, the artificial ant agents have many properties that differentiate them from the real ants and thus involve various ant algorithms based systems (Bonabeau et al, 1999; Blum, 2005). Along with these unique features that enhance the capabilities of the artificial agents there are other governing parameters such as the optimum number of ants, the pheromone decay rate, and the constants that make the solution to converge to the experimental results (Blum, 2005). As the main interest is not in the simulation of ant colonies, but in the use of artificial ant colonies as an optimization tool in the field of image retrieval, the proposed system will have some major differences with a real (natural) one that will be discussed next.

CBIR WITH THE USE OF ANT COLONIES

Feature Extraction

The three features extracted in order to simulate the ants seeking the closest "food" (images) surrounding the nest, are a spatially-biased color histogram, a color histogram inspired by the attributes of the human visual system and a simple histogram resulting from the L*a*b* color space. Although these particular descriptors were chosen for use in this chapter based on our previous research and due to the diversity that they contribute to the method, it is imperative to point out that the modified ant colony algorithm can employ a variety of features depending on the implementer or user; from simple color histograms to more complex image descriptors.

This might increase the accuracy of the system but will also increase the computational complexity of the system as a whole.

Spatially-Biased Histogram

This histogram creation method (Konstantinidis et al, 2007) has a two stage straightforward algorithm where only the hue component is enriched with spatial information so as to maintain the original histogram speed.

In the first stage a 256 bin histogram is created with the hue component being divided into 16 regions, whereas saturation and value into 4 each. This unbalance is due to the fact that the hue component carries the majority of color information from the three in the HSV color space and is hence considered more important in this method. In the second and most important part of this method the spatial information is inserted into the final histogram via the use of the mask M illustrated below. This mask is used to collect the color information from a 5 pixel "radius" neighborhood for each pixel in the manner of a shattered cross in order to increase the speed of the system.

Thus the whole image is convolved with the M matrix as illustrated in Eq.1, resulting in a new hue component H_{conv} which contains the color information for the neighborhood of each pixel.

$$
M = \begin{matrix}
0 & 0 & 0 & 0 & 0 & 1 & 0 & 0 & 0 & 0 & 0 \\
0 & 0 & 0 & 0 & 0 & 0 & 0 & 0 & 0 & 0 & 0 \\
0 & 0 & 0 & 0 & 0 & -1 & 0 & 0 & 0 & 0 & 0 \\
0 & 0 & 0 & 0 & 0 & 0 & 0 & 0 & 0 & 0 & 0 \\
0 & 0 & 0 & 0 & 0 & 1 & 0 & 0 & 0 & 0 & 0 \\
1 & 0 & -1 & 0 & 1 & 1 & 1 & 0 & -1 & 0 & 1 \\
0 & 0 & 0 & 0 & 0 & 1 & 0 & 0 & 0 & 0 & 0 \\
0 & 0 & 0 & 0 & 0 & 0 & 0 & 0 & 0 & 0 & 0 \\
0 & 0 & 0 & 0 & 0 & -1 & 0 & 0 & 0 & 0 & 0 \\
0 & 0 & 0 & 0 & 0 & 0 & 0 & 0 & 0 & 0 & 0 \\
0 & 0 & 0 & 0 & 0 & 1 & 0 & 0 & 0 & 0 & 0
\end{matrix}
$$

$$
H_{conv}(i, j) = \sum_{r=0}^{m} \sum_{c=0}^{m} M(r,c) \cdot H(i-r, j-c)
$$

(1)

where m is the height and width of the mask and r and c are the horizontal and vertical coordinates of the mask. If the pixels which are included in the vicinity of the full length of the cross possess a color similar to the one of the central pixel, then an additional hue value is added to the extension of the final histogram resulting in 272 bins (256+16).

Center-Surround Histogram

This method is based on the retinal signal processing of the human visual system. The advantage of this histogram extraction method is that it reduces the processed visual information by using only the colored area surrounding the zero-crossings of an image as well as altering the significance of this information depending on its position in the image (Panitsidis et al, 2006). The previously mentioned colored areas are defined by the center-surround operator *CS* shown below (through 2-dimensional convolution), analogous to the ganglion cells of the retina.

$$
CS = \begin{matrix}
-0.013889 & -0.013889 & -0.013889 & -0.013889 & -0.013889 & -0.013889 & -0.013889 \\
-0.013889 & -0.041667 & -0.041667 & -0.041667 & -0.041667 & -0.041667 & -0.013889 \\
-0.013889 & -0.041667 & 0.111111 & 0.111111 & 0.111111 & -0.041667 & -0.013889 \\
-0.013889 & -0.041667 & 0.111111 & 0.111111 & 0.111111 & -0.041667 & -0.013889 \\
-0.013889 & -0.041667 & 0.111111 & 0.111111 & 0.111111 & -0.041667 & -0.013889 \\
-0.013889 & -0.041667 & -0.041667 & -0.041667 & -0.041667 & -0.041667 & -0.013889 \\
-0.013889 & -0.013889 & -0.013889 & -0.013889 & -0.013889 & -0.013889 & -0.013889
\end{matrix}
$$

The descriptor contains only the chromatic information of these areas. Hence it is defined as a Center Surround Histogram (CSH). The CSH is a histogram of 256 bins, containing visual information only from the Hue component of the HSV color space. For every pixel *(i,j)* of an image of size $m \times n$, the output of the center-surround operator *CS(i,j)* is used as a function to define the degree of membership of the Hue component *h(i,j)* to the CSH. This is described by Eq. 2, where $\delta(\cdot)$ is the unitary impulse response.

$$hist(H) = \sum_{i=1}^{n}\sum_{j=1}^{m} |CS(i,j)| \cdot \delta\left(h(i,j) - H\right) \tag{2}$$

Although the CSH includes information from the whole image, it is not global in a sense that only a subset of the pixels in the image is taken into account. As a result, the proposed method significantly reduces the volume of the data, thus improving the execution time and minimizes the storage demands.

L*a*b* Color Space Histogram

The third image descriptor is a simple histogram which is produced through interlinking of the three components from the L*a*b* color space in a manner that the color components a* and b* receive more weight than the Lightness one (Konstantinidis et al. 2007). The L component is quantized into 3 regions, whereas the a* and b* components into 9 parts each, thus resulting in a 243 (3x9x9) bin histogram. The selection of 3 and 9 is not random; it was made for two reasons: the first is that the a* and b* components would receive more attention than the L component and the second reason is that significant information lies exactly in the middle of the three components and so the numbers should necessarily be odd. The significant information is the grey level shading, as black, grey and white can only be expressed when a* and b* are around 0.

ANT COLONY ALGORITHM

The proposed ant colony algorithm is represented by the generalized block diagram (Gane-Sarson) of Fig. 2. The problem is defined in the form of a network.

First Stage

Following the extraction of the three descriptors described beforehand from the images in the database and considering each histogram bin to be a virtual ant, a query is posed by mobilizing a sum of 771 (272+256+243) ants.

The terrain of the "ground" where the ants "walk" depends strictly on the query in a way that it is the one which, through comparison with the other images, provides the information about the relative position and distance of the surrounding "food". In this first stage of the algorithm, a comparison is performed using all the bins of the three features, in other words the whole population of the ants, and an initial ranking of the images takes place. Following numerous tests and simulations, it was concluded that the most efficient similarity metric in order to compare the features was the Matusita distance (Matusita, 1955). This distance is a separability measure which provides a reliable criterion presumably because as a function of class separability it behaves much more like probability of correct classification. It is expressed by Eq. 3 shown below:

$$M(H_Q, H_C) = \sqrt{\sum_i \left(\sqrt{H_Q(i)} - \sqrt{H_C(i)}\right)^2} \tag{3}$$

where H_Q is the query histogram, H_C is the histogram to be compared and (*i*) is the number of bins.

Following the calculation of the distance (Matusita) of all the images in the database (surrounding food) from the query image (nest), the smallest 1,000 distances are normalized in respect to the 1,000[th] maximum distance; in other words the food that is farthest away in the region is regarded as less similar. This ranking is then inverted in

Figure 2. Block diagram of the ant colony image retrieval system. ©*2008 Konstantinos Konstantinidis. Used with permission.*

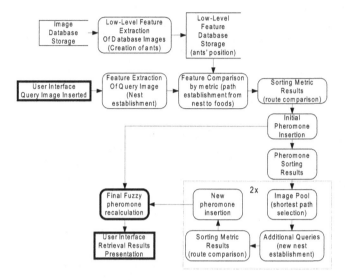

a manner that the most similar image acquires the highest value which will always be 1. Accordingly, pheromone (ranging from 0 to 1) is laid on each of the 1,000 first most popular paths in a descending manner according to its relative distance, meaning that the highest ranked path, in other words the food closest to the nest, acquires the most pheromone. The aggregate pheromone deposition from all the ants results in the creation of a pool which consists of only 1,000 images, thus creating a new much smaller sub-terrain, in the vicinity of which the second stage takes place. The amount of 1,000 images was selected after extensive experiments and is considered to be large enough to include all the ground truth images from the query (i.e. 100% recall), but on the other hand is concise enough to retain a high speed for the proposed system.

Another matter regarding the ants and the pheromone that they deposit is that when a path is not popular to a colony, which means that the particular path is farther away than others, then the pheromone deposit seems to evaporate in order for the path not to be followed again. This matter is dealt with in the fuzzy pheromone fusion section later on.

Second Stage

Having completed the image database pre-classification which results to the creation of a 1,000 image pool; the second stage of the ant colony algorithm is initiated. For each one of these images, the path to the nest is covered with a specific amount of pheromone in respect to the relative distance of each image from the query. Taking into consideration the possibility that the initial ant search can result in false positive results, the terrain is slightly altered by substituting the initial query with the second highest ranked image from the pool, i.e. the next closest food becomes the nest, and a new query takes place. The second image is selected since in most CBIR systems the query is performed by selecting an image from the database, which means that the first image to be retrieved is the query image itself. In this second query, a new group of 771 ants is mobilized and the process from the first stage is repeated, although instead of having the whole database as a terrain, the ants are constrained strictly in the vicinity of the pool, thus resulting to a second amount of pheromone attached to each of the previously ranked images. In order to restrain the overall time cost and to avoid false terrain alterations caused by false positives in the first stage, this new process is repeated for two iterations meaning that the sub-terrain of the pool is altered twice and that the first three images of the initial query in total are used as queries themselves, resulting in three pheromone values for each image. Hence for every image in the pool there are three pheromone values; one from every terrain change. However, since each number belongs to a sequential query, their importance varies from one another. On the other hand, a single value is needed in order to finally index the pool of images, and one way to analyze and fuse such imprecise data is with the use of fuzzy logic. As a result the pheromone corresponding to each image for each query is considered to be a fuzzy set.

FUZZY PHEROMONE FUSION

The fuzzy system described here has three inputs (phero1, phero2, and phero3) corresponding to the three pheromone values which result from the queries in the first and second stages described in the previous section and one output (phero out) which is the final pheromone value requested. A model of the system is shown in Fig. 3.

The fuzzification of the input is accomplished by using three triangular-shaped built-in membership functions (MF), namely: low, medium and max, for each of the three input components which represent the pheromone as shown in Fig. 4a. On the other hand, the output consists of five triangular-shaped MFs, namely: lower, low, medium, high and higher, as illustrated in Fig. 4b.

The inputs are routed to the output through a Mamdani type of fuzzy inference (Mamdani & Assilian, 1999) which uses 24 rules (Table 1). The reason why there are only 24 rules when there are 27 possible combinations (3x3x3) is that in extreme situations some combinations are eliminated. Through these rules and the exceptions which lie in these rules, the evaporation aspect in real ants is also regarded. Consider another example where although the first amount of pheromone (first stage) is a maximum, the next two pheromone deposits are low, and the final aggregate deposition is low. The difference in the input (max) and output (low) is due to the fuzzy system which simulates the evaporation.

In a Mamdani type of fuzzy inference, the fuzzy sets from the consequent of each rule are combined through the aggregation operator and the resulting fuzzy set is defuzzified to yield the output of the system. The aggregation operator in this case is set to maximum and the defuzzification method is that of the Center of Gravity

(CoG). The mathematical expression for the CoG is $\sum y_i \mu(y_i) / \sum \mu(y_i)$ where y_i is the output variable and $\mu(y_i)$ is the corresponding degree of membership (Chiueh, 1992).

The final retrieval is not based upon the value produced by the metric stating the distance between the features of the images, but on the final amount of pheromone that has accumulated on each image at the conclusion of the two stages.

Figure 3. Fuzzy Pheromone Extraction System. ©2008 Konstantinos Konstantinidis. Used with permission.

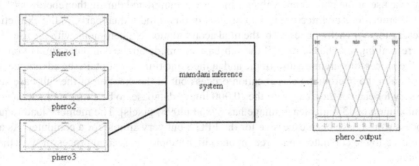

Figure 4. Fuzzy reference for variables: a) input phero1, phero2, and phero3 and b) output phero_out. ©2008 Konstantinos Konstantinidis. Used with permission.

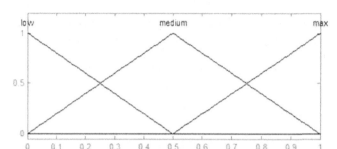

(a)

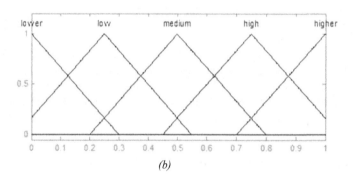

(b)

H/W ARCHITECTURE

The ant colony processor has the ability of executing calculations for the derivation of the three descriptors, the comparison between them using the Matusita distance and the final fuzzy accumulation of pheromone. The proposed architecture and the design of the individual circuits of the processor are based on pipelining and on parallel processing to achieve fast system operation.

The processor structure includes seven basic operational modules: a) the derivation of the spatially-biased color descriptor, b) the derivation of the center-surround descriptor, c) the derivation of the L*a*b* histogram, d) the comparison of the descriptors, e) the knowledge-based module, g) the rule control module and h) the defuzzification module. The ant colony algorithm is divided in two parts: a) the initial classification of all the database images from which a new much smaller sub-base is generated and b) the iterative reordering of the images in the sub-base through the use of the pheromone values which are accumulated during the repetitions.

As a result, the processor's architecture is also divided into two individual parts: a) the extraction and comparison of the descriptors for each image and b) the final accumulation of pheromone with the use of fuzzy logic. All the ranking, re-ranking and the creation of the sub-base are made on the computer and not on the processor in order to keep the processor's architecture simple and at the same time to maintain the advantage of speed. The problem does not lie in the pheromone classification process but in the creation of the sub-base since it would have been necessary for each of the images, in the 10,000 image database, to be associated with a number which may reach the maximum of 13 digits [each image has 64x64 (4096) pixels]. The memory load required for this very simple process would have been excessive for the FPGA but very simple for a computer. As a result there is one output fed back to the computer and three inputs which supply the second processor with the pheromone values for each stage.

Table 1. The Fuzzy inference rules which bind the pheromone fuzzy system

#	If phero1 is	and phero2 is	and phero3 is	then phero_out is
1	low	low	not max	lower
2	low	low	max	low
3	low	medium	low	lower
4	low	medium	medium	low
5	low	medium	max	low
6	low	max	low	low
7	low	max	medium	medium
8	low	max	max	high
9	medium	low	low	lower
10	medium	low	medium	low
11	medium	low	max	medium
12	medium	medium	low	low
13	medium	medium	medium	medium
14	medium	medium	max	high
15	medium	max	not max	medium
16	medium	max	max	high
17	max	low	low	low
18	max	low	medium	medium
19	max	low	max	high
20	max	medium	low	high
21	max	medium	medium	high
22	max	medium	max	higher
23	max	max	low	high
24	max	max	not low	higher

Descriptor Extraction and Comparison

For each image, the system inputs are the values of the h, s, v and L^*, a^*, b^* components. Initially, these values are inserted serially into the first three processing units. For this reason the number of the required input terminals for the first stage is 50 (47 input terminals for the values of the h, s, v, L^*, a^*, b^* components and 3 input terminals for the clock and the necessary control signal). The output of the first stage is the total pheromone value which is laid between the nest and each food and has 16 terminals.

At this point it should be noted that in order to achieve the correct delivery of data between the components of the circuit, an appropriate series of registers has been used which buffer the data at the input, in between and at the output of the unit.

Spatially-Biased Color Descriptor Extraction Module

The operation of the module for the extraction of the spatially-biased color descriptor is to execute the necessary arithmetic operations between the system inputs and to produce a histogram of 272 bins which will contain the chromatic information of the image and also information as to which colors form concentrations. The inputs to the module, which are the same with those for the derivation of the Center-Surround descriptor, are the h, s, v components of each image. For example the value of Hue h for an image pixel with a 8-bit depth is indicated by h[7..0] and the value of the Value v with a 4-bit depth by v[3..0].

The values of h, s, and v are therefore inserted in the first unit, each of which has a size of 8 bits [0,255]. Subsequently, the quantization of the components is performed in order for h to acquire a size of 4 bits while the s and v a size of 2 bits respectively.

By connecting the bits of the h, s, v triplet so that one and only number represents every possible combination (v[7..6]s[7..6]h[7..4]), a histogram of 256 elements is created which describes the distribution of each color. Information is derived from the h component as to which colors create concentrations. In Fig. 5, a more analytical block diagram of the extraction of the descriptor is provided.

The method by which each and every simple histogram is generated in this chapter is as follows: following the linking of the components of the respective color space, multiple discrete combinations result each of which

Figure 5. Block diagram of the module for the extraction of the spatially-biased color descriptor. ©2008 Konstantinos Konstantinidis. Used with permission.

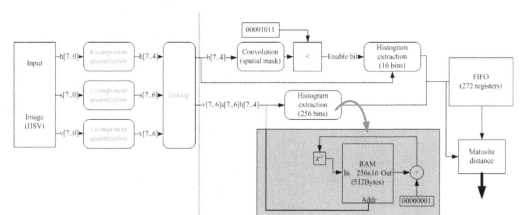

is described by an integer. With the use of RAM memory and by reserving a number of slots equal to the number of the corresponding elements of any given histogram, the memory address which is accessed is equal to the number which describes every unique combination. The depth of the memory corresponds to the maximum possible size which a histogram element can obtain. This happens when an image is dominated by a single color; then the total in that particular element will represent the total number of pixels in the image.

However, the basic function of this module is the extraction of the spatially-biased color information. The spatial mask is applied on the *h* component as its values are inserted and moved serially in a FIFO memory.

The data values slide within this memory and the whole process is actuated as soon as the first value reaches the last memory position. The sum from the addition of all the values on each clock pulse is compared to a single number and through that a decision is made as to whether the concentration of the same color exists or not. That number is the value which the total should have, if all the surrounding pixels were of the same color with that of the central one. In real images however this is not feasible and thus there is a tolerance of three pixels. In accordance to the absolute difference of the two sets and in order for a concentration to exist, the two numbers must not be more than three units apart. In the case where a concentration is detected, the process of a histogram generation is actuated for that particular color. The detailed diagram of the architecture of the histogram generation module is depicted in Fig. 6.

In this circuit, the value of the control signal "Input_1" specifies the moment when the input of the image components is terminated; this actually means that the process of storing it in the RAM is complete and the reading from the memory begins in order to create the histogram. Once the image input and the storage in memory have been stopped, the counter "Counter[7..0]" is activated starting with a value of 0 and reaching up to 255 thus substantially extracting the values of the simple HSV histogram into a new area of RAM memory. However, from the moment of actuation of the input, another procedure is also initiated: that of the "Comparator", which controls when the extraction of the first part of the histogram will finish. When the first counter reaches and becomes bigger than 256 then automatically another counter starts "Counter[3..0]", concurrently changing the flow of data and finally the values of the spatially-biased color are extracted from the RAM. These new values augment the previous ones in the output RAM, which holds the values of the whole histogram until it receives new ones for a new image.

Center-Surround Descriptor Extraction Module

The module for the extraction of the Center-Surround descriptor is very similar to the one of the spatially-biased color descriptor; both use masks for the extraction of the characteristics required. The operation of this module

Figure 6. Architecture of the module for the extraction of spatially-biased color descriptor. ©2008 Konstantinos Konstantinidis. Used with permission.

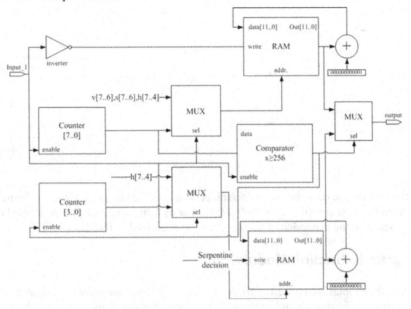

Figure 7. Diagram of the operation of the module for the extraction of the Center-Surround descriptor. ©2008 Konstantinos Konstantinidis. Used with permission.

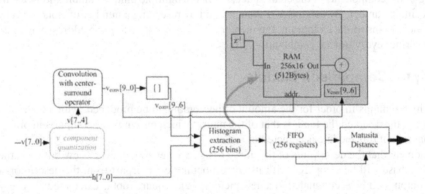

is to execute the necessary mathematical operations between the system inputs and subsequently to produce an adaptive histogram of 256 bins.

The inputs are the h and v components of each image, from which v is used to extract the edges and their intensity, while h is used in the generation of the histogram. Each component has a size of 8 bits [0,255] similarly to the previously mentioned descriptor. Subsequently the quantization of the components is performed in order to acquire a size of 4 bits [0,15].

During the next step, the convolution of the component v with the center-surround operator mask is performed. This operator, alike all the operators of its category, have one characteristic: the sum of the centre and the surround is zero and through this it exhibits sensitivity only to transitions in intensity and not to uniform regions. Furthermore, the symmetry of the operator allows a non-directional extraction of the zero-crossings and of the regions that surround them. In this module, the mask is applied to the image through a serpentine FIFO memory (width: 64 words, depth: 4 bits), similarly to that of the spatially-biased color descriptor. Each histogram bin is

Figure 8. Diagram of the operation of the module for the extraction of the L*a*b* histogram. ©2008 Konstantinos Konstantinidis. Used with permission.

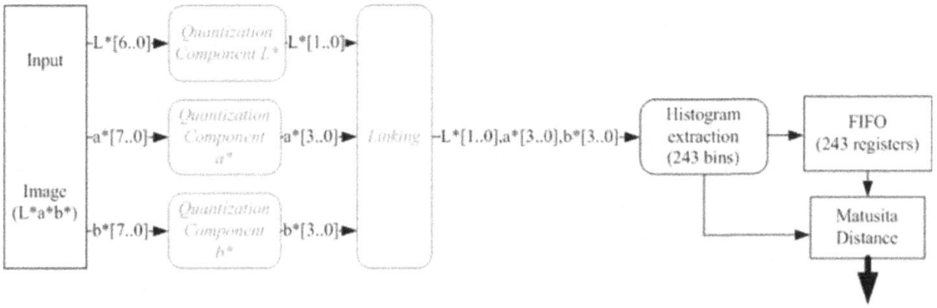

incremented by the result of the convolution for each pixel instead of the classic single unit. The maximum result that might be derived from the convolution is 1080 (15x8x9) or its respective negative. A detailed diagram of the operation of the module for the extraction of this descriptor is presented in Fig. 7.

L*a*b* Histogram Extraction Module

This third module is the simplest and fastest of them all. It is fastest from the point of view that every single one of the histogram extraction modules could be used as standalone devices. It uses the L* (7 bits), a* (8 bits) and b* (8 bits) components of an image as inputs, which after quantization result in 2, 4 and 4 bits respectively. A detailed diagram of the module's operation for the extraction of this descriptor is illustrated in Figure 8.

The linking of the components of the color-space, results in multiple unique combinations, each of which are described by a single number. By using RAM memory and by reserving a number of slots equal to the number of the corresponding bins of the histogram, the memory is accessed by using the address which is equal to the number that describes every unique combination.

The Descriptor Comparison Module

The module which remains in order for the amount of pheromone to be produced, which is proportional to the transition between the nest and the food, is that of the metric which executes the comparison of the descriptors. The general diagram of this module is depicted in Fig. 9.

From the moment that the descriptors of the query image are generated, every new bin from the descriptors of the image data base will be compared with its corresponding counterpart from the descriptors of the query image and the output will be accumulated in a new memory. The square root is calculated for every bin and the square of their difference is produced. Finally, the accumulation of all the comparisons between the bins of the descriptors results as the output.

The maximum output value which the amount of pheromone can reach for each stage is of 16-bit size, hence the output terminals from the processor to the computer are 16 in total.

Once the process for the extraction of the pheromone for each descriptor is completed, then they are all added together and are output to the computer to begin the classification. For each query, the pheromone extraction part of the algorithm has three steps: the first step is the initial classification of the complete image database (initial nest to surrounding food); the second, where the second most similar image from the first stage is used as a query image in the sub-base (nest change), and the third step where the third most similar image from the first stage is used as query image (nest change). Each of these steps produces an amount of pheromone, which results in every image from the sub-base having three values. In order to minimize the number of input terminals to the fuzzy logic module, these values are normalized in such a way so that they are all integers and all in the range [0,1000], clearly as many as the images.

Figure 9. Generalized diagram of the module for the comparison of the descriptors. ©2008 Konstantinos Konstantinidis. Used with permission.

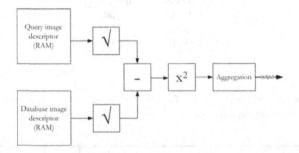

Figure 10. Architecture of the fuzzy logic processor. ©2008 Konstantinos Konstantinidis. Used with permission.

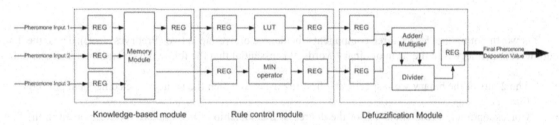

Pheromone Fusion with the Use of Fuzzy Logic

The proposed architecture and the design of the individual circuits of the processor are based on pipelined data supply and parallel processing in order to achieve a fast system operation. The processor has internal memory, which includes the fuzzy sets and the membership functions. These are used for the fuzzification of the three pheromone values produced by the descriptor extraction modules. The fuzzy logic rules are also stored in the same way. The pheromone values lie within the range [0, 1000] and as each image owns a triplet of values then the system has three inputs of 10 bits which results in 30 input terminals.

The architecture of the fuzzy logic processor, the procedure for the processing of data and the calculation of the results are presented in Fig. 10.

Knowledge-Based Module

The Knowledge-based module constitutes the internal memory of the processor which includes the fuzzy sets and the membership functions used for the fuzzification of the pheromone amount. The module inputs are the three normalized values of pheromone which were estimated in the first part of the processor and the outputs are the fuzzy sets and their corresponding degrees of membership. Three fuzzy sets are used in total for the fuzzification of the pheromone amount from the three stages. In fact, the three fuzzy sets used are represented with the use of three, triangular shaped, embedded membership functions. They are namely described as LOW, MEDIUM and HIGH and are codified into corresponding binary words of 2 bits. The manner of codification is presented in Table 2.

The selection of the number of bits used for the storage of the membership functions in memory defines the accuracy of the membership function and it influences the results produced from the activation of the fuzzy rules to a considerable degree.

Table 2. Codification of the fuzzy sets for the pheromone values

Fuzzy Set	Binary Word
Low	00
Medium	01
High	10

Figure 11. Data output from memory, which is used for the fuzzification of the pheromone values. ©2008 Konstantinos Konstantinidis. Used with permission.

2 bits	6 bits	2 bits	6 bits
1st Fuzzy Set	Degree of Membership of 1st Fuzzy Set	2nd Fuzzy Set	Degree of Membership of 2nd Fuzzy Set

It is worth noting that for all three components the degree of overlap is two (Predrycs, 1993). Thus, the data output from memory is in the form of binary words. It is essential that the following information is contained:

- The 2 bits of the binary word specify the first fuzzy set in which the value of the component participates, (see Table 2).
- Correspondingly, 6 bits are used for the degree of membership of the value of the component in the first fuzzy set.
- The next two bits of the binary word specify the second fuzzy set in which the value of the component participates (Table 2).
- In a similar manner, 6 bits are used for the degree of membership of the value of the component in the second fuzzy set.

Hence, the data output from the memory compartments of the circuit, which are used for the fuzzification of the pheromone values, are 16-bit binary words. The general format of such a word is illustrated in Fig. 11.

Rule Control Module

The rule control module is responsible for the activation of the correct rules for every combination of the three pheromone values. Every rule corresponds to a different combination of fuzzy sets. The combinations produced are used for the fuzzification of the values into a different output fuzzy set. The rule control module determines their contribution in the final output fuzzy set. The fuzzy rules triggered contain sentences which are linked by a logical AND operator. During the procedure for the extraction of the fuzzy conclusion, these sentences are combined using the Minimum operator thus selecting the smallest of the corresponding degrees of membership. For every combination of the fuzzy sets a rule is triggered and since the degree of overlap for all three inputs is two, then as a consequence the maximum number of rules that can be activated concurrently is eight ($2^3=8$). The eight output fuzzy sets are then composed into a single fuzzy set through a union operation.

The active fuzzy rules are determined using a procedure based on the coding of the linguistic variables. Each combination of the binary words from Table 2 forms a binary word of six bits (two bits for each fuzzy set). The fuzzy set that corresponds to every combination is one of the five output fuzzy sets. As $5_D = 101_B$, three bits are required for the representation of the output set. In the design of the rule control unit, a LUT using 6-bit input and 3-bit output is used for the selection of the active fuzzy rules. The minimum of the degrees of membership, used for the truncation of the output fuzzy sets, is selected by a 3-input MIN module implemented for 6-bit data.

Defuzzification Module

In this stage, defuzzification of the output fuzzy set is performed in order to obtain a crisp output value. It should be pointed out that even though there are 3 input fuzzy sets in the given system, which are of the order of 10 bits (1000_D), the output fuzzy sets are 5 and can obtain a value of 12 bits in order to render the difference between the images compared more distinct, since the range of the values will be four times wider.

The centroid defuzzification method (COG) has been selected, which happens to be the most widely used defuzzification method in systems that employ fuzzy logic.

The defuzzification module consists of three main parts:

i.   In the first part, the numerator of the mathematical expression $\sum y_i \mu(y_i)$ is computed with the use of appropriate multiplier/adder devices.
ii. The denominator $\sum \mu(y_i)$ is computed.
iii. In the third part, a divisor is used to perform the division of the two sums.

The output of the divisor is the final accumulated amount of pheromone for the three consecutive stages and it is a binary 12-bit word which corresponds to the particular values of the input triplet.

IMPLEMENTATION CHARACTERISTICS

The proposed structure was designed, compiled and simulated using the software package using the Altera Corporation software package: Quartus. For the implementation of the processor, FPGA technology was selected taking into account its characteristics. The main advantage of the FPGA devices is that they allow change of the logic operation of a system through simple reprogramming, in contrast to other technologies which do not allow any changes following the implementation. Furthermore, the implementation cost in FPGA is significantly smaller in comparison to the corresponding ones in ASIC. For these reasons, FPGAs are a widely used implementation technology, providing the possibility for the design of digital systems with high efficiency and low cost and furthermore combining versatility with ease of use (Ali, 1996; Kotoulas & Andreadis, 2003).

The two devices used for the implementation of the processor are the EP2C35F484C6 and the EP2C35F672C7 from the Altera Cyclone II device family. The particular FPGA device family is appropriate for hardware structures with a large number of typical gates and input-output terminals, which execute memory operations and complex logical operations, just like the digital signal processing applied in this chapter. The total used in this circuit is 81 input terminals and 28 output terminals.

The typical maximum operating clock frequency of the system is 76 MHz. The presented fuzzy processor exhibits a level of inference performance of 800 KFLIPS (Fuzzy Logic Inferences per Second) with 24 rules and can be used in real time applications where fast data processing is required. As an example, for the comparison of a thousand color images with dimensions 64x64 pixels with a query image with the same size, the total time required is about 1 sec. In comparison, the corresponding time required using the software package Matlab® in a Pentium IV 3GHz Windows XP computer system is about 2664 seconds, thus presenting a huge speed increase.

PERFORMANCE EVALUATION

We evaluate the total performance of the system in terms of query accuracy and precision versus recall. Two databases were used to measure the system's effectiveness and efficiency. The first one is a large part (80,000 images) of the LabelMe database (Russell et al, 2005) which was selected due to its immensity in volume as it consists of 250,000 images (and increasing). Its size makes it extremely adequate for CBIR testing and moreover it is one of the largest databases available freely on the internet. The queries performed were 120 and the datasets consisted of images with a wide variety of context. The number of images in each set varied from 20 to 1520.

This extensive variation in dataset size is due to the fact that all the images in the LabelMe database are actually a selection of personal photos of various users over the web. The second database is none other than the Corel database. This database is unequivocally the most frequently used in CBIR as it has a wide range of image classes and is also a priori categorized into groups. However, this database is not freely distributed on the internet and thus a portion of 10,000 images was obtained in order for the tests to be performed. Nevertheless, such a number is regarded as sufficient for the purpose of comparing methods and proving the effectiveness of an algorithm. The queries performed were 100 and the datasets used all consisted of 100 images. The images are of size 384x256 or 256x384 pixels. The retrieval outcome in our system is presented through a query session which produces images ranked in similarity according to the pheromone laid by the ants. The larger that the amount of pheromone aggregation is, the higher the similarity of that specific image will be. The measurement used in order to evaluate the system is presented through the graphs in Figs. 12 and 13: average precision versus recall (Muller et al 2001).

Precision is the proportion of relevant images retrieved R (similar to the query image) in respect to the total retrieved A (Eq. 4), whereas recall is the proportion of similar images retrieved in respect to the similar images that exist (Eq. 5).

$$Precision = Similar\ Retrieved\ /\ Total\ Retrieved = |A \cap R|/A \qquad (4)$$

$$Recall = Similar\ Retrieved\ /\ Similar\ Exist = |A \cap R|/R \qquad (5)$$

Generally, precision and recall are used together in order to point out the change of the precision in respect to recall (Muller et al., 2001). In most typical systems the precision drops as recall increases, hence, in order for an image retrieval system to be considered effective the precision values must be higher than the same recall ones, which is mostly the case in the current system.

In order to provide a sense of the proposed method's performance, the average precision versus recall factor for the total of queries is compared to the well established one of Swain and Ballard's method (1991), secondly to Pass and Zabih's joint histogram method (1999) due to the fact that they use a number of features, similarly to the proposed method, in order to produce results, and thirdly to the Scalable Color feature (Manjunath et al, 2001) which is actually part of the MPEG-7 standard. Finally the performance of each of the descriptors used in order to obtain the final ant feature is also illustrated, thus demonstrating the increase in effectiveness provided, by introducing the fuzzy ant algorithm.

A retrieval example from the Corel database is displayed in Fig. 14; the first image on the top left is also the query image.

As concluded from the average precision vs. recall graphs for the two databases, the proposed method performed satisfyingly, despite the bulk of images, dominating the other methods. In addition, one might notice the difference in precision between the fuzzy ant method and the features which form the basis for it, thus proving the increase in performance provided by the newly proposed algorithm.

CONCLUSION

In this chapter, a two-stage content-based image retrieval system based on the modified behavior of ant colonies is presented. Considering the images in the database as food, the ant colony is modified in a manner that the ants search for the shortest paths from the nest to the surrounding foods. The entities of these ants are represented through the basic elements of three low-level image descriptors through which the relative distance between the images is discovered and pheromone is dispersed on each separate path. Although these particular descriptors are proposed for use in this chapter it is imperative to point out that the modified ant colony algorithm can employ a variety of features depending on the implementer or user. The resulting aggregate pheromone deposition is extracted with the use of a Mamdani type fuzzy inference system through which the final retrieval is performed. Although the tedious computations required render the system fairly slow; through its implementation in hardware using

Figure 12. Average Precision versus recall graph for the LabelMe database. ©2008 Konstantinos Konstantinidis. Used with permission.

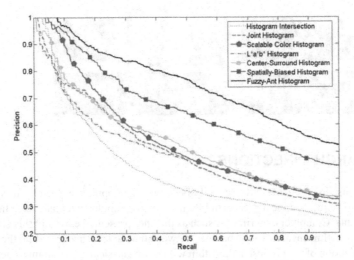

Figure 13. Average Precision versus recall graph for the Corel database for 100% recall. ©2008 Konstantinos Konstantinidis. Used with permission.

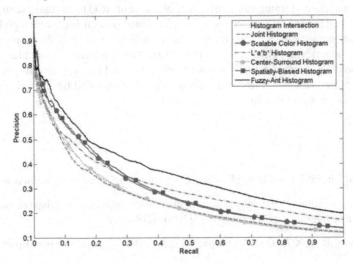

FPGA technology its speed was greatly increased. In order to test and compare the performance of the proposed method to other popular methods, two databases were used; the LabelMe database and a sufficiently large part of the Corel database. Despite the bulk of the two databases, average precision versus recall graphs prove that the proposed system exhibits a more effective performance than other popular and contemporary methods such as the histogram intersection and the scalable color histogram of the MPEG-7 standard.

Figure 14. Retrieval example of a query in the Corel database. ©2008 Konstantinos Konstantinidis. Used with permission.

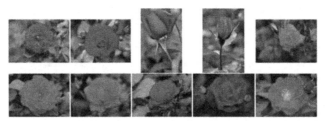

FUTURE RESEARCH DIRECTIONS

It is a fact that agent-based approaches have recently become very popular; especially in systems design and software development. The initial appeal of Swarm Intelligence to computer scientists was almost entirely due to their fascination with ants. Computer experiments such as the ones presented earlier in this chapter have attested that the proposed ant algorithm ensures a good balance between the retrieval accuracy and the optimization time. In addition, the hybridization of the proposed algorithm with more classical artificial intelligence and operations research methods appears to be very appealing. The main reason for using such techniques is largely due to the need for reduction of the search space that has to be explored by the algorithm. This can be especially useful when large scale image databases are considered. Other hybridization examples could be the application of ACO for solution refinement in multilevel frameworks, and the application of ACO to auxiliary search spaces. Another bright new prospective could be the advancement of the proposed method by using recent high level features such as emotions, colour emotions, semantics, etc focusing on the possible increment of the proposed image retrieval robustness as well as its adaptability. Finally, the resulting fuzzy ant algorithm was implemented in hardware based on the presumption that it would actually boost the efficiency and the operational speed of the proposed system. As a result, the aforementioned research directions offer many possibilities for valuable future research in the fields of image retrieval with the help of ACO algorithms.

REFERENCES

Ali, K. S. (1996). Digital Circuit Design Using FPGAs. *Computers and Industrial Engineering, 31*, 127-129.

Alupoaei, S., & Katkoori, S. (2004). Ant colony system application to marcocell overlap removal. *IEEE Transactions on Very Large Scale Integration (VLSI) Systems, 12*(10), 1118–1122.

Bilodeau, G., & Bergevin, R. (2007). Qualitative part-based models in content-based image retrieval. *Mach. Vision Appl., 18*(5), 275-287.

Del Bimbo, A. (1999). *Visual Information Retrieval.* San Francisco, California: Morgan Kaufman.

Beckers, R., Deneubourg, J. L., & Goss, S. (1992). Trails and U-turns in the selection of the shortest path by the ant Lasius Niger. *J. Theoretical Biology, 159*, 397–415.

Blum, C. (2005). Ant colony optimization: Introduction and recent trends. *Physics of Life Reviews, 2*, 353–373.

Bonabeau, E., Dorigo, M., & Theraulaz, G. (1999). *Swarm intelligence: from natural to artificial systems.* New York, NY: Oxford University Press, Inc.

Cheng, Y. C., & Chen, S.Y. (2003). Image classification using color, texture and regions. *Image and Vision Computing, 21*, 759-776.

Chen, S. Y., & Li, Y. F. (2004). Automatic Sensor Placement for Model-Based Robot Vision, *Systems, Man and Cybernetics-B, 34*(1), 393-408.

Chiueh, T. C. (1992). *Optimization of Fuzzy Logic Inference Architecture.* Prentice Hall.

Deneubourg, J. L., & Goss, S. (1989). Collective patterns and decision-making. *Ethology, Ecology & Evolution, 1,* 295–311.

Dorigo, M. (1992). *Optimization, Learning and Natural Algorithms.* PhD thesis, Politecnico di Milano, Italy.

Dorigo, M., Maniezzo, V., & Colorni, A. (1996). The Ant System: Optimization by a colony of cooperating agents. *IEEE Transactions on Systems, Man, and Cybernetics-Part B,* 26(1), 29–41.

Dorigo, M., & Gambardella, L.M. (1997). Ant Colony System: A Cooperative Learning Approach to Traveling Salesman Problem. *IEEE Transactions on Evolutionary Computation, 1,* 53–66.

Dorigo, M., & Stützle, T. (2004). *Ant Colony optimization.* Cambridge, MA: MIT Press.

Gonzalez, R. C., & Woods, R. E. (2002). *Digital Image Processing.* Reading, MA: Addison-Wesley.

Grassé, P. P. (1959). La reconstruction du nid et les coordinations interindividuelles chez *Bellicositermes natalensis et Cubitermes sp.* La th´eorie de la stigmergie: Essai d'interpr´etation des termites constructeurs. Insect Sociaux 6, 41–83.

Hamid, G., (1994). An FPGA-Based Coprocessor for Image Processing. IEE *Colloquium, Integrated Imaging Sensors and Processing, 6,* 1-4.

Huang, X., Zhang, S., Wang, G., & Wang, H. (2006). A new image retrieval method based on optimal color matching. In *Proceedings of the 2006 International Conference on Image Processing, Computer Vision, & Pattern Recognition (IPCV 2006)* (pp. 276-281). Las Vegas, Nevada.

Konstantinidis, K., Gasteratos, A., & Andreadis, I. (2007). The Impact of Low-Level Features in Semantic-Based Image Retrieval. In Yu-Jin Zhang (Ed.), *Semantic-Based Visual Information Retrieval,* (pp 23-45).

Konstantinidis, K., Sirakoulis, G. C., & Andreadis, I. (2007). An Intelligent Image Retrieval System Based on the Synergy of Color and Artificial Ant Colonies. In 15th Scandinavian Conference on Image Analysis, June 2007, Aalborg, Denmark, *Lecture Notes in Computer Science, 4522,* 868-877. Berlin, Heidelberg: Springer-Verlag.

Kotoulas, L., & Andreadis, I. (2003). Colour Histogram Content-based Image Retrieval and Hardware Implementation. *IEE Proc. Circuits, Devices and Systems, 150*(5), 387–393.

Kouzas, G., Kayafas, E., & Loumos, V. (2006). Ant Seeker: An Algorithm for Enhanced Web Search. In Maglogiannis, I., Karpouzis, K., Bramer, M., (Eds.), *Artificial Intelligence Applications and Innovations (AIAI 2006) 204* (618-626). Boston, MA: IFIP International Federation for Information Processing, Springer.

Mamdani, E. H., & Assilian, S. (1999). An experiment in linguistic synthesis with a fuzzy logic controller, *Int. J. Hum.- Comput. Stud., 51*(2), pp. 135–147.

Manjunath, B. S., Ohm, J.-R., Vasudevan, V. V., & Yamada, A. (2001). Color and texture descriptors, *IEEE Trans. on Circuits and Systems for Video Technology, 11*(6), 703-715.

Matusita, K. (1955). Decision rules based on the distance for problems of fit. *Ann. Math. Statist., 26,* 631-640.

Muller, H., Muller, W., Squire, D., McG., Marchand-Maillet, S., & Pun, T. (2001). Performance Evaluation in Content-Based Image Retrieval: Overview and Proposals. *Patt. Rec. Lett., 22,* 593-601.

Nakano, K., & Takamichi, E. (2003). An Image Retrieval System Using FPGAs. In *Proc. Asia and South Pacific Design Automation Conference* (pp. 370-373). New York, NY: ACM.

Panitsidis, G., Konstantinidis, K., Vonikakis, V., Andreadis, I., & Gasteratos, A. (2006). Fast Image Retrieval Based on Attributes of the Human Visual System. In *Proceedings of 7th Nordic Signal Processing Symposium (NORSIG 2006)*, (pp. 206-209) Reykjavik, Iceland.

Pass, G., & Zabih, R. (1999). Comparing Images Using Joint Histograms. *Multimedia Systems, 7*(3), 234-240.

Predrycs, W. (1993). *Fuzzy Control and Fuzzy Systems*. New York, NY: Wiley.

Ramos, V., Muge, F., & Pina, P. (2002). Self-Organized Data and Image Retrieval as a Consequence of Inter-Dynamic Synergistic Relationships in Artificial Ant Colonies. In Ruiz-del-Solar, J., Abraham, A., Köppen, M. (Eds.): *Hybrid Intelligent Systems, Frontiers of Artificial Intelligence and Applications, 87,* 500-512. IOS Press.

Russell, B. C, Torralba, A., Murphy, K. P., & Freeman, W. T. (2005). *LabelMe: A database and web-based tool for image annotation.* MIT AI Lab Memo AIM-2005-025.

Shmygelska, A., & Hoos, H. H. (2005). An ant colony optimisation algorithm for the 2D and 3D hydrophobic polar protein folding problem. *BMC Bioinformatics, 6*(30), 1–22.

Swain, M. J., & Ballard, D. H. (1991). Color Indexing. *Int. Journal of Computer Vision, 7,* 11-32.

Woodrow, E. & Heinzelman, W. (2002). Spin-it: A Data Centric Routing Protocol for Image Retrieval in Wireless Networks. In *Proceedings IEEE International Conference on Image Processing, 3,* 913-916.

Yang, Y., Lin, H., Zhang, Y. (2007). Content-Based 3-D Model Retrieval: A Survey. *IEEE Systems, Man and Cybernetics-C, 37*(6), 1081-1098.

KEY TERMS

Ant Colony Optimization: A probabilistic technique for solving computational problems which can be reduced to finding good paths through graphs. They are inspired by the self-organizing abilities of real ants.

Feature Extraction: The process of detection, isolation and extraction of various desired portions or features of a digitized image.

Field Programmable Gate Arrays: Semiconductor devices containing programmable logic blocks and programmable interconnects. Logic blocks can be programmed to perform the function of basic logic gates or more complex combinational functions such as decoders or simple mathematical functions.

Fuzzy Logic: Is derived from fuzzy set theory dealing with reasoning that is approximate rather than precisely deduced from classical predicate logic. It can be thought of as the application side of fuzzy set theory dealing with well thought out real world expert values for a complex problem.

Hardware: A general term that refers to the physical components of a computing system.

Image Retrieval: The process of browsing, searching and retrieving images from a large database of digital images.

Image Processing: A technique through which various mathematical operations are applied to the data of a digital image in order to enhance its quality or to extract information from its content.

Chapter XIX
Ant Colonies and Data Mining

Miroslav Bursa
Czech Technical University in Prague, Czech Republic

Lenka Lhotska
Czech Technical University in Prague, Czech Republic

ABSTRACT

The chapter concentrates on the use of swarm intelligence in data mining. It focuses on the problem of medical data clustering. Clustering is a constantly growing area of current research. Medicine, market, trade, and meteorology belong to the numerous fields that benefit of its techniques. First an introduction into data mining and cluster validation techniques is presented, followed by a review of ant-inspired concepts and applications. The chapter provides a reasonably deep insight into the most successful ant colony and swarm intelligence concepts, their paradigms and application. The authors present discussion, evaluation and comparison of these techniques. Important applications and results recently achieved are provided. Finally, new and prospective future directions in this area are outlined and discussed.

INTRODUCTION

This chapter concentrates on the use of swarm intelligence in data mining. It focuses on the problem of data clustering in biomedical data processing. Clustering is a constantly growing area of current research. Medicine, market, trade, and meteorology are some of the numerous fields that benefit of its techniques.

The objective of this chapter is to introduce the methods for clustering together with the methods for evaluation of different clusterings. It presents the fundamentals of ant inspired methods, followed by a compact review of the basic ant clustering models together with the most successful variations and modifications. In the second part, it presents the application of ant-colony clustering in biomedical data processing.

In the last two decades, many advances in computer sciences have been based on the observation and emulation of processes of the natural world.

Copyright © 2009, IGI Global, distributing in print or electronic forms without written permission of IGI Global is prohibited.

The coordination of an ant colony is of local nature, composed mainly of indirect communication through pheromone (also known as *stigmergy*; the term has been introduced by Grassé et al. (1959)), although direct interaction communication from ant to ant (in the form of antennation) and direct communication have also been observed (Trianni, Labella, & Dorigo, 2004). In studying these paradigms, we have high chance to discover inspiring concepts for many successful metaheuristics. More information on the ant colony metaphors can be found in the section *Ant Colony Optimization*.

The author himself specializes on the use of such kind of methods in the area of biomedical data processing. The application is described in the section *Applications*.

The chapter is organized as follows: First, an introduction to data mining and clustering is presented together with a brief survey on ant colony inspired methods in clustering. Then, a natural background of applied methods is presented. It summarizes the most important properties of ant colonies that served as an inspiration source for many algorithms that are described in the following part. The next section describes the most successful methods in data clustering: first, the pioneering ant-inspired clustering algorithms are described followed by the evolution of further ant-inspired algorithms for clustering. Finally, applications of the algorithms and paradigms published by the author are presented, followed by conclusion and future directions. At the end, relevant literature has been carefully selected to provide the reader with additional resources containing the state-of-the-art information in the area.

BACKGROUND

About Data Mining

This section provides more thorough introduction into data mining and reasons the use of methods that provide only approximate results (with an acceptable error) in much more reasonable time.

In many industrial, business, healthcare and scientific areas we can see still growing use of computers and computational appliances. Together with the boom of high-speed networks and increasing storage capacity of database clusters and warehouses, a huge amount of various data can be collected. Such data are often heterogeneous and seldom come without any errors (or noise). *Data mining* is not only an important scientific discipline, but also an important tool in industry, business and healthcare, that is concerned with discovering (hidden) information in the data.

Many data-mining algorithms with growing number of modifications exist nowadays. Such modifications aim at speeding up the data mining process, increase its robustness and stability. But even with rapidly increasing computational power of modern computers, the analysis of huge databases becomes very expensive (in terms of computer time and/or memory – and therefore also financially). This is why scientists instantly create, develop and evaluate novel approaches to analyze and process these data. In contrast to classical methods, nature inspired methods offer many techniques that can increase speed and robustness of classical methods. Clustering techniques inspired by nature already exist – self-organizing maps, neural networks, evolutionary algorithms, etc. This chapter concentrates on techniques, inspired by ant colonies, where various branches can be distinguished: (1) methods inspired solely by ant behavior, and (2) hybrid methods (combining ant-colony approach with traditional methods).

Clustering belongs to the most useful data-mining techniques. It significantly reduces the amount of data to be processed. Data clustering can significantly help in the case of electrocardiogram (ECG) processing. Clustering of long-term ECG record should reduce expert's (cardiologist's) work and furthermore reduce his load and fatigue. Some methods can produce structures, which can reveal the inherent structure of the data.

Clustering

As the application section is targeted towards the task of data clustering, this part provides a general introduction into the clustering problem with an overview of cluster validation techniques, which can be used in the case the correct classification is not known.

Data clustering, in literature referred as *cluster analysis* (P. Rousseeuw & Kaufman, 1990), numerical taxonomy, typological analysis, etc., is a common unsupervised learning technique. Cluster analysis is concerned with the division of data into homogeneous groups so that data within one cluster are similar to each other, and those within different clusters are dissimilar. (We are minimizing intra-cluster distance while maximizing the inter-cluster distance.) Many clustering techniques are available nowadays, differing not only in the principles of the underlying algorithm, but also in other characteristics, such as types of attributes handled or the shapes of identifiable clusters. A survey on clustering techniques can be found in the publication of Jain, Murty, & Flynn (1999).

The data clustering problem is an NP-hard problem when the number of clusters is larger than three, according to Welch (1983) and Forgey (1965). Therefore the search for approximative methods is reasonable. Approximative methods do not provide exactly the best results, but provide reasonably acceptable solutions, significantly reducing computational time.

Basic Taxonomy of Clustering Algorithms

The clustering algorithms can be classified as *stochastic* or *deterministic*. The clustering optimization (minimization of an objective function) can be accomplished using traditional techniques or through a randomized state space search. The state space consists of all possible clusterings (class assignments).

According to their characteristics, clustering techniques can be classified as follows:

- *Hierarchical* clustering technique creates a tree of clusters, where clusters near the root of the tree are more generic, and those near the leaves are more specific. *Non-hierarchical* clustering techniques produce clusters that do not possess an explicit relation to each other.
- *Agglomerative* clustering technique creates the clusters by the bottom-up approach, starting at individual data level and joining them together, while *Divisive* clustering techniques work top-down, starting with a single cluster and decomposing it furthermore.
- *Hard* clustering methods put each data unit in only one cluster, while *Soft* (fuzzy) clustering can place the data vector into multiple clusters.

Ant-based clustering algorithms, in the basic form (see section *Ant Colony Clustering: Basic Model*), can be considered as non-hierarchical, hard and agglomerative. However, many combinations exist and the underlying mechanism determines the final classification.

Metrics Considered

A key part in the clustering process is to properly determine the distance measure to be used. A simple measure as Minkowski (Manhattan, Euclidean) distance is often used.

Many other distance metrics have been proposed in the literature, for example the Chi-square metrics (Wilson & Martinez, 1997), the Mahalanobis metric (Mahalanobis, 1936), the Cosine Similarity Metric (Salton & McGill, 1983), Hausdorff metrics (Huttenlocher, Klanderman, & Rucklige, 1993), Dynamic Time Warping (Myers & Rabiner, 1981), and many others.

In this paper we use the L2 metrics (Euclidean, also called Minkowski L2) and DDTW (Derivative Dynamic Time Warping). The DDTW metrics provides better results for raw signals in the case the time axis is slightly moderated.

Ant Colony Methods in Clustering

Several species of ant workers have been reported to form piles of corpses (cemeteries) to clean up their nests. For example, the *Messor sancta* ants organize dead corpses into clusters; brood sorting has been studied in ant colony of *Leptothorax unifasciatus*. This aggregation phenomenon is caused by attraction of the dead items collected by the ant workers. The workers deposit (with higher probability) these items in the region with higher similarity (when more similar items are present within the range of perception).

This approach has been modeled by Deneubourg et al. (1990) and Lumer & Faieta (1994) to perform a clustering of data. This approach (as all the clustering methods) is very sensitive to the similarity measure used and the range of agent perception. Note, that no pheromone is used in this method.

For more compact review refer to section *Clustering by Ant Colonies.*

Inspiration in Nature

This section states the motivation for the development of nature inspired methods together with relevant success stories. We start with an introduction to the natural fundamentals of swarm societies, followed by the best optimization strategies, which are based on these observations.

Computational modeling of the swarm behavior shows its usefulness in various application domains, such as function optimization (Socha & Dorigo, 2005), finding the optimal routes (Caro, Ducatelle, & Gambardella, 2005), (Dorigo, Caro, & Gambardella, 1999), scheduling (Dorigo & Stutzle, 2004), biomedical data processing and classification (Bursa & Lhotska, 2006), and many more. Different applications originate from the study of different swarms and therefore different behavioral strategies.

Cemetery formation and brood sorting are two prominent examples of insects' collective behavior. However, other types of ant behavior have been observed, for example predator-prey interaction, prey hunting, etc.

By replicating the behavior of the insects, the underlying mechanisms may be found and a better understanding of nature may be furthermore achieved. Applying the social insect behavior in computer science leads to more effective techniques.

Social Insect

Social insect societies consist of individuals with simple behavior. However, at the collective level the societies are capable of solving complex tasks, for example finding the best food source, constructing optimal nest structure, brooding, protecting the larvae, guarding, etc. The complex behavior emerges from the interactions of individuals that each performs simple behavioral patterns. These collective behaviors span a wide range of tasks from foraging and nest construction to thermoregulation and brood sorting (Bonabeau et al., 1999), (Camazine et al., 2001).

Cemetery Formation

Cemetery formation has been observed (and furthermore modeled) in different ant species, such as *Pheidole pallidula*, *Lasius niger* and *Messor sancta* (Bonabeau, Dorigo, & Theraulaz, 1999), (Deneubourg et al., 1990). The model of Deneubourg et al. (1990) does not accurately model the way the real ants cluster corpses around heterogeneities, so Martin, Chopard, & Albuquerque (2002) proposed a minimal model to simulate cemetery formation behavior where clusters are formed around heterogeneities.

Brood Sorting

Brood sorting in *Leptothorax unifasciatus* ant species has been studied and published in the work of Deneubourg et al. (1990) and by Franks and Sendova-Franks (1992). Deneubourg et. al. (1990) described the behavior together with robotic implementation: "*...the eggs are arranged in a pile next to a pile of larvae and a further pile of cocoons, or else the three categories are placed in entirely different parts of the nest.*"

The brood sorting in the *Leptothorax species* has been described by Franks and Sendova Franks (1992): "*The standard pattern is for eggs and micro-larvae to be in the middle, with the larger larvae further from the center in order of increasing size. Pre-pupae and pupae are distributed in positions between the outer ring of the largest larvae and those of the next largest size.*"

Self-Assembling Behavior

Ants are able to build mechanical structures by a *self-assembling behavior*. Building of chains of ants (Lioni, Sauwens, Theraulaz, & Deneubourg, 2001) or formation of drops of ants (Theraulaz et al., 2001) have been observed by biologists. These types of self-assembly behavior patterns have been observed with *Linepithema humiles* Argentina ants (droplets) and African ants of gender *Oecophylla longinoda* (chain building).

The purpose of the droplets is still obscure; however the formation has been experimentally demonstrated (Theraulaz et al., 2001). The chains (built by the *Oecophylla longinoda* ants) serve for two objectives: for crossing an empty space and for building the nest of ants.

In both cases, the structures disaggregate after a given time, which is certainly the mechanism for adapting to dynamic problems.

Aggregation Behavior

Aggregation behavior has been observed in ant species. These include foraging-site marking and mating, finding shelter and defense.

Cockroaches, after finding safe shelter, produce a specific pheromone with their excrement, which attracts other members of their species (Sukama & Fukami, 1993). Based on similar property, ants need to find comfortable and secure environment to sleep, Chen, Xu, & Chen (2004) proposed *Sleeping Ant Model*, which makes ants group with those that have similar physiques.

Ant Colony Optimization

Ant Colony Optimization is a very successful concept for combinatorial optimization problems. As these methods are the best known solution for some NP hard problems, the applications are briefly discussed.

Marco Dorigo (1992) presented an optimization algorithm inspired by the ants' foraging behavior in his PhD thesis. The work has been formalized into the framework of *Ant Colony Optimization* (ACO) (Dorigo et al., 1999). One of the basic ideas underlying ACO metaheuristics is to use an algorithmic counterpart to the *pheromone trail*, used by real ants, as a medium for communication inside the colony of artificial ants. In this manner the ants communicate indirectly, solely by modifying their environment. The best results have been obtained for the Traveling Salesman Problem (TSP). For the Quadratic Assignment Problem (QAP), the results are, however, rather negative (Balaprakash, Birattari, Stutzle, & Dorigo, 2006).

Several versions of the ACO strategy have been proposed, but they all follow the same basic ideas:

- search performed by a population of individuals
- incremental construction of solutions
- probabilistic choice of solution components based on stigmergic information
- no direct communication between the individuals

The performance of ACO algorithms can be significantly enhanced by adding a local search phase in which the solutions are improved by a local search procedure (Dorigo & Gambardella, 1997), (Stutzle & Hoos, 1997). Lee, Lea, & Su (2002) used concept from immune systems to improve the local search efficiency of ACO by vaccination and immune selection.

Study on the invariance of Ant System can be found in the work of Birattari, Pellegrini, & Dorigo (2006). Also a niching metaphor for ACO has been published (Angus, 2006).

Approaches to perform an optimization in continuous domain exist, the closest to the ant colony metaphor is the method presented by Socha (2004). In his work, a probabilistic density function (PDF) is used to estimate the distribution of Gaussian function.

A review of ACO-related methods can be found in the work of Blum (2005) and Dorigo & Blum (2005).

Parallel variants also exist, as the Ant Colony Optimization approaches are naturally suited for parallel processing: see for example the work of Stützle (1998) and Manfrin, Birattari, Stutzle, & Dorigo (2006) and others (e.g. Albuquerque & Dupuis (2002), Chen & Zhang, (2005)). Also fuzzy modifications exist, see for example the work of Jensen & Shen (2004), Kanade & Hall (2003; 2004), Parpinelli, Lopes, & Freitas (2005), Schockaert, Cock, Cornelis, & Kerre (2004), Schockaert, Cock, Cornelis, & Etienne (2004).

Clustering by Ant Colonies

This section concentrates on the field of ant colony inspired clustering. It describes the pioneering approach that served as a base for many improvements. Then, following algorithms are described, in order of their publication to keep the reader informed about the development timeline in the area of ant clustering.

Ant Colony Clustering: Basic Model

The clustering of dead bodies by ants inspired Deneubourg et al. (1990). In their article they published biologically inspired model for clustering by a group of homogeneous agents. The ants possess only local perceptual capabilities – they can sense the objects immediately surrounding them, and they can also compare whether the objects are similar or not to the object they are carrying.

The basic model can be described as follows: First the data vectors are randomly scattered onto a two-dimensional grid (usually a toroidal one) (which is an analogy of the real world of an ant in the nature). Ants (also called agents) are then randomly placed onto the two-dimensional grid. In each iteration step an ant searches its neighborhood and computes a probability of picking up a vector (if the ant is unloaded and steps onto a vector) or of dropping down a vector (if the ant is loaded and steps onto a free grid element). The ant moves randomly. Intuitively the search process can be speed up by traversing the data vectors or guided by pheromone deposited (Dorigo & Stutzle, 2004). The probability of the ant to pick up an object is given by the following equation:

$$P_p = \left(\frac{k_1}{k_1 + f} \right)^2$$

(1)

where f is the perceived fraction of items in the neighborhood of the agent (3), and k_1 is a threshold constant. If f is much lower than k_1, the probability is close to a value of 1, thus the probability of picking up the item is high. The probability of dropping down the carried object is given by the following equation:

$$P_d = \left(\frac{f}{k_2 + f} \right)^2$$

(2)

where k_2 is a similar threshold constant. Again with high values of f (much greater than k_2) the probability is close to the value of 1, thus the probability of dropping the vector is high. The function f (usually called a similarity measure) is computed as follows: Assume agent located at site r finding a vertex v_i at that site. Then the similarity is measured for each object in the (square) neighborhood (denoted as $Neigh(s{\times}s)(r)$, where s denotes the neighborhood size (one side)):

$$f(v_i) = \begin{cases} \frac{1}{s^2} \sum_{v_j \in Neigh(s{\times}s)(r)} \left[1 - \frac{d(v_i, v_j)}{\alpha} \right] & \text{if } f > 0 \\ 0 & \text{otherwise} \end{cases}$$

(3)

where $f(v_i)$ is a measure of the average distance within the graph of element v_i to other elements v_j present in the neighborhood of the element v_i. The function $d(v_i, v_j)$ is a distance measure between the two parameters (Euclidean, Manhattan, Mahalanobis, DTW, or any other). Parameter α defines the scale for dissimilarity. If (for example) the neighborhood contains vectors identical to v_i, then the function $f(v_i) = 1$, thus the vertex should not be picked up. On the other hand, when the surrounding area contains no vertices, the vector will be picked up with high probability ($f(v_i) = 0$). For ant carrying a data vector, the same equation (3) is used. The v_i parameter in such case denotes the vector being carried by the ant agent.

Ant Colony Clustering: Improved Versions

Gutowitz (1993) improved the basic model by giving the ants the capacity to sense the complexity (or entropy) of their vicinity. The entropy level of perceived area was determined by the presence (or absence) of objects. These so-called complexity-seeking ants are able to avoid actions that do not contribute to the clustering process.

Lumer and Faieta (1994) have generalized Deneubourg's model to apply it to exploratory data analysis. In contrary to Deneubourg's model, Lumer and Faieta used a continuous similarity function to judge the similarity between different objects. The proposed algorithm has been called *Ant Colony Clustering*. Its drawback is that it has a number of parameters that must be set empirically and can produce more clusters than the optimal number is in reality.

In the model proposed by Lumer and Faieta, the ants carrying isolated corpses (outlier data items) will make never-ending move since they never find a proper location to drop them. This consumes a large amount of computation time. To speed up convergence and to reduce complex parameter settings, Monmarché et al. (1999) proposed an interesting hybridization of this algorithm with k-means called *AntClass* to improve the convergence of the ant algorithm.

Ramos et al. (2002) developed an ant clustering system called *ACluster,* which targeted textual document clustering and retrieval of digital images. Unlike *Ant Colony Clustering* algorithm, the ants do not move randomly in the *ACluster* algorithm, but rather according to the transition probabilities depending on the spatial distribution of the pheromone across the environment. This eliminated the need of short term memory which was required for storing past movements of the ants in the model of Lumer and Faieta.

Handl, Knowles, & Dorigo (2003b) published an article on the strategies for increased robustness of ant-based clustering and also a study on the performance of the algorithm (comparative study of the ant-based clustering with k-means, average link and 1d-som) (Handl, Knowles, & Dorigo, 2003a). The work is summarized in the book of Handl, Knowles, & Dorigo (2003c).

Azzag, Guinot, & Venturini (2004) presented a model for document hierarchical clustering called *AntTree*. It is inspired by the self-assembly behavior of some ant species. For a given objective, or to overcome a difficulty, the ants create chains by fixing themselves one on the other. The first ants fix themselves on a support and others get attached to the already fixed ants. A countermeasure to overcome initial support selection is also considered.

Schockaert et al. (2004) proposed a clustering method where the desired behavior of artificial ants (and more precisely, their stimuli for picking up and dropping items) is expressed by fuzzy IF-THEN rules. The algorithm is inspired by the work of Monmarché (2000).

To improve performance, stability and convergence of the *Ant Colony Clustering* algorithm, Vizine et. al (2005) proposed an adaptive algorithm called A^2CA (*An Adaptive Ant Clustering Algorithm*) which improves the standard ant-clustering algorithm. The A^2CA algorithm was inspired by the fact that termites, while building their nests, deposit pheromone on soil pellets. This behavior serves as a reinforcement signal to other termites placing more pellets on the same region in the space (Camazine et al., 2001).

Handl et al. (2006) published a comparative study and experimental evaluation of the *ATTA* algorithm. Authors more thoroughly describe and evaluate the *ATTA* algorithm in two versions: *ATTA-C* for clustering and *ATTA-TM* for topographic mapping. The results demonstrate the ability of ant-based clustering and sorting to automatically identify the number of clusters inherent in a data collection, and to produce high quality solutions. The results regarding the robustness in the case of clusters of different sizes and overlapping clusters are also promising. However, the results obtained for topographic mapping are disappointing.

Tan et al. (2006) presented a deterministic version of the ATTA algorithm. Authors remove the ant metaphor from the model and use a randomized partitioning method followed by an agglomerative clustering procedure. The results obtained are comparable to the ant-based model.

Bursa et Lhotska (2007) presented a novel approach for classification tree construction called *ACO_DTree*. The algorithm uses a population of classification trees that is evolved using an evolutionary approach. Creation of the trees is driven by a pheromone matrix, which uses the ACO paradigm.

In the recent paper of Handl and Knowles (2007), a discussion on multiobjective clustering approach is presented. The algorithm is called MOCK, (*Multi Objective Clustering with automatic k-determination*). It consists of two phases: in clustering phase it uses a multi-objective evolutionary algorithm to optimize two complementary clustering objectives. In the second phase, model-selection phase, the algorithm analyzes the shape of the tradeoff curve and compares it to the tradeoffs obtained for an appropriate null model (i. e., by clustering random data). Based on this analysis, the algorithm provides an estimate of the quality of all individual clustering solutions, and determines a set of potentially promising clustering solutions.

APPLICATION OF SWARM METAHEURISTICS TO BIOMEDICAL DATA PROCESSING

As the author and his research group specialize on the field of biomedical data processing, the applications to biomedical signals are presented. As the proposing author has also improved the classical ant colony clustering algorithm (Bursa, Huptych, & Lhotska, 2006) and proposed a new ant-colony based algorithm for clustering (Bursa & Lhotska, 2007b), observations from this work are included.

Biomedical Data Processing

Data

Preliminary tests with artificial data sets have to be performed, mainly with two and four clusters generated using Gaussian distributions for different dimensions in order to correctly evaluate the behavior of the clustering algorithm. The real data are not general enough, as they form a subset of the more general random data sets. For basic parameter estimation and implementation testing, the well-known *iris dataset* (Asuncion & Newman, 2007) can be used (the database is freely available). This dataset contains three classes, each containing 50 vectors and the dataset contains one well separable class, the remaining two are more difficult to separate. Also other data set from the database can be used for preliminary parameter estimation.

Real Electrocardiogram Data

Real electrocardiogram (ECG) signals come from widely used MIT-BIH database (Goldberger et al., 2000) that contains annotated records. In the work of Goldberger et al. (2000) and Chudacek & Lhotska (2006), certain description of the data can also be found (together with basic anonymous description of the patients and their medication). For the sake of simplicity, only two major distinct classes are often used. The classification into more classes is nearly impossible due to lack of the data (specific abnormal heart action signal) in some signals.

Feature extraction

From the ECG signal, the following eight features have been automatically extracted (see the work of Chudacek & Lhotska (2006) for more details):

- amplitudes of Q, R, S, positive T and negative T wave
- amplitude ratio of Q/R, R/S and R/T waves

For data clustering, the features should be normalized into interval $\langle 0.0;1.0 \rangle$. Along with the features a signal window of 401 samples has been stored (containing the beat that was used for feature extraction) thus making it available to perform a DTW (Dynamic Time Warping) distance evaluation.

Figure 1. Electrical recording of a heart action (an electrocardiogram, ECG). The most important features are marked. The graph shows amplitude dependency on time (on record samples). ©2008 Miroslav Bursa. Used with permission.

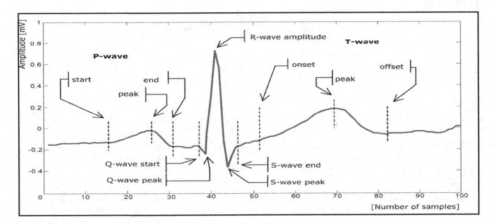

BioDat laboratory also possesses the AHA database. It is in general good idea to perform training of the method on one database (i.e. MIT-BIH) and test on the other (i.e. AHA). This approach has been agreed in our laboratory as the most beneficial. However, many authors still lack the professional approach to achieve objective results.

Application Examples

Bursa et al. (2006) presented an application of the use of ant based clustering to biomedical data clustering, where the comparison with another nature inspired approaches is presented. In the work of Bursa & Lhotska (2006), the authors presented an application of ant-colony inspired clustering to the interpretation of an ECG signal, merging the algorithm with the DTW algorithm (Myers & Rabiner, 1981) and the wavelet transform (Daubechies, 1992). The drawback of wavelet feature extraction is that the extracted features do not have clinical relevance. For the ant colony approach the accuracy has been 69.5 % and the k-means accuracy 44.7 % for the task of ECG classification.

Bursa et al. (2007) presented a novel approach for classification tree construction called ACO_DTree. The algorithm uses a population of classification trees that is evolved using an evolutionary approach. Trees are constructed using a pheromone matrix which represents probability of creating successive nodes. An application to the neonatal sleep classification (which is used to study the maturation stage of neonatal brain) can be found in the work of Gerla et al. (2007). Also the application of an improved ant colony clustering model to long-term ECG processing has been presented in the work of Bursa & Lhotska (2007).

ACO_DTree Method

The ACO_DTree method (Bursa, Lhotska, & Macas, 2007) uses an evolutionary approach combined with ant colony optimization approach. The ACO_DTree method works with a population of classifier trees (a decision-tree like structure): a hierarchical binary structure of nodes where each node divides data set into two parts using a single if-rule (e.g. if (feature(i) < value) then pass_data_left else pass_data_right). The population is continuously evaluated, new individuals are continuously added and worst solutions removed. Only the best individuals can contribute in pheromone laying process (in compliance with the work of Dorigo et al. (1999)). New individuals are inductively created using the pheromone matrix, preferring important features (features selected by the best individuals).

Figure 2. Typical history of pheromone values for a subset of 4×7 elements of the square pheromone matrix. It can be observed that at the end, we obtain saturated pheromone values which determine the importance of features. Each sub-rectangle displays pheromone values ⟨0.05;1.05⟩. during time (iterations). ©2008 Miroslav Bursa. Used with permission.

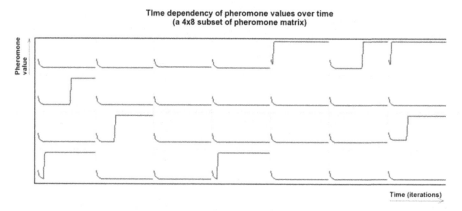

By a classification tree we mean hereby a tree-like structure composed of similar nodes. Each node can have left and right sub node. Each node is represented by a decision rule with two parameters (feature index $feature_j$ and decision value *decVal*). The same applies to the root node. The tree is constructed as follows: first, a random feature index is selected (for the root node). The decision value is also chosen randomly. Then, for each subnode, the subnode is created with certain probability (a cooling strategy is applied). The feature index is selected using the pheromone matrix: the edges that have proved to be successful are preferred. The decision value is determined randomly. The random selection of decision value does not present a problem, because even the randomly selected values provided acceptable solution. However, the population (decision values *decVal*) is furthermore optimized.

Figure 2 shows a typical history of pheromone in the pheromone matrix. Only a subset of the whole matrix is presented. The figure presents view on the pheromone matrix during the evaluation of the algorithm.

Using the classification tree, the data are divided into subgroups that should have similar properties (minimization of intra-cluster distance) and the classes should be different (maximization of inter-cluster distance). This process is known as data clustering.

Decision Tree Evaluation

Each tree can be assigned a real number which can be called fitness function. Such number represents the classification efficiency of the tree. In the method this number is determined by the ratio of incorrectly classified data to the total data in the class (hence it is called error ratio). The goal of our method is to obtain tree with the lowest error ratio on the data set.

The trees are constructed using training data set. Validating data set is used to indicate the robustness of the solution: if the tree performs well on training data and poorly on the validation data, the generalization of the tree is low (and vice-versa). Finally, the testing data set is used to evaluate the tree on the unknown data (data which have never been presented to the tree). If the classification of the testing data is not known, cluster validation techniques can be used.

Parameter Estimation and Adaptation

The most important parameters of the proposed method are: population size, number of new solutions added in each step, maximal number of iterations, max. tree height, pheromone lay/evaporate rate and the percent of ants which can deposit pheromone (elitist ratio). The overall results are better when the first four parameters increase, but the computational time rises (an exchange exists). For other parameters, an optimum must be determined. For more thorough evaluation of the parameters refer to (Bursa, M., Lhotska, L., & Macas, M. (2007)).

In order to avoid premature convergence and maintain diversity in the population of solutions, adaptive techniques have been used. The balanced process diversifies the population and avoids getting stuck in local minima.

Tree Optimization

In the ACO_DTree method, we have presented an optimization strategy (local search) that optimizes the decision value of each node in the tree. Newly added solutions (trees) are optimized before they are added to the population. This improves the overall fitness of the population.

Also after certain period (experimentally determined), the population is re-optimized (not the structure, but decision values in the nodes). We have used the Particle Swarm Optimization (Kennedy & Eberhart, 1995), but any other kind of local search can be used.

Overall Results

We have evaluated nature inspired methods (Kohonen Self-organizing map, Ant Colony Clustering, the ACO_DTree method) and classical methods (k-means) and agglomerative clustering. The Ant Colony Clustering method has been evaluated using L2 (Euclidean) measure and DDTW (Derivative Dynamic Time Warping) measure.

Table 1 shows an average sensitivity and specificity for all methods evaluated. Sensitivity has been computed as $Se = TP/(TP + FN)$, specificity as $Sp = TN/(FP + TN)$. These measures are commonly used in clinical statistics. (Note that L2 measure implies the use of feature extraction, the DDTW measure works with raw signal.)

The best results have been achieved by the hierarchical agglomerative method, which is the only method not using centroid approach. However, this approach requires much more computation time and memory than all the other algorithms.

The nature inspired methods (Ant Colony Clustering (L2 and DDTW), Kohonen SOM), however, outperformed the basic k-means algorithm both in specificity and sensitivity and achieved more stable results (in term of standard deviation).

Final results with comparison to the Dynamic Time Warping over the test runs in general improved sensitivity about 0.7 % and Specificity about 0.9 % when compared to classical feature extraction. It is an important aspect: by combining the processing of the raw signal (DTW) and feature extraction, there is a chance that the overall result will improve.

Using the ACO_DTree method we have obtained an accuracy of 97.11 % in the task of EEG clustering, and 91.32 % accuracy in the noise removal of an EEG sleep signal. These results are very promising and together with the structure produced could be used in the field of EEG clustering.

Table 1. Method comparison. Table provides results for the task of ECG clustering for nature inspired methods (Ant Colony Clustering, Kohonen SOM) and classical methods (k-means, agglomerative). The Ant Colony Clustering is evaluated using L2 and DDTW measure.

Method/Result	Measure	Sensitivity	Specificity
K-Means	L2	77	65
Agglomerative	L2	96	74
Ant Colony Clustering	L2	79	68
Kohonen SOM	L2	79	66
Ant Colony Clustering	DDTW	79	69

CONCLUSION

The basic ant clustering method is more related to the nature and offers very good robustness and speed. Their ability to form (and thus discover) natural clusters in data is also interesting.

The soft-computing methods often suffer from the need of parameter tuning during the run. It is not rare, that the algorithm parameters are also tuned using the optimization algorithm itself (as a secondary optimization task).

The PSO optimization in the ACO_DTree method must be carefully considered. When it is excessively used, it can lead to overfitting of the tree (as it is trained only on the subsection of the whole training dataset).

Previous research on ant-inspired clustering methods and sorting raises several questions, related to the algorithm's performance. Many authors do not use common technique to evaluate their algorithms; they often use data sets, which are not general enough. They should be first evaluated on artificial data sets, and furthermore on benchmark data sets, for example the UCI database (Newman et al., 1998).

The results have shown that the performance of the nature inspired method is comparable and in some cases outperforms the classical methods, but it depends on the type of clustering method.

FUTURE RESEARCH DIRECTIONS

The scientists should not only concentrate on the clustering performance (comparison with classical approaches, resource consumption), but should also consider the quality of their solutions and sensitivity to data properties. They should also consider trying high-dimensional and large data sets.

The main directions in this field are mainly the high dimensional data analysis, which is still considered a problem for the modern computers (or grids).

However the real scientific work should lead towards the generalization of the concepts from different methods, leading to selection of the best methodics, which can be incorporated in general into any optimization algorithm. Also the mathematical backgrounds of the methods are not studied thoroughly, leaving many areas of interest open for future research.

ACKNOWLEDGMENT

The research has been supported by the research program No. MSM 6840770012 "Transdisciplinary Research in the Area of Biomedical Engineering II" of the CTU in Prague, sponsored by the Ministry of Education, Youth and Sports of the Czech Republic and by the FP6-IST project No. 13569 NiSIS (Nature-inspired Smart Information Systems).

REFERENCES

Adami, C. (1998). *Introduction to artificial life*. Springer Verlag.

Albuquerque, P., & Dupuis, A. (2002). A parallel cellular ant colony algorithm for clustering and sorting. *In Proceedings of the Fifth International Conference on Cellular Automata for Research and Industry, Springer-Verlag, Heidelberg, Germany, LNCS 2492, 2492*, 220–230.

Angus, D. (2006). Niching for population-based ant colony optimization. In *E-science '06: Proceedings of the second ieee international conference on e-science and grid computing* (p. 15). Washington, DC, USA: IEEE Computer Society.

Asuncion, A., & Newman, D. J. (2007). UCI Machine Learning Repository [http://www.ics.uci.edu/~mlearn/ML-Repository.html]. Irvine, CA: University of California, School of Information and Computer Science.

Azzag, H., Guinot, C., & Venturini, G. (2004, September 5-8). How to Use Ants for Hierarchical Clustering. In M. Dorigo, M. Birattari, C. Blum, L. Gambardella, F. Mondada, & T. Stutzle (Eds.), *Proceedings of ants 2004 – fourth international workshop on ant colony optimization andswarm intelligence, 3172*, 350–357. Brussels, Belgium: Springer Verlag.

Balaprakash, P., Birattari, M., Stutzle, T., & Dorigo, M. (2006). Incremental local search in ant colony optimization: Why it fails for the quadratic assignment problem. *M. Dorigo et al (Eds.), ANTS 2006 LNCS, 4150*, 156–166.

Birattari, M., Pellegrini, P., & Dorigo, M. (2006). On the invariance of ant system. *M. Dorigo et al. (Eds.), ANTS 2006, LNCS 4150, Spriner-Verlag Berlin Heidelberg 2006*, 215–223.

Blum, C. (2005). Ant colony optimization: Introduction and recent trends. *Physics of Life Reviews, 2*(4), 353–373.

Boley, D. (1998). Principle direction divisive partitioning. *Journal on Data Mining and Knowledge Discovery, 2*, 325–344.

Bonabeau, E., Dorigo, M., & Theraulaz, G. (1999). *Swarm intelligence: From natural to artificial systems.* Oxford University Press, New York, NY.

Bursa, M., Huptych, M., & Lhotska, L. (2006). The use of nature inspired methods in electrocardiogram analysis. *International Special Topics Conference on Information Technology in Biomedicine [CD-ROM]. Piscataway: IEEE.*

Bursa, M., & Lhotska, L. (2006a). Electrocardiogram signal classification using modified ant colony clustering and wavelet transform. *In: Analysis of Biomedical Signals and Images – Proceedings of Biosignal 2006. Brno: VUTIUM Press ISBN 80-214-3152-0*, 193–195.

Bursa, M., & Lhotska, L. (2006b). The use of ant colony inspired methods in electrocardiogram interpretation, an overview. *In: NiSIS 2006 – The 2nd European Symposium on Nature-inspired Smart Information Systems [CD-ROM]. Aachen: NiSIS.*

Bursa, M., & Lhotska, L. (2007a). Ant colony cooperative strategy in biomedical data clustering. *Studies in Computational Intelligence, Springer-Verlag.*

Bursa, M., & Lhotska, L. (2007b). Automated classification tree evolution through hybrid metaheuristics. *E. Corchado, J.M. Corchado, A. Abraham (Eds.), Innovations in Hybrid Intelligent Systems, Advances in Soft Computing, 44*, 191–198.

Bursa, M., & Lhotska, L. (2007c). Modified ant colony clustering method in long-term electrocardiogram processing. *Proceedings of the 29th Annual International Conference of the IEEE EMBS*, 3249–3252.

Bursa, M., Lhotska, L., & Macas, M. (2007). Hybridized swarm metaheuristics for evolutionary random forest generation. *Proceedings of the 7th International Conference on Hybrid Intelligent Systems 2007 (IEEE CSP)*, 150–155.

Camazine, S., Deneubourg, J.-L., Franks, N. R., Sneyd, J., Theraulaz, G., & Bonabeau, E. (2001). *Self-organization in biological systems.* Princeton University Press, New Jersey.

Caro, G. D., Ducatelle, F., & Gambardella, L. M. (2005). Anthocnet: An adaptive nature-inspired algorithm for routing in mobile ad hoc networks. *Telecommunications (ETT), Special Issue on Self Organization in Mobile Networking, 16*(2).

Chen, L., Xu, X. H., & Chen, Y. X. (2004). An adaptive ant colony clustering algorithm. *Proceedings of The Third International Conference on Machine Learning and Cybernetics*, 1387–1392.

Chen, L., & Zhang, C. (2005). Adaptive parallel ant colony optimization. *Y.Pan et al. (Eds.): ISPA 2005, LNCS, 3758*, 275–285.

Chudacek, V., & Lhotska, L. (2006). Unsupervised creation of heart beats classes from long-term ecg monitoring. *Conference: Analysis of Biomedical Signals and Images. 18th International EURASIP Conference Biosignals 2006. Proceedings., 18*, 199–201.

Daubechies, I. (1992). *Ten lectures on wavelets.* Society for Industrial and Applied Mathematics.

Davies, D. L., & Bouldin, D. W. (1979). A cluster separation measure. *IEEE Transactions on Pattern Recognition and Machine Intelligence, 1*(2), 224–227.

Deneubourg, J. L., Goss, S., Franks, N., Sendova-Franks, A., Detrain, C., & Chretien, L. (1990). The dynamics of collective sorting robot-like ants and ant-like robots. In *Proceedings of the first international conference on simulation of adaptive behavior on from animals to animats* (pp. 356–363). Cambridge, MA, USA: MIT Press.

Dorigo, M. (1992). *Optimization, learning and natural algorithms.* Unpublished doctoral dissertation, Dipartimento di Elettronica, Politecnico di Milano, Italy.

Dorigo, M., & Blum, C. (2005). Ant colony optimization theory: A survey. *Theoretical Computer Science Issues 2–3, 344*, 243–278.

Dorigo, M., Caro, G. D., & Gambardella, L. M. (1999). Ant algorithms for discrete optimization. *Artificial Life, 5*(2), 137–172.

Dorigo, M., & Gambardella, L. M. (1997). Ant colony system: A cooperative learning approach to the traveling salesman problem. *IEEE Transactions on Evolutionary Computation, 1, 1*, 53–66.

Dorigo, M., & Stutzle, T. (2004). *Ant colony optimization.* MIT Press, Cambridge, MA.

Dunn, J. C. (1973). A fuzzy relative of the isodata process and its use in detecting compact wellseparated clusters. *Journal of Cybernetics, 3*, 32–57.

Forgey, E. (1965). Cluster analysis of multivariate data: Efficiency vs. interpretability of classification. *Biometrics, 21*, 768.

Franks, N. R., & Sendova-Franks, A. (1992). Brood sorting by ants: Distributing the workload over the work-surface. *Behavioral Ecology and Sociobiology, 30*, 109-123.

Gerla, V., Bursa, M., Lhotska, L., Paul & Krajca. (2007). Newborn sleep stage classification using hybrid evolutionary approach. *International Journal of Bioelectromagnetism – Special Issue on Recent Trends in Bioelectromagnetism. Tampere: International Society for Bioelectromagnetism*, 28–29.

Goldberger, A. L., Amaral, L. A. N., Glass, L., Hausdorff, J. M., Ivanov, P. C., Mark, R. G., et al. (2000). PhysioBank, PhysioToolkit, and PhysioNet: Components of a new research resource for complex physiologic signals. *Circulation, 101*(23), e215–e220. Available from Circulation Electronic Pages: http://circ.ahajournals.org/cgi/content/full/101/23/e215

Grasse, P.-P. (1959). La reconstruction du nid et les coordinations inter-individuelles chez bellicositermes natalensis et cubitermes sp. la thorie de la stigmergie: Essai d'interprtation des termites constructeurs. *Insectes Sociaux, 6*, 41–81.

Gutowitz, H. (1993). *Complexity-seeking ants.*

Handl, J., & Knowles, J. (2007). An evolutionary approach to multiobjective clustering. *IEEE Transactions on Evolutionary Computation, 11*(1).

Handl, J., Knowles, J., & Dorigo, M. (2003a). *Ant-based clustering: a comparative study of its relative performance with respect to k-means, average link and 1d-som* (Tech. Rep.). Technical Report TR/IRIDIA/2003-24, IRIDIA, Universit Libre de Bruxelles.

Handl, J., Knowles, J., & Dorigo, M. (2003b). On the performance of ant-based clustering. In *Design and application of hybrid intelligent systems*, 104, 204–213. Amsterdam, The Netherlands: IOS Press. Available from http://dbkgroup.org/handl/his2003.pdf

Handl, J., Knowles, J., & Dorigo, M. (2003c). Strategies for the increased robustness of ant-based clustering. In *Self-organising applications: Issues, challenges and trends*, 2977, 90–104. Springer-Verlag.

Handl, J., Knowles, J., & Dorigo, M. (2006). Ant-based clustering and topographic mapping. *Artificial Life 12*(1), *12*, 35–61.

Huttenlocher, D., Klanderman, D., & Rucklige, A. (1993, September). Comparing images using the Hausdorff distance. *IEEE Transactions on Pattern Analysis and Machine Intelligence, 15*(9), 850–863.

Jain, A., Murty, M. N., & Flynn, P. J. (1999). Data clustering: A review. *ACM Computing Surveys, 31*, 264–323.

Jensen, R., & Shen, Q. (2004). Fuzzy-rough data reduction with ant colony optimization. *Informatics Research Report, EDI-INF-RR-0201.*

Kanade, P. M., & Hall, L. O. (2003). Fuzzy ants as a clustering concept. *Proceedings of the 22nd International Conference of the North American Fuzzy Information Processing Society, NAFIPS*, 227–232.

Kanade, P. M., & Hall, L. O. (2004). Fuzzy ant clustering by centroid positioning. *Proceedings of the IEEE International Conference on Fuzzy Systems 2004, 1*, 371–376.

Kennedy, J., & Eberhart, R. C. (1995). Particle swarm optimization. *Proceedings IEEE International Conference on Neural Networks, IV*, 1942–1948.

Lee, Z.-J., Lea, C.-Y., & Su, F. (2002). An immunity-based ant colony optimization algorithm for solving weapon-target assignment problem. *Applied Soft Computing, 2(1),39*, 39–47.

Lioni, A., Sauwens, C., Theraulaz, G., & Deneubourg, J.-L. (2001). The dynamics of chain formation in oecophylla longinoda. *Journal of Insect Behavior, 14*, 679–676.

Lumer, E. D., & Faieta, B. (1994). Diversity and adaptation in populations of clustering ants. *From Animals to Animats: Proceedings of the 3th International Conference on the Simulation of Adaptive Behaviour, 3*, 501–508.

Mahalanobis, P. (1936). On the generalised distance in statistics. *Proceedings of the National Institute of Science of India, 12*, 49–55.

Manfrin, M., Birattari, M., Stutzle, T., & Dorigo, M. (2006). Parallel ant colony optimization for the travelling salesman problem. *M. Dorigo et al. (Eds.), ANTS 2006 , LNCS, 4150*, 224–234.

Martin, M., Chopard, B., & Albuquerque, P. (2002). Formation of an ant cemetery: swarm intelligence or statistical accident? *Future Generation Computer Systems, 18*, 951–959.

Monmarche, N. (1999). On data clustering with artificial ants. *A. A. Freitas (Ed.) AAAI-99 and GECCO-99 Workshop on Data Mining with Evolutionary Algorithms: Research Directions, Orlando, Florida*, 23–26.

Monmarche, N. (2000). *Algorithmes de fourmis artificielles: Applications a la classification et a l'optimisation.* Unpublished doctoral dissertation, Laboratoire d'Informatique, Univeriste de Tours, France.

Monmarche, N., Slimane, M., & Venturini, G. (1999). On improving clustering in numerical database with artificial ants. *D. Floreano, J. D. Nicoud, and F. Mondala (Eds.) Advances in Artificial life, 5th European Conference ECAL 99, Lecture Notes in Artificial Intelligence, 1974,* 626–635.

Myers, C. S., & Rabiner, L. R. (1981). A comparative study of several dynamic time-warping algorithms for connected word recognition. *The Bell System Technical Journal, 607,* 1389–1409.

Parpinelli, R. S., Lopes, H. S., & Freitas, A. A. (2005). Classification-rule discovery with an ant colony algorithm. *Encyclopedia of Information Science and Technology, Idea Group Inc.*

Ramos, V., & Merelo, J. J. (2002). Self-organized stigmergic document maps: Environment as a mechanism for context learning. *E. Alba, F. Herrera, and J. J. Merelo (Eds.), Proceedings of the 1st International Conference on Metaheuristic, Evolutionary and Bio-Inspired Algorithms,* 284–293.

Ramos, V., Muga, F., & Pina, P. (2002). Self-organized data and image retrieval as a consequence of inter-dynamic synergistic relationships in artificial ant colonies. *J. R. del Solar, J. Abraham, and M. Koppen (Eds.) Soft-Computing Systems- Design, Management and Applications, Frontiers of Artificial Intelligence and Applications, IOS Press, 87,* 500–509.

Rousseeuw, P., & Kaufman, L. (1990). *Finding groups in data: An introduction to cluster analysis.* John Wiley & Sons.

Rousseeuw, P. J. (1987). Silhouettes: a graphical aid to the interpretation and validation of cluster analysis. *Journal of Computers and Applied Mathematics, 20,* 53–65.

Salton, G., & McGill, M. (1983). *Introduction to modern information retrieval.* New York: McGraw-Hill.

Schockaert, S., Cock, M. D., Cornelis, C., & Etienne, E. E. K. (2004). Fuzzy ant based clustering. *ANTS 2004, LNCS 3172, Springer-Verlag Berlin Heidelberg,* 342–349.

Schockaert, S., Cock, M. D., Cornelis, C., & Kerre, E. E. (2004). Efficient clustering with fuzzy ants. In *Applied computational intelligence, world scientific publishing co. pte. ltd.*

Socha, K. (2004). Aco for continuous and mixed-variable optimization. *Proceedings of ANTS 2004 Lecture Notes in Computer Science, Springer, 3172,* 25–36.

Socha, K., & Dorigo, M. (2005). Ant colony optimization for continous domains. *IRIDIA − Technical Report Series, 037.*

Strehl, A., Ghosh, J., & Mooney, R. (2000). Impact of similarity measures on web-page clustering. pp. *7th National Conference on Artificial Intelligence: Workshop of Artificial Intelligence for Web Search, AAAI, Austin, Texas, USA,* 58–64.

Stutzle, T. (1998). Parallelization strategies for ant colony optimization. *Lecture Notes in Computer Science, 1498,* 722–731.

Stutzle, T., & Hoos, H. (1997). The max-min ant system and local search for the traveling salesman problem. *IEEE Conference on Evolutionary Computing,* 309–314.

Stutzle, T., & Hoos, H. (2000). Max-min ant system. *Future Generation Computer Systems 16, 8,* 889–914.

Sukama, M., & Fukami, H. (1993). Aggregation arrestant pheromone of the german cockroach, blattella germanica (l.) (dictyoptera: Blattellidae): isolation and structure elucidation of blasttellastanoside-a and b. *Journal of Chemical Ecology, 19,* 2521–2541.

Tan, S. C., Ting, K. M., & , S. W. T. (2006). Reproducing the results of ant-based clustering without using ants. *CEC 2006. IEEE Congress on Evolutionary Computation,* 1760–1767.

Theraulaz, G., Bonabeau, E., Sauwens, C., Deneubourg, J.-L., Lioni, A., Libert, F., et al. (2001). Model of droplet formation and dynamics in the argentine ant (linepithema humile mayr). *Bulletin of Mathematical Biology.*

Trianni, V., Labella, T. H., & Dorigo, M. (2004). Evolution of direct communication for a swarm bot performing hole avoidance. *Ant Colony Optimization and Swarm Intelligence, Springer.*

Vizine, A. L., Castro, N. L. de, Hruschka, E. R., & Gudwin, R. R. (2005). Towards improving clustering ants: An adaptive ant clustering algorithm. *Informatica, 29,* 143–154.

Welch, J. W. (1983). *Journal of Statistics and Computer Simulation, 15,* 17–25.

Wilson, D., & Martinez, T. (1997). Improved heterogeneous distance functions. *Journal of Artificial Intelligence Research, 6,* 1–34. Available from http://www.jair.org.

KEY TERMS

Bioinspired Informatics: Scientific branch with industry applicability that tries to reproduce the mental processes of the brain and biogenesis respectively, in a computer environment. These methods are used to solve NP-hard problems with exponential complexity.

Cluster Validity Measures: Indices to measure the quality of clustering obtained. When the correct classification is known, SSE measure (sum of square of errors) or accuracy can be used. If it is not known, other measures can used, such as Davies-Bouldin index, Dunn Index, Silhouette index, Mutual information, etc.

Clustering: Automated process for grouping similar data together. It minimizes the intra-cluster distance while maximizing the inter-cluster distance. It is a multi-objective optimization, some instances are NP hard (when the number of classes is higher than two).

Data Mining: Important branch in industry and market, retrieving important information from a huge amount of data. It is usually considered with huge amount of heterogeneous data, where the use of computers is inevitable.

Pheromone: Chemical substance deposited by ants to mark their path and the importance of prey found. The ants are nearly blind, they mainly sense the amount of the pheromone deposited.

Social Insect: Insect which is not able to survive on its own; however in colonies it provides astonishing solutions. Usually, the behavior of an individual is very simple, however, on the colony level it shows interesting behavior (traverse open spaces, determine shortest path, etc.).

Stigmergy: Indirect communication in social insect communities via changing the environment. The term has been introduced by Grasse et al.

Section II.III
Artificial Life, Optimizing Society, and Ethology

In this section, we can see the diverse inspiration sources of nature for solving engineering problems. Artificial life can be seen as a kind of artificial nature. Society and ethology are from human being society and animal world. All of them can inspire us to design optimization method or new learning strategy.

Chapter XX
Artificial Life Optimization
Algorithm and Applications

Bo-Suk Yang
Pukyong National University, South Korea

ABSTRACT

This chapter describes a hybrid artificial life optimization algorithm (ALRT) based on emergent colonization to compute the solutions of global function optimization problem. In the ALRT, the emergent colony is a fundamental mechanism to search the optimum solution and can be accomplished through the metabolism, movement and reproduction among artificial organisms which appear at the optimum locations in the artificial world. In this case, the optimum locations mean the optimum solutions in the optimization problem. Hence, the ALRT focuses on the searching for the optimum solution in the location of emergent colonies and can achieve more accurate global optimum. The optimization results using different types of test functions are presented to demonstrate the described approach successfully achieves optimum performance. The algorithm is also applied to the test function optimization and optimum design of short journal bearing as a practical application. The optimized results are compared with those of genetic algorithm and successive quadratic programming to identify the optimizing ability.

INTRODUCTION

Firstly, we describe an optimization algorithm (ALA) to compute the global solutions of function optimization problem based on artificial life algorithm. Emergent colonies which are a fundamental mechanism use to search the optimum solution can be accomplished through the metabolism, movement and reproduction among artificial organisms which appear at the optimum locations in the artificial world (AWorld). In this case, the optimum locations mean the optimum solutions in the optimization problem. Then, the ALA focuses on searching for the optimum solution in the location of emergent colonies and can lead to a more accurate global optimum. The ALA has a demerit that after it congregates at the neighborhood of optimum solutions, not only the convergent speed becomes very slow, but also the solution accuracy is poor. Moreover, to decide the locations where a waste

Copyright © 2009, IGI Global, distributing in print or electronic forms without written permission of IGI Global is prohibited.

of metabolism in random movement and the offspring in the reproduction having an important influence on the efficiency are the remaining problems must be improved in ALA.

Secondly, we describe an enhanced hybrid algorithm (ALRT) which introduces the random tabu search method into the ALA to solve the remaining location problems mentioned above. This technique can improve the convergent speed and accuracy, and can be applied to enhance the distinguished efficiency in the multivariable and the multi-modal problems. The hybrid algorithm is not only faster than the conventional ALA, but also gives a more accurate solution. In addition, ALRT can find all global optimum solutions. The optimization results using different types of test functions are presented to demonstrate the ability of the described approach in achieving good performance successfully.

Finally, ALRT is applied to the test function optimization and optimum design of short journal bearing as practical application. The results are compared with those of conventional methods such as ALA, genetic algorithm and successive quadratic programming, and the optimizing ability is identified.

BACKGROUND

There are two types of modeling approaches for studying natural phenomena; namely, the top-down approach involving a complicated, centralized controller that makes decisions based on access to all aspects of the global state; and the bottom-up approach, which is based on parallel, distributed networks of relatively simple, low-level agents that simultaneously interact with each other. Most traditional artificial intelligence (AI) research focuses on the former approach (Kim & Cho, 2006).

Artificial life (ALife), as a scientific term, was first stated in 1987 by Langton, who has contributed significantly to ALife. *ALife is the study of man-made systems that exhibit behavior characteristics of natural living systems* (Langton, 1989; Assad & Packard, 1992). The research motive of ALife was originated from the intent to understand the true meaning of life through the synthesis of life that makes it superior to the existing life in nature. ALife includes computational simulations such as virtual places where animated characters interact with the environment and with other virtual beings of the same or distinct categories.

A general property of ALife is that the whole system's behavior is represented only directly, and arises out of interactions of individuals with each other. In this context, known as the philosophy of decentralized architecture, ALife shares important similarities with some new trends such as connectionism (Haykin, 1998), multi-agent AI (Ferber, 1999) and evolutionary computation (EC) (Goldberg, 1989). Technologies in ALife research include cellular automata, the Lindenmayer system (L-system), genetic algorithm (GAs), and neural networks (NNs).

The two most important characteristics of ALife are *emergence* and *dynamic interaction* with the environment. Namely, the micro-interaction with each other in the ALife's group results in emergent colonization in the whole system. It is the concept of emergence that highlights the nature of ALife research. Emergence is exhibited by a collection of interacting entities whose global behaviors cannot be reduced to a simple aggregate of the individual contributions of the entities. Conventional methods of AI have to struggle to reveal and explain emergence because they are generally reductionist. That is, they reduce systems to constituent subsystems and then study them in isolation (the top-down approach). In contrast, ALife adopts the bottom-up approach which starts with a collection of entities exhibiting simple and well-understood behavior and then synthesizes more complex systems (Kim & Cho, 2006).

The concrete study method using the above characteristics consists of mainly two steps. First, the essence of ALife system, which shows the behavior characteristics of living organisms in the natural world such as growth, adaptation, multiplication, self-preserving, self-control, and evolution, which is realized through several theoretical models. Second, the ALife organisms which are called real living organisms are created in the computer through simulation. This process can be defined as the informationization process. Therefore, the research object of ALife is not the physical system of life itself but the function as the information. In the ALA for the function optimization, the emergent colonization is accomplished through the metabolism and the reproduction in the artificial world. The optimum solutions are found on the emergently colonized region (Yang & Lee, 2000).

According to Bedau (2003), there are three branches of ALife. *Soft ALife* creates simulations or other purely digital constructions that exhibit lifelike behavior. *Hard ALife* produces hardware implementations of lifelike systems. Finally, *wet ALife* synthesizes living systems out of biochemical substances. Most articles that apply to ALife fall under one of the soft and hard branches (Kim & Cho, 2006).

EC is a model of machine learning derived from the evolution process in nature. There are several different types of ECs; such as GAs, evolutionary programming (EP), and evolutionary strategies (ESs). They are all population-based search algorithms which have different representation or coding schemes and search operators. For example, GAs, originally conceived by Holland (1975) and is the most popular method. They normally use crossover and mutation as search operators, while EP only uses mutation (Yao, 1996). GAs are executed by creating a population of individuals that are represented by strings. The individuals in the population go through an evolutionary process in which individuals compete for resonances in the environment. Stronger individuals are more likely to survive and propagate their genetic material to offspring. They evolve a population of competing individuals using fitness-biased selection, random mating and a gene-level representation of individuals together with simple genetic operators for modeling inheritance of traits. GAs have been successfully applied to a wide variety of problems including optimization, machine learning and the evolution of complex structures such as neural networks. At the same time, difficulties can and do arise in forcing every problem domain into this traditional GA model.

Evolutionary algorithms (EAs) are global search procedures based on the evolution of a vector of solutions viewed as a population of interacting individuals. EAs are used to refer to any probabilistic algorithm whose design is inspired by evolutionary mechanisms found in biological species. The most widely known algorithms are GAs, simulated annealing (SA) and EP. In applying evolutionary strategies, one of the most frequently encountered difficulties is convergence toward an undesired attractor. This phenomenon occurs when the populations get trapped in a suboptimal state such that the variation operators cannot produce an offspring which outperforms its parents. The relationships between convergence to a global optimum, the parameters of the strategy such as population size or mutation probabilities, and the geometry of the optimization problem are crucial to understand (Francois, 1998).

Popular iterative approximation algorithms for combinatorial optimization are algorithms that use EA, SA and tabu search (TS). GA, SA, and TS have been found to be very effective and robust in solving numerous problems from a wide range of application domains. Also, they are even suitable for ill-posed problems where some of the parameters are not known before hand. These properties are lacking in all traditional optimization techniques (Youssef et al., 2001). These three optimization algorithms have several similarities as follows (Sait & Youssef, 1999):

- They are approximation (heuristic) algorithm, i.e., they do not guarantee finding an optimal solution
- They are blind, in that they do not know when they reached an optimal solution. Therefore they must be told when to stop
- They have *hill climbing* property, i.e., they occasionally accept uphill (bad) moves
- They can easily be engineered to implement any combination of optimization problem; all that is required is to have a suitable solution representation, a cost function and a mechanism to traverse the search space, and
- Under certain conditions, they asymptotically converge to an optimal solution.

ALife emerged through the interaction of biology and computer sciences (Adami, 1998). The ALife system is a computational model of organisms in an artificial ecology where colonization emerges through a process of resource gathering and exchange amongst an evolving population. However, except some works done by Hayashi et al. (1994; 1996), Satoh et al. (1999; 2004), Yang & Lee (2000), Yang et al. (2001), Yang & Ye (2002), Ahn et al. (2003; 2005), Guo & Kong (2004) and Song & Yang (2005), the Alife system has not been widely applied to optimization problem.

Assad & Packard (1992) described the ALife as represented by a two-dimensional discrete-value system. Hayashi et al. (1994) have considered the nonlinear optimization problem and have extended Alife to a multidimensional continuous system. It has been verified that emergent colonization is also generated in the multidimensional continuous space (Satoh et al., 1999). Also, they present an evaluation function which can generate emergent colonization in a promising area including the global optimal solution (Hayashi et al., 1996). The author proposed the artificial life optimization algorithm (ALA) as an optimization algorithm that can be applied to the irregular function and do not depend on the initial value (Yang & Lee, 2000) and used a new emergent colonization algorithm for optimum design of short journal bearings (Yang et al., 2001).

Although colonization emerges in the optimum area in that approach, the Alife system cannot always give reliable a solution because it is chosen from a limited number of artificial organisms. Also, ALA has a demerit that after it has congregated, not only does the converge speed become very slowly, but also the solution accuracy is poor. Also, the choice of location of the next generation in reproduction and the waste in metabolism has a very important influence on the efficiency of ALA. Therefore, some researches have proposed the optimization approach that combines the ALife system with other artificial algorithms. Yang & Song (2001) proposed an enhanced optimization algorithm (ALRT) which combined the random tabu search method with the existing artificial life algorithm. Using this approach, the converging speed and accuracy can be improved, and the ALRT can be enhanced to have distinguished efficiency in the multivariable and the multi-modal problems. This algorithm have applied the optimum design for engine mount to obtain the desired notch frequency and notch depth (Ahn et al., 2003), and for short journal bearing (Song & Yang, 2005).

Satoh et al. (2004) further extends artificial world (AWorld) to a two-level ALife system and introduces a predator for the artificial organisms. It was verified that by introducing such a predator, the formation of emergent colonization is accelerated and the solution can be found with high speed. Yang & Ye (2002) have proposed an optimization approach that combines the ALife system with ant algorithm to improve the searching speed. Also, they proposed a hybrid ALife system for function optimization that combines ALife colonization with genetic algorithm (Yang et al., 2002).

ARTIFICIAL LIFE OPTIMIZATION ALGORITHM (ALA)

Definition of Nonlinear Optimization Problem

Here we consider a nonlinear optimization problem with the box constraint as follows:

Minimize $f(\mathbf{x})$
subject to $\mathbf{x}_{min} \leq \mathbf{x} \leq \mathbf{x}_{max}$ (1)

where $f: R^n \rightarrow R$ is the objective function to be minimized.

No assumption, such as continuity, differentiability, or convexity is made except for the calculation of the function value. $\mathbf{x}_{min}$ and $\mathbf{x}_{max}$ are the minimum and maximum values that the variable $\mathbf{x}$ can take. It is rare in engineering problems for the solution to be completely unknown. Instead, the rough location of the solution is usually known. Consequently, it is not a problem in practice to set such a box constraint.

The Artificial World (AWorld)

The AWorld in a two-dimensional discrete-valued system considered and is defined as the space where the lowest and the highest limits are x_i^{min} and $x_i^{max} \in R^n$ ($i = 1, 2, \cdots, n$), respectively. The AWorld in this case is a square plane with $N \times N$ discrete cells. Each cell in the AWorld may contain a food or a resource. It may happen that individuals of several species, called artificial organisms (Artorgs), live in a cell. A cell can contain at most one resource unit and one Artorg individual. Assad & Packard (1992) reported emergent colonization in such a two-dimensional discrete-valued system, which is also verified by Hayashi et al. (1996).

However, when Eq. (1) is applied to the nonlinear optimization problems, the number of cells increases exponentially in the multivariable case if the discrete-valued system is used directly and a mesh is formed for each variable (Satoh et al., 2004). Consequently, it extends the AWorld which has been defined on discrete cells to a multidimensional continuous space. In other words, the permissible area in the problem of Eq. (1), namely,

$$X = \{\mathbf{x} \in R^n \mid \mathbf{x}_{\min} \leq \mathbf{x} \leq \mathbf{x}_{\max}\} \subset R^n \tag{2}$$

is defined as the AWorld.

Food Chain of Artificial Organisms (Artorg)

The appreciate number of Artorg species is determined by a preliminary calculation. Based on the results, it is assumed that there are four different Artorg species (white, red, green and blue). In the AWorld space, it is supposed that there are four kinds of resources (white, red, green and blue) and four species of Artorg (white, red, green and blue) as shown in Fig. 1.

These species form a food chain of ring form, which metabolizes a resource that can be an object of metabolism if it is obtained. The resource that can be an object of metabolism is determined for each kind of Artorg. After metabolizing, the Artorg generates waste at a random nearby site, and the waste can serve as a resource for another kind of Artorg. Artorgs can move about in the AWorld consuming energy resources and producing waste. The four species of Artorg compose a circular food chain where one species' waste is another's food (see Fig. 1). Artorg can only metabolize the resources they want. The demanded resources are determined according to the four species of Artorg. When they metabolize resources, their internal energy is increased by G_e. After metabolizing it, they produce waste at the random location of their neighborhood region. A white Artorg metabolizes a blue resource which it wants and produces waste. Then this waste becomes a white resource which is then metabolized by red Artorg. This relation is carried out among the four species of Artorg.

Internal Energy

Artorgs have a sensory system which enables them to see resources as well as other Artorgs in the AWorld. They are also able to determine the location of the nearest resources and other Artorgs from their present location. This nearest location of resource becomes the goal which drives them to move forward. Artorgs must maintain a minimum internal energy level, L_p, in order to exist. Once an Artorg's energy level drops below L_p, it is considered to be "dead" and removed from the AWorld. Whenever Artorg's age is increased by 1, its internal energy is decreased

Figure 1. A circular food chain of an artificial organism (Artorg). ©2008 Bo-Suk Yang. Used with permission.

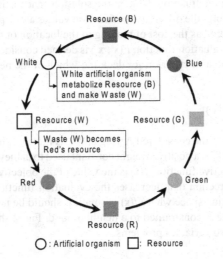

Table 1. Trading strategy (Satoh et al., 2004)

	White	Red	Green	Blue
White	0	1	1	0
Red	1	0	0	1
Green	0	1	0	1
Blue	1	0	1	0

by L_e. Therefore, although Artorgs do not have a pre-specified lifespan, they are subject to the consuming rate of energy which is proportional to their age. Thus, as an Artorg grows older, it should be supplied with energy to maintain its existence. Eventually, if it doesn't have enough chance to metabolize resources and get energy, it is supposed to die. This condition effectively imposes a finite lifespan on Artorgs.

Resource Exchange

It is assumed that an Artorg can carry a unit of resource that cannot be metabolized. An Artorg can exchange the carried resource for a resource carried by another Artorg. It has its own strategy for the exchange. As shown in Table 1, the exchange strategy of an Artorg is composed of a 16-bit table. The Artorg exchanges resources with another Artorg existing nearby. Each row of the table indicates the type of resource carried at present by the Artorg and each column indicates the type of resource that the exchange counterpart can offer. A "1" bit in the table indicates that the Artorg performs the exchange and a "0" indicates that the exchange is rejected.

For example, in the exchange strategy shown in Table 1, an Artorg carrying a red resource, corresponding to the second row of the table, exchanges the resource for a white or blue resource (the first or fourth column), but rejects an exchange with an Artorg offering a red or green resource (the second or third column). In order for the exchange to occur, both parties to the exchange must agree.

Perception System

Assad & Packard (1992) reported that macroscopic emergent colonization occurs in the system as a whole as a result of microscopic interactions. The purpose is to utilize emergent colonization in the optimization of the nonlinear function, and to generate emergent colonization in an area with small function values. For this, the perceptual systems of the Artorg, into which the function value in the solution space is introduced, is considered. In other words, for a resource near the Artorg, the difference of function values at the present point of the Artorg and the location of the resource is considered as the cost of moving to the location of the resource (Satoh et al., 2004).

Consequently, the following evaluation function $F(\mathbf{x}_s, \mathbf{x}_r)$ is defined considering the distance to be moved and the value of the objective function, as a criterion for deciding which of the nearby resources the Artorg should move:

$$F(\mathbf{x}_s, \mathbf{x}_r) = \| \mathbf{x}_r - \mathbf{x}_s \| + W\{f(\mathbf{x}_r) - f(\mathbf{x}_s)\} \tag{3}$$

where $\mathbf{x}_s$ is the present coordinate of the considered Artorg and $\mathbf{x}_r$ is the coordinate of the resource under consideration. $\|\cdot\|$ is the Euclidean norm. W is a positive weight constant used to achieve a balance between the distances traveled and the values of the objective function. $f(\mathbf{x})$ is the value of the objective function at $\mathbf{x}$. It is expected that when the Artorg moves in the direction that decreases the evaluation function, emergent colonization will be generated more easily in the solution space where $f(\mathbf{x})$ is small. It should be noted that in this process the range of Artorg movement in a unit time is constrained to a neighborhood. Fig. 2 shows an example of the definition of a neighborhood region using two variables problems.

Figure 2. Definition of a neighborhood region. ©2008 Bo-Suk Yang. Used with permission.

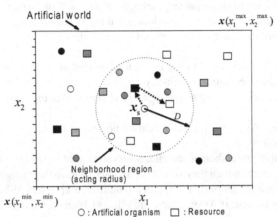

The location $\mathbf{x}_s$ of an arbitrary Artorg is considered as the center. Based on this point, the neighborhood region C of $\mathbf{x}_s$ is the space within the Euclidean length and C is defined as

$$C = \{\mathbf{x} \in R^n \mid \|\mathbf{x} - \mathbf{x}_s\|^2 \le D\} \tag{4}$$

where D is the possible movement range of Artorg per generation given by,

$$D = D_0 e^{-(t/T)a} \tag{5}$$

where D_0 is the initial value, t is the generation number, T is the last generation number, and α is the constant.

Artorgs use this defined neighborhood region for their movement and reproduction. They can only see and find the resources and other Artorgs within this area for each generation. D can be considered as a constant for the whole generation or as a variable according to increasing generation. In this chapter, Artorgs can only move about and find other Artorgs within the neighborhood region defined above per generation. If there are no resources in the neighborhood region, they can move randomly within the neighborhood region.

Artificial Life Optimization Algorithm (ALA)

In case of optimization problem, the AWorld becomes the space of the design variables $\mathbf{x}$. Every location has its own fitness. After searching the neighborhood region randomly, they produce their offspring finally at the location which has higher fitness than that of themselves.

In order to introduce the micro-interaction among Artorgs for the optimum design problem, we need to produce an emergent colonization at the location where has the optimum value. For this purpose, we introduce Artorgs and resources to have their own optimizing values which substitute their coordinate value for their location into the objective function. Also, the sensory system is introduced to enable Artorgs to see and find the optimum value in the AWorld. These resources become the goal which drives an Artorg to move towards a destination. Thus, all Artorgs move to the resources which have the optimum value. Eventually, it is more likely to produce an emergent colonization at the location of the resources in the AWorld.

The location of both Artorgs and resources becomes the variables of the objective function to be optimized. Therefore, the objective function values of Artorgs and resources can be obtained by substituting the location into the objective function. An Artorg compares its objective function value with the resources within the neighborhood region. It moves to the location of the resource having the higher fitness within the neighborhood region. Therefore, Artorgs can produce an emergent colonization at the location that has the optimum objective functions.

The calculation procedure of the algorithm is summarized as follows:

- **Step 1 Initialization:** Equal numbers of each of the four species of Artorg are placed at random locations in the AWorld. Each artificial organism is initially given by the internal energy, I_e. Equal numbers of each of the four kinds of resources, as many as Artorgs, are also placed at the random locations where Artorgs do not exist.

- **Step 2 Search resources:** Artorgs search the location nearest to the resource from their present location within their neighborhood region.

- **Step 3 Movement:** Artorgs move about using elite reservation strategy in the AWorld. First, if they find the location of the nearest resource which they want to metabolize within their neighborhood region, they move to it. Second, if not, they move randomly within their neighborhood region. When they move randomly, the elite reservation strategy is used. If Artorgs have high fitness, then they move the least distance in order to change their fitness slightly and they even get as much energy as E_e. Therefore, the Artorgs which have a high fitness have a higher chance of survival.

- **Step 4 Metabolism:** If Artorgs find the nearest resource that they want to metabolize, they metabolize it gaining the energy of G_e and produce waste at the random location in the neighborhood region.

- **Step 5 Increasing age:** In this process, Artorg's age is increased by 1.

- **Step 6 Reproduction:** If an Artorg reaches the age of R_a and has the energy more than R_{er}, it mates with the closest Artorg which has the same species and satisfies the conditions for reproduction. If Artorg A mates with Artorg B which has the same species and the nearest location and both Artorg A and B are satisfied with the condition $A, B \geq R_a, A, B \geq R_{er}$, they decide to reproduce according to the reproduction probability R_p which decides whether they reproduce themselves or not.

- **Step 7 Reducing energy:** All Artorgs' energy is decreased by L_e. If an Artorg's energy drops below L_i, it is considered to be dead and is removed from the AWorld.

- **Step 8 Increasing generation:** Generation is increased by 1. In returning to step 2, this artificial life algorithm is iterated until the final generation.

In the ALA, the emergent colony is the fundamental mechanism to search the optimum solution. Emergent colonies are accomplished through the metabolism, movement and reproduction among Artorgs which appeared at the optimum locations in the AWorld. The locations are optimum solutions in the optimization problem. The ALA then focuses on stochastic searching for the optimum solution in the location of emergent colonies and can achieve a more accurate global optimum.

HYBRID ARTIFICIAL LIFE OPTIMIZATION ALGORITHM (ALRT)

Conventional ALA has an advantage that it has good searching ability for the global optimum solution. However, it has a demerit that after it has congregated at the neighborhood of optimum solutions, not only does the convergent speed become very slow, but also the solution accuracy is poor. Moreover, to decide on the location is a waste of metabolism in random movement and the offspring in the reproduction having an important influence on the efficiency of the ALA which remained to be improved (Yang & Song, 2001).

In the ALA, the speed of the colonies at the location for optimum solution can be made, that is one of the most important factors in determining the performance of optimization. Also, the amount of individual density located in the colonies is an important factor which determines the accuracy of the solution. These are not only to determine the efficiency of the concentrate search but also the level of solution accuracy. The timing of colonies formation and the individual density basically depend on the following three decisions of location problem. The bottom line is how to decide the new location efficiently.

- To decide the location of the waste in metabolism
- To decide the location of random movement, if the individuals did not find the wanted resources
- To decide the location of the next generation in reproduction

Thus, in this section a hybrid artificial life optimization algorithm (ALRT) which introduced the random tabu search method (RT) into the ALA is aimed to solve the remaining location problems mentioned above. The technique can improve the convergent speed and accuracy, and can be applied to enhance the distinguished efficiency in the multivariable and the multi-modal problems. We compare the performance of the ALRT with the results of the ALA for the optimum design of a short journal bearing. The results show the superiority of the technique and illustrate the performance of the ALRT.

Random Tabu Search Method (RT)

RT, which was proposed by Hu (1992), is a learning algorithm. It prevents from converging to the local minima, and with respect to precision and converging speed, it is superior to other methods. But, it has a demerit that in the broad search space or multivariable problem, its optimum solution's searching ability may not be good.

The RT was extended to function optimization in the domain of continuous variables with general constraints (Yang et al., 1999). In RT with random moves, a set of steps h_1, $\mathbf{H} = \{h_1,..., h_{Ns}\}$ is given. For an initial feasible point x, the search moves are made over a set of active steps l, $l \in \{1, N_s\}$, where the step $h_1 \in \mathbf{H} - \mathbf{T}$ and $\mathbf{T}$ is the tabu list of accepted steps, which is initially empty. For each active step one feasible random move is generated as $x_i^{k+1} = x_i^k + r\, h_{i,\,p}$, where r is a random number$(-1 \leq r \leq 1)$. If there is a decrement in the objective function, the random move is saved as the current solution x and the step h_1 is added to $\mathbf{T}$. When $\mathbf{H} - \mathbf{T}$ is empty, $\mathbf{T}$ is updated empty and the total process is repeated, otherwise the above procedure is repeated. As mentioned by Hu (1992), there is a probability for each point of the search space which is exploited. In this procedure, the moves in neighbors $(x_i^k - h_i \leq x_i^{k+1} \leq x_i^k + h_i)$ of different sizes prevent it from trapping at a local optimum. The procedure used to calculate $\mathbf{H}$ is:

First, assume that the objective function is defined as a function of n continuous variables x_i, $i \in \{1, ..., n\}$ in a box $\mathbf{R}$,

$$\mathbf{R} = \{\mathbf{x} \mid a_i \leq x_i \leq b_i ..., a_n \leq x_n \leq b_n\} \tag{6}$$

Then, the N_s steps of $\mathbf{H}$ can be calculated as follows:

$$h_{i,1} = (b_i - a_i) / c, h_{i,2} = h_{i,1} / c,..., h_{i,Ns} = h_{i,Ns-1} / c \tag{7}$$

where c is a factor greater than 1, for example $c = 2$.

Features of RT are summarized as follows. First, it can reduce an iteration number and promote the efficiency of searching, because each searching solution is located at different searching domain. Second, with this method it is possible to obtain a global optimum and to avoid trapping in local optimum because of utilizing random searching. Finally, it is possible to get the optimum solution fast and accurately if the method is combined with other optimization methods.

Hybrid Algorithm

As stated above, the accuracy of existing ALife algorithm is affected by the location of the resource and the next generation. Therefore, for an effective search, we used the RT's merit which it searches the optimum solution by dividing the neighboring region into several steps. Therefore, the resource is wasted at the nearest step region to the optimum point within the neighboring region. Thus, the colonization can be achieved quickly and accurately. According to Artorgs which are forming the colonization in neighborhood of optimum solution point, the Artorgs, which have the highest fitness and the nearest location with optimum solutions, can search for the

Figure 3. Flowchart of hybrid optimization algorithm (ALRT)

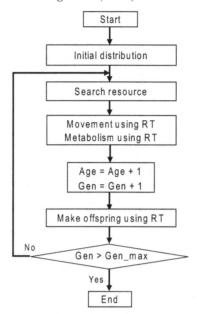

solution accurately with minimum step numbers, hence increasing the total accuracy. In addition, the outer part of the colonized group, which is belong to the colonization, but relatively farther from the optimum, can also make the resources in the step having large radius and being nearest to optimum point. So, it makes it possible to make a dense colonization. Therefore, this algorithm has good features with high converging speed and the solution is more accurate.

The calculation procedure of the ALRT is shown in Fig. 3. Basically, the calculation procedure is same with that of ALA except Artorgs movement strategy using the RT. In step 3 of the calculation procedure for ALA, if they cannot find the location of the nearest resource, the RT is applied to its moving method. If Artorgs have high fitness, then they move the least distance in order to change their fitness slightly and they even get as much energy as E_e. Therefore, the Artorgs having the highest fitness have a higher chance of survival.

Example: Function Optimization

Test Functions

In this section, there are eight benchmark test functions with different complexities chosen to validate the algorithm (Table 2, Fig. 4). In Table 2, N is the dimension of the function.

The simulations were conducted for the 2-dimensional case. All evaluations of the test functions had been cast as maximization problems. The original minimization problems had been changed to maximization problems by negation. Comparisons were made with other algorithms such as ALA, standard genetic algorithm (GA), random tabu search method (RT) and exact solution. We computed the function evaluations using the other algorithms.

The function evaluations by GA used for bit accuracies in the range of 9-18 and population sizes in the range of 15-50 and took the best results for comparing with ALRT. Single point crossover and binary coding were employed for all GA simulations. For each function, 50 different runs with different initial seeds were taken to observe the effect of reproducibility and reliability.

Table 2. Test functions and optimization results

Test functions	Variable constraints	Global optimum $(x_1, x_2), f(x_{opt})$	Reference
$f_1(x_1, x_2) = 100.0(x_2 - x_1^2)^2 + (1.0 - x_1^2)^2$	$-2.0 \le x_1, x_2 \le 2.0$	(1.0, 1.0), 0.0	Rosenbrock function (Cardoso, et al., 1996)
$f_2(x_1, x_2) = (\cos 2\pi\, x_1 + \cos 2.5\pi\, x_1 - 2.1) \times$ $(2.1 - \cos 3\pi\, x_2 - \cos 3.5\pi\, x_2)$	$-1.0 \le x_1, x_2 \le 1.0$	(0.4388, 0.3058), (0.4388, −0.3058), (−0.4388, 0.3058), (−0.4388, −0.3058) −16.09172	Multimodal function (Homaifar et al., 1994)
$f_3 = -\cos(2\pi \|\mathbf{x}\|) + 0.1\|\mathbf{x}\| + 1$	$-100 \le x_1, x_2 \le 100$	(0.0, 0.0), 0.0	Salomon function (Salomon, 1996)
$f_4 = \sum_{i=1}^{2} i \cdot x_i^2$	$-10 \le x_1, x_2 \le 10$	(0.0, 0.0), 0.0	Ellipsoid function (Salomon, 1998)
$f_5 = \sum_{i=1}^{2} \left[\sum_{j=1}^{i} x_j \right]^2$	$\mathbf{x} = (-65.536, 65.536)$	(0.0, 0.0), 0.0	Schwefel function (Salomon, 1998)
$f_6 = x_1^2 + A\sum_{i=2}^{N} x_i^2,\ A = 10 \sim 10{,}000$	$-100 \le x_1, x_2 \le 100$	(0.0, 0.0), 0.0	Cigar function (Salomon, 1998)
$f_7 = \sum_{i=1}^{2} \left[x_i^2 - 10\cos(2\pi x_i) + 10 \right]$	$-10 \le x_1, x_2 \le 10$	(0.0, 0.0), 0.0	Rastrigin function (Salomon, 1998)
$f_8 = -20\exp\left(-0.2\sqrt{\dfrac{1}{N}\sum_{i=1}^{2} x_i^2} \right)$ $-\exp\left(\dfrac{1}{2}\sum_{i=1}^{2}\cos(2\pi x_i) \right) + 20 + e$	$-30 \le x_1, x_2 \le 30$	(0.0, 0.0), 0.0	Ackley function (Jin et al., 2002)

Four kinds of species of Artorg were used in searching the optimum solution. The boundaries to which the Artorg can move during one generation were calculated with Eq. (5). Where, $D_0 = 1.0$, $\alpha = 12$. Each number of the initial Artorg and the initial resources is 160. The parameters of the updated algorithm were adopted as shown in Table 3 (Yang & Lee, 2000).

Performance of the Emergent Colonization for Searching the Global Optimum Solution

Ackley test function has been chosen to compare the performance of the emergent colonization for searching the global optimum solution with that of ALA. Fig. 5 shows the initial and final Artorgs' distributions after 3,000 generations. Artorgs are initially placed at random locations in the solution space and gradually move towards the global optimum. The Artorgs that survived lastly comprised of an emergent colonization together with the contour line of solution. After 3,000 generations, all final Artorgs of ALRT have converged at the optimum solution while many Atrorgs of ALA cannot yet found the optimum solution.

The elapsed time and the calculated optimum solutions for Rosenbrock function and multimodal function are shown as Table 4. The Rosenbrock function has only one global optimum while the multimodal function has four global and four local optima. The calculation error E is estimated by

$$E = \frac{1}{N}\sum_{j=1}^{N}\ \sum_{i=1}^{P} \left| \frac{(x_{opt,i} - x_j)}{x_{opt,i}} \right| \tag{8}$$

where N is the total number of Artorgs, and P is the number of the global optimum solutions, and x_{opt} is the optimal variables.

Table 3. Parameters of algorithms

Symbol	Value	Symbol	Value
E_e	10	α	12
G_e	50	P_e	1
I_e	150	R_a	3
L_e	5	R_e	150
R_r	10	R_p	0.0002
L_i	125	N_c	3
N_s	5		

Figure 4. Test functions. ©2008 Bo-Suk Yang. Used with permission.

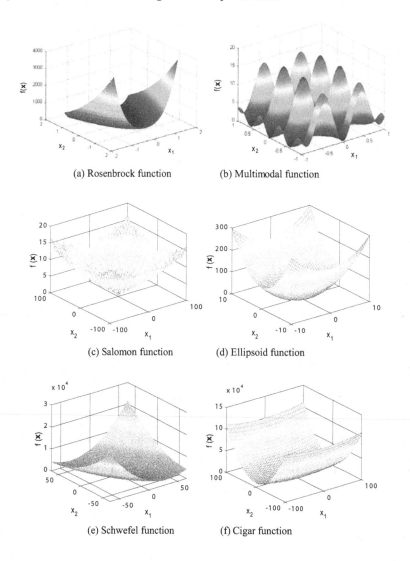

(a) Rosenbrock function

(b) Multimodal function

(c) Salomon function

(d) Ellipsoid function

(e) Schwefel function

(f) Cigar function

continued on following page

Figure 4. continued

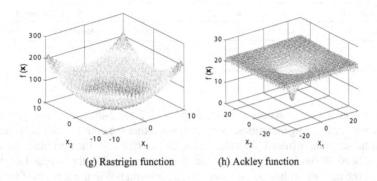

(g) Rastrigin function   (h) Ackley function

Figure 5. Initial and final distribution of organisms for Ackley's function. ©2008 Bo-Suk Yang. Used with permission.

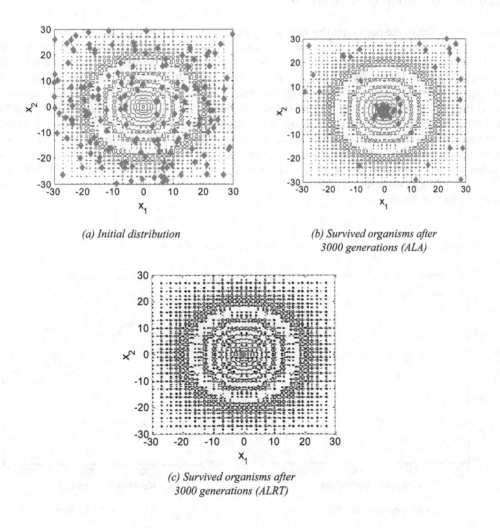

(a) Initial distribution

(b) Survived organisms after 3000 generations (ALA)

(c) Survived organisms after 3000 generations (ALRT)

Table 4. Parameters of used algorithm

Methods	Optimum value		No. of generation		Computing time (s)	
	Rosenbrock	Multimodal	Rosenbrock	Multimodal	Rosenbrock	Multimodal
ALA	0.0	-16.09172	3000	3000	49	48
ALRT	0.0	-16.09172	10	10	1	1

Fig. 6 shows the convergence characteristics of ALA and ALRT for 2-dimensional Rosenbrock function and multimodal function according to generations. We can confirm that the convergence accuracy of proposed algorithm is superior to the existing artificial algorithm. Also, in searching for the optimum solution of Rosenbrock function, the ALA needs 49 seconds, but the enhanced algorithm needs only 1 second as shown in Table 4. In other test functions, the new algorithm also has very good performance in the aspects of time for reaching the required precision. The solution accuracy after 3,000 generations, which the proposed algorithm reached is better than before existing algorithm.

Effect on Performance of RT Parameters

Fig. 7 shows the effect of the parameter that has an impact on the calculation time and the converging accuracy in RT, such as the step number N_s, and the count number (i.e., maximum search number at each step) N_c. If N_c is 1, the trial number of search in each step is so small that the probability of the successful search is low. Through above, we can know that if N_s is small, many Artorgs fail to find the optimum solution. In conclusion, the neighborhood region decreases before Artorgs converge sufficiently, so it cannot be expected that the accuracy is better. However, if it is more than 2 in number, the search efficiency is similar to the various N_s. So, we find that the search succeed before and after 3 times. In detail, let us consider the two-dimensional AWorld, with 2 variables, then there is a contour line that lies on each Artorg, and it is reasonable that the line is supposed to be concave toward the optimum point in probability. In each step, the probability of the successful search has the geometric distribution. It can be defined as $\sum pq^i$ ($i = 0,..., N-1$). Where p is the probability of success, which defined by the ratio of the area of the superior region with superior fitness to the area of the total region in each step region, and q is the probability of failure.

Figure 6. Convergence characteristics of colonization to optimum solution

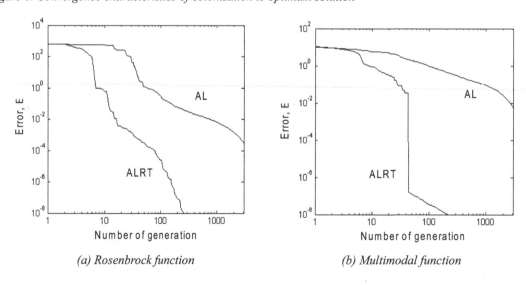

(a) Rosenbrock function	(b) Multimodal function

Figure 7. Effect of step and count numbers

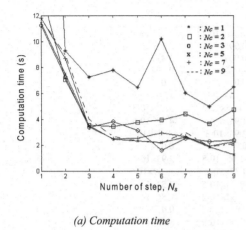

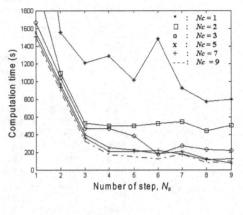

(a) Computation time   (b) Number of generation

Let us assume that the contour line around the optimum is the circle. If each Artorg's maximum radius crosses the optimum point, in the most outer step the probabilities of the success are approximately 0.33, 0.56, 0.70, 0.80, and 0.87 when N_s are 1, 2, 3, 4, and 5, respectively. And also in the internal steps, each success probability increases as the corresponding ratio of area p increases. If N_c is more than 2, the success probability is more than 50%. In case that N_c is 3, its probability is more than 70%. But if N_c is more than 3, it doesn't increase any further.

If N_s is 1, the efficiency is the same as when RT is not applied, so the proposed method is not expected to be better than the ALA. But, if it increases, the neighborhood region is divided into more parts, so the effects of RT become larger in this proposed algorithm. But if it is more than 5, the performance is not improved any more because if N_s is large, the size of internal small regions is greatly reduced, therefore the result exceeds the computational precision provided by the desk top computer used in these simulations. Also, the meaningless outer steps deteriorates the efficiency, because the colonization having shorter colonization radius it is meaningless as outer steps is already achieved near the optimum close to the optimum than the radius of the meaningless outer steps. The optimum values for the most efficient algorithm are 5 for N_s, 3 for N_c, and 12 for α.

Performance Comparisons of Test Functions

In this section, the ALRT is tested using six benchmark test functions ($f_3 - f_8$) as listed in Table 2. These functions have different characteristics: high dimensionality, large search area, uni-modal/multimodal, determinism/stochastic, and quadratic/nonquadratic. These functions have two-dimensions such that they may have numerous local minima. Hence, these functions are often utilized as test functions in optimization methods. The function f_2 is to be maximized, and the others are to be minimized. The optimized values of objective function and design variables by the ALRT with three different algorithms (ALA, SGA and RT) and the exact solutions are listed in Table 5. In ALRT, the parameters are unchanged as listed in Table 3. The stop criterion is when the search optimum value is better than the given accept value or the maximum generation number is complete.

For all six functions, the ALRT always produces the best results when comparing with the results of other algorithms and exact solutions. This shows that the ALRT has a better global search ability for optimum values. The number of function call is the number of function evaluation to evaluate the function value during the execution of the algorithm and it is often used to represent the execution time of the algorithm. For all test functions, the number of function call is best for RT, and next is SGA. This means that RT is superior to other algorithms with respect to precision and converging speed. But, RT has a demerit that its optimum solution's searching abil-

Table 5. Comparison of optimization results for various test functions

Test function	Method	No. of function call	Objective function $f(\mathbf{x}_{opt})$	Design variables x_1	x_2
f_3	ALRT	2933730	$2.01\times10-12$	$-1.41\times10-11$	$1.43\times10-11$
	ALA	254135	0.100	0.995	0.129
	GA	2750	0.0999	0.907	0.415
	RT	517	0.100	-0.720	0.694
	Exact	-	0.0	0.0	0.0
f_4	ALRT	119824	$1.34\times10-18$	$1.14\times10-9$	$1.36\times10-10$
	ALA	246926	$7.93\times10-5$	$-4.95\times10-3$	$5.23\times10-3$
	GA	3050	$4.43\times10-10$	$1.99\times10-5$	$4.85\times10-6$
	RT	359	$1.03\times10-5$	$2.98\times10-3$	$-8.45\times10-4$
	Exact	-	0.0	0.0	0.0
f_5	ALRT	93914	$4.64\times10-16$	$-1.05\times10-8$	$2.93\times10-8$
	ALA	261053	$3.28\times10-3$	$4.37\times10-2$	$-6.69\times10-3$
	GA	5100	$1.05\times10-9$	$-3.23\times10-5$	$3.53\times10-5$
	RT	424	$2.03\times10-4$	$-1.37\times10-2$	$9.86\times10-3$
	Exact	-	0.0	0.0	0.0
f_6	ALRT	125001	$8.13\times10-16$	$-7.60\times10-9$	$8.69\times10-9$
	ALA	235310	$6.75\times10-3$	$6.30\times10-2$	$-1.67\times10-2$
	GA	4550	$7.68\times10-9$	$3.03\times10-5$	$2.60\times10-5$
	RT	312	$7.14\times10-4$	$2.31\times10-2$	$-4.24\times10-3$
	Exact	-	0.0	0.0	0.0
f_7	ALRT	116483	0.0	$-7.47\times10-10$	$1.28\times10-9$
	ALA	185268	$2.26\times10-2$	$1.06\times10-2$	$1.23\times10-3$
	GA	6900	$2.54\times10-9$	$5.36\times10-8$	$-3.58\times10-6$
	RT	263	1.99	$-9.93\times10-1$	$9.91\times10-1$
	Exact	-	0.0	0.0	0.0
f_8	ALRT	2267080	$3.76\times10-12$	$-7.25\times10-13$	$-1.11\times10-12$
	ALA	260169	$2.96\times10-2$	$4.84\times10-3$	$-8.30\times10-3$
	GA	2950	$1.85\times10-4$	$-2.41\times10-6$	$-6.52\times10-5$
	RT	350	$1.67\times10-2$	$-3.45\times10-3$	$4.41\times10-3$
	Exact	-	0.0	0.0	0.0

ity maybe not be good in the broad search space or multivariable problem. The convergence speed is faster than that of the conventional artificial algorithm (ALA) except for the Salomon functions f_3 and Ackley function f_8. Therefore, the ALRT could improve significantly the drawbacks of ALA after it is congregated, not only does the converge speed become very slow, but also the solution accuracy is poor. In other words, the ALRT needs to be more efficient and effective since all optimal solutions for multimodal function can be found sequentially.

APPLICATION: OPTIMUM DESIGN OF SHORT JOURNAL BEARING

Generally, the selection of design variables in bearing design is based on a trial and error method using a number of design charts. However, it is not easy to successfully select a set of optimum design variables using such a method. A considerable amount of working time and cost is required to complete the optimum design of bearings. Therefore, a better scientific and well-organized optimum design method for bearing design is essential.

In this section, the model established by Hashimoto (1997) is used. According to this model, heating and leakage flow rate in laminar and turbulent flow are considered. The optimization here is carried out using the ALRT and the results are compared with the results by the ALA and successive quadratic programming (SQP).

Figure 8. Geometry of a hydrodynamic journal bearing

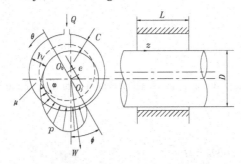

Definition of State Variables and Constraints

The journal bearing for optimum design is shown in Fig. 8. The radial clearance C (µm), length to diameter ratio λ (= L/D) and average viscosity μ (Pa·s) are chosen as the design variables, which are expressed by the design variable vector as

$$X^T = (C, \lambda, \mu) \tag{9}$$

The state variables are the physical quantity that varies with the given operating conditions of the bearings such as static load W (N) and rotational speed n_s (rps). It may include the eccentricity ratio ε_0, film pressure p (MPa), film temperature T (°K), friction force on the journal surface F_j (N), supply lubricant quantity (leakage lubricant flow rate) Q (m³/s), and whirl onset velocity ω_{cr} (1/s). These state variables are generally determined by the design variables. The following constraints are employed:

$$g_i(X) \leq 0, \quad (i = 1 \sim 10) \tag{10}$$

where

$$g_1 = C_{min} - C, g_2 = C - C_{max}, g_3 = \lambda_{min} - \lambda, g_4 = \lambda - \lambda_{max}, g_5 = \mu_{min} - \mu, g_6 = \mu - \mu_{max}$$
$$g_7 = h_a - C\{1 - \varepsilon_0(X)\}, g_8 = \Delta T(X) - \Delta T_a, g_9 = \omega - \omega_{cr}(X), g_{10} = p_{max}(X) - p_a \tag{11}$$

In Eq. (11), the subscripts min and max refer to the lower limit and the upper limit value of state variables, respectively.

Definition of Objective Function

The following weighted sum of temperature rise $\Delta T(\mathbf{x})$ in the fluid film and supply lubricant quantity $Q(\mathbf{x})$ is employed as the objective function. The artificial life algorithm is applied to find the optimum variables that minimize the objective function in Eq. (12) under the constraints in Eq. (10).

Minimize: $f(\mathbf{x}) = \alpha_1 \beta_1 \Delta T(\mathbf{x}) + \alpha_2 \beta_2 Q(\mathbf{x})$ \hfill (12)

where α_1, α_2 are the weighting factors and β_1, β_2 are the scaling factors, respectively.

The design equation of state parameter using in the objective function, Eq. (12) is formulated as follows.

The modified Sommerfeld number S, which is the most important parameter in the bearing design, and the eccentricity ratio ε_0 expressed by the function of Sommerfeld number is given by

$$S = \frac{n_s \mu D^3 \lambda}{48 G_\theta^* C^2 W} \tag{13}$$

$$\varepsilon_0 = \exp(-2.236 \alpha_m \lambda \sqrt{S}) \tag{14}$$

where α_m and G_θ^* are the correction coefficients defined as a function of the average Reynolds number R_e ($= \rho C U / \mu$).

$$R_e < 510: \qquad \alpha_m = 1, \qquad G_\theta^* = 1/12$$

$$510 \le R_e < 1125: \quad \alpha_m = 5.914 R_e^{-0.285}, \quad G_\theta^* = 2.915 R_e^{-0.57}$$

$$1125 \le R_e < 13500: \quad \alpha_m = 0.798, \qquad G_\theta^* = 2.915 R_e^{-0.57}$$

$$R_e \ge 13500: \qquad \alpha_m = 0.756, \qquad G_\theta^* = 14.45 R_e^{-0.75}$$

$$\tag{15}$$

The maximum film pressure under the steady state condition is obtained as:

$$P_{\max} = \frac{\pi n_s \mu D^2 \alpha_m^2 \lambda^2}{8 G_\theta^* C^2} \frac{\varepsilon_0 \sin \theta_0}{(1 + \varepsilon_0 \cos \theta_0)^3} \tag{16}$$

$$\theta_0 = \cos^{-1}\left(\frac{1 - \sqrt{1 + 24 \varepsilon_0^2}}{4 \varepsilon_0}\right) \tag{17}$$

For short journal bearings, the friction force on the journal surface is approximately given as:

$$R_e < 1125: \; F_j \cong \frac{\pi^2 \mu n_s D^3 \lambda}{48 G_\theta^* C} \left\{ \frac{1}{\sqrt{1 - \varepsilon_0}} + \frac{1 - \varepsilon_0}{(1 - \varepsilon_0^2)^{3/2}} \right\} \tag{18a}$$

$$1125 \le R_e < 13500: \; F_j \cong \frac{\pi^2 \mu n_s D^3 \lambda}{48 G_\theta^* C} (1.109 \varepsilon_0^2 - 1.490 \varepsilon_0 + 2.748) \tag{18b}$$

$$R_e \ge 13500: \; F_j \cong \frac{\pi^2 \mu n_s D^3 \lambda}{48 G_\theta^* C} (1.792 \varepsilon_0^3 - 1.523 \varepsilon_0^2 - 3.697 \varepsilon_0 + 8.734) \tag{18c}$$

The supply lubricant quantity, Q and the temperature rise in fluid film, ΔT are defined by Eq. (19).

$$Q = \frac{\pi}{4} n_s C D^2 \varepsilon_0, \; \Delta T = \frac{F_j R \omega}{\rho C_p Q} = \frac{2 F_j}{\rho C_p D C \varepsilon_0} \tag{19}$$

Table 6. Input parameters for optimum design

Minimum radial clearance	$C_{min} = 40\ \mu m$
Maximum radial clearance	$C_{max} = 300\ \mu m$
Minimum length to diameter ratio	$\lambda_{min} = 0.2$
Maximum length to diameter ratio	$\lambda_{max} = 0.6$
Minimum lubricant viscosity	$\mu_{min} = 0.0001\ Pa\cdot s$
Maximum lubricant viscosity	$\mu_{max} = 0.001\ Pa\cdot s$
Allowable minimum film thickness	$h_a = 10\ \mu m$
Allowable maximum film pressure	$p_a = 10\ MPa$
Allowable film temperature rise	$\Delta T_a = 70\ °K$
Density of lubricant	$\rho = 860\ kg/m^3$
Specific heat of lubricant	$C_p = 4.19 \times 103\ J/kg\cdot °K$
Journal diameter	$D = 0.1\ m$
Journal rotational speed	$n_s = 40 \sim 240\ rps$
Applied load to bearing	$W = 10\ kN$
Scaling factor	$\beta_1 = 1,\ \beta_2 = 10^5$
Weighting factor	$\alpha_1/\alpha_2 = 5/1$

Optimization Results and Discussion

Table 6 shows the input parameters for optimum design. The optimum results of radial clearance, C and length to diameter ratio, λ according to rotating speed, when the static load is 10 kN and 20 kN, are shown in Fig. 9. The result of average viscosity, μ is not shown in Fig. 9 because it converged to the lower limit of design range. It is identified that as increasing rotating speed, the radial clearance tend to increase and length to diameter ratio tend to decrease. The trend of optimization result is nearly the same with those of Hashimoto (1997) and ALA.

Comparison of Performance with the ALA

In order to compare the optimization performance with the ALA, the calculation time and the approximate E_{rms} (root mean square) of objective function for all survived individuals at final generation according to rotating speed are shown in Fig. 10. The E_{rms} is calculated by

$$E_{rms} = \left[\frac{1}{N} \sum_{i=1}^{N} (f_{opt} - f_i) \right]^{1/2} \tag{20}$$

where, N is the total number of survived individuals at the final generation, f_{opt} is the minimum value of objective function obtained not by exact solution but by the ALA and/or ALRT, because the exact solution is not known. f_i is the fitness (objective function) value of the ith survived individual at final generation.

In this work 30,000 and 6,000 generations were used in the ALA and ALRT, respectively. In the ALA, the numbers of total generation and individuals were increased for the accuracy of solution. Therefore, the ALRT is better than the ALA in the calculation time from a minimum of 3 times to a maximum of 100 times. In case with

Figure 9. Results of optimum design

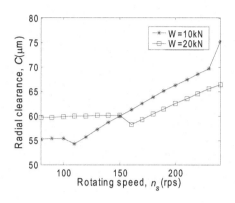

(a) Radial clearance vs. rotating speed

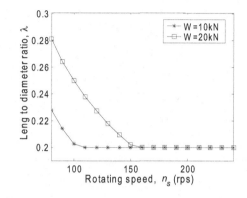

(b) Length to diameter ratio vs. rotating speed

Figure 10. Comparison with the ALRT and ALA

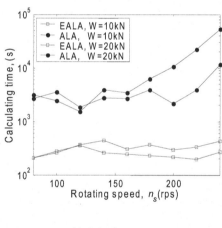

(a) Calculating time

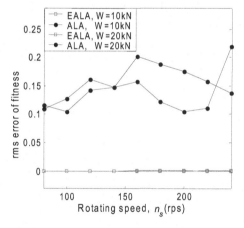

(b) rms error of fitnness

a static load of 10 kN and the rotating speed was 240 rps, the ALA achieved a maximum point in the calculation time. At this point, 52,784 s and 5,284 s were taken by using 30,000 and 6,000 total generations respectively. The iteration required 424 s in the ALRT with 6,000 generations. So, the ALA is 10 times more than the ALRT in calculation time though using the same total generation. But in case with a static load of 10 kN and rotating speed was 120 rps and 367 s is taken for the ALRT while 221 s was required in the ALA using same generation (6,000). In most of the cases, using the same generation, the ALRT is slightly better than the ALA in calculation time because the number of the produced individuals in the ALA is much greater than that the ALRT. The calculation times in the ALRT depends on the selection of N_c. Also, the number of searching in a neighboring region in the ALA is restricted. Therefore, the calculation time of each generation can be controlled in the ALA. As a result of the above discussion, the calculation time is estimated by considering the accuracy of solution and it is validated in Fig. 10 that the ALRT can search the solutions more accurately and faster than the ALA.

Figure 11. Comparison of the variations of variables by the ALRT and ALA

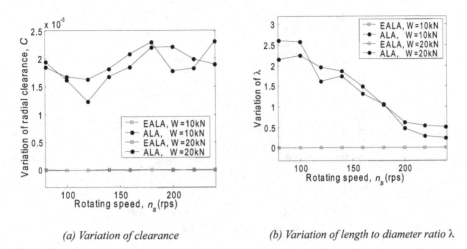

(a) Variation of clearance (b) Variation of length to diameter ratio λ

Estimation of the Variation of Colonies

Fig. 11 shows the variation of colonies for two variables using Eq. (8). It is identified that the ALRT have lower value than the ALA in the variation of colony for all design variables in Fig. 11. It means that the group having very high density of individuals is built up and more accurate and fast search is possible in the ALRT.

Comparison of the Optimum Results with ALA and SQP

Fig. 12 shows the comparison of the optimized objective function of the ALRT with those of the conventional artificial life algorithm (ALA) and the successive quadratic programming (SQP). As seen in Fig. 12, the results of the ALRT, ALA and SQP are very similar for high journal rotational speed which is in the turbulent flow regime. But the results of SQP in the laminar and transient flow regimes cannot find the global optimum solution. The design variables at the optimum points are indicated in Fig. 13. The optimum variables of ALA and SQP have many variations especially for low journal rotational speed compared to that of ALRT. As shown in Fig. 13(a), the radial clearance decreases rapidly and increases slowly in the laminar and transient flow regimes. Since the flow condition changes from laminar to turbulent, the discontinuities are observed in the optimum design variables. Fig. 14 shows the state variables at the optimum solutions. As SQP fails to find the global optimum solution in laminar and transient flow regimes, the state variables of SQP have some differences with those of ALRT and ALA. The maximum film pressure p_{max} and the fluid temperature rise ΔT at the optimum points are satisfied with each maximum allowable value shown in Table 6.

CONCLUSION

In this chapter, a complete study of the simple ALife optimization algorithm and an integrated optimization algorithm which combined the conventional ALife optimization algorithm with random tabu search algorithm for multimodal function optimization have been deeply studied. Some basic theories were reviewed to give preliminary understanding in optimum design procedure. The effectiveness of the algorithm was evaluated using eight benchmark test functions and a real optimum design for short journal bearing. The optimized results were

Figure 12. Comparison of the objective function

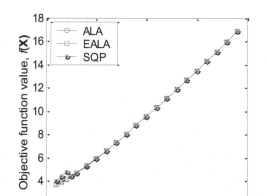

Figure 13. Comparison of the design variables

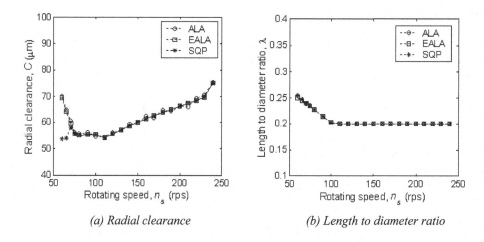

(a) Radial clearance   (b) Length to diameter ratio

compared with those of conventional ALife algorithm, standard genetic algorithm, random tabu search algorithm and exact solutions. The results show that the ALRT reaches the optimum solution faster and closer to exact solution than the conventional ALife algorithm, and will give all global optimum solutions in a solution space. The algorithm reduced the time needed for searching and leads to do accuracy of optimum solutions, because the proposed algorithm improved the method of making decision of new points for offspring and its own waste by using random tabu search method.

FUTURE RESEARCH DERECTIONS

ALife optimization techniques have many possibilities, because they can provide methods for generating complex situations with simple rules. However, it is relatively rare to find a complete study that presents the methodology of optimization and real applications for optimum design using ALife algorithm. Most applications are still at

Figure 14. Comparison of the state variables

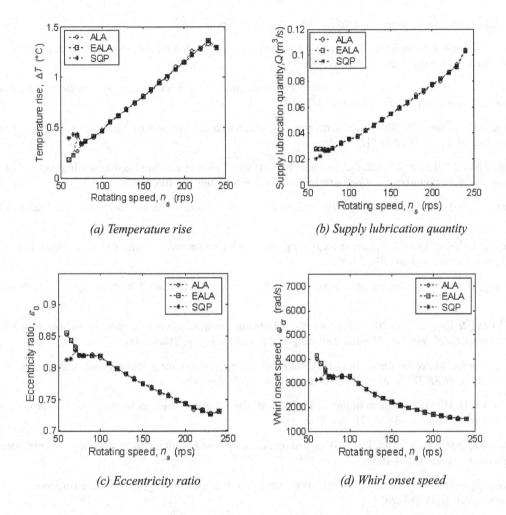

(a) Temperature rise

(b) Supply lubrication quantity

(c) Eccentricity ratio

(d) Whirl onset speed

the laboratory level, but a few of them are already being used in the real world. Although the emphasis of ALife is still a scientific discovery of the meaning of life, the outcomes of the research can be fruitful in the real world. Alife provides potential for generating real-world applications by reducing tedious human effort. Traditional methodologies based on mathematics can provide good solutions for real-world problems. However, people demand more advanced or complicated applications that provide interesting and optimized behavior.

A hybrid of ALife methodologies and traditional optimization methods may be used in future application design techniques. Most real-world problems inherently contain multiple, frequently conflicting objectives. The approach adopted by multi-objective optimization (MOO) is to assume nothing about the problem and generate a list of viable alternatives that represents the best available trade-offs between the conflicting objectives (commonly referred to as the Pareto optimal front). Thus, multi-objective optimizers represent an excellent tool for the design phase of real-world projects, enabling the experts to examine trends in the Pareto optimal front, test possible solutions or develop an understanding of the relationship between objectives. Therefore, it is an encouragement to contribute a novel optimum design technique which is applicable in real system.

REFERENCES

Adami, C. (1998). *Introduction to artificial life*. New York, Springer-Verlag.

Ahn, Y. K., Song, J. D., & Yang, B. S. (2003). Optimal design of engine mount using an artificial life algorithm. *Journal of Sound and Vibration, 261*, 309-328.

Assad A. M., & Packard, N. H. (1992). Emergent colonization in artificial ecology. *Proceedings of the first European Conference on Artificial Life* (pp. 143-152).

Bendau, M. A. (2003). Artificial life: Organization, adaptation and complexity from the bottom up. *Trends in Cognitive Sciences, 7*(11), 505-512.

Cardoso, M. F., Salcedo, R. L., & De Azevedo, S. F. (1996). The simplex-simulated annealing approach to continuous nonlinear optimization. *Computers Chemical Engineering, 20*, 1065-1075.

Ferber, J. (1999). *Multi-agent systems: an introduction to distributed artificial intelligence*. CA, Addison-Wesley.

Francois, O. (1998). An evolutionary strategy for global minimization and its Markov chain analysis. *IEEE Trans. Evolutionary Computation, 2*(3), 77-80.

Goldberg, D. E. (1989). *Genetic algorithms in search, optimization, and machine learning*. CA, Addison-Wesley.

Guo, D. W., & Kong, C. L. (2004). A new artificial life algorithm to solve time-varying optimization problem. *International Conference on Machine Learning and Cybernetics* (pp. 2146-2148).

Jin, Y., Olhofer, M., & Sendhoff, B. (2002). An evolutionary strategy for global minimization and its Markov chain analysis. *IEEE Trans. Evolutionary Computation, 2*(3), 481-494.

Hashimoto, H. (1997). Optimum design of high-speed, short journal bearings by mathematical programming. *STLE Tribology Transaction, 40*(2), 283-293.

Hayashi, D., Satoh, T., & Okita, T. (1994). Global optimization using artificial life (in Japanese). *Joint Conference of Information Society*, 164-165.

Hayashi, D., Satoh, T., & Okita, T. (1996). Distributed optimization by using artificial life (in Japanese). *Trans. IEE Japan, 116-C*(5), 584-590.

Haykin, S. (1998). *Neural networks: a comprehensive foundation*. 2nd ed., Upper Saddle River, NJ, Prentice-Hall.

Holland, J. H. (1975). *Adaptation in natural and artificial systems*. Ann Arbor, MI, University of Michegan Press (2nd ed., MIT Press, 1992).

Homaifar, A., Qi, C., & Lai, S. (1994). Constrained optimization via genetic algorithm simulation. *Electronics Letter, 62*(4), 242-254.

Hu, N. (1992). Tabu search method with random moves for globally optimal design. *International Journal of Numerical Methods in Engineering, 35*, 1055-1070.

Kim, K. J., & Cho, S. B. (2006). A comprehensive overview of the applications of artificial life. *Artificial Life, 12*, 153-182.

Langton, C. G. (Ed.). (1989). *Artificial Life*. Addison-Wesley Publishing Co.

Sait, S.M., & Youssef, H. (1999). *VLSI physical design automation: Theory and practice*. World Scientific

Salomon, R. (1996). Re-evaluating genetic algorithm performance under coordinate rotation of benchmark functions: A survey of some theoretical and practical aspects of genetic algorithms. *BioSystems, 39*, 263-278.

Salomon, R. (1998). Evolutionary algorithms and gradient search: similarities and differences. *IEEE Trans. Evolutionary Computation, 2*(2), 45-55.

Satoh, T., Uchibori, A., & Tanaka, K. (1999). Artificial life system for optimization of nonconvex functions. *International Joint Conference on Neural Networks, 4*, 2390-2393.

Satoh, T., Mizukami, Y., Tanaka, K., & Nara, K. (2004). A two-level ALife system with predator. *Electronics and Communication in Japan, 87-2*(8), 53-59.

Song, J. D., & Yang, B. S. (2005). Optimum design of short journal bearing by using enhanced artificial life optimization algorithm. *Tribology International, 38*(4), 403-411.

Yang, B. S., Choi, B. G., Yu, Y. H., & Nan, H. T. (2002). Optimum design of a damping plate with an unconstrained viscoelastic damping layer using combined genetic algorithm. *KSME International Journal, 13*(5), 387-396.

Yang, B. S., & Lee, Y. H. (2000). Artificial life algorithm for function optimization. *Proceedings of ASME Design Engineering Technical Conferences and Computers and Information in Engineering Conference.* DETC2000/DAC-14524.

Yang, B. S., Lee, Y. H., Choi, B. K., & Kim, H. J. (2001). Optimum design of short journal bearings by artificial life algorithm. *Tribology International, 34*(7), 427-435.

Yang, B. S., & Song J. D. (2001). Enhanced artificial life algorithm for fast and accurate optimization search. *Asia-Pacific Vibration Conference* (pp. 732-736).

Yang, C., Ye, H., Wang, J. C., & Wang, L. (2002). An artificial life and genetic algorithm based on optimization approach with new selecting methods. *International Conference on Machine Learning and Cybernetics, 2*, 684-688.

Yao, X. (1996). An overview of evolutionary computation. *Chinese Journal of Advanced Software Research, 3*(1), 12-29.

Youssef, H., Sait, S. M., & Adiche, H. (2001). Evolutionary algorithms, simulated annealing and tabu search: a comparative study. *Engineering Applications of Artificial Intelligence, 14*, 167-181.

ADDITIONAL READING

Annunziato, M., Bertini, I., Lucchetti, M., Pannicelli, A., & Pizzuti, S. (2004). The evolutionary control methodology: an overview, *Lecture Notes in Computer Science, 2936*, 331-342.

Brooks, R. (2001). The relationship between matter and life, *Nature, 409*, 409 - 411.

Coello C., Carlos A., Van V., David A., & Gary B. (2002). *Evolutionary Algorithms for Solving Multi-objective Problems*, Kluwer Academic Publishers, New York.

Dessalegne, T., & Nicklow, J. W. (2004). Optimal operation of multi-reservoir river systems using an artificial life algorithm. *Proceedings of the 2004 World Water and Environmental Resources Congress*, Critical Transitions in Water and Environmetal Resources Management (pp. 1840-1849).

Goldberg, D. E. (1989). *Genetic Algorithms in Search, Optimization, and Machine Learning, Reading*, MA, Addison-Wesley.

Holland, J.H. (1992). *Adaptation in Natural and Artificial Systems*, 2nd Ed., The MIT Press, Cambridge, MA.

http://www.faqs.org/faqs/ai-faq/alife/i

http://alife.santafe.edu/alife

http://http1.brunel.ac.uk:8080/depts/Al/alife/al-life.htm

http://www.webslave.dircon.co.uk/alife

http://www.newscientist.com/nsplus/insight/ai/ai.html

http://www.swarmintelligence.org/

Kuntz, P., & Snyers, D. (1994). Emergent colonization and graph partitioning. *Proceedings of the 3rd International Conference on Simulation of Adaptive Behavior: From Animal to Animats*, 3, MIT Press, Cambridge, MA.

Langton, C.G. (Ed.). (1995). *Artificial Life: An Overview*, The MIT Press, Cambridge, MA.

Maniezzo, V., & Carbonaro, A. (2001). *Ant Colony Optimization: an Overview, Essays and Surveys in Metaheuristics*, Kluwer Academic Publishers (pp. 21-44).

Mitchell, M., & Forest, S. (1995). *Genetic Algorithms and Artificial Life*. In C.G. Langton (Ed.), Artificial Life: An Overview (pp. 267-182).

Raidl, G. R. (2006). A unified view on hybrid metaheuristics. http://www.ads.tuwien.ac.at/ publications/ bib/ pdf/raidl-06.pdf

Ray, T. S. (1992). An Approach to the Synthesis of Life. In C.G. Langton et al. (Ed.), *Artificial Life II* (pp. 371-408). Reading, MA, Addison-Wesley.

Satoh, T., Kuwabara, H., Kanezashi, M., & Nara, K. (2002). Artificial life system and its application to multiple-fuel economic load dispatch problem. *IEEE paper*, 1432-1437.

Scogings, C. J., Hawick, K. A., & James, H. A. (2006). Tools and techniques for optimisation of microscopic artificial life simulation models. *Conference on Modelling, Simulation, and Optimization*, Gaborone, Botswana (pp. 1-6).

Thro, E. (1993). *Artificial Life Explorer's Kit*, Sams Publishing, Indiana.

Wang, Q., & Zhang, H. (2005). Artificial life for pavement distress. *Key Engineering Materials*, 295-296, 507-512.

Yakhno, T., & Ekin, E. (2002). Ant systems: another alternative for optimization problems? *Lecture Notes in Computer Science, 2457*, 324-326.

Yang, B.S., & Song, J.D. (2001). Enhanced artificial life algorithm for fast and accurate global optimization search, *Proceedings of Asia-Pacific Vibration Conference*, China (pp. 732-736).

Yu, H. F., & Wang, D. W. (2006). Food-chain algorithm and its application to optimizing distribution network. *Journal of Northeastern University, 27*(2), 146-149.

KEY TERMS

Artificial Life (ALife): The study of man-made systems that exhibit behavior characteristics of natural living systems. A field of study and an associated art form which examine systems related to life, its processes, and its evolution through simulations. ALife is the name given to a new discipline that studies "natural" life by attempting to recreate biological phenomena from scratch within computers and other "artificial" media. ALife complements the traditional analytic approach of traditional biology with a synthetic approach in which, rather than studying biological phenomena by taking apart living organisms to see how they work, one attempts to put together systems that behave like living organisms (Chris G. Langton).

Artificial Organisms: Individuals of several species which live in an artificial world.

Artificial World (AWorld): The space where the lowest and the highest limits are ximin, ximax $\in$ Rn (i = 1, 2, ···, n), respectively. The artificial world is the world encompassing all things that are man-made. The ALife environment is a two or three-dimensional space where the artificial individuals can move around. During the single iteration (life cycle) all the living individuals move in the space interacting with other individuals exchanging information.

Food Chain: The flow of energy from one organism to the next. Organisms in a food chain are grouped into trophic levels based on how many links they are removed from the primary producers.

Metabolism: The complete set of chemical reactions that occur in living cells. These processes are the basis of life, allowing cells to grow and reproduce, maintain their structures, and respond to their environments.

Optimization: The study of problems in which one seeks to minimize or maximize a real function by systematically choosing the values of real or integer variables from within an allowed set.

Reproduction: The biological process by which new individual organisms are produced. Reproduction is a fundamental feature of all known life; each individual organism exists as the result of reproduction.

Chapter XXI
Optimizing Society:
The Social Impact Theory Based Optimizer

Martin Macaš
Czech Technical University in Prague, Czech Republic

Lenka Lhotská
Czech Technical University in Prague, Czech Republic

ABSTRACT

A novel binary optimization technique is introduced called Social Impact Theory based Optimizer (SITO), which is based on social psychology model of social interactions. The algorithm is based on society of individuals. Each individual holds a set of its attitudes, which encodes a candidate solution of a binary optimization problem. Individuals change their attitudes according to their spatial neighbors and their fitness, which leads to convergence to local (or global) optimum. This chapter also tries to demonstrate different aspects of the SITO's behavior and to give some suggestions for potential user. Further, a comparison to similar techniques – genetic algorithm and binary particle swarm optimizer – is discussed and some possibilities of formal analysis are briefly presented.

INTRODUCTION

This chapter focuses on a novel binary optimization method called Social Impact Theory based Optimizer (SITO). One of its precursors is social psychology. However, evolutionary computation, cellular automata or artificial life can be also understood as precursors of the method. The algorithm is based on a population of simple cells. These cells are inhabited by individuals representing candidate solutions - binary vectors. Each such binary vector is a counterpart to set of binary attitudes held by real people. These attitudes are changed over time according to external influences and internal processes. This process leads to a convergence and optimization.

In the chapter, we first describe a background of the method and its several precursors. After, the SITO algorithm is introduced. The main part of the chapter discusses various aspects of the algorithm and its parameters on the basis of experimental results. Next, the relationship between SITO and other selected methods is examined and finally some sources and inspirations for theoretical approach are suggested. The main objective of the chapter is to present the SITO method and to give advices how to set its parameters.

Copyright © 2009, IGI Global, distributing in print or electronic forms without written permission of IGI Global is prohibited.

BACKGROUND

The connections between social and natural sciences have mostly laid in the use of natural sciences for a formal description of social phenomena. A particular case is the use of physical and mathematical models of society and social interaction, whose historical roots date back to 17th century (Ball, 2002).

The main source of inspiration for the SITO development comes from the area of models of social interactions. One of characteristics shared by these models is the presence of many, more or less simple, individuals representing the participants of the social processes. These individuals, sometimes called agents, form an artificial society. They are very often situated in an environment which could be defined as a medium separate from the agents, on which the agents operate and with which they interact (Epstein, 1996). There is wide variety of such models differing in their purpose or structure of agents and environment.

Epstein and Axtell describe a number of experiments with a virtual ecosystem (Epstein, 1996). The computer simulation techniques are presented, which show how social structure and group behaviors arise from simple local interactions of simple individuals. They follow a particular instance of the artificial society concept that has come to be known as "The Sugarscape Model". Actually, it is a two-dimensional grid on which agents interact and move on the basis of agent's rules. Such model of artificial society is an example of analysis study, which could help the social scientists to model and explore the behavior of a society from the bottom-up point of view. However the sugarscape model is not the first agent-based computer model of social interactions.

The first computer simulation of social interaction was the checkerboard model introduced by Sakoda (Sakoda, 1971). The checkerboard represented an environment (a square lattice) on which two groups of individuals (checkers) are situated. The individuals have different attitudes to members of their own group and different attitudes to members of the other group. The individuals are moving on the board on basis of positive, neutral or negative attitudes toward one another. The model has been capable of demonstrating the intimate connection between attitudes of group members toward their own group and toward others to a social interactional process and to the resulting social structure. The resulting social structure is a consequence of local interactions defined by simple attitude combinations. Another model, very similar to the Sakoda's one, is the Schelling's model of segregation (Schelling, 1969). The two types of individuals prefer that at least some fraction of their neighbors is of their own group. If this condition is not met, the individuals move to the nearest site where it is. The results explain and describe the emergence of segregation.

In this chapter, the main inspiration comes from social interaction models slightly differing from that described above. The individuals are scattered over a grid that defines their environment. However, contrary to previously mentioned model, the individuals are not movable and one individual occupied one cell of the grid for the whole time of simulation. Moreover, each individual change their properties on bases of some rules taking into account the individual's neighborhood. These features can be found not only in models from social sciences. In physics, the Ising model of ferromagnetic interactions deals with a grid of different interacting spins. Similar to Ising spins, people can sometimes choose between two different opinions. This perspective has been used in some economical applications (e.g. Da Silva, 2001).

Another very wide area connected with such models is study of opinion dynamics, where computer simulation can be used as tool for theory construction and validation (Schnell, 1992). An example is the computer simulation of dynamic theory of social impact known from social psychology. According to Latané (1981a), social impact is any of a great variety of changes in physiological states and subjective feelings, motives and emotions, cognitions and beliefs, values and behavior, that occur in an individual, human or animal, as a result of the real, implied, or imagined presence or actions of other individuals. The social impact theory formulates a mathematical model concerning how social processes operate at a given point in time. It specifies principles how individuals are affected by the society Social impact theory has been applied to various social processes (Latané, 1981b; Jackson, 1981). Dynamic social impact theory is based on a view of society as a self-organizing complex system composed of interacting individuals each obeying simple principles of social impact (Latané, 1996). It tries to describe and predict the diffusion of beliefs through social systems. It views society as a self-organizing complex system composed of interacting individuals each obeying simple principles of social impact. It states that the likelihood that a person will respond to social influence will increase with three factors: strength, immediacy and number. *Strength* is a property of influencing individuals which indicates how important the influencing individual is to an influenced individual. *Immediacy* represents the spatial closeness of the influencing individuals from you. *Number* describes how many individuals are influencing a specific person. This structure was simulated by Andrzej Nowak and Chris Szamrej (Nowak, 1990; Nowak, 1993).

Social Impact Theory Simulation

The simulations represented each individual as four parameters: the individual's attitude, two indicators of strength (persuasiveness and supportiveness) and the individual's location in the social structure. The attitude (or opinion) was binary parameter and could take just one of two values, regardless of its interpretation. (Possible interpretation could be that the people are for or against a given idea - "guilty/not guilty", "supporting EU/not supporting EU.) Each individual had just one attitude. Strength factors of an individual described the relative importance of the individual in the society. The first one was persuasiveness, the ability to persuade people with opposing beliefs to change their minds. The second one, supportiveness indicated the ability to provide social support for people with similar beliefs. The persuasiveness and supportiveness took values from <0, 100>, were independent and reassigned randomly after each attitude change. The concept of immediacy was established by organizing the group (or society) into a square rectangular grid where each cell represented one individual. The immediacy of two individuals was defined using the Euclidean distance between the corresponding cells.

According to the social impact theory, magnitude of impact $\hat{I}$ is a multiplicative function of these factors: $\hat{I} = f(strength, immediacy, number)$. In Nowak (1990), the total persuasive and supportive impacts are computed according to:

$$\hat{I}_p = N_0^{1/2}[\sum(p_i/d_i^2)/N_0]$$

(1)

$$\hat{I}_s = N_s^{1/2}[\sum(s_i/d_i^2)/N_s]$$

(2)

where p_i and s_i is the persuasiveness and supportiveness of an individual i, respectively. N_0 and N_s is the number of individuals with beliefs that are opposing or equal to the current individual's opinion, respectively. Finally, d_i is Euclidean distance of individual i from the current influenced individual.

In the SITO algorithm, we do not follow the original simulation, where the persuasiveness and supportiveness are independent factors of strength. Instead of this, we merge these to factors into one - the strength q. There could be different assumptions corresponding to real world and from such assumptions, different behavior of the persuasiveness and supportiveness can be derived. Nowak and Latané (Nowak, 1993) argue that "if strength is just a function of such objective characteristics as education or intelligence, the persuasiveness and supportiveness should be positively correlated. On the other hand, someone who is especially influential to one group of partisans may have become discredited by the other side, which implies the negative correlation". In our optimization tasks, the fitness function can be understood as such objective characteristics and thus we decided for the positive correlation and even for equality of the persuasiveness and supportiveness. Obviously, some different approaches can be considered, which can be the topic for some future works.

SOCIAL IMPACT THEORY BASED OPTIMIZER

Description of SITO

Consider the following binary optimization problem: find a binary vector $\vec{x}_i = (x_i^1,...,x_i^D)$ that extremizes a fitness function $f(\vec{x}_i)$. Consider a society of individuals. An individual i has associated a binary vector $\vec{x}_i = (x_i^1,...,x_i^D)$ representing candidate solution of the D-dimensional binary optimization problem, which can be evaluated using

Figure 1. The structure of the society in SITO algorithm. ©2008 Martin Macaš. Used with permission.

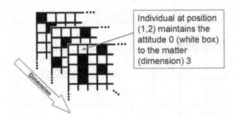

the fitness function. Further, each individual has its position in population topology (here, the rectangular lattice will be considered), which makes it possible to define distance between two individuals i and j, $d_{i,j}$. Concretely here, $d_{i,j}$ will be the Euclidean distance between positions of individual i and individual j.

At the beginning, the binary values x_i^p, where $i = (1, ..., N)$, $p = (1, ..., D)$ are randomly initialized with uniform probability. At each time step, all vectors are evaluated ($f(\vec{x}_i)$ is computed for all i). Let $f_{\min}$ and $f_{\max}$ is minimum and maximum fitness value respectively. Now, for a maximization optimization problem, the strength of the individual i is determined as follows:

$$q_i = (f(\vec{x}_i) - f_{\min})(f_{\max} - f_{\min})$$

(3)

This reflects the natural fact that the fitter the individual, the higher its influence on the others. Obviously, this definition of the strength implies that $q_i \in <0,1>$. Now, there is the same model as in the original social simulation – we have the topology (consisting of a rectangular lattice), on which individuals holding some attitudes are scattered. Moreover, each individual has its strength. The only difference is the number of attitudes, which is the dimension D of the optimization problem. This can be solved by considering D societies sharing the strength values and existing and being updated in parallel.

Further, each individual i inverts the bit (change the attitude) x_i^p if

$$\sum_{j \in O}(q_j^p / d_{i,j}^2)/\sqrt{N_O} > (\sum_{k \in S}(q_k^p / d_{i,k}^2) + q_i^p / \delta^2)/\sqrt{N_S + 1}$$

(4)

where O is the set of indices j of individuals for which $x_j^p \neq x_i^p$ (opponents) and S is the set of indices k of individuals for which $x_k^p = x_i^p$ (supporters) and $k \neq i$. Because of the simplicity and reduction of the computational costs, O and S sets are determined from a neighborhood of the current individual only. The types and size of the neighborhood will be specified and discussed below. The term on the right-hand side of the inequality (4) is the total supportive impact and the term on the left-hand side is the total persuasive impact. Note that both terms use the strength q instead of distinguishing the persuasiveness and supportiveness. The term q_i^p / δ^2 represents the self-influence. Parameter δ is a constant self-distance parameter, which determines the relative importance of the self.

The inversion of a particular bit can occur even if the persuasive impact is less than the supportive one. On the other hand, if the persuasive impact predominates, the change may not occur. It is enabled by an additional probabilistic parameter κ which represents the probability of spontaneous change. Thus, if persuasive impact is greater, the change takes place with probability $1 - \kappa$, else, the change takes place with probability κ. It can improve the explorative capability and prevent loss of diversity. Actually, this parameter is an analogy to the mutation rate in genetic algorithms. Obviously, there can be some other ways of introducing randomness. For example, a so called temperature can be defined as a random variable drawn with a mean of 0 and a standard deviation corresponding to the temperature level. This temperature, generated for each individual at each time step and each dimension is added to the persuasive impact. However, meanwhile, normal mutation rate κ will be considered. Finally, we can present the list of SITO pseudocode:

Algorithm: Social Impact Theory based Optimization

```
1    Initialize attitudes by random assigning binary values from (0,1) to society.attitudes;
2    Iter:=0;
3    WHILE (iter<max_iter) DO
4          society.fitness:=evaluate(society.attitudes);
5          fmax:=max(society.fitness);
6          fmin:=min(society.fitness);
7          society.strength:=(society.fitness-fmin)/(fmax-fmin);
8          iter=iter+1;
9          FOR each individual i and each dimension d DO
10               Find sources and supporters in neighborhood of i;
11               Compute number of sources and supporters (No,Ns) in
                 neighborhood of individual i with respect to dimension d
12               Compute total persuasive impact lp
13               Compute total supportive impact ls
14               IF lp>ls,
15                    invert the attitude of individual i in dimension d with
                      probability 1-kappa
16               ELSE,
17                    invert the attitude of individual i in dimension d with
                      probability kappa;
18               END (IF)
19          END (FOR)
20    END (WHILE)
```

Experiments with SITO Settings

One of most important challenge after the development of the SITO algorithm is an examination of different aspects of the algorithm, especially of an influence of particular parameters and settings on the method's behavior. For the purpose of parameter setting examination, two experimental sets were carried out differing in the dimension of the target problem and number of iterations only. For each set, several different parameter settings were tested on three benchmark problems – Bipolar6, Maxcut and Ppeaks.

The first testing problem is the Bipolar order-6 problem (Bipolar6). The fitness function is computed as follows:

$$f_{Bipolar6}(\vec{x}) = \sum_{i=1}^{D/6} f_6(\vec{x}_i),$$

where $\vec{x}_i$ is the ith disjoint substring of $\vec{x}$ of dimension D. The maximum values of $f_6(\vec{x}_i)$ are $f_6(000000) = f_6(111111) = 1$, local optima is $f_6(\vec{x}_i) = 0.8$ if $|\vec{x}_i| = 3$, these local optima are surrounded by $f_6(\vec{x}_i) = 0.4$ if $|\vec{x}_i| = 2$ or 4, and $f_6(\vec{x}_i) = 0.0$ if $|\vec{x}_i| = 1$ or 5 where $|\vec{x}_i|$ is the unitation of $\vec{x}_i$. This problem has been specially designed to be difficult for evolutionary techniques (Goldberg, 1992).

The second testing problem is the maximum cut of problem (Maxcut), which consists in partitioning the set of vertices of a weighted graph into two disjoint subsets such that the sum of the weights of the edges with one endpoint in each subset is maximized (Khuri, 1994). This problem is NP-complete. The representation of a candidate solution is binary vector of length D, where each component corresponds to a vertex. If a particular digit is 1, than the corresponding vertex is in the first set, if it is 0 then the corresponding vertex is in the second set.

Figure 2. The instance type of P-Peaks problem used in underlying experiments. ©2008 Martin Macaš. Used with permission.

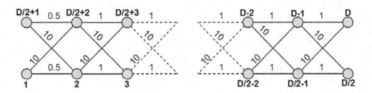

Table 1. Description of problem instances

Exp. set	Bipolar6	Maxcut	Ppeaks	Iterations
1	D=180	D=180, V=180	D=100,P=100	200
2	D=300	D=300, V=300	D=300,P=200	500

Thus, one string $\vec{x}_i$ represents a partition of the vertices. For testing, we used just two different instances of the Maxcut problem differing just in their size (graphs from figure with 180 or 300 vertices respectively).

The third testing problem is the multimodal problem generator (Ppeaks) (De Jong, 1997), where P random D-bit strings are generated that represent the location of P peaks in the D dimensional search space. The fitness value $f_{Ppeaks}(\vec{x})$ is the number of bits which the string $f_{Ppeaks}(\vec{x})$ shares with the nearest peak in the search space. An advantage is that a new instance is generated (and solved) each time the algorithm runs, which increases the predictive power of the results for the problem class as a whole. Ppeaks problem represents epistatic problem with easily tuneable degree of epistasis (through the number P of peaks). We used two types of the generator, one type for each dimension. For dimension 100, 100 peaks were used, for dimension 300, 200 peaks were used.

For all three testing problems and their particular instances, we used the default parameter setting, which is described in Table 2. For each experiment, the default setting for parameters was used with the only exception – the value of the parameter which was examined. Subsequently, the following settings were inspected: the initial value of parameter κ from which κ linearly decreases to 0, the behavior of self-distance δ, shape of the society (map size), geometry of the society and neighborhood type and radius.

Setting the Stochasticity – Parameter κ

The stochastic component is one of most important of the algorithm. In optimization algorithms generally, it prevents loss of diversity and generates new solutions. In SITO, randomness causes that individuals are sometimes not governed by the relationship of supportive and persuasive impact. The parameter κ and its temporal behavior greatly affect the behavior of optimization and its result (Macaš, 2007; Macaš, in press). It seems purposeful to

Table 2. Default parameter setting

Parameter	Default setting
κ	Decreasing from 0.05 to 0
Self-distance δ	Increasing from 1 to 7
Shape(Map size)	10x10
Lattice geometry	Bounded
Neighborhood radius	1
Neighborhood type	Moore

Figure 3. The influence of parameter κ *on the final fitness value for (a) experimental set 1, (b) experimental set 2.* ©*2008 Martin Macaš. Used with permission.*

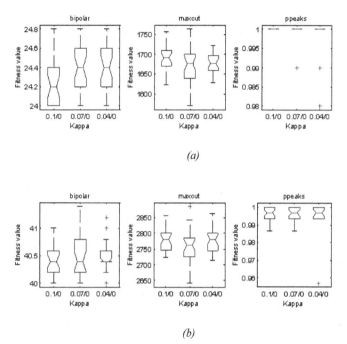

(a)

(b)

decrease the parameter linearly over the time from a higher value down to a smaller value to support the exploration at the beginning and exploitation at the end of the optimization process. The proper setting of the initial and final value depends on the particular optimization problem, however, previous preliminary experiments have shown that it is suitable to set the initial κ to a number between 0.01 and 0.15 and the final κ value to a number close to 0. Anyway, all preliminary experiments have shown that the use of a non-zero value for the parameter is necessary and essential for majority of optimization problems. In underlying experiments, we have investigated three possible settings of the initial κ (the final value was always set to 0). The particular values of initial κ were 0.1, 0.07 and 0.04. The results depicted using box-plots on Figure 3 shown that any of these values did not lead to significantly better final fitness, although there were some differences especially for Bipolar6 and Maxcut problem for both problem dimensions. Whereas for the Bipolar function and dimension $D = 180$, it is quite worst to set the initial κ to 0.1, the situation is opposite for the Maxcut problem. As it has been already stated, the use of randomness is necessary and critical point for the SITO algorithm. However, the underlying experiments imply that the proper setting of the initial κ depends on the particular optimization task. The fact that the randomness helps to prevent the loss of diversity can be seen from the Figure 4 where the temporal progress of diversity measure (averaged over 30 runs) is depicted. The diversity is evaluated using the following measure: diversity = number of different fitness values/population size. The higher is the initial κ value, the longer the time to start of the diversity degradation. However, at the end of the optimization, the diversity is same for all curves corresponding to different initial κ. The probable reason is the same final value κ, which is zero.

Figure 4. The influence of parameter κ on the temporal evolution of average diversity for experimental set 1.
©2008 Martin Macaš. Used with permission.

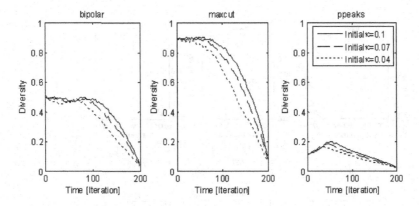

Self-Confidence – Parameter δ

Another phenomenon, which should be examined, is the self-confidence. This factor is introduced using the self-distance parameter δ in the update equation 4. It determines a relative importance of the self. The higher is the self distance parameter δ, the smaller the confidence in one's own attitude. Actually, this factor adds a bias to the total supportive impact and its inversion can be understood as inertia. From a psychological simulation point of view it could be reasonable to set δ inversely proportional to time of keeping a particular opinion. However, in the area of optimization, inertia helps to overcome local optima and to control the exploration of the search space. High inertia value enables better exploration, however can prevent accurate approach of an optimum. Thus, it seems judicious to decrease inertia through the time, which corresponds to increasing self-distance parameter. This fact corresponds with some preliminary experiments, where decreasing self-distance parameter led to quite poor results. The Figure 5 depicts box plots describing results for 5 different behaviour of δ-setting δ constant δ=0.001 and δ=1 and linearly increasing with time from initial value δ=1 to final value δ=3, 5 or 7. The Figure 6 shows the time progress of the best-so-far fitness (averaged over 30 runs). It is clear from both figures that it is significantly better to use the linearly increasing δ. Moreover, for the three particular test problems, it is not as important, if the final value is 3, 5 or 7. The only exception is the result for the Ppeaks problem of dimension 300, where it is better to use higher values. It can be seen from Figure 6 that the parameter δ has a great influence on the rate of convergence and we can conclude that δ increasing from 1 to 7 (or higher value) is a good option. Unfortunately, we did not measure some more options (like setting the self-distance to much higher values or even infinity) and thus it is still probable that it is better κ remove the self-influence from the total supportive impact.

Society in Space - Topology

As it is stated above, the individuals in SITO algorithm are distributed over a topological structure. This enables to define spatial position and neighborhood of the individuals. The first version of SITO follows the same type of topology as the social impact theory simulation – the rectangular lattice. First, we compare the bounded/unbounded rectangular grid (see figure 7), where the marginal individuals cannot/can communicate with individuals on the other side of the lattice. Box plots for the experimental set 1 are not depicted, because there has been practically no difference for the lower dimensions of the test problems. Figure 8 shows the box plots for experimental set 2, where the unbounded topology is significantly better for Ppeaks problem. However, the results for the Maxcut problem (bounded topology slightly better) and for the Bipolar6 problem (no difference) is indicative of the task dependency of the optimal topology.

Figure 5. The influence of parameter δ on the final fitness value for (a) experimental set 1, (b) experimental set 2. For example, the notation 1/3 represents linear increase of δ from 1 to 3. ©2008 Martin Macaš. Used with permission.

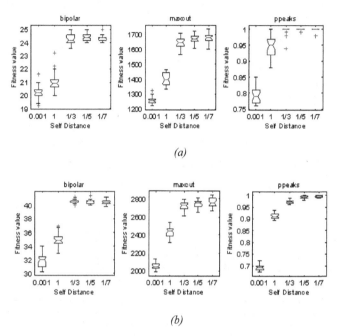

Figure 6. The influence of parameter δ on the temporal evolution of average best-so-far fitness for experimental set 1. ©2008 Martin Macaš. Used with permission.

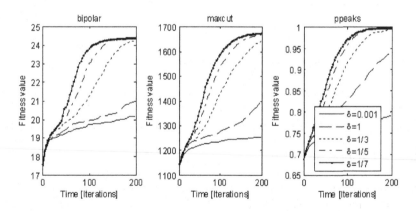

Figure 7. Two types of the topology. All lines represent connections. Unbounded topology is a toroidal structure. ©2008 Martin Macaš. Used with permission.

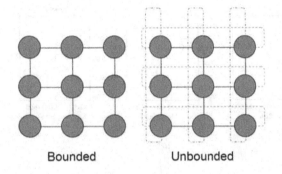

Figure 8. The influence of the topology on the final fitness value for experimental set 2. (There has been no difference for experimental set 1.). ©2008 Martin Macaš. Used with permission.

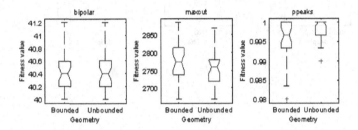

Another thing connected with the spatial structure of the society is the size of the lattice – the map size. For all experiments, we used 100 individuals. There are however different possibilities, how to organize these individuals into a rectangular grid. We tested this aspect by using three possible settings of map proportions – 10x10, 5x20 and 4x25 individuals. It can be seen from figure 9 that for all experiments, the 10x10 map is at least slightly better than the others and the difference is significant for the Maxcut problem of lower dimension (180). We can thus recommend the use of the square lattices.

Neighborhood – Type and Size

Each individual in the SITO algorithm computes the two social impacts from a predefined neighborhood. The main motivation for using a limited neighborhood is the limited computational capacity. Here, we will experimentally prove that there is also a second reason – the limited neighborhood also leads to significantly better optimization result. The figure 10 gives us the proof. Three different sizes neighborhood radius were tested – 1, 2 and 4. For Moore neighborhood, these settings correspond to 8, 24 and 48 neighbors respectively. The sums in equation 4 are computed through all neighbors and thus a big neighborhood leads to much higher computational requirements. From the figure 10, we can see that for all experiments, the widest neighborhood led to much worst results. A possible explanation is that information from many neighbors may include conflicts since the different neighbors could have found different regions of the search space. In the case of a wide neighborhood, the information is averaged through many individuals and it leads to retardation of the optimization process. In figure 10, especially 10b, we can see also a difference between the results for neighborhood radius 1 and 2. The

Figure 9. The influence of map proportions on the final fitness value for (a) experimental set 1, (b) experimental set 2. The bounded topology has been used. ©2008 Martin Macaš. Used with permission.

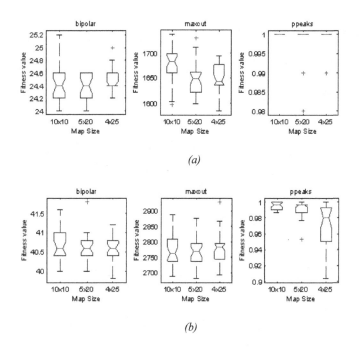

(a)

(b)

latter setting seems better, for experimental set 2 even significantly better than the former one. Thus, it looks suitable to set the neighborhood radius to 2.

It is evident that the definition of neighborhood plays very important role in the SITO algorithm. This fact is also supported by following experiments with two different types of neighborhood – Von Neumann and Moore (Figure 11).

Figure 12 shows the box plots for all results. It is evident that better results were obtained for Von Neumann neighborhood in all experiments. The difference is even higher for higher dimension (figure 12b) where for Max-cut and Ppeaks problems it is significant. These results are obtained for the default neighborhood radius, which was 1. Figure 13 shows the temporal behavior of best-so-far fitness value (averaged over 30 runs). Obviously, the information transfer and propagation is less intensive in the case of Von Neumann neighborhood, which leads to slower convergence and probably less sensitivity on local optima. We can summarize that the definition of the neighborhood significantly influence the SITO's behavior and optimization result.

Now, we can conclude this subsection with a brief summary of suggestions resulting from previous experiments. Although it is important to introduce a randomness using non-zero value of κ, its optimal value depends on particular optimization task to be solved. However, experiments included in previous studies shown that it is practical to set κ linearly decreasing from a value between 0.02 and 0.15 and a value close to 0. On the other hand, the value of self confidence δ should increase over time and its final value should reach more than 5. On the basis of our experimental results, we can recommend the square shape of the society. However there is no preference for bounded/unbounded geometry. Its optimal setting seems to be task-dependent. Finally, the optimization result is highly influenced by particular definition of neighborhood. We suggest the use of Von-Neumann neighborhood with radius 1 or 2.

Figure 10. The influence of neighborhood radius on the final fitness value for (a) experimental set 1, (b) experimental set 2. The Moore neighborhood was used. ©2008 Martin Macaš. Used with permission.

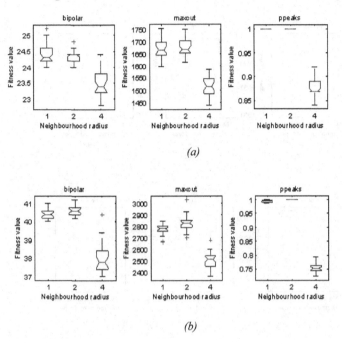

(a)

(b)

Figure 11. Two types of neighborhood with radius 1, lines represent neighborhood relation. ©2008 Martin Macaš. Used with permission.

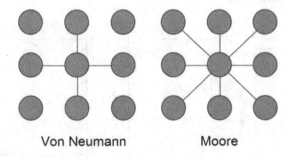

SITO and Other Methods

SITO algorithm is social-psychology-inspired, stochastic and population based method intended for optimization of generally non-linear, multimodal and analytically non-optimizable binary functions. It is therefore apparent, that it will share many properties with other optimization techniques of such type. It is important to consider a similarity with a family of evolutionary computation techniques. The main operators involved in these techniques are selection, crossover and mutation. Is it possible to find any analogy to these operators in SITO? It is obvious that in the original version, the individuals are not selected and all of them survive into the next generation. However, each individual has its own strength, which weights its relative importance. This can be understood as a special type of selection. If we understand the crossover of two individual in evolutionary techniques as a form

Figure 12. The influence of neighborhood type on the final fitness value for (a) experimental set 1, (b) experimental set 2. The neighborhood with radius 1 was used. ©2008 Martin Macaš. Used with permission.

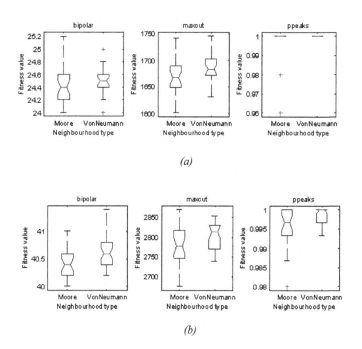

(a)

(b)

Figure 13. The neighborhood type on the temporal evolution of average best-so-far fitness for experimental set 1. ©2008 Martin Macaš. Used with permission.

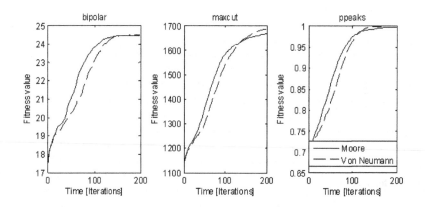

of influential process, this influence is reciprocal and each individual influence the other one at the same rate (simple change of chromosome substring). This is not true in SITO, where the fitter individual has higher impact on the worse one. Finally, the mutation is the only operator, which takes place in the same manner for both the evolutionary techniques and the SITO algorithm. In this point of view, the parameter k has the same function as the mutation rate. One interesting aspect of SITO is that the society of individuals is spatially distributed. This phenomenon is typical in spatial co-evolution (Williams, 2005), where the populations are spatially embedded on a predefined lattice and selection is performed locally in space – each individual competes for survival against the surrounding individuals in its neighborhood.

Another population based techniques, which should be mentioned here is the binary particle swarm optimization (bPSO) (Kennedy, 1997). In contrast to the continuous particle swarm optimization inspired by movement of swarms of creatures, the bPSO has quite different real-world analogy - a model of binary decision, where individuals are represented by the decision vector and the goal is to find an optimal binary pattern of some choices. The decision vector can be understood as the set of binary attitudes and the main mechanism propelling the optimization is the social impact of the individuals in the society. The socio-cognitive metaphor forms the main common element shared by particle swarms and SITO algorithm (Kennedy, 2001).

Actually, in the original PSO, each individual is influenced by its individual experience (its own best-so-far position) and its social knowledge (position reached by its best neighbor). If one wants to find a parallel in SITO algorithm, the individuals do not memorize their best-so-far solution, however, there is rich social knowledge, which comes from all members of the neighborhood. In fully-informed PSO (Kennedy, 2003), each individual uses information drawn from all neighbors, not just the best one. Obviously there are many other methods similar to SITO algorithm. An example of comparison of SITO with basic versions of genetic algorithm and binary PSO can be seen in Table 3. The detail description of results and algorithms can be found in Macaš (2007). Methods have been compared on 6 problems – three deceptive problems (namely Mühlenbein's order-5 problem (Mühlenbein, 1999), Goldberg's order-3 problem (Goldberg, 1990), bipolar order-6 problem (Goldberg, 1993)) and three binary encoded continuous functions from the DeJong test suit (De Jong, 1975) - Rastgrigrin, Griewank and Rosenbrock. 2 instances for each problem differing in dimension were used.

For all experiments, 30 runs were launched. The population size was the same for all methods and problems and was set to 100 individuals. The maximum number of iterations was 800. The results have been compared using final fitness values obtained for 30 runs. Furthermore, two-sample t-test (significance level 0.05) was used to investigate the significance of difference between the methods. The Table 3 describes the results of the statistical testing (using the two-tailed t-test) of the differences between particular results. The third column describes the comparison of GA and SITO and the fourth column describes the comparison of bPSO and SITO. Thus, the SITO was compared to both remaining methods. The "0" means, that there is no significant difference between the two results. The "+" says that SITO performed significantly better than the corresponding method (GA or bPSO) and the "-" says that SITO was significantly worse then the other method.

Some interesting conclusions can be drawn from these results. One can see that the SITO performed significantly better than GA in 7 of 11 tests and just in one test it was significantly worse. On the other hand, the SITO outperformed the bPSO algorithm just in two tests and was worse than the bPSO in 3 cases. One can observe quite good results obtained for deceptive problems that are treated as difficult for GA. Furthermore, there is no apparent correlation between dimensionality of the binary search space and the SITO's performance. Parameters of the two methods (GA, bPSO) were not tuned before experiments and settings recommended in literature were used. However, no tuning was performed for SITO too. The parameters were set empirically by following some preliminary experiments. Thus, the SITO optimizer seems to be comparable to the other examined methods.

Looking for Theory

Much work on nature inspired and population based algorithms aimed on experimental studies deducing some characteristics of a particular method from experimental observations. It is however important to be able to confront the experimental results with a theory. The lack of a well established theory is main problem of majority of nature-inspired, population based and stochastic optimization techniques. Most studies simply take some metaphors from nature and apply it directly. The theory, however, could help us to inspect and predict an influence

Table 3. Results of statistical t-test (significance level 0.05). "0" means no significant difference, "+" or "-" denotes better or worse performance of SITO, respectively

Function	D	SITO vs. GA	SITO vs. bPSO
Mühlenbein5	30	0	0
Mühlenbein5	150	+	+
Goldberg3	30	+	-
Goldberg3	150	+	0
Bipolar6	90	+	0
Bipolar6	300	0	0
Rastrigrin	34	+	0
Rastrigrin	170	0	-
Griewank	34	+	0
Griewank	170	-	-
Rosenbrock	40	+	+
Rosenbrock	200	0	0

of method's parameters and thus find a proper parameter setting. Formal proof of method's convergence can also help us to present and propagate the SITO. Thus, the need for a good theory is not just on account of scientific manners, nothing is more practical than a good theory.

The SITO algorithm is inspired and based on the model of social influence. It can be thus very practical to look for some formal theoretical approaches to the area of social psychology. An early example can be French's and Raven's attempt for an early formalization of the social influence (French, 1956). One of very promising theoretical approaches could be taken from the attempts for theoretical description of social simulation using statistical physic (Lewenstein, 1992). Statistical physics, particcularly the statistical mechanics allows to predict macro-level phenomena resulting from micro-level rules. It is commonly used for formal description of physical systems, (e.g. random ferromagnets that are composed of various species of magnetically active atoms). Lewenstein (1992) formulated the statistical mechanics of a class of models of cellular automata that describe the dynamics of social impact and explained qualitatively the results obtained in numerical simulations. This approach could be used in SITO algorithm, at least for formal description of its dynamics.

Another interesting approach is the concept of sociodynamics (Weidlich, 2002), a general concept, which allows setting up mathematical models for stochastic and quasi-deterministic dynamic processes in social systems. Its basis is the master equation for the probability distribution over macrovariables in the society.

CONCLUSION

In this chapter, we have presented the Social Impact Theory based Optimizer – novel binary optimization algorithm inspired by social psychology. Some precursors from different research area were first summarized and on the basis of these precursors, the SITO algorithm was explained. Further, the most important aspects of the algorithm were examined using various experiments. From the results, some recommendations were extracted, giving advices how to set the most critical parameters and properties. Next, discussion about connections and differences between SITO algorithm and some other selected methods has been presented and finally, a brief suggestion about formal description of SITO model was outlined. The SITO algorithm is a new model for binary optimization which opens space for new theoretical and practical research. Our results show that the algorithm is not as sensitive on its various settings.

FUTURE RESEARCH DIRECTIONS

The basic SITO algorithm has been already tested and compared to other methods on several problems. Most of them were artificial benchmarks. The SITO is comparable (not statistically better or worse than the others) to the basic version of genetic algorithm and to the binary particle swarm optimizer. However, just one practical application has been implemented – the feature subset selection (Macaš, in press). The results have shown purposeful and successful application of the SITO in the field of dimensionality reduction for pattern classification. However, it could be good to find an application where the benefit of adopting SITO is clear, which is one of most important future challenges.

The SITO algorithm is a novel and immature technique. It has been developed and its first implementation was performed during 2006/2007. The early form of the method is strongly associated with the social simulation of Latané social impact theory. However, there is no special reason why to keep the original form. Thus, many options for changing the original paradigm appear. The modifications can be connected with different aspects of the algorithm, no matter if it will be a modification of the topological structure of the society, different type of the update rule or different fitness-strength mapping. Another important challenge is a transfer of the basic model into the continuous optimization field.

ACKNOWLEDGMENT

This work has been supported by the Ministry of Education, Youth and Sports of the Czech Republic (under project No. MSM6840770012 "Transdisciplinary Biomedical Engineering Research II").

REFERENCES

Ball, P. (2002). The physical modelling of society: A historical perspective. *Physica A, 314,* 1-14.

De Jong, K. A. (1975). *Analysis of behavior of a class of genetic adaptive systems.* Unpublished doctoral dissertation, University of Michigan, Ann Arbor, Michigan.

De Jong, K. A., Potter, M. A., & Spears, W. M. (1997). Using problem generators to explore the effects of epistasis. In T. Bäck (Ed.), *Proceedings of the Seventh International Conference on Genetic Algorithms,* (pp. 338-345). Morgan Kaufmann, San Francisco, CA.

Epstein, J. M., & Axtell, R. (1996). *Growing artificial societies: Social science from the bottom up.* The Brookings Institution/Washington DC, USA: The MIT Press.

French, J. R. P., Jr. (1956). A formal theory of social power. *Psychological Review, 63,* 181-194.

Goldberg, D. E., Deb, K., & Korb, B. (1990). Messy genetic algorithms revisited: Studies in mixed size and scale. *Complex Systems, 4,* 415-444.

Goldberg, D. E., Deb, K., & Horn, J. (1992). Massive multimodality, deception, and genetic algorithms. In *Parallel Problem Solving from Nature, 2,* 37-46.

Jackson, J. M., & Latané, B. (1981). All alone in front of all those people: Stage fright as a function of number and type of co-performers and audience. *Journal of Personality and Social Psychology, 40,* 73-85.

Kennedy, J., & Eberhart, R. C. (1997). A discrete binary version of the particle swarm algorithm. In *Proceedings of the World Multiconference on Systemics, Cybernetics and Informatics.* (pp. 4104-4109).

Kennedy, J., Eberhart, R. C., & Shi, Y. (2001). *Swarm intelligence.* San Francisco: Morgan Kaufmann Publishers.

Kennedy, J., & Mendes, R (2003). Neighborhood topologies in fully-informed and best-of-neighborhood particle swarms. In *Proceedings 2003 IEEE SMC Workshop on Soft Computing in Industrial Application (SMCia03).* Binghamton, NY.

Khuri, S., Bäck, T., & Heitkötter J. (1994). An evolutionary approach to combinatorial optimization problems. In *Proceedings of the 22nd ACM Computer Science Conference* (pp. 66-73). ACM Press: Phoenix, AZ.

Latané, B. (1981a). The psychology of social impact. *American Psychologist, 36,* 343-356.

Latané, B., & Nida, S. (1981b). Ten years of research on group size and helping. *Psychological Bulletin, 89,* 308-324.

Latané, B. (1996). Dynamic social impact: The creation of culture by communication. *Journal of Communication, 4,* 13-25.

Lewenstein, M., Nowak, A., & Latané, B. (1992). Statistical mechanics of social impact. *Physical Review A* 45(2), 763-775.

Macaš, M., & Lhotská, L. (2007). Social impact theory based optimizer. In F. A. e Costa, L. M. Rocha, E. Costa, I. Harvey A. Coutinho (Eds.), *Advances in Artificial Life: LNAI Vol.4648, 9th European Conference on Artificial Life* (pp. 634-644). Springer.

Macaš, M., Lhotská, L., & Křemen, V. (in press). Social impact based approach to feature subset selection. In *International Workshop on Nature Inspired Cooperative Strategies for Optimization,* Studies in Computational Intelligence, Springer.

Mühlenbein, H., Mahnig, T. & Rodrigues, A. O. (1999). Schemata distribution and graphical modes in evolutionary optimization. *Journal of Heuristics, 5.*

Nowak, A., & Szamrej, J., & Latané, B. (1990). From private attitude to public opinion: A dynamic theory of social impact. *Psychological Review, 97* (3), 362-376.

Nowak, A., & Latané, B. (1993). Simulating the emergence of social order from individual behaviour. In N. Gilbert & J. Doran (Eds.), *Simulating Societies: The Computer Simulation of Social phenomena,* London: UCL Press.

Sakoda, J. M. (1971). The checkerboard model of social interaction. *Journal of Mathematical Sociology, 1,* 119-132.

Schelling, T. (1969). Models of segregation. *American Economic Review, 59,* 488-493.

Schnell, R. (1992). Artificial intelligence, computer simulation and theory construction in the social science. In F. Faulbaum (Ed.), *Advances in Statistical Software, 3,* 335-342. Stuttgart.

Da Silva, L. R., & Stauffer, D. (2001). Ising-correlated clusters in the Count-Bouchad stock market model. *Physica A, 294,* 235-238.

Weidlich, W. (2002). *Sociodynamics – a systematic approach to mathematical modelling in the social sciences.* Harwood Academic Publishers.

Williams, N. L., & Mitchell, M. (2005), Investigating the success of spatial coevolutionary learning, In *Proceedings of the 2005 Genetic and Evolutionary Computation Conference, GECCO-2005* (pp.523-530). New York: ACM Press.

ADDITIONAL READING

Bordogna, C. M., & Albano, E. V. (2007). Statistical methods applied to the study of opinion formation models: A brief overview and results of a numerical study of a model based on the social impact theory. *Journal of Physics: Condensed Matter*, 19(6).

Galam, S., & Moscovic, S. (1991). Towards a theory of collective phenomena: Consensus and attitude changes in groups. *European Journal of Social Psychology, 21*, 49-74.

Galam, S. (2006). When humans interact like atoms. In E. White, J. H. Davis (Eds.), *Understanding Group Behvior, 1*, 293-312. Lawrence Erlbaum Ass., New Jersey.

Hegsellman, R., & Flache, A. (1998). Understanding complex social dynamics: A plea for cellular automata based modelling. *Journal of Artificial Societies and Social Simulation, 1*(3).

Kuznetsov, D. V., & Mandel, I. (2006). Statistical physics of media processes: Mediaphysics. *Physica A, 377*, 253-268.

Macaš, M. & Lhotská, L. (2006). *Social Impact and Optimization*. Paper presented at the 2nd European Symposium on Nature-inspired Smart Information Systems, from www.nisis.de.

Schelling, T. (1971). Dynamic models of segregation. *Journal of Mathematical Sociology, 1*, 143-186.

Schelling, T. (1978). *Micromotives and macrobehavior*. New York: Norton.

Stauffer, D. (2004). Introduction to statistical physics outside physics. *Physica A, 336*, 1.

Weidlich, W. (1991). Physics and social science - the approach of synergetics. *Phys Rep, 204*, 1-163.

Wolfram, S. (1984). Universality and complexity in cellular automata. *Physica D, 10,* 1-35.

Wolfram, S. (1986). Theory and applications of cellular automata. *World Scientific:* Singapure.

Xie, X. F., & Liu, J. (2005). A compact multiagent system based on autonomy oriented computing. In *IEEE/WIC/ACM International Conference on Intelligent Agent Technology* (pp. 38-44).

KEY TERMS

Neighborhood: The set of cells that are considered to be sources of social influence. The social impact is computed purely from the neighboring cells. In this chapter, von Neumann and Moore neighborhood is considered. The more general neighborhood types can be time dependent or random.

Social Impact: Any of a great variety of changes in physiological states and subjective feelings, motives and emotions, cognitions and beliefs, values and behavior, that occur in an individual, human or animal, as a result of the real, implied, or imagined presence or actions of other individuals.

Social Impact Theory: Formulates a mathematical model concerning how social processes operate at a given point in time. It specifies principles how individuals are affected by the society.

Social Impact Theory Based Optimizer: A binary optimization technique inspired by psychological phenomena, namely the processes of social influence.

Social Psychology: Discipline dealing with formation and changes of human's mentation and personality under the influence of social stimulation. It addresses influence of groups and societies on individual.

Statistical Physics: Deals with general laws of macroscopic systems compound of a large number of particles. A macro-process does not depend on the particular types of the particles, but depends on mean numbers of these particles. In statistical physics, the too complex problem of solving the equations of motion is solved using calculus of probabilities and mathematical statistics.

Topology (Social Topology): Describes the spatial structure of the society. It can be understood as a non-oriented graph structure, where nodes are the cells (on which the individuals are situated) and the edges symbolize the relation of neighborhood.

Chapter XXII
Ethology–Based Approximate Adaptive Learning:
A Near Set Approach

James F. Peters
University of Manitoba, Canada

Shabnam Shahfar
University of Manitoba, Canada

ABSTRACT

The problem considered in this chapter is how to use the observed behavior of organisms as a basis for machine learning. The proposed approach for machine learning combines near sets and ethology. It leads to novel forms of Q-learning algorithm that have practical applications in the controlling the behavior of machines, which learn to adapt to changing environments. Both traditional and new forms of adaptive learning theory and applications are considered in this chapter. A complete framework for an ethology-based approximate adaptive learning is established by using near sets.

INTRODUCTION

The problem considered in this paper is how learning by a machine can adapt its behaviour to changing environmental conditions to achieve a better result. The solution to this problem hearkens back to the work of ethologist Niko Tinbergen (1940, 1942, 1948, 1951, 1953, 1963), starting in the 1940s. Tinbergen (1953b) suggested that the behaviour of swarms of interacting organisms and their environment make swarms be seen as individual. Of course, the insight in Tinbergen's work augurs later by those who were interested in adaptive learning by societies of interacting machines. The work by Tinbergen and Konrad Lorenz (1981) led to the introduction of ethology, a comparative science of behaviour. The basic idea in the proposed approach to adaptive learning is to look behaviour of an organism as episodic and to record observed behaviours ethograms. An ethogram is a tabular representation of observed behaviours. An ethogram is a tabular representation of observed behaviours during an episode. Let s_i, a_i, r_i denote the ith state, action, reward, respectively. Reward r_i results from performing action a_i, where $0 \leq i \leq n$ for some finite, positive integer n. Each episode consists of a finite state-action-reward sequence of the form $s_0 \xrightarrow{a_0, r_0} s_1 \xrightarrow{a_1, r_2} s_2 \cdots$. In this chapter, adaptive learning itself is observed at the individual level as well as at the society level.

Copyright © 2009, IGI Global, distributing in print or electronic forms without written permission of IGI Global is prohibited.

The fundamental of the proposed adaptive learning approach is the notion of perception. It was pointed out by Ewa Orłowska (1982) that an approximation space provides a formal framework for perception. This is especially important in establishing a formal basis what has come to be known as approximate adaptive learning (Lockery and Peters, 2008; Peters 2007d), which is the capstone of a new approach of machine learning based on ethology (Lockery, Peters 2007), which was based on earlier work on ethology and machine learning (see Peters 2005b; Peters, Henry, Ramanna, 2005a; Peters and Henry, 2005). It should also be noted that the solution to the ethology-based machine learning problem has been further aided by the recent introduction of near sets (see Peters 2007a, 2007b, 2007c, 2006e; Peters, Skowron, Stepaniuk 2006, 2007) and its applications (Anwar, Patnaik, 2008; Henry and Peters, 2007; Lockery and Peters 2007). A *near set* is a collection of objects that have matching descriptions to some degree. One set X is considered *near* another set X' in the case where there is at least one x in X with a description that matches the description of x' in X' (Peters, 2008a; Peters, 2008b; Peters and Wasilewski, 2008; Peters, 2007b, 2007e). Near sets can be looked as an extension of the original model for rough sets introduced by Zdzislaw Pawlak (1981) during the early 1980s.

The near set approach, the approximation of sets of behaviours of organisms, provides a basis for a biologically-inspired approach for approximate adaptive learning. Organism behaviour descriptions are stored in a form of short term memory called ethogram. An ethogram is a set of comprehensive descriptions of the characteristic behaviour patterns of a species. In this chapter, it focuses on learning by organisms such as E coli bacteria, silk moths, ants and tropical fish called glowlight tetra. Both the basic theory and sample applications of ethology-based study of approximate adaptive forms of machine learning are introduced. It introduces short-term and long-term memory models for biologically-inspired adaptive learning that is quite different from reinforcement learning (Sutton and Barto, 1998). In the observed behaviour of biological organisms, learning produces a durable modification of behaviour in response to information (e.g., intensity of perfume emitted by a female silk moth that leads to changing flight path of a male silk moth) acquired by an organism (Alcock, 1995). Hence, the term *adaptive* rather than *reinforcement* has been suggested to describe biologically-inspired learning by machines (Labella, 2007). The proposed approach of machine learning has many practical applications, such as target tracking by monocular vision systems, learning to recognize objects in sequences of images, and in studies of how learning by organisms can beneficially influence their environment.

BACKGROUND

Adaptive Behaviour by Machines

The proposed adaptive learning approach is a variant of the usual approach of adaptive behaviour in robotic systems, where the control of robotic behaviour relies on sensor values as a means of adapting to 'perceived' situations to accomplish a system goal. For example, in Salter (2006), a robot adapts its behaviour depending on the type of motion its sensors record, e.g., a sensor-equipped ball that relies on its sensors to determine if it is spinning, being carried, not moving to verbalize its perceived situation with pre-recorded spoken messages to attract the attention of nearby humans, such as handicapped children. An approach for adaptive systems behaviour has also been proposed by Labella (2007), where reinforcement learning by groups of robots (artificial swarms) cooperating to pick up and move sticks is aided proximity sensors. Depending on the elevation of a stick, a robot determines if a stick is being help up another robot or not. These forms of adaptive learning differ from the proposed approach inasmuch as robot behaviour itself is observed, not just robot sensor values and resulted measurements, such as the Euclidean distances between sensed objects. In addition, the proposed approach differs from recent work on adaptive learning by groups of robots (see, e.g., Labella (2007)) in its use of a form of short-term memory provided by ethograms to influence action selection. The proposed approach is closer to what is known as *social learning* found in animals (see, e.g., Braithwaite (2006); Heyes (1994)), where an animal acquires a new behaviour by watching or interacting with other animals. In this way, an animal (or a robot) quickly adapts locally to its environment by observing the successes and failures of others without incurring the costs often associated with trial-and-error learning. The correspondence between learning by animals and ethology-based adaptive learning by machines has been investigated by Peters, Henry and Gunderson (2007).

Behaviour Description

Objects are known by their descriptions. An *object description* is defined by means of a tuple of function values $\phi(x)$ associated with an object $x \in X$ (see (1)). The important thing to notice is the choice of functions $\varphi i \in B$ used τo describe an object of interest. Assume that $B \subseteq \Im$ is a given set of functions representing features of sample objects $X \subseteq O$. Let $\phi\iota \in B$, where $\phi_i : O \rightarrow \Re$. In combination, the functions representing object features provide a basis for an *object description* $\phi : O \rightarrow \Re^L$, a vector containing measurements (returned values) associated with each functional value $\phi\iota(x)$ in (1), where the description length $|\phi| = L$.

Object Description : $\phi(\xi) = (\phi 1(\xi), \phi 2(\xi), \ldots, \phi\iota(\xi), \ldots, \phi\wedge(\xi))$. 　　　　　(1)

The intuition underlying a description $\varphi(x)$ is a recording of measurements from sensors, where each sensor is modeled by a function $\phi\iota$. By way of illustration, consider the behavior of an organism (living object) represented by a tuple

$(s, a, r, V(s), \ldots)$,

where $s, a, r, V(s)$ denote organism functions representing state, action, reward for an action, and value of state, respectively. Value of state $V(s)$ in state s is the expected value of the return R from a sequence of actions. Let $\gamma \in [0, 1]$ denote the discount rate on actions performed. The return R_t (i.e., *cumulative future discounted rewards*, Watkins (1989), Sutton and Barto (1998)) on actions defined in (2).

$$R_t = \gamma^0 r_{t+1} + \gamma^1 r_{t+2} + \gamma^2 r_{t+3} + \ldots = \sum_{k=0}^{T} \gamma^k r_{t+k+1},$$ 　　　　　(2)

where R_t is summed over the first T rewards, where R_t is assumed to be a random variable. Let $E[R_t]$ denote the expected value of return R_t. The model for R_t in (2) is an example of what has been called *imminence weighting* from Sutton and Barto (1990) and also found in Watkins (1989). That is, there is a tendency to weight immediate rewards more strongly than delayed reinforcements. In the real world, this expected value of the return R cannot be computed, since the probability $Pr(R)$ is not known. Hence, it is common practice to use Monte Carlo methods to estimate $E[R]$ using (3).

$$V(s) \approx \frac{1}{n} \sum_{i=1}^{n} r_i, \lambda = 1,$$ 　　　　　(3)

where r_i is the ith reward for an action belonging to a sequence of actions leading to state s. In combination, tuples of behavior function values form the following description of an object x relative to its observed behavior:

Organism Behaviour : $\varphi(x) = (s(x), a(x), r(x), V(s(x))$.

For example, in Peters (2005b), a set of objects X with observed interesting (i.e., acceptable) behavior is approximated after the set of available sample objects has been granulated using rough set approximation methods. Observed organism behavior is episodic and behavior tuples are stored in a decision table, which is called an ethogram, where each observed behavior is assessed with an acceptability decision[1], i.e., $d(x) = 1$ (acceptable) and $d(x) = 0$ (unacceptable) based on the evaluation of organism behaviour.

Table 1. Near set notation

NEAR SETS AND ADAPTIVE LEARNING

The basic idea in the near set approach to adaptive learning is to compare behaviour descriptions. In general, sets X, Y are considered near each other if the sets contain objects with at least partial matching descriptions. That is, set X is near Y if, and only if there exists $x \in X$, $y \in Y$, $\phi_i \in B$ such that $y \sim_B x$ (Peters, 2007e). For example, let $X, Y \subseteq O$, $X \neq Y$ (i.e., a pair of different images), where $B \subseteq \Phi$ is a set of functions representing features of segmented images. An image segmentation is a partition of an image into its constituent parts. Assume $x/\sim_B \in X/\sim_B$ and $y/\sim_B \in Y/\sim_B$ contain pixel windows with matching descriptions, e.g., matching average grey level of the pixels in each window in $x/\sim_B$ and $y/\sim_B$. The notation

Object recognition problems, especially in machines that learn adaptively, adaptive gaming (*e.g.*, gaming with therapeutic applications), and image processing (*e.g.*, near images in medical imaging), and the problem of the nearness of objects has motivated the introduction of near sets (see, *e.g.*, Peters (2007e). To set up an ethological approach to adaptive learning, put $\mathbb{C} = \{[x]_B \mid x \in O\}$, a set of classes that "represent" adaptive behaviours where x is an object with a behavioural description constructed using values of probe functions in B. Let D denote a decision class, e.g., $D = \{x \mid d(x) = 1\}$, a set of objects with acceptable behaviours. Let v denote the degree of overlap between near sets. Assume that $v = 1$, if $B_*D = \varnothing$. Then define $\overline{v}$ (average near coverage) in (4)

$$\overline{v} = \frac{1}{|\mathbb{C}|} \sum_{[x]_B \in \mathbb{C}} v\big([x]_B, B_*D\big), \text{ where } v = \frac{\left|[x]_B \cap B_*D\right|}{\left|B_*D\right|}. \tag{4}$$

$\overline{v}$ is computed at the end of each behavioural episode using an ethogram that is part of an adaptive learning life cycle. From (4), it is possible to design various families of adaptive learning algorithms (see, *e.g.*, Patnaik, Peters, and Anwar (2008); Lockery and Peters (2008); Peters (2008b); Peters (2007a, 2007d), Peters and Henry (2006), Peters, Henry and Gunderson (2007)).

Nearness Approximation Space

During every the episode in a behavioural life cycle, a highly specialized approximation space is constructed (see Fig. 1). Each approximation space provides a framework for perception about the efficacy of chosen actions during a behavioural episode. This approach to "perceiving" episodic behaviour stems from an observation by Ewa Orłowska (1982), i.e., an approximation space is the formal counterpart of perception or observation. The important thing to notice about this is that perception is viewed on the level of classes of objects, not on the level of individual objects. This is the secret underlying the a near set approach to adaptive learning and other applications of near sets already mentioned.

A nearness approximation space is an extension of the original approximation space introduced by Zdzislaw Pawlak (1981a) during the early 1980s as part of rough set theory (see Pawlak and Skowron, 2007a, 2007b,

Figure 1. Derivation of an approximation space. ©2008 James F. Peters. Used with permission.

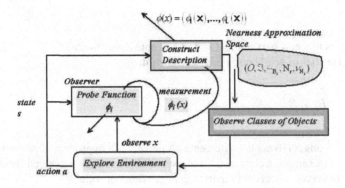

2007c). The original generalized approximation space model (Skowron and Stepaniuk, 1995) has recently been extended as a result of recent work on the nearness of objects (see, e.g., Peters, J.F. , Skowron, A., Stepaniuk, J. (2006, 2007), Peters, (2007e)). A nearness approximation space (NAS) is a tuple given in (5).

$$NAS = \left(O, \Im, \sim_{B_r}, N_r, v_{N_r} \right), \tag{5}$$

where NAS is defined with a set of perceived objects O, set of probe functions $\Im$ representing object features, indiscernibility relation $\sim_{B_r}$ defined relative to $B_r \subseteq B \subseteq \Im$, collection of partitions (families of neighbourhoods) $N_r(B)$, and neighbourhood overlap function v_{N_r}. This form of an approximation space stems from earlier work on approximation (see, e.g., Pawlak 1981, Orlowska 1982, Stepaniuk 1998, Polkowski, 2002, Skowron and Stepaniuk, 2995, Skowron, Swiniarski and Synak, 2005). The relation $\sim_B$ is the usual indiscernibility relation specialized relative to $B_r \subseteq B$. The subscript r denotes the cardinality of the subset B_r, where we consider

$$\binom{|B|}{r},$$

i.e., |B| functions $\phi_i \in \Im$ taken r at a time to define the relation $\sim_{B_r}$, where $\sim_{B_r} = \{(x, y) \mid f(x) = f(y) \ \forall \ f \in B, r = |B|\}$.

This relation defines a partition of O into non-empty, pairwise disjoint subsets that are equivalence classes denoted by $[x]_{B_r}$ and defined in (6).

$$[x]_{B_r} = \left\{ y \in O \mid x \sim_{B_r} y \right\}. \tag{6}$$

The partition defined by $\sim_{B_r}$ forms a new set, namely, the quotient set $O/\sim_{B_r}$ defined in (7).

$$O/\sim_{B_r} = \left\{ [x]_{B_r} \mid x \in O \right\}. \tag{7}$$

Every choice of B_r leads to a new partition of O. Let ξ denote a partition in $O/\sim_{B_r}$. Next, define a collection of partitions $N_r(B)$ (families of neighbourhoods) as shown in (8).

$$N_r(B) = \left\{ \zeta_{B_r} \in O/\sim_{B_r} \mid B_r \in B \right\}. \tag{8}$$

A family of neighbourhoods $N_r(B)$ contains percepts. A percept is a byproduct of perception, i.e., something that has been observed. For example, a class in ζ_{B_r} represents what has been perceived about objects belonging to a neighbourhood, i.e., observed objects with matching probe function values.

Approximation Space-Based, Adaptive Learning Rate

A fairly detailed model for the construction of approximation space at the end of each episode during the life cycle of a machine that learns adaptively is shown in Fig. 2. A detailed example of how an approximation space is extracted from an ethogram is given in this section. It focuses on the production of the terms (feature values for the behaviour of the sample objects $x_1, ..., x_n$, classes $[x]_i$, B, perceptual judgements, estimated coverage values v_i, and average cover $\overline{v}_i$). The process starts with the construction of an ethogram (tabular record of a machine's own observed behaviours). Table 2 is an example of a specialized form of ethogram. Following Tinbergen (1963), an ethogram reflects what we have observed about the behaviour of an organism, namely, actions, proximate causes of actions, ontogeny (origin of a behaviour), and evolution (changes in observed behaviours over very short periods of time).

In this study, it focuses on the construction behaviour observation tables (*i.e,* ethograms) that make it possible for us to trace 3 of the things of interest to ethologists, namely, actions and rewards (column 2 in Table 2) proximate causes of actions, survival value of a behaviour (value of state V(s) and decision d), and ontogeny (knowledge gained in the form of approximation spaces from the study of episodic behaviour from a single ethogram). The evolution of behaviour can be gleaned from a study of a sequence of ethograms.

We are interested in the classes that correspond to a selected action. In Table 2, notice that the set S = {0, 1} represents behaviour states, A = {h, i, j} represents behaviour actions, where A(0) = {h, i} and A(1) = {i, j}. Then define B_a to be the set of blocks corresponding to a particular action a as shown in (9).

Figure 2. Basic, ethology-based, adaptive learning cycle. ©2008 James F. Peters. Used with permission.

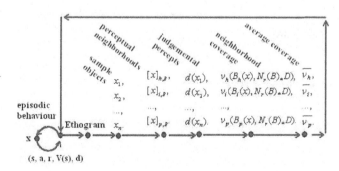

Table 2. Sample ethogram

xi	s	a	V(s)	r	d
x0	0	h	0.1	0.75	1
x1	0	h	0.1	0.75	0
x2	1	i	0.05	0.1	0
x3	1	j	0.056	0.1	1
x4	0	h	0.03	0.75	1
x5	0	i	0.02	0.75	0
x6	1	i	0.01	0.9	1
x7	1	j	0.025	0.9	0

$$B_a = \left\{ [x]_{j,B} \mid j = a, x \in O \right\}. \tag{9}$$

Then we can specialize the measure of overlap in (4) relative to action a as shown in (10).

$$\overline{v}_a = \frac{1}{|\mathbb{C}_a|} \sum_{[x]_{j,B} \in \mathbb{C}_a} v\left([x]_{j,B}, B_*D\right) \; where \; v = \frac{\left| [x]_{j,B} \cap B_*D \right|}{|B_*D|}. \tag{10}$$

From Table 2, we can construct an approximation space, starting with the classes in the partition of X.

$[x_0]_B = \{x_0, x_1\}, [x_2]_B = \{x_2\}, [x_3]_B = \{x_3\}, [x_4]_B = \{x_4\}, [x_5]_B = \{x_5\}, [x_6]_B = \{x_6\},$
$[x_7]_B = \{x_7\},$

The lower approximation is $B_*D = \{ x_3, x_4, x_6 \}$, the overlap measurements are then computed as follows:

$$v([x_0]_B, B_*D) = 0, \quad v([x_2]_B, B_*D) = 0, \quad v([x_3]_B, B_*D) = \frac{1}{3}, \quad v([x_4]_B, B_*D) = \frac{1}{3},$$

$$v([x_5]_B, B_*D) = 0, \quad v([x_6]_B, B_*D) = \frac{1}{3}, \quad v([x_7]_B, B_*D) = 0.$$

Then we can compute the degree of overlap $\overline{v}_a$ for each action a from Table 2 as follows:

$$B_h = \left\{ [x_0]_{h,B}, [x_4]_{h,B} \right\}, \overline{v}_h = \left(0 + \frac{1}{3} \right) \cdot \frac{1}{2} = \frac{1}{6}, \qquad B_i = \left\{ [x_2]_{i,B}, [x_5]_{i,B}, [x_6]_{i,B} \right\}, \overline{v}_i = \left(0 + 0 + \frac{1}{3} \right) \cdot \frac{1}{3} = \frac{1}{9},$$

$$B_j = \left\{ [x_3]_{j,B}, [x_7]_{j,B} \right\}, \overline{v}_j = \left(\frac{1}{3} + 0 \right) \cdot \frac{1}{2} = \frac{1}{6}.$$

The averages $\overline{v}_h$, $\overline{v}_i$, $\overline{v}_j$ provide a basis for estimating an adaptive learning rate during an episode in the life cycle of a machine or an organism that learns.

Value of State and Watkins-Selfridge Adaptive Control Mechanism

Recall from (3) that the value of state V(s) is approximated using the average reward During approximate adaptive learning, an action policy π(s) maps state s to an action a relative to an optimal (greedy) value of V(s). The value of state V(s) is defined using average $\overline{v}_a$ as shown in (11) .

$$V(s) \leftarrow V(s) + \overline{v}_a \cdot \left[r + \max_{a \in A(s)} \{V(s') = V(s)\} \right],$$ (11)

where *A(s)* denotes the set of possible actions that can be performed state s and s' denotes the next state as a result of performing action a. The value of state V(s) makes it possible to implement the Selfridge-Watkins approach to learning with delayed rewards in Selfridge (1984) and Watkins (1989, 1992). That is, an episode continues as long as (12) holds true.

V(s) ≤ V(s'), Selfridge-Watkins run-and-twiddle adaptive control mechanism (12)

Whenever V(s) > V(s'), an episode ends. At the end of each episode, a new approximation space is constructed and a value of $\overline{v}_a$ is derived for each action a before beginning a new episode.

Before we begin using $\overline{v}_a$ in approximate adaptive learning, we first consider a simplified model for adaptive learning that mimics familiar behaviour of biological organisms. In nature, the stopping mechanism provided by (12) is what Selfridge calls "run-and-twiddle" (i.e., adjust a failing action strategy in an attempt to achieve a better result). This approach to adaptive learning leads to Alg. 1.

The while-loop in Alg. 1 implements the Selfridge-Watkins adaptive control strategy, stopping an episode as soon as V(s) in state s exceeds V(s') in the next state s'. Notice, however, that Alg. 1 does not implement the ethogram-form of adaptive learning. The intent given in Alg. 1 is to establish a basis for comparing more advance, ethology-based algorithms with a more standard model for adaptive learning with delayed rewards.

Notice that Alg. 1 implements what is known as an ε-soft policy. Let ε denote the probability that an action a will be chosen. Let a* denote the action that is most likely to produce the highest reward. Policy π(s, a) is ε-soft stochastic policy used to select an action a in state s and is defined in (13).

Algorithm 1: Adaptive Learning Method

```
Input  : States s ∈ S, Actions a ∈ A(s) , V(s)
Output: Policy π(s, a)
while True do
    Begin episode;
    Initialize policy π(s, a), s, V(s) ⟵ 0;
    episode = true;
    Estimate V(s') = E[R_a] for all a in state s;
    while (V(s) ≤ V(s')) do
        Take action a, observe r(t) signal;
        Choose new a from new s using π(s, a);
        Estimate V(s), V(s');
        if (V(s) > V(s') for all a) then
        |   episode = false;
        else
        |   episode continues;
        end
    end
end
```

$$\pi(s,a) = \begin{cases} 1-\varepsilon+\dfrac{\varepsilon}{|A(s)|}, & \text{if } a=a^*, \\ \dfrac{\varepsilon}{|A(s)|}, & \text{otherwise.} \end{cases}$$

(13)

The policy π is deterministic in the case where $\varepsilon = 0$ and $a = a^*$. Let policy $\pi(s)$ denote an action policy that selects the same action a in a given state s. The ε-soft policy $\pi(s, a)$ implemented in Alg. 1.

Ethology vs. Near Ethology

Traditionally, ethology focuses on the observation of the behaviour of animals. The methodology for tabulating observations is fairly standard. An ethogram is a tabular representation of observations of various features of animal behaviour. In the context of a near set approach to adaptive learning by a machine, ethograms are also used. However, the focus shifts from observing the behaviour of other machines to observe the efficacy of actions by the machine performing the actions. In addition, the features of interest in observing a machine's own behaviour are inspired by Tinbergen's 4 whys proposed 40 years ago (Tinbergen, 1963). Each why is a question to be answered during the observation of animal behaviour. For conciseness, let *beh, envir, tab* denote behaviour, environment, ethogram, respectively. A comparison of the 4 whys and the features that have been used in what is known as near ethology (NE) is given in Table 3.

For an ethologist, the study of causation focuses on preceding events that be shown to contribute the occurrence of a *beh* and survival value of an organism (Tinbergen, 1963). This matches the intuition in near ethology, namely, that use of value of state

$$V(s) \approx \frac{1}{n}\sum_{i=1}^{n} r_i$$

Table 3. Tinbergen's four whys and features used in near ethology

Why	Explanation	NE Feature	NE Explanation
causation	causal analysis based on *beh* patterns, complexity of *beh*, influence of internal factors on *beh*.	action *a*, reward *r*	action performed, r = signal from envir
survival value	actions that lead to survival of an organism	value of state V(s)	V(s) = expected return on *beh*, approximated as average *r*
ontogeny	origin of development of an individual	ethogram tab	record of episodic *beh*
evolution	study of convergence of episodic beh	*tab* sequence	record of sequence of episodes

(i.e., approximating the expected return used to define value of state s using a Monte Carlo method) as a basis for evaluating the activity that has led to the current state. Each action performed leads to a new state during the life cycle of a machine that learns to adapt and survive in its changing environment. It is also fairly obvious that the reward signal from the environment (namely, *r*) will influence current and future *beh* of a machine that relies on trial-and-error (exploration) and choice of high-yield actions (exploitation) during its lifetime. The meaning of survival value of a *beh* in the context of adaptable machines is quite different from the survival value of *beh* in biological organisms. That is, survival value of a *beh* for a machine is measured relative to the ability of a machine to accomplish its system goals, e.g., target tracking, navigating, recognizing specific classes of objects. The designer of an adaptive system will probably interrupt and redesign parts of a machine in the case where a machine fails to adapt and accomplish its system goals in a changing environment. In the context of NE, ontogeny (origin of a behaviour) and evolution of a *beh* can be discovered by using traditional data mining methods on ethograms generated during a succession of episodes in the life cycle of an adapting machine.

ADAPTIVE LEARNING

1. Issues, Controversies, Problems Associated with Adaptive Learning

Adaptive learning by an intelligent system is associated with the availability of sufficient energy (power source) to perform required actions, survival value of a chosen behaviour (sufficient expected value of a return). This is perhaps the most nettlesome problem in the design of any machine that functions and learns in a hostile environment. A significant part of the design of such a machine must include methods for sustaining adequate energy levels to perform required actions. For example, this is a serious issue for robotic devices that must function in environments such as Antarctica, where there is a six month period of darkness each year (Antarctica, 2008; Lansing,1959). During the 6 month, 24 hour nighttime period in Antarctica, it is necessary to rely on some form of fossil fuel instead of solar panels to recharge batteries. The line-crawling robotic system called ALiCE II (see, e.g., Lockery and Peters, 2007; Lockery, 2007) described in this chapter relies on solar panels to recharge its batteries. The acronym ALiCE stands for Autonomous Line Crawling Equipment. ALiCE II has been designed to operate in a cold climate, e.g., winter day time temperatures can reach -40 oC, if there is any wind. Since ALiCE II functions mainly as an inspector of electric power transmission equipment while suspended an average of 20 m above the ground, it ordinarily lives in a very hostile environment. Depending on the season and temperature, the effective operating range for ALiCE II batteries can be as short as 3 hours. This means that ALiCE II must position itself so that it can absorb solar radiation whenever the charge on its batteries approaches a preset threshold. Bots able to initiate exploratory as well as exploitive actions in a synchronous manner in response to changes in their environment are more likely to survive.

In addition to the survival value of a behaviour, another issue that underlies adaptive learning is proximate cause of a behaviour (*e.g.*, policy, action-reward). The term proximate is understood to mean close in time. In adaptive learning by intelligent machines, the focus is on near-term stimuli observed over short periods of time. Periods of time are partitioned into episodes. Typically, an organism continues what is doing ("running") as long as the return for a selected sequence of actions is sufficiently high. Whenever the return drops below some threshold, an organism tends to twiddle (deciding what to do next), and then starts a new episode that is associated with a new, promising action sequence. This run-and-twiddle phenomenon was observed in the behaviour of organisms such ants and male silk moths (Selfridge, 1984) and was formalized relative to value-of-state by Watkins (1989). It has been found that this form of biologically-inspired learning carries over in the types of adaptive learning reported in this chapter. It leads to very promising results both in simulations of swarm intelligence as well as in embedded systems that learn (see, e.g., Peters, J.F., Henry, C, 2005; Peters, J.F., Henry, C., 2006; Peters, Henry, Gunderson, 2007). One of the principal problems associated with the run-and-twiddle approach to adaptive learning is the formulation of a stochastic policy that can be used in the choice of an effective action in a sequence of states. We illustrate how this can be done in a brief presentation of adaptive incremental reinforcement comparison (see Alg. 4) using average coverage $\bar{v}_a$ for each action as defined in (10).

Another issue in design of robots, which live in colonies and cooperate to survive, is to achieve effective synchronous behaviour (swarming, distributed responsibility) . It is a serious issue. An approach solving this problem has been suggested for robots that couple (attach) and uncouple themselves from each other to navigate over, around, and across obstacles (see, e.g., Nouyan and Dorigo, 2004; Monada et al., 2004). To solve this problem for line-crawling robots that cooperate, the design of each bot includes a mechanism for coupling between bots so that one bot can push or pull another bot around an obstacle (this is basic idea suggested but not shown in detail in Fig. 6).

2. Solutions and Recommendations

Epicycle in Episodic Behaviour

Viewed from the perspective of an episodic life cycle as shown in Fig. 3, each episode resembles an epicycle (small circle that moves around the circumference of a larger circle, which can figuratively viewed as the overall, adaptive learning life cycle).   A life cycle during adaptive learning begins with an episode that continues as long as the approximate value of each state $V(s)$ is greater than or equal to some threshold *th*. At the end of each episode, an ethogram is available.   In the case where $V(s) < th$, the ethogram byproduct of an episode provides the basis for the construction of an approximation space NAS.   The details of the NAS construction are shown in Fig. 2. Each new NAS leads to a new average coverage $\overline{v}_i$ associated with each action *i*. The policy function $\pi(s) = a$ maps state *s* to a new action *a* that ushers in a new episode shown in Fig. 3.

Short-Term Memory Model for Approximate Adaptive Learning Algorithm

In a short-term memory model of episodic, approximate adaptive learning, the value of $\overline{v}_a$ from (10) is derived from an approximation space constructed from an ethogram built during the previous episode and passed to the next episode. This idea leads to Algorithms 2 and 3.
   Alg. 2 is an extension of the basic model for adaptive learning given in Alg. 1. Now an ethogram is assembled during each episode. The Selfridge-Watkins stopping mechanism is at work by terminating each episode as soon

Figure 3. Epicycle model for episodic life cycle. ©2008 James F. Peters. Used with permission.

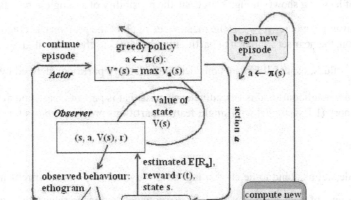

Algorithm 2: Approximate Adaptive Learning Method

Input   : States $s \in S$, Actions $a \in A$, $V(s)$
Output: Policy $\pi(s, a)$
while *True* **do**

    Begin episode;
    Initialize $\bar{\nu}_a$ for each action a, policy $\pi(s, a)$, s, $V(s) \leftarrow 0$;
    Estimate $V(s') = E[R_a]$;
    while $(V(s) \leq V(s'))$ **do**

        Take action a, observe $r(t)$ signal, compute γ ;
        Choose new a from new s using $\pi(s, a)$;
        Estimate $V(s), V(s')$;
        $V(s) \leftarrow V(s) + (\bar{\nu}_a)[r + \gamma max_a V(s') - V(s)]$;
        if $(V(s) > V(s') \, for \, all \, a)$ **then**

            episode = false;
            Compute $\bar{\nu}_a$ for each action a;
            Clear ethogram;

        else

            episode continues;

        end

    end

end

---

as V(s) > V(s'). In Alg. 2, $\bar{\nu}_a$ acts as learning rate. It is a part of the traditional Q-learning model, learning with delayed rewards, which was introduced by Watkins (1989). The computation of $\bar{\nu}_a$ in the *then*-part of if-statement in Alg. 2 is the result of construction an approximation space from the ethogram built during an episode.

Because $\bar{\nu}_a$ is derived from the ethogram obtained at the end of each episode, Alg. 2 is considered a short-term memory model for approximate adaptive learning. Alg. 3 is defined relative to single-feature neighbourhoods that result from a near set approach to approximation of a set, namely, the decision class that is associated with each ethogram constructed during an episode. Either the short-term or the long-term memory model can provide a basis for computing $\bar{\nu}_a$ after each episode. Things change (actually improve), if we the results from all previous ethograms from earlier episodes. Then we obtain a long-term memory model for approximate adaptive learning.

Long-Term Memory Model for Adaptive Learning

The epicyle view of learning shown in Fig. 3 suggests the possibility of saving the results of each episode in the form of a running average, where $avg\bar{\nu}_{a_v}$ is the mean value of all of the previous, average coverage values for an action a. In addition, the near set approach to partitioning becomes useful, since it gives a wide range of choices in deriving $avg\bar{\nu}_{a_v}$ values, especially, if we consider single-feature partitions defined by the relation $\sim_{B_1}$ for r = 1. A single-feature neighbourhood is an equivalence class that is part of a partition defined by $\sim_{B_1}$ for r = 1. The long-term memory (LTM) model with single-feature partitions provides a basis for Alg. 3.

Dynamic Stability

During each episode, actions tend to be chosen that have the greatest promise of returning a high reward. By computing $\bar{\nu}_a$ at the end of each episode, we quickly learn which actions to favour in a succeeding episode. The combination of the Selfridge-Watkins stopping mechanism and the use of $\bar{\nu}_a$ in estimating the value of each state provide a basis for optimal behaviour patterns. In effect, Alg. 2 and Alg. 3 provide a basis for optimal behaviours. These algorithms approximate what is known as dynamic stability as formulated by Yeung and

Algorithm 3: Approx. Adaptive Learning, LTM Model

Input : States $s \in S$, Actions $a \in A$.
Output: Ethogram resulting from Policy $\pi(s,a)$.
Initialize $\overline{v}_{a_v}$ wrt 1-feature nbds, $\pi(s,a), s, V(s) \leftarrow 0$;
while *True* **do**
  Begin episode;
  episode = true;
  Estimate $V(s') = E[R_{a_v}]$;
  while $(V(s) \leq V(s'))$ **do**
    Take action a_v, observe $r(t)$ signal, compute γ ;
    Choose new a_v from new s using $\pi(s,a)$;
    Estimate $V(s), V(s')$;
    Pick action a_v using policy $\pi(s,a)$;
    $V(s) \leftarrow V(s) + (\overline{v}_{a_v})[r + max_a V(s') - V(s)]$;
    if $(V(s) > V(s') for all a)$ **then**
      episode = false;
      Compute new $\overline{v}_{a_v}$ for 1-feature nbds;
      Clear ethogram;
    else
      episode continues;
    end
  end
end

Figure 4. Ecosystem testbed for simplified pattern-based learning. ©2008 James F. Peters. Used with permission.

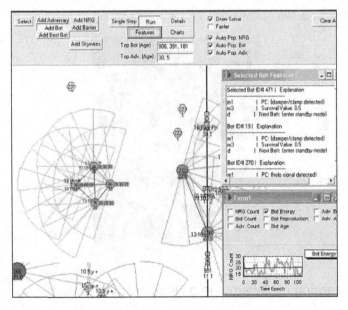

Petrosyan (2006). Dynamic stability results from the enforcement of a stringent condition that ensures that behaviours will proceed along a chosen trajectory as long as the Selfridge-Watkins condition is satisfied.   In other words, a course of action continues as long as long as acceptable value of state V(s) is achieved as a result of performing each action.

Table 4. Ecosystem symbols

Symbol	Meaning	Symbol	Meaning
	Vibration damper.		Bot with ID 45, energy level 110.
	Tower clamp attached to wire.		Swarm (line shows wireless connection between bots).
	Energy source, ID 263, level 8		Energy radiating from bot proximity sensors.

Figure 5. Cooperating Bots. ©2008 James F. Peters. Used with permission.

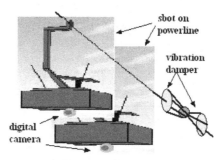

Figure 6. Line-crawling bot details. ©2008 James F. Peters. Used with permission.

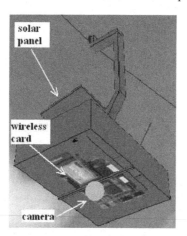

Pattern-Based Learning by Swarms in a Hostile Environment

This section briefly introduces briefly introduces a testbed for pattern-based learning (see Henry (2004)) by swarms of cooperating bots that live in a hostile environment. The bots in the ecosystem represented in Fig. 4 are designed to crawl along the sky wire stretched between electric power transmission lines. An explanation of the symbols in Fig. 4 is given in Table 4.

An idealized, Open-GL view of a line-crawling robot is shown in its environment in Fig. 5 and a closeup of a bot with computer vision system, wireless card, and solar panel is shown in Fig. 6.

The ecosystem testbed shown in Fig. 5 represents the behaviour of groups of bots that operate in a hostile

Figure 7. System performance monitoring window. ©*2008 James F. Peters. Used with permission.*

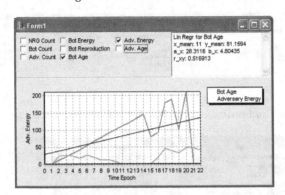

environment (sources of adversity are, for example, severe weather, electromagnetic field strength, lightning strikes). Both varying numbers of adversity and inspection bots can be started by a user. A bot must avoid adversaries, periodically charge its batteries, and carry out its objectives (climbing towers, crawling along power lines, finding a place to park when sunlight is available whenever its batteries are low, responding to wireless messages, archiving and forwarding images showing faulty equipment). In pattern-based mode, the testbed in Fig. 5 generates an ethogram for each swarm (defined by neighbouring bots communicating with each other). This testbed has a Charts button that makes it possible to monitor system performance (see Fig. 8).

Advanced Robot Swarm Testbed

The menu option for an advanced robot swarm testbed (see Henry (2005)) is shown in Fig. 9. Operation of the testbed begins after a learning method is chosen (*e.g.*, the actor critic method choice is approximation space-based (see Peters, J.F., Henry, C. (2006)).

The learning algorithms implemented in this testbed are explained in detail in Peters and Henry, 2005; Peters and Henry, 2006; Peters, Henry, Gunderson, 2007. Except for incremental reinforcement comparison, the testbed learning algorithms are not repeated, here. This testbed generates a ethogram for each group of cooperating bots. Each ethogram is associated with a leader bot chosen by a group of cooperating bots. The average energy level of a swarm member is represented by an integer, e.g., 99.5 for the central swarm in Fig. 10.

Adaptive Incremental Reinforcement Comparison

The main idea behind reinforcement learning is that actions followed by positive rewards should be reinforced, and actions followed by negative rewards should be discouraged. A reinforcement is a stimulus that increases or decreases the likelihood that an action will be selected in the future. The question is how to adapt this idea to machine learning. One solution is to use a standard or reference level, called a *reference reward*, to gauge the value of an action (see, e.g., Sutton and Barto,1998). It is common to use average action rewards as a basis for estimating action values. Let r denote a reward signal from the environment as a result of performing a chosen action a. Also, let $p(s, a)$ denote an action-preference in state s. Using the incremental reinforcement comparison method (IRC), a reference reward (denoted $\bar{r}$). In addition, let α, β denote positive, step-size parameters in the interval [0, 1] that influence the learning rate. Preference and reference reward are computed

using $p(s,a) = p(s,a) + \beta(r - \bar{r})$ and $\bar{r} = \bar{r} + a(r - \bar{r})$, respectively. After each time step, the preference $p(s, a)$ is incremented by the difference (error) between the reward ρ, and the reference reward $\bar{r}$ (a form of incremental comparison in Sutton and Barto (1998)).

Figure 8. Robot swarm testbed menu options. ©2008 James F. Peters. Used with permission.

Figure 9. Sample individual bots and swarmbots. ©2008 James F. Peters. Used with permission.

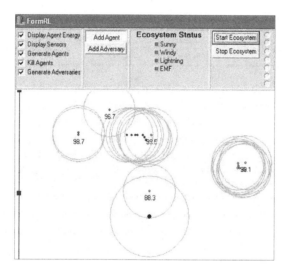

In the conventional IRC method, the reference reward $\bar{r}$ is an average formed incrementally from rewards obtained in all states. An agent's policy is represented by π(s, a) that maps an agent's state s to a probability of selecting an action a. For the IRC learning method, π(s, a) is defined in terms of preferences using the softmax function (Gibbs, 1960) shown in (14).

$$\pi(s,a) = \frac{e^{p(s,a)}}{\sum_{b=1}^{|A(s)|} e^{p(s,b)}}, \tag{14}$$

where *A(s)* denotes the set of actions in state *s*. The next step in designing an adaptive IRC method is to view learning as episodic and extract an ethogram from each episode while an agent is coping with its environment.

Using a near set approach, we define $\bar{r}$ in terms of $\bar{v}_a$ as defined in (10) for each possible action *a* in state *s*. In Alg. 4, value of state V(s) is defined by (3). The conventional form of the IRC method is not repeated here, since that method is essentially the same as the Adaptive Incremental Reinforcement Comparison (AIRC) method given

in Alg. 4 with the exception that $\bar{r}$ is used instead of $\bar{v}_a$ and ethograms are not considered. Sample results for the IRC and AIRC methods are given in Fig. 11. For β = 0.5 and α = 0.1 or α = 0.9, the adaptive form of the IRC method consistently does better than the conventional method. Similar results are obtained for β = 0.9 and α = 0.1 or for β = 0.1 and α = 0.9. However, for the extreme cases where β = 0.1 and α = 0.1 or β = 0.9 and α = 0.9, the conventional IRC method does better than the adaptive method. At this point, it is only possible to conclude that the results obtained for the adaptive form of IRC method are promising.

Algorithm 4: Adaptive Incremental Reinforcement Comparison

Input : States $s \in S$, Actions $a \in A(s)$, Initialized β, threshold th.

Output: Policy $\pi(s,a)$ //where $\pi(s,a)$ is a policy in state s that controls the selection of a particular action in state s.

for $(all \ s \in S, a \in A(s))$ **do**
$\quad$ $p(s,a) \longleftarrow 0;$
$\quad$ $\pi(s,a) \longleftarrow \frac{e^{p(s,a)}}{\sum_{b=1}^{|A(s)|} e^{p(s,b)}};$
end
$\bar{v}_a \longleftarrow 0;$
while *True* **do**
$\quad$ Initialize $s, V(s);$
$\quad$ **while** *(V(s) \geq th)* **do**
$\quad\quad$ Choose a from s using $\pi(s,a);$
$\quad\quad$ Take action a, observe $r, s';$
$\quad\quad$ $p(s,a) \longleftarrow p(s,a) + \beta \left[r - \bar{v}_a\right];$
$\quad\quad$ $\pi(s,a) \longleftarrow \frac{e^{p(s,a)}}{\sum_{b=1}^{|A(s)|} e^{p(s,b)}};$
$\quad\quad$ $s \longleftarrow s';$
$\quad\quad$ estimate $V(s);$
$\quad$ **end**
$\quad$ Extract ethogram table IS_{swarm} ;
$\quad$ Discretize feature values in ethogram IS_{swarm} ;
$\quad$ Compute $\bar{v}_a$ for each a using ethogram IS_{swarm};
end

Figure 10. Sample results for IRC and AIRC methods. ©2008 James F. Peters. Used with permission.

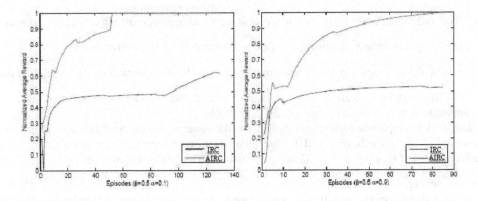

Sample Results from Glowlight Tetra Simulation

This section briefly presents the results of the adaptive learning algorithms used in the simulation of the behaviour of a single species of fish (see Fig. 12), Glowlight tetra (Hemigarmmus erythozonus) reported by Shahfar (2007). The actions are exploring, resting, searching, hiding, suspend (no motion). The states are no hunger, medium hunger, acute hunger. The reward function is defined relative to fish energy level.

In this study, short- and long-term memory models were used to implement Algorithms 1, 2, and 3. With the short-term memory model, average coverage $\overline{v}_a$ is computed in the current episode using the ethogram con-

structed during the previous episode. With the long-term, $\overline{v}_a$ denotes the average coverage for an action a over all of the episodes prior to the current episode (see Fig. 13).

A comparison of a combination of Alg. 3 short-term memory model used to compute average reward for individual fish (see Figures 13 and 14). This is followed by a comparison of a combination of Alg. 3 and long-term memory model to compute average V(s) for individual fish (see Figures 15 and 16). In both cases, it can be

Figure 11. Glowlight tetra. ©2008 James F. Peters. Used with permission.

observed that both average reward and V(s) values are highly volatile in the case where the short term memory model (see Fig. 13) provides a basis for computing $\overline{v}_a$. This volatility sharply diminishes when the long term memory model (see Fig. 13) provides a basis for computing $\overline{v}_a$.

From a swarm intelligence point-of-view, learning on the level of a group of fish of the same species can be viewed in terms of averages. That is, instead of considering average reward and value-of-state for individuals, it helps to consider how well a population as a whole learns. For the short-term memory model for a swarm of organisms, this is done by computing $\overline{v}_a$ relative to the most recent ethogram constructed by each organism (see Fig. 18, where the ethograms from k organisms are used to estimate $\overline{v}_a$ at the swarm level). The design of a long-term memory model in computing $\overline{v}_a$ for a swarm is similar to the short-term memory model for a swarm shown in Fig. 19. It makes sense to consider $\overline{v}_a$ at the swarm level because it has been observed that swarms of organisms appear to behave as an individual (Tinbergen, 1953b).

At the swarm level, a comparison of the use of the short- and long-term memory models in computing average reward is shown in Fig. 19. It can be observed that the initial volatility of swarm average reward values sharply diminishes after a period of time (by episode 42 in Fig. 19) using the long-term swarm memory model as a basis for computing $\overline{v}_a$ for Alg. 3.

Notice that things do not improve over time in the case where the short-term swarm memory model provides a basis for learning by a swarm using Alg. 3. Similarly, it can also be observed that a very high volatility in the fluctuation of average V(s) values as a result of using the short-term swarm memory model as a basis for learning (see Fig. 20). This is not the case for the experimental results of the application of the long-term swarm memory model as a basis for learning by a swarm as shown in Fig. 20. The root-mean-square error (RMSE) results, which are given in Fig. 21, show very RMSE V(s) values from starting to end in the case of the long-term swarm memory model. By contrast, the RMSE values for swarm V(s) are highly volatile for the short-term swarm memory model. These results suggest that the long-term memory model either at the individual organism level or at the swarm level provides an effective means of approximate adaptive learning.

CONCLUSION

This chapter reports recent work on various approaches for adaptive learning mainly inspired by the work by Oliver Selfridge in 1989 and Chris J.C.H. Watkins in 1989. It has been found that the inclusion of a stopping

Figure 12. Short term and long term memory basis for $\overline{v}_a$. ©2008 James F. Peters. Used with permission.

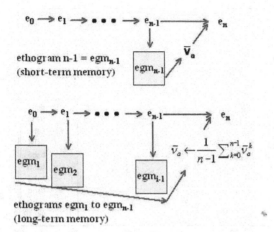

Figure 13. Alg. 3 average reward (Short term memory model). ©2008 James F. Peters. Used with permission.

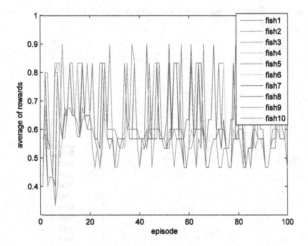

mechanism using value of state V(s) does lead to a form of dynamic stability.   This is the case because the trajectory represented by actions favored during an episode is only maintained as long as the estimated value of the next state is a least as high the value of the current state.   In addition, by estimating the learning rate at the end of each episode, it is possible to adjust the estimated value of state based on experience gained from a previous episode.   In this work, a near set approach has been used in deriving the learning rate from ethograms put together during life cycle episodes. There is considerable interest in both short-term and long-term memory models for approximate adaptive learning.   From our preliminary results, it seems that the short-term memory model provides a more efficacious basis for adaptive learning.

Figure 14. Alg. 3 Average reward (Long term memory model). ©2008 James F. Peters. Used with permission.

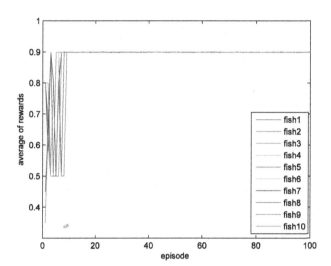

Figure 15. Alg. 3 Average Value-of-State (Short term memory model). ©2008 James F. Peters. Used with permission.

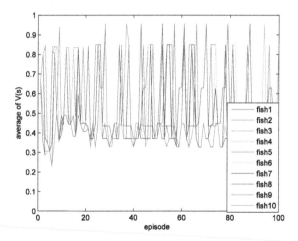

FUTURE RESEARCH DIRECTIONS

Further work concerning a near set approach to adaptive learning will include a study behavioural ecology (see, e.g., Davidson-Hunt, 2003; Davey, 1989; Dieckmann, Law, Metz, 2000; Drayson, 2002; Fiennes, 2002; Holldobler and Wilson, 1990, 1994; Hosler, 2000; Krebs and Davies, 1984; Lansing, 1979; Sloman, Wilson and Balshine, 2006; Tinbergen , 1972).   From the work of Selfridge (1984) and Watkins (1989), it is apparent a better understanding of adaptive learning results from observing the behaviour of biological organisms. An informal view of survival behaviour of calling frogs (Drayson, 2002), migrating birds (Fiennes, 2002) or members of a population no longer able to function (Lansing, 1959) suggests a rationale for retiring adaptive machines that perform some

Figure 16. Alg. 3 Average Value-of-State (Long term memory model). ©2008 James F. Peters. Used with permission.

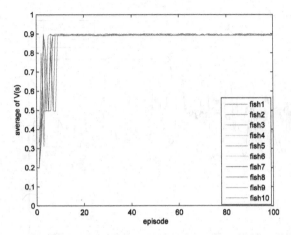

Figure 17. Short term swarm memory model. ©2008 James F. Peters. Used with permission.

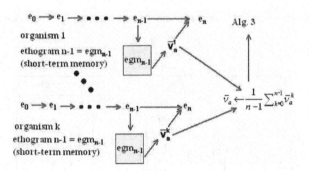

needed service for a limited time and then are no longer needed. Again, for example, visual signals by fish (Sloman, Wilson and Balsine, 2006) or sound and chemical signals by ants (Holldobler and Wilson, 1990, 1994) are part of our current research on communication between members of robot societies. Yet another aspect of our study of ecological systems is the geometry of interactions between organisms (this applies to both plant as well as animal behaviour, Dieckmann, Law and Metz, 2000). This leads to useful models of spatial allocation and separation by competing autonomous, mobile robots. Evidence of the benefits of biologically-inspired adaptive learning can found in a number of studies (see, e.g., Huntsberger, 2001; Huntsberger, Aghazarian and Tunstel, 2005; Lockery, 2007; Lockery and Peters, 2007; Peters, Henry and Gunderson, 2007). It is also fairly obvious that non-biologically inspired adaptive learning methods (see, e.g., Auer, Cesa-Bianchi and Genile, 2002; Baird, 1999; Burgsteiner, 2005; Fahle and Poggio, 2002; Ferrari, 2002; MacKay, 2003; Olsen, Leonard and Teller, 2007; Sailer, 2006) can be improved by considering refinements inspired by ecology.

Figure 18. Alg. 3 Average Reward (memory model comparison). ©2008 James F. Peters. Used with permission.

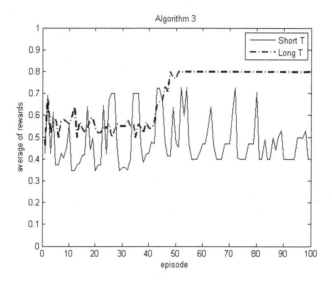

Figure 19. Alg. 3 Average Value-of-State (memory model comparison). ©2008 James F. Peters. Used with permission.

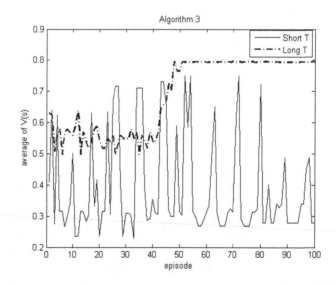

Figure 20. Alg. 3 RMSE Value-of-State (memory model comparison)

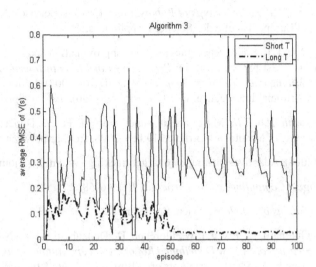

ACKNOWLEDGMENT

This research was supported by Natural Sciences & Engineering Research Council of Canada (NSERC) grant 185986 and Manitoba Hydro grant T277.

REFERENCES

Alcock, J. (1995). *Animal Behavior*, 5th Ed. Sinauer, Sunderland, MA.

Antarctica (2008). Retrieved 19 Feb. 2008, from http://www.vb-tech.co.za/Antartica/

Anwar, S., Patnaik, K. S. (2008). Actor critic learning: A near set approach. In C. Chien-Chung, J.W. Grzymala-Busse, W. Ziarko, (Eds.), *The Sixth Int. Conf. on Rough Sets and Current Trends in Computing (RSCTC 2008)*, Akron, Ohio, 23-25 Oct. 2008, *in press*.

Braithwaite, V. A. (2006). *Cognitive ability in fish*. In Sloman, K.A., Wilson, R.W., Balshine, S., (Eds.), *Behaviour and Physiology of Fish*. Elsevier, Amsterdam, 1-38.

Gibbs, J.W. (1960). *Elementary Principles in Statistical Mechanics*. NY, U.S.A., Dover.

Henry, C., & Peters, J. F. (2007). Image Pattern Recognition Using Approximation Spaces and Near Sets, In: *Proceedings of Eleventh International Conference on Rough Sets, Fuzzy Sets, Data Mining and Granular Computing* (RSFDGrC 2007), Joint Rough Set Symposium (JRS 2007). *Lecture Notes in Artificial Intelligence*, vol. 4482 (pp. 475-482). Berlin: Springer.

Henry, C. (2004). *Ecosystem Testbed*. Computational Intelligence Laboratory, Retrieved 17 Feb. 2008, from http://130.179.231.200/cilab/ [Downloads].

Henry, C. (2005). *Advanced Swarm Intelligence Testbed*. Computational Intelligence Laboratory, Retrieved 19 Feb. 2008, from http://wren.ece.umanitoba.ca/ [Downloads].

Heyes, C. M. (1994). Social learning in animals: Categories and mechanisms. *Biol. Rev.* 69, 207-231.

Labella, T. H. (2007). *Division of Labour in Groups of Robots.* Ph.D. thesis, supervisor: M. Dorigo, Universite libre de Bruxelles, Universite d'Europe, Faculte des Sciences Appliquees.

Lockery, D., & Peters, J. F. (2007). Robotic target tracking with approximation space-based feedback during reinforcement learning, Springer best paper award, in: *Proceedings of Eleventh International Conference on Rough Sets, Fuzzy Sets, Data Mining and Granular Computing* (RSFDGrC 2007), Joint Rough Set Symposium (JRS 2007). Lecture Notes in Artificial Intelligence, vol. 4482 (pp. 483-490). Berlin: Springer.

Lockery, D. (2007). *Learning with ALiCE II.* M.Sc. Thesis, supervisor: J.F. Peters, Department of Electrical & Computer Engineering, University of Manitoba. Retrieved 19 Feb. 2008, from http://wren.ece.umanitoba.ca/

Lockery, D., & Peters, J. F. (2008). Adaptive learning by a target tracking system, Best journal

article award. *Int. J. of Intelligent Computing and Cybernetics, 1*(1), 46-68.

Lorenz, K. (1981). *The Foundations of Ethology.* Wien: Springer.

Monada, F., Pettinaro, G. C., Guignard, A., Kwee, I. W., Floreano, D., Deneubourg, J.-L., Nolfi, S., Gambardella, L. M., & Dorigo, M. (2004). S*warm-bot: A New Distributed Robotic Concept. Autonomous Robots, 17*(2-3), 193-221. Retrieved 19 Feb. 2008, from http://www.swarm-bots.org/dllink.php?id=667&type=documents

Nouyan, S., & Dorigo, M. (2004). Chain Formation in a Swarm of Robots. Retrieved 19 Feb. 2008, from http://www.swarm-bots.org/dllink.php?id=565&type=documents

Orlowska, E. (1982). Semantics of Vague Concepts, Applications of Rough Sets, Institute for Computer Science, Polish Academy of Sciences, Report 469. See, also, E. Orlowska (1985). Semantics of Vague Concepts. In G.Dorn, P. Weingartner (Eds.), Foundations of Logic and Linguistics. Problems and Solutions, Plenum Press, London/NY, 465-482.

Patnaik, K. S., Peters, J. F., & Anwar, S. (2008). Influence of temperature on swarmbots that learn. *Cybernetics and Systems: An International Journal* 39, 1-18. DOI: 10.1080/01969720802069831.

Pawlak, Z. (1981a). *Classification of Objects by Means of Attributes.* Institute for Computer Science, Polish Academy of Sciences Report 429. Polish Academy of Sciences, Warsaw, Poland.

Pawlak, Z., & Skowron, A. (2007a). Rudiments of rough sets, *Information Sciences, 177*(1, 3-27).

Pawlak, Z., & Skowron, A. (2007b). Rough sets: Some extensions, Information Sciences, 177(1), 28-40.

Pawlak, Z., & Skowron, A. (2007c). Rough sets and Boolean reasoning, *Information Sciences,* 177(1), 41-73.

Peters, J. F. (2008a). Discovery of perceptually near information granules. In J.T. Yao, (Ed.), Novel Developments in Granular Computing: Applications for Advanced Human Reasoning and Soft Computation, Hersey, NY: Information Science Reference, 2008, *in press.*

Peters, J. F. (2008b). Approximation and perception in ethology-based reinforcement learning. In Pedrycz, W., Skowron, A., Kreinovich, V. (Eds.), *Handbook on Granular Computing.* Wiley, NY., 671-688.

Peters, J. F., Shahfar, S., Ramanna, S., & Szturm, T. (2007). Biologically-inspired adaptive learning: A near set approach. In *Proc. Frontiers in the Convergence of Bioscience and Information Technologies* (FBIT07), 10.1109/FBIT.2007.39, IEEE Computer Society, 403-408.

Peters, J. F. (2007a). Granular computing in approximate adaptive learning. *International Journal of Information Technology and Intelligent Computing, 2*(4), 1-25.

Peters, J. F. (2007b). Near sets. Special theory about nearness of objects, *Fundamenta Informaticae,* 75(1-4), 407-433.

Peters, J. F. (2007c). Near Sets. Toward Approximation Space-Based Object Recognition. In Yao, Y., Lingras, P., Wu, W.-Z, Szczuka, M., Cercone, N., \'{S}l\c{e}zak, D., (Eds.), *Proc. of the Second Int. Conf. on Rough Sets and Knowledge Technology* (RSKT07), Joint Rough Set Symposium (JRS07), Lecture Notes in Artificial Intelligence 4481 (pp. 22-33). Springer, Berlin.

Peters, J. F. (2007d). Toward approximate adaptive learning. In Kryszkiewicz, M. Peters, J.F. Rybinski, H., Skowron, A. (Eds.), *Int. Conf. on Rough Sets and Emerging Intelligent Systems Paradigms in Memoriam Zdzislaw Pawlak, Lecture Notes in Artificial Intelligence 4585*, Springer, Berlin Heidelberg, 57-68.

Peters, J. F. **(2007e)**. Near sets. General theory about nearness of objects. *Applied Mathematical Sciences, 1*(53), 2609-2629.

Peters, J. F., & Wasilewski, P. (2008). *Foundations of near sets, Information Sciences.* submitted, pending publication.

Peters, J. F., Skowron, A., & Stepaniuk, J. (2006). Nearness in approximation spaces. In G. Lindemann, H. Schlingloff et al. (Eds.), *Proc. Concurrency, Specification & Programming*, Informatik-Berichte Nr. 206 (pp. 434-445). Berlin: Humboldt-Universitat zu Berlin.

Peters, J. F., Skowron, A., & Stepaniuk, J. (2007). Nearness of objects: Extension of approximation space model. *Fundamenta Informaticae, 79*(3-4), 497-512.

Peters, J. F., Henry, C., & Ramanna, S. (2005a). Rough Ethograms: Study of Intelligent System Behavior. In M.A. Kłopotek, S. Wierzchoń, K. Trojanowski (Eds.), *New Trends in Intelligent Information Processing and Web Mining* (pp. 117-126). Berlin: Springer.

Peters, J. F. (2005b). Rough ethology: Towards a Biologically-Inspired Study of Collective Behavior in Intelligent Systems with Approximation Spaces. *Transactions on Rough Sets*, III, 153-174.

Peters, J. F., Henry, C., & Gunderson, D. S. (2007). Biologically-inspired adaptive learning control strategies: A rough set approach. *Int. J. of Hybrid Intelligent Systems, 4*(4), 203-216.

Peters, J. F., & Henry, C. (2005). Reinforcement learning in swarms that learn. In *Proc. IEEE/WIC/ACM Int. Conf. on Intelligent Agent Technology* (pp. 400-406). Compiègne, France: Compiègne Univ. of Tech.

Peters, J. F., Henry, C. (2006). Reinforcement learning with approximation spaces. *Fundamenta Informaticae, 71*(2-3), 323-349.

Peters, J. F., Skowron, A., Synak, P., & Ramanna, S. (2003). Rough sets and information granulation. In Bilgic, T., Baets, D., Kaynak, O. (Eds.), *Tenth Int. Fuzzy Systems Assoc. World Congress, Lecture Notes in Artificial Intelligence*, 2715, 370-377, Instanbul, Turkey. Heidelberg, Germany: Physica-Verlag.

Peters, J. F., & Skowron, A. (2006). Zdzislaw Pawlak: Life and Work. Transactions on Rough Sets, V, 1-24.

Polkowski, L. (2002). *Rough Sets. Mathematical Foundations.* Heidelberg, Germany: Springer-Verlag.

Salter, T. (2006). *Navigational And Proprioceptive Sensor-Based Recognition Of Interaction Patterns Between Children And Mobile Robots*, Ph.D. thesis, University of Alberta. Edmonton, Alberta, Canada: University of Alberta Press.

Selfridge, O. G. (1984). Some themes and primitives in ill-defined systems. In Selfridge, O.G., Rissland, E.L., Arbib, M.A. (Eds.), *Adaptive Control of Ill-Defined Systems* (pp. 21-26). London, UK: Plenum Press.

Shahfar, S. (2007). *Glowlight Tetra Freshwater Fish*. Research Report, Computational Intelligence Laboratory, University of Manitoba.

Skowron, A., & Stepaniuk, J. (1995). Generalized approximation spaces. In Lin, T.Y.,Wildberger, A.M. (Eds.), *Soft Computing* (pp. 18-21). San Diego, CA, U.S.A.: Simulation Councils.

Skowron, A., Swiniarski, R., & Synak, P. (2005). Approximation spaces and information granulation. *Transactions on Rough Sets*, III, 175-189.

Stepaniuk, J. (1998). Approximation spaces, reducts and representatives. In Polkowski, L., Skowron, A.: (Eds.), *Rough Sets in Knowledge Discovery* 2: Studies in Fuzziness and Soft Computing 19 (pp. 109-126). Heidelberg, Germany: Springer-Verlag.

Sutton, R. S., & Barto, A.G. (1998). *Reinforcement Learning: An Introduction.* Cambridge, MA, U.S.A.: The MIT Press.

Tinbergen, N. (1940). Die Ubersprungbewegung. *Zeitschrift für Tierpsychologie*, 4, 1-40.

Tinbergen, N. (1942). An objectivistic study of the innate behaviour of animals, *Bibliotheca Biotheoretica*, set D, I(2), 39-98.

Tinbergen, N. (1948). Social releasers and the experimental method required for their study. Wilson Bull., 160, 6-52.

Tinbergen, N. (1951). *The Study of Instinct.* Oxford, UK: Oxford University Press.

Tinbergen, N. (1953a). The Herring Gull's World. A Study of the Social Behavior of Birds. London, UK: Collins.

Tinbergen, N. (1953b). *Social Behaviour in Animals With Special Reference to Vertebrates.* London, UK: The Scientific Book Club.

Tinbergen, N. (1963). On aims and methods of ethology, *Zeitschrift für Tierpsychologie*, 20, 410--433.

Watkins, C. J. C. H. (1989). *Learning from Delayed Rewards*, Ph.D. Thesis, supervisor: Richard Young, King's College. Cambridge, UK: University of Cambridge.

Watkins, C. J. C. H., Dayan, P. (1992). Technical note: Q-learning. *Machine Learning*, 8, 279-292.

KEY TERMS

Adaptive Learning: Behaviour modification in response to changes in the environment.

Episode: A finite state-action-reward sequence.

Ethogram: A tabular representation of observed behaviours.

Near Sets: At least one object in a set has a description matching that of an object in another set.

Object Description: Tuple of function values.

Organism Behaviour: Tuples of behavior function values.

Return: Cumulative future discounted rewards.

Social Learning: Acquiring a new behaviour by watching or interacting with other animals.

ENDNOTE

[1] In the robotic systems that have reported in Lockery and Peters (2007), Peters and Henry (2006), Peters and Henry (2005), decision d is computed by a machine, not by an expert, where $d = 1$, if an action is chosen and $d = 0$, otherwise.

Section II.IV
Parallel Computing and Neural Networks

Parallel computing is an important feature of natural computing. And it is especially needed when the problem is very complex and has heavy computing cost. Parallel computing inspired by nature is used for designing virtual city in the section, which is a very interesting research direction. Neural network is a classical method of natural computing. Although a lot of work had been done for it, there are still many directions to be exploited. We can see some new ideas for developing new types of neural networks in this section.

Chapter XXIII
Nature Inspired Parallel Computing

Dingju Zhu
Chinese Academy of Sciences, China

ABSTRACT

Parallel computing is more and more important for science and engineering, but it is not used so widely as serial computing. People are used to serial computing and feel parallel computing too difficult to understand, design and use. In fact, they are most familiar with nature, in which all things exist and go on in parallel. If one learns parallel computing before learning serial computing, even if he or she has not read this chapter, they can find that serial computing is more difficult to understand, design and use than parallel computing, for it is not running in the way as the nature we are familiar with. Nature is composed of a large number of objects and events. Events are the spirit of objects; objects the body of events. They are related with each other in nature. Objects can construct or exist in parallel and events can occur or go on in parallel. The parallelism mainly exists in four dimensions including space dimension, application dimension, time dimension, and user dimension. After reading this chapter, even if you have been used to serial computing, you can find that the parallel computing used in your applications is just from nature. This chapter illustrates NIPC (Nature Inspired Parallel Computing) and its applications to help you grasp the methods of applying NIPC to your applications. The authors hope to help you understand and use parallel computing more easily and design and develop parallel software more effectively.

INTRODUCTION

We illustrate nature inspired parallel computing in this chapter with eight paragraphs:

1. Parallel Phenomenon in Nature
2. Nature Inspired Parallel Computing
3. Problems with Parallelisms
4. Decomposition and Communication Schemes of NIPC
5. Parallel Schemes of NIPC

Copyright © 2009, IGI Global, distributing in print or electronic forms without written permission of IGI Global is prohibited.

In the first paragraph, some phenomenon in nature is given to help readers to understand parallel computing; in the second paragraph, what is nature inspired parallel computing is discussed with readers; in the third paragraph, three typical problems can be solved faster and in larger scales via parallel computing are listed; in the fourth paragraph to the seventh paragraph, four schemes of NIPC including decomposition and communication schemes, parallel schemes, distribution schemes and mapping schemes are illustrated and applied to the three problems. At the last paragraph, the architecture of NIPC is given to integrate the four schemes and to provide readers an overall blueprint of NIPC.

BACKGROUND

Background of Parallel Computing

The term parallel computing refers to the use of (parallel) supercomputers and computer clusters (Wikipedia 2008; J. Dongarra, T. Sterling, H. Simon, & E. Strohmaier 2005).Parallel computing is a form of computing in which many instructions are carried out simultaneously (G.S. Almasi, & A. Gottlieb 1989). It operates on the principle that large problems can almost always be divided into smaller ones, which may be solved concurrently ("in parallel"). It has been used for many years, but interest in it has become greater in recent years due to physical constraints preventing frequency scaling (Wikipedia 2008). Parallel computing exists in several different forms: bit-level parallelism, instruction-level parallelism, data parallelism, and task parallelism. Parallelism is a primary method for accelerating the total power of a supercomputer. Computational physics applications have been the primary drivers in the development of parallel computing over the last 20 years. Languages (e.g., Fortran and C) and libraries (e.g., message passing interface (MPI) (M. Snir, S. Otto, S. Huss-Lederman, D. Walker, & J. Dongarra 1996) and linear algebra libraries, i.e., LAPACK (E. Anderson, Z. Bai, C. Bischof, S. Blackford, J. Demmel, J. Dongarra,J. Du Croz, A. Greenbaum, S. Hammaring, A. McKenney, & D. Sorensen 1999)) allow the programmer to access or expose parallelism in a variety of standard ways (J. Dongarra 2006).

Background of Parallel Simulation

Parallel and distributed simulation has been a research topic of interest for over twenty years. Most of the work in the area is motivated by the desire to execute simulations faster than on a serial computer which is unable to provide answers fast enough, and/or is unable to hold the simulation state in memory (Nicol,D.M 2003). Parallel and distributed simulation is concerned with issues introduced by distributing the execution of a discrete event simulation program over multiple computers. Parallel discrete event simulation is concerned with execution on multiprocessor computing platforms containing multiple central processing units (CPUs) that interact frequently, e.g., thousands of times per second. Distributed simulation is concerned with the execution of simulations on loosely coupled systems where interactions take much more time, e.g., milliseconds or more, and occur less often (Richard M. Fujimoto 2001).

MAIN THRUST OF THE CHAPTER

Parallel Phoneomenon in Nature

Animals, humans, plants live in parallel; physical and chemical reactions occur and go on in parallel; persons work in parallel to complete projects. Things in nature are independent and connected, so they can run independently at the most of time but need to react with each other at some time.

There are a large number of parallel phenomenons in nature. For example, when one person eats a watermelon, he bites the watermelon about 300 times and needs about 300 seconds; when 10 persons eat the watermelon, each person only need bites the watermelon about 30 times and needs about 30 seconds; when 30 persons eat the watermelon, each person only need bites the watermelon about 10 times and needs about 10 seconds; and when 100 persons eat the watermelon, each person only need bites the watermelon about 3 times and needs about 3 seconds. However, how can so many heads get together to eat one watermelon with heads colliding with each other? So it is necessary to cut the watermelon into many divisions according to the person number and distribute these divisions to every person. If cut through axis, the watermelon can be cut into n divisions in n/2 times. If cutting the watermelon a time costs 1 second, and distributing a division of the watermelon costs 0.1 second, cutting and distributing the watermelon to 10 persons at least costs 6 seconds via formula 10/2*1+10*0.1, cutting and distributing the watermelon to 30 persons at least costs 18 seconds via formula 30/2*1+30*0.1, cutting and distributing the watermelon to 100 persons at least costs 60 seconds via formula 100/2*1+100*0.1. The biting time, the cutting time and the distributing time considered together, 10 persons eating the watermelon costs 36 seconds via formula 30+6, 30 persons eating the watermelon costs 28 seconds via formula 10+18, 100 persons eating the watermelon costs 63 seconds via formula 3+60. Obviously, eating the watermelon in parallel is faster than eating the watermelon in serial, and in parallel way, eating the watermelon by 30 persons   is faster than eating the watermelon by 10 persons or by 100 persons.

We can learn from nature that parallel way is more effective than serial way, and solving a same problem has different efficiency in different parallel way. Correspondingly, parallel computing is more effective than serial computing, and granularity of parallel computing should design according to applications. For example, when simulating family activities, the activities need to be distributed on different computing nodes in order to make use of parallel computing to speed up the simulation, and it is vital to know how to distribute different activities onto different processors to get the greatest benefit of parallel computing. The reactions in a family are much more frequent than the reactions between different families, and correspondingly the communications within a family is much more than between different families. At the same time, communication within a computing node is much faster than between different computing nodes. When simulating reactions between families, the time the communication cost is less than the time saved by distributing and simulating different families on different computing nodes in parallel, while when simulating reactions within a family, the time the communication cost is more than the time saved by distributing and simulating activities within a family on different computing nodes in parallel. So it is wise to simulate different families on different computing nodes and avoid simulating a family on different computing nodes.

Nature Inspired Parallel Computing (NIPC)

All things in nature can be simulated using computer, and the parallel phenomenon in nature can be simulated by parallel computing technology using HPC (high performance computer), which consists of many computing nodes with CPUs and kernels, different from traditional computer with single computing node. Things in nature can be simulated in parallel on different computing nodes or different CPUs or different CPU kernels in HPC.

Nature is composed of a large number of objects and events. Events are the spirit of objects; objects the body of events. They are related with each other in nature. Objects can construct or exist in parallel and events can occur or go on in parallel. The parallelism mainly exists in four dimensions including space dimension, time dimension, application dimension, and user dimension. We can design and use NIPC according to the four dimensions.

In space dimension, objects at different locations can construct or exist in parallel, and all events at different locations can occur or go on in parallel. For an example in vertical direction, one house is repaired in Nanshan, Shenzhen China, and at the same time another house is repaired in FUtian, Shenzhen China. Another example, men are walking on roads, and at the same time buses are running on roads. For an example in vertical direction, planes are flying in the sky, at the same time cloud drifting in the sky, at the same time rain is dropping onto the earth surface, at the same time water is flowing on the earth surface, and at the same time groundwater is flowing in the earth.

In time dimension, objects can construct or exist in parallel in different time, and all events can occur or go on in parallel in different time. For example, a boy sat on a chair previously, and his father sits on the same chair at present.

In application dimension, objects in different applications can construct or exist in parallel and all events in different applications can occur or go on in parallel. For example, underground objects and events can be processed by mine monitoring application, underwater monitoring application and other underground applications in parallel; objects and events on the earth surface can be processed by city planning application, ecological resource monitoring application, tour application and other earth surface applications in parallel; objects and events in the sky can be processed by climate monitoring application, air pollution monitoring application and other sky applications in parallel.

In user dimension, objects and events can be used or watched by users in parallel. For example, Jack watches buildings from one angle, and at the same time John watches buildings from another angle.

Problems with Parallelisms

The first example: illegal building detection which is a problem that needs parallel computing:

The discussions about illegal building mainly concern about the legal definition of illegal building (Kaize Zhang 2004) or the epidemic of illegal building (Justus Reid Weiner 2003; Expatica 2006), the ways of illegal building monitoring include on-site monitoring (Zhanjiang Evening News 2008), expert interpretation of remote sensing image and computer-aided expert interpretation of remote sensing image (Sohu 2006). These technologies have not applied digital city technology and HPC technology to illegal building monitoring for the realization automatic and fast building monitoring.

The concept "digital city" is derived from the concept "digital earth" brought forward firstly by Al Gore (Al Gore 1998). The notions, technologies, strategies of digital earth applied to city and thus lead to digital city (Li Qi and Lin Shaofu 2001). There are some web sites named digital city in USA, Europe, China and other countries and areas on the internet (TORONTO, Ont 2006; Escapenet GMBH 2008; Virtual City 2008), and many famous digital cities such as Virtual Los Angeles (Urban Simulation Team at UCLA 2000), Model City Philadelphia (Bobby J 1997), Google earth (Google company. 2008), and virtual earth (Microsoft company 2008). These digital cities mainly used in E-Commerce, E-Government and other desktop applications without illegal building monitoring. However illegal building monitoring is vital for city construction and city's economic development, so illegal building monitoring should be an important application of digital city.

There are some researchers concerning the applications of HPC in Vision and image process (Cho-Li Wang, P.B. Bhat, &V.K. Prasanna 1996; Y. Kawasaki, F. Ino, Y. Mizutani, N. Fujimoto, T. Sasama, Y. Sato, N. Sugano, S. Tamura, &K. Hagihara 2004). Computer vision has applications in a wide variety of fields such as vehicle navigation, medical diagnosis, HPC-assisted surgery, aerial photo interpretation, and automatic target recognition (Cho-Li Wang, P.B. Bhat, &V.K. Prasanna 1996). Parallel processing is an attractive approach to satisfy the Computational requirements of vision applications (Y. Kawasaki, F. Ino, Y. Mizutani, N. Fujimoto, T. Sasama, Y. Sato, N. Sugano, S. Tamura, &K. Hagihara 2004). However, not much work has been found about HPC applications in the vision or image processing of illegal buildings monitoring in digital city.

Every year city planners spend a large amount of money and time to monitor illegal buildings by officials on site. In this way, all illegal buildings in a city can be identified in about 2 years. Due to such slowness, some city planners ask experts to look for illegal buildings by interpreting remote sensing image. By using this approach, the illegal buildings can be found out in about 6 months. Considering the high cost of human resource, some city planners start to use computer as an aid to the experts. In the way, the illegal buildings can be found out in about 2 months. Still, the cost and the time can not satisfy the need for large-scale city monitoring. In order to realize automatic and fast building monitoring, parallel computing is needed. In parallel computing all illegal buildings in a city can be found out in several minutes by comparing buildings-image or buildings change image with the official city planning graph of a digital city.

The second example: building reconstruction which is a problem that needs parallel computing:

The concept "digital city" is derived from the concept "digital earth" brought forward firstly by Al Gore (Al Gore 1998; Li Qi and Lin Shaofu 2001). There are some famous digital cities including Virtual Los Angeles (Urban Simulation Team at UCLA 2000), Model City Philadelphia (Bobby J 1997), Google earth (Google company. 2008) and virtual earth (Microsoft company 2008). Currently digital city mainly used in e-commerce, e-government and other desktop applications out of sync with reality. However a digital city out of sync with reality always provides users wrong information, for example, the buildings have been destroyed in an earthquake can still exist in the digital city.

In order to achieve the goal of synchronous update, how to automatically reconstruct buildings is studied recently. There are four existing approaches of automatic 3D building reconstruction. The first approach is based on urban aerial stereo pair (Zenbo Qian, etc 2000; Aijun Chen, etc 2002); the second based on airborne laser scanning data (Hongjian You, etc 2005; Hongjian You, etc 2005); the third based on some relative control condition such as the inner element and the length of building, and also, collinear equation and parallel lines condition (Yi Lin, etc 2005); the fourth method based on building shadow in single image (Guojin He, etc 2001). Obviously, the first approach needs image pairs and the other three only need single image.

3D models of buildings can be reconstructed much faster by automatic reconstruction approach than by hands. However it is still too slow automatically to reconstruct buildings one by one in serial computing for synchronous update. So parallel computing is needed to speed up the automatic 3D building reconstruction significantly. Parallel processing is an attractive approach to satisfy the computational requirements of large scale automatic 3D building reconstruction in digital city.

3D digital city is paid more and more attention on for they are expected to make life and business more convenient, but traditional 3D digital city are out of sync with reality for non-automatic 3D digital city reconstruction. Automatic 3D building reconstruction is vital for automatic 3D digital city reconstruction, for city mainly consists of buildings. Serial computing based automatic 3D building reconstruction from stereo-pair images and from single image studied recently still is too slow for synchronously updating 3D digital city. So parallel computing is needed to speed up automatic 3D building reconstruction.

The third example: city generation and simulation which is a problem that needs parallel computing:

The concept "digital city" is derived from the concept "digital earth" brought forward firstly by Al Gore (Al Gore 1998; Li Qi and Lin Shaofu 2001). There are some famous digital cities including Virtual Los Angeles (Urban Simulation Team at UCLA 2000), Model City Philadelphia (Bobby J 1997), Google earth (Google company. 2008) and virtual earth (Microsoft company 2008). These digital cities are generated and simulated in serial computing and mainly used in E-Commerce, E-Government and other desktop applications. These digital cities almost do not update in large scale once they have been generated, which leads to these digital cities can not synchronize with the corresponding real cities. If only generating and simulating digital cities in small scale, it is impossible to satisfy the requirements of some applications such as detecting and dealing with all illegal buildings in cities. What's more, the functions of these digital cities mainly focus on browsing and searching, which can not meet the need of some applications such as city emergency. These problems can be solved by applying parallel computing to the generation and simulation of digital city. Parallel processing is an attractive approach to satisfy the computational requirements of the generation and simulation of digital city in large scale.

Digital cities are paid more and more attentions on for they are expected to make life, business, travel, city planning and so on more convenient and more effective. Existing digital cities are generated and simulated based on serial computing. However, the speed of generating digital city in serial computing is so slow that digital cities can not update in sync with reality, and the limited computing power of serial computing can not simulate a digital city in large scale and the complex functions in a digital city. Since parallel computing is more powerful and faster than serial computing, parallel computing is needed to speed up and enhance the scale and the complexity of the generation and simulation of digital city.

Decomposition and Communication Schemes of NIPC

The four dimensions can be organized into different decomposition and communication schemes of NIPC. Communication scheme is always combined with decomposition and communication scheme, and in NIPC, communication always happened among the divisions of each dimension, which helps to manage and reduce communications. For example, the decomposition and communication scheme shown in Figure 1 can be expressed as (space, application, time, user) which means in order to solve problems, the problems can be firstly decomposed in the space dimension, and then the problems of each space can be decomposed in the application dimension,

Figure 1. A decomposition and communication scheme of NIPC

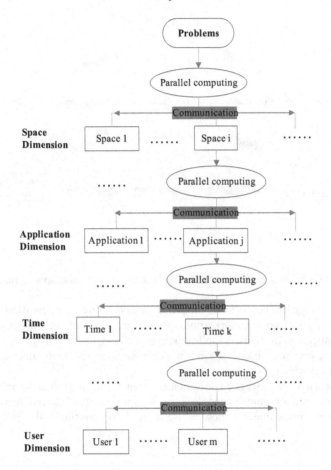

and then the problems of each application can be decomposed in the time dimension, and finally the problem of each time can be decomposed in the user dimension.

Sometimes only 1 dimension of the 4 dimensions is needed for solving problems and sometimes 2, sometimes 3, sometime 4.

Four dimensions can be organized into 4*3*2*1=24 kinds of decomposition and communication schemes including: (space, time, application, user), (space, time, user, application), (space, application, time, user), (space, application, user, time), (space, user, application, time), (space, user, time, application),(time, space, application, user), (time, space, user, application), (time, application, space, user), (time, application, user, space), (time, user, space, application), (time, user, application, space),(application, time, space, user), (application, time, user, space), (application, space, user, time), (application, space, time, user), (application, user, space, time), (application, user, time, space),(user, application, time, space), (user, application, space, time), (user, time, application, space), (user, time, space, application), (user, space, application, time), (user, space, time, application).

Three dimensions can be organized into 4*3*2=24 kinds of decomposition and communication schemes including: (space, time, application), (space, time, user), (space, application, time), (space, application, user), (space, user, application), (space, user, time),(time, space, application), (time, space, user), (time, application, space), (time, application, user), (time, user, space), (time, user, application),(application, time, space), (application, time, user), (application, space, user), (application, space, time), (application, user, space), (application, user, time),(user, ap-

Figure 2. Decomposition and communication scheme for detecting illegal buildings

plication, time), (user, application, space), (user, time, application), (user, time, space), (user, space, application), (user, space, time).

Two dimensions can be organized into 4*3=12 kinds of decomposition and communication schemes including: (space, time), (space, application), (space, user), (time, space), (time, application), (time, user),(application, time), (application, space), (application, user),(user, application), (user, time), (user, space).

One dimension can be organized into 4=4 kinds of decomposition and communication schemes including: (space), (application), (user), (time).

When we use NIPC, each of the above decomposition and communication schemes can be selected for guiding parallel programming and parallel running according to the requirements of the problems.

The following three examples illustrate how to use these decomposition and communication schemes of NIPC to solve problems.

Example 1:

The problem is to detect all illegal buildings in a city.

The parallelism of automatic illegal building monitoring is derived from real city. Real city is composed of buildings. For example, Buildings in Shenzhen always belong to one of the six county-level administrative districts known as Luohu, Futian, Nanshan, Yantian within the Shenzhen Special Economic Zone (SEZ) and Bao'an and Longgang outside the SEZ. We can divide Digital Shenzhen into six districts, every district into some blocks, and every block into some areas.

The granularity of division can be coarse, middle or fine. If the granularity is coarser than necessary, parallelism can not be exploited fully; if the granularity is finer than necessary, communication consumption among HPC processors will ruin the benefit of parallel computing.

The granularity was selected according to images scale and HPC capacity, and designed in parallel programs. It was measured by spatial scales in the longitude and latitude direction. For example: in the longitude direction and latitude, each part can be at a spatial scale of kilometer, meter or decimeter.

By reasonable division, illegal buildings can be detected from city images in parallel. If we divided digital Shenzhen into 6 districts and every district into 10 blocks, Shenzhen image was divided into 60 images. Each division was processed by same steps as used in serial computing.

The decomposition and communication scheme used in detecting illegal buildings is shown in Figure 2. Obviously, the decomposition and communication scheme is derived from the decomposition and communication scheme (space, application) of NIPC.

Figure 3. Decomposition and communication scheme for reconstructing buildings

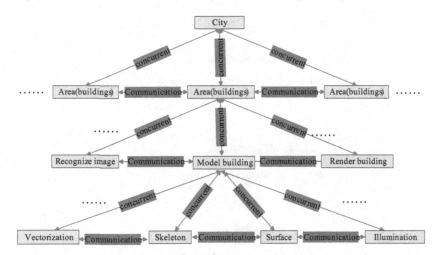

Example 2:

The problem is to reconstruct all buildings in a city.

If we divided Digital Shenzhen into 6 districts and every district into 10 blocks, so the input was divided into 60 images. Each division was processed by the same three steps as used in serial computing: recognizing images, modeling and rendering 3D buildings, which consumed one minute in the first step, two minute in the second step and one minute in the third step. The second step was the bottleneck in the process. We break the bottleneck by splitting every division in the second step into two smaller divisions.

The decomposition and communication scheme used in reconstructing buildings is shown in Figure 3. Obviously, the decomposition and communication scheme is also derived from the decomposition and communication scheme (space, application) of NIPC, although there are two layers in the application dimension.

Via the reasonable division, buildings can be recognized from city images, and then modeled and rendered in parallel. And different divisions need to communicate with each other in the longitude and latitude dimension. The communication mainly happens between neighboring divisions.

Example 3:

The problem is to generate and simulate digital city.

A digital city is divided into different horizontal scales in horizontal dimension for data parallel computing in the first layer; into different vertical scales in vertical dimension for task parallel computing in the second layer; into different applications in application dimension for task parallel computing in the third layer; into different time in time dimension for pipeline parallel computing in the fourth layer; and into different user services in user dimension for grid computing in the fifth layer.

The first communication layer includes the communications among processes of the objects and events in different horizontal scales; the second communication layer includes the communications among processes of the objects and events in different vertical scales; the third communication layer includes the communications among processes of the objects and events in different applications; the fourth communication level includes the communications among processes of the objects and events in different times; the fifth communication level includes the communications among processes of the objects and events used by different users.

For example, in the horizontal dimension, the processes of the objects and events in different scales need to communicate with each other when persons and buses move from one place to another; in the vertical dimension, the processes of the objects and events in the underground need to communicate with the processes of the objects

Figure 4. Decomposition and communication scheme for generating and simulating digital city

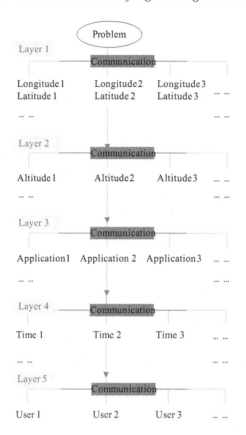

and events in the earth's surface when earthquakes happen; in the application dimension, the processes of the objects and events in city planning application need to communicate with the processes of the objects and events in resource monitoring application for city planning depends on the data obtained from resource monitoring; in the time dimension, the processes of the objects and events in a year need to communicate with the processes of the objects and events in the previous year for analyzing the economy development relationship between the two years; in the user dimension, the processes of the objects and events used by different users need to communicate with each other when users watch objects and events from different angles.

The decomposition and communication scheme used in generating and simulating digital city is shown in Figure 4. Obviously, the architecture is derived from the decomposition and communication scheme (space, application, time, user) of NIPC, and there are two layers in the space dimension.

Synchronization mechanism for generating and simulating digital city is shown in Figure 5. Synchronization is a kind of special communication. There are conservative protocols used among logic processes of a district on different CPU kernels within a computing node, and optimistic protocols used among logic processes of different districts on different computing nodes. The principal task of any conservative protocol is to determine when it is "safe" to process an event, i.e., when can one guarantee no event containing a smaller time stamp will be later received by this logic process (Richard M. Fujimoto 2001). A logic process cannot process an event until it has been guaranteed to be safe (Richard M. Fujimoto 2001). In contrast to conservative protocols that avoid violations of the local causality constraint, optimistic protocols allow violations to occur, for example it can process an event, even if events containing a smaller time stamp will be later received by this logic process, but optimistic protocols are able to detect and recover from them (Richard M. Fujimoto 2001).

Figure 5. Synchronization for generating and simulating digital city

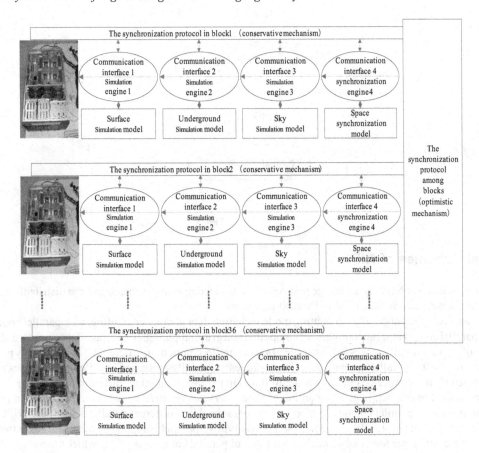

Figure 6. Parallel scheme for detecting illegal buildings

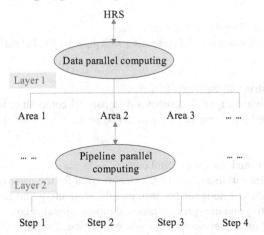

Figure 7. Parallel scheme for reconstructing buildings

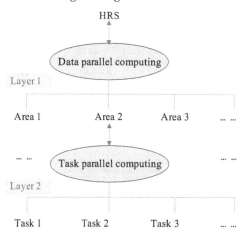

Parallel Schemes of NIPC

The parallel scheme of NIPC is the bridge that connects the decomposition scheme and the distribution scheme. The distribution scheme is illustrated in the next paragraph.

There are five types of parallel computing mode including data parallel computing, task parallel computing, pipeline parallel computing, function parallel computing and grid computing. In data parallel computing, different divisions of data are usually processed in parallel; in task parallel computing, different tasks are usually processed in parallel; in pipeline parallel computing, different phases are usually processed in different processes and data are processed by these processes little by little; in function parallel computing, different functions in a task are usually processed in parallel; in grid computing, different services required by users are processed in parallel.

The four types of parallel computing mode can be organized into different parallel schemes of NIPC. Some types of parallel schemes of NIPC can composed of one type of parallel computing mode, and some two types, and some three, and some four, and some five. All types of parallel computing mode, which a parallel scheme of NIPC contains, can be organized in a certain order, which is illustrated in the following examples.

Example 1:
The problem is to detect all illegal buildings in a city.
The parallel scheme combines data parallel computing with pipeline parallel computing, as shown in Figure 6.

Example 2:
The problem is to reconstruct all buildings in a city.
The parallel scheme shown in Figure 7 combines data parallel computing, in which the example shows 60 images are distributed onto 60 processes for data parallel computing, with task parallel computing.

Example 3:
The problem is to generate and simulate digital city.
Different computing nodes within each SMP-Cluster are used for the data parallel computing and different processors within each computing node for the task parallel computing and the pipeline computing. Coarse-grained data parallel computing and fine-grained task and pipeline parallel computing are used together to get a high parallel efficiency and provide services for the grid computing. The parallel scheme is shown in Figure 8.

Figure 8. Parallel scheme for generating and simulating digital city

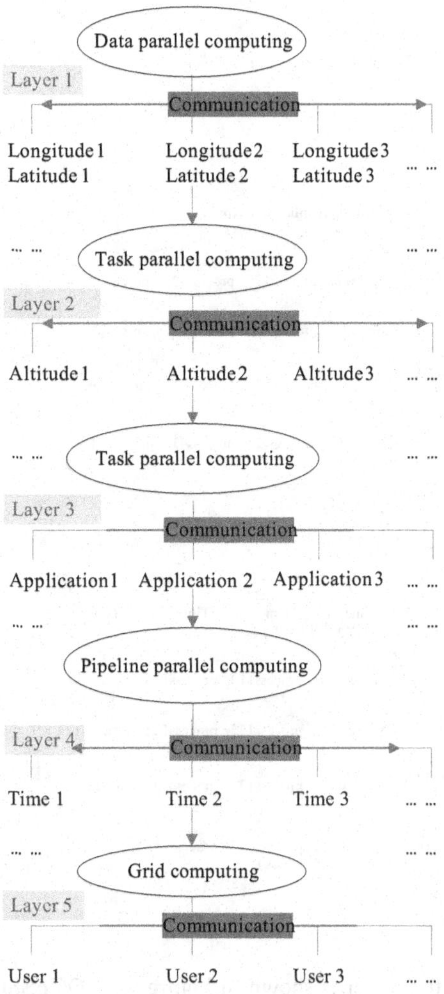

Distribution Scheme of NIPC

The distribution schemes are consistent with the parallel schemes. Each parallel scheme can have different distribution schemes according to the conditions of hardware platform for different number of divisions can be assigned to one process.

For example, the distribution scheme in Figure 8-11 corresponds to the parallel scheme (space, application, time, user).

In the space dimension, processes of objects and events in different spaces in the space dimension are distributed onto processes, and run in parallel.

In the application dimension, different processes of objects and events in different applications in the application dimension are distributed onto different processes, and run in parallel.

In the time dimension, different processes of objects and events in different time in the time dimension are distributed onto different processes, and run in parallel.

In the user dimension, processes of objects and events in different user services are distributed onto different grid nodes, and run in parallel.

Figure 9. Distribution in the first layer

	Space S1	Space S2	Space S3	Space S4
Problem	process1	process2	process3	process4

Figure 10. Distribution in the second layer

	Application A1	Application A2	Application A3	Application A4
process1	process11	process12	process13	process14
process2	process21	process22	process23	process24
process3	process31	process32	process33	process34
process4	process41	process42	process43	process44

Figure 11. Distribution in the third layer

	Time T1-T2	Time T2-T3	Time T3-T4	Time T4-T5
process11	process111	process112	process113	process114
process12	process121	process122	process123	process124
process13	process131	process132	process133	process134
process14	process141	process142	process143	process144

An example of distribution in the first layer is shown in Figure 9. PROCESSi in the matrix represents the processes of the objects and events in the space Si. In the matrix, logical processes of the objects and events in the space from S1 to S4 are distributed onto 4 processes.

The example of distribution in the second layer is shown in Figure 10. PROCESSij in the matrix represents processes of objects and events in the space Si and the application Aj. In the matrix, all logical processes of the objects and events in the space from S1 to S4 and the application from A1 application to A4 application. Obviously the matrix shown in Figure 9 can be divided into four matrixes with the same number of nodes as the matrix shown in Figure 10, so all logical processes of the objects and events in the space from S1 to S4 and the applications from A1 application to A4 application can be distributed onto 16 processes now

The example of distribution in the third layer is shown in Figure 11. PROCESSijk in the matrix represents processes of objects and events in the space Si and the application Aj and the time from Tk to Tk+1. In the matrix, all logical processes of the objects and events in the space S1 and the application from A1 to A4 and the time from T1 to T5. Obviously the matrix shown in Figure 10 can be divided into four matrixes with the same number of nodes as the matrix shown in Figure 11, so all logical processes of the objects and events in the space from S1 to S4 and the applications from A1 to A4 and the time from T1 to T5 can be distributed onto 64 processes now

The example of distribution in the fourth layer is shown in Figure 12. PROCESSijkl in the matrix represents processes of objects and events in the space Si and the application Aj and the time from Tk to Tk+1 and used by

Figure 12. Distribution in the fourth layer

$$\begin{array}{c} & \begin{array}{cccc} \text{User} & \text{User} & \text{User} & \text{User} \\ \text{U1} & \text{U2} & \text{U3} & \text{U4} \end{array} \\ \begin{array}{c} \text{process111} \\ \text{process112} \\ \text{process113} \\ \text{process114} \end{array} \left(\begin{array}{cccc} \text{process1111} & \text{process1112} & \text{process1113} & \text{process1114} \\ \text{process1121} & \text{process1122} & \text{process1123} & \text{process1124} \\ \text{process1131} & \text{process1132} & \text{process1133} & \text{process1134} \\ \text{process1141} & \text{process1142} & \text{process1143} & \text{process1144} \end{array} \right) \end{array}$$

Figure 13(a). Distribution scheme for detecting illegal building

$$\begin{array}{c} & \begin{array}{cccc} \text{Block 0} & \text{Block 1} & \text{...\,...} & \text{Block9} \end{array} \\ \begin{array}{c} \text{District 0} \\ \\ \text{District 1} \\ \vdots \\ \vdots \\ \text{District 5} \end{array} \left(\begin{array}{cccc} \text{image-group00} & \text{image-group01} & \text{...\,...} & \text{image-group09} \\ \text{image-group10} & \text{image-group11} & \text{...\,...} & \text{image-group19} \\ \vdots & \vdots & \vdots & \vdots \\ \vdots & \vdots & \vdots & \vdots \\ \text{image-group50} & \text{image-group51} & \text{...\,...} & \text{image-group59} \end{array} \right) \end{array}$$

Figure 13(b). Distribution scheme for detecting illegal buildings

$$\begin{array}{c} & \begin{array}{cccc} \text{Image 1} & \text{Image 2} & \text{...\,...} & \text{Image 60} \end{array} \\ \begin{array}{c} \text{Step 1} \\ \text{Step 2} \\ \text{Step 2} \\ \text{Step3} \end{array} \left(\begin{array}{cccc} \text{Process 1} & \text{Process 5} & \text{...\,...} & \text{Process 237} \\ \text{Process 2} & \text{Process 6} & \text{...\,...} & \text{Process 238} \\ \text{Process 3} & \text{Process 7} & \text{...\,...} & \text{Process 239} \\ \text{Process 4} & \text{Process 8} & \text{...\,...} & \text{Process 240} \end{array} \right) \end{array}$$

users U1. In the matrix, all logical processes of objects and events in the space S1 and the application A1 and the time from T1 to T5 and used by users from U1 to U4. Obviously the matrix shown in Figure 11 can be divided into four matrixes with the same number of nodes as the matrix shown in Figure 12, so all logical processes of the objects and events in the space from S1 to S4 and the applications from A1 to A4 and the time from T1 to T5 and the users from U1 to U4 can be distributed onto 256 processes no.

The following three examples illustrate how to use these distribution schemes of NIPC to solve problems.

Figure 14. Distribution scheme for reconstructing buildings

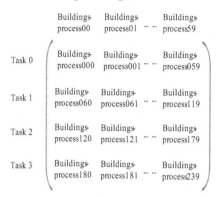

Example 1:

The problem is to detect all illegal buildings in a city.

In the distribution scheme shown in figure 6, 60 images are distributed onto 240 processes. The 240 processes are divided into 60 groups, in each group the first node is in charge of the first step of the pipeline, the second for the second step, and so on. The distribution scheme for detecting illegal buildings is shown in Figure 13.

Example 2:

The problem is to reconstruct all buildings in a city.

Base on the parallel scheme in Figure 7, 60 images are distributed onto 60 processes for data parallel computing, and each image are divided into 4 tasks with task parallel computing. In the distribution scheme shown in figure 14, 60 images are distributed onto 240 processes.

Example 3:

The problem is to generate and simulate digital Shenzhen.

Based on the parallel scheme in Figure 8, 36 blocks of digital Shenzhen are distributed onto 32 computing nodes; one of the remained computing nodes manages the synchronization of different computing nodes. Each block uses 2 parallel processes to generate and simulate the surface of the block including its applications, periods and users, 2 parallel processes to generate and simulate the underground of the block including its applications, periods and users, 2 parallel processes to generate and simulate the sky of the block including its applications, periods and users, and 1 parallel process to manage the synchronization of the different parallel processes within each block. The distribution scheme corresponds to the decomposition and communication scheme (space, application, time, user).

Mapping Schemes of NIPC

When the distribution scheme has been designed for a problem, there are many processes need to be mapped to computing nodes. The mapping scheme of NIPC should consider the architecture of parallel computing platform. If there are several CPUs in a computing node, the processes can be mapped to CPUs. If there are several kernels in a CPU, the processes can be mapped to CPU kernels. And the mapping scheme of NIPC should consider the communications among different processes. If the communications are frequent among pi (process i) and pj and so on, pi and pj and so on can be mapped to different CPUs or CPU kernels within a computing node; and if the communications are few among pi and pj and so on, pi and pj and so on can be mapped to different computing nodes. MPI the most popular parallel environment is preferred for parallel programming.

The typical architecture of parallel computing platform is shown in Figure 15. And a supercomputer with 17.6TB storage disks, delivering 1.5 Teraflop/s peak-rates, is shown in Figure 16.

Figure 15. Typical architecture of parallel computing platform

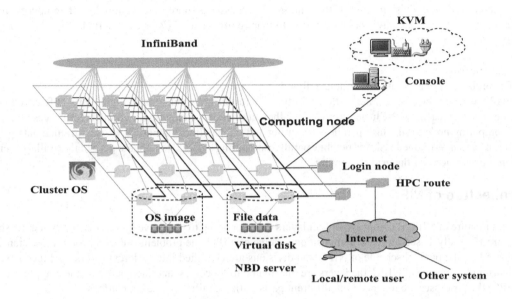

Figure 16. Parallel computer

Example 1:

The problem is to detect all illegal buildings in a city.

SMP-Cluster is the best parallel platform for illegal building monitoring in digital city. Different computing nodes of SMP-Cluster are used for data parallel computing of different images and different processors within each computing node for pipeline parallel computing of different steps. Coarse-grained data parallel computing and fine-grained pipeline parallel computing are used together to get a higher parallel efficient.

Example 2:

The problem is to reconstruct all buildings in a city.

Different computing nodes of SMP-Cluster are used for data parallel computing of different images. And the different tasks can be mapped to different computing nodes or different CPUs or CPU kernels within a computing node according to the division grain. If the number of processes is more than the number of computing nodes, different tasks of each data division maybe need to map to different CPUs or CPU kernels within a computing node.

Example 3:

The problem is to generate and simulate digital city.

SMP-Cluster is the best parallel platform for the generation and simulation of digital city. Different computing nodes within each SMP-Cluster are used for the data parallel computing, and different processors within each computing node for the task parallel computing and the pipeline computing. Coarse-grained data parallel computing and fine-grained task and pipeline parallel computing are used together to get a high parallel efficiency and provide services for the grid computing.

Architecture of NIPC

The architecture of NIPC is composed of four layers corresponding to the above four kinds of scheme. As shown in Figure 17, firstly, based on the decomposition scheme of NIPC, the problem is decomposed to divisions, and then based on the parallel scheme of NIPC, the divisions are classified into different layers, and then based on the distribution scheme of NIPC, the layers are distributed to processes, and then based on the mapping scheme of NIPC, the processes are mapped onto different parts of the parallel computing platform.

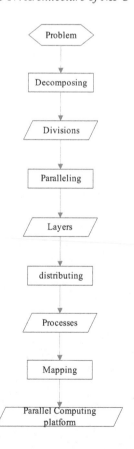

Figure 17. Architecture of NIPC

Example 1:

The problem is to detect all illegal buildings in a city.

Architecture shown in Figure 18 consists of four main layers: the first layer is data parallel computing layer, in which remote sensing images are divided into a large amount of images for data parallel computing; the second layer is pipeline parallel computing layer, in which monitoring process is divided into a number of steps for pipeline parallel processing; the third layer is HPC layer providing parallel environment; and the fourth layer is client layer managing users.

The input is remote sensing images, which are obtained through RS (remote sensing) satellite or RS (remote sensing) plane. The output is an illegal building vector graph.

SMP-Cluster is the best HPC platform for detecting illegal buildings. Different computing nodes of SMP-Cluster are used for data parallel computing; Different processors within the each computing node are used for pipeline parallel computing.

Example 2:

The problem is to reconstruct all buildings in a city.

The Architecture is shown in Figure 19, which consists of four main layers: the first layer is image acquisition layer providing city images to the second layer; the second layer parallel computing layer including three sub-layers: data parallel computing layer, pipe parallel computing layer and task parallel computing layer, this layer reconstructing 3D buildings from the images in parallel; the third layer HPC layer providing parallel environment; and the fourth layer client layer managing users.

The input is city images, which can be obtained through RS (remote sensing) satellite or RS (remote sensing) plane or sensor or camera, the longitude and latitude scale of the images is measured by GPS (Global Posi-

Figure 18. Architecture for detecting illegal buildings

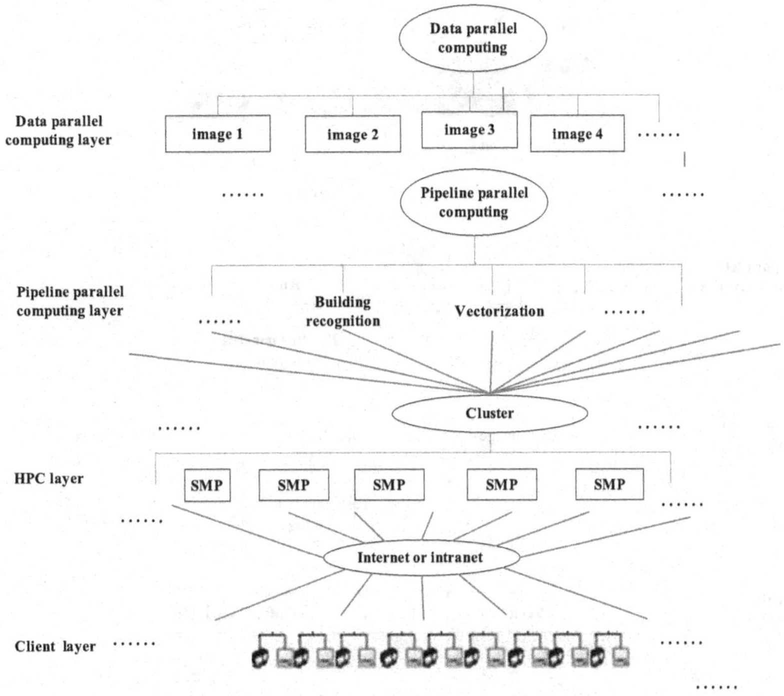

tioning System), and the data of image and coordinate are managed by GIS. The output is digital 3D buildings.

SMP-Cluster is the HPC platform for reconstructing buildings. Different computing nodes of SMP-Cluster are used for the data parallel computing; Different processors within the each computing node are used for the task and pipeline parallel computing.

Example 3:

The problem is to generate and simulate digital city.

There are three layers, as shown in Figure 20.

The first layer is parallel computing layer, in which, digital city is divided into many blocks for data parallel computing in the horizontal dimension, the each block into many altitude scales for task parallel computing in the vertical dimension, the each altitude scale into many applications for task parallel computing in the application dimension, the each application into many periods for pipeline computing in the time dimension, the each period into many types of users for grid computing in the user dimension.

The second layer is platform layer. SMP-Cluster is the best parallel platform for the simulation of digital city.

The third layer is device layer. The input includes the Shenzhen images obtained from real city by RS (Remote sensing), sensor or camera, the location of the images identified by GPS (Global Positioning System) and city vector graph. The input data and the computing data are managed by GIS (Geographic Information System).The output is sent to clients linked with users.

CONCLUSION

In fact, in the last century, the performance of the parallel computer is the main goal of parallel computing and in this century the capacity of using parallel computing to solve problems is more cared about. Now the parallel

Figure 19. Architecture for reconstructing buildings

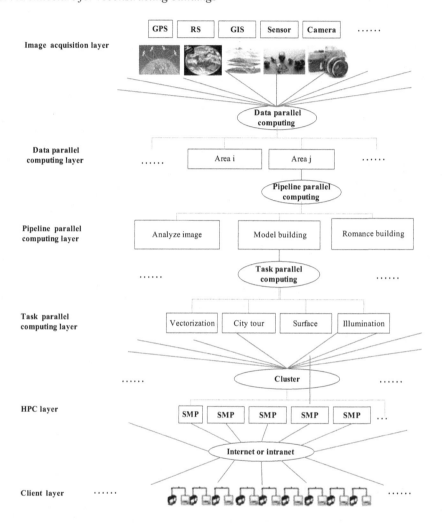

computer is very powerful, but the parallel efficiency is low and parallel computing is used less than serial computing. Maybe the situation need a long time to change, but an easier and more effective way for programmers and users to understand the parallel computing is very necessary. The way is NIPC which regards parallel computing just as a simulation of the parallel way in nature based on computing technology and electronic information technology.

We illustrate the nature inspired parallel computing by analyzing the phenomenon and the four dimensions of the parallel way in nature. The four steps in the architecture of NIPC and the corresponding four schemes of NIPC can give the programmers and users more clear guides to parallel computing.

Based NIPC, the problem is analyzed to dig its parallelism and then decomposed, paralleled, distributed and mapped step by step. Then three problems including illegal building monitoring, 3D building reconstruction, generation and simulation of digital city, are solved step by step using NIPC.

In a word, NIPC can be used to promote the efficiency of parallel programming and parallel applications, and to create new parallel applications.

Figure 20. Architecture for generating and simulating digital city

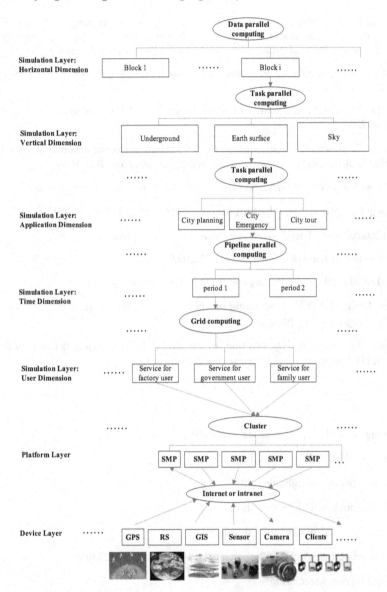

FUTURE RESEARCH DIRECTIONS

Future research directions should focus on studying how to use parallel computing to solve all kinds of problems in all kinds of fields. Although the theory of NIPC is vital to the development of parallel computing, using NIPC to solve problems is more important. NIPC paves the parallel computing way passers prefer to design and use parallel computing based on.

REFERENCES

Almasi, G. S., & Gottlieb A.(1989). *Highly Parallel Computing*. Benjamin-Cummings publishers, Redwood city, CA. Anderson, E., Bai, Z., Bischof, C., Blackford, S., Demmel, J., Dongarra, J. J., Croz, D., Greenbaum, A., Hammaring, S., McKenney, A.,& Sorensen, D. (1999). *LAPACK Users' Guide, 3rd ed*. Philadelphia, PA: SIAM.

Bobby, J. (1997). Modelcity Philadelphia . *Retrieved December 5, 2007, from* Bobby, J. (1997). Modelcity Philadelphia . *Retrieved October 25, 2007, from*

Dongarra, J. (2006). Trends in parallel computing: A historical overview and examination of future developments. *Circuits and Devices Magazine, 22*(1), 22-27.

Dongarra, J., Sterling, T., Simon, H., & Strohmaier, E. (2005).High-performance computing: clusters, constellations, MPPs, and future directions. *Computing in Science & Engineering, 7*(2), 51-59

Escapenet GMBH (2008). VirtualCity. *Retrieved October 25, 2007, from* http://www.virtualcity.ch/

Expatica (2006).**Illegal building: The expat nightmare.** *Retrieved October 20, 2007, from*

Google company. (2008).Google Earth. *Retrieved December 5, 2007, from*

Google company. (2008).Google Earth. *Retrieved October 25, 2007, from*

Gore, A. (1998). The Digital Earth: Understanding our planet in the 21st Century.

Gore, A. (1998).The Digital Earth:Understanding our planet in the 21st Century. *Retrieved October 20, 2007, from* http://www.isde5.org/al_gore_speech.htm

He, G. J. (2001). Extracting Buildings Distribution Information of Different Heighs in a City from the Shadows in a Panchromatic SPOT Image. *Journal of Image and Graphics, (5)*.

http://earth.google.com/

http://earth.google.com/

http://en.wikipedia.org/wiki/High-performance_computing

http://en.wikipedia.org/wiki/Parallel_computing

http://members.aol.com/bobbyj164/bjhome01.htm

http://members.aol.com/bobbyj164/bjhome01.htm

http://news.sohu.com/20060405/n242654025.shtml

http://www.expatica.com/actual/article.asp?subchannel_id=87&story_id=27308

http://www.isde5.org/al_gore_speech.htm

http://www.microsoft.com/virtualearth/default.mspx

http://www.microsoft.com/virtualearth/default.mspx

http://www.ust.ucla.edu/ustweb/

http://www.ust.ucla.edu/ustweb/

Justus Reid Weiner (2003). The Global Epidemic of illegal building and Demolitions: Implications for Jerusalem. *Jerusalem Letter / Viewpoints(498)*.

Kawasaki, Y., Ino, F., Mizutani, Y., Fujimoto, N., Sasama, T., Sato, Y., Sugano, N., Tamura, S., & Hagihara, K. (2004). High-performance computing service over the Internet for intraoperative image processing.Information *Technology in Biomedicine*, IEEE Transactions. 8(1):36 – 46.

Li ,Q.,& Lin , S.F. (2001). Research on digital city framework architecture. *ICII Conference 1, 30-36.*

Lin, Y. (2005). Three-dimensional building reconstruction based on single image vision. *Journal of Shandong Jianzhu University,* (2).

Microsoft company (2008). *Retrieved December 5, 2007, from*

Microsoft company (2008). *Retrieved October 25, 2007, from*

Nicol, D. M (2003).Utility analysis of parallel simulation. *PADS Conference, 123-132*

Qi, L., &Lin, S.F.2001). Research on digital city framework architecture. *ICII Conference, 1, 33-36.*

Qian, Z. B. (2000).Total-automatically Image Matching of Stereoscopic Pair of Aerial Photograpgy. *Journal of Zhengzhou Institute of Surveying and Mapping,* (4).

Richard, M. F. (2001). PARALLEL AND DISTRIBUTED SIMULATION SYSTEMS. *WSC Conference, 147-157.*

Snir, M., Otto, S., Huss-Lederman, S., Walker, D., &Dongarra, J. (1996). *MPI: The Complete Reference.* Cambridge, MA: MIT Press.

Sohu (2006). Beijing monitoring illegal buildings by the two satellites every two-month with 90 percent accuracy rate. *Retrieved October 20, 2007, from*

TORONTO, Ont(2006). VirtualCity. *Retrieved October 25, 2007, from* http://www.virtualcity.ca/

Urban Simulation Team at UCLA (2000). Applications for fast visual simulation in design, urban planning, emergency response, and education. *Retrieved October 25, 2007, from*

Urban Simulation Team at UCLA (2000). Applications for real-time visual simulation in design, urban planning, emergency response, and education. *Retrieved December 5, 2007, from* Virtual City (2008).VirtualCity. *Retrieved October 25, 2007, from* http://www.virtualcity.co.ke /

Wang, C.L., Bhat, P.B.,& Prasanna, V.K. (1996). High-performance computing for vision.*Proceedings of the IEEE 84(7):931 – 946.*

Wikipedia (2008). High-performance computing. *Retrieved October 10, 2007, from*

Wikipedia (2008). Parallel computing. *Retrieved October 10, 2007, from*

You, H. J. (2005). 3D Building Reconstruction Based on Scanning Laser Rangerfinder Data. *Remote Sensing Technology and Application,* (4).

You, H. J. (2005). The research status of building extraction based on airborne laser scanning data. *Science of Surveying and Mapping,* (5).

Zhang, K. Z. (2004). Legal Definition for Illegal Building. *Academic Exploration (11).*

Zhanjiang Evening News (2008).illegal buildings existed 15 years demolished once. *Retrieved October 20, 2007, from* http://zjphoto.yinsha.com/file/200804/2008040716332642.htm

ADDITIONAL READING

Papers:

[1]Yao, X.; Burke, E.; Lozano, J.A.; Smith, J.; Merelo-Guervós, J.J.; Bullinaria, J.A.; Rowe, J.; Tino, P.; Kabán, A.; Schwefel, H.-P. (2004).Parallel Problem Solving from Nature, Lecture Notes in Computer Science , Vol. 3242

[2] D Schluter, LM Nagel (1995). Parallel Speciation by Natural Selection. American Naturalist. UChicago Press.

Parallel Information Sites

- NHSE - National HPCC Software Exchange
- Netlib Repository at UTK/ORNL
- BLAS Quick Reference Card
- LAPACK
- ScaLAPACK
- GAMS - Guide to Available Math Software
- Center for Research on Parallel Computation (CRPC)
- Supercomputing & Parallel Computing: Conferences
- Supercomputing & Parallel Computing: Journals
- High Performance Fortran (HPF) reports
- High Performance Fortran Resource List
- Fortran 90 Resource List
- Major Science Research Institutions from Caltech
- Message Passing Interface (MPI) Forum
- High Performance Fortran Forum
- OpenMP
- PVM
- Parallel Tools Consortium
- DoD High Performance Computing Modernization Program
- DoE Accelerated Strategic Computing Initiative (ASCI)
- National Computational Science Alliance

Related On-line Textbooks

- **Templates** for the Solution of Linear Systems: Building Blocks for Iterative Methods, SIAM Publication, Philadelphia, 1994.
- **PVM** - A Users' Guide and Tutorial for Networked Parallel Computing, MIT Press, Boston, 1994.
- **MPI** : A Message-Passing Interface Standard
- **LAPACK** Users' Guide (Second Edition), SIAM Publications, Philadelphia, 1995.
- **MPI: The Complete Reference**, MIT Press, Boston, 1996.
- Using MPI: Portable Parallel Programming with the Message-Passing Interface by W. Gropp, E. Lusk, and A. Skjellum
- Parallel Computing Works, by G. Fox, R. Williams, and P. Messina (Morgan Kaufmann Publishers)
- Computational Science Education Project
- Designing and Building Parallel Programs. A dead-tree version of this book is available by Addison-Wesley.
- High Performance Fortran (HPF), a course offered by Manchester and North High Performance Computing Training & Education Centre, United Kingdom

KEY TERMS

Application Dimension of NIPC: In application dimension, objects in different applications can construct or exist in parallel and all events in different applications can occur or go on in parallel. For example, underground objects and events can be processed by mine monitoring application, underwater monitoring application and other underground applications in parallel; objects and events on the earth surface can be processed by city planning application, ecological resource monitoring application, tour application and other earth surface applications in parallel; objects and events in the sky can be processed by climate monitoring application, air pollution monitoring application and other sky applications in parallel.

In the application dimension, different processes of objects and events in different applications in the application dimension are distributed onto different processes, and run in parallel.

Digital City: The concept "digital city" is derived from the concept "digital earth" brought forward firstly by Al Gore . Digital city simulate real cities by computer science and geographic science to help government for city planning and transportation simulation. There are some famous digital cities including Virtual Los Angeles, Model City Philadelphia, Google earth and virtual earth .

Nature Inspired Parallel Computing(NIPC): Use the parallel method in nature to solve computing problems. All things in nature can be simulated using computer, and the parallel phenomenon in nature can be simulated by parallel computing technology using HPC (high performance computer), which consists of many computing nodes with CPUs and kernels, different from traditional computer with single computing node. Things in nature can be simulated in parallel on different computing nodes or different CPUs or different CPU kernels in HPC.

Nature is composed of a large number of objects and events. Events are the spirit of objects; objects the body of events. They are related with each other in nature. Objects can construct or exist in parallel and events can occur or go on in parallel. The parallelism mainly exists in four dimensions including space dimension, time dimension, application dimension, and user dimension. We can design and use NIPC according to the four dimensions.

Parallel Computing: The term parallel computing refers to the use of (parallel) supercomputers and computer clusters. Parallel computing is a form of computing in which many instructions are carried out simultaneously. It operates on the principle that large problems can almost always be divided into smaller ones, which may be solved concurrently ("in parallel"). It has been used for many years, but interest in it has become greater in recent years due to physical constraints preventing frequency scaling. Parallel computing exists in several different forms: bit-level parallelism, instruction-level parallelism, data parallelism, and task parallelism. Parallelism is a primary method for accelerating the total power of a supercomputer. Computational physics applications have been the primary drivers in the development of parallel computing over the last 20 years. Languages (e.g., Fortran and C) and libraries (e.g., message passing interface (MPI) and linear algebra libraries, i.e., LAPACK) allow the programmer to access or expose parallelism in a variety of standard ways.

Space Dimension of NIPC: In space dimension, objects at different locations can construct or exist in parallel, and all events at different locations can occur or go on in parallel. For an example in vertical direction, one house is repaired in Nanshan, Shenzhen China, and at the same time another house is repaired in FUtian, Shenzhen China. Another example, men are walking on roads, and at the same time buses are running on roads. For an example in vertical direction, planes are flying in the sky, at the same time cloud drifting in the sky, at the same time rain is dropping onto the earth surface, at the same time water is flowing on the earth surface, and at the same time groundwater is flowing in the earth.

In the space dimension, processes of objects and events in different spaces in the space dimension are distributed onto processes, and run in parallel.

Time Dimension of NIPC: In time dimension, objects can construct or exist in parallel in different time, and all events can occur or go on in parallel in different time. For example, a boy sat on a chair previously, and his father sits on the same chair at present.

In the time dimension, different processes of objects and events in different time in the time dimension are distributed onto different processes, and run in parallel.

User Dimension of NIPC: In user dimension, objects and events can be used or watched by users in parallel. For example, Jack watches buildings from one angle, and at the same time John watches buildings from another angle.

In the user dimension, processes of objects and events in different user services are distributed onto different grid nodes, and run in parallel.

Chapter XXIV
Fuzzy Chaotic Neural Networks

Tang Mo
Automation College, Harbin Engineering University, China

Wang Kejun
Automation College, Harbin Engineering University, China

Zhang Jianmin
Automation College, Harbin Engineering University, China

Zheng Liying
Automation College, Harbin Engineering University, China

ABSTRACT

An understanding of the human brain's local function has improved in recent years. But the cognition of human brain's working process as a whole is still obscure. Both fuzzy logic and dynamic chaos are internal features of the human brain. Therefore, to fuse artificial neural networks, fuzzy logic and dynamic chaos together to constitute fuzzy chaotic neural networks is a novel method. This chapter is focused on the new ways of fuzzy neural networks construction and its application based on the existing achievement in this field. Four types of fuzzy chaotic neural networks are introduced, namely chaotic recurrent fuzzy neural networks, cooperation fuzzy chaotic neural networks, fuzzy number chaotic neural networks and self-evolution fuzzy chaotic neural networks. Chaotic recurrent fuzzy neural networks model is developed based on existing recurrent fuzzy neural networks through introducing chaos mapping into the membership layer. As it is a dynamic system, the input of neuron not only processes the information of former monument but also contains chaos maps information which is provided by dynamic chaos. Cooperation fuzzy chaotic neural network is proposed on the basis of simplified T-S fuzzy chaotic neural networks and Aihara chaotic neuron. It realizes fuzzy reasoning process by a neural network structure in which the rule inference part is realized by chaotic neural networks. Then enlightened by fuzzy number neural networks we propose a fuzzy number chaotic neuron, which is obtained by blurring the Aihara chaotic neuron. Using these neurons to construct fuzzy number chaotic neural networks, the mathematical model and weight updating rules are also given. At last, a self-evolution fuzzy chaotic neural network is proposed according to the principle of self-evolution network, which unifies the fuzzy Hopfield neural network constitution method.

Copyright © 2009, IGI Global, distributing in print or electronic forms without written permission of IGI Global is prohibited.

INTRODUCTION

There is appreciable understanding of some partial functions of the human brain. The researches of perceptrons, visual processing network, and memory and so on, have attained certain levels of success. Unfortunately despite these successes the overall function of the human brain remains a real challenge to understand. At present scientists have already accumulated massive knowledge of basic and essential facts about brain composition, brain contour and cerebrum function, but are still unable to explain substantively, the question of brain information processing.

But the integrated function is in no way a simple combination the partial function. The consciousness and cognition process of the brain involves a complex dynamic system to carry on the massive neuron activity. The fact that people do not have a complete understanding of the human brain and work process, underscores a need for qualitative leap in this research (Zhu, D.Q., 2004).

It is well known, that neural network is an attempt to simulate the human brain's structure and primary function. Fuzziness is a remarkable characteristic of human brain. The synergy of neural network and the fuzzy theory helps to address more complex questions in wider application domains with a solution model usually called the fuzzy neural network.

Chaos has been discovered to be a characteristic of the dynamics present in the brain. In the cranial nerve system, from the microscopic neuron and neural network, to the macroscopic brain wave and the brain magnetic wave, chaos were discovered in two aspects (Huang, R. S., 2000; Wang, Y. N, Yu, Q. M., & Yuan, X. F., 2006). Chaos theory could help understand certain irregular activities in the brain, thus the chaos dynamics provide people a new turning point to study the neural network. The chaos phenomenon is has inherently a non-linear dynamics, and the neural network is also a highly non-linear dynamics system, so that both have a close correlation.

At present, the fuzzy neural network technology have been well developed, and widely applied in many kinds of domains. The chaos dynamics and the chaos neural network technology is an exciting emerging research area which yielded encouraging results from theory to application. From the existed literature, it can be seen that the proposed fuzzy neural network models (whether the static or dynamic models) do not consider the chaos characteristic of actual biological neural network (Liu, C. J., Liao, X. Z., & Zhang, Y. H. 2000; Juang, C. F., 2004; Yang, G., & Meng, J. E., 2005; Abdulhamit, S., 2006; Theocharis, J. B., 2006; Gu, L. L., & Deng, Z. L., 2006; Shashi, K., Sanjeev, K., Prakash, Ravi, S., Tiwari, M. K., & Shashi B. K., 2007). The chaotic neural network technology stems from chaos dynamic do not consider the fuzzy characteristic of actual biological neural network, and cannot process the fuzzy information. From the exist literature, the research of fuse fuzzy logic, chaos and artificial neural networks is extremely few at present.

There is an emerging interdisciplinary science that combines fuzzy logic, chaos dynamics and artificial neural networks paradigms. These three sciences individually reflect some aspects of the human brain information processing mechanism. From the existing literature however, a synergized approach which combines fuzzy logic, chaos and artificial neural networks is extremely few at present. Such a hybrid facilitates an overlapping of individual capabilities to establish a more robust system that has fuzzy reasoning ability, auto-adaptation ability, and chaos search ability.

The structure of the chapter is organized as follows: **Backgrounds and Previous Research Work** provides a detailed review and a background of the existing fuzzy, chaos, and neural networks theory development. **The Main Thrust of the Chapter** consists of four types of fuzzy chaotic neural networks. **Concluding Remarks** concludes the whole chapter with the special emphasis on the advantage of the four models. Finally, the future directions are addressed in **Future Research Directions**. The terms and definitions, as well as an additional reading list, can be found at the end of the chapter.

BACKGROUND AND PREVIOUS RESEARCH WORK

The fuzzy logic and the neural network study human's cognition question from the different angle respectively. Fuzzy neural network is developed based on neural network and fuzzy system. Complimenting neural network and fuzzy systems yield a system that can handle language computation, logical reasoning, distributional processing and the non-linear dynamics. The literature on fuzzy logic and neural network reveals two main areas (Zhang, D., 2004). One is based on making neural network to constitute a fuzzy reasoning system; while the other kind is introducing the fuzzy concept and the fuzzy reasoning mechanism to neuron, thus constituting a fuzzy neural network. The former also called neural fuzzy system, been widely applied. The second kind of fuzzy neural network adds the fuzzy ingredient into the traditional neural network. The present methods of a fuzzified neuron is one which has any of its components fuzzified, such as the inputs, weights, or outputs and then carries on the maximum and minimum operation with the fuzzy set (Pedrcy, W., & Recha, A. F.,1993; Kosko, B., 1992; Jou, C. C., 1992). Although the application of second kind of fuzzy neural network is not as widespread as the first, incomparable superiority in functions, like fuzzy classification, fuzzy information storage and memory usage and so on.

There was an upsurge in the exploration of chaos phenomenon, in the 20th century beginning in the 70's, with increasing research interest today (Wu, X. X., & Chen, Zh., 2001). American meteorologist *E.Lorenz* (1963), when analyzing climate data, discovered that the outcome of two curves with extremely close starting values can differ finally in a big way, thus giving an insight into the first example of chaos. Since the birth of chaos science, it has developed rapidly. Chaos has a rich physical background of great interest to mathematicians and physicist, and seeps gradually to the natural and social sciences. At present, chaos already obtained widespread application as astronomy, meteorology, physiology, mathematics, physics, information science, economic even art. The understanding of chaos phenomenon is one of most important achievements in non-linear science. At present, brain wave research is a major research area that applies the chaos phenomenon to brain studies.

The brain nerve system is a complex system which is composed by non-linear neurons. A research approach which is basically a mutual fusion of neural network and chaos began in the 1990s, and has developed very quickly. Its main research aim is to clarify the cerebrum chaos phenomenon, establish the dynamics of neural network model including chaos, and use it in intelligent information processing. Thus, chaos dynamics research provides a turning point and an exciting research frontier for researchers in the field of neural networks. The chaotic neural network has its foundation in both chaos theory and artificial neural networks. It not only has the artificial neural networks characteristic, but also has the chaos search and association memory ability, and can better simulate the human brain information process.

The fuzzy neural network technology and the chaotic neural network technology have attracted wide research interest in recent times. But, the existing fuzzy neural network and the chaotic neural network still have the following areas that require further research namely:

(1) Existing fuzzy neural network algorithms easily fall into the partial minimum;
(2) Fuzzy neural network models are mainly static models, its dynamic chaos characteristic has not been considered;
(3) Insufficient analysis of the chaos characteristic of dynamic fuzzy neural network;
(4) Chaotic neural network does not posses the fuzzy language information ability.

In order to address the above listed problems, a research method which fuses fuzzy logic, chaos theory and artificial neural networks is explored. This method is scarcely reported in the literature, and the technology is still in a preliminary exploration phase. Hubert, Y. (1999) proposed a method, with fuzzy logic rule control branch parameter in chaotic neural network, thus enhancing the chaotic neural network performance; Pan, Y. X. *et al.* introduced chaos optimization method into fuzzy controller or fuzzy neural network model, thus enhancing the network performance (Pan, Y. X., Xu, Q. F., & Gao, H. M., 2000; Tang, W., & Li, D. P., 2000; Liao, Y. F., & Ma, X. Q., 2005; Zou, E., Li, X. F., & Liu, Y. G., 2004; Zou, E., Liu, J. P., Li, X. F., & Zhang, T. S., 2006; Wang, S. X., Jiang, Y., & Li, Y. G., 2006). But these models themselves don't have both the fuzzy reasoning ability and chaos characteristic. The fusion of fuzzy logic, artificial neural networks and chaos theory is a new method, which aims at forming a *fuzzy chaotic neural network* that not only has the fuzzy reasoning ability but also has auto-adaptation, self-learning and chaos search ability, so as to enhance the neural network information-handling capacity. It is helpful to simulate the whole function of the human brain, and very meaningful in modeling nonlinear and associative memory problems from the view of both theory and reality.

Based on the above research results, this article carries on further studies to the fuzzy chaotic neural network fusion technology and the application domain.

THE MAIN THRUST OF THE CHAPTER

There are mainly four types of fuzzy chaotic neural networks to be introduced in this section, namely *chaotic recurrent fuzzy neural networks, cooperation fuzzy chaotic neural networks, fuzzy number chaotic neural networks* and *self-evolution fuzzy chaotic neural networks*. Among them, the former two networks are constructed based on fuzzy neural networks and the last two are on the basis of chaotic neural networks which are fuzzified.

Chaotic Recurrent Fuzzy Neural Networks

Chaotic Recurrent Fuzzy Neural Networks Model

By now, most widely used dynamic fuzzy neural networks (DFNN) are constituted based on T-S fuzzy neural network. Dynamic fuzzy neural networks could also be called *recurrent fuzzy neural networks (RFNN)*, and it appears as a powerful approach to solve many engineering problems in the field of nonlinear system identification and control.

Wang, Y. *et al.* (2003) proposed a multi-layer recurrent fuzzy network model. Based on this model, this chapter proposes a *chaotic recurrent fuzzy neural network (CRFNN)*, which introduces chaos mapping into the membership layer of recurrent fuzzy neural networks. The topological diagram of the proposed CRFNN structure is as shown in fig 1.1.

There are four layers in *chaotic recurrent fuzzy neural networks*, namely input layer, membership function layer, rule layer and output layer. There are m input nodes, p output nodes and $n \times m + m$ membership function nodes. Each input node corresponding with m linguistic nodes, each chaotic mapping corresponding with a linguistic nodes either. Define u_i^k represent the *ith* input node of the *kth* layer; O_i^k represent the *ith* output node of the *kth* layer. The semantic meaning and function of the neurons in the proposed chaotic recurrent fuzzy neural network are as follows.

Layer 1 (input layer): Each neuron in this layer represents one input variable. And the input variables are transfer to the next layer directly.

Figure 1.1. Chaotic recurrent fuzzy neural networks model

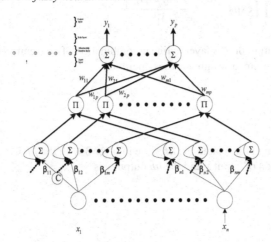

$$O_i^1(k) = x_i^1(k).$$ (1-1)

where x_i^1 represent the *ith* input node of this layer, and O_i^1 represent the *ith* output.

Layer 2 (membership layer): Each node in this layer represents the membership function of a linguistic variable, serve as memory unit. The Gaussian function is adopted here as a membership function of neuron. Then,

$$O_{ij}^2(k) = \mu_{A_{ij}}(u_{ij}^2) = \exp\left\{-\frac{[u_{ij}^2(k) - m_{ij}(k)]^2}{[\sigma_{ij}(k)]^2}\right\}.$$ (1-2)

Where m_{ij} is the mean, σ_{ij} is the variance of the Gaussian function. Subscript *ij* represents the *jth* node of the *ith* input variable x_i corresponding to.

In this layer, we introduce chaotic map as mentioned before. But this map could only realize in the interval [0,1]. In order to mapping between [0,*N*], it could be rewritten as

$$x(k) = \gamma(k)x(k-1)(N - x(k-1))/N.$$ (1-3)

When $\gamma \in (3,6,4)$, system (1-3) is a chaotic system.

Therefore, at disperse moment *k*, the input variable of layer 2 becomes

$$u_{ij}^2(k) = \beta_{ij}(k)x_i^1(k) + \theta_{ij}(k)O_{ij}^2(k-1) + x_{ij}^c(k).$$ (1-4)

Where

$$x_{ij}^c(k) = \gamma_{ij}(k)x_{ij}^c(k-1)(N - x_{ij}^c(k-1))/N.$$

In (1-4), $O_{ij}^2(k-1)$ is the feedback of the *jth* node of the *ith* input, and θ_{ij} is the feedback link weight. There are five parameters to adjust, namely m_{ij}, σ_{ij}, β_{ij}, θ_{ij} and γ_{ij}.

Layer 3 (rule layer): Nodes in this layer are called rule nodes, and each of them denotes a term of rule. These neurons accomplish and operation.

$$O_j^3(k) = \prod_{i=1}^n O_{ij}^2(k) = \prod_{i=1}^n \mu_{A_{ij}}(u_{ij}^2) = \prod_{i=1}^n \exp\left\{-\frac{[u_{ij}^2(k) - m_{ij}(k)]^2}{[\sigma_{ij}(k)]^2}\right\}.$$ (1-5)

Layer 4 (output layer): The output of this layer is linear combination of consequences of last layer. That is to say, this layer accomplishment summed-weight defuses operation.

$$y_j(k) = O_j^4(k) = \sum_{i=1}^m w_{ij}^4(k) \cdot u_i^4(k).$$ (1-6)

Where w_{ij}^4 denotes the link weight associated the *ith* node in layer 3 with the *jth* node in layer 4.
Finally, the overall representation of input *x* and the *lth* output *y* is

$$y_l(k) = O_l^4(k) = \sum_{j=1}^{m} w_{jl} \cdot O_j^3 = \sum_{j=1}^{m} w_{jl} \prod_{i=1}^{n} \exp\left\{-\frac{[\beta_{ij}x_i^1 + \theta_{ij}O_{ij}^2(k-1) + \gamma_{ij}x_{ij}^c(k-1)(M-x_{ij}^c(k-1))/M - m_{ij}]^2}{[\sigma_{ij}]^2}\right\}, \quad l = 1, \cdots, p$$

(1-7)

Where

$$O_{ij}^2(k-1) = \exp\left\{-\frac{\left[\beta_{ij}x_i^1 + \theta_{ij}O_{ij}^2(k-2) + \gamma_{ij}x_{ij}^c(k-2)(M-x_{ij}^c(k-2))/M - m_{ij}\right]^2}{[\sigma_{ij}]^2}\right\}.$$

(1-8)

This proposed *CRFNN* is equivalence to a digital quantity fuzzy system from perspective of structure. The general fuzzy if-then rule is as followings

R^j : if u_{1j} is A_{1j},... u_{nj} is A_{nj}, then $y = w_j$ $i = 1, \cdots n$.

Where $u_{ij} = \beta_{ij}u_i^1 + \theta_{ij}O_{ij}^2(k-1) + x_{ij}^c$. $A_{1j} \ldots A_{nj}$ are the linguistic terms of the precondition part with membership function. w_j is the fuzzy singleton, which implies the matching degree of *jth* control rule. n is the dimension of input vectors.

Thus the fuzzy rules expressed in (1-8) can be implemented with the following nonlinear equation

$$y^* = \sum_{j=1}^{m} w_j \cdot \alpha_j = \sum_{j=1}^{m} w_j \cdot \prod_{i=1}^{n} \mu_{A_{ij}}(u_{ij}).$$

(1-9)

where α_j is define as the fire strength of the *jth* rule, which is obtained from the product of the grades of the membership function $\mu_{A_{ij}}(\mu_{ij})$. $\mu_{A_{ij}}$ is the membership function of fuzzy set of A_{ij}.

When we use the CRFNN above-mentioned as a system identifier, take no account of the systemic structure learning phase. Namely, the number of fuzzy division and the initial value of system acquits as a matter of experience.

The following learning algorithm based on gradient descent. The deviation is the same as that of the back-propagation learning law. Seen from (1-2) and (1-4), the input of feedback unit includes the output of hidden neuron at the previous moment. Since the output $O_{ij}^2(k-1)$ is the function of $m_{ij}(k-1)$, $\sigma_{ij}(k-1)$, $\theta_{ij}(k-1)$, $\beta_{ij}(k-1)$ and $\gamma_{ij}(k-1)$, the gradient of $O_{ij}^2(k-1)$ with respect to these parameters must be considered as a whole, when using BP learning method. Consequently, BP learning method turns to be a dynamic BP (DBP) arithmetic. When the single output case is considered for clarity, the cost function $E(k)$ which we want to minimize is defined as

$$E(k) = \frac{1}{2}\left(y^d(k) - y(k)\right)^2 = \frac{1}{2}\left(y^d(k) - O^4(k)\right)^2.$$

(1-10)

where $y^d(k)$ and $y(k)$ are, respectively, the desire output and current output for on discrete time k. According to the famous negative gradient and chain law, the update rule of weight defined as follows

$$W(k+1) = W(k) + \Delta W(k) = W(k) + h\left(-\frac{\partial E(k)}{\partial W(k)}\right).$$

(1-11)

Where $\mathbb{W}$ denotes $m, \sigma, \theta, \beta, \gamma$ or w, η is learning rate. Let $e(k) = y^d(k) - y(k)$ be the training error. So that, the gradient of error $E(\cdot)$ in (10) with respect to a weight vector $\mathbb{W}$ is

$$\frac{\partial E(k)}{\partial \mathbb{W}(k)} = -e(k) \cdot \frac{\partial O^4(k)}{\partial \mathbb{W}(k)} \qquad (1\text{-}12)$$

The adjusting parameters w could be updated using (1-11) and (1-12) directly. While, for m, σ, θ, β and γ, (1-12) should be modified as

$$\frac{\partial E(k)}{\partial \mathbb{W}(k)} = -e(k) \cdot \left(\left. \frac{\partial O^4(k)}{\partial \mathbb{W}(k)} \right|_* + \frac{\partial O^4(k)}{\partial O^2(k-1)} \cdot \frac{\partial O^2(k-1)}{\partial \mathbb{W}(k)} \right) \qquad (1\text{-}13)$$

Suppose there is just a slight modification each time, so that $\mathbb{W}(k)$ can be substitute by $\mathbb{W}(k-1)$. Therefore, (1-13) can be approximated as

$$\frac{\partial E(k)}{\partial \mathbb{W}(k)} \approx -e(k) \cdot \left(\left. \frac{\partial O^4(k)}{\partial \mathbb{W}(k)} \right|_* + \frac{\partial O^4(k)}{\partial O^2(k-1)} \cdot \frac{\partial O^2(k-1)}{\partial \mathbb{W}(k-1)} \right) \qquad (1\text{-}14)$$

Where

$$\frac{\partial O^2(k-1)}{\partial \mathbb{W}(k-1)} \approx \left. \frac{\partial O^2(k-1)}{\partial \mathbb{W}(k-1)} \right|_* + \frac{\partial O^2(k-1)}{\partial O^2(k-2)} \cdot \frac{\partial O^2(k-2)}{\partial \mathbb{W}(k-2)} \qquad (1\text{-}15)$$

Where

$$\left. \frac{\partial O^4(k)}{\partial \mathbb{W}(k)} \right|_* \quad \text{and} \quad \left. \frac{\partial O^2(k-1)}{\partial \mathbb{W}(k-1)} \right|_*$$

denote local derivation with respect to $\mathbb{W}$. From (1-11), (1-14) and (1-15), it is easy to derive the update rule.
Then

$$\frac{\partial E(k)}{\partial w_{ij}(k)} = -e(k) \cdot O_i^3(k) \qquad (1\text{-}16)$$

$$\frac{\partial E(k)}{\partial m_{ij}(k)} = e(k) w_j(k) O_j^3(k) \frac{2\left[\beta_{ij}(k) x_i^1(k) + \theta_{ij}(k) O_{ij}^2(k-1) + x_{ij}^c(k) - m_{ij}(k) \right]}{\left[\sigma_{ij}(k) \right]^2} \left[\frac{\partial O_{ij}^2(k-1)}{\partial m_{ij}(k-1)} \theta_{ij}(k) - 1 \right]$$

$$(1\text{-}17a)$$

where

$$\frac{\partial O_{ij}^2(k-1)}{\partial m_{ij}(k-1)} = -O_{ij}^2(k-1) \cdot \frac{2\left[\beta_{ij}(k-1)x_i^1(k-1)+\theta_{ij}(k-1)O_{ij}^2(k-2)+\gamma_{ij}(k-1)x_{ij}^c(k-2)(N-x_{ij}^c(k-2))/N - m_{ij}(k-1)\right]}{\left[\sigma_{ij}(k-1)\right]^2}$$

$$\left(\cdot\left[\frac{\partial O_{ij}^2(k-2)}{\partial m_{ij}(k-2)}\theta_{ij} \; k-1)-1\right]\right.$$

$$(1\text{-}18)$$

$$\frac{\partial E(k)}{\partial \sigma_{ij}(k)} = 2e(k)w_j(k)O_j^3(k) \cdot \left[\frac{-\left[\beta_{ij}(k)x_i^1(k)+\theta_{ij}(k)O_{ij}^2(k-1)+x_{ij}^c(k)-m_{ij}(k)\right]^2}{\left[\sigma_{ij}(k)\right]^3}\right.$$

$$\left.(+\frac{\left[\beta_{ij}(k)x_i^1(k)+\theta_{ij}(k)O_{ij}^2(k-1)+x_{ij}^c(k)-m_{ij}(k)\right]}{\left[\sigma_{ij}(k)\right]^2}\frac{\partial O_{ij}^2(k-1)}{\partial \sigma_{ij}(k-1)}\theta_{ij} \; k)\right]$$

$$(1\text{-}17\text{b})$$

$$\frac{\partial E(k)}{\partial \theta_{ij}(k)} = 2e(k)w_j(k)O_j^3(k)\frac{\left[\beta_{ij}(k)x_i^1(k)+\theta_{ij}(k)O_{ij}^2(k-1)+x_{ij}^c(k)-m_{ij}(k)\right]}{\left[\sigma_{ij}(k)\right]^2}$$

$$\left(\cdot\left[\theta_{ij} \; k)\frac{\partial O_{ij}^2(k-1)}{\partial \theta_{ij}(k-1)}+O_{ij}^2(k-1)\right]\right.$$

$$(1\text{-}17\text{c})$$

$$\frac{\partial E(k)}{\partial \beta_{ij}(k)} = 2e(k)w_j(k)O_j^3(k)\frac{\left[\beta_{ij}(k)x_i^1(k)+\theta_{ij}(k)O_{ij}^2(k-1)+x_{ij}^c(k)-m_{ij}(k)\right]}{\left[\sigma_{ij}(k)\right]^2}\left[x_i^1(k)+\theta_{ij}(k-1)\frac{\partial O_{ij}^2(k-1)}{\partial \beta_{ij}(k-1)}\right]$$

$$(1\text{-}17\text{d})$$

$$\frac{\partial E(k)}{\partial \gamma_{ij}(k)} = 2e(k)w_j(k)O_j^3(k)\frac{\left[\beta_{ij}(k)x_i^1(k)+\theta_{ij}(k)O_{ij}^2(k-1)+x_{ij}^c(k)-m_{ij}(k)\right]}{\left[\sigma_{ij}(k)\right]^2}\left[x_{ij}^c(k)+\theta_{ij}(k)\frac{\partial O_{ij}^2(k-1)}{\partial \gamma_{ij}(k-1)}\right]$$

$$(1\text{-}17\text{e})$$

Where

$$\frac{\partial O_{ij}^2(k-1)}{\partial \sigma_{ij}(k-1)},\; \frac{\partial O_{ij}^2(k-1)}{\partial \theta_{ij}(k-1)},\; \frac{\partial O_{ij}^2(k-1)}{\partial \beta_{ij}(k-1)},\; \frac{\partial O_{ij}^2(k-1)}{\partial \gamma_{ij}(k-1)}$$

can be adjust according to update rule similar to (1-18) by (1-15).

Chaotic Recurrent Fuzzy Neural Networks Characteristic

When adjust parameters using *dynamic BP algorithm* (DBP), how to choose learning rate η play an important role. The update rule of (1-11) calls for a proper choice of the learning rate η. For a small value of η the convergence is guaranteed but the speed is very slow; on the other hand if η is too big, the algorithm becomes unstable (Chen, Y., & Teng, C., 1995; Zhou, Y. F., Li, S. J., & Jin, R. C., 2002; Wu, W., Shao, H. M., & Qu, D., 2005). This part develops a guideline in selecting the learning rate properly, which leads to adaptive learning rate.

Using Lyapunov stability theorem, the authors such as Wang, Y. (2003) has analyzed the influence of learning rate η on convergence before. And finally, they gave a general parameter adjusting method in DBP algorithm. The definition of discrete Lyapunov function is as follows

$$V(k) = E(k) = \frac{1}{2}\left[e(k)\right]^2 .$$

(1-19)

Where $e(k)$ denote the error in the learning process.

During the training procedure, the change of Lyapunov function is obtained by

$$\Delta V(k) = V(k+1) - V(k) = \frac{1}{2}\left[e^2(k+1) - e^2(k)\right].$$

(1-20)

Lemma 1: Let $\boldsymbol{\eta} = \begin{bmatrix} \eta_1 & \eta_2 & \eta_3 & \eta_4 & \eta_5 \end{bmatrix}^T = \begin{bmatrix} \eta^\sigma & \eta^c & \eta^\theta & \eta^\beta & \eta^w \end{bmatrix}^T$ which represents the learning rate of adjusting parameters. The vector $\mathbf{P}_{max}$ is defined as

$$\mathbf{P}_{max} \equiv \begin{bmatrix} P_{1,max} & P_{2,max} & P_{3,max} & P_{4,max} & P_{5,max} \end{bmatrix}^T$$
$$= \begin{bmatrix} \max_k \left|\frac{\partial y(k)}{\partial \sigma}\right| & \max_k \left|\frac{\partial y(k)}{\partial c}\right| & \max_k \left|\frac{\partial y(k)}{\partial \theta}\right| & \max_k \left|\frac{\partial y(k)}{\partial \beta}\right| & \max_k \left|\frac{\partial y(k)}{\partial w}\right| \end{bmatrix}^T .$$

(1-21)

where $y(k)$ is the output of RFNN.

If

$$0 < \eta_i < 2/(P_{i,max})^2, \quad i = 1,2,3,4,5 .$$

(1-22)

Then, *DBP* algorithm is convergent.

Next, introduce the conclusion of lemma 1 into the update rule of learning rate, and we can get the following deduction.

Deduction 1: Let η^σ, η^m, η^θ, η^β, η^γ and η^w represents the learning rate of weights σ, m, θ, β, γ and w. For $|\sigma| > 1$, $|\theta| < 1$, $|x_i^1| < 1$, $i = 1,2,\cdots,n$. x_i^1 represents the input term of CRFNN, Then the convergence is guaranteed if the learning rate are chosen as

$$0 < \eta^w < 2/R$$

(1-23)

$$0 < \eta^\sigma, \eta^c, \eta^\beta < 2/\left(W_{max} M_{max}\right)^2$$

(1-24a)

$$0 < \eta^\theta < 1/2\left(W_{max} M_\sigma\right)^2$$

(1-24b)

$$0 < \eta^\gamma < 2/\left(P_{5,max}\right)^2 = 2/\left(W_{max} M_{max} T\right)^2$$

(1-24c)

where $W_{max} = \sqrt{R}\,|w_{max}|$, $M_{max} = \sqrt{N_{max}}/(|\sigma_{min}| - 1)$, R is the number of fuzzy rules in the CRFNN, N_{max} is the maximum quantity of fuzzy set related to CRFNN, and N is chaos variable.

Figure 1.2. Phase diagram of the chaotic system (1-25)

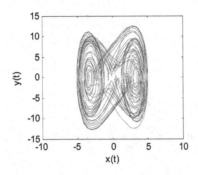

Application

In this section Duffen system is studied as the plant. It is a typical chaotic system characterized by second order differential equation, including a cube item. This system behaves as periodic motion or chaotic motion when meeting with external drive. The difference equation is

$$\dot{x}(t) = y(t) \,. \tag{1-25a}$$

$$\dot{y}(t) = -ay(t) - x^3(t) + b\cos(t) \,. \tag{1-25b}$$

where a, b are system nonlinearity parameters. $0 < a < 1$, $0 < b < 250$ and $\cos t$ is an exterior inspirit.

When the parameters a, b and initial condition change, the solutions of (1-25) switch among different attractors. The trajectory of solutions turn to chaos from cycle when the value of b gradually increases between interval [0, 250]. Set initial conditions $x0 = 0.3$, $y0 = 0.5$, $a = 0.3$, $b = 31.5$, then the Duffing system has a chaotic solution. The phase diagram is as shown in Fig 1.2.

The two input terms are $x(t)$ and $\cos(t)$, the output is $y(t)$. Pick 1000 pairs of data except the initial 1000 pairs of data. Identifying the plant uses *ANFIS (Adaptive Neuro-Fuzzy Interference System), RFNN, CRFNN* and *CRFNN with adaptive learning rate* separately.

Figure 1.3. Phase diagram of system using ANFIS

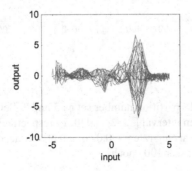

Figure 1.4. Phase diagram of system using RFNN

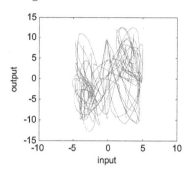

Figure 1.5. Phase diagram of system using CRFNN

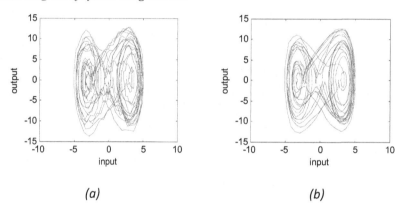

(a)   *(b)*

Figure 1.6. Error curve of CRFNN

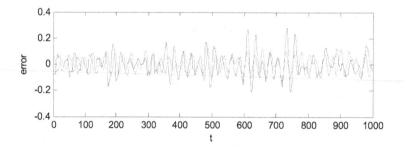

The two-input single-output ANFIS partition number set as 5 and 3. Set RFNN learning rate $\eta = 0.02$, m_{ij} and σ_{ij} are initialized randomly between interval $[-2, 2]$ and $[0, 1]$, respectively. β_{ij} and θ_{ij} are initialize randomly between interval $[-1, 1]$. Set CRFNN learning rate $\eta = 0.02$ or adaptively according to deduction 1, γ_{ij} is initialize randomly between interval $l[0, 4]$. Train for 100 epochs.

Figure 2.1. Cooperation fuzzy chaotic neural networks model

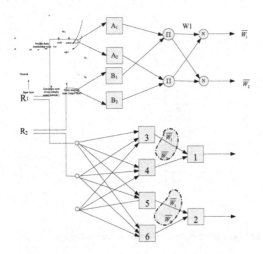

The identification results of ANFIS and RFNN, CRFNN and CRFNN with adaptive learning rate are as shown in Fig 1.3, Fig 1.4, Fig 1.5. Hereinto, Fig 1.5(a) is CRFNN with fixed learning rate; Fig 1.5(b) is CRFNN with adaptive learning rate according to according to deduction 1. The error between them is shown is Fig 1.6.

As seen from the simulation result, we can conclude that the *CRFNN* model we proposed is better at identifying capacity than *ANFIS* and *RFNN* when dealing with chaos system approximation. That is because of CRFNN model is a dynamic system, it not only process the information of former monument but also contains a chaos map which provide dynamic chaos information. Thus it is more appropriate for dynamic chaotic system identifying. Moreover, the adaptive learning rate could improve network capacity and accelerate convergence speed though it still takes a long training time.

Cooperation Fuzzy Chaotic Neural Networks

Cooperation Fuzzy Chaotic Neural Networks Model

In this section a *cooperation fuzzy chaotic neural network (CFCNN)* is proposed on the basis of simplified T-S fuzzy chaotic neural networks (Zhang, Z. X., 2000) and *Aihara* chaotic neuron (Inoue, M., & Fukushima, S., 1992; Li, Z., Zhang, B., & Mao, Z. Y., 2000). This cooperation fuzzy chaotic neural network realize fuzzy reasoning process including membership function production, normalization, rule inference and fuzzlized by a neural network structure, in which the rule inference part is realized by chaotic neural networks.

The mathematic model of chaotic neural networks constitute by chaotic neuron is as follows

$$x_i(t+1) = kx_i(t) + \sum_{j=1}^{n} T_{ij} h_j \left(f\left(x_j(t)\right)\right) + \sum_{j=1}^{q} \omega_{ij} A_j(t) - \alpha \left(f_i\left(x_i(t)\right)\right) - \theta_i(1-k) \quad i=1,2,...n \tag{2-1}$$

$$y_i(t+1) = f_i\left(x_i(t+1)\right) \quad i=1,2,\cdots,n \tag{2-2}$$

A double-input double-output *cooperating fuzzy chaotic neural network* model which is made up of precondition and conclusion part is shown in Fig 2.1. The precondition part comprises three segments, namely membership function layer, production layer and normalization layer. The conclusion is also made up of three parts, which are input layer, rule conclusion layer and output layer. The rule conclusion layer is constituted by chaotic neural network, which could be one layer or multi-layers.

Figure 2.2. State diagram of cooperation fuzzy chaotic neural networks

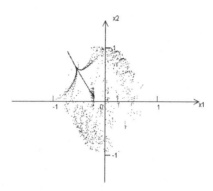

Figure 2.3. Structure diagram of m regular of F_j output neural imprison with j piece

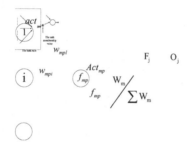

The state chart of *cooperation fuzzy chaotic neural network* system is shown in Fig 2.2, when it has single input, single output and two internal states. Where $k_1 = k_2 = 0.55$, $A(t) = \sin t$, $T_{11} = 0.8$, $T_{12} = 0.5$, $T_{21} = 0.4$, $T_{22} = 0.4$, $w_1 = 0.5$, $w_2 = 0.8$, $\alpha_1 = \alpha_2 = 5$, $\beta_2 = \beta_2 = 3.5$.

The graphs above show that the system has chaotic characteristics.
The mathematic model of preconditions part is as follows.
The function of membership function layer is

$$u_{qm}\left(R_q(\tau+1)\right) = \exp\left(-\left(\left(R_q(\tau+1) - st_{qm}\right)/\sigma_{qm}\right)^2\right) \qquad (2\text{-}3)$$

Output of product layer is

$$W_m(\tau+1) = \prod_q u_{qm}(\tau+1) \qquad (2\text{-}4)$$

Output of normalization layer is

$$\overline{W}_m(\tau+1) = W_m(\tau+1) / \sum_m W_m(\tau+1) \qquad (2\text{-}5)$$

Let O_j and F_j are the *jth* output and *jth* neural function of system final output layer, separately. The structure diagram of the *mth* rule is shown in fig 2.3.
So that, input of conclusion layer is

$$net_{mp}(\tau+1) = \sum_{l} w_{mpl}(\tau+1)act_{ml}(\tau+1) \qquad (2\text{-}6)$$

Output of conclusion layer is

$$Act_{mp}(\tau+1) = f_{mp}\left[x_{mp}(\tau+1)\right] \qquad (2\text{-}7)$$

$$f_{mp}(x) = 1/\left(1+e^{-\beta_{mp}x}\right) \qquad (2\text{-}8)$$

Entire status of conclusion layer is

$$x_{mp}(\tau+1) = kx_{mp}(\tau) + \sum_{rt} T_{mprt} h_{rt} f_{mp}(x_{rt}(\tau)) + net_{mp}(\tau) - \alpha f_{mp}(x_{mp}(\tau)) - \theta_{mp}(1-k) \qquad (2\text{-}9)$$

Input of the output layer is

$$NET_j(\tau+1) = \frac{\sum_m W_m(\tau+1)Act_{mp}(\tau+1)}{\sum_m W_m(\tau+1)} = \frac{W_1(\tau+1)Act_{1j}(\tau+1) + W_2(\tau+1)Act_{1j}(\tau+1) + \ldots + W_m(\tau+1)Act_{mp}(\tau+1) + \ldots}{W_1(\tau+1) + W_2(\tau+1) + \ldots + W_m(\tau+1) + \ldots} \qquad (2\text{-}10)$$

Output of the network is

$$O_j(\tau+1) = F_j\left(NET_j(\tau+1)\right) \qquad (2\text{-}11)$$

$$F_j = 1/\left(1+e^{-\beta_j NET_j}\right) \qquad (2\text{-}12)$$

The study algorithm of *cooperation fuzzy chaotic neural network* system is considering the two part precondition and conclusion at the same time. Therefore, the study algorithm is dynamic learning algorithm.

Update precondition parameter s(*st* or σ) as followings

$$\Delta s(\tau) = -\eta_s \frac{\partial E(\tau)}{\partial s(\tau)} = -\eta_s \frac{\partial E(\tau)}{\partial O_j(\tau)} \cdot \frac{\partial O_j(\tau)}{\partial s(\tau)} = -\eta_s \frac{\partial E(\tau)}{\partial O_j(\tau)} \cdot \frac{\partial O_j(\tau)}{\partial NET_j(\tau)} \cdot \frac{\partial NET_j(\tau)}{\partial W_m(\tau)} \cdot \frac{\partial W_m(\tau)}{\partial s(\tau)}$$

$$\left(= -\eta_s \frac{\partial E(\tau)}{\partial O_j(\tau)} \cdot F_j'\left(NET_j(\tau)\right)\right) \cdot \left[\frac{\partial}{\partial W_m} \cdot \frac{\sum_m W_m Act_{mp}(\tau)}{\sum_m W_m}\right] \cdot \frac{\partial W_m(\tau)}{\partial s(\tau)}$$

$$\left(= -\eta_s \left\{\left(\overline{O}_j(\tau) - O_j(\tau)\right) F_j'\left(NET_j(\tau)\right)\right\} \frac{Act_{mp}(\tau) - NET_j(\tau)}{\sum_m W_m} \cdot \frac{\partial W_m(\tau)}{\partial s(\tau)}\right) \qquad (2\text{-}13)$$

Where, η_s is learning rate, $\overline{O}_j$ is expect output.

For the sake of simple and convenient writing ω_l substitute for ω_{mpl}, T_{rt} substitute for T_{mprt}.

Figure 2.4. Characteristic of cooperation fuzzy chaotic neural networks to candy alcoholysis chaos oscillator

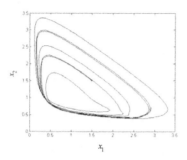

(a) phase plane trajectory

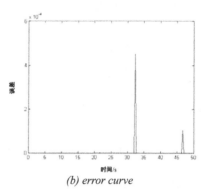

(b) error curve

$$\Delta\omega_l = -\eta_{\omega_l} \frac{\partial E(\tau)}{\partial \omega_l} = -\eta_{\omega_l} \frac{\partial E(\tau)}{\partial NET_j(\tau)} \cdot \frac{\partial NET_j(\tau)}{\partial \omega_l}$$

$$= -\eta_{\omega_l} \frac{\partial E(\tau)}{\partial O_j(\tau)} \cdot \frac{\partial O_j(\tau)}{\partial NET_j(\tau)} \cdot \frac{\partial NET_j(\tau)}{\partial x_{mp}(\tau)} \cdot \frac{\partial x_{mp}(\tau)}{\partial net_{mp}(\tau)} \cdot \frac{\partial net_{mp}(\tau)}{\partial \varphi}$$

$$= -\eta_{\omega_l} \frac{\partial E(\tau)}{\partial O_j(\tau)} \cdot F_j^{'}\left(NET_j(\tau)\right) \frac{W_m}{\sum_m W_m} f_{mp}^{'}\left(x_{mp}(\tau)\right) \cdot \frac{\partial x_{mp}(\tau)}{\partial net_{mp}(\tau)} \cdot \frac{\partial}{\partial \varphi} \sum \omega_l act_{mp}$$

$$= -\eta_{\omega_l} \left\{ \left(\overline{O}_j(\tau) - O_j(\tau)\right) \right\} F_j^{'}\left(NET_j(\tau)\right) \frac{W_m}{\sum_m W_m} \cdot f_{mp}^{'}\left(x_{mp}(\tau)\right) \frac{\partial x_{mp}(\tau)}{\partial net_{mp}(\tau)} act_{mp}$$

(2-14)

And

$$\frac{\partial x_{mp}(\tau)}{\partial net_{mp}(\tau)} = k \frac{\partial x_{mp}(\tau-1)}{\partial net_{mp}(\tau-1)} + 1 - \alpha f_{mp}^{'}\left(x_{mp}(\tau-1)\right) \cdot \frac{\partial x_{mp}(\tau-1)}{\partial net_{mp}(\tau-1)}$$

(2-15)

According to (2-15), the training process is a dynamic adjusting process.

$$\Delta T_{rt} = -\eta_{T_{rt}} \frac{\partial E(\tau)}{\partial T_{rt}} = -\eta_{T_{rt}} \frac{\partial E(\tau)}{\partial NET_j(\tau)} \cdot \frac{\partial NET_j(\tau)}{\partial T_{rt}} = -\eta_{T_{rt}} \frac{\partial E(\tau)}{\partial O_j(\tau)} \cdot \frac{\partial O_j(\tau)}{\partial NET_j(\tau)} \cdot \frac{\partial NET_j(\tau)}{\partial Act_{mp}(\tau)} \cdot \frac{\partial Act_{mp}(\tau)}{\partial T_{rt}}$$

$$:= -\eta_{T_{rt}} \frac{\partial E(\tau)}{\partial O_j(\tau)} \cdot F_j^{'}\left(NET_j(\tau)\right) \frac{W_m}{\sum_m W_m} \frac{\partial Act_{mp}(\tau)}{\partial x_{mp}(\tau)} \cdot \frac{\partial x_{mp}(\tau)}{\partial T_{rt}}$$

$$:= -\eta_{T_{rt}} \frac{\partial E(\tau)}{\partial O_j(\tau)} \cdot F_j^{'}\left(NET_j(\tau)\right) \cdot \frac{W_m}{\sum_m W_m} f_{mp}^{'}(x_{mp}(\tau)) \cdot \frac{\partial x_{mp}(\tau)}{\partial T_{rt}}$$

(2-16)

Where

$$\frac{\partial x_{mp}(\tau)}{\partial T_{rt}} = k \frac{\partial x_{mp}(\tau-1)}{\partial T_{rt}} + \sum_n h_{rt} \left(f_{mp}\left(x_{rt}(\tau-1)\right)\right) - \alpha f_{mp}^{'}\left(x_{mp}(\tau-1)\right) \cdot \frac{\partial x_{mp}(\tau-1)}{\partial T_{rt}}$$

(2-17)

According to (2-17), the update of T_n is also a dynamic.

Application

The mathematics model and characteristics of candy ferment chaos oscillator is

$$\dot{x}_1(t) = -x_1(t)x_2^2(t) + 0.999 + 0.42\cos(1.75t) \qquad (2\text{-}18)$$

$$\dot{x}_2(t) = x_1(t)x_2^2(t) - x_2(t) \qquad (2\text{-}19)$$

Approximate the candy alcoholysis chaos oscillator using chaotic neural fuzzy system model. The conclusion layer is realized by chaotic neural network which constituted by four chaotic neurons. The parameters are set as $m=1\backslash2$, $j=1\backslash2$, $t=1\backslash2$, $q=1$, $l=1$, $p=1\backslash2$, $r=1\backslash2$.

The phase plane trajectory of candy alcoholysis chaos oscillator acquired by *cooperation fuzzy chaotic neural networks* is shown in fig.2.4.(a), and the error curve between outputs of real candy ferment chaos oscillator and *cooperation fuzzy chaotic neural networks* are shown in Fig 2.4.(b). Choosing parameters as $k_1 = k_2 = k_3 = k_4 = 0.55$, $\alpha_1 = \alpha_2 = \alpha_3 = \alpha_4 = 5$.

In the structure, the *cooperation fuzzy chaotic neural networks* is neural network, which has chaos characteristic; while in the function, it is a fuzzy system, which unify blur, chaos, artificial neural network three together and simulate the human brain intelligent behavior fully.

Fuzzy Number Chaotic Neural Networks

Fuzzy Number Chaotic Neuron Model

Fuzzy number is used to describe the inaccurate and uncompleted general affairs and phenomenon, such as "about 20 years old" (James D., & Donald W., 1999). *Fuzzy number neural networks* whose link weights are all fuzzy numbers is an extension of general neural networks. One of fuzzy number neural networks proposed by James P.Dunyak calculate the output of fuzzy number neuron according to the λ-cut set of fuzzy number and then generate networks. Enlightened by this in this section we propose a fuzzy chaotic neuron.

Dynamics equations of chaos neuron model which putted forward by *Aihara* can be simplified as follows (Hubert, Y. C., 1999):

$$y(t+1) = ky(t) - \alpha g(f(y(t)) + a(t)$$
$$x(t+1) = f(y(t+1))$$

Set $g(x)=x$, $f(x)$ to continuous increasing function, then

$$y(t+1) = ky(t) - \alpha x(t) + a(t)$$
$$x(t+1) = f(y(t+1)) \qquad (3\text{-}1)$$

The fuzzy neuron of system (3-1) is

$$\tilde{Y}(t+1) = k\tilde{Y}(t) - \alpha \tilde{X}(t) + \tilde{A}(t)$$
$$\tilde{X}(t+1) = f(\tilde{Y}(t+1)) \qquad (3\text{-}2)$$

when $\forall \lambda \in [0,1]$, we can get

535

$$(Y_1(t+1))_\lambda = k(Y_1(t))_\lambda - \alpha(X_2(t))_\lambda + (A_1(t))_\lambda$$

$$(Y_2(t+1))_\lambda = k(Y_2(t))_\lambda - \alpha(X_1(t))_\lambda + (A_2(t))_\lambda$$

$$(X_1(t+1))_\lambda = f((Y_1(t+1))_\lambda)$$

$$(X_2(t+1))_\lambda = f((Y_2(t+1))_\lambda) \tag{3-3}$$

where: $(Y_1(t+1))_\lambda$—left-hand end point of λ-cut set of $\widetilde{Y}(t+1)$

$(Y_2(t+1))_\lambda$—right-hand end point of λ-cut set of $\widetilde{Y}(t+1)$

To different $\lambda \in [0,1]$, we can calculate each zone of state $\widetilde{Y}$ and output $\widetilde{X}$ respectively. So the fuzzy neuron can be seen equivalence to a two-dimension system (3-3). That is to say we can study the character of fuzzy neuron (3-2) through system (3-3).

$\forall \lambda \in [0,1]$, the Jacobian matrix of system (3-3) is

$$J_{FC} = \begin{bmatrix} \dfrac{\partial(Y_1(t+1))_\lambda}{\partial(Y_1(t))_\lambda} & \dfrac{\partial(Y_1(t+1))_\lambda}{\partial(Y_2(t))_\lambda} \\[2mm] \dfrac{\partial(Y_2(t+1))_\lambda}{\partial(Y_1(t))_\lambda} & \dfrac{\partial(Y_2(t+1))_\lambda}{\partial(Y_2(t))_\lambda} \end{bmatrix} = \begin{bmatrix} k & -\alpha\dfrac{\partial(X_2(t))_\lambda}{\partial(Y_2(t))_\lambda} \\[2mm] -\alpha\dfrac{\partial(X_1(t))_\lambda}{\partial(Y_1(t))_\lambda} & k \end{bmatrix} \tag{3-4}$$

The trace of matrix J_{FC} is the divergence of system (3-3)

$$divV = 2k \tag{3-5}$$

Since $k>0$, the divergence of system (3-3) $divV > 0$, that is to say there is no chaotic attractor in system (3-3).

System (3-3) can be changed as follows to construct a *fuzzy number chaotic neuron* model which can generates chaotic attractor for $\forall \lambda \in [0,1]$

$$(Y_1(t+1))_\lambda = k(Y_1(t))_\lambda - \alpha f((Y_1(t))_\lambda + (Y_2(t))_\lambda) + (A_1(t))_\lambda$$

$$(Y_2(t+1))_\lambda = k(Y_2(t))_\lambda - \alpha f((Y_1(t))_\lambda + (Y_2(t))_\lambda) + (A_2(t))_\lambda$$

$$(X_1(t+1))_\lambda = (Y_1(t+1))_\lambda$$

$$(X_2(t+1))_\lambda = (Y_2(t+1))_\lambda \tag{3-6}$$

Fuzzy Number Chaotic Neuron Characteristic

In this section we will analyze fuzzy character, scattering and *Lyapunov exponent (LE)* index of *fuzzy number chaotic neuron* system (3-6) as follows.

Theorem 3.1: System (3-6) can and only can generate the fuzzy number whose shape of membership function is symmetrical.

Prove: Assume the initial state and control performance parameter are fuzzy numbers. First prove any λ-cut set of $\widetilde{Y}(t)$ is closed interval.

$\forall \lambda \in [0,1]$, then

$$(Y_2(t+1))_\lambda - (Y_1(t+1))_\lambda = k((Y_2(t))_\lambda - (Y_1(t))_\lambda) + (A_2(t))_{\overline{\lambda}}(A_1(t))_\lambda \tag{3-7}$$

$\widetilde{Y}(0), \widetilde{A}(t)$ are both fuzzy numbers, so right hand of above formula is greater than 0 when t=0, viz.

$$(Y_2(1))_\lambda - (Y_1(1))_\lambda > 0 \tag{3-8}$$

assume $t = t1$, then

$$(Y_2(t))_\lambda - (Y_1(t))_\lambda > 0 \tag{3-9}$$

when $t = t1 + 1$, then

$$(Y_2(t))_\lambda - (Y_1(t))_\lambda > 0 \tag{3-10}$$

and the like, for $\forall t \in [0, \infty)$ and $\forall \lambda \in [0,1]$, then

$$(Y_2(t))_\lambda - (Y_1(t))_\lambda > 0 \tag{3-11}$$

so any λ-cut set of $\widetilde{Y}(t)$ is closed interval.

We'll prove the membership function of $\widetilde{Y}(t)$ possesses convexity as follows.
Assume $0 \le \lambda_1 < \lambda_2 \le 1$, then

$$(Y_1(t+1))_{\lambda 1} - (Y_1(t+1))_{\lambda 2} = k((Y_1(t))_{\lambda 1} - (Y_1(t))_{\lambda 2}) +$$
$$(A_1(t))_{\lambda 1} - (A_1(t))_{\lambda 2} + \alpha[f(Y_1(t))_{\lambda 2} + Y_2(t))_{\lambda 2}) - f(Y_1(t))_{\lambda 1} + Y_2(t))_{\lambda 1})] \tag{3-12}$$

$$(Y_2(t+1))_{\lambda 1} - (Y_2(t+1))_{\lambda 2} = k((Y_2(t))_{\lambda 1} - (Y_2(t))_{\lambda 2}) +$$
$$(A_2(t))_{\lambda 1} - (A_2(t))_{\lambda 2} + \alpha[f(Y_1(t))_{\lambda 2} + Y_2(t))_{\lambda 2}) - f(Y_1(t))_{\lambda 1} + Y_2(t))_{\lambda 1})] \tag{3-13}$$

To satisfy the convexity, (3-12) must be less than 0 and formula (3-13) is greater than 0.
To let formula (3-12) less than 0, there must be

$$f((Y_1(t))_{\lambda 2} + (Y_2(t))_{\lambda 2}) - f((Y_1(t))_{\lambda 1} + (Y_2(t))_{\lambda 1}) \le 0 \tag{3-14}$$

$f(x)$ is continuous increasing function, so only need

$$f((Y_1(t))_{\lambda 2} + (Y_2(t))_{\lambda 2}) - f((Y_1(t))_{\lambda 1} + (Y_2(t))_{\lambda 1}) \le 0 \tag{3-15}$$

To let formula (3-13) greater than 0, there must be

$$(Y_1(t))_{\lambda 2} + (Y_2(t))_{\lambda 2} - [(Y_1(t))_{\lambda 1} + (Y_2(t))_{\lambda 1}] \ge 0$$

Thereby, to satisfy convexity of fuzzy number, there must be

$$(Y_1(t))_{\lambda 2} + (Y_2(t))_{\lambda 2} - ((Y_1(t))_{\lambda 1} + (Y_2(t))_{\lambda 1}) = 0 \tag{3-16}$$

We can learn from (3-16) that membership function of fuzzy number $\widetilde{Y}(t)$ is symmetrical.
Prove over.

Theorem 3.2: The shape of membership functions of fuzzy numbers, which are generated by system (3-6), are affected by parameter k, when system tend to stable, the shape of membership functions of fuzzy numbers which are generated by it are same.

Prove: $0 \leq \lambda_1 < \lambda_2 \leq 1$, learn from formula (3-13)

$$\frac{[(Y_1(t+1))_{\lambda 1} - (Y_1(t+1))_{\lambda 2}] - [((Y_1(t))_{\lambda 1} - (Y_1(t))_{\lambda 2}]}{[(Y_1(t))_{\lambda 1} - (Y_1(t))_{\lambda 2}] - [(Y_1(t-1))_{\lambda 1} - (Y_1(t-1))_{\lambda 2}]} = k \qquad (3-17)$$

Assume

$$[(Y_1(t+1))_{\lambda 1} - (Y_1(t+1))_{\lambda 2}] - [(Y_1(t))_{\lambda 1} - (Y_1(t))_{\lambda 2}] = M(t) \qquad (3-18)$$

$$[(Y_1(t))_{\lambda 1} - (Y_1(t))_{\lambda 2}] - [(Y_1(t-1))_{\lambda 1} - (Y_1(t-1))_{\lambda 2}] = M(t-1) \qquad (3-19)$$

Then

$$M(t) = kM(t-1) = k^t M(0) \qquad (3-20)$$

For $0 < k < 1$, when $t \to \infty$ there must be $M(t) \to 0$. So when system (3-6) tends to stable, the left shape of membership functions of fuzzy numbers that generated by it are same.

Prove over.

Theorem 3.3: When input and control parameter $\widetilde{A}(t)$ are distinct number, then output of system (3-6) is distinct too; when input and control parameter $\widetilde{A}(t)$ are fuzzy number, then output of system (3-6) is fuzzy number too.

Prove: When input and control parameter $\widetilde{A}(t)$ are distinct number, for $\forall \lambda$ there are

$$(Y_1(0))_\lambda = (Y_2(0))_\lambda) = y(0), A_1(0)_\lambda = A_2(0)_\lambda = a(0) \qquad (3-21)$$

Learn from system (3-6), $\forall t$ and $\forall \lambda$ then

$$(Y_1(t))_\lambda = (Y_2(t))_\lambda) = y(t), A_1(t)_\lambda = A_2(t)_\lambda = a(t) \qquad (3-22)$$

System (3-6) can be written as follows

$$\begin{aligned} y(t+1) &= ky(t) - \alpha f((2y(t)) + a(t) \\ x(t+1) &= y(t+1) \end{aligned} \qquad (3-23)$$

Obviously, output of formula (3-23) is distinct.

Learn from theorem 3.1 and 3.2, output is fuzzy number when input and control parameter $\widetilde{A}(t)$ are fuzzy number.

Prove over.

Next prove the scattering of system.
Jacobian matrix of system (3-6) is

$$
J_{FC} = \begin{bmatrix} k - \alpha \dfrac{\partial f((Y_1(t))_\lambda + (Y_2(t))_\lambda)}{\partial (Y_1(t))_\lambda} & -\alpha \dfrac{\partial f((Y_1(t))_\lambda + (Y_2(t))_\lambda)}{\partial (Y_2(t))_\lambda} \\ -\alpha \dfrac{\partial f((Y_1(t))_\lambda + (Y_2(t))_\lambda)}{\partial (Y_1(t))_\lambda} & k - \alpha \dfrac{\partial f((Y_1(t))_\lambda + (Y_2(t))_\lambda)}{\partial (Y_2(t))_\lambda} \end{bmatrix}
$$

(3-24)

and

$$
\frac{\partial f((Y_1(t))_\lambda + Y_2(t))_\lambda)}{\partial (Y_1(t)_\lambda)} = \frac{\partial f((Y_1(t))_\lambda + Y_2(t))_\lambda)}{\partial (Y_2(t)_\lambda)} = \frac{\partial f((Y_1(t))_\lambda + Y_2(t))_\lambda)}{\partial ((Y_1(t))_\lambda + Y_2(t))_\lambda)} = m(t)
$$

(3-25)

Thereby, formula (3-24) can be written as follow:

$$
J_{FC} = \begin{bmatrix} k - \alpha m(t) & -\alpha m(t) \\ -\alpha m(t) & k - \alpha m(t) \end{bmatrix}
$$

(3-26)

We'll analyze whether system (3-6) can be a scattering system as follows.
Learn from formula (3-26), divergence of system (3-6) is

$$
div V = 2(k - \alpha m(t))
$$

(3-27)

If system (3-6) is a scattering system, then

$$
div V = 2(k - \alpha m(t)) < 0
$$

(3-28)

$$
k < \alpha m(t)
$$

(3-29)

If $f(x)$ is monopole Sigmoid function, then

$$
f(x) = 1/1 + \exp(-x/\varepsilon)
$$

(3-30)

Learn from formula (3-25), then

$$
m(t) = \frac{1}{\varepsilon} f((Y_1(t))_\lambda + Y_2(t))_\lambda)(1 - f((Y_1(t))_\lambda + Y_2(t))_\lambda))
$$

(3-31)

So $\forall t, m(t) \in [0, 0.25/\varepsilon)$.
We can conclude as follows through inferences above.

Conclusion 3.1: The essential condition that let system (3-6) to be a scattering system is $k < \alpha/4\varepsilon$.
Learn from formula (3-26), character value of matrix J_{FC} is

$$
\mu_1 = k
$$

$$
\mu_2 = k - 2\alpha m(t)
$$

(3-32)

Since $\mu_1 = k$ and $0 < k < 1$, the first *Lyapunov exponent* index of system (3-6) is

$$LE_{FC1} = \lim_{n \to \infty} \frac{1}{n} \sum_{t=0}^{n-1} \ln k < 0 \qquad (3\text{-}33)$$

To let system (3-6) generate chaos, another *Lyapunov exponent* index of system (3-6) must be greater than 0. There must be

$$LE_{FC2} = \lim_{n \to \infty} \frac{1}{n} \sum_{t=0}^{n-1} \ln |k - 2\alpha m(t)| > 0 \qquad (3\text{-}34)$$

Essential condition for formula (3-34) is for $\exists t$, let $|k - 2\alpha m(t)| > 1$, $k < 2\alpha m(t) - 1$ or $k < 2\alpha m(t) + 1$ viz. So we can achieve following conclusion.

Conclusion 3.2: The essential condition to generate chaotic phenomenon of system (3-6) is $k < 2\alpha m(t) - 1$ or $k < 2\alpha m(t) + 1$.

For $0<k<1$, if $f(x)$ is monopole Sigmoid function, then $f(x)$ satisfy formula (3-34). There is a conclusion as follow.

Conclusion 3.3: If conclusion 3.2 is succeed, then $k < \alpha/2\varepsilon - 1$.

Simulation Analysis

In the simulation process, set parameters of *fuzzy number chaotic neuron* system (3-6) $\varepsilon = 0.04$, $\alpha = 0.07$, $k = 0.8$; set control parameter $\widetilde{A}(t) = \widetilde{A}(a_1, a_2, a_3)$, initial state $\widetilde{Y}(0) = (y_1(0), y_2(0), y_3(0))$, initial output $\widetilde{X}(0) = (x_1(0)\ x_2(0)\ x_3(0)$ to triangular fuzzy number and $a_1 = a_2 - 0.6$, $a_3 = a_2 + 0.6$, $y_1(0) = y_2(0) - 0.6$, $y_3(0) = y_2(0) + 0.6$, $x_1(0) = x_2(0) - 0.6$, $x_3(0) = x_2(0) + 0.6$, $y_2(0) = x_2(0) = 0.5$. Every membership function of fuzzy number can be expressed by 11 λ-cut sets, set $\lambda_i = 0.1 * i (i = 0 ... 10)$. Since the fuzzy numbers are triangular, λ_i-cut sets of fuzzy number can be calculated by formula (3-6). Then we can get a set of initial values of state, output and control parameter to calculate system (3-6). When $\lambda_i = 0.1, 0.5$, the LE_{FC2}- Layapunov character index of system (3-6) changes against parameter a_2 is shown in table 3.1; when $\lambda_i = 0.1$, the curve of *Lyapunov exponent* index LE_{FC1}, LE_{FC2} change against parameter a_2 is shown in Fig 3.1. Bifurcation diagram of the system (3-6) state $(Y_1(t))_{\lambda_i}$ is show in Fig 3.2.

Table 3.1. LE_{FC2} with a_2 (triangular fuzzy number)

λ_i	0.1								
a_2	0.0	0.05	0.1	0.25	0.4	0.45	0.6	0.65	0.7
LE_{FC2}	-2.08	0.285	-0.01	0.3	-0.17	0.3	0.00	0.25	-2.08
λ_i	0.5								
a_2	0.0	0.05	0.1	0.25	0.4	0.45	0.6	0.65	0.7
LE_{FC2}	-2.08	0.285	-0.01	0.3	-0.17	0.3	0.00	0.25	-2.08

Figure 3.1. LEFC plotted against a2

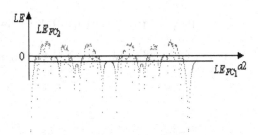

Fig.3.2 Bifurcation diagram of $(Y_1(t))_{\lambda_i}$

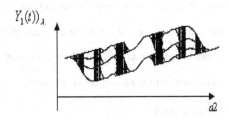

Figure 3.3. Fuzzy chaotic neural network

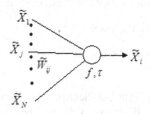

From table 3.1, it is shown that *Lyapunov exponent* index of system (3-6) are same when λ=0.1 and λ=0.5. So any λ-cut set of *fuzzy number chaotic neuron* allows same dynamic equation.

As shown in table 3.1, fig.3.1 and fig.3.2, the Lyapunov exponent index of fuzzy number chaotic neuron is bigger than zero, when the parameters λ and a_2 acquire certain values. And the bifurcation diagram also testified the chaotic feature of *fuzzy number chaotic neuron*.

Fuzzy Number Chaotic Neural Networks Model

Using fuzzy chaotic neurons construct *fuzzy number chaotic neural networks*. When we try to do this, the first problem we confront is the coupling relationship of neurons. Generally, this relationship is achieved by the connection of two neurons.

As shown in fig3.3, suppose there are N neurons connect with the *ith* neuron, and weight between the *ith*

neuron and *jth* neuron is $\widetilde{W}_j$. The control parameter of all neurons is $\widetilde{A}$. So dynamic model of the *ith* neuron can be written as follow:

$$(Y_{i1}(t+1))_\lambda = k(Y_{i1}(t))_\lambda - \alpha f((Y_{i1}(t))_\lambda + (Y_{i2}(t))_\lambda) + (A_1(t))_\lambda - (\Gamma_2)_\lambda + \sum_{j=1}^{N} \min\{(W_{ij1})_\lambda (X_{j1}(t))_\lambda, (W_{ij1})_\lambda (X_{j2}(t))_\lambda,$$

$$(W_{ij2})_\lambda (X_{j1}(t))_\lambda, (W_{ij2})_\lambda (X_{j2}(t))_\lambda\}(Y_{i2}(t+1))_\lambda = k(Y_{i2}(t))_\lambda - \alpha f((Y_{i1}(t))_\lambda + (Y_{i2}(t))_\lambda) + (A_2(t))_\lambda$$

$$(-\Gamma_1)_\lambda + \sum_{j=1}^{N} \max\{(W_{ij1})_\lambda (X_{j1}(t))_\lambda, (W_{ij1})_\lambda (X_{j2}(t))_\lambda, (W_{ij2})_\lambda (X_{j1}(t))_\lambda, (W_{ij2})_\lambda (X_{j2}(t))_\lambda\}_\lambda$$

$$(X_{i1}(t+1))_\lambda = f(Y_{i1}(t+1))_\lambda$$
$$(X_{i2}(t+1))_\lambda = f(Y_{i2}(t+1))_\lambda \qquad\qquad (3\text{-}35)$$

Where,

$(Y_{i1}(t)_\lambda$—left endpoint of the *ith* neuron state's λ-cut set at the moment of t

$(Y_{i2}(t)_\lambda$—right endpoint of the *ith* neuron state's λ-cut set at the moment of t

$(X_{i1}(t)_\lambda$—left endpoint of the *ith* neuron output's λ-cut set at the moment of t

$(X_{i2}(t)_\lambda$—right endpoint of the *ith* neuron output's λ-cut set at the moment of t

$(W_{j1})_\lambda$—left endpoint of weight $\widetilde{W}_j$'s λ-cut set

$(W_{j2})_\lambda$—right endpoint of weight $\widetilde{W}_j$'s λ-cut set

$f(\cdot)$—continuous differentiable function, simply adopt Sigmoid function

$(\Gamma_1)_\lambda$—left endpoint of threshold value Γ 's λ-cut set

$(\Gamma_2)_\lambda$—right endpoint of threshold value Γ 's λ-cut set

For $(x_1{}^P, x_2{}^P, \cdots x_N{}^P)$ $p = 1, 2, \cdots, p$ is the *pth* clear pattern that need to be remembered. To non-fuzzy neural network, if the connection weight is W_{ij} between the *ith* and *jth* neuron, according to Hebb rules, the principle of updating W_{ij} is:

$$W_j = \frac{1}{P} \sum_{p=1}^{P} x_i{}^p x_j{}^p \qquad\qquad (3\text{-}36)$$

For $(x_1{}^P, x_2{}^P, \cdots x_N{}^P)$ $p = 1, 2, \cdots, p$ is the *pth* clear pattern that need to be remembered. To (3-35), if the connection weight is $\widetilde{W}_j$ between the *ith* and *jth* neuron, according to Hebb rules (3-36), the principle turns into:

$$(W_{ij1})_\lambda = \frac{1}{P} \sum_{p=1}^{P} \min\{(x_{i1}{}^P)_\lambda (x_{j1}{}^P)_\lambda, (x_{i2}{}^P)_\lambda (x_{j1}{}^P)_\lambda, (x_{i1}{}^P)_\lambda (x_{j2}{}^P)_\lambda, (x_{i2}{}^P)_\lambda (x_{j2}{}^P)_\lambda\} \qquad (3\text{-}37)$$

$$(W_{ij2})_\lambda = \frac{1}{P} \sum_{p=1}^{P} \max\{(x_{i1}{}^P)_\lambda (x_{j1}{}^P)_\lambda, (x_{i2}{}^P)_\lambda (x_{j1}{}^P)_\lambda, (x_{i1}{}^P)_\lambda (x_{j2}{}^P)_\lambda, (x_{i2}{}^P)_\lambda (x_{j2}{}^P)_\lambda\}$$

$$(3\text{-}38)$$

Figure 4.1. Structure diagram of FuzzyHN

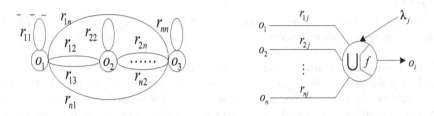

| (a) Topological structure of FuzzyHN | (b) FuzzyHN neuron model |

In summary, the fuzzy number chaotic neuron constructed here is based on fuzzy number neural network constitution method, which is obtained by blurring the Aihara chaotic neuron. This fuzzy chaotic neuron not only has fuzzy number but chaos characteristic. Therefore, the fuzzy number chaotic neural network constitute by these neurons has fuzzy association memory function.

Self-Evolution Fuzzy Chaotic Neural Networks

Self-Evolution Fuzzy Chaotic Neural Networks Model

This section constituted a *self-evolution fuzzy chaotic neural networks* model based on the fuzzy Hopfield neural networks and self-evolution neural networks.

Ruan, X. G. (1997) proposed a *fuzzy Hopfield neural network model (FuzzyHN)*, the Topological structure of fuzzy Hopfield neural networks is shown in Fig 4.1.

Where $node(i)(1 \leq i \leq n)$ represent the ith neuron of FuzzyHN, r_{ij} represent the linking degree from $node(i)$ to $node(j)$, $o_i(1 \leq i \leq n)$ represent the output of $node(i)$, $\lambda_i(1 \leq i \leq n)$ represent the threshold vector of $node(i)$, $\cup$ represent collateral operation, f is non-linear inspire function.

The set of neurons in *FuzzyHN* corresponds to the domain $X = \{x_i | 1 \leq i \leq n\}$, and the fuzzy relation $R = \{r_{ij}\}_{n \times n}$ is regarded as the weighting matrix between neurons in *FuzzyHN*. Then FuzzyHN is a mathematical mode executing the computation of fuzzy logic.

Ruan, X. G. (2000) defined the fuzzyHN model as follows.

Definition 4.1 A *fuzzy Hopfield network FuzzyHN* is defined as 5-tuple

$$FuzzyHN = \langle NS, R, \Lambda, O, Oper \rangle \tag{4-1}$$

where

(1)   The set of neurons is $NS = \{node(i) | 1 \leq i \leq n\}$;

(2)   The weighting matrix between neurons is $R = \{r_{ij}\}_{n \times n} \in [0,1]^{n \times n}$;

(3)   The threshold vector is $\Lambda = (\lambda_1, \lambda_2, \cdots, \lambda_n)^T \in (0,1]^{n \times 1}$;

(4)   The output vector of neurons is $O = (o_1, o_2, \cdots, o_n)^T \in \{0,1\}^{n \times 1}$. $O(t)$ is the state vector in time t of neurons in FuzzyHN;

(5)   A complete parallel computation model is used in FuzzyHN, where Oper $O(t+1) = f(R \circ O(t) - \Lambda)$. $\circ$ is synthesize operation, normally adopt max-min, max-product and so on. The output $O(t)$ is 0 or 1.

In most of the neural models discussed, the input-output transform functions of the neurons are all supposed to be monotonic, e.g, sigmoid functions. Shuai, J. W. *et al.* (1996) pointed out that the effective transform functions will take a variety of shapes and should exhibit nomonotonic behavior. On the basis of this, Shuai, J. W. *et al.* (1997) propose a chaotic neural network, which has chaotic odd-symmetric nonmonotonic function as

$$f(x) = \tanh(\alpha x)\exp(-\beta x^2),\ \alpha, \beta \geq 0 \tag{4-2}$$

Where α, $\beta \geq 0$, with the increasing of β, the iteration dynamics of the function $f(x)$ goes to the chaos through bifurcation.

The N chaotic neurons can compose a chaotic neural network. The dynamics of the *ith* chaotic neuron is

$$S_i(t+1) = f(\sum_{j=1}^{N} W_{ij} S_j(t)) \tag{4-3}$$

Here W is the synaptic connection matrix. One can see that the model becomes the analogue Hopfield model if $\beta = 0$, and becomes the discrete Hopfield model if $\alpha \to \infty$ and $\beta = 0$. Given fixed values for α and β, which are bigger than the thresholds, the network often has chaotic solutions.

For large β, the neuron states are more strongly determined by $\exp(-\beta x^2)$ and approach zero, i.e. quiescent states. We call the nonmonotonic exponential $\exp(-\beta x^2)$ the degree of calm. One can see that not only chaos but also other features of the brain can be simulated with the model. When the calm degree $\beta = 0$ or very small, the network falls into the fixed state and the states of neurons $|S| \to 1$. In other words, the network is active and can associate the input correctly. Like the brain in a state of thinking with a high activity and reasonable association ability, the network can be interpreted to be in the clear-headed state. As β increases, bifurcation occurs while p decreases. Similar to the brain in the rest state, the network seems to be somewhat in rest and the imaginative faculty is rich. When β increases further, the chaotic solution appears. We may think that the network with small activity wandering chaotically is in the deep rest state and simulates the sleeping state of the brain in appearance. Actually periodical windows with a low activity rate also appear intermittently in the chaotically region. They are called the dream-time states.

According to the principle of self-evolution network, and unifies the fuzzy Hopfield neural network constitution method, in this section we proposed an improvement of the self-evolution chaotic neural network. The self-evolution neural network carries on fuzzy processing, causes it to turn from the self-evolution fuzzy chaotic neural network. The new established self-evolution fuzzy neural network can work under two kind of active statuses and complete different function. When $\beta = 0, \alpha \to \infty$, the network turns to fuzzy Hopfield network; increase network tranquility parameter, the network under chaotic state and has association memory function.

The fuzzy processing of system (4-2), (4-3)

(1)   Replaces traditional product and sum operator with the fuzzy maximum and fuzzy minimum operator,

namely takes $\sum \to \vee (\max),\ \cdot \to \wedge(\min)$;

(2)   Adds the threshold value vector $\Lambda = (\lambda_1, \lambda_2, \cdots, \lambda_n)^T \in (0,1]^{n \times 1}$.

Thus, we obtained one *self-evolution fuzzy chaotic neural network* composed by N chaos neuron, the *ith* dynamic equation of neuron is

$$S_i(t+1) = f(\bigvee_{j=1}^{N}(W_{ij} \wedge S_j(t) - \lambda_i)) \tag{4-4}$$

$$f(x) = \tanh(\alpha x)\exp(-\beta x^2), \; \alpha, \beta \geq 0 \tag{4-5}$$

When the degree of calm $\beta = 0, \alpha \to \infty$, the self-evolution fuzzy chaotic neural network above turns into an N-rank fuzzy Hopfield neural network, the dynamic equation of the *ith* neuron is

$$S_i(t+1) = f(\bigvee_{j=1}^{N}(W_{ij} \wedge S_j(t) - \lambda_i)) \tag{4-6}$$

$$f(x) = \tanh(\alpha x), \; \alpha \to \infty \tag{4-7}$$

This N step fuzzy Hopfield neural network (FuzzyHN) also define as followings

$$FuzzyHN = \langle NS, R, \Lambda, O, Oper \rangle \tag{4-8}$$

Where $N, R, \Lambda, O, Oper$ represent the same meaning as in definition 4.1, the operation relations is

$$Oper : O(t+1) = f(R \circ O(t) - \Lambda)$$

Where $\circ$ represent max-min compound operation, $R = W$, $f(x) = \tanh(\alpha x)$, $\alpha \to \infty$, the value of $O(t)$ is 1 or -1

$$Oper : O(t+1) = f(R \circ O(t) - \Lambda)$$

Self-Evolution Fuzzy Chaotic Neural Network Characteristic

In this section, we analyze the fuzzy clustering characteristic and association memory characteristic.

Theorem 4.1: Let n-rank $FuzzyHN = \langle NS, R, \Lambda, O, Oper \rangle$ and model set $X = \{x_1, x_2, ..., x_n\}$. If R is a fuzzy relation on $X \times X$ with anti-reflexivity, then for time t

$$\Delta o(t) \equiv o_i(t) - o_i(t-1) \leq 0 \qquad (1 \leq i \leq N) \tag{4-9}$$

Proof: By the reflexivity of R, $\vee i \in \{1, 2, ..., N\}$,

$$r_{ii} = 1(r_{ii} \in R) \tag{4-10}$$

For anytime t, if $o_i(t-1) = 1$, then

$$\delta_i(t) = \bigvee_{j=1}^{n}(r_{ij} \wedge o_j(t-1)) = 1 \tag{4-11}$$

$$o_i(t) = F(\delta_i(t) - \lambda_i) = 1 \qquad (4\text{-}12)$$

so $o_i(t-1) = 1$, and $\Delta o_i(t) = 0$.

If $o_i(t-1) = -1$, then

$$\Delta o_i(t) = o_i(t) - o_i(t-1) = o_i(t) + 1 \geq 0 \qquad (4\text{-}13)$$

Therefore, $\forall t$

$$\Delta o_i(t) = o_i(t) - o_i(t-1) \geq 0, \ 1 \leq i \leq N \qquad (4\text{-}14)$$

Theorem 4.2: Let n-rank fuzzy Hopfield network $FuzzyHN = \langle NS, R, \Lambda, O, Oper \rangle$ and model set $X = \{x_i | 1 \leq t \leq N\}$, R is a fuzzy relation on $X \times X$ with anti- reflexivity, then

(1) FuzzyHN is stable;
(2) FuzzyHN reaches a stable state if energy function E(t) can converge to some energy value;
(3) FuzzyHN converges to a stable state from initial state in N time at most.

Proof: Because

$$E(t) = O^T(t)RO(t) + \Lambda^T O(t) \leq N^2 + N = N(N+1) \qquad (4\text{-}15)$$

So E(t) has a upper boundary. Moreover

$$
\begin{aligned}
\Delta E &= E(t) - E(t-1)O^T(t)RO(t) + \Lambda^T O(t) - O^T(t-1)RO(t-1) - \Lambda^T O(t-1) \\
&= O^T(t)RO(t) + \Lambda^T O(t) - O^T(t-1)RO(t-1) - \Lambda^T O(t-1) \\
&\quad + O^T(t)RO(t-1) - O^T(t)RO(t-1) \\
&= O^T(t)R(O(t) - O(t-1)) + \Lambda^T(O(t) - O(t-1)) \\
&\quad + O^T(t)RO(t-1) - O^T(t-1)RO(t-1) \\
&= O^T(t)R\Delta O(t) + \Lambda^T \Delta O(t) + O^T(t-1)R^T O(t) - O^T(t-1)R^T O(t-1) \\
&= O^T(t)R\Delta O(t) + \Lambda^T \Delta O(t) + O^T(t-1)R^T \Delta O(t)
\end{aligned}
\qquad (4\text{-}16)
$$

By the theorem 4.1, we have $\Delta O(t) \geq 0$, so $\Delta E(t) \geq 0$, $E(t)$ can convergence to a constant value. Therefore

(1) if $\forall i \in 1, 2, ..., N, \Delta o_i(t) = 0$, then the system is stable;

(2) if $\exists i \in 1, 2, ..., N, \Delta o_i(t) \neq 0$, then by theorem 4.1 we know $o_i(t) = 1$, it is easy to deduce $o_i(t+1) = 1$, therefore $\Delta o_i(t+1) = 0$.

Lemma 4.1: Let n-rank fuzzy Hopfield network $FuzzyHN = \langle NS, R, \Lambda, O, Oper \rangle$ and model set $X = \{x_i | 1 \leq t \leq N\}$, R is a fuzzy relation on $X \times X$ with anti- reflexivity, $\lambda_i = \lambda (\lambda \in \Lambda, 1 \leq i \leq N; \lambda \in (0,1])$,

Table 4.1. The cluster result of FuzzyHN with λ = 0.5

Initial state $O(0)$	Stable state $\tilde{O} \in O_s$	Clustering result
$e_1 = (1\,0\,0\,0\,0)$	(1 -1 1 1 1)	$\{x_1, x_3, x_4, x_5\}$
$e_2 = (0\,1\,0\,0\,0)$	(-1 1 -1 -1 -1)	$\{x_2\}$

Table 4.2. The cluster result of FuzzyHN with λ = 0.6

Initial state $O(0)$	Stable state $\tilde{O} \in O_s$	Clustering result
$e_1 = (1\,0\,0\,0\,0)$	(1 -1 1 -1 -1)	$\{x_1, x_3\}$
$e_2 = (0\,1\,0\,0\,0)$	(-1 1 -1 -1 -1)	$\{x_2\}$
$e_4 = (0\,0\,0\,1\,0)$	(-1 -1 -1 1 1)	$\{x_4, x_5\}$

set $O(0) = e_k$ is the initial state of FuzzyHN, then FuzzyHN can convergence to a stable state $\tilde{O} \in O_s$, thus the elements whose value are one in $\tilde{O}$ are clustered into one class, namely the elements whose value are one in $\tilde{O}$ are in the same class with the elements in x_k, when take λ as the cluster standard.

Simulation Analysis

Let $X = \{x_1, x_2, x_3, x_4, x_5\}$, and R is a fuzzy relation with anti-reflexivity on X,

$$R = \begin{bmatrix} 1 & 0.1 & 0.8 & 0.5 & 0.3 \\ 0.1 & 1 & 0.1 & 0.2 & 0.4 \\ 0.8 & 0.1 & 1 & 0.3 & 0.1 \\ 0.5 & 0.2 & 0.3 & 1 & 0.6 \\ 0.3 & 0.4 & 0.1 & 0.6 & 1 \end{bmatrix}$$

Set $N = 5$, $\beta = 0$, $\alpha = 10000$, then the *self-evolution fuzzy chaotic neural network* we proposed above turns to a 5-step fuzzy Hopfield network $FuzzyHN = \langle NS, R, \Lambda, O, Oper \rangle$.

(1)   Set $\lambda = 0.5$, the cluster results are as shown in table 4.1

From table 4.1, for $\lambda = 0.5$ we know elements in X are classified into two class $\{x_1, x_3, x_4, x_5\}$ and $\{x_2\}$

Table 4.3. The cluster result of FuzzyHN with λ = 0.7

Initial state $O(0)$	Stable state $\tilde{O} \in O_s$	Clustering result
$e_1 = (1\ 0\ 0\ 0\ 0)$	$(1\ \text{-}1\ 1\ \text{-}1\ \text{-}1)$	$\{x_1, x_3\}$
$e_2 = (0\ 1\ 0\ 0\ 0)$	$(\text{-}1\ 1\ \text{-}1\ \text{-}1\ \text{-}1)$	$\{x_2\}$
$e_4 = (0\ 0\ 0\ 1\ 0)$	$(\text{-}1\ \text{-}1\ \text{-}1\ 1\ \text{-}1)$	$\{x_4\}$
$e_5 = (0\ 0\ 0\ 0\ 1)$	$(\text{-}1\ \text{-}1\ \text{-}1\ \text{-}1\ 1)$	$\{x_5\}$

(2)   Set λ = 0.6, the cluster results are as shown in table 4.2

From table 4.2, for λ = 0.6 we know elements in X are classified into three class $\{x_1, x_3\}$, $\{x_2\}$ and $\{x_4, x_5\}$.

(3)   Set λ = 0.7, the cluster results are as shown in table 4.3

From table 4.3, for λ = 0.7 we know elements in X are classified into four class $\{x_1, x_3\}$, $\{x_2\}$, $\{x_4\}$ and $\{x_5\}$

After the fuzzy clustering function completes, takes the stable state set $O_s = \{\tilde{O}_1, \tilde{O}_2, ... \tilde{O}_r\}$ as the memory patterns. The connection power matrix of network is required through Hebbian rule. According to Hebbian rule, if the *ith* neuron and the *jth* neuron excited at the same time, then the connection power between them increases, the weight adjustment formula is

$$\begin{cases} w_{ij} = \dfrac{1}{N} \sum_{n=1}^{r} o_{ni} o_{nj} & i \neq j \\ w_{ii} = 1 & i = j \end{cases} \tag{4-17}$$

Set $w_{ii} = 0$ when $i = j$, the reason is that according to self-evolution neural network own characteristic as well as indicated many times by simulation experiments, when the self-feedback connection is weak namely the self-feedback connection power is small, the network is easy to fall into the state zero. Therefore, we set self-feedback connection power $w_{ii} = 1$.

Make threshold value vector $\Lambda = (\lambda_1, \lambda_2, \cdots, \lambda_n)^T = 0$, when β = 0, α is big enough (for example α = 10000), the network behavior and the ordinary Hopfield network association memory characteristic is approximate. When inputs r memory pattern or their distortion, the network can associate one of r correctly patterns and stabilizes in certain pattern throughout certain iterations.

In certain scope, increases β gradually, the self-evolution neural network enters chaotic state gradually from periodic motion, and becomes a chaotic neural network. This time, input patterns that already remembered, the network can not only recollect current pattern but also could recollect other patterns once restored. That is because chaotic neural network has association memory function which is realized in chaos movement. Besides, the memory state is a non-cyclical behavior which changes continuously.

Below are some simulations to explain the association process of self-evolution fuzzy chaotic neural network.

Set λ = 0.5, 0.6, 0.7 separately, the stable state O_s ={ (1 -1 1 1 1), (1 -1 1 -1 -1), (-1 1 -1 -1 -1), (-1 -1 -1 1 1), (-1 -1 -1 1 -1), (-1 -1 -1 -1 1) }. Make all the stable states to be memory patterns, retrain the network according to Hebbian rule, we can obtain a 5×5 weight matrix.

$$W = \begin{bmatrix} 1.0 & 0 & 6/5 & 0 & 0 \\ 0 & 1.0 & 0 & -2/5 & -2/5 \\ 6/5 & 0 & 1.0 & 0 & -2/5 \\ 0 & -2/5 & 0 & 1.0 & 2/5 \\ 0 & -2/5 & 0 & 2/5 & 1.0 \end{bmatrix}$$

Carry on confirmation the association memory ability of *self-evolution fuzzy chaotic neural network* through experiment.

(1)   Fuzzy association memory

When β = 0, α = 10000, the self-evolution fuzzy chaotic neural network has similar association memory characteristic to Hopfield neural network.

Figure 4.2. Fuzzy associative memory with noise

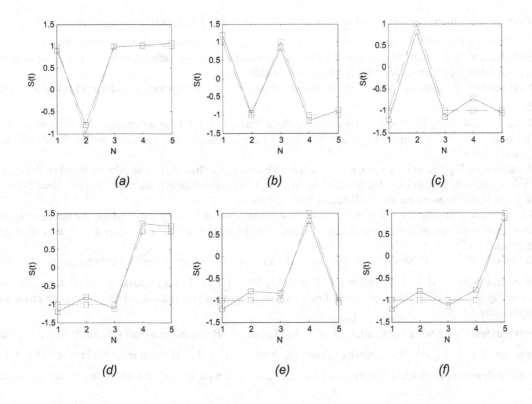

Table 4.4. LLE variation with changement of parameters

α	60						
β	2	3	4	4.3	4.37	6	8
LLE	-0.6204	-3.9064	-0.0020	-0.0023	-0.0084	0.3411	0.0252
β	10	15	20	30	60	80	100
LLE	0.5588	0.1499	0.2057	-0.1547	-0.5421	-1.6135	-2.1139

Input a set of memory patterns includes noise signal to the network, where S1=(0.9 -0.8 0.97 1.02 1.0567), S2=(1.2 -0.95 0.85 -1.157 -0.875), S3=(-1.2 0.8 -1.135 -0.72 -1.0567), S4=(-1.2 -0.8 -1.135 1.22 1.15), S5=(-1.2 -0.8 -0.835 0.82 -1.0567), S6=(-1.2 -0.8 -1.135 -0.767 0.875). Simulation result as shown in Fig 4.2, in which the blue color solid line expression noise pattern, red dashed line expression stable state pattern.

Seen from fig 4.2, when the input is S1, the network can associate the correct pattern(1 -1 1 1 1) and stain in this pattern; when the input is S2, the network can associate the correct pattern(1 -1 1 -1 -1) and stain in this pattern; when the input is S3, the network can associate the correct pattern (-1 1 -1 -1 -1) and stain in this pattern and so on.

Briefly stated, in spite of deviations in the input signal, the network still can associate the correct pattern and stabilize in this pattern. This indicates that the network has fuzzy association memory characteristic and good fault tolerance.

(2)   Chaotic association memory

Takes several groups of β values in the scope of α = 60, β∈ [1,100]. Computing *Largest Lyapunov Exponent (LLE)* of system, the initial value set S=(1 -1 1 1 1). The computing results are as shown in table 4.4.

Seen from table 4.4, increasing β gradually causing the attractor of the network to be period attractor from fixed point throughout bifurcation, and finally arrives at chaos.

Next confirm the association memory ability of self-evolution neural network under cyclical and chaotic state.

Takes β = 2, 4, 4.3, 4.37 separately, take inputs pattern S(0)=(1 -1 1 1 1) as an example, the network motion results as shown in Fig 4.3, in which blue color solid line expression input pattern, red dashed line expression stable state pattern.

As seen from Fig 4.3, when α = 60, β = 2, the network finally stabilizes in two steady states; when β = 4, the network finally stabilized in four steady states; when β = 4.3, the network finally stabilized in eight steady states; when β = 4.37, the network finally stabilized in 16 steady states.

Increasing β gradually, we discover the network stabilizes in more steady states which are not necessarily at the already remembered patterns. In addition, input other patterns that had been remembered can obtain the same conclusion.

When α = 60, β = 10, the self-evolution fuzzy chaotic neural network becomes a chaotic neural network. Input pattern S(0)=(1 -1 1 -1 -1), S(0)=(-1 -1 -1 1 -1), S(0)=(-1 -1 -1 -1 1) separately, simulation result as shown in Fig 4.4. Where the blue color solid line expression input pattern, red dashed line expression chaos association pattern.

As seen from Fig 4.4, when input pattern (1 -1 1 -1 -1), the network also can associate pattern (1 -1 1 1 1); with input pattern (-1 -1 -1 1 -1), the network can associate pattern (-1 -1 -1 1 1); with input pattern (-1 -1 -1 -1 1), the network also can associate pattern (-1 -1 -1 1 1). This indicates, the self-evolution fuzzy chaotic neural

Figure 4.3. Periodic behavior of networks

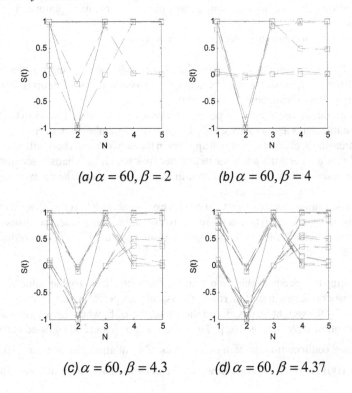

(a) $\alpha = 60, \beta = 2$ (b) $\alpha = 60, \beta = 4$

(c) $\alpha = 60, \beta = 4.3$ (d) $\alpha = 60, \beta = 4.37$

Figure 4.4. Chaos associative memory

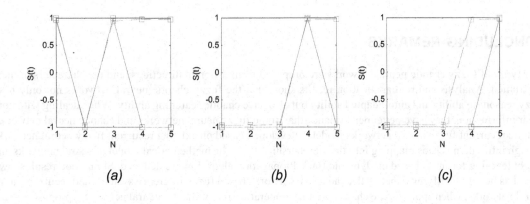

(a)   (b)   (c)

network can recollection the classified results of $\lambda = 0.5$ and $\lambda = 0.6$ according to the classified results of $\lambda = 0.7$ under chaos conditions. But, the network state cannot pause in some fixed pattern; it walks randomly during the different patterns.

Summary the simulation results in the following conclusion:

1) When $\beta = 0$, α big enough, the network has fuzzy association memory characteristic. When inputs r memory patterns or their distortion, the network can associate one of r correctly patterns, and stabilizes in this memory pattern throughout certain iterations.

2) Increases β gradually, the network appears in periodic motion and stabilizes in the fixed pattern state finally. But, these stable states are not necessarily the already remembered patterns.

3) Further increasing β, chaotic movement appears in the network and chaos attractor appears. The self-evolution neural network becomes a chaotic neural network which has chaos association memory function. But its dynamic association memory is realized in chaotic movement, the memory condition is a non-cyclical behavior which changes continuously.

4) The fuzzy association memory ability of the network enables it to remember all classified results when the threshold value λ takes 0.5, 0.6, and 0.7 respectively. At the same time, the chaos association memory ability of the network enables it recollect classified results when λ takes 0.7 according to the classified results when λ takes 0.5 and 0.6.

There is one thing that needs explanation namely; the controlled variable value α, β in self-evolution fuzzy chaotic neural network takes an important role in the association performance. Because the network characteristic is decides together by the weight matrix W and the parameter α, β, when the weight matrix is fixed, the network characteristic is controlled by variables α, β. Thus, the value α, β must be adjusted corresponding as the simulation demands. After confirmation through many times of simulation, the interval $[10,30)$ is determined for β and interval $[50,100]$ for α as intervals in which the network association memory functions can obtain good effect.

In summary, the work process of self-evolution fuzzy chaotic neural network that is proposed in this section is: in initial phase, the tranquility parameter β establishes as the zero, the self-evolution fuzzy chaotic neural network becomes a fuzzy Hopfield network which can realize fuzzy clustering function; Then reset network weight, lets the network remember all cluster patterns; Increases the tranquility parameter β until the chaos characteristic of the network appears, and the network can realize chaos association memory function.

CONCLUDING REMARKS

Four types of fuzzy chaotic neural networks are proposed from different directions; and the characters of them are studied. Analysis and real application results show that the fuzzy chaotic neural networks not only have fuzzy reasoning ability and auto-adapted ability but also have chaotic searching ability. When dealing with non-linear information, they have better performance than some fuzzy neural networks and chaotic neural networks. Chaotic recurrent fuzzy neural networks model is developed based on existing recurrent fuzzy neural networks through introducing chaos mapping into the membership layer. The mathematical model of neural networks and weight learning formulas based on dynamic Back-Propagation algorithm are deduced. Simulation result shown that it has better identifying capacity than adaptive networks based fuzzy inference systems and recurrent fuzzy neural networks, when approximate chaos system. Cooperation fuzzy chaotic neural network is proposed on the basis of simplified T-S fuzzy chaotic neural networks and Aihara chaotic neuron. In the structure, the cooperation fuzzy chaotic neural networks is a neural network, which has chaos characteristic; while in function, it is a fuzzy system, which unifies both chaos and artificial neural network together. The mathematical model and weight learning algorithms are given, and results of a simulation test are presented. When dealing with non-linear chaotic system approximation, the new networks have higher precision because of combining fuzzy reasoning and chaotic optimizing function together. Fuzzy number chaotic neuron and fuzzy number chaotic neural networks are obtained by blurring the Aihara chaotic neurons. Three theorems are deduced, which signified that fuzzy number chaotic neuron not only has fuzzy number but also chaos characteristic. At last, a self-evolution fuzzy chaotic neural network is proposed. It can work under two kind of active statuses and complete different function. When $\beta = 0, \alpha \rightarrow \infty$, the network turns to fuzzy Hopfield network; increasing network tranquility parameter, the network under chaotic state has association memory function.

FUTURE DIRECTION

The combination of fuzzy logic, artificial neural networks and chaos theory is a new method; the aim is to construct *fuzzy chaotic neural networks* that have both the fuzzy reasoning ability and auto-adapted, self-learning and chaos search ability, in order to enhance the neural network information-handling capacity. But the study on this field is relatively new, and a so practical application of the theory is quite few. This chapter we introduced four types of models. There is however need for further research to address unresolved problems.

Firstly, the chaotic recurrent fuzzy neural networks and cooperation fuzzy chaotic neural networks models themselves are extremely complex; they take too long time for non-linear chaos system modeling and thus have some difficulty in practical application. Here, there is need for algorithm improvement, for example introduction of intelligent optimization algorithm and so on.

Secondly, we have tested that fuzzy number chaotic neural networks can carry on simple pattern association. However, in complex patterns for example image, writing and memory issues, there is need for further research.

Besides, it is meaningful of propose self-evolution fuzzy chaotic neural networks which combine fuzzy clustering and memory associated to the cluster results. While, the capability of self-evolution fuzzy chaotic neural networks are excessively dependent on the choice of parameters, these parameter values are obtained by experiment, which lack of theorem support.

Other methods to fuse fuzzy logic, chaos with neural networks should be considered. For example, blur other chaotic neural networks to construct new fuzzy chaotic neural networks; choose new fuzzy neural network to combine with chaotic neural networks; analyze the essence chaotic characteristic of dynamic fuzzy neural networks and so on.

REFERENCES

Abdulhamit, S. (2006). Automatic detection of epileptic seizure using dynamic fuzzy networks. *Expert Systems with Applications, 31,* 320-328.

Chen, Y., & Teng, C. (1995). A model reference control structure using a fuzzy neural network. *Fuzzy Sets and Systems, 73,* 291-31.

Dong, Z. (2004). *A study on new methods of fuzzy and neural network modeling.* Unpublished doctoral dissertation, Beijing Technology and Business University, China.

Gu, L. L., & Deng, Z. L. (2006). Application of dynamic fuzzy neural network in ship dynamic positioning system. *SHIP ENGINEERING, 28*(2), 43-46.

Huang, R. S. (ed.). (2000). *Chaos theory and its application.* Wuhan: Wuhan University Press.

Hubert, Y. C. (1999). Chaotic neural fuzzy associative memory. *International Journal of Bifurcation and Chaos, 9*(8), 1597-1617.

Hubert, Y. C. (1999). Chaotic neural fuzzy associative memory. *International Journal of Bifurcation and Chaos, 9*(8), 1597-1617.

Inoue, M., & Fukushima, S. (1992). A neural network of chaotic oscillators. *Prog Theor Phys, 88*(3), 128-133.

James, D., & Donald, W. (1999). Fuzzy number neural networks. *Fuzzy Sets and Systems, 108,* 49-58.

Jou, C. C. (1992). A fuzzy cerebella medd articulation controller. *Proceedings of IEEE International Conference of Fuzzy Sets* (pp.1171-1178).

Juang, C. F. (2004). Temporal problems solved by dynamic fuzzy network based on genetic algorithm with variable-length. *Fuzzy Sets and Systems, 142*, 199-219.

Kosko, B. (ed.). (1992). *Neural Networks and Fuzzy Systems: A Dynamical Systems Approach to Machine Intelligence.* NJ: Prentice Hall Inc.

Li, Z., Zhang, B., & Mao, Z. Y. (2000). Analysis of the chaotic phenomena in permanent magnet synchronous motors based on Poincare map. *The 3rd World Congress on Intelligence Control and Intelligent Automation* (pp. 3255-3258). Hefei, P.R China.

Liao, Y. F., & Ma, X.Q. (2005). Application of Fuzzy Neural Network-Based Chaos Optimization Algorithm to Coal Blending. *Journal of South China University of Technology (Natural Science Edition), 34*(6), 117-126.

Liu, C. J., Liao, X. Z., & Zhang, Y. H. (ed.). (2000). Simplified Dynamical Neuro-fuzzy Network Controller and Application. *Proceedings of the 3rd World Congress on Interlligent Control and Automation*(pp. 998-1001). Hefei, P.R China.

Pan, Y. X., Xu, Q. F., & Gao, H. M. (2000).The Research of t he Fuzzy Control Algorithm Optimization Based on Chaos. *Control Theory and Applications, 17*(5), 703-706.

Pedrcy, W., & Recha, A. F. (1993).Fuzzy-set based models of neurons and knowledge-based networks. *IEEE Transations on Fuzzy System, 1*(4), 254-266.

Ruan, X. G. (1997).Research on fuzzy Hopfield network and its fuzzy clustering function. *Fuzzy system and mathematic, 11*(1), 88-94.

Ruan, X. G. (2000). A Neuro-Fuzzy Recognition System based on fuzzy Hopfield network. *Pattern Recognition and Artificial Intelligence, 13*(4), 387-394.

Shuai, J.W., Chen, Z. X., Liu, R. T., & Wu, B. X. (1996). Self-evolution neural model. *Physics Letters A, 221*,311-316.

Shuai, J. W., Chen, Z.X., Liu, R. T., & Wu, B. X. (1997) .Maximum hyperchaos in chaotic nonmonotonic neuronal networks.*PHYSICAL REVIEWE, 56*(1), 890-893.

Shashi, K., Sanjeev, K., Prakash, Ravi, S., Tiwari, M. K., & Shashi B. K. (2007).Prediction of flow stress for carbon steels using recurrent self-organizing neuro fuzzy networks. *Expert Systems with Applications, 32*(3), 777-788.

Tang, W., & Li, D. P. (2000).Chaos Optimization Method for Fuzzy Controller. *Journal of Harbin Engineering University, 21*(2), 6-9.

Theocharis, J. B. (2006). A high-order recurrent neuron-fuzzy system internal dynamics. Application to the adaptive cancellation. *Fuzzy Sets and Systems, 157,* 471-500.

Wang, S. X., Jiang, Y., & Li, Y. G. (2006). Chaos Optimization Strategy on Fuzzy-immune-PID Control of Turbine Regulating System. *Journal of System Simulation, 18*(6), 1729-1732.

Wang, Y. N., Yu, Q. M., & Yuan, X. F. (2006). Progress of Chaotic Neural Networks and Their Applications. *Control and Decision, 21*(2), 121-128.

Wang, Y., Wang, G. F., & Dong, H. (2003).Stability Analysis of the Dynamic BP Algorithm for a Recurrent Fuzzy Neural Network. *Journal of Harbin Engineering University, 24*(1), 262-268.

Wu, W., Shao, H. M., & Qu, D. (ed.). (2005). Strong Convergence of Gradient Methods for BP Networks Training. *Proceedings of Neural Networks and Brain, 1*, 332- 334).

Wu, X. X., & Zhong, C. (ed.). (2001). *Introduction of Chaos*. Shanghai, P.R China: Shanghai Science Technology Document Press.

Yang, G., & Meng, J. Er (2005). Narmax time series model prediction: feedforward and recurrent fuzzy neural network approaches. *Fuzzy Sets and Systems, 150*, 331–350.

Zhang, Z. X. (ed.). (2000). *Neuro-Fuzzy and soft Computer*. USA :Prentice-Hall Press.

Zhou, Y. F., Li, S. J., & Jin, R. C. (2002). A new fuzzy neural network with fast learning algorithm and guaranteed stability for manufacturing process control. *Fuzzy Sets and Systems, 132*, 201–216.

Zhu, D. Q. (2004). The Research Progress and Prospects of Artificial Neural Network. *Journal of Southern Yangtze University(Natural Science Edition), 3*(1),103-110.

Zou, E., Li, X. F., & Liu, Y. G. (2004).Optimization design for fuzzy neural network- chaos simulated annealing algorithm. *Journal of center south University (SCIENCE AND TECHNOLOGY), 35*(3), 443-447.

Zou, E., Liu, J. P., Li, X. F., & Zhang, T. S. (2006). A chaos optimization design of fuzzy controller-inverted pendulum system. *J. CENT. South University (SCIENCE AND TECHNOLOGY), 37*(3), 567-571.

KEY TERMS

Fuzzy Chaotic Neural Networks: It is a new network which combine fuzzy logic, chaos and neural networks together. It has fuzzy reasoning ability, auto-adapted, self-learning as well as chaos search ability, in order to enhance information-handling capacity.

Chaotic Recurrent Fuzzy Neural Network: It is based on recurrent fuzzy neural networks, and has four layers, namely input layer, membership function layer, rule layer and output layer. Chaotic mapping is introduced into the membership layer, via addition of chaotic neurons into the recurrent fuzzy neural networks.

Cooperation Fuzzy Chaotic Neural Networks: It is an improvement of T-S fuzzy neural networks by introducing chaotic neurons or chaotic neural networks. The rule conclusion layer is constituted by chaotic neural networks, which could be one layer or multi-layers.

Fuzzy Number Chaotic Neural Networks: Fuzzy number chaotic neural networks are constituted by fuzzy number chaotic neurons and have associate memory ability.

Self-Evolution Neural Networks: In the mathematical model of self-evolution neural network, the inspiring function is a chaotic odd-symmetric nonmonotonic function differing from normal neural network. It has periodic trait and chaos trait under certain circumstances.

Self-Evolution Fuzzy Chaotic Neural Networks: It is proposed according to the principle of self-evolution network, and unifies the fuzzy Hopfield neural network constitution method. It can work under two kind of active status and completely different function.

Compilation of References

Abbas, A. K., Lichtman, A. H., & Pober, J. S. (2000). *Cellular and Molecular Immunology*. 4th edn. W B Saunders Co., New York.

Abdulhamit, S. (2006). Automatic detection of epileptic seizure using dynamic fuzzy networks. *Expert Systems with Applications, 31*, 320-328.

Adamatzky, A. (1994). *Identification of Cellular Automata*. London: Taylor & Francis.

Adami, C. (1998). *Introduction to artificial life*. New York, Springer-Verlag.

Adami, C. (1998). *Introduction to artificial life*. Springer Verlag.

Aditya, G. (2001). *Learning strategies in multi-agent systems - applications to the herding problem*. Unpublished master's thesis, Virginia Polytechnic Institute and State University.

Agnati, L. F., Fuxe, K. G., Goncharova, L. B., & Tarakanov, A. O. (2008). Receptor mosaics of neural and immune communication: possible implications for basal ganglia functions. *Brain Research Reviews,* (in press).

Agnati, L. F., Tarakanov, A. O., & Guidolin, D. (2005a). A simple mathematical model of cooperativity in receptor mosaics based on the "symmetry rule". *BioSystems, 80*(2), 165-173.

Agnati, L. F., Tarakanov, A. O., Ferre, S., Fuxe, K., & Guidolin, D. (2005b). Receptor-receptor interactions, receptor mosaics, and basic principles of molecular network organization: possible implication for drug development. *Journal of Molecular Neuroscience, 26*(2-3), 193-208.

Ahmed, E., & Elettreby, M. F. (2006). On combinatorial optimization motivated by biology. *Applied Mathematics and Computation, 172*(1), 40-48.

Ahn, Y. K., Song, J. D., & Yang, B. S. (2003). Optimal design of engine mount using an artificial life algorithm. *Journal of Sound and Vibration, 261*, 309-328.

Aho, A. V., & Corasick, M. J. (1975). Efficient string matching: An aid to bibliographic search. *Communications of the ACM, 18*(6), 333-340.

Aho, A. V., Hopcroft, J. E., & Ullman, J. D. (1976). *The Design and Analysis of Computer Algorithms*. Reading, MA: Addison-Wesley P.C.

Ahuja, A., Das, S., & Pahwa, A. (2007). An AIS-ACO hybrid approach for multi-objective distribution system reconfiguration. *IEEE Transactions on Power Systems, 22*(3), 1101-1111.

Akbarzadeh M. R., Kumbla, K., Tunstel, E., & Jamshidi, M. (2000). Soft computing for autonomous robotic system. *Computers and Electrical Engineering, 26*(1), 5-32.

Albuquerque, P., & Dupuis, A. (2002). A parallel cellular ant colony algorithm for clustering and sorting. *In Proceedings of the Fifth International Conference on Cellular Automata for Research and Industry, Springer-Verlag, Heidelberg, Germany, LNCS 2492, 2492*, 220–230.

Alcock, J. (1995). *Animal Behavior,* 5th Ed. Sinauer, Sunderland, MA.

Ali, K. S. (1996). Digital Circuit Design Using FPGAs. *Computers and Industrial Engineering, 31*, 127-129.

Almasi, G. S., & Gottlieb A.(1989). *Highly Parallel Computing*. Benjamin-Cummings publishers, Redwood city, CA.

Almuallim, H., & Dietterich, T. G. (1991). Learning with many irrelevant features. In *Proceedings of the Ninth National Conference on Artificial Intelligence*, (pp. 547-552). San Jose, CA: AAAI Press.

Alonso, O. M., Nino, F., & Velez, M. (2004). A game-theoretic approach to artificial immune networks. In G. Nicosia et al, (Ed.), *Third International Conference on Artificial Immune Systems, number 3239 in LNCS* (pp. 143-151). U.K.: Springer-Verlag.

Copyright © 2009, IGI Global, distributing in print or electronic forms without written permission of IGI Global is prohibited.

Alupoaei, S., & Katkoori, S. (2004). Ant colony system application to marcocell overlap removal. *IEEE Transactions on Very Large Scale Integration (VLSI) Systems, 12*(10), 1118–1122.

Anchor, K. P., Zydallis, J. B., Gunsch, G. H., & Lamont, G. B. (2002). Extending the Computer Defense Immune System: Network Intrusion Detection with a Multiobjective Evolutionary Programming Approach. In J. Timmis, & P.J. Bentley (Ed.) *1st International Conference on Artificial Immune Systems* (pp. 12-21).

Anderson, E., Bai, Z., Bischof, C., Blackford, S., Demmel, J., Dongarra, J. J., Croz, D., Greenbaum, A., Hammaring, S., McKenney, A., & Sorensen, D. (1999). *LAPACK Users' Guide, 3rd ed*. Philadelphia, PA: SIAM.

Angus, D. (2006). Niching for population-based ant colony optimization. In *E-science '06: Proceedings of the second ieee international conference on e-science and grid computing* (p. 15). Washington, DC, USA: IEEE Computer Society.

Ansheng Q., & Chanying D. (Ed.) (1998). *Nonlinear Model of Immunology*. Shanghai, CN: Science and Technology Education Press Shanghai.

Antarctica (2008). Retrieved 19 Feb. 2008, from http://www.vb-tech.co.za/Antartica/

Anwar, S., Patnaik, K. S. (2008). Actor critic learning: A near set approach. In C. Chien-Chung, J.W. Grzymala-Busse, W. Ziarko, (Eds.), *The Sixth Int. Conf. on Rough Sets and Current Trends in Computing (RSCTC 2008)*, Akron, Ohio, 23-25 Oct. 2008, *in press*.

Aplevich, J. D. (1973). Gradient methods for optimal linear system reduction. *International Journal of Control, 18*(4), 767-772.

Arce, I., & Levy, E. (2003). An analysis of the Slapper worm. *IEEE Security & Privacy, 1*(1), 82-87.

Arroyo, J. M., & Conejo, A. J. (2000). Optimal Response of a Thermal Unit to an electricity Spot Market. IEEE Transaction on Power Systems, 15(3), 1098-1104.

Arroyo, J. M., & Conejo, A. J. (2004). Modeling of Start-up and Shout-down Power Trajectories of Themal Units. IEEE Transaction on Power Systems, 19(3), 1562-1568.

article award. *Int. J. of Intelligent Computing and Cybernetics, 1*(1), 46-68.

Asama, A. (1994) *Distributed Autonomous Robotic Systems I , 0*, Springer-Verlag,

Assad, A. M., & Packard, N. H. (1992). Emergent colonization in artificial ecology. *Proceedings of the first European Conference on Artificial Life* (pp. 143-152).

Asuncion, A., & Newman, D. J. (2007). UCI Machine Learning Repository [http://www.ics.uci.edu/~mlearn/MLRepository.html]. Irvine, CA: University of California, School of Information and Computer Science.

Atreas N., Karanikas, C., & Tarakanov, A. (2003). Signal processing by an immune type tree transform. *Lecture Notes in Computer Science, 2787*, 111-119.

Atreas, N., Karanikas, C., & Polychronidou, P. (2004). Signal analysis on strings for immune-type pattern recognition. *Comparative and Functional Genomics, 5*, 69-74.

Avizienis, A. (1978). Fault-Tolerance: The Survival Attribute of Digital Systems. *Proceedings of the IEEE, 66*(10), 1109-1125.

Ayara, M., Timmis, J., Lemos, R. d., Castro, L. N. d., & Duncan, R. (2002, September). *Negative Selection: How to Generate Detectors*. Paper presented at the 1st International Conference on Artificial Immune Systems, Canterbury, UK.

Azzag, H., Guinot, C., & Venturini, G. (2004, September 5-8). How to Use Ants for Hierarchical Clustering. In M. Dorigo, M. Birattari, C. Blum, L. Gambardella, F. Mondada, & T. Stutzle (Eds.), *Proceedings of ants 2004 – fourth international workshop on ant colony optimization and swarm intelligence, 3172*, 350–357. Brussels, Belgium: Springer Verlag.

Back, T., Fogel, D. B., & Michalewicz, Z. (Eds.) (1997). *Handbook of Evolutionary Computation*. Oxford University Press.

Bakirtzis, A., Ziogos, N., & Tellidou, G. (2007). Electricity Producer Offering Strategies in Day-Ahead Energy Market With Step-Wise Offers. IEEE Transaction on Power Systems, 22(4), 1804-1818.

Balachandran, S. (2005). *Multi-shaped detector generation using real-valued representation for anomaly detection*. Masters Thesis, University of Memphis.

Balaprakash, P., Birattari, M., Stutzle, T., & Dorigo, M. (2006). Incremental local search in ant colony optimization: Why it fails for the quadratic assignment problem. *M. Dorigo et al (Eds.), ANTS 2006 LNCS, 4150*, 156–166.

Balicki, J. (2004). Multi-criterion Evolutionary Algorithm with Model of the Immune System to Handle Constraints for Task Assignments. In L. Rutkowski, J.H. Siekmann, R. Tadeusiewicz, & L.A. Zadeh (Ed.), *7th International Conference on Artificial Intelligence and Soft Computing* (pp. 394-399).

Balicki, J. (2005). Immune systems in multi-criterion evolutionary algorithm for task assignments in distributed computer system. In *3rd International Atlantic Web Intelligence Conference* (pp. 51-56).

Balicki, J., & Kitowski, Z. (2003). Model of the Immune System to Handle Constraints in Evolutionary Algorithm for Pareto Task Assignments. In M.A. Klopotek, S.T. Wierzchon, & K. Trojanowski (Ed.), *International Intelligent Information Processing and Web Mining* (pp. 3-12).

Ball, P. (2002). The physical modelling of society: A historical perspective. *Physica A, 314,* 1-14.

Balthrop, J., Forrest, S., & Newman, M. E. J., et al. (2004). Technological Networks and the Spread of Computer Viruses. *Science, 304*(5670), 527-52.

Baraldi, A., & Blonda, P. (1999). A survey of fuzzy clustering algorithms for pattern recognition, *IEEE Transactions on Systems, Man and Cybernetics, 29B,* 786-801.

Barber, D. G., & LeDrew, E. F. (1991). SAR sea ice discrimination using texture statistics: a multivariate approach. *Photogrammetric Engineering & Remote Sensing, 57*(4), 385–395.

Barker, I. (2005). *Information scent: helping people find the content they want.* Retrieved February 7, 2008, from http://www.steptwo.com.au/papers/kmc_information-scent/index.html

Basar, T., & Olsder, G. J. (1998). *Dynamic non-cooperative game theory.* New York: Academic Press.

Bates, J., & Gautier, C. (1989). Interaction between net shortwave flux and sea surface temperature. *Journal of Applied Meteorology, 28(1),* 43-51.

Beckers, R., Deneubourg, J. L., & Goss, S. (1992). Trails and U-turns in the selection of the shortest path by the ant Lasius Niger. *J. Theoretical Biology, 159,* 397–415.

Becks, A. (2001). Visual knowledge management with adaptable document maps. Sankt Augustin, *GMD Research Series, 15.*

Bell, G. I. (1970). Mathematical model of clonal selection and antibody production. *J Theor Biol, 29*(2), 191-232.

Bendau, M. A. (2003). Artificial life: Organization, adaptation and complexity from the bottom up. *Trends in Cognitive Sciences, 7*(11), 505-512.

Berek, C., & Ziegner, M. (1993). The maturation of the immune response. *Immunology Today, 14*(8), 400-402.

Berry, M.W. (1992). Large scale singular value decompositions. *International Journal of Supercomputer Applications, 6*(1), 13-49.

Bersini H., & Varela F. J. (1990). Hints for adaptive problem solving gleaned from immune networks. *Parallel Problem Solving from Nature. Springer-Verlag,* 343-354

Beyer, H. G. & Schwefel, H. P. (2002). Evolution Strategies: A Comprehensive Introduction. *Natural Computing, 1*(1), 3-52.

Bezdek, J. C., & Pal, S. K. (1992). *Fuzzy models for pattern recognition: Methods that search for structures in data.* New York: IEEE.

Bezerra, G. B., de Castro, L. N., & Zuben, F. J. V. (2004). A hierachical immune network applied to gene expression data. In Nicosia, G., Cutello, V., Bentley, P., & Timmis, J. (Eds.), *Proc. 3rd Int. Conf. Artif. Immune Syst.,* Catania, Italy, (pp. 14–27).

Bhalla, U. S., & Lyengar, R. (1999). Emergent properties of networks of biological signaling pathways, *Science, 283*(5400), 381-387.

Bilodeau, G., & Bergevin, R. (2007). Qualitative part-based models in content-based image retrieval. *Mach. Vision Appl., 18*(5), 275-287.

Birattari, M., Pellegrini, P., & Dorigo, M. (2006). On the invariance of ant system. *M. Dorigo et al. (Eds.), ANTS 2006, LNCS 4150, Spriner-Verlag Berlin Heidelberg 2006,* 215–223.

Blake, C., Keogh, E., & Merz, C. J. (1998). *UCI repository of machine learning databases* [http://www.ics.uci.edu/~mlearn/MLRepository.html], Department of Information and Computer Science, University of California, Irvine, CA.

Blum, A. L., & Langley, P. (1997). Selection of relevant features and examples in machine learning. *Artificial Intelligence, 97*(2), 245–271.

Blum, C. (2005). Ant colony optimization: Introduction and recent trends. *Physics of Life Reviews, 2,* 353–373.

Blum, C. (2005). Ant colony optimization: Introduction and recent trends. *Physics of Life Reviews, 2*(4), 353–373.

Bobby, J. (1997). Modelcity Philadelphia . *Retrieved December 5, 2007, from* Bobby, J. (1997). Modelcity Philadelphia . *Retrieved October 25, 2007, from*

Boley, D. (1998). Principle direction divisive partitioning. *Journal on Data Mining and Knowledge Discovery, 2,* 325–344.

Bonabeau, E., Dorigo, M., & Theraulaz, G. (1999). *Swarm Intelligence: From Natural to Artificial Systems.* Oxford University Press.

Bonabeau, E., Dorigo, M., & Theraulaz, G. (1999). *Swarm intelligence: from natural to artificial systems.* New York, NY: Oxford University Press, Inc.

Bonabeau, E., Dorigo, M., & Theraulaz, G. (1999). *Swarm intelligence: From natural to artificial systems.* Oxford University Press, New York, NY.

Bonnafous, D., Lacroix, S., & Simeon, T. (2001). Motion generation for a rover on rough terrains. In *Proceedings of the IEEE/RSJ International Conference on Intelligent Robots and Systems* (pp. 784-789). New York, NY: IEEE Press.

Börner, K., Chen, Ch., & Boyack, K. (2003). Visualizing knowledge domains. In B. Cronin (Ed.), *Annual Review of Information Science & Technology,* 37, 179-255. Medford, NJ: Information Today, Inc./American Society for Information Science and Technology.

Bradley, D. W., & Tyrrell, A. M. (2000, April). *Immunotronics: Hardware Fault Tolerance Inspired by the Immune System.* Paper presented at the 3rd International Conference on Evolvable Systems: from Biology to Hardware, Edinburgh.

Bradley, D. W., & Tyrrell, A. M. (2001, July 12-14). *The Architecture for a Hardware Immune System.* Paper presented at the 3rd NASA/DoD Workshop on Evolvable Hardware, Long Beach, Cailfornia.

Bradley, D. W., & Tyrrell, A. M. (2002a). *A Hardware Immune System for Benchmark State Machine Error Detection.* Paper presented at the 2002 Congress on Evolutionary Computation, Honolulu, USA.

Bradley, D. W., & Tyrrell, A. M. (2002b). Immunotronics - Novel Finite-State-Machine Architectures with Built-In Self-Test Using Self-Nonself Differentiation. *IEEE Transactions on Evolutionary Computation,* 6(3), 227-238.

Bradley, D. W., Ortega-Sanchez, C., & Tyrrell, A. M. (2000, July). *Embryonics + Immunotronics: A Bio-Inspired Approach to Fault Tolerance.* Paper presented at the 2nd NASA/DoD Workshop on Evolvable Hardware, Silicon Valley.

Braithwaite, V. A. (2006). *Cognitive ability in fish.* In Sloman, K.A., Wilson, R.W., Balshine, S., (Eds.), *Behaviour and Physiology of Fish.* Elsevier, Amsterdam, 1-38.

Brucker, P. (1998). *Scheduling algorithms.* Berlin, Heidelberg: Springer-Verlag.

Burgin, M. (1983). Multiple computations and Kolmogorov complexity for such processes. *Notices of the Academy of Sciences of the USSR,* 269(4), 793-797

Burgin, M. (2003) Nonlinear Phenomena in Spaces of Algorithms, *International Journal of Computer Mathematics,* 80(12), 1449-1476.

Burgin, M. (2005). *Superrecursive Algorithms.* Springer, New York.

Burgin, M. (2005a). *Measuring Power of Algorithms, Programs, and Automata.* In Artificial Intelligence and Computer Science. Nova Science Publishers, New York, 1-61.

Burnet, F. M. (1959). *The Clonal Selection Theory of Acquired Immunity.* UK: Cambridge at the University Press,

Burnet, F. M. (1959). *The Clonal Selection Theory of Acquired Immunity.* Cambridge, MA, UK: Cambridge Univ. Press.

Burnet, F. M. (1978). Clonal selection and after. *Theoretical Immunology.* New York: Marcel Dekker. (pp. 63-85).

Bursa, M., & Lhotska, L. (2006a). Electrocardiogram signal classification using modified ant colony clustering and wavelet transform. *In: Analysis of Biomedical Signals and Images – Proceedings of Biosignal 2006. Brno: VUTIUM Press ISBN 80-214-3152-0,* 193–195.

Bursa, M., & Lhotska, L. (2006b). The use of ant colony inspired methods in electrocardiogram interpretation, an overview. *In: NiSIS 2006 – The 2nd European Symposium on Nature-inspired Smart Information Systems [CD-ROM]. Aachen: NiSIS.*

Bursa, M., & Lhotska, L. (2007a). Ant colony cooperative strategy in biomedical data clustering. *Studies in Computational Intelligence, Springer-Verlag.*

Bursa, M., & Lhotska, L. (2007b). Automated classification tree evolution through hybrid metaheuristics. *E. Corchado, J.M. Corchado, A. Abraham (Eds.), Innovations in Hybrid Intelligent Systems, Advances in Soft Computing,* 44, 191–198.

Bursa, M., & Lhotska, L. (2007c). Modified ant colony clustering method in long-term electrocardiogram processing. *Proceedings of the 29th Annual International Conference of the IEEE EMBS,* 3249–3252.

Bursa, M., Huptych, M., & Lhotska, L. (2006). The use of nature inspired methods in electrocardiogram analysis. *International Special Topics Conference on Information Technology in Biomedicine [CD-ROM]. Piscataway: IEEE.*

Bursa, M., Lhotska, L., & Macas, M. (2007). Hybridized swarm metaheuristics for evolutionary random forest generation. *Proceedings of the 7th International Conference on Hybrid Intelligent Systems 2007 (IEEE CSP)*, 150–155.

Byeon, E. S., David, W. S., & Robert, H. S. (1998). Decomposition Heuristics for Robust Job-shop Scheduling. *IEEE Transactions on Robotics and Automation, 14*(2), 303-313.

Cai, Z. X., & Peng, Z. H. (2002). Cooperative coevolutionary adaptive genetic algorithm in path planning of cooperative multi-mobile robot systems. *Journal of Intelligent and Robotic systems, 33*(1), 61-71.

Cai, Z. X., & Wang, Y. (2006). Multiobjective optimization based evolutionary algorithm for constrained optimization. *IEEE Trans. on Evolutionary Computation, 10*(6), 658-675.

Cai, Z. X., & Xu, G. Y. (2004). Artificial Intelligence: Principles and Applications (Third Edition, Graduate Book), Beijing: Tsinghua University Press.

Caire, R., Retiere, N., Morin, E., Fontela, M., & Hadjsaid, N. (2003). Voltage management of distributed generation in distribution networks. In IEEE Power Engineering Society General Meeting, 1, 282-287..

Caldon, A. T. R. (2004). Optimisation algorithm for a virtual power plant operation. In 39th International Universities Power Engineering Conference, 3,1058-1062.

Camazine, S., Deneubourg, J.-L., Franks, N. R., Sneyd, J., Theraulaz, G., & Bonabeau, E. (2001). *Self-organization in biological systems*. Princeton University Press, New Jersey.

Campelo, F., Guimarães, F. G., & Igarashi, H. (2007). Overview of artificial immune systems for multi-objective optimization. In *4th International Conference on Evolutionary Multi-Criterion Optimization* (pp. 937-951).

Campelo, F., Guimarães, F. G., Saldanha, R. R., Igarashi, H., Noguchi, S., Lowther, D. A., & Ramirez, J. A. (2004). A novel multiobjective immune algorithm using nondominated sorting. In *11th International IGTE Symposium on Numerical Field Calculation in Electrical Engineering*.

Canham, R. O., & Tyrrell, A. M. (2002, September). *A Multi-layered Immune System for Hardware Fault Tolerance within an Embryonic Array*. Paper presented at the 1st International Conference on Artificial Immune Systems, Canterbury.

Canham, R. O., & Tyrrell, A. M. (2003a). A Hardware Artificial Immune System and Embryonic Array for Fault Tolerant Systems. *Genetic Programming and Evolvable Machines, 4*(4), 359-382.

Canham, R. O., & Tyrrell, A. M. (2003b). *A Learning, Multi-Layered, Hardware Artificial Immune System Implemented upon an Embryonic Array*. Paper presented at the 5th International Conference on Evolvable Systems (ICES 2003), Trondheim, Norway.

Canham, R. O., Jackson, A. H., & Tyrrell, A. M. (2003, July). *Robot Error Detection Using an Artificial Immune System*. Paper presented at the NASA/DoD Conference on Evolvable Hardware.

Canova, A., Cavallero, C., Freschi, F., Giaccone, L., Repetto, M., & Tartaglia, M. (2007). Comparative Economical Analysis of a Small Scale Trigenerative plant: A Case Study. In Conference Record of IEEE 42nd IAS Annual Meeting (pp. 1456-1459).

Canova, A., Freschi, F., & Tartaglia, M. (2007). Multiobjective optimization of parallel cable layout. *IEEE Transactions on Magnetics, 43*(10), 3914-3920.

Card, S. K., Robertson, G. G., & York, W. (1996). The WebBook and the WebForager: An information Workspace for the World Wide Web. Retrieved February 7, 2008, from http://www.sigchi.org/chi96/proceedings/acmcopy.htm

Cardoso, M. F., Salcedo, R. L., & De Azevedo, S. F. (1996). The simplex-simulated annealing approach to continuous nonlinear optimization. *Computers Chemical Engineering, 20*, 1065-1075.

Caro, G. D., Ducatelle, F., & Gambardella, L. M. (2005). Anthocnet: An adaptive nature-inspired algorithm for routing in mobile ad hoc networks. *Telecommunications (ETT), Special Issue on Self Organization in Mobile Networking, 16*(2).

Carpaneto, E., Freschi, F., & Repetto, M. (2005). Two stage optimization of a single CHP node. In Symposium on Power Systems with Dispersed Generation: Technologies, Impacts on Development, Operation and Performances.

Carpinelli, G., Celli, G., Mocci, S., Pilo, F., & Russo, A. (2005). Optimisation of embedded generation sizing and siting by using a double trade-off method. IEE Proceedings-Generation, Transmission and Distribution, 152(4), 503-513.

Carter, J. H. (2000). The Immune System as a model for Pattern Recognition and classification. *Journal of the American Medical Informatics Association, 7*(3), 28-41.

Castro, L. N. d., & Timmis, J. (2002). *Artificial Immune Systems: A New Computational Intelligence Approach*. London: Springer-Verlag.

Cazangi, R. R., & Von Zuben, F. J. (2006). Immune Learning Classifier Networks: Evolving Nodes and Connections. In *IEEE Congress on Evolutionary Computation* (pp. 7994-8001).

Celli, G., Ghiani, E., Mocci, S., & Pilo, F. (2005). A multiobjective evolutionary algorithm for the sizing and siting of distributed generation. IEEE Transactions on Power Systems, 20(2), 750-757.

Chakrabarti, S. (2002) *Mining the Web: Analysis of hypertext and semi structured data.* San Fransisco, CA: Morgan Kaufmann.

Chan, F. T. S., Swarnkar, R., & Tiwari, M. K. (2005). Fuzzy goal-programming model with an artificial immune system (AIS) approach for a machine tool selection and operation allocation problem in a flexible manufacturing system. *International Journal of Production Research, 43*(19), 4147-4163.

Chao, D. L., Davenport, M. P., & Forrest, S., et al. (2004). Modelling the impact of antigen kinetics on T-cell activation and response. *Immunology and Cell Biology, 82*(1), 55-61.

Chao, D. L., Davenport, M. P., Forrest, S., & Perelson, A. S. (2004). A stochastic model of cytotoxic T cell responses. *Journal of Theoretical Biology, 228*, 227-240.

Chen, J., & Mahfouf, M. (2006). A population adaptive based immune algorithm for solving multi-objective optimization problems. In *5th International Conference on Artificial Immune Systems* (pp. 280-293).

Chen, J., & Mahfouf, M. (2006). A Population Adaptive Based Immune Algorithm for Solving Multi-objective Optimization Problems. In H. Bersini and J. Carneiro (Ed.), *ICARIS 2006, LNCS 4163* (pp. 280-293). Springer Berlin/Heidelberg.

Chen, J., & Mahfouf, M. (2008). An Immune Algorithm Based Fuzzy Predictive Modeling Mechanism using Variable Length Coding and Multi-objective Optimization Allied to Engineering Materials Processing. In *Proceedings of the 2009 IEEE International Conference on Granule Computation (GrC 2008)*. China.

Chen, L., & Zhang, C. (2005). Adaptive parallel ant colony optimization. *Y.Pan et al. (Eds.): ISPA 2005, LNCS, 3758*, 275–285.

Chen, L., Xu, X. H., & Chen, Y. X. (2004). An adaptive ant colony clustering algorithm. *Proceedings of The Third International Conference on Machine Learning and Cybernetics*, 1387–1392.

Chen, S. Y., & Li, Y. F. (2004). Automatic Sensor Placement for Model-Based Robot Vision, *Systems, Man and Cybernetics-B, 34*(1), 393-408.

Chen, Y., & Teng, C. (1995). A model reference control structure using a fuzzy neural network. *Fuzzy Sets and Systems, 73*, 291-31.

Cheng, S. L. & Hwang, C. (2001). Optimal Approximation of Linear Systems by a Differential Evolution Algorithm. *IEEE Transactions on systems, man, and cybernetics-part A, 31*(6), 698-707.

Cheng, T., & Wang, J. (2007). Application of a dynamic recurrent neural network in spatio-temporal forecasting. *Lecture Notes in Geoinformation and Cartography, XIV*, 173-186.

Cheng, Y. C., & Chen, S.Y. (2003). Image classification using color, texture and regions. *Image and Vision Computing*, 21, 759-776.

Chiueh, T. C. (1992). *Optimization of Fuzzy Logic Inference Architecture*. Prentice Hall.

Choi, B. K., & Yang, B. S. (2001). Multiobjective optimum design of rotor-bearing systems with dynamic constraints using immune-genetic algorithm. *Journal of Engineering for Gas Turbines and Power, 123*(1), 78-81.

Chudacek, V., & Lhotska, L. (2006). Unsupervised creation of heart beats classes from long-term ecg monitoring. *Conference: Analysis of Biomedical Signals and Images. 18th International EURASIP Conference Biosignals 2006. Proceedings., 18*, 199–201.

Chueh, C. H. (2004). *An Immune Algorithm for Engineering Optimization*. Unpublished doctoral dissertation, Department of Mechanical Engineering, Tatung University, Taipei, Taiwan.

Ciesielski, K., & Kłopotek, M. A. (2007). Towards adaptive Web mining. Histograms and contexts in text data clustering. In M.R. Berthold, J. Shawe-Taylor, N. Lavrac (Eds.), *Advances in Intelligent Data Analysis* VII IDA 07 (pp. 284-295), LNCS 4723, Berlin Heidelberg, Springer.

Ciesielski, K., Kłopotek, M. A., & Wierzchoń, S. T. (in press). Term distribution-based initialization of fuzzy text clustering. In *The Seventeenth International Symposium on Methodologies for Intelligent Systems (ISMIS'08)*, Toronto, Canada, LNCS, Springer.

Ciesielski, K., Wierzchoń, S. T., & Kłopotek, M. A. (2006). An immune network for contextual text data clustering. In H. Bersini, J. Carneiro (Eds.), *Artificial immune systems. Proceedings of the 5th International Conference, ICARIS-2006* (pp. 432-445) LNCS 4163, Berlin Heidelberg, Springer.

Clausi, D. A. (2002). An analysis of co-occurrence texture statistics as a function of grey level quantization. *Canadian Journal of Remote Sensing, 28*(1), 45–62.

Clausi, D. A., & Yue, B. (2004). Comparing cooccurrence probabilities and Markov Random Fields for texture analysis of SAR sea ice imagery. *IEEE Trans. Geoscience and Remote Sensing, 42*(1), 215-228.

Clausi, D. A., & Zhao, Y. (2002). Rapid extraction of image texture by co-occurrence using a hybrid data structure. *Computers & Geosciences, 28*(6), 763–774.

Coelho, G. P., & Von Zuben, F. J. (2006). omni-aiNet: an immune-inspired approach for omni optimization. In *5th International Conference on Artificial Immune Systems* (pp. 294-308).

Coello Coello, C. A., & Cruz Cortés, N. (2002). An Approach to Solve Multiobjective Optimization Problems Based on an Artificial Immune System. In J. Timmis, & P.J. Bentley (Ed.), *1st International Conference on Artificial Immune Systems* (pp. 212-221).

Coello Coello, C. A., & Cruz Cortes, N. (2005). Solving Multiobjective Optimization Problems Using an Artificial Immune System. *Genetic Programming and Evolvable Machines, 6*(2), 163-190. Springer Netherlands.

Coello Coello, C. A., & Cruz Cortés, N. (2005). Solving multiobjective optimization problems using an artificial immune system. *Genetic Programming and Evolvable Machines, 6*(2), 163-190.

Coello Coello, C. A., Cortes Rivera, D., & Cruz Cortes, N. (2003). Use of an Artificial Immune System for Job Shop Scheduling. In *Proceeding of Second International Conference on Artificial Immune Systems,* Napier University, Edinburgh, UK.

Coello Coello, C. A., David, A., Van, V., & Lamont, G. B. (2002). *Evolutionary Algorithms for Solving Multi-objective Problems.* London, New York: Kluwer Academic.

Cordon, O., Gomide, F., Herrera, F., Hoffmann, F., & Magdalena, L. (2004). Ten years of genetic fuzzy systems: Current framework and new trends. *Fuzzy sets and Systems, 141*(1), 5-31.

Cover, T. M., & Hart, P. E. (1967). Nearest neighbor pattern classification. *IEEE Transactions on Information Theory, 13(1),* 21-27.

Cruz Cortés, N., & Coello Coello, C. (2003a). Multiobjective Optimization Using Ideas from the Clonal Selection Principle. In E. Cantú-Paz (Ed.), *Genetic and Evolutionary Computation* (pp. 158-170).

Cruz Cortés, N., & Coello Coello, C. A. (2003b). Using Artificial Immune Systems to Solve Optimization Problems. In A. Barry (Ed.), *Workshop Program of Genetic and Evolutionary Computation Conference* (pp. 312-315).

Cuesta, F., & Ollero, A. (2005). *Intelligent Mobile Robot Navigation.* Berlin: Springer.

Cui, X., Li, M., & Fang, T. (2001). Study of population diversity of multiobjective evolutionary algorithm based on immune and entropy principles. In *IEEE Conference on Evolutionary Computation* (pp. 1316-1321).

Cutello, V., Narzisi, G., & Nicosia, G. (2005). A class of Pareto Archived Evolution Strategy algorithms using immune inspired operators for Ab-Initio Protein Structure Prediction. In F Rothlauf (Ed.), *EvoWorkshops* (pp. 54-63).

Cutello, V., Narzisi, G., Nicosia, G., & Pavone, M. (2005). Clonal Selection Algorithms: A Comparative Case Study Using Effective Mutation Potentials. In *Proceedings of 4th International Conference on Artificial Immune Systems, Lecture Notes in Computer Science, 3627,* 13-28.

Cutello, V., Nicosia, G., & Pavone, M. (2004). Exploring the Capability of Immune Algorithms: A Characterization of Hypemutation Operators. In *Proceedings of Third International Conference on Artificial Immune Systems, Lecture Notes in Computer Science, 3239,* 263-276.

D'haeseleer, P. (1995). *Further Efficient Algorithms for Generating Antibody Strings* (No. Technical Report CS95-3). Albuquerque, New Mexico: Department of Computer Science, University of New Mexico.

D'haeseleer, P., Forrest, S., & Helman, P. (1996). *An Immunological Approach to Change Detection: Algorithms, Analysis and Implications.* Paper presented at the 1996 IEEE Symposium on Security and Privacy, Los Alamitos, CA.

Da Silva, L. R., & Stauffer, D. (2001). Ising-correlated clusters in the Count-Bouchad stock market model. *Physica A, 294,* 235-238.

Darmoul, S., Pierreval, H., & Gabouj, S. H. (2006). Scheduling using artificial immune system metaphors: a review. In *International Conference on Service Systems and Service Management* (pp. 1150-1155).

Das, S., Natarajan, B., Stevens, D., & Koduru, P. (2008). Multi-objective and constrained optimization for DS-CDMA code design based on the clonal selection principle. *Applied Soft Computing Journal, 8*(1), 788-797.

Dasgupta D., & Forrest S. (1999). *Artificial Immune Systems in Industrial Applications.* Paper presented at the

2nd International Conference on Intelligent Processing and Manufacturing of Materials, Honolulu.

Dasgupta, D. (2006). Advances in artificial immune systems. *IEEE Computational Intelligence Magazine, 1(4)*, 40-49.

Dasgupta, D. (2006, November). Advances in Artificial Immune Systems. *IEEE Computational Intelligence Magazine,* 40-49.

Dasgupta, D. (Ed.). (1999). *Artificial Immune Systems and Their Applications.* Berlin: Springer.

Dasgupta, D.(1999). Artificial Immune Systems and Their Applications. Springer-Verlag.

Dasgupta, D., & Gonzalez, F. (2005). Artificial immune systems in intrusion detection. In V. Rao Vemuri (Ed.), *Enhancing Computer Security with Smart Technology* (pp. 165-208). Boca-Raton, FL: Auerbach Publications.

Dasgupta, D., & Gonzalez, F.A. (2002). An immunity-based technique to characterize intrusions in computer networks. *IEEE Trans. Evol. Comput., 6*, 281–291.

Dasgupta, D., & Nino, F. (2008). *Immunological Computation: Theory and Applications.* Auerbach Publications.

Dasgupta, D., Krishna-Kumar, K., Wong, D., & Berry, M. (2004). Negative selection algorithm for aircraft fault detection. *Lecture Notes in Computer Science, 3239*, 1-13.

Dash (2008). Xpress [computer software]. http://www.dashoptimization.com.

Dash, M., & Liu, H. (1997). Feature selection for classification. *Intelligent Data Analysis, 1*(3), 131–156.

Daubechies, I. (1992). *Ten lectures on wavelets.* Society for Industrial and Applied Mathematics.

Davidor, Y. (1991). *Genetic algorithms and Robotics: A Heuristic Strategy for Optimization.* Singapore: World Scientific.

Davidson, A., & Kita, N. (2001). 3D simulation and map-building using active vision for a robot moving on undulating terrain. In *Proceedings of the 2001 IEEE Computer Society Conference on Computer Vision and Pattern Recognition* (pp. 784-789). New York, NY: IEEE Press.

Davies, D. L., & Bouldin, D. W. (1979). A cluster separation measure. *IEEE Transactions on Pattern Recognition and Machine Intelligence, 1*(2), 224–227.

Davis, M., & Weyuker, E. (1983). *Computability, Complexity and Languages.* Orlando: Academic Press.

de Castro, L. N. & Timmis, J. (2002). *Artificial Immune Systems: A New Computational Intelligence Approach.* Springer-Verlag, Berlin Heidelberg New York.

de Castro, L. N. & Timmis, J. (2002). *Artificial immune systems: A new computational approach.* London, UK: Springer-Verlag.

de Castro, L. N. & Von Zuben F.J. (2002). Learning and Optimization Using the Clonal Selection Principle. *IEEE Transactions on Evolutionary Computation, 6*(3), 239-251.

de Castro, L. N. & Von Zuben, F. J. (2000). The clonal selection algorithm with engineering applications. In L. D. Whitley; D. E. Goldberg; E. Cantú-Paz; L. Spector; I. C. Parmee, & H. Beyer (Ed.), *GECCO'00, Workshop on Artificial Immune Systems and Their Applications* (pp. 36-37). Las Vegas, USA: Morgan Kaufmann.

de Castro, L. N. & Von Zuben, F. J. (2002). Learning and optimization using the clonal selection principle, *IEEE Transactions on Evolutionary Computation, 6*(3), 239-251.

de Castro, L. N. & Von Zuben, F. J. (2002). Learning and optimization using the clonal selection principle. *IEEE Trans. Evol. Comput., 6.* 239–251.

de Castro, L. N., & Timmis, J. (2002). An Artificial Immune Network for Multimodal Function Optimization. *Proc. of the IEEE Congress on Evolutionary Computation (CEC' 2002), 1,* 699-704. Honolulu, Hawaii.

de Castro, L. N., & Timmis, J. (2002). An Artificial Immune Network for Multimodal Function Optimization. In Congress on Evolutionary Computation, 1, 699-704.

de Castro, L. N., & Timmis, J. (2002). *Artificial immune systems: A new computational intelligence approach.* London Berlin Heidelberg, Springer.

de Castro, L. N., & Timmis, J. (2002). *Artificial Immune Systems: A New Computational Intelligence Paradigm.* London, UK: Springer-Verlag.

de Castro, L. N., & Timmis, J. (2002). *Artificial immune systems: A new computational intelligence approach.* Springer-Verlag, London.

De Castro, L. N., & Timmis, J. (2002). *Artificial Immune Systems: A New Computational Intelligence Approach.* London: Springer-Verlag.

De Castro, L. N., & Timmis, J. (2002). *Artificial Immune Systems: A New Computational Intelligence Approach.* London: Springer.

de Castro, L. N., & Von Zuben, F. J. (1999). *Artificial Immune Systems: part I-basic theory and applications.* FEEC/Univ. Campinas, Campinas, Brazil.

de Castro, L. N., & Von Zuben, F. J. (2000). Clonal selection algorithm with engineering applications. In *Proc GECCO's* (pp. 36–37). Las Vegas, NV.

de Castro, L. N., & von Zuben, F. J. (2001). aiNet: An artificial immune network for data analysis. In: H. A. Abbass, R.A. Sarker, and Ch.S. Newton (Eds.), *Data mining: A heuristic approach* (pp. 231-259). Hershey, PA: Idea Group Publishing.

de Castro, L. N., & Von Zuben, F. J. (2002). Learning and Optimization Using the Clonal Selection Principle. *IEEE Transactions on Evolutionary Computation, 6*(3), 239-251.

De Castro, L. N., & Von Zuben, F. J. (2002). Learning and optimization using the clonal selection principle. *IEEE Trans on Evolutionary Computation, 6*(3), 306-313.

De Castro, Leandro, N., & Timmis, J. (2002). *Artificial Immune System: A New Computational Intelligence Approach.* 1st ed. 2002, Springer-Verlag.

De Castro, Leandro, N., & Von Zuben, F. (2001) *aiNET: An Artificial Immune Network for Data Analysis, in Data Mining: A Heuristic Approach.* (Eds). Idea Group Publishing.

De Jong, K. A. (1975). *Analysis of behavior of a class of genetic adaptive systems.* Unpublished doctoral dissertation, University of Michigan, Ann Arbor, Michigan.

De Jong, K. A., Potter, M. A., & Spears, W. M. (1997). Using problem generators to explore the effects of epistasis. In T. Bäck (Ed.), *Proceedings of the Seventh International Conference on Genetic Algorithms,* (pp. 338-345). Morgan Kaufmann, San Francisco, CA.

Deb, K. (2001). *Multi-Objective Optimization using Evolutionary Algorithms.* Chichester, UK: Wiley.

Deb, K., & Agrawal, B. R. (1994). *Simulated Binary Crossover for Continuous Search Space* (Technical Reports IITK/ME/SMD-94027). Convenor: Indian Institute of Technology, Department of Mechanical Engineering.

Deb, K., Reddy, A., & Singh, G. (2003). Optimal scheduling of casting sequences using genetic algorithms. Journal of Materials and Manufacturing Processes 18(3), 409-432.

Deb, K., Thiele, L., Laumanns, M., & Zitzler, E. (2001). *Scalable Test Problems for Evolutionary Multi-Objective Optimization* (TIK-Technical Report 112). Zurich:

Swiss Federal Institute of Technology (ETH), Computer Engineering and Networks Laboratory (TIK).

Del Bimbo, A. (1999). *Visual Information Retrieval.* San Francisco, California: Morgan Kaufman.

deLope, J., & Maravall, D. (2003). Integration of reactive utilitarian navigation and topological modeling. In C. Zhou, D. Maravall, & D. Ruan (Eds.), Autonomous Robotics Systems: Soft Computing and Hard Computing Methodologies and Applications (pp. 122-138) Heidelberg: Physica-Verlag.

Deneubourg, J. L., & Goss, S. (1989). Collective patterns and decision-making. *Ethology, Ecology & Evolution, 1,* 295–311.

Deneubourg, J. L., Goss, S., Franks, N., Sendova-Franks, A., Detrain, C., & Chretien, L. (1990). The dynamics of collective sorting robot-like ants and ant-like robots. In *Proceedings of the first international conference on simulation of adaptive behavior on from animals to animats* (pp. 356–363). Cambridge, MA, USA: MIT Press.

Deng, Y., & Korobka, A. (2001) Performance of a supercomputer built with commodity components. *Parallel Processing, 27*(12), 91-108.

Deutsch, D. (1985). Quantum theory, the Church-Turing principle, and the universal quantum Turing machine. *Proc. Roy. Soc.,* Ser. A, *400,* 97-117.

Dinabandhu, B., Murthy, C. A., & Sankar, K. P. (1996). Genetic algorithm with elitist model and its convergence. *International Journal of Pattern Recognition and Artificial Intelligence, 10*(6), 731-747.

Ding, Y. S., & Ren, L. H. (2000). Artificial immune systems: Theory and applications. *Pattern Recognition and Artificial Intelligence, 13*(1), 52-59. (in Chinese).

Ding, Y. S., & Ren, L. H. (2003). Design of a bio-network architecture based on immune emergent computation. *Control and Design, 18*(2), 185-189. (in Chinese)

Doak, J. (1992). *An evaluation of feature selection methods and their application to computer security* (Tech. Rep.). Davis, CA: University of California, Department of Computer Science.

Dong, W. S., Shi, G. M., Zhang, L. (2007). Immune memory clonal selection algorithms for designing stack filters. *Neurocomputing, 70*(4-6), 777-784.

Dong, Z. (2004). *A study on new methods of fuzzy and neural network modeling.* Unpublished doctoral dissertation, Beijing Technology and Business University, China.

Dongarra, J. (2006). Trends in parallel computing: A historical overview and examination of future developments. *Circuits and Devices Magazine, 22*(1), 22-27.

Dongarra, J., Sterling, T., Simon, H., & Strohmaier, E. (2005).High-performance computing: clusters, constellations, MPPs, and future directions. *Computing in Science & Engineering, 7*(2), 51-59

Dongmei F., & Deling Zh. (2005). *Design and Analysis of a Biological Immune Controller Based on Improved Varela Immune Network Model.* Paper presented at the 2005 international Conference on Machine Learning and Cybernetics.

Dongmei F., & Deling Zh. (2005). *The Analysis of Stability of Immune Control System Based on Small Gain Theorem.* Paper presented at the International Conference on Communications, Circuits and Systems, HKUST, Hong Kong, China.

Dongmei F., & Deling Zh. (2006). An Anamnestic and Integral Two-cell Immune Controller and Its Characteristic Simulation. *Journal of University of Science and Technology Beijing, 27*(2), 190-193.

Dongmei F., Deling Zh., & Yaoguang W. (2006). Design,Realization and Analysis of Immune Controller Based on Two-cell Adjustment. *Information and Control, 35*(4), 526-531.

Dongmei F., Deling Zh., & Ying C. (2005). *Design and Simulation of a Biological Immune Controller Based on Improved Varela Immune Network Model. Artificial Immune Systems.* Paper presented at the 4th International Conference, ICARIS 2005.

Dongmei F., Deling Zh., Yaoguang W., Ying Zh., & Lei J. (2004). Design for Biological Immune Controllers and Simulation on Its Control Feature. *Journal of University of Science and Technology Beijing, 26*(4), 442.

Dongqiang Q., & Yaqing T. (2001). Present Situation and Future Development of Neural Network-based Control. *Journal of Automation & Instrumentation, 27*(1), 1-7.

Dorigo, M. (1992). *Optimization, Learning and Natural Algorithms.* PhD thesis, Politecnico di Milano, Italy.

Dorigo, M. (1992). *Optimization, learning and natural algorithms.* Unpublished doctoral dissertation, Dipartimento di Elettronica, Politecnico di Milano, Italy.

Dorigo, M., & Blum, C. (2005). Ant colony optimization theory: A survey. *Theoretical Computer Science Issues 2–3, 344*, 243–278.

Dorigo, M., & Gambardella, L. M. (1997). Ant colony system: A cooperative learning approach to the traveling

salesman problem. *IEEE Transactions on Evolutionary Computation, 1, 1*, 53–66.

Dorigo, M., & Gambardella, L.M. (1997). Ant Colony System: A Cooperative Learning Approach to Traveling Salesman Problem. *IEEE Transactions on Evolutionary Computation, 1*, 53–66.

Dorigo, M., & Stützle, T. (2004). *Ant Colony optimization.* Cambridge, MA: MIT Press.

Dorigo, M., & Stutzle, T. (2004). *Ant colony optimization.* MIT Press, Cambridge, MA.

Dorigo, M., Caro, G. D., & Gambardella, L. M. (1999). Ant algorithms for discrete optimization. *Artificial Life, 5*(2), 137–172.

Dorigo, M., Maniezzo, V., & Colorni, A. (1996). The Ant System: Optimization by a colony of cooperating agents. *IEEE Transactions on Systems, Man, and Cybernetics-Part B, 26*(1), 29–41.

Doyle, L. B. (1961). Semantic road maps for literature searchers. *Journal of ACM, 8*, 553-578.

Du, H. F., Gong, M. G., Jiao, L. C., & Liu, R. C. (2005). A novel artificial immune system algorithm for high-dimensional function numerical optimization. *Progress in Natural Science, 15*(5), 463-471.

Du, H. F., Jiao, L. C., Gong, M. G., & Liu, R. C. (2004). Adaptive dynamic clone selection algorithms. In Shusaku Tsumoto, Roman Sowiński, Jan Komorowski, et al, (Ed.), *Proceedings of the Fourth International Conference on Rough Sets and Current Trends in Computing* (pp. 768–773). Uppsala, Sweden.

Du, H. F., Jiao, L.C., & Wang, S. A. (2002). Clonal operator and antibody clone algorithms. In Shichao, Z., Qiang, Y. & Chengqi, Z. (Ed.), *Proceedings of the First International Conference on Machine Learning and Cybernetics* (pp. 506-510). Beijing.

Dunn, J. C. (1973). A fuzzy relative of the isodata process and its use in detecting compact wellseparated clusters. *Journal of Cybernetics, 3*, 32–57.

Ebbinghaus, H. -D., Jacobs, K., Mahn, F. -K., & Hermes, H. (1970). *Turing Machines and Recursive Functions,* Springer-Verlag, Berlin/Heidelberg/New York.

Eberbach, E. (2005a). Toward a theory of evolutionary computation. *BioSystems, 82*, 1-19.

Eberbach, E. (2005b). \$-Calculus of Bounded Rational Agents: Flexible Optimization as Search under Bounded Resources in Interactive Systems. *Fundamenta Informaticae, 68*(1-2), 47-102.

Eberbach, E., & Wegner, P. (2003). Beyond Turing Machines, *Bulletin of the European Association for Theoretical Computer Science* (EATCS Bulletin), *81*, 279-304.

Eberhart, R. C., & Kennedy, J. (1995). A New Optimizer Using Particle Swarm Theory. *The 6th International Symposium on Micro Machine and Human Science* (pp. 39-43).

Efatmaneshnik, M., & Reidsema, C. (2007). Immunity as a design decision making paradigm for complex systems: A robustness approach. *Cybernetics and Systems, 38*(8), 759-780.

Einstein, A. (1920). *Relativity: the Special and General Theory*. Three Rivers Press, New York.

Elfes, A. (1989). Using occupancy grids for mobile robot perception and navigation. *IEEE Computer, 22*(1), 46-57

El-Khattam, W., Bhattacharya, K., Hegazy, Y., & Salama, M. M. A. (2004). Optimal investment planning for distributed generation in a competitive electricity market. IEEE Transactions on Power Systems, 19(3), 1674-1684.

El-Khattam, W., Hegazy, Y. G., & Salama, M. M. A. (2005). An integrated distributed generation optimization model for distribution system planning. IEEE Transactions on Power Systems, 20(2), 1158-1165.

Endoh, S., Toma, N., & Yamada, K. (1998). Immune algorithm for n-TSP. *1998 IEEE International Conference on System, Man and Cybernetics, 4*, 3844-3849. Oct 11-14, San Diego, California, USA.

Epstein, J. M., & Axtell, R. (1996). *Growing artificial societies: Social science from the bottom up*. The Brookings Institution/Washington DC, USA: The MIT Press.

Escapenet GMBH (2008). VirtualCity. *Retrieved October 25, 2007, from* http://www.virtualcity.ch/

Esponda, F., Forrest, S., & Helman, P. (2004). A Formal Framework for Positive and Negative Detection Scheme. *IEEE Transaction on Systems, Man, and Cybernetics, 34*(1), 357-373.

EU (2003). Directive 2003/54/Ec of the European Parliament and of the Council of 26 June 2003 concerning common rules for the internal market in electricity and repealing Directive 96/92/EC, Retrieved February 11, 2008, from http://eur-lex.europa.eu/en/index.htm.

Everitt, B. S. (1993). *Cluster analysis*. Halsted Press.

Expatica (2006). **Illegal building: The expat nightmare.** *Retrieved October 20, 2007, from*

Fan, Y. S., Luo, H. B., & Lin, H. P. (2001). *Workflow management technology foundation*. Beijing: Tsinghua University Press, Springer-Verlag.

Farmer, J. D., & Packard, N. H. (1986). The Immune System, Adaptation, and Machine Learning. *Physica, 22D*, 187-204. North-Holland, Amsterdam.

Farmer, J. D., Packard, N. H., & Perelson, A. S., (1986). The immune system, adaptation, and machine learning. *Physica, 22D*, 187-204.

Fauci, S. A. (2003). HIV and AIDS: 20 years of science. *Nature Medicine, 9*(7), 839-843.

Ferber, J. (1999). *Multi-agent systems: an introduction to distributed artificial intelligence*. CA, Addison-Wesley.

FIPA agent management specification, http://www.fipa.org/specs/fipa00023/XC00023H.html.

FIRA official Web page. (2007) (*www.fira.net*)

Fogel, D. B. (1995). *Evolutionary Computation: Toward a New Philosophy of Machine Intelligence*. IEEE Press.

Fogel, D. B. (2000). *Evolutionary Computation: Toward a New Philosophy of Machine Intelligence*. New York, NY: IEEE Press.

Fogel, D. B. (2001). *An Introduction to Evolutionary Computation, Tutorial, Congress on Evolutionary Computation (CEC'2001)*, Seoul, Korea.

Fonseca, C. M., & Fleming, P. J. (1993). Genetic Algorithms for Multi-objective Optimization: Foundation, Discussion, and Generalization. *Proc. Of the 5th International Conference on Genetic Algorithms* (pp. 416-423).

Forgey, E. (1965). Cluster analysis of multivariate data: Efficiency vs. interpretability of classification. *Biometrics, 21*, 768.

Forrest, S., Perelson, A. S., Allen, L., & Cherukuri, R. (1994). Self-nonself discrimination in a computer. In *Proceedings of the IEEE Symposium on Research in Security and Privacy*. Los Alamitos, CA: IEEE Computer Society Press. (pp. 202-212).

Forrest, S., Perelson, A. S., Allen, L., & Cherukuri, R. (1994). Self-nonself discrimination in a computer. In *Proc. IEEE Symp. Research in Security and Privacy*, Oakland, CA, (pp. 202–212).

Forrest, S., Perelson, A. S., Allen, L., & Cherukuri, R. (1994). *Self-Nonself Discrimination in a Computer*. Paper presented at the 1994 IEEE Symposium on Research in Security and Privacy, Los Alamitos, CA.

Francois, O. (1998). An evolutionary strategy for global

minimization and its Markov chain analysis. *IEEE Trans. Evolutionary Computation, 2*(3), 77-80.

Franks, N. R., & Sendova-Franks, A. (1992). Brood sorting by ants: Distributing the workload over the work-surface. *Behavioral Ecology and Sociobiology, 30,* 109-123.

French, J. R. P., Jr. (1956). A formal theory of social power. *Psychological Review, 63,* 181-194.

Freschi, F. (2006). *Multi-Objective Artificial Immune Systems for Optimization in Electrical Engineering.* Unpublished doctoral dissertation, Department of Electrical Engineering, Politecnico di Torino, Torino, Italy.

Freschi, F., & Repetto, M. (2005). Multiobjective optimization by a modified artificial immune system algorithm, In *4th International Conference on Artificial Immune Systems* (pp. 248-261).

Freschi, F., & Repetto, M. (2005). Multiobjective Optimization by a Modified Artificial Immune System Algorithm. In: Christian Jacob et al. (eds.), *ICARIS 2004, LNCS 3627* (pp. 248-261). Springer Berlin/Heidelberg.

Freschi, F., & Repetto, M. (2006). VIS: an artificial immune network for multi-objective optimization. *Engineering Optimization, 38*(8), 975-996.

Freschi, F., Carpaneto, E., & Repetto, M. (2005). Application of a Double Stage Optimization to Integrated Energy Management In 22nd IFIP TC 7 Conference on System Modeling and Optimization (pp. 30).

Freund, Y., & Schapire, R. E. (1997). A decision-theoretic generalization of on-line learning and an application to boosting. *Journal of Computer and System Sciences, 55*(1), 119-139.

Fries, T. P. (2004). Fuzzy genetic motion planning under diverse terrain conditions for autonomous robots. In *Proceedings of the IASTED International Conference on Circuits, Signals, and Systems* (pp. 449-454). Calgary, Canada: ACTA Press.

Fries, T. P. (2005). Autonomous robot motion planning in diverse terrain using genetic algorithms. In *Proceedings of the 2005 Genetic and Evolutionary Computation Conference.* New York, NY: ACM Press.

Fries, T. P. (2006a). Autonomous robot motion planning in diverse terrain using soft computing. In *Proceedings of the 2006 IEEE SMC Workshop on Adaptive and Learning Systems.* New York, NY: IEEE Press.

Fries, T. P. (2006b). Evolutionary robot navigation using fuzzy terrain conditions. In *Proceedings of the 2006 Conference of the North American Fuzzy Information Processing Society* (pp. 535-540). New York, NY: IEEE Press.

Fritzke, B. (1995). *Some Competitive Learning Methods.* Draft available from http://www.neuroinformatik.ruhr-uni-bochum.de/ini/VDM/research/gsn/JavaPaper/.

Fukuda, S., & Hirosawa, H. (1999). A Wavelet-Based Texture Feature Set Applied to Classification of Multifrequency Polarimetric SAR Images. *IEEE Trans. on Geoscience and Remote Sensing, 37,* 2282–2286.

Fukuda, T., Mori, K., & Tsukiyama, M. (1993). Immune networks using genetic algorithm for adaptive production scheduling. In Proceedings of the 15th IFAC World Congress. (pp. 57-60).

Fukuda, T., Mori, K., & Tsukiyama, M. (1998). Parallel Search for Multi-Modal Function Optimization with Diversity and Learning of Immune Algorithm. *Artificial Immune Systems and Their Applications* (pp. 210-220). Springer Berlin/Heidelberg.

Galeano, C., Veloza, A., & Gonzales, F. (2005). *A Comparative Analysis of Artificial Immune Network Models.* GECCO '05: Proceedings of the 2005 conference on Genetic and evolutionary computation. Washington, DC, USA.

Galeano, J. C., Veloza-Suan, A., & González, F. A. (2005). A comparative analysis of artificial immune network models. In *Proceedings of the 2005 Conference on Genetic and Evolutionary Computation, GECO2005,* (pp. 361-368) Washington DC, USA.

Gandomkar, M., Vakilian, M. & Ehsan, M. (2005). Optimal Distributed Generation Allocation in Distribution Network Using Hereford Ranch Algorithm. In 8th International Conference on Electrical Machines and Systems, 2, 916-918.

Gao Xiujuan, M. (2005). *The theories, methods and applications of image segmentation.* Master's thesis, Jilin University, Changchun.

Gao, F., (2000). Optimal design of piezo-electric actuators for plate vibroacoustic control using genetic algorithms with immune diversity. *Smart Materials and Structures, 8,* 485-491

Gao, L., Ding, Y. S., & Ren, L. H. (2004). A novel ecological network-based computation platform as grid middleware system. *Int. J. Intelligent Systems, 19*(10), 859-884.

García-Pedrajas, N., & Fyfe, C. (2007). Immune network based ensembles. *Neurocomputing, 70*(7-9), 1155-1166.

Garrett, S. M. (2004). Parameter-free, Adaptive Clonal Selection. In *Proceedings of IEEE Congress on Evolutionary Computing, CEC 2004,* Portland, Oregon. (pp. 1052-1058).

Garrett, S. M. (2005). How Do We Evaluate Artificial Immune Systems. *Evolutionary Computation, 13*(2), 145-178.

Georgakis, D., Papathanassiou, S., Hatziargyriod, N., Engle, A., & Hardt, C. (2004). Operation of a prototype microgrid system based on micro-sources quipped with fast-acting power electronics interfaces. In 35th Annual IEEE Power Electronics Specialists Conference, 4 2521-2526.

George, A. J. T., & Gray, D. (1999). Receptor editing during affinity maturation. *Immunology Today, 20*(4), 196.

Gerla, V., Bursa, M., Lhotska, L., Paul & Krajca. (2007). Newborn sleep stage classification using hybrid evolutionary approach. *International Journal of Bioelectromagnetism – Special Issue on Recent Trends in Bioelectromagnetism. Tampere: International Society for Bioelectromagnetism,* 28–29.

Gibbs, J.W. (1960). *Elementary Principles in Statistical Mechanics.* NY, U.S.A., Dover.

Girvan, M., & Newman, M. E. (2002). Community structure in social and biological networks. *Proc. Natl Acad. Sci., 99,* 7821-7826.

Glover, K. (1984). All optimal Hankel-norm approximations of linear multivariable systems and their error bounds. *International Journal of Control, 39*(6), 1115-1193.

Goldberg, D. E. (1989). *Genetic Algorithms for Search, Optimization, and Machine Learning.* MA: Addison-Wesley.

Goldberg, D. E. (1989). *Genetic algorithms in Search, Optimization and Machine Learning.* New York, NY: Addison-Wesley.

Goldberg, D. E. (1989). *Genetic algorithms in search, optimization, and machine learning.* CA, Addison-Wesley.

Goldberg, D. E., Deb, K., & Horn, J. (1992). Massive multimodality, deception, and genetic algorithms. In *Parallel Problem Solving from Nature, 2,* 37-46.

Goldberg, D. E., Deb, K., & Korb, B. (1990). Messy genetic algorithms revisited: Studies in mixed size and scale. *Complex Systems, 4,* 415-444.

Goldberger, A. L., Amaral, L. A. N., Glass, L., Hausdorff, J. M., Ivanov, P. C., Mark, R. G., et al. (2000). PhysioBank, PhysioToolkit, and PhysioNet: Components of a new research resource for complex physiologic signals. *Circulation, 101*(23), e215–e220. Available from Circulation Electronic Pages: http://circ.ahajournals.org/cgi/content/full/101/23/e215

Gomez-Villalva, E., & Ramos, A. (2003). Optimal energy management of an industrial consumer in liberalized markets. IEEE Transactions on Power Systems, 18(2), 716-723.

Goncharova, L. B., & Tarakanov, A. O. (2007). Molecular networks of brain and immunity. *Brain Research Reviews, 55(1),* 155-166.

Goncharova, L. B., & Tarakanov, A. O. (2008a). Nanotubes at neural and immune synapses. *Current Medicinal Chemistry, 15(3),* 210-218.

Goncharova, L. B., & Tarakanov, A. O. (2008b).Why chemokines are cytokines while their receptors are not cytokine ones? *Current Medicinal Chemistry, 15(13),* 1297-1304.

Goncharova, L. B., Jacques, Y., Martin-Vide, C., Tarakanov, A. O., & Timmis, J. I. (2005). Biomolecular immune-computer: theoretical basis and experimental simulator. *Lecture Notes in Computer Science, 3627,* 72-85.

Gong, M. G., Du, H. F., & Jiao, L. C. (2006). Optimal approximation of linear systems by artificial immune response. Science in China. *Series F Information Sciences, 49*(1), 63-79.

Gong, M. G., Du, H. F., & Jiao, L. C. (2006). *Optimal approximation of linear systems by artificeal immune response,* Science in China: Series F Information Sciences. Science in China Press, co-published with Springer-Verlag GmbH, *49*(1), 63-79.

Gong, M. G., Jiao, L. C., Du, H. F., & Bo, L. F. (2006). *Multi-objective Immune Algorithm with Pareto-optimal Neighbor-based Selection* (Technical Report (IIIP-06-05)). China: Xiandian University, Institute of Intelligent Information Processing.

Gong, M. G., Jiao, L.C., Liu, F., & Du, H.F. (2005). The Quaternion Model of Artificial Immune Response. In *Proceedings of the fourth international conference on Artificial Immune Systems, Lecture Notes in Computer Science, 3627,* 207-219.

Gong, T., & Cai, Z. X. (2003) Parallel evolutionary computing and 3-tier load balance of remote mining robot. *Trans Nonferrous Met Soc China, 13*(4), 948-952.

Gonzalez, F., & Dasgupta, D. (2003). Anomaly detection using real-valued negative selection. *Journal of Genetic Programming and Evolvable Machines, 4*(4), 383-403.

Gonzalez, F., Dasgupta, D., & Kozma, R. (2002). Combining Negative Selection and Classification Techniques for Anomaly Detection. In *Proceedings of the special sessions on artificial immune systems in Congress on Evolutionary Computation*, Honolulu, Hawaii.

Gonzalez, F., Dasgupta, D., & Nino, L. F. (2003, September 1-3). *A Randomized Real-Valued Negative Selection Algorithm*. Paper presented at the 2nd International Conference on Artificial Immune Systems (ICARIS 2003), LNCS 2787, Edinburgh, UK.

Gonzalez, R. C., & Woods, R. E. (2002). *Digital Image Processing*. Reading, MA: Addison-Wesley.

Google company. (2008).Google Earth. *Retrieved December 5, 2007, from*

Google company. (2008).Google Earth. *Retrieved October 25, 2007, from*

Gore, A. (1998). The Digital Earth: Understanding our planet in the 21st Century.

Gore, A. (1998).The Digital Earth:Understanding our planet in the 21st Century. *Retrieved October 20, 2007, from* http://www.isde5.org/al_gore_speech.htm

Grassé, P. P. (1959). La reconstruction du nid et les coordinations interindividuelles chez *Bellicositermes natalensis et Cubitermes sp.* La th´eorie de la stigmergie: Essai d'interpr´etation des termites constructeurs. Insect Sociaux 6, 41–83.

Grasse, P.-P. (1959). La reconstruction du nid et les coordinations inter-individuelles chez bellicositermes natalensis et cubitermes sp. la thorie de la stigmergie: Essai d'interprtation des termites constructeurs. *Insectes Sociaux, 6*, 41–81.

Gu, L. L., & Deng, Z. L. (2006). Application of dynamic fuzzy neural network in ship dynamic positioning system. *SHIP ENGINEERING, 28*(2), 43-46.

Guimarães, F. G., Campelo, F., Saldanha, R. R., Igarashi, H., Takahashi, R. H. C., & Ramirez, J. A. (2006). A multiobjective proposal for the TEAM benchmark problem 22. *IEEE Transactions on Magnetics, 42*(4), 1471-1474.

Guimarães, F. G., Palhares, R. M., Campelo, F., & Igarashi, H. (2007). Design of mixed H_2/H_∞ control systems using algorithms inspired by the immune system. *Information Sciences, 177*(29), 4368-4386 .

Guo, D. W., & Kong, C. L. (2004). A new artificial life algorithm to solve time-varying optimization problem. *International Conference on Machine Learning and Cybernetics* (pp. 2146-2148).

Guo, T. Y., & Hwang, C. (1996). Optimal reduced-order models for unstable and nonminimum-phase systems. *IEEE Transactions on Circuits and Systems-I, 43*(9), 800-805.

Gupta, S.K., & Hubble, J.M. (2002). Minutes from the CERES science team meeting. *The Earth Observer, 14(1)*, 1-13.

Gutowitz, H. (1993). *Complexity-seeking ants.*

Haag, C. R. (2007a). *An Artificial Immune System-inspired Multiobjective Evolutionary Algorithm with Application to the Detection of Distributed Computer Network Intrusions.* Unpublished master's thesis, Department of Electrical and Computer Engineering, Graduate School of Engineering and Management, Air Force Institute of Technology, Dayton, Ohio, USA.

Haag, C. R., Lamont, G. B., Williams, P. D., & Peterson, G. L. (2007b). An artificial immune system-inspired multiobjective evolutionary algorithm with application to the detection of distributed computer network intrusions. In *6th International Conference on Artificial Immune Systems* (pp. 420-435).

Haag, C. R., Lamont, G. B., Williams, P. D., & Peterson, G. L. (2007c). An artificial immune system-inspired multiobjective evolutionary algorithm with application to the detection of distributed computer network intrusions, *In Genetic and Evolutionary Computation Conference* (pp. 2717-2724).

Hait, A., & Simeon, T. (1996). Motion planning on rough terrain for an articulated vehicle in presence of uncertainties. In *Proceedings of the IEEE/RSJ International Conference on Intelligent Robots and Systems* (pp. 1126-1133). New York, NY: IEEE Press.

Hajela, P., Yoo, J., & Lee, J. (1997). GA Based Simulation of Immune Networks-Applications in Structural Optimization. *Journal of Engineering Optimization.*

Hajri, S., Liouane, N., Hammadi, S., & Borne, P. (2000). A controlled genetic algorithm by fuzzy logic and belief functions for job-shop scheduling. *IEEE Transactions on System, Man, and Cybernetics Part B: Cybernetics, 30*(5), 812-818.

Hamid, G., (1994). An FPGA-Based Coprocessor for Image Processing. IEE *Colloquium, Integrated Imaging Sensors and Processing, 6*, 1-4.

Han, S., & Wang, L. (2002). A survey of thresholding methods for image segmentation. Systems Engineering and Electronics, 24(6), 91-102

Handl, J., & Knowles, J. (2007). An evolutionary approach to multiobjective clustering. *IEEE Transactions on Evolutionary Computation, 11*(1).

Handl, J., Knowles, J., & Dorigo, M. (2003a). *Ant-based clustering: a comparative study of its relative performance with respect to k-means, average link and 1d-som* (Tech. Rep.). Technical Report TR/IRIDIA/2003-24, IRIDIA, Universit Libre de Bruxelles.

Handl, J., Knowles, J., & Dorigo, M. (2003b). On the performance of ant-based clustering. In *Design and application of hybrid intelligent systems*, 104, 204–213. Amsterdam, The Netherlands: IOS Press. Available from http://dbkgroup.org/handl/his2003.pdf

Handl, J., Knowles, J., & Dorigo, M. (2003c). Strategies for the increased robustness of ant-based clustering. In *Self-organising applications: Issues, challenges and trends*, 2977, 90–104. Springer-Verlag.

Handl, J., Knowles, J., & Dorigo, M. (2006). Ant-based clustering and topographic mapping. *Artificial Life 12*(1), *12*, 35–61.

Harada, K., & Kinoshita, T. (2003). The emergence of controllable transient behavior using an agent diversification strategy. *IEEE Transactions on Systems, Man and Cybernetics - Part A: Systems and Humans, 33*(5), 589-596.

Haralick, R. M., Shanmugam, K., & Dinstein, I. (1973). Textural Features for Image Classification. *IEEE Trans. on System, Man, and Cybernetics, 3*, 610–621.

Hart, E., & Ross, P. (1999). The Evolution and Analysis of a Potential Antibody Library for Use in Job-Shop Scheduling. In *New Ideas in Optimization*. McGraw-Hill.

Hart, E., & Timmis, J. (2005). Application Areas of AIS: The Past, The Present and The Future. In C. Hacob et al. (Ed.), *ICARIS 2005, LNCS 3527* (pp. 483-497). Springer-Verlag Berlin/Heidelberg.

Hart, E., & Timmis, J. (2005). Application Areas of AIS: The Past, The Present and The Future. In *Proceedings of the 4th International Conference on artificial immune systems, Lecture Notes in Computer Science, 3627*, 483-497.

Hashimoto, H. (1997). Optimum design of high-speed, short journal bearings by mathematical programming. *STLE Tribology Transaction, 40*(2), 283-293.

Hawking, S., & Penrose, R. (1996). *The nature of space and time*, Princeton University Press.

Hayashi, D., Satoh, T., & Okita, T. (1994). Global optimization using artificial life (in Japanese). *Joint Conference of Information Society*, 164-165.

Hayashi, D., Satoh, T., & Okita, T. (1996). Distributed optimization by using artificial life (in Japanese). *Trans. IEE Japan, 116-C*(5), 584-590.

Haykin, S. (1994). *Neural Networks a comprehensible Foundation*. Ed College Publishing Company.

Haykin, S. (1998). *Neural networks: a comprehensive foundation*. 2nd ed., Upper Saddle River, NJ, Prentice-Hall.

He, G. J. (2001). Extracting Buildings Distribution Information of Different Heighs in a City from the Shadows in a Panchromatic SPOT Image. *Journal of Image and Graphics, (5)*.

He, J., & Yao, X. (2004). A study of drift analysis for estimating computation time of evolutionary algorithms. *Nat. Comput. 3*, 21-25.

He, S., Luo, W., & Wang, X. (2007). A Negative Selection Algorithm with the Variable Length Detector. *Journal of Software, 18*(6), 1361-1368.

Hegel (2006). Official website of the EU sponsored research Project HEGEL, Retrieved February 11, 2008, from http://www.hegelproject.eu.

Henry, C. (2004). *Ecosystem Testbed*. Computational Intelligence Laboratory, Retrieved 17 Feb. 2008, from http://130.179.231.200/cilab/ [Downloads].

Henry, C. (2005). *Advanced Swarm Intelligence Testbed*. Computational Intelligence Laboratory, Retrieved 19 Feb. 2008, from http://wren.ece.umanitoba.ca/ [Downloads].

Henry, C., & Peters, J. F. (2007). Image Pattern Recognition Using Approximation Spaces and Near Sets, In: *Proceedings of Eleventh International Conference on Rough Sets, Fuzzy Sets, Data Mining and Granular Computing* (RSFDGrC 2007), Joint Rough Set Symposium (JRS 2007). *Lecture Notes in Artificial Intelligence*, vol. 4482 (pp. 475-482). Berlin: Springer.

Hernandez-Aramburo, C. A., Green, T. C. & Mugniot, N. (2005). Fuel Consumption Minimization of a Microgrid. IEEE Transaction on Industry Applications, 41(3), 673-681.

Hespanha, J., Prandini, M., & Sastry, S. (2000). Probabilistic pursuit-evasion games: A one-step Nash approach. In *IEEE Conference on Decision and Control: Vol. 3* (pp. 2272–2277). Sydney: IEEE Press.

Heyes, C. M. (1994). Social learning in animals: Categories and mechanisms. *Biol. Rev.* 69, 207-231.

Ho, S. Y., Shu, L. S., & Chen, J. H. (2004). Intelligent Evolutionary Algorithms for large Parameter Optimization Problems. *IEEE Transactions on Evolutionary Computation, 8*(6), 522-540.

Hoffmann, G. W. (1986). A neural network model based on the analogy with the immune system. *J. Theoretical Biology, 122*, 33-67.

Holland, J. H. (1975). *Adaptation in Natural and Artificial Systems*. Univ. of Michigan Press, Ann Arbor: MIT Press, 2nd ed.

Holland, J. H. (1975). *Adaptation in Natural and Artificial Systems*. Ann Arbor, MI: University of Michigan Press.

Holland, J. H. (1975). *Adaptation in natural and artificial systems*. Ann Arbor, MI, University of Michegan Press (2nd ed., MIT Press, 1992).

Holland, J., Holyoak, K., Nisbett, R., & Thagard, P. (1989). *Induction, Processes of Inference, Learning and Discovery. MA*: MIT Press.

Homaifar, A., Qi, C., & Lai, S. (1994). Constrained optimization via genetic algorithm simulation. *Electronics Letter, 62*(4), 242-254.

Hopcroft, J. E., Motwani, R., & Ullman, J. D. (2001). *Introduction to Automata Theory, Languages, and Computation*, Addison Wesley, Boston/San Francisco/New York.

Horn, R., & Johnson, Ch. (1986). *Matrix Analysis*. London: Cambridge University Press.

http://earth.google.com/

http://earth.google.com/

http://en.wikipedia.org/wiki/High-performance_computing

http://en.wikipedia.org/wiki/Parallel_computing

http://members.aol.com/bobbyj164/bjhome01.htm

http://members.aol.com/bobbyj164/bjhome01.htm

http://news.sohu.com/20060405/n242654025.shtml

http://www.expatica.com/actual/article.asp?subchannel_id=87&story_id=27308

http://www.isde5.org/al_gore_speech.htm

http://www.microsoft.com/virtualearth/default.mspx

http://www.microsoft.com/virtualearth/default.mspx

http://www.ust.ucla.edu/ustweb/

http://www.ust.ucla.edu/ustweb/

Hu, N. (1992). Tabu search method with random moves for globally optimal design. *International Journal of Numerical Methods in Engineering, 35*, 1055-1070.

Hu, X., & Vie, C. (2007). Niche Genetic algorithm for Robot Path planning. In *Proceedings of the Third International Conference on Natural Computation* (774-778). New York, NY: IEEE Press.

Huang, R. S. (ed.). (2000). *Chaos theory and its application*. Wuhan: Wuhan University Press.

Huang, S. (1999). Enhancement of thermal unit commitment using immune algorithms based optimization approaches. *Electrical Power and Energy Systems, 21*, 245-252.

Huang, S. (2000). An immune-based optimization method to capacitor placement in a radial distribution system. *IEEE Transaction on Power Delivery, 15*(2), 744-749.

Huang, S. (2000). An immune-based optimization method to capacitor placement in a radial distribution system. *IEEE Transaction on Power Delivery, 5*(2), 744-749.

Huang, T. Y., Hsiao, Y. T., Chen, C. P., & Chang, C. H. (2006). Fuzzy modeling with immune multi-objective algorithm to optimal allocate of capacitors in distribution systems. *In 9th Joint Conference on Information Sciences* (pp. 289-292).

Huang, X., Zhang, S., Wang, G., & Wang, H. (2006). A new image retrieval method based on optimal color matching. In *Proceedings of the 2006 International Conference on Image Processing, Computer Vision, & Pattern Recognition (IPCV 2006)* (pp. 276-281). Las Vegas, Nevada.

Hubert, Y. C. (1999). Chaotic neural fuzzy associative memory. *International Journal of Bifurcation and Chaos, 9*(8), 1597-1617 .

Hubert, Y. C. (1999). Chaotic neural fuzzy associative memory. *International Journal of Bifurcation and Chaos, 9*(8), 1597-1617.

Huo, F. M. (2004). *Optimal problems research based on artificial immune algorithm*. Master's thesis ,Daqing Petroleum Institute, Daqing.

Huttenlocher, D., Klanderman, D., & Rucklige, A. (1993, September). Comparing images using the Hausdorff distance. *IEEE Transactions on Pattern Analysis and Machine Intelligence, 15*(9), 850–863.

Iagnemma, K., & Dubowsky, S. (2004). *Mobile Robots in Rough Terrain*. New York, NY: Springer.

Iagnemma, K., Kang, S., Brooks, C., & Dubowsky, S. (2003). Multi-sensor terrain estimation for planetary rovers. In *Proceedings of the 7th International Symposium on Artificial Intelligence, Robotics, and Automation in Space* (pp. 542-549). Nara, Japan: Japan Aerospace Exploration Agency.

Il-Seok Oh, Jin-Seon Lee, & Byung-Ro Moon (2004). Hybrid genetic algorithms for feature selection, *IEEE Trans. Pattern Analysis and Machine Intelligence, 26*(11), 1424-1437.

Inoue, M., & Fukushima, S. (1992). A neural network of chaotic oscillators. *Prog Theor Phys, 88*(3), 128-133.

Isaacs, R. (1965). *Differential games*, New York: John Wiley & Sons, Inc.

Ishida, Y. (1990). Fully Distributed Diagnosis by PDP Learning Algorithm: Towards Immune Network PDP Model. In *Proceedings of International Joint Conference on Neural Networks*, San Diego, 777-782.

Ishiguro, A., Ichikawa, S., & Uchikawa, Y, (1994). A gait acquisition of 6-legged walking robot using immune networks. *Proceedings of the IROS'94, 2*, 1034-1041.

Ishiguro, A., Kuboshiki, S., Ichikawa, S., & Uchikawa, Y. (1996). Gait control of hexapod walking robots using mutual-coupled immune networks. *Advanced Robotics, 10*(2), 179-195.

Ishiguro, A., Watanabe, Y., Kondo, T., Shirai, Y., & Uchikawa (1997). *A robot with decentralized concensus-making mechanism based on the immune system.* Proceeding of the ISADS'97, (pp. 231-237).

Isidori A., Ben W., & Shengxian Zh Translation. (Ed.) (2005). *Nonlinear Control System.* Beijing, CN: Electronic Publishing Industry.

Isler, V., Kannan, S., & Khanna, S. (2004). Randomized pursuit-evasion with limited visibility. In J. I. Munro (Ed.), *ACM-SIAM Symposium on Discrete Algorithms (SODA)* (pp. 1053–1063). New Orleans, USA: SIAM.

Jackson, J. (1994). An efficient membership-query algorithm for learning DNF with respect to the uniform distribution. In *proceedings of the IEEE Symposium on Foundations of Computer Science*.

Jackson, J. M., & Latané, B. (1981). All alone in front of all those people: Stage fright as a function of number and type of co-performers and audience. *Journal of Personality and Social Psychology, 40*, 73-85.

Jackson, J. T., Grunsch, G. H., Claypoole, R. L., & Lamont, G. B. (2003). Blind Steganography Detection Using a Computational Immune System: A Work in Progress. *International Journal of Digital Evidence, 4*(1), 1-19.

Jain, A. K., & Zongker, D. (1997). Feature selection: evaluation, application, and small sample performance. *IEEE Trans. Pattern Analysis and Machine Intelligence, 19*(2), 153-158.

Jain, A., Murty, M. N., & Flynn, P. J. (1999). Data clustering: A review. *ACM Computing Surveys, 31*, 264–323.

James, D., & Donald, W. (1999). Fuzzy number neural networks. *Fuzzy Sets and Systems, 108,* 49-58.

Jang, J. R. (1993). ANFIS: Adaptive-Network-Based Fuzzy Inference System. *IEEE Transaction on Systems, Man and Cybernetics, 23*(3), 665-685.

Jensen, M. T. (2003). Generating robust and flexible job shop schedules using genetic algorithms. *IEEE Transactions on Evolutionary Computation, 7*(3), 275-288.

Jensen, R., & Shen, Q. (2004). Fuzzy-rough data reduction with ant colony optimization. *Informatics Research Report, EDI-INF-RR-0201.*

Jerne N. K. (1973). The Immune System. *Scientific American, 229*(1), 52-60.

Jerne N. K. (1974). Towards a Network Theory of the Immune System. *Annual Immuno- logy,* 125C, 373-389.

Jerne, N. K. (1973). The immune system. *Scientific American, 229*(1), 52-60.

Jerne, N. K. (1974). Towards a Network Theory of the Immune System. *Ann. Immunology (Inst. Pasteur), 125C,* 373-389.

Jerne, N. K. (1974). Towards a network theory of the immune system. *Annals of Institute Pasteur/Immunology, 125C,* 373-389.

Jerne, N. K. (1974). Towards a network theory of the immune system. *Annual Immunology, 125C,* 373-389.

Jerne, N. K. (1974). Towards a network theory of the immune system. *Annual Immunology, 125C,* 373-389.

Jerne, N. K. (1974). Towards a network theory of the immune system. *Ann Immunol, 125C,* 373-389.

Ji, Z., & Dasgupta, D. (2004, June 19-23). *Augmented Negative Selection Algorithm with Variable-Coverage Detectors.* Paper presented at the 2004 Congress on Evolutionary Computation (CEC '04).

Ji, Z., & Dasgupta, D. (2007). Revisiting Negative Selection Algorithms. *Evolutionary Computation, 15*(2), 223-251.

Jiao, L. C., & Wang, L. (2000) Novel genetic algorithm based on immunity. *IEEE Trans on Systems, Man and Cybernetics — Part A: Systems and Humans, 30*(5), 552-561.

Jiao, L. C., & Wang, L. (2000). A novel genetic algorithm based on immunity. *IEEE Transactions on Systems, Man and Cybernetics, Part A, 30*(5), 552-561.

Jiao, L., Gong, M., Shang, R., Du, H., & Lu, B. (2005). Clonal selection with immune dominance and anergy based multiobjective optimization. In *3rd International Conference on Evolutionary Multi-Criterion Optimization* (pp. 474-489).

Jin, Y., Olhofer, M. & Sendhoff, B. (2001). Dynamic Weighted Aggregation for Evolutionary Multi-Objective Optimization: Why Does It Work and How? *Proc. GECCO 2001 Conf.* (pp. 1042-1049).

Jin, Y., Olhofer, M., & Sendhoff, B. (2002). An evolutionary strategy for global minimization and its Markov chain analysis. *IEEE Trans. Evolutionary Computation, 2*(3), 481-494.

Jingzhen Zh., & Zengji H. (1997). Development of Fuzzy Control Theory and its Applications. *Journal of Technological advances, 19*(3), 156-159.

Joachims, T. (2003). *Learning to Classify Text Using Support Vector Machines: Methods, Theory, and Algorithms.* Kluwer Academic Publishers.

Joachims, T. (2004). *SVM-light: Support Vector Machine,* from http://svmlight.joachims.org

John, G. H., Kohavi, R., & Peger, K. (1994). Irrelevant features and the subset selection problem. In *proceedings of the Eleventh International Conference on Machine Learning* (pp. 121-129). New Brunswick, NJ: Morgan Kaufmann.

Johnson, J. E. (2005). Networks, Markov Lie monoids, and generalized entropy. *Lecture Notes in Computer Science, 3685,* 129-135.

Jou, C. C. (1992). A fuzzy cerebella medd articulation controller. *Proceedings of IEEE International Conference of Fuzzy Sets* (pp.1171-1178).

Juang, C. F. (2004). Temporal problems solved by dynamic fuzzy network based on genetic algorithm with variable-length. *Fuzzy Sets and Systems, 142,* 199-219.

Jung, I.K., & Lacroix, S. (2003). High resolution terrain mapping using low altitude aerial stereo imagery. In *Proceedings of the Ninth IEEE International Conference on Computer Vision* (pp. 946-953). New York, NY: IEEE Press.

Justus Reid Weiner (2003). The Global Epidemic of illegal building and Demolitions: Implications for Jerusalem. *Jerusalem Letter / Viewpoints(498).*

Kachroo, P. (2001). Dynamic programming solution for a class of pursuit evasion problems: the herding problem. *IEEE Transactions on Systems, Man, and Cybernetics, Part C: Applications and Reviews, 31*(1), 35–41.

Kamei, K., & Ishikawa, M. (2004). Determination of the Optimal Values of Parameters in Reinforcement Learning for Mobile Robot Navigation by a Genetic algorithm. In *Brain-Inspired IT: Invited papers of the 1st Meeting Entitled Brain IT 2004* (pp. 193-196). New York, NY: Elsevier.

Kanade, P. M., & Hall, L. O. (2003). Fuzzy ants as a clustering concept. *Proceedings of the 22nd International Conference of the North American Fuzzy Information Processing Society, NAFIPS,* 227–232.

Kanade, P. M., & Hall, L. O. (2004). Fuzzy ant clustering by centroid positioning. *Proceedings of the IEEE International Conference on Fuzzy Systems 2004, 1,* 371–376.

Kapur, J. N., Sahoo, P. K., & Wong, A. K. C. (1985). A new method of gray level picture thresholding using the entropy of the histogram. *Computer Vision, Graphics and Image Processing, 29*(2), 273-285

Kawasaki, Y., Ino, F., Mizutani, Y., Fujimoto, N., Sasama, T., Sato, Y., Sugano, N., Tamura, S., & Hagihara, K. (2004). High-performance computing service over the Internet for intraoperative image processing. Information *Technology in Biomedicine,* IEEE Transactions. 8(1):36 – 46.

Kazarlis, S. A., Papadakis, S. E., Theocharis, J. B., & Petridis, V. (2001). Microgenetic algorithms as generalized hill-climbing operators for GA optimization. *IEEE Transactions on Evolutionary Computation, 5*(2), 204-217.

Kelly, A., & Stentz, A. (1998). Rough terrain autonomous mobility—part 2: an active vision predictive control approach. *Journal of Autonomous Robots, 5*(2), 163-198.

Kelsey, J., & Timmis, J. (2003). Immune Inspired Somatic Contiguous Hypermutation for Function Optimization. In Cantupaz, E. et al. (ed.), *Proc. Of Genetic and Evolutionary Computation Conference (GECCO).* Lecture Notes in Computer Science, *2723,* 207-218. Springer Berlin/Heidelberg.

Kelsey, J., & Timmis, J. (2003). Immune inspired somatic contiguous hypermutation for function optimisation. In *Proceedings of the Genetic and Evolutionary Computation Conference,* 207-218.

Kennedy, J., & Eberhart, R. (1995). Particle Swarm Optimization. In *Proc. of the 1995 IEEE Int. Conf. on Neural Networks,* 1942-1948.

Kennedy, J., & Eberhart, R. C. (1995). Particle swarm optimization. *Proceedings IEEE International Conference on Neural Networks, IV,* 1942–1948.

Kennedy, J., & Eberhart, R. C. (1997). A discrete binary version of the particle swarm algorithm. In *Proceedings of the World Multiconference on Systemics, Cybernetics and Informatics.* (pp. 4104-4109).

Kennedy, J., & Mendes, R (2003). Neighborhood topologies in fully-informed and best-of-neighborhood particle swarms. In *Proceedings 2003 IEEE SMC Workshop on Soft Computing in Industrial Application (SMCia03).* Binghamton, NY.

Kennedy, J., Eberhart R., & Shi Y. (2001). *Swarm Intelligence*, Morgan Kaufmann.

Kennedy, J., Eberhart, R. C., & Shi, Y. (2001). *Swarm intelligence.* San Francisco: Morgan Kaufmann Publishers.

Kesheng L., Jun Zh., & Xianbing C. (2000). An Algorithm Based on Immune Principle Adopted in Controlling Behavior of Autonomous Mobile Robots. *Computer Engineering and Applications*, 36(5), 30-32.

Khan, M. E. (2007). *Game theory models for pursuit evasion games* (Tech. Rep. No. 2). Vancouver, University of British Columbia, Department of Computer Science.

Khuri, S., Bäck, T., & Heitkötter J. (1994). An evolutionary approach to combinatorial optimization problems. In *Proceedings of the 22nd ACM Computer Science Conference* (pp. 66-73). ACM Press: Phoenix, AZ.

Kim D. H. (2001). *Tuning of a PID Controller Using an Artificial Immune Network Model and Local Fuzzy Set.* Paper presented at the meeting of IEEE International Symposium on Industrial Electronics, Seoul Korea.

Kim D. H., & Lee K. Y. (2002). *Neural Networks Control by Immune Network Algorithm Based Auto-Weight Function Tuning.* Paper presented at the International Joint Conference on Neural Networks, Hawaii USA.

Kim D.W. (2002). *Parameter Tuning of Fuzzy Neural Networks by Immune Algorithm.* Paper presented at the 2002 IEEE International Conference on Fuzzy Systems, Japan.

Kim D.W. (2003). Intelligent 2-DOF PID Control for Thermal Power Plant Using Immune Based on Multiobjective. *Neural Network and Computational Intelligence, 22(2),* 215-220.

Kim D.W., & Cho J. H. (2002). *Auto-tuning of Reference Model Based PID Controller Using Immune Algorithm.* Paper presented at the meeting of Evolutionary Computation, CEC '02. Honolulu, HI, USA.

Kim D.W., & Cho J. H. (2004). *Intelligent Tuning of PID Controller with Robust Disturbance Rejection Function Using Immune Algorithm.* Paper presented at the 8th International Conference on Knowledge-Based Intelligent

Information & Engineering System KES, Wellington, New Zealand.

Kim D.W., & Horg W. P. (2004). *Tuning of PID Controller of Deal Time Process Using Immune Based on Multiobjective.* Paper presented at the 8th International Conference on Knowledge-Based Intelligent Information & Engineering System KEMS, Wellington, New Zealand.

Kim, D. H. (2003a). Tuning of PID controller of dead time process using immune based on multiobjective. In *7th IASTED International Conference on Artificial Intelligence and Soft Computing* (pp. 368-373).

Kim, D. H. (2003b). Intelligent 2-DOF PID control for thermal power plant using immune based multiobjective. In *IASTED International Conference on Neural Networks and Computational Intelligence* (pp. 215-220).

Kim, D. H. (2004). Robust PID control using gain/phase margin and advanced immune algorithm. *WSEAS Transactions on Systems, 3(9),* 2841-2851.

Kim, D. H. (2005). Tuning of PID controller for dead time process using immune based multiobjective. In *IEEE Mid-Summer Workshop on Soft Computing in Industrial Applications* (pp. 63-68).

Kim, D. H., & Cho, J. H. (2004a). Robust PID controller tuning using multiobjective optimization based on clonal selection of immune algorithm. In *8th International Conference on Knowledge-Based Intelligent Information and Engineering Systems* (pp. 50-56).

Kim, D. H., & Cho, J. H. (2004b). Robust tuning for disturbance rejection of PID controller using evolutionary algorithm. In *Annual Conference of the North American Fuzzy Information Processing Society* (pp. 248-253).

Kim, D. H., & Cho, J. H. (2005). Robust control of power plant using immune algorithm. In *2nd IASTED International Multi-Conference on Automation, Control, and Information Technology* (pp. 105-110).

Kim, D. H., & Hong, W. P. (2003). Tuning of PID controller of dead time process using immune based on multiobjective. In *IASTED International Conference on Neural Networks and Computational Intelligence* (pp. 221-226).

Kim, D. H., & Lee, H. (2004). Intelligent control of nonlinear power plant using immune algorithm based multiobjective optimization. In *IEEE International Conference on Networking, Sensing and Control* (pp. 1388-1393).

Kim, D. H., Jo, J. H., & Lee, H. (2004). Robust power plant control using clonal selection of immune algorithm based multiobjective. In *4th International Conference on Hybrid Intelligent Systems* (pp. 450-455).

Kim, D. J., Lee, D. W., & Sim, K. B. (1997). Development of Communication System for Cooperative Behavior in Collective Autonomous Mobile Robots. *Puoc. of 2nd ASCC.*

Kim, K. J., & Cho, S. B. (2006). A comprehensive overview of the applications of artificial life. *Artificial Life, 12,* 153-182.

Kira, K., & Rendell, L. (1992). A practical approach to feature selection. In *proceedings of the Ninth International Conference on Machine Learning* (pp 249-256). Aberdeen, Scotland: Morgan Kaufmann.

Kira, K., & Rendell, L. A. (1992). The feature selection problem: Traditional methods and a new algorithm (pp. 129-134). In *proceedings of Ninth National Conference on AI.*

Kłopotek, M. A. (2003). Reasoning and learning in extended structured Bayesian networks. *Fundamenta Informaticae, 58*(2)2003, 105-137.

Kłopotek, M. A., Dramiński, M., Ciesielski, K., Kujawiak, M., & Wierzchoń, S. T. (2004). Mining document maps. In M. Gori, M. Celi, M. Nanni (Eds.), *Proceedings of Statistical Approaches to Web Mining Workshop* (SAWM) at PKDD'04 (pp. 87-98), Pisa, 2004.

Kłopotek, M. A., Wierzchoń, S. T., Ciesielski, K., Draminski, M., & Czerski, D., (2007b). *Conceptual Maps of Document Collections in Internet and Intranet. Coping with the Technological Challenge.* IPI PAN Publishing House, Warszawa, 139 pages.

Kłopotek, M. A., Wierzchoń, S. T., Ciesielski, K., Dramiński, M., & Czerski, D. (2007a). Techniques and technologies behind maps of Internet and Intranet document collections. In J., Lu, D. Ruan, G., Zhang (Eds.), *E-Service intelligence – Methodologies, Technologies and Applications* (pp. 169-190). Series: Studies in Computational Intelligence, 37, Berlin Heidelberg, Springer.

Knowles, J. D., & Corne, D. W. (2000). Approximating the Nondominated Front Using the Pareto Archived Evolution Strategy. *Evolutionary Computation, 8*(2), 149-172.

Kohavi, R., & John, G. H. (1997). Wrappers for Feature Subset Selection. *Artificial Intelligence Journal, 97,* 273-324.

Kohavi, R., & Sommereld, D. (1995). Feature subset selection using the wrapper method: Overtting and dynamic search space topology. In *proceedings of First International Conference on Knowledge Discovery and Data Mining* (pp. 192-197). Morgan Kaufmann.

Kohonen, T. (1987). *Content-Addressable Memories* (2nd ed.). Berlin, Germany: Springer-Verlag.

Kohonen, T. (2001). Self-organizing maps. *Springer Series in Information Sciences, 30.* Berlin, Heidelberg, New York, Springer.

Kohonen, T., Kaski, S., Lagus, K., Salojärvi, J., Honkela, J., Paatero, V., & Saarela, A. (2000). Self organization of a massive document collection. *IEEE Transactions on Neural Networks, 11*(3), 574-585.

Koller, D., & Sahami, M. (1994). Toward optimal feature selection. In *proceedings of International Conference on Machine Learning* (pp. 171-182).

Konstantinidis, K., Gasteratos, A., & Andreadis, I. (2007). The Impact of Low-Level Features in Semantic-Based Image Retrieval. In Yu-Jin Zhang (Ed.), *Semantic-Based Visual Information Retrieval*, (pp 23-45).

Konstantinidis, K., Sirakoulis, G. C., & Andreadis, I. (2007). An Intelligent Image Retrieval System Based on the Synergy of Color and Artificial Ant Colonies. In 15th Scandinavian Conference on Image Analysis, June 2007, Aalborg, Denmark, *Lecture Notes in Computer Science, 4522,* 868-877. Berlin, Heidelberg: Springer-Verlag.

Kosko, B. (1997). *Fuzzy Engineering.* Prentice Hall, Upper Saddle River, NJ.

Kosko, B. (ed.). (1992). *Neural Networks and Fuzzy Systems: A Dynamical Systems Approach to Machine Intelligence.* NJ: Prentice Hall Inc.

Kotoulas, L., & Andreadis, I. (2003). Colour Histogram Content-based Image Retrieval and Hardware Implementation. *IEE Proc. Circuits, Devices and Systems, 150*(5), 387–393.

Kouzas, G., Kayafas, E., & Loumos, V. (2006). Ant Seeker: An Algorithm for Enhanced Web Search. In Maglogiannis, I., Karpouzis, K., Bramer, M., (Eds.), *Artificial Intelligence Applications and Innovations (AIAI 2006) 204* (618-626). Boston, MA: IFIP International Federation for Information Processing, Springer.

Koza, J. (1992). *Genetic Programming I, II, III,* MIT Press, 1992, 1994, 1999.

Kozyrev, S.V. (2002). Wavelet theory as p-adic spectral analysis. *Izvestia: Mathematics, 66(2),* 367-376.

Kristjansson, J.E., Staple, A., Kristiansen, J., & Kaas, E. (2002). A new look at possible connections between solar activity, clouds and climate. *Geophysical Research Letters, 29(23),* 2107-2110.

Kurapati, A., & Azarm, S. (2000). Immune network simulation with multiobjective genetic algorithms for multidisciplinary design optimization, *Engineering Optimization, 33*(2), 245-260.

Labella, T. H. (2007). *Division of Labour in Groups of Robots*. Ph.D. thesis, supervisor: M. Dorigo, Universite libre de Bruxelles, Universite d'Europe, Faculte des Sciences Appliquees.

Labrou, Y., Finin, T., & Peng, Y. (1999). Agent communication languages: The current landscape. *IEEE Intelligent Systems, 14*(2), 45-52.

Langley, P. (1994). Selection of relevant features in machine learning. In *Proceedings of the AAAI Fall Symposium on Relevance* (pp. 1-5).

Langton, C. G. (Ed.). (1989). *Artificial Life*. Addison-Wesley Publishing Co.

Lasseter, R. H. (2002). Microgrids. In IEEE Power Engineering Society Winter Meeting, 1, 305-308).

Lasseter, R. H., & Paigi, P. (2004). Microgrid: A Conceptual Solution. In 35th Annual IEEE Power Electronics Specialists Conference, 6,4285-4290.

Lasseter, R., Akhil, A., Marnay, C., Stephens, J., Dagle, J., & Guttromson, R., et al. (2002). The CERTS MicroGrid concept. Retrieved February 11, 2008, from http://certs.lbl.gov/certs-der-micro.html.

Latané, B. (1981a). The psychology of social impact. *American Psychologist, 36*, 343-356.

Latané, B. (1996). Dynamic social impact: The creation of culture by communication. *Journal of Communication, 4*, 13-25.

Latané, B., & Nida, S. (1981b). Ten years of research on group size and helping. *Psychological Bulletin, 89*, 308-324.

Latombe, J. C. (1991). *Robot motion planning*. Norwell, MA: Kluwer Academic.

Laubach, S., & Burdick, J. (1999). An autonomous sensor-based path planner for microrovers. In *Proceedings of the IEEE International Conference on Robotics and Automation* (pp. 347-354). New York, NY: IEEE Press.

Lee, D. W., Jun, H. B., & Sim, K. B. (1999). Artificial immune system for realization of cooperative strategies and group behavior in collective autonomous mobile robots. In *Fourth International Symposium on Artificial Life and Robotics* (pp. 232-235). Oita, Japan.

Lee, D.-W., & Sim, K.-B. (1997) *Artificial immune network-based cooperative control in collective autonomous*

mobile robots. Proceedings of the IEEE International Workshop on Robot and Human Communication. (pp. 58-63).

Lee, P. A., & Anderson, T. (1990). *Fault Tolerance Principles and Practice, Dependable Computing and Fault-Tolerance Systems* (2 ed. Vol. 3). Berlin, Germany: Springer-Verlag.

Lee, T., & Wu, C. (2003). Fuzzy motion planning of mobile robots in unknown environments. *Journal of Intelligent and Robotic Systems, 37*(2), 177-191.

Lee, Z.-J., Lea, C.-Y., & Su, F. (2002). An immunity-based ant colony optimization algorithm for solving weapon-target assignment problem. *Applied Soft Computing, 2(1),39*, 39–47.

Leon, V. J., Wu, S. D., & Storer, R. H. (1994). Robustness measures and robust scheduling for job shops. *IIE Transactions, 26*(5), 32-43.

Lesteven, S., Poincot, P., & Murtagh, F., (1996). Neural networks and information extraction in astronomical information retrieval. *Vistas in Astronomy, 40*(3), 395-400.

Leung, Y. W., & Wang, Y. P. (2001). An Orthogonal Genetic Algorithm with Quantization for Global Numerical Optimization. *IEEE Transactions on Evolutionary Computation, 5*(1), 41-53.

Levy, E. (2005). Worm Propagation and Generic Attacks. *IEEE Security and Privacy, 3*(2), 63- 65.

Levy, R. & Rosenschein, J. S. (1992). A game theoretic approach to distributed artificial intelligence and the pursuit problem. In Y. Demazeau & E. Werner (Ed.), *Decentralized Artificial Intelligence III* (pp. 129-146). North-Holland: Elsevier Science Publishers B.V.

Lewenstein, M., Nowak, A., & Latané, B. (1992). Statistical mechanics of social impact. *Physical Review A* 45(2), 763-775.

Li ,Q.,& Lin , S.F. (2001). Research on digital city framework architecture. *ICII Conference 1*, 30-36.

Li, Q., Tong, X., Xie, S., & Zhang, Y. (2006). Optimum Path planning for Mobile Robots Based on a Hybrid Genetic algorithm. In *Proceedings of the Sixth International Conference on Hybrid Intelligent Systems* (53-56). New York, NY: IEEE Press.

Li, R., Bhanu, B., & Dong, A. (2005). Coevolutionary Feature Synthesized EM Algorithm for Image Retrieval. In *proceedings of the Application of Computer Multimedia* (pp. 696–705).

Li, X., Pu, Q., & Mastorakis, N. (2006). The immune algorithm and its application to blood pressure measuring. *WSEAS Transactions on Electronics, 3*(5), 288-292.

Li, Y. D. (2002). *Hybrid intelligent computing techniques and its application.* Doctoral dissertation, Xidian University, Xi'an.

Li, Y., & Jiao, L. (2007). Quantum-inspired immune clonal multiobjective optimization algorithm. In *11th Pacific-Asia Conference on Advances in Knowledge Discovery and Data Mining* (pp. 672-679).

Li, Z., Zhang, B., & Mao, Z. Y. (2000). Analysis of the chaotic phenomena in permanent magnet synchronous motors based on Poincare map. *The 3rd World Congress on Intelligence Control and Intelligent Automation* (pp. 3255-3258). Hefei, P.R China.

Liao, Y. F., & Ma, X.Q. (2005). Application of Fuzzy Neural Network-Based Chaos Optimization Algorithm to Coal Blending. *Journal of South China University of Technology (Natural Science Edition), 34*(6), 117-126.

Lin, C. H., Chen, C. S., Wu, C. J., & Kang, M. S. (2003). Application of immune algorithm to optimal switching operation for distribution-loss minimisation and loading balance. *IEE Proceedings: Generation, Transmission and Distribution, 150*(2), 183-189.

Lin, X. X., Janak, S. L., & Floudas, C. A. (2004). A new robust optimization approach for scheduling under uncertainty: I bounded uncertainty. *Computers and Chemical Engineering, 28*, 1069-1083.

Lin, Y. (2005). Three-dimensional building reconstruction based on single image vision. *Journal of Shandong Jianzhu University,* (2).

Lin, Y., & Bhanu, B. (2005). Evolutionary Feature Synthesis for Object Recognition. *IEEE Trans. on Systems, Man, and Cybernetics–Part C, 35*, 156–171.

Lioni, A., Sauwens, C., Theraulaz, G., & Deneubourg, J.-L. (2001). The dynamics of chain formation in oecophylla longinoda. *Journal of Insect Behavior, 14*, 679–676.

Liu, C. J., Liao, X. Z., & Zhang, Y. H. (ed.). (2000). Simplified Dynamical Neuro-fuzzy Network Controller and Application. *Proceedings of the 3rd World Congress on Interlligent Control and Automation*(pp. 998-1001). Hefei, P.R China.

Liu, H., & Yu, L. (2005). Toward Integrating Feature Selection Algorithms for Classification and Clustering. *IEEE Trans. Knowledge and Data Engineering, 17*(4), 491–502.

Liu, H., Ma, Z., Liu, S., & Lan, H. (2006). A new solution to economic emission load dispatch using immune genetic algorithm. In *IEEE Conference on Cybernetics and Intelligent Systems* (pp. 1-6).

Lockery, D. (2007). *Learning with ALiCE II.* M.Sc. Thesis, supervisor: J.F. Peters, Department of Electrical & Computer Engineering, University of Manitoba. Retrieved 19 Feb. 2008, from http://wren.ece.umanitoba.ca/

Lockery, D., & Peters, J. F. (2007). Robotic target tracking with approximation space-based feedback during reinforcement learning, Springer best paper award, in: *Proceedings of Eleventh International Conference on Rough Sets, Fuzzy Sets, Data Mining and Granular Computing* (RSFDGrC 2007), Joint Rough Set Symposium (JRS 2007). Lecture Notes in Artificial Intelligence, vol. 4482 (pp. 483-490). Berlin: Springer.

Lockery, D., & Peters, J. F. (2008). Adaptive learning by a target tracking system, Best journal

Lorenz, K. (1981). *The Foundations of Ethology.* Wien: Springer.

Lu, B., Jiao, L., Du, H., & Gong, M. (2005). IFMOA: immune forgetting multiobjective optimization algorithm. In *1st International Conference on Advances in Natural Computation* (pp. 399-408).

Lu, J., & Yang, D. (2007). Path planning Based on Double-layer Genetic algorithm. In *Proceedings of the Third International Conference on Natural Computation* (357-361). New York, NY: IEEE Press.

Lucińska, M., & Wierzchoń, S. T. (2007). An immune-based system for herding problem. In T. Burczyński, W. Cholewa, & W. Moczulski (Ed.), *Recent Developments in Artificial Intelligence Methods* (pp. 107-121). Gliwice: Silesian University of Technology.

Luh, G. C., & Chueh, C. H. (2004). Multi-objective optimal design of truss structure with immune algorithm. *Computers and Structures, 82*(11-12), 829-844.

Luh, G., Chueh, C., & Liu, W. (2003). MOIA: Multi-Objective Immune Algorithm. *Engineering Optimization, 35*(2), 143-164.

Luh, G., Wu, Ch., & Liu, W. (2006) *Artificial Immune System based Cooperative Strategies for Robot Soccer Competition.* Strategic Technology, The 1st International Forum on. (pp. 76-79).

Lumer, E. D., & Faieta, B. (1994). Diversity and adaptation in populations of clustering ants. *From Animals to Animats: Proceedings of the 3th International Conference on the Simulation of Adaptive Behaviour, 3*, 501–508.

Luo, W., Wang, X., & Wang, X. (2007, August 26-29). *A Novel Fast Negative Selection Algorithm Enhanced by State Graphs*. Paper presented at the 6th International Conference on Artificial Immune Systems (ICARIS 2007), LNCS 4628, Santos/SP, Brazi.

Luo, W., Wang, X., Tan, Y., & Wang, X. (2006, September 9-13). *A Novel Negative Selection Algorithm with an Array of Partial Matching Lengths for Each Detector*. Paper presented at the 9th International Conference on Parallel Problem Solving From Nature (PPSN IX), LNCS 4193, Reykjavik, Iceland.

Luo, W., Wang, X., Tan, Y., Zhang, Y., & Wang, X. (2005, September 12-14). *An Adaptive Self-Tolerant Algorithm for Hardware Immune System*. Paper presented at the 6th International Conference on Evolvable Systems (ICES 2005), LNCS 3637, Sitges, Spain.

Luo, W., Zhang, Z., & Wang, X. (2006, September 4-6). *A Heuristic Detector Generation Algorithm for Negative Selection Algorithm with Hamming Distance Partial Matching Rule*. Paper presented at the 5th International Conference on Artificial Immune Systems (ICARIS 2006), LNCS 4163, Instituto Gulbenkian de Ciência, Oeiras, Portugal.

Luo, X. D. (2002). *The research on artificial immune genetic learning algorithm and its application in engineering*. Doctoral dissertation, Zhejiang University, Hangzhou.

Luus, R. (1980). Optimization in model reduction. *International Journal of Control, 32*(5), 741-747.

Lydyard P M., Whelan A., & M.W.Panger. (Ed.) (2001). *Instant Notes in Immunology*. Beijing, CN: Science Press (The introduction of photoprint).

Ma, W., Jiao, L., Gong, M., & Liu, F. (2005). An novel artificial immune systems multi-objective optimization algorithm for 0/1 knapsack problems. In *International Conference on Computational Intelligence and Security* (pp. 793-798).

Macaš, M., & Lhotská, L. (2007). Social impact theory based optimizer. In F. A. e Costa, L. M. Rocha, E. Costa, I. Harvey A. Coutinho (Eds.), *Advances in Artificial Life: LNAI Vol.4648, 9th European Conference on Artificial Life* (pp. 634-644). Springer.

Macaš, M., Lhotská, L., & Křemen, V. (in press). Social impact based approach to feature subset selection. In *International Workshop on Nature Inspired Cooperative Strategies for Optimization*, Studies in Computational Intelligence, Springer.

Madjidi, H., Negahdaripour, S., & Bandari, E. (2003). Vision-based positioning and terrain mapping by global alignment for UAVs. In *Proceedings of the IEEE Conference on Advanced Video and Signal Based Surveillance* (pp. 305-312). New York, NY: IEEE Press.

Mahalanobis, P. (1936). On the generalised distance in statistics. *Proceedings of the National Institute of Science of India, 12*, 49–55.

Mahfouf, M., Chen, M., & Linkens, D. A. (2005). Design of Heat-treated Alloy Steels Using Intelligent Multi-objective Optimization. *ISIJ International, 45*(5), 694-699.

Mamdani, E. H., & Assilian, S. (1999). An experiment in linguistic synthesis with a fuzzy logic controller, *Int. J. Hum.- Comput. Stud., 51*(2), pp. 135–147.

Manfrin, M., Birattari, M., Stutzle, T., & Dorigo, M. (2006). Parallel ant colony optimization for the travelling salesman problem. *M. Dorigo et al. (Eds.), ANTS 2006, LNCS, 4150*, 224–234.

Mange, D., Goeke, M., Madon, D., Stauffer, A., Tempesti, G., & Durand, S. (1996). Embryonics: A new family of coarse-grained FPGA with self-repair and self-reproduction properties. In E. Sanchez & M. Tomassini (Eds.), *Toward Evolvable Hardware: The Evolutionary Engineering Approach* (pp. 197-220): Springer-Verlag.

Manjunath, B. S., Ohm, J.-R., Vasudevan, V. V., & Yamada, A. (2001). Color and texture descriptors, *IEEE Trans. on Circuits and Systems for Video Technology, 11*(6), 703-715.

Manning, C. D., Raghavan, P., & Schütze, H. (2008). *Introduction to Information Retrieval*, New York: Cambridge University Press.

Mardaneh, M., & Gharehpetian, G. B. (2004). Siting and sizing of DG units using GA and OPF based technique. In IEEE Region 10 Conference, 3, 331-334.

Martin, M., Chopard, B., & Albuquerque, P. (2002). Formation of an ant cemetery: swarm intelligence or statistical accident? *Future Generation Computer Systems, 18*, 951–959.

Matusita, K. (1955). Decision rules based on the distance for problems of fit. *Ann. Math. Statist., 26*, 631-640.

Matzinger, P. (2001). The Danger model in its historical context. *Scandinavian Journal of Immunology, 54*.

Maynard-Smith, J. (1982). *Evolution and the theory of games*. U.K.: Cambridge University Press.

MC8051 IP Core - User Guide. (2002). Vienna: Oregano Systems - Design & Consulting GesmbH.

MCS®51 Microcontroller Family User's Manual. (1994). Intel Corporation.

Meiri, R., & Zahavi, J. (2006). Using simulated annealing to optimize the feature selection problem in marketing applications. *European Journal of Operational Research, 171*(3), 842–858.

Meng, H., & Liu, S. (2003). ISPEA: improvement for the strength Pareto evolutionary algorithm for multiobjective optimization with immunity. In *5th International Conference on Computational Intelligence and Multimedia Applications* (pp. 368-372).

Meng, H., Zhang, X., & Liu, S. (2005). Intelligent multiobjective particle swarm optimization based on AER model. In *12th Portuguese Conference on Artificial Intelligence* (pp. 178-189).

Michalewicz, Z. (1996). *Genetic Algorithms + Data Structures = Evolution Programs.* Springer-Verlag.

Michalewicz, Z. (2002). Genetic algorithms + data structure = evolution programs. New York, NY, USA: Springer-Verlag.

Michalewicz, Z., & Fogel D. B. (2004). *How to Solve It: Modern Heuristics.* Springer-Verlag.

Michelan, R., & Von Zuben, F. J. (2002). Decentralized control system for autonomous navigation based on an evolved artificial immune network. In *Congress on Evolutionary Computation* (pp. 1021-1026).

Microsoft company (2008). *Retrieved December 5, 2007, from*

Microsoft company (2008). *Retrieved October 25, 2007, from*

Monada, F., Pettinaro, G. C., Guignard, A., Kwee, I. W., Floreano, D., Deneubourg, J.-L., Nolfi, S., Gambardella, L. M., & Dorigo, M. (2004). *Swarm-bot: A New Distributed Robotic Concept. Autonomous Robots, 17*(2-3), 193-221. Retrieved 19 Feb. 2008, from http://www.swarm-bots. org/dllink.php?id=667&type=documents

Monmarche, N. (1999). On data clustering with artificial ants. *A. A. Freitas (Ed.) AAAI-99 and GECCO-99 Workshop on Data Mining with Evolutionary Algorithms: Research Directions, Orlando, Florida*, 23–26.

Monmarche, N. (2000). *Algorithmes de fourmis artificielles: Applications a la classification et a l'optimisation.* Unpublished doctoral dissertation, Laboratoire d'Informatique, Univeriste de Tours, France.

Monmarche, N., Slimane, M., & Venturini, G. (1999). On improving clustering in numerical database with artificial ants. *D. Floreano, J. D. Nicoud, and F. Mondala (Eds.) Advances in Artificial life, 5th European Conference ECAL 99, Lecture Notes in Artificial Intelligence, 1974*, 626–635.

Mori, K., Kitamura, S., & Shindo, S. (2004). Simulation-based scheduling system for saving energy consumptions. In *SICE Annual Conference* (pp. 657-660).

Mori, K., Tsukiyama, M., & Fukuda, T. (1998). Adaptive scheduling system inspired by immune system. *1998 IEEE International Conference on System, Man and Cybernetics, 4*, 3833-3837, Oct 11-14, San Diego, California, USA, .

Mühlenbein, H., & Dirk, S. (1993). Predictive Models for the Breeder Genetic Algorithm. *Evolutionary Computation, 1*(1), 25-49.

Mühlenbein, H., Mahnig, T. & Rodrigues, A. O. (1999). Schemata distribution and graphical modes in evolutionary optimization. *Journal of Heuristics, 5.*

Muller, H., Muller, W., Squire, D., McG., Marchand-Maillet, S., & Pun, T. (2001). Performance Evaluation in Content-Based Image Retrieval: Overview and Proposals. *Patt. Rec. Lett., 22*, 593-601.

Munoz, F., Nino, L., & Quintana, G. (2008). Object Transportation with an Agent Inspired by the Innate and Adaptive Immune Responses. *ISA'08: Proceedings of the Intelligent Systems and Agents 2008 Conference.* Amsterdam, The Netherlands. (pp. 135-142).

Myers, C. S., & Rabiner, L. R. (1981). A comparative study of several dynamic time-warping algorithms for connected word recognition. *The Bell System Technical Journal, 607*, 1389–1409.

Nakano, K., & Takamichi, E. (2003). An Image Retrieval System Using FPGAs. In *Proc. Asia and South Pacific Design Automation Conference* (pp. 370-373). New York, NY: ACM.

Narendra P. M., & Fukunaga K. (1977). A branch and bound algorithm for feature subset selection. *IEEE Trans. on Computers, C-26*(9), 917–122.

NASA (2007). *Ocean Color Time-Series Online Visualization and Analysis,* from http://reason.gsfc.nasa. gov/Giovanni

Nash, J. F. Jr. (1950). Equilibrium points in n-person games. *Proceedings of the National Academy of Sciences, 36*(1), 48–49.

Neal, M., Feyereisl, J., Rascunà, R., & Wang, X. (2006). *Don't Touch Me, I'm Fine: Robot Autonomy Using an Artificial Innate Immune System.* ICARIS 349-361.

Nearchou, A. C. (1998). Path planning of a mobile robot using genetic heuristics. *Robotica, 16*(5), 575-588.

Nearchou, A. C. (1999). Adaptive navigation of autonomous vehicles using evolutionary algorithms. *Artificial Intelligence in Engineering, 13*(2), 159-173.

Nehrir, H., Caisheng, W., & Shaw, S. R. (2006). Fuel cells: promising devices for distributed generation. IEEE Power and Energy Magazine, 4(1), 47-53.

Nelder, J. A., & Mead, R. (1965). *Computer Journal, 7,* 308-313.

Nicol, D. M (2003).Utility analysis of parallel simulation. *PADS Conference, 123-132*

Nicosia, G., Castiglione, F., & Motta, S. (2001). Pattern recognition by primary and secondary response of an artificial immune system. *Theory in Biosciences, 120*(2), 93–106.

Nouyan, S., & Dorigo, M. (2004). Chain Formation in a Swarm of Robots. Retrieved 19 Feb. 2008, from http://www.swarm-bots.org/dllink.php?id=565&type= documents

Nowak, A., & Latané, B. (1993). Simulating the emergence of social order from individual behaviour. In N. Gilbert & J. Doran (Eds.), *Simulating Societies: The Computer Simulation of Social phenomena*, London: UCL Press.

Nowak, A., & Szamrej, J., & Latané, B. (1990). From private attitude to public opinion: A dynamic theory of social impact. *Psychological Review, 97* (3), 362-376.

Oates, R., Greensmith, J., Aickelin, U., Garibaldi, J., & Kendall, G. (2007). The application of a dendritic cell algorithm to a robotic classifier. In *ICARIS 2007.*

Oguz, T., Dipper, J.W., & Kaymaz, Z. (2006). Climatic regulation of the Black Sea hydro-meteorological and ecological properties at interannual-to-decadal time scales. *Journal of Marine Systems, 60,* 235-254.

Orlowska, E. (1982). Semantics of Vague Concepts, Applications of Rough Sets, Institute for Computer Science, Polish Academy of Sciences, Report 469. See, also, E. Orlowska (1985). Semantics of Vague Concepts. In G.Dorn, P. Weingartner (Eds.), Foundations of Logic and Linguistics. Problems and Solutions, Plenum Press, London/NY, 465-482.

Orman, H. (2003). The Morris Worm: A Fifteen-Year Perspective. *IEEE Security & Privacy, 1*(5): 35-43.

Ortega-Sanchez, C., Mange, D., Smith, S., & Tyrrell, A. (2000). Embryonics: A Bio-Inspired Cellular Architecture with Fault-Tolerant Properties. *Genetic Programming and Evolvable Machines, 1*(3), 187-215.

Pagello, E., D'angelo, A., Ferrari, C., Polesel, R., Rosati, R., & Speranzon, A. (2003). Emergent behaviors of a robot team performing cooperative tasks. *Advanced Robotics, 17*(1), 3-19.

Pai, D., & Reissel, L. M. (1998). Multiresolution rough terrain motion planning. *IEEE Transactions on Robotics and Automation, 14*(1), 19-33.

Palle, E., Butler, C.J., & O'Brien, K. (2004). The possible connection between ionization in the atmosphere by cosmic rays and low level clouds. *Journal of Atmospheric and Solar-Terrestrial Physics, 66,* 1779-1790.

Pan, Y. X., Xu, Q. F., & Gao, H. M. (2000).The Research of t he Fuzzy Control Algorithm Optimization Based on Chaos. *Control Theory and Applications, 17*(5), 703-706.

Pan, Z. J., & Kang, L. S. (1997). An adaptive evolutionary algorithms for numerical optimization. In *Proceedings of the International Conference on Simulated Evolution and Learning*, Berlin, Germany, 27-34.

Pang, C. K., & Chen, H. C. (1976). Optimal short-term thermal unit commitment. IEEE Transaction on Power Apparatus and Systems, 95(4), 1336-1346.

Panitsidis, G., Konstantinidis, K., Vonikakis, V., Andreadis, I., & Gasteratos, A. (2006). Fast Image Retrieval Based on Attributes of the Human Visual System. In *Proceedings of 7th Nordic Signal Processing Symposium (NORSIG 2006)*, (pp. 206-209) Reykjavik, Iceland.

Parker, P. J., & Anderson, B. D. (1987). Unstable rational function approximation. *International Journal of Control, 46*(5), 1783-1801.

Parpinelli, R. S., Lopes, H. S., & Freitas, A. A. (2005). Classification-rule discovery with an ant colony algorithm. *Encyclopedia of Information Science and Technology, Idea Group Inc.*

Pass, G., & Zabih, R. (1999). Comparing Images Using Joint Histograms. *Multimedia Systems, 7*(3), 234-240.

Passino, K. M., & Yurkovich, S. (1998). *Fuzzy Control.* MA: Addison-Wesley.

Patnaik, K. S., Peters, J. F., & Anwar, S. (2008). Influence of temperature on swarmbots that learn. *Cybernetics and Systems: An International Journal* 39, 1-18. DOI: 10.1080/01969720802069831.

Pawlak, Z. (1981a). *Classification of Objects by Means of Attributes*. Institute for Computer Science, Polish Academy of Sciences Report 429. Polish Academy of Sciences, Warsaw, Poland.

Pawlak, Z., & Skowron, A. (2007a). Rudiments of rough sets, *Information Sciences*, *177*(1, 3-27).

Pawlak, Z., & Skowron, A. (2007b). Rough sets: Some extensions, Information Sciences, 177(1), 28-40.

Pawlak, Z., & Skowron, A. (2007c). Rough sets and Boolean reasoning, *Information Sciences*, *177*(1), 41-73.

Pedrcy, W., & Recha, A. F. (1993).Fuzzy-set based models of neurons and knowledge-based networks. *IEEE Transactions on Fuzzy System, 1*(4), 254-266.

Peleg, S., Naor, J., Hartley, R., & Avnir, D. (1984). Multiple Resolution Texture Analysis and Classification. *IEEE Trans. on Pattern Analysis and Machine Intelligence, 6*, 518–523.

Percus, J. K., Percus, O. E., & Perelson, A. S. (1993). Probability of Self-Nonself Discrimination. In A. S. Perelson & G. Weisbuch (Eds.), *Theoretical and Experimental Insights into Immunology* (pp. 63-70). New York: Springer-Verlag.

Perelson, A. S. (1986). Immune Network Theory. *Immunological Review, 110*, 5-36.

Perelson, A. S. (1989). Immune network theory. *Immunological Review, 10*, 5-36.

Perelson, A., Hightower, R., & Forrest, S. (1996). Evolution (and learning) of v-region genes. *Research in Immunology, 147*, 202-208.

Peters, J. F. (2005b). Rough ethology: Towards a Biologically-Inspired Study of Collective Behavior in Intelligent Systems with Approximation Spaces. *Transactions on Rough Sets*, III, 153-174.

Peters, J. F. (2007a). Granular computing in approximate adaptive learning. *International Journal of Information Technology and Intelligent Computing, 2*(4), 1-25.

Peters, J. F. (2007b). Near sets. Special theory about nearness of objects, *Fundamenta Informaticae, 75*(1-4), 407-433.

Peters, J. F. (2007c). Near Sets. Toward Approximation Space-Based Object Recognition. In Yao, Y., Lingras, P., Wu, W.-Z, Szczuka, M., Cercone, N., \'{S}l\c{e}zak, D., (Eds.), *Proc. of the Second Int. Conf. on Rough Sets and Knowledge Technology* (RSKT07), Joint Rough Set Symposium (JRS07), Lecture Notes in Artificial Intelligence 4481 (pp. 22-33). Springer, Berlin.

Peters, J. F. (2007d). Toward approximate adaptive learning. In Kryszkiewicz, M. Peters, J.F. Rybinski, H., Skowron, A. (Eds.), *Int. Conf. on Rough Sets and Emerging Intelligent Systems Paradigms in Memoriam Zdzislaw Pawlak, Lecture Notes in Artificial Intelligence 4585*, Springer, Berlin Heidelberg, 57-68.

Peters, J. F. **(2007e)**. Near sets. General theory about nearness of objects. *Applied Mathematical Sciences, 1*(53), 2609-2629.

Peters, J. F. (2008a). Discovery of perceptually near information granules. In J.T. Yao, (Ed.), Novel Developments in Granular Computing: Applications for Advanced Human Reasoning and Soft Computation, Hersey, NY: Information Science Reference, 2008, *in press*.

Peters, J. F. (2008b). Approximation and perception in ethology-based reinforcement learning. In Pedrycz, W., Skowron, A., Kreinovich, V. (Eds.), *Handbook on Granular Computing*. Wiley, NY., 671-688.

Peters, J. F., & Henry, C. (2005). Reinforcement learning in swarms that learn. In *Proc. IEEE/WIC/ACM Int. Conf. on Intelligent Agent Technology* (pp. 400-406). Compiègne, France: Compiègne Univ. of Tech.

Peters, J. F., & Skowron, A. (2006). Zdzislaw Pawlak: Life and Work. Transactions on Rough Sets, V, 1-24.

Peters, J. F., & Wasilewski, P. (2008). *Foundations of near sets, Information Sciences*. submitted, pending publication.

Peters, J. F., Ahn, T. C., Borkowski, M., Degtyaryov, V., & Ramana, S. (2003). Line-crawling robot navigation: a neurocomputing approach. In C. Zhou, D. Maravall, & D. Ruan (Eds.) *Autonomous Robotics Systems: Soft Computing and Hard Computing Methodologies and Applications* (pp. 141-164) Heidelberg: Physica-Verlag.

Peters, J. F., Henry, C. (2006). Reinforcement learning with approximation spaces. *Fundamenta Informaticae, 71*(2-3), 323-349.

Peters, J. F., Henry, C., & Gunderson, D. S. (2007). Biologically-inspired adaptive learning control strategies: A rough set approach. *Int. J. of Hybrid Intelligent Systems, 4*(4), 203-216.

Peters, J. F., Henry, C., & Ramanna, S. (2005a). Rough Ethograms: Study of Intelligent System Behavior. In M.A. Kłopotek, S. Wierzchoń, K. Trojanowski (Eds.), *New Trends in Intelligent Information Processing and Web Mining* (pp. 117-126). Berlin: Springer.

Peters, J. F., Shahfar, S., Ramanna, S., & Szturm, T. (2007). Biologically-inspired adaptive learning: A near set approach. In *Proc. Frontiers in the Convergence of Bioscience and Information Technologies* (FBIT07), 10.1109/FBIT.2007.39, IEEE Computer Society, 403-408.

Peters, J. F., Skowron, A., & Stepaniuk, J. (2006). Nearness in approximation spaces. In G. Lindemann, H. Schlingloff et al. (Eds.), *Proc. Concurrency, Specification & Programming*, Informatik-Berichte Nr. 206 (pp. 434-445). Berlin: Humboldt-Universitat zu Berlin.

Peters, J. F., Skowron, A., & Stepaniuk, J. (2007). Nearness of objects: Extension of approximation space model. *Fundamenta Informaticae, 79*(3-4), 497-512.

Peters, J. F., Skowron, A., Synak, P., & Ramanna, S. (2003). Rough sets and information granulation. In Bilgic, T., Baets, D., Kaynak, O. (Eds.), *Tenth Int. Fuzzy Systems Assoc. World Congress*, *Lecture Notes in Artificial Intelligence, 2715*, 370-377, Instanbul, Turkey. Heidelberg, Germany: Physica-Verlag.

Pierre, H., & Nenad, M. (2001). Variable neighborhood search: principles and applications. *European Journal of Operational Research, 130*, 449-467.

Pirolli, P. (2007). *Information Foraging Theory: Adaptive interaction with information*. Oxford: Oxford University Press.

Player project official web page. (2006) (http://playerstage.sourceforge.net/)

Polkowski, L. (2002). *Rough Sets. Mathematical Foundations*. Heidelberg, Germany: Springer-Verlag.

Polycity (2006). Official website of the EU sponsored research Project Polycity, Retrieved February 11, 2008, from http://www.polycity.net.

Pratihar, D. K., Deb, K., & Ghosh, A. (1999). A genetic-fuzzy approach for mobile robot navigation among moving obstacles. *International Journal of Approximate Reasoning, 20*(2), 145-172.

Predrycs, W. (1993). *Fuzzy Control and Fuzzy Systems*. New York, NY: Wiley.

Prieto, C., Nino, F., & Quintana, G. (2008). A Goalkeeper Strategy in Robot Soccer Based on Danger Theory. In *2008 IEEE World Congress on Computational Intelligence*, Hong Kong.

Qi, L., & Lin, S.F. 2001). Research on digital city framework architecture. *ICII Conference, 1, 33-36.*

Qian, Z. B. (2000). Total-automatically Image Matching of Stereoscopic Pair of Aerial Photograpgy. *Journal of Zhengzhou Institute of Surveying and Mapping*, (4).

Ramos, V., & Merelo, J. J. (2002). Self-organized stigmergic document maps: Environment as a mechanism for context learning. *E. Alba, F. Herrera, and J. J. Merelo (Eds.), Proceedings of the 1st International Conference on Metaheuristic, Evolutionary and Bio-Inspired Algorithms*, 284–293.

Ramos, V., Muga, F., & Pina, P. (2002). Self-organized data and image retrieval as a consequence of inter-dynamic synergistic relationships in artificial ant colonies. *J. R. del Solar, J. Abraham, and M. Koppen (Eds.) Soft-Computing Systems- Design, Management and Applications, Frontiers of Artificial Intelligence and Applications, IOS Press, 87*, 500–509.

Ramos, V., Muge, F., & Pina, P. (2002). Self-Organized Data and Image Retrieval as a Consequence of Inter-Dynamic Synergistic Relationships in Artificial Ant Colonies. In Ruiz-del-Solar, J., Abraham, A., Köppen, M. (Eds.): *Hybrid Intelligent Systems, Frontiers of Artificial Intelligence and Applications, 87*, 500-512. IOS Press.

Raymer, M.L., Punch, W.F., Goodman, E.D., Kuhn, L.A., & Jain, A.K. (2000). Dimensionality reduction using genetic algorithms. *IEEE Trans. Evolutionary Computation, 4*(2), 164–171.

Read, D.W. (2003). Emergent properties in small scale societies. *Artificial life, 9*(4), 419-428.

Reid, G.C. (1991). Solar total irradiance variation and the global sea surface temperature record. *Journal of Geophysical Research, 96*, 2835-2844.

Ren, L. H., & Ding, Y. S. (2002). A new network simulation platform based on ecological network computation. *J. System Simulation, 14*(11), 1497-1499, 1503. (in Chinese).

Renyi, A. (1961). On measures of entropy and information. *Fourth Berkeley Symposium on Mathematics, Statistics and Probability: Vol. 1* (pp. 547-561). London: Cambridge University Press.

Richard, M. F. (2001). PARALLEL AND DISTRIBUTED SIMULATION SYSTEMS. *WSC Conference, 147-157.*

Ripeanu, M., Foster, I., & Iamnitchi, A. (2002). Mapping the Gnutella network: Properties of large-scale peer-to-peer systems and implications for system design. *IEEE Internet Computing Journal, 6*(1).

Rogers, H. (1987). *Theory of Recursive Functions and Effective Computability*. Cambridge, MA: MIT Press.

Romero, D. A., & Niño, L. F. (2006). An Immune-based Multilayered Cognitive Model for Autonomous Navigation. *Proceedings of the IEEE Congress on Evolutionary Computation* (pp. 1115–1122).

Rosenschein, J. S. (1985). *Rational interaction: Cooperation among intelligent agents*. Unpublished doctoral dissertation, Stanford University, CA.

Rousseeuw, P. J. (1987). Silhouettes: a graphical aid to the interpretation and validation of cluster analysis. *Journal of Computers and Applied Mathematics, 20*, 53–65.

Rousseeuw, P., & Kaufman, L. (1990). *Finding groups in data: An introduction to cluster analysis*. John Wiley & Sons.

Ruan, X. G. (1997).Research on fuzzy Hopfield network and its fuzzy clustering function. *Fuzzy system and mathematic, 11*(1), 88-94.

Ruan, X. G. (2000). A Neuro-Fuzzy Recognition System based on fuzzy Hopfield network. *Pattern Recognition and Artificial Intelligence, 13*(4), 387-394.

Rudolph, G. (1994). Convergence analysis of canonical genetic algorithms. *IEEE Transactions on Neural Networks, 5*, 96-101.

Rudolph, G. (1994). Convergence analysis of canonical genetic algorithms. *IEEE Trans. Neural Networks: Special Issue on EC, 5*(1), 96-101.

Russell, B. C, Torralba, A., Murphy, K. P., & Freeman, W. T. (2005). *LabelMe: A database and web-based tool for image annotation*. MIT AI Lab Memo AIM-2005-025.

Sait, S.M., & Youssef, H. (1999). *VLSI physical design automation: Theory and practice*. World Scientific

Sakoda, J. M. (1971). The checkerboard model of social interaction. *Journal of Mathematical Sociology, 1*, 119-132.

Salomon, R. (1996). Re-evaluating genetic algorithm performance under coordinate rotation of benchmark functions: A survey of some theoretical and practical aspects of genetic algorithms. *BioSystems, 39*, 263-278.

Salomon, R. (1998). Evolutionary algorithms and gradient search: similarities and differences. *IEEE Trans. Evolutionary Computation, 2*(2), 45-55.

Salter, T. (2006). *Navigational And Proprioceptive Sensor-Based Recognition Of Interaction Patterns Between Children And Mobile Robots*, Ph.D. thesis, University of Alberta. Edmonton, Alberta, Canada: University of Alberta Press.

Salton, G., & McGill, M. (1983). *Introduction to modern information retrieval*. New York: McGraw-Hill.

Sasaki M., & Kawakuku M., & Takahashi K. (1999) *An Immune Feedback Mechanism Based Network controller.*

Paper presented at the 6th IEEE International Conference on Neural Information Processing(ICONIP '99), Perth, Australia.

Sathyanath, S., & Sahin, F. (2002). AISIMAM – An artificial immune system based intelligent multi agent model and its application to a mine detection problem. In *International Conference on Artificial Immune Systems* (pp. 3-11), U.K.: Canterbury Printing Unit.

Sathyanath, S., & Sahin, F. (2002). *AISIMAM – An Artificial Immune System Based Intelligent Multi Agent Model and its Application to a Mine Detection Problem*. ICARIS 2002, Session I, pp. 22-31.

Satoh, T., Mizukami, Y., Tanaka, K., & Nara, K. (2004). A two-level ALife system with predator. *Electronics and Communication in Japan, 87-2*(8), 53-59.

Satoh, T., Uchibori, A., & Tanaka, K. (1999). Artificial life system for optimization of nonconvex functions. *International Joint Conference on Neural Networks, 4*, 2390-2393.

Schaffer, J. D., & Grefenstette, J. J. (1985). Multi-objective Learning via Genetic Algorithms. *Proc. Of the Ninth International Joint Conference on Artificial Intelligence*. Morgan Kaufmann (pp. 593-595).

Schelling, T. (1969). Models of segregation. *American Economic Review, 59*, 488-493.

Schlimmer, J. C. (1993). Efficiently inducing determinations: A complete and systematic search algorithm that uses optimal pruning. In *proceedings of Tenth International Conference on Machine Learning* (pp. 284–290).

Schnell, R. (1992). Artificial intelligence, computer simulation and theory construction in the social science. In F. Faulbaum (Ed.), *Advances in Statistical Software, 3*, 335-342. Stuttgart.

Schockaert, S., Cock, M. D., Cornelis, C., & Etienne, E. E. K. (2004). Fuzzy ant based clustering. *ANTS 2004, LNCS 3172, Springer-Verlag Berlin Heidelberg*, 342–349.

Schockaert, S., Cock, M. D., Cornelis, C., & Kerre, E. E. (2004). Efficient clustering with fuzzy ants. In *Applied computational intelligence, world scientific publishing co. pte. ltd.*

Scholtes, J. C. (1993). *Neural networks in natural language processing and information retrieval*. Unpublished doctoral dissertation, University of Amsterdam.

Sedghisigarchi, A. (2006). Impact of Fuel Cells on Load-Frequency Control in Power Distribution Systems. IEEE Transactions on Energy Conversion, 21(1), 250-256.

Selfridge, O. G. (1984). Some themes and primitives in ill-defined systems. In Selfridge, O.G., Rissland, E.L., Arbib, M.A. (Eds.), *Adaptive Control of Ill-Defined Systems* (pp. 21-26). London, UK: Plenum Press.

Seraji, H., & Howard, A. (2002). Behavior based robot navigation on challenging terrain: a fuzzy logic approach. *IEEE Transactions on Robotics and Automation, 18*(3), 308-321.

Sergei G., & Yuri M. (2003). A Simple Non-linear Model of Immune Response[J]. *Chaos. Solitons and Fractals, 16* (1), 125-132.

Shahfar, S. (2007). *Glowlight Tetra Freshwater Fish.* Research Report, Computational Intelligence Laboratory, University of Manitoba.

Shang, R., & Ma, W. (2006). Immune clonal MO algorithm for ZDT problems. In *2nd International Conference on Advances in Natural Computation* (pp. 100-109).

Shang, R., Jiao, L., Gong, M., & Lu, B. (2005). Clonal selection algorithm for dynamic multiobjective optimization. In *International Conference on Computational Intelligence and Security* (pp. 846-851).

Shang, R., Ma, W., & Zhang, W. (2006). Immune clonal MO algorithm for 0/1 knapsack problems. In *2nd International Conference on Advances in Natural Computation* (pp. 870-878).

Shashi, K., Sanjeev, K., Prakash, Ravi, S., Tiwari, M. K., & Shashi B. K. (2007).Prediction of flow stress for carbon steels using recurrent self-organizing neuro fuzzy networks. *Expert Systems with Applications, 32*(3), 777-788.

Sheppard, J.W. (1996). Multi-Agent Reinforcement Learning in Markov Games, Ph.D. Dissertation, The Johns Hopkins University, Baltimore, Maryland.

Shibata, T., & Fukuda, T. (1993). Intelligent motion planning by genetic algorithm with fuzzy critic. In *Proceedings of the 8th IEEE Symposium on Intelligent Control* (pp. 565-569). New York, NY: IEEE Press.

Shmygelska, A., & Hoos, H. H. (2005). An ant colony optimisation algorithm for the 2D and 3D hydrophobic polar protein folding problem. *BMC Bioinformatics, 6*(30), 1–22.

Shoham, Y., & Leyton-Brown, K. (2008). *Multi agent systems.* U.K.: Cambridge University Press.

Shuai, J. W., Chen, Z.X., Liu, R. T., & Wu, B. X. (1997) .Maximum hyperchaos in chaotic nonmonotonic neuronal networks.*PHYSICAL REVIEWE, 56*(1), 890-893.

Shuai, J.W., Chen, Z. X., Liu, R. T., & Wu, B. X. (1996). Self-evolution neural model. *Physics Letters A, 221,*311-316.

Shutler, P. M. E. (2004). A priority list based heuristic for the job shop problem: part 2 tabu search. *Journal of Operational Research Society, 55*(7), 780-784.

SIDC (2007). *Solar Influences Data Analysis Center,* form http://sidc.oma.be

Siedlecki, W. & Sklansky, J. (1988). On automatic feature selection. *International Journal of Pattern Recognition and Artificial Intelligence, 2,* 197–220.

Simpson, S. G. (2006). *What is Foundations of Mathematics?* (http://www.math.psu.edu/simpson/hierarchy.html)

Singh, Ch., & Fair, Sh. (2005). An Artificial Immune System for a MultiAgent Robotics System. *Transactions on Engineering, C V6,* 308-311.

Singh, S., & Thayer, S. (2002). A foundation for kilorobotic exploration. In *IEEE World Congress on Evolutionary Computational Intelligence*: *Vol. 2.* Honolulu: IEEE Press.

Singhal, A. (2001). Modern information retrieval: A brief overview. *Bulletin of the IEEE Computer Society Technical Committee on Data Engineering, 24*(4), 35-43.

Skowron, A., & Stepaniuk, J. (1995). Generalized approximation spaces. In Lin, T.Y.,Wildberger, A.M. (Eds.), *Soft Computing* (pp. 18-21). San Diego, CA, U.S.A.: Simulation Councils.

Skowron, A., Swiniarski, R., & Synak, P. (2005). Approximation spaces and information granulation. *Transactions on Rough Sets,* III, 175-189.

Snir, M., Otto, S., Huss-Lederman, S., Walker, D., &Dongarra, J. (1996). *MPI: The Complete Reference.* Cambridge, MA: MIT Press.

Socha, K. (2004). Aco for continuous and mixed-variable optimization. *Proceedings of ANTS 2004 Lecture Notes in Computer Science, Springer, 3172,* 25–36.

Socha, K., & Dorigo, M. (2005). Ant colony optimization for continous domains. *IRIDIA – Technical Report Series, 037.*

Sohu (2006). Beijing monitoring illegal buildings by the two satellites every two-month with 90 percent accuracy rate. *Retrieved October 20, 2007, from*

Solberg, A. H. S., & Jain, A. K. (1997). Texture Fusion and Feature Selection Applied to SAR Imagery. *IEEE Trans. on Geoscience and Remote Sensing, 35,* 475–479.

Song, J. D., & Yang, B. S. (2005). Optimum design of short journal bearing by using enhanced artificial life optimization algorithm. *Tribology International, 38*(4), 403-411.

Spero, D., & Jarvis, R. (2002). Path planning for a mobile robot in a rough terrain environment. In *Proceedings of the Third International Workshop on Robot Motion and Control* (pp. 417-422). New York, NY: IEEE Press.

Stackelberg, H. (1952). *The theory of the market economy.* London, U.K.: Oxford University Press.

Stafylopatis, A., & Blekas, K. (1998). Autonomous vehicle navigation using evolutionary reinforcement learning. *European Journal of Operational Research, 108*(2), 306-318.

Stepaniuk, J. (1998). Approximation spaces, reducts and representatives. In Polkowski, L., Skowron, A.: (Eds.), *Rough Sets in Knowledge Discovery* 2: Studies in Fuzziness and Soft Computing 19 (pp. 109-126). Heidelberg, Germany: Springer-Verlag.

Stepney, S., Smith, R. E., Timmis, J., & Tyrrell, A. M. (2004). Towards a Conceptual Framework for Artificial Immune Systems. In *Proceedings of Third International Conference on Artificial Immune Systems,* 53-64.

Stevens, D., Natarajan, B., & Das, S. (2004). Multiobjective artificial immune systems based complex spreading code sets for DS-CDMA. In *4th IASTED International Multi-Conference on Wireless and Optical Communications* (pp. 364-368).

Stewart, J., & Varela, F. J. (1990). Dynamics of a class of immune networks. Oscillatory activity of cellular and humeral component. *Theo. Biol., 144,* 103-115.

Strehl, A., Ghosh, J., & Mooney, R. (2000). Impact of similarity measures on web-page clustering. pp. *7th National Conference on Artificial Intelligence: Workshop of Artificial Intelligence for Web Search, AAAI, Austin, Texas, USA,* 58–64.

Stutzle, T. (1998). Parallelization strategies for ant colony optimization. *Lecture Notes in Computer Science, 1498,* 722–731.

Stutzle, T., & Hoos, H. (1997). The max-min ant system and local search for the traveling salesman problem. *IEEE Conference on Evolutionary Computing,* 309–314.

Stutzle, T., & Hoos, H. (2000). Max-min ant system. *Future Generation Computer Systems 16, 8,* 889–914.

Sugihara, K., & Smith, J. (1997). Genetic algorithms for adaptive motion planning of an autonomous mobile robot. In *Proceedings of the 1997 IEEE International Symposium*

on Computational Intelligence in Robotics and Automation (pp. 138-143). New York, NY: IEEE Press.

Sukama, M., & Fukami, H. (1993). Aggregation arrestant pheromone of the german cockroach, blattella germanica (l.) (dictyoptera: Blattellidae): isolation and structure elucidation of blasttellastanoside-a and b. *Journal of Chemical Ecology, 19,* 2521–2541.

Sun, Y. D. (2004). *The research on model, algorithm and application of artificial immune system.* Doctoral dissertation, Zhejiang University, Hangzhou.

Sun, Z. H., Yuan, X. J., Bebis, G., & Louis, S. J. (2002). Neural-Network-based Gender Classification Using Genetic Search for Eigen-Feature Selection. *IEEE International Joint Conference on Neural Networks, 3,* 2433–2438.

Suresh, V., & Chandhuri, D. (1993). Dynamic scheduling--A survey of research. *International Journal of Production Economics, 32*(1), 53-63.

Sutton, R. S., & Barto, A.G. (1998). *Reinforcement Learning: An Introduction.* Cambridge, MA, U.S.A.: The MIT Press.

Svensmark, H., & Friis-Christensen, E. (1997). Variation of cosmic ray fux and global cloud coverage – a missing link in solar-climate relationships. *Journal of Atmospheric and Solar-Terrestrial Physics, 59,* 1225-1232.

Swain, M. J., & Ballard, D. H. (1991). Color Indexing. *Int. Journal of Computer Vision, 7,* 11-32.

Swinburne, R. (2002). *Bayes's Theorem.* Oxford: Oxford University Press.

Takahashi K., & Yamada T. (1997). *A Self-Tuning Immune Feedback Controller for Controlling Mechanical System.* Paper presented at the meeting of IEEE Advanced Intelligent Mechatronics, USA.

Takahashi K., & Yamada T. (1998). Application of an Immune Feedback Mechanism to Control Systems. *JSME International Journal, Series C,* 41(2), 184-191.

Takahashi, K., & Yamada, T. (1997). A self-tuning immune feedback controller for controlling mechanism systems. *IEEE/ASME International Conference on Advanced Intelligent Mechatronics'97, June 16-20, Tokyo, Japan,* 101-104

Tan, G. X., & Mao, Z. Y. (2005). Study on Pareto front of multi-objective optimization using immune algorithm. In *International Conference on Machine Learning and Cybernetics* (pp. 2923-2928).

Tan, K. C., Goh, C. K., Mamun, A. A., & Ei, E. Z. (2008). An evolutionary artificial immune system for multi-objective optimization. *European Journal of Operational Research, 187*(2), 371-392.

Tan, S. C., Ting, K. M., & , S. W. T. (2006). Reproducing the results of ant-based clustering without using ants. *CEC 2006. IEEE Congress on Evolutionary Computation,* 1760–1767.

Tang, N., & Vemuri, V. R. (2005). An artificial immune system approach to document clustering. In *Proceedings of the 2005 ACM Symposium on Applied Computing* (pp. 918-922), Santa Fe, New Mexico.

Tang, W., & Li, D. P. (2000).Chaos Optimization Method for Fuzzy Controller. *Journal of Harbin Engineering University, 21*(2), 6-9.

Tao L. (Ed.) (2004). *Computer Immunology.* Beijing, CN: Electronic Publishing Industry.

Tarakanov A., & Dasgupta D. (2000). A Formal Model of an Artificial Immune System. *Biosystems, 55*(8), 151-158.

Tarakanov, A. O. (2007a). Formal immune networks: self-organization and real-world applications. In M. Prokopenko (Ed.), *Advances in Applied Self-Organizing Systems* (pp. 269-288). Berlin: Springer.

Tarakanov, A. O. (2007b). Mathematical models of intrusion detection by an intelligent immunochip. *Communication in Computer and Information Science, 1,* 308-319.

Tarakanov, A. O. (2008). Immunocomputing for intelligent intrusion detection. IEEE Computational Intelligence Magazine, 3(2), 22-30.

Tarakanov, A. O., & Tarakanov, Y. A. (2004). A comparison of immune and neural computing for two real-life tasks of pattern recognition. *Lecture Notes in Computer Science, 3239,* 236-249.

Tarakanov, A. O., & Tarakanov, Y. A. (2005). A comparison of immune and genetic algorithms for two real-life tasks of pattern recognition. *International Journal of Unconventional Computing, 1*(4), 357-374.

Tarakanov, A. O., Goncharova, L. B., & Tarakanov, O. A. (2005a). A cytokine formal immune network. *Lecture Notes in Artificial Intelligence, 3630,* 510-519.

Tarakanov, A. O., Kvachev, S. V., & Sukhorukov, A.V. (2005b). A formal immune network and its implementation for on-line intrusion detection. *Lecture Notes in Computer Science, 3685,* 394-405.

Tarakanov, A. O., Skormin, V. A., & Sokolova, S. P. (2003). *Immunocomputing: Principles and Applications.* New York: Springer.

Tarakanov, A. O., Sokolova, L. A., & Kvachev, S. V. (2007c). Intelligent simulation of hydrophysical fields by immunocomputing. *Lecture Notes in Geoinformation and Cartography, XIV,* 252-262.

Tarakanov, A., & Adamatzky, A. (2002). Virtual clothing in hybrid cellular automata. *Kybernetes, 31*(7-8), 394-405.

Tarakanov, A., & Dasgupta, D. (2000). A formal model of an artificial immune system. *BioSystems, 55*(1/3), 151-158.

Tarakanov, A., & Nicosia, G. (2007). Foundations of immunocomputing. *First IEEE Symposium on Foundations of Computational Intelligence (FOCI'07)* (pp. 503-508). Madison, WI: Omnipress.

Tarakanov, A., & Prokaev, A. (2007). Identification of cellular automata by immunocomputing. *Journal of Cellular Automata, 2*(1), 39-45.

Tarakanov, A., Goncharova, L., Gupalova, T., Kvachev, S., & Sukhorukov, A. (2002). Immunocomputing for bioarrays. In: Timmis, J., & Bentley, P. (Eds.), *Proceedings of the 1st International Conference on Artificial Immune Systems ICARIS'02* (pp. 32-40). University of Kent at Canterbury, UK.

Tarakanov, A., Kryukov, I., Varnavskikh, E., & Ivanov, V. (2007a). A mathematical model of intrusion detection by immunocomputing for spatially distributed security systems. *RadioSystems, 106,* 90-92 (in Russian).

Tarakanov, A., Prokaev, A., & Varnavskikh, E. (2007b). Immunocomputing of hydroacoustic fields. *International Journal of Unconventional Computing, 3*(2), 123-133.

Tarokh, M. (2008). Hybrid Intelligent Path planning for Articulated Rovers in Rough Terrain. *Fuzzy sets and Systems, 159,* 1430-1440.

Tavakkoli-Moghaddam, R., Rahimi-Vahed, A., & Mirzaei, A. H. (2007a). Solving a bi-criteria permutation flow shop problem using immune algorithm. In *IEEE Symposium on Computational Intelligence in Scheduling* (pp. 49-56).

Tavakkoli-Moghaddam, R., Rahimi-Vahed, A., & Mirzaei, A. H. (2007b). A hybrid multi-objective immune algorithm for a flow shop scheduling problem with bi-objectives: Weighted mean completion time and weighted mean tardiness. *Information Sciences, 177*(22), 5072-5090.

Tchikou, M., & Gouraderes, E. (2003). Multi-agent model to control production system: A reactive and emergent approach by cooperation and competition between agents. *Lecture notes in computer sciences, 2606*, 105-118.

Tefatsion, L. (2001). Economic agents and markets as emergent phenomena. *Proceedings of the National Academy of Sciences of the United States of America, 99(10),* 7191-7192.

Theocharis, J. B. (2006). A high-order recurrent neuron-fuzzy system internal dynamics. Application to the adaptive cancellation. *Fuzzy Sets and Systems, 157,* 471-500.

Theraulaz, G., Bonabeau, E., Sauwens, C., Deneubourg, J.-L., Lioni, A., Libert, F., et al. (2001). Model of droplet formation and dynamics in the argentine ant (linepithema humile mayr). *Bulletin of Mathematical Biology.*

Timmis, J. (2001). aiVIS: Artificial immune network visualization. In *Proceedings of EuroGraphics UK 2001 Conference,* (pp. 61-69), London, University College London,

Timmis, J., & Neal, M. (2001). A recourse limited artificial immune system for data analysis. *Knowledge Based Systems, 14*(3–4), 121–130.

Timmis, J., Neal, M., & Hunt, J. (2000). An artificial immune system for data analysis. *Biosystems, 55*(1/3), 143-150.

Tinbergen, N. (1940). Die Ubersprungbewegung. *Zeitschrift für Tierpsychologie,* 4, 1-40.

Tinbergen, N. (1942). An objectivistic study of the innate behaviour of animals, *Bibliotheca Biotheoretica,* set D, I(2), 39-98.

Tinbergen, N. (1948). Social releasers and the experimental method required for their study. Wilson Bull., 160, 6-52.

Tinbergen, N. (1951). *The Study of Instinct.* Oxford, UK: Oxford University Press.

Tinbergen, N. (1953a). The Herring Gull's World. A Study of the Social Behavior of Birds. London, UK: Collins.

Tinbergen, N. (1953b). *Social Behaviour in Animals With Special Reference to Vertebrates.* London, UK: The Scientific Book Club.

Tinbergen, N. (1963). On aims and methods of ethology, *Zeitschrift für Tierpsychologie,* 20, 410--433.

Toma, N., Endoh, S., & Yamada, K. (1999). Immune algorithm with immune network and MHC for adaptive problem solving. *Fourth International Symposium Autonomous Decentralized Systems,* 4, 271-276. March 21-23, Tokyo, Japan.

TORONTO, Ont(2006). VirtualCity. *Retrieved October 25, 2007, from* http://www.virtualcity.ca/

Trepes, D. (2008). *Information foraging theory.* Retrieved 1 February, 2008 from Interaction-Design.org: http://www.interaction-design.org/encyclopedia/information_foraging_theory.html

Trianni, V., Labella, T. H., & Dorigo, M. (2004). Evolution of direct communication for a swarm bot performing hole avoidance. *Ant Colony Optimization and Swarm Intelligence, Springer.*

Tsiropoula, G. (2003). Signatures of solar activity variability in meteorological parameters. *Journal of Atmospheric and Solar-Terrestrial Physics, 65,* 469-482.

Tsutsui, S., Yamamure, M., & Higuchi, T. (1999). Multi-parent recombination with simplex crossover in real coded genetic algorithms. in *Proc. Genetic and Evol. Comput. Conf.,* 657–664.

Tunstel, E., Howard, A., Huntsberger, T., Trebio-Ollennu, A., & Dolan, J. M. (2003). Applied soft computing strategies for autonomous field robotics. In C. Zhou, D. Maravall, & D. Ruan (Eds.), *Autonomous Robotics Systems: Soft Computing and Hard Computing Methodologies and Applications* (pp. 75-102) Heidelberg: Physica-Verlag.

Tyrrell, A. M. (1999, September). *Computer Know Thy Self!: A Biological Way to Look at Fault Tolerance.* Paper presented at the 2nd EuroMicro / IEEE Workshop Dependable Computing Systems.

U. S. Department of Energy, (2000). Strategic Plan for Distributed Energy Resources.

U. S. Department of Energy, (2001). Transmission Reliability Multi-Year Program Plan FY2001-2005.

Urban Simulation Team at UCLA (2000). Applications for fast visual simulation in design, urban planning, emergency response, and education. *Retrieved October 25, 2007, from*

Urban Simulation Team at UCLA (2000). Applications for real-time visual simulation in design, urban planning, emergency response, and education. *Retrieved December 5, 2007, from* Virtual City (2008).VirtualCity. *Retrieved October 25, 2007, from* http://www.virtualcity.co.ke /

Urdiales, C., Bandera, A., Perez, E., Poncela, A., & Sandoval, F. (2003). Hierarchical planning in a mobile robot for map learning and navigation. In C. Zhou, D. Maravall, & D. Ruan (Eds.) *Autonomous Robotics Systems: Soft Computing and Hard Computing Methodologies and Applications* (pp. 165-188) Heidelberg: Physica-Verlag.

Vadakkepat, P., Lee, T. H., & Xin, L. (2003). Evolutionary artificial potential field – applications to mobile robot planning. In C. Zhou, D. Maravall, & D. Ruan (Eds.), *Autonomous Robotics Systems: Soft Computing and Hard Computing Methodologies and Applications* (pp. 217-232) Heidelberg: Physica-Verlag.

Valckenaers, P., Brussel, H., Hadeli, O., Bochmann, B., Germain, S. and Zamfirescu, C. (2003). On the design of emergent systems: An investigation of integration and interoperability issues, *Engineering applications of artificial intelligence, 16*(4), 377-393.

Vallem, M., & Mitra, J. (2005). Siting and sizing of distributed generation for optimal microgrid architecture. In 37th Annual North American Power Symposium (pp. 611-616).

van Rijsbergen, C. J. (1979). *Information retrieval.* London: Butterworths.

Vapnik, V. (1995). *The Nature of Statistical Learning Theory.* Springer-Verlag, New York.

Varela F.J. (1994). The Immune Learning Mechanisms: Reinforcement, Recruitment and Their Application. *Computing with Biological Metaphors, 1*(1), 37-45.

Varela F.J., & Stewart J. (1990). Dynamics of a Class of Immune Networks- I: Global Behavior. *Theory Biology, 144*(1), 93-101.

Varela, F. J., & Stewart, J. (1990). Dynamics of a class of immune networks. *Global behavior. Theo. Biol., 144,* 93-101.

Varela, F. J., & Stewart, J.(1990). Dynamics of a class of immune networks. *Global behavior. Theo. Biol., 1*(144), 93-101.

Varotsos, C., Dris, N., Asimakopoulos, D., & Cartalis, C. (1992). On the relationship between the 10.7 cm solar flux, surface pressure and air temperature over Greece. *Theoretical and Applied Climatology, 46(1),* 27-32.

Vertosick, F. T., & Kelly, R. H. (1989). Immune network theory: A role for parallel distributed processing? *Immunology, 66,* 1-7.

Villalobos-Arias, M., Coello Coello, C. A., & Hernández-Lerma, O. (2005). Asymptotic convergence of some metaheuristics used for multiobjective optimization. In *Revised Selected Papers of 8th International Workshop on Foundations of Genetic Algorithms* (pp. 95-111).

Villalobos-Arias, M., Coello Coello, C. A., & Hernández-Lerma, O. (2004). Convergence analysis of a multiobjective artificial immune system algorithm. In *3rd International Conference on Artificial Immune Systems* (pp. 226-235).

Vizine, A. L., Castro, N. L. de, Hruschka, E. R., & Gudwin, R. R. (2005). Towards improving clustering ants: An adaptive ant clustering algorithm. *Informatica, 29,* 143–154.

Wang Lei, D. (2004). *Immne evolutionary computation and its application.* Doctoral dissertation, Xidian University, Xi'an.

Wang, C.L., Bhat, P.B.,& Prasanna, V.K. (1996). High-performance computing for vision.*Proceedings of the IEEE 84(7):931 – 946.*

Wang, J. Q., Qin, J., & Kang, L. S. (2006). A new QoS multicast routing model and its immune optimization algorithm. in *3rd International Conference on Ubiquitous Intelligence and Computing* (pp. 369-378).

Wang, L., Pan, J. & Jiao, L. (2000). The immune algorithm. *ACTA Electronica Sinica, 28*(7),74-78

Wang, S. X., Jiang, Y., & Li, Y. G. (2006). Chaos Optimization Strategy on Fuzzy-immune-PID Control of Turbine Regulating System. *Journal of System Simulation, 18*(6), 1729-1732.

Wang, X. L., & Mahfouf, M. (2006). ACSAMO: An Adaptive Multiobjective Optimization Algorithm using the Clonal Selection Principle. In *2nd European Symposium on Nature-Inspired Smart Information Systems* (pp. 1-12).

Wang, X., Gao, X. Z., & Ovaska, S. J. (2004). Artificial Immune Optimization Methods and Applications-A Survey. *2004 International Conference on Systems, Man and Cybernetics.*

Wang, X., Luo, W., & Wang, X. (2006a, September 4-6). *A Comparative Study on Self-tolerant Strategies for Hardware Immune Systems.* Paper presented at the 5th International Conference on Artificial Immune Systems (ICARIS 2006), LNCS 4163, Instituto Gulbenkian de Ciência, Oeiras, Portugal.

Wang, X., Luo, W., & Wang, X. (2006b). Research on an Algorithm with Self-Tolerant Ability in Hardware Immune System. *Journal of System Simulation, 18*(5), 1151-1153.

Wang, Y. N., Yu, Q. M., & Yuan, X. F. (2006). Progress of Chaotic Neural Networks and Their Applications. *Control and Decision, 21*(2), 121-128.

Wang, Y., Wang, G. F., & Dong, H. (2003).Stability Analysis of the Dynamic BP Algorithm for a Recurrent Fuzzy Neural Network. *Journal of Harbin Engineering University, 24*(1), 262-268.

Watanabe Y., Ishiguro A., Shirai Y., & Uchikawa Y. (1998). Emergent Construction of Behavior Arbitration Mechanism Based on the Immune System. Paper presented at the meeting of ICEC'98, Seoul, Korea.

Watanabe, Y., Ishiguro, A., Shirai, Y., & Uchikawa, Y. (1998). Emergent Construction of a Behavior Arbitration Mechanism Based on Immune System. *Advanced Robotics, 12*(3), *227-242.*

Watkins, C. J. C. H. (1989). *Learning from Delayed Rewards,* Ph.D. Thesis, supervisor: Richard Young, King's College. Cambridge, UK: University of Cambridge.

Watkins, C. J. C. H., Dayan, P. (1992). Technical note: Q-learning. *Machine Learning, 8,* 279-292.

WCCI 2008 Proceedings (2008). 2008 IEEE Congress on Evolutionary Computation. *IEEE Computational Intelligence Society.* ISBN: 978-1-4244-1823-7

Weibing G. (Ed.) (1988). *Nonlinear Control System Introduction.* Beijing, CN: Science Press.

Weidlich, W. (2002). *Sociodynamics – a systematic approach to mathematical modelling in the social sciences.* Harwood Academic Publishers.

Weiss, G. (Ed.) (1999). *Multiagent Systems.* The MIT Press

Welch, J. W. (1983). *Journal of Statistics and Computer Simulation, 15,* 17–25.

Whitbrook. A., M. (2005). *An Idiotypic Immune Network For Mobile Robot Control.* School of Computer Science and information and Information Technology, University of Nottingham. (www.cs.nott.ac.uk/~uxa/papers/05amanda_thesis.pdf)

White, J. A. & Garrett, S. M. (2003). Improved Pattern Recognition with Artificial Clonal Selection. In *Proceedings of Second International Conference on Artificial Immune Systems,* Napier University, Edinburgh, UK.

Wikipedia (2008). High-performance computing. *Retrieved October 10, 2007, from*

Wikipedia (2008). Parallel computing. *Retrieved October 10, 2007, from*

Williams, N. L., & Mitchell, M. (2005), Investigating the success of spatial coevolutionary learning, In *Proceedings of the 2005 Genetic and Evolutionary Computation Conference, GECCO-2005* (pp.523-530). New York: ACM Press.

Willy, H., & Roel, L. (2005). Project scheduling under uncertainty: survey and research potentials. *European Journal of Operational Research, 165,* 289-306.

Wilson, D. R., & Martinez, T. R. (2000). Reduction techniques for instance-based learning algorithms. *Machine Learning, 38,* 257-286.

Wilson, D., & Martinez, T. (1997). Improved heterogeneous distance functions. *Journal of Artificial Intelligence Research, 6,* 1–34. Available from http://www.jair.org.

Wolpert, D. H., & Macready, W. G. (1997). No free lunch theorems for optimization. *IEEE Trans. Evol. Comput., 1*(1), 67-82.

Wolpert, D. H., & Tumer, K. (2000). An Introduction to Collective Intelligence. In *Handbook of Agent Technology.* AAAI/MIT Press.

Wolsey, L. A., & Nemhauser, G. L. (1999). Integer and Combinatorial Optimization. New York, NY, USA: Wiley-Interscience.

Woodrow, E. & Heinzelman, W. (2002). Spin-it: A Data Centric Routing Protocol for Image Retrieval in Wireless Networks. In *Proceedings IEEE International Conference on Image Processing, 3,* 913-916.

Wu, J., Qin, D.-X., & Yu, H.-P. (2006). Nonholonomic Motion planning of Mobile Robot with Ameliorated Genetic algorithm. In *Proceedings of the 2006 International Conference on Intelligent Information Hiding and Multimedia Signal Processing* (219-222). New York, NY: IEEE Press.

Wu, W., Shao, H. M., & Qu, D. (ed.). (2005). Strong Convergence of Gradient Methods for BP Networks Training. *Proceedings of Neural Networks and Brain, 1,* 332- 334).

Wu, X. X., & Zhong, C. (ed.). (2001). *Introduction of Chaos.* Shanghai, P.R China: Shanghai Science Technology Document Press.

Xiong, H. and Cheng, H. (2006). Multi-objective optimal reactive power flow incorporating voltage stability. *WSEAS Transactions on Power Systems, 1*(3), 613-618.

Xiong, H., Cheng, H., Zhang, W., Xu, Y., & Jia, D. (2006). Optimal reactive power compensation planning with improving voltage stability margin in deregulated environment. *WSEAS Transactions on Circuits and Systems, 5*(1), 104-110.

Xu, W., Liang, B., Li, C., Qiang, W., Xu, Y., & Lee, K. (2006). Non-holonomic Path planning of Space Robot Based on Genetic algorithm. In *Proceedings of the 2006 IEEE International Conference on Robotics and Biometrics* (1471-1476). New York, NY: IEEE Press.

Yahja, A., Stentz, A., Singh, S., & Brumitt, B. (1998). Framed-quadtree path planning for mobile robots operating in sparse environments. In *Proceedings of the IEEE*

International Conference on Robotics and Automation (pp. 650-655). New York, NY: IEEE Press.

Yan, X., Wu, Q., Yan, J., & Kang, L. (2007). A Fast Evolutionary Algorithm for Robot Path planning. In *Proceedings of the IEEE International Conference on Control and Automation* (pp. 84-87). New York, NY: IEEE Press.

Yang, B. S., & Lee, Y. H. (2000). Artificial life algorithm for function optimization. *Proceedings of ASME Design Engineering Technical Conferences and Computers and Information in Engineering Conference.* DETC2000/DAC-14524.

Yang, B. S., & Song J. D. (2001). Enhanced artificial life algorithm for fast and accurate optimization search. *Asia-Pacific Vibration Conference* (pp. 732-736).

Yang, B. S., Choi, B. G., Yu, Y. H., & Nan, H. T. (2002). Optimum design of a damping plate with an unconstrained viscoelastic damping layer using combined genetic algorithm. *KSME International Journal, 13*(5), 387-396.

Yang, B. S., Lee, Y. H., Choi, B. K., & Kim, H. J. (2001). Optimum design of short journal bearings by artificial life algorithm. *Tribology International, 34*(7), 427-435.

Yang, C., Ye, H., Wang, J. C., & Wang, L. (2002). An artificial life and genetic algorithm based on optimization approach with new selecting methods. *International Conference on Machine Learning and Cybernetics, 2,* 684-688.

Yang, G., & Meng, J. Er (2005). Narmax time series model prediction: feedforward and recurrent fuzzy neural network approaches. *Fuzzy Sets and Systems, 150,* 331–350.

Yang, J., & Honavar, V. (1998). Feature Subset Selection Using a Genetic Algorithm. *IEEE Trans. on Intelligent Systems, 13,* 44–49.

Yang, S. X., & Wang, D. W. (2001). A new adaptive neural network and heuristics hybrid approach for job-shop scheduling. *Computer & Operations Research, 28,* 955-971.

Yang, Y., Lin, H., Zhang, Y. (2007). Content-Based 3-D Model Retrieval: A Survey. *IEEE Systems, Man and Cybernetics-C, 37*(6), 1081-1098.

Yao, X. (1996). An overview of evolutionary computation. *Chinese Journal of Advanced Software Research, 3*(1), 12-29.

Yingqi X., & Jie C. (Ed.) (2002). *Nonlinear Dynamics Mathematical Methods.* Beijing, CN: Meteorological Press.

Yingzi T., Jiong S., & Zhengzhong L. (2003). A Study of the Immune Evolutionary Algorithm-based Self-tuning PID Control of Superheated Steam Temperature. *Power Engineering Department, 18*(1), 58-62.

Yongsheng D., & Lihong R. (2006). An Algorithm Based on Immune Principle Adopted in Controlling Behavior of Autonomous Mobile Robots. *Journal of Control And Decision.*

Yoo, J., & Hajela, P. (1999). Immune network simulations in multicriterion design. *Structural Optimization, 18,* 85-94.

Yoo, J., & Hajela, P. (2001). Fuzzy Multicriterion Design Using Immune Network Simulation. *Structural and Multidisciplinary Optimization, 22*(3), 188-197.

You, H. J. (2005). 3D Building Reconstruction Based on Scanning Laser Rangerfinder Data. *Remote Sensing Technology and Application,* (4).

You, H. J. (2005). The research status of building extraction based on airborne laser scanning data. *Science of Surveying and Mapping,* (5).

Youssef, H., Sait, S. M., & Adiche, H. (2001). Evolutionary algorithms, simulated annealing and tabu search: a comparative study. *Engineering Applications of Artificial Intelligence, 14,* 167-181.

Zadeh, L. (1965). Fuzzy sets. *Information and Control, 8*(3), 338-353.

Zadeh, L. (1983). Commonsense knowledge representation based on fuzzy logic. *IEEE Computer, 16*(1), 61-65.

Zavrel, J. (1995). *Neural information retrieval - An experimental study of clustering and browsing of document collections with neural networks.* Unpublished doctoral dissertation, University of Amsterdam.

Zeng, C., Saxena, N., & McCluskey, E. J. (1999, September 28-30). *Finite State Machine Synthesis with Concurrent Error Detection.* Paper presented at the International Test Conference.

Zhang, B. T., & Kim, S. H. (1997). An evolutionary method for active learning of mobile robot path planning. In *Proceedings of the 1997 IEEE International Symposium on Computational Intelligence in Robotics and Automation* (pp. 312-317). New York, NY: IEEE Press.

Zhang, H., Wu, L., Zhang, Y., & Zeng, Q. (2005). An Algorithm of r-Adjustable Negative Selection Algorithm and Its Simulation Analysis. *Chinese Journal of Computers, 28*(10), 1614-1619.

Zhang, K. Z. (2004). Legal Definition for Illegal Building. *Academic Exploration (11)*.

Zhang, L. M. (2004). *The research and application on artificial immune system*. Master's thesis, Nanjing University of Technology, Nanjing.

Zhang, T., Ramakrishan, R., & Livny, M. (1997). BIRCH: Efficient data clustering method for very large databases, in: *Proceedings ACM SIGMOD International Conference on Data Management* (pp. 103-114).

Zhang, X., Lu, B., Gou, S., & Jiao, L. (2006). Immune multiobjective optimization algorithm for unsupervised feature selection. In *10th Pacific-Asia Conference on Advances in Knowledge Discovery and Data Mining* (pp. 484-494).

Zhang, X., Meng, H., & Jiao, L. (2005a). Improving PSO-based multiobjective optimization using competition and immunity clonal. In *International Conference on Computational Intelligence and Security* (pp. 839-845).

Zhang, X., Meng, H., & Jiao, L. (2005b). Intelligent particle swarm optimization in multiobjective optimization. In *IEEE Congress on Evolutionary Computation* (pp. 714-719).

Zhang, X., Tan, S., & Jiao, L. (2004). SAR Image Classification Based on Immune Clonal Feature Selection. In Proceedings of International Conference on Image Analysis and Recognition (pp. 504–511).

Zhang, Z. (2006). Constrained Multiobjective Optimization Immune Algorithm: Convergence and Application. *Computers and Mathematics with Applications, 52*(5), 791-808.

Zhang, Z. (2007). Immune optimization algorithm for constrained nonlinear multiobjective optimization problems. *Applied Soft Computing Journal, 7*(3), 840-857.

Zhang, Z. X. (ed.). (2000). *Neuro-Fuzzy and soft Computer*. USA : Prentice-Hall Press.

Zhanjiang Evening News (2008). illegal buildings existed 15 years demolished once. *Retrieved October 20, 2007, from* http://zjphoto.yinsha.com/file/200804/2 008040716332642.htm

Zhao, W. (2005). Review of "Immunocomputing: Principles and Applications". *ACM SIGACT News, 36*(4), 14-17.

Zhengshan L. (Ed.) (2003). *The Study of Non-linearity Science and its Application in the Geosciences*. Beijing, CN: Meteorological Press.

Zhong, W. C., Liu, J., Xue, M. Z., & Jiao, L. C. (2004). A multiagent genetic algorithm for global numerical optimization. *IEEE Transactions on Systems, Man and Cybernetics, Part B, 34*(2), 1128-1141.

Zhou, F., & Deng, L. (2004). *Compatison of immune algorithm with genetic algorithm* (Tech. Rep. No. 6). Danjiangkou, Hubei: Yunyang Teachers College.

Zhou, G. (2000). *Principles of Immunology*. Shanghai: Scientific and Technical Documents Publishing House.

Zhou, Q. M. (2005). *The research on aritificial immune system theory and immune clone optimization algorithm*. Master's thesis, Hunan University, Changsha.

Zhou, Y. F., Li, S. J., & Jin, R. C. (2002). A new fuzzy neural network with fast learning algorithm and guaranteed stability for manufacturing process control. *Fuzzy Sets and Systems, 132*, 201–216.

Zhou, Y., Li, B., Yang, J., & Wang, Q. (2006). An immune algorithm for batch job-shop scheduling with multi-objectives. In *International Technology and Innovation Conference* (pp. 1642-1646).

Zhu, D. Q. (2004). The Research Progress and Prospects of Artificial Neural Network. *Journal of Southern Yangtze University(Natural Science Edition), 3*(1), 103-110.

Zio, E., Baraldi, P., & Pedroni, N. (2006). Selecting features for nuclear transients classification by means of genetic algorithms, *IEEE Trans. Nuclear Science, 53*(3), 1479–1493.

Zitzler, E., Laumanns, M., & Thiele, L. (2001). *SPEA2: Improving the Strength Pareto Evolutionary Algorithm* (TIK-Report 103). Zurich: Swiss Federal Institute of Technology (ETH), Computer Engineering and Networks Laboratory (TIK).

Zixing C. (Ed.) (2004) *Intelligent Control* (pp. 312-318). Beijing, CN: Electronic Publishing Industry.

Zou, C. C., Gong, W., & Towsley, D. (2002). Code Red Worm Propagation Modeling and Analysis. In: Atluri V. eds. *Proc of the 9th ACM Conf on Computer and Communications Security*, ACM Press, New York, 138-147.

Zou, E., Li, X. F., & Liu, Y. G. (2004). Optimization design for fuzzy neural network- chaos simulated annealing algorithm. *Journal of center south University (SCIENCE AND TECHNOLOGY), 35*(3), 443-447.

Zou, E., Liu, J. P., Li, X. F., & Zhang, T. S. (2006). A chaos optimization design of fuzzy controller-inverted pendulum system. *J. CENT. South University (SCIENCE AND TECHNOLOGY), 37*(3), 567-571.

Zuo, X. Q., Fan, Y. S. et al. (2006). Workflow simulation scheduling model with application to a prototype system of cigarette factory scheduling. In Koji, K.,

Shinasuke, T., & Osamu, O. (Ed.), *Systems Modeling and Simulation: Theory and Applications* (pp. 158-162). Springer-Verlag.

Zuo, X. Q., Fan, Y. S., & Mo, H. W. (2007). Variable neighborhood immune algorithm. *Chinese Journal of Electronics, 16*(3), 503-508.

About the Contributors

Hongwei Mo was born in 1973. He receiced BS and PhD degrees from Automation College of Harbin Engineering University in 2002 and 2005. He is presently a professor of Automation College of Harbin Engineering University. He was a visiting scholar of UCDavis, CA, USA from 2003-2004. His main research interests include: natural computing, artificial immune system, data mining, intelligent system, artificial intelligent. He had published 30 papers and two books on AIS. He is a director of the Biomedicine Engineering Academy of Heilongjiang Province, commissioner of China Neural network committee, and senior member of computer academy of China. He is secretary-general chairman and associate chairman of organization committee of 16th China Neural Network Conference and 1st conference of special topic on artificial immune system,and member of program committee of 2nd international conference on natural computing--fuzzy system and knowledge discovery(ICNC-FSKD2006), 1st international conference on rough set and knowledge discovery,6th international conference on simulation learning and evolution, 13th IEEE International Conference on Mechanics and Automation(ICMA2007), Biology Inspired Computing 2008 and numerous other conferences. He served as a member of the editorial board for the *International Journal on Information Technology Research*.

* * *

Ioannis Andreadis received the Diploma Degree from the Department of Electrical & Computer Engineering, Democritus University of Thrace (DUTH), Greece, in 1983 and the MSc and PhD degrees from the University of Manchester Institute of Science & Technology, UK, in 1985 and 1989, respectively. His research interests are mainly in electronic systems design, intelligent systems and machine vision. In these areas he has published more than 150 referred publications in book chapters, international journals and conferences. He joined the Department of Electrical & Computer Engineering, DUTH in 1993. Professor Andreadis is a fellow of the Institute of Engineering and Technology, (IET - Formerly IEE), an associate editor of the *Pattern Recognition Journal* (1996 - Present) and a member of the Technical Chamber of Greece.

Xiaojun Bi received bachelor's degree in electrical engineering from Harbin Engineering University in 1987, the MSC in Signal and Information Processing from Harbin Institute of Technology in 1990 and the PhD in Signal and Information Processing from Harbin Engineering University in 2003. As a Professor she is working in the College of Information and Communication, Harbin Engineering University. She has made research in the fields of image processing, speech recognition and Intelligent Processing of Information for 28 years, and meanwhile is the author of more than 30 papers in these subjects. She is the recipient of the prestigious of the awards from both province and nation many times.She is the executive director both in Heilongjiang society of biomedical engineering and Heilongjiang society of Artificial Intelligence, and is the member of China Society of Image and Graphics.

Copyright © 2009, IGI Global, distributing in print or electronic forms without written permission of IGI Global is prohibited.

Mark Burgin is currently a visiting scholar at University of California, Los Angeles. Previously he occupied various senior research and teaching positions in Ukraine and Russia, including Professor at Kiev State University, chief scientist and director of a Laboratory at the National Academy of Sciences of Ukraine, and professor at International Solomon University. Dr. Burgin's current work in computer science is in the areas of distributed systems and concurrent processes, evolutionary computations, theory of super-recursive algorithms, process algebras, information studies, knowledge management, testing, complexity and software correctness. His general topics of interest in computer science are new computing paradigms, languages and architectures, computer simulation, concurrency and interaction, network architectures, knowledge representation and processing, and grid computations. His main contributions to computer science are: theory of inductive Turing machines, theory of inductive algorithmic complexity, axiomatic complexity theory and mathematical models of knowledge and information. Dr. Burgin is the author of more than 300 papers and books in different areas of computer science, artificial intelligence and mathematics.

Miroslav Bursa is a researcher in the biomedical data processing group at the Gerstner Laboratory. He graduated in computer science at the Faculty of Electrical Engineering of the Czech Technical University in Prague in 2005. His research area is interpretation of an ECG signal using AI methods, namely ant colony optimization, Ant Colony Clustering, Particle Swarm optimization, Neural Networks and others. He directs his research towards the field of Nature inspired methods.

Jun Chen received the BEng (Hons) in electrical engineering from Nanjing University of Science & Technology, Nanjing, China, in 2001, MEng (Hons) degree in software engineering from Tongji Univeristy, Shanghai, China, in 2004, and MSc (with distinction) in control systems engineering from the University of Sheffield, Sheffield, UK in 2005. He is currently working toward his PhD at the Intelligent Systems Research Laboratory, and the Institute of Microstructural and Mechanical Process Engineering: The University of Sheffield (IMMPETUS), Department of Automatic Control and Systems Engineering, the University of Sheffield. His research interests include Artificial Immune Systems, evolutionary multi-objective optimization algorithms, fuzzy systems modelling, modelling uncertainty, Bayesian modelling, and neural networks.

Krzysztof Ciesielski, DrEng in computer science, received his MSc degree (2003) in computer science from Warsaw University, Poland, and BSc degree in mathematics (1998) from the same university. In January 2008 he received his PhD degree (cum laude) from the Institute of Computer Science, Polish Academy of Sciences. Currently Assistant Professor at the Institute of Computer Science. He also works as data mining expert for StatConsulting Ltd. His main research areas include: text and web mining, high dimensional data clustering and classification and modeling of cooperation patterns in multiagent systems. He participated in several research projects concerning these topics. He is an author or co-author of more than 30 scientific publications in national and international journals and conference proceedings.

Carlos Artemio Coello Coello received an MSc and a PhD in computer science from Tulane University, USA in 1993 and 1996, respectively. He has published over 200 papers in international peer-reviewed journals and conferences. He has also co-authored the book *Evolutionary Algorithms for Solving Multi-Objective Problems* which is now in its second edition (Springer, New York, 2007) and has co-edited the book *Applications of Multi-Objective Evolutionary Algorithms* (World Scientific, 2004). He has delivered invited talks, keynote speeches and tutorials at international conferences held in Spain, USA, Canada, Switzerland, UK, Chile, Colombia, Brazil, Uruguay, India, Argentina, and Mexico. He currently serves as associate editor of the journals *IEEE Transactions on Evolutionary Computation, Evolutionary Computation, Journal of Heuristics, Pattern Analysis and Applications* and *Computational Optimization and Applications*, and as a member of the editorial boards of the journals *Soft Computing, Engineering Optimization*, and the *International Journal of Computational Intelligence Research*.

Yongsheng Ding is a full professor at College of Information Sciences and Technology, Donghua University, Shanghai, China. He obtained the BS, MS and PhD degrees in electrical engineering from Donghua University, Shanghai, China in 1989, 1994 and 1998, respectively. From 1996 to 1998, he was a Visiting Scientist at Biomedical

Engineering Center, The University of Texas Medical Branch, TX, USA. From March 2003 to May 2003, he was a Senior Visiting Scientist at Ecole Nationale Supérieure des Arts et Industries Textiles, Roubaix, France. From February 2005 to April 2005, he was a Visiting Professor at Department of Electrical and Computer Engineering, Wayne State University, MI, USA. From September 2007 to February 2008, he was a visiting professor at Harvard Medical School, Harvard University, MA, USA. He serves as senior member of Institute of Electrical and Electronics Engineers (IEEE). He has published more than 300 technical papers, and three research monograph/advanced textbooks entitled *DNA Computing and Soft Computing* (2002), *Computational Intelligence* (2004), and *Natural Computing and Network Intelligence* (2008). His scientific interests include computational intelligence, network intelligence, nature-inspired technologies, bio-computing and bio-informatics, intelligent decision-making, and digitized textile & garment technology.

Zhu Dingju, PhD, studied at the Institute of Computing Technology, CAS, being a member of the High Performance Computing professional Commission of China Computer Institute, director of transfer and industrial transformation forum and director of Digital City Research Group in Shenzhen Institute of advanced technology, Chinese Academy of Sciences, vice chairman of Organization Committee of HPC China2007, finance director of GCC2008, PC member of CW2008, main researches include high-performance computing and digital city, responsible for two 863 funds and four municipal projects, and taken part in one 863 project and one institute project, published 17 papers and 9 patents, and developed five software systems.

Eugene Eberbach is a clinical associate professor at Department of Engineering and Science, Rensselaer Polytechnic Institute, Hartford, USA. Previously he was an associate professor at Computer and Information Science Department and Intercampus Graduate School of Marine Sciences and Technology, University of Massachusetts Dartmouth, USA; a professor with tenure at School of Computer Science, Acadia University and an adjunct professor at Faculty of Graduate Studies, Dalhousie University, Canada; senior scientist at Applied Research Lab, The Pennsylvania State University; visiting professor at The University of Memphis, USA; research scientist at University College London, UK; assistant professor in Poland, and he also has industrial experience. Dr. Eberbach's current work is in the areas of process algebras, resource bounded optimization, autonomous agents and mobile robotics. General topics of interest are new computing paradigms, languages and architectures, distributed computing, concurrency and interaction, evolutionary computing and neural nets. Dr. Eberbach is the author of more than 140 publications in the above areas and he has been a recipient of 17 external research grants. More information about projects, publications, courses taught can be found at http://www.ewp.rpi.edu/~eberbe

Fabio Freschi was born in Torino, Italy, in 1976. He received the Laurea degree and a PhD degree in electrical engineering from the Politecnico di Torino, Turin, Italy in 2002 and 2006, respectively. He is currently working as assistant professor in fundamentals of electrical engineering at the Politecnico di Torino. His main research interests are related to optimization and inverse problems in electromagnetism, numerical computation of electromagnetic fields, environmental electromagnetic fields. He published more than 40 papers on these topics.

Terrence P. Fries earned a PhD in computer science and engineering from the University of Louisville in 1998. He also received an MS in computer science and engineering and a BS in engineering from Oakland University in Rochester, Michigan. He is a senior member of the ACM and the IEEE. Terry's research in artificial intelligence includes fuzzy sets, evolutionary computation, and multiple agent systems with applications in robot navigation, network security, and manufacturing systems. He has published numerous papers in international conferences and journals, and is the author of several book chapters. He is a reviewer for many international computer science journals and conferences including the *IEEE Transactions on Systems, Man and Cybernetics*. He has been on the program committees of IEEE workshops.

Dongmei Fu works in the University of Science & Technology Beijing (USTB). In 1984 and 1987, she earned a bachelor's and master's degree from the University of Northwest Technology. She earned her doctor from USTB in 2006. She was a teacher and taught automatic control principle, theory of modern control, computer control system, adaptive control system, theory and application of artificial neural network, intelligence algorithm and control methods since 1987. Her interesting researches are in intelligence control methods, data analyses and its models, image processing (especially in infrared image which include image segment, image recognition, image fusion), etc.

Maoguo Gong is currently an associate professor with the Institute of Intelligent Information Processing at Xidian University, Xi'an, China. He received his BSc in electronic engineering from Xidan University in 2003 with the highest honor. He was a master's student in the Institute of Intelligent Information Processing, Xidian University, from August 2003 to August 2004. He took the Fund of Excellent Doctor's Dissertation of Xidian University in April 2007. He is a member of the IEEE. His research interests are broadly in the area of computational intelligence. His areas of special interest include artificial immune systems, evolutionary computation, image understanding, data mining, optimization, and some other related areas. He has published round about 30 papers in journals and conferences. More information at http://gong.ipiu.org.cn.

Tao Gong is with College of Information Science and Technology, Donghua University, China, and has been a full member of Sigma Xi, The Scientific Research Society since 2002. He got his master's degree in AI and PhD in computer application techniques at Central South University, China in respectively 2003 and 2007. He has published over 45 papers on artificial intelligence and computer science and over 20 books on computers. His research interests include artificial immune systems, computational intelligence and intelligent networks. He has attained grants on his research on artificial immune systems and applied two inventing patents on artificial immune systems.

Licheng JIAO received the BS degree from Shanghai Jiao Tong University, Shanghai, China, in 1982, the MS and the PhD degree from Xi'an Jiao Tong University, Xi'an, China, in 1984 and in 1990, respectively. Now, he is the dean of School of Electronic Engineering (SEE) and the director of Institute of Intelligent Information Processing (IIIP), Xidian University. His current research interests include signal and image processing, natural computation and intelligent information processing. He is an IEEE senior member, member of IEEE Xi'an Section Executive Committee, and the Chairman of Awards and Recognition Committee, executive committee member of Chinese Association of Artificial Intelligence, councilor of Chinese Institute of Electronics, committee member of Chinese Committee of Neural Networks, and expert of Academic Degrees Committee of the State Council. He has charged of and completed about 40 important scientific research projects which win many science and technology awards, published more than 10 monographs and a hundred papers in international journals and conferences.

Mieczysław A. Kłopotek (DrEng, Habil. in Computer Science) received an MSc in 1983 and PhD in computer science in 1984 from Dresden University of Technology, Germany. Dr.Eng.habil. from Institute of Computer Science, Polish Academy of Sciences in 1998. Currently Associate Professor at the Institute of Computer Science of Polish Academy of Sciences; also Extraordinary Professor and Head of AI Department of Computer Science Institute at the University of Podlasie. Member of the Editorial Board of the International Journal Machine Graphics and Vision. Main research areas are: artificial intelligence, especially expert systems, management of uncertainty, machine learning, machine vision, intelligent information systems. More than 200 scientific publications in national and international journals and conference proceedings. Cooperates with industry and medical centers in the area of intelligent information systems and knowledge discovery in databases. Participated and participates in national and international research projects, recently concerning construction of document map based internet search engines.

Konstantinos Konstantinidis was born in Sheffield, England. He received the BSc and MSc Degrees from the Department of Automatic Control and Systems Engineering, The University of Sheffield, UK in 1999 and 2000 respectively and his PhD from the Department of Electrical and Computer Engineering, Democritus University of Thrace (DUTH), Greece in 2008. His research interests include content-based image retrieval, artificial intelligence, image processing, machine vision and robotics. He is a member of the Technical Chamber of Greece (TEE).

Lenka Lhotska is associate professor at the Department of Cybernetics at Czech Technical University and head of the biomedical processing group. She obtained an MSc in technical cybernetics at the Czech Technical University in Prague, thesis: "Application of an Expert System for Acupuncture Therapy" and PhD in Technical Cybernetics at the Czech Technical University in Prague, with thesis "Blackboard Control Architecture at the FEL-EXPERT System". Her main research interests focus on intelligent biomedical data and signal processing, decision support systems in medicine, knowledge representation, machine learning.

Zhifang Li was born in 1982. He received the BS from Department of Computer Science and Technology, University of Science and Technology of China, Hefei, China, in 2005. He is presently a PhD student of Department of Computer Science and Technology, University of Science and Technology of China. His current research interests include evolvable hardware and nature inspired computation.

Fang Liu is currently a professor with the School of Computer Science at Xidian University, Xi'an, China. She received the BS degree in computer science and technology from the Xi'an Jiaotong University, Xi'an, China, in 1984, and the MS degree in computer science and technology from the Xidian University, Xi'an, China, in 1995. She is a senior member of IEEE. Her current research interests include natural computation, optimization problems, data mining, and image processing. She has charged of and completed about 20 scientific research projects in the related areas, and published about one hundred papers in journals and conferences.

Małgorzata Lucińska graduated with the MSc in physics from Jagiellonian University, Krakow, Poland, in 1989 and PhD from System Research Institute Polish Academy of Sciences, Warsaw, Poland, in 2006 for research in artificial immune systems. She is currently a Lecturer in the Department of Management and Computer Modeling University of Technology, Kielce, Poland. She has been active in the area of nature-inspired computing since 2003. She has published a number of papers in the fields of artificial immune systems and multi-agent systems. Her research interests include optimization of complex systems, optimization in dynamic environments and agent-based modeling.

Wenjian Luo was born in 1974. He received the BS and PhD degrees from Department of Computer Science and Technology, University of Science and Technology of China, Hefei, China, in 1998 and 2003. He is presently an associate professor of Department of Computer Science and Technology, University of Science and Technology of China. His current research interests include artificial immune system, evolvable hardware, computational intelligence and nature inspired computation.

Wenping MA is currently a lecturer with the Institute of Intelligent Information Processing at Xidian University, Xi'an, China. She received the PhD in pattern recognition and intelligent system from Xidian University in 2008. Her research interests include artificial immune systems, evolutionary computation, and image processing.

Martin Macaš received his MSc degree in technical cybernetics from the Czech Technical University in Prague. Currently, he is employed as a PhD student of artificial intelligence and biocybernetics in the Biomedical Data Processing Group, FEE, CTU. His topics of interest include optimization algorithms, pattern recognition and biomedical signal applications.

Mahdi Mahfouf has received the degrees of MPhil (1987) and PhD (1991) from the University of Sheffield (UK). He was a post-doctoral research fellow (1992-1996) in the Department of Automatic Control and Systems Engineering, The University of Sheffield. In January 1997 he was appointed as a Lecturer of Industrial Control in the Department of Mechanical Engineering, The University of Manchester. In October 1997 he joined the Department of Automatic Control and Systems Engineering, The University of Sheffield, as a lecturer in systems and control engineering and was promoted to senior lecturer in 2000, reader in 2003, and to a personal chair in Intelligent Systems Engineering in 2005. Professor Mahfouf has worked in the areas of Intelligent Control and Modelling in Biomedicine and Process Industries for more than 18 years and is the author of more than 150 papers in these subjects and has authored/co-authored books and book chapters. He is the recipient of the prestigious

IEE HARTREE Premium Award for a paper published in the IEE Proceedings on Control Theory and Applications. His research interests include Predictive Control, Fuzzy/Neuro-Fuzzy Systems, Intelligent Systems based Modelling and Control, Evolutionary Computing, Modelling and Control for Biomedicine, and Modelling and Optimisation in the Metal Processing Industry.

Jose Guillermo Guarnizo Marín is an electronic engineer who obtained his bachelor's degree from Francisco Jose de Caldas University. His undergraduate project was an Artificial Neural Control Applied to Buck Converter. He is currently a student of the Industrial Automation Master Program and an assistant professor in the Department of Electrical and Electronic Engineering at National University of Colombia. He is a member of the Intelligent Systems Research Laboratory (LISI) at the same university and his master's thesis deals with a Cognitive Model Inspired by Immunology for Object Recognition and Transportation. He also works as a professor of electronic engineering and is a member of the Alternative Energy Sources Research Laboratory (LIFAE) at Francisco Jose de Caldas University. Topics of interest: automatic control systems, power electronics, robotics, intelligent control, soft computing, artificial immune systems.

Tang Mo received the BE in automation from Harbin University of Science and Engineering, Harbin, China, in 2003. She received the ME in control theorem and control engineering and PhD in pattern recognition and intelligence system from Harbin Engineering University, Harbin, China, in 2006 and 2008 respectively. She is currently a lecture at Automation Academy of Harbin Engineering University, Harbin. She is also a research fellow of Pattern Recognition and Intelligence System Laboratory. Her research interests are intelligent control system modeling, fuzzy logic, chaos, and pattern recognition.

Fredy Fernando Muñoz Mopan received a bachelor's degree in electronic engineer from National University of Colombia and is a student of the Industrial Automation Master Program at the same university. Mr. Muñoz is a member of the Intelligent Systems Research Laboratory (LISI) and has received a scholarship awarded to young researchers countrywide by COLCIENCIAS, the main Colombian Research Funding Institution. He works at an important international organization, Corona in Colombia, and his work at Corona is focused on implementing machine vision systems. His master's thesis is a research on how to model the innate and adaptive immune responses and to apply those cognitive models in a multi-agent system object transportation. Muñoz's topics of interests are artificial immune systems, neural networks, pattern recognition, robotics, multi-agent systems, swarms.

Alexander Olegovich Tarakanov received a PhD in computer science (1988) and a DrSci in physics & mathematics (1999). As a Ret. Lt. Col. of Russian Space Forces, he has 20 years experience in space navigation. He is currently leading researcher at St. Petersburg Institute for Informatics and Automation, Russian Academy of Sciences. He took part in work on the unique Ecological Atlas of Kaliningrad city (formerly Koenigsberg), for which he received Honor Appreciation from Greenpeace Russia (Moscow, 2001). He was team leader of EU project IST-2000-26016 "Immunocomputing" (2001-2003) and Project Manager of EOARD project #017007 "Mathematical models of immune networks for information security" (2002-2005). He is main author of the immunocomputing book (Springer NY, 2003) which got the Book of the Year Award of the International Institute for Advanced Studies in Systems Research and Cybernetics (Baden-Baden, 2004).

James F. Peters, PhD, *Constructive Specification of Communicating Systems* (1991), postdoctoral fellow, Syracuse University, and Rome Laboratories (1991), assistant professor, University of Arkansas and researcher in the Mission Sequencing and Telecommunications Divisions at the Jet Propulsion Laboratory/Caltech, Pasadena, California (1992-1994), is now a full professor in the Department of Electrical and Computer Engineering (ECE) at the University of Manitoba. In April, 2008, Dr. Peters received the *International Journal of Intelligent Computing and Cybernetics* best journal article award. In 2007, He received a Best Paper Award from Springer, Berlin and Joint Rough Set Symposium 2007 (JRS 2007) Program Committee, for a paper on robotic target tracking with approximation space-based feedback and approximate adaptive learning capability. In 2007, Dr. Peters was a plenary speaker on image pattern recognition and biologically-inspired adaptive learning at two international conferences (JRS 2007, Toronto and RSEISP 2007, Warsaw). He is the recipient of the IEEE Gold Medallion

Award Medal (2000) and an IFAC Best Paper Award (1998) for a paper on rough control. Currently, he research group leader in the Computational Intelligence Laboratory, University of Manitoba. He also is co-editor-in-chief of the *Transactions on Rough Sets Journal* published by Springer-Verlag, co-founder and research group leader, Computational Intelligence Laboratory in the ECE Department (1996-), current member of the steering committee, International Rough Sets Society, and current member of the executive board of IFAC Canada. He was also a Plenary speaker at the Symposium on Methods of Artificial Intelligence (AIMETH 2005) where Prof. Lotfi A. Zadeh was the Honorary Chair, Keynote speaker at the International Workshop on Monitoring, Security and Rescue Techniques in Multiagent Systems (MSRAS 2004), P_lock, Poland, June 2004, Plenary speaker at the 9th Int. Conf. on Rough Sets, Fuzzy Sets, Data Mining and Granular Computing (RSFDGrC2003), October 2003, Chongqing, China, Program Co-Chair, Rough Sets and Knowledge Technology (RSKT 2006) and RSFDGrC 2005, Program Chair for North America for the 3rd Int. Conf. on Rough Sets and Current Trends in Computing (RSCTC'02), Workshop Co-Chair of COMPSAC'02 Workshop on the Foundation of Data Mining via Granular and Rough Computing, Program Committee Member of RSCTC 2000 and numerous other conferences. He served as Guest Editor for the International Journal on Intelligent Systems, 1999, 2001 and 2002. Since 1997, he has published over 300 articles in refereed journals, edited volumes, international conferences and workshops. His current research interests are in near sets, perceptual systems (*e.g.*, perceptual information systems that result from sample percepts), pattern recognition, and therapeutic telegaming in pervasive computing environments. He has also done considerable research in ethology and image processing, rough set theory, adaptive learning, biologically-inspired designs of intelligent systems (vision systems that learn), the extension of ethology (study of behaviour of biological organisms) to the study of intelligent system behaviour.

Lihong Ren is an associate professor at College of Information Sciences and Technology, Donghua University, Shanghai, China. She obtained the BS, MS and PhD degrees in electrical engineering from Donghua University, Shanghai, China in 1989, 1992 and 2000, respectively. She has published more than 60 technical papers, and two research monograph/advanced textbooks entitled *DNA Computing and Soft Computing* (2002), and *Electric and Electronics* (2004). Her scientific interests include computational intelligence, network intelligence, nature-inspired technologies, bio-computing, and bio-informatics.

Maurizio Repetto was born in Genova, Italy, in 1960. He received the degree in electrical engineering in 1985 and the PhD in electrical engineering in 1989, both from the University of Genova, Genova, Italy. He was a researcher at the University of Genova from 1990 to 1992. In 1992, he joined the Politecnico di Torino, Torino, Italy, where he is now full professor of fundamentals of electrical engineering. His main research interests are related to the numerical computation of electromagnetic fields in the area of power devices; in particular, he is involved in research projects about the analysis of ferromagnetic hysteresis and the automatic optimization of electromagnetic devices, environmental electromagnetic fields, and shielding. He is author of more than 100 publications on these topics.

Camilo Eduardo Prieto Salazar holds a bachelor's degree from Surcolombiana University and a specialization's degree from National University of Colombia. His undergraduate project was a control system applied to servomotors and during his specialization project he developed a computational model to obtain direct kinematics from manipulator robots. Currently, he is a master's student at National University of Colombia and his master's thesis deals with a bio-inspired computational model applied to robot soccer games. Since 2006, Prieto is a member of the LISI at National University of Colombia and his research is focused on intelligent systems applied to robotics and control systems.

Georgios Ch. Sirakoulis received the Dipl. Eng. and PhD in electrical and computer engineering from the Democritus University of Thrace, Greece, in 1996 and 2001, respectively. He joined the Department of Electrical and Computer Engineering, Democritus University of Thrace, Greece, as a non tenured faculty member, in 2002, where he serves as assistant professor. He has published more than 60 technical papers and he is the co-author of one book. His current research emphasis is on automated electronic systems design, cellular automata theory and applications, CAD and Technology CAD systems, physical design automation of VLSI systems, bioengineering and biocomputation. Dr. Sirakoulis received a prize of distinction from the Technical Chamber of Greece (TEE) for his Diploma Thesis in 1996. He is a member of the Institution of Engineering and Technology (IET), of the European Geosciences Union (EGU), of the International Society of Computational Biology (ISCB) and of the TEE. He was also founding member and vice president of the IEEE Student Branch of Thrace for the period 2000-2001.

Luis Fernando Niño Vasquez is an associate professor and the academic coordinator of the Computer Science and Industrial Engineering Department at National University of Colombia Niño holds an MSc in mathematics from National University of Colombia, an MSc in computer science from The University Of Memphis, USA, where Associative Storage of Information Using n-Dimensional Dynamical Dystems was developed as his master's thesis. He also received a PhD in computer sciencie from The University Of Memphis in 2000. Currently, Niño is the director of the Intelligent Systems Research Laboratory at Nacional University of Colombia. Dr. Niño's research interests center around computer science, cognitive models, mathematics and general biology.

Kejun Wang received the BE from Institute of Northeast Heavy Machinery, 1980, and the ME, PhD degrees from Harbin Engineering University, Harbin, in 1987 and 1995, respectively. He was the first doctor in ship and ocean engineering special assist device system in China. He completed his research work in liquid transmission and control from Harbin Institute of Technology as a post doctor, 1998. From 1987 to 1991, he was a lecture of the computer center in the Institute of ship engineering, Harbin Engineering University. From 1992 to now, he is working in the Institute of Automation, Harbin Engineering University, and was award associate professor in 1992, award professor in 1998. He is currently a doctoral advisor and subdecanal in the Institute of Automation. He joined Electronics Inc. China as senior member. He serves as the chairman of Intelligent Acad. and automation Acad., Heilongjiang Province, China. His research interests are in pattern recognition and intelligent system, control theory and engineering, fuzzy chaotic neural network, network intelligent control, adaptive inverse control, extension control, multi-mode biology character identifier and micro robot systems. Dr. Wang is the recipient of the NSF CAREER Award and Doctoral Foundation of Ministry of Education, China, for research in intelligent control. He is also a subject editor for the *IEEE Journal of Image and Graphics*, *Journal of Automation Technology and Application*, *Journal of Motor and Control*, *Journal of Applied Science*, *Journal of Harbin Engineering University*, *Journal of Jilin University*, and *Journal of Xian Jiatong University*.

Xin Wang was born in 1981. He received the PhD from Department of Computer Science and Technology, University of Science and Technology of China, Hefei, China, in 2008. He is presently an assistant of School of Computer Science and Technology, Southwest University of Science and Technology, Mianyang, China. His current research interests include artificial immune system, evolvable hardware and nature inspired computation.

Xufa Wang was born in 1948. He is a professor of Department of Computer Science and Technology, University of Science and Technology of China, Hefei, China. His main research interests include signal processing, pattern recognition, computational intelligence, computer network, intelligent information processing and nature inspired computation. He has published more than 100 professional papers, authored and edited five books.

Sławomir T. Wierzchoń received MSc (1974) and PhD degree in computer science (1979) from Technical University of Warsaw, Poland. He holds Doctor of Science (Habilitation) degree in computer science from the Polish Academy of Science (1997). In June 2003 he received the title of Professor from the President of Poland. Currently Full Professor and Head of AI Department at the Institute of Computer Science of Polish Academy of Sciences. Also Full Professor and Head of Computational Intelligence Department at the University of Gdansk. Main research areas are: biologically inspired computation, artificial intelligence, especially management of uncertainty, expert systems and machine learning, intelligent information systems. More than 200 scientific publications in national and international journals and conference proceedings. He cooperated with medical centers in the area of statistical analysis and knowledge discovery in databases. Participated and participates in national and international research projects, recently concerning construction of document map based internet search engines.

Bo-Suk Yang is the director of the Intelligent Machine Condition Monitoring & Diagnostics Centre and the dean of academic affairs at the Puyong National University in Korea. He received a PhD in mechanical engineering from Kobe University, Japan in 1985. Presently he is a professor in Mechanical Engineering Department, Pukyong National University since 1996. His main research fields cover machine dynamics and vibration engineering, intelligent optimum design, and condition monitoring and diagnostics in rotating machinery. He has published well over 170 research papers in the research areas of vibration analysis, intelligent optimum design and diagnosis of rotating machinery. He is a member of international steering committee for APVC and a director of International Society of Engineering Asset Management. He is listed in Who's Who in the World, Who's Who in Science and Engineering, among others.

Jianmin Zhang received the ME degree in control theorem and control engineering from Northeast University, Jilin, China in 1999 and the PhD in pattern recognition and intelligence system from Harbin Engineering University, Harbin, China in 2006. From 1988 to 1995, she was a lecture in the Institute of Automation, Jilin Higher Associate College of Electrification, Jilin. And later is an associate professor at the Electrification Department of the Beihua University, Jilin, from 1999 to 2006. Her research interests are intelligent control system modeling and chaos.

Xiangfeng Zhang is an assistant professor at Shanghai Dianji University, Shanghai, China. She obtained the BS, MS, and PhD degrees in electrical engineering from Donghua University, Shanghai, China in 1999, 2004, and 2007, respectively. She has published more than 20 technical papers. Her scientific interests include network intelligence, nature-inspired technologies, and multi-agent systems.

Xiangrong ZHANG is currently an associate professor with the Institute of Intelligent Information Processing at Xidian University, Xi'an, China. She received the BS and MS degrees from the School of Computer Science at Xidian University, Xi'an, China, in 1999 and 2003 respectively, and the PhD from the School of Electronic Engineering at Xidian University, Xi'an, China, in 2006. She is a member of IEEE. Her current research interests include pattern recognition, machine learning, natural computation, and SAR image analysis and understanding. She has published about 30 papers in journals and conferences.

Liying Zheng received the BE, ME and PhD degrees in pattern recognition and intelligent system from Harbin Engineering University, Harbin, China, in 1997, 2000, and 2002 respectively. From 1999 to 2002, she was a lecture in the Institute of Automation and later is an associate professor, Harbin Engineering University, Harbin. Her research interests are intelligent control system modeling, fuzzy control, image processing, pattern recognition and chaos.

Xingquan Zuo was born in 1971. He is currently associate professor of Information Engineering School of Beijing University of Posts and Telecommunications. He received the PhD in control theory and control engineering from Harbin Institute of Technology, Harbin, China, in 2004. From April 2004 to March 2006, he was Postdoctal Research fellow in Automation Department of Tsinghua University. His research interests include artificial immune system, production scheduling, and optimization computation. He published more than 20 research papers in journals and conferences.

Index

Copyright © 2009, IGI Global, distributing in print or electronic forms without written permission of IGI Global is prohibited.